JESUS

AND THE

VICTORY OF GOD

CHRISTIAN ORIGINS AND THE QUESTION OF GOD

Volume Two

JESUS

AND THE

VICTORY OF GOD

N. T. Wright

FORTRESS PRESS
Minneapolis

for M.E.A.W.

JESUS AND THE VICTORY OF GOD
Christian Origins and the Question of God, vol. 2

First North American edition published 1996 by Fortress Press.

Cover graphic: *Christ Eleemon* mosaic, Constantinople, 1100-1150 (Staatliche Museen, Berlin)

The Library of Congress has catalogued this series as follows:
Wright, N. T. (Nicholas Thomas)
    Christian origins and the question of God / N. T. Wright – 1st
Fortress Press ed.
        p. cm.
    Includes bibliographical references and indexes.
    Contents: v. 1. The New Testament and the People of God
    ISBN 0-8006-2681-8 (v.1; alk. paper)
    1. God—Biblical teaching. 2. God—History of doctrines—Early
church ca. 30—600. 3. Bible. N.T.—Theology. 4. Christianity—
Origin. 1. Title.
BS2398.W75 1992
225.6—dc20   92–19348
                                                                       CIP

ISBN 0-8006-2682-6 (paper); 0-8006-3089-0 (cloth)

8   9   10

Printed in the U.S.A.

SUMMARY OF CONTENTS

CONTENTS

PREFACE

I

'The historian of the first century . . . cannot shrink from the question of Jesus.' That was the conclusion I came to near the end of the first volume in this series, on whose shoulders the present work rests all its weight.[1] I argued that the study of first-century Judaism and first-century Christianity forces us to raise certain specific questions about Jesus: who was he? what were his aims? why did he die? and why did early Christianity begin in the way that it did? The present book is my attempt to answer the first three of these questions, and to point towards an answer to the fourth.

I am still sometimes embarrassed when people ask me what the present book is about, and I say 'Jesus'. It seems pretentious. How can anyone have anything *new* to say about Jesus without being a crank or a maverick, or, worse, making Jesus himself into one? I have come to believe that these questions about Jesus are vital, central, *and as yet not fully answered*; and that a clearly worked out historical method, and a fresh reading of first-century Judaism and Christianity, will point us in the right direction.

Questions about Jesus possess, I believe, enormous intrinsic interest, no matter what the standpoint of the questioner. They are worth asking, whether one is a historian, a philosopher, a theologian, a cultural critic, or simply someone interested in the human condition with all its joys and sorrows, its high and low points, its perils and possibilities. But there is no point pretending that such questions are not also of very specific relevance for those who profess some sort of Christian faith. A recent survey of the Church of England, discussing the manifold reasons why people do not go to church, comments wryly:

---

[1] *The New Testament and the People of God* (hereafter referred to as *NTPG*), 468.

Part of the reason is simply a lack of belief that the death of Christ was the turning-point of history . . . It all seems less and less likely to be true, the more you discover about those maniacs in the first century who were expecting a Messiah and getting ready for the end of the world.[2]

Unless one can at least address this question, one might as well give up and go home. The same point is made from a different angle by the veteran philosopher of religion John Hick.[3] What you say about Jesus affects your entire worldview. If you see Jesus differently, everything changes. Turn this small rudder, and the whole ship will change tack. To put it bluntly: what if the maniacs turned out to be right?

There are some, of course, who would rather not mix up history and faith. I shall have quite a bit to say about this dilemma as the book progresses. For the moment it is enough to say that I come to this work as a practising historian and as a practising Christian, and that my experience of both worlds suggests – to put it no stronger – that neither of them need feel compromised by intimate association with the other.

II

In one sense, I have been working on this book on and off for most of my life. Serious thought began, however, when I was invited in 1978 to give a lecture in Cambridge on 'The Gospel in the Gospels'. The topic was not just impossibly vast; I did not understand it. I had no real answer, then, to the question of how Jesus' whole life, not just his death on the cross in isolation, was somehow 'gospel'. Fifteen subsequent years of teaching in Cambridge, Montreal and Oxford have convinced me that this question, and the detailed sub-questions which go with it, are worth asking; and that answers are available, if we keep to the high road of historical enquiry and refuse to be sidetracked into the superficially more attractive country lanes of much modern gospel study, where we are often brought to a halt by the hermeneutical equivalent of a hay-waggon or a herd of sheep.

Further stimulus to persevere with the historical task has come from the new wave of scholarly Jesus-studies which I describe in Part I. I invented the phrase 'Third Quest' to denote one particular type of contemporary Jesus-research, namely, that which regards Jesus as an eschatological prophet announcing the long-awaited kingdom, and which undertakes serious historiography around that point (see chapter 3). Some writers have used the

[2] Maxtone Graham 1993, 129.
[3] Hick 1993, esp. chs. 2, 3.

phrase subsequently to denote *all* current study of Jesus, but I see no need to abandon my original sharper meaning. It is to colleagues within this branch of the 'Quest' that I owe most in terms of signposts towards the solutions I propose. At the same time, those Jesus-scholars who pursue very different lines of enquiry (described in chapter 2) have forced me to articulate much more clearly than I would otherwise have had to do why I disagree with them, and I am genuinely grateful for this, as also for emphases and nuances which they rightly highlight and which I and others might otherwise have missed.

All writers about Jesus have to live with the old jibe that the historian is inclined to see his or her own face at the bottom of a deep well and mistake it for the face of Jesus. I have to say that the face I describe in this book always was, and still remains, disturbingly unlike my own. I have not tried to make Jesus in the image either of a university lecturer or of an Anglican priest; he continues to challenge and disturb both of those worlds and those who live in them, myself included. This does not mean, of course, that the portrait is thereby validated; only that it is not a self-portrait. I wish it were.

This book argues, in fact, for conclusions which were quite simply not in view from the start of the exercise. Nor were they worked out even early on in the process of teaching, or even when, thinking I had settled them, I began to write. At every stage I found myself coming face to face with historical problems, and (since I could not abandon my basic Christian beliefs without becoming a totally different person) with the question of how, if at all, history and belief might cohere. In the process, my view of Jesus within his historical context has substantially developed and changed. So, inevitably, has my understanding of what Christianity itself actually is, and the nature of my belief in it. This process, which continues, is neither easy nor comfortable. (Again, this does not validate the conclusions, but merely refutes the suggestion that they were in view from the start.)

The book inevitably carries overtones of current situations in the land where the story of Jesus is set, where I was staying in 1989 when I wrote the first draft. From my room I could hear distant gunfire; on the street one could sense Jewish anxiety and Palestinian frustration in about equal measure. To have a riot dispersed with tear gas outside my window while I was writing the chapter on the cross gave me, to say the least, food for thought. To watch the events of late 1995 and early 1996 while rewriting it for the last time was no less painful. The multiple ambiguities and tensions of that beautiful country are now forever bound up in my mind with the subject-matter of the book itself, as is perhaps appropriate. If what I write could help in any way towards the establishment of justice and peace there, or indeed anywhere else, I would be deeply grateful.

III

Seven small points, and one not so small. First, I have continued to use the lower case 'g' in 'god', and to refer to Jesus as 'Jesus' rather than 'Christ'. The reasons for this are explained in the Preface of *NTPG* (xivf.).

Second, I have taken it for granted that Jesus of Nazareth existed. Some writers feel a need to justify this assumption at length against people who try from time to time to deny it. It would be easier, frankly, to believe that Tiberius Caesar, Jesus' contemporary, was a figment of the imagination than to believe that there never was such a person as Jesus. Those who persist in denying this obvious point will probably not want to read a book like this anyway.

Third, this book is largely based on the synoptic gospels. What about John?[4] Someone who spends most of his time studying Paul and the synoptics, rather than John, may come to feel like an Alpine climber who from time to time hears tales of the Himalayas. I am aware that there is a large range of mountains still waiting for me; aware, too, that they may offer views, prospects and of course risks yet more breathtaking than the ones I habitually climb. I hope I shall be spared to explore them in due course, and I beg the indulgence of those who wish that a guidebook to the Alps had included their senior cousins as well. However, the debate to which I wish to contribute in this book has been conducted almost entirely in terms of the synoptic tradition. Even if, in the long term, this is judged a weakness, it sets a limit for which readers of an already long book may perhaps be grateful.

Fourth, what I said about secondary literature in the Preface to *NTPG* is even more the case here. The huge quantity of contemporary writing about Jesus and the gospels means that any serious attempt to engage in dialogue with even a small proportion of it would result in a hopeless morass of footnotes. One must choose one's conversation partners, referring to others only where necessary for the argument. If one were to try even to 'catch up' with everything that had been written at the time of going to press, one would put off for ever going to press. I apologize to those colleagues whose work I have not been able to discuss in detail.

Fifth, there is a problem of scale which I have not really attempted to solve. In some cases a particular saying has snatched a few pages all to itself, while elsewhere a whole complex episode has had to make do with the same or less. The only alternative would have been to give the saying less than it seemed to need within that particular argument, or perhaps to swell the discussion of the episode into a young monograph. Perhaps, like vineyard-

---

[4] For the further question, 'What about Thomas and the others?', cf. ch. 2 below.

owners, authors may choose to pay the same wages to those who appear to deserve differently, or vice versa. The argument as a whole has, I think, a certain proportion, but some of its parts do not. That is just the way it is.

Sixth, a word about method. In reading the sayings of Jesus, we must of course guard against over-exegesis. Under-exegesis, though, is also risky, sometimes even more so. Historical exegesis is not simply a matter of laying out the lexicographical meanings of words and sentences. It involves exploring the resonances those words and sentences would have had in their contexts. Like anthropologists learning a language and a culture simultaneously, we have to be prepared to hear more in a word or phrase than could be caught by a dictionary equivalent. A small saying can function like a spyglass through which one can glimpse a large and turbulent world. To object to this exercise, whether through pedantry or positivism, is like protesting that houses, fields and ships cannot be contained within the physical body of a telescope.

Seventh, the book does not attempt to follow the synoptic accounts of Jesus' life straight through, but rather arranges the material by themes. This involves a certain amount of repetition: the parable of the wicked tenants (for instance) is discussed at different points in connection with different issues. The alternative would, of course, involve another sort of repetition: one would (for instance) constantly be saying similar things about the 'kingdom of god' in connection with yet another group of texts. Each chapter is therefore meant to function like a transparent layer laid over a basic map or picture. The eventual aim is that the underlying picture, set out at the start of Part II, should be seen through all the layers at once, even though for the sake of clarity they must of course be added one by one.

Eighth, I argued in *NTPG* that most first-century Jews would have seen themselves as still, in all sorts of senses, 'in exile'.[5] This is not an idiosyncratic view, as the notes there make clear; and many colleagues, in person and in their writings, have encouraged me to persist.[6] Nevertheless, some have remained unconvinced. Without wishing to labour the point further, I would ask critics to face the question: would any serious-thinking first-century Jew claim that the promises of Isaiah 40–66, or of Jeremiah, Ezekiel, or Zechariah, had been fulfilled? That the power and domination of paganism

---

[5] *NTPG* 268–70; to the refs. there add Ezra 9.8–9, which emphasizes that (what we call) 'post-exilic' Israel is still in 'slavery'. Danby's comment (306 n.9) on mSot. 9.15 (the passage about the 'footsteps of the Messiah' and the accompanying woes in Israel; cf. 347f. below) is to the point: these are 'the signs which herald the coming of the Messiah at the end of the time of exile.'

[6] In addition to those listed in *NTPG* ad loc., note Garnet 1977, 1980a & b, 1982, 1983; Ackroyd 1968, ch. 13; Harvey 1982, 143–5; Scott 1993; Ito 1995.

had been broken? That YHWH had already returned to Zion? That the covenant had been renewed, and Israel's sins forgiven? That the long-awaited 'new exodus' had happened? That the second Temple was the true, final and perfect one? Or – in other words – that the exile was really over? The closest we come, I think, is the grandiose biblical language used in 1 Maccabees 3.3–9 to refer to the victory of Judas Maccabaeus. Various books of the period explicitly question or challenge the adequacy, or even the god-givenness, of the second Temple.[7] The writings at Qumran see the sect as *the secret advance guard* of the real return from exile, which of course implies that the rest of Israel is exiled still.

The point of all this is not that the exile functioned in this period as an *example*, an illustration from the past of the way in which YHWH might perhaps work; nor was it just an *idea*, a type or image that might have been useful in formulating a soteriology that 'really' consisted in something else. The point is that Jewish eschatology in the second-Temple period focused on the hope that that which had happened in the Babylonian exile, the triumph of paganism over Israel because of her sins, was still the dominant state of affairs, but would at last be undone. Ironically, at this point one normal would-be Christian viewpoint – that the Bible contains proof-texts for a time-less and non-historical system of salvation – has combined with the non-eschatological viewpoint of the post-135 rabbis to mislead those who come from either tradition of reading. If we are to be historians of Jesus' own period we must think our way back from those subsequent rereadings to the very historically concrete worldview of the second-Temple period itself. This whole point of view is presupposed in what follows, and it will, I think, be very substantially supported by the excellent sense it makes of a good deal of the tradition about Jesus. I must stress, in particular, that when I say 'end of exile' and similar things I am not attempting to reduce everything to a single theme. Rather, I use the phrase as a shorthand, wishing thereby to draw attention to the richly textured and many-layered second-Temple Jewish expectation that Israel's god would once again act *within her history*.

IV

To acknowledge all the help I have received in the many years of writing this book would be impossible. But some debts must be noted specifically.

George Caird was my teacher during my doctoral years at Oxford. During the time I studied with him we always talked about Paul, never about Jesus;

---

[7] e.g. *1 En.* 89.73–7; *Ass. Mos.* 4.5—6.9; 1QpHab. 9.3–7; 12.7–9; 4QTest. 25–30. Cf. e.g. Rowland 1991.

but, when I later came to look more seriously at the gospels, it was his little book *Jesus and the Jewish Nation*[8] that provided the clue to a fresh line of thought. Alas, we had only one exchange of letters between my thinking these thoughts after him and his tragically early death. He would certainly not have agreed with all my conclusions, but I would certainly not have reached them without his work.

Another remarkable scholar who is no longer with us, but whose influence on me will be obvious, is Ben Meyer. News of his death, after a long illness, reached me as I was bringing this book to completion. His writings, friendship, example and encouragement remain as a wonderful legacy of Christian scholarship.

Professor Charlie Moule has generously read a good deal that I have written over the years, including various parts of this book. His comments have always been shrewd, wise, learned and extremely helpful – even where I persist in disagreeing with him. Bishop Rowan Williams discussed most of the relevant issues with me when we taught a seminar together on Jesus in the late 1980s; there are many things I know I learned from him, and I suspect there are many others that I have made my own without acknowledgment. Professor Oliver O'Donovan discussed many of the issues with me over a number of years, providing wisdom and learning of a sort otherwise unavailable, at least to me. The Reverend Michael Lloyd and Dr Brian Walsh have likewise discussed the subject-matter of the book with me on many occasions, and have given invaluable help and support. The (then) Dean of St George's Cathedral, Jerusalem, the Very Reverend Hugh Wybrew, provided me with a room in his flat, and sustained me with cheerful friendship and encouragement, during the summer of 1989 when the main first draft of the book, along with *NTPG*, was written. Large sections of the typescript were read at that stage by Professors Paul Achtemeier and Richard Hays, and Dr Francis Watson, all of whom made very helpful comments.

My stay in Jerusalem was made possible by the generosity of the Leverhulme Trust, without whose financial help this book would not have been able to take proper shape. I am grateful, too, to Oxford University, and to Worcester College, for granting me the two sabbaticals, in 1989 and 1993, when a good deal of the spadework for the book was done; and to the Revds Michael Lloyd and Andrew Moore, and Dr Susan Gillingham, who looked after the different aspects of my job in my absence.

Other friends and colleagues have helped notably in various ways. Some have read and commented on bits of the book; some have discussed it with me in public. In the former category, I think particularly of Drs Anthony

---

[8] Caird 1965. Much of the substance of this has found its way into Caird and Hurst 1994.

Cummins, Andrew Goddard, Sylvia Keesmaat, Thorsten Moritz, and Peter Head, the Revd Grant LeMarquand, and Professor Walter Wink; in the latter, of Professors Marcus Borg, Colin Brown, Christopher Rowland, Ed Sanders, Dominic Crossan, John Riches, Paula Fredriksen, John P. Meier, and Elisabeth Schüssler Fiorenza. None of them, of course, is responsible for the result; some will be frustrated that I did not listen more closely to their advice. I am deeply grateful to them all.

The chance to try out parts of the material on audiences in Bonn, Cambridge, Durham, Jerusalem, Lichfield, London, Los Angeles, Montreal, Oxford, Sheffield, Toronto, Vancouver, and several other locations in Britain and North America has been wonderfully stimulating and challenging. I am deeply grateful to audiences in all of these places for their questions, criticisms and encouragement. I have been overwhelmed by the support of many around the world who have written to me following the publication of *NTPG* and my popular-level book *Who Was Jesus?* They have sustained me at many times when the present task seemed massive and daunting. I hope they will not be too disappointed with the result.

In the detailed labour of research, Jayne Cummins, Elisabeth Goddard, Lucy Duffell, Kathleen Miles, Catherine Wilson, and Alison Taylor have all helped at various stages. I wish once again to record my deep gratitude to the friends around the world who provided the funds to make such assistance possible.

I never expected to be moving house, and job, in the final stages of writing this book. Nor, when the move was decided upon, did I foresee (despite what some of my friends said to me) the extent of the delay in the present project that would result. I am grateful to the Canons of Lichfield Cathedral, to the Cathedral administration, particularly Mr David Wallington, and to the many others who have enabled me to make the transition to a totally new type of work, and who have encouraged me, difficult though it has been, to fulfil the expectations of those who appointed me by continuing with serious research and writing. The support and inspiration I have received from the Bishop of Lichfield, the Right Reverend Keith Sutton, is beyond praise.

I must again thank the staff of SPCK and Fortress, especially Mr Philip Law, Mr Simon Kingston, and Dr Marshall Johnson, for their enthusiasm for the whole project, their help in carrying it forward, and their remarkable patience with its delays. Mr David Mackinder's copy-editing has once again sharpened up the text, and saved me from numerous infelicities. I must also pay tribute to Steve Siebert and his colleagues, who produce the *Nota Bene* software which has greatly streamlined the process of writing and producing a complex work such as this.

V

The book is dedicated, with the author's gratitude and love, to his wife. She has borne its griefs and carried its sorrows for a long time, and has continued, despite everything, to be enthusiastic and encouraging about it. She has given to this work far more than I (and probably it) deserve, and certainly more than these words can hope to indicate.

N. T. Wright

The Deanery, Lichfield
14 August 1996

With a further reprinting of the book, I have taken the opportunity to correct a few small misprints. I am grateful to those who have pointed them out to me.

N. T. W.
1 May 1999

Part One

Introduction

Chapter One

JESUS THEN AND NOW

1. Angels, Giants and Jigsaws

The silhouette has obvious advantages over the full-face portrait. It is appealing and evocative. The onlooker needs room for imagination, and loses interest if the artist leaves no room for it. This is perhaps partly why, in our century, most scholars who have concerned themselves with Jesus have shied away from the classical attempts at full-face portraits. They were not only massively anachronistic, busily dressing Jesus in borrowed, and highly unsuitable, clothes. They proved too much; they left (it seemed) no room for imagination, reflection, or even perhaps for faith. Not merely wrong: boring.

In their place, we have seen a new kind of *via negativa*:

He comes to us as one unknown . . .[1]

I do indeed think that we can now know almost nothing concerning the life and personality of Jesus . . .[2]

Jesus Christ in fact is . . . historically so difficult to get information about . . .[3]

The form of the earthly no less than of the heavenly Christ is for the most part hidden from us . . . we trace in [the gospels] but the outskirts of his ways.[4]

No one is any longer in the position to write a life of Jesus.[5]

There should be no mistaking the evocative, dramatic power of the silhouettes thus produced. They cannot be dismissed as the products merely of cynical unbelief. They appear to possess the proper, indeed reverent, caution of the angel rather than the blundering haste of the fool (in this case, the

---

[1] Schweitzer 1954 [1906], 401.
[2] Bultmann 1958a [1926], 8.
[3] Barth 1936–1969, 1.1.188.
[4] Lightfoot 1935, 225.
[5] Bornkamm 1960 [1956], 13. Compare Bowden 1988, 32: 'There is a good deal that we probably do know about Jesus; the trouble is that we can rarely, if ever, be sure precisely what it is.' For discussion of individual writers, see below.

heavy-handed historian). Just as many Jewish scholars have preferred to study Talmud rather than Tanakh, the rabbis instead of the Bible, so twentieth-century Christian theologians have expended more and more energy on the early church and less and less upon Jesus. It appeared, after all, safer.

This almost instinctive, and quite understandable, reticence has been considerably fortified by a whole string of other more subtle motivations. Albert Schweitzer was passionately concerned to restore the conception of Jesus' *'overwhelming historical greatness'* against those who, like Renan and Schopenhauer, had 'stripped off his halo and reduced him to a sentimental figure'.[6] Schweitzer tore down the sentimental portraits of Jesus and, like a revolutionary replacing the monarch's portrait on the schoolroom wall with that of the new leader, put up instead the sharp, indeed shocking, drawing of Jesus the towering prophetic genius, the enigmatic hero-figure, totally unlike 'modern man', yet strangely summoning him to follow in the noble path that would bring in the kingdom. One might point out that Blake had said similarly iconoclastic things eighty years before; but now it was being said by a highly learned and respected teacher in one of the strongholds of academic theology.[7]

Bultmann wrestled mightily with the multiple ambiguities of German theology after the First World War, and achieved the status of a prince among exegetes, even if his theology limps as a result of the struggle. He and his followers in their way, and Barth in his, found this Jesus too remote, and actually a *misguided* hero (since he hoped for a kingdom that never came). They therefore determined to strip off the layers of paint which even Jesus himself, as a child of his time, could not help superimposing on his real message, and to uncover the original fresco, which turned out to be a message whose etiolated content seemed to be a necessary condition of its required timelessness: a constant invitation from the creator to live in faith and obedience, open to the future. With that, the bulk of the gospel records can safely be put on one side as relevant merely for establishing the views of the early church or the evangelists, whose apparent desire to express their faith by telling stories about Jesus we cannot, or must not, emulate.[8] The powerful theological constructs of Barth and Bultmann formed an alliance with the fears of ordinary people as to what might happen to orthodox

---

[6] Schweitzer 1925 [1901], 274; italics original.

[7] See Blake, *The Everlasting Gospel* [c. 1818], in Bronowski 1958, 73–86, containing the memorable couplet: 'I am sure this Jesus will not do/ Either for Englishman or Jew' (84). (It perhaps needs adding that Blake's own Jesus was highly idiosyncratic and imaginary.)

[8] See esp. Bultmann 1958a [1926], 1958b, 1968 [1921]. For recent treatments cf. Thiselton 1980, chs. 8–10; Painter 1987; Jones 1991; Fergusson 1992.

Christianity if history was scrutinized too closely. The icon and the silhouette ruled, and ruled powerfully, at the popular and at the academic level.[9]

Schweitzer and Bultmann are of vital, if negative, importance to contemporary work on the New Testament. This is not merely because of their direct influence. Schweitzer, in fact, has never had a 'school' of disciples. One could argue that he deserved one more than Bultmann, whose children and grandchildren are yet with us, reinforcing their ancestral heritage by telling and retelling their story (sometimes wrongly called 'the history of modern New Testament Studies' or some such) as though it were the only family story, or tracing, in the fashion of those Jewish apocalyptic works they are so careful to disdain, the line of great events from the founding of their clan up to the present moment, when by implication the final revelation is about to dawn in some grand seminar or colloquium. No: Schweitzer and Bultmann are important because they saw, arguably more clearly than anyone else this century, the fundamental shape of the New Testament jigsaw, and the nature of the problems involved in trying to put it together. They thus established fundamental hypotheses for lesser lights to test, elaborate and modify. They are the giants, a pair of Colossi bestriding the narrow world of learned articles, seminar papers, and textual variants.

The jigsaw they perceived is first and foremost an historical one. The oddity of this particular puzzle consists in the fact that the shape of the pieces is indeterminate: each must be cut and trimmed to fit with the others, with none being automatically exempt from the process. The outside limits – themselves a matter of fierce debate – are pre-Christian Judaism and the second-century church; and the puzzle involves fitting together the bits in the middle to make a clear historical sequence all the way across. How did this new movement arise, and why did it arise in this way? The central pieces are, of course, John the Baptist (or does he belong with pre-Christian Judaism?), Jesus, the earliest church, Paul, the churches he and others founded, and the other writers of the New Testament, particularly John (or do some of them belong with the second-century church?). The way in which we shape any one bit of the puzzle will determine, and/or be determined by, the shape we give the others. What we say about Jesus is thus inextricably intertwined with what we say about the first century as a whole. That is why I dealt with the first century in some detail in *NTPG* Parts III and IV.

Twentieth-century scholarship has at least one great advantage over its predecessors. Since Weiss and Schweitzer at the turn of the century, it has been realized that Jesus must be understood in his Jewish context. The only

---

[9] See the accounts of this period in e.g. Baillie 1948, 34–9; Tatum 1982, 71–4.

sense in which the old nineteenth-century 'Quest' had really attempted this was by producing a sharp contrast. The Jews had the wrong sort of religion; Jesus came to bring the right sort.[10] The game was then to cut off all those bits of the 'Jesus' piece that appeared too Jewish, too ethnically restricted, leaving the hero as the founder of a great, universal, 'spiritual' religion, so nobly recaptured now by Protestantism, at least since Kant and Hegel. The other bits of the puzzle would then drop into place. Weiss and Schweitzer, however, rightly insisted that the historical jigsaw must portray Jesus as a credible and recognizable first-century Jew, relating comprehensibly in speech and action to other first-century Jews. No solution which claims to be talking about history can ever undo this basic move.

But what does it involve? Here there is still no agreement. We shall see below that the relation of Jesus to his Jewish context is the first question that faces any serious attempt to understand him historically. I shall suggest that there are possibilities that have not been sufficiently explored, and which can give a more rigorously historical shape to the central piece of the jigsaw and, ultimately, a new and more satisfactory solution to the entire puzzle.

The giants who set us this puzzle, and offered such cautious and apparently negative answers to it themselves, were not interested in history simply for its own sake. Though several scholars have claimed to write as 'mere historians', there is, as we saw in *NTPG*, no such thing as 'mere history'. Schweitzer and Bultmann both had in mind a reconstruction of first-century Christian origins which would possess significance for contemporary Christian faith and life. Schweitzer's Jesus set the example for all those who (like Schweitzer himself) would devote themselves to the cause of the kingdom, crazy though it might seem. History itself, in which Jesus' message was an apparent failure, prompts us (he said) to take this unhistorical step of active reinterpretation.[11] Schweitzer thus anticipated by a matter of decades one key element in Bultmann's famous 'demythologization' programme: the historical husk of the 'real' message must be identified *and then thrown away*. But if for Schweitzer Jesus was 'as one unknown', one could be forgiven for thinking that for Bultmann he was even less: Bultmann's Jesus was

[10] Contrast Reimarus 1970 [1778], who set Jesus in his Jewish revolutionary context, casting him as an unsuccessful would-be reformer, and tried to keep him there.

[11] Schweitzer 1954 [1906], 249ff. See esp. 251f.: 'Theology is not bound to graze in a paddock. It is free, for its task is to found our Christian view of the world solely upon the personality of Jesus Christ, irrespective of the form in which it expressed itself in his time. He himself has destroyed this form with his death. History prompts theology to this unhistorical step.' The question of whether Schweitzer succeeded in Christianizing Nietzsche's idea of the Superman is worth pursuing, but not here; see O'Neill 1991a, ch. 19. Weiss (1971 [1892]), too, portrays Jesus as a Jewish apocalyptic prophet, while retaining for himself a fundamentally Ritschlian liberal theology.

'unknown' in the sense that one could not know his 'personality' at all, whereas for Schweitzer it was precisely his 'personality' that was unexpectedly shocking. Schweitzer claimed that his predecessors had painted the portrait wrong; Bultmann, that no portrait was possible. Bultmann therefore drew his silhouette: Jesus the preacher of existentialist decision, calling to all those who (like Bultmann himself) lived in the midst of social chaos, and who needed to trust and follow their god day by day without being able to see, in the darkness of the present, what was going to happen in the future. Both Schweitzer and Bultmann, to complete their schemes, needed to show how Paul in particular had taken Christianity in the form in which Jesus left it (about which they disagreed) and had made it relevant for the gentile world.

Even where neither of these solutions has held any appeal, almost every book on Jesus has carried the implicit presupposition that when we 'really' find what Jesus was like we will have discovered the pearl of great price, the buried treasure that will set us up for life – even if the treasure turns out to be the truth that Jesus was quite an ordinary and unremarkable person and that we are thus set free from the church's arrogant claims about him. History, not least this bit of history, can never be done in a vacuum. There is thus a second jigsaw, connected somehow or other to the first, consisting this time of the questions asked not only by Christians but by all who seek a worldview which might include so obviously attractive a figure as Jesus: what should we believe, and how should we behave, in the modern world? I have no desire to avoid, or to pretend to be uninterested in, such questions; I shall attempt to address them when appropriate. But we must recognize that, for all the necessary interconnections, they are not the *same* questions as the first ones.[12]

The legacy of the giants has meant, however, that the relation between the two jigsaws ('Who was Jesus?' and 'So what?') appears very tenuous. *That* we must relate them is clear (at least, to all writers on the subject known to me, without exception): *how* we are to do so is not. This has meant a lot of split-level writing about Jesus. A good example is the massive book of Edward Schillebeeckx, who spends hundreds of pages investigating a merely human Jesus, only to move at the end, without much help from the preceding argument, to a confession of faith in Jesus as the Son of God.[13] It is a measure of the extent to which the split between history and theology has dominated recent western Christian thought that writers of all shades of opinion, from extreme orthodox to extreme radical, have tacitly affirmed that it is difficult, if not impossible, to hold the two together, especially in talking

---

[12] I have explored some of the links between them in *NTPG* ch. 1.
[13] Schillebeeckx 1979 [1974], 575–674.

about Jesus.[14] Either we 'know' ahead of time that Jesus is 'divine' (it is usually assumed that the force of this predicate is already understood), in which case the writing of the history of his life 'must' reflect this fact: the portrait then becomes an icon, useful for devotion but probably unlike the original subject. Alternatively, we commit ourselves to ruthless historical investigation, and expect, whether gladly or fearfully, that we will thereby 'disprove', or at least seriously undermine, orthodox theology. If we dislike these two options, we can still withdraw to the silhouette, lest we compromise or damage our faith; or we can leap, without explanation, from one side to the other. The underlying argument of this book is that the split is not warranted: that rigorous history (i.e. open-ended investigation of actual events in first-century Palestine) and rigorous theology (i.e. open-ended investigation of what the word 'god', and hence the adjective 'divine', might actually refer to) belong together, and never more so than in discussion of Jesus. If this means that we end up needing a new metaphysic, so be it. It would be pleasant if, for once, the historians and the theologians could set the agenda for the philosophers, instead of vice versa.[15]

A note must be entered at this point, echoing an argument advanced in *NTPG* Part II. It is often suggested that 'faith' must bridge the gap between what can be known or 'proved' by 'history' and what 'must be true' if Christianity is to survive – or, *mutatis mutandis*, if it is to be modified or transformed. History, it is said, can take us only so far; we have to travel the rest of the journey by faith. But this is a misconception. All history involves imaginative reconstruction. We seldom, if ever, 'know' enough, in terms of positive indubitable proof, to give the kind of account we want to give of any period, incident or character from the past. There is always a leap to be made between the actual evidence and the fully-blown reconstruction. This move *could* be called 'faith'; but it has very little to do with any specifically Christian meaning of that word. The really interesting relation, then, is not between 'history' (conceived positivistically as a provable series of events, a collection of mathematically certain data) and 'faith' (conceived as a leap in

---

[14] See, among recent writers, Hick 1993.

[15] By 'open-ended investigation' I mean an investigation whose results are not determined in advance, not an investigation that might in principle go on until midnight or beyond, though the latter might be true as well. It may be as well to note here that the picture often painted by both exegetes and theologians, in which the exegetes do the 'neutral, objective' historical work, and pass on their results to the theologians, is completely without warrant. What this usually means in practice is that the exegetes are unaware of their own presuppositions, and that the theologians simply choose to employ those exegetical 'results' which are conditioned by the very philosophical or theological beliefs they are invoked to support. For examples at rather different levels, cf. Macquarrie 1990, Hick 1993; for a way out of this dilemma, see *NTPG* Part II.

the dark over the gap where such data is not available). It is between real history, in all its complexity of hypothetical reconstruction, and real faith, in all its glory as the constant exploration of, and trust in, a god whom Christians believe to be, among other things, intimately and passionately involved in the historical process itself. And that relationship (between real history and real faith) is not something that can be settled in advance of the quest as a whole. It must be left to be explored as the actual historical task gets under way.

Whether we like it or not, then, we are all heirs and successors to the giants and their jigsaws. If we renounce the apparent angelic caution of their classic silhouettes, it is not because we reject their questions but because we choose to take seriously the apparently foolish road of historical investigation. We are, in due awareness of the risks involved, attempting a portrait. I have argued in *NTPG* that this is not in fact so foolish as twentieth-century scholarship has usually thought. As we shall see, there are today more fools of this sort than there have been for some while; I shall be in good company for much of the journey. To those who still say, enlarging somewhat the scope of Nathanael's objection to the provenance of the Messiah, 'Can any good thing come out of History?', the best answer I can give is Philip's: 'Come and see.'[16]

An alternative metaphor could be found in one of Jesus' best-known stories. The wastrel son, representing the Enlightenment, has rejected traditional Christian orthodoxy, and has set off for the apparently far country of historical scepticism. The elder brother, representing the would-be 'orthodox' Christian who has never troubled much with history and has never abandoned traditional belief, is both angry and suspicious. But supposing the younger brother suddenly comes home again? Supposing – even more shocking – that there is to be a celebration of his return?

Among the modern elder brothers are those who insist on neither a portrait nor a silhouette, but (as I hinted a moment ago) an icon. The Divine Saviour to whom they pray has only a tangential relationship to first-century Palestine, and they intend to keep it that way. He can, it seems, be worshipped, but if he ever actually lived he was a very strange figure, clothed in white while all around wore drab, on his face a perpetual faraway expression

---

[16] Jn. 1.46. At a late stage in the production of this book there appeared Johnson 1995, which does its best to hold history and theology apart. It would take us too far afield to enter into detailed debate with Johnson in the present work. Suffice it to note that when he speaks of the 'fateful link' between history and theology (69), the opposition between the 'historical' and the 'real', or the disjunction of 'fact' and 'meaning' (160), I find myself in such total disagreement that I wonder if we are even talking the same language. In one sense, actually, we are not; Johnson limits 'history' and its cognates to 'that which people write about the past' rather than 'that which happened in the past' (cf. *NTPG* ch. 4, esp. 81f.).

of pious solemnity. This icon was one means by which Victorian devotion tried to cope with Enlightenment rationalism, though arguably its use conceded the main point at issue (the non-identity of Jesus with the worshipped Christ). Sometimes such a view is combined with a form of the silhouette-view, 'We worship the icon ("the Christ of Faith") because we know that, if we look for the portrait ("the Jesus of History"), there is nothing more to be had than an irrelevant silhouette, or, worse, a misleading pseudo-picture.'[17] At a popular level, the icon is sustained by an ahistorical reading of the gospels (so that, for instance, the phrase 'son of god' is read as if the disciples, and indeed Caiaphas at the trial, understood it in the fully Nicene sense, and 'son of man' is regarded as simply referring to Jesus' 'humanity' as opposed to his 'divinity'). It is true, of course, that icons can sustain faith when other aids fail. But they must never be mistaken for the real thing. Real iconographers know this, and paint accordingly. My task is not to outlaw iconography, but (among other things) to remind it of what it is, and is not.

This book, then, is unashamedly about Jesus. The question 'who was Jesus?' has taxed people's minds and imaginations a good deal of late: in theatre and cinema, in scholarship and popular writing, sketches and portraits have been pouring out, mostly more or less alarming to the ordinary Christian, who prefers the icon or the silhouette that the mainline theologians (or some of them) have supplied.[18] Jesus is almost universally approved of, but for very different and indeed often incompatible reasons. He is wheeled in to give support to social or political programmes of one persuasion or another, to undergird strict morality here or to offer freedom from constricting regulations there. But the question as to *which* Jesus we are talking about will not go away.[19] Nor will the impression that this question contains the deeper question as to which *god* we are talking about. That is why, as we shall see presently, the question of Jesus has in some way or other been of vital importance in modern theology and church life. An appeal to him is thought to settle a dispute, even if only by implication.

But when both parties in the dispute make the appeal, where can they turn for Solomonic judgment? The point of having Jesus at the centre of a religion or a faith is that one has *Jesus*: not a cypher, a strange silhouetted Christ-figure, nor yet an icon, but the one Jesus the New Testament writers know, the one born in Palestine in the reign of Augustus Caesar, and crucified out-

[17] See the interesting polemic against 'historical Jesus' research in C. S. Lewis' famous *Screwtape Letters*, no. 23 (Lewis 1955 [1942]). For a recent example of a similar position, cf. Johnson 1995; in a more cautious form, Schnackenburg 1995 [1993].

[18] I first wrote this sentence in 1989; the events of 1992 merely confirmed it (see Wright 1992c, and the 'popular' writers there discussed); the story continues.

[19] See Bowden 1988, *passim*.

side Jerusalem in the reign of his successor Tiberius. Christianity appeals to history; to history it must go.[20] The recognition that the answers we may find might change our views, or even our selves, cannot and must not prevent us from embarking on the quest.

2. Procedure

We shall begin, in the rest of this chapter, with a brief review of some of the significant writing on Jesus within the last hundred or so years. This story has been told many times, and I have comparatively little to add to what has been written elsewhere.[21] However, the outline is necessary, both to give orientation to those coming to the subject for the first time and to show old hands where my suggested hypothesis fits on the map. I shall then, in the second and third chapters, home in on the last twenty years or so of scholarship. Here there has been an impressive turning of the tide, away from the *via negativa* and towards historical realism, though often enough with a differently negative result: the full-face portraits are now commonplace, but we search in vain in several of them for an explanation of why the early church not only revered Jesus' memory but made striking and unique claims about him. This will lead us, in the fourth chapter, to examine, by means of an initial study of a single parable, some of the key issues which will occupy us in the rest of the book. These four chapters complete Part I, clearing the ground for the positive reconstruction which follows.

The second and third Parts form the bulk of the book, and consist of a step-by-step argument about Jesus' ministry. I shall argue, first, that Jesus' public persona within first-century Judaism was that of a prophet, and that the content of his prophetic proclamation was the 'kingdom' of Israel's god. This is discussed at some length in Part II, in terms of the categories developed in *NTPG*: praxis (chapter 5), story (chapters 6–8), symbol (chapter 9) and question (chapter 10). With this, we trace the fundamental contours of Jesus' mindset, his own particular variation on the overarching first-century Jewish worldview.[22] Here a good deal of the material in the synoptic

---

[20] See Caird 1965, 3: 'Anyone who believes that in the life and teaching of Christ God has given a unique revelation of his character and purpose is committed by this belief, whether he likes it or not, whether he admits it or not, to the quest of the historical Jesus.'

[21] cf. the note at the start of section 3 below.

[22] I am well aware, as *NTPG* Part III demonstrates, that first-century Judaism is a highly complex and pluriform entity. This does not mean (cf. *NTPG* 118f.) that it does not possess an overall worldview which distinguishes it from first-century paganism. For there to be many 'Judaisms', there must still be something, however generalized, that one can call 'Judaism'. Nor does the recognition of this worldview mean that we are lapsing back into the caricature of *Spätjudentum*, 'late Judaism', after the manner of some earlier scholarship. The

gospels comes up for initial review. I shall then argue (Part III) that, within this public proclamation, and this basic mindset, Jesus held to a complex but thoroughly coherent network of aims and beliefs. There was not just one 'Messianic secret', as has sometimes been imagined, but three interlocking secrets. The first of these, his belief about his own role *vis-à-vis* Israel (chapter 11), the disciples more or less grasped. The second, his belief about how his mission would be achieved, they did not, though Jesus tried to teach it to them (chapter 12). The third secret, Jesus' belief about himself, could not even be spoken except under a thick veil. We can, however, hypothesize that Jesus himself held this belief, on the grounds of actions which make sense only on this assumption (chapter 13).

This historical argument leads us to the moment of Jesus' death. The historian must then face the question: why did the early church begin, and why did it take the shape it did? I initially intended to address this topic, not least the whole question of Easter, in the present volume. Space, or rather the lack of it, has decreed that it be postponed for the time being. I do not think this weakens the argument of the rest of the book, which is after all about Jesus' mindset, aims and beliefs prior to the crucifixion.

There remains the awesome task of suggesting ways in which this historically particular, timebound and in some ways alien portrait of Jesus can be relevant for the church and world of a later day. (Some will see the raising of this question as a sign of academic weakness. I can only say that all writers about Jesus I have ever read know that their work has contemporary relevance, one way or another, and that it is better to face the fact than to pretend to a spurious detachment or 'objectivity'.) Having lived with this as a serious problem for many years, I now feel that I see some ways at least in which the necessary moves can be made, and I shall hint in the concluding chapter of this book at the way in which they might begin, in the hope that sooner or later I may be able to develop them further.[23]

It may be that some will have different interpretative suggestions to make, even if they follow my historical argument. I shall welcome such suggestions; my own conclusions are somewhat worrying for my liking. I hope their uncomfortableness (to myself at least) is a measure of the seriousness with which I have attempted the task of thinking through the argument wherever it may lead. This ambition is sometimes caricatured: the irresponsible academic dreaming up arguments in an ivory tower. But precisely when 'taking the argument as far as it will go' forces one to look beyond the ivory tower and into the purposes of the creator for the world as a

---

possibility of spurious analyses does not automatically render all analyses invalid.

[23] For a preliminary statement, cf. Wright 1992d.

whole, and to face the possibility that these purposes might call into question a good deal that comfortable academic theologians take for granted, the caricature seems less true to life. The very concern for actuality, for life in the 'real' world, which produces the objection in the first place, can scarcely be advanced *against* an argument that claims to take history, ancient as well as modern, with full seriousness.

We are thus committed to the historical argument. And, since it has been in full swing for some little while, it is necessary that we find out what has been going on.

3. The 'Quests' and their Usefulness[24]

(i) Jesus Through History

Since Schweitzer, it has been customary to think that the 'Quest of the Historical Jesus' began with Hermann Samuel Reimarus in the eighteenth century. There is some truth in that. But quite a long time before Reimarus, and at least as important in the overall history of the subject, is the work and the theological position of the sixteenth-century reformers.[25] Despite their desire for a church based on 'scripture alone', and their insistence on the literal sense of those scriptures, it may be questioned whether they ever found a satisfactory way of making the literal sense of the *gospels* yield worthwhile theological results.[26] If what one needed was clear, 'timeless' doctrinal and ethical teaching, one must go (so it seemed) to the epistles. The gospels must then be turned into repositories of the same 'timeless truth'. This was achieved by treating them, not literally, as stories which were there for their own sake, but as collections of sayings of Jesus which then became, as it were, mini-epistles; or of events which showed the clash between false religion (here represented by sixteenth-century legalists or formalists thinly disguised as Pharisees) and the true one offered by Jesus. All this culminates, of course, in the event to which the gospels really do point, the death and resurrection of Jesus, which is to be understood not as the execution of an

[24] On this section see further, as a selection from an enormous range available: Schweitzer 1954 [1906]; Meyer 1979, ch. 2; Tatum 1982; Brown 1988 [1985]; Sanders 1985, 23–58; Neill & Wright 1988 [1964], 379–403; Wright 1992b. Reumann 1989, remarkably, manages virtually to ignore the serious work of the previous ten years. Many writers surveyed below have become subjects of research in their own right; it is impossible here to enter into discussion at this level. For detailed bibliography, see Evans 1989c.

[25] For all of the succeeding argument, see the standard treatments, e.g. Kümmel 1972/3 [1970].

[26] See *NTPG* 19f.; and cf. now Noble 1993.

awkward figure who refused to stop rocking the first-century Jewish or Roman boat, but as the saving divine act whereby the sins of the world were dealt with once and for all.

This divine act, however, did not have very much to do with what went before. The fact that the gospels reached their climax with the death of Jesus seemed to have little to do with any significance to be drawn from his life, except that the conflict he engendered by preaching about love and grace was the proximate reason for his death, which the redeemer god then 'counted' in a redemptive scheme which had nothing to do with that historical reason. The reformers had very thorough answers to the question 'why did Jesus die?'; they did not have nearly such good answers to the question 'why did Jesus live?' Their successors to this day have not often done any better. But the question will not go away. If the only available answer is 'to give some shrewd moral teaching, to live an exemplary life, and to prepare for sacrificial death', we may be forgiven for thinking it a little lame. It also seems, as we shall see, quite untrue to Jesus' own understanding of his vocation and work.

It would not, then, be much of a caricature to say that orthodoxy, as represented by much popular preaching and writing, has had no clear idea of the purpose of Jesus' ministry. For many conservative theologians it would have been sufficient if Jesus had been born of a virgin (at any time in human history, and perhaps from any race), lived a sinless life, died a sacrificial death, and risen again three days later. (In some instances the main significance of this would be the conclusion: the Bible is all true.) The fact that, in the midst of these events, Jesus actually said and did certain things, which included giving wonderful moral teaching and annoying some of his contemporaries, functions within this sort of orthodox scheme merely as a convenience. Jesus becomes a composite figure, a cross between Socrates defeating the Sophists and Luther standing up against the Papists. His ministry and his death are thus loosely connected. The force of this is lost, though, when the matter is thought through. If the main purpose of Jesus' ministry was to die on the cross, as the outworking of an abstracted atonement-theology, it starts to look as though he simply took on the establishment in order to get himself crucified, so that the abstract sacrificial theology could be put into effect. This makes both ministry and death look like sheer contrivance.

For the same reasons, as we have already suggested, the reformers and their successors have seemed to be much better exponents of the epistles than of the gospels. Although Luther and the others did their best to grasp the meaning of (say) Galatians as a whole, and to relate it to their contemporary setting, little attempt was made to treat (say) Matthew in the same way, or to ask what the evangelists thought they were doing in not merely collecting interesting and useful material about Jesus but actually stringing it together in what looks for all the world like a continuous narrative, a story. My later argument will, I hope, indicate that these two weaknesses – the failure to ask about the theological significance of the ministry of Jesus, and the failure to treat the gospels with full seriousness as they stand, that is, as *stories* – are among the chief causes of much present confusion, and that they can and must be remedied.

The reformers, then, focused not on the Jesus of history for his own sake, but on the results, the 'benefits', of his work. 'This is to know Christ, to know his benefits . . . unless one knows why Christ took upon himself human flesh and was crucified, what advantage would accrue from having learned his life's history?'[27] Though this does not exactly say that one cannot or must not 'learn his life's history', it certainly directs attention away from it, and towards an abstract – and therefore, it seems, a more easily applicable – doctrine of incarnation and atonement. The emphasis on the *pro me* of the gospel seemed to be threatened by the specificity, the historical unrepeatableness, of the gospels. Some of the reformers, at least, intended, and all effected, a break with history: they founded essentially new churches, in supposed continuity with Christ and the apostles (and perhaps the Fathers), but in decided discontinuity with the mediaeval church. Along with this there came about, at least in principle, another break with history, this time at the very heart of the faith. Continuity with Christ meant sitting loose to the actuality of Jesus, to his Jewishness, to his own aims and objectives. This is not the place to explore why the reformers made the moves they did, nor have I the competence for such an enquiry. Suffice it to note here that the claim of later Lutherans such as Kähler and Bultmann to be standing in the reformation tradition when they put forward the 'historic, biblical Christ' over against the 'so-called historical Jesus', or when they stripped away the layers of Jewish apocalyptic mythology to uncover the timeless call to decision, has solid ground under its feet. There may also be a disquieting note: a hint of the theologian spurning the historian, of the elder brother rejecting the rehabilitated prodigal.[28]

Within post-reformation circles, both Catholic and Protestant, there has been a general use of the gospels as sourcebooks for ethics and doctrine, for edifying tales or, smuggled in behind the back of the *sensus literalis*, allegory. What else was there to do with them? Attention was directed elsewhere: to the creation of 'Christian' societies, and their maintenance and

[27] Philipp Melanchthon, *Loci Communes*, 1521; in the English tr. of Melanchthon's Works, 2.7, (ed. Hill, 1944), 68. Cf. the one-volume edition of Melanchthon: 1982 [1555].
[28] See Kähler 1964 [1892], and the accounts in Kümmel 1972/3 [1970], 222–5; McGrath 1994 [1986], 111–14; cf. now Braaten 1994; Johnson 1995.

defence by argument and war; to the burning theological and practical issues of the day. For the church, which one way or another still held much of Europe in its control, Jesus was the divine Christ who redeemed the world and whose derivative authority, whether through pope or preacher, was exercised to the supposed benefit of that world. The icon was in place, and nobody asked whether the Christ it portrayed – and in whose name so much good and ill was done – was at all like the Jesus whom it claimed to represent. Nobody, that is, until Reimarus.

The hypothesis I shall propose shares the reformers' concern for theology, but not their uncertainty about the value of the history of Jesus' life in relation to the theological and hermeneutical task. From that point of view I cannot but welcome the rise of the critical movement, which drew the attention of the reformation churches to that history which had, for two centuries at least, been conveniently ignored.

(ii) The Rise of the Critical Movement: from Reimarus to Schweitzer

Reimarus (1694–1768) was the great iconoclast. His *Fragments* (published posthumously by Lessing in 1778) do not constitute the greatest of the 'Lives of Jesus' chronicled by Schweitzer, but he usually gets the credit for being the first to challenge the ruling myth, or at least the first whose challenge was heard.[29] As Colin Brown has recently shown, Reimarus himself must be seen in the light of English Deism, which created a favourable climate for the questioning upon which he embarked.[30] He was not writing in, or to, a vacuum. He was, on the contrary, reacting sharply to the mainline tradition of his day. That tradition – of European Christianity, and particularly continental Protestantism – had its own view of Jesus and the gospels, and Reimarus was determined to prove them wrong. His aim seems to have been to destroy Christianity (as he knew it) at its root, by showing that it rested on historical distortion or fantasy. Jesus was a Jewish reformer who became increasingly fanatical and politicized; and he failed. His cry of dereliction on the cross signalled the end of his expectation that his god would act to support him.

[29] cf. Reimarus 1970 [1778], and the discussions in Schweitzer 1954 [1906], 13–26; Meyer 1979, 27–31; Brown 1988 [1985], ch. 1.

[30] See Brown 1988 [1985], chs. 1–3; and Kümmel 1972/3 [1970], 51ff. English Deism in the late C17 and early C18 created a climate of anti-supernaturalism, in which the NT was seen as wrong in some respects, and Jesus was understood to be bringing the true spiritual religion over against the hidebound Jews. The work of Semler and Michaelis, and particularly Lessing, in the late C18 suggested that the NT was only relevant for its time: real religion was somewhere else, not in history (Kümmel 62–73, with references and full quotations).

The disciples fell back on a different model of Messiahship, announced that he had been 'raised', and waited for their god to bring the end of the world. They too were disappointed, but instead of crying out in despair they founded the early Catholic church, which to Reimarus may have looked like much the same thing. The thesis is devastatingly simple. History leads away from theology. Cash out the ancestral inheritance, and you will end up feeding the pigs. Jesus was no more than a Jewish revolutionary; the gospels hushed this up in the interests of the new religion. Go back to the beginning, and you will find your faith (and the European way of life which was based on it) resting on a failed Messiah and a fraudulent gospel. The 'Quest' began as an explicitly anti-theological, anti-Christian, anti-dogmatic movement. Its initial agenda was *not* to find a Jesus upon whom Christian faith might be based, but to show that the faith of the church (as it was then conceived) could not in fact be based on the real Jesus of Nazareth.

We should be clear that the post-reformation church had laid itself wide open to this attack. Reimarus was simply exploiting the split between history and faith implicit in the emphasis of Melanchthon's dictum, quoted above. He claimed that the gospels were records of early Christian faith, not transcripts of history, and that when we study the actual history we discover a very different picture. It simply will not do to say that such a question ought not even to be raised. Schweitzer's objection to Reimarus was that he should not have thought of Jesus' eschatology in a purely political sense, though he was right to emphasize Jesus' claim that the hope of Israel was about to be fulfilled. My own objection would be similar, only wider: Jesus did not support the Jewish national resistance to Rome, but rather opposed it. But Jesus must certainly be understood within his own historical context. In so far as the reformers and their successors did not understand him thus, Reimarus, or somebody like him, must be seen, not just as a protester against Christianity, but, despite his intentions, as a true reformer of it. This is not to side with Reimarus and other Enlightenment thinkers against Christian orthodoxy; it is to acknowledge that the challenge of the Enlightenment might, despite itself, benefit Christianity as well as threatening it. The elder brother had better not be too snooty if and when the prodigal returns.

Let us be clear. People often think that the early 'lives of Jesus' were attempting to bring the church back to historical reality. They were not. They were attempting to show what historical reality really was, in order that, having glimpsed this unattractive sight, people might turn away from orthodox theology and discover a new freedom. One looked at the history in order then to look elsewhere, to the other side of Lessing's 'ugly ditch', to the eternal truths of reason unsullied by the contingent facts of everyday events, even extraordinary ones like those of Jesus.[31] The fascinating thing, looking back two hundred years later, is that the appeal to history against itself, as it were, has failed. History has shown itself to contain more than the idealists believed it could. It is in this sense that Reimarus was, despite himself, a genuine reformer of the faith. He pulled back the curtain, thinking to expose the poverty of Christian origins. But the invitation to look more closely, once issued, could not be withdrawn; and within the unpromising historical specificity of the story of Jesus we can now, I believe, discern after all the buried treasure of the gospel. We may have to sell all – not least Lessing's metaphysic – in order to be able to buy it; but the one thing we cannot do is to tug the veil back into place. Reimarus has, it seems, done us a great service. His historical approach may have had its faults, but the fault may ultimately be a happy one.

The same could not be said of all those who came between Reimarus and Schweitzer. Their story is well enough known, and often enough told, to need little elaboration here. The famous *Life of Jesus Critically Examined* of David Friedrich Strauss (1835) tried to bring Christianity into line with rationalism, and with speculative Hegelian philosophy, ruling out the miraculous by means of an *a priori* (and having no difficulty in showing that many of the orthodox rationalizations of miracles were simply laughable).[32] Ernest Renan's equally celebrated *Vie de Jésus* (1863) represents the high-point of the liberal 'lives', offering the world the pale and timeless Galilean whom the next generation would reject as too ephemeral, almost too effeminate, for the needs of a brave new age.[33]

It was Schweitzer himself, of course, who rejected the liberal portraits most sharply and effectively. For Schweitzer, Reimarus was right to see Jesus in the context of first-century Judaism, but wrong to see him as a

---

[31] There are two streams at least within the C19 'Quest', and it is no part of my present purpose to disentangle them. Some writers followed the Enlightenment's split of history from 'meaning'; others followed Hegel and Schleiermacher in criticizing this, though without thereby producing a better historical portrait of Jesus. On all this, see Brown 1988 [1985]; O'Neill 1991a; Theissen 1996.

[32] Strauss (1808–74): 'If I know myself rightly, my position in regard to theology is that what interests me in theology causes offence, and what does not cause offence is indifferent to me.' (Quotation, and discussion, in Kümmel 1972/3 [1970], 122).

[33] On Renan (1823–92) see the acid comments of Schweitzer 1954 [1906], 180–92: Renan's work 'lacks conscience' (quoting C. E. Luthardt); it is insincere; it offers, in place of an historical solution, 'the highly-coloured phrases of the novelist'; in order to feel at home in the New Testament, Renan 'must perfume it with sentimentality'. 'Men's attention was arrested, and they thought to see Jesus, because Renan had the skill to make them see blue skies, seas of waving corn, distant mountains, gleaming lilies, in a landscape with the Lake of Gennesareth for its centre, and to hear with him in the whispering of the reeds the eternal melody of the Sermon on the Mount' (191f.; 181). It was a Jesus like this which Nietzsche rejected, and which evoked from Swinburne the taunt of the 'pale Galilean'.

revolutionary. Instead, the first-century phenomenon which Jesus shared with his contemporaries was 'apocalyptic', the expectation of the imminent end of the world. Schweitzer's brilliant exposition and critique of the work of others is matched only by the daring and boldness of his own silhouette of Jesus. We cannot know him except by obeying his summons; he is the totally different Jesus, the Jesus unlike all our expectations. He believed himself to be the Messiah while the onlookers thought he might be Elijah; he confidently expected that his god would step in and bring the world to an end during the course of his ministry. He dreamed the impossible dream of the kingdom, bringing about the end of world history. When this did not happen, and the great wheel of history refused to turn, he threw himself upon it, was crushed in the process, but succeeded in turning it none the less. He thus took upon himself the Great Affliction which was to break upon Israel and the world. The bridge between his historical life and Christianity is formed by his *personality*: he towers over history, and calls people to follow him in changing the world. The very failure of his hopes sets them free from Jewish shackles, to become, in their new guise, the hope of the world. The main lines of Schweitzer's silhouette remain stark and striking nearly a century later.[34]

In a measure, Schweitzer succeeded. Almost all western thought about Jesus has taken his basic ideas on board in some way or another. In their very strangeness they carried, perhaps, more conviction than they should have done. People's attention was arrested, and they thought to see Jesus, because Schweitzer had the skill to make them see darkening apocalyptic skies, secrets being hidden and revealed, the strange shadow of a coming cataclysm, and the silhouette of a cross upon a hill, and to hear with him, in the strange summons to the disciples, the eternal vocation to obedience, conflict, suffering and, finally, knowledge. Those who have drawn back from the full implications of Schweitzer's Jesus have done so, perhaps, just as much because of the total demand such a Jesus makes as because the work failed to meet the exacting standards of historical scholarship. Many other works that have become far more popular fare no better by that criterion. The race is not always to the swift.

My own hypothesis stands in an ambiguous relation to the Old Quest; hardly surprising, considering the ambiguities inherent in that movement itself. On the one hand, the nineteenth-century writers were, in the main, attempting to meet the critical challenge by writing lives of Jesus which seemed to have some historical grounding and yet maintained a semblance of theological, or at least religious, significance. I too wish to write history

---

[34] See esp. Schweitzer 1954 [1906], 328–401; and cp. Schweitzer 1968a [1967], 68–130. For a recent discussion of Schweitzer's work see O'Neill 1991a, ch. 19.

without forgetting the possible 'meaning' the events may possess.[35] On the other hand, nineteenth-century historians frequently ignored the Jewishness of Jesus, trying as hard as they could to universalize him, to make him the timeless teacher of eternal verities. This strand of their work, which served the interests of the romantic-idealist interpretation of Jesus, means that very few of their historical judgments can now stand unaltered. I share their desire to do both history and theology; but their governing hermeneutical programme, and consequent historical method, mean that I cannot in the end proceed in the same direction as they did.

Schweitzer himself recognized very clearly that, at the turn of the century, the scholar researching into Jesus was faced with quite a stark choice. His label for this forms the title of his last main chapter: 'Thoroughgoing Scepticism and Thoroughgoing Eschatology'. Or, to put it personally, the choice between the view of William Wrede and that of Schweitzer himself.[36] Since this antithesis, in one form or another, still faces us at the end of the twentieth century, it is worth sketching it out a little more.

Wrede and Schweitzer both, in their own way, offered a development of Reimarus' basic position. Both thought that serious historical study of Jesus would come up with something very different to what mainstream orthodoxy had supposed or wanted.[37] But there the ways divided. Wrede's book on the 'Messianic secret' in Mark went further than Reimarus: all we know of Jesus is that he was a Galilean teacher or prophet who did and said some striking things and was eventually executed.[38] Mark's gospel, from which the others derive, is a theologically motivated fiction, devised from within an early church that had already substantially altered direction away from Jesus' own agenda. Schweitzer, however, while agreeing with Reimarus that Jesus belongs within his first-century Jewish context, insisted that the Jewish context that mattered was not revolution, but apocalyptic. On this basis he was able to include within his own sketch far more gospel material than Wrede, and to suggest a far more nuanced development from Jesus, through the early church, to the writing of the gospels.

Once the distinction between these two positions is fully grasped, we can understand the two main highways of critical writing about Jesus in the late

---

[35] See particularly *NTPG* ch. 4, esp. 109–18.

[36] Schweitzer 1954 [1906], ch. 19.

[37] So Schweitzer 329: 'Thoroughgoing scepticism and thoroughgoing eschatology may, in their union, either destroy, or be destroyed by modern historical theology; but they cannot combine with it and enable it to advance, any more than they can be advanced by it.' For theology not to recognize this would be foolish: 'Theology comes home to find the broker's marks on all the furniture and goes on as before quite comfortably, ignoring the fact it will lose everything if it does not pay its debts' (330).

[38] See Schweitzer's summary, 336.

twentieth century. The *Wredestrasse* insists that we know comparatively little about Jesus, and that the gospels, in outline and detail, contain a great deal that reflects only the concerns of the early church. The *Schweitzerstrasse* places Jesus within the context of apocalyptic Judaism, and on that basis postulates far more continuity between Jesus himself, the early church, and the gospels, while allowing of course for importantly different historical settings in each case. The two approaches are sufficiently distinct for us to be able to categorize current writings in two main groups, discussed respectively in chapters 2 and 3 below. Of course, these days the *Strasse* has in each case turned into an *Autobahn*, with a lot of people going, at different speeds, in a lot of different lanes and indeed directions.[39] This development, in turn, has spawned a good many side-roads, service-stations and picnic-areas. Several writers, also, have tried to erect new link-roads and junctions between the two main routes. But the distinction between them remains illuminating, as we shall see in due course. Do we know rather little about Jesus, with the gospels offering us a largely misleading portrait (Wrede)? Or was Jesus an apocalpytic Jewish prophet, with the gospels reflecting, within their own contexts, a good deal about his proclamation of the kingdom (Schweitzer)?

(iii) No Quest to New Quest: Schweitzer to Schillebeeckx

Schweitzer is thus the turning-point in the history of the 'Quest'. He demolished the old 'Quest' so successfully – and provided such a shocking alternative – that for half a century serious scholarship had great difficulty in working its way back to history when dealing with Jesus. This was the period of the great *via negativa*, when theologians applied to Jesus that tradition of reverent silence which in other traditions had been reserved for speaking about the one god.[40] Martin Kähler had already issued his protest in this direction in 1892: the preached Christ should be the focal point of theology, and if Jesus and hence the true god are to be known only through history, then the historians will become the priests.[41] (Instead, Kähler seems to leave

[39] I am grateful to Dominic Crossan for this development of the metaphor.

[40] This *via negativa* is odd. Earlier theologians, such as Aquinas, who used this (originally Neoplatonic) idea, tended then to stress that silence about the true god was compensated for by speech about Jesus (cp. Schillebeeckx 1979 [1974], 669; and, evocatively, Williams 1994, 101f.). But if we are to be silent about Jesus, of what shall we speak? It is clear, looking at the last hundred years, that quite definite answers have been given to this question; but we should not underestimate the novelty of the overall theological method thus emerging.

[41] Kähler (1964 [1892]) does not say that nothing can be known of Jesus: his criticism is aimed at those who think they can do history 'purely objectively', with no axe to grind. With this basic point I have, of course, no quarrel (see *NTPG* Part II); my disagreement with Kähler is at another level altogether, to do with his apparent downplaying of history.

the preacher in control.) In 1926 Bultmann published a book in which he discarded the apocalyptic trappings of the preaching of Jesus, and the 'wishful thinking about the world to come', and translated the eschatology of Jesus into the existentialist call for decision.[42] Like Schweitzer, he rejected the nineteenth-century liberal Protestant Jesus;[43] unlike Schweitzer, he insisted that Jesus' 'personality' could not be recovered from the records, and would in any case have been of no interest for theology.[44] The stories which looked like stories of the historical Jesus were mostly faith-statements about the 'risen Christ' read back into his lifetime, expressing therefore the current faith of the church rather than historical memory. In any case, Jesus shared the primitive and mythological outlook of his day, and one would have to get back behind that (by 'demythologization') if one wished to uncover the 'real' import of his message. The bridge between Jesus and the life of the church was then to be found simply in the preaching of the Word.[45] Bultmann trod the fine line between having no interest in the historical Jesus and wanting to keep him on his own side just in case. Separated from both his Jewish context and the post-Easter church (a separation reinforced by the 'criterion of dissimilarity'), such a Jesus is almost as lonely a figure as Schweitzer's, though for a different reason.

Bultmann in his way, and Karl Barth in his, ensured that little was done to advance genuine historical work on Jesus in the years between the wars. Attention was focused instead on early Christian faith and experience, in the belief that there, rather than in a dubiously reconstructed Jesus, lay the key to the divine revelation that was presumed to have taken place in early Christianity. Form-criticism, the tool usually associated with Bultmann, was not, at its heart, designed to find out about Jesus. It was part of the other great 'Quest', which still goes on despite being in principle even harder than the Quest for Jesus: the Quest for the Kerygmatic Church, the attempt to reconstruct movements of thought and belief in the first century, and in particular to recapture (in both senses) the early Christian faith.[46] The gospels are faith-documents, not history-books. The echoes of Melanchthon are not far away: Bultmann intended to direct attention to faith rather than 'bare facts'; but the echoes of Reimarus and Wrede are there too, in the distinction

---

[42] Bultmann 1958a [1926], 52. The book, ironically, was part of a series entitled 'Great Heroes of the Past', which was precisely how Bultmann thought one should *not* regard Jesus.

[43] Bultmann 93f., against ethical idealism.

[44] Schweitzer anticipated Bultmann in several ways, however: cf. Schweitzer 1954 [1906], 399f., including e.g. a 'Bultmannian' reading of 2 Cor. 5.16.

[45] Bultmann 218f. (the conclusion of the book).

[46] See *NTPG* Part IV, esp. ch. 14. Cf. Perrin 1970, 79: the locus of revelation is in the present.

between 'what really happened' and the beliefs of the church, including those of the gospel-writers. The difference is that Reimarus was directing attention to the history in order to undermine the theology. Bultmann, in effect, rejected the challenge by denying the premises. History had nothing to do with faith.[47]

Books about Jesus, of course, continued to be written. Some of them were, so to speak, nineteenth-century 'lives' written a little too late, not really taking Schweitzer's challenge on board. Others, exemplified by a scholar like T. W. Manson, attempted to take the historical questions seriously but without integrating the detailed work into a large picture that would have given direction to further study. In this phase too one might put the work of J. Jeremias and C. H. Dodd, neither of whom fit too easily into any of the 'movements' so beloved of scholars.[48] But, on the continent, it turned out that a vow of silence was not easy to maintain. Despite all the pressing theological reasons for not wanting to enquire about Jesus, the boldest of Bultmann's pupils realized that this time the master had gone too far. On 23 October 1953, Ernst Käsemann gave a now-famous lecture to a group of former Bultmann students on 'The Problem of the Historical Jesus', thereby beginning a significantly new phase, which quickly styled itself 'The New Quest for the Historical Jesus'.[49] Käsemann, aware (as in all his work) of the dangers of idealism and docetism, insisted that if Jesus was not earthed in history then he might be pulled in any direction, might be made the hero of any theological or political programme. Käsemann had in mind, undoubtedly, the various Nazi theologies which had been able, in the absence of serious Jesus-study in pre-war Germany, to construct a largely unJewish Jesus. Without knowing who it was who died on the cross, he said, there would be no solid ground for upholding the gospel of the cross in all its sharpness, which he saw as especially needed in post-war Germany. However, this very definite theological agenda, for all its worth (which would scarcely be questioned today), meant that the New Quest, ironically enough, did not represent a turning to history in the fullest sense. The best

[47] I have discussed this at various points in *NTPG*, e.g. ch. 4, and esp. p. 94. It is significant that many conservative critics who trumpet loud disapproval of Bultmann's anti-supernaturalism share his basic premise at this point.

[48] See Jeremias 1958 [1956], 1971; Dodd 1961 [1935], 1971 (for a famous account of a debate between Dodd and Tillich, cf. Dillistone 1977, 241-3). Probably here, too, belong Betz 1968 [1965]; Hengel 1981b [1968]; Goppelt 1981 [1975]; though these three are in other ways part of the 'Third Quest', as are Caird 1965, 1982 and Moule 1967. See below, ch. 3.

[49] ET in Käsemann 1964 [1960], 15-47. See the survey in Robinson 1959, and discussions in the more recent writers, e.g. Meyer 1979, 51-4; Sanders 1985, 34ff., Reumann 1989, 506ff.

known of the books to appear during this phase, that of G. Bornkamm, begins with words already quoted: 'No one is any longer in the position to write a life of Jesus.'

The main productions of the New Quest are, in fact, of little lasting value.[50] Its practitioners, or would-be practitioners, have not shaken off the outdated view of apocalyptic as meaning simply the expectation of the end of the world, in a crudely literalistic sense. Nor have they managed to escape from the constraining shackles of form- and tradition-criticism, which, being mainly designed to discover the early church, not Jesus himself, have caused considerable difficulty when it comes to serious historical reconstruction. For this reason, much time has been devoted to method, and in particular to discussing the appropriate criteria for reconstructing the life of Jesus – a concern which leads, with a sad inevitability, to books filled with footnotes, in which the trees are so difficult to discern that one never even glimpses the forest itself.[51] Attention has been focused on sayings of Jesus, both within and outside the synoptic tradition. This, again, is true to the reformation emphasis: the purpose of Jesus' life was to *say* things, to teach great truths in a timeless fashion. It was also true to idealist philosophy: what matters ultimately is ideas, not events.

One of the largest works from this period – that is, between Schweitzer and the Third Quest which has arisen in the last fifteen years – is that of the Dominican theologian Edward Schillebeeckx. His prodigious book on Jesus builds on the traditio-historical criticism whereby the synoptic gospels have been combed for evidence of this or that 'early Christian community', and between whose faith-statements glimpses of Jesus may emerge. Such an argument is necessarily both tortuous and tenuous, since different sets of traditio-historical critics will come out with different sets of answers. Schillebeeckx takes a position which is the mirror-image of Bultmann's: the resurrection accounts are stories from Jesus' lifetime, brought forwards. His eventual leap from a purely historical Jesus to the incarnate Son of God is based on little or nothing in the main part of the book itself.[52] He seems to lend considerable tacit support to the notion that history and theology are two worlds which must be kept entirely separate. His book bravely attempts to combine the multiple hypotheses required to postulate both a divided 'Q community', as a key matrix of early traditions, and some sort of normative theological interest. But his work seems to me to have shown the barrenness of the New

---

[50] Two substantial pieces of work which now look very dated are those of Perrin 1967 and Braun 1984 [1969].

[51] See the survey in Epp & MacRae 1989, part 2.

[52] Schillebeeckx 1979 [1974], Part Four.

Quest in just as devastating, though not as readable, a way as Schweitzer's did in relation to the Old.

Not that the New Quest is finished. (Perhaps I should state at this point that I do not actually believe in rigid 'periods' in the history of scholarship, except as heuristic aids to help us grasp currents of thought. In the present matter, it would be silly to imagine that all scholars suddenly gave up one kind of work and took up another – just as silly, in fact, as the impression given by many surveys of gospel scholarship this century, in which suddenly 'everyone' is doing form-criticism, redaction-criticism, or whatever.[53]) Followers of the Wrede-Bultmann line are numerous, and, after a comparatively quiet period in the 1980s, they are again back in business. They have not given up trying out the combinations and permutations of the master's arguments, endlessly discussing criteria, reconstructing Q, and, most recently, setting up a new Seminar. This work has now produced quite substantial results, and in the next chapter we must look at them in some detail. First, however, a summary of where we have got to so far.

(iv) Two Hundred Years of Questing

What did the Quest achieve in the two hundred years between Reimarus and Schillebeeckx? It put the historical question firmly and irrevocably on the theological map, but without providing a definite answer to it. Theologians cannot honestly ignore the questions of who Jesus was, whether he said and did roughly what we find in the gospels, the reasons for his death, and the reasons for the rise of Christianity. This is by no means to imply that the historical study of Jesus is designed simply for the benefit of the church and theology. Those who wish to demonstrate the unbelievability of Christianity, as did Reimarus and some of his followers, are likewise bound to take these questions seriously. But have the historians enabled either side, or indeed those in the middle, to get very far?

Looking simply, for now, at the period between Schweitzer and Schillebeeckx, we find many notable works in the field of systematic theology, and particularly christology. All of them have made use, to a lesser or greater extent, of the figure of Jesus. The massive schemes of writers like

---

[53] For the continuation of New Quest work on the Jesus-traditions in Germany see particularly the collection of studies in Kümmel 1985. In a paper at the British New Testament Studies Conference in September 1990, Dr W. R. Telford of Newcastle University warned of the sense of academic disenfranchisement that New Questers might feel if Third Questers pretended they no longer exist. I intend no such thing, though one might equally draw attention to the sense of academic disenfranchisement that serious historians of Jesus have felt for decades when facing the often dismissive and scornful proponents of *Traditionsgeschichte*.

Barth and Tillich, the provocative and seminal works of Pannenberg, Jüngel and Moltmann, and the great Catholic works of Rahner, Kasper, Schoonenberg and Schillebeeckx himself – not to mention Hans Küng's famous *On Being a Christian* – all bear witness to the importance of the question of the historical Jesus within their respective schemes.[54] But at no point, I suggest, has the full impact of the historical evidence been allowed to influence very much the dogmatic conclusions reached; when it has, it is only perhaps as a concession. This may seem an over-hasty judgment: some of these theologians (one thinks particularly of Pannenberg) have made very serious and thorough use of parts of Jesus' Jewish context; but I remain convinced that there is a good deal more to be said about the perceptions, worldviews and mindsets of first-century Jews that will have considerable importance, as yet unimagined, for systematic theology. The exception to this might be the liberation theologians, among whom Segundo in particular has produced an impressive study.[55] But there again the conclusions, though very different from the normal dogmatic ones, seem to have been at least outlined in advance; the detailed historical work has not really been taken with full seriousness.

The years of the silhouette were by no means all negative. Even if they did not reach firm results about Jesus, they provided new pictures of the early church. These turn out to be the twentieth-century equivalent of the nineteenth-century lives of Jesus:[56] fanciful, theory-laden and agenda-driven hypotheses about the early church, with only tangential relation to the sources, and to the actual history of first-century Palestine, Asia Minor, and elsewhere. But, again like their nineteenth-century analogue, they bear witness both to the complexity of the task, to its potential theological importance, and, negatively, to the wrongness of many theories which, having now been tried and found wanting, ought to be consigned to the scrap-heap. Out of all this there might perhaps grow a new awareness of first-century history and its potential theological significance.[57]

Two hundred years, then – surveyed swiftly here, because the story has been told so often – have demonstrated that the Quest is vital, but difficult. The sources are no less tricky to use now than they were at the start. The

---

[54] For details, see McGrath 1994 [1986]. Tillich, of course, gave a minimalist answer to the question (admitting that he based his view of Jesus on the work of Schweitzer and Bultmann: see Tillich 1967, 49, a reference I owe to Brown 1969, 197); but this is itself highly significant within his theology. On the place of Jesus in contemporary ethical discourse, see the works discussed in McGrath 1989.

[55] Segundo 1985. I very much regret not being able in the present volume to discuss this and similar works in any detail.

[56] cf. *NTPG* ch. 11.

[57] See *NTPG* Parts IV and V.

questions are no less pressing. From time to time one hopes that a few false trails may have been closed off for good, but, just when one allows oneself a sigh of relief at the thought, there arises another cunning variation on an old theme.[58] From time to time one believes that some aspect of first-century Jewish history is now firmly established, so that it can be used as a fixed point in future work; but there always seems to be enough scope within the complex sources for strikingly different interpretations to emerge. Nevertheless, the last twenty years (1975 to 1995) have seen a remarkable flurry of research, addressing all these questions with renewed vigour and enthusiasm. It is to these newer movements that we now turn. Perhaps the prodigal is coming back home.

---

[58] e.g. Reimarus' revolutionary theory, revived by Brandon in 1967 and demolished in Bammel & Moule 1984. (Variations still appear: e.g. Buchanan 1984, and, in a sense, Horsley 1987.) See below, ch. 3.

Chapter Two

HEAVY TRAFFIC ON THE WREDEBAHN: THE 'NEW QUEST' RENEWED?

1. Introduction

Albert Schweitzer, as we saw, bequeathed two stark alternatives to posterity: the 'thoroughgoing scepticism' of William Wrede, and his own 'thoroughgoing eschatology'. As we turn to the current scene in Jesus-studies, we discover that these two streets have become broad highways, with a good deal of traffic all trying to use them at once.[1] In the present chapter we shall consider those who, in some senses at least, have followed Wrede; in the following chapter, those who have followed Schweitzer.

It should be noted at once that this distinction is not hard-and-fast, and that several of the most important writers incorporate elements of both positions. At the same time, there is a distinction which can be made clearly, and is visible most obviously at the extremes. On the one hand, there are those who think we can know very little about Jesus, and that the synoptic gospels (and, *a fortiori*, John) are little more than theological fiction. Thus, for instance, in form though not in content, Burton Mack (see below) stands more or less exactly in line with Wrede. On the other hand, some have continued to place Jesus within Jewish apocalyptic eschatology, and have in consequence placed a far higher value on the synoptic record, which offers more or less this position. Thus, again in form though not in content, A. E. Harvey and E. P. Sanders stand alongside Schweitzer. In between, just for the sake of showing the spectrum, two recent writers (Borg and Crossan) have a far less minimal Jesus than Wrede (or Mack), and insist on the importance of 'eschatology', in some sense, within Jesus' work. This makes them far harder to classify, though in their major emphases I would still place them, in the last analysis, as heavily modified Wrede-followers rather than in the Schweitzer-stream. Again, Vermes, whose whole project is to insist on the Jewishness of Jesus, makes so little of eschatology that his Jesus remains, in some ways, more like that of Wrede.

---

[1] The metaphor is taken from Perrin's 1966 article, entitled 'The *Wredestrasse* becomes the *Hauptstrasse* . . .'

It would be possible, in principle, to map the various options in far more detail than is necessary or desirable here. My own study has led me to conclude that, however many details may need adjusting, it is Schweitzer's route that is in principle to be preferred. Accordingly, I regard his contemporary followers, whose work I shall discuss in the next chapter, as my main conversation-partners. But, since the proponents of the minimal-Jesus-and-fictional-gospels line have become once again more vocal of late, it is important to say what they are claiming, and why I disagree with them. Hence the present chapter.

2. The 'Jesus Seminar'

The late 1970s and early 1980s saw a decline in the 'New Quest', and, as we shall see presently, the rise of a quite different approach. But in the mid-1980s a serious move was made to put new life into what remains basically the post-Bultmannian study of Jesus. In 1985 Robert W. Funk, then Professor in the University of Montana, founded the 'Jesus Seminar', bringing together scholars in North America to discuss sayings of Jesus piece by piece and to vote on their authenticity or otherwise. The agenda and practice of this Seminar contains three important features. First, all relevant Jesus-material is to be included. The net is cast far wider than the canonical gospels, bringing in *Thomas* and numerous other works, several of them fragmentary. Second, voting takes place in four categories, using coloured beads which symbolize different grades of probability: red means authentic, pink probably authentic, grey probably inauthentic, black definitely inauthentic.[2] Third, the Seminar

---

[2] The full official meaning of the four colours is set out in various places, with (confusingly) two options. The first option concerns which items one might include in a database for determining who Jesus was: red means that the item is included unequivocally, pink that the item is included with reservations or modifications, grey that the item would not be included, but some of its content might be made use of, black that the item would simply not be included. The second option is simpler: red means 'Jesus undoubtedly said this or something very like it', pink means 'Jesus probably said something like this', grey means 'Jesus did not say this, but the ideas contained in it are close to his own', and black means 'Jesus did not say this; it represents the perspective or content of a later or different tradition'. (This is set out in e.g. Funk, Scott & Butts 1988, 21; Funk 1991, xxii; Funk & Hoover 1993, 36f.) Put still more simply,
red: That's Jesus!
pink: Sure sounds like Jesus.
gray: Well, maybe.
black: There's been some mistake.
(Funk 1991, xx). Whether or not the Seminar ever faced the question of how politically correct such a colour-scheme might be is not recorded.

publishes its results as widely as possible, recognizing that it is not only scholars who may be interested in the results. The eventual product is a multi-coloured edition of the gospels, including *Thomas*, in which one may see at a glance how the various sayings have been evaluated.[3] The Seminar has produced a new translation which combines colloquial Americanisms with a somewhat pretentious title ('The Scholars Version').[4] The possibility has also been mentioned of producing a completely revised equivalent of Rudolf Bultmann's *History of the Synoptic Tradition*, tracing the development of Jesus-sayings through their various hypothetical stages. There are also plans for a film.[5]

A certain amount of gentle mockery of the Jesus Seminar has been the custom among scholars not directly involved. This, however, though no doubt invited by the somewhat pompous tones of early pronouncements, misses the point. Each of the features mentioned above can be defended in itself. The inclusion of non-canonical material is simply good scholarly practice; how one evaluates it is a second step, but to have it on the table cannot be faulted. Here various members of the Seminar, including its Chairman, are to be thanked for their sterling work in producing study texts.[6] The practice of voting on individual sayings has a close analogy with the standard practice among, for instance, the editors of critical texts such as the United Bible Societies' edition of the Greek Testament – though with the significant difference, not always acknowledged, that whereas the latter committee is weighing the evidence of actual manuscripts, in most instances the Jesus Seminar is not voting on anything half so tangible.[7] The fact that the polls have not always given a clear answer, and obviously depend on the mood and presuppositions of certain North American scholars at a particular time, is not in itself an argument for not attempting the exercise. And the determination to make the results of the work available to a wide audience is clearly laudable, even though the sense of knowing in advance what may be good for that audience to hear creeps into the Seminar's pronouncements –

---

[3] Funk & Hoover 1993; for detailed analysis and criticism, cf. Wright 1995a.

[4] cf. Miller 1992; Funk & Hoover 1993. The introduction to the latter work makes a great point of how this version is independent of church control, and concludes (xviii) 'the Scholars Version is authorized by scholars'. Were there, I wonder, any wry smiles in the Seminar at this explicit statement of the papacy of the scholars?

[5] The Seminar's work is chronicled in its journal, *Foundations and Facets Forum*. A journalistic account of its beginnings and praxis can be found in various places, e.g. Funk 1991, xiii–xix.

[6] Cameron 1982; Funk 1985b & c; Kloppenborg 1988; Crossan 1991b [1986]; Miller 1992 [1991].

[7] Crossan 1991a, 424–6; cp. Metzger 1971, xxviii, explaining the use of the letters A, B, C and D to describe textual variants, in terms very similar to the Jesus Seminar's explanation of its four colours.

just as it does, of course, into those of pretty well everybody else.[8] Since a certain cross-section of North American biblical scholarship is represented in the Seminar, we may reasonably hope that interesting and potentially worthwhile material will emerge.

There are two points in particular, however, at which criticism must be levelled.[9] The underlying presuppositions of the enterprise are systematically unclear; and the way the system actually operates gives cause for concern.

First, the initial flyer advertising the seminar spoke in classic positivist terms of 'the quest for fact and history, for honesty and candour, for the truth and its consequences'. It invited as participants those who preferred 'facts rather than fancies', 'history rather than histrionics', and 'science rather than superstition'. It even used the old phrase 'the assured results of historical-critical scholarship'; this ought, by the 1980s, to have become a stock joke, since many beliefs which were labelled thus as recently as the 1960s have already been consigned to scholarly oblivion, not least by some of those involved in the Jesus Seminar itself. But this positivistic mood is, as I argued in *NTPG* Part II, quite out of place in serious historical scholarship. It also accords ill with the actual practice of the Seminar, and the methodological pronouncements of some of its leading members. It quickly became clear with the first voting that, as Burton Mack wrote, 'we have no common categories for actually making sense of things even among ourselves';[10] a common enough scholarly predicament, but one that tempers somewhat the notion of being able to tell a waiting America what Jesus actually said. And the best-known writer in the Seminar, Dominic Crossan, has (as we shall see) explicitly eschewed the positivism of the Seminar's early pronouncements. The Seminar appears, then, to hover uneasily between a positivistic public image and an inner methodological uncertainty.

But do not the 'results' show that there is in fact an emerging consensus? Yes and no. This is the second point: the way the system operates, we may suggest, demonstrates simply that a certain swathe of modern American

[8] Two examples, more or less at random. Funk's opening remarks to the Seminar suggested, *inter alia*, that the group could 'undertake to advise our president [i.e. Ronald Reagan] . . . about the perils of apocalyptic foreign policy' (Funk 1985a, 10). So too, in an interesting recapitulation of Bultmann's anti-heroic stance, we are told that 'Jesus, updated or not, is not what American society needs. The Jesus Tradition, on the other hand, may be a bit more helpful, because it chronicles a dramatic . . . accomplishment of social formation within cultural chaos' (Taussig 1986, 76). The extent to which the shadow of Reaganism falls across the page is remarkable, and makes some parts of the agenda look quite dated from the perspective of 1996: see Mack 1985, 27; Carter & Hutchison 1985. The dream of a radical critique of western society based on some aspect of early Christianity lives on, however: see Mack 1993, 11, 249–58, and elsewhere.

[9] For a much fuller critique, see Wright 1995a.

[10] Mack 1985, 23f.

scholarship has opted, largely *a priori* in terms of the present exercise, for one particular way of understanding who Jesus was and how the early church developed.[11] This fairly recent tradition has been enthusiastically embraced by the Chairman of the Seminar, Robert Funk, who touchingly describes his own sense of a beckoning destiny and his own invigorating challenge to the first Fellows of the Seminar. He promises that he will himself write a book about Jesus, when the Seminar has completed its work; we may be forgiven for suggesting that there will be few surprises when it comes.[12] In the meantime, the laudable desire to communicate the results of the Seminar's deliberations has led to some astonishing oversimplifications. In the Introduction to the red-letter text of Mark (presented again in *The Five Gospels*), we are told that scholars are united on the major premises that underlie all critical work on the gospels. Unfortunately, the whole point of a premise is that it is not a conclusion, whereas most of the statements offered as 'premises' in what follows are conclusions, many of them very dubious. In the discussion of some recent Jesus- and gospels-research, sixty-four of these 'premises' are distilled, ranging from the uncontroversial ('Premise 2: Jesus taught his disciples orally; Jesus wrote nothing') to the highly contentious ('Premise 4: Oral tradition is fluid'; 'Premise 24: Thomas represents an earlier stage of the tradition than do the canonical gospels'; 'Premise 44: The earliest sources are Q^1 and Thomas[1]. The second and third editions of Q follow closely') and the downright polemical ('Premise 45: Only a small portion of the sayings attributed to Jesus in the gospels was actually spoken by him').[13] To call these 'premises' is to invite the charge of cooking the discussion in advance. To suggest that scholars are united on these so-called 'premises' is simply to ignore the work of a great many contemporary scholars who are every bit as 'critical' as the members of the Seminar.[14]

Alongside the text where this sequence of would-be 'premises' is expounded are some other highlighted definitions. Again, some are simply uncontroversial ('*Parchment* is made from the skins of animals, usually sheep or goats, prepared to receive writing'); others are misleading in the extreme,

[11] The background to this line of thought can be studied in e.g. Robinson & Koester 1971.

[12] See the 'Story of the Jesus Seminar' in Funk 1991, xiii–xix, at xv, xvi, xix. Funk's call to fearless discipleship (xvi: 'We are about to embark on a momentous enterprise . . . the course we shall follow may prove hazardous. We may well provoke hostility. But we will set out, in spite of the dangers, because we are professionals and because the issue of Jesus is there to be faced.') is strangely reminiscent of Mark 8.34f., which in the Seminar's voting came out heavily black, i.e. inauthentic. Perhaps the real allusion is more contemporary: boldly going where no one has gone before? Funk's earlier work included major grammatical and hermeneutical studies, e.g. Funk 1966, 1973 [1961].

[13] Ibid., 5, 11, 16, 17.

[14] cf. ch. 3 below.

reflecting viewpoints now abandoned by most serious students of the subject-matter concerned ('*Apocalypticism* is the view that history will come to an end and a new age begin following a cosmic catastrophe').[15] This sort of popularization serves no one's interests except those determined to push through a viewpoint at all costs.

This impression is confirmed by the voting records of the Seminar. In the voting on the sayings, set out in volumes 6 and 7 of *Foundations and Facets Forum*, it is notable that the heavy weight of 'red' votes – i.e. 'authentic' – falls on sayings which occur in either Q or *Thomas* or both. Luke puts in a brief appearance, with the parables of the good Samaritan (10.29–37) and the incompetent manager (16.1–9) being voted authentic. But the Q-and-Thomas pattern continues to predominate. The main reason why these sayings are considered 'authentic' is clearly not that each one has been tested individually against some abstract criteria, but that they have been judged to fit into the picture of Jesus *which has already been chosen*. Again, Burton Mack: 'we may have to give up on [the criterion of dissimilarity] in favor of the criterion of plausibility, given what can be reconstructed of social life and thought in the Galilee of the times'.[16] Let it be noted that I am not dismissing this move as a false one: I am actually endorsing it. What I am doing is pointing out that it completely relativizes the Jesus Seminar's apparent purpose and stated claim. What is afoot, at least in the 'results' available thus far, is not the detailed objective study of individual passages, leading up to a new view of Jesus and the early church. *It is a particular view of Jesus and the early church, working its way through into a detailed list of sayings that fit with this view.* Once this is recognized, it should also be seen that the real task, still awaiting all students of Jesus, is that of major hypothesis and serious verification, not pseudo-atomistic work on apparently isolated fragments. About this I have already written in some detail elsewhere.[17] In this particular case, the view which has already been chosen contains, as one of its major elements, a set of assumptions about 'apocalyptic' and 'eschatology', about 'prophecy' and 'wisdom', which we have challenged in part already and will continue to argue against in the present work.[18]

The last point about the Seminar's actual practice concerns its assigning 'weighted averages' to the different votes cast. Obviously, if 25% of Fellows

[15] Ibid., 17, 13; a similar misleading 'definition' is found in Miller 1992, 430. On 'apocalyptic' etc. cf. *NTPG* ch. 10; and below, esp. chs. 6, 8.

[16] Mack 1985, 24. This effectively renders redundant most of the other 'criteria' of the 'New Quest', so painstakingly reassembled and developed by, among others, Boring 1985, Patterson 1989, Vaage 1989, and Funk 1989. It should be noted that Mack's own reconstruction of Galilee in this period is highly idiosyncratic: cf. Mack 1993, ch. 4.

[17] *NTPG* ch. 4, esp. 99–104.

[18] cf. e.g. Funk 1991, 52; and see *NTPG* ch. 10, and below, on Q.

vote in each category, there will be a stalemate, and no colouring will be possible; so some system for deciding how to proceed is necessary. But in several instances a high percentage – sometimes a clear majority – voted either red or pink, i.e. either authentic or probably authentic, but the 'weighted average' came out grey because of the high proportion of black votes cast on the other side.[19] A voting system like this, allied to a publicity machine that purports to tell America 'what Jesus really said', has nothing whatever to commend it. If, even within the restricted group of the Jesus Seminar itself, a majority of scholars thinks that a saying is probably or certainly authentic, for a minority to vote black and so make the saying 'probably inauthentic' simply cannot make sense.

Does this flurry of activity belong with the older 'New Quest', or with what I have called the 'Third Quest', which I shall discuss in the next chapter? From one point of view this is a mere matter of labels. It does not much matter whether we think of the 'Jesus Seminar', and its key players such as Mack and Crossan, as being on the radical wing of the 'Third Quest', or whether we recognize the major differences between them and those to be discussed in chapter 3 by placing them, as I have now done, in a different category altogether. Briefly, the position may be stated as follows. The 'New Quest' was an explicitly Bultmannian movement, an attempt by some of Bultmann's followers to recover something of the historical Jesus, by building outwards from the Bultmannian understanding of the kerygma of the cross and resurrection.[20] The 'Jesus Seminar', and Mack and Crossan (to be discussed presently) as representatives of it, work with somewhat different premises and methods; they are quite unBultmannian in their concern to find out about Jesus, to discover what he actually said (Bultmann would have regarded this as a very unsound preoccupation). They are concerned to locate Jesus within his social and cultural milieu. Crossan at least is concerned to link together history and theology in a way foreign to mainstream Bultmannianism. In these respects they are indeed closer to the 'Third Quest'. But the links between them and the older Bultmann school still seem to me obvious. Mack's whole programme grows quite explicitly out of Bultmann and Wrede, with its emphasis on the fictitious (in every sense) work of Mark.[21]

---

[19] e.g. Funk & Hoover 232 (on Mt. 21.28–31a; 28.31b); 213 (on Mt. 18.3); 250 (on Mt. 24.32f.).

[20] See esp. Robinson 1959.

[21] Interviewed in the *National Catholic Register* for 9 May 1993, Mack stated: 'In fact, there's very little we can know about Jesus historically in any case.' Asked 'You say in your book that you're not very interested in the historical Jesus', Mack replied, 'That's right.' (Quite an admission for a member of the 'Jesus Seminar'.) He went on, 'What's important to me are the early Christians . . .' This is as clear a Bultmannian agenda as one might ever hear. See too Mack 1993, 239: Mark has combined the Pauline 'Christ myth' with 'various traditions about Jesus from the Jesus movement' – Bultmann's position more or less exactly.

His (Mack's) emphasis on primitive Palestinian Christianity as quite unlike the Christ-cult of Paul is straight out of Bultmann and Bousset, and has little in common with the 'Third Quest', which is more likely to be combined (as, for instance, in the work of Sanders) with a robustly Jewish reading of Paul.[22] The reconstruction of Q, and the attempt to assign it a vital role in the search for Jesus, is far more reminiscent of the 'New Quest' and its attendant *Traditionsgeschichte* than of the 'Third Quest', which has distanced itself from such movements. Crossan's relation to the Bultmann tradition I shall discuss presently; there is enough evidence, I believe, to place him in the same general category of a renewed 'New Quest'. If anyone wishes to suggest that this renewal overlaps with some of the 'Third Quest', I shall be happy to agree, provided that the points of clear distinction are also noted. In that case, the purpose of the present chapter would be simply to introduce the 'Third Quest' by, as it were, the back door.

Mack and Crossan have been, within the last decade, two of the most influential writers on Jesus and the gospels in North America. We must now discuss them in more detail.[23]

3. Burton L. Mack (and the Question of Q)

I have already quoted Burton Mack more than once, and it is his work in particular that has given the Jesus Seminar one of its strong directional impulses. In his book *A Myth of Innocence: Mark and Christian Origins*[24] he argues trenchantly, and often quite brilliantly, for a view of Jesus, of Christian origins and of Mark's gospel which are in sharp contrast to normal received wisdom. Mark, he urges, created a myth of Christian beginnings in which Jesus, the innocent son of god, announced the end of the world. This legitimated a particular second-generation way of being Christian – which was then canonized, with disastrous results down to the present day:

At the same time, Mack distances himself from the perspective of Bultmann 1968 [1921], in that there Bultmann gave priority to apocalyptic sayings and regarded wisdom sayings as the invention of the early church – a judgment which Mack reverses (Mack 1993, 32f.). He notes, though, that in Bultmann's book *Jesus* (Bultmann 1958a [1926]), the two themes are regarded as compatible.

[22] See e.g. Mack 1993, 3-5.

[23] Some English colleagues have questioned whether one should give so much space to these authors, since their views appear, from East of the Atlantic, unbelievable to many. My reasons for persisting are (a) that they represent two versions of a powerful and seemingly growing movement within North American scholarship; (b) that they raise most of the crucial issues which face us in assessing this renewal of the 'New Quest'; and (c) that they and their followers represent the major current alternative to what I call the 'Third Quest'.

[24] Mack 1988. Subsequent references without date are to this work.

A brilliant appearance of the man of power, destroyed by those in league against God, pointed nonetheless to a final victory when those who knew the secret of his kingdom would finally be vindicated for accepting his authority.

Neither Mark's fiction of the first appearance of the man of power, nor his fantasy of the final appearance of the man of glory, fit the wisdom now required. The church canonized a remarkably pitiful moment of early Christian condemnation of the world. Thus the world now stands condemned. It is enough. A future for the world can hardly be imagined any longer, if its redemption rests in the hands of Mark's innocent son of God.[25]

The pedigree of Mack's work runs clearly back to two seminal figures from the start of the century: Wrede and Bultmann. Like Wrede, Mack thinks that the story-line of Mark's gospel is Mark's own handiwork, a fiction invented for theological reasons at the end of the first generation of Christianity, in which the original message of Jesus, and the beliefs of most of his early followers, were radically revised in the interests of a quite different scheme of thought.[26] For Wrede, this scheme centred upon the 'secret' of Jesus' Messiahship; for Mack, it focuses on the negative apocalyptic message in which the world stands condemned by the son of god. Like Bultmann, Mack conceives the development of early Christianity in two strands, which Mark has then brought together: there are the (early, mostly Jewish) followers of Jesus himself, continuing his own line of teaching, and there are the members of the Hellenistic Christ-cult, of which Paul represents one strand.[27] But, whereas for Bultmann Mark's fusion of the two strands was a brilliant and creative move, for Mack it was and is a disaster.

What then is the truth about Jesus? One must pick and choose among the material in the gospels, since so much is inconsistent with itself: 'casting out demons is difficult to imagine for one adept at telling parables'.[28] In particular, 'an aphoristic social critique suggests one stance, an apocalyptic pronouncement of doom another, yet both kinds of sayings are included in the collection known as Q'.[29] This gives Mack his particular focus, along with the proponents of the two-stage Q:[30]

[25] Mack 323, 376 (cf. also 14, 24). The second quotation concludes the main text of the book.

[26] See Mack's endorsement (54) of Wrede 1971 [1901].

[27] cf. e.g. Mack 97. Mack's Jesus (a social reformer) is of course very different from Bultmann's (a preacher of individual existential decision); but Mack's endorsement of Bultmann's overall programme emerges at numerous points, e.g. 355n.: 'Bultmann's preference for the kerygma over the gospels as the myth more adequate to modern times is due, no doubt, to his Lutheran tradition. It was also, however, intuitively correct.' This also provides a clear insight on the underlying agenda behind Mack's own work.

[28] Mack 55.

[29] Mack 56. This is the easy either/or that has dominated so much of the Jesus Seminar's work.

[30] cf. *NTPG* 435–43. On Q see Mack 1993, discussed below.

Aphoristic wisdom is characteristic for the earlier layer [of Q]. This turns the table on older views of Jesus as an apocalyptic preacher and brings the message of Jesus around to another style of speech altogether.[31]

Jesus, it appears, belonged in the largely gentile environment of Galilee. (Mack cites with approval Freyne's detailed study of Galilee, but then disagrees with him on the question of how Jewish Galilee still was.[32]) His teaching, once it has been properly reconstructed, resembles most closely that of a Cynic sage, spinning aphorisms designed to subvert his hearers' social and cultural worlds.[33] He had little or nothing to say about the 'kingdom of god', or at least not in any Jewish sense – not that, in any case, the idea was especially prominent in the Judaism of the time.[34] In fact,

One seeks in vain a direct engagement of specifically Jewish concerns. Neither is Jesus' critique directed specifically toward Jewish institutional issues, nor do his recommendations draw upon obviously Jewish concepts and authorities . . . Jesus' kingdom was not the fulfillment of old epic ideals that history had failed to realize. The social critique was general; the invitation was specific in its address to individuals. The invitation would have been to something like the Cynic's 'kingdom,' that is, to assume the Cynic's stance of confidence in the midst of confused and contrary social circumstances. Simply translated, Jesus' 'message' seems to have been, 'See how it's done? You can do it also.'[35]

As a result, 'what Jesus set in motion was a social experiment'.[36] This of itself is insufficient to explain the movements that told their stories of origins as beginning with him, and so we must look further, to the group experience of his followers. Much of Mack's work is an essay in the social history of early Christianity, and at this point he plots a multiple division within the movement. There are 'the followers of Jesus', represented partly by the Q material. They 'kept the memory of Jesus alive and thought of themselves in terms of Jewish reform'.[37] They thought of Jesus as a teacher, sage or charismatic reformer. They lacked the features of the 'Christ cult': no eucharist,

[31] Mack 59.

[32] Mack 66f., n.9, and Mack 1993, ch. 4; cf. Freyne 1980b, 1988b. This topic was discussed in detail in the 1993 Annual Meeting of the Society of Biblical Literature, where papers by Eric M. Meyers ('Jesus and his Galilean Context') and Freyne ('The "Jews" of the Galilee') made it clear that Mack's view, which has become a major plank in the 'Jesus Seminar' platform, is largely without foundation.

[33] Mack 68f. On the Cynic possibility see Downing 1987a & b, 1988, 1992; and below, 66–75. Mack does not note the parallels between some of Jesus' aphoristic sayings and similar sayings in Jewish texts: see Dalman 1929, 225–31, a reference I owe to Colin Brown.

[34] Mack 70–3.

[35] Mack 73. On this quite thorough deJudaizing of Jesus, in line with so much German scholarship in the first half of the century, see the remarks at the end of the present chapter.

[36] Mack 76.

[37] Mack 96.

no belief in resurrection, no idea of Jesus as god or saviour. For them, 'Jesus did not become the Lord of a new religious society that called for abrogation of the past in order to be transformed and enter a new creation.'[38] The 'Christ cult', however, embraced all those things in a burst of syncretism that had comparatively little to do with Jesus himself.[39] In the ensuing multiple developments of early Christianity, conflict between different groups gave rise to new forms of the tradition in each case. The question of authority became important. Into this scenario came the evangelist Mark:

> Mark defined his group apocalyptically by severing the ties with Judaism, as well as ties with the past history of the group, and with other competitive forms of early Jesus-Christ movements . . . The gospel he composed addressed the issue of authority in a very provocative way. All contenders were crushed or subsumed in the single figure of Jesus.[40]

This thesis about Jesus is then complemented in two ways: with a detailed consideration of the various types of material in Mark's gospel, and then with a discussion of the way in which Mark actually composed his work, making the stories of Jesus 'memorable' on the one hand and, on the other, turning the Christ myth into a 'myth of origins'.[41] Mark has written an apocalypse with a totally negative outlook: he 'gave up on the possibility of imagining a society fit for the real world'.[42] The bulk of Mack's book is thus about Mark and his reworking of traditions, and thus falls strictly within the scope of a later volume. But his picture of Jesus is so striking, and has been so influential in some contemporary discussion, that it merits further consideration here.

Mack's work is itself, of course, a would-be authoritative presentation of early Christianity, created by combining different streams of (scholarly) tradition to form a radically new alternative. Ironically, he has himself provided a new 'myth of origins'. First there is Jesus: not now either the 'son of god' or the 'son of man', but the Cynic wordsmith, 'softly spoken but extremely engaging',[43] setting in motion a more or less non-Jewish tradition of social protest and transformation. The Opponent in Mack's scheme, taking the place occupied in Mark by the wicked authorities, who act diabolically to get rid of the innocent divine one, is of course Mark himself, who writes the real Jesus out of history and squashes his genuine followers under the weight of his soon-to-be-canonized authority. Instead of Mark's radical rejection of

---

[38] For all this, cf. Mack 96f.
[39] Mack 98–123.
[40] Mack 130f.
[41] Mack 312.
[42] Mack 349.
[43] Mack 69. This sounds like a silhouette of Dominic Crossan.

Judaism and the world, we have Burton Mack's radical rejection of that which became, and has continued as, mainstream Christianity, with its focal points as Jesus' saving death, the resurrection, the eucharist, and the church. This tradition, founded by Mark, has done untold damage to the world, and especially to America, which has clung on to its own 'myth of innocence'.[44] Christianity now stands condemned. A future for it can hardly be imagined any longer, if the truth rests with Mack's innocent Cynic wordsmith.

Given the lack of eschatology within Mack's reconstruction of Jesus, it is appropriate that there should be little within his own programme. But there is a hint of it. Instead of Mark's expectation that those who cling to his mythic Jesus will be vindicated, we have, at least by implication, Mack's expectation that the true, Cynic Jesus will vindicate (by historical memory) those who reject the whole Markan 'Christian' tradition, not least as it has appeared in modern American politics. And it appears that the Jesus Seminar has been quick to take the hint. Mack outlined his argument in advance, in a paper to the Seminar, published in 1987.[45] The Seminar then voted on the kingdom sayings, and produced – or rather endorsed – a non-apocalyptic Jesus. The Markan sayings were, quite literally, black-balled. Mack's influence, appealing as it did to an alternative American myth, came in on the tide of anti-Reaganism. The Seminar announced to its public that the real Jesus was innocent of the wicked apocalypticism with which so many Christians, not least in the conservative American churches against which American academics react so strongly, had for so long associated him.[46]

Mack's brilliant *tour de force* has breathed new life into the Bultmannian paradigm of Christian origins.[47] He has seen the range of questions to be addressed if one is to rewrite the history of Jesus and early Christianity, and he has tackled them with thoroughness and vigour. He has recognized many of the ways in which Christians down the years have supposed they were serving a crucified and risen Lord when in fact they were serving their own interests.[48] But, if our suspicions are aroused by the ease with which his Jesus, and his early Christianity, conform to one particular agenda, our critical faculties must likewise reject his proposal both in outline and in detail.[49]

[44] Mack 365–76.
[45] Mack 1987. The influence of this paper on the Seminar exemplifies the significance of Mack within the movement.
[46] cf. Butts 1987, esp. 108f.
[47] cf. now Mack 1995.
[48] See, for instance, his deconstruction of the C16 reformation, 364: 'The text . . . gave power to those in charge of it . . . The preacher became the priest of the pulpit, presiding over the enactment of the new liturgy, a liturgy of linguistic transformations. Christian experience now took place in the aural imagination of the listener. It was called salvation by faith based solely on scripture.'
[49] For critiques of Mack cf. Overman 1990; Witherington 1995, ch. 3; Boyd 1995.

I have already argued that the proposal of a 'Q-and-*Thomas*' early form of Christianity is extremely tenuous.[50] I have demonstrated in some detail (a) that popular Judaism in the first century was eagerly expecting Israel's god to act decisively to get rid of the Roman overlord,[51] (b) that this expectation regularly expressed itself in terms of Israel's god becoming king,[52] and (c) that the apocalyptic language of some of its favourite writings, not least the book of Daniel, had nothing to do with a supposed end to the space-time order, and everything to do with the great climax of Israel's history, the final liberation of Israel from her pagan enemies.[53] I have argued that, though Mark is indeed in some sense a Christian 'apocalypse', this has nothing to do with a negative attitude to the world or to history.[54] In particular, I have shown in some detail that the whole synoptic tradition, both in its pre-literary and in its literary forms, carried the intention to refer to the actual Jesus of Nazareth, not to some cult-figure, nor to some quasi-mythical figure to whom could be attributed words of prophecy that the original Jesus could not have spoken.[55] This point could be amplified further by a full consideration of the nature of oral tradition in the middle-eastern village life of the period.[56] We may add, in advance of a fuller demonstration, that the evidence for a Cynic presence in Galilee is slight to the point of invisibility; that Jesus' claim to be fulfilling the scriptures, and indeed the whole history, of Israel, can only be written out of the text by major and drastic surgery comparable to cutting off an arm and a leg; that the vital split between 'prophetic' and 'wisdom' traditions, or between 'apocalyptic' and 'sapiential' sayings, is warranted by nothing stronger than frequent repetition in certain limited scholarly circles; and that the attempt to discover social contexts within which the tradition could undergo the huge developments necessary for Mack's theory to work is almost entirely (since there is no real evidence for it whatsoever) an exercise in creative imagination. We just do not have the evidence to be able to postulate with any hope of accuracy the groups, the locations, the cultural influences and so forth which Mack presents to our dazzled gaze. We actually know very little about early Christianity. What we do know points in a very different direction.[57]

---

[50] *NTPG* 435–43. See below for discussion of Mack and Kloppenborg.

[51] Full details and refs. in *NTPG* ch. 7.

[52] *NTPG* 302–7: e.g. Jos. *Ant.* 18.23f., *War* 7.323–36. For the biblical background cf. e.g. Ps. 145.10–13; Isa. 33.22; 52.7; Zeph. 3.14–20; etc.; and in the post-biblical writings e.g. *T. Mos.* 10.1–10; 1QM 6.4–6.

[53] *NTPG* 280–99.

[54] *NTPG* 390–6.

[55] *NTPG* chs. 13, 14; esp. 396–403.

[56] cf. esp. Bailey 1991; and Kelber 1983; Ong 1970, 1982. See below, ch. 4.

[57] cf. *NTPG* Part IV, esp. chs. 11–12 and 15. Mack rivals Koester (1982b [1980]) in his easy certainty as to which early Christians were doing what, and when and where they were doing it, without any basis in actual evidence.

A further note may be in place here about the status of Q within the Jesus Seminar, and in the work of Mack and Crossan in particular.[58] Great reliance has been placed on the work of John Kloppenborg, who has painstakingly analysed the Q material into its supposed three stages of composition.[59] I described this hypothesis, and argued somewhat briefly against it, in chapter 14 of *NTPG*.[60] To that argument we must now add the following.

First, to treat Q as a 'gospel' runs way beyond the evidence. Even if it did exist as a separate document, the word 'gospel' means 'good news', and the force of that phrase comes precisely from the sense of Israel's god bringing her history to its appointed goal – which, according to Kloppenborg and his followers, was precisely what the early stages of Q did not believe.[61]

Second, even those who firmly believe in a reconstructable document Q, rather than merely fragments of oral and/or written 'Q material' (let alone those very serious scholars who believe that Q is a modern fiction from start to finish[62]), are by no means agreed either on its historical, geographical or theological location within early Christianity or on its supposed stages of redaction. The relegation of eschatological, prophetic and apocalpytic material to a secondary stage, leaving the early ground free for a non-apocalyptic, and indeed a largely non-Jewish, 'sapiential' early Christianity and Jesus, is not shared by most Continental and British Q scholars, nor indeed by all North Americans.[63] The massive study of Q by Siegfried Schulz came to conclusions almost exactly opposite to those of Kloppenborg and his followers: for him, the first stage of Q was very Jewish, and focused on Jesus as the son of man, and the second stage was more Hellenistic, introducing sapiential ideas for the first time.[64] The article on Q in the *Anchor*

---

[58] Though this discussion relates to the whole chapter, it is particularly appropriate here because of Mack 1993 – a popularized and highly tendentious account of Q as though it were a 'lost gospel' whose recent 'discovery' compels a complete re-evaluation of Jesus and early Christianity, generating a new contemporary agenda.

[59] See esp. Kloppenborg 1987, followed closely by e.g. Koester 1990, 133-71; Mack 1993 *passim*; Vaage 1994; and many others.

[60] pp. 435-43.

[61] See the restrained language of Catchpole 1993, 1ff. On the meanings of 'gospel' see Wright 1994.

[62] e.g. Farmer 1982; Goulder 1989.

[63] cf. e.g. Webb 1991, 322-32, discussing 'sapiential prophets' – a category which, if the prevailing 'Jesus Seminar' view were correct, ought not to exist (which is perhaps why Horsley & Hanson 1985 try to play it down; on this, see Webb's comments, 329f.). See too e.g. Allison 1994, 661-3.

[64] Schulz 1972, heavily drawn on by Schillebeeckx 1979 [1974], e.g. 100-2, 410-14. On Schulz see the remarks of Riches 1980, 57: this precision 'in locating the communities in time and space is surprising, but without firm foundations'. The same, I suggest, is true of Kloppenborg's mirror-image theory.

Bible Dictionary, written by Christopher Tuckett, one of the current world authorities on the subject, likewise takes a very different line from Kloppenborg.[65] One of the most recent serious scholarly works on Q reaches the following conclusions, which are also very different from the North American Q school, and which rule out Mack's and some other uses of Q altogether:

> . . . there will not be . . . reluctance on the part of the advocates of Q to accept that the boundaries of this hypothetical document remain indistinct.[66]

> Whatever may have been the message of the historical John [sc. the Baptist] for his contemporaries, the message of the John of Q for his audience is clear. That message recurs in Q and is there from the beginning. It is that the people of God must be prepared in the fullest sense for the eschatological crisis which will, in spite of delay, occur imminently and centre on the coming of the Son of man to judge and save.[67]

> The inaugural discourse of Jesus in Q is an integrated whole in respect of both formal construction and theological texture . . . Given the key role of an inaugural discourse, this is extremely important for the understanding of Q. This is a text for persons belonging to the community of Israel.[68]

> The results of the investigation [of the 'mission charge' in Luke 10 and parallels] are more modest than those recommended by, for example, John Kloppenborg and Risto Uro. In essence, the distinctions which form the basis of a reconstruction of a four-stage evolution in the tradition seem unduly fine, and the associated premise that Mark and Q were independent appears unduly hazardous. In place of such a reconstruction this study has suggested two conclusions. The first is that an original mission charge, which is an integrated whole stemming from Jesus himself, can be recovered . . . The second is that a single layer of additional material was added by the Q editor.[69]

> The Q material studied so far has brought to light a community whose faith was personally centred on Jesus as Son of man, but whose commitment to the message proclaimed by Jesus as prophet was intense . . . The Q Christians held on to, and indeed proclaimed, the imminence of the kingdom of the God they knew as Father.[70]

Q provides prefaces to some collections of sayings; in each case these address

> a problem peculiar to the period some thirty years before the Jewish War, the problem of the charismatic prophets with their preoccupation with particular places where the great act of liberation would occur. Against that whole pattern of thought the Q community

---

[65] Tuckett 1992, warning (568f.) against oversimplified theories.

[66] Catchpole 1993, 6, supported by a detailed note. The implied triple negative of this sentence reflects quite appropriately, in my view, the degree of uncertainty involved.

[67] Ibid., 78.

[68] Ibid., 133; cf. 172f., where the mission implied in Q is described as 'thoroughly prophetic'.

[69] Ibid., 188.

[70] Ibid., 201, 228.

sets the coming Son of man, the one whose coming would be visible anywhere and every-where.[71]

We have a picture of a community whose outlook was essentially Jerusalem-centred, whose theology was Torah-centred, whose worship was temple-centred, and which saw (with some justice) no incompatibility between all of that and commitment to Jesus.[72]

My point is not that every one of these statements is to be taken without further debate. I am not sure, myself, that we can know all the things that even Catchpole thinks we can know (and no doubt he would say the same of me). The point is simply that scholars who have immersed themselves in the study of Q every bit as much as Kloppenborg, Mack and some other North Americans have returned with a rather different tale to tell. Gone is the firm support, in Q, for an early, non-apocalyptic, largely non-Jewish, non-prophetic form of Christianity, into which such elements are introduced as secondary deviations or corruptions. Gone is the Cynic-like community intent simply on 'living with verve in troubled times'.[73] It disappears back whence it came, which turns out to be the mythology of the counter-cultural movements of the 1960s and the environmental protests of the 1980s.[74] Gone, in particular, is the sense of certainty that Q was a 'gospel' whose omissions (the crucifixion, for instance) were as significant as its inclusions.[75]

Mack's proposal, in short, is a historical hypothesis, to be verified according to the normal canons; and by those canons it fails.[76] It does not do justice to the data: it chops up texts with cheerful abandon and relocates them all over the place, radically misreading first-century Judaism and completely marginalizing the theology and religion of Paul – which is the one body of literature we not only actually possess but which we know for certain was produced within thirty years of the crucifixion. Mack's scheme has no simplicity of design, except in regard to Jesus himself, who is grossly *over*simplified. The only area on which it seems to shed light is the analysis of twentieth-century American religion. Ironically, the rejection of the Great Man cultural myth in the American academy of the 1980s paralleled the rejection of the Great Man myth in the German Academy of the 1920s, just in time to revive Bultmann's hypothesis before it disappeared off the map altogether. But when these particular socio-cultural conditions change, the wallpaper that presently covers the large cracks in this historical theory will

---

[71] Ibid. 255.

[72] Ibid. 279.

[73] cf. Mack 1993, 4.

[74] Ibid., 117.

[75] cf. esp. Kloppenborg 1992, 117–19. I shall deal with the question of the crucifixion in Part III of the present volume.

[76] cf. *NTPG* 98–109.

start to peel off. Those who want to continue with serious research on Jesus will need different foundations and building materials. They may conclude that they require a different architect as well.

4. J. Dominic Crossan

(i) Introduction

John Dominic Crossan is one of the most brilliant, engaging, learned and quick-witted New Testament scholars alive today. He has been described by one recent friendly critic as a 'rather skeptical New Testament professor with the soul of a leprechaun'.[77] He seems incapable, in his recent work at least, of thinking a boring thought or writing a dull paragraph.[78] His major work *The Historical Jesus: The Life of a Mediterranean Jewish Peasant* is a book to treasure for its learning, its thoroughness, its brilliant handling of multiple and complex issues, its amazing inventiveness, and above all its sheer readability. The book is based on many years of careful and painstaking research, and stands on the shoulders of previous books that won acclaim in their own right.[79] Crossan represents, far more than Burton Mack, the high-point of achievement in the new wave of the New Quest.[80]

It is all the more frustrating, therefore, to have to conclude that the book is almost entirely wrong.[81] In order to substantiate this judgment we must do our best to summarize and criticize a work whose whole direction is entirely different from the present one. It may be simplest if we note first the ways in which Crossan stands as a fairly typical representative of the Jesus Seminar, in the same stream as Mack, before turning to the things that mark his book out from them.

Like Mack, Crossan follows Wrede in believing that Mark (and, following him, Matthew and Luke) have bequeathed to subsequent history an account

[77] van Beeck 1994, 97.

[78] Though some would dissent from this when it comes to Crossan 1988a, whose preface apologizes quite rightly for the density of the detailed argument.

[79] See particularly Crossan 1973, 1983, 1988a, 1988b [1975]. Subsequent references without date are to Crossan 1991a. A shorter, and in some ways more openly provocative, statement of the same position can be found in Crossan 1994; Crossan's view of the passion and resurrection narratives is presented in a more popular form in Crossan 1995.

[80] I wish to record my deep gratitude to Crossan for his willingness to enter into friendly and, I hope, continuing debate, following my public discussion with him (see Wright 1993). I am also grateful to some other participants in the discussions of Crossan 1991a at the 1992 SBL meeting in San Francisco, and the 1993 symposium at DePaul University, for letting me have copies of their then unpublished critiques.

[81] A brief but fairly devastating critique can be found in Meyer 1993.

of Jesus which, though beguilingly attractive, is fundamentally fictitious. Mark, like a brilliant script-writer, shows us a story-line so compelling that he lures us into imagining that it is really historical.[82] Unlike Mack, however, Crossan does not think that Mark is raising the banner of an unworldly, dualistic apocalyptic perspective. Crossan sees that eschatology, and even the idea of something being 'world-denying', have to do not with the abandonment of the world to its fate but with the subversion of the world. Crossan uses the term 'eschatological' and 'world-negation' in a wide-ranging way, denoting 'views which find this world radically and profoundly corrupt or corrupting'.[83] This allows him to share with Mack, and many others in the Jesus Seminar, the view that apocalyptic sayings have been introduced into the Jesus-traditions without authority from Jesus himself. He has, however, a far more nuanced way of reading that development. Mark was being subversive, not (in Mack's sense) world-denying.[84] Nevertheless, the tradition which Mark initiated led to sad consequences, as Catholic Christianity argued itself into the position where the Constantinian settlement embraced a different sort of kingdom, and a different sort of common meal, to that envisaged by Jesus.[85]

Like Mack again, Crossan follows Bultmann in certain key respects which justify our placing of him within the revived Bultmannian 'New Quest'. True, he actually thinks, against Bultmann, that we can know a good deal about Jesus, and that what we can know is significant for Christian faith and practice.[86] By implication at least, Crossan's Jesus sets standards against which subsequent developments in the tradition can be judged.[87] Crossan also thinks, against Bultmann, that history must be read politically rather than existentially, and that the Bultmannian hermeneutic never engages (as he wants to do) with systemic evil, but only with personal evil. He studies not only Jesus' words, but also his deeds; indeed, the words themselves are 'performance', so that the very opening sentence of Crossan's largest work,

---

[82] This image, and some of what now follows, comes from a private conversation with Crossan on 5 February 1993.

[83] Private correspondence, 18 September 1995.

[84] See the discussion in Crossan 238, and my comments below.

[85] Crossan 424; cf. Mack 1988, 361f. To suggest that debates about authority in the first two centuries were simply a foretaste of the Constantinian settlement is, in my view, a gross oversimplification.

[86] On the former point, see the implicit criticism of Bultmann in Crossan xxvii: 'There were always historians who said [historical Jesus research] could not be done because of historical problems. There were always theologians who said it should not be done because of theological objections. And there were always scholars who said the former when they meant the latter.' On the contemporary relevance of the 'Quest', cf. Crossan 422–4.

[87] See e.g. Crossan 263.

in which this is highlighted, is intended to distance himself from Bultmann.[88] His Jesus, in short, is radically different from Bultmann's lonely existentialist preacher. As Crossan himself insists, his own background and inspiration is Irish and Catholic, not German and Protestant.[89] But, as earlier phases in Crossan's work would suggest, the same underlying concerns emerge.[90] Who, within twentieth-century scholarship, did most to promote a view of Jesus as a wise aphoristic teacher, generating an early tradition in which his short sayings became steadily elaborated, not least within an increasingly gnostic setting? The answer is of course Bultmann. Crossan's own admission that he is primarily interested in the Jesus-tradition, not in Jesus himself, tells in the same direction:

> I am not seeking a moment in the Galilean past, not even one fixed and frozen in surety and certainty. I am seeking an understanding of the Jesus tradition, of what must have been done and said to generate such immediate diversity of interpretation. What is of supreme interest to me is not the content of the Jesus voice but the nature of the Jesus tradition. But I do not really know how to comprehend the tradition without asking also about its origins with Jesus.

This Jesus-tradition, moreover, is not merely one to be remembered but one that demands that we come to terms with it: it

> is not a mnemonic but a hermeneutical tradition. It is one which challenges us not to obedient repetition but to interpretive decision.[91]

The voice may be Celtic and Catholic – there are echoes, indeed, of liberal Catholicism in the emphasis on the tradition rather than its founder, and in the evocations of Loisy – but the sentiments expressed are not far removed from those of the Teutonic Protestant master.

There are other interesting echoes as well. Indeed, it has been argued that Crossan's book places itself firmly in the company of the great line of writers, from Schleiermacher through Renan to Schweitzer himself, who

> try to make [Jesus] theologically appealing by cultivating universalism – that is, by casting him as the historic proponent of the most attractive humanism imaginable.[92]

[88] xi: 'In the beginning was the performance; not the word alone, not the deed alone, but both, each indelibly marked with the other forever.' If this is directed to Bultmann, the next sentence is obviously aimed at Schweitzer: 'He comes as yet unknown into a hamlet of Lower Galilee . . .'

[89] See Crossan 1985, 61.

[90] At the Society of Biblical Literature meeting in Leuven in August 1994, Crossan himself distinguished his more Bultmannian earlier work, which was close to that of the arch-Bultmannian Perrin, from his more recent phase. I suggest that some traces of Early Crossan are still clearly visible in Late Crossan. The problem of plotting such things in the work of our contemporaries should make us wary when dividing up, for instance, Q or *Thomas*.

[91] Crossan 1985, 61.

[92] van Beeck 1994, 88. As van Beeck points out, this impression is confirmed by Cros-

Crossan, in short, is to be located well and truly on the map of nineteenth- and twentieth-century seekers after Jesus – even if the manner of his pursuing the Quest, and the results he achieves, are in some ways strikingly different from those of his predecessors.

(ii) Basic Features

So to the book itself. Three basic features call for immediate discussion: the treatment of sources, the historical method, and the implicit epistemology. In each case Crossan is original, clear, and highly provocative.

The sources are discussed and handled in as thoroughgoing a fashion as has ever been attempted. Crossan sets out a substantial 'inventory of the Jesus tradition'.[93] This is arranged first by chronological stratification, and second by independent attestation; the aim, of course, is to be able to see which parts of the material are both early and well attested. Chronologically, Crossan divides the material into four: AD 30–60, 60–80, 80–120, and 120–150. The first stratum contains some of the Pauline correspondence,[94] the hypothetical first version of *Thomas*, the so-called 'Egerton Gospel', two fragmentary papyri, the *Gospel of the Hebrews*, the so-called 'Sayings Gospel' Q, a collection of miracles reconstructed from Mark and John, a hypothetical source standing behind *Didache* 16 and Matthew 24 and different to Mark 13, and what Crossan calls the 'Cross Gospel', reconstructed out of the *Gospel of Peter*. The second chronological stratum (60–80) contains the *Gospel of the Egyptians* (not extant, but reconstructed from six patristic citations), two versions of the Gospel of Mark – the first including the so-called 'secret gospel of Mark' – another fragmentary papyrus (*P. Oxy.* 840), the fuller (second) version of *Thomas*, a 'dialogue collection' now embedded in the gnostic tract called *Dialogue of the Saviour*, a 'signs gospel' now incorporated in the gospel of John, and the letter to the Colossians. The

---

san's frequent quotations from Renan and Schweitzer. What we have in Crossan, says van Beeck, is 'a twentieth-century version of a Romantic preconception: true religiosity is a matter of the *inner* experience of human authenticity alone; articulate worship of a transcendent God and positive engagement in socio-political structures are inauthentic and alienating. No wonder Crossan's work is reminiscent of Strauss, Renan, Schweitzer' (96: italics original).

[93] Appendix 1, 427–50. Frustratingly, Crossan does not say at this point where one may find all the texts he lists. Most of them, however, are helpfully included in Funk 1985b & c and/or Miller 1992 [1991]. A painstaking, and in parts devastating, critique of this inventory is provided by Neirynck 1994.

[94] Namely, 1 Th., Gal., 1 Cor., and Rom. One might have thought that 2 Cor. and Phil. deserved to be included. Col. is placed in the 60–80 bracket: apart from the Pastorals, the other Paulines are, surprisingly, not mentioned.

third stratum (80-120) contains somewhat better-known works: Matthew, Luke, Revelation, *1 Clement*, *Barnabas*, parts of the *Didache*, the *Shepherd of Hermas*, the letter of James, the first edition of John's gospel, the letters of Ignatius, 1 Peter, chs. 13-14 of Polycarp's *Letter to the Philippians*, and 1 John. The fourth and final stratum (120-150) concludes the list with John's gospel (second edition), Acts, the *Apocryphon of James*, 1 and 2 Timothy, 2 Peter, chs. 1-12 of Polycarp's *Letter to the Philippians*, 2 Clement, the *Gospel of the Nazoreans*, the *Gospel of the Ebionites*, some more fragments of the *Didache*, and the full version of the *Gospel of Peter*.

Clearly, this catalogue is of immense importance for Crossan's whole project. If he is right, not least in placing all sorts of works quite unlike the synoptic gospels chronologically so close to the time of Jesus, and the synoptic gospels themselves so comparatively late, then almost all the research on Jesus undertaken in the last two hundred and fifty years has been labouring under a great delusion. This is of course quite possible; but is it likely?

It is only fair to say that all but a few within the world of New Testament scholarship would regard this list as extremely shaky, and all except Crossan himself would have at least some quite serious points of disagreement with it. Almost all the list, except for the early Paulines, could well be challenged. We must look briefly at some aspects, stratum by stratum.

1st stratum. To place *Thomas* within this stratum, albeit distinguishing between two separate layers, is highly tendentious. To state baldly that one layer 'was composed by the fifties C.E., possibly in Jerusalem, under the aegis of James' authority', with only the reference to *Thomas* 12 as justification, is a remarkable piece of bravado.[95] And the other sources in the first stratum are equally problematic. It is hard enough to be sure of our ground in reconstructing the life-setting of whole gospels such as Matthew or Luke; infinitely harder when dealing with fragmentary papyri, or works known only from patristic citation. To treat Q as a document at all is controversial. To treat it as a *gospel* (Crossan insists emphatically on this) is more so; to postulate two or three stages in its development is to build castles in the air; to insist that the document was 'composed by the fifties, and possibly at Tiberias in Galilee', is to let imagination run riot.[96] Early collections of Jesus' sayings, or deeds, or apocalyptic words, may have existed, but to reconstruct them with any certainty is extremely risky. As for the so-called 'Cross Gospel', which Crossan himself reconstructed from parts of the

---

[95] Crossan 427. The case has of course been argued (e.g. Koester 1982a [1980], 150-4). On *Thomas* see further *NTPG* 435-43, and other literature cited there.

[96] Crossan 429. On Q see the discussion, and further literature, in *NTPG* 435-43; and above, 41-3.

(clearly much later) *Gospel of Peter*,[97] its very existence as a separate document has not been accepted yet by any other serious scholar, and its suggested date ('by the 50s C.E.') and provenance ('possibly at Sepphoris in Galilee') are purely imaginary. To suggest, further, that it is 'the single source of the intracanonical passion narrative' is one of the most breathtaking moves Crossan makes in an already strikingly original book.[98] Like so many of the judgments made in the inventory, this one depends wholly on Crossan's prior convictions both about Jesus himself and about the nature of early Christianity. (This is not to say that they are thereby disproved, merely that the real debate must take place elsewhere.[99])

2nd stratum. Crossan dates here the *Gospel of the Egyptians* and a dialogue collection supposedly embedded in the *Dialogue of the Saviour*, on the grounds that their dialogue formats are 'more developed' than material already assigned to the first stratum. These reconstructions, though, are both extremely shaky, as is the underlying notion of development. The same holds for the dating of Oxyrhynchus Papyrus 840, which Crossan claims is also 'more developed'. 'Secret Mark', which Morton Smith claimed to have discovered in 1958, is regarded by most scholars as, at the very best, a considerably later adaptation of Mark in a decidedly gnostic direction.[100] The existence of a pre-Johannine 'signs source' is only one possible interpretation, out of many, of the prehistory of the gospel of John.[101]

3rd & 4th strata. If almost all these sources are dubious candidates for a date before 80, are there others which should replace them? Almost certainly. Leaving Paul aside, a good many would want to place Matthew and Luke no later than 80, and even those who would demur at this might suggest that plenty of their distinctive material may well go back into the second period if not the first.[102] Once again, the very strong argument that can be made on the basis of oral tradition must be invoked, not as a *deus ex machina* but as a serious historical point about the kind of society in which early Christianity was born and nurtured.[103] To relegate material in Matthew

---

[97] cf. Crossan 1988a. To speak, then, of the 'lost opening' to this already hypothetical work, and to suggest that this lost opening is the source for one of Matthew's traditions (Crossan 394), is to attempt to climb a ladder without rungs.

[98] Crossan 429; cf. Crossan 1995, *passim*. The 'Jesus Seminar' voted against Crossan's hypothesis in its 1996 Spring meeting. Cf. too Brown 1994, 1317–49.

[99] For more discussion of this point, see the start of the next chapter.

[100] cf. Smith 1973. See now the detailed discussion in Gundry 1993, 603–23.

[101] For alternatives, cf. e.g. Hengel 1989b; Ashton 1991; Bauckham 1993a; and other literature cited by all three.

[102] Crossan's cut-off points for dating are of course arbitrary. The first two strata consist of twenty years each, the third forty, thus enabling him to imply, say, that a document written in 81 belongs with one written in 119 rather than with one written in 79.

[103] See above, n.56; and the discussion in ch. 4 below.

and Luke (other than Q) to a date after 80 is simply unwarranted. And to insist that the second edition of John's gospel is later than 120 is to fly in the face of strong evidence: the material most likely to be added later seems to reflect the recent death of the 'beloved disciple', and, difficult of course though it is to know how to date such an event, it is especially problematic to place it later than around 100 at the outside.

In fact, Crossan's chronological strata must be seen for what they are. Though he offers them as *starting*-points, they are in fact *conclusions* drawn from his basic thesis about Jesus and early Christianity. They are none the worse for that. They are part of the overall hypothesis which he is advancing, and all hypotheses are, as we have seen, ultimately circular.[104] But, despite the postmodern tone which predominates in the book, the massive inventory of material is bound to look like a thoroughly modernist piece of work, appearing to lay firm, almost positivist, foundations for the main argument of the book. Though in some cases Crossan has adjusted his presentation to fit with the canons he has set up (omitting the parable of the good Samaritan, for instance, on the grounds that it only appears once, and that in the third stratum), I submit that his inventory is the *result*, not the *ground*, of a position about early Christianity adopted for quite other reasons. This is where the real debate must take place, as we shall see. Many will regard the inventory, for all its massive learning, care and ingenuity, as the *reductio ad absurdum* of the thesis. To conclude thus at this stage would be to beg the question, but not to note the possibility would be irresponsible.

Crossan's second way of slicing the cake, that is, of dealing with the source material, is his arrangement of it according to 'independent attestation'. He lists the items which appear in each of the chronological strata, subdividing them further into 'multiple independent attestation' (i.e. occurring more than three times), then triple, then double, and finally those with single attestation only. Once one has grasped the quite considerable complexities of the system – which of course faithfully reflect the complexities of the material – one can see almost at a glance how Crossan is able to 'grade' a particular item or cluster of items. If something occurs in the first chronological stratum, and possesses multiple attestation, it stands a good chance of being accepted as genuine; the further one moves down the chronological scale, and the fewer attestations we find, the less chance there may be. This does not prevent many judgments going in the opposite direction. The prediction of 'Jesus' apocalyptic return' occurs in the first stratum, and is multiply attested,[105] but is regarded as 'from the later Jesus tradition'

---

104 See Crites 1989 [1971], 72 n.6, and *NTPG* 31f., 98–109.

105 Crossan's list (434): 1 Th. 4.13–18; *Did.* 16.6–8; Mt. 24.30a; Mk. 13.24–7 = Mt. 24.29, 30b–31 = Lk. 21.25–8; Rev. 1.7; Rev. 1.13; Rev. 14.14; Jn. 19.37. Several passages from the Pauline corpus are strangely absent from this list, such as 2 Th. 2.1–12. If (as I

rather than from Jesus himself, because Crossan has decided that such 'apocalyptic' material is uncharacteristic of Jesus.[106] The same is true of the Lord's Prayer.[107] Conversely, the parables of the lost coin, the prodigal son and the unjust steward (Luke 15.8–10, 11–32, 16.1–7) are judged to be from Jesus, even though they are in the third chronological stratum and only singly attested.[108] Despite these and many other exceptions, however, Crossan sticks quite faithfully to his programme, and throughout the book he reminds the reader of the status, on both scales, of the material under consideration.

The exceptions just noted, however, force us to place two important caveats here. First, the number of times a saying happens to turn up in the records is a very haphazard index of its likely historicity or otherwise. By historical accident, we happen to have certain sources and not others. If we had a few more extra-canonical gospels, we might easily have several more parallels for material that at the moment appears unique to one document. Second, if, as I have argued elsewhere, one likely scenario of Jesus' ministry is that he said the same or similar things in many places at many times,[109] it is highly likely that we would have what look like similar or even dependent accounts which are in fact independent. All hinges on what view we take of the wider synoptic problem (i.e. the question of the mutual interrelationship not only of Matthew, Mark and Luke but also *Thomas* and the rest). The question of what counts as 'independent' is therefore very difficult to settle, and harder still to use with any security as an index of historical probability. It is small comfort to note, as we have, that Crossan himself does not use it with any great strictness, but relies, as we all must, on the larger question: does this saying cohere with the overall historical hypothesis being advanced? Once that question has been admitted to be the vital one, we are back where we started. The appearance of great scientific and methodological rigour given by this long Appendix is just that, an appearance. The inventory has

---

guess) Crossan does not regard 2 Th. as Pauline, it surely functions as a further independent witness?

[106] cf. Crossan's discussions at 238–59, 284–7; and below, chs. 6, 8.

[107] Crossan 293f.; see Harvey 1993, 227. Crossan believes that there are in fact three independent versions of the prayer, and that some of them belong to the earliest stratum; but, he says, 'I do not think that such a coordinated prayer was ever taught by [Jesus] to his followers' (294). That, he says, would have resulted in wider attestation and more unanimity on the contents. 'Also . . . the establishment of such a prayer seems to represent the point where a group starts to distinguish and even separate itself from the wider religious community, and I do not believe that point was ever reached during the life of Jesus.' The decision rests, therefore, not on the inventory at all, but on one's overall reconstruction of what Jesus' ministry was actually like.

[108] Crossan 449; he obeys his own self-restriction, though, by refraining from using the material in the positive reconstruction.

[109] cf. *NTPG* 422f.

been put together with immense care and skill, but it does not help much when we come to make large historical judgments. Nor, I submit, has Crossan actually used it in *this* way – i.e. to affect his major historical reconstruction – to any great extent. It has conditioned the *presentation* of his case, but not the underlying case itself.[110]

We now turn to the second area for preliminary discussion, namely Crossan's historical method itself. Here there are three levels of operation. The treatment of the sources, just outlined, is the small-scale level (the 'microcosmic'). The regular task of ancient history, the reconstruction of the world of the Eastern Mediterranean in the first century, is the middle level (the 'mesocosmic'). Overarching both of these, at the 'macrocosmic' level, comes an analysis at the level of social anthropology.

We have already discussed the microcosmic level. With the mesocosmic level there can be no problem in principle; all agree that the serious task of historical reconstruction, applied to first-century Palestine, is the essential setting for any study of Jesus.[111] Crossan brings to the task a refreshing grasp of a wide range of sources, drawing freely on Josephus, on various papyri, and on classical authors such as Cicero. But with the macrocosmic level further difficulties arise.

No one should doubt the great value of social anthropology as part of the equipment of the historian. Indeed, from one point of view social anthropology is simply one vital aspect of the historical task: it is a way of avoiding anachronisms by recognizing that different societies operate with different worldviews and social norms.[112] Without this, for instance, the conversation between Mary, Martha and Jesus becomes simply a matter of Mary being a more 'spiritual', and Martha a more 'practical', sort of person. The passage (Luke 10.38–42) has thus been the subject of millions of homilies on the priority of prayer over housework. But as soon as we get inside the culture of a first-century Palestinian village, a much more subversive note is struck. Mary has refused to be confined to the women's quarters:

> Jesus' remark to Martha serves to vindicate Mary's exceptional presence in space not expected of her; the story consciously upsets the native perception of how things ought to be.[113]

[110] cf. Harvey 1993, 227f.

[111] cf. *NTPG* Part III; Crossan Part II.

[112] See esp. Neyrey 1991, e.g. the programmatic statements in x–xv. Cp. Crossan 6: study of even a modern, but traditional, Mediterranean village 'is an excellent therapeutic against presuming that an ancient Galilean village is like, say, a modern American one, only much smaller, older, and without electric utilities or electronic toys.' On the relation between sociology, history and theology see now esp. Milbank 1990.

[113] Malina and Neyrey, in Neyrey 1991, 62. I was first alerted to the point about Mary and Martha through an unpublished paper by Dr Kenneth Bailey.

And if Mary, in Luke's narrative, is abandoning the serving of tables to concentrate on the word of God, this may have wider overtones yet.[114] This is the kind of insight that the social scientist can and must contribute to historical reconstruction, necessarily involving the question of why people do and say the things they do.[115]

The application of social science to the historical study of the New Testament is still in comparative infancy, and it is to Crossan's credit that he has done so much to bring its necessary insights to the task of setting Jesus in his own world, instead of in a world imagined simply by analogy with our own. In particular, he has highlighted the situation of the peasant within Mediterranean culture.[116] Following various anthropologists, he plots the all-important sense of 'honour' and 'shame', which function as basic and pivotal values, determining not least the expectations of gender roles. Following Lenski, he suggests that the aristocratic classes and their retainers formed about 10% of the population, with the rest being peasants and artisans, at the bottom of which large group came those generally regarded as expendable, the 'nobodies'. There was no real 'middle class'. Power and influence were 'brokered' through the informal but all-important patron/client system, in which well-placed clients of wealthy and powerful patrons became patrons to others in their turn. Society hinges upon these 'brokers' who sustain a double relationship, 'one as client to a patron and another as patron to a client';[117] and Crossan's argument in turn will hinge vitally on this analysis. Thus

> In the Roman Mediterranean . . . the web of patronage and clientage, with accounts that could never be exactly balanced because they could never be precisely computed, was the dynamic morality that held society together.[118]

And what if the patronage system does not deliver the goods? The alternatives are, basically, destitution and banditry. There are stages *en route* to both, but neither is far away. From this point there is a clear line into the history of first-century Palestine, as I tried to show earlier.[119] Thus the 'macrocosmic' social-anthropological model gives, in principle, depth and greater accuracy to the 'mesocosmic' historical work.

Questions remain, though, about Crossan's actual use of the social sciences. Following Neyrey's critique, we may note the following.[120] First, Crossan has not given as detailed an analysis of the peasant class as was

[114] Neyrey 1991, 379. Cf. Ac. 6.2.
[115] cf. *NTPG* 109–12.
[116] Crossan ch. 3.
[117] Crossan 60.
[118] Crossan 65.
[119] *NTPG* 167–81.
[120] Neyrey 1992.

really needed. In particular, his use of the social sciences to describe this group is selective, and the materials 'seem to have been chosen from an ideological point of view: they will yield the results desired', i.e. of portraying Jesus as some sort of a revolutionary.[121] Though he notes that artisans form a lower class than peasants, he never considers the possibility that Jesus might have been part of this group.[122] Nor, second, has he supplied a 'sociology of deviance' such as would fill out his portrait of a political and dangerous Jesus.[123] And, third, had Crossan gone more thoroughly into the notion of purity as it functioned within peasant societies, he would have been restrained 'from celebrating sexual ambiguity or homosexuality',[124] and would have found his notion of 'egalitarianism' called into question.[125] Other criticisms could also be levelled, not least against Crossan's use (following Horsley) of Hobsbawm's work on bandits.[126] But in general, these criticisms apart, his macrocosmic essay in social anthropology serves as a vital backdrop to the historical account. It opens a door for further research down the same line.

In the middle, between the social anthropology and the textual inventory, there comes the historical reconstruction. Here we reach our third set of introductory comments, relating now to basic epistemology.[127]

Crossan insists, in good postmodern style, that he is rejecting the old modernist historiography, with its pretensions to objectivity and its carefully masked social and cultural programme and agenda:

> Need I say . . . that the way in which the nineteenth century [and much of the twentieth, we might add] dreamed of uncommitted, objective, dispassionate historical study should be clearly seen for what it was, a methodological screen to cover various forms of social power and imperialistic control?[128]

He is aware (more, perhaps, than some of his colleagues in the 'Jesus Seminar') of the danger of 'positivistic simplicities' in the labelling of material as either authentic or inauthentic. He is clear that his methodology

---

[121] Neyrey 1992, 4f. One aspect of peasant society that Crossan has not examined is precisely its functioning as an *oral* society with a strong local folk memory not just for aphorisms but for narratives. See ch. 4 below.

[122] So Harvey 1993, 227f.

[123] Neyrey 1992, 5.

[124] Ibid., 6, referring to Crossan 330ff.

[125] Neyrey 1992, 7, on Crossan 263, 298, 346, 361.

[126] See further ch. 4 below.

[127] On this point see esp. Wright 1993.

[128] Crossan 423. Crossan, here and elsewhere, is interestingly in line with Nietzsche, who in his own aphoristic philosophy insisted that there is 'only interpretation'. Cf. Nietzsche 1909–13, 15.2.12, aphorism 481 (a reference I owe to Thiselton 1995, 15f.).

does not claim a spurious objectivity, because almost every step demands a scholarly judgment and an informed decision.

He is thus concerned

not with an unattainable objectivity, but with an attainable honesty.[129]

This, I think, coheres very well with the programme I set out in *NTPG* Part II, and as such Crossan's book falls into a different league from those that persist in the pursuit of the old-style objectivity.[130] When Crossan speaks of 'honesty' here I sense that he means fundamentally the same thing as I mean when I speak of the 'public' nature of the enquiry.[131] Rejection of spurious objectivity cannot mean collapsing back into the private world, the closed circle, of mere subjectivism. The honesty of the critic is correlated to the publicness of the discourse. Without honesty there can be no genuine publicness, only publicity.

At the same time, building on what we noted above about Crossan's inventory of Jesus-material, it should be clear that his book still tacitly appeals to the old 'objectivist' values that he explicitly repudiates. The inventory itself, in its content and manner of presentation, bears witness to this, as does the striking claim on the book's jacket: 'The first comprehensive determination of who Jesus was, what he did, what he said.' It is clear that the book possesses a certain inner tension: the stated claim to avoid spurious objectivism sits uncomfortably alongside the implicit claim that here at last is the solid historical ground that generations of Jesus-researchers have been waiting for. Even if the latter emphasis represents simply the publisher's determination to market the book to an audience that it perceives, no doubt correctly, to be hungry for 'objective' results, there is still an unresolved tension at the philosophical, specifically the epistemological, level. Crossan sees the need for appropriate reconstruction,[132] but has not yet articulated a way by which this can actually be achieved. Unless we can do this – and I submit that a serious 'critical realism' goes at least some way towards such a goal[133] – then history will remain a matter of brokerage, of the historian as patron and the reader as client. 'Critical realism', in other words, is an attempt to provide, in the sphere of historical method, what Crossan thinks Jesus was offering in the sphere of first-century peasant life: a brokerless kingdom.

---

[129] Crossan xxxiv.

[130] e.g. Meier 1991, 1f. Cf. van Beeck 1994, 85f.

[131] *NTPG* Part II, esp. 135f.

[132] cf. Crossan 426: 'One cannot dismiss . . . the search for the historical Jesus as *mere* reconstruction, as if reconstruction invalidated somehow the entire project. Because there is *only* reconstruction' (italics original).

[133] cf. *NTPG* Part II.

(iii) Historical Reconstruction of Jesus

What then does Crossan have to offer at the level of historical reconstruction? Bearing in mind the all-important notion of 'brokerage' discussed earlier, he divides the material into three: 'Brokered Empire' (the Roman world of late antiquity, with its highly developed networks of master–slave and patron–client relationships), 'Embattled Brokerage' (the Palestinian world of the first century, with its crescendo of protest, brigandage and revolution leading up to the war of 66–70), and 'Brokerless Kingdom' (Jesus' own agenda and work).

Four points among many in the first two sections stand out to me as needing comment. First, Crossan is absolutely right to stress that when Tacitus says 'all was quiet under Tiberius' he does *not* mean that there were no movements of protest, no social groundswell of anti-Roman feeling. All he means, importantly, is 'that under Tiberius there were no revolts in Palestine *necessitating intervention from the Syrian legate backed by his legionary forces*'.[134] Second, however, he is in my estimation wrong to follow Horsley in regarding the Sicarii as an aristocratic, scribal group whose revolutionary aspirations were of a totally different order to those of the peasant bandits, and who only resorted to violence in the AD 50s and thereafter, having previously embraced a nonviolent form of revolt.[135] It may well be the case that the Sicarii on the one hand, and those who wrote and/or read apocalyptic literature on the other, came from a better-educated class than the average peasant. But to limit the slogan 'no king but god', or the revolutionary reading of books like Daniel, to such a group seems to me to fly in the face of the evidence.[136] Third, Crossan, like Mack and others, invokes the hypothesis that Jesus was some kind of a Cynic. I shall have more to say about this presently.[137] For the moment we may note that Crossan himself has to indicate a key distinction between Cynics (who carried a wallet as part of their regular kit, almost of their uniform) and Jesus' followers, who were expressly forbidden to do so; and between regular Cynicism, which was a Hellenistic and urban phenomenon, and Jesus' sort, which was Jewish and rural.[138] Fourth, I believe that Crossan, in common (be it said) with the great majority of New Testament scholars, has misunderstood the nature of

---

[134] Crossan 101f. (quote at 102: italics original). This corroborates my argument in *NTPG* 171f. The Tacitus line is from *Hist.* 5.9.

[135] Crossan 103–23. On this point, cf. ch. 11 below.

[136] cf. esp. *NTPG* 177–81.

[137] Below, 66–74.

[138] Crossan 338f., 340, 421f.. Crossan's solution – to use one of these problems to explain the other – is admirably ingenious, but historically implausible. Cf. too van Beeck 1994, 95.

apocalyptic. Just as Crossan 'reads' Jesus' healings, and his open table-fellowship, as indicating a profoundly subversive intent within the world of his day, so I have argued elsewhere that 'apocalyptic' writings, and Daniel in particular, were read in the first century as describing *not* 'the darkening scenario of an imminent end to the world'[139] but the radical subversion of the present world order.[140] This necessitates a thorough redrawing of Crossan's antithesis (in line with the Jesus Seminar) between 'apocalyptic' and 'sapiential'. 'Apocalyptic' is not about a god doing something and humans merely spectating. It invests human political and social action with its full theological significance.[141]

Turning to Jesus himself, Crossan argues that he was trying to inaugurate 'the brokerless kingdom of God'. Jesus was encouraging all and sundry, but especially the 'nobodies', to rely on god alone, subverting the whole patron/client system. He was not setting himself up as a new sort of 'patron'; that was why he kept on the move, lest any one town or village would regard him as such and set itself up as his intermediaries in a renewed patronage system, brokering his religious authority.[142]

The heart of Jesus' activity is seen in the highly subversive combination of 'magic and meal'. 'Magic', Crossan argues, is a loaded term, just like 'brigandage': a 'brigand' (like a 'hooligan' in former Communist parlance) is simply someone doing things of which the authorities disapprove, and 'magic' is simply a miracle done by the wrong sort of person. Jesus' invocation of the kingdom of god is to be seen 'not as an apocalyptic event in the imminent future but as a mode of life in the immediate present'.[143] It is a social programme which

is pointed directly and deliberately at the intersection of patronage and clientage, honor and shame, the very heart of ancient Mediterranean society.[144]

Miracles of healing (some of which Crossan takes to be definitely historical) are not simply evidence of Jesus' care for those in physical need. The fact that he did them at all carried enormous social implications: exorcisms and healings 'were what the Kingdom looked like at the level of political reality'.[145] Commensality, the sharing of food, was equally powerful as a socially and spiritually subversive action. It represented 'a strategy for building or rebuilding peasant community on radically different principles from

---

[139] Crossan 238.
[140] See above all *NTPG* ch. 10.
[141] cf. *NTPG* 459–64.
[142] Crossan 346ff., 422.
[143] Crossan 304.
[144] Crossan 304.
[145] Crossan 332.

those of honor and shame, patronage and clientage'.[146] Jesus thus 'sets the Kingdom against the Mediterranean'.[147] This is Crossan's basic and fundamental vision of what Jesus was about; and it becomes his major criterion for deciding which parts of the tradition are authentic, and which represent a declining away from the original vision in subsequent generations.[148] 'The heart of the original Jesus movement' was 'a shared egalitarianism of spiritual and material resources'. Crossan adds:

> I emphasize this as strongly as possible, and I insist that its materiality and spirituality, its facticity and symbolism cannot be separated. The mission we are talking about is not, like Paul's, a dramatic thrust along major trade routes to urban centres hundreds of miles apart. Yet it concerns the longest journey in the Greco-Roman world, maybe in any world, the step across the threshold of a peasant stranger's home.[149]

As a result, Jesus is to be seen as a *peasant Jewish Cynic*, like and unlike other Cynics of the period:

> His strategy, implicitly for himself and explicitly for his followers, was the combination of *free healing and common eating*, a religious and economic egalitarianism that negated alike and at once the hierarchical and patronal normalcies of Jewish religion and Roman power . . . Miracle and parable, healing and eating were calculated to force individuals into unmediated physical and spiritual contact with God and unmediated physical and spiritual contact with one another. He announced, in other words, the brokerless kingdom of God.[150]

What can be said about this remarkable vision of Jesus and his work? Certainly not that it illegitimately turns Jesus' concern in a social direction. I am convinced that the social and material dimensions of Jesus' ministry must be brought to the fore, as indeed they are in many contemporary writings. My anxiety, rather, is this: in grasping the way in which Jesus' programme cut against the normal social expectations of Mediterranean peasant culture, Crossan, like Mack (though not so blatantly), has radically and consistently underplayed the specifically Jewish dimension both of the culture itself and of Jesus' agenda for it. (Here some may trace a parallel with a great German writer of nearly a century ago. It was Adolf von Harnack who offered a deJudaized Jesus with a social programme.[151])

The lines of this basic criticism will emerge gradually as the present book unfolds. But certain markers may be put down at this stage. First, Crossan's rejection of apocalyptic, as incommensurate with Jesus' agenda, shows

---

[146] Crossan 344.
[147] Crossan 302.
[148] cf. e.g. Crossan 341–53.
[149] Crossan 341.
[150] Crossan 422 (italics original). This is the book's final basic summary.
[151] I owe this point to Professor Christopher Rowland.

through in his dismissal of the Jewish hope which, in my reading (and that of several others), Jesus claimed to fulfil. There is nothing incompatible with the cherishing of this hope, the claim both that it is being fulfilled and will be fulfilled, and the acting out of it in terms of a new agenda, a new way of celebrating being the people of god. Just because Jesus may well have had what may be described as a *social* programme, this does not mean he did not have a *Jewish* programme, stemming from the belief that Israel's god was the one true god and would vindicate his people at last. Crossan's reliance on Mack at this point, to demonstrate that language about the 'kingdom' may have had less to do with Jewish apocalyptic hope than with ethical and 'sapiential' ideals, speeds him on his way into a cul-de-sac.[152]

Second, Crossan's reconstruction enables us to understand perfectly well why there would be opposition to Jesus. Anyone who shatters the prevailing worldview as thoroughly as his Jesus did would be bound to incur hostility. But he never explains why there would be hostility from Jews *qua* Jews, from those who saw themselves as guardians of Israel's beliefs, hopes and way of life. And yet, if Jesus was claiming in any sense that by these socially explosive actions he was bringing about the promised time when Israel's god would become king, he was also clearly implying that the present structures of Judaism, and the present non-official movements within Judaism that still looked to those structures as their framework, were being challenged. Like so many other writers, Crossan is happy to leave the controversy stories to a later stage in the gospel tradition. But if we add to his socially subversive Jesus the possibility of his being also *Jewishly* subversive, other options will have to be considered.[153]

It ought to be possible, therefore, to add in all sorts of other dimensions, most particularly from a more specifically Jewish background, theology and expectation, without detracting from the social and cultural picture Crossan has painted. This will have the effect of relativizing some of the bold claims he makes, without (I trust) blunting the force of some of his main points.

If Jesus' work concentrated on articulating and enacting a 'brokerless kingdom', a 'kingdom of nobodies', then why did he die, and why did the early church come to attribute to his death the significance it did? Here we come to perhaps the boldest, and in my view the least satisfactory, aspect of the whole book, and, indeed, of Crossan's whole *oeuvre*. In Crossan's view, the earliest followers of Jesus knew nothing whatever about the details of why or how Jesus died, except that he had been crucified. They did not know where his body was buried. One 'very literate and highly sophisticated

---

[152] Crossan 287f., quoting Mack 1987, and 1988, 73f. See below, ch. 6.
[153] See below, ch. 9.

stream of tradition'[154] then began to search the Jewish scriptures to find texts which spoke of suffering and vindication, and to meditate on them in much the way we find in the *Epistle of Barnabas*. Then someone put these together into a narrative. The first such narrative is the so-called 'Cross Gospel', which, as we saw, Crossan himself has reconstructed out of the (admittedly much later) *Gospel of Peter*. All the other accounts of Jesus' death, he suggests, are dependent upon this – and upon their own further reflection on the scriptures. At some stage in the process from meditation to narrative the mood changes from focusing on suffering-and-vindication to death-and-resurrection: and the 'resurrection narratives' are born as well, though in the form in which we have them they concentrate, according to Crossan, on the legitimation of certain power-centres in the early church.

This is Crossan at his most ingenious, and, most will say, unconvincing. Crossan's ultra-suspicion of the texts (his neat slogan for their *modus operandi* is 'hide the prophecy, tell the narrative and invent the history'[155]) produces a complete *tour de force*, which has not so far persuaded many others in the discipline, and, in my judgment, ought not to do so.

It is clearly the case that the earliest interpretations we have of the death of Jesus see that event in the light of Jewish scripture. Christ died for our sins, says Paul quoting very early tradition, *according to the scriptures* (1 Corinthians 15.3). But if this means that all evidence of scriptural interpretation of Jesus' death is to be read as a sign of early Christian scribal activity, inventing narratives to cover a historical void, then Crossan has placed the texts in a quite spurious Catch-22 situation. There is, of course, no such thing as uninterpreted historical narrative; Crossan knows that as well as anyone. But if the sign of interpretative activity is the give-away clue that the history has been invented, how then can there ever be any history at all? Would Crossan have been more convinced of possible historicity if the passion narratives had consisted of obvious two-level writing, with 'historical facts' supplemented on occasion by 'interpretative glosses' that one could easily peel away? That may be what Matthew did ('all this happened to fulfil what was spoken by the prophet . . .'), but it is not the only way to write about actual events and invest them with the meaning that in these events the story of Israel has come to its goal. That, after all, is what 'according to the scriptures' means.[156]

Let us suppose that the earliest followers of Jesus *did* know what had happened to Jesus. Suppose, too, that they *did* associate these events with the

[154] Crossan 375. The whole phrase is italicized.

[155] Crossan 372. Van Beeck 1994, 92 comments that this line must have been written in 'a moment of inattention to the demands of both critical scholarship and sensitivity', and that it 'marks the end of careful historical scholarship'.

[156] cf. *NTPG* 241–3.

expectations which were cherished, not just by sophisticated scribes, but by thousands of ordinary Jews. Suppose that, from very early on, they told the story of Jesus and his death in a way which was designed *both* to refer to the actual events *and* to allude to the scriptural traditions which, they believed, had not merely been exemplified in Jesus (Jesus as simply a type of the righteous sufferer), but had actually reached their climax in him. There are strong signs that this was how some of the earliest Christian writings saw the matter.[157] But how would such a possibility ever come through Crossan's hermeneutic of suspicion and establish itself as historically probable?

Crossan's deep scepticism about our knowledge concerning Jesus' crucifixion is all the more ironic, since early in the relevant chapter he comes close to what I believe is the correct reading of the events that precipitated it. Crossan thinks, and I fully agree with him, that Jesus' action in the Temple was a symbolic destruction; that some words of Jesus about this destruction are original; and that these words and this action followed with a close logic from the rest of Jesus' agenda, the programme enacted in healings and meal-sharings.[158] This is a vital move, to be embraced in contrast with some other recent readings of the Temple-incident.[159] Crossan sees what many ignore, a crucial link between Jesus' programme in Galilee and his action in Jerusalem.[160] (Of course, I want to fill both halves of this equation with a different content and meaning to that postulated by Crossan.) Crossan faces the possibility that these words, and this action, led more or less directly to Jesus' death, but draws back from affirming it as more than a possibility. I think, and I shall argue later on, that at this point we are on very firm historical ground indeed.[161]

With Crossan's reconstruction of the genesis of the passion narratives, we are back again in the realm of William Wrede. Once you doubt everything in the story, and postulate a chain of events by which someone might have taken it upon themselves to invent such a narrative from scratch, all things are possible. But not all things are probable. I shall argue in the appropriate place that Crossan's reading of Jesus' death is far less likely than a reading in

---

[157] See Wright 1991, esp. ch. 7.

[158] Crossan 354–60.

[159] e.g. that of Chilton 1992b: see below, ch. 3.

[160] 'No matter . . . what Jesus thought, said, or did about the Temple, he was its functional opponent, alternative, and substitute' (355). Has Crossan reflected on the theological, and indeed the historical, implications of this stunning – and, I believe, entirely accurate – statement? Contrast Vermes 1993, 155 n.2 (Jesus' interest in Temple matters 'appears to have been rather peripheral'); 185.

[161] Crossan's anxiety (359) about the lack of this connection in *Thomas* 71 (the saying about destroying the Temple) is odd, since, as Crossan himself emphasizes so often, *Thomas* never makes narrative connections of any sort, and in any case has no account of the passion.

which the synoptic and Johannine traditions, though of course replete with theological and scriptural allusion, intend to describe things that actually happened, and basically succeed in this intention.[162] This hypothesis, I submit, makes better sense of the data, and does so with far more simplicity, than the complex and convoluted speculation offered by Crossan.

(iv) The Early Church

Nowhere is this speculation more intricately spun than in Crossan's account of the early church and its concern with Jesus of Nazareth. This is not the subject of the present book, any more than it was of Crossan's; but, as all writers on Jesus know, any theory about gospel traditions is also a theory about how the early church developed.[163] Crossan's theory is present at many points in the book, not least in the presuppositions behind the inventory of material. He elaborated it further in a paper given in Chicago on 4 February 1993. It runs as follows.

First, there is 'Thomas Christianity'. The opponents faced by Paul in Corinth represent this position: an early group, concerned with asceticism, with little need for reminiscences about Jesus (sayings, yes; deeds, no). They are opposed to an even earlier Christian apocalyptic movement; as far as they are concerned, paradise (a pre-sexual paradise, hence the asceticism) has been regained, and there is no End to be awaited. This group quickly shades off into early Christian gnosticism, represented by the *Gospel of Thomas* in its various hypothetical forms.

Second, there is 'Pauline Christianity'. This group, like its apostle, insists on the mode, not just the fact, of Jesus' death: hence the folly, the sheer lunacy, of the preaching of the cross. The historical Jesus, especially as the crucified one, is a part of Christian faith for Paul, as it was not for the hypothetical 'Thomas Christians'. So, too, a belief in the risen Jesus is absolutely central.

Third, there is 'Q Christianity'. Those who embraced this, in its early version, showed no interest in the death and resurrection of Jesus. They were, instead, living and acting in continuity with Jesus, maintaining his practice of open commensality. Like Jesus, they embraced the lifestyle of a wisdom which would continue its strange practice even if the world turned its back. They wandered about as early preachers, perhaps in husband-and-wife teams (thereby creating social scandal; women did not do such things). Later, the Q

---

[162] cf. *NTPG* chs. 13, 14; and below, ch. 12.
[163] cf. *NTPG* Part IV; cp. Crossan 422.

community reinstated the sort of apocalyptic against which the Thomas group had initially reacted.

Fourth, there is 'exegetical Christianity'. This consists of a group with scribal learning and the ability to manipulate scriptural texts to contribute to an early apologetic. It was they who wrote the passion and resurrection narratives, 'not as history remembered, but prophecy historicized'. They were learned, and therefore – unlike Jesus and his closest followers, and the Q community – they were not peasants. 'Their faith in the historical Jesus was so strong that they were constantly inventing more of it all the time.'[164]

This fascinating, brilliant, mind-blowing reconstruction is clearly at the heart of a great deal in Crossan's work. Without it, his use of the sources makes no sense; nor does his highly idiosyncratic reading of the passion and resurrection narratives. It gives to his whole work a completeness which it would otherwise lack. Yet it is, arguably, the most threadbare part of his whole rich tapestry. There is no space here to criticize it in detail. Suffice it to note the following points.

First, the belief that we can identify Paul's opponents in 1 Corinthians as a distinct group is not one that would be shared by many scholars. The suggestion that we can identify them *as Thomas Christians*, adhering to the ideology seen in the *Gospel of Thomas* – or at least an early form of it – is tenuous in the extreme.[165] It is of course true that some of Paul's language in that letter seems to indicate some use of 'gnosis' at Corinth. But most Pauline scholars have come to reject any form of a fully-blown 'gnostic' hypothesis as the explanation of the Corinthian problems.[166] In any case, to imagine that the Corinthian opponents were a recognized group who can be identified with a document reflecting an ideology which we only know for certain to have been embraced a century later, and then in Egypt, is straining credibility way beyond breaking point.

Second, Crossan is of course right to see the Pauline churches as forming a significant group within early Christianity. But were they as strongly bounded as he implies? Were they really an entirely separate body, without intertwining with other forms of Christianity? The incidental mention, in the letters and Acts, of all sorts of comings and goings in the early church, across geographical and cultural boundaries, suggests the contrary. In addition, to separate Paul from 'exegetical Christianity' seems to me quite extraordinary. Paul, as much as any writer in the first generation, had searched the Jewish scriptures and seen them fulfilled in Jesus.

[164] Crossan, in an oral presentation, February 1993.
[165] See Koester 1982b, 121f., on whom Crossan relies (228).
[166] For a recent discussion cf. Baird 1990.

Third, Crossan is of course being deliberately provocative in insisting that Q is not just a source but a gospel, and that we can postulate the praxis of a group of Christians by means of it. I have responded to this proposal already.[167] Even if there was such a source, even such a single document, as Q, to which we had access through the material in which Matthew and Luke overlap – and a good many scholars today doubt even this much – we have no evidence that it did not contain much besides, which either Matthew or Luke, or both, omitted, or which happens also to overlap with Mark. If that is so, its extent is quite literally unknowable. It could perfectly easily have contained a passion and/or resurrection narrative. Whether it did or not – and again there is no agreement on this, except among a very limited group of scholars, mostly committed to the reconstruction of Q as part of a particular way of reconceiving early Christianity – there is no particular reason to suppose that this document represents the beliefs and lifestyle of a substantial group within early Christianity. What we know of other groups that told and retold stories about Jesus – the second-century church, for example, and still more the church under Constantine – does not encourage us to think that the story-telling group modelled its lifestyle on its Jesus-stories with any degree of accuracy. The existence of Q Christians, like that of Thomas Christians, may well turn out to be a modern myth: a story told, without basis in real history, to support a particular way of construing contemporary reality.

Finally, the 'exegetical Christianity' which Crossan needs so badly as the perpetrator of the passion and resurrection narratives, and much else besides, is another simple fiction. True, the *Epistle of Barnabas* has clearly ransacked the Jewish scriptures for proof-texts to explain some of the subtler points about Jesus. But that text actually demonstrates the problem: it is so different from Paul or Matthew or any of the others that we have no particular reason to suppose that it reflects a way of thinking which was current in the first generation. It looks much more like a second- or third-generation attempt to fill in some gaps in Christian exegesis of the Jewish scriptures, but without the more thoroughgoing sense, which we find in Paul and in the synoptic tradition as a whole, that these scriptures were telling a great *story* that has now reached its climactic moment. In addition, to suppose (as Crossan has to) that only a few of Jesus' early followers would have any idea about, or interest in, the Jewish scriptures, and that nobody until after Jesus' death would have thought that the events they were witnessing could be part of the divinely promised fulfilment of Israel's history, and hence of her scriptures too, is way out of line with the evidence. Josephus tells us that it was scriptural oracles which incited the majority of Jews to rise against Rome.[168]

---

[167] *NTPG* 435–43; and cf. above, 41–3.
[168] *War* 6.312–15; see the discussion in *NTPG* 312–14.

Crossan will no doubt respond that this is what we should expect of Josephus, (a) because he is blaming the war on the lower orders, and (b) because he is himself the sort of scribally trained man who might think like that.[169] But this would miss the point. Josephus is concerned to *correct* the idea that Israel's scriptures prophesied the rise of a Jewish world ruler. He transfers the prediction to Vespasian. It is highly unlikely that he would invent a popular belief, so apparently damaging to his attempt to explain away the hotheaded attitudes of his countrymen, in order then to turn it in a new direction. Far more likely that the belief was well known and widespread, and that he was attempting to make the best of it. It was not only scribes who believed that Israel's god would act, in accordance with the scriptures which ordinary Jews would hear read week by week, to rescue his people. It was not only 'scribal' Christians who believed, starting most likely before Jesus' death, that the events they were witnessing were the fulfilment of those prophecies.

I began this analysis of Crossan's work by saying that he is one of the most brilliant New Testament scholars alive today. Sharp disagreement should not make the praise sound faint. Crossan has attempted to reconstruct the whole of early Christianity, with massive labour and attention to detail, with scintillating hypotheses right, left and centre, with a sense of the big picture as well as the little detail, with an eye open for contemporary implications of his historical work, and, perhaps most of all, with a deft, shrewd, and impish writing style that make us smile with appreciation at the very moment when we most want to disagree. We may say of Crossan, as he says of Mark, that he is such a gifted script-writer that we are lured into imagining that his scheme is actually historical.

Like Odysseus, however, we must resist the siren's voice. The rest of the present book offers an alternative hypothesis which, I claim, does far more justice to the evidence. This book was not originally conceived as a reply to Crossan, since its earliest draft was written two years before *The Historical Jesus* was published. But I have had to think through everything again after reading him; and it is by no means every book of which that can be said. Crossan towers above the rest of the renewed 'New Quest', in just the same way as Schweitzer and Bultmann tower above most of twentieth-century scholarship, and for much the same reasons. He, like them, has had the courage to see the whole picture, to think his hypothesis through to the end, to try out radically new ideas, to write it all up in a highly engaging manner, and to debate it publicly without acrimony. With foes like this, who needs friends? May the debate continue.

[169] cf. Crossan 91–100.

5. Jesus the Cynic?

A constant strand throughout the renewed 'New Quest' has been the finding of parallels to the sayings of Jesus within the corpus of material that reflects the Cynic philosophy. We have seen that Mack and Crossan both lean quite heavily in this direction, and they are by no means alone.[170] A major contribution has also been made, from a different angle, by Abraham J. Malherbe.[171] But the most thorough background work, and the fullest presentation of the case, has been made by the English scholar F. Gerald Downing.

In a steady stream of books and articles, Downing has advocated his bold thesis: the broad range of popular philosophy loosely known as Cynicism finds a great many echoes in the teaching of Jesus, in the early church, and within the synoptic tradition in particular. These echoes are not accidental. Jesus deliberately chose to couch his teaching in Cynic-style aphorisms and challenges. Those in the early church with the courage to follow his lead continued to teach in this way – though some, such as Paul, modified this into a much less socially critical stance. In the patristic period Christianity was known, by its advocates as well as its detractors, to share several features with Cynicism. As well as presenting as strong a historical case as anyone has ever done for this sort of position, Downing is quite clear that it has considerable implications for the present day.[172]

Who were the Cynics?[173] The answers are always fuzzy, since it was of the essence of the movement that its adherents sat loose to formal structures. Everybody's definition, in the ancient as in the modern world, would carry some problematic aspects. They were, more or less, popular philosophers operating within the Greco-Roman world. Their basic line of argument, or at least assertion, was that society as it now is is corrupt and worthless, and that the best thing for humans to do is radically to re-evaluate their attitudes to themselves, their property, their whole lives. The word 'Cynic' itself comes from the Greek *kyon*, meaning 'dog': the Cynics barked at society, snapped

---

[170] Mack 1988, 67–74, 179–92, and *passim*; Crossan 1991a, 72–88, 338–41, and *passim*; and cf. e.g. Vaage 1987, 1994; and other studies listed in Mack 1988, 69.

[171] e.g. Malherbe 1977, 1989. Malherbe 1976 offers a good, brief, clear account of the Cynics, as does Hock 1992.

[172] See now esp. Downing 1992, in which some previous material is re-presented and/or summarized. Cf. too the collection of texts in Downing 1988; the earlier articles, esp. Downing 1984, 1987b; and the more popular presentation, with bracing conclusions, in Downing 1987a.

[173] In addition to the other works referred to, see above all Goulet-Cazé 1990, 1993. The chief sources are the Cynic Epistles, and the works of Dio Chrysostom, Diogenes Laertius, Epictetus, Lucian of Samosata, Musonius Rufus, Plutarch, and Seneca, on all of which see Downing 1988, 192–5; 1992, 340–2. A lively impression of the movement may be gained easily from Crossan 1991a, ch. 4.

at its heels (we must remember that dogs were normally scavengers, not family pets, in the Greco-Roman world[174]), warning people, waking them up, harrying them into thinking differently about their lives. Clearly, with such a broad agenda, there was plenty of room for local and personal variation.[175]

Traditionally, Cynicism goes back to one Antisthenes, a pupil of Socrates who supposedly lived in the fifth and fourth centuries BC. He was followed, according to tradition, by Diogenes of Sinope (fourth century BC), who is portrayed as witty and acerbic. He in turn was followed by Crates of Thebes (c.360–280 BC; Zeno, the founder of Stoicism, was a pupil of his); he, by Menippus of Gadara in the first half of the third century BC. These, and others of the period, are described by Diogenes Laertius in his *Lives of the Eminent Philosophers*, written around 200 BC. Diogenes of Sinope is especially important, being regarded by subsequent Cynics as setting something of a pattern in his shameless disregard for social convention. After 200 BC the evidence is more patchy, for want of a contemporary historian rather than for lack of Cynics. Some first-century AD Cynics are known, such as Demetrius the friend of Seneca; Seneca himself, as well as his near-contemporary, the ex-slave-turned-philosopher Epictetus, have plenty to say about the Cynic way of life.[176] Fuller specific evidence comes, however, in the second century AD, partly because Lucian of Samosata wrote an account of two Cynics in particular, Demonax and Peregrinus. Evidence continues for three hundred or more years beyond this, ending with the sixth-century Sallustius.[177] There thus appears to be a continuity of Cynic presence and teaching within the Mediterranean world over roughly a millennium.[178]

The Cynics could be recognized not least by their immediate outward appearance. A Cynic would most likely wear a threadbare cloak, and carry a begging bag and a staff. Long hair was common, going barefoot a regular option. They lived by their wits from day to day, surviving the rigours of the weather, eating and drinking what they could find or beg. Their teaching eschewed the complexities of the more serious education of the day, and aimed simply at challenging received opinions, 'altering the currency' in the phrase attributed to Diogenes,[179] and advocating a life lived in harmony with nature rather than with the enslavements and immorality that accompany

---

[174] cf. Firmage 1992, 1143f.

[175] cf. Malherbe 1989, ch. 1; Downing 1992, ch. 2.

[176] cf. Epict. 3.22, a somewhat idealized portrait of a way of life that Epictetus clearly regards as a more extreme, out-and-out version of the popular Stoicism he himself represents. Other important first-century figures are Musonius Rufus and Attalus.

[177] More details on all the above in Hock 1992, 1221–3; Downing 1992, 57–84, 326–39.

[178] On the question of whether this suffered a relapse in the first century BC or AD, see Downing 1992, 63f.

[179] Diogenes Laertius, *Lives of Eminent Philosophers* (hereafter *LEP*) 6.20–21, 71.

wealth. Freedom, self-sufficiency, and self-control: these were the Cynic's goals, and almost any means to express them for oneself, or to shock others into seeing their value, was acceptable. Anecdotes about Cynics abounded, often in the short, clipped form known as the *chreia*.[180]

There are obvious parallels between some Cynic sayings and actions and some passages in the New Testament. Diogenes has a child teach a philosopher a lesson, just as Jesus exalts the child in the presence of the disciples.[181] Malherbe has argued that Paul's hearers would have recognized some features of his self-description, not least in his writing to the Thessalonians, as an echo of some aspects of the Cynic style.[182] What is new in the recent wave of study is the suggestion that Jesus himself, in some important senses, actually *was* a Cynic: that he deliberately chose a style of life and teaching which embodied Cynic ideals, and that this would have been clearly recognized by his contemporaries.

There are differences of approach between the various advocates of Jesus-the-Cynic, but as it is Downing who has presented by far the fullest argument it is best to proceed in terms of his contribution. Downing immerses the reader in the supposed parallels between Cynic teaching and that of Jesus (or at least Q).[183] A few examples at random. Jesus remarks on the birds' carefree life, to show the divine providential care over all; so does Musonius.[184] Jesus declares that a good tree cannot bear evil fruit, nor vice versa; Seneca observes that evil no more gives birth to good than an olive tree produces figs.[185] Jesus is reported to have spoken of coming as a shepherd to the lost sheep; Dio declares that a king must, like a good shepherd, give full attention to looking after the flock.[186] Jesus spoke of the doctor being needed for the sick, not for the healthy; Antisthenes, of doctors visiting the sick without catching the fever.[187] These examples and dozens of similar ones, urges Downing, demonstrate that the Q community in the 50s saw itself, and expected to be seen, in 'Cynic' terms. Evidence suggests that in the second and subsequent centuries many Christians appeared to many outsiders much like Cynics, and were happy to be seen that way.[188]

[180] cf. *NTPG* 428, 432, 435.

[181] *LEP* 6.37; Mk. 9.33-7, 10.14-16.

[182] cf. Malherbe 1989. Malherbe is careful, however (48, 66, etc.), not actually to identify Paul as a Cynic. For alternative readings of the evidence cf. Horbury 1982b; Stowers 1984.

[183] See Downing 1988; and, for discussion, 1992 ch. 5.

[184] Mt. 6.25-33 par.; Musonius 15: Downing 1988, 68-71 (with several other parallels); discussed in Downing 1992, 137f.

[185] Mt. 7.16-21 par.; Seneca *Ep. Mor.* 87.25: Downing 1988, 31f.

[186] Mt. 15.24; Dio 3.41: Downing 1988, 104.

[187] Mk. 2.16f.; *LEP* 6.6, cp. also Dio 8.5: Downing 1988, 122.

[188] Downing 1992, chs. 7-10.

So what of Jesus? Here the inquiry sometimes turns on the question, first, whether there might have been Cynics in Galilee in the relevant period, and, second, whether Cynics would have been found in the villages and countryside – where Jesus seems to have conducted his ministry – or whether, conversely, Jesus could have come into contact with city- or town-based teachers. Downing acknowledges that these questions need more research than has been offered so far, but stresses various points in favour of Jesus coming into contact with Cynics and choosing to identify himself with their style.[189] There is evidence of one Cynic living in Gadara in the third century BC, and another in the second century AD. Sepphoris, only four miles away from Nazareth, may well have been an important place for Jesus as he was growing up, so that even if he confined his public ministry to the countryside and villages there is still the possibility of his having met them earlier on. In any case, Cynics were not confined to towns.[190] So what are we to conclude? That Jesus was a Jewish teacher through and through, and that after his death his followers reinterpreted him in a Cynic direction? This, says Downing, is difficult to imagine.[191] Better, he suggests, to take Josephus' 'fourth philosophy' as indicating the presence of Cynic teaching within Jewish society.[192] So Jesus was

a Jewish Cynic from Galilee who created his own distinctive amalgam out of elements of both traditions as he encountered them in his own formative years.[193]

He teaches on his own authority. He engages in banter with a foreign woman who accepts the designation 'dog'. He refuses flattering respect. His parables subverted the conventional norms. He travelled light, trusting his god to provide. 'He comes as a physician for social misfits.' He repudiated the conventional wisdom about authority structures and the importance of money: 'Jesus maintains a Cynic disparagement of wealth as such – while giving it a Jewish name, Mammon.' He urges his hearers to live as if the rule of god were already a reality: 'again his terminology is Jewish, but what Jesus presses is an absurd Cynic trust in the possibility of living fully by living simply, as

---

[189] See the cautionary note in Downing 1992, 146f. – and Downing's criticism of Mack and Crossan for assuming that the case can stand without much argument.

[190] Downing 1992, 82f., 148f. Hengel 1989a, 44 agrees with Downing: 'Why should not the craftsman Jesus, who grew up in the neighbourhood of Sepphoris, have made contact with Cynic itinerant preachers, especially as he himself spoke some Greek? . . . These affinities between Gospel tradition and Cynic religious and social criticism go right back to Jesus himself.'

[191] Downing 1992, 151, 161f.

[192] Ibid., 150–4. I confess that I find this attempt to make the Jewish rebels into Cynics one of the least plausible parts of Downing's case. On the 'fourth philosophy' cf. *NTPG* 170–81.

[193] Downing 1992, 154.

things are'.[194] Jesus, then, stands at the fountain-head of the tradition that Downing finds most clearly in Q:

> The tradition was Jewish-Cynic from the start, in an individual selection of ideas, attitudes and practices that by and large goes back to the original Jesus himself.[195]

Downing notes that several other pictures of Jesus are currently available (he lists several writers whom I shall discuss in the next chapter), but argues that the popular impression of early Christianity, and of Jesus himself, must have been that this was some kind of Cynic movement. The most likely response of hearers would be, he claims, 'This sounds pretty Cynic to me, and a lot more like the Cynics than like anyone else I've heard.'[196]

Downing's bracing style and clear argument is refreshing; his parallels are often striking; his fine-tuning of the argument is impressive;[197] his learning is prodigious; his present-day conclusions are as challenging as Schweitzer's.[198] Downing is right, I believe, to highlight the fact that Jesus, and his earliest followers, challenged their hearers to understand themselves and their world in an entirely different way. They subverted the normal way of looking at things, as much by their behaviour as by their teaching, casting suspicion on received wisdom, and offering an alternative self-awareness. Since postmodernism has been offering a hermeneutic of suspicion-of-everybody for some little while, it is paradoxically comforting to find that this stands in a tradition which goes back to Jesus and beyond. Any open-minded historian is bound to give the theory a good run for its money. And yet, for historical reasons, I am convinced that, as a whole, it will not do.

Objections have been raised: the absence of evidence for Cynics in Palestine in the first century; their being largely townsfolk;[199] the difference between the standard Cynic dress (including a bag) and the standard early-Christian-missionary one (without a bag);[200] the reliance on a reconstructed Q; the fact that many of the parallels are not as close as they appear at first sight; and Downing's bringing together of sources, many of which are not so

---

[194] Downing 1992, 154–62; quotations from 159f.

[195] Downing 1992, 162.

[196] Downing 1992, 165.

[197] I particularly like his demonstration of the serious differences between the worldview of the Cynics and that of *Thomas*: Downing 1988, xi; 1992, 135 n.99.

[198] Downing 1987a; 1992 ch. 11. I am myself suspicious, however, of his claim (1988, xii) that, whereas apocalyptic is so alien to us, the down-to-earth ethical reflection of the Cynic will be less so. A strange modernization, but modernization none the less; in parallel, perhaps, with the tone of Crossan's conclusion that Jesus and his followers were 'hippies in a world of Augustan yuppies' (Crossan 1991a, 304, 421). The 'Jesus' of the 1960s is alive and well after all.

[199] cf. Liefeld 1967, 213 (quoted in Crossan 1991a, 340).

[200] cf. Crossan 1991a, 338f., on which see above, n.138.

much Cynic as part of a far wider popular philosophy, a kind of low-grade Stoicism.[201] All these are valid, but do not present a completely compelling case against Downing's hypothesis.

The real objections lie deeper. I have already argued in some detail that when we find solid historical ground under our feet in the first century of Christianity, we find ourselves still in a very Jewish world, even if transplanted to Rome, Smyrna or Thessalonica. There is one true god who challenges all the other gods, and those who worship this one true god must offer allegiance to no others. Thus

> The Roman authorities found the Christians (as they found the Jews) a social and political threat or nuisance, and took action against them. The Christians, meanwhile, do not seem to have taken refuge in the defence that they were merely a private club for the advancement of personal piety. They continued to proclaim their allegiance to a Christ who was a 'king' in a sense which precluded allegiance to Caesar, even if his kingdom was not to be conceived on the model of Caesar's. This strange belief, so Jewish and yet so non-Jewish (since it led the Christians to defend no city, adhere to no Mosaic code, circumcise no male children) was . . . a central characteristic of the whole movement, and as such a vital key to its character.[202]

It is this essential Jewishness that I find totally absent in Downing's portrait. For him, the worldview is Cynic, the incidentals Jewish. In my reading, this is, to say the least, the wrong way round.[203]

As Downing himself notes, finding Cynic traits in a Christian writer does not mean a Cynic worldview. The obvious example is Paul. Malherbe has provided a suggestive portrait: Paul was well able to evoke Cynic echoes, but the drift of his thought and argument remains within the Jewish and apocalyptic world of early Christianity.[204] Downing regards this as a sign that Paul had compromised and was settling down into a less confrontational existence – a position which ill accords with such passages as 1 Corinthians 4.8-13, 2 Corinthians 6.3-10 and 2 Corinthians 11.16-33, where Paul ironically celebrates the fact of his becoming 'like the rubbish of the world, the dregs of all things' (1 Corinthians 4.13). It is a mark precisely of the Jewish-

---

[201] cf. Tuckett 1989; Harvey 1989. Downing's replies are not always very convincing. In 1992, 135 he allows that he has cast the net quite wide for parallel texts. Cf. too Denaux 1996, 138, likening Vaage's use of disparate Cynic sources to the uncritical pulling together of rabbinic material represented by Strack-Billerbeck.

[202] *NTPG* 355.

[203] On the non-Jewishness of the portrait, see Downing 1988, xi. We could also point out that many of the parallels adduced could be explained with reference to a much more general folk-wisdom on which Jewish sages and Cynic philosophers were both able to draw for their very different purposes. Professor Colin Brown points out to me that the Steward's dilemma in Lk. 16.3 ('I cannot dig; to beg I am ashamed') could be an allusion to Cynicism and at the same time a repudiation of it.

[204] Malherbe 1989. See above, n.182.

ness of early Christianity that it claims to fly in the face of all paganism – including the gods whom the Cynics were happy to acknowledge, or the one god of pantheism who emerges often enough in the pages of a writer like Epictetus. There is a fundamental difference in worldview.[205] If Christianity shares some features with Cynicism, which seems to be the case, I submit that this is essentially superficial, and comes about because its essential Jewishness led it to confront the world of paganism, and to do so with all the subversive weapons available, rather than because an essential Cynicism led it to abandon the world of Judaism. It was because of their essentially Jewish beliefs, in the kingdom of Israel's god having come in the person of Jesus, that the early Christians became deeply nonconformist, to the point of persecution and martyrdom.[206]

This relates especially to Jesus' own announcement of the kingdom of Israel's god. This is a theme which Downing consciously marginalizes.[207] The Jesus-tradition, unless of course emasculated by those determined to leave no 'apocalyptic' in sight, is replete not just with the timeless challenge of the Cynic but with the very specific note that Israel's god, the creator of the world, is bringing Israel's and the world's history to an awesome climax, so that urgent action is called for if Israel is to escape cataclysmic judgment. This is totally different from the very occasional note of judgment found in Cynic traditions,[208] which focus in an ahistorical way on the individual and his or her future. One should not be surprised at such a difference. A philosophy which was content to leave untouched the worldview system of

---

[205] My reading of Epictetus does not incline me to endorse Crossan's description of him as 'saintly' (1991a, 304).

[206] Downing 1992, 95 acknowledges that the book of Revelation is highly nonconformist, while showing no Cynic traits at all. This should perhaps have alerted him to the danger of thinking that a lack of Cynic features implied a conformist Christianity.

[207] Most clearly in Downing 1987a, 113; cf. too Vaage 1994, e.g. 56; Mack 1988, 69–74, esp. 69 n.11: 'Most of these scholars [i.e. those who have pointed to some parallels between Jesus' teaching and that of the Cynics] have been cautious not to draw conclusions about the historical Jesus based on their observations of Cynic parallels [with the synoptic tradition]. The Cynic hypothesis gains in credibility, however, as soon as the view of Jesus as an apocalyptic prophet is recognized as problematic.' This is heavily ironic: Downing (1988, xi), Mack (*passim*), and others squeeze out the most Jewish of material not least because of their contemporary agendas. Yet it is the gnosticism of the *Gospel of Thomas*, so beloved of the Jesus Seminar, that is the really world-denying and dualist philosophy, not the Jewish apocalyptic of Jesus and Mark. If Downing really desires a contemporary social critique, I submit that a serious kingdom-theology is a far better ground for it than loose and individualized Cynic teaching. If Mack really wants to avoid a world-denying philosophy, I submit that the new world order held out in Jewish apocalyptic, rightly understood, offers a better prospect for him than a slap in the face from a wandering Cynic – or the escapist antiworld theology of the gnostic texts.

[208] See the attempt made to avoid this point in Downing 1992, 140f.

paganism, with its tendency towards a loosely Stoic pantheism, would never generate a sense of eschatological urgency such as we find, as I shall argue, not only in early Christianity but also in the teaching of Jesus himself. So, too, there is no real room in the ministry of Downing's Jesus for healing as a regular thematic activity, or for the open commensality, and its significance, of which Crossan has made so much. These fit, as I shall try to show, with a far more Jewish proclamation of the kingdom. Crossan's attempt to marry the two remains unconvincing.[209]

Above all, there is a basic incongruity in Downing's noble attempt to draw as much of the Jesus-tradition as he can into the world of popular Cynicism. What he totally fails to explain is why *this* Cynic teacher should have started a movement that so quickly spread throughout the known world, with results significantly different from those either of Cynicism as a whole or of any particular Cynic teacher. There is no explanation of why Jesus should have been executed; no suggestion of why his first followers spoke of his being raised from the dead. The apparent integration of Jesus and early Christianity which Downing offers by reducing both to the level of a variant within Cynicism is achieved by huge and vital omissions from what we actually know of early Christianity itself.[210]

One final note, about the use of 'Jesus the Cynic' within the portrait of Jesus (and early Christianity) drawn by the majority of 'Jesus Seminar' scholars. One of the reasons why the Cynic model has appealed to this group seems to be the possibility that it offers of evading the 'horizontal' eschatology of traditional Judaism (i.e. the belief that Israel's god would act within history in the future). Instead, we are offered the 'vertical eschatology' in which *Thomas* and other writings 'translate' eschatological language into the 'vertical' dimension of an escape from the space-time world. This is sometimes written up in ways which clearly seek to make it sound attractive.[211] There is a great irony in this. First, *Thomas* is a fine example of a genuine dualism, truly rejecting the world in a way that 'apocalyptic' actually does not. If we imagine for a moment a genuine Cynic being presented with a copy of *Thomas*, it does not take much thought to envisage him responding

---

[209] Crossan 1991a, 340f.: 'call it, if you will, Jewish and rural Cynicism rather than Greco-Roman and urban Cynicism'. Call it, in other words, something for which we have no other evidence, and which is far more easily and thoroughly explained in other categories.

[210] cf. *NTPG* Part IV.

[211] cf. e.g. Miller 1992, 304, speaking of the work's 'counter-cultural wisdom', sharing a concern 'for personal identity within a world which was widely perceived as brutal and mean', and portraying a Jesus 'whose words call one from out of the chaos into a quest, to seek and to find, and finally to discover one's true identity as a child of God'. The attempt to interpret Jesus' use of Jewish eschatological language as expressing a timeless call for decision is of course a major characteristic of Bultmann, e.g. 1958b, 1961.

with a fairly caustic put-down. Second, neither *Thomas*' supposed 'vertical eschatology' nor its esoteric musings would cut any ice with someone like Epictetus, let alone with those he regarded as genuine Cynics, more serious than himself. If we really mean business in attempting to plot trajectories within early Christianity, we cannot possibly get away with lumping together Cynics, *Thomas* and Q as though they were all saying more or less the same thing. (One sometimes gets the impression that anything will do, in this strangely mixed set of bedfellows, as long as it is nothing like orthodoxy.) Third, we cannot label this odd amalgam as 'sapiential', or as articulating a 'vertical eschatology', with any hope of achieving historical accuracy. Nor, fourth, can we play it off against 'apocalyptic' as though the latter is world-denying while Cynicism and *Thomas* are somehow not. Fifth and finally, we cannot take any or all of this strange mixture and apply it to Jesus, or to any movement in first-generation Christianity of which we possess any actual solid evidence.

Perhaps the most important thing that this new movement of scholarship has done is to alert us to the fact that to make Jesus a first-century Palestinian Jew does not *necessarily* mean that he will be, so to speak, recognizably 'Jewish' through and through. We no longer think (or at least we should no longer think) of Palestine in this period as encircled with an invisible steel curtain that kept out ideas and influences that were circulating in the ancient near east in general. It may well be that, when scholarship has got over the determination to make Jesus as apparently 'Jewish' as possible, it may have to weave in other factors as well.[212] That said, however, there are extremely serious weaknesses in all the various manifestations of the view now before us. It seems to me far more likely that sayings of a Jewish kingdom-prophet (as some perceived him) were taken up and transmitted in a context of wider cultural influences, and, having their rough (and perhaps Jewish) edges knocked off them from time to time, ended up looking occasionally like some aphorisms spoken by some Cynics.[213] This is not to say that the parallels are unimportant. I shall do my best to allow their echoes to be heard. It is to say that to make Jesus a Cynic as such, and to treat that identification as a Procrustean bed in order to lop off other bits that do not fit, is historically unjustified. As Demonax nearly said, 'Don't vote for this resolution, men of Athens, until you've pulled down the altar of Clio.'[214]

---

[212] cf. Hengel 1989a.

[213] See *NTPG* 427-32 on the form-critical implications of this.

[214] Lucian, *Demonax* 57. In the original, the altar was to Mercy; Demonax was objecting to the innovation of gladiatorial shows. Clio is, of course, the muse of history.

6. Marcus J. Borg

The last writer to be considered in this chapter is in fact a bridge between it and the next. He belongs in a kind of middle position, straddling the Jesus Seminar on the one hand and the post-Schweitzer 'Third Quest' on the other.[215] As Burton Mack's influence in the 'Jesus Seminar' has faded, so the name of Marcus J. Borg has become increasingly heard not only in the Seminar but much wider. Borg has written several books about Jesus, at various different levels. He has also attempted to locate Jesus within models taken from a wider history-of-religions context, and at the same time to integrate his findings with a positive restatement of Christian experience and theology. Unlike some in the 'Jesus Seminar', he is clear and positive about his own Christian commitment, which by his own account has grown stronger as his work on Jesus has progressed.

In Borg's first book, he argues for the integration of political, social and theological themes in Jesus' work.[216] Resistance to Rome went hand in hand with the quest for holiness, particularly the Pharisaic agenda; Jesus opposed this entire programme with a new paradigm of holiness, characterized by mercy rather than by exclusion. The threatening sayings in the synoptic tradition are then to be read, not as predictions of the end of the space-time universe, but as Jewish-style prophecies of the destruction, by Rome, of Jerusalem and the Temple.[217] Following the work of G. B. Caird and others, Borg argues that the apocalyptic *language* of these sayings has been wrongly assumed to denote 'the end of the world', whereas in Jewish prophecy it actually *invests* (what we call) historical and political events with their theological significance.[218] Borg thus follows Schweitzer in setting Jesus within Jewish apocalyptic, while disagreeing radically with Schweitzer about what apocalyptic language actually denotes.[219] This means that he frequently finds himself poles apart from many of his colleagues in the 'Jesus Seminar',

---

[215] Hence my placing him in the latter category in Neill & Wright 1988 [1964], 387–91 (where I carelessly placed Borg in the University of Oregon rather than Oregon State, a lapse for which I apologize to him and both institutions), and Wright 1992b, 800f. It is his recent work in particular that has convinced me to place him now in the non-eschatological 'New Quest renewed' category, rather than in the essentially post-Schweitzer and eschatological 'Third Quest'. This illustrates the point I would stress in any case, that the categories are heuristic rather than watertight – though the distinction between a non-eschatological Jesus and an eschatological one remains vital.

[216] Borg 1984.

[217] Ibid., *passim*, esp. ch. 8 and the Appendix (265–76).

[218] For my own argument in the same vein, cf. *NTPG* ch. 10. Allison 1994 claims to have disproved this line of thought; I do not think he has understood it. See below, ch. 8, esp. 321f.

[219] cf. Borg 1994a, chs. 3 and 4.

committed as they are to a completely non-apocalyptic Jesus and hence to voting black on sayings with an apocalyptic character.[220]

Since his original work, Borg's own portrait of Jesus has developed within categories taken from cross-cultural analysis of religion.[221] In contrast to the severely minimalist Jesus-pictures of some of his Seminar colleagues, he offers a sketch in five strokes.[222] Jesus was a *religious ecstatic*, such as has been known in most cultures: that is, he had frequent and vivid experiences of other layers of reality than the space-time world. Jesus was a *healer*, both of illness (the social consequences of disease) and of disease itself. He was a *wisdom teacher*, not so much of conventional but of subversive wisdom.[223] He was a *social prophet*, not predicting some distant future event, nor speaking of the end of the world, but, like the ancient Hebrew prophets, protesting against injustice and oppression within the society of his day. He uttered prophetic oracles, and engaged in prophetic actions, threatening divine judgment (of a this-worldly nature) against those who persisted in the evils he denounced. Finally, he was a *movement-founder*, or perhaps a *movement-catalyst*: a movement, that is, came into existence around Jesus during his lifetime, and this was not foreign to his intentions. This found expression in the table-fellowship which he shared with his followers, cutting across traditional social boundaries, and embodying the divine compassion.

Borg does not think of Jesus the man as the 'divine son of God'; he does not suppose that he deliberately died for the sins of the world; nor did he focus his message on himself. But Borg nevertheless sketches the rudiments of a portrait which is far more positive than that of the 'Jesus Seminar' as a whole, and a writer like Mack in particular. In addition, Borg's Jesus is thoroughly Jewish, and, despite some criticisms, his Jesus engages in an essentially inner-Jewish debate.[224]

On the basis of this reconstruction, Borg sees in Jesus, at the level of cross-cultural analysis, clear evidence of the multi-layered nature of all existence, and a clear pointer to the fact that (in his words) the ultimate reality is one with which we can be in a transforming relationship.[225] As a result of the historical study of Jesus, we are summoned to a life centred in Spirit, through which we can grow in relationship and in deeper levels of prayer.

---

[220] Borg remains, however, an apologist for the 'Jesus Seminar': see Borg 1994a, ch. 8.

[221] An important signpost on the way is Borg 1987a.

[222] What follows is dependent partly on Borg's writings, not least 1994b, and partly on an oral presentation in Vancouver on 11 February 1995, in which the first 'stroke' of the 1994 sketch (Jesus as 'spirit person') was divided into the first two categories immediately following.

[223] See further Borg 1994b, ch. 4.

[224] cp. Fredriksen 1995a & b, on which see ch. 9 below.

[225] Oral presentation, 11 February 1995.

The primary fruit of this life is compassion, and the endeavour to bring this compassion to birth more and more in the world. And this life is to be lived in a community which, precisely as a community, holds on to this total vision. Borg describes movingly the difference that this portrait has made to him personally, a difference between believing the dogmas about Jesus and believing in the following sense: 'to give one's heart, one's self at its deepest level, to the post-Easter Jesus who is the living Lord, the side of God turned toward us, the face of God, the Lord who is also the Spirit'.[226]

It might seem perverse, from the point of view of my previous criticism of the 'Jesus Seminar', to criticize also one who, from within its ranks, offers such a very different portrait. Let me simply offer, in a spirit of collegial appreciation and friendship, four of the many questions which have occurred to me, in debate with Borg, over the last few years.

First, the cross-cultural categories Borg brings to Jesus are refreshing. But are they necessarily the most sharply accurate? Why, once we have agreed that Jesus was an ecstatic, a healer, a teacher, a prophet, and a movement-founder, should we systematically exclude some more obvious Jewish ones, such as Messiah? If we found a person in, say, Josephus' story who fitted the first five categories, would we be surprised to find him thought of as a potential Messiah?[227] And, if not, why should Borg's would-be Jewish Jesus not fit that category too?

Second, what did Borg's Jesus think would happen next? He did not, evidently, think he would die an atoning death (whatever that might mean at this stage of the argument). Did he think that more and more people might come to embrace his way of compassion? If so, is he not in all sorts of ways just as much a failure as Reimarus' Jesus? Does this matter, and if so why?

Third, and perhaps most important: is Borg's Jesus really an eschatological figure, or does he after all use the language of eschatology to express, within his own context, the essentially timeless truth that God is always available to human beings, and requires compassion rather than exclusive and oppressive ways of life? In other words, did Borg's Jesus (like, say, Sanders') suppose that Israel's god was actually *doing* something climactic and unique, in and through which Israel's (and perhaps the world's) story would be brought to some kind of fulfilment? Or did this Jesus pick up that language but use it to teach, sharply and locally no doubt, a general truth? From Borg's first book one might have supposed that he favoured the former; now, I think, he has clearly embraced the latter. But will this quasi-Bultmannian position really do, as an analysis either of eschatological language or of Jesus?

---

[226] Borg 1994b, 137.
[227] On Messianic figures and expectations cf. *NTPG* 307-20.

Fourth, Borg seems to me to be offering a new version of the split between the Jesus of history and the Christ of faith. How convincing is his jump from the pre-Easter Jesus who 'was not God'[228] to the post-Easter Jesus who is 'the side of God turned toward us'? I can see only too well how the dogmatism against which he reacted in his earlier years (Borg's writing has sometimes been deliberately autobiographical) has closed off for him the route to traditional affirmations. But is he not in danger of making his warm and devout faith into a bridge which, perhaps, those who do not share such faith will after all find themselves unable to cross? If so, does he perceive this as a problem?

In short, there is a great deal that I find congenial in Borg's fresh portrait, and in the spirit with which it is offered. If I part company from him, it is in order to set his many shrewd and well-worked points into a context where I think they will fit, historically, even better (and, of course, to suggest that what I see as his weak points may be avoided). As this is done, however, some of the things Borg finds himself obliged to deny will come up for question again, from a different angle; and I venture to hope that, in this guise, they may not after all appear so unacceptable. But the best way to advance the debate beyond this point will be to mount the positive argument contained in Parts II and III of this book.

7. Conclusion: the New 'New Quest'

Ten years ago it seemed possible to write off the 'New Quest' as a spent force. I did so.[229] I was wrong. I still believe that the future of serious Jesus-research lies with what I have called the 'Third Quest', within a broadly post-Schweitzerian frame of reference, and to this we must presently turn. But these artificial distinctions do not do justice to the manysidedness of contemporary scholarship.[230] It is increasingly clear that there are cross-over points between different schools, and that those who immerse themselves most thoroughly in the material, especially the historical sources, are most likely to move to and fro across what had seemed a firm Green Line into what some of their colleagues may still regard as no-go areas. Crossan himself is a good example of this: witness his full and detailed use of Josephus, something which earlier New Questers had never quite got around to. Borg, too, happily straddles the divide, though eventually coming down, I think, on the New Quest side. Likewise, some of the writers to be reviewed presently,

---

[228] Borg 1994b, 37.
[229] Wright 1982.
[230] See above, p. 24f.

though I have categorized them as Third Questers, have a good claim to belong with Mack, Crossan and the Jesus Seminar. If the categories crumble in the next decade or so, that will be an excellent thing for the discipline.

But that will only happen if the residual weaknesses in the New Quest are seriously addressed. I have already highlighted several, and merely list the obvious ones in conclusion. First, there is the continued Bultmannian reliance on the sayings of Jesus as the primary material. Against that, set Borg's shrewd comment:

> Ironically, twentieth-century scholarship has sought to distance itself from the later nineteenth-century focus on Jesus as teacher; yet our preoccupation with his words suggests that the understanding of Jesus as primarily a teacher remains.[231]

But what other models are open? For serious answers we must go to the Third Quest.

This reliance on sayings leads, second, to a spurious idea that history can be done by assessing these sayings through 'criteria' of various sorts. Crossan's own work, though far more sophisticated than that, still operates with two quite basic criteria: date and attestation. Both, as we saw, are extremely difficult to assess, despite the confident feel of Crossan's inventory, and are open to the charge that they simply reflect decisions reached on quite other grounds. All the current New Questers point, despite themselves, to the correct solution: the scholar must work with a large hypothesis, and must appeal, ultimately, to the large picture of how everything fits together as the justification for smaller-scale decisions. That is the real criterion that operates the system whereby, in dealing with gospel pericopae, many are called but few are chosen. I shall work with the same basic criterion, with the differences that I am not claiming to do something else at the same time, and that I shall not need to jettison data with the same cheerful abandon.

The renewed New Quest works, third, with an overall picture of Christian origins that ought now to be abandoned.[232] It is the Bultmannian picture, with variations: a deJudaized Jesus preaching a demythologized, 'vertical' eschatology;[233] a crucifixion with no early theological interpretation; a 'resurrection' consisting of the coming to faith, some time later, of a particular group of Christians; an early sapiential/gnostic group, retelling the master's aphorisms but uninterested in his life story; a Paul who invented a Hellenistic Christ-cult; a synoptic tradition in which rolling aphorisms, as

---

[231] Borg 1987b, 91 n.28.

[232] cf. *NTPG* Part IV.

[233] Have the New Questers, and the advocates of the Cynic Jesus, come to terms with the politically problematic analogy between themselves and those German scholars who, in the 1920s and 1930s, reduced almost to nil the specific Jewishness of Jesus and his message?

they slowed down, gathered the moss of narrative structure about themselves, and gradually congealed into gospels in which the initial force of Jesus' challenge was muted or lost altogether within a fictitious pseudo-historical framework. This modern picture, in fact, is the real fiction. For a time it seemed to be a helpful fiction. I suggest that that time has come to an end.

In terms of method, we are back at the point which Schweitzer chronicled at the start of the century. Writing about his own work alongside Wrede's book on Mark, which appeared the same day, he declared that

> [These two books] are written from quite different standpoints, one from the point of view of literary criticism, the other from that of the historical recognition of eschatology.[234]

Schweitzer saw this as in one sense a combined movement, with the two approaches joining forces to gang up on the false 'historical' pictures that had been offered before, and the spurious orthodox schemes that had used such pictures. Since a good part of Schweitzer's own purpose was the negative one of demolishing previous 'Lives' of Jesus, this was all very satisfactory. But when the two new approaches stop celebrating their joint triumph and turn to face each other, they discover that they are fundamentally incompatible:

> Here the ways divide . . . There is, on the one hand, the eschatological solution, which at one stroke raises the Marcan account as it stands, with all its disconnectedness and inconsistencies, into genuine history; and there is, on the other hand, the literary solution, which regards the incongruous dogmatic element as interpolated by the earliest Evangelist into the tradition and therefore strikes out the Messianic claim altogether from the historical Life of Jesus. *Tertium non datur.*[235]

Schweitzer therefore expounds and sharply criticizes Wrede's view, before setting out his own at greater length.[236]

Now, at the end of the century, one might suggest that the renewed 'New Quest' finds itself in a traffic jam on the *Wredebahn*, while what I have called the 'Third Quest' is poised to accelerate down the *Schweitzerbahn*. This is, of course, a considerable oversimplification, but I believe that, when all allowances and caveats have been made, there remains a major and

---

[234] Schweitzer 1954 [1906], 328.

[235] Ibid., 335.

[236] Ibid., 336–48; 348–95. Cf. too 400, which might apply as well to the 'Jesus Seminar' as to Schweitzer's contemporaries: 'Men feared that to admit the claims of eschatology would abolish the significance of His words for our time; and hence there was a feverish eagerness to discover in them any elements that might be considered not eschatologically conditioned. When any sayings were found of which the wording did not absolutely imply an eschatological connexion there was great jubilation – these at least had been saved uninjured from the coming *débâcle*.'

important difference between the two basic approaches, and that the latter has the far greater chance of achieving lasting success. The 'Jesus Seminar' has rejected Jewish eschatology, particularly apocalyptic, as an appropriate context for understanding Jesus himself, and in order to do so has declared the Markan narrative a fiction. The 'Third Quest', without validating Mark in any simplistic way, has placed Jesus precisely within his Jewish eschatological context, and has found in consequence new avenues of secure historical investigation opening up before it.

It is not, of course, as though nothing has changed in the intervening century. Both positions have undergone significant development and modification. The attempt to follow Wrede has resulted not only in the scepticism of his basic position becoming even more 'thoroughgoing', but also in an extremely thoroughgoing *credulity* regarding other matters. History, abhorring the vacuum left by the dismissal of Mark as pure fiction, has come up with new fictions which seem harder to attack only because they are based on nothing at all. The blithe 'reconstruction' not only of Q, not only of its different stages of composition, but even of complete communities whose beliefs are accurately reflected in these different stages, betokens a naive willingness to believe in anything as long as it is nothing like Mark (let alone Paul). Wrede's own basic thesis has been found wanting, but instead of being abandoned it has been developed into still more extraordinary forms. At the same time, the attempt to follow Schweitzer has resulted in a major refinement of what precisely Jewish eschatology and apocalyptic really was. One of the things for which Schweitzer has become most famous is now increasingly questioned: 'apocalyptic' was for him, and for the ninety years since he wrote, almost synonymous with the end of the space-time universe, but it is now clear that this is a bizarre literalistic reading of what the first century knew to be thoroughly metaphorical.[237] Things have not stood still in the research which Wrede and Schweitzer generated.

But if the teams have changed a bit, the same basic game goes on. Once the necessary readjustments have been made, many elements in Schweitzer's reconstruction can in turn be salvaged. His basic position (Jewish eschatology as the context for Jesus, joining forces with scepticism to confront naive traditionalism, but then defeating scepticism with appropriate historical reconstruction) survives intact, and the present work intends to promote it further. Like Schweitzer, we shall be met by the anxious demand for relevance: how can a first-century apocalyptic prophet have anything to say in the twentieth century? I think there are better ways of answering this question than those which Schweitzer offered, and I shall come to them in due course. They will not be found, though, by rejecting his basic position.

---

[237] cf. *NTPG* ch. 10 (including references to others who had already made this point).

It is the 'Third Quest' that has done most to revive Schweitzer's position, while refining it so that its very serious weaknesses can be eliminated. Having therefore followed in his footsteps by arguing, in this chapter, against the revival of thoroughgoing scepticism, we now turn to the new form taken by thoroughgoing eschatology. The time was ripe ten years ago for a Schweitzerian 'Third Quest'. The failings of the revived 'New Quest' make it all the more imperative than ever that this 'Third Quest' be put into as good a running order as possible.

Chapter Three

BACK TO THE FUTURE: THE 'THIRD QUEST'

1. Breaking out of the Straitjacket

The 'New Quest' was the first sign that the wall of resistance to serious study of Jesus had begun to crack. Now the dam has burst altogether, allowing a flood of scholarly and seriously historical books on Jesus to sweep the market in the space of a very few years.[1] Instead of the Old Quest brought to a close by Schweitzer, and the New Quest inaugurated by Käsemann (and revived by the Jesus Seminar), we now have a phenomenon which is arguably sufficiently distinct to deserve the title of a 'Third Quest'.[2] There are, as we saw in the last chapter, some writers who straddle the revived 'New Quest' and the 'Third Quest'. Instances would include Vermes (who stresses the Jewishness of Jesus, but ends up with an existentialist teacher), and Borg (who puts Jesus firmly in his Jewish social and cultural context, but ends up with Jesus as a non-apocalyptic sage, teacher, prophet and movement-founder). There are considerable affinities, too, between Crossan and Horsley, such as to make the placing of them in different categories dubious. Let me stress again that, though there are vital distinctions to be drawn, the categories are

[1] The movement consists at present mostly of books, not as yet articles: why might this be? Because the journal editors are too unready for change? Or because, until the new paradigm has become fully established, it is almost impossible to say anything about one detail without setting out an entire argument, including some discussion of method, and showing at least in outline how the whole hypothesis works? I think the latter is the more likely: cf. Schweitzer 1954 [1906], 396: 'Henceforth it is no longer permissible to take one problem out of the series and dispose of it by itself, since the weight of the whole hangs upon each.'

[2] Neill & Wright 1988 [1964], 379–403; and see further above, 75, 78–82. Despite some who see the present movement as part of the (now old) New Quest (e.g. Reumann 1989), the substantial differences between the two movements are quite clear, as is recognized by e.g. Meyer 1979, 48–59; Charlesworth 1988, ch. 1 and e.g. 163 n.61, 204f.; Freyne 1988b, 3; Holmberg 1993. Meyer, almost prophetically, provided a thought-out methodological basis for the Third Quest which all intending writers on Jesus would do well to study carefully. It is sad to state that some writers continue to pretend that no such movement exists: e.g. Drury 1985, 3; Bowden 1988 – the latter insisting that answers are impossible, while continuing to publish books which offer them.

heuristic attempts to describe recent writing, not watertight compartments. However, I have come to the view that the distinction which Schweitzer drew between himself and Wrede still has a lot to commend it; that those who follow Schweitzer in placing Jesus within apocalyptic Jewish eschatology belong in a category distinct from those who do not;[3] and that this category is where the real leading edge of contemporary Jesus-scholarship is to be found.

There are, to date, twenty writers that I regard as particularly important within this Third Quest. In chronological order of publication in English, they are Caird (1965), Brandon (1967), Betz (1968 [1965]),[4] Hengel (1971, 1973, 1981b [1968]), Vermes (1973, 1983,[5] 1993), Meyer (1979, 1992a & b), Chilton (1979, 1984a, 1992b), Riches (1980), Harvey (1982, 1990), Lohfink (1984), Borg (1984, 1987a, 1994b), Sanders (1985, 1993), Oakman (1986), Theissen (1987), Horsley (1987), Freyne (1988b), Charlesworth (1988), Witherington (1990, 1994, 1995), Meier (1991, 1994), and de Jonge (1991a).[6] Anyone familiar with these books will at once see how very different many of them are from each other, and yet how similar are the sets of questions being addressed – which are the questions that we shall ourselves be addressing throughout this book.

I have already discussed several of these works elsewhere. The reader may be glad to know that there is nothing to be gained by repeating myself at this point, or by attempting to go through the list, author by author, offering exposition and critique.[7] A better method of reviewing the Third Quest, as a prelude to my own exposition, will be to examine the questions that all these writers are addressing, drawing out their particular emphases as we do so. More detail, and more debate, will of course emerge as the book proceeds.

First, though, some general remarks about the Third Quest.[8] There is now a real attempt to do history seriously. Josephus, so long inexplicably ignored,

---

[3] Even if the latter continue to speak of Jesus' message as in some other sense 'eschatological', as (for instance) Crossan does.

[4] cf. too Betz 1987, esp. Part II.

[5] Containing some material previously published in Vermes 1981.

[6] Charlesworth gives a useful annotated list (187–207) of writing on Jesus in the 1980s. See also, in various slightly different categories: Dodd 1971; Yoder 1994 [1972]; Bowker 1973; Derrett 1973; Maccoby 1980 [1973]; Dunn 1975; O'Neill 1980, 1995; Farmer 1982 (building on Farmer 1956, a work which could have precipitated the Third Quest earlier if more notice had been taken of it); Schüssler Fiorenza 1983, 1994; Bammel & Moule 1984; Rivkin 1984; Buchanan 1984; Riesner 1984 [1981]; Goergen 1986a & b; Leivestad 1987; Zeitlin 1988; Stanton 1989; Neusner 1993; Brown 1994; Johnson 1995 (though this work denies the propriety of any 'quest' at all, it nevertheless makes oblique contributions to it); O'Collins 1995. Mention should also be made of the Hensley Henson lectures of Professor Colin Brown, delivered in Oxford in 1993, building on his previous work in various places e.g. Brown 1984.

[7] cf. Neill & Wright 1988 [1964], 379–403; Wright 1992b.

[8] Some of which apply also, of course, to parts of the revived 'New Quest', described in the previous chapter.

is suddenly and happily in vogue. There is a real willingness to be guided by first-century sources, and to see the Judaism of that period in all its complex pluriformity, with the help now available from modern studies of the history and literature of the period.[9] Qumran and the apocalyptic writings are not merely part of the dark backcloth against which the great light of the gospel shines the more brightly; they are part of the historical evidence for the world of first-century Palestine. Certain basic questions emerge: Jesus' message is evaluated, not for its timeless significance, but for the meaning it must have had for the audience of his own day, who had their minds full of poverty and politics, and would have had little time for theological abstractions or timeless verities. The crucifixion, long recognized as an absolute bedrock in history, is now regularly made the centre of understanding: what must Jesus have been like if he ended up on a Roman cross? The answer given by S. G. F. Brandon (himself one recent representative in a long line) is now usually rejected: Jesus was not the would-be instigator of a violent Jewish uprising.[10] But Brandon's mistake was not as silly as some have supposed. It cannot be dismissed by means of the old division of politics and theology, reflecting the expensive luxury of post-Enlightenment dualism. The question still presses, as to whether Jesus in any way sided with those who wanted to overthrow Rome.

If we start out with historical questions such as these, there are important consequences for our method. We do not need to detach Jesus' sayings from the rest of the evidence, and examine them in isolation. The words of Jesus in the gospel tradition have been studied endlessly without hearing the *ipsissima vox Jesu* any the clearer, and without resolving the enigma of the christological titles. This is the burden of Sanders' section on method, and I think he is right.[11] The Old Quest was determined that Jesus should look as little like a first-century Jew as possible. Bultmann was determined that, though Jesus was historically a first-century Jew, his first-century Jewishness was precisely not the place where his 'significance' lay. The renewed 'New Quest', following this line, has often played down the specifically Jewish features of Jesus, stressing instead those which he may have shared with

[9] Cf. *NTPG* Part III. Vermes' *Jesus the Jew* (1973) seemed to offer a novel idea when it came out; since then almost all the Jesus-pictures (except some within the renewed New Quest) have been Jewish, though still quite different from each other.

[10] See Bammel & Moule 1984, offering a wide range of counter-evidence both Christian and non-Christian (summarized e.g. by Sweet (9) and Horbury (192, 195))).

[11] Sanders 1985, 3–13, and esp. 133: 'analysis of the sayings material does not succeed in giving us a picture of Jesus which is convincing and which answers historically important questions'. This is Sanders' verdict on 'most of the exegetical efforts of the last decades'; contrast the revived Bultmannianism reviewed in ch. 2 above. 'Words' and 'deeds' are not, of course, ultimately different sorts of things, a point well made by Downing 1995.

other Mediterranean cultures; it has also downplayed to a large extent the significance of Jesus' death, stressing that we know very little about it and suggesting that the earliest Christians were not particularly interested in it – a feature, of course, which marks a break with Bultmann himself. The present 'Third Quest', by and large, will have none of this. Jesus must be understood as a comprehensible and yet, so to speak, crucifiable first-century Jew, whatever the theological or hermeneutical consequences.

To this extent, the old so-called 'criterion of dissimilarity' may still be applied, though with great caution. Plenty of Jews were not, in this sense, crucifiable; plenty of early Christians were less comprehensibly Jewish. There were, of course, thousands of other Jews crucified in Palestine in the same period, but few if any were handed over by Jewish authorities, as Jesus seems to have been.[12] There were many 'Jewish Christians' in the first generation of the movement; to begin with, of course, all Christians were Jewish. But their allegiance to Jesus made them, from very early on, far less comprehensible as mainstream Jews.[13] This way of setting up a 'criterion of dissimilarity' is substantially different from the way in which something by that name has been used in the past, i.e. to distance Jesus from Judaism and from the early church. Instead, it locates him firmly within Judaism, though looking at the reasons why he, and then his followers, were rejected by the Jewish authorities. Likewise, it assumes a major continuity between him and his followers, while respecting the fact that, unlike him, they were from very early on not perceived as simply one more movement within Judaism. This revived 'criterion of dissimilarity' cannot be simply applied, as used to be attempted, to saying after saying with any hope of 'validating' individual words or sentences. Historians do not live by sayings alone. Instead, the criterion works on a larger scale altogether, to check the lines of a fully historical portrait, including actions and words within the wider treatment of Jesus' aims. This, as we saw in the first volume, is what serious history is all about.[14]

In writing and rewriting the present book I have sometimes wished that the substance of this present argument – and indeed of *NTPG* chapter 4 – could be included in the running head for every page on which synoptic material is under discussion. Perhaps all one can do at this stage is to quote Bultmann and Sanders: 'One can go on asking questions like this about one saying after another, without getting any further';[15] the conviction 'that a

---

[12] cf. ch. 12 below.

[13] See now Alexander 1992. The myth that the split between Jews and Christians only really began after AD 70 must be abandoned: cf. *NTPG* 161–6.

[14] *NTPG* ch. 4. On this point see further ch. 4 below.

[15] Bultmann 1968 [1921], 105.

sufficiently careful exegesis of the sayings material will lead to "a correct decision", has led many a New Testament scholar into a quagmire from which he has never emerged'.[16] If someone replies that we should therefore be content never to know anything, perhaps the best answer is that of Charlesworth, who tells of how he abandoned his previous admiration for New Testament scholars who were 'cautiously reticent until they [could] defend virtually infallible positions'. It is, he says, 'wise and prudent to be cautious; but, pushed to extremes, even a virtue can become a vice. As the rabbis stated, timidity is not a virtue in pursuing truth.'[17]

And the pursuit of truth – historical truth – is what the Third Quest is all about. Serious historical method, as opposed to the pseudo-historical use of home-made 'criteria', is making a come-back in the Third Quest. The much-vaunted 'normal critical tools', particularly form-criticism, are being tacitly (and in my view rightly) bypassed in the search for Jesus; enquiry is proceeding by means of a proper, and often clearly articulated, method of hypothesis and verification.[18] As we saw in the first volume, and again in the previous chapters, much of the impetus for form-critical and redaction-critical study came from the presupposition that this or that piece of synoptic material about Jesus *could not* be historical; in other words, that *an historical hypothesis about Jesus could already be presupposed* which demanded a further tradition-historical hypothesis to explain the evidence. If, however, a viable alternative historical hypothesis, whether about Jesus or about the early church, is proposed, argued out, and maintained, the need for tradition-criticism within the search for Jesus (to say nothing about its undoubted value in other historical enterprises) could in principle be substantially reduced and altered in shape. This is exactly what happens in the hypotheses of (say) Sanders and Meyer: all sorts of things in the gospels which, on the Bultmannian paradigm, needed to be explained by complex epicycles of *Traditionsgeschichte* turn out, after all, to fit comfortably within the ministry of Jesus.

It is vital that this point of method be grasped from the outset. Within the Third Quest, which is where I locate this present book, the task before the serious historian of Jesus is not in the first instance conceived as the

[16] Sanders 1985, 131.

[17] Charlesworth 1988, 17f. Compare the remark of an eminent historian in another field: 'I believe that the literary sources exaggerate when I can catch them out, but otherwise I give them the benefit of the doubt . . . One should not approach any of them in a spirit of resistant scepticism' (Wallace-Hadrill 1974, 8).

[18] See particularly Meyer 1979, ch. 4, esp. 87–92; Sanders 1985, 10, 18–22; and compare Harvey's notion of 'historical constraint', on which see Wright 1986. On the continuing perfectly valid place of 'form-criticism', as a tool to study early Christianity rather than Jesus, cf. *NTPG* ch. 14. Vermes stands out from the newer articulation of historical method, preferring to describe himself (1993, 4, 7) in thoroughly positivist and pragmatist terms.

reconstruction of traditions about Jesus, according to their place within the history of the early church, but the advancement of serious historical hypotheses – that is, the telling of large-scale narratives – about Jesus himself, and the examination of the *prima facie* relevant data to see how they fit. I am only too aware of how controversial this will seem in certain quarters (also, of how obvious and commonsensical it will seem in others). I am, however, optimistic that the point is being grasped within the Third Quest, which is by no means a narrowly confined movement, since it encompasses scholars of widely differing background and outlook. I am, after all, suggesting no more than that Jesus be studied like any other figure of the ancient past. Nobody grumbles at a book on Alexander the Great if, in telling the story, the author 'harmonizes' two or three sources; that is his or her job, to advance hypotheses which draw together the data into a coherent framework rather than leaving it scattered.[19] Of course, sources on Alexander, like sources on Jesus, Tiberius, Beethoven, Gandhi or anybody else, have their own point of view, which must be taken carefully into account. But the object of the exercise is to produce a coherent synthesis which functions as a hypothesis and must be treated as such.[20] As I tried to show in *The New Testament and the People of God*, the problem has been that so-called 'radical' criticism has not been radical enough, but has remained largely content with the hypotheses about Jesus (and the early church) that were advanced by Schweitzer and Bultmann, making only minor modifications to them. If we are to create new hypotheses we cannot assume any fixed points taken from the history of scholarship. All must be questioned. This is why it is irrelevant and inappropriate to discuss, at every point in the historical argument, those views that arise from quite different paradigms.[21] Of course Third Quest writers – myself included – are interested in what people from different movements of scholarship made, or make, of this or that parable, aphorism or whatever. The detailed work of the renewed 'New Quest', and Crossan in particular, must be kept in mind throughout. But the essential argument must take place at a different level.

[19] See e.g. Lane Fox 1986.

[20] See the wise remarks on *Tendenzkritik* in Moule 1984 – an article which, like its author, is short but full of wisdom. Cf. too, on the task of writing a narrative, *NTPG* 113–15; and, on the task of a biographer in particular, Solomon 1988, 114: '. . . the biographer's task appears to be not only to establish a documentary record but constantly to clear away the accumulated fantasies and rumours which have filled the void created by ignorance'. What is there said of Beethoven applies, without many *mutanda*, to Jesus.

[21] There is a basic oddity in debating, in detail, with scholars whose aims and methods are quite different from one's own. Quoting Bultmann (for instance) 'in favour of' or 'against' this or that saying proves nothing whatever if one has already emphatically disagreed with him at the more fundamental level of aim, method and overall hypothesis. Cf. e.g. Sanders 1985, 368 n.66 and frequently.

If today there is a new wave of historical seriousness about Jesus, there is also a new sense, well beyond what early redaction-criticism envisaged, that the gospels are to be seen as texts, works of literary art, in their own right. This has sometimes misled scholars into supposing that they are therefore of less historical value. However, there are signs that a more mature approach is beginning to emerge.[22] It is becoming apparent that the authors of at least the synoptic gospels, which still provide the bulk of the relevant source material, intended to write about Jesus, not just about their own churches and theology, and that they substantially succeeded in this intention.[23]

The attempt to set Jesus credibly within his historical context, then, is once again widely regarded as a reputable scholarly task.[24] Within this, the Third Quest can claim certain solid advantages. First, it takes the total Jewish background extremely seriously. Second, its practitioners have no united theological or political agenda, unlike the quite monochrome New Quest and its fairly monochrome renewal; the diverse backgrounds of the scholars involved serve to provide checks and balances, so that one scholar's reading of a particular passage (say) in Josephus is balanced by another's, and a measure of critical realism is both possible and increasingly actual. Third, there has increasingly been a sense of homing in on the key questions which have to be asked if we are to make progress. All these things have enabled the study of Jesus to rejoin the mainland of historical work after drifting, for more years than was good for it, around the archipelago of theologically motivated methods and criteria.

2. The Questions

What, then, are the key questions that have emerged, and how are they being handled within the Third Quest?[25] There are, I suggest, five major questions,

[22] Mack (1988) provides an example of the false antithesis; Freyne (1988b), of how it may be overcome. Cf. esp. *NTPG* chs. 13, 14.

[23] cf. *NTPG* ch. 13, esp. 396–403.

[24] Not, however, universally: there will always be some in orthodox Christian circles who regard it with grave suspicion, and prefer the (often seemingly almost docetic) Christ of faith. (A recent example is Johnson 1995.) Käsemann, at the start of the New Quest, rightly saw that such a Christ is unlikely to be disturbing and hence unlikely to have anything to do with genuine Christianity. It is still difficult to persuade some colleagues in the discipline that there is anything worth doing in the Third Quest area, for instance by doctoral students – or that, if there is, there are ways forward that bypass the log-jam of endless *Traditionsgeschichte*. I look forward to the day when there will be less over-cautious conservatism on this point and more genuine openness to the real historical task.

[25] In what follows, reference to an author without date indicates the book(s) mentioned in the previous section.

with a sixth always waiting in the wings. It is important to realize that these questions are not independent or isolated, but overlap and interlock at various points. Indeed, the interaction between them is one of the most complex and interesting features of the whole discussion. These questions are all raised explicitly within the Third Quest; in fact, no work on Jesus can get off the ground without a position being taken, at least by implication, in relation to them all, though many earlier writers simply presupposed particular answers and carried on from there. However, within the Third Quest itself, different writers have focused on different sets of these questions, and no single writer has given them all, and their integration, equal prominence, as I hope eventually to do (though this lies beyond the scope of the present volume).

The five questions are all subdivisions of the larger question which, I submit, all historians of the first century, no matter what their background, are bound to ask, namely: how do we account for the fact that, by AD 110, there was a large and vigorous international movement, already showing considerable diversity, whose founding myth (in a quite 'neutral' sense) was a story about one Jesus of Nazareth, a figure of the recent past? How do we get, in other words, from the pluriform Judaism that existed within the Greco-Roman world of 10 BC to the pluriform Judaism and Christianity of AD 110 – from (roughly) Herod the Great to Ignatius of Antioch?[26] In every generation there are one or two scholars who think this can be done without reference to Jesus. There are also a few dozen who try to do it with only minimal reference to him. In both cases the weight of counter-probability is enormous. Radical innovation has to be ascribed elsewhere, and the only strength of such suggestions is that, since they build on no evidence at all, they are hard to attack.[27] This forces us, simply as historians, to ask: who then was Jesus, what was he trying to do, what happened to him, and why? And, just as we can ask such questions about Paul, or the emperor Claudius, or Tiberius' hatchet-man Sejanus (all figures of the first century about whom we have a certain amount of historical evidence), there is every reason to ask them about Jesus as well. So, sharpening up these issues into our five main questions: How does Jesus fit into the Judaism of his day? What were his aims? Why did he die? How did the early church come into being, and why did it take the shape it did? and Why are the gospels what they are?[28] The

---

[26] cf. *NTPG* Part IV.

[27] The lines of thought here tend to be: 'Christianity' was founded by Paul and others with little relation to Jesus (e.g. Vermes, Maccoby); 'Christianity' is the work of the myth-making communities and evangelists, with little continuity with Jesus (Bultmann; Mack; and beyond). See *NTPG* ch. 14.

[28] It will readily be apparent that my list of questions is close to that of Sanders 1985, 1. However, as we proceed it will also be clear that he and I understand several of the questions in interestingly different ways. Sanders claims to have a non-theological agenda (1985, 333f.; though cf. Charlesworth 1988, 26–9). He is at least right in this respect, that he is not

sixth question is something of a joker in the pack, though every writer on Jesus is quite well aware of it: So What?

These questions are emphatically not the mere private concern of Christians and/or theologians. They belong – all of them, including the sixth – in the public arena. They are not 'slanted' towards a particular theology, as is clear from the very different answers they receive within the Third Quest itself. To this diversity we now turn.

(i) How does Jesus fit into Judaism?

The first question (together with the second, which sharpens it to a point) arises naturally from the whole movement of historical investigation of Jesus. If he belongs anywhere in history, it is within the history of first-century Judaism. But how does he belong there? Was he a typical Jew, really quite unremarkable? Or, at the opposite extreme, was he so totally different that he stood out completely, following an entirely different set of aims, obedient to a different vision of reality? Or, if we renounce these two extremes, did he share the perspective of his people to a large extent, adjusting it only at a few points (however significant) here and there? Or did he have a major programme for reform? Where did he fit *vis-à-vis* the various revolutionary groups, or the Pharisaic movement? Was he a Hasid? a prophet? Did he in any way either encourage or tolerate armed resistance to Rome, or did he speak out against it, or did he ignore the issue? Did he appear in any sense as a Messiah-figure? Where, in short, do we place Jesus within first-century Judaism?[29]

The list of possible answers is of course enormous. To make some sense of them, we may divide them into three, each of which is capable of considerable variation. The first two can be seen side by side before we turn to the third.

First, we can put Jesus so thoroughly within his context as almost to camouflage him into invisibility. Thus we have Jesus the thoroughly Jewish wandering Hasid (Vermes) and Jesus the Jewish revolutionary (Brandon). Second, we can put him at the other extreme, and minimize his Jewishness (thus moving beyond the boundaries of the Third Quest). Thus we have Jesus the preacher of timeless (and non-Jewish) truths (Bultmann), or Jesus the Cynic (Downing, Mack, and much of the Jesus Seminar). There are some

---

attempting to provide a Christian apologetic. This gives the lie to a criticism I received orally from Professor Geza Vermes, that these questions are specifically 'Christian'.

[29] This all depends, of course, on one's view of that complex and pluriform entity, first-century Judaism: cf. *NTPG* Part III.

interesting ways in which the opposite ends of this chain can be twisted round so as to meet. Vermes' Jesus, for all he is supposed to be so very Jewish, preaches in fact a liberal and timeless form of Judaism which is itself fairly thoroughly existentialist.[30] Crossan's Jesus, for all he is fairly non-Jewish (his message of the kingdom has little to do with classic Jewish expectation), preaches a message opposed to Roman domination, and thus aligns himself, almost by accident, with some very Jewish movements.

These two extreme positions can of course be modified. Perhaps, on the one hand, Jesus was really hoping for violent revolution, but rested content, for the moment, with secretly gathering support, waiting for the day when force could and should be used (Buchanan). Perhaps he was aligned with a non-violent social revolution, rooted in the peasant society of his day, at the same time implicitly supporting the 'social bandits' who subsequently, when all else had failed, took to violence to oppose the system that had systematically brutalized them (Horsley).[31] Perhaps, on the other hand, Jesus was indeed a wandering Cynic-style teacher, but addressed his aphorisms and world-shattering parables to a specifically Jewish context which modified the style and content of the Cynic image, though still aiming its basic thrust at the larger Mediterranean world (Crossan).

The historian is thus faced with a bewildering range of options. One well-worn traditional Christian position is to say that the Jewish background is a mass of legalism and formalism, and that Jesus came to teach a different sort of religion, namely, an interior spiritual sort. This is clearly no good.[32] If it were true, Jesus would have been simply incomprehensible, a teacher of abstract and interior truths to a people hungry for God to act within history. The people were asking for bread and freedom, not thin air. Nor did he simply come to found the church, giving the Sermon on the Mount as its charter.[33] In the search for alternatives to these distortions, scholars and

---

[30] cf. Vermes 1993, in which there are more references to Bultmann – mostly in agreement – than to any other modern writer except Sanders. Cf. e.g. 137: 'Jesus, the existential teacher, was more concerned with man's attitude and behaviour towards the Kingdom than with its essence or structure', cp. 153, 161, 193. See too 180: Vermes repeats the old Bultmannian idea, now heavily criticized by Sanders and others, that Jesus proclaimed 'the near and approachable God' as opposed to 'the eternal, distant, dominating and tremendous Creator'.

[31] cf. the discussion in *NTPG* 177–81.

[32] For a full critique, see Sanders 1985 *passim*, e.g. 23–47, 331–4, even though he is sometimes open to the charge of unfairness.

[33] Nor – especially – did he come to give a list of things one had to do in order to go to heaven after death. That view is based, I think, simply on the misreading of 'inherit the kingdom of heaven' in Matthew (understanding 'kingdom' as a place and 'heaven' as saying where that place is) instead of as a periphrasis for 'reign of God'. See *NTPG* 302ff., and below, Part II.

exegetes have tried ways of closer integration, usually involving Jesus in some form of affirmation of basic Jewish expectations, with minor modifications here and there. We have Jesus the prophet of 'restoration eschatology'.[34] We have Jesus the charismatic of charismatics, the great spiritual leader who shared so completely the aspirations of the Pharisees.[35] In these portraits, and many others like them, Jesus has little or no quarrel with (what is seen as) mainline Judaism, but only with the official Jerusalem aristocracy, who are then seen as the proximate cause of his death.

If the first two forms of solution are the near-identification and the near-dislocation between Jesus and Judaism, the third explores the confrontation between Jesus and Judaism in terms of Jesus' reclamation of a key part of the Jewish heritage itself. One of the clearest exponents of this point of view is Marcus Borg.[36] For him, Jesus claims the high ground of fulfilment of the Jewish scriptures, in particular the prophets, while challenging head-on several aspects of the actual Judaism of his time. The challenge comes, *not* because he has a different, non-Jewish sort of religion, but because first-century Judaism, including Pharisaism, is in his view disobedient to Israel's god and consequently likely to reap disaster. I do not follow Borg's thesis all the way, and indeed, as noted in the previous chapter, I take a different direction on several vital issues; but this general thrust, of a very Jewish Jesus who was nevertheless opposed to some high-profile features of first-century Judaism, seems to me the most viable one if we are to do justice, not just to the evidence of the synoptic gospels (they, after all, are easy game for any critic who wants to avoid their implications) but more particularly to the requirements of consistency and clear historical line in our historical reconstruction of Jesus himself.

We have already noted more than once that 'Judaism' is as difficult to describe as Jesus himself (see *NTPG* Part III), so that putting the two together is like climbing from one moving boat into another. The history of research indicates how easy it is to fall into the water. The more specific questions, which bring the first of our main questions into sharper focus, concern especially Jesus' relationship with the Pharisees, and here the two boats sometimes seem close to capsizing altogether. Some theories try to keep the conflict to a minimum: according to Sanders, the Pharisees of Jesus' day were a small, Jerusalem-based group, and the narratives which portray Jesus in conflict with them reflect simply the church-versus-synagogue controversies of a later period.[37] Rivkin, however, for all his desire to show that

---

[34] Sanders 1985, 1993.

[35] Rivkin 1984; cf. too Maccoby 1980.

[36] See esp. Borg 1984, on which see Neill & Wright 1988, 387-91.

[37] For discussion and critique, see *NTPG* 181-203. Sanders seems to have modified his position in his more recent book on Judaism (1992b), and his second one on Jesus (1993).

the Roman imperial system was responsible for Jesus' death, allows that the 'Scribes-Pharisees' (he considers the two groups identical) would have had difficulty with much that Jesus said and did, even though his religious ideals coincided with theirs to a large extent.[38] Other theories allow for considerable conflict. Riches sees Pharisaic Judaism as offering a wrong, or at least deficient, view of the true god, with Jesus 'transforming' this view into the right one (particularly important in his treatment is the 'transformation' of the vision of a wrathful god into that of a merciful one).[39] Borg is equally concerned to maintain the historicity of Jesus' challenge to basic Jewish symbols and institutions, the Torah and the Temple being central. His Jesus therefore comes into quite sharp conflict with the Pharisees. But this is not because Judaism is the wrong sort of religion; it is because Israel has forgotten her vocation.

A further point at which our answer to the first question depends upon a careful reconstruction of one aspect of first-century Judaism is the question of Jesus' relation to the hopes and aspirations of Israel. Neither Sanders nor Borg deals at all with the question of Jesus' Messiahship in its relation to Israel. If, however, it is true that the Temple was bound up in Jewish thought with the true king,[40] then Sanders' argument that Jesus' attitude to the Temple is the best starting-point for the historical quest is *ipso facto* an argument for the centrality of Messiahship within Jesus' self-understanding, or at the very least within his contemporaries' understanding of him. And 'Messiahship' in this context is not (as, surprisingly, even Vermes seems to think) a 'divine' category. It is an 'Israel' category. Jesus as 'king of the Jews' is the one in whom Israel's destiny is summed up, as Pilate knew very well when he caused the *titulus* to be nailed to the cross, offering thereby an insult to the nation, as much as to its supposed (and now supposedly failed) Messiah.[41]

Sharpening up still further the question of Jesus and Jewish aspirations, we continually meet the question: did Jesus, or did he not, expect the end of the world, i.e. of the space-time universe? Here the two boats are again in

---

[38] Rivkin 1984, 44 (the spiritual teaching of the Scribes-Pharisees), 96–9 (their objection to Jesus' behaviour). See too Neusner 1993.

[39] Riches 1980, e.g. 130–5 (133: 'the system of rigid boundaries is replaced by a set of personal standards which are at once more demanding and more fulfilling'), 142–4, 166f. ('Jesus must effectively recast the Jewish doctrine of rewards and punishments because his view of God's mercy and bounty cannot countenance the limits which such a doctrine imposes on God's dealings with man'), and esp. 168–89 (187: 'the central importance of Jesus' life and work is . . . to be found . . . in his reworking of fundamental assumptions about God, man and the world').

[40] See *NTPG* Part III, esp. 224–6, 307–20; below, ch. 11; and e.g. Runnalls 1983.

[41] See Part III below.

choppy water. Did Jews expect the end of the world? If so, did Jesus share that expectation, or react against it? If not, did he introduce the idea? Some, such as Harvey, follow Schweitzer and Bultmann in saying 'yes' in both cases: Jesus, like first-century Jews, did expect the end of the world. Others, such as Mack, say 'yes' and 'no': many Jews did cherish 'apocalyptic' expectations (meaning by that an end-of-the-world expectation), but Jesus took a different line. Others, such as Borg,[42] echo the protests of writers like Caird and Glasson, with a double negative: neither Jesus nor his Jewish contemporaries expected the end of the world.[43] This leaves yet a further question: did he then use apocalyptic imagery in his preaching, and if so how are we to understand it? One can deny the authenticity of the 'apocalyptic' sayings, or one can reinterpret them: Perrin does the first, Borg the second.[44] Sanders, in his book on Jesus, leaves this issue finely balanced; in his more recent work he seems to me to be coming down more on the side of Borg and others.[45] This whole problem, of course, has a sting in its tail in the form of an implication for the sixth question: if Jesus expected the end of the world, then he was mistaken, so was he perhaps mistaken about all sorts of other things as well? (This last suggestion usually, as a matter of fact, devalues the debate. Anyone who says that Jesus did not expect the end of the world may find themselves suspected of having cooked the evidence to 'protect' Jesus' reputation – unless, of course, the conclusion is advanced within the 'Jesus Seminar', where it is evidence of a desire for a non-apocalyptic, and hence non-fundamentalist or non-Reaganite, Jesus!) We need here to be sure what exactly we are talking about; we need to be on firm ground in our reading of apocalyptic language and literature. A brief word on both, by way of recapitulation from the first volume, is appropriate at this stage.[46]

First, what are we talking about in discussing first-century Jewish hopes? It has commonly been assumed, at least since Weiss and Schweitzer, that Jesus and many of his contemporaries expected the imminent end of the present space-time order altogether, the winding up of history and the ushering in of a new age in radical discontinuity with the present one. It is possible, however, to take the idea in quite a different sense: that Jesus and some of his contemporaries expected the end of the present *world order*, i.e. the end of the period when the Gentiles were lording it over the people of the true god, and the inauguration of the time when this god would take his power and reign and, in the process, restore the fortunes of his suffering people.[47]

[42] Borg 1984, 1986, 1987c.
[43] cf. Caird 1965; 1980, chs. 12–14; Glasson 1984 [1977].
[44] Perrin 1967, 202–6; Borg *passim*.
[45] cf. Sanders 1992b; and the discussion in *NTPG* 333f.
[46] For detail, and argument, cf. esp. *NTPG* 280–99, 342f., 459–64; and chs. 6, 8 below.
[47] Even this way of putting it is not, I realize, unambiguous. Sanders speaks of 'the end of the present world order' in a subtly different way, retaining both the idea of an imminent

Clarity at this point is imperative. One can either opt for extreme discontinuity, or extreme continuity, or find some way (as Sanders tries to do) of holding both together.

Second, how does apocalyptic language and literature work? In the post-Bultmannian New Quest it was assumed that talk of the 'kingdom of god', or of the 'son of man coming on the clouds of heaven', was to be taken as a literal prediction of events, shortly to take place, which would close the space-time order. But not only is it unnecessary to read apocalyptic language in this way: it is actually necessary, as historians, that we refuse to do so. Apocalyptic language was (among many other things, to be sure) an elaborate metaphor-system for investing historical events with theological significance. This understanding of the literature has at any rate a good *prima facie* claim to be historically on target, in contrast with the contrived literalism in which the Bultmann school find themselves as uncomfortable bedfellows of mainstream fundamentalism.

What then was Jesus talking about? It is time, as I shall argue in detail later on, to reject the old idea that Jesus expected the end of the space-time universe – though this does not mean, as the 'Jesus Seminar' has imagined, that Jesus did not use 'apocalyptic' language.[48] Nor does it mean, as I find myself accused of saying by some colleagues, that we have hereby 'abandoned eschatology'. Far from it. I wish to stress that, in my view, first-century Judaism, and Jesus as firmly within it, can be understood only within a climate of intense eschatological expectation, whose character I have

---

future, *dis*continuous with present space-time events, and the suggestion of considerable continuity. Cf. Sanders 1985, e.g. 93, 123ff., 130, 306 ('a new world order, whether "in the air" or in a new Jerusalem'), 371 n.2, and esp. 376 n.3: 'I use "eschatology" to refer to the expectation of an imminent end to the current order.' What we need to decide is: what is this 'order', and what is involved in its 'end'? Cf. again *NTPG* 333f.; and, recently, Sanders' further cautious remarks (1993, 30f.). His clearest statements come in his work on Judaism (1992): e.g. 298: 'Many Jews looked forward to a new and better age . . . The hopes centred on the restoration of the people, the building or purification of the temple and Jerusalem, the defeat or conversion of the Gentiles, and the establishment of purity and righteousness'; cf. 303.

[48] Vermes 1993 has, in my view, radically misread Jesus' apocalyptic eschatology. He speaks (188f.) of 'Jesus' eschatological Judaism', but I am not convinced that he has understood how that system of thought works. Here Vermes is at his most Bultmannian: 'In a real eschatological atmosphere the change is total. The future to all intents and purposes is abolished and replaced by imminence, immediacy and urgency . . . Instead of a search for society's progress and improvement, single [i.e., presumably, 'individual'] men and women have to face up at once to an ultimate choice and decision . . . In a world in which the *now* is sacrosanct, all dawdling is banned' (189, 193). Vermes builds a great deal on Jesus' supposed belief in the imminent approach of the kingdom, as a great event which did not in fact materialize (147, 211, 214), even though he admits his own puzzlement as to what exactly Jesus meant by this language (146).

already tried to make clear.[49] If this position is taken, it becomes possible to move, as Caird did, to the claim that Jesus' warnings about imminent judgment were intended to be taken as denoting (what we would call) socio-political events, *seen as the climactic moment in Israel's history*, and, in consequence, as constituting a summons to *national* repentance. In this light, Jesus appears as a successor to Jeremiah and his like, warning Israel that persistence in her present course will bring political disaster, which in turn should be *understood as* the judgment of Israel's own god.[50] But Jesus is not merely a successor, one in a continuing line of prophets. His warnings include the warning that he is the last in the line. This is, I think, what Jesus' eschatology is all about. Israel's history is drawing to its climax.

The events of AD 70 thus once again become significant in the argument. If the Romans do this (i.e. the crucifixion of Jesus) when the wood is green, what will they do when it is dry, when thousands of young Jews are crucified outside Jerusalem, guilty of the 'crime' of which Jesus was innocent?[51] But the question as to whether Jesus preached judgment at all is itself one of the many controversial areas in the Third Quest. Borg thinks he did, and makes this fact central. Sanders thinks he approved of John the Baptist's message of judgment, but did not find it necessary to repeat it.[52] One aspect of Sanders' book that I find strange at this point is his treatment of the Temple sayings. Though only one of the sayings attributed to Jesus by the evangelists even mentions the *rebuilding* of the Temple (John 2.16; the other sayings which mention this aspect are put in the mouth of *false* witnesses), Sanders passes very quickly over the overwhelmingly negative aspect of all the other sayings about the Temple, and focuses attention instead on restoration as though this were the main explicit theme.[53]

These various levels in the discussion of eschatology reveal one final and vital feature of the Jesus-and-Judaism discussion. It will not do to drive a wedge between politics and theology, between national and 'eschatological' expectation. We cannot either insist *a priori* on a non-political Jesus in order

---

[49] cf. *NTPG* 268–79, 280–338.

[50] This theme is emphasized by Matthew (cf. Knowles 1993), but this should not be taken automatically to mean that it is unhistorical.

[51] cf. Caird 1963, 249f.; 1965, 22. An interesting parallel to Caird's thought is found in Downing 1963. See below, ch. 12.

[52] Sanders 1985, 322, 326.

[53] cf. Borg 1984, ch. 7. See particularly the quite sudden transition in Sanders 1985, 71: 'The *obvious answer* is that destruction, in turn, looks towards restoration' (my italics). The parallel between the Temple-incident (which, as Sanders rightly stresses, had nothing to do with the superiority of inner worship over the sacrificial cult, or with fraud on the part of the traders) and the cursing of the fig tree makes this answer far from obvious. (This is not to say that the word about rebuilding is inauthentic; see Meyer 1989, ch. 8, esp. 162–6.) See Part III below.

to reject a revolutionary reading, or expose the weaknesses in the revolutionary case and imagine that we have thereby argued for a non-political Jesus.[54] One of the great merits of Borg's first book is its grasping of this nettle. He explains that by 'politics' he means 'the concern about the structure and purpose of a historic community'. Jesus' message was addressed to Israel, and

> to be a religious figure in this tradition was quite different from being a religious figure in a tradition which defines religion as, for example, what persons do with their solitude. It meant to face questions about the purpose, structure and destiny of the historic community of Israel. What did it mean to be the people of God? In particular, in a setting in which Israel's sovereignty was denied and her very existence threatened by the imperial combination of Hellenistic culture and Roman military power, what did it mean to be Israel, the people of promise destined to rule Yahweh's created order?[55]

In such a world, to be non-political is to be irrelevant.

Borg's definition of 'political' may still, however, be too wide for some. He shows, I think, that Jesus is concerned with *society*; but, if 'politics' refers to the detailed mechanisms of actual power ('the science and art of government' is the definition offered by the *Concise Oxford Dictionary*), one could still say either that Jesus held aloof from it (he did not try to get himself appointed to the Sanhedrin), or, perhaps better, that he challenged the whole power-system of first-century Israel by setting up himself and the twelve in a new and highly paradoxical position of *alternative* political 'power' – which turned out to redefine the meanings of both politics and power.[56] In this sense he was indeed 'political': such an adjective by no means indicates that one is underwriting anyone else's particular programme. We have seen in our own generation what happens to those who refuse to run with the hares or hunt with the hounds. To tell all sides that their vision for the nation is wrong, and to act as if one has glimpsed, and is implementing, a different vision, is to invite trouble. The strength of this analysis, applied to Jesus, is that it makes him, as we said before, both comprehensible and crucifiable. Out of the morass of discussion in the Third Quest, an increasingly clear answer to the first question is emerging: Jesus cannot be separated from his Jewish context, but neither can he be collapsed into it so that he is left without a sharp critique of his contemporaries. I shall do my best to clarify and develop this insight throughout much of the present book.

---

[54] The latter line is taken, for apparently Christian reasons, by some of the contributors to Bammel & Moule 1984, and for Jewish reasons by e.g. Rivkin 1984. When Sanders (1985, 294) argued that Jesus was 'non-political', it is clear that he simply meant non-revolutionary.

[55] Borg 1984, 3f.

[56] See the interesting discussion of 'power' in Riches 1980, 171f.

(ii) What were Jesus' Aims?

The second question follows naturally from the first. What was Jesus seeking to *do* within Judaism? What event or sets of events would mean, from the perspective of his ministry, that he could say 'I have succeeded in my aim'? From the viewpoint of conservative orthodoxy the answer would be 'he aimed to die as a sacrifice for the sins of the world'; for Reimarus or Brandon, it would be 'he aimed to liberate Jews from their Roman over-lords'. Granted that both of these, in different ways, are as they stand simplistic and misleading, how can we sketch an alternative which is not?

Was Jesus trying to change individuals, to change society, to change the world, or all of the above – and if so how? In particular, was his death accidental to the purpose of his life, or did he in any sense intend it? Theology has usually been content to jump from the question of why Jesus was born to the question of why he died, leaving the field clear for romantic or political reconstructions of the ministry. At best, some Catholic writing has suggested that his one aim was to found the church – which of course he did simply by calling the disciples (especially Peter), teaching them what they needed to know, and then dying for their sins. This solution has the merit that it tries to take the life of Jesus seriously from a theological point of view. It has the drawback, however, that it leaves the first of the five questions out of consideration, except in so far as it requires Judaism to be the dark backdrop against which all this could be understood. This problematic position must not remain unchallenged. Instead, we must stress the central importance of questions concerning Jesus' aims, desires, aspirations and goals.[57]

An objection to this set of questions was lodged two generations ago by Cadbury, who suggested that the whole idea of a person having consistent and life-directing aims was anachronistic.[58] This, however, is spurious. Paul was clearly motivated by a long-held overarching aim which he followed consistently. So, as far as we can tell, was John the Baptist. So were many figures in the Greco-Roman world about whom we have reliable information.[59] Similarly, it has often been supposed that the intentions of human beings, not least in ancient history, are bound to be opaque to us. It is so

[57] On the discussion of aims, etc., cf. *NTPG* 110f., 125f. 'Desires', 'aspirations' and 'goals' are introduced here as less specific terms, fleshing out some aspects of 'aims'.

[58] Cadbury 1962 [1937].

[59] Sanders' answer to Cadbury (1985, 19f.) can thus be strengthened (against e.g. Bowden 1988, 141-3). Ancient persons whose aims can be studied include Pericles, Socrates and Cicero, and several Roman emperors, not least Augustus, Vespasian, and Hadrian. Our inability to study everybody in this way arises from lack of information, not from the fact that having consistent life-directing aims is a 'modern' phenomenon.

hard to reconstruct what went on in somebody's head in another period of history, so impossible to be sure we have got it right. And yet this is in fact the stuff of which history is made. When we look for explanations of events in the world of human affairs, we are seeking for human motivations.[60]

How may we go about this perilous search? How, in other words, may we engage in the full historical task? There are two things to look for in particular.[61] First, we must study the *worldview* of the society or culture, or subculture, concerned. We must understand the way people looked at the world, what they hoped for, what they were afraid of. We can assume some continuity with other human societies with which we are more familiar, but we had better not assume too much. If, for instance, a future historian of the Second World War were to study the Japanese Kamikaze pilots, she would fail to understand the whole phenomenon unless she managed to get inside the worldview of the Japanese of that period, in which human life, including one's own, was counted cheap in comparison with the coming victory of the race as a whole – not an idea that would necessarily occur at once to a modern western historian. If, as another example, one tried to understand the Desert Fathers, one would have to get inside the whole worldview of early Egyptian Christianity. One could at no point presume that a transfer of ideas would be possible. If, finally, coming closer to our subject, we were to read the parable of the prodigal son without realizing that the son's initial request for his share of the inheritance would be 'heard', within peasant village culture, as expressing the shocking wish that his father were dead, the entire reading of the parable would get off on the wrong foot.[62] We can only avoid such problems by painstaking historical and cultural research.

Second, we must study the *mindset* of the individual concerned. This will normally be a variation – sometimes a mutation – on the worldview as a whole. Worldviews themselves are necessarily large and overarching, and there is plenty of room for local and individual variation. Most human beings possess a mindset which retains a fair degree of consistency over time. Mavericks do arise, and people do odd things without – even to themselves –

---

[60] See *NTPG* Part II, esp. 109–12, particularly the emphasis that this does not commit us to the attempt to psychoanalyse figures from the past (see further Part III below). On this point, see the well-known protest of Schweitzer 1954 [1906], 331f.: 'Formerly it was possible to book through-tickets at the supplementary-psychological-knowledge office which enabled those travelling in the interests of Life-of-Jesus construction to use express trains, thus avoiding the inconvenience of having to stop at every little station, change, and run the risk of missing their connexion. This ticket office is now closed. There is a station at the end of each section of the narrative, and the connexions are not guaranteed.' Schweitzer himself, however, clearly booked some through-tickets at offices dealing in aims, goals and motivations – as, I suggest, he had every right to do. This is what history is about.

[61] On what follows see *NTPG* ch. 4.

[62] cf. Bailey 1983 [1976, 1980], 1.161–9; and below, ch. 4.

apparent motivation. But where an individual seems to have made up his or her mind on an issue, and be acting with a measure of consistency, in accordance with a particular plan (even if the actual plan remains opaque to onlookers), it makes sense to ask what it is that motivates that individual, what his or her particular aims may be. Moreover – and this is the point I wish to make here – this set of questions applies just as much in ancient as in modern history. We can ask, perfectly meaningfully, why Hannibal wanted to march on Rome, and why he chose to go the way he did. We can understand his mindset as a mutation of the regular Carthaginian one. We can ask, perfectly meaningfully, why Seneca committed suicide, and answer the question by reconstructing the worldview of Roman Stoics under Nero, and the particular mindset of Seneca himself as a variant or mutation of that worldview. There is nothing odd about this; it is actually what historians do all the time, though New Testament scholars often talk as if it were not. There is nothing in principle magical or mystical, nothing in principle inaccessible, about the settled intentions, aims, or ambitions of an individual. Even if little is said about them, they will gradually become apparent in actions performed, in choices made, in lifestyles adopted. In searching for the aims of Jesus, we are looking for a particular mindset within a particular worldview, quite possibly challenging that worldview in some ways, but with intentions that make sense in relation to it. This quest is in principle possible; I hope to show that it can be realized in practice.

What options have been offered on this question? The traditional pre-critical view was, as we have said, that Jesus came to die for the sins of the world, and/or to found the church. The Old Quest, by contrast, tended to assume – and this is still followed in much of the New Quest – that Jesus was basically a *teacher*: hence the concentration on his sayings, and the continual attempt to make them into timeless proclamations of truths about a god, or about human relationships.[63] Jesus intended, on this view, to tell people something new, to impart information they did not previously possess. This viewpoint is still reflected in the work of Vermes. But most Third Quest writers have homed in on more specific aims, almost always taking for granted that Jesus' aims had to do with the kingdom, and proceeding from there. Thus we find that Jesus intended to foment revolution of one sort or another (Brandon and others); or, again, that he intended to oppose revolutionary zeal (Hengel, Borg). We read that Jesus intended to bring to birth the 'restoration eschatology' that he, like some others, believed in, involving the

---

[63] cf. ch. 2 above. An example taken nearly at random: Evans 1990, 589 asks what the parable of the prodigal son is 'intended to teach', and is surprised at how difficult this is to establish. Perhaps this is because the better question would be: what is the parable intended to *do*?

destruction and rebuilding of the Temple (Sanders). Or, again, he intended to bring about a radical reform in the sacrificial cult of Jerusalem; only when this failed to come about did he alter his focus and regard his fellowship-meals with his followers as an *alternative* to the Temple (Chilton). Again, Jesus intended to establish a nexus between Israel and himself, such that Israel was already being restored in his words, his acts, and finally in his death (Meyer).[64] Or Jesus intended to announce to Israel a new way of being the people of God, which would involve finding the way through vicarious suffering to the 'vindication of the son of man', which would include the destruction of the Temple (Caird).

There are two interlocking questions which emerge from this brief survey. First, did Jesus remain true to one set of aims throughout his life, or did he change his mind at a particular stage? Second, did Jesus go up to Jerusalem with the intention of dying there? A third question, concerning Jesus' sense of personal vocation, is usually also waiting in the wings as these ones are under discussion.

There are various ways of postulating a change of mind. The classic form is that of Renan:[65] the 'Galilean springtime', in which Jesus is popular and successful, is followed by a cooler, and darker, period when it seems as though his demands are too heavy to be met. Subsequent forms of the theory include those of Buchanan (Jesus wanted to be a subversive revolutionary, and then changed his mind in order to go to the cross) and Chilton (Jesus wanted to reform the Temple and its sacrificial system; having failed, he treated his followers as a counter-Temple movement).[66] The change of mind, clearly, relates directly to the second of the interlocking questions: did Jesus go to Jerusalem in order to die?

Schweitzer declared long ago that one could in fact divide up Lives of Jesus into two categories: did Jesus go to Jerusalem to work, or to die?[67] Schweitzer himself firmly took the latter option, though he too postulated a change of mind: Jesus did not originally intend to die, but to prepare the way for the victorious 'coming of the son of man'. It was only after the apparent failure of his mission – the failure of the son of man to appear – that he took it upon himself to force the divine hand. So, in a famous passage, Schweitzer saw Jesus putting into operation his revised aim (the added italics indicating where the change of mind occurred):

In the knowledge that He is the coming Son of Man [Jesus] lays hold of the wheel of the world to set it moving on that last revolution which is to bring all ordinary history to a

---

[64] cf. esp. Meyer 1979, 221f., 251–3.
[65] cf. Schweitzer 1954 [1906], 185ff., discussing Renan 1863.
[66] Buchanan 1984; Chilton 1992b.
[67] Schweitzer 1954 [1906], 333, 389 n.1; O'Neill 1980, ch. 4.

close. *It refuses to turn, and He throws Himself on it.* Then it does turn; and crushes Him. Instead of bringing in the eschatological conditions, He has destroyed them. The wheel rolls onward, and the mangled body of the one immeasurably great Man, who was strong enough to think of Himself as the spiritual ruler of mankind and to bend history to his purpose, is hanging upon it still. That is His victory and His reign.[68]

A softer version of this position is taken by Meyer: Jesus, having always reckoned with the possibility of violent death, built this more firmly into the structure of his aims quite early on in the course of the ministry.[69] Sanders pronounced this whole view, of Jesus going to Jerusalem to die, 'weird';[70] but this, I think, fails to take fully into account the major differences of worldview between first-century Palestine and modern America.[71] Moule, with a far more nuanced account, suggests that, although Jesus did not seek death,

> he did pursue, with inflexible devotion, a way of truth that inevitably led him to death, and he did not seek to escape . . . He knew he was, in fact, bound to die, and he made no attempt either to escape or to defend himself.[72]

If we push both the options (going to work, or to die) into a more clear-cut form, we find the following antithesis. For Vermes, Jesus simply died in despair and with a broken heart, his life-aim in ruins.[73] For Caird, conversely,

> not only in theological truth but in historic fact, the one bore the sins of the many, confident that in him the whole Jewish nation was being nailed to the cross, only to come to life again in a better resurrection.[74]

Thus the question, whether Jesus intended to die, and if so whether he gave his death any particular theological interpretation, remains firmly open within Third Quest study. I hope that the later chapters of the present book will advance the matter significantly.

The further question, whether Jesus intended to found a church (or even *the* church), clearly needs more refinement. The question is often asked, and answered, with some scorn, on the assumption that, if the answer is 'yes',

---

[68] Schweitzer 1954 [1906], 368f.

[69] Meyer 1979, 252. Cf. too Schillebeeckx 1979 [1974], 298–302; Witherington 1990, 262.

[70] Sanders 1985, 333; the whole passage is interesting, though perhaps skewed because Sanders is, as often, anxious to ward off the supposedly extreme position of Jeremias. I think my argument in Part III, in which I take a view very different from that of Jeremias, meets Sanders' objections.

[71] cf. Neyrey 1991, xiv and elsewhere.

[72] Moule 1977, 109. Moule refers here to Downing 1963.

[73] Vermes 1993, 207.

[74] Caird 1965, 22.

we must think of Jesus envisaging cathedrals, cardinals, popes, processions, Archbishops of Canterbury and all. Thus Vermes:

> if [Jesus] meant and believed what he preached . . ., namely that the eternal Kingdom of God was truly at hand, he simply could not have entertained the idea of founding and setting in motion an organized society intended to endure for ages to come.[75]

If, however, we follow either Meyer or Sanders, and see Jesus' aim as the restoration, in some sense, of Israel, beginning with the highly symbolic call of twelve disciples, then the apparently peculiar idea of Jesus 'founding' a community designed to outlast his death gives way to a more nuanced, and perfectly credible, first-century Jewish one: that of Jesus restoring the people of God, and doing so in some sense around himself. Anyone who cherished such a goal was *ipso facto* intending to leave behind a community, a renewed Israel, that would continue his work.[76] One must assume that, *mutatis mutandis*, this was true of the Teacher of Righteousness, of Judas the Galilean, of Hillel and Shammai, and of the ill-fated Simeon ben Kosiba. This is a thoroughly Jewish intention, which cannot be dismissed by hinting sarcastically that one can hardly envisage Jesus envisaging the contemporary church.

A third question that is aroused by the wave of current study is, of course, whether Jesus' aims included a sense of personal vocation: in other words, whether he believed himself to possess a special role in the kingdom he was proclaiming. Again, the pre-critical idea that Jesus knew himself to be the divine Messiah was well and truly rejected in the Old Quest and, largely, in the New. The Third Quest has quite rightly separated out the question of Messiahship from that of 'divinity', focusing almost exclusively on the former. Many Third Questers are happy to say that Jesus saw himself as having a key role, probably the Messianic role, within the divine purposes that he aimed to put into operation. Harvey, scaling down the meaning of 'Christ' more than a little, is able to conclude that Jesus was known by this title during his lifetime.[77] Sanders regards it as 'highly probable' that 'Jesus' disciples thought of him as "king", and that he accepted the role, either implicitly or explicitly.'[78] Witherington goes further still: Jesus clearly

---

[75] Vermes 1993, 214f.; Vermes' original position (1973) is expanded by Wilson 1992. Vermes thus again appeals to the old Bultmannian position: Jesus expected the world to end, therefore he could not have envisaged his followers continuing as a community.

[76] So e.g. Lohfink 1984.

[77] Harvey 1982, 80–2, 120–51.

[78] Sanders 1985, 326, summarizing 234. Cf. too 321f.: 'the hard evidence is this: he talked about a kingdom; his disciples expected to have a role in it; they considered him their leader; he was crucified for claiming to be king'.

believed himself to be Messiah.[79] At the same time, of course, there are still plenty who stand firm on the older view, that Jesus saw himself, at most, as a prophet.[80] We have come a long way from Wrede's shallow identification of Messianic status with a heavenly son of man figure and with the later Christian claim about Jesus' 'divinity'. But we are still a long way from agreement.

What then did Jesus aim to do, and how did this work out in specific intentions?[81] The answer, from within most of the Third Quest, seems to have something to do with the kingdom; something to do with the Temple;[82] something to do with Jesus himself; just possibly something to do with his death; conceivably something to do with a group of people continuing his work after his death. Can we move further? I shall argue that we can. In each case, of course, we meet a further form of the familiar problem: since the first generation of Jesus' followers regarded themselves as in some senses continuing his work and mission, and as in some sense the heirs of his teaching and actions, and the beneficiaries of his death, it is natural that they would tell stories about him which made it appear that he had indeed intended all of this. If the stories provide the legitimation for aspects of the early church, how can we trust them to tell us about Jesus? This problem can, however, be resolved, in principle at least, by the resolute pursuit of a serious historical hypothesis about Jesus himself. Otherwise, 'critical history' becomes mere paranoia, insisting on conspiracy theories and unable to see the way that the real evidence is pointing.[83]

The question of Jesus' aims, therefore, is nowhere near as simple as either pre-critical Christianity thought, or as some within the various Quests have imagined. There are several avenues of enquiry which the question opens up; and we cannot retreat from them as though there were nothing much more to be said. Out of the many lines that positively demand to be pursued at this point, there is one in particular to which all these questions point forward, and with which they are all significantly integrated. This is the next major question to be addressed: why did Jesus die?

---

[79] Witherington 1990, *passim*: see the conclusion, 267–75.

[80] e.g. Vermes 1973, ch. 4.

[81] cf. *NTPG* 110f.

[82] So e.g. Meyer, Sanders, Chilton; rejected (of course) by Vermes, e.g. 1993, 155, 185. Even Crossan (1991, 355, 359f.) allows that Jesus' action in the Temple is highly significant as an index of his aims, though he doubts a direct link with the crucifixion.

[83] cf. van Beeck's comments (1994, 89–93) on Crossan; e.g. 90: 'What will prevent prejudice from rushing in to take charge of the reconstruction, under cover of acumen?'

(iii) Why did Jesus die?

Whether or not one concludes that Jesus himself intended to die, it does not follow that this intention was a sufficient cause of his crucifixion. Ignatius fully intended to die as a martyr, but envisaged the possibility that meddling Christians in Rome might prevent him.[84] Paul knew he might well be called upon to face execution, but kept an open mind about whether and when this would come to pass.[85] Even if we take the strong view that Jesus fully intended to die, and that he invested this death, in advance, with some sort of theological interpretation, we still need to know what the Romans thought they were doing when they crucified him. Granted that they crucified quite a lot of people, it is still only the extreme historical sceptic who will suggest that there was anything random or accidental about their execution of Jesus.[86]

What, then, were the circumstances which led to this event? What were the aims and intentions, expressive of worldviews and mindsets, of the various actors involved? At this level, of course, the question is on a par with other (comparatively) straightforward questions: why did John the Baptist die? Why did Julius Caesar die? And, if we wish to include cases in which the subject's own intentionality was clearly involved, why did Seneca die?[87] Why did Ignatius die? Why did Eleazar, the leader of the Sicarii on Masada, die?[88] These rough parallels demonstrate that, though it is of course difficult, the question can in principle be addressed by regular historical means.

This historical question, searching for the human motivations that led to Jesus' death, has regularly been confused with a quite different one. 'Why did Jesus die?', if asked in many Christian circles, would elicit a range of 'theological' answers: he died for the sins of the world, to defeat the devil, to save people from eternal death, or whatever.[89] The two sorts of answers appear to be in watertight compartments. The evangelists only hint at an answer of the second type (the theological), and appear to concentrate on the first (the historical); it is thus often assumed that they do not have what is called a 'theology of the cross' – though it has also been held that their

---

[84] Ign. *Rom.* 2.
[85] Phil. 1.20-6; and cp. 1 Th. 4.17; 1 Cor. 15.51 with 2 Cor. 1.9, 4.16-5.10.
[86] cf. Harvey 1982, 16: 'It could have been an accident . . . but a moment's reflection shows that [such a theory] will not fit this particular case.'
[87] cf. Tac. *Ann.* 14.52-6, 65, 15.45, 60 (where Tacitus recognizes the same set of questions in his 'forte an prudens' ('whether accidentally or on purpose'), 61-4.
[88] cf. Schürer 1.511f., following Jos. *War* 7.25-8, 320-401 (cf. *NTPG* 326f.). It is, of course, an open question whether Eleazar and the others really perished by mass suicide; but that simply confirms my point, that the question of *why* they died is worth asking.
[89] This is perhaps why Vermes thought this list of questions to be specifically 'Christian' (see above, 90f. n.28).

apparent 'history' is fairly worthless, precisely because it reads the theological viewpoint of the church back into the narrative! For these reasons, it is vital that we enquire carefully what precisely an 'historical' explanation of the cross might consist in, and that we then attempt to offer exactly that. In other words, we must entertain the serious possibility that the 'theological' accounts of the crucifixion that we find in early and subsequent Christianity – already, for instance, in Paul – may have nothing to do with what actually happened; and also that the apparently 'historical' accounts of the evangelists are themselves the reading back of later theological, or even political, interests.[90] This third question is thus very firmly set within the overall historical task of the book.

What, then, is the range of possible answers to the third question, at a 'historical' level? One obvious answer, given among Jews from at least the time of the Talmud, is that Jesus died because he was perceived as a deceiver of the people.[91] Another, given among historians since at least the time of Reimarus, is that he was executed simply because he was a revolutionary. Jesus, in other words, clearly offended either official Israel or official Rome, possibly both. But the long and tragic legacy of anti-semitism within a soi-disant Christian culture has meant that scholars are now rightly sensitive about even appearing to say 'the Jews crucified Jesus';[92] and the pressure of historical evidence has led almost all scholars to doubt whether Jesus was in fact executed by the Romans on a straightforward, and manifestly deserved, charge of stirring up sedition.[93] The old views, that Jews espoused a corrupt form of religion and therefore hated Jesus for preaching a better one, and that Jesus posed a straightforward revolutionary threat to (Roman) public order, are to be rejected.[94] Someone, or more likely some group, wanted Jesus out of the way for somewhat less obvious reasons.

But what were those reasons? That there was a 'political' element to it – in other words, that the Romans were convinced, or at least persuaded, that Jesus was some sort of a trouble-maker – seems clear. But who convinced, or persuaded, them? Here there have been two mainstream alternatives: the Pharisees, and the Temple hierarchy. It used to be thought that Jesus' clashes with the Pharisees, as recorded in the synoptic tradition (e.g. Mark 2.23—3.6), consisted of his standing up against the 'petty legalism' of the Pharisees; that they reacted, to protect their own interests, by plotting against

---

[90] The fact that we have seen good reasons to reject Crossan's version of this theory (ch. 2 above) is no reason to suppose *a priori* that all such theories are wrong.

[91] See ch. 9 below.

[92] See e.g. the shrill protest of Rivkin 1984, and the sustained polemic of Crossan 1994.

[93] e.g. Harvey 1982, ch. 2; on the whole question cf. Brown 1994.

[94] cf. Sanders 1985, 296–306 (against the latter); 331 (against the former).

him; that these plots reached a crescendo, culminating in Jesus' trial before Jewish authorities; and that this essentially 'religious' charge was then turned neatly into a 'political' one, enabling him to be handed over to the pagans. This produces an answer to the question which purchases its clarity (Jesus constantly provokes the Pharisees to kill him, which they eventually succeed in doing) at the cost of historical plausibility. There is no historical verisimilitude in the picture of the Pharisees as petty, and perhaps Pelagian, legalists. There is no evidence that the Pharisees as such were directly involved in the events which led to Jesus' actual death. And there is no connection, in this scheme, between the Pharisees' reaction to Jesus and the Temple incident, which looms so large in the narratives leading to the crucifixion.

Against this simplistic line, Sanders in particular has argued that Jesus probably never disputed with the Pharisees anyway; that it was his action in the Temple which caused all the trouble; that those who were offended by this action, and who responded by (somehow) handing him over to the Romans, were not Pharisees at all, but were the chief priests and rulers.[95] This reaction, though perhaps necessary, has in my judgment gone too far. Many serious scholars still hold out for Jesus having had serious disputes with the Pharisees. But to argue for a third, quite different, position will take some little while, and must not be anticipated at this stage. Once again, however, we may note that in the Third Quest one particular strand is emerging as vital and central, namely Jesus' attitude to the Temple, and the possible connection of that with his death. Chilton, indeed, argues that what Judas betrayed, and what Jesus was crucified for, was not his action in the Temple but his regarding of himself and his followers as a counter-Temple movement;[96] but this simply confirms the current tendency, which I believe to be profoundly correct, to associate the Temple with Jesus' death. The precise nature of that association, however, must remain for the moment *sub judice.*

There is still, of course, the question of the 'trial' which Jesus may have undergone. In the synoptic tradition, this consists of a hearing before the chief priests, followed by a hearing before the governor, Pilate. Most recent scholars who have discussed these narratives have expressed considerable scepticism; once again the shadow of anti-semitism rears up, as various writers do their best to exonerate 'the Jews' from any complicity whatever in Jesus' death. The various questions this has raised in turn (whether the Jewish authorities had the right to execute people; whether the 'trial' before the high priest could have taken place according to Jewish law; whether there

---

[95] Sanders 1985, 309–18. Cf. too Vermes 1973, 36f.
[96] Chilton 1992b, 150–5.

was a charge of 'blasphemy' levelled at Jesus, etc.) have been debated this way and that without any of the issues being resolved. Nevertheless, in so far as there is any consensus within the Third Quest at the moment, it is that Jesus was handed over to the pagan rulers by the official Jewish authorities. Clearly there remains a good deal of work to do in this area if we are to give the third question anything like a clear answer.

If we manage, by whatever means, to arrive at a satisfactory answer to the historical question as to why Jesus died, there remains still the theological question. This forces itself upon the historian, willy-nilly, because very early within the Christian tradition a theological interpretation was given to Jesus' death. 'Christ died *for our sins*' was already a traditional formula within a few years of the crucifixion; Paul could write not long afterwards that 'the son of god loved me and gave himself for me'.[97] Part of the explanation for Jesus' death, therefore, must include its sequel: why did the early church come to attach to Jesus' execution such far-reaching significance? This, however, already trespasses on the territory of the fourth major question.

(iv) How and Why did the Early Church Begin?

The understanding of any event is not only bound to involve, but may well be enhanced by, the understanding of its sequel.[98] Thus (for instance) one of the merits of Sanders' work is that he reasons backwards from the fact that, after Jesus' death, the disciples were not, as one might have expected, rounded up and arrested, and perhaps executed, in their turn. But, as well as negative arguments such as this, there are positive questions: what (if anything) actually happened on Easter morning? Like Bach's Passion music, the current studies of Jesus are perfectly valid even if, like this one, they come to a halt on Good Friday. But the Third Quest cannot for that reason put off for ever the question of the resurrection. I shall return to it myself in due course.

Nor can it escape from the (perfectly virtuous) circle of (a) studying Jesus in the light of the gospels, and hence of the early church, and (b) studying the early church, including the gospels, in the light of Jesus. Hypotheses at the one point have to dovetail, and routinely within the discipline do dovetail, with hypotheses at the other point. That is why I spent an entire Part of the previous volume (*NTPG* Part IV) discussing the early church, and the gospels as arising within it. But the question now before us focuses quite narrowly on one particular moment. I argued earlier that

---

[97] 1 Cor. 15.3 (quoting a very early formula); Gal. 2.20.
[98] Meyer 1979, 249–53; cf. *NTPG* 115; and Downing 1992, 167: 'It is only in the light of what happens next that you can hope to understand and explain what has been happening.'

What united early Christians, deeper than all diversity, was *that they told, and lived, a form of Israel's story which reached its climax in Jesus and which then issued in their spirit-given new life and task* . . .

The church appropriated for itself the Jewish belief that the creator god would rescue his people at the last, and interpreted that rescue in terms of a great lawcourt scene . . . The major underlying difference between the Christian and the Jewish views at this point was that the early Christians believed that *the verdict had already been announced* in the death and resurrection of Jesus . . .

First-century Jews looked forward to a public event . . . in and through which their god would reveal to all the world that he was not just a local, tribal deity, but the creator and sovereign of all . . . The early Christians . . . looked back to an event in and through which, they claimed, Israel's god had done exactly that.[99]

How, as historians, are we to describe this event, which resulted in the church believing that the eschaton had now arrived, but which was not itself the eschaton as they had imagined it? Though this question has not been seriously addressed within Third Quest studies, there are several pointers to it. This is perhaps clearest in the work of Sanders:

Without the resurrection, would [Jesus'] disciples have endured longer than did John the Baptist's? We can only guess, but I would guess not.[100]

So would I. One might add, for good measure, the followers not only of John the Baptist but of Judas the Galilean, Simon, Athronges, Eleazar ben Deinaus and Alexander, Menahem, Simon bar Giora, and bar-Kochba himself.[101] Faced with the defeat of their leader, followers of such figures would either be rounded up as well or melt away into the undergrowth. The other possibility was to latch on to a new leader: in the case of the apparent dynasty that ended up being known as the Sicarii, when one leader was killed they simply chose another from the same family. In not one case do we hear of any group, after the death of its leader, claiming that he was in any sense alive again, and that therefore Israel's expectation had in some strange way actually come true. History therefore spotlights the question: what happened to make Jesus' followers, from the very start, articulate such a claim and work out its implications? Sanders again:

We have every reason to think that Jesus had led [the disciples] to expect a dramatic event which would establish the kingdom. The death and resurrection required them to adjust their expectation, but did not create a new one out of nothing.[102]

[99] *NTPG* 456, 458, 476: italics original.

[100] Sanders 1985, 240.

[101] On all these, cf. *NTPG* 170–81, and other refs. there. Vermes would dispute the claim that these movements were similar to that of Jesus; but he can only sustain this objection by divorcing Jesus' teaching about the kingdom from the popular expectation (Vermes 1993, 130 ('an entirely different politico-religious view of the Kingdom of God'), 148–50). I have argued the contrary case in *NTPG* ch. 10; and see below, Part II.

[102] Sanders 1985, 320. Sanders points out that Apollonius of Tyana was reputed to have

Again, I totally agree; but what content do we then give to the resurrection itself? Here Sanders leaves the argument pointing forward towards the key question, but without addressing it:

> [Jesus'] followers, by carrying through the logic of his own position *in a transformed situation*, created a movement which would grow and continue to alter . . .[103]

Quite so. But what changed the situation?

If the question of the origin of the early church thus pushes us relentlessly back towards the problem of Easter, the same question broadens out to include all sorts of features which appear in the early church, claiming continuity of some sort with Jesus himself. Thus we must ask: why and how did the early disciples, shattered as they had been by the crucifixion of their master, regroup and go out to face persecution for declaring that in him the hope of Israel had quite literally come to life? Why did they then organize themselves and act in the way that they did, and, in particular, why (granted their abiding commitment to Jewish-style monotheism) did they begin very early on to *worship* Jesus, and to include him in Jewish-style monotheistic formulae?[104] Why did their communities take the form they did, which as it turns out was very different from any of the standard models available in the ancient world, being neither an ethnic group worshipping a tribal deity nor a private religious club? So different was it, after all, that the early Christians sometimes had to argue to the authorities, against apparent appearances, that they were in some sense or other a 'religious' organization. It was perhaps almost as much their socio-cultural oddness as their denial of the pagan deities that earned them the title 'atheists'. There were no other groups in the ancient world going around claiming to *be* the human race.[105] And, since the answer which the early Christians themselves seem to have given to the question has to do both with Jesus of Nazareth prior to his death and with their belief that he had been raised from the dead, the historian is bound to ask whether we are forced to reject either of these answers. If, for instance, the Q community – supposing there to have been such a thing – was composed of wandering radicals, from whom did they get the idea? And why did they still think it worth pursuing after Jesus' death?

The impetus towards including this fourth question within the study of Jesus comes partly from the sense of incompleteness (both historical and

---

appeared to a doubting young philosopher to convince him of the soul's immortality (Philostratus, *Life of Apollonius* 8.31), but rightly notes that the story is scarcely a parallel to the experience of the early Christians.

[103] Sanders 1985, 340 (italics added).

[104] cf. *NTPG* 362, 448; and Wright 1991, chs. 4–6. See further Hurtado 1988; Bauckham 1992, and other bibliography there.

[105] I owe this whole point to Bishop Rowan Williams.

theological) that may be felt when some of the current quest is reviewed. Some of the pieces of the jigsaw appear to be still in the box; studying the sequel to the event may perhaps bring them to light. Some of the Third Quest authors, implicitly addressing these questions, have to postulate a large gap between Jesus and the early church; having located Jesus, supposedly, within his native Judaism, they have the early church located nowhere in particular, certainly not in any very direct connection to Jesus.[106] This book will aim to avoid such a *prima facie* weakness (the reverse, more or less, of Bultmann's), and to demonstrate, at least preliminarily, the continuity, as well as the clear discontinuities, between Jesus and the early church.

All pictures of Jesus, then, depend to a lesser or greater extent on a complementary picture of the early church. Again we are faced with the problem of the interrelation of history and theology. In the standard Bultmannian paradigm the history of the early church (as opposed to the history of Jesus) provided the context and explanation for the rise of particular theological beliefs. Some of these were then regarded as valid, either because of their history-of-religions pedigree, or because they cohered with some other external standard.[107] I hope I shall be spared to address this whole problem, which I regard as urgent, not only theologically but also historically.

(v) Why are the Gospels what they Are?

It is a commonplace of gospel study that we have in Matthew, Mark and Luke[108] a new genre of literature. It is not quite this and not quite that; neither simply biography nor simply religious propaganda, yet sharing the main characteristics of both.[109] No one is quite sure how to account for this genre, but there it is. And yet the gospels clearly stand in some sort of relation to Jesus himself, and their existence is in some way or other derived from what he was and did and said. Why, then, are they what they are? This question is of course a subset of the previous one, but it is so specialized as to be worth setting out on its own, without forgetting its links with what has preceded. With this question, in fact, we have reached the other side of the jigsaw whose central piece is Jesus. First-century Judaism, and the gospels, are opposite edges, and all discourse about Jesus must take place between them.

---

[106] cf. esp. Vermes, who drives a fat wedge between Jesus himself and subsequent Christianity (1993, ch. 8, esp. 212: 'Is it an exaggeration to suggest that oceans separate Paul's Christian Gospel from the religion of Jesus the Jew?'). Cf. too Maccoby 1986, 1991.

[107] See *NTPG*, esp. Parts I and V; Neill & Wright 1988 [1964], 439–46.

[108] For John, see *NTPG* 410–17, and the Preface to the present volume.

[109] cf. *NTPG* ch. 13; and esp. Burridge 1992.

One can thus see at a glance the reason for the complexity of such discourse, since both edges are themselves so difficult to describe accurately and hence to work within.[110] Answering this fifth question will take at least another whole book. But it will be an enormous strength for any hypothesis about Jesus if it can at least indicate why, if Jesus was as the hypothesis suggests, the gospels are what they are.[111]

(vi) The Five Questions Together

It should be noted once more that the five questions fit together very closely, so that answers to any of them have repercussions elsewhere. It is comparatively easy to find an answer to one of them, but fitting it with answers to the rest is not. Together they form the jigsaw of Jesus himself, which is itself a piece in the larger jigsaw of the rise of Christianity as a whole. The five questions can, in fact, be drawn together under two headings: Jesus' relation to Judaism on the one hand and to the early church on the other.[112]

Different schools of thought have emphasized one or another question and ignored the rest; sometimes the solution advanced to one has meant a particularly awkward and ill-fitting answer to the others. Wrede and Schweitzer, once again, provide paradigms: Wrede analysed Jesus in a fairly minimal way, and in consequence put a good deal of weight first on the early church and then on the gospels. Schweitzer's apocalyptic Jesus generated an apocalyptic early church – including Paul and the gospels – which nevertheless can be seen as the beginning of the later, wider, Hellenistic developments.

Perhaps the best example of the integration of the questions, in terms of twentieth-century scholarship, is Rudolf Bultmann. Bultmann put all the weight on question 4 (the rise of the early church). The early church began with a tremendous burst of creative energy, finding, in the proclamation of the crucified Jesus as the living Lord, the key to unlock the prison of human existence. It expressed this faith in language that, to the untrained eye, can be mistakenly thought to refer to Jesus, but which in fact is, strictly, 'mythological', i.e. a projection on to 'history' of the present experience of 'faith'. This view, however, has grave difficulties with questions 1–3. Jesus is not really related to Judaism at all, except by a contrast of abstract ideals; his own aims were extremely generalized and only marginally related to the

[110] Not to mention the question of the non-canonical gospels, on which see *NTPG* ch. 14, and 29f., 48f. above.
[111] See *NTPG* ch. 13, 14.
[112] See Neill & Wright 1988, 398–401.

concerns of most Jews of his day; the historical reasons for his death, which are in any case hidden from us, have nothing whatever to do with the theological interpretation which the early church gave that event. Question 5 also causes problems. Within the usual form-critical paradigm, the evangelists were simply collectors of stories which they strung together without much regard for sequence. But redaction-criticism and subsequent literary-critical study of the gospels have cut off this branch (although some redaction-critics, perhaps out of deference to their scholarly tradition, still claim to be sitting on it). The gospels are revealed as quite sophisticated documents, and if we wish to retain the Bultmannian paradigm we must invent ever more cunning sub-theories to account for them as they actually are. The great irony of this total position, seen from the perspective I shall advance, is that it regards genuinely mythological language (apocalyptic) as though it were understood 'literally' by those who first used it, and regards genuinely literal language (talk about Jesus) as though it were intended 'mythologically' by those who first used it.[113]

Within the Bultmannian scheme, and within the New Quest that retained at least some of his framework, critical methods became a means of maintaining a discreet reticence, or even silence, about Jesus, in the face of the threat that history might undermine faith (or, in the case of the 'Jesus Seminar', the threat that history might somehow create or support orthodox faith). And, as we have seen, the emphasis on the history of the early church has led to ever more detailed, and unprovable, speculative hypotheses in the realm of tradition-criticism. Such exercises would only be valuable if we knew a lot more about the early church than we actually do. Remythologization has replaced demythologization. The Bultmann school still needs history – but this time it is the history of the early church. And this requires a far greater effort of unsupported imagination from the historian than even the old liberal 'lives' of Jesus did.[114] Starting with an apparently solid answer to question 4 has ended up in a cul-de-sac.

Just to be even-handed to the 'giants', we may point out here that Schweitzer's theory is weakest, ironically, where it claimed to be strongest, i.e. in its treatment of question 1. It is not at all clear that there ever was such a thing as the 'late-Jewish apocalyptic worldview' upon which Schweitzer built so much.[115] He was right to insist on putting Jesus into his Jewish context; right to see that context as inescapably apocalyptic; but wrong to interpret that apocalyptic eschatology in the way he did. This weakness is the

---

[113] So *NTPG* 297.
[114] *NTPG* ch. 11.
[115] cf. Schweitzer 1954 [1906], esp. 364–8; and cf. *NTPG* ch. 10, esp. 333f..

fatal flaw which ultimately vitiates his fascinating answers to questions 2 and 3, and calls his answers to 4 and 5 into question as well.

It is a residual weakness even within the Third Quest that one or other question tends to be highlighted at the expense of the rest. This does not (in my view) result in such a dramatic failure as that of Bultmann, but it still needs to be addressed. The attempt to answer questions 1 and 2 (Jesus' aims) has sometimes resulted, as we have seen, in a picture of Jesus the revolutionary, whether military (Brandon, Buchanan) or social (Horsley); this never really comes to grips with questions 4 and 5 (the church and the gospels), except in terms of a massive failure of nerve, or at least a total change of direction, on the part of the early church. And, since we only know about questions 1-3 (the supposed strengths of such a view) through the gospels which are the subject of question 5 and grow out of the early church discussed in question 4, the theories seem once more to be sitting on branches that are mostly sawn through. Vermes' picture of Jesus the Hasid (his answer to questions 1 and 2) fails altogether to explain why Jesus was crucified (question 3), and only explains the rise of the early church (question 4) by an enormous leap into a religion completely different from that of Jesus. By the content of his very thorough answer to the first two questions, he has made it very difficult to answer 3 at all, and has been forced to produce very strained answers to 4 and 5. Conversely, Downing has offered a provocative and fascinating study of Jesus as a Cynic preacher, which achieves its new angle on question 2 (Jesus' aims), and possible implicit solution to 3 (his death), at the enormous cost of an all-but-incredible answer to question 1 (his relation to Judaism), and a failure to explain 4 (the church) and 5 (the gospels) except, again, as a massive *volte-face*.[116] Horsley offers an answer to question 2 (Jesus' aims), and to some extent 1 (his relation to Judaism), which make 3, 4 and 5 somewhat difficult: it is not clear from his book why Horsley's Jesus got crucified, or why the church would have taken the line, and written the books, that it did. Freyne addresses 1 and 5 superbly: his social history of Galilee, and his sensitive reading of the gospels, is exemplary. But his placing of Jesus and the earliest Christians into this framework – his answer, in other words, to questions 2, 3 and 4 – is as yet not full enough to do justice to the complex issues involved.[117]

Among the other prominent Third Quest writers, Harvey's stated historical method insists on the primacy of placing Jesus within the 'constraints' of his own time and setting. This, clearly, is a way of addressing the first

---

[116] He, and the others discussed in ch. 2 above, attempt an answer here in terms of the purely hypothetical Q community, and those parts of the subsequent church which kept the 'Cynic' vision alive. See above, 47-55.

[117] cf. Freyne 1988b. Horsley has now written elsewhere about Jesus' death (1994).

two questions.[118] He nevertheless, in my judgment, never totally takes on board the subtleties of the Jewish context and Jesus' aims in relation to it. He has an extensive explanation of the crucifixion (question 3), which nevertheless does not explain why the early church came to give it the significance it did (i.e. the point at which questions 3 and 4 overlap and interact). Why, in other words, did the early church move so quickly from their leader's execution to the belief that his death was 'for our sins'? Harvey likewise never, at least in his book on Jesus, addresses question 5. Borg's reconstruction of Jesus' aims within his Jewish setting provides a fascinating and inviting set of answers to questions 1 and 2. But he does not directly address questions 3, 4 or 5; I find his indirect statements in these areas as yet unsatisfactory, though I believe that this is partly because he has not followed through his earlier arguments (in his 1984 book) as far as they will go. Sanders, who sees as clearly as anyone what the issues are, explicitly disavows 'theological' interest, and thus avoids the challenge of integrating what happened in Jesus' ministry and death with the question of what the early church came to believe, and how they began to live and worship, after his death.[119] In particular, as we saw, he avoids the sharp edge of question 4 (the rise of the early church), by referring simply to 'a changed situation'. Borg and Sanders, despite their clear intention of answering question 1 as fully as they can, never really get to grips with the first-century Jewish reading of Daniel 7 which forms an essential part of the background.[120] Borg persists with the view – which originates in a period in which question 1 was answered quite differently! – that Messiahship was not a major category for Jesus. Meyer, whose major book is one of the most learned, patient and methodologically thorough of any in the last fifteen years – perhaps in the last 150 – has likewise seen clearly the full range of issues. His reading of the Jewish context is sensitive, and his outlining of Jesus' aims well nuanced; his understanding of the cross goes far further than most other Third Quest writers. I find his accounts of Jesus' apocalyptic eschatology, and of the early church, less satisfying.[121] At each point, despite my admiration for his work, I shall suggest possible improvements to his overall solution.

[118] Harvey 1982; cf. Wright 1986, and Neill & Wright 1988 [1964], 384–7.

[119] Sanders 1993, 176 seems to me a fairly inadequate summary of Borg's thesis, and 1990, 336 n.20 seems to me a fairly inadequate answer to it.

[120] See Sanders' candid disclaimer about the use of 'son of man': 1985, 308 ('I have no answer to the question of precisely how Jesus saw the relationship between himself, the Son of man, and the Father'), 324.

[121] On apocalyptic, cf. Meyer 1992a, chs. 3, 9; on the early church, Meyer 1986 (discussed at various points in *NTPG* Part IV).

(vii) The Sixth Question: Agenda and Theology

There is, of course, a sixth question, always in mind although different in character. How does the Jesus we discover by doing 'history' relate to the contemporary church and world? This question cannot ultimately be bracketed out, though it is assumed here that it cannot be allowed to exercise leverage over the course of historical study. As we saw in *NTPG*, all history is of course a dialogue between student and sources, not a positivist's fantasy in which a 'purely objective' point of view is attained by an observer who is, for the purposes of the argument, a negligible mathematical point. This does not mean, however, that the observer is allowed to inflict his or her point of view on to unwilling material. If the dialogue is to be an exercise in real history, the observer has to be prepared to change his or her mind. Instead of the spurious antithesis between 'objective' and 'subjective', we must hold to the proper distinction between public and private. We can debate in public; if we refuse to do so, we are left with private opinion. The historian is committed to working in public. If the historian is also committed, in whatever sense, to living in some sort of continuity with certain features of the past, that of course gives to the whole exercise a peculiar sense of risk; but it should not mean that the historical task is reduced to terms of the historian's own antecedent beliefs or worldview.

There are, of course, huge issues at stake here. One of the major reasons for dialectical theology's refusal to continue the Old Quest was the belief that historical research would be of no theological use.[122] The prodigal (Enlightenment historiography) is not welcome within the ancestral home. To put it bluntly, if one locates Jesus in first-century Palestine, one risks the possibility that he might have little to say to twentieth-century Europe, America or anywhere else – except, of course, by happy, or maybe contrived, coincidence.[123] We have already seen how Schweitzer and Bultmann got round this problem. It was not a problem for the New Quest, since the hermeneutical and theological answers were implicitly built-in to it from the start: the gospels became 'meaningful' by various means, of which form- and redaction-criticism were but two.[124]

[122] See Wright 1992b, 798; and above, ch. 1.

[123] Thus, Harvey tries to get over the problem of historical relativity by suggesting that we have in our day faced once more the sense that the world might come to an end. This, I think, concedes the point it is trying to avoid, by implying that Jesus' eschatology only became relevant once more after Hiroshima.

[124] It is a good question whether structuralist interpretation of the gospels aims at making them 'meaningful' in the same sense. On the various methods and their hermeneutical significance, see *NTPG* ch. 3, and Neill & Wright 1988, 439–46.

The Third Quest has no predetermined route to follow here. That is just as well, if it is to retain its status as a major public enterprise, instead of collapsing (as the renewed New Quest is in danger of doing) into a private game. This is not to say that various Third Questers have not tried their hand at stating the results of their work for contemporary reflection. Harvey hints at a preacher's answer which he does not develop: the challenge of Jesus to his contemporaries 'is capable of being presented with as much force today as it ever has been in the past'.[125] Meyer hints at a Catholic solution: 'it is above all in the tradition generated by Jesus that we discover what made him operate in the way he did, what made him epitomize his life in the single act of going to his death'.[126] Sanders boldly confronts would-be interpreters, telling them that if the history is done right the theology will look after itself. His own frequent mocking of various theological positions, however, leads one quickly to the conclusion, which he eventually confirms, that he has his own theological position (that of 'a liberal, modern, secularized Protestant'), and that, even if Jesus did not die for this position, he certainly lived up to it.[127] Vermes, who protests too much in his 'historian's reading of the gospels', ends up with Jesus as (in the title of Henry Chadwick's BBC Radio 3 review when the book came out) 'a rather pale Galilean', whose significance for today is not least that the church since Paul and John has, in 'divinizing' him, radically misunderstood him.[128] Some (Horsley, Downing, Mack) have thinly disguised social agendas which, worked out in terms of first-century Palestine, have clear implications for the modern world, but little to say about theology as such. Reading between the lines of Borg's main book one may hear a more subtle theme: Jesus' challenge to his contemporaries was a call to abandon nationalist or militarist political aspirations, and to imitate God in being merciful, rather than in maintaining a dualistic separation from the wicked world.[129]

Such implications have not been discussed very explicitly or thoroughly within the Third Quest.[130] This should not be taken to imply that this wave of studies has after all achieved 'neutral' or 'objective' results. One does not have to look very far beneath the surface to discover all sorts of implicit conclusions and recommendations. For Horsley, Jesus is on the side of at least a

---

[125] Harvey 1982, 173.

[126] Meyer 1979, 252f.

[127] Sanders 1985, 334. See the criticisms in Charlesworth 1988, 28f.

[128] Vermes 1993, ch. 8. Vermes does allow (214) that sometimes Christianity can still retain 'fundamental elements of the piety of Jesus': he cites Francis of Assisi, Albert Schweitzer and Mother Theresa as examples.

[129] This agenda comes out more explicitly in Borg 1987a, esp. in its concluding chapter.

[130] For an attempt by a Third Quest writer to relate Jesus' teaching to contemporary ethics, cf. Harvey 1990.

moderate revolution. For Meyer, Jesus points forward cryptically to something like mainstream Christianity.[131] Even those who (like Sanders and Vermes) claim to avoid theology reach conclusions which, as they very well know, present a challenge to a number of different theological positions, including those formerly held by those two scholars themselves. They are as aware as anyone of ways in which their work could affect the way people actually think and behave in the modern world.[132] Since the Third Quest has, in my opinion, a better chance than any of its predecessors of achieving solid answers to the five main questions about Jesus, it is important that in concluding this chapter we should explore where some of the theological and practical possibilities may lie.

The first and sometimes most noticeable feature here is the use being made of answers to question 1, that is, of Jesus' relation to Judaism. One of the initial impulses (not the only one) towards the Third Quest has, I suspect, been the desire to make Jesus more Jewish; this has been reflected in a tendency towards a rather self-conscious philo-semitism. The incoming tide of post-holocaust reaction has reached the study of Jesus. The Pharisees were not, after all, the hardened legalists of Matthew's gospel, and they did not engage in controversy with Jesus (Sanders). Jesus did not teach, or believe, his own Messiahship, for so long a stumbling-block to Jews: so Vermes, with Bultmann (but for very different reasons) on his side. The 'constraint of monotheism' meant that Jesus could not have thought of himself as divine, but only as 'son of god' in the sense of the accredited agent of the one god (Harvey). Rivkin's theological axe-grinding is the most marked: the blurb on the cover makes no pretence about neutral historical scholarship, but hails the book as 'an important bridge of reconciliation between Jews and Christians'. (I hope that the present work will be that too; the serious search for historical foundations cannot but be healthy and air-clearing.) One of the notable features in some of the books I have listed is thus a response – sometimes implicit, sometimes loud and clear – to the charges of anti-semitism laid at the door of Christianity by a whole line of writers.[133]

In the Jewish writers (Vermes, Rivkin) this comes across as an attempt, in line with earlier writers such as Klausner, to reclaim Jesus.[134] In some of the Christian writers (Harvey, Sanders) the implication (reading between the lines, in good form-critical manner) is one of contrition. Borg's striking thesis manages to have Jesus oppose the main lines of first-century Jewish aspirations without giving off the unpleasant odour of anti-Judaism, since he

---

[131] Meyer 1979, 253.

[132] e.g. Vermes 1993, 214f.

[133] For an obvious example, cf. Ruether 1974.

[134] Klausner 1947 [1925]; on the Jewish reclamation of Jesus cf. Hagner 1984.

takes care to show that Jesus grounded his critique in mainstream Jewish traditions rooted in the Hebrew scriptures. Riches, albeit armed with much modern learning, leans more towards an old-fashioned, almost an Old Quest, view of Judaism as a religion of judgment, in contrast with which Jesus taught a religion of mercy.

It is important to see this variety of positions on the question of the significance of Jesus' relation to Judaism not just as a series of knee-jerk reactions from different theological standpoints, but as part of a wider problem.[135] The early years of this century saw history-of-religions research being conducted among Christians on the principle that Judaism was merely the dark background against which the bright light had shone, so that if Christianity wanted reputable ancestry it had better look elsewhere. The postwar reaction, in line with Barthian neo-orthodoxy, took the opposite line: Jewish ideas were 'good', non-Jewish ones 'bad'. We are now at an interesting point of possible advance. What if (a) it is in fact much harder to distinguish between Jewish and non-Jewish ideas than used to be thought, and (b) we reject the belief that one can evaluate ideas by associating them with one culture or the other? The Third Quest has come to birth at a period of methodological indecision on such matters, and a variety of approaches is hardly surprising. But further progress is not to be expected unless the issue is squarely faced. Otherwise we will merely witness shadow-boxing, with historical argument as a cover for contemporary theologizing. That would reduce the present quest to the lowest level ever reached by its predecessors.

Probably the most sensitive theological issue to be discovered within the Third Quest, and certainly the one on which many will focus instant attention, is christology. Is it possible to proceed, by way of historical study, to a portrait of Jesus which is sufficient of itself to evoke, or at least legitimate, that worship which Christianity has traditionally offered to him? If not, is this because we merely lack sufficient biographical information, or because we know *a priori* that anything in the gospel accounts which might seem to present Jesus as worthy of worship must, for that reason if no other, be reckoned a later accretion? And, in the light of answers to these questions, how do we view the church's continuing use of the gospels? Do we read them to find out more about Jesus 'as he really was', or to reinforce the faith of the gospel writers that, no matter who or what Jesus was in his earthly life, he is in fact the incarnate son of god, who died for us? Can these two levels of reading be combined, or are they mutually self-contradictory?

Three recent attempts to write about Jesus have offered ways in which history may be thought to lead to a positive christological conclusion. We saw

---

[135] For all this, see Neill & Wright 1988, 439–46.

earlier that Edward Schillebeeckx, at the end of his massive work, declares that he chooses to say, 'Jesus is the Son of God.' It may be doubted, however, whether the argument of the book actually leads to this conclusion. It seems that Schillebeeckx himself has merely jumped from a complex historical thesis to a theological judgment without any visible connection between the two. Anthony Harvey, in his briefer and more stimulating work, speaks of an historical enquiry, for which materials are now available,

> which will enable us to understand better what it might mean to claim that 'God was with' a person of history in such a unique and decisive way that he could be regarded as an actual agent of the divine, and become thereby an object, not only of our endless and fascinated study, but of our love and worship.[136]

Again, it may be doubted whether Harvey has produced an argument that will carry all his readers with him. But the attempt to move from Jesus to christology calls for further reflection.[137] Witherington, having argued in detail that Jesus believed himself to be Messiah, opts for a cautious but open-ended possibility: that Jesus saw himself 'not merely as a greater king than David but in a higher and more transcendent category'.[138] A lot more work is clearly required if such questions are to be addressed satisfactorily.

Though several of the practitioners of the Third Quest (e.g. Sanders) leave the christological question more or less explicitly out of consideration, it cannot in fact be put off for ever, and the present work will attempt eventually to address it head on. The Third Quest may look, to some suspicious eyes, as though it is bound to end up with an old-fashioned 'liberal' Jesus, really just a human being and nothing more. From the other end of the telescope, of course, anything that *did* end up with an argument, based on history, that showed a continuous line between Jesus' own understanding of himself and the early church's high christology would be at once, for that very reason, suspect in many quarters. But, if we play the game properly – if, that is, we leave the meanings of 'divine' and 'human' as unknowns until we have looked at the material – then there can be no advance prediction of what the result may look like.[139]

3. Conclusion: Future Directions of the Third Quest

Where, then, is the Third Quest going? Some of its practitioners, it seems, are similar in outlook to Reimarus: if we study the history for all it is worth,

---

[136] Harvey 1982, 10; cf. too his ch. 7, and 1976, 88–92; 1987.
[137] Such an attempt (not, I think, wholly successful) may be seen in Fredriksen 1988.
[138] Witherington 1990, 276.
[139] cf. *NTPG* xiv–xv, 12, 248–59, 456–8, 471–6.

we shall find that Christian theology can safely be downgraded. Others are more like some of the Old Questers: we must integrate a historical portrait of Jesus with a rediscovery of his religious significance. I wish in the present work to share the concern of the former for rigorous historical construction, and also to work towards a new integration of history and theology which will do justice, rather than violence, to both. The Third Quest has produced tools that enable us to attempt this task with high hopes.

There will, of course, be varied reactions to the Third Quest in general. Many will echo the reaction of dialectical theology to the Old Quest and to Schweitzer himself: give us something of instant use for theology, or we shall declare your work irrelevant.[140] The older brother is not going to like it if the prodigal tries to come back home. Old memories die hard; Reimarus' revolutionary Jesus, Schweitzer's apocalyptic visionary, and Vermes' Galilean Hasid have all caused consternation among theologians. One might even foresee a new 'demythologization' programme, designed to free Jesus from the political entanglements which Horsley and others get him into, just as Bultmann's programme tried to liberate him from Jewish apocalyptic thought. One can certainly foresee that many will take what is useful to them from the current debate and fit it into a framework of their own devising, however inappropriately; this disease is endemic to scholarship, my own no doubt included, and there is no reason to imagine that the present wave of studies will be exempt. Nor is this problem confined to those who want to find a Jesus on whom they can base their own brand of faith. Others are just as good at finding a Jesus on whom they can base their own brand of agnosticism. But we should not be put off from undertaking, and advancing, the Third Quest by the fears of those who say it will be useless for the practice or the theology of the church. (Sometimes, of course, this simply means that it will prove too challenging, and so is to be left aside.) Having lived with this dilemma for several years, I am convinced that the way out is forward, not backwards. We must take the historical questions and challenges on board; we cannot retreat into a private world of 'faith' which history cannot touch (what sort of a god would we be 'believing' in if we did?). The forward direction may not be comfortable, either for scholarship or the church. Forward directions seldom are; and I do not say that with the glee of

---

[140] This question – of the relevance of the 'historical Jesus' for preaching, for 'New Testament Theology' and for systematics – is not to be downplayed: see the penetrating article (1987) by Robert Morgan. As we saw in ch. 1, a surprisingly Bultmannian position on the issue is offered by C. S. Lewis in *The Screwtape Letters*, letter no. 23 (1955 edn., 116–20) – surprising, that is, in view of Lewis' anti-Bultmannian bluster in 1967, 155f., where he fails to see that Bultmann's discussion of Jesus' 'personality' was a response to Schweitzer's very specific proposal.

the scholar who sees that his own agenda will be uncomfortable *for every-body else*, though not for him. If there is discomfort here, I share it.

The Third Quest, then, is the basic starting-point of this book. It correctly highlights Jewish eschatology as the key to understanding Jesus: hence the title of this chapter. By following up and sharpening its questions, and honing and using its methods, we can attain real advance in our understanding of Jesus within his historical context, and thus raise in new ways the vital questions of continuity and discontinuity between Jesus of Nazareth and Christian faith – and between the *agenda* of Jesus of Nazareth and the contemporary *task* of the church. As we look at the history, we discover that we are also, and at the same time, looking at the traditional subject-matter of Christian theology, and that such theology is not to be separated from Christian praxis. To put it the other way round: when the New Testament writers speak of their encounter with Jesus as an encounter with Israel's god, they are redefining what 'god' (or even 'God') means at least as much as they are redefining who Jesus was and is. The dichotomies between event and interpretation, between fact and value, are not ultimate, and it is precisely when we are studying Jesus that they break down in disarray.[141] This relativizes some Third Quest work, to be sure, with its potential for materialist reductionism. But it hits far harder, as Schweitzer saw, at the anti-historical idealism of the iconographers on the one hand and the silhouette-makers on the other. To put it bluntly, we can know quite a lot about Jesus; not enough to write a modern-style biography, including the colour of the subject's hair, and what he liked for breakfast, but quite a lot. What we know, with the kind of 'knowledge' proper to all historical enquiry, may turn out to generate theological and practical significance far in excess of, and perhaps quite different from, anything that recent scholarship, and recent Christianity, has imagined or wanted. The renewed New Quest has sometimes implied that it and only it can make the study of Jesus relevant, at least to contemporary North America. I suggest that a far greater relevance will result from a more serious historical enterprise, although we cannot predict in advance what this relevance may be. As the first Christian century discovered, whole-hearted discipleship of Jesus by no means leads to unthinking support for the *status quo*, whether in religion or in politics.[142]

Authentic Christianity, after all, has nothing to fear from history. Rather, scholars of all backgrounds now have the opportunity, given us not least by the massive wave of discoveries about and research into first-century Judaism, to answer the questions raised by Reimarus, Schweitzer, Bultmann, Sanders, Crossan and the others, and even perhaps those raised by Luther

---

[141] cf. the suggestive remarks of Thatcher 1993.
[142] cf. *NTPG* Part IV.

and Melanchthon. The opportunity is at hand to respond appropriately to the challenge of the Enlightenment, and in so doing to issue some counter-challenges from the perspective of a history which, however rigorous, has not abandoned theology, but has rather rediscovered theological possibilities hidden under the pile of icons or behind the stack of silhouettes. History, even if bedraggled from its sojourn in the far country, may yet come home to a celebration. And that points us to the next chapter.

Chapter Four

PRODIGALS AND PARADIGMS

1. Jews, Peasants and Prodigals

History proceeds by telling stories. Here is one of the best known:

> There was a man who had two sons. The younger of them said to his father, 'Father, give me the share of the property that will belong to me.' So he divided his property between them. A few days later the younger son gathered all he had and travelled to a distant country, and there he squandered his property in dissolute living. When he had spent everything, a severe famine took place throughout that country, and he began to be in need. So he went and hired himself out to one of the citizens of that country, who sent him to his fields to feed the pigs. He would gladly have filled himself with the pods that the pigs were eating; and no one gave him anything. But when he came to himself he said, 'How many of my father's hired hands have bread enough and to spare, but here I am dying of hunger! I will get up and go to my father, and I will say to him, "Father, I have sinned against heaven and before you; I am no longer worthy to be called your son; treat me like one of your hired hands."' So he set off and went to his father. But while he was still far off, his father saw him and was filled with compassion; he ran and put his arms around him and kissed him. Then the son said to him, 'Father, I have sinned against heaven and before you; I am no longer worthy to be called your son.' But the father said to his slaves, 'Quickly, bring out a robe – the best one – and put it on him; put a ring on his finger and sandals on his feet. And get the fatted calf and kill it, and let us eat and celebrate; for this son of mine was dead and is alive again; he was lost and is found!' And they began to celebrate.
>
> Now his elder son was in the field; and when he came and approached the house, he heard music and dancing. He called one of the slaves and asked what was going on. He replied, 'Your brother has come, and your father has killed the fatted calf, because he has got him back safe and sound.' Then he became angry and refused to go in. His father came out and began to plead with him. But he answered his father, 'Listen! For all these years I have been working like a slave for you, and I have never disobeyed your command; yet you have never given me even a young goat so that I might celebrate with my friends. But when this son of yours came back, who has devoured your property with prostitutes, you killed the fatted calf for him!' Then the father said to him, 'Son, you are always with me, and all that is mine is yours. But we had to celebrate and rejoice, because this brother of yours was dead and has come to life; he was lost and has been found.'[1]

---

[1] Lk. 15.11–32.

Son, or father? The prodigal son, it is often called; but the son is not the only prodigal in the story. This is an explosive narrative, designed to blow apart the normal first-century reading of Jewish history and to replace it with a different one. Just as we saw in *NTPG* that some retellings of the Jewish story were designed to subvert others (the book of Susannah being a case in point),[2] so this tale subverts the telling of the story which one might expect from mainstream first-century Jews, not least those claiming to be the guardians of Israel's ancestral heritage. The story will serve, as we conclude the Introduction to this book, as a case-study to whet the appetite, to point forward to some of the main themes that will emerge, and to underscore the points of method that emerged from the previous chapter.

Years of scholarship have produced many commentaries on Luke, and many books on the parables. But none that I have been able to consult has noted the feature which seems to me most striking and obvious. Consider: here is a son who goes off in disgrace into a far country and then comes back, only to find the welcome challenged by another son who has stayed put.[3] The overtones are so strong that we surely cannot ignore them. This is the story of Israel, in particular of exile and restoration. It corresponds more or less exactly to the narrative grammar which underlies the exilic prophets, and the books of Ezra and Nehemiah, and a good deal of subsequent Jewish literature, and which must therefore be seen as formative for second-Temple Judaism. The exodus itself is the ultimate backdrop: Israel goes off into a pagan country, becomes a slave, and then is brought back to her own land. But exile and restoration is the main theme. This is what the parable is about.[4]

Babylon had taken the people into captivity; Babylon fell, and the people returned. But in Jesus' day many, if not most, Jews regarded the exile as still continuing. The people had returned in a geographical sense, but the great prophecies of restoration had not yet come true.[5] What was Israel to do? Why, to repent of the sin which had driven her into exile, and to return to YHWH with all her heart.[6] Who would stand in her way, to prevent her

[2] cf. *NTPG* 215-23; on Susannah, 220f.

[3] In the story the son chooses to leave. But, as will shortly become clear, a peasant audience would know he was in disgrace.

[4] The great merit of Drury 1985 is that he takes seriously the Jewish context of the parables, not least (what later writers would see as) their quasi-allegorical intent. The pity is that he fights shy of letting Jesus use them in this way. For a fascinating window on Jewish expectations of such stories, strongly confirming the exilic reference here, cf. Magonet 1988, 143f. (I owe this reference to Dr Bruce Longenecker.)

[5] *NTPG* 268-72, 299-301, and ch. 10 *passim*; and above, xvif.

[6] cf. Dt. 30.1-10; Ezra 9.5-10.5; Neh. 1.4-11; 9.6-38; Jer. 3.11-15, 19-25; 24.4-7; 29.10-14; Dan. 9.3-19; Hos. 5.15-6.2; 13.14; 14.1-7; etc. See below, ch. 7.

return? The mixed multitude, not least the Samaritans, who had remained in the land while the people were in exile.[7] But Israel would return, humbled and redeemed: sins would be forgiven, the covenant renewed, the Temple rebuilt, and the dead raised. What her god had done for her in the exodus – always the crucial backdrop for Jewish expectation – he would at last do again, even more gloriously. YHWH would finally become king, and would do for Israel, in covenant love, what the prophets had foretold.[8]

Exile and restoration: this is the central drama that Israel believed herself to be acting out. And the story of the prodigal says, quite simply: this hope is now being fulfilled – but it does not look like what was expected. Israel went into exile because of her own folly and disobedience, and is now returning simply because of the fantastically generous, indeed prodigal, love of her god. But this is a highly subversive retelling. The real return from exile, including the real resurrection from the dead, is taking place, in an extremely paradoxical fashion, in Jesus' own ministry. Those who grumble at what is happening are cast in the role of the Jews who did not go into exile, and who opposed the returning people. They are, in effect, virtually Samaritans. The true Israel is coming to its senses, and returning to its father, as Jeremiah had foretold;[9] and those who oppose this great movement of divine love and grace are defining themselves as outside the true family. There are, perhaps, other echoes, of quarrels between two brothers which left the younger vindicated and the elder angry and disinherited.[10] These give to the story a sense of depth and resonance. But the main line remains clear. Israel's history is turning its long-awaited corner; this is happening within the ministry of Jesus himself; and those who oppose it are the enemies of the true people of god.[11]

[7] cf. 2 Kgs. 17.24–41; Ezra 4.1–24; 9.1–2; Neh. 4.1–8; 6.1–19; 13.23–9; etc. On the historical questions surrounding Samaritan opposition to the restoration of Israel and the rebuilding of the Temple, cf. R. T. Anderson 1992, 941f. Cp. also the invective against the Jews who remained in the land during the exile, Jer. 24.8–10. To the possible response, that in Luke the Samaritans are invariably cast in a good light, the obvious reply is that this was not the understanding of the first-century Jews who are the parable's supposed first audience. Luke's rehabilitation of the Samaritans will have been a surprise to many of his readers; they would have remained well aware of the overtones which this story would generate.

[8] cf. *NTPG* 268–338; and cp. Ezek. 36–37; Hos. 11.1–9, Isa. 40–55, etc. Anyone who supposes that all these things had happened by the time of Jesus, or that any devout Jews of the period would have imagined that they had, has simply not learned to think historically.

[9] Jer. 31.18–20. This passage is seen by some (Quell 1967, 973, followed by Marshall 1978, 604) as the background to the parable, though without observing the narrative context. This enables e.g. Evans 1990, 589 to dispute the link.

[10] Gen. 4; 27; 32f. Dr A. Goddard points out to me that Lk. 15.20 echoes Gen. 33.4.

[11] This shows beyond a doubt the folly of attempting to split the parable up into its two sections, as though one were original and the second added later: so, rightly, Bultmann 1968 [1921], 212; Marshall 1978, 605, against e.g. Wellhausen, Weiss and J. T. Sanders 1969. Evans 1990, 588 suggests that vv. 25–32 seem 'a somewhat lame appendix'; this simply misses the point, reducing the parable to a shallow moralistic tale.

Luke, to be sure, has used the story within his own larger story. There is an interesting parallel, again not always observed, between Luke 15 and Acts 15. In both, people are being welcomed in from beyond the boundaries of normal acceptability. In both, this provokes grumbles from the guardians of the ancestral traditions. In both, the grumbles are answered by the claim that Israel is entering, has indeed already entered, the time of renewal, of return from exile, of the kingdom of her god. That is the appointed time for outcasts to be welcomed.[12] The crucial passage in Acts 15 is the quotation from Amos 9.11f.:

> After this I will return,
> and I will rebuild the dwelling of David, which has fallen;
> from its ruins I will rebuild it, and I will set it up,
> so that all other peoples may seek the Lord –
> even all the Gentiles over whom my name has been called.
> Thus says the Lord, who has been making these things known from long ago.[13]

In other words, it is time for the Gentiles to come in, because Israel's exile is at last over, and she has been restored. The Temple has been rebuilt; the Messiah has come at last. But where did Luke get that idea from? As I argued earlier, it was a major theme within his whole work, but he did not invent it. It was something he held in common with all the other major early Christian writers. Israel's Messianic restoration, and the consequent theological rationale of the mission to the world, are to be found (to look no further) as striking themes within Matthew and Paul as well, and for that matter in story after story of the pre-synoptic tradition.[14]

Like a great pincer movement, therefore, we can work inwards towards Jesus, from the Jewish context of his own work and from the Christian theology of the early church. Israel has been waiting for redemption, for the return from exile. The early Christians are behaving as though it has already happened, and are justifying this by telling stories about Jesus himself. The simplest solution (not that New Testament scholars usually opt for the simplest solution) is that Jesus himself believed that he was the agent of this strange return from exile, and that he lived and acted accordingly. His welcome to all and sundry, that free commensality of which Crossan writes so movingly, was a sign that resurrection – forgiveness – restoration – return from exile – the reign of YHWH – were all happening under the noses of the elder brothers, the self-appointed stay-at-home guardians of the father's

---

[12] cf. *NTPG* 223, 267f.; cp., as one example among many, Tob. 13.9–11.
[13] Ac. 15.16f.
[14] cf. *NTPG* Part IV, esp. chs. 13, 14. On Lk. cf. esp. 381f.

house. The covenant was being renewed, and Jesus' welcome to the outcasts was a vital part of that renewal.

And, in the middle of it, the father himself was being reckless, prodigal, generous to a fault. Careful study of the peasant context in which the story makes fullest sense offers the following striking points.[15] For the younger son to ask for his share of the inheritance is almost unthinkable: it is the functional equivalent of saying to his father, 'I wish you were dead.' The father should have beaten him, or thrown him out. Instead, he agrees. The son ends up doing the job beyond which it was impossible, in Jewish eyes, to sink: feeding pigs for a gentile master. He then does a further unthinkable thing: he returns home, threatening to disgrace the whole family in the eyes of the village. The father *runs* to meet him; senior members of families never do anything so undignified at the best of times, let alone in order to greet someone who should have remained in self-imposed ignominy. The party is for the whole village, like a big family wedding; a fatted calf would be far too much for a single household. The elder brother, meanwhile, also shames his father, by quarrelling with him in public, and in his turn suggesting that he wished the father dead so that he could at last enjoy his share of the property; but again the father is astonishingly, unbelievably, gentle. The story ends, within its cultural context, too soon: it demands a last scene, preferably a reconciliation.

Most commentators have focused on the welcome home as the great sign of the father's love. Helmut Thielicke, famously, wrote a book called *The Waiting Father*.[16] But the thrust of the story, the emphasis on the prodigal love of the father, is felt much sooner, and sustained much longer. Exile, as some of the greatest prophets had seen, was itself part of the strange covenant purposes of Israel's father-god. Israel could be allowed to sin, to follow pagan idolatry, even to end up feeding the pigs for a pagan master, but Israel could not fall out of the covenant purposes of her god. She could say to her god 'I wish you were dead', but this god would not respond in kind. When, therefore, Israel comes to her senses, and returns with all her heart, there is an astonishing, prodigal, lavish welcome waiting for her. Equally, the same generous love is still extended to those who, hurt and upset, cannot at the moment understand how it can possibly be right to welcome the prodigal home.

Each of these levels of meaning resonates appropriately when we envisage Jesus telling the story – and telling it in pretty much the setting Luke has given it (Luke 15.1–2). Jesus is acting, as an increasingly large number of

[15] Here as elsewhere the work of Bailey 1983 [1976, 1980] has been eyes to the blind. On this parable cf. 1.158–206.

[16] Thielicke 1960.

scholars admit, as if he is simply bypassing the Temple system altogether. He is claiming to admit all and sundry into the renewed people of Israel's god. In telling this story, he is explaining and vindicating his own practice of eating with sinners: his celebratory meals are the equivalent, in real life, of the homecoming party in the story. They are the celebration of the return from exile. What is more, Jesus is claiming that, when he does all this, Israel's god is doing it, welcoming sinners no matter whether they have passed all the normal tests for membership, as long as they will accept the welcome of Jesus. What, is Israel's holy god likely to behave in such a way? Yes, replies the parable, just as the prophets foretold: just like a father who . . . For Israel's god to act in this way is not an innovation; it is consistent with his character as revealed throughout Israel's long and chequered history. This is who he is, who he will be.

Despite the elder brother. The parable does not 'teach', in the sense of teaching abstract or timeless truth; it *acts*. It creates a new world. Those who object to what Jesus is doing are warned of the role they are in fact playing in this new world, in the great climactic drama of Israel's history. Resurrection, the return from exile, is happening, and they cannot see it. The battle-lines are drawn. It is not a matter (as has often been imagined, and now quite often refuted) of Jesus offending some petty scruples here or there, or of an abstract challenge offered by one timeless religious system to another. Jesus is claiming to be ushering in Israel's long-awaited new world; and he is doing it, apparently, in all the wrong ways. Jesus is enacting the great healing, the great restoration, of Israel. And he interprets his own actions in terms of the fulfilment, not of a few prophetic proof-texts taken atomistically, but of the entire story-line which Israel had told herself, in a variety of forms, over and over again.[17] His opponents find themselves standing under a new sort of spotlight. If this is the new exodus, those who are objecting to it are cast as Pharaoh. If it is the real return from exile, the objectors are the Samaritans. If Jesus is in some sense building the real Temple, the objectors – ironically, since their own worldview focuses so strongly on the Temple in Jerusalem – are cast as those who resolutely opposed its rebuilding.[18] They, in their turn, are saying to Israel's covenant god that they wish he were dead. This, however, merely underlines the wish that the elder brother be reconciled. In Luke's gospel the Samaritans are given a new hope, a new possibility. The elder brother in the story is, implicitly, condemned, in order then to be offered a new chance. The parable creates a new situation, in which the hearers are confronted with a choice, a warning, and an invitation.

[17] cf. *NTPG* 241–3.
[18] cf. Ezra 4.1–3.

Dramatically, historically, theologically, the parable fits perfectly into the ministry of Jesus, as we shall be studying it in the rest of this book. Jesus is reconstituting Israel around himself. This is the return from exile; this, in other words, is the kingdom of Israel's god. Those with vested interests in different visions of the kingdom are bound to disapprove strongly. The strange announcement of resurrection, twice within the parable (verses 24, 32), makes excellent sense in this context. Jesus' actions, and his words, themselves stand in need of vindication. Is his offer merely a reckless gesture, which the hard realities of history will prove to have been empty? Are his celebratory meals simply an empty charade? He is making a claim, a claim to be the one in and through whom Israel's god is restoring his people. The claim is highly controversial. It points, within his own teaching, to a final clash with the authorities, who will wish him dead and act on that wish. Like any good Jew, he believes that if he faces this, in obedience to the divine plan, he will be vindicated. And the word for that is 'resurrection'.

2. From Parable to Paradigm

(i) Towards a Hypothesis

One swallow does not make a summer; one parable does not necessarily reveal a paradigm, a full outline of Jesus' aims and career. But it gives a clear indication of certain vital points, both of content and of method. Of content I have given an indication in the previous paragraph. Of method there is more which should be said at this point.

We have seen, in one small instance, that the double context of Judaism and the early church – the great complex entities which we studied in *NTPG* Parts III and IV – does indeed provide a pincer movement by which we can go back towards Jesus himself with an excellent chance of finding solid historical ground. We have also seen the clear value of reading the material in terms of the relevant worldviews, and of the stories in which they were regularly expressed, sustained, or subverted. The parable only makes sense as a retelling of Israel's story; but it also only makes sense as a profoundly subversive retelling of that story. When we examine the particular sort of subversion in question, it turns out to be one which is *presupposed* from the very earliest days of the church. As a parable, not least in its manner of concluding one scene too early, it makes sense precisely at that moment in history when the possibility of Israel's redemption happening in this fashion is being controversially mooted, not when it is being climactically and publicly celebrated. The parable thus fits exactly into the gap between Judaism and early Christianity, into the intertextual and intercommunal space between the worldviews we studied in the previous volume. It is thus decisively *similar* to both the Jewish context and the early Christian world, and at the same time importantly *dissimilar* – in just that sense which we saw highlighted in some recent Third Quest work.[19] It is vital to recognize this double movement. Without it, one is in the difficult position of working simply from later and Christianized texts, or from complex reconstructions of Judaism. Along with the much-discussed 'criterion of dissimilarity' must go a criterion of double similarity: when something can be seen to be credible (though perhaps deeply subversive) within first-century Judaism, *and* credible as the implied starting-point (though not the exact replica) of something in later Christianity, there is a strong possibility of our being in touch with the genuine history of Jesus. This powerfully reinforces the method which the Third Quest, explicitly, and the renewed New Quest, despite itself, are employing.

It sets up, in other words, a basic hypothesis which addresses the five major questions we studied in the last chapter. (1) Jesus fits believably into first-century Judaism, retelling its stories in new but thoroughly comprehensible ways. He speaks and acts, and is perceived to be speaking and acting, prophetically, challenging his hearers to recognize that in him the new thing for which they have longed is, however paradoxically, coming to pass. (2) He believes himself, much as John the Baptist had done, to be charged with the god-given responsibility of regrouping Israel around himself. But this regrouping is no longer a preliminary preparation for the return from exile, the coming of the kingdom; it *is* the return, the redemption, the resurrection from the dead. As a result, it is also a counter-Temple movement, and is perceived as such. It also puts Jesus in a different position to John. (3) For all these reasons, it will arouse hostility. During the course of Jesus' ministry, this may well come from the Pharisees. If the message is ever to be spoken or acted in Jerusalem itself, hostility will come from the Temple authorities. If the Romans hear of a major renewal movement among the Jews, they too will want to stamp it out. (4) If this proclamation were to end simply with the shameful death of its proclaimer, that would be that: a beautiful dream, with all the charm, and the brief life-span, of a butterfly. But if it were vindicated after that shameful death, there would be every reason to continue to believe that the kingdom had indeed arrived, in however paradoxical a fashion. Every reason, too, for the all-embracing welcome then to be extended in a new way to Gentiles; and (5) for a writer like Luke to retell the original story with an eye to this new, but theologically consistent, setting. Thus, in a nutshell, the parable of the prodigal father

---

[19] Above, p. 85f.

points to the hypothesis of the prophetic son: the son, Israel-in-person, who will himself go into the far country, who will take upon himself the shame of Israel's exile, so that the kingdom may come, the covenant be renewed, and the prodigal welcome of Israel's god, the creator, be extended to the ends of the earth.

How does a hypothesis like this work in practice, and gain its own vindication? As we have said, by showing how its essentially simple line works out in detail, and by showing, conversely, how the manifold details fit within it. It helps, too, if one can show that the strengths of other scholarly hypotheses are retained, and the weaknesses eliminated. It does not help very much at all to take each saying, each parable, and work through a multiply hypothetical history of traditions as though aiming thereby to peel the historical onion back to its core. That is the way of tears and frustration, a new form of scholarly exile, reflected in the wild carob-pods of the prodigal, which, being neither gastronomically nor nutritionally satisfying, may drive the eater to repentance.[20] Such a diet serves only as a reminder that there is such a thing as serious history, and that this is not the way to do it. The hypothesis must be explored as a hypothesis. Its vindication will come, like that of all hypotheses, in its inclusion of the data without distortion; in its essential simplicity of line; and in its ability to shed light elsewhere.[21] To that task we shall presently proceed.

(ii) Of the Telling of Stories

The powerful resonances of the parable with the context of peasant society provide the basis for a hypothesis of a different sort, to do with the nature of story-telling within peasant communities.[22] Part of the thrust of the parable within peasant society comes from the fact that the whole village would know what the younger son had done, and would have told the awful and shocking story of his behaviour over and over again. When he returned, it would not be to a modern-style middle-class suburb where everybody (in theory at least) minded their own business, but to a peasant village which thrived on narrative. Not mere gossip, either: the community would order its life and thought by telling and retelling important events which had made them who

---

[20] Bailey 1983 [1976, 1980], 1.171-3; Safrai 1994, 141f.

[21] cf. *NTPG* 98–109.

[22] Again I acknowledge my debt to the work of Kenneth Bailey, this time in his 1991 article. This needs to be put alongside Wansbrough 1991 in future discussions of oral tradition within the culture of Jesus and the early church. Since Bailey's work is not well known, and not easily accessible, I shall summarize it briefly.

they were. This provides a window on a world of which, perhaps surprisingly, Crossan says nothing, for all his repeated emphasis on Jesus and his early followers as coming from peasant stock. It is the world of *informal but controlled oral tradition.*

Bailey has argued effectively for a position midway between the extremes represented by Bultmann and Gerhardsson. Bultmann proposed that the oral traditions about Jesus were *informal* and *uncontrolled.*[23] The community was not interested in preserving or controlling the tradition; it was free to change this way and that, to develop and grow. Gerhardsson and Riesenfeld, by contrast, suggested that Jesus taught his disciples fixed forms of teachings which functioned as *formal* and *controlled.*[24] From his wide and prolonged first-hand study of middle-eastern peasant culture, undertaken while working as a theological teacher in various countries in that part of the world, Bailey allows that there are such things as informal and uncontrolled traditions: they occur when rumours, for instance of atrocities, spread like wildfire and become grossly enlarged and reshaped in the process. There is also, to this day, a middle-eastern tradition of formal and controlled tradition, as when Muslims learn the entire Koran by heart, or when Syriac-speaking monks can recite all the hymns of St Ephrem. In between the two, however, Bailey identifies *informal* and *controlled* oral traditions. They are informal in that they have no set teacher and students. Anyone can join in – provided they have been part of the community for long enough to qualify. They are controlled in that the whole community knows the traditions well enough to check whether serious innovation is being smuggled in, and to object if it is.[25]

Bailey divides the traditions that are preserved, in this informal yet controlled way, into five categories. There are proverbs, thousands of them (in comparison with the average modern westerner's knowledge of maybe a few dozen). There are narrative riddles, in which a wise hero solves a problem. There is poetry, both classical and contemporary. There is the parable or story. Finally, there are accounts of important figures in the history of the village or community. The control in each case is exercised by the community. Again Bailey has categorized this into its different patterns. Poems and proverbs allow no flexibility. Some flexibility is allowed within parables, and recollections concerning historical people: 'the central threads of the

---

[23] Bultmann 1968 [1921], etc.

[24] Gerhardsson 1961, 1964, 1979, 1986; Riesenfeld 1970. Cf. too Riesner 1984 [1981].

[25] If the nearest a modern western person can approach to a pre-literary culture is through the eyes of a child, an anachronistic analogy might be allowed. Supposing a parent, reading a Beatrix Potter story for the twentieth time to a three-year-old, decides to skip or change a word, a line, or a page – what will happen next?

story cannot be changed, but flexibility in detail is allowed'.[26] More complete flexibility is allowed when '*the material is irrelevant to the identity of the community*, and is not judged *wise* or *valuable*'.[27]

Bailey finally categorizes the methods used by the community to fix important material in the communal memory. New and important stories are repeated over and over until the basic pattern of their telling is indelibly imprinted on the village mind. This, he suggests, is precisely what happened with the early Jesus-traditions. We find that

> the assumption that the early Christians were not interested in history becomes untenable. To remember the words and deeds of Jesus of Nazareth was to affirm their own unique identity. The stories had to be *told* and *controlled* or everything that made them who they were was lost.[28]

This, Bailey argues, is the process presupposed by the phrase 'eye-witnesses and ministers [*hyperetai*] of the word' in Luke 1.2. A *hyperetes* is an official: in Luke 4.20, a synagogue official in charge of the scrolls, but in the early Christian community, without buildings and formal institutional structures, most likely an accredited witness to vital traditions.[29] Several persons in a village are qualified to retell the village's key stories, and the same is true within early Christianity. Paul reflects this: having himself received traditions, he passes them on (1 Corinthians 11.2, 23; 15.1–3). He is not himself a *hyperetes tou logou*, an eye-witness who can himself be an authentic original source. But he belongs within an extended network in which the traditions, the stories, would be told and retold, under conditions of informal but quite definite control. It was only with the major social disruption of the Jewish-Roman war that the normal life, and story-telling, of the primitive Palestinian Christian communities would have been broken up. That, of course – rather than the usual explanation that the world had not after all come to an end – provides the perfect reason, sociologically and historically, for the committing of the traditions to writing.[30]

There is, no doubt, plenty more to be said on the subject of oral tradition.[31] The study of different contemporary cultures, and of different ancient societies and texts, may well result in further fine-tuning. But Bailey's proposal has, to my mind, the smell of serious social history about it. It allows for different shaping of material within a framework. It enables us to

---

[26] Bailey 1991, 42.

[27] Bailey 1991, 45: italics original.

[28] Bailey 1991, 51: italics original.

[29] Bailey 1991, 50, 53, citing Safrai 1976c, 935.

[30] Another reason would be, of course, the need for the traditions to be available in missionary settings way beyond the original communities.

[31] cf. *NTPG* 422–4; and e.g. Ong 1982; Kelber 1983; and esp. Wansbrough 1991.

explain, without as yet having recourse to complex theories either of synoptic relationships or of a freely expanding tradition, the way in which again and again the story comes out slightly differently, but the *sayings* remain more or less identical.[32] It shows that the narrative form is unlikely to be a secondary accretion around an original aphorism: stories are fundamental. It enables us to understand how divergent traditions could arise, particularly in communities which, after the disaster of the two wars, found themselves free from the informal control of the original community and wished, for whatever reason, to take a different theological or practical line.[33] It enables us, in other words, to understand the material before us, without invoking extra epicycles of unwarranted assumptions. These are great strengths. Until it is shown that the process Bailey envisages is historically impossible, I propose that it be taken as a working model.

Ironically, therefore, by agreeing with Crossan upon the vital importance of setting Jesus in his Mediterranean peasant culture, we have reached a conclusion which radically undermines Crossan's own historical reconstruction.[34] The community's vital interest in affirming its identity by means of telling Jesus-stories, so long regarded within some critical circles as a good reason for reducing the stories to terms of the community, is in fact nothing of the kind. That reductionism turns out to be an ahistorical assumption, based on a flawed epistemology[35] and a misreading of the Jewish worldview,[36] and characterized by an over-active zeal for detecting conspiracies. If we wish to object to the historicity of some part of the tradition, we must do so on good historical grounds, that is, in terms of putting forward serious hypotheses about the whole subject-matter, not on the assumption that the stories were never intended to refer to anything other than the community that told them. The stories of Jesus that circulated in the first generation are in principle to be taken as just that: stories of Jesus.

The story we are now telling, therefore, must itself subvert the story told by the strand of New Testament criticism that runs from Wrede to Crossan. According to that story, the evangelists were radical innovators, who spun their tales with such art that they deceived, if possible, even the elect. Early Christianity was made to stand on its head as first Mark, then Matthew and Luke, reshaped and rewrote it according to their own ideologies. Subsequent Christianity canonized the mistake, and built upon it all manner of grievous

---

[32] Allowing, also, for the fact that in an itinerant ministry Jesus must inevitably have said similar, but slightly different, things on numerous occasions; see ch. 5 below.

[33] Thus explaining the non-canonical gospels: so Bailey 1991, 50.

[34] A similar point is urged by van Beeck 1994, 89–93.

[35] cf. *NTPG* chs. 2, 3, esp. 77f.

[36] cf. *NTPG* 77–9, and Part III *passim*.

distortions.[37] But if I am anywhere near the mark in my discussion of early Christianity (*NTPG* Part IV), and if Bailey is anywhere near the mark in his analysis of Mediterranean peasant oral culture, then the case for Mark-the-film-script-writer melts away like morning dew. In Crossan's reading, it is orthodox Christianity that should be banished to the far country, where in post-Constantinian Europe it has wasted its substance on dissolute imperial living. But supposing mediaeval 'orthodoxy', realizing its mistake, its use of Jesus as an idol to serve its own prosperity, were to come to its senses and return home? Who would then appear in the role of the elder brother?

From another point of view, of course, as I suggested earlier, the historical task itself is the suspect prodigal. There is still a soi-disant 'orthodoxy' that wishes to have nothing more to do with history, in view of the shame that it has brought on the family in the past.[38] But, as I have now argued, the historical task is just as possible, in principle, when we approach Jesus, as it is anywhere else – and just as necessary. As long as history comes to its senses, and forswears the dissolute methodologies that have made it appear so bankrupt, there is every reason why it should be welcomed home. The Quest may have begun with people studying history in order to disprove Christianity, in order to declare that the Christian god was now dead; but there is no reason to suppose that this state of affairs will be permanent. For Christian theology to take that elder-brother line would, in fact, be the ultimate folly. It would itself be wishing that the creator god, the god of history, were dead. Of course, if history is to be welcomed back into the fold, there will be no room, either, for an inverted arrogance, with the older brother (theology) left out in the cold. But the long story of chilly relationships between history and theology, or between serious questioning and serious faith, cannot be allowed to end with mutual suspicion, recrimination and hostility. Precisely because we are studying Jesus himself, we may perhaps hope, despite all the problems still to be worked through, that by this means the reconciliation of the brothers may at last take place.

(iii) Worldviews and Mindsets

In *The New Testament and the People of God*, I set out a plan whereby one might study the worldview of a particular society and the mindset of particular individuals within it. I then put this to work in studying the worldviews of first-century Judaism on the one hand and first-century Christianity on the

---

[37] For this suggestion, cf. e.g. Crossan 423f., speaking of the possibility of 'ultimate betrayals' at this stage of the historical development.
[38] cf. now Johnson 1995.

other. In doing so, I also began to explore, through the literature they produced, the mindsets of some within both of those groups.[39] We now return to this model in order to set up the terms of reference with which to tackle the historical task in such a way as to avoid provoking again the sibling rivalry we have just discussed.

It will be as well briefly to recapitulate the outline of the model itself.[40] Worldviews are the lenses through which a society looks at the world, the grid upon which are plotted the multiple experiences of life. Worldviews may be studied in terms of four features: characteristic stories; fundamental symbols; habitual praxis; and a set of questions and answers (who are we? where are we? what's wrong? what's the solution? and what time is it?[41]). These features interact with each other in a variety of complex and interesting ways.

By 'mindset' I mean a worldview as held by a particular individual person. Its structure and functioning are basically the same as those of a worldview, except that it relates to its parent worldview in a number of ways: it is routinely sustained by interaction with other persons who share the worldview, but it may be subverted, generating variations and mutations, under particular circumstances. In extreme cases, this can involve a major personal crisis in which the worldview is abandoned altogether and a different one adopted. More often, the same worldview is retained, but with local and personal differences.[42]

Worldviews and mindsets generate a set of 'basic beliefs' and 'aims', which in turn reach day-to-day expression in what I have termed 'consequent beliefs' and 'intentions'. My intention to practise the trombone this afternoon gives expression to my aim to become a proficient orchestral performer. I do not often stop to think about the worldview of western culture within which such strange behaviour makes sense, or about my own mindset, my variation on that worldview, incomprehensible no doubt even to some who share the worldview itself, whereby I will play classical music one day and jazz the next. But this worldview and this mindset exist, and they can be summoned up, if required, to explain actions otherwise inexplicable. One cannot explain worldviews and mindsets themselves in terms of anything else: if challenged, a worldview generates the answer 'that's just the way things are', and a mindset replies to critics with 'that's just the sort of person I am' (or perhaps, more poetically, 'what I do is me; for that I came'[43]).

[39] *NTPG* Parts II (method); III (Judaism); IV (Christianity).

[40] cf. esp. *NTPG* 109–12, 122–6. For a different, though ultimately compatible, account of worldviews see Wink 1992a, 3–10.

[41] I have added the fifth question to those listed in *NTPG*; see ch. 10 below.

[42] cf. Funk 1991, 21: everybody is unique, but nobody can be wrenched out of context.

[43] Hopkins, 'As kingfishers catch fire' (Phillips 1986, 129).

The historical study of an individual such as Jesus, no different in principle from the historical study of other individuals, consists of the assembly and interpretation of evidence which contributes as fully as possible to the understanding of the person at all these levels – worldview, mindset, basic beliefs, aims, consequent beliefs, and intentions. This process is of course complex. In it, the historian moves continually in two basic directions.

First, we can move from event to mindset. When we see an expert chess-player making a move which seems to us incomprehensible, we assume that it is not an accident, but rather that it forms part of a strategy which at the moment we cannot grasp, but whose eventual aim – winning the game – is already known. (If someone asks 'but why do you want to win the game?', we have reached the chess equivalent of worldview: that is simply what the exercise is all about.) Where some action or activity of Jesus is securely established, we can ask what beliefs, aims and intentions it reveals, granted the prevailing Jewish worldview whose basic shape, it is assumed, he shared. This move, from event to mindset-within-worldview, is not in principle problematic, even allowing for development or change within the subject. The alternative is to regard the action as random, unthinking, or accidental.

Second, we can move from an already established mindset-within-worldview to hypotheses about actions. Where some feature of chess is so basic as to be immutable – for instance, that one does not sacrifice a Queen without very obvious good reason – one can deduce that a report of the game may be mistaken if it claims that an excellent player, never before known as a Queen-sacrificer, has done just that. In the same way, when some element of the Jewish worldview, such as the god-givenness of male and female within the created world, is regarded as immutable, we can assume that it formed part of Jesus' mindset, and weigh such sayings as *Thomas* 114 in the balance against it, and find them wanting.[44] Since most historical characters worth studying are so because they held mindsets that formed significant variations on the parent worldview, this latter move will always be risky. (The Queen sacrifice may after all have taken place, obedient to some extraordinary new strategy. Perhaps Jesus did say and do things that challenge some fundamental aspects of the Jewish worldview.) But it is in principle the sort of move that critical historians make all the time.

These two sorts of enquiry – from action to mindset, from mindset to action – form the constant process by which history does its work. It is no surprise, then, to find that the entire story of the Quest, as recounted in the

---

[44] 'Jesus said, "Look, I will guide [Mary] to make her male, so that she too may become a living spirit resembling you males. For every female who makes herself male will enter the kingdom of heaven."' For a recent discussion of this, cf. Meyer 1985. Of course, in chess every pawn wants to become a Queen.

first three chapters of this book, could be arranged under these heads. All scholars start off with a few very basic facts about Jesus. They move quite quickly, often immediately, to a hypothetical reconstruction of his mindset: for Reimarus, Jesus had the mindset of a Jewish reformer; for Schweitzer, that of an apocalyptic prophet; and so on, though in each case still within the parent first-century Jewish worldview.[45] This then forms the basis for the reflex process, reasoning from mindset-within-worldview to deeds and words, as the scholar wrestles with the puzzling data of the gospel tradition, writing sentences of the form 'Jesus would never have said . . .', or 'Jesus must have realized . . .' or perhaps 'Jesus could not have done . . .' Again, for Reimarus this meant that Jesus could not have acted as if he thought of himself as the later church came to think of him; for Schweitzer, it meant that Jesus must have thought of himself as facing, alone, the apocalyptic climax of Israel's history; and so on. This in turn may give rise to modifications in the hypothesis about the mindset: some events and sayings turn out to be less easy to incorporate, or to jettison, than one might have thought, and so we have to rethink the hypothetical worldview. Thus history proceeds in a spiral of knowledge, or at least guesswork. This process, in general terms, has been common to all historiography from Herodotus to the present, and hence also of course to all serious writing about Jesus from Reimarus to the present. Recognizing it for what it is will help us to evaluate arguments, and to advance new ones, with some hope of success.[46]

Variations within a worldview, in the form of particular mindsets, can and do occur at all levels (symbol, story, praxis, questions, beliefs, aims, and intentions), but they become especially public and visible when they emerge in words or actions. If somebody in modern western society walks into a bank and makes a show of cutting up a set of credit cards, we may deduce that they are registering a subversive protest against a significant element within the modern western worldview, without necessarily abandoning that worldview altogether. When one man in ancient Roman society crossed the Rubicon with an army at his heels, onlookers readily and correctly concluded that he was acting on a set of beliefs and aims that indicated a significant shift within, and ultimately a deep subversion of, the standard republican worldview. If somebody in ancient Palestine rode into Jerusalem on a donkey amidst an excited pilgrim crowd, and performed symbolic actions in the Temple, onlookers would deduce, before any words had been spoken, that he

---

[45] Even those who make Jesus a Cynic, or a proto-gnostic, agree that Jesus was a Jew and should be studied as such: cf. e.g. Funk 1991, 19f., with 'premise 59', which reads 'Jesus was not a Christian; he was a Jew'.

[46] Basic historical method is thus not new, as suggested in Funk 1991, 20f. Cf. *NTPG* ch. 4.

was acting on a set of beliefs and aims which indicated a particular variation, a particular mindset, within the larger first-century Jewish worldview. We can thus use particular actions to deduce particular intentions, and from there work back, with suitable caution, to the entire model of a mindset within a worldview. One of the first tasks, therefore, is to examine the known actions of the subject (not to exclude words, but to set them in their fullest context), and to see what may be deduced from them. Actions, especially symbolic actions, speak louder than words. Studying actions, especially symbolic actions, is a far better starting-point for the historian than studying isolated sayings.[47]

When, however, the subject is (as often in historiography) someone who has taken a lead in a new movement of whatever sort, or who has deliberately set out to subvert a dominant worldview, we may find that elements of the worldview or mindset will emerge into the light which in more normal circumstances, or persons, would probably remain hidden. We are here on similar ground to Thomas Kuhn when he described the difference between 'normal science' and 'paradigm shifts'.[48] Most people live most of the time within the worldview which characterizes their society at large ('normal science'); some people sometimes challenge their surrounding worldview with a significant new variation ('paradigm shift'). When Isaiah went about naked and barefoot for three years, this *praxis* was intended to function as a *symbol* which told a *story* about the people of Israel, answering the basic worldview *questions* in new and startling ways. Instead of Israel's problem being a lack of military strength, and the solution being reliance on Egypt and Ethiopia, such reliance was in fact the problem, and the solution was a fresh trust in YHWH.[49] Precisely because Isaiah was challenging the existing construal of the Jewish worldview, the main features of his own mindset, as a radical variation on that worldview, came into view. His settled *aim*, to be a faithful mouthpiece of Israel's god to his people, dovetailed with his basic *belief* in this god and his long-term purposes, producing *consequent beliefs* such as the futility of trusting one set of pagan nations for support against another set, and specific *intentions* – such as, on this particular occasion, that of behaving in this otherwise bizarre and inexplicable fashion.

The task of the historian, faced with figures who are not content to live quietly within a particular worldview, but who seem bent on challenging it with their own proposed variation, is therefore to plot as far as possible the

---

[47] On the danger of isolating 'sayings', cf. Sanders 1985, 4, 8, and frequently. See too Meyer 1979, 19.

[48] Kuhn 1970 [1962]. Sometimes, of course, a paradigm shift involves abandoning a worldview entirely and adopting a new one.

[49] Isa. 20.1–6.

full range of worldview features. This need not, but often can, take something like the following form. (a) We are quite often in a position to begin with *actions and words* (recognizing, again, the close link between them, producing our twentieth-century phrases 'body language' and 'speech-acts'). (b) Where these become habitual and characteristic, they regularly reveal the *praxis* of the subject, and so introduce us to the first quadrant of the worldview. (c) When actions/words are examined carefully, in the light of this praxis, they are frequently found to tell *stories*, the second quadrant. (d) Actions/words and stories will frequently evoke, transform or generate *symbols* – the third quadrant; and (e) they will regularly, particularly when all these elements are put together, address by implication at least the fourth quadrant, the deep *questions* to which all worldviews offer some sort of answers. (f) In the light of this plotting of the worldview/mindset of the person concerned, we can move to an analysis of *beliefs* and *aims*, and (g) of *consequent beliefs* and *intentions*, which will (h) bring us back, at least in theory, to where we started, now knowing the place for the first time. It is this daunting task that now faces us as we turn to the study of Jesus himself:

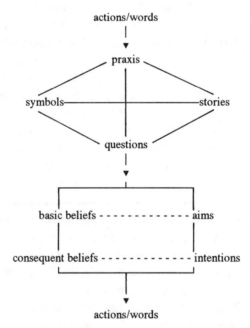

The aim of the next Part of the book will thus be to plot Jesus' distinctive mindset within the Jewish worldview of his day. We shall first set out the basic material we know, by more or less common consent, about Jesus; this leads directly to the praxis which his contemporaries regarded as characteristic of him, which we shall study in chapter 5. We shall then examine the stories Jesus told, including of course the parables (chapters 6–8); his attitude towards the symbols of Judaism, and the conflict which this brought about (chapter 9); and the answers he gave to the basic worldview questions (chapter 10). Once we have thus completed the four quadrants of the worldview, we will be able, in Part III, to explore the beliefs and aims in which this found particular expression, and so see our way back towards the particular consequent beliefs and intentions which generated the central actions through which his public career gained its particular shape and came to its particular conclusion. In the course of this we will look in particular at Jesus' own sense of vocation and identity, and his attitude to his own approaching death.

How does this agenda relate to the five questions which the Third Quest has been raising, which we discussed in chapter 3? It is a way of coming at the first three questions (Jesus and Judaism; Jesus' aims; the reasons for Jesus' death) from an unusual and, I hope, fruitful angle. The fourth and fifth questions must be put on hold for the time being; one eventual test of the hypothesis will of course be the extent to which it makes sense precisely at those points.

I should emphasize again, in case of possible objections, that this study of worldview and mindset, of aims and beliefs, is a matter of history, not of psychology. We can sometimes say more or less *what* happened (Caesar was murdered). We can sometimes also find out more or less *why* it happened (his imperial ambitions made staunch republicans anxious). The second of these questions involves us in the study of human motivation, which can be approached ultimately through the full worldview model; this full-scale study is necessary if we are to avoid the danger of anachronism, of projecting current preoccupations backwards into earlier times. But this remains a matter of history, not covert psychology. Our claim about the conspirators' motivations does not imply that we have interrogated Brutus and Cassius on the psychiatrist's couch.

Two other final notes. First, there is a problem as to the general word we should use to describe what Jesus was up to. If we were to speak of Jesus' 'ministry', we might envisage him as a Protestant pastor preaching from a pulpit. 'Ministry' is certainly now too 'religious' a word to do justice to Jesus within the highly integrated worldview of first-century Judaism. 'Career' is better, but, by contrast, it may seem too 'secular'; we might find ourselves thinking of Jesus as a young executive on the way up.[50] 'Work' and 'activity' are too general, and seem to spotlight deeds to the exclusion of words; 'teaching', also too general, makes the opposite mistake. 'Vocation' strikes an important note, but relates to Jesus' inner attitude to what he was

---

[50] Though cf. Meyer 1979, frequently, e.g. 220f.

doing, rather than to the activity itself. 'Campaign' is in some sense as close as we can come to what Jesus was doing, but suffers from the severe drawback of evoking the picture of either a military operation or the preparation for an election. One cannot simply say 'life', because we shall be focusing almost exclusively on the last short period of Jesus' life, during which he went about doing and saying things that, so far as we know, he had not been doing and saying up to that time. I am not aware of a good solution to this problem, and shall therefore use a variety of these terms, always with this proviso: that, if it is true that Jesus ultimately fits no known pattern within the first century,[51] it is more or less bound to be true that he fits none within the twentieth. I hope that by the end of this book the various inadequate words will be seen as what they are: pointers to a different reality for which at the moment we have no very suitable vocabulary. We should not be surprised, still less alarmed, at such a possibility.[52]

Second, a word about the relationship between my arrangement of material (in which the 'mindset' (Part II) is followed by the 'aims and beliefs' (Part III)), and Ben Meyer's clear and important distinction between the 'public' and the 'esoteric', the open and the secret, aspects of Jesus' work.[53] I endorse the appropriateness of Meyer's programme as one way of going about the necessary analysis. In a sense it may look as though my Parts II and III correspond straightforwardly to his 'public' and 'esoteric'. In Part II, however, though the main focus is on what could be known or inferred of Jesus' mindset from his public proclamation of the kingdom, we shall necessarily be examining some aspects which remained more or less private to him and his disciples. In Part III, likewise, though we shall be looking at the more private beliefs and aims of Jesus, we shall also be examining some very public incidents, such as the entry into Jerusalem, the action in the Temple, and of course the crucifixion. Meyer's distinction remains important, but I have not made it an exact organizing principle in the present work. The model I hammered out in *NTPG* is different, though certainly complementary, and that is the one I have followed.

By such means, I suggest, history may be written: a penitent history, I hope, not arrogantly seeking to take over the family home, but a history that should be welcomed as what it is. The historical method I have described offers itself as the long and dusty road back to reality, to confrontation, and perhaps to reconciliation.

---

[51] So Harvey 1982, 113, with reference to Jesus' healings.

[52] On the problem of language and its reference cf. *NTPG* 63.

[53] cf. Meyer 1979, chs. 7 and 8; cf. his 129, 174f., 220-2; and frequently in Meyer's other work on Jesus, e.g. 1992a & b.

Part Two

Profile of a Prophet

Chapter Five

THE PRAXIS OF A PROPHET

1. Jesus' Career in Outline

What would the average Galilean have perceived as Jesus came through the village? What categories would have been available for understanding what was going on? How did Jesus himself regard these basic categories? Only when we have asked these questions is it safe, historically speaking, to work forwards and ask about the other aspects of his mindset, and hence also about his beliefs and his aims.

It is quite easy to lay out a brief list of things that few will deny about Jesus' life and public activity.[1] He was most likely born in what we now call 4 BC (the calculation of the BC/AD divide took place in the sixth century, based on limited information).[2] He grew up in Galilee, in the town of Nazareth, close to the major city of Sepphoris. He spoke Aramaic, some Hebrew, and probably at least some Greek.[3] He emerged as a public figure in around AD 28, in the context of the initially similar work of John the Baptist.[4] He summoned people to repent (in some sense, to be discussed later), and announced the kingdom, or reign, of Israel's god, using parables in particular to do so. He journeyed around the villages of Galilee, announcing his message and enacting it by effecting remarkable cures, including exorcisms, and by sharing in table-fellowship with a socio-culturally wide group. He called a group of close disciples, among whom twelve were given special status.[5] His activities, especially one dramatic action in the Temple, incurred

[1] Cp. the summary accounts in works as divergent as Perrin & Duling 1982 [1974], 411f.; Sanders 1985, 11, 326f.; Crossan 1991a, xi–xiii; Meier 1991, 406f. Perrin's summary, which takes less than a page, concludes with a now notorious phrase: 'that, or something very like it, is all we can know; it is enough'. There are, of course, still some who deny that Jesus existed, and others who try out speculative theories without much regard for the evidence: e.g. Clayton 1992.

[2] cf. Sanders 1993, 11f.; Meier 1991, 375f.

[3] Full discussion: Meier 1991, 255–68; cf. Porter 1993. mSot. 9.14 assumes that C1 Jews normally learned at least some Greek at home.

[4] On the chronology, see esp. Meier 1991, 372–433; and e.g. Robinson 1985, ch. 3.

[5] cf. Meyer 1979, 153f.; Sanders 1985, 95–106; and below, 169, 299–301. The evidence is found in 1 Cor. 15.5; Mt. 19.28; Ac. 1.16–20; the lists of names, not identical, are in Mt.

the wrath of some elements in Judaism, notably (at least towards the end) of the high-priestly establishment. Partly as a result of this, he was handed over to the Romans and executed in the manner regularly used for insurrectionists. His followers claimed, soon afterwards, that he had been raised from the dead. They carried on his work in a new way, and some of them were persecuted for doing so, both by Jews and by pagans.

Some would question this or that detail of this list, and we will discuss these problems as they arise. Some would include more at this basic level. What we have here is enough – not for us to say everything that can and must be said about Jesus, but for us to find our necessary starting-point for further investigation.

We can fill in the bare outline with a few more details, most of which are comparatively non-controversial.[6] All through the gospels we find Jesus performing certain habitual actions, which, taken individually and together, contribute in no small way to our total picture of his career. Part of his paradoxical persona consisted of certain styles of activity that cannot be reduced to terms either of teaching (though they often provided the occasion for teaching) or of mighty works (though they were sometimes associated with, or closely parallel to, mighty works of one sort or another). This activity formed the basic raw material of the ministry, the context within which teaching and mighty works took place.

Jesus engaged in an itinerant ministry. This took him into synagogues, into private houses, into the open countryside, including non-Jewish territory. Sometimes he met with his followers in secret, sometimes he appeared in public. At least once, but possibly quite frequently, he travelled to Jerusalem and carried on his activities there, and on the last occasion the journey took on something of a new overtone. He was often to be found in prayer, not merely on formal and public occasions, i.e. when attending the synagogue,[7] but informally and in private contexts, sometimes in lonely places.[8] Among the characteristics of his prayer-life we must of course note his use of 'Abba' as an address for Israel's god. It used to be thought that

---

10.2–4; Mk. 3.16–19; Lk. 6.14–16; Ac. 1.13. Cf. too the texts in Funk 1985b, 476–81. The story of the five-year-old Jesus making twelve clay sparrows on the sabbath, and causing them to fly, seems to reflect the same knowledge of Jesus' use of the symbolism of the number 12: cf. *In. Thom.* 2.1–5.

[6] i.e. this list is no more tendentious than most, and certainly less so than e.g. Crossan 1991a, xi–xxvi. Parts of it depend, of course, on arguments yet to be advanced.

[7] Mk. 1.21, 29/Lk. 4.33, 38; Mt. 4.23; 9.35/Mk. 1.39; Mt. 12.9/Mk. 3.1/Lk. 6.6; Mt. 13.54/Mk. 6.2; Lk. 4.16 ('as was his custom'); 4.44.

[8] Not, of course, that this, any more than the formal sort of prayer, was or is unknown in Judaism. Cf. Mk. 1.35/Lk. 4.42; Lk. 6.12; Mt. 11.25–7/Lk. 10.21–2; Mt. 14.23/Mk. 6.46; Mk. 9.29; Lk. 9.28. On Jewish prayer-customs see e.g. Safrai 1976b, 800f.

this address was unique, and that it was a child's familiar term, meaning 'Daddy'. Both of these ideas have been shown to be misleading.[9] 'Abba' remains, however, a form of address which, if not unique, is particularly distinctive of Jesus. Apart from an early period in the wilderness[10] he did not fast – which distinguished him and his followers from other pious Jews.[11] He sat loose to family commitments, in a way which must have been felt and perceived by both family and onlookers as puzzling and offensive.[12] This attitude to his own family was reflected in the shocking demands for family disloyalty that he made on his followers.[13]

In particular, he ate and drank with all sorts and conditions of people, sometimes in an atmosphere of celebration.[14] He ate with 'sinners', and kept company with people normally on or beyond the borders of respectable society – which of course, in his day and culture, meant not merely social respectability but religious uprightness, proper covenant behaviour, loyalty to the traditions and hence to the aspirations of Israel.[15] This caused regular offence to some of the pious, and we will consider in due course why this was so. For the moment we note that his table-fellowship was a sufficiently well-known and striking feature of his regular style to be commented on, and for him to respond to such comment in various ways. Like many other of his actions, this table-fellowship became seen as a further way in which the kingdom was actually being inaugurated.

It is, of course, possible in theory that this whole picture is pure fabrication. Someone in the very early church might conceivably have started rumours of Jesus behaving in this way when in fact his style and conduct was quite different. But this can be confidently ruled out as highly improbable. (a) All our sources, however we analyse them, point back in this direction. (b) This activity carries the marks of the appropriate similarities and appropriate dissimilarities of which we spoke earlier. Jesus' actions make sense within his Jewish context, and within the socio-cultural world of Galilee in particular, and they make sense also as the precursor of some

[9] For other Jewish uses of 'Abba', cf. Vermes 1973, 210f., citing mBer. 5.1 and bTaan. 23b; for 'Abba' as not meaning 'Daddy' cf. Barr 1988. See below, 262f., 648f.
[10] Mt. 4.1-11/Mk. 1.12-13/Lk. 4.1-13, on which see below, 457-9.
[11] Mt. 9.14-17/Mk. 2.18-22/Lk. 5.33-9.
[12] Mt. 12.46-50/Mk. 3.31-5/Lk. 8.19-21/*Thom.* 99/*GEbi.* 5; Lk. 11.27-8/*Thom.* 79.
[13] Mt. 8.21f./Lk. 9.59-62; Mt. 10.37/Lk. 14.26/*Thom.* 55.1f. (cf. *Thom.* 101.1-3); Mt. 19.29/Mk. 10.29/Lk. 18.29; etc.
[14] Mt. 9.10-13/Mk. 2.15-17/Lk. 5.29-32; Mt. 11.16-19/Lk. 7.31-4; Lk. 15.1-2; 19.1-10. 'All sorts and conditions' here includes not only outcasts but also Pharisees: Lk. 7.36-50; 14.1-6.
[15] Against Horsley 1987, 212-23. Horsley's picture of Jesus as sharing the social agenda of the Jewish peasants does not allow him to entertain this possibility.

aspects of the early mission of the church.[16] At the same time, these actions presented a challenge to certain aspects of the Jewish worldview, and were not imitated easily or readily by the church as a whole. (c) For what it is worth, almost all serious contemporary writers about Jesus would agree that something like this activity was indeed characteristic of him.[17] We may therefore safely conclude that Jesus habitually went about from village to village, speaking of the kingdom of the god of Israel, and celebrating this kingdom in various ways, not least in sharing meals with all and sundry. These actions and words must therefore be seen not as incidental behaviour, irrelevant to his worldview or mindset, but as part at least of the praxis through which we can bring that worldview into focus.

What sort of worldview, then, might such praxis reveal? And what sort of mindset begins to emerge as Jesus' own variant on that worldview? I want now to argue that the best initial model for understanding this praxis is that of a prophet; more specifically, that of a prophet bearing an urgent eschatological, and indeed apocalyptic, message for Israel. This, of course, corresponds to many 'Third Quest' studies, as opposed to some within the renewed 'New Quest', for whom the specific hope of Israel has been set aside in favour of a 'sapiential' outline of Jesus as simply a teacher of wisdom. The model of Jesus as prophet also, as we shall see, has the capacity to function as a basis for further study which will draw in many other features of Jesus' life and work which may otherwise remain on the margins.

One of the strongest arguments for the prophetic portrait is the sense it makes in the total context of Judaism in general, of popular movements in particular, and of John the Baptist above all. We must look briefly at each before proceeding further.

2. Jesus' Context

(i) First-Century Judaism

We have already studied the wider context within which what Jesus was doing would have made whatever sense it did (*NTPG* Part III). First-century Judaism, with all its pluriformity, had certain dynamics running through it, not least an undercurrent of potential or actual revolution. This was not confined to the lowest social classes, but enjoyed the support of at least some Pharisees and, eventually, even some aristocrats.[18] Tacitus says that in

---

[16] cf. Theissen 1978.

[17] So Boring 1992, 498.

[18] cf. *NTPG* 170-81 (movements of revolt); 185-95 (Pharisaic involvement); 210 (aristocratic involvement).

Tiberius' reign (AD 14–37) all was quiet in Palestine; what he means, as we have seen, is that there was no major war such as would necessitate calling for intervention from the legions, stationed in Syria.[19] But there is plenty of evidence for revolutionary movements smouldering away throughout the period, coming into explicit confrontation with the authorities from time to time as opportunity offered or pressure to revolt became intense. The extent to which these movements were automatically committed to violence is very difficult to assess. Sometimes violent intent was there from the start. Sometimes those who followed a new leader seemed to assume that their god would intervene on their behalf, as had happened when the walls of Jericho fell before Joshua and his company. But at least we can be sure of this: anyone who was heard talking about the reign of Israel's god would be assumed to be referring to the fulfilment of Israel's long-held hope.[20] The covenant god would act to reconstitute his people, to end their exile, to forgive their sins. When that happened, Israel would no longer be dominated by the pagans. She would be free. The means of liberation were no doubt open to debate. The goal was not.

What would a *prophet* be doing in such a setting?[21] It used to be common to say that in the first century prophecy was regarded as having ceased, and there is some evidence which points in this direction.[22] Jews in the second century BC spoke of waiting for a prophet to come, in the tone of voice of people who do not imagine that this will happen very soon. In 1 Maccabees 4.46, Judas and his companions store the stones of the defiled altar in a convenient place 'until a prophet should come to tell what to do with them'. In 14.41 of the same book, Simon is appointed leader and high priest 'until a trustworthy prophet should arise'. In both cases the prophet is seen as the one who would reveal the will of YHWH on matters of the highest importance. In the former passage, the prophet will effectively have authority over the Temple; in the latter, over the present royal and priestly regime. Both of these might be thought to point to a more-than-prophetic role, namely that of the coming king who would have authority over the Temple and, naturally, over any temporary royal house. At the same time, there is no obvious reference to Deuteronomy 18, and no suggestion that this prophet would

---

[19] Tac. *Hist.* 5.9; cf. *NTPG* 172, and, rightly, Crossan 1991a, 100–2. Until AD 66 the Roman army in Palestine was small: see e.g. Safrai 1992, 104. For a full treatment of the Roman presence in the middle east, stressing the political turbulence and the Roman problems in controlling it, see now Millar 1993, esp. chs. 2, 10.

[20] On the meaning of 'kingdom of god' in this period cf. *NTPG* 302–7, and below, 202–9. The hope goes back to such classic passages as Isa. 52.7–12.

[21] On the following cf. esp. Hill 1979; Aune 1983; Boring 1992; Gray 1993, with other bibliography.

[22] cf. Meyer 1992a, 29; Gray 1993, ch. 1; Sommer 1996.

necessarily be the only one who would arise in the future.[23] As far as these texts are concerned, then, prophecy is not available in the present time, and when it returns all sorts of crucial elements in Israel's life will be differently ordered. Some rabbinic texts, too, seem to indicate a sense that prophecy had come to a stop.[24] The phenomenon of the *Bath Qol*, the 'daughter of a voice', should not be taken as counter-evidence, since it is a more indirect phenomenon, a substitute for the direct revelation to the true prophet.

However, in each of these cases we are right to be a little suspicious of the evidence.[25] 1 Maccabees, written to undergird the authority of the Hasmonean regime, would be unlikely to acknowledge as truly prophetic any oracles that challenged this upstart royal house, and the nod in the direction of a possible future prophet is most likely to be seen as a pious gesture. (It should not be pressed into service, either, as evidence for a lively expectation of a specific prophet, perhaps the one spoken of in Deuteronomy 18.18.) The rabbis, not least in the second century (when their traditions began to take written form), were concerned above all with the supremacy of Torah (and of themselves as its accredited interpreters), and with the renunciation of revolution in favour of Torah-piety. It suited this double agenda to declare, or imply, that old-fashioned prophecy, especially if it carried revolutionary overtones, had come to an end.[26]

One grain of truth in the idea of the cessation of prophecy is no doubt to be found in the absence, at least since Daniel, of written prophetic material being included within the developing canon.[27] This certainly seems to be what Josephus means when he writes of the failure of an exact succession of prophets in the second-Temple period. He is thinking specifically of the prophets as historians, and explaining that, though the history of Israel right up to his own time has indeed been written, the more recent material is not accorded equal weight with the work of the 'former prophets', i.e. the historical books of the Hebrew Bible.[28] To this extent at least, a form of 'prophecy' had ceased.

Prophecy of various sorts, however, seems to have continued unchecked in the second-Temple period.[29] Among the best and most recent analyses is

---

[23] For the postponement of important decisions until the arrival of a prophet, cf. Ezra 2.63, Neh. 7.65. The Maccabaean expectation of a prophet is linked to the theme of the cessation of prophecy by e.g. 1 Macc. 9.27.

[24] e.g. mAb. 1.1; bYom. 9b.

[25] cf. e.g. Aune 1983, 103–52.

[26] cf. Leivestad 1973.

[27] This does not depend on any particular view of the process and date of the canonization of the OT. For differing views cf. Beckwith 1985; Barton 1986; J. A. Sanders 1992.

[28] cf. *Apion* 1.41.

[29] cf. Horsley & Hanson 1985, ch. 4, and esp. Webb 1991, ch. 9.

that of Robert Webb, who discusses the sources and possible categorizations very thoroughly, and offers his own variation. He distinguishes three basic types. First, there were 'clerical prophets', holders of priestly (and perhaps also royal) office, possessing prophetic powers apparently in virtue of their office. This applies particularly to John Hyrcanus, and to Josephus himself.[30] Second, there were 'sapiential prophets', wise men belonging to various sectarian groups such as the Essenes,[31] or the Pharisees.[32] We may perhaps add in this cluster a reference to Philo and the author of Wisdom, for whom prophecy was still a live possibility, and occurred as and when 'wisdom' inspired people.[33] Third, there were 'popular prophets', with a further subdivision: 'leadership popular prophets' and 'solitary popular prophets'.

These last two categories denote prophets who emerged from, and appealed to, the ordinary people of Palestine, without the benefit of office or scribal learning. They are described by Josephus in various places.[34] First, he uses the term to describe revolutionary leaders such as Theudas, 'the Egyptian', and the prophet who, towards the end of the siege in 70, persuaded 6,000 Jews to stay in a portico of the Temple, hoping in vain for 'the signs of salvation'.[35] Josephus comments bitterly that there were many prophets at this time in the pay of 'the tyrants', promising salvation in order to stop people deserting to the Romans, and so blinding the inhabitants of Jerusalem to the signs, both natural and supernatural, that their doom was near.[36] A

---

[30] cf. *War* 1.68f./*Ant.* 13.282f., 299f., 322 (John Hyrcanus); *War* 3.351–4; 3.399–407; 4.622–9; cp. *Life* 208–11 (Josephus writing of himself, possibly on the model of Jeremiah; cf. e.g. Daube 1980; Gray 1993, ch. 2; on *War* 3.352 cf. Rajak 1983, 18f., 169–72, 185–92; Gray 1993, 52–70). Cf. also *Ant.* 11.333 (the High Priest Jaddus); 17.345, 352 (Archelaus and his wife Glaphyra).

[31] e.g. *War* 1.78–80; 2.159; *Ant.* 13.311; 15.373–9; 17.345–7. For the community reflected in the Scrolls, the Teacher of Righteousness functioned in some ways as a prophet, though his role was more, like that of Daniel, as an interpreter of mysteries. The word 'prophet' is not used of the Teacher, but he is said to have received words 'from the mouth of God' (1QpHab. 2.2f.), which amounts to much the same thing. On his interpretation of mysteries cf. 1QpHab. 7.4–7.

[32] *Ant.* 17.41–5, with Webb 1991, 326f.; *Ant.* 14.172–6 (cf. the similar account in 15.3f.), with Webb 327–31.

[33] Wis. 7.27; Philo, *Heres* 259 (speaking of Abraham and the other patriarchs, but implying that the gift of prophecy continues).

[34] cf. Horsley & Hanson 1985, 135f., 160–89; Webb 1991, 333–46; Gray 1993, chs. 4–5.

[35] *Ant.* 20.97–8; *War* 2.261–3, *Ant.* 20.169–72; *War* 6.284–5. Webb 1991, 340 cautiously classifies the last of these as a 'solitary', partly because he did not start an actual 'movement'; but anyone who leads 6,000 people, even for a short time, is hardly solitary. Clearly the categories must be allowed flexibility. Cf. too the groups described in *War* 2.258–60; 6.286, 288; on the former (including the possibility that they were Pharisees), see *NTPG* 192; on the latter, Webb 341; on the wider issue, cf. esp. *NTPG* 170–81.

[36] *War* 6.286–8.

second, different sort of prophet, promising no salvation, gathering no following, but only announcing disaster, is typified in Jesus the son of Ananias,
who despite punishment proclaimed the coming doom throughout the war
until he was himself killed in the Roman attack.[37] These, then, are Webb's
two types, 'leadership popular prophets' and 'solitary popular prophets'.
(Webb points out that Horsley's distinction of 'action prophets' and 'oracular
prophets' ignores the fact that the 'action prophets' also uttered oracles in
order to gain, and give directions to, their following.)

The first type, copying Moses or Joshua, attempted, with promises of salvation, to initiate and lead a movement of liberation. The second, copying
some parts at least of the work of the classical Hebrew prophets, announced
oracles which warned of impending doom. From the examples already given
it is clear that all the above categories could and did overlap. It is risky to
project artificially clear twentieth-century distinctions (e.g. those between
scribal and peasant activity) back on to the screen of what was clearly a very
confused social setting.

In some technical senses, then, 'prophecy' might be held to have ceased in
the second-Temple period, but in all sorts of ways it was still very much
alive and well.[38] Certainly the general populus thought so. And it is in this
context, I shall argue presently, that we can credibly locate both John the
Baptist and Jesus of Nazareth. The gospels fit them both into this context and
setting, and it is highly unlikely that the early church, which had come to
evaluate Jesus in several other more important ways, made this up. Both
belong here, even though both, in different ways, broke the moulds from
which they came. Somebody announcing a message from Israel's god, which
might include both warnings of coming disaster and promises of coming
deliverance, belongs broadly in a context that was not unknown, even if the
precise contours of their message differed somewhat from what other
prophets had offered.

One feature of 'leadership prophets', and also of some of the others
described above, is of enormous importance for the subsequent argument of
this book. We have seen that the prophets who gained a following often
engaged not only in teaching and oracular pronouncements, but also in symbolic actions. These regularly involved leading people into the wilderness,
often around the Jordan. They sometimes appear to have focused on a stylized symbolic entry into the land, with the apparent expectation and promise
that Israel's god would act dramatically as he had done at the time of the
exodus. These symbolic actions were not random. No historical purpose is

---

[37] *War* 6.300–9.

[38] This conclusion is, I think, only tangentially at odds with Sommer 1996; it all depends
on a precise definition of 'prophecy' itself.

served by ignoring the fact that people who act in this way, as leaders or as led, do so in obedience to a controlling story, a metanarrative which underlies their whole programme and agenda. The sense of expectation which induced this strange behaviour is, quite simply, only explicable if we understand those involved to have been obedient to an underlying story within which their actions made sense. Nor do we have to look very far to see what sort of story this might be. It was a story in which Israel's long night of suffering and misery would soon be over, and the new day would dawn in which Israel's god would act, at last, as king of all the world:

> These movements were oriented toward the deliverance of those peasants from the oppression and dissatisfaction they felt toward their lot. These prophetic figures called the people to gather together and participate in a symbolic action reminiscent of their past religious heritage, especially the events associated with the Exodus and Conquest. The prophetic figures evidently promised the people that the deliverance would take place by divine intervention. These prophetic movements appear to have had an eschatological dimension.[39]

Retelling, or re-enacting, the story of the exodus, then, was a classic and obvious way of pre-telling, or pre-enacting, the great liberation, the great 'return from exile', for which Israel longed. Moreover, the 'popular' prophets in particular seem to have been informed by the memory of the great classical prophets, not least the prophetic ministry of Moses and Joshua.[40] We are here in touch with part of what we will later see to be bedrock within the Jesus-tradition. It was as a prophet in this basic mould, acting symbolically in ways that would be understood, and were designed to be understood, according to this basic metanarrative, that Jesus made his decisive impact on his contemporaries.

All this, however, raises the question: what exactly was the social context in which such prophetic movements could thrive? Some recent work has given great prominence to the concept of 'banditry', and to that we now turn.

(ii) Bandits, Peasants and Revolt

One particular manifestation of the drive towards revolution is seen in the sociological fact of banditry. The word 'bandit' (*lestes* in Greek) was, of course, loaded: it meant someone doing something of which the present authorities, and perhaps the writer, disapproved. As far as Josephus was concerned, the normal Roman definition worked quite well: any opposition to the governing forces which did not require a major military operation to put

---

[39] Webb 1991, 347.
[40] So Horsley & Hanson 1985, 136–46, followed by Webb 1991, 348.

it down was 'banditry'.[41] An enemy whom one does not deign to acknowledge as such is a 'bandit'; putting down such an enemy counts as glorified police action, rather than the more serious business of actual 'war'. This enabled the official line to remain intact: bandits were simply common criminals, and could be treated as such, rather than with the grudging respect accorded a noble foe.[42]

So far, so good. But the undoubted fact of first-century banditry has been given a new twist by Richard Horsley, building on the work of the British social historian Eric Hobsbawm, and followed, though with modifications, by Dominic Crossan. In this reading, the banditry is actually 'social banditry'. This phrase has come to mean three things in particular. (a) It refers, first, to a 'Robin Hood' type of banditry: the outlaws are supported and encouraged by the local peasant community, since they are seen as fighting the community's battles against their social, political and economic oppressors.[43] (b) In Horsley's reading, second, this produces a scenario in which the Jewish Palestinian peasant population, though not themselves involved in violence, were tacitly supporting the violence of the bandits. This violence, Horsley stresses, was a second stage in the 'spiral of violence', following the first-order violence whereby Rome, like so many before her, was holding her subjects in check. Setting Jesus within this context enables Horsley to suggest that he basically supported the peasants in their attitude, and was himself inaugurating a new form of social, though as yet non-violent, protest. In order to sustain this thesis Horsley has to argue, further, (i) that there was no serious movement of violent revolution in Jesus' lifetime, so that he cannot be imagined to be protesting against such a thing, and (ii) that Jesus, in supporting the social protest of the peasantry, would not have offered any support or welcome to those, such as tax-collectors and prostitutes, who were flouting the tight-knit and basically anti-Roman communal stance of the peasantry. (c) Third, Crossan has developed the idea of 'social banditry' in such a way as to make the phrase denote, not so much the 'Robin Hood' style of life in which the noble bandits were supported by a grateful peasantry, but the sociological phenomena in which the bandit moves ambiguously 'between unpower and power, between the peasant class and the governing class'.[44]

What are we to make of all this?[45] It is seriously misleading, as I have

---

[41] Crossan 1991a, 452 gives a useful summary of key references to banditry in Josephus.

[42] So Crossan 1991a, 171–4, following Shaw 1984; on Josephus' use of the idea, Crossan 174–206.

[43] cf. Hobsbawm 1965, 1972, 1973a & b, and esp. 1985 [1969]; Horsley 1979, 1981, 1986, 1987; Horsley & Hanson 1985; Crossan 1991a, ch. 9.

[44] Crossan 1991a, 170.

[45] I am very grateful to my former student Paula Gooder for letting me borrow from her as yet unpublished research in this area.

already shown, to imagine that serious violent revolution was not on the agenda in the 20s of the first century AD. The 'Zealots' themselves emerged as a clear-cut group later on, in the 60s; but this did not represent a major change of direction, a turning to serious paramilitary violence by a group previously committed only to 'social banditry'.[46] Further, Horsley's suggestion that Jesus did not after all welcome social outcasts into the kingdom flies in the face not only of most recent study, but of the strong historical argument that the early church would have been most unlikely to invent such a theme, and to weave it so thoroughly into the traditions about Jesus, were it not firmly grounded.

Hobsbawm's own thesis, developed in any case in relation to data from quite different periods and settings to those of first-century Palestine, has been subjected to damaging objections even in its own terms. Blok pointed out that Hobsbawm's theories about social bandits were based more upon poems and ballads than upon the actual study of bandits in real-life situations, and were thus, though more broadly based than specific case-studies could be, flavoured with a romanticism which tended to pull the actual history quite severely out of shape.[47] He points out that actual bandits are quite capable of abandoning the peasants from whom they are supposed to have emerged, and siding with the oppressors.[48] Others have argued that banditry does not arise merely from peasant communities, but can take root in a wide variety of settings,[49] and that, when the phenomenon of banditry is studied in relation to Africa, Hobsbawm's model is of only limited use in a far more complex situation.[50] Hobsbawm, responding to Blok, said that his main point was the social *ambiguity* of the bandits – a point also stressed by B. D. Shaw and, as we saw, developed by Crossan.[51] But this reduces significantly the usefulness of the theory as a support for Horsley's argument; and the actual case-studies of bandits in Galilee reveal this problem quite clearly.[52] Horsley's apparent neat identifications (a) of bandits as social bandits, (b) of social bandits as noble heroes of a grateful peasantry, (c) of Jesus as a peasant social revolutionary who, by implication, would have supported such banditry, and (d) of the fundamentally non-revolutionary nature of such

---

[46] cf. *NTPG* 170-81.

[47] Blok 1972, 1988 [1974].

[48] This point is strongly supported by Taylor 1987, e.g. 113; Perez 1989.

[49] O'Malley 1979.

[50] Austen 1986, esp. 101-3. Cf. too Fernyhough 1986, on northern Ethiopia: 'banditry in Ethiopia appeared as a form of rebellion at once more primitive and more sophisticated than that described by Eric Hobsbawm' (165).

[51] Shaw 1984; Crossan 1991a, 171-4.

[52] cf. esp. Freyne 1988a.

banditry until just before the war in the mid-60s AD, falls apart at every seam.[53] Crossan's more nuanced use of Hobsbawm and Shaw does not seriously stitch these identifications together again, but concentrates on ramming home a somewhat different point, that the rhetoric of power and its legitimation sound mightily ambiguous when the brutal force of empire is confronted with the sporadic violence of the bandit:

> What was a bandit but an emperor on the make, what was an emperor but a bandit on the throne? . . . The line between the personalized violence of the bandit gangs and the institutionalized violence of the state armies was far harder to justify in theory than to maintain in practice . . . Rural banditry holds up to agrarian empire its own unpainted face, its own unvarnished soul.[54]

This, it seems to me, carries a self-evident truth, even though Crossan, like all passionate rhetoricians, may have oversimplified things somewhat. His point certainly helps to explain why the Romans took the phenomenon of banditry so seriously. But it does not support the Hobsbawm-Horsley line, according to which the bandits were in implicit and constant league with the peasant population. Indeed, the 'corrosive ambiguity' of banditry 'on social, economic, political, and juridical levels'[55] demonstrates precisely the impossibility of sustaining a definite and lasting bandit-peasant link, far less a theory about Jesus based on such a foundation.

In addition, as Freyne says, 'it would be ironic if, having dismantled one construct, the Zealots, we were to replace it by another, that of social banditry'.[56] By no means all the 'bandits' we meet in Josephus were in fact outlaws; Josephus was indulging in the ancient art of polemical definition. In particular, not every actual bandit was a *social* bandit, a quasi-Robin Hood, supported by the peasants, and perceived by them to be acting in their interests.[57] In fact, serious banditry is more characteristic of Judaea than Galilee in the period under consideration. This is not to say that Galilee did not produce its revolutionary movements; merely that the pressure in that direction was not as strong as it was further south.[58]

---

[53] As Crossan 1991a, 184 suggests, 'the First Roman-Jewish War almost started in 52 C.E., and it almost started among peasants and bandits rather than among aristocrats and retainers'. His evidence is a critical reading of Jos. *War* 2.239–46 and *Ant.* 20.125–36.

[54] Crossan 1991a, 172, 174. Crossan suggests that Blok is superficially correct (in denying Hobsbawm's romantic Robin-Hood picture of social bandits) but profoundly wrong (in that banditry does in fact 'rob the monopoly of violence from the rich and distribute it to the poor', 304f.). I take his point; but we are then no longer talking about *social* banditry, which was the focus of Hobsbawm's work, and of Horsley's use of it, but banditry in general. We are then moving, also, further and further away from a probable scenario for Jesus.

[55] Crossan 1991a, 174.

[56] Freyne 1988a, 51.

[57] Freyne 1988a, 62.

[58] So Freyne 1988a, 54f., following his earlier argument (1980b). Together, Freyne's two major books (1980b, 1988b) and his various articles (1980a, 1987, 1988a, 1992) form

We may conclude as follows:

(a) The situation was confused enough at the time, and may only become more so by the partial application of social theories based on other times and places.[59]

(b) There was indeed widespread banditry of various sorts in the Palestine of Jesus' day.

(c) Some but not all of this banditry was supported for some but not all of the time by some but not all peasants.

(d) The line between banditry and serious revolutionary violence is artificial, and at best very blurred and easy to cross.

(e) Though serious revolution was more likely to occur in Judaea, it was by no means impossible in Galilee.

(f) The Romans, and the Jewish authorities, took banditry seriously as a force to be reckoned with.

(g) The relationship between banditry as such and other popular movements was likely to have been extremely fluid.

In other words, though Horsley and Crossan are right to highlight the social context of the various movements in the period, it is impossible to use the sociological category of banditry, whether 'social' or otherwise, to set up a rigid grid of categories into which Jesus must be made to fit. In particular, it would be wrong to suggest that there was no undercurrent of violent revolutionary intentions in the world addressed by Jesus, and hence to deduce that Jesus could not have been speaking of, or to, such violent movements. It would be equally misguided to insist that, in speaking of the kingdom, Jesus must have been aligning himself with the peasant aspirations that may have led some within that class to support, for some of the time, such actual 'banditry' as there was. Jesus cannot be pinned down that easily.

Equally, if it was heard that someone was proclaiming that Israel's god was at last becoming king, it makes no sense at all to imagine the average

---

the best possible answer to the suggestion of Mack (1993, ch. 4) and others that the interests of Galileans would only be marginally or minimally Jewish: see esp. e.g. Freyne 1987, 607, speaking of 'an old and deep-seated attachment to Jerusalem and its temple' and 'a shared symbolic world-view, of which the Jerusalem temple was the central focal point' as characterizing Galilean Jews. (See further the collection of essays edited by Levine (1992a).) In fact, Mack's arguments point in the opposite direction from his own conclusions: precisely because Galilee was a heavily mixed-race area, the Jews who lived there would be more, not less, likely to cling fiercely to their ancestral traditions, and to maintain as best they could the symbols of their distinctiveness.

[59] Crummey 1986 demonstrates the wide variety of types of social protest in contemporary Africa, and the difficulty of applying any one model to that continent in our own century. How much more should we be wary of taking a simplistic thesis based on folk-legends and transferring it wholesale to the Palestine of the first century.

Palestinian Jew, of whatever locality, enquiring diligently what manner of movement this might be. If the kingdom was really coming, it made sense to join in. So, at least, we may judge from the two movements to which we now turn: those of John and Jesus.

(iii) John the Baptist

All agree that Jesus began his public work in the context of John's baptism. This has been recently studied in great depth, and we do not need to repeat this work here.[60] The major features are now mostly uncontroversial. John was clearly a figure of some importance and notoriety in the late 20s of the first century, a well-known, puzzling and disturbing phenomenon. He was an 'oracular' prophet, in that he was announcing oracles of woe upon Israel if she did not repent. At the same time, unlike some other oracular prophets, he gathered followers around him and gave them sufficient coherence to continue as a group after his death. Josephus takes note of him, as he does of other prophetic figures.[61] John announced imminent judgment on the nation of Israel, and urged her to repent, warning that her status as YHWH's covenant people would not be enough, by itself, to deliver her from the coming disaster.

This activity was, clearly, 'political' as well as 'religious', partly in that Herod Antipas may well have been a prime target of John's invective,[62] but also because anyone collecting people in the Jordan wilderness was symbolically saying: this is the new exodus. Anybody offering water-baptism for the forgiveness of sins was saying: you can have, here and now, what you would normally get through the Temple cult.[63] Anybody inviting those who wished to do so to pass through an initiatory rite of this kind was symbolically saying: here is the true Israel that is to be vindicated by YHWH. By implication, those who did not join in had forfeited the right to be regarded as the covenant people. In these ways, completely credibly within the history of first-century Judaism, what John was doing must be seen, and can only be seen, as a prophetic renewal movement within Judaism – a renewal, however, that aimed not at renewing the existing structures, but at replacing them. Though the synoptic gospels give John's attack on Herod Antipas' marital arrangements as the reason for his arrest, it is likely that there were

---

[60] cf. above all Webb 1991; and cp. e.g. Scobie 1964; Wink 1968; Meyer 1979, ch. 6; Hollenbach 1992. Crossan 1991a, 227–38 is flawed but none the less highly suggestive.

[61] *Ant.* 18.116–19, fully discussed by Webb 1991, ch. 2.

[62] cf. Hollenbach 1992, 894f.

[63] cf. Webb 1991, 203–5.

wider reasons as well. 'Desert and Jordan, prophet and crowds, were always a volatile mix calling for immediate preventive strikes.'[64]

From a strictly historical point of view, then, we are bound to see John as more than simply an oracular prophet. As Webb sees, John had begun to put together the two types of prophecy distinguished by Horsley and others ('oracular' and 'leadership') into a new and explosive combination. Oracles of doom coupled with a movement for renewal spoke of eschatological events, of divine promises and warnings at last coming true, and of the need to be part of the true people of YHWH when the great moment came. In addition, though John does not seem to have been associated directly with any sect or school of scribal activity, his location and some aspects of his praxis give at least a hint of parallels with the Essenes. He is not, in Webb's classification, a 'sapiential' prophet, but he is not as far removed from that group as some 'leadership' prophets.[65] Moreover, John's family was priestly, and his activity of offering a baptism for forgiveness out in the desert presented a clear alternative to the Temple. Though he was not a 'clerical' prophet like those figures in Josephus whom Webb characterizes thus, this background, and this aim, at least suggest that he was what we might call a 'counter-clerical' prophet.[66] There are senses, then, in which John could at least be associated with all three types of second-Temple prophet (clerical, sapiential, and popular), though he belongs most exactly within the first sub-type within the latter category (leadership).[67]

As we shall see, it is clear that Jesus regarded John as an important fixed point at the beginning of his own ministry. The early church, faced with a group of continuing Baptist disciples, would hardly have invented the connection. There is good reason to think that John himself did indeed prophesy a coming figure who would complete the work that he had begun, and that Jesus applied this to himself.[68] Though John seems at a later stage, while in prison, to have been puzzled by what Jesus was doing (and more particularly, it appears, by what he was not doing), Jesus continued to regard him as the

[64] Crossan 1991a, 235. For the attack on Herod's marriage to his brother's wife, cf. Mk. 1.14; 6.17f./Mt. 14.3f.; Lk. 3.19-20. Cf. too Mk. 10.1/Mt. 19.1f., which, setting the divorce pericope (Mk. 10.2-12/Mt. 19.3-9) in the region where John had been preaching, may indicate that the question was a political trap, inviting Jesus to make a rash comment about Herod's marital arrangements. I owe this point to Professor Colin Brown.

[65] cf. Webb 1991, 351.

[66] cf. Webb 1991, 350f.; Horsley & Hanson 1985, 178f.

[67] See above, 152-4. Cf. Webb 1991, 350-5, disagreeing with Horsley & Hanson 1985, 175-81, who classify John as 'oracular', and hence as solitary. Horsley and Hanson are at least, in my judgment, correct to plot the socio-political significance of John in the way they do, though Webb is obviously correct, not least in view of the continuance of a group of John's disciples (Ac. 19.1-7), to see John as a leader rather than a solitary.

[68] cf. Webb 1991, 196f., 261-306; more cautiously, Hollenbach 1992, 895f.

advance guard for his own work, both as the chronological and theological starting-point for his own ministry, and as in some senses the role model for his own style, the pattern with which he would begin.[69] This leads us to set out the major category of Jesus' public persona, which forms the setting for everything else that follows. Though his followers came to regard him as more than a prophet, they never saw him as less.

3. Jesus as 'Oracular' and 'Leadership' Prophet

The early church is highly unlikely to have invented the many sayings, isolated but telling, scattered throughout the gospels, which call Jesus a prophet. Several of them are on his own lips. By the time the gospels were written down, the church had come to believe that Jesus was much more than a prophet. It might well have seemed risky theologically to refer to him in this way: it might have appeared that he was simply being put on a level with all the other prophets. It is therefore extremely probable that these sayings represent thoroughly authentic tradition. The arguments advanced in chapter 2 above should be sufficient to make us wary of accepting the main alternative reading currently available, namely that Jesus was a teacher of aphoristic wisdom only, and that the 'prophetic' traits in the gospel portraits are to be ascribed to a stage in the development of the early church.[70]

Before we look at the sayings in question, there are two other lines of thought which we must leave to one side. First, was Jesus in any sense a 'charismatic', or even a 'charismatic of charismatics'?[71] He attracted crowds. He was dynamic, exciting, and offered people new hope and a new focus for their aspirations. He was powerfully aware of the divine spirit at work in him, as in prophets of former days. This picture certainly has some appeal, and considerable historical plausibility. But by itself it is too unspecific.[72] For a start, it is possible to distinguish far more sharply between different Jewish figures of the period than the 'charismatic' label suggests: in the title of a recent book, there were 'bandits, prophets and messiahs', whose movements can be systematically differentiated and categorized, who may all in some senses have been 'charismatic', and who cannot usefully be lumped

---

[69] On John's puzzlement: Mt. 11.2-6/Lk.7.18-23; Jesus' view of John in relation to himself: Mt. 11.7-19/Lk. 7.24-35, cf. Mk. 9.11-13; *Thom.* 46, 78; Lk. 16.16; Mk. 11.27-33/Mt. 21.23-7/Lk. 20.1-8; Jesus being seen as John *redivivus*: Mk. 6.14; 8.27f.; 9.11-13/Mt. 17.9-13. On all this see the suggestive remarks of Meyer 1992a, ch. 2.

[70] cf. Boring 1992, 498. Cf. too Riesner 1984 [1981], 276-98.

[71] Vermes 1973, ch. 3; Dunn 1975, ch. 4; Rivkin 1984.

[72] cf. Harvey 1982, 107.

together in one vague general group.[73] Second, discussions of Jesus as prophet have often focused too soon, and too exclusively, on whether Jesus was perceived to be, or whether he perceived himself to be, '*the* prophet' – that is, the one like Moses predicted in Deuteronomy 18.18-19, who was to be the new deliverer.[74] This seems to have been what we would now call a type of messianic expectation, and is a much more limited category than those discussed above, following Horsley and Hanson and in particular Webb. The best evidence for Jesus being seen as *the* prophet, on the lines of Deuteronomy 18, is not in the synoptic gospels, but in John 1.21, 6.14, and 7.40, and in Acts 3.22.[75] There is no particular reason why this should not be historical, and indeed it may well be that, in the midst of the confused state of things, different observers would have come up with all kinds of different ideas about who Jesus was and what his movement signified, of which this would just be one. But the great bulk of the relevant evidence does not point to Jesus being seen in terms of Deuteronomy 18.

Rather, I suggest that Jesus was seen as, and saw himself as, *a* prophet; not a particular one necessarily, as though there were an individual set of shoes ready-made into which he was consciously stepping, but a prophet like the prophets of old, coming to Israel with a word from her covenant god, warning her of the imminent and fearful consequences of the direction she was travelling, urging and summoning her to a new and different way. This is not to say that Jesus did not regard his prophetic ministry as in some way unique, and able to be combined with other roles. It certainly does not rule out the possibility of him, and/or his followers, regarding his work as in some way climactic within Israel's long story. As we shall see, this is in fact highly likely to have been the case. It is simply to stress that we cannot confine the investigation to the use, explicit or implicit, of Deuteronomy 18 and the figure of 'the prophet' mentioned there; and that the initial impression made on Jesus' hearers would not have been that Jesus was claiming to be a particular figure, of whom they had had advance expectations. Rather, I shall now suggest that he was announcing a prophetic message after the manner of 'oracular' prophets, and that he was inaugurating a renewal movement after the manner of 'leadership' prophets. He was, in fact, to this extent very like John the Baptist, only more so.

[73] Horsley & Hanson 1985.

[74] See e.g. Vermes 1973, 86-99. Vermes, noting correctly that Jesus is regarded as a prophet in the gospels, passes on to consider the question of Dt. 18, without probing further into the actual role and task of the ordinary prophet. By regarding Elijah as the role model for the Hasid, rather than for other types of Jewish holy men (e.g. 102), Vermes effectively removes the ministry of announcing judgment from the role of the prophet.

[75] cf. too 1QS 9.11; 4Q175 5-8.

Was he also in any sense a 'clerical' prophet? There is no evidence of his belonging to the priestly class. Webb's classification of 'clerical' prophets, however, includes kings and other rulers. Since there is *prima facie* evidence, which we will discuss later on, to connect Jesus with some kind of kingly claim or perception, it may be that we should not entirely rule this category out altogether.[76] Also, Jesus, like John, was doing and saying things which posed a challenge of sorts to the current Temple hierarchy. Pending discussion of the relevant material, we should perhaps hold open for the moment the possibility of his being seen as a counter-clerical prophet.

Was he also in any sense a 'sapiential' prophet? It is very unlikely that Jesus belonged to any of the sects of his day. Attempts to make him a Pharisee or an Essene have not proved convincing. Nevertheless, both in style and in content a good deal of his teaching shares the features that Webb lists as characteristic of 'sapiential' prophets. Jesus seems to have made the interpretation of scripture, not least of the biblical prophets, a significant part of his work; based on this, he warned of a threat hanging over the Israel of his day, not least over her rulers; his time spent in prayer, and the report of his visionary experiences,[77] testify to his being at least regarded as the sort of person, who, like the devout Essenes, might be expected to possess the gift of prophecy.

Since the prophetic aspect of Jesus' work is often surprisingly ignored, it will be as well to set the texts out *in extenso*, with very brief comments:

> Jesus said, 'A prophet is not without honour except in his own country and in his own house'.[78]
>
> In reply to Jesus' question, 'Who do people say that I am?', the disciples replied, 'Some say John the Baptist, others say Elijah, others one of the prophets.'[79] Though Jesus goes on to ask a further question, it is clear from the present list that he regarded this answer not as wrong or misleading but as the first level of true understanding.
>
> When Jesus arrived in Jerusalem, Matthew, in the midst of making it quite clear that he thinks Jesus is coming as Messiah, has the pilgrim crowds respond to the Jerusalemites' question, 'Who is this?', by, 'This is the prophet Jesus from Nazareth of Galilee.'[80]
>
> After the parable of the wicked tenants, in which Jesus portrayed himself as, by implication, the last in the line of the prophets, Matthew says that those who wished to arrest Jesus feared the crowds, 'because they held him to be a prophet'.[81]

---

[76] See below, ch. 11.

[77] e.g. Lk. 10.18. Cf. the analyses offered by Borg (1987a, 1994a & b).

[78] Mt. 13.57/Mk. 6.4; cf. Lk. 4.24 (the latter, in context, comparing Jesus with Elijah and Elisha).

[79] Mk. 8.28/Mt. 16.14 (adding Jeremiah to the list)/Lk. 9.19 (with 'one of the old prophets has arisen' instead of the last phrase). Cf. too Mt. 10.40–1.

[80] Mt. 21.11.

[81] Mt. 21.46.

When Herod hears about Jesus and what he is doing, his instant reaction is that John the Baptist has been raised to life; others in his retinue suggest that he is Elijah or one of the other prophets of old.[82]

The response of the crowds to the healing of the widow's son at Nain is not (as we might have expected, if the story had been 'written up' with the full colours of later christology) that Jesus is the Messiah, the son of god, or whatever, but that 'a great prophet has arisen among us'.[83]

When the Pharisee sees the woman 'who was a sinner' worshipping Jesus lavishly, he says to himself, 'if this man were a prophet, he would have known . . .'; in other words, the incident is casting doubt on whether Jesus really is the prophet he is claiming to be. The claim is thus common coin; Jesus' response shows that he knows not only all about the woman, but all about the Pharisee too. The claim is thus implicitly vindicated.[84]

When warned about Herod's threats, Jesus replies to 'that fox' that it is impossible for a prophet to perish away from Jerusalem. He here accepts not only the role, but also the fate, of the prophet.[85]

We may add, too, the references in John, to which the same comment applies. The Samaritan woman perceives 'that Jesus is a prophet'; the rulers mock at Jesus, saying that 'no prophet comes from Galilee'; the man healed from blindness says of Jesus, 'he is a prophet'.[86]

The mocking of the guards consists partly in their invitation to Jesus to prophesy who it is that is hitting him. This makes sense only if Jesus is known to be regarded as a prophet, and is charged with being a false one.[87]

When the disciples on the road to Emmaus are asked why they are sad, they begin to speak about Jesus, 'a prophet mighty in word and deed'.[88] Whatever the historical status of the story, this detail has certainly not been invented to suit a later christology.

This accumulation of evidence is already impressive. In terms of hypothetical source-criticism, we have material here from triple tradition, from Matthew's special material, from Luke's special material, and from John. Apart from Acts 3.22 there is nothing in the New Testament, outside the gospels, about Jesus as a prophet.[89] It appears that the early church quickly left this category behind in their understanding of Jesus and his work. The only alternative conclusion is to suggest that Jesus and his very first followers did not think in this way; that quite soon a widespread tradition of Jesus as a prophet grew up in several different circles, represented in these texts but not in Paul; and that it just as quickly died away again. This, I submit, strains historical credibility past breaking point. It is far more likely that we are here in touch with firmly authentic tradition, preserved against all the tendencies that may be presumed

[82] Mk. 6.14–16/Mt. 14.1–2/Lk. 9.7–9.

[83] Lk. 7.16.

[84] Lk. 7.39–50.

[85] Lk. 13.33: see ch. 12 below.

[86] Jn. 4.19; 7.52; 9.17. Cf. the other Jn. refs. noted above in relation to Dt. 18.

[87] Mk. 14.65/Mt. 26.68/Lk. 22.64.

[88] Lk. 24.19.

[89] cf. too Ac. 7.37. There is nothing, either, in *Thomas* or Q. This is perhaps why the theme has been marginalized in the 'Jesus Seminar'.

to have been at work. Even though the gospels quite often hint at a 'Moses-typology',[90] there is, as we have seen, only tangential allusion to the specific idea of a 'prophet like Moses'. This portrait of Jesus as a prophet seems the most secure point at which to ground our study of Jesus' public career, and in particular of his characteristic praxis.

Equally impressive are the strong hints, throughout the gospels, that Jesus was modelling his ministry not on one figure alone, but on a range of prophets from the Old Testament. Particularly striking is his evocation of the great lonely figure Micaiah ben Imlach (1 Kings 22), who, when asked about the coming battle, predicted the death of Ahab, king of Israel, by saying, 'I saw all Israel scattered upon the mountains, as sheep that have no shepherd.'[91] Jesus, looking at the crowds, takes pity on them, because that is what they remind him of: leaderless sheep.[92] Like Ezekiel, Jesus predicts that the Temple will be abandoned by the Shekinah, left unprotected to its fate.[93] Like Jeremiah, Jesus constantly runs the risk of being called a traitor to Israel's national aspirations, while claiming all the time that he nevertheless is the true spokesman for the covenant god. This, as we shall see, lies behind a good part of the story of Jesus' action in the Temple, and his subsequent 'trial': Jesus has predicted the destruction of the Temple, and is on trial not least as a false prophet.[94] Jesus replies to earlier critics and questioners with the sign of the prophet Jonah. Jonah was predicting imminent judgment on Nineveh, following his adventure with the fish; Jesus is predicting imminent judgment on Israel, and a similar sign will validate his message too.[95] He is constantly redefining what the coming day will mean for Israel, warning her, like Amos, that it will be a day of darkness, not of light.[96] Like Amos, too, he implies that the people of god are to be judged as the climax of the divine judgment upon all nations. The judgment which he announces upon Israel is

---

[90] e.g. Mt. 2–4; cf. *NTPG* 388f.

[91] 1 Kgs. 22.17.

[92] Mt. 9.36/Mk. 6.34; cf. Mt. 10.6; 15.24; Mk. 14.27; Lk. 15.6; etc., and of course Jn. 10. The image of sheep and shepherd evokes Ezek. 34 as well: see ch. 11.

[93] Ezek. 10.1–5, 15–22; 11.22–3; cf. Mt. 23.38/Lk. 13.35.

[94] Jer. 7, esp. v. 11; cf. Mt. 21.12–13/Mk. 11.15–19/Lk. 19.45–8, cp. Jn. 2.13–22. For the charge of 'false prophet', cf. Dt. 13.1–3; for the 'trial', including the charge relating to a prophecy of the Temple's destruction: Mt. 26.57–68/Mk. 14.53–62/Lk. 22.54–71; Jn. 2.19; *Thom.* 71. See below, chs. 9, 12. Further echoes of Jer. may be found in the tradition: cf. Jer. 11.16 and Lk. 23.31, with ref. to the context of Jer. 11.18–20.

[95] Mt. 12.38–42/Lk. 11.29–32. This may suggest a model for one particular aspect of Jesus' proclamation, namely the time-span of a generation. There are other reasons for this as well, which we will see later; but, as Jonah was saying, 'Yet forty days, and Nineveh shall be overthrown,' so Jesus was saying, by implication, 'Yet forty years, and Jerusalem shall be overthrown.'

[96] Amos 5.18–20. For the redefinition and the resulting warning, see ch. 8 below.

sketched with the help of prophetic passages relating to the judgment of Jerusalem by Babylon, and also, more terrifyingly, passages which speak of the divine judgment upon Babylon itself.[97]

Above all, Jesus adopts the style of, and consciously seems to imitate, Elijah. Here we are again in an interesting position *vis-à-vis* the sources. It is clear from all three synoptics that they, and presumably with them the early church as a whole, regarded John the Baptist as in some sense Elijah *redivivus*.[98] They nevertheless portray Jesus as acting in Elijah-like ways, and show that the disciples were thinking of Elijah-typology as giving them a blueprint for his, and their own, activity.[99] Jesus himself, explaining the nature of his work, is portrayed using both Elijah and Elisha as models.[100] Again, it is highly unlikely that the early church, seeing Jesus as the Messiah and hence John as Elijah, created this identification out of nothing. However, at the same time, though John himself seems to have thought that Jesus was to be the new Elijah, Jesus actually returned the compliment.[101] We begin here to see both parallel and distinction. Jesus' ministry is so like that of Elijah that they can be easily confused. He too is announcing to the faithless people of YHWH that their covenant god will come to them in wrath. But at the same time he is also acting out a different message, one of celebration and inauguration, which bursts the mould of the Elijah-model.

From all of this it should be clear that Jesus regarded his ministry as in continuity with, and bringing to a climax, the work of the great prophets of the Old Testament, culminating in John the Baptist, whose initiative he had used as his launching-pad. Though not a solitary prophet, as we shall see presently, he was certainly an oracular prophet. This is how his contemporaries must have seen him, and did in fact see him. Like Elijah or Jeremiah, Jesus was proclaiming a message from the covenant god, and living it out with symbolic actions. He was confronting the people with the folly of their ways, summoning them to a different way, and expecting to take the consequences

---

[97] Judgment of Jerusalem: Lk. 19.41–4; of Babylon (cf. Isa. 13.10): Mk. 13.24f. Cf. ch. 8.

[98] In addition to Mt. 3.1–12/Mk. 1.2–8/Lk. 3.1–20 (whose echoes of Elijah-symbolism emerge in e.g. Webb 1991, 250–4), cf. Mt. 17.12f./Mk. 9.13.

[99] Lk. 7.11–17 is very close to 1 Kgs. 17.17–24; 2 Kgs. 4.32–7. In Lk. 9.51–5, James and John want to call down fire from heaven, as Elijah had done. This shows that, though ultimately the identification was not endorsed (Jesus rebuked them), it was one which he had to risk by many similarities. See too the instructive parallel between Mt. 8.21f and 1 Kgs. 19.20. On this theme cf. Robinson 1962, 28–52.

[100] Lk. 4.25–7. The proposal of Bostock 1980, that Jesus saw himself as the new Elisha, following John's Elijah, is in some ways suggestive; but there is no sense that Jesus regarded himself as John's *junior* partner, once his own ministry had been launched.

[101] Mt. 3.11–12/Lk. 3.16–17, cf. Jn. 1.21; Mt. 11.2f./Lk. 7.18f.; Mt. 17.12f./Mk. 9.13.

of doing so. We are here, historically speaking, on certain ground. And the picture is indeed a striking one. John the Baptist had said it was not enough to be a physical child of Abraham, and had denounced the ruling Herod. Elijah had stood alone against the prophets of Baal, and against the wickedness of King Ahab. Jeremiah had announced the doom of the Temple and the nation, in the face of royalty, priests and official prophets. Though all had followers, all were politically lonely figures. All were accused of troubling the *status quo*. When people 'saw' Jesus as a prophet, this was the kind of model they had in mind.

4. A Prophet Mighty in Word and Deed

(i) Jesus as a 'Leadership' Prophet

We may, then, start on firm ground: Jesus' public career was that of an 'oracular' prophet. As soon as we develop the picture, however, we see that he also clearly belongs in the other category of 'popular' prophets. He gathered around him a group of followers, and acted in various symbolic ways which indicated, for those with eyes to see, that the great exodus, the real return from exile, was at last on its way. Israel's god would act powerfully within history, and Jesus would lead his people to salvation. He was, in Horsley's terms, an 'action' prophet; in Webb's, a 'leadership' prophet; or, as Luke would have it, 'a prophet mighty in word and deed'.[102]

He conducted his work by going from village to village in Galilee, gaining support there while apparently omitting the larger centres of population like Tiberias or Sepphoris, for reasons which we will look at later.[103] Sometimes he assembled large groups of his followers in the wilderness, and on at least one occasion performed symbolic actions there reminiscent of the events of the exodus.[104] His work thus has close analogies with that of some of the other 'leadership' prophets, not least John. It is quite possible that Jesus copied John, to begin with at any rate, in baptizing those who adhered to his teaching; the disciples encouraged people to be baptized at the beginning of Acts, but there is no record of their having undergone such a baptism themselves except, by implication, at the time of John. This point should not be overplayed, since a baptism in Galilee would not have had the same geographically symbolic function (that of evoking the exodus) as one in, or near, the Jordan, in the wilderness. Anyway, Jesus seems to have intended

---

[102] Lk. 24.19 (cf. Ac. 7.22, a similar phrase describing Moses).
[103] Below, ch. 9.
[104] Mt. 14.15–21/Mk. 6.35–44/Lk. 9.12–17/Jn. 6.1–15; cf. Mt. 15.32–9/Mk. 8.1–10.

that what he was doing should be seen as in continuity with what John had been doing. Again, the early church, for whom a continuing movement associated with John was an embarrassment, continued to stress Jesus' close ties with John himself. Luke emphasizes *both* that Jesus' followers dated their point of origin from John's baptism *and* that they were clearly distinguished from the continuing groups of John's disciples.[105]

That Jesus had followers, and regarded them in some ways as a 'leadership' prophet would, is completely secure in the tradition. Nobody doubts that Jesus called disciples, and regarded them as a distinct group.[106] This creates a context in which it makes sense, despite some recent doubts, for Jesus to give his followers a special prayer, and to speak of them as a new community, a 'little flock'.[107] He explained what he was doing, as we shall see in more detail later, in terms of the *reconstitution of Israel*.[108] This again echoes the work of John, who saw his disciples, we may certainly suppose, as the nucleus of the renewed people of God; and the tradition of this sort of thing goes back at least as far as Isaiah of Jerusalem.[109] The wilderness setting of some of Jesus' actions fits this picture well; this, again, is not the sort of thing that the early church, aware of the political implications of such activities, would readily have made up without some solid base in the life of Jesus.

Already, therefore, we find Jesus deliberately adopting a praxis which can function in our investigation as the way in to the discovery of his mindset, his own variant on the worldview of those around him. He was combining in a new way the prophetic styles of oracular prophets on the one hand and leaders of renewal movements on the other. John had combined them already, but not like this. Jesus went further in at least three directions: he was itinerant; he gave extensive teaching which, as we shall see, carried a note of even greater urgency than that of John; and he engaged in a regular programme of healing. We must look at each of these in turn as we fill in this initial prophetic portrait. At each point the double criteria of similarity and dissimilarity can be invoked. This outline of Jesus' praxis is thoroughly credible within a first-century Jewish context, and makes good sense as part of the presupposition of the early church; at the same time, this praxis breaks the moulds of the Jewish context, and is, in detail, significantly unlike the characteristic activity of most of the early Christians. Mozart's music is

---

[105] Ac. 1.22; 10.37; 13.24f.; 18.25; 19.1–7.

[106] Sanders 1985, 326 includes this as one of the basic 'key facts' about Jesus. Cf. too Riesner 1984 [1981], ch. 5.

[107] Prayer: Mt. 6.9–13/Lk. 11.2–4/*Did.* 8.2. Flock: Lk. 12.32.

[108] cf. Meyer 1979 and Sanders 1985, *passim.*

[109] cf. e.g. Isa. 8.16–18. Cf. Meyer 1979, 210–19.

incredible without Bach and Haydn as its predecessors, yet it is strikingly different from both; it is the necessary presupposition for Beethoven and Schubert, yet is still gloriously distinct. Jesus' prophetic work makes historical sense, yet remains in a class of its own.

(ii) An Itinerant Prophet

The fact that Jesus was an *itinerant* prophet meant, clearly, that he went from village to village, *saying substantially the same things* wherever he went.[110] Local variations would no doubt abound. Novelty would spring up in response to a new situation, or a sharp question or challenge. But the historical likelihood -- and it is very likely indeed – is that if he told a parable once he told it dozens of times, probably with minor variations; that if he gave a list of (what we call) 'beatitudes' once, he gave such a list, probably with minor variations, dozens of times; that he had regular phrases with which he urged repentance, commended faith, encouraged the desperate, rebuked those he considered hard-hearted, spoke words of healing. The chances of his finding totally new things to say all the time, so that everything he said he said once and once only, must be reckoned at nil. Theissen's picture, of those who had heard him comparing memories and coming up with similar, though not identical, ways of retelling his stories, rings thoroughly true.[111]

We have already mentioned the enormous implications that this has for synoptic criticism. Within the peasant oral culture of his day, Jesus must have left behind him, not one or two isolated traditions, but a veritable mare's nest of anecdotes, and also of sentences, aphorisms, rhythmic sayings, memorable stories with local variations, and words that were remembered because of their pithy and apposite phrasing, and because of their instantly being repeated by those who had heard them. Again and again he will have said cryptic words about having ears to hear, about the first being last and the last first, about salt and light, and particularly about Israel's god and his coming kingdom. My guess would be that we have two versions of the great supper parable, two versions of the talents/pounds parable, and two versions of the beatitudes, not because one is adapted from the other, or both from a single common written source, but because these are two out of a dozen or more possible variations that, had one been in Galilee with a tape-recorder, one might have 'collected'. Anyone who suggests that this is not so must, I think, either be holding on doggedly to the

---

[110] For this point, cf. *NTPG* 422–4.
[111] Theissen 1987; cf. again Bailey 1991.

picture of the early church which I criticized in the first volume, or be in thrall to a highly dogmatic view of scripture, or simply have no historical imagination for what an itinerant ministry, within a peasant culture, would look like. Even the anachronistic semi-parallel of a modern travelling lecturer or preacher will make the point: once one hears the lecture or sermon two or three times, even if it is delivered impromptu with local variations, one will be able to reproduce considerable parts of it. One may accurately guess that any of Jesus' followers who had been with him for even a few days could have told some of Jesus' stories, or announced some of his characteristic words of welcome and warning, with close accuracy to the original.

Remembering that Jesus was an itinerant prophet should help us to keep the different aspects of his work in their proper balance. Sayings and deeds form a single whole, and must be studied as such.[112] The different artificially divided parts of the ministry must be allowed to be mutually informative. The distinction of 'word' and 'deed' has clear warrant in Luke 24.19, and we shall follow it in setting out the material in the remainder of this chapter. But we should not suppose that it represents a sharp disjunction between two unrelated entities. Jesus' contemporaries would have found that very odd indeed.

(iii) Mighty in Word

(a) Authority and the Kingdom

Jesus was known, among many other things, as someone who could speak with power and authority. But it is the *sort* of things he said which marked him out in particular. When the synoptic evangelists say that 'he taught as one having authority, and not as the scribes', they are not merely referring to his tone of voice. Nor are they simply saying that, instead of quoting learned authorities upon which he relied (or even debating the rights and wrongs of the opinions of some rabbinic school), he appeared to be founding a new school of his own, a new branch of Torah-interpretation. Rather, they are saying something, backed up by all the words they record, about the actual *content* of his proclamation. Jesus was announcing a message, a word from Israel's covenant god. He was not simply reshuffling the cards already dealt, the words of YHWH delivered in former times. Modern western culture does not have too many obvious models for the kind of thing he was doing, and that may be just as well; if we did, we might be tempted to make them fit

[112] cf. Downing 1995.

despite residual anachronisms. But we may catch something of the required flavour if we say that Jesus was more like a politician on the campaign trail than a schoolmaster; more like a composer/conductor than a violin teacher; more like a subversive playwright than an actor. He was a herald, the bringer of an urgent message that could not wait, could not become the stuff of academic debate. He was issuing a public announcement, like someone driving through a town with a loudhailer. He was issuing a public warning, like a man with a red flag heading off an imminent railway disaster. He was issuing a public invitation, like someone setting up a new political party and summoning all and sundry to sign up and help create a new world. He was, in short, in some respects though not all, quite similar to the other 'leadership' prophets of the first century. The fact that he was not arrested sooner was due to his itinerant style, and to his concentration on villages rather than major cities, not to anything bland or unprovocative about the content of his message.[113]

For this reason (among others), the old picture of Jesus as the teacher of timeless truths, or even the announcer of the essentially timeless call for decision, will simply have to go. His announcement of the kingdom was a warning of imminent catastrophe, a summons to an immediate change of heart and direction of life, an invitation to a new way of being Israel. Jesus announced that the reign of Israel's god, so long awaited, was now beginning; but, in the announcement and inauguration itself, he drastically but consistently redefined the concept of the reign of god itself. In the light of the Jewish background sketched in *NTPG* Part III, this cannot but have been heard as the announcement that the exile was at last drawing to a close, that Israel was about to be vindicated against her enemies, that her god was returning at last to deal with evil, to right wrongs, to bring justice to those who were thirsting for it like dying people in a desert. We are bound to say, I think, that Jesus could not have used the phrase 'the reign of god' if he were not *in some sense or other* claiming to fulfil, or at least to announce the fulfilment of, those deeply rooted Jewish aspirations. The phrase was not a *novum*, an invention of his own. It spoke of covenant renewed, of creation restored, of Israel liberated, of YHWH returning. It can be reduced neither to a general existential state of affairs, unrelated to Israel's national hope, nor to a hypothetical 'parousia' hope (which the early church first invented, then cherished, then projected back on to Jesus, and then finally abandoned), nor to the offer of a new type of private spirituality.[114]

---

[113] For attempts to arrest Jesus cf. e.g. Lk. 13.31.

[114] Against the general tenor of the 'Jesus Seminar': see above, ch. 2, and Funk 1991, 52; and also against e.g. Vermes 1993, ch. 5, esp. 130, 137, 146–50. See further below, chs. 6–9.

At the same time, of course, a good deal of the preaching of Jesus, at least as set out in the synoptic tradition, consists of parables and other sayings in which he is patiently, but often cryptically, redefining the meaning of the term 'kingdom of god'. *This* is what the reign of Israel's god is like: it is like seed growing secretly, like treasure hidden in a field, like leaven in a lump, like a net full of all sorts of fish. This presents us with a puzzle. Is Jesus simply changing the meaning of the term entirely, like somebody saying 'this is what Beethoven's Fifth Symphony really means', and handing us a wet fish, or perhaps a hand grenade?[115] Or is he (as Buchanan argues) offering a cryptic programme of revolution: this is how the kingdom will come, the violent revolution for which you have been waiting – with small beginnings, with plans kept secret until the harvest time when at last we shall put in the sickle?[116]

The answer, I believe, is neither of these. I shall spell this out in much more detail in the following chapters; but it is important at the moment to get an idea of the general picture. Jesus was affirming the basic beliefs and aspirations of the kingdom: Israel's god is lord of the world, and, if Israel is still languishing in misery, he must act to defeat her enemies and vindicate her. Jesus was not doing away with that basic Jewish paradigm. He was reaffirming it most strongly – and, as I shall argue later, in what he saw as the only possible way. He was, however, redefining the Israel that was to be vindicated, and hence was also redrawing Israel's picture of her true enemies. This, after all, has good historical parallels; it was the basic move made in some way or other by every Jewish sect, including the followers of John, and the Essenes, and the various factions during the war of 66–70. Jesus, then, was offering the long-awaited renewal and restoration, but on new terms and with new goals. He was telling the story of Israel, giving it a drastic new twist, and inviting his hearers to make it their own, to heed his warnings and follow his invitation.

But what would this involve? George Caird, in a private letter written in 1982, declared: 'It must be possible to see what course Israel should follow if she were to heed the warning.' Jesus' moral teaching, so-called, cannot be reduced to the level of timeless ethics. At that level, it apparently made some stringent demands, but much of it was not particularly new. Nor can it be seen simply as instruction for the ongoing life of 'the church', in the sense of

---

[115] cf. Sanders 1985, 329: 'If [Jesus] meant [kingdom] only symbolically (it represents the call to submit oneself to God), then we would have to conclude that he completely deceived his disciples, who continued to expect a kingdom. The view that Jesus was entirely deceptive and misled his disciples into false hopes, while spinning parables which can be unravelled only by twentieth-century literary analysis, must be rejected.'

[116] Buchanan 1984, 208–12.

a new community to be founded after Jesus' death; no Galilean villager would have known what to make of such an idea. Nor was it simply, at the opposite extreme, an *Interimsethik* (Schweitzer's term), a sort of martial law relevant only for the short time between the start of Jesus' public ministry and the end of the world. If we take seriously the public persona of Jesus as a prophet, the material we think of as 'moral teaching', which has been categorized as such by a church that has made Jesus into the teacher of time-less dogma and ethics, must instead be thought of as *his agenda for Israel.* This is what the covenant people ought to look like at this momentous point in their long story.

The gospels portray Jesus as 'teaching' in a variety of ways. Sometimes, of course, in parables; sometimes in shorter epigrammatic sayings, nuggets of wisdom or summaries of complex issues; sometimes, it seems, in more extended discourses. There is no reason *a priori* why Jesus could not have taught in extended discourses; indeed, there is quite good reason to suggest that he did. The attempt to make one of these various styles of teaching the norm, and to question the historicity of the others on that basis, stands on very thin historical ice. This is not to say, of course, that the discourses as we have them are by any means stenographic reproductions of what was said on this or that particular occasion. The reasons why Jesus' followers at the time, and after Easter, remembered, collected, and edited such material, and transmitted it in circumstances which materially shaped it and gave it, per-haps, new focal points, must be studied elsewhere. But, within the persona of a prophet, who was engaged in carrying out new ways of *being* a prophet, there is no reason to deny, and every reason to affirm, that the different genres of sayings and teachings that we find in the gospels present in princi-ple a coherent overall picture. In worldview terms, this total praxis relates directly to the broad category of 'story'. Jesus made a regular practice of retelling the story of Israel in such a way as to subvert other tellings, and to invite his hearers to make his telling of the story their own. That will be the theme of the next three chapters of this book.

(b) Parables

The best-known form of Jesus' proclamation is of course his use of explicit stories, namely the parables.[117] We will look at the parables in some detail

---

[117] This discussion builds on that in *NTPG* 433f. A recent highly provocative treatment of the parables has emerged from the 'Jesus Seminar': Funk, Scott & Butts 1988. Students of that work will note several interesting contrasts between it and the present discussion, result-ing from the fundamental differences of approach outlined in ch. 2 above.

during the course of the next four chapters; at this stage we must say something about their form and style, by way of continuing our initial sketch of Jesus as he would have been perceived by his contemporaries, the bemused villagers who stood in doorways, who gathered round in little clumps, brought their sick people on stretchers to be healed, and swarmed out to the countryside to hear him talk about Israel's consolation. Scholarly interpretation of the parables tends always – and surely rightly – to be a function of a particular view of Jesus' career (and/or of the nature and purpose of the gospels), rather than a free-standing entity. It is therefore important to include a general consideration of them at this stage, within the treatment of Jesus' characteristic praxis.[118]

The first thing to be said is that the parables followed well-known Jewish lines. Several of them are taken from Old Testament models: the vine or vineyard is a regular image for Israel, the sheep and shepherd speaks of Israel and her king, and so on. Several have analogies with other more contemporary Jewish sources: a steward and a master, or a son and a father, speaks at once of Israel and her god.[119] Several are, in their present form in the synoptic tradition, quite close to apocalyptic discourse: a strange story is interpreted so that its secret symbols may be understood by those with ears to hear. This means, as we saw in the previous chapter, that the stories would already be functioning at a variety of levels. They are not totally new; their message sounds in some ways familiar; yet they tend to have new twists within the uncomfortable familiarity. They seem designed, within the worldview of the Jewish village population of the time, as tools to break open the prevailing worldview and replace it with one that was closely related but significantly adjusted at every point. Jesus was not saying 'throw away your Jewish aspirations, and think about music, or philosophy, or pie in the sky when you die'. Nor was he simply declaring a plague on all houses

---

[118] The literature on parables is of course vast, including piecemeal but important discussions in commentaries, in most books about Jesus and/or the kingdom (cf. chs. 1–3 above), and in innumerable articles. I have found the following works helpful, though disagreeing with all of the authors at some points and with some of them at most points: Dodd 1961 [1935]; Jeremias 1963a [1947]; Wilder 1971 [1964], esp. ch. 5; 1982; Crossan 1973; 1992; Boucher 1977; Bailey 1983 [1976, 1980]; Drury 1985; Wenham 1989. Other recent useful works include Kissinger 1979 (a full history of interpretation, with bibliography); Perkins 1981; Stein 1981; Lambrecht 1983 [1976]; Donahue 1988; Young 1989; Blomberg 1990. Detailed mapping of, or navigation within, this great river of tradition is clearly impossible in a work such as this.

[119] cf. Magonet 1988, 143, discussing the Hasidic parable of the king whose son, the prince, goes mad and has to be rescued by a wise man: 'The king in such parables is usually God, and the prince would thus be the Jewish people, so far destroyed by exile as to forget their royal rank and status as the children of God. The wise man [is] perhaps the messiah . . .'

except those of radical-minded peasants, as one might think from reading some contemporary scholars. Jesus was articulating *a new way of understanding the fulfilment of Israel's hope*. He had radicalized the tradition. This, as has often been remarked in recent years, is how stories work. They invite listeners into a new world, and encourage them to make that world their own, to see their ordinary world from now on through this lens, within this grid. The struggle to understand a parable is the struggle for a new world to be born.

Talking about Israel's god by means of telling stories is, in fact, a peculiarly good way of going about such a task. Most of the Old Testament consists of stories about Israel and her god, and cannot be reduced to terms of formulae, to be studied or put into test-tubes. This is not accidental. The main Jewish traditions have to do with the *story* of the creator and the cosmos, of the covenant god and his people. Old Testament thought does not fall easily into detached abstractions or timeless verities. Though, of course, its rich traditions encompass a wide variety of genres, it is narrative, not the unstoried world of the detached aphorism or the mystical insight, that is its underlying mode.[120]

It should therefore be clear that the parables, by their very form, place Jesus firmly within his Jewish context. The genre itself puts into effect that double-edged message of welcome and warning which is the parables' regular actual theme. The parables are not simply *information about* the kingdom, but are part of the *means of* bringing it to birth. They are not a second-order activity, talking about what is happening at one remove. They are part of the primary activity itself. They do not merely give people something to think about. They invite people into the new world that is being created, and warn of dire consequences if the invitation is refused. Jesus' telling of these stories is one of the key ways in which the kingdom breaks in upon Israel, redefining itself as it does so. They also function, for the same reason, as explanation and defence of what Jesus is doing. As Meyer argues, the parables are not merely *theme*, they are also *performance*. They do not merely talk about the divine offer of mercy; they both make the offer, and defend Jesus' right to make it.[121]

This understanding of how stories, and particularly parables, work does not mean, as has often been suggested, that the purpose of the parables was simply to break open worldviews without having anything definite to put in their place.[122] The *means by which* they 'work', which can be and has been

---

[120] cf. Frei 1974; Alter 1981; and many other recent works.

[121] Meyer 1979, 162. On the functioning of parables cf. too Riches 1988.

[122] See, e.g., Perrin 1976, 196: 'The challenge of the message of Jesus was to recognize the reality of the activity of God in the historicality of the hearer's existence in the world.' This is explicitly a dehistoricized, deJudaized, existential reading, like that of Bultmann (so

analysed with various modern tools, cannot of itself tell us the *purpose towards which* they are directed. That would be like analysing a human being into physical, chemical and biological components, leaving us still with no idea of who the person actually *is*. When this point is added to the recent correct recognition that the so-called 'allegory' form of some of the parables is neither necessarily late nor necessarily non-Jewish, but actually belongs in the most intimate way within Judaism,[123] the parables can and must be understood as falling within precisely the *Jewish prophetic tradition*. This was how Isaiah, Ezekiel and Jeremiah had been known on occasion to articulate their message, usually a message of warning to the nation. They wanted, after all, to change their contemporaries' worldview: stories were one of the best ways of doing so. And sometimes, particularly but not exclusively within 'apocalyptic', we find what we can only call allegories. By this, speaking generally, I mean stories which, within the multiple resonances that any good story will have, make use of an extended metaphor in which different features (a) represent different elements in the 'real' world and (b) evoke a larger world of story, myth and symbol. By this means, the teller of apocalyptic allegory within the Jewish tradition can say: what I am describing is a new exodus, a new world, a new creation. Jesus' parables, as we saw in the previous chapter, continue the long Jewish tradition of telling the story of Israel herself, and showing how it is arriving at its paradoxical conclusion.

The closest parallel to the parables thus turns out to be the world of Jewish apocalyptic and subversive literature – when properly understood. In Qumran, the message of the prophets is interpreted by the Teacher of Righteousness, resulting in a 'pesher' reading which applied old words to the current situation.[124] In apocalyptic visions, the seer is asked by an angel whether he understands the vision, usually replies that he does not, and then has the 'mystery' revealed to him by the angel, explaining in a quasi-allegorical manner that the woman is Jerusalem, the beast is the king of Greece, or whatever.[125] In Jesus' parables, the disciples play the role of the

---

Perrin 1976, 199). Similarly Breech 1983; Scott 1983, on which cf. Sanders 1985, 7: according to these two writers, Jesus was 'offering things which, though mysterious then, are seen, when finally puzzled out twenty centuries later, to be striking in manner but not especially in matter.' Sanders concludes, I think rightly: 'The Jesus of [Breech and Scott] . . . could not have been an important historical figure.' Cf. too Sanders 329.

[123] So Boucher 1977; Caird 1980, 160–7; Drury 1985; against Jülicher 1910 [1899]; Dodd 1961 [1935]; Jeremias 1963a [1947]. The theories of the last three all presuppose the old rejection (a) of allegory as Hellenistic and (b) of apocalyptic as the kind of Jewish thought Jesus forswore. The irony is (a) that allegory and apocalyptic are very close to each other and (b) that Jesus, as we shall see, used allegory within a Jewish framework, and apocalyptic language and themes in a way which broke open the Jewish worldview.

[124] cf. *NTPG* 242.

[125] cf. *NTPG* 280–99. The seers in this literature tended to be male, hence the pronoun.

seers, with Jesus himself as both revealer and interpreter of the 'mystery'. As in the scrolls and other apocalyptic writings, this revelation is not the unveiling of abstract truth *per se*, but the disclosure of a subversive and dangerous message. Israel's history is moving swiftly towards its climax – but it is happening in *this* way, not as expected. It is a message designed to encourage those who 'have ears to hear' to believe that they really are the true Israel of the covenant god, and that they will soon be vindicated as such – while the rest of the world, *including particularly the now apostate or impenitent Israel*, is judged. This is how apocalyptic literature works; this is the characteristic message it conveys. I suggest that Jesus' parables worked in much the same way, and conveyed (at this level of generality) much the same message.[126]

This means that we must give up the false distinction between allegory and parable, and the false dichotomy between steno- and tensive symbols.[127] Just because a story can be 'cashed out' in terms of particular 'applications' intended by the writer or speaker, that does not rule out all sorts of other resonances. In the parable of the wicked tenants, Israel is the vineyard, her rulers the vineyard-keepers; the prophets are the messengers, Jesus is the son; Israel's god, the creator, is himself the owner and father.[128] But this 'allegorical' meaning allows fully for much wider implications. Jesus is claiming to be developing a story already used by Isaiah (5.1-7); the present moment is the moment of crisis, the end of exile; behind the covenant stands a god who cannot be blackmailed by its supposed terms; Israel was made for YHWH's will and not vice versa, since he is after all the creator who called her into being in the first place; he will return to his vineyard, to judge his wicked tenants. And, in particular, the story is not told in such a way as to leave these implications as 'truths' or 'messages' to be cashed out as 'ideas' and filed away safely for any time when need might arise. The parable, allegory and all, functions as an urgent summons which attempts to break open the worldview of the present tenants and replace it with a new one. Specifically, it tells them that their implicit controlling story has reached its

---

[126] Among many other corollaries, this rules out Bultmann's divide (1968 [1921], 199; followed e.g. by Wilder 1982, 91) between Mk. 4.10-12 and 4.14-20 on the grounds that the former treats parables as esoteric utterances and the latter as an 'interpretation'.

[127] Perrin (1976) argued that Jesus' symbols were 'tensive' (having multiple layers of meaning), rather than 'steno-symbols' (with only one main referent). It is perfectly possible, and within the Jewish context very likely, that a symbol could have one main, overarching referent, while evoking various echoes and allusions. Perrin's all-too-neat scheme seems designed to highlight the symbolic nature of the parables while retaining the scholarly orthodoxy of his day by holding 'allegory' at bay, a task now rendered unnecessary by subsequent scholarship.

[128] Mt. 21.33-46/Mk. 12.1-12/Lk. 20.9-19/*Thom.* 65. See below, ch. 11.

crisis point, threatening some of their cherished symbols and praxis, and offering new and startling answers to the underlying worldview questions. Such parables (and most of Jesus' parables fit this model one way or another) are Israel's-story-in-miniature, Jesus' telling of the Israel-story in order to undermine the present way of understanding the nation's identity. It is as though someone were to tell the story of the development of America, or of the British Empire, not, as the Americans and British normally tell them, as the stories of freedom and civilization and how they were achieved, but as stories of Promethean ambition achieving deeply ambiguous power, handling it with irresponsible self-righteousness, and facing imminent disaster as a result.

This explains something about parables which has puzzled many, if not most, readers and scholars. Someone who is telling strangely familiar stories and *meaning the wrong things by them* will land up in trouble.[129] The parable about defilement, about the things which come out of or go into a person, in which the former defile and the latter do not, is a cryptic invitation to abandon one of the most cherished cultural boundary-markers of Israel, a social and religious symbol which people in recent memory had adhered to even when the result was torture and death.[130] It is as though someone, claiming to represent the real hope for Polish Roman Catholics at a time of foreign domination, were to tell a short story in which, cryptically and sym-bolically, the figure of Mary was quietly downgraded or set aside. If people really understood what was being said, a lynching would always be on the cards. This ties in, of course, with the use of apocalyptic, which (as we now know) is at least in part to be understood as the literature of subversion, of the cryptic undermining of a dominant and powerful worldview, and the encouraging and supporting of a revolutionary one.[131] If one had asked Jesus, after the parable in Mark 7, why he spoke so cryptically, he might well have replied with the famous and (otherwise) puzzling words from Mark 4.11–12: so that they may look and look but never see, and hear and hear but never understand.[132] If they were really to see or understand there might be a riot. Those who have ears will hear; for the moment it is just as well that those who do not will not. The 'Nazareth Manifesto' of Luke 4.16–30 was a bit

---

[129] cf. Bailey 1991, 45, 47f. What is true simply at the level of any peasant community's control over its regular stories is true *a fortiori* of the community's reaction to a story which does not just alter, but actually subverts, the story's normal meaning.

[130] Mt. 15.10–20/Mk. 7.14–23; cp. *Thom.* 14. For the symbol and its importance cf. *NTPG* 227–30, 237–41; and below, ch. 9. On the torturing of those who refused to eat unclean food cf. e.g. 2 Macc. 6.18–31; 7.1–42.

[131] See *NTPG* ch. 10.

[132] Mk. 4.11f./Mt. 13.13/Lk. 8.10. Cf. below, 236–8. Cf. too Mk. 10.10, on which see 000.

too clear, perhaps: if the prophet is not to perish away from Jerusalem, his subversive message must be clothed in a disguise which only the seeing eye will penetrate. Jesus' parables, then, belong with, rework, reappropriate and redirect Israel's prophetic and apocalyptic traditions. They belong substantially, as they stand, within the specific period of his public career and ministry, of his work as a prophet of judgment and renewal.

They do not properly belong, in fact, anywhere else. Once the early church was established, the secret was an open one. The very form, the parable-as-apocalyptic-allegory, belongs only at the time when the warning and summons must needs be cryptic and veiled: that is, to the time of Jesus' public career. Mark and Matthew have their own way of keeping other things cryptic: 'let the reader understand'.[133] The evangelists, in their own situations, do not need to be cryptic in their use of the parables. They are talking about the situation of Jesus' ministry; secrecy of that sort was necessary then, but now is not. Form-criticism of the parables should drive us to conclude that the only appropriate *Sitz im Leben* (life-setting) for the parable-plus-interpretation form is in the ministry of Jesus itself.

The parables, therefore, are not simply 'teaching', with each parable making one and only one moral or 'religious' point (Jülicher). Such a theory is totally anachronistic. Nor are they merely announcing a realized eschatology, with allegorization introduced subsequently to make different points for a different generation, producing a new and 'inauthentic' meaning for the parable (Dodd).[134] Nor are they allegorical, with several points each, but directed simply from evangelists to communities with little relation to Jesus (Drury). Nor are they word-events without definite 'content', so that anyone

---

[133] Mt. 24.15/Mk. 13.14. Cf. *NTPG* 390–6; 396–403.

[134] cf. *NTPG* 434: the parables in *Thom.* have been shorn of their allegorical, and Israel-specific, elements, in order to conform to a different, radically Hellenized, worldview (contra Perrin 1976, 189). *Thomas* thus did for the parables in the second century what Jülicher, Dodd and Jeremias did in the twentieth, and perhaps for similar reasons, namely, the attempt to get away from their historical, and very Jewish, specificity. The irony of Jülicher's position, which has been among the most influential this century, is this: he assumed that the parables were basically timeless teachings, which the early church then directed into some particular cultural setting, different from that of Jesus, by adding to them and variously 'interpreting' them. The opposite is likely to have been the case. The parables were originally highly 'situational', highly specific to Jesus' unique ministry. The early church is likely to have made them more 'timeless', in order to 'translate' them for different situations. Jülicher and others, finding the specific and situational material non-universalizable and hence apparently useless, yet wanting to follow Jesus rather than the early church, have drawn the picture upside down, attributing the 'usable', generalized versions to Jesus, and the 'situational', and hence apparently useless, material to the early church. The question of how one might then 'use' Jesus' highly context-specific work within a different context and culture must (as Dodd saw, 1961 [1935], ch. 7) be addressed as a whole, not picked off piecemeal, parable by parable.

who thinks he has found a 'meaning' will have missed the point (Perrin).[135] They are the ideal vehicle for the paradoxical and dangerous campaign which Jesus was undertaking, expressing the very heart of his message in their form as well as their content, in their style and language as well as their particular imagery and apocalyptic or allegorical meaning.

We may sum up this discussion of the parables in eight points, as follows.

1. The most immediate literary background to the parables is that of apocalyptic. The parables are not just 'about' the return of Israel's god into her history, to judge, redeem and restore her; they are also agents of that all-important event.[136]

2. Jesus used parables a good deal. We should expect to find (and we do in fact find) local variations, in which he used similar stories on several different occasions, represented by some different versions in our sources.

3. The parables made sense only within the whole context of Jesus' career. They echoed, reflected, interpreted and indeed defended the main thrusts of Jesus' work, and themselves set up other echoes in turn.

4. The parables functioned the way all (good) stories function, by inviting hearers into the world of the story. They were designed to break open worldviews and to create new ones, encouraging listeners to identify themselves in terms of the narrative. To see the point of the parable was to make a judgment on oneself.

5. The parables were therefore, like the apocalyptic genre to which in some senses they belong, subversive stories, told to articulate and bring to birth a new way of being the people of god.

6. The parables were therefore essentially secretive. Jesus was not a 'universal teacher' of timeless truths, but the starter of a movement which was to grow like an unobserved seed turning into a plant before anyone had realized.[137] There was something necessarily cryptic about the parables.

---

[135] cf. too Crossan 1992, 152: 'It is a parable's destiny to be interpreted and those interpretations will necessarily be diverse. When the diversity ceases, the parable is dead and the parabler is silent.' (Cf. too Wilder 1982, 99f.) Without wishing to deny the polyvalence of all stories, we must insist that such radical postmodern pluralism is unhelpful within serious historiography.

[136] The best examples of the parables as apocalyptic allegory are the wheat and the tares, the seed growing secretly, the sheep and the goats, etc.; and the clearest background may be found not only in Nathan's parable (2 Sam. 12.1-15), which broke open David's mindset with a vengeance, but also e.g. Ezek. 17.1-24; Dan. 7.1-27; Zech. 14, and others discussed in e.g. Drury 1985, ch. 1.

[137] The parable which breaks this rule actually proves it. When Jesus told the 'wicked tenants', the time had come to abandon the earlier secrecy and force a showdown. Historically speaking, the parable belongs precisely with the action in the Temple, the moment when Jesus at last acted in a way that the authorities could not ignore. See below, ch. 11.

Their import was so explosive that they could not necessarily be explained in public. One had to have ears to hear the message.

7. The secretive function of the parables worked by analogy with other Jewish hermeneutical models, not least those of Qumran and the apocalyptic literature.

8. Narrative analysis of the parables is as yet in its infancy. But in principle detailed analysis of the parables would be an excellent project, and might yield very fruitful results – once, and only once, their total context, and setting within the ministry of Jesus, is fully understood.[138]

Jesus' tellings of Israel's story, then, fit extremely well as part of the prophetic praxis he adopted. He drew on many models from the Hebrew prophets, and brought them together in a new synthesis appropriate to his perception of the particular moment that the nation now faced. This meant, in turn, that he shared another characteristic with the canonical prophets and with his immediate predecessor John: that of issuing solemn warnings about imminent judgment.

(c) Oracles of Judgment

The prophetic work of John the Baptist included, it appears, a major element of *warning*. Like several of the old Hebrew prophets, John solemnly announced that Israel's god would shortly judge his people, unless they repented. This tradition of warning finds other echoes within the first century.[139] It has often been thought that Jesus avoided speaking in this fashion, but this, in my judgment, is incorrect.[140] Instead, I agree with Borg that the tradition of judgment sayings has a good claim to be historical.[141]

What does this note of warning sound like in practice? Prophets in the Jewish tradition characteristically announced the judgment of the covenant god upon his rebellious people, and (sometimes) announced also the inauguration of a new movement, a time when Israel's god would again act graciously for his people. Part of Jesus' prophetic persona was that he did

---

[138] For a start, cf. Crossan 1973; *NTPG* ch. 3.

[139] cf. e.g. Jos. *War* 6.300-9.

[140] Sanders 1985, esp. 115-17. Sanders uses a fairly heavy version of the criterion of dissimilarity: warnings about imminent judgment, and the summons to national repentance, either conform the message to that of John or look suspiciously like the activity of the early church. In my view this is one of the places where this criterion needs to be abandoned in favour of a criterion of appropriate similarity. At the same time, Jesus' warnings are neither exactly like John's, nor yet exactly like the theology of early Christianity.

[141] Borg 1984, 201-27, 265-76. Though I shall go beyond Borg at some points, I regard his survey as essentially on the right lines.

both. In order to gauge the full weight of this tradition, it is worth setting out some of the salient features of it as we find it in the synoptics:

Leave the dead to bury the dead (Mt. 8.22/Lk. 9.60);

Do not put the new wine into old wineskins (Mt. 9.17/Mk. 2.22/Lk. 5.37-8);

Israel is a lost sheep, without a shepherd (Mt. 9.36);

Those who do not repent will soon reach a time when it will be more tolerable for Sodom and Gomorrah than for them (Mt. 10.15/Lk. 10.12, cf. Mt. 11.20-24/Lk. 10.13-15);

Abraham, Isaac and Jacob will welcome Gentiles into the kingdom, while the sons of the kingdom will be cast out (Mt. 8.11-12/Lk. 13.28-9);

Israel must make friends quickly with her accuser, lest she be hauled off to prison (Mt. 5.25-6/Lk. 12.58-9);

Israel is like salt which has lost its savour, and is now good for nothing but to be cast out and trodden underfoot (Mt. 5.13/Mk. 9.50/Lk. 14.34-5);

Whoever denies or is ashamed of the Son of Man, of him will the Son of Man be ashamed (Mk. 8.38/Lk. 9.26);

It is better to sacrifice precious parts of the body than to go whole into Gehenna (Mt. 5.29-30/Mk. 9.43-8);[142]

There is a narrow gate that leads to life, and there are few that find it, but the gate to destruction is broad and well-travelled (Mt. 7.13-14/Lk. 13.24);

Israel at present is like a field with wheat and weeds mixed, but there will come a day of separation and judgment (Mt. 13.24-30, 36-43);[143]

Israel is like fish in a drag-net, good and bad together, and soon the net will be on shore and the bad fish thrown away (Mt. 13.47-50);[144]

The master of the house will come and punish those servants who were not faithful (Mt. 24.45-51/Lk. 12.42-6);[145]

The first will be last, and the last first (Mt. 19.30/Mk. 10.31/Lk. 13.30);

Nineveh will condemn this generation, because it repented at the preaching of Jonah, and a greater than Jonah is here (Mt. 12.39-41/Lk. 11.29-32);[146]

This generation will be like an exorcised man reoccupied by worse demons than before (Mt. 12.43-5/Lk. 11.24-6);

Those to whom tragedies had occurred were not greater sinners than the rest; unless Israel repents, all will likewise perish, mown down by Roman guards or crushed under falling buildings (Lk. 13.1-5);

Unless the tree bears fruit this year, it will be cut down (Lk. 13.6-9);

In the messianic banquet, those who insist on the best places will be humiliated (Lk. 14.7-11);[147]

In the coming great wedding feast, those invited were not worthy (Mt. 22.1-14/Lk. 14.15-24/*Thom.* 64);

Jerusalem will end up like chickens without a mother hen, unprotected in the farm-yard fire (Mt. 23.37/Lk. 13.34);[148]

[142] cf. Mt. 18.8-9. Gehenna was Jerusalem's smouldering rubbish-heap, and thence became a metaphor for the place of fiery judgment after death. Cf. Bailey 1986; Milikowsky 1988; Watson 1992.

[143] cf. *Thom.* 57.

[144] cf. *Thom.* 8.

[145] cf. Mk. 13.33-7.

[146] cf. Mt. 16.4.

[147] cf. Mt. 20.28 in the long variant (D).

[148] cf. Isa. 31.5.

The Temple has been abandoned by YHWH, and faces its fate unprotected (Mt. 23.38/Lk. 13.35);[149]

Just as the flood swept Noah's contemporaries away, so will this generation be destroyed (Mt. 24.37-9/Lk. 17.26-7);

Just as Lot's wife was overtaken by sudden judgment, so will this generation be (Lk. 17.32);

There will be foolish maidens unprepared when the bridegroom comes (Mt. 25.1-13);

There will be foolish servants who hide their talent in the earth, or bury their pound in a napkin (Mt. 25.14-30/Lk. 19.11-27);[150]

There will be unwilling subjects who will pay the price when the rightful king comes to reign (Lk. 19.14, 27);

There will be goats as well as sheep (Mt. 25.31-46);

Upon this generation will come all the righteous blood shed on earth, from Abel to Zechariah; it will all come on this generation (Mt. 23.35/Lk. 11.51);

The Temple will be destroyed, and (perhaps) rebuilt (Mk. 14.58/Mt. 26.61; cf. Mk. 13.2/Mt. 24.2/Lk. 21.6, etc.; Lk. 19.43f.; Mk. 15.29/Mt. 27.40; *Thomas* 71; cp. Ac. 6.14);

If they do not hear Moses and the prophets, neither will they believe even if one should rise from the dead (Lk. 16.31).

This, by any reckoning, is a pretty devastating catalogue of threats and warnings. It will, of course, be objected at once that these passages, or most of them, are well known within the traditions of New Testament scholarship to belong to a later date than the ministry of Jesus. All we can say at this stage is that this remains to be seen. Arguments have been advanced for the authenticity of this or that group (it will be noted that the sayings are spread across triple tradition, Q, special Matthew, special Luke, and *Thomas*); and matters are by no means as settled as some scholars would like to make out. In addition, the new paradigm I am proposing is to be built from the ground up, and we cannot assume anything one way or the other except the usual requirements: to get in the data, to do so as simply as possible, and to shed light on further questions. Here the point I wish to make is straightforward. If Jesus' public persona was that of an oracular prophet, then such warnings as these, or most of them, would be perfectly natural, and indeed might be expected. Part of the prophetic vocation and role was to announce to Israel that she was pursuing a path that led to ruin. It would be surprising if Jesus were seen as a prophet if he had said nothing of the kind.[151]

The warnings, moreover, are of the classic prophetic type. Eschewing the misreading of the texts which sees Jesus' language as referring to the end of the world *per se*,[152] we may regard these warnings as threatening the end of

---

[149] cf. 1 Kgs. 9.7f.; Jer. 12.7; 22.5; Ezek. 10.18f.; 11.22f.; Tob. 14.4.

[150] cf. *G. Naz.* 18.

[151] cf. Knowles 1993.

[152] cf. *NTPG* ch. 10, following the work of Collins and others on apocalyptic literature in general, and Caird and Borg on the sayings in the gospels.

the present nation of Israel, if they do not repent. In the sad, noble, and utterly Jewish tradition of Elijah, Jeremiah and John the Baptist, Jesus announced the coming judgment of Israel's covenant god on his people, a judgment consisting of a great national, social and cultural disaster, ultimately comprehensible only in theological terms. At the heart of the disaster would be the ruin of the Temple. (The charge that Jesus was a Samaritan looks as though it belongs to this theme,[153] since the Samaritans were, notoriously, opposed to the Jerusalem Temple; Jesus risked identification with them if he spoke out against it too – though of course others, such as the Essenes, had denounced it as well.) Actually, it hardly took a prophet to foresee a major disaster if Israel kept up her present attitude to Rome.[154] Jesus, it seems, was warning against false prophets who, like those that Jeremiah opposed, were telling the people to trust in the Temple;[155] or who, like those opposed by Micaiah ben Imlach, were telling the people to fight, to resist, because they would win. Jesus, like Micaiah, saw all Israel scattered on the mountains, like sheep without a shepherd, and interpreted this coming judgment not as a coincidental and unfortunate political happening but as the coming of YHWH's wrath on his people. It is this that distinguishes the prophet from the mere political analyst.[156] 'If they do this when the wood is green, what will they do when it is dry?'[157] Jerusalem is the city that kills the prophets, and stones those sent to her; Jesus comes as the last in the prophetic line,[158] expecting no better than his predecessors, and indeed worse. Indeed, Jesus' anticipation of his own death falls so well within the prophetic mould that, once we see the data as a whole, it becomes another part of the evidence which is now all pointing in the same direction: that his habitual praxis marked him out as a prophet, in the sense of one announcing to Israel an urgent message from the covenant god.

The warnings were, as we saw, balanced by the welcome to those who heeded the message. Jesus gathered around him the motley crew who answered his call. This too was part of his prophetic ministry, taken as a whole. The total effect is clear. Jesus was seen, by the public at large, as a great prophet, like one of the prophets of old, announcing to Israel her imminent

---

[153] Jn. 8.48.

[154] Compare the predictions of Josephus, e.g. *War* 5.399-419.

[155] Jer. 7.1-34. For the lingering attempt to trust in the Temple even at the end of the siege in AD 70, cf. Jos. *War* 6.285. Once the Temple was destroyed, those who had defended it so valiantly asked to be allowed to leave the city: *War* 6.351.

[156] 1 Kgs. 22. The critique is spelled out in e.g. Mt. 12.31-50; Mt. 23, etc., and their parallels. See Borg 1984 in particular, esp. ch. 8 and the Appendix (265-76); and ch. 8 below.

[157] Lk. 23.31; cf. below, 567-70.

[158] cf. Mk. 12.6 pars.; Mt. 23.34-9/Lk. 11.49-52; 13.34-5.

doom and vindication, and putting his message into operation around himself.

Jesus' tellings of Israel's story, and his prophetic announcement of judgment, exactly match the other side of his prophetic work. He acted out that of which he spoke. At the heart of his characteristic praxis there stand two elements in particular, described by Crossan as 'Magic and Meal'. We shall look further at Jesus' table-fellowship when considering his reshaping of the symbols of Israel's life in chapter 9 below. Here we must turn our attention to what Crossan calls 'magic', more traditional exegesis 'miracle', and what I prefer to describe as 'mighty works'.

(iv) Mighty in Deed

(a) Introduction

The present Third Quest has seen something of a quiet revolution in relation to the 'mighty works' or 'works of power' that Jesus is said to have performed.[159] Pre-critical readings of the Bible regarded these not only as actual events, but as primary evidence for the 'divinity' of Jesus. The older liberalism, dating back at least to the eighteenth century and in particular to Hume, claimed that 'miracles' never happened, or at any rate that there could never be sufficient evidence to believe that they had; hence, that Jesus probably never performed any; hence, that perhaps he was not after all 'divine'. Both of these lines of thought, in fact, contain the same *non sequitur*: the strongest incarnational claims in the New Testament (e.g. those in Paul) have nothing to do with Jesus' mighty works, and the accounts of mighty works in the gospels are not usually offered as 'proof' of Jesus' 'divinity'. If we are to discuss Jesus' deeds seriously, we must set that older question aside.

More thoroughgoing recent history has been coming to the conclusion that we can only explain the evidence before us if we reckon that Jesus did indeed perform deeds for which there was at the time, and may well be still, no obvious 'naturalistic' explanation – to use that terminology for the moment.[160] To say this is not, of course, to advance for ourselves any kind

[159] On this whole subject see esp. Aune 1980; Brown 1984; Kee 1983, 1986; Remus 1992 (with full bibliography, 869).

[160] See Vermes 1973, ch. 3; Meyer 1979, 153–8 (esp. 158); Goppelt 1981 [1975], 138–57; Harvey 1982, ch. 5; Sanders 1985, ch. 5; Borg 1987a, ch. 4; Crossan 1991a, ch. 13, esp. 310f. It is naive to suppose that first-century Galilean villagers were ready to believe in 'miracles' because they did not understand the laws of nature, or did not realize that the space-time universe was a closed continuum. Cf. esp. Harvey 1982, 101f., with refs. As has often been pointed out, in Mt. 1.18f. Joseph was worried about Mary's unexpected preg-

of actual explanation, reductionist or otherwise. It is still possible that, if one were to adopt a worldview in which, strictly speaking, 'the miraculous does not occur', one might find satisfactory explanations, no doubt of the 'psychosomatic' kind, for many if not all of the healing stories, and of the 'mythical' or similar kind for many if not all of the 'nature miracles'. But we must be clear that Jesus' contemporaries, both those who became his followers and those who were determined not to become his followers, certainly regarded him as possessed of remarkable powers. The church did not invent the charge that Jesus was in league with Beelzebul; but charges like that are not advanced unless they are needed as an explanation for some quite remarkable phenomena.[161]

It is prudent, methodologically, to hold back from too hasty a judgment on what is actually possible and what is not within the space-time universe.[162] There are more things in heaven and earth than are dreamed of in post-Enlightenment philosophy, as those who have lived and worked in areas of the world less affected by Hume, Lessing and Troeltsch know quite well. This is not to say that there are not such things as gullibility, credulity, culpable ignorance, and self-deception. Nor is it to deny, what is manifestly true, that the evangelists have written their stories of Jesus, not least their accounts of his extraordinary deeds, in such a way as to make particular theological points, by echoes of the Old Testament, juxtaposition with other stories, highlighting of certain elements. Nor, we should stress, is this to say that, if we reject Hume's stance on miracles, we are bound to embrace a non-Humean worldview in which a (normally absent?) god intervenes in the world in an apparently arbitrary and irrational fashion. The appeal for suspension of judgment, then, cannot be used as a Trojan horse for smuggling in an old-fashioned 'supernaturalist' worldview under pretence of neutrality; this is sometimes done by conservative apologists, who are often interested at this point, not in Jesus himself, but in miracles as test cases for whether the Bible is believed to be 'true' or not – a position that brings its own nemesis. To insist at the beginning of an enquiry, whose results (like those of all important enquiries) may call basic worldviews into question, that some particular contemporary worldview is the only possible one, is simply to beg the question, to show that all we really want to do is to hear the echo of our own voices.

The very word 'miracle' itself, and for that matter the words 'natural' and 'supernatural', are in fact symptomatic of a very different range of possible

---

nancy not because he did not know where babies came from but because he did.
[161] Mt. 12.24–32/Mk. 3.20–30/Lk. 11.14–23; cp. *Thom.* 35. See below, ch. 9.
[162] cf. Meyer 1979, 99–104; Brown 1984.

worldviews from those which were open to Galilean villagers in the first century. The evangelists used words like *paradoxa*, things one would not normally expect; *dunameis*, displays of power or authority; *terata* or *semeia*, signs or portents. The closest we come to 'miracle' is the single occurrence of *thaumasia*, 'marvels', in Matthew 21.15. These words do not carry, as the English word 'miracle' has sometimes done, overtones of invasion from another world, or from outer space. They indicate, rather, that something has happened, *within* what we would call the 'natural' world, which is not what would have been anticipated, and which seems to provide evidence for the active presence of an authority, a power, at work, not invading the created order as an alien force, but rather enabling it to be more truly itself. And that describes equally well the impression that other aspects of Jesus' ministry made on people: here was an unexpected phenomenon, a prophet apparently questioning the nationalist hope – and yet announcing the kingdom of Israel's god. This was not what would have been anticipated, yet it none the less carried the note of fulfilment.

The word 'miracle', by contrast, has come to be associated with two quite different questions, developed not least in the period of the Enlightenment: (a) Is there a 'supernatural' dimension to the world? (b) Which religion, if any, is the true one? 'Miracles' became, for some, a way of answering 'yes' to the first and 'Christianity' to the second. Jesus' 'miracles' are, in this scheme, a 'proof' that there is a god, who has 'intervened' in the world in this way. Hume and his followers, as we saw, put it the other way round: granted that 'miracles' do not occur, or at least cannot be demonstrated to occur, does this mean that all religions, including Christianity, are false, and the Bible untrue? This posing of the question precipitated two possible answers from those wishing to preserve something of the tradition: a non-miraculous 'Christianity' on the one hand, and a rearguard anti-critical reaction on the other. Today these questions seem a little lame. Few serious historians now deny that Jesus, and for that matter many other people, performed cures and did other startling things for which there was no obvious natural explanation. But Christian apologetics has moved on as well: 'miracles' are not advanced as a 'proof' of anything much. What matters far more is intention and meaning. What did Jesus think he was doing, and why? What did his deeds mean to those involved, and to those who passed on the tradition?

This latter question raises another: what contribution, in turn, has the tradition made to the stories of Jesus' mighty works? Here opinions divide. Some think that the post-Easter community invented stories in which Jesus appeared in the guise of a Hellenistic wonder-worker; others, that the post-Easter community toned down the aspects of Jesus' activity which made him look like a magician. These two, of course, more or less cancel one another out. Within the stories as they stand at the moment, i.e. within the gospels as a whole, the mighty works do not in any way protrude from the rest of the narrative, as they ought to if they had been added to the tradition by people interested in telling stories of a Hellenistic-style wonder-working hero-figure.[163] Rather, they fit remarkably well into the complete picture of Jesus' ministry. There is no dividing line, enabling us to bracket off different aspects, isolating the mighty works, so as then, perhaps, to declare them later accretions. Equally, it is of course possible (as we shall see in a moment) that our sources have been thoroughly 'purged' of 'magical' elements, though if that had been the intention it is hard to see why the most damaging thing of all, the accusation of black magic, should have been left untouched, and indeed highly prominent, in all three synoptic gospels.[164] But it is far more likely that, as a matter of history, 'the miraculous activity of Jesus conforms to no known pattern'.[165] The new pattern that we find, however, fits into the prophetic profile of Jesus that we are building up.

A sharper-edged question, historically, is: should we then think of the deeds of Jesus as in some sense 'magic'? The distinction between miracle and magic has been commonly made, and in some cases argued quite closely.[166] There are two quite different ways of approaching the question. The first is to find some apparently neutral criteria: for instance, that miracles have to do with the gracious act of a god, while magic is all about human manipulation of divine or quasi-divine forces. On that basis many have concluded that the things Jesus did were not magic; or that, if they were, the actual evidence for the magical element has been carefully suppressed by the church.[167] Another apparently neutral criterion, advanced by MacMullen, runs thus: miracle produces beneficent results, whereas magic is harmful.[168] This criterion, however, quickly generates the second, very different, approach which Crossan adopts, following Robert Grant and others: 'magic is to religion as banditry is to politics'.[169] Who, after all, is to judge whether a particular act

---

[163] There have of course been many theories about collections of miracle stories which predate the present forms of the gospels. The best known is the hypothesis of a 'signs source' lying behind the miracles in John: cf. Fortna 1970, 1988, 1992, and the discussions in commentaries on John. On the possibility of pre-Markan 'miracle catenae' cf. Achtemeier 1970.

[164] cf. too *Thom* 35; 44. This theory is analogous to Reimarus's: the gospels have been 'purged' of Jesus' 'revolutionary' teaching - except for blunders like the two swords in Lk. 22.38.

[165] Harvey 1982, 113.

[166] MacMullen 1981, 95-7; Sanders 1985, 167f. (following MacMullen); Kee 1986, esp. 1-8, 126-31; Crossan 1991a, 304-20; Remus 1992, 858f.

[167] So Smith 1978, on which cf. Kee 1986, 115-17; cp. Meyer 1979, 158.

[168] So MacMullen 1981, discussed by Sanders 1985, 168f.

[169] Crossan 1991a, 305; cf. Grant 1966 [1959], 93: 'In polemical writing, your magic is my miracle, and vice versa' (quoted in Remus 1992, 859); Remus 1983, 182f.

is beneficial or not? Who is to say whether a particular act is the work of a god graciously acting within the world, or whether it is the result of secret, and probably deceptive, black arts? Crossan pours scorn on those who refuse to recognize that Jesus – and for that matter the Jewish charismatics Honi and Hanina, and the prophets Elijah and Elisha – were in some such sense 'magicians'. Magic is 'subversive, unofficial, unapproved, and often lower-class religion'; magic is 'what any socioreligious ascendancy calls its deviant shadow'.[170] Crossan has, in other words, widened the earlier meaning of 'magic' so as to include any mighty work performed outside an official context.

This may actually clarify the issue somewhat, without necessarily leading to all the conclusions Crossan intends. The evidence, it seems to me, is actually quite straightforward: Jesus performed mighty deeds, which did in fact call forth the charge that he was a magician, in league with demonic forces.[171] But what does this charge *mean*? It means, not least, that Jesus was perceived to be posing a serious threat to the social, cultural and religious world of his day. His whole career raised a deeply problematic question, analogous to the question Jesus himself asked about John the Baptist.[172] Either these things are the work of none other than YHWH himself, Israel's god acting in a new way within his people's history; or they are the work of the arch-deceiver, leading the people astray. It is beyond question that Jesus was acting subversively, as John the Baptist had been. However we categorize his actions in terms of *technique*, in terms of *social and religious significance* there is no question. He was going outside the system. He was acting without any official sanction. If that is part of what we mean by 'magic', then Jesus was indeed, though only in this extended sense, a magician.

It will not do, then, simply to define the mighty works as non-magical, therefore 'miraculous', and leave it at that. But nor will it do simply to assert that, because they were 'magical' in one particular sense, that Jesus is to be identified as one Hellenistic-style wonder-worker among many others, Jewish and pagan alike.[173] The mighty works possess, it seems to me, exactly the same kind of troubling ambiguity that characterized Jesus' whole career. Either he was indeed inaugurating the long-awaited time of liberation, the return from exile, the kingdom of Israel's god – or he was leading the people astray, deluding them with a programme and an agenda that radically subverted Israel's true destiny. Our twentieth-century question as between magic

---

[170] Crossan 1991a, 305, 309.
[171] Mt. 12.24–32/Mk. 3.20–30/Lk. 11.14–23; cp. *Thom.* 35.
[172] Mk. 11.27–33/Mt. 21.23–7/Lk. 20.1–8.
[173] cf. Hull 1974, with the discussion in Kee 1986, 117f.

and miracle simply reflects the first-century question posed by Jesus to his onlookers. And that question is not resolvable in terms of parallels in the history of religion. Despite occasional glimpses of Jesus using techniques that may have parallels in some magical practices,[174] for the most part his actual practice seems to have been distinct from that of his contemporaries, both Jewish and pagan.[175]

Thus, from the perspective of a follower of Jesus at the time, his mighty works will have been interpreted within the context of his overall proclamation: they would be seen as signs that the kingdom of Israel's god was indeed coming to birth. From the perspective of anyone with vested interests in the kingdom coming in different ways, or indeed in not coming at all, the same events will have appeared as dangerous and subversive, i.e. as 'magic'. How might one decide? Not, clearly, by further scrutiny of the mighty works themselves. One could only decide by seeing what else this strange prophet was up to, and what he was saying. In that sort of an investigation, Jesus' contemporaries, just like the modern historian, would pay attention to the stories Jesus told and the way he treated the national symbols. That, as we shall see, was indeed how the matter was tackled.

(b) 'Mighty Works': Interpretation

One way in which Jesus' mighty works were evidently understood by some was that they were the signs of the long-awaited fulfilment of prophecy.[176] For a first-century Jew, most if not all of the works of healing, which form the bulk of Jesus' mighty works, could be seen as the restoration to membership in Israel of those who, through sickness or whatever, had been excluded as ritually unclean. The healings thus function in exact parallel with the welcome of sinners, and this, we may be quite sure, was what Jesus himself intended. He never performed mighty works simply to impress. He saw them as part of the inauguration of the sovereign and healing rule of Israel's covenant god. We may therefore examine briefly the various elements of the tradition in order to see, in line with the rest of this chapter, how the prophetic praxis of Jesus would have been perceived by some at least of his contemporaries.

The evidence from Qumran suggests that, in some Jewish circles at least, a maimed Jew could not be a full member of the community.[177] In addition

---

[174] e.g. Mk. 8.23.

[175] cf. Harvey 1982, ch. 5.

[176] Meyer 1979, 157f.

[177] 1QSa 2.3-11 (Vermes 1995 [1962], 121). The material seems to be an expansion and extension of Dt. 23.1-6.

to the physical burden of being blind, or lame, or deaf, or dumb, such a Jew was blemished, and unable to be a full Israelite.[178] How far this was taken by Jewish society in Jesus' day it is difficult to assess. But we know that at least in Qumran it was a very serious matter. This means that Jesus' healing miracles must be seen clearly as bestowing the gift of *shalom*, wholeness, to those who lacked it, bringing not only physical health but renewed membership in the people of YHWH.

Many of the people Jesus healed came into one of these banned categories. There were blind people,[179] deaf and dumb,[180] lepers (who were not only ritually excluded, but also, of course, socially ostracized),[181] a woman with an issue of blood, which rendered not only her, but anything she sat on, or anyone or anything she touched, unclean,[182] a crippled woman 'whom Satan bound for eighteen years'.[183] By extension of the same point, Jesus' touching of the dead and raising them to life should certainly have brought him uncleanness, but in fact had the effect of restoring them.[184] So too his miracles performed for Gentiles,[185] and for a Samaritan,[186] bear witness to the inclusion within the people of YHWH of those who had formerly been outside.

The effect of these cures, therefore, was not merely to bring physical healing; not merely to give humans, within a far less individualistic society than our modern western one, a renewed sense of community membership;[187] but to reconstitute those healed as members of the people of Israel's god. In other words, these healings, at the deepest level of understanding on the part of Jesus and his contemporaries, would be seen as part of his total ministry, specifically, part of that open welcome which went with the inauguration of the kingdom – and, consequently, part of his subversive work, which was likely to get him into trouble. The vindication for which Israel looked to her god was being brought forward into the present, close up, in the case of these individuals. They were being reintegrated into the worshipping community, like those psalmists who began with lament and ended with thanksgiving.[188]

---

[178] On purity and related matters cf. the sensitive discussion of G. Wenham 1982.

[179] Mt. 9.27–31; Mt. 12.22; Mk. 8.22; Mt. 20.29–34/Mk. 10.46–52/Lk. 18.35–43; Mt. 21.14.

[180] Mt. 9.32–3; Mt. 12.22/Lk. 11.14; Mk. 7.32.

[181] Mt. 8.1–4/Mk. 1.40–5/Lk. 5.12–16/*P.Eger.* 2.1–4; Lk. 17.11–14.

[182] Mt. 9.20–2/Mk. 5.24–34/Lk. 8.42–8.

[183] Lk. 13.10.

[184] Mt. 9.18–19, 23–6/Mk. 5.21–4, 35–43/Lk. 8.40–2, 49–56; Lk. 7.11–17.

[185] Mt. 8.5–13/Lk. 7.1–10; Mt. 15.21–8/Mk. 7.24–30; and perhaps the feeding of the 4,000 in Mt. 15.32–8/Mk. 8.1–10/Lk. 9.12–17.

[186] Lk. 17.11–19.

[187] cf. Malina & Neyrey 1988, 145–7.

[188] e.g. Ps. 22.

Jesus' mighty works thus had the effect of gathering the community of 'all Israel', in accordance with ancient prophecy.[189] They were linked very closely with the great blessing of the renewed covenant, namely, the forgiveness of sins.[190]

Other signs of covenant renewal include the multiplication of the bread in the wilderness, and the stillings of the storms, both carrying overtones of the exodus.[191] Negatively, this covenant renewal meant judgment falling on the nation: the parable of Luke 13.6–9 (the fig tree that eventually bears no fruit) becomes an acted parable in Matthew 21.18–20/Mark 11.12–25, where it clearly symbolizes the same as the action in the Temple, i.e. the imminent judgment that will fall on impenitent Israel.[192] The evangelists, in their editorial notes, sometimes highlight the fact that in first-century terms the main thing that would be 'seen' in the mighty works was not a supernatural display of power for its own sake but the coming of Israel's god in power to save and heal, to do for these individuals what had been promised (it was thought) to the nation as a whole. As Matthew puts it, 'They glorified the god of Israel.'[193] The works of power were a vital ingredient in the inauguration of the kingdom.[194]

As such, they might also be seen as the breaking in of the new order planned by the creator god. In the healing miracles in general, but also in several other actions, we glimpse something beyond the simple reconstitution of Israel. As we saw in *NTPG*, Israel believed herself to be the linchpin of what the creator god was doing, and would do, for the world as a whole; when Israel was restored, the whole creation would be restored.[195] Thus it is not surprising that we find echoes in the gospels of strange events in which Jesus exercises power over the natural order, bringing it into a new harmony with itself and with the divine saving purpose only previously seen at odd

[189] Mt. 8.17; Mt. 11.2–6/Lk. 7.18–23 (cp. Isa. 35.5–6); cf. Mt. 15.29–31; Mk. 7.37; Lk. 4.18–19 (cp. Isa. 61.1).

[190] Mt. 9.1–8/Mk. 2.1–12/Lk. 5.17–26 (cp. Jer. 31.34); see below, 268–74.

[191] Feedings: Mt. 14.15–21/Mk. 6.35–44/Lk. 9.12–17/Jn. 6.1–15; Mt. 15.32–9/Mk. 8.1–10 (cp. Ex. 16; Num. 11; 2 Kgs. 4.42–4); Storm: Mt. 8.23–7/Mk. 4.35–41/Lk. 8.22–5 (cp. Ex. 14.21–2; Isa. 43.16; 51.9–11; Ps. 65.5–8; 77.16–20; 107.23–32).

[192] Cf. too the story of the fish with the coin (Mt. 17.24). Jesus was, at least, the sort of figure of whom it might very well be asked whether he paid the Temple-tax; and his cryptic answer to Peter shows both that he regarded himself and his followers as not beholden to do so and that, for the moment, he did not wish to force a confrontation on such a relatively small issue. He sat loose to the obligation *de jure*, but avoided *de facto* offence for the moment; i.e. he saw his movement as the start of the renewed Israel, and the Temple-system as implicitly redundant. Cf. Horbury 1984b.

[193] Mt. 15.31.

[194] cf. below, 469f., on Mt. 12.28/Lk. 11.20.

[195] *NTPG* 259–68.

moments such as the crossing of the Red Sea. The extraordinary catch of fish,[196] the stilling of storms, the desert feedings, and, negatively, the cursing of the fig tree, must all be included here. The resurrection itself, of course, properly belongs to this series, but it raises all kinds of other issues and must be dealt with separately.[197] In all of these, as in the 'mighty works' as a whole, what was 'seen' within the first-century Jewish worldview would be the restoration of creation, which Israel had expected to happen when her god became her king and she was vindicated by him.

It is, of course, open to anyone to question whether any of the supposed events referred to here actually took place. It is no part of my purpose to argue about them individually.[198] Rather, I have a threefold suggestion. (a) Many scholars from widely differing backgrounds now accept that Jesus did remarkable 'mighty works'; this consensus is strong enough to sustain the point at least that Jesus' contemporaries, friend and foe alike, believed him to be doing such things, and that the best and simplest explanation of this is that it was more or less true. (b) Interpretations of the sort I have suggested would be highly likely to emerge, not only within the minds of the post-Easter community or the evangelists, but in the minds of the original spectators and the very early story-tellers. (c) The echoes of prophecy, and the theme of fulfilment, belong therefore not simply in later theological reflection, but as part of the answer to the question, what did people 'see' when they saw Jesus at work? The praxis of the prophet invited the interpretation: he was announcing the great fulfilment, the great renewal, the time when Israel's god would at last become king.

As will become clear in subsequent chapters, these 'mighty works' dovetail in to the other themes. They belong with the story which Jesus is telling; they take place in the context of what is called 'faith',[199] which turns out to be the recognition that Israel's god is active in and through Jesus; they raise the question of Jesus' authority and status;[200] they are the occasion of controversy, as the symbols of the Jewish worldview are called into question by Jesus' activity.[201] They appear to be a vital part of what Jesus describes as

[196] Lk. 5.4–11; cp. Jn. 21.1–14.

[197] See below, ch. 14.

[198] For a recent discussion cf. e.g. Wenham & Blomberg 1986.

[199] See below, ch. 7; and cp. Mt. 8.10/Lk. 7.9; Mt. 9.2/Mk. 2.5/Lk. 5.20; Mt. 9.22/Mk. 5.34/Lk. 8.48; Mt. 9.28; Mk. 10.52/Lk. 18.42; Mt. 13.58/Mk. 6.6, cf. Lk. 4.23; Mt. 17.17, 19–20/Mk. 9.19/Lk. 9.41; Lk. 17.19; Mt. 21.21–2/Mk. 11.23–4; cf. Lk. 17.5–6.

[200] Authority: Mt. 13.54/Mk. 1.27/Lk. 4.36; Mt. 8.5–13/Lk. 7.1–10; Jesus' identity: Mt. 8.23/Mk. 4.41/Lk. 8.25; Jesus as prophet: Lk. 7.16; Mt. 14.2/Mk. 6.14–16/Lk. 9.7–9; cp. Jn. 6.1–15; Jesus as Messiah: Mt. 9.27, cf. Mt. 11.2–6/Lk. 7.18–23; Mt. 12.22–3; Mt. 20.30–1/Mk.10.47–8/Lk. 18.38–9.

[201] See ch. 9 below, with refs. there.

the breaking-in of the kingdom, not least in terms of the battle with the satan, the accuser. Thus the exorcisms,[202] in particular, are not simply the release from strange bondage of a few poor benighted souls. (Nor are they all to be explained away with a rationalistic reductionism.) For Jesus and the evangelists, they signalled something far deeper that was going on, namely, the real battle of the ministry, which was not a round of fierce debates with the keepers of orthodoxy, but head-on war with the satan. This belief made perfect sense within the first-century Jewish worldview that Jesus shared. The exorcisms are especially interesting, in that they formed a part neither of the regular Old Testament predictions, nor of first-century Jewish expectations, concerning healing and deliverance associated with the coming of the kingdom; nor were they a major focus of the life and work of the early church. They therefore stand out, by the criterion of dissimilarity, as being part of a battle in which Jesus alone was engaged. He seems to have seen himself as fighting a battle with the real enemy, and to have regarded the exorcisms – or healings of those whose condition was attributed to the work of the satan – as a sign that he was winning the battle, though it had not yet reached its height. 'If I by the finger of god cast out demons, then the kingdom of god has come upon you.'[203]

One particular account is worth a closer look at this point. In Mark 5.1–20 and the parallel passages, the evangelists give a good deal of space to Jesus' healing of the man who had the legion of demons, whose 'inhabitants' left him and entered a herd of pigs, which rushed into the sea and were drowned.[204] Various elements of this narrative appear significant. The location is on the non-Jewish side of the lake: Jesus is among Gentiles. The demoniac (in Matthew, there are two of them; it seems the singular/plural ambiguity was not confined to the sufferer's state of mind) lives among tombs. Herdsmen are nearby feeding pigs. The demons identify themselves as 'legion'. All these features point in the same direction: the situation is about as unclean, from a Jewish point of view, as it could be. All the indications are that Jesus is surrounded by places, people and influences that belong to the enemies of YHWH and his people. The driving of the pigs into the sea may well be regarded, at least by Mark, as symbolic of what the Jews desired to do with the unclean Romans. The exorcism then takes on the following connotation. Jesus is fighting a battle against the enemies of the

---

[202] Mk. 1.23-7/Lk. 4.33-5; Mt. 4.24/Mk. 1.39; Mt. 8.28-33/Mk. 5.1-14/Lk. 8.26-34; Mt. 9.32-4; Lk. 8.1-3; Lk. 11.14-15; Mt. 12.22-32/Mk. 3.20-30/Lk. 11.14-23, cf. Mt. 10.25; Mt. 15.21-8/Mk. 7.24-30; Mt. 17.14-18/Mk. 9.14-27/Lk. 9.37-43; Lk. 13.10-17 (cf. v. 16).

[203] Mt. 12.28/Lk. 11.20 (cf. 469f. below).

[204] See the discussions in Theissen 1991a, 109–11, referring also to earlier work; Wink 1986, 43–50; Myers 1990 [1988], 190–4. The pars. are Mt. 8.28-34/Lk. 8.26-39.

people of YHWH. But Rome is not the enemy; it is the satan and his hordes, who are deceiving Israel into thinking that Rome is the real enemy, so that she (Israel) will not notice the reality. Jesus is going into what was thought of as enemy territory, taking on (from the Jewish point of view) the demon of uncleanness and hostile paganism, and defeating the real enemy instead, demonstrating that victory in the acted symbolism of the death of the pigs. The story is, to be sure, strange, but all the signs are that these are the resonances that it would have carried at the time. This points forward to several aspects of the mindset, not only of the early church, but also of Jesus himself.[205]

Within the public career of Jesus, therefore, the mighty works were not simply showy magic, nor the attempt to win support from crowds, and certainly not in themselves indications or hints that Jesus was 'divine' (whatever that might be deemed to mean). They were signs which were intended as, and would have been perceived as, the physical inauguration of the kingdom of Israel's god, the putting into action of the welcome and the warning which were the central message of the kingdom and its redefinition. They were an integral part of the entire ministry, part of the same seamless robe as the parables, and on a level with Jesus' other characteristic actions. They were indications of a prophetic ministry to be ranked at the very least with those of Elijah and Elisha.

All this reinforces and fills out the conclusion to which this chapter has been arguing. Jesus believed himself called to work as a prophet, announcing the word of Israel's god to his wayward people, and grouping around himself a company who, according to all the partial precedents and parallels, would be regarded as the true people of YHWH. This, however, is not the end of the story. There are plenty of indications that he saw himself, not just as one prophet among many, nor simply as the prophet spoken of in Deuteronomy 18, but as the prophet through whose work Israel's history would finally reach its climactic moment.

5. More Than a Prophet?

How then was Jesus perceived by the villagers who saw and heard him? All the evidence so far displayed suggests that he was perceived as a *prophet*. His speech and action evoked, even while they went beyond, contemporary pictures of prophetic activity. Furthermore, we must conclude that Jesus was conscious of a *vocation* to be a prophet; it is in no way 'modernizing' him to

---

[205] See ch. 10 below.

point out that he would not have acted like this unless he believed himself called by Israel's god to do so.[206] In particular, he acted in ways that had some analogy at least to the praxis of other 'leadership' prophets in second-Temple Judaism. As such, it is already possible to explain a good deal of his career, not least its dramatic conclusion, from this basis. Other 'leadership' prophets spoke and acted in ways which evoked the whole story-line of Israel's chequered history, and implied that this story was coming to a climactic point with their own work. They came into sharp conflict with the authorities, for good and comprehensible reasons.

Jesus, then, had the public persona of a prophet, and we can understand a good deal of his ministry, at least in a preliminary fashion, simply on this basis. But this historical analysis inevitably points beyond itself. We can be sure that the early church did not invent the saying according to which John the Baptist is said to be 'more than a prophet';[207] but if that is said of John, what must be said for Jesus himself? At this point some will want to jump without more ado into a full Nicene christology, and will, not for the last time, have to be severely restrained. It will not do for the elder brother (orthodoxy) to set terms and conditions for the return of the younger (history). But the question 'Who then is this?', or at least 'Who does he think he is?', will not go away. It comes to a sharp point in the questions asked of the disciples at Caesarea Philippi, where the public persona of the prophet proved insufficient to do justice to the disciples' developing perceptions of Jesus. But for that we must wait a little longer. Before the secret, the story. And the story, or rather the stories, that Jesus told indicate well enough that he did not see himself as a prophet entrusted with a task simply for his own generation, one member of a long, continuing line. None of the 'leadership' prophets who have left traces in Josephus thought of themselves in that way, either. The stories he told, and acted out, made it clear that he envisaged his own work as bringing Israel's history to its fateful climax. He really did believe he was inaugurating the kingdom.

---

[206] Against Cadbury 1962 [1937]: cf. Sanders' proper critique (1985, 19–22).
[207] Mt. 11.9/Lk. 7.26.

Chapter Six

STORIES OF THE KINGDOM (1): ANNOUNCEMENT

1. Introduction

'It's going to rain.' This is a fairly clear statement, but its meaning varies with the context.[1] The context supplies an implicit narrative, and the force of the statement depends on the role that it plays within those different potential narratives. If we are about to have a picnic, the statement forms part of an implicit story which is about to become a minor tragedy instead of (as we had hoped) a minor comedy. If we are in East Africa, fearing another drought and consequent crop failure, the statement forms part of an implicit story in which imminent tragedy will give way to jubilation. If I told you three days ago that it would rain today, and you disbelieved me, the statement forms part of an implicit story in which my ability as a meteorologist is about to be vindicated, and your scepticism proved groundless. If we are Elijah and his servant on Mount Carmel, the sentence invokes a whole theological story: YHWH is the true god, and Elijah is his prophet.[2] In each case, the single statement demands to be 'heard' within the context of a full implicit plot, a complete implicit narrative. The meaning of a word is the job it performs in a sentence; the meaning of a sentence is the job it performs within a *story*.[3]

It would be tedious to have to spell this out, were it not for the fact that the principle itself is often doubted, not least by those who cherish suspicions about the recent fashion for 'story' as a category, and about the whole idea that submerged narratives (or 'metanarratives') provide the context of meaning for actions and statements. Since I intend to argue in this and the next two chapters that a good deal of what is generally called the 'teaching' of

---

[1] This depends, of course, on the meaning of 'meaning'. If 'meaning' means simply 'denotation', 'it's going to rain' means 'water is going to fall from the sky'. As I explained in *NTPG* 115–17, however, I (like a great many other people) normally intend at least to connote, and usually also to denote, the meaning 'connotation' as well as 'denotation'.

[2] 1 Kgs. 18.41–6.

[3] cf. *NTPG* 115–17. There is a splendid statement of this point in Maitland 1995, 141f.

Jesus is best characterized in terms of implicit, and sometimes explicit, story, it is vital that the general point be grasped in advance. Jesus' explicit stories (the parables) are well enough known as such. But their very existence can become an excuse for seeing all the non-parabolic sayings of Jesus as something other than stories, explicit or implicit. That, at the level of theory, is what I wish to challenge in the present and subsequent chapters, while advancing, at the level of content, a new reading of what Jesus meant by Israel's god becoming king.

In particular, I intend to demonstrate two things: first, that when Jesus spoke of the 'reign' or 'kingdom' of Israel's god, he was deliberately evoking an entire story-line that he and his hearers knew quite well; second, that he was retelling this familiar story in such a way as to subvert and redirect its normal plot. This can in fact be seen even without considering the parables themselves, in which the point is more obvious. The basic announcement carries, by implication, the complete story in its new form.

Such implicit narratives are familiar enough in writings from roughly the same period. Josephus claimed that Israel's god was now exalting Vespasian as world ruler.[4] The Habakkuk *pesher*, by contrast, declared that 'God will not destroy His people by the hand of the nations; God will execute the judgment of the nations by the hand of his elect'.[5] The same story (Israel exalted over the world) has here been retold in two radically different ways. For Josephus, Israel's scriptures have come true in a pagan ruler, while Israel herself is punished for her brigandry; for the author of the Habakkuk commentary, the elect few, i.e. the tiny group of sectarians, are the true Israel, and the rest of the nation joins the pagans in the *massa damnata*. In both cases the retelling makes sense only in a context of shared meaning; readers or hearers would assume the normal story-line (or 'metanarrative'), and register the significance of the variation. Such retellings of the national story, we may be sure, played a key role in revolutionary or renewal movements. It was because prophets promised their followers such things as the parting of the Jordan, or the walls of Jerusalem falling down, that people followed them, eager for a new Joshua, a new Conquest.[6]

It should be no surprise, then, that Jesus retold Israel's story, both explicitly and implicitly, as part of his prophetic work. To refuse to see this is, ultimately, to refuse to think historically.[7] Nor should we be surprised, when we remember the other 'leadership' prophets, that Jesus would place himself, as the kingdom-announcer, at the centre of the redrawn narrative.

---

[4] *War* 6.312-15.
[5] 1QpHab 5.3f. (Vermes 1995 [1962], 342).
[6] *Ant.* 20.169-71.
[7] So, rightly, Meyer 1992a, e.g. 15-17.

Like several others roughly contemporary with himself, he believed that he was called to spearhead the movement of Israel's renewal and salvation. Israel's true god was becoming king; Jesus claimed to be his true prophet.[8] Though this claim was no doubt bold (most who made it did not live very long afterwards), it was not in any way bizarre or incomprehensible. On the contrary. It was precisely because its meaning was all too clear that the life-expectancy of such prophets was short.

The argument I wish now to mount must be advanced in five stages, which we will tackle in successive chapters. First (the present chapter), Jesus' announcement of the kingdom is best seen as evoking the story of Israel and her destiny, in which that destiny was now rapidly approaching its fulfilment. Second (chapter 7), the story therefore summoned Israel to follow Jesus in his new way of being the true people of god. Third (chapter 8), the story included a great, climactic ending: judgment would fall upon the impenitent, but those who followed the true path would be vindicated. Fourth (chapter 9), the story generated a new construal of Israel's traditional symbols. Like all readjustment of worldview-symbols, this was seen as traitorous, and involved Jesus in conflict with those who had alternative agendas, both official and unofficial. Fifth (chapter 10), this retelling of the story, and readjustment of the symbols, betokened Jesus' fresh answers to the key worldview questions. Behind his conflict with rival agendas, Jesus discerned, and spoke about, a greater battle, in which he faced the real enemy. Victory over this enemy, Jesus claimed, would constitute the coming of the kingdom.

Jesus' announcement of the kingdom was, in short, the articulation of a new variant upon Israel's basic worldview. The different elements of his announcement, which we study one by one in this Part of the book, should not therefore be conceived either as separate stages or as discrete themes within his work. They are more like a set of lenses, each of which needs careful individual cleaning, but all of which must eventually be held together in a line if the true picture is to be seen through them. As we do this, what we are looking at, in increasing detail, is *the mindset of Jesus*: his variation on Israel's worldview, his subversion of rival interpretations.

It is important to stress that the story as Jesus retold it, with its reworked praxis, symbols and answers-to-questions, fits exactly into the overall grid of second-Temple retellings of Israel's controlling narrative.[9] Other retellings, too, involved substantial adjustments at the level of praxis, symbol and

---

[8] cf. Sanders 1993, 239, 248. The old liberal idea that Jesus in no way included reference to himself as part of his proclamation is increasingly abandoned within the 'Third Quest'.

[9] e.g. the Maccabaean literature; Susannah; Tobit; the implicit stories of the Scrolls (with explicit moments like 1QpHab, cited above). Cf. *NTPG* ch. 8.

questions-and-answers. One has only to think of John the Baptist, offering people forgiveness down by the Jordan, and warning that racial descent from Abraham would count for nothing in the coming judgment; or (once again) of Josephus' breathtaking rewriting of Israel's metanarrative, ending with the Temple in ruins, and with Vespasian enthroned by YHWH in Rome, and all as the fulfilment of prophecy. Some recent scholarship has searched for a Jesus who had no conflict with his fellow Jews, producing a Jewish Jesus who nevertheless founded a religion that had more or less nothing to do with Judaism (Neusner), a Jesus whose Judaism was only skin-deep and whose mindset was an amalgam of Cynic and proto-gnostic wisdom (Mack), or a Jesus who was so Jewish that he had no real or substantial quarrel with the Pharisees (Maccoby, Rivkin). Historical study, I suggest, leads to the more complex result: a Jesus who engaged in that characteristically Jewish activity of subversively retelling the basic Jewish story, and adjusting the other worldview-elements accordingly.

We may anticipate here the completion of this Part, and set out a preliminary version of the full narrative that results from it all. Jesus was announcing that the long-awaited kingdom of Israel's god was indeed coming to birth, but that it did not look like what had been imagined. The return from exile, the defeat of evil, and the return of YHWH to Zion were all coming about, but not in the way Israel had supposed. The time of restoration was at hand, and people of all sorts were summoned to share and enjoy it; but Israel was warned that her present ways of going about advancing the kingdom were thoroughly counter-productive, and would result in a great national disaster. Jesus was therefore summoning his hearers to *be* Israel in a new way, to take up their proper roles in the unfolding drama; and he assured them that, if they followed him in this way, they would be vindicated when the great day came. In the course of all this, he was launching the decisive battle with the real satanic enemy – a different battle, and a different enemy, from those Israel had envisaged. The conflicts generated by his proclamation were the inevitable outworking of this battle, which would reach its height in events yet to come, events involving both Jesus himself and the Temple. As will be apparent, much of what has just been said could also be said about Jewish leadership prophets other than Jesus. None of it is out of place in Palestine in the first century; none of it smells of a later 'Christian' perspective read back spuriously into the lifetime of Jesus.

It would be comparatively straightforward to begin where we were in *NTPG* Part III and move forwards from there, to see how Jesus took the Jewish stories of his day (discussed in *NTPG* chapter 8) and subverted them. Things are complicated by three problems, which we must examine right away. (a) There has been considerable confusion about the nature of the

Jewish kingdom-stories, and we shall have to restate the historical position briefly. (b) The early Christians continued to speak of the kingdom, and to act accordingly; but the sense which they gave to the phrase seems to be shorn of many of the crucial overtones which we find within first-century Judaism. Have they simply picked up a slogan and incorporated it into a quite different story? (c) Twentieth-century writers, both scholarly and popular, have had quite a lot to say about the kingdom as Jesus announced it. This too presents us with some necessary preliminary ground-clearing.

In all three cases there is likely to be continuity and discontinuity. Jesus' usage (which can be set out in various ways; for a start, see the Appendix) certainly had some element of meaning in common with that of his contemporaries, otherwise his use of the phrase would simply be maverick or malicious – and incomprehensible. Equally, it seems *a priori* unlikely that the early church, in its use of the phrase, had completely misunderstood Jesus' meaning. We should therefore expect some continuity at this point, despite obvious discontinuities caused by the difference of perspective. Finally, it is similarly unlikely that *all* modern interpreters are *totally* wrong; we cannot simply discount serious debates and go back to the sources as though nothing of value had been said in the last hundred years or so.

We must, then, familiarize ourselves with these three contexts of meaning before plunging into the gospels themselves. This can be done fairly swiftly in the light of earlier discussion.[10]

2. Contexts

(i) The Jewish Hope

(a) Eschatology

The most important thing to recognize about the first-century Jewish use of kingdom-language is that it was bound up with the hopes and expectations of Israel. 'Kingdom of god' was not a vague phrase, or a cipher with a general religious aura. It had nothing much, at least in the first instance, to do with what happened to human beings after they died. The reverent periphrasis 'kingdom of heaven', so long misunderstood by some Christians to mean 'a place, namely heaven, where saved souls go to live after death', meant nothing of the sort in Jesus' world: it was simply a Jewish way of talking

---

[10] See *NTPG* Parts III and IV, esp. 280–307; 369f.; 456–64. On contemporary discussions of Jesus and the kingdom, see also chs. 1–3 above.

about Israel's god becoming king.[11] And, when this god became king, the whole world, the world of space and time, would at last be put to rights. This is the Jewish eschatology that I have attempted to describe elsewhere.[12]

The idea of Israel's god being, or becoming, king cannot therefore be understood without a sense of what I have described elsewhere: the anguished longing of Israel for her covenant god to come in his power and rule the world in the way he had always intended. A great many Jews of Jesus' day lived, implicitly at least, under the story that ran as follows:[13] YHWH, committed to Israel by an unbreakable covenant, was delaying his decisive act, for reasons best known to himself, though earnestly inquired after by the pious. He was holding back from putting into practice the plan that Israel knew he really had. Since he was the god of all the earth, it was clearly his will to keep his promises to Israel by vindicating her at last over her enemies, and by thus reordering the whole world.

The phrase 'kingdom of god', therefore, carried unambiguously the *hope* that YHWH would act thus, within history, to vindicate Israel; the *question*, why he was taking so long about doing so; and the *agenda*, for those with watchful hearts, not only to wait for him to act, but to work, in whatever way was deemed appropriate, towards that day. Furthermore, the idea of YHWH's being king carried the particular and definite revolutionary connotation that certain other people were due for demotion. Caesar, certainly. Herod, quite probably. The present high-priestly clan, pretty likely. When YHWH was king, Israel would be ruled properly, through the sort of rulers YHWH approved of, who would administer justice for Israel and judgment on the nations.

We therefore find, in Josephus particularly, that the idea of the true god being king was tied in with the dream of holy revolution.[14] 'No king but

---

[11] This misunderstanding, I believe, has been accidentally fostered by the position of Matthew at the start of the NT. Mt.'s fondness for 'kingdom of heaven' has played into the hands of those who come to the gospels with the assumption that their message concerns simply the attainment of *post mortem* bliss.

[12] *NTPG* ch. 10. What follows now will fill in some more details in this picture; cf. too ch. 13 below.

[13] Several of the relevant texts (e.g. Ps. 145.10-13; Isa. 33.22; 52.7; etc.) are set out and discussed in *NTPG* 302-7; cf. also *NTPG* 270-2. Many other significant refs. could be added, e.g. Zech. 14.9: 'And YHWH will become king over all the earth; on that day YHWH will be one and his name one'; Tob. 13.1, 15: 'Blessed be God who lives forever, because his kingdom lasts throughout all ages . . . My soul blesses the Lord, the great king! For Jerusalem will be built as his house for all ages' (in the context of the explicit *story* set out in Tob. 13.1-14.7). Cf. further Num. 23.21; Ps. 5.2; 22.28; 24.7-10; 47.2, 7; Isa. 41.21; 43.15; 44.6; Jer. 8.19; 10.7; 10.10-16; 46.18; 48.15; 51.57; Dan. 2.27; 2.44f.; 4.3; 4.32-5; 5.21; 6.26f.; 7.14; 7.18; 7.27f.; Mic. 2.12f.; 4.6f.; Zeph. 3.15; Zech. 14.16f.; Mal. 1.14. The same overall theme re-emerges in e.g. *1 En.* 84.2; 103.1, etc.

[14] On this para., cf. *NTPG* Part III, esp. 170-81, 302-7.

God!' was the slogan that fired the revolutionaries. It gave them courage to do the unthinkable: to tear down the eagle from outside the Temple, or to assemble *en masse* in risky protest at the latest indignity threatened or inflicted by a crass governor or a megalomaniac emperor. Monotheism and election, the Jews' twin beliefs, focused themselves into a story which issued in a great hope: there was one god, he was Israel's god, and he would soon act to reveal himself as such. Israel would at last return from exile; evil (more specifically, paganism, and aberrant forms of Judaism) would finally be defeated;[15] YHWH would at last return to Zion. Meanwhile, there were heavy taxes to be paid, a living to be eked out, Torah to be kept (if one could afford the time and energy).[16] There were sabbaths, to remind one that at the end of the present 'week' of Israel's story there would be a coming day of rest, when she would enjoy peace and prosperity. There were festivals, particularly Passover, at which Israel celebrated the fact that she was the free people of the sovereign god, who had given her the land in perpetuity and who specialized in defeating pagan tyrants. Symbolic actions kept the story fresh.[17]

Thus, week after week, and year after year, Israel kept alive the memory of what YHWH had done in the past to show that he was king, both of Israel and of the whole world, and so kept alive the hope that his kingdom would soon come, and his will be done, on earth as it was (they believed) in heaven. God's kingdom, to the Jew-in-the-village in the first half of the first century, meant the coming vindication of Israel, victory over the pagans, the eventual gift of peace, justice and prosperity. It is scarcely surprising that, when a prophet appeared announcing that this kingdom was dawning, and that Israel's god was at last becoming king, he found an eager audience. This was the story they were waiting to hear; or, better, this was the proper and fitting conclusion to the story in which they were already living. The story itself, though enormously varied in its several expressions, basically ran as follows:[18]

1. The first Temple, built by Solomon, was the place where YHWH chose to dwell. He had formerly revealed his glory in the tabernacle set up in the

---

[15] cf. e.g. Chilton 1982, 20, on Tg. Isa.'s rage (28.1, 10–13) against pagan practices in the Temple.

[16] Sanders 1992b, ch. 9 has tried to show that the tax problem was not as intense as is sometimes made out. It is true, as he says (168f.), that what created the revolutionary climate among the Jews was not taxes but 'the Jewish combination of theology and patriotism'; but this does not mean that the burden was not great, as is implied by Tac. *Ann.* 2.42. See e.g. Millar 1993, 48; Edwards 1992; Safrai 1992; 1994, 340–52.

[17] On Israel's symbolic actions cf. *NTPG* 224–41; on the keeping of the story fresh in Jesus' day, cf. e.g. Farmer 1956.

[18] On this whole theme see also *NTPG* 224–6, and bibliography there.

wilderness; now he had done so in Solomon's Temple.[19] The Psalms, which formed the staple diet of Jewish worship throughout the period, continually celebrated the fact that Israel's god was Lord of the whole earth, and that he had chosen to dwell in the Temple in Jerusalem, whence he would hear his people's prayers and come to their aid.[20]

2. Temple and royalty belonged closely together. When David was establishing his rule, one key move (at least in retrospect) was his bringing of the ark of the covenant to Jerusalem, and his consequent planning of the Temple.[21] When Solomon built the Temple, he established the pattern that would remain true for all subsequent generations up to and including the first century: the Temple-builder was the true king, and vice versa.[22]

3. The symbolism of the Temple was designed to express the belief that it formed the centre not only of the physical world but also of the entire cosmos, so that, in being YHWH's dwelling-place, it was the spot where heaven and earth met.[23]

4. The destruction of the Temple by the Babylonians was a catastrophe at every level, theological as well as political. It could only be explained in terms of YHWH's having abandoned the Temple to its fate. The glory, the Shekinah, had departed;[24] the Davidic monarchy had been cast aside;[25] heaven and earth had been pulled apart, so that worship became impossible.[26]

5. The longing for *return from exile* thus contained, as a major component, the equal longing for *the return of YHWH to Zion*, with, as its concomitants, the defeat of evil (i.e. paganism, typified by Babylon), the rebuilding of the Temple, and the re-establishment of the true Davidic monarchy. This hope for the future sustained itself with retellings of YHWH's mighty acts in the past, notably the exodus. As YHWH had been with his

---

[19] Tabernacle: Ex. 29.43; 40.34; Lev. 9.4, 6, 23; Num. 14.10; 16.19, 42; 20.6. Temple: 1 Kgs. 8.10f.; 2 Chr. 5.13f.; 7.1-3. Cf. also Isa. 6.4; Rev. 15.8, in which the cloud/smoke theme is repeated from Ex. 40.34f., etc. The stories of the wilderness tabernacle are, of course, normally regarded as, at least in part, retrojections from later Temple-ideology.

[20] e.g. Ps. 3.4; 5.7; 9.11; 14.7; 15.1; 20.2; 24.3, 7-10; 26.8; 27.4-6; 42.4; 43.3f.; 46.4-7; 47.8; 48.1-14; 50.1-3; 53.6; 65.1-4; 68.5, 16, 24, 35; 74.2; 76.2; 78.54, 68f.; 84.1-12; 87.2; 93.5; 99.2; 110.2; 118.19-29; 122.1-9; 125.1f.; 128.5; 132.1-18; 134.1-3; 135.21.

[21] 2 Sam. 6—7; 1 Chron. 21—2, 28—9; cf. e.g. Ps. 132.

[22] cf. esp. Meyer 1992a, ch. 11, with copious references to primary and secondary literature; and cf. below, ch. 11.

[23] cf. Barker 1991, *passim*; Meyers 1992, 359f. Thus, in (for example) Ps. 20, YHWH's help comes *both* from Zion (v. 2) *and* from heaven (v. 6); cp. Ps. 93.1-5.

[24] Ezek. 10.1-22; 11.22f.

[25] e.g. Ps. 89.38-51.

[26] e.g. Ps. 137.4-6; cf. Ps. 80.14-19.

people in the wilderness, as he had come to dwell in the first Temple, so he would come back at last to settle permanently in the midst of Israel.[27]

If, then, someone were to speak to Jesus' contemporaries of YHWH's becoming king, we may safely assume that they would have in mind, in some form or other, this two-sided story concerning the double reality of exile. Israel would 'really' return from exile; YHWH would finally return to Zion. But if these were to happen there would have to be a third element as well: evil, usually in the form of Israel's enemies, must be defeated. Together these three themes form the metanarrative implicit in the language of the kingdom. Together they sustain the concomitant hopes for the re-establishing of David's house and rebuilding of the Temple. It cannot be stressed too strongly that the 'kingdom of god', as a theme within second-Temple Judaism, connoted first and foremost this complete story-line. Any attempt to deJudaize it, whether or not in the interests of 'relevance' to another age, is bound to result in the dissolution into multiple elements of what first-century Jews would have perceived as a complex but coherent whole, in the consequent mutilation of each element, and (last but not least) in the serious misreading of the relevant texts.

Once we grasp this, it is not hard to see how the symbols and praxis associated with Temple, Torah, Land and Jewish identity sustained and reinforced the narrative of hope.[28] Although 'kingdom of god' referred more to the *fact* of Israel's god becoming king than to a localized *place*, the sense of Holy Land was invoked by the phrase as well, since YHWH had promised this country to his people. And the focus of the land was of course Jerusalem, with the Temple at its centre. YHWH would eventually restore the fortunes of Jerusalem; in the meantime, Israel was to show whose side she was on by following Torah as best she might. Different views as to what this would mean in practice are the demarcating factors between the different groups (Pharisees and Essenes in particular) that have been so intensively studied in recent years.[29]

This complex metanarrative explains further phenomena that might otherwise be puzzling. It has often been pointed out that there is no single clearly defined 'messianic expectation' in second-Temple Judaism. The reason for this was that such hopes formed simply one part of a larger expectation, and could be pulled this way or that within different tellings of the overall story. Conversely, however, we should not conclude, from the comparative scarcity

---

[27] cf. ch. 13 below.

[28] cf. *NTPG* ch. 8.

[29] cf. *NTPG* ch. 7. This shows, of course, that the legal or other emphases of certain groups were not an *alternative* to this apocalyptic and revolutionary eschatology, but were one way in which it found expression.

of reference to Messiah-figures in the literature of the period, that the idea of a coming king was largely unknown. The point is that such ideas took their place within a much wider-ranging narrative, which could be evoked in a number of ways that appear quite distinct until one grasps their overall coherence.[30]

In particular, we must stress that those among Jesus' Jewish contemporaries who were looking for a great event to happen in the immediate future were *not* expecting the end of the space-time universe.[31] This 'cosmic meltdown' (the phrase is Borg's) has regularly been supposed to be the event predicted or expected by second-Temple Jews and by Jesus himself. This assumption has been made by scholars from Schweitzer to the present day, and equally by literalists and/or fundamentalists. Though I have argued the case quite thoroughly elsewhere, subsequent debate suggests that the position I have taken needs to be clarified further before we can proceed.

Part of the problem, of course, is the slippery word 'eschatology'.[32] Out of a large number of various uses, we can distinguish at once two opposite ends of a scale. Some still use the word unambiguously to mean 'the end of the space-time universe'. Because I deny that second-Temple Jews (including Jesus) characteristically believed in this, one or two colleagues have, amusingly enough, accused me of 'abandoning eschatology'. Others, however, use 'eschatology' to refer to 'those views which find this world radically and profoundly corrupt or corrupting', and which offer a critique and solution.[33] In this sense, all serious social reformers and revolutionaries are 'eschatological'; so, for example, is Buddhism; but that does not mean they expect the space-time universe to come to a sudden end. In this sense, it is possible to argue, as Crossan does, that Jesus is 'eschatological', while firmly denying that he belongs within 'apocalyptic'. Crossan uses the phrase 'world-negating' along with this broader sense of 'eschatological', and (as we shall see presently) argues that Jesus belonged with a strictly non-apocalyptic *sapiential* 'eschatology'. Only when we are aware of this sliding semantic scale can we keep our footing in the current discussion.

The most critical distinction seems to me as follows. Did second-Temple Jews, including Jesus, expect a great event, within a generation or so, through and after which, quite literally, the world, especially Israel's world, would be a radically different place? Did they, moreover, expect such an

---

[30] *NTPG* 307-20; cf. below, ch. 11. Among literature to have appeared since *NTPG*, pride of place surely goes to Charlesworth 1992c; cf. too Collins 1995.

[31] cf. *NTPG* ch. 10.

[32] cf. Caird 1980, ch. 14; Caird & Hurst 1994, 243-67. One would never guess the depth and subtlety of Caird's analysis from the writings of some of his critics: see below.

[33] Crossan, in private correspondence, 18 September 1995.

event as the climax of Israel's long chequered career, her covenant story? Or did they not? I shall argue that they did, and that Jesus did. That, as I shall show in a minute, puts me in a completely different category from (for instance) Crossan, for whom Jesus' 'eschatology', for all the sharpness and specificity of its social critique, had no sense of a great coming event, still less of such an event as the climactic moment in a story, still less of such an event as the climax of *Israel's* story.

We might tabulate the options (they are not the only ones, but one cannot include everything in a map) as follows:[34]

1. Eschatology as the end of the world, i.e. the end of the space-time universe;
2. Eschatology as the climax of Israel's history, involving the end of the space-time universe;
3. Eschatology as the climax of Israel's history, involving events for which end-of-the-world language is the only set of metaphors adequate to express the significance of what will happen, but resulting in a new and quite different phase *within* space-time history;
4. Eschatology as major events, not specifically climactic within a particular story, for which end-of-the-world language functions as metaphor;
5. Eschatology as 'horizontal' language (i.e. *apparently* denoting movement forwards in time) whose *actual* referent is the possibility of moving 'upwards' spiritually into a new level of existence;
6. Eschatology as critique of the present world order, perhaps with proposals for a new order;
7. Eschatology as critique of the present socio-political scene, perhaps with proposals for adjustments.

The traditional reading has been (1), though Schweitzer himself would, I think, have insisted on (2). Bultmann advocated view (5), which is basically a way of expressing a kind of gnosticism in more or less Jewish language. Crossan's view is a combination of (6) and (7) (allowing for hints of (5); hence his favourable attitude towards *Thomas*); he distinguishes this quite sharply from 'apocalyptic', by which he, like the 'Jesus Seminar', mean (1). Borg, who thinks that Jesus did predict some drastic political events if Israel did not change her ways, belongs at (4) (on Crossan and Borg, see the next section of this chapter). The view for which I argued at some length in *NTPG* is (3), which I suppose was always liable to be criticized from both sides as if it were something it is not.[35]

The strengths of view (3) are quite simple. First, it retains the sense of urgency and imminence which pervades so much of the teaching of Jesus.[36]

[34] This analysis is in many ways parallel to that offered by Caird 1980, ch. 14. I have not attempted to line up his and my various senses exactly.

[35] C. H. Dodd, in many works, advocated a significantly different form of (3), in which, though he retained the Israel-context, the future had so completely arrived in the present as to be redefined much more radically than I am suggesting. Cf. Caird 1980, 252–4.

[36] Thus retaining the strong points of e.g. Meyer 1992, ch. 3; Allison 1994.

Second, it takes very seriously the actual referent of the Jewish 'apocalyptic' language which Jesus seems to have shared. Starting with passages such as Isaiah 13, it insists that language about sun, moon and stars being darkened or shaken has as its primary referent a set of cataclysmic events *within* the space-time universe, not an event which will bring that universe to its utter end. Even the great vision of the lion and the lamb lying down together continues with a state of affairs 'in which justice still needs to be administered and the rights of the poor protected'.[37] This view cannot, then, be accused of collapsing into timeless teaching or mere social critique. However sharp the latter might be, it still needs a theological dimension if it is to be authentic to Jewish eschatology. Nor can it be misunderstood as though it were reasserting a Schweitzer-like end of the world, whether or not as the climax of Israel's story. It retains the strengths of both Schweitzer's view and the 'social critique' view, while, I suggest, eliminating their outstanding weaknesses.[38]

Many if not most second-Temple Jews, then, hoped for the new exodus, seen as the final return from exile. The story would reach its climax; the great battle would be fought; Israel would truly 'return' to her land, saved and free; YHWH would return to Zion. This would be, in the metaphorical sense, the end of the world, the ushering in at last of YHWH's promised new age. From the perspective of covenant history, this complex event would be climactic, and not merely a paradigmatic example of a general principle (such as the importance of social justice). Moreover, this whole set of ideas and themes belongs together as a whole, not as a collection of abstract ideas, but precisely as a *story*.[39] And the whole story clearly has to do with the kingdom of god, even when that phrase itself, or something like it, does not occur. This, I suggest, is the proper and historically appropriate context in which to understand Jesus' sayings about the kingdom, or kingship, of Israel's god.

[37] Caird & Hurst 1994, 249, referring of course to Isa. 11.1–9.

[38] Allison 1985, 84–90 attempts a critique of Caird, but fails to understand what Caird was saying. His main criticisms (88f.) amount simply to a restatement of his own position. Caird spent a fair amount of time pointing out, in numerous contexts, that to describe something as metaphorical is not to say that it is 'merely' metaphorical. For him (unlike, perhaps, some of his followers), reading 'end-of-the-world' language as metaphorical did *not* mean that nothing dramatically climactic was going to happen; only that the language referring to that event was not to be taken with flat literalness – a point which Allison himself acknowledges, both in the passage cited and in e.g. 1994, 651 n.2. I totally agree with Allison (and Schweitzer) that Jesus 'was a man whose imagination dwelled in a world akin to the imaginative worlds of the old Jewish apocalypses'. But I think he has not grasped what that world was actually like, particularly its deeply revolutionary tendency.

[39] cf. again Meyer 1992a, 17.

(b) A Non-Apocalyptic Kingdom?

A very different view of the proper historical background for understanding
the language of the kingdom has recently been proposed by Burton Mack,
and developed and supported by Dominic Crossan and the Jesus Seminar as a
whole. Since this line of thought appears to be quite influential in some
quarters, it is important to show, building on chapter 2 above, why I believe
it to be completely wrongheaded.[40]

Rejecting the eschatological hope of Israel in its 'apocalyptic' form or
expression as the true context of Jesus, these writers have suggested that the
proper context is instead one that falls more within the general Hellenistic
culture of the day, evidenced in a couple of Hellenistic-Jewish sources and in
some pagan writers. Instead of 'apocalyptic' thought, we have 'sapiential'.
Jesus' sayings bore no relation to the specific expectations or aspirations of
Israel; rather, they teased people into looking at their lives and social situations in a new way. Instead of a future dream, they were encouraged to discover a present reality. Instead of an other-worldly expectation, they were to
understand his language to refer to actual social situations. Instead of the
view that 'the age was about to come to an abrupt end', Jesus held to a vision
that was 'more subtle, less bombastic and threatening'.[41]

The most obvious problem with this line of thought is that it perpetuates
the classic false reading of 'apocalyptic' which I have already argued to be
historically inadmissible.[42] But there are subsidiary problems as well. For a
start, it is not easy – as Crossan, I think, implicitly recognizes – to think of
Jesus-the-*peasant* embracing a style of thinking known to us, within Judaism,
only in Philo.[43] Nor is it easy to imagine a 'non-apocalyptic' Jesus giving

[40] cf. the 'cameo essay' on 'God's Imperial Rule: Present or Future?' in Funk & Hoover
1993, 136f. (on this work as a whole, see above, ch. 2, and Wright 1995a). Cf. too e.g.
Funk 1991, 52; Miller 1992, 428f. (also printed in Funk & Hoover 1993, 76f.); Vaage
1994, ch. 3. Koester 1992, 6 speaks of 'a new consensus' in Jesus-scholarship according to
which 'the eschatological character of Jesus' preaching of the kingdom' (he means
'eschatological', it seems, in sense (1) or (2) above, not in Crossan's sense (5)) is eliminated.
As a statement of the current situation in scholarship this is simply absurd.

[41] Funk & Hoover 1993, 137: the implicit but unsubtle value-judgment meant that 'The
Jesus Seminar awarded a pink designation to all the sayings and parables in which the kingdom is represented as present; the remaining sayings, in which the rule of God is depicted as
future, were voted black.' Cf. too Mack 1987; 1988, 69–74; Crossan 1991a, ch. 12. Downing goes further (1987a, 113–15): Jesus only occasionally spoke of the kingdom, and when
he did he would be echoing the meaning found in e.g. Epictetus 3.22.63, 72. (In Downing
1992 the 'kingdom'-theme is virtually ignored.)

[42] *NTPG* ch. 10, summarized at the end of the previous section of this chapter.

[43] cf. Philo *Spec. Leg.* 1.207; 4.135–6; *Op. Mund..* 148; *Somn.* 2.243–4; *Abr..* 261;
Quod Omn. 125–6; cf. Crossan 1991a, 287–91; Mack 1988, 72–4, with supposed parallels
from literature outside Jewish or Christian tradition. On Wis. 6.3–4, 17–20; 10.10 see
below.

birth to an early Christianity which (unless we beg the question by cooking the evidence) was thoroughly 'apocalyptic', and which then rediscovered the 'non-apocalyptic' meaning of Jesus at a later stage.[44] Far easier, I suggest, to start with an 'apocalyptic' Jesus (with the true understanding of 'apocalyptic', of course); to proceed to an early Christianity which was also 'apocalyptic', again in the proper sense; and to move from there, as Christianity grew and developed, to the non-historical, indeed sometimes gnostic, understanding of the kingdom that we find, for instance, in *Thomas* – an understanding which, though I think Philo would have repudiated it, bears more resemblance to him than to the major Jewish texts, such as Daniel, which are echoed so strongly in the synoptic material.

One other text has been advanced in support of the Mack/Crossan thesis, but the evidence crumbles away upon inspection. The Wisdom of Solomon, as we had occasion to remark in another context, is not so Hellenized as is sometimes supposed.[45] The passages which speak of the kingdom of Israel's god do not, as Crossan asserts, describe a kingdom which is 'eternally present, available . . . to anyone who heeds her call'.[46] Wisdom 6.3–4, the passage which Crossan quotes first in this connection, warns the kings of the earth that their sovereignty comes to them from the one true god (an idea in itself not far removed from the theology of the book of Daniel). This passage is flanked by other sections which, if they were not found in a book already deemed to belong to 'wisdom' literature, would unhesitatingly be labelled 'apocalyptic'.[47]

> The Lord will take his zeal as his whole armour,
> and will arm all creation to repel his enemies;
> he will put on righteousness as a breastplate,
> and wear impartial justice as a helmet;
> he will take holiness as an invincible shield,
> and sharpen stern wrath for a sword,
> and creation will join with him to fight against his frenzied foes.
> Shafts of lightning will fly with true aim,
> and will leap from the clouds to the target, as from a well-drawn bow,
> and hailstones full of wrath will be hurled as from a catapult;
> the water of the sea will rage against them,

[44] This is Crossan's interpretation of *Thomas*: a reaction against an earlier apocalyptic, resulting in the rediscovery of the even earlier message of Jesus. My argument here is parallel in form to that of Downing 1992, 151, 161f., but opposite in content.

[45] *NTPG* 329f., on resurrection. The relevant passage in Wis. (3.7f.) is closely parallel to the very Jewish, and very 'apocalyptic', 4Q246 2.1–8 (GM 138).

[46] Crossan 1991a, 290.

[47] Duling 1992, 55: Wis. combines both sorts of material. It belongs, in fact, to a central Jewish reading of the world and history, that easily embraces what *we* call 'apocalyptic' and what *we* call 'wisdom' within one overall worldview. Cf. Wright 1996a.

and rivers will relentlessly overwhelm them;
a mighty wind will rise against them
and like a tempest it will winnow them away.
Lawlessness will lay waste the whole earth,
and evil-doing will overturn the thrones of rulers.
Listen therefore, O kings, and understand;
learn, O judges of the ends of the earth.
Give ear, you that rule over multitudes,
and boast of many nations.[48]

There then follows at once the passage quoted by Crossan and Mack as evidence of a non-apocalyptic, 'sapiential' kingdom:

For your dominion was given you from the Lord,
and your sovereignty from the Most High;
he will search out your works and inquire into your plans.
Because as servants of his kingdom you did not rule rightly,
or keep the law,
or walk according to the purpose of God,[49]

which is again followed immediately by a note of apocalyptic judgment:

he will come upon you terribly and swiftly, because severe judgment falls on those in high places . . .[50]

If we were looking for passages in Jewish literature to compare with all this, the obvious ones would surely be Psalm 2 and Daniel 1—6. If Wisdom 6 offers a non-apocalyptic, sapiential kingdom, then words have indeed lost their meaning. In the same way, we are bound to see the other references to the kingdom in Wisdom[51] within the context of the work as a whole. There we find, after the initial praise of Wisdom and the warning to the rulers of the earth (chapters 1-9), a long historical survey, describing the history of the world, and of Israel, in terms of the activity of Wisdom. The final chapters of the book (15-19) deal in great detail with the plagues visited on pagan Egypt at the time of the exodus, and the sufferings of the people as they wandered, and sinned, in the wilderness. This is, in other words, *a retelling of Israel's story* under the category of 'Wisdom' – not an abstract treatise about a Hellenistic 'Wisdom', with occasional (and Jewish) historical footnotes.

The ending of the work may appear something of a puzzle, since the catalogue of Israel's sufferings and divine judgments simply comes to a stop. The puzzle is resolved, however, when we discover that the whole book

---

[48] Wis. 5.17—6.2. On the last few lines cp. Ps. 2.10-12.
[49] Wis. 6.3-4.
[50] Wis. 6.5.
[51] Wis. 6.17-20; 10.10.

speaks powerfully of *the divine judgment working its way out in history*, specifically the history of Israel. By telling the story of Israel in Egypt, and the great judgments which Israel's god poured out upon the pagan nations, the writer is presenting a none-too-subtle message to the Jews of his day: remain faithful to this god in the face of pagan (perhaps Egyptian) opposition, and you will be vindicated at the last. Like Daniel, in fact, the Wisdom of Solomon is designed to strengthen and encourage the Israelites when they are suffering. They are to hold fast to Wisdom, which is to be found in Torah, and their god will deliver them, judging the nations and exalting Israel as his people. This is substantially the same message as can be found in much apocalyptic writing. There is simply no way in which the Wisdom of Solomon can be invoked as evidence for a kingdom-theology which has bypassed the story of Israel, the covenant, and the coming vindication.[52] It belongs with classic (and non-dualist) 'apocalyptic', rather than with the dualistic world of *Thomas*. It is part of the mainstream kingdom-theology of first-century Judaism.

What happens if we take away the Wisdom of Solomon from the list of supposed non-apocalyptic kingdom-texts? We are left with Philo, the *Sentences of Sextus*, and various popular philosophical texts which speak of the wise man, the Sage, being like a king.[53] Are we seriously being invited to think that Jesus, rather than being a prophet in the mould of the great Hebrew prophets, was in fact more like the Alexandrian allegorist Philo, or that his characteristic sayings really resembled the generalized ascetic teaching of the second-century AD pagan moralist 'Sextus'?[54] Such a conclusion could only be reached if we were first to screen out with great care almost all the kingdom-sayings which we find in the gospels. This, of course, is exactly what Mack in particular does, leading with him into the ditch the majority of the 'Jesus Seminar'.[55] But this argument falls, it seems to me, by its own weight. Any hypothesis which fits Jesus more credibly into his Palestinian context, and does so with less violence to the actual evidence, must score highly over such a dubious proposal. I am reminded of Schweitzer's comment on those who try to explain Paul's very Jewish thought on the basis of Hellenism: they are, he says, 'like a man who should bring water from a long distance in leaky watering-cans in order to water a garden lying beside a stream'.[56]

---

[52] Against Duling 1992, 55.

[53] For Philo cf. n.43 above; *Sextus* 41-4, 307-11 (cf. Crossan 1991a, 290f.; Mack 1987).

[54] On *Sextus* and its problematic provenance cf. Chadwick 1959. On the Coptic MSS of part of the work (non-gnostic, despite being found at Nag Hammadi), cf. Wisse 1992.

[55] Mack 1988, 72; see above, ch. 2.

[56] Schweitzer 1968b [1930], 140.

Ironically, of course, once we understand 'apocalyptic' writings and sayings in their proper historical context, we can see that the emphasis which Mack, Crossan and Downing are all eager to preserve – the element of sharp and often quizzical social critique – is not only retained but enhanced. If, however, we take the ahistorical route pioneered by *Thomas*, we are left in a world of private dualistic piety. The world of first-century Jewish expectation, expressed in a wide variety of forms of which 'apocalyptic' is one, gives us far and away the most obvious context within which to understand Jesus' retelling of the story of Israel and her god, and of how, in particular, this god would become king. If, in that context, Jesus were to have addressed his contemporaries with stories, or even aphorisms, designed to make the non-historical, non-apocalyptic point imagined by Mack, Crossan, and the *Gospel of Thomas*, he would have been heard, if at all, to be contradicting himself. He would have been speaking, apparently, about what Israel's god was going to do within history – in order to warn his puzzled hearers not to focus their minds upon what this god was going to do within history.

We may conclude, therefore, that when we come upon a first-century Jew talking about the kingdom of god, we are correct to assume, at least to begin with and until solid evidence is produced to the contrary, that the language must take its meaning from the traditional Jewish story. Within that story, the meaning was not escapist or dualist, but revolutionary. The only apparent alternative is simply not viable.

We should therefore be able to understand fairly well the mood of Galilean villagers when Jesus began his proclamation. When it became known that there was a prophet roaming the countryside announcing that YHWH's kingdom was dawning, the reaction was entirely comprehensible. Many villagers would be thrilled to the core. Some would have been sceptical: there had been other prophets before, and things had got worse, not better. Herod and Pilate might have been disturbed, but as long as the prophet kept to villages there was little to worry about. The Jewish leaders, real and self-appointed, might also have been alarmed, as we shall see. Sufficient for the moment to note what people would have *heard* when Jesus talked about the kingdom of Israel's god. The extent to which he reaffirmed their expectations, and the extent to which he redefined them and indeed replaced them with new proposals, is a main theme of this whole Part of the book.

(ii) The Christian Reappropriation

If one starting-point for discussing Jesus' kingdom-language is second-Temple Judaism, the other must be early Christianity. This is properly the subject of a whole other book, and we must treat it briefly here.[57] Kingdom-language is spread fairly evenly across a wide range of early Christian writings, and even a cursory study of the relevant passages reveals the following highly interesting results.[58]

First, the early Christians spoke of the kingdom quite frequently, and apparently with an assumed reference. Kingdom-language seems to have functioned as a kind of shorthand summary for the preaching and apologetic message of the church, or indeed for the whole of what Christianity was about. To this extent, it almost functions like 'the Way' in Acts: it was a means whereby Christians could identify themselves and their very *raison d'être*.[59]

Second, this language still possesses the major features it had had in Judaism. The 'god' in question, in the phrase 'kingdom of god' and its cognates, is still, without a doubt, the god of Abraham, Isaac and Jacob, the one true god of Jewish monotheism, who claims an allegiance that excludes the worship of idols and the absolute claims of pagan rulers. The people of the kingdom are called to holiness: what we would call the 'ethical' claims of the kingdom loom large in several of the relevant early Christian passages.[60] The god who was thus becoming king had a true people, who would be vindicated when the kingdom finally appeared; for the moment this chosen people would suffer, but their god would win a mighty victory in which they would be vindicated.[61] They would then be established, as Israel had hoped to be, as the vicegerents of the creator god, ruling over his world.[62] This familiar combination of monotheism and election gave rise, as naturally as did the Jewish expressions of the same beliefs, to eschatology: the creator would act again within history, to bring the kingdom fully to birth.[63] All of this locates early Christian kingdom-language firmly on the first-century Jewish map.

Third, however, the early Christian use indicates that a substantial redefinition has taken place *within* this basic Jewish framework. Four key points, all closely related, must be noted:

[57] Following the introductory discussion in *NTPG* Part IV, esp. chs. 12, 15.

[58] cf. the Appendix (663–71 below).

[59] For 'The Way' as a shorthand for the Christian movement cf. Ac. 9.2; 16.17; 19.9, 23; 22.4, 22. Examples of 'kingdom' in this shorthand sense, where the summary meaning is assumed to be obvious, are Ac. 28.31 and Rom. 14.17.

[60] e.g. 1 Cor. 6.9f.; Gal. 5.21; Eph. 5.5; *2 Clem.* 9.6; Ign. *Philad.* 3.3; Pol. *Phil.* 5.3; *Barn* 4.13; Herm. *Sim* 9.15.3, 9.29.2.

[61] e.g. Ac. 14.22; 1 Cor. 15.23-8; Col. 1.13; 1 Th. 2.12; 2 Th. 1.5; 2 Tim. 4.18; Jas. 2.5; Rev. 1.6, 9; 12.10; 17.14; *1 Clem.* 50.3.

[62] cf. Ac. 1.6; Rom. 5.17, 21; 1 Cor. 4.8f.; Heb. 12.28; Rev. 5.10; 20.4, 6; 22.5; and perhaps *Thom.* 2.3f.

[63] Among many refs., cf. e.g. 1 Cor. 15.23-8, on which see below; 2 Pet. 1.11; *1 Clem.* 42.3; etc. *Thom.* is of course largely an exception: see below.

1. From time to time, but without any explanation such as we would expect had the point been unfamiliar, the kingdom is referred to as belonging not only to the true god but also to the Messiah. Sometimes this is an explicit conjunction, as in Ephesians 5.5 ('the kingdom of the Messiah and of God');[64] sometimes it is implicit, as when, in Acts, Paul teaches about the kingdom of god in close conjunction with teaching about Jesus.[65] Sometimes the kingdom is simply said to belong to Jesus as Messiah.[66]

2. In one key passage, this joint kingdom of the creator god and the Messiah is given a detailed chronological explanation, indicating that a decisive new element has entered into what still remains essentially the Jewish framework:

> But now the Messiah has been raised from the dead, the first-fruits of those who have slept. For since through a human came death, through a human has come also the resurrection of the dead. For as in Adam all die, so also in the Messiah shall all be made alive. But each in their proper order: the Messiah as first-fruits, then those who belong to the Messiah, at his appearing. Then comes the end, when he hands over the kingdom to the god who is the father, when he shall have suppressed all rule and all authority and power. For he must reign until 'he has put all his enemies under his feet'.[67] Death is the last enemy to be destroyed. For 'he has put all things in subjection under him'.[68] When, however, it says that all things are subjected, it is clear that this does not include the one who subjected all things to him. So when all things are subjected to him, then the son himself will be subjected to the one who subjected all things to him, so that God may be all in all.[69]

This passage, the earliest Christian writing about the kingdom that we possess, retains the essential Jewish framework. Not only in the explicit biblical quotations, but in the entire sequence of thought, the point is that the creator god is completing, through the Messiah, the purpose for which the covenant was instituted, namely, dealing with sin and death, and is thereby restoring creation under the wise rule of the renewed human being. The vital difference between this view and those we find in non-Christian second-Temple literature is that the kingdom is in a sense already present, as well as in another sense still future. Here the shorthand of Ephesians 5.5, cited above, is spelled out: the 'kingdom of the Messiah' is already established, while the 'kingdom of God', in this stricter sense, is yet to come.[70] We see here

---

[64] cf. too e.g. Rev. 11.15; 12.10; and cp. 2 Tim. 4.1.

[65] Ac. 28.23, 31.

[66] e.g. Col. 1.13; 2 Pet. 1.11; *1 Clem.* 50.3; cf. Jn. 18.36f.

[67] Alluding to Ps. 110.1 (a passage about the king's god-given authority).

[68] Alluding to Ps. 8.7 – the passage about the god-given authority of the human being over creation.

[69] 1 Cor. 15.20–8. On the whole chapter cf. Wright 1991, ch. 3.

[70] This terminological distinction is not, of course, maintained across the board: cf. e.g. 2 Pet. 1.11 (the *future* 'kingdom of the Messiah'; similarly *1 Clem.* 50.3 (unless the v.l. is correct)); Mt. 12.28/Lk. 11.20 (the *present* 'kingdom of god'). The discussion of all this in

exactly that tension between present realization and future hope which is so utterly characteristic of early Christianity as a whole and so puzzlingly opaque to generations of modern scholars. Of course there is a broader sense in which the 'kingdom of the Messiah' is itself part of the sovereignty, the wise saving rule, of the creator god. But the distinction made here enables Paul to locate himself and his readers at a point in the covenant plan of the creator god where the future hope remains clearly future (ruling out any suggestion that the full resurrection has already happened)[71] while equally emphasizing that a new phase in the plan has been fully inaugurated in and through the messianic events of Jesus' death and resurrection.

3. This new phase is therefore to be seen in terms of a kingdom realized in the present, something for which Judaism longed but which it never saw (unless we are to count Ben-Sirach's grandiose vision of the high priest in the Temple[72]). The 'kingdom of [god's] beloved son'[73] is already a reality in which the Messiah's people partake. They have already been created as 'a kingdom, and priests',[74] precisely through the work of the Messiah. But we can now see what that present kingdom actually is. It is not simply a private, secret, 'spiritual' experience shared by believers. Nor is it defined in terms of a hidden *gnosis*, a knowledge revealed to the elect. Nor is there any indication that by stressing the *present* nature of this kingdom one has left behind the world of Jewish apocalyptic, properly conceived. Those various ways of construing a kingdom in the present, as opposed to one in the future, tend inevitably towards a dualism in which the created order is devalued. What we find across the board in early Christianity (ironically, in view of current debates) is a firm belief in the presentness of the kingdom, *alongside* an equally firm belief in its futurity, these two positions being held together within a redefined apocalyptic schema.

Jewish apocalyptic, then, has been rethought, not abandoned, within early Christianity. But this rethinking of apocalyptic has nothing to do with a demythologization in which apocalyptic *language* conveys a gnostic or similar *meaning*, substituting the so-called 'vertical eschatology' of private piety or revelation (or, indeed, a 'world-denying' social critique) for the so-called 'horizontal eschatology' of Jewish thought.[75] The early Christian

---

Schweitzer 1968b [1930], ch. 5 is still of interest.

[71] cf. 2 Tim. 2.17f., in addition to 1 Cor. 15.12–19. The latter can of course be read differently, as referring to a denial of 'resurrection' altogether.

[72] Sir. 50.1–21: cf. *NTPG* 217.

[73] Col. 1.13.

[74] Rev. 1.6; 5.10; cf. Rom. 5.17.

[75] *Thom.* is obviously an exception; but, as I argued above (48, 72, 180), it is best understood as a serious deviation away from widespread mainstream early Christianity. *2 Clem.* 12.1–7 is probably to be understood as an attempt to supply an orthodox reading of the saying found variously in Clem. *Strom.* 3.13 (citing a passage from *G. Eg.*, which can be

rethinking has taken place because the crucified and risen Jesus has turned out to be the central character in the apocalyptic drama. The point of the present kingdom is that it is the first-fruits of the future kingdom; and the future kingdom involves the abolition, not of space, time, or the cosmos itself, but rather of that which threatens space, time, and creation, namely, sin and death. The vision of 1 Corinthians 15 thus coheres neatly with that of Romans 8.18–27, and, for that matter, Revelation 21. The creation itself will experience its exodus, its return from exile, consequent upon the resurrection of the Messiah and his people.[76]

4. Within this redefined but still thoroughly Jewish-monotheistic vision of the kingdom we find the most remarkable of the redefinitions. At the level of worldview, the regular Jewish *symbols* are completely missing. The *story* of the new movement is told without reference to the national, racial or geographical liberation of Israel. The *praxis* of the kingdom (holiness) is defined without reference to Torah. The answers to the worldview *questions* can be given in terms of a redeemed humanity and cosmos, rather than in terms simply of Israel and her national hope. This picture, which could be amplified in detail in terms of a study of early Christianity as a whole,[77] can be seen in reference to specific 'kingdom' texts, as follows. John stresses that Jesus' kingdom is 'not from this world', distinguishing it explicitly (in context) from the kingdom sought by the Jewish revolutionaries of the time.[78] Paul stresses that the kingdom is not defined in terms of food laws, but in terms of 'righteousness, peace, and joy in the holy spirit'.[79] Luke stresses that the newly inaugurated kingdom claims as its sacred turf, not a single piece of territory, but the entire globe.[80] In the vision of the Apocalypse, it is the heavenly Jerusalem that counts, not the earthly one; in that new city, where the Messiah's people 'will reign for ever and ever', there will be no Temple.[81] The symbolic world of first-century Judaism has been rethought from top to bottom, even while its underlying theology (monotheism, election, and eschatology) has been explicitly retained.

Early Christianity thus poses an obvious question for the historian, at this point as elsewhere. How are we to explain the way in which, from our very

---

found in *NTA* 1.168 (not 2.168 as Crossan 1991a, 295)) and in *Thom.* 22.1–7 (cf. too *Thom.* 106.1); cf. also Hippol. *Haer.* 5.2f. On 'kingdom' in *Thom.* cf. Davies 1983; King 1987; Duling 1992, 61f.

[76] For this theme in Romans 8 cf. Keesmaat 1994, chs. 2–4.

[77] cf. *NTPG* ch. 12 for a brief survey.

[78] Jn. 18.36f. The saying should not be read in a dualist or 'gnostic' sense; cf. e.g. Schnackenburg 1990 [1975], 249.

[79] Rom. 14.17.

[80] Ac. 1.6–8, on which cf. *NTPG* 374f.

[81] Rev. 22.5; 21.22. Cp. Gal. 4.25f.

earliest documents, kingdom-language is used in this fashion, at once so Jewish and yet so innocent of national and ethnic worldview-markers? We have seen that early Christian kingdom-language shared the theological lineaments of the Jewish usage. Yet, even at a surface reading, this early Christian kingdom-language has little or nothing to do with the vindication of ethnic Israel, the overthrow of Roman rule in Palestine, the building of a new Temple on Mount Zion, the establishment of Torah-observance, or the nations flocking to Mount Zion to be judged and/or to be educated in the knowledge of YHWH. A major redefinition has taken place.

The clue to this redefinition lies in the controlling story itself. We are not faced with a new story altogether, but with *a new moment in the same story*. The shape of the narrative is recognizably the same as that of the Jewish stories: it is the story of the creator god fulfilling his purposes for Israel. The difference is this: the Jewish tellings of the story locate themselves in what I suggested was Act 3 of the overall drama, whereas Christian tellings locate themselves in Act 5.[82] The all-important fourth Act, in which the problems of Act 3 are dramatically resolved, has taken place, and it has generated in turn a new Act, in which the symbols appropriate to the third Act are now deemed inappropriate. Specifically, the new Act self-consciously sees itself as the time when the covenant purpose of the creator, which always envisaged the redemption of the whole world, moves beyond the narrow confines of a single race (for which national symbols were of course appropriate), and calls into being a trans-national and trans-cultural community. Further, it sees itself as the time when the creator, the covenant god himself, has returned to dwell with his people, but not in a Temple made with hands. Once we understand how the whole story works, we can understand how it is that the actors have been given new lines to speak, that new praxis is now deemed appropriate, and that new symbols have been generated which perform, *mutatis mutandis*, the equivalent functions within the new Act to those performed by the former symbols within the earlier Act. We cannot, in other words, take the easy way out and suggest that the early Christians used kingdom-language in a completely non-Jewish sense. Their thorough reworking of symbol, praxis, and answers to questions was generated, not by the *abandonment* of the classic Jewish story, but by the belief *that they were living in its long-awaited new phase*.[83] There is all the difference in the world between a new story and a new Act within the same story.

---

[82] cf. *NTPG* 140–3. The 'Acts' are: creation, fall, Israel, Jesus, the church.

[83] It is true that, because they believed that this new phase was the final Act in the drama, they spoke sometimes of living in 'the last days' (e.g. Ac. 2.17; 1 Tim. 4.1; 2 Tim. 3.1; Jas. 5.3; 2 Pet. 3.3; Jd. 18). But, equally importantly, they were conscious of living in the *first* days of this new Act.

All the signs are that this major redefinition of kingdom-language was achieved well before AD 70. Other redefinitions were happening after 70, but not this one.[84] This redefined story, about a god who was king of the whole world, and whose kingdom was being established through Jesus of Nazareth, was being told throughout earliest Christianity as part of the constitutive story of the whole movement. It was already well established long before Paul. When we seek an explanation for this, there is only one which even begins to look like fitting the bill: that Jesus himself in his proclamation, and the very earliest Christians in their reflection on his death and resurrection, were responsible for the basic redefinition. Any viable hypothesis about the meaning of 'kingdom of god' must therefore show, at least in principle, both how Jesus reconceived and spoke of the kingdom, and why his earliest followers came to construe the extraordinary events of his death and resurrection in the way they did. These twin tasks are the major concerns of the present and following Parts of this volume.

(iii) The Kingdom in recent Scholarship

So: what *would* first-century Galilean villagers have heard if a prophet came into their area announcing that the true god was becoming king? A good deal of recent writing has attempted to clarify this question and to plot possible answers to it. We have already examined, in chapters 2 and 3, the current state of the various 'quests', which all address this issue one way or another. Within the present chapter, we have looked at one option in particular, that of Mack and Crossan, and found it wanting. Turning to the more serious contenders, time would fail us to tell of Schweitzer, Bultmann, Dodd, Jeremias, Ladd and others.[85] This story has been rehearsed many times;[86] one fears that students may know it better than they know the story of Jesus himself. What we must do, rather, is to focus on the key questions that have been discussed.

---

[84] As a good example, consider the reworking of 'kingdom'-language in *Thomas*: e.g. 3 (cf. *P. Oxy. 654*.3); 22; 113; 114. These passages are best seen as later attempts to rework the *Christian* meaning of 'kingdom'-language, not the Jewish one; thus e.g. *Thom.* 113 seems a clear reworking of Lk. 17.20f.

[85] Schweitzer 1925 [1901]; 1954 [1906]; 1968a [1967]; Bultmann 1957; 1958a [1926]; Dodd 1961 [1935]; 1971; Jeremias 1963a [1947]; 1971; Ladd 1966; 1974a; 1974b. Cf. too e.g. Cranfield 1972 [1959]; Allison 1985; Beasley-Murray 1986; Meyer 1992a. An older work which is still of considerable value is that of Dalman 1903.

[86] cf., recently, Perrin 1963, 1976; Chilton 1984b, 1-26; Beasley-Murray 1986; Willis 1987; Duling 1992; and the various writers discussed in ch. 3 above. These works give full details of the huge range of secondary literature.

We have already commented on the debate as to whether the kingdom Jesus announced was in any way 'political'.[87] Much ink has been spilled over a different question, that of the *timing* of the kingdom. Is it future (Schweitzer, Weiss), present (Dodd),[88] or in some sense both (Jeremias, Ladd)? Sometimes this has been expressed in terms of the 'nearness of God', as opposed (presumably) to his distance, or absence.[89] Likewise, there has been a good deal of concentration on the implicit *christology* within Jesus' kingdom-language. Where does the Messiah-figure fit into the announcement of the kingdom? Again, attempts have often been made to align kingdom-language with church-language, as though 'the church' is the real meaning of the kingdom. Thus politics, timing, distance, christology, and ecclesiology have been among the focal points of debate.

None of these questions is idle or useless. They all spotlight issues that must eventually be dealt with. But they do not lie at the heart of the matter. Historically speaking, all of them appear in some way or other quite anachronistic.[90]

(1) The word 'politics' carries, of course, all kinds of overtones from the contemporary world in which many scholars do their work, namely, the world of modern western democracies. Politics in the contemporary western world is often thought to have nothing to do with 'religion'. This is, of course, part of the legacy of the Enlightenment; in most periods of history, and in most countries in the world to this day, the two have been inextricably intertwined. Certainly first-century Palestine, with its ruling high-priestly family, its politically active Pharisees, its holy revolutionaries, and its devout but politically frustrated peasantry, would have been puzzled by the distinction. Attempts to make Jesus 'non-political' were always bound to fail. More nuancing is necessary: anyone who was announcing god's kingdom, even if they had only meant it in a Cynic sense, was engaging in political activity. The question is, rather, what sort of politics they were undertaking, and with what end in view.

(2) As to timing, the texts often thought of as referring to the end of the world have a much more precise, and Jewish, meaning. This suggests that the crucial question is not so much that of the kingdom's *timing* as of its *content*. Until we know what is being spoken of, how can we tell whether it is

---

[87] Above, ch. 3.

[88] Bultmann, too, comes in at this point, proposing that Jesus used end-of-the-world language to *mean* the call for urgent existential decision. The similarity in theological *content* between Bultmann and Dodd should not go unnoticed behind the clear dissimilarity in *form* and in individual exegetical and historical decisions (cf. Caird 1980, 252-5).

[89] Recently, Vermes 1993, 180, following a long German tradition.

[90] See Caird 1980, 111.

present or future?[91] This points back once more, therefore, to the question of the nature of Jesus' proclamation, and the aims which he cherished in making it.

(3) So it is, too, with the thought of the nearness or distance of Israel's god. There may have been first-century Jews who speculated about such things in the abstract, but our evidence suggests that the more important question would have concerned the imminent *arrival* of this god, after the long exile, in judgment and/or mercy. The strong evidence for this expectation, which we shall review in more detail in chapter 13, is severely distorted if it is used to suggest that Israel's god was perceived to be ontologically or metaphysically remote. That idea belongs more in the world of eighteenth-century Deism, or of Epicureanism, than in first-century Palestine.[92] The crucial issue was: when would YHWH return to Zion, to dwell with his people fully as he had promised them and restore them, to forgive them and restore them?

(4) There is indeed a good deal of implicit christology within kingdom-language, but we cannot read it off the surface. It will only emerge (as we shall see in the next Part of the book) when we have fully understood what exactly was being said by Jesus in his kingdom-language itself. It is vital that this discussion should not be short-circuited. As I argued earlier,[93] the announcement of the kingdom carried a clear, if implicit, self-reference, as it would have done for any 'leadership' prophet or would-be Messiah in the first century. The old idea that 'Jesus proclaimed God, and the Church proclaimed Jesus' simply misses the point, reflecting the unhistorical dogma that Jesus could not have held any particular beliefs about his own unique role. The way in which Jesus' understanding of his own *vocation* belonged closely with an implicit understanding of his own *self* demands careful thought that takes us beyond the announcement of the kingdom to the question of its fulfilment, which we shall study in Part III.

(5) To equate kingdom and church is at best putting the cart before the horse, and at worst a complete anachronism. True, there is a sense in which the community of Jesus' people was part of the overall meaning of his announcement of the kingdom. But this idea needs checking and modifying in far too many ways for us to be able to assert that when Jesus walked around the Galilean villages announcing the kingdom he was telling people about the church he was trying to found. Put baldly like that, it is bound to seem as out of place as the attempt to discover what sort of computer Paul used to write his letters. Again, as we saw in chapter 3, we should not be

[91] See below, ch. 10.
[92] cf. *NTPG* 161, and above, 205f., on the sense of divine absence after the destruction of the Temple.
[93] Above, 199f.; see too ch. 11 below.

thrown out of gear by the anti-ecclesiastical mood of some contemporary writers, who have amused themselves by creating a straw man ('Jesus came to found the church, complete with buildings, bishops, cardinals and candlesticks') and then knocking it down with a supposedly neutral and disinterested historical enquiry.[94] What this exercise ignores is the fact that there were plenty of leadership prophets in the second-Temple period (we know of several, and there were probably others as well); that the point of being a leadership prophet is that one should lead people; and that the people one leads will form some sort of community, which can in principle have a long subsequent history. The Essenes are the best second-Temple example. The Essenes lived on for two centuries after the Teacher of Righteousness; had it not been for the Romans in AD 70, they might be there still. The Samaritans, who survived AD 70, still are.[95]

What, then, is central to the understanding of the kingdom? That which we saw a moment ago: the Jewish expectation of the saving sovereignty of the covenant god, exercised in the vindication of Israel and the overthrow of her enemies. As far as first-century Jews were concerned, most of the redefinitions offered in modern scholarship would have been simply irrelevant. Inner peace of mind would not enable one to eke out a living under heavy taxation. The end of the space-time universe could scarcely be the sign that YHWH, the creator of heaven and earth, had vindicated himself and his people, and cleansed their land. Jewish hope was concrete, specific, focused on the people as a whole. If Pilate was still governing Judaea, then the kingdom had not come. If the Temple was not rebuilt, then the kingdom had not come. If the Messiah had not arrived, then the kingdom had not come. If Israel was not observing the Torah properly (however one might define that), then the kingdom had not come. If the pagans were not defeated and/or flocking to Zion for instruction, then the kingdom had not come. These tangible, this-worldly points of reference (the strength of those who present Jesus as a Jewish revolutionary) are all-important. Most modern scholars who have attempted redefinitions of the kingdom have considered such essentially Jewish ideas to be already moribund, and have passed them by on the other side, anxious to avoid contamination as they hurry to worship at the shrine of intellectual respectability.

Why so? After all, in western scholarship since (at least) Schweitzer it has been felt important to ground what one says about Jesus in terms of actual history. But the history offered by Schweitzer has in turn generated increasingly unhistorical developments. Schweitzer's Jesus, who prophesied the end of the cosmos, seemed so remote, so unlike modern perceptions of

---

[94] Wilson 1992 is one of the latest in a long line of such writers.

[95] On the Samaritans today cf. R. T. Anderson 1992, with bibliography.

reality, that his picture gained acceptance more by force of its strangeness than by any actual historical plausibility. At the same time, it opened up all kinds of interpretative possibilities, particularly once it was said that, since Jesus was mistaken, there was good reason to move beyond what he said into new ways of thinking. Schweitzer's view thus lent itself to the existentialism of Bultmann and the moralism of Dodd, for all that both disagreed with Schweitzer himself. It appealed, too, to popular millenarian piety, with the proviso that the texts which seemed to say that the end should have come within a generation did not in fact mean that literally.[96] But if we are to be true to first-century history we must chart a new course, and set it by the actual beliefs and expectations of the time, plotting Jesus' challenge to his contemporaries not in terms of a totally different message (they asked for the bread of liberation; was he offering them the stone of existentialism?) but in terms of his redefinition of the kingdom itself. The question is *not*, did 'kingdom of god', for Jesus, still mean 'Israel's god, the creator, at last asserting his sovereign rule over his world', with the connotation of the return from exile, the return of YHWH to Zion, the vindication of Israel by this covenant god, and the defeat of her enemies? That simply *was* its basic, irreducible meaning within first-century Palestine. The question is, *in what sense* did Jesus affirm this meaning, and how did he redefine the concept in such a way as to give rise to the meanings that emerge among his earliest followers?

This leads to a vital point of method. The *story* which can be evoked by the phrase 'kingdom of god' may well be present even though the phrase itself is absent.[97] Clearly, when revolutionaries talk of having 'no king but god', they are moving in the same world of thought as someone who says 'the kingdom of god is coming'.[98] They are appealing to the same underlying *narrative*. Similarly, when someone talks about the renewal of the Temple and its worship, about the cleansing of the Land, about the vindication of Israel over her enemies, or about dying rather than being forced to transgress Israel's law, they are telling the story of the coming kingdom of Israel's god, even though the phrase itself is not used. If, without a word, they *act as if* they mean to achieve these ends, or as if they are in some way coming to pass (even in a paradoxical manner), such symbolic praxis evokes the same

---

[96] Producing the interesting spectacle of fundamentalist interpreters taking the metaphorical language in Mk. 13.26, 30 ('the coming of the son of man') literally, and literal language ('within a generation') metaphorically. See the positions discussed in e.g. Gundry 1993, 466–70, 783–92. On Dodd as a moralist cf. e.g. Dodd 1961 [1935], 82f.

[97] cf. Meyer 1992a, ch. 1.

[98] To object, then, that Josephus does not use the phrase 'kingdom of god' itself, and that therefore he cannot be cited as part of the background of the concept (e.g. Duling 1992, 63), is to miss the point.

basic story. We must beware, therefore, of limiting our study to the strict occurrences of the word 'kingdom' and its obvious cognates as they occur in dictionaries and concordances. Much relevant material would thereby be omitted.

It is still, of course, vital to examine the places where the phrase does occur. But how might one organize such a mass of material? One way of calling up these sayings is according to the different hypothetical sources in which they occur: triple tradition, Q, special Mark, special Matthew, special Luke, and, quite ungrudgingly of course, *Thomas*. Alternatively, one might list them by rough categorization of content. Both of these tasks are undertaken in the Appendix.[99] A third possibility, sometimes adopted, is to take certain well-known and highly controversial passages and to attempt an exegesis based on each verse by itself, working eventually towards some kind of synthesis. This, which can look fine to begin with, actually puts the cart before the horse. It is unhelpful simply to begin with tough, gritty aphorisms;[100] we cannot expect to make sense of them as they stand without examining Jesus' work as a whole. Even those who make these aphorisms central do so, quite explicitly, on the basis of a prior notion of what Jesus' whole career looked like.[101] Such passages are not 'pillars', as is sometimes thought. If we begin with them, they are in danger of becoming millstones.

The rest of this Part of the book, then, offers a broad classification of the major emphases of Jesus' ministry in relation to his reaffirmation and redefinition of the Jewish expectation of the kingdom of God. I have organized the material, not without some difficulty, owing to its intricate complexity and the impossibility of breaking it up into separate categories, along the lines of the worldview model discussed earlier. Having begun with praxis, we continue with story, leading to symbols and questions. Throughout this process we will be able to draw on the parables, in which actual small-scale narratives again and again evoke and illuminate the underlying metanarrative or some part of it. This will lead us to the point where, in Part III, we can put the entire picture together, and plot the aims

[99] Below, 663–71.

[100] e.g. especially Mt. 11.12/Lk. 16.16; Mt. 16.28/Mk. 9.1/Lk. 9.27; Mt. 12.28/Lk. 11.20; Lk. 19.11. To be specific: in Mk. 1.15 ('the kingdom of god is at hand'), we might worry endlessly about the precise meaning of *engiken*, 'is at hand'; in Lk. 17.21 ('the kingdom of god is *entos hymon*'), we could argue for ever whether to translate that phrase as 'within you', 'in your midst', 'in your reach', or 'in your power'. One can only come at texts like this in the light of a more global discussion. Cf. ch. 10 below.

[101] Thus e.g. Mack 1988, 72: 'Given the predominantly aphoristic character of his utterance, [Jesus] *must have* used [the term] in a way that agreed with that style' (italics added); Funk, Scott & Butts 1988, 43: the Matthaean modifications to the 'great supper' parable are 'alien to Jesus' (so too Funk & Hoover 1993, 235).

and intentions of Jesus, and his basic and consequent beliefs, in their complex relation to his mindset.

3. Kingdom Redefined: The Announcement

(i) Introduction: Summary Announcements

We saw in the last chapter that the obvious features of Jesus' work, to any casual observer, would be certain styles of action and teaching that marked him out as a prophet. We are now in a position to see that the crucial element in his prophetic activity was the story, both implicit and explicit, that he was telling and acting out. It was Israel's story reaching its climax: the long-awaited moment has arrived! The kingdom has come! These statements, repeated (especially by Matthew) as summaries of what Jesus was saying, can only be understood as statements-in-context. They are like saying 'Frodo and Sam have reached Mount Doom', or 'They're coming into the home straight', or 'Jayne has had her baby': the hearer is assumed to know the context, the previous acts in the drama. To say 'the kingdom of god is at hand' makes sense only when the hearers know 'the story so far' and are waiting for it to be completed.

This recognition of the nature of the kingdom-announcement as part of an assumed larger *story* enables us to make a preliminary assessment of historicity. We may remind ourselves that if Jesus' announcement of the kingdom is to make historical sense it must make sense *both* as something that would be clearly understood within its Jewish context *and* as the presupposition for the significantly different resonances of 'kingdom' in the early church. At the same time it would clearly *both* challenge some prevailing assumptions within that Jewish context *and* retain a special focus which would be characteristic only of Jesus' career, not of the work of his post-Easter followers. It must be set within Judaism, but as a challenge; it must be the presupposition for the church, but not the blueprint. As we argued earlier, double similarity and double dissimilarity must characterize any analysis that claims historicity.[102]

How does this affect our reading of the opening statement of Jesus' public career reported in Matthew and Mark?

> From then on Jesus began to make an announcement, saying, 'Repent! For the kingdom of heaven is at hand.'
>
> Jesus came, announcing the good news of god, and saying, 'The time is fulfilled; the kingdom of god is at hand. Repent, and believe in the good news.'[103]

[102] cf. 131–3 above.
[103] Mt. 4.17/Mk. 1.15.

No one in Judaism had said quite that before,[104] but the sayings make no sense except in a firmly Jewish context. Equally, the early church, venturing beyond the borders of Judaism, did not announce the kingdom in these terms – they would have meant nothing to Gentiles – and yet the announcement they made, and the life they led, are unthinkable without this kingdom being believed to have come in a still very Jewish sense. They were not, after all, offering 'a different religious option' to a world already sated with such things. They were announcing that the one true god, the creator, had fulfilled his purpose for Israel and was now, in consequence, addressing the whole world. That is why the evangelists stressed Jesus' announcement of the kingdom. They were not simply reading their own communities' preaching back into an imagined 'history'; recent studies have shown that part of what they wanted to convey, as their message to their own communities, was the fact that in the unique and unrepeatable career of Jesus Israel's history had reached its climactic moment.[105] Thus, without as yet going into the finer detail of the sayings, the preliminary indications are that we have substantial historical ground under our feet in saying that Jesus' characteristic message was the announcement of the kingdom. This conclusion, indeed, is not particularly controversial except where dogma has gained total control over history.

This sort of announcement is presumably what Matthew means when he refers, later, to Jesus 'preaching the gospel of the kingdom'.[106] It is also presumably what Luke has in mind when he has Jesus refer to 'preaching the good news of the kingdom of god'.[107] The disciples, too, are sent out with the same message, both as a group[108] and as individuals.[109] We must stress, again, that this message is *part of a story*, and only makes sense as such. And there is only one story that will do. Israel would at last 'return from exile'; evil would be defeated; YHWH would at last return to 'visit' his people. Anyone wishing to evoke and affirm all this at once, in first-century Palestine, could not have chosen a more appropriate and ready-made slogan than 'kingdom of god'.

---

[104] Apart, perhaps, from John the Baptist: Mt. 3.2, cf. Mt. 11.11–12/Lk. 16.16, on which see below. John, in any case, would be the exception that proved the rule. No doubt other prophetic and revolutionary movements had announced the coming of the kingdom, but we have no reason for thinking they produced the same combined message as Jesus had done; in particular, we have no record of them calling Israel to *repent* at the same time as announcing the kingdom.

[105] cf. esp. *NTPG* ch. 13, with details of secondary discussions.

[106] Mt. 4.23; 9.35.

[107] Lk. 4.43; 8.1.

[108] Mt. 10.7/Lk. 9.2/Lk. 10.9, 11.

[109] Lk. 9.60.

This means, of course, that the announcement of the kingdom of god could never, in the nature of the case, be heard as a 'timeless' message, an incidental example or occurrence of some general truth.[110] The whole point of it was that Israel's dream was coming true *right now*. Equally important, it could never be divorced from the person and deeds of the proclaimer. This will have been as true for John the Baptist as for Jesus. *This* baptism is the 'getting-ready-for-the-kingdom' baptism; *this* proclamation is the one that is actually inaugurating the kingdom. The two are, it seems, very closely linked; Jesus regarded the work of John as the launching-pad for his own work, and it is historically probable that he saw John's arrest as the appropriate time to begin his own independent career of kingdom-proclamation.[111] The link of message and messenger is, of course, part of the scandal: the scandal of particularity (that YHWH should act *here and now* rather than at other times and places); the scandal that *this* was how the kingdom was coming; the scandal, too, of just who it was that YHWH was using, and the methods that he was employing. Like Salieri in Shaffer's *Amadeus*, scandalized that his god should choose the disreputable Mozart as the vehicle for divine music, Jesus' hearers could not but be struck, if they realized what was going on, at his extraordinary and shocking implicit claim.[112]

The significance of the kingdom-announcement, as reported in the short synoptic summaries, is strongly reinforced by certain elements of Jesus' praxis which we studied in the previous chapter. In particular, the exorcisms carry with them the haunting word: 'If I by the finger of god cast out demons, then the kingdom of god has come upon you.'[113] This evokes the same implicit narrative: Israel's god will one day become king; the establishment of this kingdom will involve the defeat of the enemy that has held Israel captive; there are clear signs that this is now happening; therefore the kingdom is indeed breaking in. YHWH really is becoming king; Israel really is being liberated.

If the short summary kingdom-announcements, even by themselves, evoke the entire story of Israel, the parables do so even more. Many of them are best understood as the retelling of precisely that story which is implicit in the

---

[110] By 'timeless' truth I do not mean necessarily a lofty philosophical abstraction. I mean something conceived to be a generally valid principle -- e.g. 'God is love' or 'oppressors must be overthrown' or 'brokered empires are bad for you' -- which could lead to political and/or revolutionary activity, and could indeed suggest some theological underpinnings for such activity, but which, crucially, would not carry the sense that the story of Israel was reaching its climax.

[111] Jn. 3.22-6; 4.1f.; Mt. 4.12, 17/Mk. 1.14. Cf. esp. Cleary 1988; Murphy-O'Connor 1990, 371f.; Meyer 1992a, 30-3.

[112] See Shaffer 1985 [1980], 27, etc. Cf. ch. 13 below.

[113] Lk. 11.20/Mt. 12.28. See above, 193-5.

summaries. We shall look at some crucial ones here, under the first of the three headings suggested by our analysis of the Jewish context of kingdom-meanings: 'return from exile', happening at last, but not in the expected way. We shall return in chapters 8, 10, and 12 to the second key element of the story (the defeat of evil, and the rescue of YHWH's people); and, in chapter 13, to the third and final one (the return of YHWH to Zion).

(ii) Stories of Israel's Paradoxical History

(a) Introduction

Several of the best-known parables find an obvious setting in the context we have sketched, as miniature stories which evoke the underlying narrative of Israel, and which show, in their different ways, how it is coming to a highly paradoxical resolution.[114] The collections of parables in Mark 4 and Matthew 13 are the obvious place to begin. These collections are clearly designed to characterize Jesus' preaching as a whole. This, the evangelists seem to be saying, is the sort of thing you would have heard Jesus say in a typical Galilean village at some stage (perhaps early on?) during his public career. These parables are the fuller tellings of the story which is implicit in the briefer kingdom-announcements.

Moreover, in explicitly describing what the kingdom is like, the parables in that very act inaugurate it, by inviting people to come and share the secret, to make this strange story their own, and to join Jesus in his new way of being Israel. The hearers are summoned to understand that their own present story – the story of Israel's dream of national liberation – is being subverted and changed into the dangerous and revolutionary story Jesus is telling. The parables offer not only information, but challenge; they are stories designed to evoke fresh praxis, to reorder the symbolic world, to break open current understandings and inculcate fresh ones.

The subversive nature of these stories, telling the story of Israel and giving it a devastating new twist, results again and again in the evocative challenge: 'If you have ears, then hear!' To add that to a public utterance implies that what has been said is cryptic, and suggests that a certain secrecy is necessary in the present circumstances.[115] This saying, which is firmly

---

[114] On the parables, cf. *NTPG* 433f., and 174–82, 229f. above.

[115] Mt. 11.15 (after declaring that John is Elijah); Mt. 13.9/Mk. 4.9/Lk. 8.8 (after the parable of the sower); Mt. 13.43 (after the explanation of the 'weeds'); Mk. 4.23 (secret things will come to light); 7.16 (what comes out of the heart is what defiles; this v. is omitted by some good MSS); Lk. 14.35 (useless salt will be thrown out). A parallel to this cryptic communication, at the level of the evangelists' own writing, is in Mt. 24.15/Mk. 13.14, 'Let the reader understand'; in other words, one cannot speak about these things

established in the tradition, reinforces the reading of the parables which I am proposing. Their frequent apocalyptic imagery reflects, of course, a characteristically Jewish mode of communicating a subversive new reading of the hope of Israel.[116] They are stories which both affirm the Jewish expectation and declare that it is being fulfilled in a radically new fashion.

(b) The Sower[117]

Of all the oddities about the parable of the sower, perhaps the strangest is this: there is still no agreement on what it was originally supposed to mean.[118] Considering the important place it occupies in all three synoptic gospels, and by common consent in the teaching of Jesus himself, this should be regarded as an indication that historians have not yet caught up with something fairly central in Jesus' career. Leaving aside at this stage the vexed question of what the parable meant to each of the synoptic evangelists, let alone to *Thomas*, I suggest that the context of the kingdom-announcement, in the form we have been studying it, provides a way forward.

I propose that, in Jesus' use of it, the parable of the sower (or whatever else it should be called; various names have been tried, and all disputed[119]) does two closely related things. Using imagery and structure which evoked 'apocalyptic' retellings of Israel's story, the parable *tells the story of Israel, particularly the return from exile, with a paradoxical conclusion*, and it *tells the story of Jesus' ministry, as the fulfilment of that larger story, with a paradoxical outcome*. Various indications point in this double direction.

---

openly just now. Cf. *NTPG* 390–6. See too Rev. 13.9, 18; *Thom.* 8.2 (the dragnet); 21.5 (seed growing secretly); 24.2 (light and darkness); 63.2 (the rich fool); 65.2 (the wicked tenants); 96.2 (leaven).

[116] On the apocalyptic background of the Mk. 4 parables in particular, cf. 4 Ezra 4.26–32; 8.41–5; 9.26–37. These are discussed by e.g. Boucher 1977, 45–53; Drury 1985, 26f., 53; and cf. *NTPG* 433f.

[117] Mt. 13.1–23/Mk. 4.1–20/Lk. 8.4–15/*Thom.* 9; cf. *Ap. Jas* 6.11; 8.1f; *1 Clem.* 24.5; Justin *Dial.* 125.1–2. In *In. Thom.* 12.1–2 the parable has become a miracle, performed by Jesus as a boy. On this parable see, in addition to the commentaries and books on parables listed on p. 175 above, Garnet 1983; Chilton 1984a, 90–8; Marcus 1986; and other bibliography in Guelich 1989, 186f., 198f., 215f.; Davies & Allison 1988–91, 2.403–6.

[118] So Boucher 1977, 47; Hooker 1991, 124; and, behind much of the modern tradition, Bultmann 1968 [1921], 199f.: 'the original meaning of many similitudes has become irrecoverable' – citing this parable as an example.

[119] e.g. 'soils', 'seeds', etc.; Mt. at least refers to it as the 'parable of the sower' (13.18). Garnet (1983, 41) suggests 'the parable of the fortunes of the seed'. In Aland's *Synopsis*, 174 (para. 122), the Latin and English titles refer to the 'sower', but the German one to the 'soils'.

First, the parable as it stands in all three synoptic versions exhibits, both in form and in content, that narrative mode which we know as 'apocalyptic', and which is used in such writings to tell the cryptic story of the creator's dealings with the world and/or Israel, and to show how that story is reaching its dramatic and surprising climax.[120] An obvious example is Daniel 2.31–45, in which the great statue has a head of gold, a chest of silver, a belly of bronze, and feet of clay. This is interpreted, in that allegorical style so typical of apocalyptic visions, to refer, not (as one might perhaps have supposed) to different features of a contemporaneous kingdom, but to successive stages, different kingdoms, in ongoing world history. At the end of the succession there will come a stone, cut from a mountain, which will smash the statue on its feet and destroy it; the stone will then become a mountain, filling the whole earth. This represents the kingdom which shall never be destroyed, which the creator god will establish in those days.

The parallel between Daniel 2 and Mark 4 is instructive. The vision in Daniel 2 concerns the kingdom of god and its triumph over the kingdoms of the world. The revelation of this vision is described as the unveiling of a 'mystery' which could not be made known any other way.[121] The 'stone' which smashed the clay feet and which then became a huge mountain was fairly certainly read as messianic by some groups in the first century, not least, perhaps, because of the well-known play between 'stone' (*eben* in Hebrew) and 'son' (*ben*);[122] and the passage offers a natural link to Daniel 7, with its four kingdoms and its 'son of man'.[123] The themes of the Daniel passage clearly have a good deal in common with themes in Mark, not least chapter 4. It will not do to object pedantically that statues and seeds (or soils) are like apples and elephants, or that Daniel sketches a chronological sequence while the parable describes different things that happen simultaneously. The point is that, just as the *form* of Mark 4.1–20 and its parallels resembles that of an apocalypse (its cryptic story, its transition passage about the revealing of mysteries, and its point-by-point interpretation), so here the *content* is so close (the failed sowings, and the kingdom of the creator god successfully set up, seen as the unveiling of the mysterious divine plan and, as we shall see, as the revelation of the Messiah) that it gives the lie to any suggestion of either forcing the evidence or mere coincidence. When we read it in its first-century Jewish context, the parable of the sower,

[120] See *NTPG* 393f., 433; and above, 231–41.

[121] Dan. 2.17–23: in vv. 18, 19 the key word is *raz*, translated *mysterion* in LXX.

[122] cf. Snodgrass 1983, 113–18; and recently Gundry 1993, 689–91, citing e.g. Ex. 28.9f., Isa. 54.11–13, and other passages. Rabbinic texts identifying the rejected stone of Ps. 118.22f. with Abraham, David and the Messiah are collected in SB 1.875f. Cf. below, 501.

[123] cf. *NTPG* 313–17, and below, 500f.

like the vision of the statue, asks to be understood as a retelling of Israel's controlling narrative about the kingdoms of the world and the kingdom of god.

The second indication that the sower is a retelling of the story of Israel is found in the fairly close parallel with the wicked tenants (Mark 12.1–12 and parallels).[124] There should be no doubt that this parable narrates the history of Israel in terms of YHWH's sending of prophets, and finally of his son. The prophets are looking for 'fruit', which is of course what the unsuccessful seeds fail to produce and what the successful seed produces in abundance.[125] They come in sequence: the first is beaten, the second wounded in the head, the third killed.[126] Finally he sends his 'son', who, in being rejected, nevertheless becomes the 'stone' spoken of in Psalm 118.22. Three sendings with no fruit; then a final sending with apparent failure but actual success, both in that the owner eventually gets the fruit and in that the son, the 'stone', though rejected, becomes the head of the corner. This is Jesus' subversive retelling of the story of Israel, which as we shall see belongs exactly with his action in the Temple.[127] It evokes Daniel 2 in various ways; I suggest that it also describes something very similar to what is going on in the parable of the sower.

The third indication that the parable is retelling the story of Israel – and this is also an indication of where, within the story, the teller and hearers belong – lies at the heart of the narrative, in the idea of the 'seed' itself. Within second-Temple Judaism, the idea of 'seed' is capable of functioning as a shorthand for the 'remnant' who will return when the exile is finally over. The 'seed' is a metaphor for the true Israel, who will be vindicated when her god finally acts, 'sown' again in her own land.[128] For someone

---

[124] cf. below, 497–501.

[125] cf. Mk. 12.2/Mt. 21.34/Lk. 20.10; Mt. 21.41.

[126] The reference to 'many others' being sent after this (Mk. 12.5/Mt. 21.36, missing from Lk. and *Thom.*) is regarded by some as an interpolation, spoiling the neat patterning of the story (cf. Gundry 1993, 685f.). But the narrative is governed more by its cryptic reference to Israel's history, in which multitudes of prophets were sent and rejected (cp. Jer. 7.25; 25.3, and frequently) than by formal laws of story-structure. It is far more likely that it has been smoothed down to regulation size in Lk. and *Thom.* than that it has been untidily 'expanded' in Mk. and Mt.

[127] Below, 497–501.

[128] The usage goes back at least to Isa. 6.13c ('the holy seed is its stump'), referring to the tree of Israel, felled in the exile. Behind that, of course, are the promises to Abraham and his 'seed' (Gen. 12.7; 13.15, etc.), reflected in e.g. Tob. 4.12. For the idea of return from exile as a 'sowing', and/or the returnees as 'seed', cf. Ezra 9.2 (cp. 1 Esdr. 8.70, 88); Ps. 126.6; Isa. 1.9 (quoted in this sense in Rom. 9.29); 31.9 LXX; 37.31f. ('the remnant that is escaped of the house of Judah shall again take root downward, and bear fruit [LXX *sperma*, "seed"] upward; for out of Jerusalem shall go forth a remnant, and out of Mount Zion those who escape'); 43.5 ('I will bring your seed from the east, and from the west I will gather you'); 44.3; 45.26; 53.10; 54.3; 60.21; 61.9; 65.23; 66.22; Jer. 24.6; 31.27; 32.41; 46.27

announcing the kingdom to tell a story about the seed being sown, then, would be to say: the remnant is now returning. The exile is over. Your god is at last sowing the good seed, creating his true Israel. It will not do to object that, in the parable's interpretation, the 'seed' is the 'word'.[129] That is precisely what we should expect, granted one of the central and classic prophecies of return from exile:

> For as the rain and the snow come down from heaven,
>   and do not return there until they have watered the earth,
> making it bring forth and sprout,
>   giving seed to the sower and bread to the eater,
> so shall my word be that goes out from my mouth;
>   it shall not return to me empty,
> but it shall accomplish that which I purpose,
>   and succeed in the thing for which I sent it.
> For you shall go out in joy,
>   and be led back in peace;
> the mountains and the hills before you shall burst into song,
>   and all the trees of the field shall clap their hands.
> Instead of the thorn shall come up the cypress;
>   instead of the brier shall come up the myrtle;
> and it shall be to YHWH for a memorial,
>   for an everlasting sign that shall not be cut off.[130]

The close thematic links between several aspects of the parable (and its interpretation) and this passage suggest strongly that we are on the right lines. The sowing of seed, resulting in a crop that defies the thorns and briers, is a picture of YHWH's sowing of his word, and the result is the return from exile and, indeed, the consequent renewal of all creation. At the heart of the story is the cryptic announcement that the time foretold by the prophets is at last coming to birth.

But if the parable informs Jesus' hearers that they are living in the days of the return, it also warns them that the final harvest will not come about in the way they had imagined. It will not simply be the case that, following previous unsuccessful 'sowings', there is now to be a thoroughly successful one. The parable does not describe a chronological sequence, but different

---

('I will save you from afar, and your seed from the land of captivity; and Jacob shall return, and shall be quiet and at rest, and none shall make him afraid'); Ezek. 17.22f.; 36.8-12 (nb. the whole context); Hos. 2.23; Amos 9.15; Zech. 10.8f.; Mal. 2.15. In post-biblical material, cf. *Jub.* 1.15-18; 21.24; *Ps. Sol.* 14.2f.; *1 En.* 62.8; 4 Ezra 8.41 (a simile very like the parable under discussion); 1QM 13.7; 1QH 8.4-26; 17.14. See esp. Garnet 1983, whose suggestive piece helped me bring this already-germinating suggestion to fruition, though I have pruned some of his ideas and grafted in others.

[129] Mk. 4.14/Lk. 8.11; Mk. 4.15/Mt. 13.19/Lk. 8.12; etc.

[130] Isa. 55.10-13.

results from simultaneous sowings. Israel's god is acting, sowing his prophetic word with a view to restoring his people, but much of the seed will go to waste, will remain in the 'exilic' condition, being eaten by birds (satanic forces, or perhaps predatory Gentiles), or lost among the rocks and thorns of the exilic wilderness.[131] The eventual harvest, though, will be great. We are here not far from Jesus' story about the great banquet. The party will go ahead, and the house will be full, but the original guests will not be there.[132] Judgment and mercy are taking place simultaneously.

The parable, therefore, not only informs, but, as has been pointed out often enough, it *acts*. It creates the situation where having ears to hear is itself one of the marks of the true remnant. Israel as she stands may look as though she had returned from exile; she may want to consider herself automatically and inalienably the true people of YHWH; but only those who hear the word as it is now proclaimed, and hold it fast, will form the remnant that Israel's god is creating. Those who do not are like those who reject the prophetic summons in the 'wicked tenants'. They are calling down judgment upon themselves.

These considerations tell strongly in favour of the 'sower' being a story about the return from exile, as it is taking place in Jesus' own work. His telling of the story forms a cryptic warning and invitation. Israel will not be re-affirmed as she stands when her god acts, as he is now doing. The parable is, obviously, self-referential; it describes its own effect.

One recent writer who came close, in outline at least, to this view, was Robert Guelich. The parable of the sower, he wrote, is about

> the outcome of God's eschatological activity in history, an outcome that is more complex than the common Jewish expectation of a final harvest . . . God's eschatological activity . . ., like scattered seed, encounters opposition and failure but also produces an abundant harvest.[133]

This, I suggest, is on the right lines, and can now be sharpened up. The parable, as I said, tells two closely related stories – or rather, the same story from two different points of view.

---

[131] Birds = Gentiles: Ezek. 17.23; 31.6, 13; Dan. 4.12; = satanic enemies, *Jub.* 11.11; *Apoc. Abr.*. 13.1–15; with Guelich 1989, 202. Thorns = exilic judgment: Isa. 5.5f.; 7.23–5; 32.13; Ezek. 28.24; Hos. 9.6; 10.8; and, behind these, of course, Gen. 3.18. Sowing among thorns is forbidden in Jer. 4.3, as part of the prophetic warning of coming judgment; cf. too Jer. 12.13.

[132] Mt. 22.1–14/Lk. 14.15–24/*Thom.* 64.

[133] Guelich 1989, 197. Cf. too Dodd 1961 [1935], 135 (expounding the secret seed): 'The parable in effect says, Can you not see that the long history of God's dealings with His people has reached its climax?' On the paradoxical results (Israel expected harvest, not seed-time; the kingdom should be manifest, not hidden) cf. Evans 1990, 374.

On the one hand, it tells the long and puzzling story of Israel, and says cryptically, but plainly for those with ears to hear, that now at last the story is reaching its goal. To say this is already to launch a stupendous claim. Jesus is implying that *his own career and kingdom-announcement* is the moment towards which all Israel's history has been leading. If we fail to see how profoundly subversive, how almost suicidally dangerous, such a claim was, it is perhaps because we have forgotten that there was another would-be king of the Jews, Herod Antipas, not too far away. People who attempted to set themselves up against that family tended to come to a bad end.

On the other hand, precisely because it is telling the story of Israel, the parable also tells the story of Jesus' own ministry as the *encapsulation*, not merely the *climax*, of that story. Jesus, as himself first and foremost a prophet, was to suffer the fate of the prophets. He was the prophetic agent through whom the recreative word of YHWH was being sown; but, like Isaiah, he would sow that seed on the path, on the rock, and among the thorns – just as he would come as a prophet to the vineyard-tenants, and himself be rejected. But (and here is the mystery indeed, which will take us some time to unpick in the next Part of this book) in this very rejection, in this very failure, there was to be seen the god-given plan for the establishment of the kingdom. The rejected stone would become the head corner-stone. The vineyard would be given to others, who would give the owner his fruit. Some seed would fall on good soil, and produce an abundant harvest.

Observe how the matter then unfolds. Jesus tells a story about a sower sowing seed in a field. Scholars have argued as to whether or not the picture fits with contemporary Palestinian farming methods,[134] but this is really beside the point. In the narrative logic of the parable (as opposed to a historicizing what-would-really-have-happened sort of reading), the sower sows in three unsuccessful places, and finally succeeds with the fourth. In the tradition of cryptic second-Temple Jewish stories, the assumption should be, until we have firm evidence otherwise, that the sower is YHWH himself, and that his desire (as the sower's desire is to plant successful seed) is to establish his kingdom. The other plantings will bear no fruit, but there will be one that will yield a large and satisfying crop.[135]

Jesus, then, in telling this story, indicates that his own work is at one and the same time the climax and the recapitulation of the story of Israel.

---

[134] cf. Fitzmyer 1981, 703 for discussion and bibliography. Among the chief protagonists are Jeremias 1963a [1947], 11f. (the parable fits with the culture) and Drury 1973; 1985, 55–8 (the parable mysteriously controverts the culture). Jeremias was following Dalman 1926.

[135] Another debate should be regarded as settled: thirtyfold, sixtyfold and a hundredfold indicates a substantial return; much better than average, but not wildly exaggerated or miraculous. Cf. Meyer 1979, 41; Guelich 1989, 195; Davies & Allison 1988–91, 2.385.

Climax: as Matthew and Luke record in a different context, the law and the prophets were until John, but since then – that is, in Jesus' own ministry – the good news of the kingdom has been proclaimed.[136] Israel's long wait is over; YHWH is at last sowing good seed which will bring forth fruit. As with the wicked tenants, the previous sowings represent the unfruitful work of the prophets, longing to bring Israel back to her god. Jesus is also rejected – by some; but ultimately he succeeds where the prophets had failed. Recapitulation: if Jesus is a prophet like the prophets of old, then the reaction they provoked – and received – will be his as well. His message will be rejected by most, and judgment will result; but YHWH's strange purposes of salvation will not thereby be thwarted, but rather fulfilled. The story is, then, about Jesus' own ministry, but not entirely in the way sometimes supposed.[137]

We are now in a position to understand the quotation from Isaiah 6.9–10 in Mark 4.12, Matthew 13.13–15, and Luke 8.10, that has given exegetes and theologians so much trouble down the years.[138] Isaiah's prophetic commission summoned him to a strange ministry which would bring Israel *through* devastating judgment to mercy. The hardening process ('keep looking, but do not see; keep listening, but do not comprehend') will lead the people to judgment:

> until cities lie waste without inhabitants, and houses without people . . . Even if a tenth part remain in it, it will be burned again, like a terebinth or an oak whose stump remains standing when it is felled . . .[139]

– but there will be mercy beyond the judgment. And the sign of mercy will be, of course, the 'seed', hidden within the charred stump: 'the holy seed is its stump'.[140] Just as the parable of the wicked tenants evokes Isaiah 5, so, I suggest, the sower evokes Isaiah 6 – not accidentally, or obliquely, but by way of *telling the story of Israel as the story of rejected prophets, consequent judgment, and renewal the other side of judgment*, and by way of describing Jesus' own ministry as the culmination, and hence encapsulation or recapitulation, of that prophetic heritage. For Jesus, Isaiah was *both* an earlier part of the story, one of his predecessors in the long line, one (moreover) whose own commission contained a most striking statement of the inevitable

---

[136] Lk. 16.16/Mt. 11.12f., on which see below, 468f.; cf. Meyer 1992a, ch. 2.

[137] For the view that the parable is simply about Jesus' ministry and the varied response it produces, cf. e.g. Guelich 1989, 192; Nolland 1989, 376; Hooker 1991, 122f.

[138] See e.g. the recent discussions in Guelich 1989, 198–215; Hooker 1991, 125–9; Gundry 1993, 195–204. Cf. too Jn. 12.40f.; Ac. 28.26f.; and cp. Rom. 11.8.

[139] Isa. 6.11–13.

[140] This last phrase of Isa. 6.13, missing from LXX, is present in 1QIs[a]. This link between Isa. 6 and Mk. 4 is explored suggestively by Bowker 1974; Evans 1981, 1985.

rejection of his message – *and* one whose ministry, and its results, were being climactically recapitulated in his own work.

This suggests a way through the puzzle of the apparently predestinarian passage in Mark 4.10–12, which seems to say that Jesus told parables *so that* people would not understand him. The problem only arises, in fact, when the historical context is not taken seriously, and when the vacuum thus created is filled with a generalized 'theology' in which Jesus is either the teacher of timeless truths or the announcer of impenetrable enigmas. Parables are neither of these. 'If you have ears, then hear'; if too many understand too well, the prophet's liberty of movement, and perhaps life, may be cut short. Jesus knew his kingdom-announcement was subversive. It would be drastically unwelcome, for different reasons, to the Romans, to Herod, and also to zealous Jews and their leaders, whether official or not. He must therefore speak in parables, 'so that they may look and look but never see'. It was the only safe course. Only those in the know must be allowed to glimpse what Jesus believed was going on.[141] These stories would get past the censor – for the moment. There would come a time for more open revelation. The parable of the wicked tenants did not need an explanation. 'They perceived that he had told this parable against them', and took appropriate action.

The second-order offence of the parable then emerges into the open. Not only was Jesus making the risky claim that the story of Israel was coming to its climax in his own work. He was claiming that this climax, so far from underwriting Israel's present life and ambitions, was radically challenging them – so much so that his proclamation would simply harden them in their ways. The son would come to the vineyard, and the tenants would reject him. They would look and look, but never see.

This insight is a 'mystery': not a 'puzzle', something merely opaque or confusing, but the secret plan of YHWH, now cryptically unveiled.[142] The disciples stand to Jesus as the seer to the angel in, for example, 4 Ezra 10.29–58, where 10.38 assures Ezra that the Most High has revealed 'many

---

[141] The parable, as is often seen, thus asks to be closely correlated with the final paragraph of Mk. 3 (Mk. 3.31–5/Mt. 12.46–50/*Thom.* 99/*G. Ebi.* 5.), in which Jesus coolly redefines his 'family': 'who are my mother and brothers? Those who hear the word of god and do it.' There are 'insiders' who are outside, and vice versa. For other cryptic and deeply subversive sayings which can only be explained when away from the crowds cf. e.g. Mk. 7.17; 10.10.

[142] Mk. 4.11 & pars. speak of Israel's god *giving* a mystery to the disciples; this is rare in Jewish literature, and some have quite reasonably doubted whether Jesus would have spoken thus (so Harvey 1980, 335f.). The passive, 'it has been given', clearly refers to divine action. But the form of words is not unknown, and in any case may well represent an attempt to express in Greek a more natural Aramaic idiom: so Gundry 1993, 197, citing *1 En.* 51.3; 68.1.

mysteries' to him[143] – mysteries concerning precisely the strange judgment that has fallen on Jerusalem. The 'mystery', the whole secret plan of Israel's god, is that *this* was how his purpose for Israel is to be worked out. He would come to rescue his people, not in a blaze of triumphant glory, but in the sowing of seed, the long-promised prophetic 'word', the god-sent agency through which Israel and the world would be renewed. (The 'word' was, after all, one of the ways in which second-Temple Jewish thought was able to express YHWH's active involvement in the world, and in Israel's history, without transgressing her basic monotheism.[144]) The method of YHWH's return, and of Israel's release from bondage, would therefore itself involve a hiddenness and a secret revelation. What was revealed was not only what the mystery was but also that the plan was indeed a mystery. It was a plan of judgment and mercy; a plan to be put into operation, not through the Herodian dynasty, nor through the Pharisaic movement, nor through high-priestly activity in the Temple, nor yet in the plottings of holy revolutionaries, but in Jesus' own proclamation and activity. As Mark indicates, this parable is thus itself *about* parables.[145]

The 'explanation' of the parable at last falls into place.[146] The paradoxical prophetic 'sowings' of the 'word' were being recapitulated in Jesus' own ministry. The satan was at work to snatch away the seed.[147] Many were called, but few chosen; many sown, few harvested – though the harvest itself would be abundant. The explanation functioned as a challenge to 'those inside', who had been grasped by Jesus' words. They must persevere, and become those that bear fruit. In them the destiny of Israel would be realized.

The evangelists are therefore correct, I suggest, to treat the sower as the classic parable of Jesus' kingdom-announcement. It claimed that Israel's history had reached its great climactic moment with the work of Jesus himself. The end of exile was at hand; the time of lost seed was passing away, and the

---

[143] The Latin is *mysteria multa*, no doubt reflecting an underlying Greek *mysteria polla*. The Ethiopic version has 'a hidden secret', and the first Arabic version 'a mighty secret'. On 'mystery' in 4 Ezra see above all Stone 1990, 332–4.

[144] cf. *NTPG* 256–9. The other ways are of course Torah, Shekinah, Wisdom and Spirit.

[145] Mk. 4.13: 'Do you not understand this parable? How then will you understand all the parables?'

[146] Among those who have stood against the tide on the matter of the explanation's belonging intrinsically with the parable are Moule 1969; Bowker 1974; Payne 1980a & b; and now Gundry 1993, 204–11. Caird's objection, that an explained parable is about as interesting as an explained joke (1980, 165f.), misses the point: explanation is not for the particularly obtuse, but for those who are to be allowed into the deeper secret. Caird, however, does go on to allow for the possibility that the content of the interpretation represents Jesus' intention.

[147] See above, n.133. I am grateful to Dr Michael Knowles for letting me see an unpublished paper of his on this subject.

time of fruit had dawned; the covenant was to be renewed; YHWH himself was returning to his people, to 'sow' his word in their midst, as he promised, and so restore their fortunes at last. The parable of the sower tells the story of the kingdom.

(c) Other Parables of Israel's Story

Space forbids a full treatment of all the parables which could be included here. We shall simply indicate the way in which some of them fall into the same pattern, of Israel's history reaching its paradoxical climax. We begin with the smaller parables in Mark 4.21-34.

The section begins with some short sayings which emphasize the same point as the sower. Mark has apparently collected them here from different places; they occur scattered in the parallels.[148] The lamp is made to be put on a lampstand, not under a cover;[149] the measure one gives is the measure one gets;[150] the one who already has will receive more, but the one who has not will lose what he has.[151] Commentators sometimes despair of being able to recover the original sense of these cryptic little sayings.[152] But the exposition of the sower offered above provides some clues. The question about the lamp is explained in verse 22:[153] 'Nothing is hidden except to be revealed, nothing secret except to be publicized.' This implies that something has already been covered up, so that the 'lamp' saying in 4.21 retrospectively gains the force: 'so, granted that the plan has been hidden, it cannot be the divine purpose to keep it so for ever'. Do not be surprised, Jesus is saying, that at last the divine plan is being revealed. There had to come a time when this would happen, otherwise Israel's god would be like someone who kept the lamp permanently under the bed. At the same time, since the secret is still a mystery (in the popular sense, i.e. a puzzle) to most of Jesus' contemporaries, this saying functions as a warning: complete disclosure is on the way, and will not long delay.[154] Mark, strangely, has Jesus speak of the light

[148] Guelich 1989, 227 speaks of a 'vast consensus' on this point, which is rare enough in gospel interpretation.

[149] Mk. 4.21-3/Mt. 5.15; Mt. 10.26/Lk. 8.16f.; Lk. 11.33; Lk. 12.2/*Thom.* 33; cf. 5, 6/*P. Oxy. 654.5.*

[150] Mk. 4.24/Mt. 7.2/Lk. 6.38.

[151] Mk. 4.25/Mt. 13.12; Mt. 25.29/Lk. 19.26/*Thom.* 41.

[152] e.g. Hooker 1991, 133: 'It is impossible for us now to recover their original application.'

[153] cf. Guelich 1989, 230.

[154] Contrast Gundry 1993, 212, who thinks the saying is explaining Jesus' practice of concealing things from the crowds and revealing them to the disciples. The immediacy of the explanation in 4.13-20, he says (214f.), rules out the possibility of Jesus' ministry remaining a riddle until his death and resurrection. But (a) 4.13-20 is still somewhat cryptic (like

as 'coming'.[155] The best explanation of this is in terms of a combination of themes: the coming of YHWH to his people,[156] the coming of the kingdom,[157] and of course the coming of Jesus himself, in the sense of the commencement of his public career.[158] Again, the saying itself is cryptic, as is indicated well enough in the warning of verse 23, repeating verse 9: 'if you have ears, then hear!'

A similar warning to hear properly introduces the saying about measuring (verse 24). Since contemporary English does not use 'to measure' with the metaphorical sense it clearly has here (and elsewhere in Jesus' world[159]), we may have to switch images, and say something like 'The attention you give will be the attention you get', where the first 'attention' picks up 'look out how you hear' at the start of the verse, and the second 'attention' alludes to the way in which Israel's god will care for those who are listening appropriately to the announcement of the kingdom. This then introduces the frequently repeated proverb about those who have and those who do not. Clearly, those who 'have' are equated with those who hear aright, who in turn are identified as Jesus' true family, those to whom is revealed the mystery of the kingdom; those who 'have not' are identified as 'those outside' (4.11, compare 3.31–5).[160] Israel's story, now reaching its climax, will be marked (as in some other second-Temple thought) by a great divide between the true Israel and the renegades. Mark's bringing together of these sayings reflects a sure instinct for the meaning of Jesus' kingdom-announcement.

Mark's section continues with the short parable of the 'seed growing secretly'.[161] Having read the sower carefully, we should be on familiar territory here. Israel's god is not working in a sudden dramatic way. He will not bring in his kingdom in the manner that Jesus' contemporaries desired. He is working in a way that is hidden and opaque, but which, nevertheless,

---

Jesus' other explanation in 7.17–23, which Mk. has had to supplement in 7.19b); (b) at this stage, the secret is only revealed to the disciples, not to outsiders.

[155] Mt., Lk. and *Thom.* speak of the lamp being 'lit', though using different terms. (On the secondary nature of the *Thom.* saying, cf. Fitzmyer 1985, 717.) It has been argued, however, that the underlying Aramaic for 'come' may mean 'to be brought': cf. Gundry 1993, 212, with refs.

[156] For Israel's god as a 'lamp' cf. 2 Sam. 22.29; Job 29.3; Ps. 27.1.

[157] So Guelich 1989, 229, 231f.

[158] With possible kingly overtones; cf. 2 Sam. 21.17; 1 Kgs. 11.36; 15.4; 2 Kgs. 8.19.

[159] cf. Chilton 1984a, 123–5, noting esp. Tg. Isa. 27.8. He comments (125) that, since this thought is part of common folk-wisdom developed by Jesus in a particular way, the gospels are probably correct to envisage him using the saying on a number of occasions. This point of method deserves wider application.

[160] With Marcus 1986, 156f. Guelich 1989, 234 thinks it impossible to be precise here.

[161] Mk. 4.26–9, with some echoes at the end of *Thom.* 21.4 and in *Ap. Jas.* 8.1f.

Israel *ought* to recognize. There is something strangely familiar about the secret seed. It sleeps and rises, just as the observer does, and yet he does not understand. There may be overtones here of resurrection: this is how the creator god raises the dead in the inauguration of the kingdom, by sowing seeds and letting them grow secretly so that only those with eyes to see can realize what is happening.[162] There are, too, clear overtones of the apocalyptic scenario that is to come: when harvest comes, he puts in the sickle. This refers directly to a passage in Joel (3.13) which speaks of the great coming judgment and harvest. Jesus is not abandoning the idea that there will be a great judgment in which Israel's destiny will at last be realized. He is reinterpreting it, declaring that, though there will come a day of clear vindication, at the moment, i.e. during Jesus' ministry, the seed is growing quietly in ways that Israel does not understand – though she should.

The parable of the mustard seed[163] is another redefinition of the kingdom. It will not appear all at once in its full splendour, but will begin inconspicuously. Those who expect Jesus to lead a march on a Roman garrison will be disappointed. Nevertheless, what he is offering remains a redefinition, not an abandonment, of the dream. YHWH has planted a small seed, which will grow into a great shrub. The ministry of Jesus, which does not look like the expected coming kingdom, is in fact its strange beginning. This time the apocalyptic image is of the birds of the air coming to nest in the tree:[164] this seems to be a hint that when the tree has grown to full height – when Israel becomes what her god intends her to become – others, presumably Gentiles, will come to share in her blessing. This was of course one part of some mainstream tellings of Israel's story;[165] but to announce it at a time of nationalist fervour was revolutionary indeed, directly cognate with the 'Nazareth Manifesto' of Luke 4.

The leaven in the lump[166] similarly declares that the kingdom is not like a new loaf, appearing suddenly as a whole. It is more like the leaven which works its way quietly through a lump of dough. Once again, this parable was not originally about the influence of Christianity on the world, but about the effect of the kingdom's inauguration within Israel. The key word in the parable is 'hidden'. This was not the natural way to describe what the woman did with the leaven; but it coheres well with the theme of all these parables, namely, that what Israel's god was doing in the ministry of Jesus was veiled and cryptic. The leaven of Jesus' message is hidden within Israel, so that it

---

[162] cf. above, 128f.

[163] Mk. 4.30–2/Mt. 13.31f./Lk. 13.18f./*Thom.* 20.

[164] cf. Dan. 4.20–2.

[165] cf. *NTPG* 267f.

[166] Mt. 13.33/Lk. 13.20f./*Thom.* 96.

may work its way through the whole people. The parable is a warning not to look (yet) for sudden dramatic events; it is an invitation to see Israel's god at work in the secret workings of Jesus' paradoxical activity.

The same theme of hiddenness is the obvious characteristic, too, of the treasure and the pearl.[167] But a new twist is added. The hiddenness means that people can, and must, seek out the treasure, and then abandon everything else in favour of it. It is within their power to grasp it. What must be abandoned? Clearly, the cherished assumptions and expectations of Jesus' contemporaries. They are challenged to realize what is going on before their eyes, and so, dropping their other aspirations, to embrace this new possibility. They may appear foolish in the eyes of their contemporaries, who are building their hopes on a kingdom which will restore the national fortunes of Israel; but they will have found something far better, over which they will rejoice, for it is they who will be vindicated when God acts. This theme projects us forward towards the developed story which we will explore in the next two chapters.

Matthew ends his particular parable-collection with the householder,[168] and, though it clearly reflects his own interests,[169] there is no very good reason for denying it to Jesus as well. The image presupposes that Israel is being reconstituted around Jesus, and goes on to suggest that those who are in on the secret ('scribes trained for the kingdom of heaven') will be like householders producing things new as well as things old. Jesus has introduced a radically new note into Israel's expectation. This does not mean a total break with the past, nor even an abandonment of the framework of Israel's hope; it means filling that framework with new content. The 'therefore' with which the parable begins indicates that it functions, and that Matthew clearly intends it to function, as a statement of what happens when people respond to the other parables.

There are, of course, many other parables which fill out the announcement of the kingdom as the story of Israel's paradoxical history. The most obvious, perhaps, is the one we have already used as a case-study, namely the prodigal son.[170] There, most clearly (in my view), Jesus was retelling the story of Israel's return from exile, and doing so in a sharp and provocative manner. We should also note the way in which this whole theme dovetailed into one aspect of Jesus' praxis, studied in chapter 5. The acts of healing were understood by the evangelists, and most probably by Jesus himself, as

---

[167] Mt. 13.44–6/*Thom.* 109; 76. In *Thom.*, the purchaser of the field does not know about the treasure until after he has made the purchase.

[168] Mt. 13.51–2.

[169] cf. *NTPG* 384.

[170] Lk. 15.11–32: cf. ch. 4 above.

the fulfilment of prophecy; but not just any miscellaneous prophecy. They fulfilled the prophecies of *return from exile*. The time when the blind would see, the deaf hear, the lame walk, and the poor hear good news was the time when Israel would return at last from Babylon.[171] This gives further indication that our reading of these stories is on the right track.

It would be possible at this stage to develop our initial treatment of Jesus' announcement of the kingdom further by examining parables which speak of other aspects of the kingdom, notably the defeat of evil and the return of YHWH to Zion. These, however, we defer for subsequent treatment in chapters 8 and 13 below, when other pieces of the puzzle are in place.

4. Conclusion: Announcing the Kingdom

We have taken some soundings within Jesus' kingdom-announcement, rather than offering a full-dress presentation. Jesus, we have seen, claimed in word and deed that the traditional expectation was now being fulfilled. The new exodus was under way: Israel was now at last returning from her long exile. All this was happening in and through his own work.

Jesus enacted this announcement in terms of *welcome* and *warning*. He welcomed those in any kind of need, thereby enacting the story of the return from exile, of repentance and restoration. All were summoned to celebrate the great restoration. At the same time, he warned those who presumed upon their ancestral heritage, and who supposed that the coming kingdom would automatically vindicate them. If the true Israel was returning from exile, some might resist. If YHWH was returning to Zion, he would judge those who refused his rule. The major kingdom-theme of the defeat of evil, of paganism, of Babylon, is to be located here within Jesus' proclamation, with a typically prophetic twist: the critique is sharpest when aimed, not at pagans, but at Israel herself.

In the next two chapters we shall examine the welcome and the warning in detail. In each case, the story of Israel's god becoming king, as Jesus told it, turned into a play in search of a cast. Jesus' hearers, whether they liked it or not, could not remain mere spectators. They were on stage. The only question was: which parts would they choose to play?

---

[171] Isa. 35.5, and the ch. as a whole; cf. Isa. 29.18f.; 32.3; Mt. 11.2–6/Lk. 7.18–23.

Chapter Seven

STORIES OF THE KINGDOM (2):
INVITATION, WELCOME, CHALLENGE AND SUMMONS

1. Introduction: The Open-Ended Story

'The kingdom of god is at hand; repent, and believe the gospel.' We have studied the first half of this saying, and have concluded that it summoned up the entire narrative of Israel's new exodus, her final return from exile. What about the second half?[1]

The thesis of this chapter is that Jesus' kingdom-announcement functioned like a narrative in search of fresh characters, a plot in search of actors. In the terms made familiar by Greimas, and studied in the previous volume, if Jesus is the 'agent' in the drama, the action is in need of some 'recipients', and apparently some 'helpers':[2]

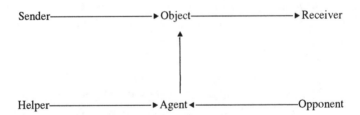

Thus far, we have an implicit story-line which runs like this:

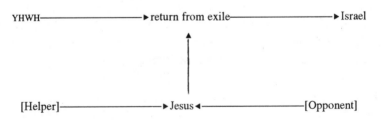

---

[1] This is the form of the saying, of course, in Mk. 1.15. The par. in Mt. 4.17 has 'repent, for the kingdom of heaven is at hand'. The arguments which caused the Jesus Seminar to print both versions of the entire saying in black, i.e. inauthentic (Funk & Hoover 1993, 40f.), have been sufficiently dealt with in ch. 2, and pp. 210-4, above.

[2] On the analysis of stories cf. *NTPG* ch. 3, esp. 69-77.

The question is, who is the 'Israel' who will benefit from this 'return from exile'? And who, if anyone, are Jesus' 'helpers'? (We shall examine 'opponents' in chapter 9.) I shall argue in the present chapter that Jesus' implicit, and explicit, kingdom-narratives carried as part of their story-line the sense that his hearers were invited to see themselves as the 'Israel' who would benefit from his work; and also, to some extent at least, as the 'helpers' who would have an active share in that work. With that invitation there went a further implication: the returned-from-exile Israel must conduct itself in a certain fashion. Nor was this simply a general set of rules, a new abstract 'ethic'. The unique and unrepeatable nature of Jesus' own sense of vocation extended to those who followed him. They were summoned to specific tasks, which had to do with his own career and project.

The *story* of the kingdom thus generated an appropriate *praxis* among those who heard it and made it their own. Within the worldview model, stories not only reinforce and cohere with the praxis and symbol of the story-teller; they address other worldviews and mindsets, and seek to elicit response in terms of changed stories, symbols, and praxis. The appeal for the last of these – changed praxis – implicitly invites a change in the entire set.[3] My case here is that Jesus' appeals, commands, and so forth are to be seen not simply as 'new teaching' in the sense of a few new moral rules or theological principles, but as part of the underlying story he told, which aimed to produce in his hearers a realignment of their own praxis, necessarily involving a realignment of the other elements of their worldview also.

In order to see how the controlling story works in this way, we shall study it in four stages. It begins with *invitation*: the kingdom-announcement necessarily included the call to 'repent and believe the good news'. This phrase has become something of a slogan over the years, and, having acquired certain anachronistic connotations as a result, has had its authenticity questioned in some quarters. It will be important to go behind this problem, and tease out its actual first-century connotations. For those invited, there was also *welcome*: Jesus' kingdom-stories made it clear that all and sundry were potential beneficiaries, with the most striking examples being the poor and the sinners. Invitation and welcome gave birth to *challenge*: those who heard Jesus' call, and understood themselves as characters in his kingdom-story, were summoned to live precisely as the renewed-Israel people, personally and corporately. Finally, the story generated a *summons*. Some at least of those who made Jesus' story their own were called to go with him on his journey to Jerusalem, to be his companions as his mission reached its strange

---

[3] On worldviews etc. cf. *NTPG* ch. 5, esp. 122–6.

climax. These four elements together make up a profile of the praxis generated by Jesus' kingdom-stories.

It should come as no surprise (though some will still feel it strange) to discover that Jesus intended consequences of this sort from his proclamation. Scholarship has moved on somewhat from the idea that Jesus' message was for the 'individual' as an isolated entity. But, when the guard is down, people still speak and write sometimes as if that were the case, as if in consequence Jesus could not have thought about a 'community' either listening to his stories or acting together to make them their own. We have, in the last forty years, 'discovered' that Matthew, Mark, Luke, and John – and even, according to some, Q and *Thomas* – had a great interest in 'community'. It ought to be just as clear, if not clearer, that Jesus himself was deeply concerned about the social and corporate effects of his kingdom-announcement. (In case this paragraph should itself be misunderstood, let me say as clearly as possible that the *corporate* meaning of the stories does not undermine, but actually enhances, the *personal* meaning for every single one of Jesus' hearers. It is *individualism* and *collectivism* that cancel each other out; properly understood, the *corporate* and the *personal* reinforce one another.[4])

Scholarship has also moved on, though not quite so thoroughly, away from the idea that Jesus expected the end of the world at any moment, and so could not have intended any 'communal' application of his stories – apart from the close fellowship created among his intimates as they awaited the end. We shall deal with this question further in the next chapter. Suffice it to say here that a good deal of evidence indicates that Jesus fully intended his stories to generate a new form of community, and that this by itself ought to be sufficient to call into question any unthinking acceptance of the old dogma of the imminent expectation of the end of the cosmos. That Jesus expected cataclysmic events very soon ought not to be doubted; what those events consisted of is a question yet to be considered.

2. Invitation: The Call to Repent and Believe

(i) Repentance

Matthew and Mark both offer, as their opening summary of Jesus' proclamation, a sentence which includes the command to 'repent' (Mark 1.15/Matthew 4.17). But can we be sure that Jesus really did make this demand? What precisely would it mean? In what way would it cohere with the kingdom-story which formed the overarching theme of his message?

[4] I owe this way of putting the point to Bishop Michael Marshall.

The older commentaries and dictionaries are more or less unanimous in treating 'repentance' as a major theme of Jesus' ministry, giving to the concept the meaning, so to speak, of the negative side of 'conversion'.[5] This forms part of a more or less ahistorical scheme, in which Jesus preached a timeless message about 'God' and 'Man', and about how the latter could be converted. Specifically, in this view, Jesus explained that 'conversion', including 'repentance', was an act of undeserved divine grace, instead of the achievement of human legalism, as the Jews had thought.[6] 'Repentance' thus belongs in the world of individual moral conduct: one of Jesus' fundamental aims, it seems, was to make people change their behaviour for the better (though without, if possible, becoming Pelagians in the process).

It is now widely recognized that this involves a complete caricature of Judaism at least, never mind Jesus, and a reaction has set in. E. P. Sanders, in particular, has argued that Jesus was not to any great extent a preacher of repentance;[7] that, even if he did hint at such a thing, the difference between what he said and what his Jewish contemporaries would have said was not great; that the passages in which he is depicted as calling for repentance are probably themselves inauthentic; and that, if he had concentrated on getting notorious sinners to mend their ways, 'he would have been a national hero', instead of incurring the opposition which his fellowship with sinners seems to have done.[8] He concludes that Jesus did not ask for *repentance in the sense in which his Jewish contemporaries would have meant it*; instead, he summoned people to follow him. This was his real offence.[9]

Sanders, clearly, takes as his starting-point the manifest excesses of the older view.[10] This, I think, has somewhat clouded his presentation, even in his more recent book in which the polemic is largely suppressed. I believe he

[5] e.g. *TDNT* 4.975-1009 (Behm, Würthwein); *NIDNTT* 1.357-9 (Goetzmann, as part of the article on 'Conversion'); *ABD* 5.671-4 (Healey, Boyd Luter).

[6] The article by Behm in *TDNT* 4 offers several choice examples of this view: e.g. 997f. on rabbinic ideas of repentance; 1003 on the difference between Jesus and Judaism; 1008 on the 'fateful relapse of post-apostolic and early Catholic Christianity into Jewish legalism'.

[7] Sanders 1985, 106-13, 203-5; 1993, 230-7. On the present point, 1985, 108, 111, 203: 'there is scant material which depicts Jesus as calling Israel to repent'; 1993, 230: 'Jesus was not a preacher of repentance: he was not primarily a reformer'. Sanders is challenged at various points by Chilton 1988.

[8] Sanders 1985, 203; cf. 1993, 232, 235. Allison 1987, 69 has challenged this last point perceptively.

[9] cf. esp. 1993, 234-7: Jesus 'regarded himself as having the right to say who would be in the kingdom' (236). Sanders has discussed the same issues in his articles of 1983b (on which see the initial comments of Young 1985), 1987, 1992a. The issues remain important, whatever one thinks of the debate in Meyer 1991 & Sanders 1991.

[10] 1985, 202, 204, 205, 208, arguing specifically against Jeremias and Perrin. As I have indicated in relation to Behm (n.6 above), there were plenty of other targets he could have chosen.

is right to see that Jesus did not ask for repentance in the normal sense, but wrong to deny that he asked for it at all. He has, I think, overlooked precisely the element of implicit narrative, and of the praxis it was designed to generate, on which the present chapter focuses attention.

We may begin once more where Jesus himself began: with John the Baptist. John had told Israel that, if she did not repent, her god would create children for Abraham from the very stones.[11] From one point of view, this treated Israel as a whole as if she were pagan, needing to repent as would a proselyte if she wished to be re-included in the people of YHWH.[12] But this event – Israel's reconversion, as it were – was not just another story about Israel and her god, yet one more chapter within an ongoing narrative. It fell within a wider Jewish notion of 'eschatological repentance'.

What was this wider Jewish notion? 'Repentance', in a good many texts, was *what Israel must do if her exile is to come to an end.*[13] Though the Greek word *metanoia* and its cognates, which occur in the gospels with this meaning, are rare in the Septuagint – and when they do occur they refer, more often than not, to YHWH himself 'repenting' – the first-century sense of the word encapsulates a range of meanings expressed in other ways in the Hebrew scriptures and their Greek translations. Deuteronomy spoke of Israel 'returning' to YHWH with her whole heart; this would be the condition of her forgiveness, and of the return from exile.[14] In Deuteronomic terms, this would mean a return to the *Shema*, to the love of YHWH alone with all the heart. The prophets regularly used the term 'repent' to denote the turning to YHWH which would result in restoration, return from exile.[15] Indeed, the words *shub* and *epistrephein*, since they mean 'return', hint constantly, particularly in Jeremiah, that for Israel to 'return' to YHWH with all her heart is the crucial thing that will enable her to 'return' to her own land. The whole point of passages like Daniel 9, Ezra 9 or Nehemiah 9 is that these great

[11] Mt. 3.9/Lk. 3.8.

[12] On the repentance of proselytes, cf. e.g. *Jos. As.* 9—10, and the discussions, with passages, in Moore 1927-30, 1.323-53.

[13] cf. the very helpful section in Sanders 1985, 106-8. In 1993, 234, however, he treats the idea of national repentance as simply a corporate version of individual repentance, and does not seem to link it with eschatology. This notion of national repentance, as part of the movement towards the End, is noted on the edge of some of the articles listed above (e.g. *TDNT* 4.992; *ABD* 5.672), but it has in no way affected the ahistorical tone of the presentation. See too Moore 1927-30, 1.520-34 (on repentance as the precondition for return from exile, 531).

[14] Dt. 30.2, 8, in the context of vv. 1-10 as a whole: the key words are Heb. *shub*, Gk. *epistrephein.* Cf. the similar passage in Lev. 26.40-5.

[15] Isa. 44.22; 45.22; 46.8; 55.7; Jer. 3.10, 12, 14, 22; 4.1; 5.3; 15.19; 18.8; 24.7; 31 [LXX 38].18; Ezek. 14.6; 18.30, 32; Hos. 3.5; 6.1; 7.10; 11.5; 12.6; 14.1, 2; Joel 2.12, 13; Hag. 2.17; Zech. 1.3-6; 10.9-10.

prayers of repentance – and we must be careful not to confine our thinking simply to occurrences of *shub* and *epistrephein* themselves – are prayers precisely designed to bring about the return from exile. (We may note once again that all three books are clearly 'post-exilic' in the normal sense, and yet are still seeking the real 'return'.)

The same theme is found within post-biblical Jewish literature.[16] Qumran is a particularly interesting case, since in the Scrolls we have evidence of a community that considered itself precisely to be the advance guard of the real 'return from exile'. 'Repentance', as a condition of entry into membership, is therefore linked inescapably with eschatology, rather than with an ahistorical or individualist piety.[17] This remains the case within the early rabbis, i.e. before the Bar-Kochba rebellion: Eliezer ben Hyrcanus spoke of Israel's 'repentance' as the condition for her redemption, and it is fairly clear that by 'redemption' he meant her liberation from the Romans, the real and final return from the exile which, still continuing at the time of AD 70, had plunged into a new Babylonian state thereafter.[18] We may well suppose that the non-eschatological, moral emphasis of the later rabbinic doctrine of repentance reflects a period when political and eschatological expectations had been put firmly on the back burner. The post-135 rabbis are unlikely to provide the best index of what the notion would have meant to devout Jews in the first century.[19] Further evidence, albeit oblique, of the strong connection between 'repentance' and eschatology is found, for what it may be worth, in some second-century Christian literature.[20]

'Repentance' in Jesus' context, then, would have carried the connotations of 'what Israel must do if YHWH is to restore her fortunes at last'. Jesus, in

[16] e.g. Bar. 2.32-4; Tob. 13.5f.; *Ps. Sol.* 18.4-7; *Jub.* 1.15-23; 23.26. I owe this list to Sanders 1985, 106f. Philo *De Praem.* 162-72 makes the same point, seemingly as an exegesis of Lev. 26.40-5 and Dt. 30.

[17] e.g. 1QS 10.20; 1QH 2.9; 6.6; 14.24; CD 4.2; 6.4f.; 8.16; 19.16; 20.17.

[18] Hengel 1981b [1968], 23 n.26, suggests that Judas and Menahem, the revolutionary leaders, may have been in some sense 'eschatological "preachers of repentance"'; he compares Judas' rebuke (*oneidisas*) of his contemporaries, for recognizing the Romans as overlords when they already had YHWH (Jos. *War* 2.433, cp. 2.118), to Jesus' rebuke (*oneidizein*) of his contemporaries for refusing to repent (Mt. 11.20).

[19] Tanch. 5.56a; jTaan. 1.1 (63d); cp. bSanh. 97b-98a (another discussion between Eliezer ben Hyrcanus and Joshua ben Hananiah, i.e. set precisely between the first and second wars, when liberation from Rome was still a very live issue); bYoma 86b: cf. Moore 1927-30, 2.351. For the transition from an eschatological/political understanding to a largely ahistorical and moral one, cf. e.g. mAb. 3.5, on which see *NTPG* 199. On Eliezer ben Hyrcanus and his particular agenda cf. *NTPG* 197-8. On 'repentance' in the later rabbis see the treatments in Moore 1.507-34; Sanders 1977, index s.v. 'repentance'.

[20] e.g. Hermas, for whom *metanoia* was an eschatological act; that was why it was hard to think of its being repeated. A second repentance could only be allowed by deeming the present situation to be a sort of second eschatological moment: cf. e.g. Herm. *Vis.* 2.2.1-6; *Mand.* 4.3.2-7.

announcing the kingdom, was declaring that Israel's fortunes were being restored. It is therefore highly likely that he would have included the demand for repentance – in this sense – within his proclamation. When, therefore, we find passages in the synoptic tradition which suggest that he did, we should take them very seriously.[21] Nor do they stand alone; once again, we must not confuse the *subject* 'repentance' with occurrences of the *word*.

Before we can consider this evidence, however, there is another point about Jesus' context which is of great significance, and which has been, I think, more or less universally overlooked. If 'repentance' carries the overtone of 'what Israel must do if her fortunes are to be restored', it can also have a much more down-to-earth ring: *to abandon revolutionary zeal*. This is found in a setting strikingly reminiscent of the major introductory passage in the gospels (Mark 1.15/Matthew 4.17). The setting is a passage in Josephus' autobiography.

Josephus is describing an incident which took place in Galilee in around AD 66 – that is, roughly when some of the synoptic traditions may have been achieving a settled shape. Josephus has gone to Galilee to sort out the turbulent factionalism there. A brigand chief called Jesus (there are twenty-one people by that name in the index to Josephus' works; originality in naming children was evidently not prized highly among first-century Jews) makes a plot against Josephus' life. Josephus manages to foil it. Then, he tells us, he called Jesus aside and told him

> that I was not ignorant of the plot which he had contrived against me . . .; I would, nevertheless, condone his actions if he would show repentance and prove his loyalty to me. All this he promised . . .[22]

'If he would show repentance and prove his loyalty to me.' The translation is accurate enough, but could just as well have been rendered 'if he would *repent and believe in me*'.[23] Josephus is requiring of this Jesus that he give up his brigandage, and trust him (Josephus) for a better way forward. 'Repentance', in this sense of abandoning revolutionary inclinations, is found elsewhere in the same narrative; so, for that matter, is 'belief', in the sense

---

[21] Sanders 1985, 109–13 has a curious heads-I-win-tails-you-lose argument. (a) We know that the passages about repentance are secondary (because it is a favourite theme of Luke (109) and because Bultmann says so (110)); (b) one would have expected Jesus to issue a call to repent; it is surprising that this does not exist (112f.); (c) the evangelists, sensing this odd deficiency, have added sayings to make it good (113). I suspect that Sanders would not have got into this twisted logic had he not been over-concerned to combat the views of Perrin and others.

[22] Jos. *Life* 110 (tr. Thackeray in LCL).

[23] *ei melloi metanoesein kai pistos emoi genesesthai.*

of trust in and loyalty to a leader.[24] I find it somewhat remarkable that, in all the literature I have read about Jesus of Nazareth, only one writer even mentions the incident involving Josephus and the brigand Jesus, and even he makes no comment about the meaning of 'repentance' and 'belief' in the light of it.[25] It is, I suggest, of considerable significance. This is what those words meant in Galilee in the 60s; by what logic do we insist that they meant something rather different, something perhaps more 'personal', 'inward' or 'religious', in Galilee in the 20s and 30s? Why should we use that 'religious' sense as the criterion for assessing whether Jesus of Nazareth could have said such a thing? He may well have meant more than Josephus; that must be seen by further historical investigation. He is highly unlikely to have meant less.

The most plausible historical reconstruction of Jesus' call to repent brings together, I suggest, the two emphases we have now sketched (returning to YHWH so that the exile may come to an end; renunciation of nationalist violence). It was an *eschatological* call, not the summons of a moralistic reformer. And it was a *political* call, summoning Israel as a nation to abandon one set of agendas and embrace another. 'Repentance' in Jesus' first-century context is not to be conceived simply as one feature within the timeless landscape of a non-historical religion. That is the mistake of many Christian writers, who, ignoring the perfectly clear place of that sort of repentance within day-to-day Jewish life and teaching, have imagined that Jesus invented the idea and so became unpopular. But it would be equally wrong to imagine that Jesus – still understood as a preacher of timeless truths – did *not* make repentance thematic, because, as a preacher of 'timeless truths', he had no need to.[26] Rather, precisely as a would-be prophet, and a prophet of the eschaton at that, he summoned Israel to a once-for-all national repentance, such as would be necessary for the exile to end at last. This was not simply the 'repentance' that any human being, any Jew, might use if, aware of sin, they decided to say sorry and make amends. It is the single great repentance which would characterize the true people of YHWH at the moment when their god became king. What is more, this repentance seems to have little to do with the official structures of the Jewish system. True

---

[24] 'Repentance': e.g. *Life* 17; 262; and 370f., where Josephus successfully persuades 4,000 followers of John of Gischala to 'repent', i.e. to lay down their arms, and to 'come to me', i.e. desert and join Josephus. Cp. too *Ant.* 2.23, where Reuben (or 'Rubel' as Jos. calls him) persuades his brothers to 'repent' of their intention towards Joseph. On 'belief/loyalty', cf. e.g. *Life* 167; and below, 258–64. The present passage is not noted in Lindsay 1993.

[25] Crossan 1991a, 190.

[26] This, in my judgment, is where Sanders fails to carry through his own basic reform: cf. 1985, 112 (Jesus' 'commitment to cherished religious abstractions'); 1993, 232 (repentance as a 'major and fundamental element in religion').

repentance, it seems, consisted rather in adherence and allegiance to Jesus himself.

What, then, of the relevant gospel texts?

We have already noted the opening summary in Matthew and Mark (4.17/1.15), which is echoed in Mark's summary of the disciples' commission (6.12): they, too, were to call people to 'repent and believe the gospel'.[27] The early church no doubt used similar language – it would be exceedingly surprising if it had not – but the burden of proof must rest firmly on those who wish to suggest that these summaries are substantially unhistorical. We find 'repentance' in a passage peculiar to Mark, in passages peculiar to Luke, in Q passages, and, as we have seen, in Matthew/Mark parallels. The fact that Luke is particularly interested in it, as witnessed by two passages in which he mentions repentance while the parallel passage does not (5.32; 15.7: see below), is no good reason for denying that it formed part of Jesus' preaching; Luke may conceivably have thought of it in a less 'eschatological' and more 'moral' fashion, but this does not remove it from Jesus' announcement.[28] The following passages indicate, *prima facie*, that Jesus was indeed summoning his hearers to a great turning, that is, not just to an individual moral repentance, but to an eschatological act which would prove the only way to escape eschatological judgment:

> Then he began to upbraid the cities where most of his mighty works had been done, because they did not repent. 'Woe to you, Chorazin! Woe to you, Bethsaida! For if the mighty works done in you had been done in Tyre and Sidon, they would have repented long ago in sackcloth and ashes. But I tell you, it shall be more tolerable on the day of judgment for Tyre and Sidon than for you. And you, Capernaum, will you be exalted to heaven? You shall be brought down to Hades. For if the mighty works done in you had been done in Sodom, it would have remained until this day. But I tell you that it shall be more tolerable on the day of judgment for the land of Sodom than for you.'[29]

> Then some of the scribes and Pharisees said to him, 'Teacher, we wish to see a sign from you.' But he answered them, 'An evil and adulterous generation seeks for a sign; but no sign shall be given to it except the sign of the prophet Jonah . . . The men of Nineveh repented at the preaching of Jonah, and behold, something greater than Jonah is here.'[30]

> There were some present at that very time who told him of the Galileans whose blood Pilate had mingled with their sacrifices. And he answered them, 'Do you think that these

---

[27] On the historical probability of Mk. 6.12 cf. Allison 1987, 72: 'with John the Baptist in prison or already dead, it would make perfect sense for Jesus to instruct his disciples to continue John's renewal movement'.

[28] cf. Sanders 1985, 109f.; 1993, 231f. In favour of authenticity: Gundry 1993, 69f., with other literature including e.g. Allison 1987.

[29] Mt. 11.20-4. The parallel in Lk. (10.13-15) is shorter. Cp. too. Mt. 10.15/Lk. 10.12.

[30] Mt. 12.38f., 41/Lk. 11.29f., 32; cf. Mk. 8.11-13; Mt. 16.1-4.

Galileans were worse sinners than all the other Galileans, because they suffered thus? I tell you, No; but unless you repent you will all likewise perish. Or those eighteen upon whom the tower in Siloam fell and killed them, do you think that they were worse offenders than all the others who dwelt in Jerusalem? I tell you, No; but unless you repent you will all likewise perish.'[31]

The Pharisees and their scribes murmured against his disciples, saying, 'Why do you eat and drink with tax collectors and sinners?' And Jesus answered them, 'Those who are well have no need of a physician, but those who are sick; I have not come to call the righteous, but sinners to repentance.'[32]

It will not do to dismiss these passages, as Sanders does, simply by referring to Bultmann.[33] Nor is the tone of these sayings 'anti-Jewish' in such a way as to force us to conclude that the sayings come from much later Christian polemic.[34] Was Jeremiah anti-Jewish? Was Amos? Was John the Baptist? I suggest that Jesus, like them, was acting as a prophet of Jewish restoration, speaking on behalf of Israel's god, summoning the nation, in view of impending judgment, to repent of its nationalist violence, and offering to all those who did so the promise that they would emerge as the vindicated people of Israel's god. Those who refused, by contrast, would be faced with devastating judgment in the form of a national disaster.

The passage from Luke 13 is especially instructive in this regard. Those who did not repent would be killed by Roman soldiers or crushed by falling masonry. This 'repentance' is not, then, simply the individual moral turning from private sin.[35] It is the sort of repentance which Josephus urged upon his fanatical and violent contemporaries. A call to repentance in this sense fits well into the prophetic persona of Jesus as we have studied it. The story he was telling, which he was inviting his hearers to make their own, was the story of Israel's exile coming to its end. Repentance was necessary for that finally to happen. Eschatological repentance, and national repentance from violent rebel activity, were joined together in Jesus' proclamation and summons. The blend was not accidental. As we shall see in chapter 10, it was precisely in her tendency to violent nationalism that Jesus saw the true depth of Israel's present exile.[36]

[31] Lk. 13.1–5; the same theme is clearly echoed in 13.6–9, to which, as Allison 1987, 70 points out, Mt. 3.10/Lk. 3.9 offers a parallel.

[32] Lk. 5.29–32. The parallels (Mt. 9.10–13/Mk. 2.15–17, cf. *P. Oxy.1224*.1) lack the phrase 'to repentance', which is retained in Justin *1 Apol*. 1.15.8.

[33] Sanders 1985, 109f. Sanders' rejection, elsewhere in the book, of the presuppositions, methods, and conclusions of Bultmann and Perrin undermines his own suggestion that their scepticism renders the sayings less than 'solid'.

[34] Sanders 1985, 110 and n.60, quoting Bultmann, who was following Fridrichsen.

[35] For a statement of the 'traditional' understanding, which I am arguing is completely inadequate, cf. e.g. Guelich 1989, 45.

[36] See below, 290f., on the call to love one's enemies.

I suggest, therefore, that Jesus was heard to be saying more or less exactly what Josephus would have been heard to be saying: give up your way of being Israel, your following of particular national and political aims and goals, and trust me for mine instead. And he was heard to be investing that call for repentance with a significance way beyond anything Josephus intended, a significance which had Deuteronomy, Jeremiah and other classic texts resonating in the background: this is the repentance which will constitute you as the returned-from-exile people, the renewed and reconstituted Israel.

This also shows that there is far more evidence for Jesus preaching 'repentance', in this sense, than merely the passages where the root *metanoia* happens to occur.[37] Much of the rest of this chapter, in fact, will review this evidence: the welcome of 'sinners'; the call to live by a different set of goals and values (not just 'ethical norms', but actual aims and intentions) to those current among Jesus' contemporaries; the offer – and requirement! – of the renewed heart (an obvious Jeremiah/Deuteronomy theme); and the call to follow Jesus in the way of the cross, rather than to follow his contemporaries in the way of violence. *Each of these themes was, in fact, a summons to repentance.* Each one showed an aspect of what Israel must be if exile were to end. One might put it like this: it is the fundamental nature of the 'repentance' theme in Jesus' proclamation which largely accounts for the relative scarcity of appearances of the term 'repentance' in the gospels.

Among the parables, too, there is copious evidence. Sanders makes great play of the fact that the sheep does not 'repent', despite Luke's implication (15.7); the shepherd has to go looking for it. He might also have added that coins do not 'repent' of being lost, and that Luke has again apparently blundered by implying that they do (15.10).[38] The reason Sanders does not spell this out is perhaps that it would give the game away: that is not how such parables work. Whatever 'repentance' Jesus' followers may have offered – just what that consisted in we must discuss presently – was already a 'given'. The point of the parable in each case was to validate and vindicate Jesus' own activity in taking the initiative and seeking out the lost. In any case, these two small parables lead up to the greater one, the prodigal son. There, as we have already seen, the turning-point in the story is just that, the turning-point: 'He came to his senses, and said, "I will arise, and go to my father, and say to him, Father, I have sinned."' However much we place this in the context of the father's own prodigal love throughout the story, it remains a classic account of one thing: repentance.[39]

[37] cf. Chilton 1988, 4: repentance 'need not be named to be operative'.

[38] Sanders 1993, 233f.; cf. 1985, 109.

[39] Lk. 15.11–32. Sanders thinks it authentic (1993, 197f.). Cf. ch. 4 above.

The other parable that stresses repentance is the rich man and Lazarus (Luke 16.19-31). The story carries clear echoes of well-known folk-tales,[40] to which Jesus is giving a fresh and startling twist. The emphasis falls at the same point that was made twice – i.e. with great stress – in the prodigal son: 'resurrection', i.e. 'return from exile', is happening all around, and the Pharisees cannot see it.[41]

The parable is not, as often supposed, a description of the afterlife, warning people to be sure of their ultimate destination.[42] If that were its point, it would not be a parable: a story about someone getting lost in London would not be a *parable* if addressed to people attempting to find their way through that city without a map. We have perhaps been misled, not for the first time, by the too-ready assumption, in the teeth of the evidence, that Jesus 'must really' have been primarily concerned to teach people 'how to go to heaven after death'. The reality is uncomfortably different.

The welcome of Lazarus by Abraham evokes the welcome of the prodigal by the father, and with much the same point. The heavenly reality, in which the poor and outcast would be welcomed into Abraham's bosom (as everyone would know from the folk-tale), was coming true in flesh and blood as Jesus welcomed the outcasts, just as the father's welcome to the returning son was a story about what Jesus was actually doing then and there. The theme of 'rich and poor', not unimportant in Luke, is here thrown into stark prominence, as recent studies have rightly stressed.[43] But the point of this, when the story is seen as a traditional tale with a new ending, was not so much what would happen to both in the end, nor yet simply a statement on the abstract 'ethical' issue of wealth and poverty, but rather what was happening to both rich and poor *in the present time*.[44] Jesus' welcome of the poor and outcast was a sign that the real return from exile, the new age, the 'resurrection', was coming into being; and if the new age was dawning, those who wanted to belong to it would (as in Deuteronomy and Jeremiah) have to repent. The story points up the true significance of what Jesus was doing, and the urgent need of those who were at present grumbling to recognize this

[40] Details in e.g. Jeremias 1963a [1947], 183; Fitzmyer 1985, 1126f.; Bauckham 1991, stressing a wider background than normally envisaged.

[41] Lk. 15.24, 32; 16.30f.

[42] Cf. Bauckham 1991, 233, 245f.: the story 'cannot claim eyewitness authority as a literal description of the fate of the dead. It has only the status of parable.' In fact, it directs attention 'away from the apocalyptic revelation of the afterlife back to the inexcusable injustice of the coexistence of rich and poor'. Contrast e.g. Marshall 1978, 633; Fitzmyer 1985, 1129; Nolland 1993, 827.

[43] Hock 1987; Bauckham 1991.

[44] This is why scholars who presuppose the real referent of the parable to be the future *post mortem* state (e.g. Nolland 1993, 827) tend to reject the importance of the known story – despite the wealth of evidence discussed by Hock and Bauckham, to look no further.

significance. The five brothers at home correspond quite closely to the older brother in the prodigal son. 'Resurrection' is happening, but they cannot see it. The story takes for granted that the poor and outcast were rightly being welcomed into the kingdom, and it turns the spotlight on to the rich, the Pharisees, the grumblers: they, too, now needed to repent if they were to inherit the new day that would shortly dawn. They were refused the extra revelation of someone going to them from the dead;[45] the message of repentance was clear enough in Moses and the prophets.

This parable is therefore further strong evidence that 'repentance', in the senses already discussed, formed a central element in Jesus' proclamation. The basic story he was telling invited his hearers to see themselves as the true Israel, returning at last from exile, and turning back to their god as an essential part of the process.

Within this broader (both eschatological and national) category of repentance, it is of course unproblematic to suggest that a form of *personal* repentance also formed part of Jesus' summons. In his more recent work, Sanders seems to acknowledge this. He notes that, were Jesus a social reformer, he would have had to face the problem of integrating reformed sinners into ordinary society, and that there is no sign of his attempting this. But he nevertheless admits that 'Jesus did not want the wicked to remain wicked in the interim' – the interim, that is, before the great event which would shortly take place.[46] Since the concept of 'repentance', with its personal dimension, was clearly well known within Judaism, it would be extraordinary if a call to an *eschatological* and *national* repentance were not perceived to include a call to personal repentance within it. This is not to say, of course, that Jesus was after all simply a 'reformer' in the sense of one advocating a new system of ethics, or urging new adherence to an old one. But that does not mean he did *not* call people to repent at every level, corporate and personal.

However, the fact that repentance involved persons as persons, not mere ciphers within a collective, does not mean that, after all, we can simply rehabilitate the notion of an 'individual' repentance which ignores the eschatological and historical dimension. Any sub-group within the parent body must be composed of persons who have decided, quite possibly one by one, to swap the solidarity of the parent body for that of the sub-group; once more, Qumran is a good example. At the moment of entry, this will look to the individualizing twentieth-century eye like 'individualism'. But the logic of the position is quite different from that of the lonely post-Enlightenment

[45] This, as Bauckham stresses, is part of the 'surprise' in Jesus' story; in the traditional versions, the request would have been granted.

[46] Sanders 1993, 234; cf. also 232.

individual bent on a quest for private salvation. It is the logic of the promise to Abraham and his family; and the key question is: who really are the children of Abraham? This raises the most telling point of all about Jesus' call to repent. It brings us back once again to John the Baptist.

The crucial thing, of course, is that for Jesus this repentance, whether personal or national, *did not involve going to the Temple and offering sacrifice.*[47] John's baptism, as we saw, already carried this scandalous notion: one could 'repent', in the divinely appointed way, down by the Jordan instead of up in Jerusalem![48] In just the same way, Jesus offered membership in the renewed people of the covenant god *on his own authority* and *by his own process*. This was the real scandal. He behaved as if he thought (a) that the return from exile was already happening, (b) that it consisted precisely of himself and his mission, and hence (c) that he had the right to pronounce on who belonged to the restored Israel. The crucial issue in the Zacchaeus episode – to take one highly relevant passage – is that, whatever Zacchaeus did or did not do with his money, Jesus declared on his own authority that Zacchaeus was a true son of Abraham, and that salvation had 'today' come to his house.[49] In other words, what Zacchaeus would normally have obtained through visiting Jerusalem and participating in the sacrificial cult, Jesus gave him on the spot. It seems likely that Zacchaeus' restitution of property had to do more with his now being accepted by his neighbours than with Jesus' verdict itself – just as the lepers who were told to show themselves to the priest, and to offer the relevant sacrifice, did so not in order to obtain their healing but in order to gain public certification, a clean bill of health.[50] What counted in each case, and what made each such act so scandalous, was not (of course) that Jews of Jesus' day were opposed to forgiveness, love, grace and so forth, but that they were not expecting these gifts to be available outside the context of Temple and cult. It came down to this: if the story which Jesus was telling by his words and actions was true, the climactic moment in Jewish history had arrived in person, and was behaving in a thoroughly unprincipled manner.

The repentance for which Jesus called, then, was not at all like the regular, *ad hoc*, repentance of individual sinners when they recognized their sin and underwent the normal Jewish practices for restitution. That could take place, in principle, at any time in Israel's history, and would not of itself indicate the coming of the kingdom or the end of exile. Nor would it be

---

[47] Sanders see this clearly: 1985, 203, 206; 1993, 235–7.

[48] cf. 160f. above.

[49] Lk. 19.1–10. Read in this way, I see no reason to deny the story's essential historicity, *pace* Sanders 1993, 235f.

[50] Mt. 8.4/Mk. 1.44/Lk. 5.14/*P. Eger.* 2.2, with Lev. 14.2–20.

likely to involve a great national turning away from one agenda and towards another. Jesus' summons was more radical by far. It had nothing to do with urging people to visit the Temple more frequently, to offer more sacrifices, to take more care over regular ritual purification. Though it included the note of (what we would call) moral repentance, this was one aspect of the main emphasis rather than the main emphasis itself. Like Josephus, Jesus was urging his compatriots to abandon a whole way of life, and to trust him for a different one. He did indeed summon people to repent, as he did indeed announce the kingdom. But in neither case did the story follow the plot that his hearers might have expected. His implied narrative continued, not with national restoration *per se* (as one might have expected from within the normal Jewish story), but with the challenge to his hearers to follow a different way of being Israel, and to await a different sort of vindication. The test of repentance was whether or not one responded to this challenge.

An analogy with a different debate may make the point clear. Sanders argued in 1985 that Jesus was not 'political', meaning that he did not advocate violent revolution. He is certainly correct in the latter point, but to say that this makes for a 'non-political' Jesus is to miss the vital political overtones of the kingdom-proclamation.[51] In the same way, I suggest, Sanders is right to say that Jesus was not primarily a 'reformer', but wrong to deny, on that basis, that Jesus 'preached repentance'. Jesus was not opposed to the steady, ongoing work of moral reformation; but he had far more urgent business in hand.

(ii) Belief

Like 'repentance', 'belief' has come to carry a good many overtones of religious experience and dogma. Theologians have discussed the meaning of 'faith', or 'belief', and have located it on a scale somewhere between the English concepts of 'trust' and 'assent', sometimes using the Latin tags *fides qua* (the faith *with which* one believes) and *fides quae* (the faith *which* one believes) to distinguish the two.

The former of these ('trust') can, in the biblical languages, be further subdivided into 'faith' and 'faithfulness'. The Hebrew *emunah* and the Greek *pistis* can both have this double sense, and it is perhaps only a residual anxiety about 'works-righteousness' being smuggled in by the back door that prevents the meaning 'faithfulness' or 'loyalty' from being heard in many New Testament passages.[52] The older dictionary articles on 'faith' reflect the

---

[51] See Borg 1984, ch. 1; Caird & Hurst 1994, 356–9 and elsewhere.

[52] cf. Moore 1927–30, 2.238: 'fidelity to God was in Jewish thought inseparable from confidence in God'. It is this inseparability that has called down so many strictures on

dogmatic as much as the historical discussion, moving swiftly on from Jesus to Paul and the debates which his writings arouse; few if any commentaries spend much time on the topic of what Jesus actually *meant* when he spoke of belief or faith.[53] It is doubtless true that the church, not least the Pauline church, retold stories in which Jesus had talked about 'faith', and did so in order to reinforce their own meaning for the term and the place which it had in their theology. But there should be no doubt that Jesus himself spoke of people 'believing' or 'having faith'.[54] What precisely did he mean by it?

Of the numerous passages in the Old Testament which speak of faith, certain ones stand out as constituting a striking appeal for a faith (or 'belief', or 'trust') which must characterize Israel in her hour of distress. The book of Isaiah offers the following:

If you will not believe, indeed you will not be established.[55]

See, I am laying in Zion a foundation stone, a tested stone, a precious cornerstone, a sure foundation: One who trusts will not panic.[56]

In returning and rest you shall be saved; in quietness and trust shall be your strength. But you refused . . .[57]

The well-known passage in Habakkuk contributes the same idea. When all other boundary-markers disappear in the great moment of judgment, the people of YHWH will be marked out by their faith:

Judaism from e.g. Bultmann *TDNT* 6.201, and which has marginalized most of the relevant evidence in e.g. Lührmann 1973, 26f., who sees 'fidelity' as a 'virtue' – and therefore, by implication, having to do with moralism rather than with justification by faith.

[53] e.g. Bultmann in *TDNT* 6.197-228; Michel in *NIDNTT* 1.587-606. Lührmann 1973 has a more historical approach, but does not address very far the issue of Jesus' own meaning. Wallis 1995 has a short section (17-23) on the background, but his main topic is the NT's reports of Jesus' *own* faith. Cf. too France in *DJG* 223-6. Here is, perhaps, a potential research topic for some brave soul.

[54] The theme occurs in all strands of synoptic tradition. Triple: Mk. 5.34/Mt. 9.22/Lk. 8.48; Mk. 2.5/Mt. 9.2/Lk. 5.20; Mt. 21.25/Mk. 11.31/Lk. 20.5. Mt./Mk.: Mt. 21.21/Mk. 11.22f.; Mt. 18.6/Mk. 9.42. Mk./Lk.: Mk. 5.36/Lk. 8.50; Mk. 10.52/Lk. 18.42. Q: Mt. 8.10/Lk. 7.9; Mt. 24.45/Lk. 12.42. Special Mk.: 1.15. Special Mt.: 8.13; 9.29. Special Lk.: 8.12, 13; 17.5f., 19. Interestingly, 'faith' seems to play no part in *Thom.*, even in the sayings (48, 106) which parallel Lk. 17.5f.

[55] Isa. 7.9. No English translation comes close to the direct and crisp link between 'believe' and 'be established': *'im lo tha'minu, ki lo theamenu*. None, that is, except the idiomatic 'trust or bust'.

[56] Isa. 28.16. Meyer (1979, 183, with 302 n.26) comments: 'The final ransoming of Israel would turn on an act of faith . . . Copestone signified Messiah; temple, the messianic remnant of believers.'

[57] Isa. 30.15. The Heb. for 'returning' is *shubah*, the regular 'repentance' root.

Look at the proud! Their spirit is not right in them; but the righteous live by their faith.[58]

'Faith', as far as these texts is concerned, is not simply to be understood as a single, miscellaneous religious quality, 'virtue', or attribute. It is the distinguishing mark of the true people of YHWH at the time of crisis. It is one of the things, predictably, that will characterize the return from exile:

> Behold, I shall restore to her soundness and health, and I shall cause them to hearken; and I shall heal her, and create for them peace and faith.[59]

When we move into post-biblical Jewish writings we find the same emphases. Lack of faith characterizes those whose membership in Israel is called into question, whereas the true Israel have faith:

> This [having quoted Habakkuk 1.5] concerns those who were unfaithful together with the Liar, in that they did not listen to the word received by the Teacher of Righteousness from the mouth of God. And it concerns the unfaithful of the New Covenant in that they have not believed in the Covenant of God and have profaned his holy name. And likewise, this saying is to be interpreted as concerning those who will be unfaithful at the end of days. They, the men of violence and the breakers of the Covenant, will not believe when they hear all that is to happen to the final generation . . .[60]

> 'But the righteous shall live by his faith': Interpreted, this concerns all those who observe the Law in the House of Judah, whom God will deliver from the House of Judgment because of their suffering and because of their faith in the Teacher of Righteousness.[61]

> For the heavens and the earth will listen to His Messiah, and all that is in them will not turn away from the holy precepts. Be encouraged, you who are seeking the Lord in his service! Will you not, perhaps, encounter the Lord in it, all those who hope in their heart? For the Lord will observe the devout, and call the just by name, and upon the poor he will place his spirit, and the faithful (*'emunim*) he will renew with his strength. For he will honour the devout upon the throne of eternal royalty, freeing prisoners, giving sight to the blind, straightening out the twisted. Ever shall I cling to those who hope . . .[62]

> Those who trust in him will understand truth, and the faithful will abide with him in love, because grace and mercy are upon his holy ones, and he watches over his elect.[63]

---

[58] Hab. 2.4. According to bMakk. 24a, this verse sums up the whole of divine revelation. On the use of this verse within subsequent Jewish thought cf. Strobel 1961. For the idea of judgment coming upon the *un*faithful cp. Ps. 78 (LXX 77).22.

[59] Jer. 40.6 (LXX). The MT (33.6) has 'peace and truth'.

[60] 1QpHab. 2.1-7 (Vermes 1995 [1962], 341 (cf. GM 198); I have not indicated lacunae in the scroll, since they do not affect the point at issue).

[61] 1QpHab. 7.17—8.3 (Vermes 344). GM 200 translates *emunah*, equally validly, as 'loyalty'.

[62] 4Q521 II.2.1-9 (GM 394).

[63] Wis. 3.9: 'those who trust' is *hoi pepoithotes*; 'the faithful', *hoi pistoi*. This concludes the description of the righteous whose souls are presently in the hands of the creator god until the time of their resurrection (cf. *NTPG* 329f.). The strong similarity between this passage and the previous one, from an apocalyptic-style Scroll, indicates once more where the book of Wisdom belongs historically (cf. above, 211-13).

Jerusalem shall no longer undergo desolation,
nor shall Israel be led into captivity,
because the Lord will be in her midst . . .
The Holy One of Israel will rule over them in humility and poverty,
and he who trusts in him shall reign in truth in the heavens.[64]

Therefore the enemy is eager to trip up all who call on the Lord, because he knows that on the day in which Israel has faith, the enemy's kingdom will be brought to an end.[65]

For this reason, you will be scattered like Dan and Gad, my brothers, you shall not know your own lands, tribe, or language. But he will gather you in faith through his compassion and on account of Abraham, Isaac and Jacob.[66]

Finally, we note that 'faith' is held up as the quality which sustained the victims of persecution in 4 Maccabees, urging its readers:

You too must have the same faith in god and not be grieved.[67]

It should be clear from this that, though the theme of 'believing' or 'having faith' occupies nowhere near as large a place in the pre-Christian Jewish world as it has across the board in early Christianity, it functions as a theme with the following connotations. First, it is the appropriate stance of the covenant people before their rightful god (and, for that matter, of creatures before their maker). Second, it is the thing which marks out the true people of Israel at a time of crisis and judgment. Third, it will characterize the people who are restored after the exile. We may add to this a fourth point, from the literature on the conversion of proselytes: faith, in the sense of belief in the one true god and the rejection of pagan idols, was of course a vital characteristic for anyone seeking to join the people of Israel. 'Faith' is thus not simply to be understood, within the world of first-century Judaism, in terms simply of religious interiority. Nor is the vital question the one which occupies so much twentieth-century writing on the subject, namely the shape of 'faith' and its role within religious experience as a whole.[68] What matters is that *faith is a crucial part of the definition of Israel at her time of great crisis.* Jesus' call for 'faith' was not merely the offering of a new religious option or dimension. It was a crucial element in the eschatological reconstitution of Israel around himself.[69]

---

[64] *T.Dan* 5.13.
[65] *T.Dan* 6.4.
[66] *T.Ash.* 7.6–7.
[67] 4 Macc. 16.22; cf. 15.24; 17.2. Cf. too e.g. Sir. 44.20.
[68] cf. e.g. Bultmann in *TDNT* 6, cited at n.52 above; the whole article is an object-lesson in asking the wrong questions.
[69] cf. Hengel 1981a, 22, with various rabbinic refs.

Once this dimension of Jesus' references to 'faith' is opened up, we can see that the characteristic sayings dovetail neatly into the call for repentance which we have studied already.[70] The 'faith' which is the concomitant of so many acts of healing is not simply 'believing that Israel's god can do this'.[71] It is believing *that Israel's god is acting climactically in the career of Jesus himself*. Both halves of this are equally important: (a) this is the moment Israel has been expecting; (b) this moment is constituted and characterized precisely by the presence and activity of Jesus. The 'healing' aspect of the prophetic praxis we studied in chapter 5 formed, as we saw, a vital part of the eschatological proclamation.[72] Now we find that the faith which reached out to grasp that healing also carried the same eschatological overtones. This was the distinguishing mark of those who grouped themselves around Jesus, just as it was the mark of those who focused their life upon the Teacher of Righteousness.

'Faith', as Jesus invited people to it, carried two particular overtones, one (in the anachronistic division of our own times) more obviously 'religious' and the other more apparently 'secular'. The 'religious' meaning, stressed at various points in the gospels, focused on the insistence that Israel's god was to be seen as the 'father' of his people. This, it must be emphasized, was not a new thought; it is found in the Old Testament and in a fair amount of subsequent Jewish writings.[73] Nor is it simply a matter of 'father' being one miscellaneous appellation among many for YHWH. Nor, yet, is it to be explained solely in terms of Jesus' 'religious experience'.[74] It is particularly

[70] This is not to decide for or against any particular sayings; merely to affirm that Jesus regularly spoke of 'faith', not least in the context of healings.

[71] Faith as the necessary accompaniment of mighty works is highlighted in e.g. mRH. 3.8; cf. Moore 1927–30, 2.206.

[72] Above 191–6.

[73] e.g. Ex. 4.22; Dt. 32.6; Isa. 63.16; 64.8; Jer. 3.4; 3.19; 31.9; 31.20; Hos. 11.1; Mal. 1.6; 2.10; Tob. 13.4; Sir. 23.1, 4; 51.10 (in the Heb.: Gk. 'the father of my lord'); Wis. 14.3 (cf. 2.16; 5.5; 11.10); 3 Macc. 5.7; 6.3, 8; *Ps. Sol.* 18.4; *Jub.* 1.24f.; 1.28; 19.29; Philo *Abr.* 12.58 (on Philo cf. Quell in *TDNT* 5.956f.); Jos. *Ant.* 5.93; mYom. 8.9 (Akiba, quoting Ezek. 36.25); mSot. 9.15 (quoting Mic. 7.6; ascribed to Eliezer ben Hyrcanus: a fascinating passage, on which see below, 347f.); mAb. 3.15 (quoting Dt. 14.1; ascribed to Akiba); bBab. Bat. 10a (debate between Akiba and a Roman; cf. Pesikta Rab. on Jer. 2.4); bTaan. 23b; 25b; bKidd. 36a; Midr. Ps. 25, on 25.14; Siphra Lev. on 20.26; Mek. Ex. on 20.25 (quoting Johanan ben Zakkai); and many others. Cf. Moore 1927–30, 1.396–8; 2.201–11 (208–11 on 'father' within liturgical address); Quell & Schrenk in *TDNT* 5.945–1022; Jeremias 1967, ch. 1; Byrne 1979, 13–78. It is remarkable that there is no article on 'Father' in the *ABD*.

[74] On this latter theme, with reference to 'Abba' for 'Father', cf. e.g. Jeremias 1967 and elsewhere; Vermes 1973, 210–13; 1983, 39–43; 1993, ch. 6; Bauckham 1978; Barr 1988; Hurtado 1992. For our present purposes it is not pressing that we resolve the debate between these writers. Suffice it to note, with Bauckham 246–53, Byrne 1979, 74 that Vermes has not, in fact, fully refuted Jeremias's argument for Jesus' usage being special. See also below, 648f.

associated, as the passages in the note indicate, with his great acts of deliverance, namely the exodus and the return from exile. To invoke this god as 'father' is to stir up associations of the great coming deliverance. Jesus, in inviting his hearers to think of their god explicitly in this way, was emphasizing a strand in Jewish tradition which implicitly carried forward his claim: those who possessed this 'faith' in YHWH as 'father' were defining themselves as the eschatological Israel.[75] Parables which echo this whole theme include the two sons;[76] gifts for the children;[77] and of course, once again, the prodigal son (or the prodigal father).

'Faith' can also carry the more 'secular' meaning which we saw in the passage from Josephus' *Life* quoted above. Josephus asked Jesus the Galilean brigand leader 'to repent and believe in me', in other words, to give up his agenda and follow Josephus' instead.[78] Jesus of Nazareth, I suggest, issued more or less exactly the same summons to his contemporaries. They should give up their way of being the people of god and trust him for his. As with repentance, so with faith: Jesus' call carried the implication that those who followed him, followed his way of being Israel, were the true Israel whom YHWH was calling into being as the real returned-from-exile ones. The call to 'believe in the gospel', or to 'believe in me', does not suggest that Jesus was inviting Galilean villagers to embrace a body of doctrine – not even a basic 'theory' about 'salvation' and how they might attain it, nor, again, very much of a christology (though presumably it involved recognizing Jesus as a god-sent prophet like John). Nor does it suggest that Jesus was offering them what we would today call a new 'religious experience'. It evokes the historical picture of one who believed that, with his work, Israel's god was inaugurating his long-awaited kingdom.

Jesus of Nazareth was not the only person who held that belief, and acted upon it, in the period. His call to 'believe' him does not, by itself, make him 'unique'. We can perfectly easily envisage other leaders – Judas the Galilean, for example, or Bar-Kochba – summoning their followers to personal loyalty in such terms.[79] Was Jesus of Nazareth, then, different? Yes, but not in this

---

[75] cf. Bauckham 1978, 249, 253.

[76] Mt. 21.28-32.

[77] Mt. 7.7-11/Lk. 11.5-8; Lk. 11.9-13. The parallels to Lk. 11.9f. in *P. Oxy.654*.2; *Thom.* 2; 92; 94 lack the parable.

[78] *Life* 110; cf. 250f. above. Thackeray in the LCL edn. (1.43) translates 'if he would . . . prove his loyalty to me'. The passage is not noted in Lindsay 1993, which constantly divides the material into 'profane use' and 'religious use', while recognizing (136f.) that the distinction does not always hold.

[79] cf. Hengel 1981b [1968], 23: 'Joining such apocalyptic "prophets" or Zealot leaders of the people . . . was conditional on *'emunah* towards the message and divine authorisation of the "charismatic".'

summons itself. The differences appear not least in the way of life to which he called his hearers. To this we must shortly turn. First, though, we move from 'invitation' to 'welcome'. Here the key question is: who precisely were the 'sinners' whom Jesus welcomed, and what did he say about them?

3. Welcome: Sinners and Forgiveness

(i) Who are the Sinners?

There is a more or less universal consensus among scholars – something as rare as snow in midsummer, and no doubt similarly transitory – that Jesus offered a welcome to, and shared meals with, 'sinners'.[80] But there agreement stops, since we run into a variety of difficult questions: who were the 'sinners'? What precisely did Jesus offer them? Did anyone object, and if so why? We must study these questions in turn, here and in what follows.

First, we should now be able to distinguish, as former generations often did not, between 'sinners' and 'non-Pharisees'.[81] In some influential older writings, the meaning of 'sinner' was drawn out of texts which spoke of the 'people of the land', the *amme-ha'aretz*.[82] But the texts appealed to in support of this identification – several rabbinic passages of various vintage – will not bear the weight. They undoubtedly tell us that many rabbis in the post-135 period regarded all those who did not adhere to their way of studying and practising Torah as something of a lesser breed, albeit still within Judaism as a whole. They undoubtedly prove that some rabbis encouraged the study and practice of Torah by saying rude things about those who refused. But they do not tell us very much about the meaning and reference of the word 'sinner' – whatever Aramaic words might have conveyed that nebulous idea – in the Palestine of Jesus' day.[83] Clearly, the word was sometimes used, as it is in some early Christian writings, to mean 'lesser breeds without the law', i.e. Gentiles.[84] If used in reference to a Jew, therefore, it would demarcate him or her as 'no better than a pagan'.[85] But, as the polemical note in such a phrase indicates, such a category would gain its content strictly in relation to the point of view of the speaker. Different varieties of

---

[80] cf. Sanders 1985, 5. The consensus is broken only by Horsley 1987, 217–23.

[81] cf. the brief discussion in *NTPG* 213f.

[82] Particularly Rengstorf in *TDNT* 1.317–35; and SB 2.494–519. On the 'people of the land' in the OT see esp. Healey 1992; for the later developments cf. Oppenheimer 1977.

[83] On the technical terms cf. Chilton 1988, 9f., correcting apparent oversimplifications in Sanders 1977, 1985; and cf. Sanders 1993, 227.

[84] e.g. Mt. 26.45/Mk. 14.41; Gal. 2.15.

[85] It seems to be used thus of Jesus in Jn. 9.16, 24f.

exceedingly scrupulous Jews hurled such anathemas at each other, for instance in the Qumran polemic against the Pharisees, and the sometimes bitter wrangling between the houses of Hillel and Shammai.[86] The language of polemic is not good soil for producing terminological accuracy.

It is therefore highly likely that, though all 'sinners' would be 'people of the land', not all 'people of the land' would be 'sinners'. The phrase 'people of the land' has its own somewhat chequered history. Beginning as the designation of a respectable group within pre-exilic Israel, the term is used in some second-Temple writings to denote those who were in the land already at the time of the return from Babylon; it thus acquires a pejorative overtone.[87] This distinction, between the returning exiles and those of dubious pedigree who were in the land already, seems then, by the rabbinic period, to have been used to highlight a quite different distinction, that between the rabbis themselves and the 'ordinary Jews', of no matter what pedigree, who did not follow their particular interpretation of Torah.

What about our particular period? Since the term does not feature in texts (including Christian ones) that we can date to the time between 63 BC and AD 70, it is difficult to determine the extent to which its rabbinic use may be a construct of post-70, or even post-135, rabbinic thought. It may well be that, before 70, the Pharisees would simply have seen their not-especially-wicked Jewish contemporaries as 'ordinary Jews', who after all made up the great bulk of the population.[88] Only after the two wars, as the rabbis consolidated their quite new position as the official leaders of the Jews, were they in a position to elevate the occasional sneering comment ('these people who don't know the Torah'[89]) into a matter of articulated policy. It is not impossible, however, that part of the pejorative tone of 'sinners' in a passage like Luke 15.2 may have been that it carried the sense of 'not quite real Jews' – which would mean, in effect, 'like those who were in the land when the exiles returned from Babylon'. This, of course, would fit very well with the subversive meaning of the parable of the prodigal son which we explored in chapter 4.

In the absence of firmer evidence, then, we can draw the following conclusions:

(i) The phrase 'people of the land' already carried a slur in some second-Temple literature, meaning in effect 'of uncertain ancestry, and therefore dubious membership in the people of Israel'.[90]

---

[86] cf. Knibb 1987, 209–19 (commenting on 4QpNah., where the Pharisees are described as 'seekers after smooth things'); *NTPG* 183f.

[87] For the background, cf. 2 Kgs. 17.24–41; Ezra 4.2, 10.

[88] cf. Bauckham 1993b.

[89] Jn. 7.49.

[90] e.g. Ezra 4.4; 9.1, 2; 10.2, 11; Neh. 10.20–31: cf. Gunneweg 1983.

(ii) 'People of the land' was a category used by the post-135 rabbis to designate those who, albeit Jewish, did not follow rabbinic observance of Torah.[91]

(iii) It is very likely that the Pharisees of the pre-70 period regarded ordinary non-Pharisaic Jews as in some ways second-class citizens who, because they did not adhere to the Pharisaic way, were *technically*, in their eyes, transgressors of the Torah.

(iv) This technical category would include those who, as well as being simply non-Pharisaic Jews, clearly and deliberately flouted the Torah. These were the 'wicked' or 'sinners', for example prostitutes. It is very unlikely that anyone in the first century drew a sharp distinction between 'people of the land' and 'sinners'; we are dealing with shadings, not clear and obvious demarcations. Perhaps a Shammaite Pharisee would have been happy with a coloured scale: Shammaites – red; Hillelites – pink; 'people of the land' – grey; 'sinners' – black. There might well have been some disagreement when it came to voting on who came into which of the latter two groups;[92] some ultra-zealous Shammaites might have elided the middle two as well.

(v) Jesus associated with both the latter categories, the ordinary non-Pharisaic Jews and the 'sinners'. (There is also evidence that he was happy to associate with Pharisees if they were happy to associate with him.[93]) It is very unlikely that he or they drew too sharp a distinction between them.

Can we then be more specific about the 'sinners'? One particular category of 'sinner' that crops up frequently in the gospels is the tax- or toll-collector (Greek *telones*).[94] It is commonly said that they were hated as collaborators with Rome; this needs nuancing somewhat, since in the Galilee of Jesus' day monies would be collected not for Rome but for Herod. This may not make too much of a difference, since Herod was scarcely a popular monarch: kept in power by Rome as a client king, his Jewish orthodoxy was widely suspect.[95] Even if, as seems to be the case with Zacchaeus in Luke 19.1–10, the real problem was simply that tax- or toll-collectors were widely regarded as dishonest and rapacious, that does not lessen the point that they had a

---

[91] Rabbinic texts regularly cited in the discussion include e.g. bSanh. 25b; mKidd. 4.14; bKidd. 82a; mAb. 5.10–19; mSot. 9.15.

[92] cf. Meyer 1979, 296 n.109: 'we should neither identify notorious sinners . . . with the ordinary run of men nor disregard the continuity which the religious *élite* considered to exist between them'. He compares Lk. 18.11, which lumps the tax-collector together with 'the rest of the people'.

[93] cf. e.g. Lk. 7.36; 13.31.

[94] cf. Horsley 1987, 212–17; Malina and Rohrbaugh 1992, 189f.; Sanders 1993, 228f.

[95] On Herod Antipas see Hoehner 1980 [1972], with other bibliography; Schürer 1.340–53; on the present point cf. Borg 1984, 310 n.46. The impurity of tax-collectors, presumably based on their contact with Gentiles, is presupposed in e.g. mHag. 3.6; mToh. 7.6.

reputation not just as 'people of the land' but as sinners, regarded not just by Pharisees but by other 'people of the land' as a class apart, almost as the moral equivalent of lepers. We are concerned as much with perceptions as with what was actually the case; and the perception is reflected even in sayings attributed to Jesus himself.[96] It is thus striking, and (to return to where we started) must be regarded as a fixed point, that Jesus welcomed 'tax-collectors and sinners' into table-fellowship with himself.[97]

The other category that is mentioned just once in this connection in the synoptic tradition is that of prostitute.[98] In Matthew 21.31 Jesus, following the parable of the two sons, comments:

> Truly I say to you, the tax-collectors and the prostitutes precede you into the kingdom of god. For John came to you in the way of righteousness, and you did not believe him – but the tax-collectors and the prostitutes believed him. But even though you saw it, you did not change your minds and believe him.

This, as it stands, is scarcely evidence that Jesus kept company with prostitutes. It refers, obviously, to John's following. Nevertheless, the story of the woman regarded as a 'sinner', whose scandalous behaviour in public so offended the Pharisee in Luke 7.36–50, indicates clearly enough that one at least of the welcomed sinners was a woman who had a low reputation to start with and made it worse by her behaviour towards Jesus.[99] And with that in mind we may hear in the passage just quoted a hint that prostitutes had followed Jesus, as they had followed John.[100] But it is no more than a hint. The reputation which Mary of Magdala has acquired in later tradition owes nothing to the synoptic or Johannine gospel texts, in which the only thing said about her is that she had had seven demons cast out of her – which puts

---

[96] e.g. Mt. 5.46; 18.17, where the *telones* is put in parallel with Gentiles; and cf. Lk. 18.10, where the point of the story is of course that the Pharisee and the *telones* are assumed to be at opposite ends of the scale.

[97] Mk. 2.15/Mt. 9.10/Lk. 5.29; cf. Mt. 11.19/Lk. 7.34; Mt. 21.31f.; Lk. 7.29.

[98] In Lk. 15.30 the older brother accuses the younger of squandering the father's property on prostitutes; this may be implied in the earlier *zon asotos* (15.13), which may be translated 'living in profligacy', with the definite connotation of sexual immorality: cf. LSJ, ad loc.

[99] Derrett 1970, 267–85 has shown that the passage only makes sense on the assumption that the woman was a prostitute.

[100] Horsley's suggestion (1987, 223) that the woman of Luke 7 was a 'debtor' rather than a 'sinner' seems to me to be straining the evidence beyond breaking point. The parable of the two debtors (Lk. 7.41–2) is, after all, a parable. Ironically, Horsley's attempt to make Jesus a social revolutionary (against Rome) ends up making him something of a social conformist (with Israel). Horsley's real point is seen in e.g. 213: he is determined to rule out any evidence that Jesus took 'a nonresistant stance toward Roman rule', such as might be hinted at in associating with collaborators. On prostitutes as collaborators, cf. Gibson 1981.

her on a level with several other characters in the gospels about whom there is no suggestion of sexual misconduct.[101]

What then, more precisely, did Jesus offer to 'sinners'? It would be all too easy to say 'forgiveness', and leave it at that. But, like many terms which have become standard in later Christian vocabulary, this one too needs further exploration if we are to locate Jesus within his historical context.

(ii) The Forgiveness of Sins

Centuries of Christian usage have accustomed readers of the New Testament to think of 'forgiveness' as primarily a gift to the individual person, which can be made at any time. It is, in that sense, abstract and ahistorical, however much it may burst upon one's consciousness with fresh delight in particular historical situations. On this basis, analyses of Jesus' offer of forgiveness have tended to focus on the piety (the *sense* of forgiveness) or the abstract theology (the *fact* of forgiveness, or the belief in it) of Jesus' hearers and/or the early church.

The entire argument of this book so far indicates that this puts the cart before the horse. What is regularly missing from analyses of forgiveness[102] is that which, arguably, stands front and centre in precisely those biblical and post-biblical Jewish texts upon which Jesus and the early church drew most heavily. *Forgiveness of sins is another way of saying 'return from exile'.*

Lest any reader, determined to remain unconvinced by my thesis about the still-awaited return from exile, should sigh in disbelief, let me begin with some texts in which the point is crystal clear. We should remember, in reading these, that the prophets of the time of the exile (in particular Jeremiah, Ezekiel, and Isaiah 40—55) saw Israel's exile precisely as the result of, or the punishment for, her sins. It should be clear from this that if the astonishing, unbelievable thing were to happen, and Israel were to be brought back from exile, this would *mean* that her sins were being punished no more; in other words, were forgiven. In this context, here is the writer of Lamentations, stating the matter about as clearly and baldly as one could wish:

> The punishment of your iniquity, O daughter Zion, is accomplished;
> He will keep you in exile no longer.[103]

---

[101] Lk. 8.2. On Mary Magdalene in the NT cf. Collins 1992; in later art, cf. Hall 1984 [1974], 202-4. Prior to 1785, the statue of Mary Magdalene in the choir of Lichfield Cathedral had 'one leg bare, to note her legendary wantonness' (Prentis 1996, 25).

[102] e.g. Shogren 1992; this is the less surprising, in that his *ABD* article follows two others, by Kselman on the OT and by Charlesworth on Early Judaism, in which the point is similarly missed.

[103] Lam. 4.22.

This is, patently, the point also of Jeremiah's famous promise, holding out the composite hope of covenant renewal, return from exile (seen as the real or new exodus), the renewal of the heart, the internalization of Torah, and the forgiveness of sins:

> The days are coming, says YHWH, when I will make a new covenant with the house of Israel and the house of Judah. It will not be like the covenant that I made with their ancestors when I took them by the hand to bring them out of the land of Egypt . . . But this is the covenant that I will make with the house of Israel after those days, says YHWH: I will put my law within them, and I will write it on their hearts; and I will be their god, and they shall be my people. No longer shall they teach one another, or say to each other, 'Know YHWH,' for they shall all know me, from the least of them to the greatest, says YHWH; for *I will forgive their iniquity, and remember their sin no more.*[104]

Within the whole context of Jeremiah, the message should be obvious. Among a good many other things, the return from exile will mean forgiveness of sins, and vice versa. This is filled out, even more explicitly, a couple of chapters later:

> Thus says YHWH, the God of Israel, concerning the houses of this city and the houses of the kings of Judah that were torn down to make a defence . . . I have hidden my face from this city because of all their wickedness. I am going to bring it recovery and healing; I will heal them and reveal to them abundance of prosperity and security. *I will restore the fortunes of Judah and the fortunes of Israel, and rebuild them as they were at first. I will cleanse them from all the guilt of their sin against me, and I will forgive all the guilt of their sin and rebellion against me.* And this city shall be to me a name of joy, a praise and a glory before all the nations of the earth who shall hear of all the good that I do for them . . . for I will restore the fortunes of the land as at first, says YHWH.[105]

Forgiveness, in other words, is not simply one miscellaneous blessing which will accompany covenant renewal. Since covenant renewal means the reversal of exile, and since exile was the punishment for sin, covenant renewal/return from exile *means* that Israel's sins have been forgiven – and vice versa.

Here, similarly, is Ezekiel:

> I will take you from the nations, and gather you from all the countries, and bring you into your own land. I will sprinkle clear water upon you, and you shall be clean from all your uncleannesses, and from all your idols I will cleanse you. A new heart I will give you, and a new spirit I will put within you; and I will remove from your body the heart of stone and give you a heart of flesh . . . Thus says the Lord YHWH: On the day that I cleanse you from all your iniquities, I will cause the towns to be inhabited, and the waste places shall be rebuilt.[106]

---

[104] Jer. 31.31–4.
[105] Jer. 33.4–11. The whole chapter provides a rich expansion and expression of the same set of themes.
[106] Ezek. 36.24–6, 33.

This, too, could hardly be clearer. Or again:

> I will take the people of Israel from the nations among which they have gone, and will
> gather them from every quarter, and bring them to their own land . . . I will save them
> from all the apostasies into which they have fallen, and will cleanse them. Then they
> shall be my people, and I will be their god.[107]

But perhaps the most obvious passages are those in Isaiah. No one will doubt
that chapters 40—55 as a whole are about Israel's promised return from
exile, coupled with YHWH's own return to Zion. But the way this message is
announced is in the language of forgiveness, of sin having been dealt with:

> Comfort, comfort my people, says your god. Speak tenderly to Jerusalem, and cry to her
> that she has served her term; that her penalty is paid; that she has received from YHWH's
> hand double for all her sins.[108]

The exile, in other words, was caused by Israel's sin; so now, if the sin has
been dealt with and forgiven, the exile must be ending. This emerges equally
clearly a few chapters later:

> I, I am he who blots out your transgressions for my own sake, and I will not remember
> your sins . . . Your first ancestor sinned, and your interpreters transgressed against me.
> Therefore I profaned the princes of the sanctuary, I delivered Jacob to utter destruction,
> and Israel to reviling. But now hear, O Jacob my servant, Israel whom I have chosen!
> Thus says YHWH . . .: Do not fear, O Jacob my servant . . . for I will pour water on the
> thirsty land, and streams upon the dry ground; I will pour my spirit upon your descend-
> ants, and my blessing on your offspring . . .[109]

Like so many other strands in Isaiah 40—55, the combination of return from
exile and the forgiveness of sins comes to its climax in chapters 52—5:

> Awake, awake, put on your strength, O Zion! . . . for the uncircumcised and the unclean
> shall enter you no more . . . For thus says YHWH: you were sold for nothing, and you
> shall be redeemed without money . . . Break forth into singing, you ruins of Jerusalem,
> for YHWH has comforted his people, he has redeemed Jerusalem . . .
>
> He was wounded for our transgressions, crushed for our iniquities; upon him was the
> punishment that made us whole, and by his bruises we are healed. All we like sheep have
> gone astray; we have all turned to our own way, and YHWH has laid on him the iniquity
> of us all . . . The righteous one, my servant, shall make many righteous, and he shall
> bear their iniquities . . . He bore the sin of many, and made intercession for the trans-
> gressors . . .
>
> Sing, O barren one who did not bear; burst into song and shout, you who have not
> been in labour! For the children of the desolate woman will be more than the children of
> her that is married, says YHWH . . . You will spread out to the right and to the left, and
> your descendants will possess the nations, and will settle the desolate towns . . . In over-

---

[107] Ezek. 37.21-3.

[108] Isa. 40.1-2.

[109] Isa. 43.25—44.3: here, clearly, YHWH is no longer counting Israel's sins against her.

flowing wrath for a moment I hid my face from you, but with everlasting love I will have compassion on you, says YHWH, your redeemer . . .

Let the wicked forsake their way, and the unrighteous their thoughts; let them return to YHWH, that he may have mercy on them, and to our god, for he will abundantly pardon . . . For you shall go out in joy, and be led back in peace . . .[110]

Similarly, the great prayers for return and restoration focus on Israel's sin as the cause of the exile, and on the need for forgiveness if restoration is to become a reality. Thus, for instance, Daniel:

O Lord, in view of all your righteous acts, let your anger and wrath, we pray, turn away from your city Jerusalem, your holy mountain; because of our sins and the iniquities of our ancestors, Jerusalem and your people have become a disgrace among all our neighbours. Now therefore, O our god, listen to the prayer of your servant . . ., and let your face shine upon your desolated sanctuary . . . We do not present our supplication before you on the ground of our righteousness, but on the ground of your great mercies. O Lord, hear; O Lord, forgive; O Lord, listen and act and do not delay! For your own sake, O my god, because your city and your people bear your name![111]

The same theme informs the great prayers of Ezra, recognizing even in the 'post-exilic' period that the exile, from a theological point of view, is still continuing, since Israel is still enslaved and sinful;[112] and, at more length, the prayer of 'Baruch'.[113]

The conclusion hardly needs restating. From the point of view of a first-century Jew, 'forgiveness of sins' could never simply be a private blessing, though to be sure it was that as well, as Qumran amply testifies.[114] Overarching the situation of the individual was the state of the nation as a whole; and, as long as Israel remained under the rule of the pagans, as long as Torah was not observed perfectly, as long as the Temple was not properly restored, so Israel longed for 'forgiveness of sins' as the great, unrepeatable, eschatological and national blessing promised by her god. In the light of this, the meaning which Mark and Luke both give to John's baptism ought to be clear. It was 'for the forgiveness of sins', in other words, to bring about the redemption for which Israel was longing.[115]

This conclusion chimes in with the analysis of 'sinners' offered above, and with the analysis of Jesus' invitation to 'repent' and 'believe'. Recent

---

[110] Isa. 52.1, 3, 9; 53.5–6, 11–12; 54.1, 3, 8; 55.7, 12. The entire passage, obviously, needs to be read as a whole; I have extracted the salient points for the present theme. Cp. too Isa. 33.24 in context; 64.8–12; and, for the wider setting, Lev. 26.27–45; Dt. 30.1–10.

[111] Dan. 9.16–19, concluding the prayer beginning at v. 4.

[112] Ezra 9.6–15; Neh. 9.6–37.

[113] Bar. 1.15—3.8.

[114] e.g. 1QS 11.11–14; the context, though, remains that of return from exile, as is argued by Garnet 1977. Cf. too the 6th of the 18 Benedictions (Schürer 2.457); *Pr. Man.* 11–13; and many other texts.

[115] Mk. 1.4/Lk. 3.3; cf. Lk. 1.77 in context.

scholarly debates have focused so much on the individual, seen in a hypothetical timeless moment of sin and/or forgiveness, that they have ignored this wider, but vital, context. It is not enough to prove, as Sanders, Charlesworth and many others have done quite satisfactorily, that first-century Jews were not in fact proto-Pelagians who thought that they could earn the divine forgiveness.[116] The point at issue was not that Jesus was offering forgiveness where the rabbis were offering self-help moralism. The point is that *Jesus was offering the return from exile, the renewed covenant, the eschatological 'forgiveness of sins'* – in other words, the kingdom of god. And he was offering this final eschatological blessing outside the official structures, to all the wrong people, and on his own authority. That was his real offence.

Jesus' 'welcome' to sinners, and the offence that it caused, therefore had everything to do with *eschatology* (in the sense I set out in the previous chapter), and little to do with (what we call) *'religion'*. That is, he welcomed people into his retinue as, by implication, *part of the restored people of YHWH*. Like David in the period between his anointing and his enthronement, Jesus collected a motley crew of followers who formed, as it were, a royal retinue-in-waiting. They were a sign that YHWH was at last restoring his people. They were not simply the recipients of a grace and mercy which had been denied them within Judaism; had they wanted to find 'forgiveness' as private individuals within the existing system, the means were available. The sacrificial system and the means of purification were in principle open to them – though how realistic it is to think of tax-collectors abandoning their despised but bread-winning job in order to seek reconciliation with Israel and her god may well be questioned. What Jesus was offering, in other words, was not a different religious system. It was a new world order, the end of Israel's long desolation, the true and final 'forgiveness of sins', the inauguration of the kingdom of god.[117]

This, I suggest, was what was implied when Jesus announced 'forgiveness of sins' to particular people. The effect was the same as his eating with 'sinners': he was celebrating the coming of the kingdom, and those who shared this celebration with him were benefiting from this great 'forgiveness of sins'. There is, in fact, no tension, no play-off, between the personal and the corporate at this point. The relevant passages are well known, though not normally read in this way. Jesus announces to the paralysed man that his sins are forgiven: the coming kingdom of YHWH has reached out to embrace him as well. It is on this basis that the man can experience his own personal

---

[116] Sanders 1985, on which see below; Charlesworth 1992a.
[117] See esp. Meyer 1979, e.g. 161, 172, 221.

'return from exile', in the form of healing from his paralysis.[118] Jesus announces to the woman who has anointed him that her sins are forgiven: again, the offence lies not least in this, that Jesus was announcing and enacting the eschatological kingdom, and including all the wrong people in it.[119] This explains, too, the cryptic saying about forgiveness which follows the Beelzebul controversy. The forgiveness of sins, Jesus insisted, was indeed coming, and sins of every kind could be forgiven when that happened; but if someone specifically denied the eschatological work of the spirit of YHWH, they were by that very act declaring themselves to be outside the eschatological Israel.[120] And, of course, Jesus enacts 'forgiveness' in many events where the word does not occur, just as he speaks of it frequently in parable and image without using the word *aphesis* and its cognates.[121]

Why then did people object to Jesus' practice?[122] Not, again, because he was preaching about love and mercy while ordinary Judaism, not least Pharisaism, remained hostile to such ideas. This is the strong point of Sanders' oft-repeated polemic against various German scholars.[123] The objection did not arise because Jesus was teaching or propagating a different religious system; nor because he was letting wicked people carry on with their

[118] Mt. 9.1–8/Mk. 2.1–12/Lk. 5.17–26.

[119] Lk. 7.36–50.

[120] Mk. 3.28–30/Mt. 12.31–7/Lk. 12.10. A later (apparently trinitarian) version occurs in *Thom.* 44; cp. too Heb. 6.4–8; 10.26–9; 1 Jn. 5.16. This eschatological reading is, I think, far and away the best solution to the old problem of the so-called 'unforgivable sin'; the closest parallel (pointed out by Shogren 1992, 838) is in *Jub.* 15.33f., where not circumcising one's child is unforgivable, because it is a declaration that one does not belong to the covenant people. For a recent discussion see Caird & Hurst 1994, 116f., with bibliography. See further above, 249 n.20.

[121] This eschatological meaning of 'forgiveness of sins' can be observed within early Christianity as well, e.g. Lk. 24.47; Ac. 2.38; 5.31; 10.43; 13.38; 26.18; Col. 1.14. Of course, once the gospel goes out to the gentile world the specifically Jewish context and echoes become progressively fainter; but, here as elsewhere, we must take it that 'restoration eschatology' was the original matrix of the idea, and that a detached, dehistoricized or privatized application came later.

[122] As in Mk. 2.16/Mt. 9.11/Lk. 5.30; Mt. 11.19/Lk. 7.34; Lk. 15.2.

[123] Sanders 1985, 200–4; 1987; 1992, 43; though cf. Meyer 1991. Interestingly, in Sanders' recent restatement of his views (1993), he seems to rehabilitate by the back door part at least of the view which he has so strongly attacked: Jesus' message, which made such a novel and striking impact on first-century Jewish hearers, was 'God loves you' (233); 'the message that God loves them anyway might transform their lives . . . perhaps [after Jesus' death] they lived out their lives in Galilee, hoping that the man who made them feel so special would be back' (234). Would this message of divine love not have been, on Sanders' own account, readily available in Judaism? And, if not, would not Jeremias and others respond that this was the substance of what they were getting at? Here, I think, Sanders has again not carried his own revolution far enough: he does not allow for the fact that 'forgiveness of sins' is one aspect of that 'Jewish restoration eschatology' to which he rightly draws attention.

sin and pretending all was well; nor because Jesus, as a private individual, was associating with people who were 'beyond the pale'. There is no reason to suppose that Pharisees, or anyone else, spied out ordinary people who were 'associating' with 'sinners' and angrily objected to them doing so. Accusations were levelled, rather, because this welcome to sinners was being offered *precisely by someone announcing the kingdom of god*, and, moreover, offering this welcome as itself a vital part of that kingdom. The question was not about the sinners, or the moral or theological niceties of whether they had repented, and, if so, in what sense. It was about the scandalous implied redefinition of the kingdom itself. Jesus was replacing adherence or allegiance to Temple and Torah with allegiance to himself. Restoration and purity were to be had, not through the usual channels, but through Jesus.

We can therefore lay to rest the debate as to whether Jesus intended sinners to 'reform'.[124] It is false to say, as Sanders has done, that had Jesus made notorious sinners mend their ways he would have been a national hero.[125] Reformed sinners are not a notably popular class; the only people who would have made Jesus a hero if he had achieved widespread moral reformation are exactly those Jewish legalists who anxiously imposed their own rigorous interpretations on the rest of the population – and whom Sanders himself has shown to be fictitious. The point about Jesus' welcome to 'sinners' was that he was declaring, on his own authority, that anyone who trusted in him and his kingdom-announcement was within the kingdom. However, the agenda that he set before not only 'sinners', but all who heeded his summons, was bracing and demanding. There is no reason to think he proposed a second-class option for those whose moral background had not prepared them for such a challenge. Precisely because Jesus welcomed people into the kingdom that was being inaugurated, he put before them the challenge of the kingdom, the call to live as the beneficiaries of the new covenant. To this we must now turn.

4. Challenge: The Call to Live as the New Covenant People

(i) Introduction: Community and Praxis

The story of the kingdom, we have seen, functioned as *invitation* and *welcome*. It was the kind of story that invites its hearers to make it their own: the story of Israel finally being released from bondage, and of YHWH returning to Zion, included the emphasis that the gates were being thrown wide

---

[124] cf. 247f. above.
[125] Sanders 1985, 203; toned down somewhat in 1993, 236; cf. Allison 1987.

open to all who would come and give loyalty to Jesus. But the story did not stop there. Precisely because it concerned the renewal of the covenant, the restoration of Israel, the fulfilment of the promises, and the realization of the hope, Jesus' retelling of Israel's story included the call and challenge to his hearers to live as the renewed Israel, the people of the new covenant.

This forms, I believe, the correct context for understanding two aspects of Jesus' 'teaching' which have often caused great problems. I refer to Jesus' view of the people who gave him their allegiance, and his intentions for their behaviour, their praxis. One of the 'characters' in the 'story' of the kingdom is the community of those who were loyal to Jesus. One of the key elements in the whole narrative is the behaviour to which he summoned them.

(ii) New Covenant, New Community

Did Jesus intend to found a 'church'? The question is hopeless. Of course he didn't; of course he did. The way the oft-repeated question puts it is impossibly anachronistic: it makes Jesus sound like a pioneer evangelist of the nineteenth century, throwing previous denominations to the winds and building his own tin tabernacle. Worse, it implies, almost with a sneer, that Jesus could hardly have envisaged the church as we know it today, or even as it has been for most of the last two thousand years; and that therefore the church stands condemned, untrue to the founder's intentions.[126]

What then did Jesus intend to do? The alternative offered by many who dismiss the church as a bad mistake is simply that Jesus came to offer individuals a new way of salvation, or perhaps a new form of religion. This, of course, is equally anachronistic; individualism is a comparatively modern, and a largely western, phenomenon.[127] More satisfactory by far, at the level of history, is to say with Gerhard Lohfink that Jesus did not intend to found a church *because there already was one*, namely the people of Israel itself. Jesus' intention was therefore to *reform* Israel, not to found a different community altogether.[128] Though there have been recent attempts to argue for a different position, that Jesus intended to establish a community which would be quite different from (what became) Judaism, Lohfink's proposal is in my judgment far more likely to be near the mark.[129]

---

[126] cf. e.g. Wilson 1992; at a serious level, Vermes 1973, 1983, 1993.

[127] A wonderful example of what happens when modern western individualism (not least as applied to evangelism) is confronted by corporate solidarity is provided in Donovan 1982, 91–3.

[128] Lohfink 1984; cf. too Borg 1984, 70–2.

[129] cf. Neusner 1989; 1991; and elsewhere. Cf. *NTPG* 472f. Neusner's proposal, of course, still involves Jesus intending to establish a community who would follow his teaching and look to him as leader and founder.

But did Jesus intend to bring the whole of Israel – say, all Jews living in Galilee and Judaea in the 20s AD – into his following? Was he aiming to mount a renewal movement that would sweep the board, propelling him into a position of undisputed national leadership? All the indications are to the contrary. That is not how the kingdom was to come, according to parables like the sower. The evidence points, I suggest, towards Jesus intending to establish, and indeed succeeding in establishing, what we might call cells of followers, mostly continuing to live in their towns and villages, who by their adoption of his praxis, his way of being Israel, would be distinctive within their local communities. (This is not, of course, to limit Jesus' ultimate intention to this activity.) From the point of view of other Jews looking on, such groups might seem in some ways like the followers of John the Baptist, or like a group of Pharisees. This, in fact, is just what we find in a key text:

> The disciples of John and the Pharisees were fasting. And they came and said to him, Why do John's disciples and the Pharisees' disciples fast, but your disciples do not fast? And Jesus said to them, How can the children of the bridechamber fast, while the bridegroom is with them? As long as they have the bridegroom with them, they cannot fast. The days will come when the bridegroom will be taken away from them; then they will fast, in that day.[130]

John's disciples, and groups adhering to Pharisaic teaching, were recognizable as small collective entities within local communities. In a world where 'private life' was virtually non-existent, everybody in the village would know what praxis they were following. The clear implication, which we would be quite wrong to locate only in the post-Easter period, is that those who gave their allegiance to Jesus, just like those who gave their allegiance to John, formed a distinct group with a distinct praxis – and that Jesus himself saw them in these terms.

What do we know about such groups, sometimes loosely called 'sects'? It will help to include the Essenes in the discussion as well.[131] They believed themselves to be in some sense the true Israel. They looked for the day when YHWH would act to vindicate them in this claim, by defeating and overthrowing not only the pagans but also the present (corrupt) Jewish regime (sects always believe that the present regime is corrupt; that is part of the very logic of their existence). They saw themselves as related ambiguously to the Temple: the Pharisees saw their own purity as an extension, the Essenes as a temporary replacement, of Temple purity, and we can assume that John the

---

[130] Mk. 2.18–20. The variations in the pars. (Mt. 9.14–15/Lk. 5.33–5) do not affect the present point.

[131] For the Essenes, cf. *NTPG* 203–9. The present paragraph is based on *NTPG* Part III as a whole, esp. ch. 7.

Baptist and his followers were somewhere on this spectrum as well. They gave loyalty either to a founder (for the Essenes, the Teacher of Righteousness; for John's disciples, obviously John) or to great recent teachers (for the Pharisees, Shammai and Hillel). They were characterized by distinctive praxis, involving reinterpretation and reapplication of the ancestral code, the Torah.

We have every reason to suppose that Jesus regarded his followers, and that they regarded themselves, in ways that bear close comparison on all these points. As we shall see in the next chapter, Jesus encouraged his followers to believe that YHWH would soon act to vindicate him and them, not least in the destruction of the evil regime that presently ruled in Jerusalem. As we shall see in chapter 9, his construal of the symbolic world of Judaism involved, as with the Essenes, a sharp critique of the Temple and the clear understanding that his movement was in some sense a replacement for it. We have already seen that Jesus, in company with all sorts of first-century Jewish leaders, looked for loyalty to himself as a major characteristic of his group; he was not simply a wandering spinner of aphorisms who merely encouraged people to go off and do their own thing. And we shall see presently that he challenged his followers to a distinctive lifestyle: they were to live as the people of the new covenant, those who were truly returning from exile, those for whom and in whom the prophecies were coming true at last.

The praxis that went with the kingdom-story cannot, then, be reduced to terms either of individual 'ethics' or of the individual response to grace. The whole point of it is that it demarcated Jesus' people as a community; scattered through various villages, maybe, as indeed some of the Essenes may have been, but a community none the less.[132] Jesus describes his followers in Israel-language: the little flock, the bridegroom's bride;[133] and he gives them their own prayer to pray, binding them together as John had his disciples (see below).

One of the most striking signs of this is found in a passage which occurs, in one form or another, in six different (and no doubt interrelated) texts. Here is Mark's version:

> [Jesus'] mother and brothers came, and, standing outside, sent to him to call him. A crowd was sitting around him, and they said to him, 'Look, your mother and your brothers and sisters are outside, looking for you.' And he answered, 'Who is my mother? Who are my brothers?' And, looking at those sitting in a circle around him, he said,

---

[132] Philo (*Quod Omn.* 75–6; *Hypoth.* 11.1) says that Essenes lived in villages and towns; Josephus (*War* 2.124), that they were to be found in 'every town' (in Palestine); cf. Schürer 2.562f. The settlement at Qumran, still itself of course the subject of controversy, was never, it seems, the only Essene establishment.

[133] Lk. 12.32; Mk. 2.19/Mt. 9.15/Lk. 5.34/*Thom.* 104.

'See, my mother and my brothers. Whoever does the will of god, that person is my brother, my sister, and my mother.'[134]

As we shall see in more detail in chapter 9, this would be remarkable enough in almost any culture. In a peasant society, where familial relations provided one's basic identity, it was shocking in the extreme. In first-century Jewish culture, for which the sense of familial and racial loyalty was a basic symbol of the prevailing worldview, it cannot but have been devastating.[135] Jesus was proposing to treat his followers as a surrogate family. This had a substantial positive result: Jesus intended his followers to inherit all the closeness and mutual obligations that belonged with family membership in that close-knit, family-based society. It also carried fairly clear negative consequences in that society: to be a member of one family meant sitting loose to membership in any other. Hence the remarkable demands for Jesus' followers to 'hate' father, mother, siblings, spouse and children – and even their own selves.[136] This was not just extraordinarily challenging at a personal level; it was deeply subversive at a social, cultural, religious and political level, as we shall see in due course.

Further, those who followed Jesus' teaching were 'those who do god's will'; in other words, they were following the true way for Israel. Here are all the signs that Jesus did indeed mean to set up groups of his followers, to regard them as a distinct group within Israel, and to encourage them to live in the new way that his kingdom-story dictated. We are again in a situation with quite close parallels in some of the Scrolls, where, for instance, the sect regarded themselves as the true 'house of Judah' *over against* the existing 'house of Judah'.[137]

What, then, was to be so distinctive about these groups of people loyal to Jesus? They were, clearly, to be committed to that retelling of Israel's *story* which focused on Jesus himself as the kingdom-bringer. This formed the basic loyalty without which none of the rest would make much sense. As we shall see in subsequent chapters, they were to live by a set of *symbols*, and to give a set of answers to the key *questions*, that would mark them out from other Jews of their day. But the most obviously distinctive thing about them, after their basic loyalty to Jesus himself, was the *praxis* which they were to adopt. This, I suggest, is the appropriate way in to the vexed question of the so-called ethical teaching of Jesus.

---

[134] Mk. 3.31–5; pars. Mt. 12.46–50/Lk. 8.19–21/*G. Ebi.* 5/*Thom.* 99/2 *Clem.* 9.11.

[135] cf. *NTPG* 230–2; Malina & Rohrbaugh 1992, 178f., 201f.

[136] cf. e.g. Mt. 10.37–8/Lk. 14.26–7/*Thom.* 55; 101.

[137] CD 4.11; cf. Schwarz 1981; Davies 1982, 103.

(iii) New Covenant, New Praxis

(a) Introduction

How did Jesus expect this community to behave? This involves what are sometimes described as 'Jesus' ethics'.[138] The danger with that phrase, and others like it, is that it can so easily imply that Jesus was simply a moral reformer, a preacher of a new, or upgraded, moral code, offering a timeless system which he just happened, as things turned out, to have applied to first-century Jews. When Jesus was talking about styles of behaviour, his teaching has been treated as just that: 'teaching', which could be abstracted from its historical setting and made timeless (though the commands to cut off hands and pluck out eyes have a habit of losing a little in the course of their long journey to the twentieth century).[139]

This problematic idea of a timeless ethical position, of course, can be stood on its head. Schweitzer, for example, supposed that because Jesus' message was through and through eschatological (in the sense that he expected the end of the world very soon), he cannot have taught any detailed 'ethics' at all. All there can have been was a kind of martial law, a tight regime, an 'interim ethic', for the short emergency period. This view has persisted even where Schweitzer's robust view as a whole has been jettisoned. It is, perhaps, appealing to those with a late-twentieth-century dislike of cold moralism to be able to say that all that 'moral teaching' in the gospels derives, not from Jesus, but from people like Matthew, who can then be safely dismissed as second-generation legalizing reinterpreters of the pure original vision. If the kingdom meant the end of the world, who needed moralism?

Our analysis of Jesus' kingdom-story provides a different starting-point. This means getting our minds round a more historical reading of eschatology (in the sense both of a reading more true to history and of a reading which indicates the historical referent of eschatological language). If this can be managed, we can avoid the Scylla of 'Jesus the mere moral teacher' and the Charybdis of 'Jesus the non-moralistic eschatological prophet'. 'Eschatology' here means, not the end of the world, but the rescue and renewal of Israel

---

[138] cf. Chilton and MacDonald 1987; Harvey 1990; older treatments such as Jeremias 1971, 203–30; Kümmel 1973, 46–58; Ladd 1974b, ch. 9; Goppelt 1981 [1975], 1.77–119; and, among recent studies of Jesus, Borg 1984, ch. 5; Crossan 1991a, ch. 12; Sanders 1993, ch. 13.

[139] They are, to be sure, intended as exaggerations: cf. Harvey 1990, 82. The dehistoricizing process can be seen, for instance, in Throckmorton's *Gospel Parallels*, where the heading for Lk. 6.43–6 is 'A Test of Goodness', as though Jesus were simply offering his hearers a rule of thumb for telling, in any time and place, who was morally good.

and hence of the world. 'Ethics' here means the god-given way of life for those caught up in this renewal. Elevate either beyond that, and tension will result; keep them within historical bounds, and they belong together. Indeed, they demand one another.

A further complication in discussing Jesus' agenda for his communities results from an over-zealous application of reformation theology to the reading of the gospels. Scholars in the Lutheran tradition in particular have agonized over how to reconcile the detailed moral teaching of the gospels with the Pauline doctrine of 'justification by faith, not works'. Should we read this teaching (it has been asked) as 'law', designed to show sinners their sinfulness, and so to drive them to repentance and faith? Or should we read it, along the lines of (what is thought of as) Luther's 'third use of the law', as detailed instruction for those who have *already* been justified by faith, and who are therefore free from the possibility of a self-help Pelagianism?[140] The one thing we must not do, on this account, is to treat Jesus' ethics as commands carrying the implication that ordinary people can keep them 'unaided' and so earn favour with their maker.

Of course not. Yet this way of discussing things, like the 'morals-versus-eschatology' debate, misses the point. Paul and justification must wait for another volume in the present series;[141] for the moment we may simply note that the question of abstract moralism, in which human beings try from scratch to make themselves good enough for acceptance with god, or to earn his favour, is not something that would have been particularly familiar to Paul, Jesus, or their hearers. For a Jew, the context of behaviour was of course the covenant.[142] For Jesus, I suggest, the context of behaviour was the renewal of the covenant. The *story* of the kingdom was designed to generate the *praxis* of the kingdom.

The puzzles noted above have made exegesis of the Sermon on the Mount, in particular, more than a little tricky.[143] To develop further the questions posed a moment ago: was the sermon a high moral code designed to instil a sense of total failure and guilt into its hearers, so that they would then flee for mercy to the gospel? Was it a blueprint for a 'special' group within Jesus' followers, such as might have been fulfilled by a few ascetics while the rest of Jesus' people settled for something more manageable? Was it to be watered down into a generalized ethic (one still hears people say that they are

---

[140] cf. e.g. Jeremias 1963b [1961]. A similar alternative, at a less doctrinaire theological level, is posed in the title of Lapide 1986: is the Sermon on the Mount a utopia or a 'program for action'? Cf. esp. Harvey 1990, e.g. 10, 19, 22. On Luther etc. cf. O'Donovan 1986, 154.

[141] Cf. too Wright 1980.

[142] cf. the already classic statement of Sanders 1977.

[143] cf. again Harvey 1990, *passim.*

'Sermon on the Mount' Christians, apparently meaning that they believe in morality without religion)? Was it in any sense a blueprint for the church, as though Jesus were to sit on a Galilean hillside teaching puzzled villagers the rule of life for an institution which had not yet been founded and which would have seemed to answer none of their felt needs and aspirations? Or was it simply a blueprint for life in a Galilean village itself, without reference to any larger programme or agenda? Was it the agenda of the 'Q people', who are so visible and vigorous in some contemporary scholarship but who remain curiously shy when serious historians go looking for them? Or was it to be regarded not primarily as Jesus' word to anyone, certainly not during his ministry, but as Matthew's word to his church, a church which already knew all about the cross and forgiveness and so could listen to moral teaching without imagining for a moment that they were to justify themselves by their good works?[144]

The answer is that the Sermon on the Mount was none of these things. None of them fit with the expectation of the kingdom, or with what we have already seen of Jesus' redefinition-in-action of that expectation. If we are to be true to the historical setting, we must ask: what sort of instructions would Jesus' contemporaries have expected to receive from someone who was announcing the inauguration of YHWH's kingdom?

Possible answers are not difficult to find. Take up arms and march on Jerusalem; quite likely. Abandon the half-committed life they had been living, with a foot in the nationalist camp and a toe at least in Greek culture or Roman collaboration; pretty certainly. Intensify the observance of Torah, so that holiness would guarantee victory and vindication by YHWH; definitely. Certainly there would be a demand, a summons. It would have something to do with the behaviour appropriate for the people of god, appropriate not just because their god happened, for reasons best known to himself, to like certain styles of behaviour, but because certain styles of behaviour were the genuine marks of covenant loyalty, the loyalty which responded to YHWH's grace and because of which YHWH, in turn, would keep his side of the covenant, i.e. would act to vindicate this group as his true people.

If Jesus belongs in this context – and if he does not, the entire Third Quest and a fair amount even of the renewed 'New Quest' are completely on the wrong track – we have a fresh chance to understand his so-called 'ethical teaching'. This teaching is, in fact, just as important for understanding the meaning of the kingdom as the kingdom is for understanding the meaning of the ethics. The fact that Jesus told people to behave as if the kingdom was

---

[144] cf. e.g. Strecker 1988; Jeremias 1963b [1961].

already present has the same function as his saying, 'If I, by the spirit/finger of god, cast out demons, then the kingdom of god has come upon you.'[145] It is as though Jesus were to say, 'If I command you to behave as those with renewed hearts, then the kingdom of god has come upon you.' To understand why this should be so, we must examine first that strand of his teaching which deals precisely with the heart and its renewal.

(b) The Renewed Heart

One of the great scriptural promises of restoration, of return from exile, concerned the renewal of the heart:

> Moreover, YHWH your god will circumcise your heart and the heart of your descendants, so that you will love YHWH your god with all your heart and with all your soul, in order that you may live . . . Then you shall again obey YHWH, observing all his commandments that I am commanding you today . . . For YHWH will again take delight in prospering you, just as he delighted in prospering your ancestors, when you obey YHWH your god by observing his commandments and decrees that are written in this book of the law, because you turn to YHWH your god with all your heart and with all your soul.[146]

> But this is the covenant that I will make with the house of Israel after those days, says YHWH: I will put my law within them, and I will write it on their hearts; and I will be their god, and they shall be my people.[147]

> They shall be my people, and I will be their god. I will give them one heart and one way, that they may fear me for all time . . . I will make an everlasting covenant with them, never to draw back from doing good to them; and I will put the fear of me in their hearts, so that they may not turn from me.[148]

> A new heart I will give you, and a new spirit I will put within you; and I will remove from your body the heart of stone and give you a heart of flesh. I will put my spirit within you, and make you follow my statutes and be careful to observe my ordinances.[149]

The same theme is visible at Qumran:

> For thou, O God, hast sheltered me
>   from the children of men,
> and hast hidden thy Law within me
>   against the time when Thou shouldst reveal
> Thy salvation to me.[150]

[145] Mt. 12.28/Lk. 11.20. On acting 'as if . . .' cf. Harvey 1990, ch. 9.
[146] Dt. 30.6–10 (cf. 10.16).
[147] Jer. 31.33; cf. 24.7. For the law in the heart cf. Ps. 37.31; Isa. 51.7.
[148] Jer. 32.38–40.
[149] Ezek. 36.26–7; cf. 11.19f.; 18.31; Ps. 51.10.
[150] 1QH 5 [=13].11–12 (Vermes 1995 [1962], 204, cf. GM 337). The crucial phrase 'within me' is partially missing in the original, but the reconstruction is not in doubt.

No man shall walk in the stubbornness of his heart so that he strays after his heart and eyes and evil inclination, but he shall circumcise in the Community the foreskin of evil inclination and of stiffness of neck that they may lay a foundation of truth for Israel, for the Community of the everlasting Covenant.[151]

In other words, renewal of covenant and renewal of heart go together. This should enable us to understand passages in the gospels which are otherwise, quite anachronistically, pulled in the direction of the Protestant works/faith divide (as though the crucial issue were whether one behaved ethically because one had *received* grace, or because one was hoping to *earn* it), or of the Platonic 'material/non-material' divide (as though what mattered was whether one was putting an idea before an object or vice versa), or the Romantic 'outward/inward' divide (as though what mattered in true religion were its essential inwardness, with all outward expression being trivial or irrelevant). In fact, as passages like those just quoted make clear, the all-important distinction is not between outward and inward, or between earning grace and expressing it, but between that outer *and* inner state which is evil all through (albeit, from time to time, appearing outwardly clean) and that outer *and* inner state which is being renewed all through.[152] The former state, according to the Hebrew scriptures, characterizes Israel in the present age; the renewal, when it comes, will be one aspect of the renewal of the covenant, which is of course one way of speaking about the return from exile. If, therefore, Jesus was announcing that the time of return and renewal was now dawning, we should actually expect that the kingdom-story he told would be designed to produce *both* the inward state *and* the outward praxis which would be appropriate for that renewal. Eschatology, rightly understood, is not antithetical to ethics. It generates them. When the kingdom comes, the will of YHWH will be done, on earth as it is in heaven.

It is therefore thoroughly consonant with the whole story-line we have been studying to suggest that Jesus demanded of, and offered to, his hearers that renewal of heart which would characterize them as the restored people of YHWH. Jesus would call into being 'a graced discipleship in which "your hardness of heart" (Mark 10.5 par.) would be cured'.[153] Indeed, Jesus' comments about his hearers' state of heart are themselves an indication that he located the problem of Israel where Deuteronomy, Jeremiah and Ezekiel had located it – that is, in the heart.[154] This should not be seen either as a late moralizing of the tradition or as a reflection of subsequent Christian polemic

---

[151] 1QS 5.4f. (Vermes 1995 [1962], 75). Cp. 1QpHab. 11.13.

[152] On different types of 'dualities' cf. *NTPG* 252-6.

[153] Meyer 1979, 173.

[154] cp. Jer. 17.9. In addition to Mk. 10.5/Mt. 19.8, cf. Mk. 7.6/Mt. 15.8; Mk. 7.20-3/Mt. 15.18-20; and cp. Mt. 13.15.

against continuing Judaism. It makes perfect sense on the lips of an eschatological prophet convinced of a mission to inaugurate the kingdom.

There are two passages in particular in which the theme of the heart becomes prominent. The first of these is Mark 7.14–23/Matthew 15.10–20, where Jesus, in the course of cryptically subverting the Jewish food laws, explains that what really matters is not physical substances that pass into someone's body, but thoughts and intentions that emerge from (what we would call) the personality.[155] This distinction between outward act and attitude of heart was quite frequent in the Hebrew Bible,[156] and there is no reason at all why Jesus should not have used the idea and indeed made it central to this part of his agenda. This does not make him a good Platonist, or for that matter a good liberal Protestant, rejecting everything 'material' or 'outward' as being irrelevant to the 'spiritual' life.[157] It makes him a good Jew, recognizing that YHWH desires to recreate human beings as wholes. In particular, it relates directly to the promises in Deuteronomy, Jeremiah and Ezekiel concerning the new covenant which YHWH will confirm with his people when he renews her fortunes. We shall discuss this passage, not least its historical setting, in chapter 9. Sufficient to note for the moment that, like some others, it suggests that Jesus believed his own time to be the time of fulfilment of eschatological prophecy.

This is strongly supported by the second passage which speaks, again cryptically, of a renewed heart: Mark 10.2–12/Matthew 19.3–12. This time the subject-matter is divorce.[158] Again Jesus' comments, which have a high degree of historical probability,[159] indicate his belief that a new day is dawning in which new things can be expected.

The question about divorce was not simply a matter of pure legal interpretation – though even at that level the issue was one that divided the Jewish sects, as is clear from Qumran.[160] In view of Herod Antipas' incestuous marriage to his sister-in-law Herodias, the question had a sharp political edge: the imprisonment and death of John the Baptist had been partly at least due to his resolute opposition to Herod's behaviour, and the geographical setting in both Mark and Matthew (Judaea, near the Jordan) suggests that echoes of the

---

[155] In addition to the commentaries, cf. esp. Booth 1986.

[156] e.g. Isa. 29.13, quoted at Mk. 7.6f.

[157] cf. Borg 1984, 99, on the peril of modernizing Jesus at this point.

[158] In addition to the commentaries, cf. e.g. Dungan 1971, 81–131; Witherington 1985; Sanders 1985, 233f., 256–60; 1993, 198–201.

[159] So, rightly, Sanders 1985, 257. The Jesus Seminar was quite evenly divided on the sayings, eventually voting them grey by a narrow margin (Funk & Hoover 1993, 88f., 219f.).

[160] cf. CD 4.19–21, discussed in e.g. Sanders 1985, 257–9; 11QTemple 57.17–19, prohibiting divorce in the case of the king (cf. Maier 1985, 126f.).

Baptist, and of his demise because of his opposition to the incestuous marriage, may have coloured the original incident.[161] Discussion of this passage has often focused on two issues: the differences between Mark and Matthew, i.e. whether Jesus really gave permission for divorce in the case of adultery, as Matthew says, and if so what 'adultery' in this case actually means; and the question of whether the discussion reflects Roman rather than Jewish law, and if so whether it properly belongs in the time of the church rather than that of Jesus.[162] These matters are important, and it is certainly possible that the discussion has been 'translated' for different audiences. But I agree with Sanders that the setting as we have it – a question from Pharisees to Jesus on a point of Torah where he was thought to be suspect, and where some political pressure could be applied or threatened, followed by an answer from Jesus about the true divine intention for human beings – is highly likely to be historical.

The crucial point for our present purposes is not only that Jesus envisages the new age, the time of renewal, as happening in his own ministry. It is that this time of renewal must contain a cure for hardness of heart. The scribes quote Deuteronomy (24.1–3) in replying to Jesus' counter-question ('What does Moses say?'). Sure enough, there is a passage permitting divorce and giving instructions as to how it is to be carried out. But Jesus responds with an assertion which reveals that he stands at a vitally different point in Israel's story. Deuteronomy, he says, is part of a *temporary phase* in the purposes of YHWH. It was necessary because of the ambiguous situation, in which Israel was called to be the people of god, but was still a people with *hard hearts*. Israel cannot be affirmed as she stands. She is still in exile, still hardhearted; but the new day is dawning in which 'the Mosaic dispensation is not adequate', since 'Jesus expected there to be a better order'.[163]

By quoting Genesis 1.27 and 2.4 to undermine Deuteronomy 24.1–3, Jesus was in fact making it clear that the story to which he was obedient was that in which Israel was called by YHWH to restore humankind and the world to his original intention. This is not quite the same as saying, as some have suggested, that the last days must correspond exactly to the first; rather, the last days must fulfil the creator's intention. For that to happen, hardness of

---

[161] So Witherington 1985. Gundry 1993, 536 is dubious about this, but his grounds are mainly lexical, which seems to me to miss the point. The fact that Herodias seems to have taken the initiative in separating from Philip (cf. Jos. *Ant.* 18.109f., 136) suggests that Mk. 10.12, prohibiting a woman from divorcing her husband, may not be so much a later comment in relation to Roman law as a direct criticism (made, it should be noted, in private) of Herodias as well as Antipas.

[162] On these questions cf. e.g. Hooker 1991, 234–7; Gundry 1993, 528–43; and cf. the previous note.

[163] Sanders 1985, 260.

heart must be dealt with. Granted that the original permission to divorce was given because of the nation's hard-heartedness, Jesus' refusal of that permission only makes sense if he envisaged his hearers' hard-heartedness somehow being dealt with. The only explanation for that, which fits like a glove with the rest of Jesus' kingdom-story, is that he believed himself to be inaugurating the great time of renewal spoken of in the prophets, when the law would be written on the hearts of YHWH's people.

The saying about hard hearts thus coheres well with Mark 7. Covenant renewal would bring about a new phase of the divine plan. Now, at last, the true people of the creator god would be demarcated by their state of heart, not by taboos; now, at last, the purpose for which Israel was called into being, namely the rescue of humanity from evil, was to be realized. Jesus told the kingdom-story in such a way as to evoke the praxis he saw as proper to the new phase, the new act in the drama.

The demand for, and implicit offer of, a new heart is also seen in Jesus' comment to the scribe who answered 'wisely'.[164] He had followed Torah to its centre, and having arrived there – the Deuteronomic command to love god and neighbour – was not far from the kingdom of god. It is precisely those commands for which, according to Deuteronomy itself, one needs a renewed heart.[165] YHWH would become king, not by vindicating Israel as she stood, but by vindicating an Israel that showed evidence of what Torah was really meant to produce.

The need for the new heart included, in Jesus' vision, the need to pass on to others the 'forgiveness of sins' which had been received.[166] This apparently 'ethical' challenge is again to be understood 'covenantally' and eschatologically. It was part of Jesus' summons to his hearers to become true Israelites by following him. As we saw earlier, Jesus' own extension of forgiveness to those in need of it was an extraordinary move, claiming by implication that he had the right to give people what could normally only be obtained through official channels; claiming, too, that the new covenant was being instituted, the new covenant in which (according to Jeremiah 31) sins would be forgiven once and for all. But if that claim was to be made good, Jesus' people would have to enact this forgiveness among themselves.

This demand must not be seen simply as a peculiarly difficult piece of ethical behaviour. It is the sign of the inauguration of the new covenant.[167] The reference to Jeremiah 31 shows conclusively that the idea of a new heart

---

[164] Mk. 12.32–4, on which see below, 434f., 566f.

[165] Dt. 30.6.

[166] See above, 268–74. Cf., e.g., Mt. 6.12/Lk. 11.4; Mt. 6.14; 18.21–35; Mk. 11.25; Lk. 6.37b.

[167] It is, to this extent, what Nehemiah was striving for (Neh. 5.1–13).

was not the invention of anti-materialistic Protestant or Romantic thought, but a central theme of a central Old Testament promise. What Jesus was demanding, and by implication offering (though the implication would remain puzzling for a while, as the disciples realized in Matthew 19.10), was the new heart *promised as part of the new covenant*. In other words, in this 'ethical' teaching he was not criticizing Judaism for being concerned with 'externals', and focusing instead on 'internals'. He was carrying through the entire kingdom-agenda we have been studying, inaugurating the kingdom by calling men and women to follow him, to discover how to be the true Israel, and to become the people whom YHWH would vindicate when he finally acted.[168] They were to be the Israel that was truly released from exile. They were to be, in other words, the Israel described in the Sermon on the Mount.

(c) The Sermon on the Mount[169]

It is impossible to think of Jesus' moral teaching without thinking of the Sermon on the Mount. Equally, it is impossible to do more in a book like this than to offer some suggestions for the way in which it might be handled historically. It has, of course, been fashionable to split up the sermon (and its Lukan counterpart) into small pieces, to assign them to places all round the Mediterranean world and times all through the first century, and to credit the evangelists with complete originality in arranging or even inventing the material.[170] I wish to question this current fashion.

The evangelists are of course responsible, one way or another, for the form the discourses now have. But arguments for the creation or serious mutation of such material within the early church must start from the known point that there is no setting in the ministry of Jesus from which it could have come; and that seems to me manifestly not to be the case.[171] Jesus' redefined

---

[168] It is probably in this category that we should place the apparently harsh longer ending to the parable of the great supper, i.e. Mt. 22.11-14. The man without the wedding garment seems to be someone who claims to belong to Jesus' people but who has not realized that following Jesus means receiving the new heart which alone qualifies one to sit at the table in the messianic banquet. Cf. Sanders 1993, 198: though the ending is secondary, it remains the case that 'Jesus demanded high moral standards of his followers'. Why are we so sure, then, that the ending is secondary?

[169] i.e. Mt. 5—7; the corresponding 'sermon on the plain' is in Lk. 6.20-40. Among the welter of literature even in the last decade, cf. e.g. Guelich 1982; Lambrecht 1985; Strecker 1988; Harvey 1990. Among older works, Davies 1964 remains a classic.

[170] cf. esp. Betz 1985, 1992. Part of the apparent strength of the argument for a non-Jewish provenance has been its alliance with the equally fashionable theory that Jesus was simply a speaker of dark riddles and Cynic wisdom.

[171] Kennedy 1984, 68 offers a striking argument for the unity of the sermon, based on rhetorical analysis.

kingdom-story, as we are analysing it, creates a perfectly plausible historical context within which Jesus not only could but, I suggest, would have said things like this. I suspect, moreover, that, as with other sayings, he said them on numerous occasions, with numerous local variations.

The sermon – to take it for the moment as a whole – is not a mere miscellany of ethical instruction. It cannot be generalized into a set of suggestions, or even commands, on how to be 'good'. Nor can it be turned into a guide-map for how to go to 'heaven' after death. It is rather, as it stands, a challenge to Israel to *be* Israel. We may follow the main lines of the sermon and observe in outline the effect of reading it this way, as Jesus' retelling of his contemporaries' story. References in what follows are to Matthew.

First, the beatitudes (5.3–13). Israel longs for YHWH's kingdom to come (5.3). She is ready to work and struggle and fight to bring it in. But the people to whom it belongs are the poor in spirit.[172] Israel longs for consolation, for *paraklesis* (5.4). But YHWH has in mind to give her, not the consolation of a national revival, in which her old wounds will be healed by inflicting wounds on others, but the consolation awaiting those who are in genuine grief. Israel desires to inherit the earth (5.5); she must do it in Jesus' way, by meekness.[173] Israel thirsts for justice (5.6); but the justice she is offered does not come by way of battles against physical enemies. It is not the way of anger, of a 'justice' which really means 'vengeance'. It is the way of humility and gentleness. Israel longs for mercy, not least the eschatological mercy of final rescue from her enemies (5.7). But mercy is reserved for the merciful, not the vengeful. Israel longs for the vision of her god (5.8); but this is the prerogative not of those who impose an external purity, but of those with purity of heart. Israel desires to be called the creator's son, being vindicated by him in the dramatic historical proof of national victory (5.9). But those whom Israel's god will vindicate as his sons will be those who copy their father; and that means peacemakers. Persecution will be inevitable for people who follow this way, Jesus' way (5.10); but those who are persecuted because they follow this way are indeed assured of a great vindication. In other words, the promise that would formerly apply to those who were faithful to Torah now applies to those who are faithful to Jesus. Whatever they have meant to subsequent hearers or readers, I suggest that the beatitudes can be read, in some such way, as an appeal to Jesus' hearers

---

[172] Despite the well-known point that Lk. 6.20 omits 'in spirit', I do not think there is much actual difference between Mt. and Lk. at this point. The contrast upon which we should focus is not between material and spiritual poverty, but between the way of the powerful and the way of the powerless – who are likely to be the poor in all senses, certainly in first-century Israel. On poverty cf. esp. Hanks 1992, with full bibliography.

[173] cp. Mt. 11.29.

to discover their true vocation as the eschatological people of YHWH, and to do so by following the praxis he was marking out for them, rather than the way of other would-be leaders of the time.

It is easy to generalize the beatitudes, and thus harder to think one's way out of anachronism. But the specific historical context I have suggested cannot be so easily avoided in the case of the words about salt and light (5.13–16). They sound a challenge to Israel: she is to be the salt of the earth, the light of the world. That always was her vocation: to be a nation of priests, to be YHWH's servant, so that his glory might reach to the ends of the earth.[174] But the salt has now forgotten its purpose. The light has turned in on itself. The city set on a hill (Jerusalem, presumably) was meant to be the place to which the nations would flock like moths to a lamp, but she has done her best to make herself, and the god to whom her very existence bears witness, as unattractive as possible. There is rebuke within the challenge. Israel, called to be a lighthouse for the world, has surrounded herself with mirrors to keep the light in, heightening her own sense of purity and exclusiveness while insisting that the nations must remain in darkness. But with Jesus' work the way is open, for any Jews who will dare, to find out what being the true Israel is all about. By following him, by putting his agenda into practice, they can at last *be* true Israel.

It will then be asked, is this simply an abandonment of the entire hope of Israel? When Israel asks for bread, is this strange prophet offering her a stone? By no means (5.17–20). The boot is on the other foot. Jesus claims the high ground: it is his interpretation of the vocation and destiny of Israel that is in ultimate continuity with the Torah and the Prophets, and the scribes and Pharisees have got it wrong. The kingdom will not override Moses and the Prophets – how could it, without the covenant god contradicting himself? – but Israel must not remain content with the shallow reading of scripture that uses it merely to bolster her own national security. There is a deeper meaning in the sacred writings than first-century Israel had grasped; it is this deeper meaning that Jesus is commending.

The deeper meaning is seen particularly in the series of five 'antitheses'[175] between 'what was said to those of old time' and 'but I say unto you' (5.21–48). The five deal, respectively, with murder, adultery, oaths, judicial revenge, and hatred of enemies. The section functions, loosely, as an application and exegesis of the beatitudes themselves: poverty of spirit, meekness and peacemaking underlie the first, fourth and fifth antitheses, purity of heart the second, hunger for true justice the fourth, and so on. The emphasis of

---

[174] So Betz 1992, 1108: salt and light are each 'a traditional metaphor of Jewish self-description'. Cf. *NTPG* 267f.

[175] Treating the word on divorce (5.31f.) as a subset of that on adultery (5.27–32).

this whole section is on a mode of Torah-intensification which is quite unlike that of the Pharisees. Instead of defining ever more closely the outward actions necessary for the keeping of Torah, thereby proving one's loyalty to YHWH's covenant, Israel was challenged to discover the meaning of the commands in terms of a totally integrated loyalty of heart and act. As we shall see in chapter 9, the real clash between Jesus and his opponents is one of *agenda*, not of petty legalistic quibbles.

The antitheses do not, then, focus on the contrast between 'outward' and 'inward' keepings of the law. They are not retrojections into the first century of a nineteenth-century Romantic ideal of religion in which outward things are bad and inward things good. They emphasize, rather, the way in which the renewal which Jesus sought to engender would produce a radically different way of being Israel in real-life Palestinian situations. There, the ruling interpretation of Torah would lead to being Israel in the wrong way, the way that would lead to destruction; the way of life he was urging would suggest a totally different approach and result. Thus: the potential accuser must be faced and reconciled (5.25-6);[176] the soldier who commandeers the services of a Galilean villager must not be resisted or resented, but must be met with astonishing generosity (5.41);[177] enemies of the state are not enemies in the eyes of YHWH, and if Israel is really to imitate her heavenly father she must learn to love them and pray for them (5.44f.). Love and mercy, as practical codes of living, are to characterize Israel as the true people of the creator god. People like that are the ones he will vindicate when he comes in his kingdom. Forgiveness is to be the hallmark of all social relationships. (One only has to live for a short time in a society where forgiveness is not even valued in theory – where, for instance, 'losing face' is regarded as one of the greatest misfortunes – to realize how revolutionary this challenge really is.) The antitheses would be perceived, within Jesus' ministry, as a challenge to a new way of being Israel, a way which faced the present situation of national tension and tackled it in an astonishing and radically new way.

In particular, as emerges in the final two antitheses, Jesus' followers were not to make common cause with the resistance movement.[178] The command

---

[176] See Lk. 16.1ff., on which see below, 332.

[177] cf. Harvey 1990, 72f.; and esp. Wink 1992b [1988], 108-12.

[178] See Yoder 1972; Weaver 1992; Wink 1992b [1988]. In a number of works, Richard Horsley (esp. e.g. 1987, 1992a [1986]) has attempted to oppose this conclusion, which he sees as allowing the dangerous corollary of first-world theologians telling oppressed third-world peoples that they must not revolt. He sees the relevant texts as referring purely to local-level disputes, not to national resistance against the occupying forces. But Horsley's historical base is not as secure as he repeatedly insists. The absence of the 'Zealots' proper in the first half of the first century AD does not mean there was not a continuing groundswell of other resistance movements, in some of which, indeed, the Pharisees were themselves involved (cf. *NTPG* 170-181; 190-5). And there are multiple inner contradictions in Horsley's own account, well exposed by Wink 1992c. Cf. too Borg 1984, esp. 130-3. One

'do not resist evil' (5.39) is not to be taken simply to refer to personal hostilities or village-level animosity. The word 'resist' is *antistenai*, almost a technical term for revolutionary resistance of a specifically military variety.[179] Taken in this sense, the command draws out the implication of a good deal of the sermon so far. The way forward for Israel is not the way of violent resistance, not the way of zeal that the Shammaite Pharisees would encourage, but the different, oblique way of creative non-violent resistance. A blow on the right cheek is given with the back of the hand, implying insult as well as injury; to offer the left is not mere passivity, but the affirmation of one's own equality with the aggressor.[180] To be sure, these guidelines would apply to local village disputes as much as anywhere else. But the overall thrust of both text and context is much wider: Jesus' people were not to become part of the resistance movement.

Moving into Matthew 6, Jesus' challenge focuses now on Israel's perception of her god as 'father'. The warnings on ostentatious almsgiving, prayer and fasting (the three key marks of Jewish observance, which, especially when away from Jerusalem, were regarded by some Pharisees as equivalent to offering sacrifices in the Temple[181]) are not, again, directed simply at the difference between outward and inward observance. They are about Israel's appropriation of the belief that YHWH is her father. She claims him as such, but apparently treats him as a faceless bureaucrat, to be bribed or wheedled into giving her what she wants. There is no place for such an attitude. Those who will be vindicated by YHWH are those who know him, and treat him, as father indeed. This is, in the last analysis, a matter of worshipping the true god as opposed to worshipping idols: Israel cannot serve the true god and mammon (6.24),[182] and anxiety about the future is a sign that she is trying to do just that (6.25–34). Those who are truly seeking the kingdom need not be afraid,[183] whereas those whose seeking of the kingdom consists in pursuing a national or personal agenda for the restoration of land, property or ancestral rights will find that they have been serving a god who cannot give them such things.[184]

The real way forward for Israel, therefore (7.1–6), is to avoid the way of condemnation, whether of Gentiles or of one another. It is unnecessary; all

---

may perhaps point out that opposing Horsley on a point of history is not the same as discounting all his contemporary agendas.

[179] cf. Wink 1992b [1988], 114f., with notes; Jos. uses the word with the sense of 'violent struggle' 15 times out of 17 uses.

[180] Wink 1992b [1988], 104f.

[181] cf. Davies 1964, 305–15.

[182] cp. Lk. 16.13; *Thom.* 47.1–2; *2 Clem.* 6.1.

[183] cf. Lk. 12.32.

[184] cp., once more, Lk. 12.13–15; 16.13–31.

that is needful will be given to those who ask (7.7–11). The Torah and the Prophets boil down to a rule of thumb, easy to be learned and practised by Israelites eager to do YHWH's will and so be part of the kingdom-movement: whatever you would have people do to you, do that to them (7.12). But there will not be many followers of this way. False prophets are on the loose, leading Israel astray, and the only way to avoid being deceived by them is to note clearly where their movements lead (7.15–20). Like the good revolutionary that he is, Jesus finishes by offering a critique of alternative movements and a dire warning that his way of being Israel is the only way by which his followers may avoid ultimate disaster (7.24–7), a disaster which will be not merely personal, but also national. The house built on the rock, in first-century Jewish terms, is a clear allusion to the Temple. Unless Israel follows the way that Jesus is leading, the greatest national institution of all is in mortal danger. One can imagine Judas the Galilean saying much the same.

The Sermon on the Mount, in short, makes excellent sense in a Palestinian setting in the first third of the first century. There is no need to force this material into a post-70, let alone a non-Jewish, setting. It addresses directly the question people were asking: how to be faithful to YHWH in a time of great stress and ambiguity, a time when many thought the climax of Israel's history was upon them. It offers a set of specific kingdom-agendas, consonant with the rest of Jesus' specific message, as the bracing answer to this question. It can, no doubt, be generalized into a universal ethic, as has happened to most of Jesus' teaching. But the question of its original meaning is not thereby resolved. I suggest that it can only be ultimately settled in some such way as I have indicated here. The question of how to apply the sermon to different times and places is another matter, and cannot be allowed to dictate the question of historical origins.

(d) The Lord's Prayer[185]

It may seem strange to include the prayer Jesus taught his disciples in a section on the challenge he issued to them. But it is actually part of the same movement of thought, as its presence in the Sermon on the Mount indicates. The challenge includes the summons to pray this extraordinary, revolutionary, and at the same time very characteristically Jewish, prayer. Equally, Jesus' provision of a special prayer for his followers fits very well with the perception of his movement outlined above: the setting for the prayer in

---

[185] Mt. 6.9–15; Lk. 11.2–4; *Did.* 8.2–3. Among a mass of literature cf. Jeremias 1967; Houlden 1992; and the full bibliography in Hagner 1993, 143. For further reflections at a different level cf. Wright 1996b.

Luke, where Jesus' disciples ask him to teach them a prayer 'as John taught his disciples' (Luke 11.1), has the ring of plausibility, not least because it is unlikely that an early Christian would have invented the implied parallel between Jesus' community and that of John the Baptist.[186] We may leave out of consideration for the moment the question of the original form of the prayer, if indeed there ever was such a thing. Liturgical use in the early church has obviously affected the texts as we now have them. But this may actually be an indication that Jesus taught, not so much an exact form of words (which, out of all his teaching, one might have expected would be the thing that would be preserved), but a shape and a pattern, a basic content.[187]

The prayer comes from within the very heart of Jewish longing for the kingdom, shot through with Jesus' own reinterpretation of what that kingdom meant. The first petition is for YHWH to sanctify his own name; as Fitzmyer points out, this evokes the prophecy of Ezekiel 36, in which the gift of the new heart and spirit to YHWH's people will be the means of his sanctifying his name in his people.[188] The prayer for the kingdom to come, in the way that YHWH wants it (as opposed to the way Israel wants it) leads into the prayer of the pilgrim, needing the supply of bread, whether day by day (Luke) or this day (Matthew; the difference, which is quite possibly insignificant in Aramaic, is slight, if after all the prayer is to be prayed day after day).[189] Prayer for forgiveness, and the accompanying promise of forgiveness within the community – an odd thing in a prayer, and consequently to be regarded as highly significant – is part of the whole emphasis on the inauguration of the new covenant. And the prayer for deliverance from the time of trial (*peirasmos*) and from the evil one (*poneros*) likewise belongs very closely with Jesus' whole kingdom-proclamation as the announcement of the great moment that Israel had been longing for. The time of great testing was coming upon Israel, and Jesus intended his people to be protected

---

[186] So Marshall 1978, 456; though Fitzmyer 1985, 897f. is uncertain. It is already notorious that the Jesus Seminar allowed only the opening phrase 'Our Father' to be certainly original to Jesus, and ruled out hints of 'apocalyptic' ideas altogether: see Funk & Hoover 1993, 148. Crossan 1991a, 294 doubts that it contains 'apocalyptic' elements, but rejects the authenticity of the prayer because of an *a priori*, seeing well enough where the real issue lies: 'The establishment of such a prayer seems to represent the point where a group starts to distinguish and even separate itself from the wider religious community, and *I do not believe* that point was ever reached during the life of Jesus' (italics added).

[187] So Hagner 1993, 145.

[188] Fitzmyer 1985, 898.

[189] cf. Fitzmyer 1985, 900f., 904–6; Hagner 1993, 149f. Matthew's version is sometimes interpreted as eschatological, i.e. the bread of the age to come (e.g. Hagner), and sometimes as the bread the wandering preacher required for one day only at a time (the Jesus Seminar: Funk & Hoover 1993, 149, 326).

from it. The real enemy was not Rome, but the evil one, who was to be watched and guarded against constantly.[190] The whole prayer fits excellently into the context of Jesus' ministry as we have been examining it. Of course it is a pastiche of thoroughly Jewish elements; what else would we expect? Those who prayed this prayer were, from Jesus' point of view, becoming true Israelites, those whom the covenant god would vindicate.

(e) Jubilee: Forgiveness of Debts

The first thing the rebels did at the start of the Jewish War in AD 66 was to burn the treasury where the records of debt were kept.[191] The modern equivalent might be the destruction of a bank's central computing system. Debt was quite a major problem in first-century Palestine, as some of Jesus' own parables indicate.[192] In the light of this, some have interpreted certain passages in Jesus' teaching, particularly the so-called 'Nazareth Manifesto' of Luke 4.16–30, as an indication that Jesus intended to summon Israel as a whole to celebrate the Jubilee, the time when, every fifty years, debts should be cancelled and people allowed to return to their ancestral property.[193] Certainly the passage from Isaiah 61 quoted in Luke 4 lends itself to this interpretation: the Hebrew word 'release' in the phrase 'release for the captives' (Isaiah 61.1, quoted in Luke 4.18) is *deror*, as in Leviticus 25.10. Is there a place for such a theme in Jesus' challenge to his followers?

Three factors, quite apart from the debatable authenticity of Luke 4, militate against thinking that Jesus intended to summon the nation as a whole to observe a Jubilee year. First, it is not at all clear that a Jubilee year had ever been celebrated; there is no mention of such a thing in the Old Testament, and the existing Mishnaic legislation, as on several other matters, has the appearance of an ideal rather than a reality.[194] This does not, of course, mean that Jesus could not have proposed it as an innovation, but it indicates

---

[190] cf. ch. 10 below.

[191] Jos. *War* 2.426–7.

[192] Lk. 7.41–2; Mt. 18.23–35. On the issue cf. Malina and Rohrbaugh 1992, 62f.

[193] The basic legislation is set out in Lev. 25; cp. e.g. Ezek. 46.17, and Jos. *Ant.* 3.280–6. Cf. recently C. J. H. Wright 1992 (= C. J. H. Wright 1995, ch. 8), with bibliography. The best-known proponent of the 'Jubilee' understanding of Jesus' work is Yoder 1972; cf. too Sloan 1977.

[194] cf. e.g. mRH. 1.1; 3.5; mArak. 7.1–5; cp. Moore 1927–30, 1.340, with note, on laws that fell into disuse after the exile, since they only applied at a time when it lay in the Jews' power to determine their own conditions. The existence of Hillel's *prosbul* (mSheb. 10.3–7) shows well enough that the *sabbatical* year (every seven years) had been observed to some degree at least (cf. Schürer 2.366f.); but the absence of similar legal wrangles over the Jubilee suggests that the institution was simply not observed.

that there would have been massive problems involved. Second, the fact that Luke has Jesus quote from Isaiah rather than from Leviticus may suggest that Jesus' programme, like Isaiah's, made use of Jubilee *imagery* rather than the fully-blown legislation itself. Third, at no point in the rest of Jesus' ministry do we find such an agenda. Rather, as we shall see, we find agendas which actually go further, beyond even the most radical social or cultural reform.

Is the Jubilee-language in Luke 4, then, just vivid imagery, a highly charged metaphorical way of speaking about a different sort of reality (say, a 'spiritual' one)? Not necessarily. There is a danger here of being trapped into a spurious either/or: *either* Jesus wanted all Israel to celebrate the Jubilee, *or* he meant it all in a purely 'spiritual' sense. This does not allow for the possibility that, as I argued above, Jesus intended his people, those who were loyal to him in the villages and towns, to form cells, groups or gatherings, much as the non-Qumran Essenes, or John's disciples, seem to have done – and, *mutatis mutandis*, much as the *Haberim*, the groups of Pharisees, must have done.[195] If this suggestion is anywhere near the mark, it opens the possibility that, although Jesus did not envisage that he would persuade Israel as a whole to keep the Jubilee year, *he expected his followers to live by the Jubilee principle among themselves.* He expected, and taught, that they should forgive one another not only 'sins' but also debts. This may help to explain the remarkable practice within the early church whereby resources were pooled, in a fashion not unlike the Essene community of goods. Luke's description of this in Acts 4.34 echoes the description of the sabbatical year in Deuteronomy 15.4.[196]

I suggest, therefore – it is only a suggestion, but I think it reasonably likely historically – that Jesus intended his cells of followers to live 'as if' the Jubilee were being enacted. They were, after all, to be the returned-from-exile people; and one of the emphases of the geographical 'return' of a few hundred years earlier had been Nehemiah's sharp dealing with the problem of debt and slavery within Israel, precisely as part of his attempt to create the true post-exilic people.[197] This brings us back to where we were at the end of section (b) above. Forgiveness was to be the central character of the life of those loyal to Jesus. Thus were they to show their belief that the kingdom of YHWH was indeed dawning. There is good reason to suppose that, after Jesus' death, his followers continued to take this command very seriously. This, indeed, functions as retrospective evidence that Jesus did indeed envisage such a community, such a praxis.

---

[195] cf. *NTPG* 185.
[196] On community of goods in the early church cf. Capper 1985.
[197] Neh. 5.1–13.

(f) Revolution, Politics, Community and Theology

This picture of the communities that Jesus intended to call into being, and the way of life that he enjoined upon them, enables us to hold together various strands that are normally kept apart. The split between politics and theology is familiar enough to us; it has dominated much western thought for the last two hundred years; but Jesus' world remained innocent of it. Less familiar, perhaps, is the split between social and political action postulated by Horsley; he claims that Jesus was propagating local social revolution rather than nationalist (or anti-nationalist) politics. This enables him to mount, in effect, a much softer version of the hypothesis made famous in our generation by S. G. F. Brandon: Jesus was implicitly in favour of the liberation of Palestine from the Romans, but the moves he actually made were towards revolution at the local, social level rather than the national or political.[198]

I suggest that both these splits are thoroughly misleading. For a start, it was precisely Jesus' commitment to the story and praxis of the kingdom – as thoroughly a 'theological' idea as there could be – that gave him the vision and the basic imagery with which to challenge his hearers to action that could not but have implications at every level of their lives. In addition, he certainly did mount what may be called a social revolution, since to persuade even small groups within the villages to change their behaviour to the extent just outlined represented a serious challenge to existing practices. So much was this the case, indeed, that the passage in Matthew 18 which gives detailed instructions for a situation where one 'brother' is reproved by another, which has usually been regarded as the creation of the later church, may in fact have a quite plausible setting within the context of Jesus' own ministry.[199] Once we even begin to imagine the real-life situation faced by people who had heard Jesus gladly but who had no choice but to remain in their villages, such possibilities are wide open. Jesus' followers needed to know how to put into practice the way of forgiveness he was advocating.

But it would be quite wrong to imagine that this social revolution had no wider political implications. Anyone announcing the kingdom of YHWH was engaging in serious political action. Anyone announcing the kingdom *but explicitly opposing armed resistance* was engaging in doubly serious political action: not only the occupying forces, but all those who gave allegiance to the resistance movement, would be enraged. And, as we saw in the previous volume, some of the most ardent revolutionaries were in fact the hard-line Pharisees.[200] This, as I shall argue in chapter 9, goes some way to explain

---

[198] cf. Horsley 1987.

[199] Mt. 18.15–18; cf. Davies & Allison 1988–91, 2.781–7.

[200] *NTPG* 189–97; cf. too e.g. Klausner 1947 [1925], 205f.: 'The Zealots were, in fact, simply active and extremist Pharisees.' He sees them as the 'violent ones' of Mt. 11.12.

the real nature of Jesus' controversies with them. It was *because* Jesus' agenda was 'theological' from first to last that it was 'social', envisaging and calling into being cells of followers committed to his way of life. Jesus, like the founder(s) of the Essenes, and like John the Baptist, apparently envisaged that, scattered about Palestine, there would be small groups of people loyal to himself, who would get together to encourage one another, and would act as members of a family, sharing some sort of common life and, in particular, exercising mutual forgiveness. It was because this way of life was what it was, while reflecting the theology it did, that Jesus' whole movement was thoroughly, and dangerously, 'political'.

And, to recapitulate, the main characteristic of the cells that Jesus called into being was of course loyalty to Jesus himself. This, I suggest, lies behind the saying in Matthew 18.19-20:

> If two of you agree on earth about any matter which they may ask, it shall be done for them by my father in heaven. For where two or three gather together in my name, I am there in their midst.

It has often been observed that this saying echoes Pirqe Aboth 3.2: 'If two sit together and words of the Law are spoken between them, the Divine Presence rests between them.'[201] The saying is, of course, normally regarded as a creation of the early church, referring to the risen and exalted Jesus. It no doubt carried that meaning, as did Matthew 28.20, for post-Easter Christians. But, as Davies and Allison point out, Paul could speak of being powerfully 'present in spirit' with his churches;[202] and there is no reason why others, including Jesus himself, should not have spoken in this way too. If, as I have argued, Jesus intended to leave behind him in the villages groups of people committed to his cause, some such saying as this is thoroughly comprehensible. Once we grasp the dynamics of Palestinian Jewish society at the time, and the inner dynamic of Jesus' kingdom-story, the picture makes historical sense. Jesus was calling for a change of lifestyle to match what he saw as the new moment in YHWH's plan of salvation.

5. Summons: The Call to be Jesus' Helpers and Associates

(i) The Summons to Follow Jesus

The story of the kingdom, then, generated invitation, welcome, and challenge. All Jesus' hearers were summoned to become characters in the drama,

---

[201] cf. e.g. the discussion in Davies 1964, 224f.; Davies & Allison 1988-91, 2.788-91.
[202] 1 Cor. 5.3-5; Col. 2.5; Davies & Allison 2.790.

to live as the people of the kingdom. But there is one further dimension to the way in which the story opened up to include its hearers within it. Jesus summoned some at least of his hearers not only to be loyal to him and his movement wherever they were, but to leave their homes and, quite literally, follow him. He had an agenda, a purpose he was eager to accomplish. For this he needed associates, and even helpers.

We can trace in the gospels several different levels of challenge and summons. There are no hard and fast lines between them, but it is clear that, while Jesus was perfectly content for some (like Mary and Martha) to remain loyal to him at a distance, he challenged some others to sell up and join him on the road.[203] Some appear to have been with him from time to time; others to have provided for him and his disciples from their private property, which assumes that they still had property from which to gain income; others to have given hospitality to the wandering party in their homes, which of course assumes that they themselves were still resident at home, not travelling the roads with Jesus. We do not know for how many months in the year Jesus and his close followers were travelling, or whether, if they stayed in one place for the winter (as is not unreasonable to assume), that place would usually be Capernaum, where at least some of them had originated.

What we do know is that Jesus issued very specific commands to some of his hearers to abandon everything and follow him. We begin with the call of the disciples.[204] Jesus commanded them, imperiously, to leave their present commitments and to follow him, to embrace his way of life and support the needs of his programme and mission. Through the different stories – Mark's is brief and simple, Luke sets his in the context of a fishing incident, and John puts it at the time of John's baptism – we trace an indubitable historical event, namely that Jesus issued a summons to Peter, Andrew, James and John, who obeyed him. To some the call seems to have been quite specific: the memory of Matthew (or Levi) being summoned from the toll-booth in Capernaum, receiving the tolls as people crossed over from Philip's territory to Antipas's, is a sharp vignette with strong historical probability.[205] To others the call seems to have come as Jesus, out of a larger number of general followers, selected a few for specific tasks.[206]

---

[203] cf. Sanders 1993, 123–7 for one way of dividing the gospel material into categories. Cf. esp. Hengel 1981b [1968], 59.

[204] Mk. 1.16–18/Mt. 4.18–20/Lk. 5.1–11 (cf. Jn. 1.35–51; *G. Ebi.* 1); Mk. 2.14/Mt. 9.9/Lk. 5.27–8.

[205] Mk. 2.14/Mt. 9.9/Lk. 5.27–8/*G. Ebi.* 1. The parallels between this story and that of the call of the first disciples (Mk. 1.16f.) are not complete, and should not be taken to imply that one story is simply derived from the other (cf. Pesch 1968; Guelich 1989, 99f.).

[206] Mk. 3.12–14/Lk. 6.13. Mt. 10.1, in some ways par. to these, presupposes the twelve as already existing.

At the wider level, the summons was shocking: Jesus' call overrode normal family obligations of the kind usually regarded as sacrosanct. 'Leave the dead to bury their dead'; only someone conscious of an all-important task could have issued such a summons, and only someone who believed him could have obeyed it.[207] This definite call offered nothing except a wandering life: foxes have holes, birds have nests, but the son of man has nowhere to lay his head.[208] But the promised long-term reward, as one might expect from a leadership prophet, let alone one who was more than a prophet, was that one would share in the blessings of the great coming new age, the age of redemption.[209]

To this strand within the kingdom-story belong those short parables that envisage people giving up everything to follow Jesus. Pearls of great price can only be bought when one has sold everything else; the buried treasure is worth all else that one might have to abandon.[210] The various mammon-sayings function in the same way: following Jesus meant abandoning other prospects and possibilities. It seems likely that Jesus included in the general category of 'mammon' an attachment to the ancestral inheritance of land; as we shall see in chapter 9, this was part of his redrawing of the symbolic world of Israel.[211] And, in a saying with clear echoes of the whole tradition of divine Wisdom calling people to trust her, to find in her the true rest, Jesus invited people to bear his easy yoke, to discover true 'rest' in following his way as opposed to all others.[212]

Within the larger number whom Jesus called to give up all and follow him, there was of course the inner circle of the twelve. There is a wide consensus in favour of the historicity of this group, even though ironically uncertainty remains as to who precisely constituted it.[213] We should not make too much of a meal of the differences between the various lists; the similarities are far more striking, and it may in fact be an incidental argument for veracity that, as with eye-witness statements, the lists do not tally in

[207] See Hengel 1981b [1968], 3–15; Sanders 1985, 252–5. Cf. below, 398–403.

[208] cf. Mt. 8.18–22/Lk. 9.57–62/*Thom.* 86.

[209] cf. Mk. 10.28–31/Mt. 19.27–30/Lk. 18.28–30, cf. Lk. 22.28–30; *Ap. Jas.* 4.1—5.5.

[210] Pearl: Mt. 13.45–6/*Thom.* 76; treasure: Mt. 13.44/*Thom.* 109.

[211] Mt. 6.24/Lk. 16.13; cf. Lk. 12.13–15; 14.33; see below, 403–5.

[212] Mt. 11.28–30; cf. *Thom.* 90; and, further, 2 *Clem.* 6.7; *Dial. Sav.* 65–8; *G. Hebr.* 4. The most obvious background is in Sir. 51.23–7; an alternative, proposed by Davies & Allison 1988–91, 2.283–7, is Ex. 33.12–14. Cf. Hagner 1993, 319–25. Betz 1967, 24 sees Mt. 11.28–30 as identical theologically with the beatitudes of Mt. 5. Neusner 1993, ch. 4 interestingly links the saying with the sabbath-controversies in the following chapter of Mt.

[213] cf. esp. Sanders 1985, 98–106, 115, 118, 156, 229–30, 233; Horsley 1987, 199f.; Meyer 1992b, 781; Caird & Hurst 1994, 382f. In addition to the gospel texts (and Ac. 1.13), cf. 1 Cor. 15.5; Rev. 21.14; these are evidence that the group as a whole, with or without Judas Iscariot, was still thought of as 'the twelve'.

all particulars.[214] The very existence of the twelve speaks, of course, of the reconstitution of Israel; Israel had not had twelve visible tribes since the Assyrian invasion in 734 BC, and for Jesus to give twelve followers a place of prominence, let alone to make comments about them sitting on thrones judging the twelve tribes, indicates pretty clearly that he was thinking in terms of the eschatological restoration of Israel.[215]

It is not so often noticed that, within the twelve, there was a group of three – Peter, James and John – who functioned regularly as Jesus' closest personal aides. It is perhaps not accidental that this is a Davidic symbol, echoing the three who were David's closest bodyguards.[216] The symbolism fits well with Jesus' persona, which we shall study in the next Part of this book, as the wandering, anointed-but-not-yet-enthroned king of Israel.[217]

The summons to follow Jesus, going beyond the challenge to be loyal to his cause in one's own setting, thus focused itself more and more narrowly. Some were summoned to abandon all and follow Jesus; within that, some were called into a special and deeply symbolic inner group; within that again, some had a further symbolic, as well as humanly supportive, function. All of this prompts the further question: what would such followers have thought they were signing on for? And what impression would the average Galilean onlooker have received of this wandering prophet gathering followers whose loyalty went so deep as to override normally binding obligations?

The obvious answer is that the onlookers, and quite probably those who were summoned, will have observed the creation of a movement, with some

---

[214] Mk. 3.13–19/Mt. 10.2–4/Lk. 6.12–14/Ac. 1.13: in each of these, the first four are the same (Peter, Andrew, James and John), though with differences in the order of the last three; the second four are the same (Philip, Bartholomew, Thomas and Matthew), though with differences in the order of the last three; the last four always begin with James son of Alphaeus, and end with Judas Iscariot (except in Acts, of course, since by then he was dead). Only in the tenth and eleventh places are there significant variations: Mt. and Mk. both have Thaddaeus and Simon the Cananaean, while Lk. and Ac. both place 'Simon the Zealot' in the tenth spot and 'Judas son of James' eleventh. By far the easiest solution is to see 'Zealot' as Luke's gloss on 'Cananaean', and to suggest that 'Judas son of James' is a second name of 'Thaddaeus'; perhaps the latter name was preferred in some circles because of the possibility of confusion with Judas Iscariot (cf. Jn. 14.22). The main other problem concerns Nathanael, who achieves sudden prominence in Jn. 1.45–9, reappears in Jn. 21.2, and is otherwise unheard of. John does not say he was one of the twelve; if he was, he might be the same person as Bartholomew, not mentioned in John. Cp. Fitzmyer 1970, 613–21; Guelich 1989, 153–64; Davies & Allison 1988–91, 2.150–9; Hagner 1993, 263–7; Sanders 1993, 120f., all with bibliog.

[215] Mt. 19.28/Lk. 22.30. Lk. omits the word 'twelve' before 'thrones', presumably through embarrassment about Judas (so Sanders 1985, 100). Cp. Jas. 1.1. For the background cf. e.g. 1 Kgs. 11.29–37; 2 Kgs. 17.5–23; Ezek. 37.15–23.

[216] 2 Sam. 23.8–23; 1 Chr. 11.10–25.

[217] cp. Mk. 2.25–6/Mt. 12.3–4/Lk. 6.3–4; cf. ch. 11 below.

analogies at least to the movements called into being by Judas the Galilean, Theudas, and others. It is remarkable that Luke, despite his own apparent agenda of showing that Christianity was not politically dangerous, allows Gamaliel a speech in which Jesus is put alongside these two.[218] His summons may well have sounded similar to the sort of summons that other visionaries and/or revolutionaries had issued. Nothing was said about taking up arms; but Peter somehow had a sword with him in Gethsemane, and it is perhaps unlikely that he had only just purchased it. The announcement that YHWH was now king, and the consequent summons to rally to the flag, had far more in common with the founding of a revolutionary party than with what we now think of as either 'evangelism' or 'ethical teaching'. 'It is quite likely that at least in part the disciples misunderstood Jesus' activity and mission, reading them, as did the mass of his Galilean audience, in terms of traditional Jewish national messianic hopes.'[219]

Jesus, then, summoned some of his hearers to a specific 'following' of him, which involved their giving up a good deal that was not required of others among his audience. One such instance in particular is given considerable prominence in all three synoptic gospels, and we must now examine it in more detail.

(ii) The 'Rich Young Ruler'[220]

Jesus' summons to follow a new way of being Israel comes to a climax, as far as the synoptics are concerned, with the story of a rich young man.

He came with a question: 'What must I do to inherit eternal life?' This was, of course, the question of the kingdom: what must I do to have a share in the age to come, to be among those who are vindicated when YHWH acts decisively and becomes king? (It is not, that is to say, the medieval or modern question: what must I do to go to heaven when I die?) Jesus' response began in the normal Jewish place. The Torah was the boundary-marker of the covenant people: those who kept it would share the life of the coming age. But the young man was not satisfied, not simply perhaps because Jesus had only quoted the second half of the ten commandments. Jesus' second challenge to him was blunt: sell up, give to the poor, follow me. This is similar to the call to the original disciples, only this time with the emphasis even more firmly on the cost.

---

[218] Ac. 5.36f.; cf. Ac. 21.38. See Hengel 1981b [1968], 40, nn.9, 10; and *NTPG* 170–7.
[219] Hengel 1981b [1968], 79.
[220] Mk. 10.17–22/Mt. 19.16–22/Lk. 18.18–25/G. *Naz.* 16. Mt. says he was young, Lk. that he was a ruler; all agree he was rich.

What was Jesus doing? Was he setting aside the Torah and outlining a new 'ethic' as a 'way of life', a timeless way to conduct oneself? Or was this merely an interim-ethic, a martial law for a short and untypical period before the world ends? Or what?

The passage suggests that none of these categories will do. The command to forsake riches and to follow Jesus appears to have been very specific to this young man. We are not told that Jesus said this sort of thing regularly, or even often (though the warnings against riches, and trust in them, is of course frequent).[221] In particular, since Jesus quoted seven out of the ten commandments, it is fair to assume that the challenges he put to the young man took the place of two that he did *not* quote (the one still missing is the command about the sabbath, for reasons that will become apparent later). The young man must sell all his possessions: that is, get rid of the idols which were holding him bound to mammon instead of to YHWH. And he must follow Jesus: that is, give total allegiance to the way of life which, like the first commandment, was YHWH's immediate and urgent summons to Israel.[222] Once again, Torah had been relativized by its real intention being fulfilled. Instead of being under Torah itself, the summons was now to be under Jesus.[223] The young man was being summoned to join an Israel that was no longer defined by Torah (nor would it be vindicated on the basis of its fidelity to Torah), but by allegiance to Jesus – an allegiance that would involve giving up all idols.

There is an important underlying theme here which runs through the entire ministry of Jesus. Some Jews assumed, perhaps on the basis of a facile reading of Deuteronomy and certain psalms, that wealth was a sign of YHWH's favour. It signalled, apparently, that one was already in receipt of covenant blessings. This explains the disciples' great surprise ('they were exceedingly astonished', Mark 10.25) at being told that rich people would have difficulty inheriting the kingdom. They *assumed* that the rich were going to be part of the kingdom; the question for them was, who else? But Jesus was saying that the rich were not only not automatically within the covenant, but very likely outside it. This completely overturned the disciples' worldview; but it was not a new thing in Jesus' preaching. There were, as we saw, other warnings

---

[221] Joseph of Arimathea remained a property-owner (Mk. 15.43–6/Mt. 27.57–60/Lk. 23.50–3/Jn. 19.38–42); Zacchaeus, an apparently fitting target for the command to give everything away, parted with only half (Lk. 19.8) – though he did restore his victims fourfold, too. For other warnings cf. e.g. Lk. 6.24; 12.13–21; 14.33; 16.1–15, 19–31.

[222] cf. Hengel 1981b [1968], 22, quoting various sources to support the point that following the messianic messenger is the equivalent to following Israel's god himself.

[223] As in Mt. 11.29, where 'take my yoke upon you' is implicitly contrasted with the 'yoke of Torah'; cf. the contrast between 'the yoke of the law' and 'the yoke of the kingdom' in a saying of R. Nehunya ben Ha-Kanah (c. AD 70–130): mAb. 3.5. Cf. *NTPG* 199.

to the rich. When 'the age to come' finally arrived, possessions and property would have nothing whatever to do with membership.

Jesus' exchange with this one young man thus contained several central aspects of his kingdom-story, which is no doubt why the synoptic evangelists all give it such prominence. It focused on to one particular person and incident three features: the implied eschatology (the age to come/'eternal life'), the place of Torah (fulfilled strangely by following Jesus), and the warning about current idolatries. It sharpened Jesus' summons to a point which the man in question found unbearable, but which, from the evangelists' point of view, encapsulated the subversive wisdom which Jesus was offering, and which we shall study further in the final main section of this chapter.

(iii) The Summons to Assist in the Proclamation of the Kingdom

First, though, we must note one more specific aspect of Jesus' summons. Some (though not all) of those who obeyed the call to follow Jesus were then organized into groups to go out and extend his work of announcement and proclamation.[224] They were to mobilize more people for the task: the harvest was plentiful, but the labourers few. They were to be agents of the kingdom, just as Jesus was, telling its story and enacting its praxis. And in the process they were to travel light, literally and metaphorically. Everything had to be done in a hurry. They would not have gone through all the towns of Israel before the 'son of man' would be vindicated.[225]

It is of course true that such 'mission charges' must have been important for the first generation of Christians, and will certainly have been shaped by them in a variety of ways.[226] But this is no reason to deny that Jesus did indeed entrust some of his followers – the twelve at least, and according to Luke a larger number as well – with a share in his own work of spreading the news of the kingdom. Again, we must stress that the itinerant work of Jesus' followers will not have looked, to their contemporaries, much like what in the modern west would be thought of as a 'religious' movement. Those sent on this commission will have looked more like what in many

---

[224] Mt. 10.1–42; Lk. 9.1–6; Mk. 6.7–13; Lk. 10.1–16 (cf. Lk. 22.35–6). Other pars. to Mt. 10 are found in various places in Lk., Mk., and *Thom.*, as the synopsis reveals.

[225] This line (Mt. 10.23), which became a corner-stone of Schweitzer's scheme, does indeed, as he rightly saw, limit the mission to a single drive with a particular, historically delimited purpose, which makes the passage effectively useless for literal translation into a subsequent generalized ethic. But Schweitzer's way of reading the saying about the 'son of man' was, as I shall argue in chs. 8 and 11, completely mistaken.

[226] cf. esp. Theissen 1978.

ways they were: enthusiasts for a new and revolutionary movement. That is why they were to expect opposition (Matthew 10.16–22).

(iv) The Summons to Take up the Cross and Follow Jesus

The summons to follow Jesus is frequently amplified, in the synoptic tradition, as the call to follow him into political danger and consequent death. This forms a major element in the 'mission discourse' of Matthew 10, with its partial parallels in Luke.[227] And it is set at a climactic and transitional moment in Mark, picked up by both Matthew and Luke.[228] Once again, the summons ('We are going up to Jerusalem; the son of man will suffer, but will be vindicated; so take up your cross and follow me!') could well have sounded like the call to revolution. Those who answered such a call would have to be prepared to act in such a way that, if they were caught, they would be likely to pay for it with their lives. One can imagine Judas the Galilean or Bar-Kochba saying similar things to their disciples. The Pharisees who urged the young hotheads to pull down the eagle from Herod's temple issued a similar call.[229] Within the context of Jewish martyr-stories, such a summons would carry as well the implication that any who died in the cause would subsequently be vindicated by YHWH.[230] The thought that Jesus actually *intended* his followers to die seems, however, no more to have entered the disciples' heads than the thought that his talk about a cross meant that he himself intended to do so. What we can say for certain is that a summons to risk all in following Jesus places him and his followers firmly on the map of first-century socially and politically subversive movements. In so far as it also indicates a 'theological' meaning (which we shall discuss later), this is found within the history, not superimposed upon it from outside.

(v) The Great Commandment[231] and the Good Samaritan[232]

A good deal of Jesus' challenge and summons, both positively and negatively, is focused in the brief discussion of which commandment is the

---

[227] Mt. 10.17–39; Lk. 6.40; 12.2–9, 11–12, 51–3; 14.25–7 (cf. 28–33); 21.12–19; 17.33.

[228] Mk. 8.34—9.1/Mt. 16.24–8/Lk. 9.23–7; cf. Jn. 12.25.

[229] Once we allow for Josephus' rendering of their speeches into philosophical language appropriate for his own audience: Jos. *Ant.* 17.149–66; *War* 1.648–55; cf. *NTPG* 172, 327.

[230] cf. *NTPG* 320–34.

[231] Mk. 12.28–34/Mt. 22.34–40/*Did.* 1.2; cf. Lk. 10.25–8.

[232] Lk. 10.25–37.

greatest (a question with which rabbis of Jesus' day, as of subsequent generations, would have been quite familiar[233]). The answer Jesus gave was
thoroughly non-controversial, quoting the most famous of Jewish prayers
('Hear, O Israel, YHWH our god, YHWH is one'). The *Shema*, the prayer
which begins with these lines, was as central to Judaism then as it is now,
and the coupling of it with the command to love one's neighbour as oneself
was not unknown, either.[234] What was new was the inference Jesus drew
from that: first, that the category of 'neighbour' was wider than most Jews
would allow, and second, that loving God with the heart meant the firm
relativization of cult and sacrifice. The scribe who drew the latter, highly
subversive, conclusion was rewarded with a rare accolade: he was 'not far
from the kingdom of god'.[235]

The same theme, that of the unrestricted love of neighbour and the consequent relativization of cult and sacrifice, is highlighted in the parable of the
good Samaritan.[236] A story like this contains so much of the significance of
Jesus' ministry, of the redefinition of the kingdom, of numerous overtones
that resonate in various directions, that it is well-nigh impossible to tie it
down to any particular theme, or indeed stereotypical literary category. What
follows can only be the beginnings of an indication of how, within the historical reconstruction I am offering, it might be treated.

Despite the scepticism of some scholars about the appropriateness of
Luke's setting of this parable (a scepticism that has more to do, in my view,
with an unwillingness to face possibilities about the actual historical setting
and nature of Jesus' public career than with anything else), its present context
is actually very telling. The lawyer asked Jesus what he must do to inherit
'eternal life' – presumably, again, the standard Jewish question about the
conditions for having a share in the age to come, *ha'olam haba'*. He may

---

[233] cf. e.g. bShab. 31a; bBer. 63a.

[234] The *Shema* itself consists of Dt. 6.4-9; 11.13-21; Num. 15.37-41. Rabbinic discussions of it include mBer. 1.1-3.5; mShab. 8.3; etc.; cf. SB 4.189-207. The command to
love the neighbour (Lev. 19.18) is cited as a commonly known saying in mNed. 9.4. The
combination is found in e.g. *T. Issach.* 5.2; 7.6; *T. Dan* 5.3, though these may be Christian
in origin. Cf. too Philo *Spec. Leg.* 2.63. Cf. Fitzmyer 1985, 879; Gundry 1993, 713f.; Nolland 1993, 581; all with other refs.

[235] Mk. 12.34. The exchange in Mk. and Mt. functions as a riddle, explaining further
Jesus' action in the Temple: see below, 434f., 566f.

[236] Lk. 10.30-5. For the massive bibliography available, cf. e.g. Nolland 1993, 586-8.
The basic parable, for all its occurrence in Luke alone, is accepted as genuine by virtually all
scholars (exceptions: Sellin 1974/75; Goulder 1989, 487-92, on which cf. Nolland 1993,
588-90). The concluding lines – the question to the lawyer, and the brief exchange that follows – are rejected by some (e.g. the Jesus Seminar: Funk & Hoover 1993, 324) as a Lukan
addition. On the question of whether it is really a 'parable' at all, and if so of what sort, cf.
e.g. Fitzmyer 1985, 883.

306 Part II: Profile of a Prophet

perhaps have already known Jesus' view on the *Shema*, so that when Jesus replied with a counter-question he was ready to make the next move, knowing it would meet with Jesus' approval. Then came the real question. If 'loving my neighbour' was part of one's duty as a good Jew – i.e. part of the boundary-marker that meant one would inherit the age to come, the blessing in store for the covenant people when Israel's god established the kingdom – then how was 'neighbour' to be delimited? If one started from the apparent purpose of Torah, to define the boundaries of Israel, then there would appear to be a natural, and quite limited, definition of 'neighbour'. If, however, one wanted to define 'neighbour' more broadly, so as to include those outside the covenant, then did one not have to give up the idea of Torah, of a boundary around the covenant people, altogether? It is in this context that Luke's introductory remark becomes very pregnant: he, *desiring to justify himself*. This is not the Pelagian 'self-justification' imagined by some in the reformation tradition. Nor should the question be understood, as in some readings, 'he, desiring not to look a fool for having asked such an easy question'. It is the justification of the Jew, seeking to draw the boundaries of the covenant at the appropriate place, with (of course) himself inside, and sundry other specifiable categories outside.[237]

Jesus' reply, one of the most brilliant miniature stories ever composed, has often been misunderstood by moralizing, existentializing, or hasty exegesis. The point was not that the Samaritan regarded the Jew in the ditch as his neighbour (he did, but that was not the thrust of the story). Nor was the story simply a moral encouragement, urging its hearers either to help people out in times of trouble or to recognize human worth in those one habitually despises.[238] The point was subtler, and more directly related to the actual agenda behind the lawyer's question. What he was really interested in was where the covenant boundary-line had to be drawn. Jesus' question at the end of the story was not simply, how then should you behave towards those you normally despise? It was sharper: which of the three turned out to be neighbour to the Jew in the ditch? In other words, which person in the story counts as the 'neighbour' whom the shorthand summary of Torah commands that you shall love as yourself?

[237] Bailey 1983, 2.43f. quotes Sir. 12.1–7, which specifically forbids going to the help of sinners and ungodly persons.

[238] Luke's setting is misunderstood to mean this by e.g. Funk & Hoover 1993, 324, who therefore accuse Luke of 'domesticating' the parable. In fact, Luke's setting actually emphasizes what, according to the same writers, the original parable intended: the redrawing of 'the map of both the social and the sacred world' (loc. cit.). Cf. Bailey 1983, 2.33: it is when we *ignore* the surrounding dialogue that the parable becomes a mere moralistic tale! Cf. e.g. Evans 1990, 467, who first assumes that the parable is a moral tale about the boundless love of neighbour, and then confesses that it is difficult to fit this precisely into its context.

The answer was obvious, though revolutionary: *the Jew in the ditch discovered that the Samaritan was his neighbour.* And, by implication, he also discovered that the two other travellers on the road were *not* his neighbours – perhaps precisely because they were anxious to keep themselves in a state of ceremonial purity, as part of the complex workings of the sacrificial cult. What we have here, then, is not a generalized moral tale *per se*, which just happens to be about a Jew and a Samaritan because they form a good example of a long-standing cultural feud. Nor yet is it a generalized and abstract example of the demolition of traditional categories or the fracturing of 'worlds of meaning'. These obvious and, in themselves, not unimportant levels of meaning and function are taken up within the larger whole, which is that the story dramatically redefines the covenant boundary of Israel, of the Torah itself, and by strong implication of the Temple cult. At stake throughout was the question: who would inherit the age to come? In other words, who would benefit when YHWH brought in the kingdom? The parable answered this question with sharp clarity. Outsiders were coming into the kingdom, and – at least by implication – insiders were being left out. More specifically, there was a way of being Israel which would be truly and radically faithful to the very centre of Torah, as summed up in the *Shema*. But this way, when pursued to the limits, would involve the redrawing of Israel's boundaries, to include those normally reckoned beyond the pale. In that process, the whole system of Temple and sacrifice would itself be called into question.

The result was, of course, a challenge to the lawyer, not unlike Jesus' challenge to the rich young man. 'What must I do to inherit *ha'olam haba'*, the age to come?' Answer: follow Jesus in finding a new and radicalized version of Torah-observance. Loving Israel's covenant god meant loving him as creator of all, and discovering as neighbours those who were beyond the borders of the chosen people. Those who followed Jesus in this way would be 'justified'; that is, they would be vindicated when the covenant god acted climactically within history. 'Go and do likewise.'

If the scribe had to learn that the Samaritan was his neighbour, one may readily suspect that Jesus would not ultimately have stopped his redefinition at that point. This parable thus points to another vital theme within the kingdom-story, seen both as announcement and as summons. The story which Jesus was retelling did not stop with Israel alone. If Jesus was announcing the arrival of the kingdom, the whole context of Jewish expectation demanded that this should have worldwide implications. What, if anything, did Jesus have to say about the non-Jewish nations?

6. Many Will Come From East and West

I argued earlier that

> The fate of the nations was inexorably and irreversibly bound up with that of Israel . . .
> This point is of the utmost importance for the understanding both of first-century Judaism
> and of emerging Christianity. What happens to the Gentiles is conditional upon, and con-
> ditioned by, what happens to Israel . . . The call of Israel has as its fundamental objective
> the rescue and restoration of the entire creation. Not to see this connection is to fail to
> understand the meaning of Israel's fundamental doctrines of monotheism and election.[239]

One could sharpen the point up this way.

1. In many strands of Jewish expectation, demonstrably current in the first
century, the fate of the gentile nations would hinge upon the fate of Israel.
What YHWH intended to do to or for the Gentiles, he would do in some sense
or other through Israel.

2. When, therefore, YHWH did for Israel whatever he was going to do for
Israel (leaving vague for the moment the content of the eschatological
expectation), then the Gentiles would share in the results.

3. In some strands of thought, this would mean judgment for the Gentiles
(and for renegade Jews); in others, it would mean that the nations would
share in Israel's blessing. Both stand together in some texts, such as
Zechariah.[240]

4. Anyone announcing that Israel's god was now at last becoming king
would be bound at least to imply that now at last the kingdom would spread,
for better or for worse, to the ends of the earth. 'YHWH will become king
over all the earth', wrote Zechariah in one of the most explicit statements
both of the coming kingdom and of the subjugation of the Gentiles.[241]
Indeed, to the extent that kingdom-language would be heard as revolutionary
language, it could hardly *not* imply the rule of YHWH (and, by implication,
the rule of Israel) over all the peoples of the earth; that was the whole point
of it. To announce the kingdom in a sense which brought Israel merely a new
dimension of religious experience, or a new sense of religious community,
but which left the rest of the world unaffected, would be radically to miss the
point.

5. In particular, we have seen that Jesus was challenging Israel to *be*
Israel; that is, to be the light of the world, the salt of the earth. He was, that

---

[239] *NTPG* 268, summing up the discussion, with copious texts, of 262–8. The point is
perhaps most obviously visible in passages such as Isa. 2.2–5 (= Mic. 4.1–5); 49.1–6;
Zech. 8.20–3; 14.12–19.

[240] Albeit in very different parts of the book (Zech. 8 & 14); but there is no reason to
suppose that first-century Jews anticipated the divisions made by historical critics.

[241] Zech. 14.9.

is, criticizing his contemporaries for being more concerned for victory over the gentile world than for bringing YHWH's healing and salvation to it.

All of this points to the provisional conclusion: from the historian's point of view, one would strongly expect that anyone announcing the kingdom, and offering this critique of his contemporaries, would envisage that part of the result of his work would be the ingathering of the nations of which the prophets had spoken. When YHWH finally acted for Israel, the Gentiles would be blessed as well.

So what do we find? The evidence is at first sight puzzling. In one well-known gospel tradition Jesus announces that Gentiles will share in the blessings of the kingdom.[242] In various others, he compares his contemporaries with various well-known pagans from biblical stories, always to the advantage of the latter.[243] However, he also insists that his own mission, and that of the disciples during his lifetime, is to be restricted to ethnic Israel.[244] In the early church, even Luke, who is obviously in favour of the gentile mission, stresses that the church was initially wary of Gentiles, with some trying to insist on pagan converts becoming proselytes – a problem we know also, of course, from the letters of Paul.[245]

The best solution to this problem is, in principle, a version of that advocated by Jeremias, and supported recently by, for instance, Meyer, and by Caird and Hurst.[246] My argument up to this point gives us every reason to suppose that Jesus would have hinted, as part of his total kingdom-story, at the vocation of Israel coming true at last: Israel would be the light of the

---

[242] Mt. 8.11-12/Lk. 13.28-9.

[243] Mt. 10.15; 11.21-4/Lk. 10.12-14; Lk. 4.25-7; 11.29-32. The par. to Mt. 10.15 in Mk. 6.11 is based on a variant reading, now generally rejected.

[244] Mt. 10.5-6; cf. Mt. 15.21-8/Mk. 7.24-30. The latter story (concerning the Syrophoenician woman) is now regularly made the basis of a fashionable theory concerning Jesus' innate prejudices and his willingness to receive rebuke and illumination from a foreign woman (cf., e.g., Theissen 1991b, 40-6). That this is not the only way to read the story is clear from e.g. Caird & Hurst 1994, 395.

[245] cf. Ac. 10—11; 15; Gal. *passim.*

[246] Jeremias 1958; Meyer 1987; Caird & Hurst 1994, 393-8. Sanders' sustained attack on Jeremias lays emphasis on the question: did Jesus, or did he not, 'favor the nation of Israel'? (Sanders 1987, 236f.). This may be the question suggested by Jeremias' picture; but, once the evidence is read within 'restoration eschatology' in the way I have suggested (following Sanders himself), I believe one can answer: yes, Jesus believed in the *election* and hence *priority* of Israel, but this does not mean he did not think the Gentiles would share Israel's blessing. It is too simplistic by far to oppose 'the destruction of Israel' to 'the affirmation of Israel' (cf. Sanders 238). As will be clear, I agree with Sanders (239) that Jesus 'saw the full redemption of Israel as the goal towards which he directed his own efforts'. In the end, Sanders' position as in 1993, 192 is not far off my own: like many second-Temple Jews, Jesus 'expected at least some Gentiles to turn to the God of Israel and to participate in the coming kingdom'. I do not think Jeremias would have been too worried about this conclusion, either.

world, so that the nations, seeing it, would come in and glorify the god of Israel.[247] Once again, the scandal inherent in this announcement lay not in its *religious* but in its *eschatological* and therefore *political* meaning. It was not so much that Jesus was condemning his contemporaries for their bad attitude to Gentiles (conveniently anticipating late-twentieth-century western political correctness), as that he was suggesting that through his work the kingdom was arriving, bringing both hope for the gentile world, and dire warning for those who failed in their vocation to be the light of the world.

The kingdom-story told by Jesus thus opened up, as from its Jewish roots it was bound to do, to embrace the world. From Jesus' point of view, the narrative of YHWH's dealings with Israel was designed to contribute to the larger story, of the creator's dealings with the cosmos. In terms of narrative analysis, Jesus' retelling of YHWH's story with Israel looks like this:[248]

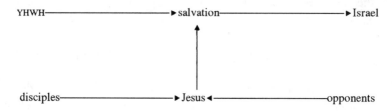

while the larger story, within which this one fits, looks like this:

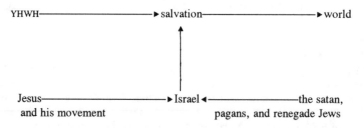

This shows, as clearly as I think one can, that Jesus' promise, implicit and explicit, to the nations beyond Israel's borders came as part of an affirmation, not a denial, of the unique elected role of Israel within the purposes of YHWH. At the same time, Jesus' challenge to his contemporaries was real, and sharp. His affirmation of Israel's elected status, and role within the creator's purposes, did not mean that he had no critique of the Jews of his day. On the contrary. He was not offering conventional wisdom, with the odd new twist here and there. He was holding out a deeply subversive wisdom, and was inviting his followers to make it their own.

---

[247] Mt. 5.14–16; cf. Mk. 4.21; Lk. 8.16; 11.33; *Thom.* 33.2-3.
[248] cf. *NTPG* 389f.; and above, 244.

7. The True Wisdom

There are, no doubt, many different lenses through which we can usefully view Jesus, and it is always good to be reminded of those which had been forgotten. I therefore welcome with enthusiasm the recent emphasis on Jesus as a 'sage', a teacher of wisdom.[249] Indeed, from one point of view the present chapter has been about little else. Jesus offered his contemporaries a challenge and summons to leave the path of received wisdom and to follow a different route, which he himself was not only offering but exemplifying. As such he was standing in a line of great wisdom teachers going back in both Jewish and pagan traditions to the book of Proverbs and beyond.

So far, so good, and fairly uncontroversial. Within this general statement, much work has been done on the way in which Jesus' teaching, by its very style, was designed to subvert the worldviews of his hearers. Teasing aphorisms, laconic and cryptic sayings, and strange subversive stories, all challenged their perceptions of reality and deftly unlocked fresh possibilities.[250] Again: so far, so good.

The problem that arises within this quite recent wave of study is that the picture of Jesus as a sage, a teacher of subversive wisdom, has regularly been played off against various other emphases. In particular, as we saw in chapter 2, the Jesus Seminar, and some (though not all) of its most prominent members, have routinely used their picture of 'Jesus the sage' as the basis for certain negative arguments: Jesus was a 'sapiential' teacher, therefore he was not a prophet; he taught about a new way of life in the present, therefore he had nothing to say about the future; his home ground was 'wisdom', therefore he had nothing to do with 'apocalyptic'.[251] Some have gone so far as to suggest that Jesus' teaching was only marginally Jewish, and had little to do with the specific aspirations, let alone the scriptures, of Israel, having its background instead in the Cynic-style wisdom that he might conceivably have met in the Galilee of his early years.[252] Others, while still wanting to highlight the category of 'sage', have tried to avoid false antitheses, and have placed Jesus, still as a 'sage', within a more recognizably Jewish context.[253]

The problem with the deJudaized Jesus offered in the more extreme versions of 'Jesus the sage' was nicely expressed a decade ago by Ed Sanders: Jesus appears to be 'offering things which, though mysterious then, are seen,

---

[249] Chronicled e.g. by Borg 1994a, 9f., and expounded in Borg 1987a, ch. 6; 1994b, ch. 4; Scott 1990; Witherington 1994, ch. 4.

[250] See e.g. Crossan 1973, 1983; Scott 1983, 1989.

[251] For all this, cf. e.g. Funk & Hoover 1993, 30-4 and *passim.*

[252] e.g. Mack 1988, 1993; Downing 1988, 1992. Crossan 1991a offers a more nuanced reading, though with the same broad emphases.

[253] Thus e.g. Borg 1984, 1987a, 1994b.

when finally puzzled out twenty centuries later, to be striking in manner but not especially in matter'.[254] Jesus' teaching boils down to cryptic advice and admonition, such as might be given at any time or place.[255] As Sanders comments on this kind of thing, 'A Jesus who was only a teacher, but as teacher did not even communicate striking ideas to his audience, surely was a person of little consequence.'[256] Putting this problem another way, if Jesus was simply a cryptic sage who did not address the urgent state of affairs within Israel, virtually all the material we have studied in this and the preceding two chapters must be deemed inauthentic, and the entire picture we have built up so far, with the historical argumentation at every point, must be set aside.

In fact, however, to recognize that Jesus stood within the 'wisdom' traditions of Israel (and her neighbours) in no way means abandoning the view that he used this broad stream of thought and style to drive home his message about YHWH's call to Israel at the critical moment in her history. Wisdom and prophecy, and wisdom and apocalyptic, do not cancel each other out, but rather belong together. Prophet and apocalyptist share the agenda of the Jewish wisdom tradition: to break open the worldly perspectives of readers and hearers, so that the truth of YHWH can be seen, and his call heard.[257]

This can easily be exemplified from various Jewish contexts. The book of Daniel, one of the most obvious examples of apocalyptic literature anywhere within or outside the biblical canon, stresses constantly that Daniel and his friends are the truly wise people who put pagan wisdom to shame (1.4, 19–20; 5.10–17; etc.). Their skills cover the whole range which compartmentalizing scholarship has liked to break up:

> To these four young men God gave knowledge and skill in every aspect of literature and wisdom; Daniel also had insight into all visions and dreams.[258]

We should not be surprised, therefore, when at the close of the book the great apocalyptic prediction of resurrection is linked at once to wisdom:

> Many of those who sleep in the dust of the earth shall awake, some to everlasting life, and some to shame and everlasting contempt. Those who are wise shall shine like the brightness of the sky, and those who lead many to righteousness, like the stars forever and ever.[259]

If we ask which of these categories is the primary one, holding the other within it, the whole book offers a clear answer. Daniel's apocalyptic visions

---

[254] Sanders 1985, 7.
[255] cf. e.g. Mack 1988, 73 (quoted above, 37).
[256] Sanders, *loc. cit.*
[257] I here draw on some arguments I have rehearsed in Wright 1996a.
[258] Dan. 1.17.
[259] Dan. 12.2.

are not an *example* of wisdom, as though the book were simply commending wisdom and using Daniel's ability to interpret dreams as a striking instance of this great quality. It is the other way round. Daniel's wisdom is the thing that enables him to grasp the secrets of *what Israel's god is doing with Israel and the world*.

To begin with, the Wisdom of Solomon looks as though it works the other way round. The book exhorts the rulers of the world to acquire true wisdom, so that they may know how to govern their people (1.1–5; 6.21–5). But the testimony and prayer which are put into the mouth of the fictitious 'Solomon' (chs. 7–9) indicate, significantly, that it is within the story of Israel, and the call of the true god to Israel, that the true wisdom is active. So it turns out in the second half of the book. What starts off in chapter 10 as a list of (biblical) heroes, exemplifying wisdom, gradually reveals itself as a polemic against pagan idolatry, and a warning of the divine judgment that it will incur. The exodus will serve as the model for this (17–19): the plagues on the Egyptians, and the rescue of Israel, will be repeated in the coming great act of deliverance. So, once again, 'wisdom' is thoroughly compatible with, and actually supports and sustains, a theology in which Israel's god acts within history to defeat evil and to vindicate and liberate his people.

The wide sweep of thought evident in Ben-Sirach, too, locates the multiple and various teachings about wisdom within a very specifically Jewish context. However far 'wisdom' may range in the earlier chapters of the book, however easily the very generalized teaching may be applied to humankind as a whole, in the end it is the story of Israel, highlighted in her great leaders and heroes, that embodies and exemplifies the way of life that has been commended; and the high priest of the writer's own day, Simon son of Onias, is the crowning glory of them all, as he blesses the people in the Temple.[260] It is not surprising, then, that at the centre of the book the great poem in praise of wisdom envisages Lady Wisdom, the creator's handmaid, coming to live in the Temple itself, being embodied in the Torah, Israel's national charter, creating Israel as another Eden.[261]

A final example, this time from the Scrolls. In the Community Rule, one of the most important works discovered at Qumran, the overarching context is covenantal and apocalyptic. The first two columns of the scroll deal with admission to membership in the covenant, the secretly renewed covenant which now exists in parallel to the 'dominion of the satan', which is still running its course (2.19). But then, in the third column, we find one of the most familiar of the many 'wisdom' motifs, traceable back to the early chapters of Proverbs: the 'two ways' that lie open before humans, and the characteristics

---

[260] Sir. 50.1–21.
[261] Sir. 24.8–29: cf. *NTPG* 217 and elsewhere.

of those who follow them. The implication is clear enough. Those who belong to the little community of the renewed covenant are those who follow the way of truth, while those who remain outside are following the way of falsehood. But then, bringing 'wisdom' and 'apocalyptic' together quite clearly, we read that

> in the mysteries of His understanding, and in His glorious wisdom, God has ordained an end for falsehood, and at the time of the visitation He will destroy it for ever. Then truth, which has wallowed in the ways of wickedness during the dominion of falsehood until the appointed time of judgment, shall arise in the world for ever . . . And he shall be plunged into the spirit of purification that he may instruct the upright in the knowledge of the Most High and teach the wisdom of the sons of heaven to the perfect of way. For God has chosen them for an everlasting Covenant and all the glory of Adam shall be theirs . . .[262]

Once again, 'wisdom' is securely grounded within the wider context of Israel's story, with its traditional motifs: the struggle between the people of the true god and the evil that still resides in the world, and the promise that this god, being the creator, will act to defeat evil and vindicate his true people.

In all of these examples, possessing 'wisdom' is potentially or actually highly subversive. Ben-Sirach is supporting the existing regime, but by implication is also challenging paganism; the others are more explicit. For none of them does 'wisdom' mean a private, esoteric or ahistorical knowledge. Rather, it means living by the true interpretation of Israel's law, and thus being vindicated by the true god when he acts. 'Wisdom' goes with 'apocalyptic'; neither category eliminates the other. Both are ways of addressing the question of Israel's strange and subversive hope, and of her call to be YHWH's people at the crucial moment of history.

Which is more likely, then? That Jesus would have taught as a 'sage', but without his wise teaching meshing in any way with the covenantal and 'apocalyptic' hopes of his contemporaries? Or that, like all other Jewish sages known to us, he would have addressed the burning issues of his day, confronting his contemporaries with a choice between wisdom and folly *seen in terms of* the choice between following the prophetic call to covenant renewal and following the merely human way, the way of the world, which would lead to ruin? The overwhelming probability, in the light of all the evidence, is that the second of these is right. 'Jesus the sage' is ultimately a subset of 'Jesus the prophet'; 'Jesus the teacher of wisdom' is one aspect of the Jesus we have been studying in the present chapter, the Jesus who challenged his contemporaries to a new way of being Israel, and summoned them to follow him in this way.

---

[262] 1QS 4.18–23 (Vermes 1995 [1962], 74f; cf. GM 7).

A fairly clear example of this whole sequence of thought – chosen almost at random out of many possibilities – is the parable of the wise and foolish maidens (Matthew 25.1–13). Here we find exactly that contrast of wisdom and folly, suitably personified, which goes back to such early forms of the wisdom tradition as the book of Proverbs, and which is re-expressed in 1QS and elsewhere. But the context of the whole passage is of course Jesus' announcement of the coming kingdom, in other words, his apocalyptic eschatology. What matters is this. Jesus was urging his followers to grasp, or perhaps to be grasped by, the true wisdom, since only those who did so would be ready for the great day which was coming, the day of judgment and vindication. Such other antitheses as the houses built on rock and sand made the same point. There were two ways (as in the traditional wisdom teaching); but the two ways led to two radically different results for Israel (as in regular apocalyptic eschatology).

Perhaps the summit of Jesus' subversive wisdom, cutting against the prevailing conventional wisdom at every point, was the challenge which, as so often, came in the form of a narrative about himself and those who followed him:

> If any want to become my followers, let them deny themselves and take up their cross and follow me. For those who want to save their life will lose it, and those who lose their life for my sake, and for the sake of the gospel, will save it. For what will it profit them to gain the whole world and forfeit their life? Indeed, what can they give in return for their life?[263]

This is as cryptic a riddle, as arcane an aphorism, as any found on Jesus' lips. Yet, in context, *it demands to be understood as part of a narrative*. It articulates, very sharply, one part of a controlling story. It is the story of how the strange purposes of Israel's god were at last to be fulfilled, and of how (as in 1QS!) anyone who wanted to belong to the community of the new covenant, during the continuing dominion of Satan, might do so. And, within that, it clearly states the choice that faced Jesus' hearers. There was the way of wisdom and the way of folly. Conventional wisdom said, of course, that the way of the Messiah would be the way of fulfilment and self-aggrandizement: those who wanted to gain their lives would have to fight for them, and the devil take the hindmost. Jesus' most subversive teaching, in both form and content, consisted in just this: that the way of wisdom meant taking up the cross, dying in order to live.

So, as Ben Witherington has rightly argued, the wisdom sayings were 'very likely grounded in Jesus' conviction that God's eschatological reign was breaking into the midst of Israel through his ministry'. Jesus' message

---

[263] Mk. 8.34–7/Mt. 16.24–6/Lk. 9.23–5; cp. *Thom.* 55.2.

'involved telling of the Good News of the inbreaking Dominion of God, using various forms of Wisdom speech specifically and especially aphorisms and narrative *meshalim*'.[264] Jesus was, in short, 'a sage who expressed his eschatological convictions in Wisdom forms'; his was 'a Wisdom tempered, indeed molded, by his eschatological convictions'.[265] Seen from the perspective of the Jewish traditions to which Jesus fell heir, the attempt to make him a sage *and therefore not concerned with the coming of the kingdom* is exposed as simply another lame attempt to get off the hook of an unwelcome theology, and perhaps an unwelcome praxis.

To the extent that the current fashion for 'Jesus the sage' is also an attempt to show how deeply subversive his message was, we must reply that nothing could have been more subversive than the apocalyptic message of the kingdom which Jesus articulated, and the invitation, welcome, challenge and summons which went along with it. This message subverted, of course, the normal power-structures of the world, the Herods, Pilates and Caiaphases of the day, and the Caesars who stood behind them. That is what all kingdom-announcements did, and do. It also subverted the kingdom-announcements of other alternative would-be prophets and messiahs. Jesus' way of revolt was radically different from the others on offer. Furthermore, in case there should be any doubt, Jesus' message would also have subverted any ahistorical and merely aphoristic wisdom teaching that might (or might not) have been found in the Galilee of his day. For him, what mattered was the story: the story of Israel's god and his dealings with Israel and the world, and the story of how that larger story was reaching its climax in his own work. In the most radical way imaginable, Jesus thus presented himself and his message as a story about an alternative order of reality that, he believed, was being accomplished through his work. And his telling of that story was designed to invite his hearers to give up their controlling metanarratives and trust him for his. Or, in the more usual language with which this chapter began, he told them to repent and believe in him.

8. Conclusion: The Renewed People of God

The story Jesus was telling, the story of the kingdom, was Israel's story. He intended those who responded to him to see themselves as the true, restored Israel. This, as we have seen, puts Jesus on the same map as a good many other people roughly contemporary with him, and we are on historically firm ground in predicating all this of him. But we must therefore allow for his

---

[264] Witherington 1994, 172, 180f.
[265] Witherington 183, 200f.

giving to his followers a way of life which would characterize them *as* his followers. If we rule out this whole sphere of Jesus' teaching as unhistorical, on the grounds that 'Jesus did not intend to found a church', we are quite simply failing to think historically. If, conversely, we treat this aspect of the kingdom-story as merely a timeless ethic, we are bound to misunderstand it, not least by ignoring its eschatological dimension. If, again, we think that Jesus, in his 'eschatological' teaching, expected the end of the space-time world, the whole point of his detailed instructions is lost. Jesus' kingdom-story was about a very different sort of eschatological fulfilment, one that was in fact far more consonant with other first-century Jewish expectations, and one which generated quite naturally and appropriately a set of community rules for those who were prepared to make the story their own.

To tell such a story was of course threatening to a good many within Israel itself. Since there was no realistic chance of all Israel responding to Jesus' radical challenge, one of two results was bound to follow: either Jesus' movement would fizzle out as a damp squib, or there would be confrontation. Jesus seems never to have contemplated the former, and always to have expected the latter. Three things follow from this, which we shall study in successive chapters.

First, Jesus consistently and continually warned his contemporaries that unless Israel repented – in the sense we studied above, i.e. gave up her militant confrontation with Rome and followed his radical alternative vision of the kingdom – then her time was up. Wrath would come upon her, in the form not so much of fire and brimstone from heaven as of Roman swords and falling stonework. In particular, Jerusalem herself, and especially the Temple and its hierarchy, had become hopelessly corrupt, and was as ripe for judgment as it had been in the days of Jeremiah. In this coming judgment the true people of YHWH – that is, Jesus' followers – would be vindicated. This is the theme of chapter 8.

Second, Jesus' vision of an alternative Israel as, in the first instance, a network of cells loyal to him and his kingdom-vision, was bound to come into conflict with other first-century visions of the kingdom. His communities were not to be content to stay in comparative secrecy, like the Essenes, nor yet to work from within the system, like the Pharisees. Had they met any Essenes, they would certainly have clashed with them, but there is no evidence of such a meeting. It was inevitable, though, that they would meet Pharisees, during Jesus' lifetime as much as subsequently; and, equally inevitably, when they did so there would be conflict, not simply over niceties of religion, cult or morals, but over the kingdom itself. And when Jesus and his followers finally confronted the Temple system itself, the battle would be well and truly joined. We shall study Jesus' clash with his rivals in chapter 9.

Third, although Jesus did intend what we have called a social revolution, in that he called people to be loyal to him in their towns and villages, and some in particular to leave all and follow him, there is never a sense that this challenge and summons constituted the be-all and end-all of his agenda and programme. The movement was going somewhere, physically and theologically: physically, to Jerusalem; theologically, to establish the kingdom. This raises the question: what precisely was Jesus' answer to the crucial third and fourth worldview questions? What, in his view, was wrong with Israel and the world, and what was the solution? This will be the subject of chapter 10, which will lead into Part III of the book.

What, then, was the immediate result of Jesus' kingdom-story – his invitation, welcome, challenge and summons? Anticipating for a moment some discussions yet to come, we may answer as follows. Jesus, during his ministry, had a following, but a deeply ambiguous one. The 'twelve', and quite a number of others, continued to follow him, and tried, with more or less muddle, uncertainty and failure, to put what he said into practice. Some at least did leave all and follow him, but their motives, as became apparent, were some way off from what Jesus had had in mind. For all he called them by Israel-titles, they evinced the ambiguity of the old Israel as well as the zeal of the new. At the last, even those who had followed him were not on hand to help as he underwent Israel's vocation alone.

But Jesus' new way of being Israel, paradoxically, was thereby vindicated, not nullified. Since his target was always greater than a mere social reform within Israel – since what he had in mind was the fulfilment of YHWH's purposes, which were not only for Israel but, through Israel, for the world – it was actually within his intention that his followers, having failed to heed the summons during his lifetime, would return to it again afterwards, and reuse his teaching, his challenge to Israel, as the basis for their self-understanding as the renewed community of YHWH's people. In the meantime, we must conclude that Jesus knew that his followers would be muddled and ambiguous, just as he knew that the nation as a whole would not repent. Both of these beliefs belonged with his awareness that what he had to do for Israel had ultimately to be done by himself alone.

But this is to run several chapters ahead of ourselves. We must postpone consideration of other questions, too, which are raised clearly enough by the present chapter, especially questions of christology (Who is this, whom to follow is to obey Israel's god, even if he seems to abrogate Torah? Who is this, belonging to whom is to belong to the true Israel? Who is this, who sovereignly administers forgiveness, who offers the new hearts that his message requires, who ends up following perfectly the summons he had issued to the others, even when they could not follow it themselves?). Before we can get to any of these issues, we must look nearer at hand, to the third major feature of Jesus' kingdom-story. If the kingdom is at hand, those who reject it will incur judgment. In and through this judgment, those who have accepted the kingdom will find their vindication.

Chapter Eight

STORIES OF THE KINGDOM (3): JUDGMENT AND VINDICATION

1. Introduction

> Jesus believed that Israel was called by God to be the agent of his purpose, and that he himself had been sent to bring about that reformation without which Israel could not fulfil her national destiny. If the nation, so far from accepting that calling, rejected God's messenger and persecuted those who responded to his preaching, how could the assertion of God's sovereignty fail to include an open demonstration that Jesus was right and the nation was wrong? How could it fail to include the vindication of the persecuted and the cause they lived and died for?[1]

If Jesus was telling a story anything like that which we have outlined so far, he must have had some idea of where it was all going to end. No one tells a new version of a story without a sense of what the new ending might be. The retellings of Jewish stories which we find in, for instance, the Psalms, the Qumran texts, the Maccabaean literature and Josephus all have a sense that the story is going somewhere; there is an end in view.

When we examine Jesus' proclamation with this in mind, two clear lines emerge. First, there are warnings of impending national disaster: a coming political, military and social nightmare, as a result of which Jerusalem will be destroyed. Second, there are assurances that those who follow Jesus will escape; they are challenged to be ready to do so at the opportune moment. These two – which we will look at separately in a moment – come together with a rush in the great passage in Mark 13 and its parallels, which must be studied as a whole. This will complete our examination of Jesus' mindset from the angle of 'story', and will lead us into the further question of the symbols of the kingdom.

The reading I am proposing of this strand within the gospel tradition is of course controversial. (a) Passages about impending judgment have regularly been seen as predictions of the end of the space-time universe. Jews of Jesus' day are supposed to have believed that the created world was about to come to an end; Jesus is supposed to have shared this belief. I shall here restate and

---

[1] Caird 1965, 20f. (= Caird & Hurst 1994, 365f.).

develop my argument against this reading. (b) Alternatively, such passages have sometimes been denied to Jesus on the grounds that he was not an 'apocalyptic' thinker of this sort; they are then accredited to the early church. I have already dealt fairly thoroughly with this problem in chapter 2. (c) Similarly, passages about the vindication of Jesus and his people have routinely been treated as later constructions of the church, on the grounds that Jesus did not envisage either his own resurrection or a community of people loyal to himself. This has been examined and found wanting in chapter 7: we can be virtually certain that Jesus, like other leadership prophets of the first century, thought of his followers as the true people of Israel, who would survive the coming moment of crisis and form the renewed people of the covenant god. (d) The idea that Jesus warned his contemporaries, and the city of Jerusalem, of impending judgment has sometimes been rejected as making Jesus somehow anti-Jewish. We shall discuss this presently.

The standard views about impending judgment can now, I think, be addressed in an historically responsible fashion. In *NTPG* I argued in detail that

> Within the mainline Jewish writings of this period, covering a wide range of styles, genres, political persuasions and theological perspectives, *there is virtually no evidence that Jews were expecting the end of the space-time universe.* There is abundant evidence that they . . . knew a good metaphor when they saw one, and used cosmic imagery to bring out the full theological significance of cataclysmic socio-political events. There is almost nothing to suggest that they followed the Stoics into the belief that the world itself would come to an end; and there is almost everything . . . to suggest that they did not.[2]

If this is so, the time is indeed ripe for a complete reassessment of the many passages in the gospels which have been read as evidence that either Jesus or the early church expected the end of the world. If Jesus and the early church used the relevant language in the same way as their contemporaries, it is highly unlikely that they would have been referring to the actual end of the world, and highly likely that they would have been referring to events within space-time history which they interpreted as the coming of the kingdom.

It will not do to dismiss this reading of 'apocalyptic' language as 'merely metaphorical'. Metaphors have teeth; the complex metaphors available to first-century Jews had particularly sharp ones, and they could be, and apparently were, reapplied to a variety of scenarios, all within this-worldly

---

[2] *NTPG* 333, in the immediate context of 331–4 and the wider context of ch. 10 as a whole. To the list of sources there in favour of the position advanced should be added Horsley 1987, 138f., 337; and (cited by Horsley) Wilder 1959. Among many passages which could be cited, the three which Allison 1985, 89 quotes, against the drift of his own argument (on which see above, 209 n. 38, and the next note, below), will do for a start: *Ps.-Philo* 11.3–5; 4 Ezra 3.18–19; and bZeb. 116a.

history. I have argued elsewhere that the early Christians reused the language of Jewish apocalyptic eschatology to describe, and hence to interpret, the events of Jesus' death and resurrection and the sending of the divine spirit. In doing so, they expressed their belief that the decisive 'end' for which Israel had longed *had already happened*, and that the consummation for which they still waited was simply the final outworking of that now-past event.[3] I now wish to suggest that the early Christians thought like this not least because Jesus himself had done so. He referred to events within the lifetime of his contemporaries, events which related closely to his own work, in language which invested those events with the significance that, in them, YHWH was indeed becoming king. It is this proposal that I now wish to state in some detail.[4]

2. The Coming Great Disaster

(i) Introduction

We begin with some further words about the message of judgment. The story Jesus told is often thought of as an invitation to experience the joys of the coming salvation, with notes of judgment screened out. Some have even suggested that Jesus believed John the Baptist to have said quite enough about coming judgment, so that he felt it unnecessary to add any words of his own on the subject, even though he did in fact agree with what John had been saying.[5] In fact, when we read through the synoptic tradition (and John, for that matter) we find a great deal of warnings of coming judgment, in all

---

[3] cf. *NTPG* 459–64. The attempt by Allison 1985, 84–90 to argue against this position, as articulated by George Caird, boils down to (a) a simple reassertion of the contrary view (87–9) and (b) a somewhat flat-footed misunderstanding of Caird's argument (88–9). Meyer 1992a, 56, professing to agree with Allison in rejecting a 'metaphorical' reading of Jesus' eschatology, nevertheless uses the category of 'symbol' in a way which corresponds closely to what Caird at least meant by 'metaphor': 'All prophecy speaks in the idiom of symbol. There is an irreducible disparity between this idiom and the actuality of events.' Caird in several places (esp. 1980, Part II) protests against the reduction of 'metaphor' to 'mere metaphor' which Allison and Meyer seem to ascribe to him; and cf. below, 341.

[4] My proposal has some affinities with those of Glasson 1963 [1945] and Robinson 1979 [1957]; many of the details, however, and some of the shape, is worked out quite differently. Recent important discussions include Aune 1992b; Witherington 1992. As with many sections of the present book, it is impossible here to enter into as much detailed debate as these and other works really deserve.

[5] So Riches 1980, 106, 168; more cautiously, Sanders 1985, 115: the message of judgment is not a warning to Israel, but rather Jesus' message to the disciples about the role they were going to play (Mt. 19.28).

strands of the traditions, and all pointing in one direction.[6] Jesus, I shall now argue, predicted that judgment would fall on the nation in general and on Jerusalem in particular. That is to say, he reinterprets a standard Jewish belief (the coming judgment which would fall on the nations) in terms of a coming judgment which would fall on impenitent *Israel*. The great prophets had done exactly the same.[7] Jerusalem, under its present regime, had become Babylon. The evangelists stressed the theme of judgment on present Israel,[8] but they certainly did not invent it. Jesus seems to have adopted the theme from John, who predicted 'wrath to come',[9] saying that membership in physical Israel was no guarantee of a share in the age to come. Very much in the mould of Amos, or indeed of Qumran, John insisted on redrawing the boundaries of Israel; for him, only those who repented and submitted to baptism would be included. The story Jesus told about Israel's immediate future seems to have developed directly from this point.[10]

The next comment ought to be unnecessary, but misunderstanding has been so long-lasting here that perhaps it is as well to be clear. The warnings already mentioned, and those about to be discussed, are manifestly and obviously, within their historical context, warnings about a coming national disaster, involving the destruction by Rome of the nation, the city and the Temple. The story of judgment and vindication which Jesus told is very much like the story told by the prophet Jeremiah, invoking the categories of cosmic disaster in order to invest the coming socio-political disaster with its full theological significance.[11] The 'normal' way of reading these passages within the Christian tradition has been to see them as references to a general *post mortem* judgment in hell; but this betrays a fairly thorough lack of historical understanding. Jesus' sayings may have wider implications. That is a topic outside the scope of the present book. But as historians we are bound to read at least the passages discussed in this chapter as warnings about a coming national disaster.[12]

Jesus' warnings thus take on a quadruple character within the context of his times. First, they fit quite naturally into the wider context of the Jewish

[6] These are listed briefly above, 183f.

[7] e.g. Isa. 1.10, likening Jerusalem to Sodom and Gomorrah. Need I add that this is not 'anti-Jewish', but the typical prophetic call to Israel to be faithful to her god?

[8] e.g. the slaughter of the innocents in Mt. 2.6-18, quoting Jer. 31.13; the fall and rise of many in Israel, Lk. 2.34.

[9] Mt. 3.7-10/Lk. 3.7-9.

[10] On all this, cf. Borg 1984, 201-27, 265-76; on Jesus and John, 269n.

[11] Jer. 4.23-8; cf. *NTPG* 298f.

[12] cf. Caird & Hurst 1994, 361: 'The disciples were not evangelistic preachers sent out to save individual souls for some unearthly paradise. They were couriers proclaiming a national emergency and conducting a referendum on a question of national survival.'

sectarianism of the day. To pronounce judgment on the present regime was not unusual; nor, it must be stressed, was it in the slightest degree a sign that one was being 'anti-Jewish'.[13] On the contrary, it was a sign of deep loyalty to Israel's true god and true vocation, and of deep distress at the corruption which seemed endemic in the national life. Of course, the possibility of false prophecy was always present. Some declared 'peace, peace' when there was no peace; some, perhaps, declared 'war, war' when there was no war. But prophecy demands to be tested by events; and that is the burden of the present discussion. For the moment, we note that Jesus' solemn announcements were completely in place within the world of first-century *inner-Jewish* polemic.

Second, Jesus' warnings fit also quite naturally into the wider context of the first century, where Rome, provoked before, remained a threatening, brooding presence.[14] The troubles of 4 BC and AD 6 remained in the powerful recent folk memory; Pilate's administration was given to sporadic bloody repression; it did not take much political wisdom to extrapolate forwards and to suggest that, if Israel continued to provoke the giant, the giant would eventually awake from slumber and smash her to pieces. Josephus came to the same conclusion thirty or so years later, which was why he issued his call to the Galilean brigands to 'repent' and to trust him instead, and why, eventually, he told a story of Israel's god going over to the Romans, so that her emperor, acclaimed in Judaea, would be the 'world ruler' predicted by Daniel. I suggest that Jesus of Nazareth proposed a change in the traditional story which in some ways, though not all, was parallel to this. The story he told was one in which Israel's intransigence led to judgment: to the judgment of angry imperial Rome, provoked once too often; and at the same time to the judgment of Israel's own god, returning to his people at last only to discover that they had been untrue to their vocation. And, instead of a reinterpretation of the Danielic story in which Vespasian would become world ruler, Jesus offered his own new twist: he himself, and his people, would be vindicated when Jerusalem, having rejected his message of peace, chose war and suffered the consequences. Jesus' warnings belong perfectly within the context of Palestine under threatening and heavy-handed Roman rule.

Third, it appears that though such warnings, echoing as they did a centuries-long prophetic tradition, could in principle have been articulated at any time in Israel's history, Jesus' own warnings carried a constant reference to the present generation. We shall enquire into the reasons for this later on. For the moment we must note that Jesus seems to have stressed 'the signs of the times': the story he was telling was not about some general or abstract

---

[13] cf. the exchange between Ahab and Elijah in 1 Kgs. 18.17f.
[14] For this paragraph, cf. *NTPG* chs. 6, 7.

truth, of which the present moment just happened to be one example. His message was specifically directed to that very moment in Israel's history.[15]

Fourth, Jesus' warnings, read in this way, cut against several strands within the complex and pluriform Judaism of the time. Most obviously, they warned, as Josephus was to do later, against violent revolution. Since revolution was part of the stricter Pharisaic agenda, he was also warning his contemporaries against them.[16] Since the chief priests controlled the Temple, which became for many in Jesus' day, as in Jeremiah's, a symbol of national inviolability, and which he, like Jeremiah, attacked as such, his warnings would provoke them as well, especially when the words were accompanied by actions. It is difficult to know how many 'ordinary Jews' of the time attached themselves to any of these agendas, but the evidence of the gospels on the one hand, and of Josephus on the other, indicates that Jesus' message was not, at this point, one that the majority of his contemporaries were particularly disposed to hear.

Putting together these four elements of Jesus' warnings, we find a classic prophetic profile, a classic example of critique from within. Israel's story is retold so as to reach a devastating climax, in which the present Jerusalem regime will be judged, and the prophet and his followers vindicated. The covenant god will use the pagan forces to execute his judgment on his people, and a new people will be born, formed around the prophet himself. This, no doubt, is part of the reason why the prophecy is specifically for the present generation: the prophet himself, and his immediate followers, bring the last word from the covenant god. In fact, this sense that the present phase of the story has reached its last page has to do not only with the extreme nature of the present crisis, but also precisely with the identity of the prophet as the bearer of the last word.

One further comment before we launch into the texts. I take it as read that apocalyptic language, including language derived from Daniel 7, would quite readily be understood in the first century as a retelling of Israel's national story, climaxing in the judgment of Israel's true enemies and the vindication of Israel's true representative(s).[17] This means that the warnings which utilize such language are not to be siphoned off as dealing only with some far-off future 'final judgment' in the sense of the end of the space-time universe.[18] Warnings of this sort are, on the contrary, exactly what we might expect on the lips of a prophet such as we have seen Jesus to be. The relevant texts may

---

[15] cf. Mt. 16.2-3/Lk. 12.54-6. The eschatological note is, predictably, muted in the parallel in *Thom.* 91.

[16] cf. *NTPG* 185-203; and below, ch. 9.

[17] cf. *NTPG* ch. 10, esp. 291-7.

[18] cf. Caird & Hurst 1994, 361f., against Kümmel.

briefly be set out as follows, leaving those in Mark 13 and its parallels to a separate section.[19]

(ii) John the Baptist

We may begin with the sayings attributed to John, since it is in fact highly likely that Jesus continued his practice of warning-oracles. We find John alerting his contemporaries about coming wrath:

> John said to [the Pharisees and Sadducees], 'You brood of vipers! Who warned you to flee from the wrath to come? Bear fruit that befits repentance, and do not presume to say to yourselves, "We have Abraham as our father"; for I tell you, God is able from these stones to raise up children to Abraham. Even now the axe is laid to the root of the trees; every tree therefore that does not bear good fruit is cut down and thrown into the fire.'[20]

Pointing towards the one who was to come, John designated him as a bringer of judgment:

> His winnowing fork is in his hand, and he will clear his threshing floor and gather his wheat into the granary, but the chaff he will burn with unquenchable fire.[21]

These warnings are to be taken in a thoroughly historical sense. Just as the wrath of YHWH, within the Hebrew scriptures, consisted as often as not of military conquest and consequent social disaster,[22] so we may assume that John's hearers would have heard, and John would have intended, a reference to a great national disaster, to be interpreted as the judgment of the covenant god.

(iii) General Warnings of Judgment on Israel

Jesus' message, so far from omitting or toning down the warning of judgment, seems from a wide variety of texts to have emphasized it continually. We might have guessed as much from the traditions which report on his public image: he was likened not only to John the Baptist but to Elijah and

[19] Borg 1984, 266–76 lists the threat/warrant tradition, but to my mind splits it up unnecessarily: he continues to read 'son of man', and sayings including that phrase, in the way now traditional among certain branches of scholarship, and therefore denies such sayings to Jesus (221–7). Cf. too Borg 1987c; 1994a chs. 3, 4.

[20] Mt. 3.7–10/Lk. 3.7–9. For parallels in the teaching of Jesus, cf. esp. Lk. 13.6–9, and the story of the fig tree in Mt. 21.18–22 and pars.

[21] Mt. 3.12/Lk. 3.17. For the idea of fire in the warnings of Jesus, cf. e.g. Mt. 5.22; 7.19; 13.40, 42, 50; 18.8f.(/Mk. 9.43); 25.41; Mk. 9.48f.; Lk. 12.49; cf. Jn. 15.6.

[22] e.g. 2 Chr. 36.16f.

Jeremiah, a conclusion that the early church, with its very different identification of Jesus, would hardly have invented.[23] Once we see Jesus in this light, a great many sayings come together and make sense:

> Unless your righteousness exceeds that of the scribes and Pharisees, you will never enter the kingdom of heaven.[24]

Jesus, in other words, was announcing that Israel's god was establishing his kingdom in a way which would leave the self-appointed guardians of Israel's tradition outside. Israel was being redefined; to be outside that company when the true god acted would mean total ruin. In that situation, Israel had better settle accounts quickly, before she was handed over to judgment:

> Make friends quickly with your accuser, while you are going with him to court, lest your accuser hand you over to the judge, and the judge to the guard, and you be put in prison; truly, I say to you, you will never get out till you have paid the last penny.[25]

This was no mere prudential moralism, advising individuals on how to escape debt and jail. Its thrust was against the nation as a whole. If they did not learn the new way of being the people of god, it would soon be too late:

> If you do not forgive people their trespasses, neither will your father forgive your trespasses.[26]

There was a different way, a way of peace, to which Jesus was summoning Israel, and those who refused it would find no victory, but instead ruin:

> Those who take the sword will perish by the sword.[27]

The way that Jesus was beckoning would pass through a narrow gate, and many who thought they were inalienably within the people of god would be proved wrong:

> Enter by the narrow gate; for the gate is wide and the way is easy, that leads to destruction, and those who enter by it are many. For the gate is narrow and the way is hard, that leads to life, and those who find it are few.[28]

Or, changing the metaphor, only the trees that bear good fruit would escape devastation:

---

[23] Mt. 16.14/Mk. 8.28/Lk. 9.19.

[24] Mt. 5.20.

[25] Mt. 5.25-6/Lk. 12.58-9.

[26] Mt. 6.15; cf. Mt. 18.35; Mk. 11.25. Cp. too Mt. 22.11-14, and the fuller discussion at 268-74 above.

[27] Mt. 26.52.

[28] Mt. 7.13-14; cf. Lk. 13.24.

Every tree that does not bear good fruit is cut down and thrown into the fire.[29]

In that context, those who thought they were the people of Abraham might find out that they were not:

I tell you, many will come from east and west and sit at table with Abraham, Isaac and Jacob in the kingdom of heaven, while the sons of the kingdom will be thrown into the outer darkness; there men will weep and gnash their teeth.[30]

The same theme emerges powerfully from the parables.[31] The seed was growing in secret, and when it was ripe the sickle would be put in, because the time of harvest had arrived.[32] The weeds would be gathered by the angels at the close of the present age, and bound and burned.[33] The net would drag in fish of every kind, which would then be separated.[34] Those who refused the invitation would be like murderers who killed the messengers sent to them with invitations to a wedding feast: the king would send his troops and deal severely with them.[35] At the banquet, those who insisted on the best seats would be humiliated; those who refused the invitation would be replaced with others; those who were not ready, or worthy, would be excluded.[36] When the king came to his people, those who failed to do his bidding would incur judgment.[37] The parable of the wicked tenants sums up this, as so much else: the present hierarchy had decided to try to keep the vineyard for themselves, but it was now to be given to others. Their rejection of Jesus meant that now they would not only not be the heirs, they would not be tenants either. Those who rejected the heaven-sent messengers would find the kingdom of god taken away from them and apportioned elsewhere; the stone which had been rejected would become the head of the corner.[38] Israel's regular stock of imagery, used traditionally to assert that when her god acted she, Israel, would be vindicated while the pagan nations received their just deserts, is here reused by the prophet from Nazareth to say: when Israel's god acts, it will be upon Israel herself that the judgment will fall.

---

[29] Mt. 7.19. On the image of the 'good and bad trees' in general cp. e.g. Mt. 12.33-7/Lk. 6.43-5; Lk. 13.6-9.

[30] Mt. 8.11-12/Lk. 13.28-9 (in a different context).

[31] cf. above, 230-43.

[32] Mk. 4.26-9, cf. *Thom.* 21.4f.

[33] Mt. 13.24-30, 36-43.

[34] Mt. 13.47-50; adjusted in *Thom.* 8.

[35] Mt. 22.7; missing from the parallels in Lk. and *Thom.*

[36] Mt. 22.1-14; 25.1-13, cf. Mk. 13.35-7; Lk. 12.35-6; 13.24-30; 14.7-11; 14.15-24; *Did.* 16.1; *Thom.* 64.

[37] Mt. 25.14-30/Lk. 19.11-27; cf. below, 632-9.

[38] Mt. 21.41-3/Mk. 12.9-11/Lk. 20.16-18. The saying about the coming judgment is missing from the par. in *Thom.* 65; *Thom.* 66, however, includes the saying about the rejected corner-stone.

Why does she look at the speck in her neighbour's eye, when there is a plank in her own?[39] If she is blind herself, how can she be the light of the world?[40] If the light in her is darkness, how great that darkness is.[41]

Israel's boundaries were thus radically redrawn by Jesus, so as to include those who 'repented' according to his own redefinition, but to exclude those who did not:

> John came to you in the way of righteousness, and you did not believe him, but the tax collectors and the harlots believed him; and even when you saw it, you did not afterward repent and believe him.[42]

Throughout the teaching, story-telling and career of Jesus, this message rang out again and again, in word and deed. Israel was being redefined; and those who failed to heed Jesus' warnings would discover themselves in the position that they had thought was reserved for the pagans.

(iv) Warnings of Imminent Judgment on 'This Generation'

The general warning is frequently made more specific: the moment in question will arrive within the next generation. Jesus' commission to the disciples, as they engage in their own work of announcing the kingdom, included severe warnings on any who rejected the message:

> If anyone will not receive you or listen to your words, shake off the dust from your feet as you leave that house or town. Truly, I say to you, it shall be more tolerable on the day of judgment for the land of Sodom and Gomorrah than for that town.[43]

Once again, this was not a prediction of a non-spatio-temporal 'last judgment'. It was a straightforward warning of what would happen if this or that Galilean village refused the way of peace which Jesus had come to bring. This was amplified in the words of woe uttered over Chorazin, Bethsaida, and even Jesus' own adopted home town of Capernaum. Judgment would fall upon them which would make the judgment of Tyre, Sidon and Sodom seem mild by comparison.[44] The horrifying thing was that Jesus was using, as models for the coming judgment on villages within Israel, images of judgment taken straight from the Old Testament, where they had to do with the

---

[39] Mt. 7.1–5/Lk. 6.39–42/*Thom.* 26/*P. Oxy. 1.1.*

[40] Mt. 15.14/Lk. 6.39/*Thom.* 34.

[41] Lk. 11.33–6, cf. Mt. 5.14–16/Mk. 4.21–3/Lk. 8.16f./*Thom.* ?4; 33/*Dial. Sav.* 8/*P. Oxy. 655.24.*

[42] Mt. 21.32.

[43] Mt. 10.14–15/Lk. 10.11–12, cf. Mk. 6.11.

[44] Mt. 11.20–4/Lk. 10.13–15.

divine judgment *on the pagan nations* (Tyre, Sidon, Sodom – and Nineveh; though Nineveh escaped the judgment, because she repented).[45] Jesus had offered these Galilean towns the way of peace. By following him, they would find the god-given golden thread to guide them through the dark labyrinth of current political aspirations and machinations, and on to vindication as the true people of the creator and covenant god. If they refused, they were choosing the way that led, inevitably, to confrontation with Rome, and so to unavoidable ruin.

The catalogue of judgment upon the scribes and Pharisees, as it appears in the material common to Matthew and Luke, concludes with a further warning that is specific to 'this generation':

> Fill up, then, the measure of your fathers. You serpents, you brood of vipers, how are you to escape being sentenced to Gehenna? Therefore I send you prophets and wise men and scribes, some of whom you will kill and crucify, and some you will scourge in your synagogues and persecute from town to town, that upon you may come all the righteous blood shed on earth, from the blood of innocent Abel to the blood of Zechariah the son of Barachiah, whom you murdered between the sanctuary and the altar. Truly, I say to you, all this will come upon this generation.[46]

Faced with this prospect, it would be better to abandon that which was most cherished rather than to go straight ahead into the conflagration:

> If your hand causes you to sin, cut it off; it is better for you to enter life maimed than with two hands to go to Gehenna, to the unquenchable fire. And if your foot causes you to sin, cut it off; it is better for you to enter life lame than with two feet to be thrown into Gehenna. And if your eye causes you to sin, pluck it out; it is better for you to enter the kingdom of god with one eye than with two eyes to be thrown into Gehenna, where their worm does not die, and the fire is not quenched. For every one will be salted with fire.[47]

The judgment was coming upon 'this generation', now caught in the act of rejecting the final messenger who had been sent to call it back to obedience.[48]

This theme of judgment upon the present generation can be seen to particularly striking effect in the long sequence from chapters 11 to 19 of Luke's gospel, with much of the material of course being paralleled in one or both of the other synoptics. Quite a bit of this sequence covers material we have already examined in detail, so we need only run through it in outline to capture the effect. Though the sequence and ordering are of course Luke's, the emerging historical hypothesis suggests strongly that this was indeed the sort of thing that Jesus regularly said, the devastating story he habitually told.

[45] Mt. 12.38–9, 41 and pars.; cf. Caird & Hurst 1994, 363f.
[46] Mt. 23.32–6/Lk. 11.45–52.
[47] Mk. 9.43–9, cf. Mt. 5.29–30; 18.8–9.
[48] Mt. 21.33–46/Mk. 12.1–12/Lk. 20.9–19.

The demons will return, and the last state of the house will be worse than the first (11.24-6). The generation that seeks a sign is rewarded only with the sign of Jonah, which will be enough to condemn them (11.29-32). If the light that is in you is darkness, the darkness is great indeed (11.33-6). Woe is called down on the heads of the Pharisees, because they are so concerned with ritual purity that they cannot see the huge disease that is growing within Israel (11.37-54).[49] The blood of all the righteous, and the prophets, will be required from this generation (11.51). Israel has reason to fear the one who can not only kill but cast into Gehenna (12.4-5). Those who acknowledge Jesus will be vindicated, but those who refuse will be cast out (12.8-9). Israel is like a rich fool, storing up investment in land and property when her world is about to collapse around her (12.13-21). The master of the house is coming, and servants who are unready for him will be 'put with the unfaithful' (12.35-46); those who are actively disobedient will be punished according to the severity of their offence (12.47-8). From now on there will be division within Israel (12.49-53), while her citizens, not reading the signs of the times, do not recognize that her hour has come (12.54-6). If they did, they would come to terms with their enemies now, rather than risk total ruin (12.57-9).

Luke 13 opens with a double solemn warning. Unless Israel repents of her headlong rush into destruction, she will suffer the same fate as those whom Pilate killed, or who were crushed by the tower of Siloam: in other words, Roman swords and falling masonry will be their fate if they persist in going the way of idolatrous nationalism (13.1-5). The warnings are at once reinforced with a parable: the fig tree had better bear fruit soon, because otherwise it is to be cut down (13.6-9). There is a narrow door; once it is shut there will be no chance to get in, and some who are first will be last, and vice versa (13.22-30). Jerusalem is about to face the equivalent of a devastating farmyard fire, seen from the point of view of the livestock; Jesus has longed to do what mother hens do in such circumstances, but the chicks are refusing to come under his wings. As a result, the Temple is abandoned by its rightful inhabitant, left to its oncoming fate, just as in the prophecies of Ezekiel (13.34-5).[50]

In view of all this, those who exalt themselves will begin with shame to take the lowest place (14.7-11). None of those who were invited will taste

---

[49] The fact that this is a Q passage ought of itself to give pause to those who insist that material of this sort must belong in the period after 70. It is completely arbitrary to force such material into a late hypothetical stratum of Q (cf. e.g. Funk & Hoover 1993, 332, on 11.29-32). In addition, Luke's placing of it in the context of sustained judgment-warnings by Jesus means that it is in no way isolated from the general tenor of his other teaching. We may include here the woe on offenders of little ones: Mt. 8.6-7/Mk. 9.42/Lk. 17.1-2.

[50] Ezek. 10; see Borg 1984, 181ff.

the messianic banquet (14.24). Israel must stop clinging to family identity and ancestral possessions, otherwise she will be like someone building a tower but unable to finish – or, in a warning whose metaphor may be a bit close for comfort, she will be like a king with a small army going to war against someone with a large one (14.25–33). At the moment, the salt of the earth is losing its taste, and when that happens it can only be thrown away (14.34–5). The characteristic phrase 'if you have ears, then hear' (14.35b) is another tell-tale sign that Luke at least understood this saying as a cryptic warning of awful judgment hanging over Israel's head.

The parables of Luke 15 and 16 point in the same direction. The older brother stays out of the party while the prodigal finds himself guest of honour (15.11–32). The steward is about to be put out of his stewardship, and if he knew his business he would be looking around for all the friends he could get while there is time (16.1–9).[51] The five brothers of Dives are worshipping mammon as devoutly as they can (16.10–15), unaware that soon they will join the eldest brother in torment (16.19–31). Israel will experience a time which will be like the days of Noah, or of Sodom (17.22–37). The elect will be vindicated, but there will be few who will be faithful on the day of the son of man (18.1–8). Those who trust in their riches will never enter the kingdom (18.18–30). The citizens who did not want the king to rule over them will be destroyed; the servant who failed to keep his commission will be ruined (19.11–27).

The same theme is reinforced as Jesus goes to the cross. The women who are bewailing Jesus' death should weep for themselves and their children. There will come a time when they will utter a terrible 'beatitude': 'Blessed are the wombs that never bore, and the breasts that never gave suck!' The great blessing of children will be turned into shame; for if they (the Romans) do this when the wood is green, when the condemned one is innocent of violent revolt, what will happen when the wood is dry, when the children at present playing in the streets grow up into a revolutionary force that will pit itself directly against Rome?[52] Jesus, knowing that Israel has now finally rejected the one road of peace, knows also that within the next generation she will find herself embroiled in a war she cannot but lose, and lose horribly. The two *lestai* crucified with him are simply a foretaste of the thousands of *lestai* – brigands, revolutionaries – who will suffer the same fate by the time the next generation is through. Israel's noble but tragic story is fast becoming a nightmare.

These warnings make a catalogue of considerable size and power. Of course, some will say, we are here dealing simply with Lukan theology, not

---

[51] For other interpretations, cf. e.g. Fitzmyer 1985, 1094–1111.
[52] Lk. 23.29–31: see below, 567–70.

at all with Jesus. This objection must be dealt with at two quite different levels. First, it is a basic mistake of method to suppose that because the evangelist, like all writers that ever existed, had reasons for selecting and arranging what was written, the material is therefore non-historical. It was because of this problem that a good part of *NTPG* Part II was necessary as a preliminary to the present volume.[53] Second, we should take careful note of the implication of saying that this whole swathe of Lukan material does not relate to Jesus. We are forced, quite frankly, to say *either* that Luke did not know anything at all about the emphases of Jesus' teaching, the plot of his story, *or* that the ministry of Jesus really did have the warning of imminent national disaster high on the list of its regular themes. No middle ground is really tenable. Two things in particular support the latter alternative: a good many of the sayings just collected occur in some form in other strands of tradition; and the picture we now have before us forms part of an overall hypothesis which, I submit, makes sense historically. These give us good grounds to proceed to the more specific warnings upon which the general category is focused, with a strong assurance that material of this sort is highly likely to go back to Jesus himself.[54]

(v) Warnings of Judgment on Jerusalem and the Temple

The warnings come to a head in Luke 19.39-44, where Jesus, riding down the Mount of Olives, bursts into tears over the beautiful city that comes into view – much the same view that Titus would have, forty years later, as he drew up his legions for the final siege:

> If you, even you, had only recognized on this day the things that make for peace! But now they are hidden from your eyes. Indeed, the days will come upon you, when your enemies will set up ramparts around you and surround you, and hem you in on every side. They will crush you to the ground, you and your children within you, and they will not leave within you one stone upon another; because you did not recognize the time of your visitation from God.[55]

[53] *NTPG* Part II, e.g. 51f.

[54] cf. e.g. Meyer 1992a, 88: the refusal to take the election of all Israel for granted 'was anything but isolated among Jesus' words . . . He consistently affirmed that the maintenance of election in the sight of God hinged on response to the final call of God. That the sanction of this claim would be the coming judgment is a theme copiously attested by the Synoptic tradition.' Cp. Meyer 1992b, 784: the coming judgment is 'a recurrent theme copiously attested by every line of transmission in the gospel literature . . . One should doubtless apply careful historical critique to all these texts; still, there is no plausibility in the view that they are *en bloc* unhistorical.'

[55] On the complex web of OT allusions here, and their making a more plausible background for the passage than the actual siege of Jerusalem in AD 70, see above all Dodd 1968, 74-7. On Titus' position on Mount Scopus, with the 10th legion on the Mount of Olives cf.

This, however, was by no means the first time that Jerusalem and the Temple had featured prominently within Jesus' frequently-told story of judgment.[56] Consider this passage, for example, remembering that, within his culture, the word 'house' could easily evoke the idea of 'Temple', and that the 'rock' or 'stone' would readily be identified as the foundation-stone of that Temple:[57]

> Every one then who hears these words of mine and does them will be like a wise man who built his house upon the rock; and the rain fell, and the floods came, and the winds blew and beat upon that house, but it did not fall, because it had been founded on the rock. And every one who hears these words of mine and does not do them will be like a foolish man who built his house upon the sand; and the rain fell, and the floods came, and the wind blew and beat against that house, and it fell; and great was the fall of it.[58]

Jesus, like some other Jewish sectarians, was inviting his hearers to join him in the establishment of the true Temple. The Jerusalem Temple was under judgment, a judgment that would fall before too long. The demons, as we saw, would return, and the last state of the 'house' would be worse than the first.[59] Falling masonry, as when the tower of Siloam fell, will be the fate of the unrepentant.[60] The 'house' is left, abandoned, desolate, unprotected against enemy attack.[61] It is in this context that Jesus' dramatic action in the Temple makes perfect sense: it was an acted parable of judgment, of destruction. The 'house' had become a den of *lestai*, brigands, and Jesus, like Jeremiah whom he quoted, was declaring divine judgment upon it.[62] The fig tree functions as a visual aid of what was really intended: Mark has made this stand out by dividing the fig-tree narrative into two and placing the Temple action in between, but there is no reason to suppose that this does any more than make explicit what was latent in the tradition, and implicit in Jesus' action itself.[63] The link is reinforced by the saying about 'this mountain' being cast into the sea.[64] The evident proverbial nature of the saying[65] should not disguise the fact that someone speaking of 'this

---

Jos. *War* 5.67-70.

[56] This whole section anticipates, and in part depends on, the fuller treatments of the material in ch. 9 and Part III.

[57] cp. Michel 1967, 120, etc.; Meyer 1979, 185f. Cf. *NTPG* 387 n.59.

[58] Mt. 7.24-7/Lk. 6.46-9.

[59] Mt. 12.43-5/Lk. 11.24-6.

[60] Lk. 13.1-5.

[61] Mt. 23.38/Lk. 13.35.

[62] Mt. 21.13/Mk. 11.17/Lk. 19.46, cf. Jer. 7.11 and, indeed, Jer. 7 as a whole. See esp. Borg 1984, ch. 7, e.g. 174; and cf. below, 419-21.

[63] Mk. 11.12-14, 20-5; cf. Mt. 21.18-22.

[64] Mt. 21.21/Mk. 11.23 cf. Mt. 17.20; *Thom.* 48, 106.

[65] cf. 1 Cor. 13.2.

mountain' being cast into the sea, in the context of a dramatic action of judgment in the Temple, would inevitably be heard to refer to Mount Zion.

The same conclusion is reached by a different route when we consider various sayings which implicitly declare the Temple to be redundant. Jesus declares, quoting Hosea, that what Israel's god desires is 'mercy, not sacrifice'.[66] The same point is implied in Jesus' dialogue with the scribe in Mark 12.28–34: Jesus was inaugurating a way of life which had no further need of the Temple. The fact that Johanan ben Zakkai is supposed to have said similar things after AD 70 is hardly surprising, and should not lead to the conclusion that Jesus could not have used Hosea 6.6 in this way.[67] And, in particular, there is a whole nexus of traditions in which Jesus actually prophesied the destruction quite explicitly, sometimes as a divine act and sometimes, astonishingly, as his own:

> We heard him say, 'I will destroy this temple that is made with hands, and in three days I will build another, not made with hands.'[68]

> Those who passed by derided him, wagging their heads, and saying, 'Aha! You who would destroy the temple and build it in three days, save yourself, and come down from the cross!'[69]

> Jesus answered them, 'Destroy this temple, and in three days I will raise it up.'[70]

> 'We heard [Stephen] say that Jesus of Nazareth will destroy this place and the customs which Moses gave us.'[71]

> Jesus said, 'I shall destroy this house, and no one will be able to rebuild it.'[72]

As we shall see, this remarkable assertion coheres completely with the theme that emerges steadily at the centre of Jesus' story. He was claiming prophetic and messianic authority to pronounce judgment on the Temple. It was for this that he was eventually accused before the authorities. With these sayings we stand, ironically enough, on the rock of history.[73]

[66] Mt. 9.13; 12.7; cf. Hos. 6.6.

[67] cf. *NTPG* 162f.; and below, 427.

[68] Mk. 14.58; Mt. 26.61 is an abbreviated version of the same saying.

[69] Mk. 15.29–30/Mt. 27.39–40.

[70] Jn. 2.19.

[71] Ac. 6.14: *topos* ('place') was a regular way of referring to the Temple. Cf. too Jn. 11.48.

[72] *Thom.* 71. *Thomas*, not surprisingly, does not envisage a rebuilding, either in the literal sense of a rebuilt Temple or in the Pauline sense of the church as the real restored Temple. This reworking is a good indication that the tradition of Jesus speaking against the Temple was very strong; we would not normally expect *Thomas* to concern itself with a Jewish institution in this way.

[73] Ironic not least because the main sayings in the groups are put in the mouths of 'false witnesses' or adversaries. Cf. above all Sanders 1985, *passim*, esp. 71–6.

Jesus, then, pronounced warnings against the nation; warnings against his own generation in particular; and warnings focused on the disaster that would befall Jerusalem and the Temple. All of this I regard as established before we even touch Mark 13 and its parallels. Throughout his public career, Jesus told a story, very much like the implicit narrative of the Scrolls, in which the judgment usually associated with YHWH's action against the pagan nations would fall upon those Jews who were refusing to follow in the way he was holding out to them. None of the sayings I have listed in this brief survey need be attributed, in their essence, anywhere other than to him. They are typically prophetic oracles, issuing, in the name of Israel's god, warnings to his rebellious people. And the judgment which was to come was conceived in classic scriptural terms: invasion and destruction by foreign armies, allowed to do what they are doing because YHWH, having warned his people beyond patience and beyond hope, has deliberately abandoned them to their fate. Assyria and Babylon had been the instruments of YHWH's wrath before; now it would be the turn of Rome.

3. Assurance of Vindication

Would this, then, be the end of the story? Would all that was left of Israel's dreams and aspirations be a heap of rubble, with Jerusalem as a whole turned into a large, smoking extension of Gehenna, her own rubbish-dump? In a sense, yes. In so far as Israel cherished nationalist ambition, it would end up on the fire. Those who took the sword would perish by the sword. But in another, most important, sense, no. The whole emphasis of Jesus' announcement of the kingdom was that Israel's god certainly would vindicate his people, his elect who cried to him day and night. If this were not so, the charge that Jesus' proclamation (as we have expounded it) was overthrowing the foundations of all things Jewish might seem, despite everything, to have some weight. This, after all, was the basic hope of Israel: that the enemies of the chosen people would be destroyed, and the chosen themselves vindicated. Jesus seems to have been reaffirming, even though radically redrawing, this expectation. How would this happen? What form would it take? How would the story proceed to its resolution?

The constant emphasis that we find here is that those who had followed Jesus (and, by implication, those who would follow his way in the future) would escape the great coming disaster, and would themselves receive the vindication that had been promised to Israel. They would be the ones who would inherit the promise, who would experience the real release from exile.

Here again there is a great concatenation of passages, at which we may simply glance to sense the shape and content of the hope.

The main point is expressed in the traditions which, in classic apocalyptic language, emphasize that those who followed Jesus would eventually be acknowledged as his true people:

> So every one who acknowledges me publicly, I also will acknowledge before my father who is in heaven; but whoever denies me publicly, I also will deny before my father who is in heaven.[74]

> Then Jesus told his disciples, 'If any one would come after me, let him deny himself and take up his cross and follow me. For whoever would save his life will lose it, and whoever loses his life for my sake will find it. For what will it profit someone, to gain the whole world and forfeit his life? Or what shall one give in return for his life? For the son of man is to come with his angels in the glory of his Father, and then he will repay every one for what he has done.'[75]

The truth will out: at the moment, no one looking at Jesus' followers would realize that they were to be vindicated as the people of the covenant god, but one day it would be manifest:

> So have no fear of them; for nothing is covered that will not be revealed, or hidden that will not be known. What I tell you in the dark, utter in the light; and what you hear whispered, proclaim upon the housetops.[76]

> For there is nothing hid, except to be made manifest; nor is anything secret, except to come to light. If anyone has ears to hear, let them hear.[77]

This vindication could be relied upon utterly: although Jesus' followers might have seemed totally unprotected and at risk in every way, they were to trust the true god for their safety and vindication:

> Are not two sparrows sold for a penny? And not one of them will fall to the ground without your Father's will. But even the hairs of your head are all numbered. Fear not, therefore; you are of more value than many sparrows.[78]

They were therefore to pray that they might not be led into the *peirasmos*, the great time of testing and tribulation which would precede the great deliverance, and that they would be rescued from the *poneros*, the evil one.[79] If they were put on trial, the spirit with which Jesus had been anointed for

---

[74] Mt. 10.32f./Lk. 12.8f. (with 'the son of man' in place of the first 'I', and 'the angels of god' instead of 'my father in heaven'). Cf. also *2 Clem.* 3.2.

[75] Mt. 16.24–8/Mk. 8.34–8/Lk. 9.23–6.

[76] Mt. 10.26f./Lk. 12.2f./*P. Oxy.1.8/Thom.* 33.

[77] Mk. 4.22f./Lk. 8.17/*P. Oxy.654.5/Thom.* 5; 6.

[78] Mt. 10.29–31/Lk. 12.6–7; cf. Mt. 6.26/Lk. 12.24; Lk. 21.18.

[79] Mt. 6.13/Lk. 11.4/*Did.* 8.2; cf. Mt. 26.41/Mk. 14.38/Lk. 22.40.

his task would be with them too, so that they would know what to say.[80] Not only would they be preserved and protected in and through tribulation and persecution; they would be given positions of responsibility, so that in the *palingenesia*, the great time of renewal, they would sit on twelve thrones judging the twelve tribes.[81] Those who had abandoned all in order to follow Jesus would receive back far more than they had lost.[82] Israel's god would speedily vindicate his elect; those who acknowledged Jesus would themselves be acknowledged on the great and terrible day.[83] Finally, if Jesus had pronounced judgment on the Temple, this made way for the balancing assertion: Jesus would build the new Temple; his people would be the real new Jerusalem.[84] The whole of the story, of judgment for those who had not followed Jesus and vindication for those who had, is summed up in the cryptic but frequently repeated saying: the first shall be last, and the last first.[85] In other words, when the great tribulation came on Israel, those who had followed Jesus would be delivered; and that would be the sign that Jesus had been in the right, and that in consequence they had been in the right in following him. The destruction of Jerusalem on the one hand, and the rescue of the disciples on the other, would be the vindication of what Jesus had been saying throughout his ministry.

What can we say as historians about this catalogue of passages? I endorse the quotation from Caird with which this chapter began: the sequence of thought just outlined makes excellent sense within the developing hypothesis.[86] Sanders dismisses the sayings material we have examined as not being like 'Jewish restoration eschatology', and hence not what Jesus was getting at.[87] But it would be better, I think, to say that these sayings look like *Jesus'* kind of Jewish restoration eschatology, i.e. that scheme of thought in which Israel's hopes have been redefined and remoulded around him and his own agenda for the kingdom. The double criterion of similarity and dissimilarity again comes into play. Sanders denies similarity and therefore authenticity. I suggest that the similarity fails at exactly the point where, if my whole hypothesis so far is correct, we should expect it to fail. Jesus is

---

[80] Mt. 10.19–20/Lk. 12.11–12; cf. Mk. 13.11/Lk. 21.14–15.

[81] Mt. 19.28/Lk. 22.30.

[82] Mt. 19.29/Mk. 10.29–30/Lk. 18.29–30; cf. *Apoc. Jas.* 4.1.

[83] Lk. 17.1ff.; Mt. 10.32/Lk. 12.8–9; and esp. Mt. 16.24–8/Mk. 8.34—9.1/Lk. 9.23–7, which Luke insists is a saying to do with the kingdom.

[84] Mt. 16.17–19; Mt. 18.15–20. Cf. esp. Meyer 1979, 185–97, with 302f.; Meyer 1992a, 258–62.

[85] Mt. 19.30/Mk. 10.31/Lk. 13.30, cf. Mt. 20.16; *P. Oxy.654.*4; *Thom.* 4.

[86] Caird, so far as I know, never published a full-dress statement of this point of view, though his commentary on Luke (1963) encapsulates its basic thrust. This may explain why the commentary is currently out of favour in some quarters.

[87] Sanders 1985, 222ff.

telling the recognizable story of Israel, with the coming judgment and vindication exactly as one might imagine it within mainline restoration eschatology; *except for the fact that,* just as we find in some of the Scrolls, Israel's official leaders (and their cherished symbol, the Temple) have been cast in the role of 'enemies', while the role of 'persecuted and vindicated Israel' is given instead to Jesus and his disciples. The story itself has not changed. Jesus is speaking of judgment and vindication, just as so many prophets had done before him. The plot is the same, the *dramatis personae* different.

It is, of course, open to anyone to respond that in mainstream scholarship since Bultmann at least almost all these sayings have been quickly ascribed to the early church. Of course; nothing could be more natural, within a movement of scholarship that, fuelled by a phenomenalist or empiricist epistemology, assumed that sayings which the early church would have found useful must therefore have been invented by them.[88] We are fairly near to a straightforward clash of worldviews at this point, and assertion will simply be met with counter-assertion. I submit that the hypothesis I am offering makes more sense of the data, does so more simply, and sheds light over a wider area, than its various Bultmannian and post-Bultmannian alternatives. In addition, it possesses that similarity and dissimilarity, both with Judaism and with the early church, which is a basic sign of historical plausibility.

This claim may now be powerfully reinforced by consideration of another central passage. This, too, is commonly ascribed to the early church. It is, however, very well embedded in early tradition of all sorts, and coheres excellently with the developing hypothesis. It should, I suggest, be allowed a strong claim to go back, in some form or other, to Jesus himself. I refer to the so-called 'little apocalypse' of Mark 13 and its parallels.

4. Mark 13 and Parallels: The Coming Destruction and Vindication

(i) Introduction

Mark 13 and its parallels have been the focus of fierce scholarly debate in discussions of the kingdom, and hence of the aims of Jesus. My own contention will now be that if we read this chapter (and its parallels in Matthew and Luke) in the light of the argument so far, and of the relevant discussions in *NTPG,* we will discover both that it possesses an inner coherence and that it draws together exactly that combination of warnings and promises which we

---

[88] cf. *NTPG* 34f., 51–4, 59, 88–96. One might equally suggest that Martin Luther wrote the letter to the Galatians – as indeed one might think, to judge from some commentaries.

have seen to characterize Jesus' ministry all through. The setting – Jesus sitting on the Mount of Olives, looking across to the Temple Mount the other side of Gethsemane and the Kidron valley – is utterly credible. The timing – during the last week, Jesus having acted out a parable of the Temple's destruction – is likewise perfect. The content – the making explicit of the warnings of imminent destruction and the promises of vindication – makes excellent sense. The language – apocalyptic metaphor and symbol, to evoke the full resonances of Old Testament prophecy and to invest the coming events with their full theological significance – is both characteristic of Jesus and utterly appropriate to the occasion. There is simply no need (as there was felt to be in the days when Jesus was being 'rescued' from apocalyptic, as though the latter were an unwelcome Jewish intrusion into his pure timeless message[89]) to treat this passage as an early Christian apocalypse which Jesus could not and would not have spoken.[90] Nor is there any real need to imagine that it has been substantially 'written up' in the light of the events of AD 70. As has been shown often enough, the language used here comes, not from descriptions of battles and sieges in the field, but from scriptural predictions of catastrophic judgment on this or that city. Here, indeed, is the real shock of this passage. Just as before Jesus had used Tyre, Sidon, Sodom and other pagan cities as types of the judgment that was to fall on this or that town or village that had rejected him, so now, faced with Jerusalem and its rejection of his message, he chose imagery that had been used to describe the greatest pagan city of the Old Testament period. The destruction coming on YHWH's chosen city would be like that which fell on Babylon.[91] The exile was coming to an end at last. The arch-enslaver was to be destroyed. The story was working its way to its proper, but shocking, conclusion.

Mark 13.5–37 and its parallels have long been described, and treated, as a 'little apocalypse', with the implication that the material is, both in style and content, appreciably different from the rest of the gospel, and from Jesus' teaching as a whole. In particular, it has been argued again and again that the chapter from verse 5 onwards must be seen as a separate entity to verses 1–4, since verses 1–4 speak of the destruction of the Temple, while from verse 5 onwards the passage consists of a long and tumultuous build-up to the coming of the son of man on a cloud.[92] This, however, radically misunderstands

[89] Koch 1972, esp. ch. 6. The Jesus Seminar still appears to be following the line of rescuing Jesus from apocalyptic; cf. above, ch. 2, and e.g. Funk 1991, 192f. In Funk & Hoover 1993, 107–14, Mark 13 appears uniformly in black or (occasionally) grey.

[90] cf. e.g. Funk & Hoover 1993, 107.

[91] cf. Dodd 1968, 69–83; see below for details.

[92] Funk 1991, 192f. is an excellent brief summary of this well-worn position. For fuller treatments cf. Beasley-Murray 1954, 1957, 1983, 1986; Moore 1966; Gaston 1970; Hooker 1982; the commentaries; and the sections on this passage in numerous books about Jesus.

the meaning of 'son of man' within first-century Jewish expectation. Instead, we must insist on a seriously historical reading:

> Here, as in the book of Daniel . . ., the coming of the Son of Man on the clouds of heaven was never conceived as a primitive form of space travel, but as a symbol for a mighty reversal of fortunes within history and at the national level . . .
>
> How odd of Mark, say the critics, to append to a question about a historical crisis a discourse which is an answer to a question about an eschatological crisis! . . . But supposing Mark was right! . . . Supposing the prediction of the coming of the Son of Man on the clouds of heaven really was an answer to the disciples' question about the date of the fall of Jerusalem! Is it indeed credible that Jesus, the heir to the linguistic and theological riches of the prophets, and himself a greater theologian and master of imagery than them all, should ever have turned their symbols into flat and literal prose?[93]

According to this view, Mark 13 has been badly misunderstood by the importation into it of ideas concerning the 'second coming' of Jesus. There has been a long tradition in mainline Christianity of reading it this way, which has found its way into sermons, books, and even into the headings in many Bibles, and thence into the bloodstream of generations of pious folk. There has been a comparatively short tradition within mainline New Testament scholarship, going back particularly to Johannes Weiss and Albert Schweitzer, of endorsing this reading, with one significant difference. Pietism supposes that, in Mark 13, Jesus was predicting his own coming at the end of time, a prediction still to be fulfilled; Weiss, Schweitzer, and their successors have thought that Jesus here predicted the imminent end of the world, and that he was proved wrong. I suggest that both traditions, the old pietist one and the more recent scholarly one, are simply mistaken.

But does not the passage speak of the 'parousia', the 'second coming'? Yes, the Greek word *parousia* does occur, in Matthew's version (24.3, 27, 37, 39; these are, surprisingly enough in view of its popularity among scholars, its only occurrences in the gospels). But why should we think – except for reasons of ecclesiastical and scholarly tradition – that *parousia* means 'the second coming', and/or the downward travel on a cloud of Jesus and/or the 'son of man'?[94] *Parousia* means 'presence' as opposed to *apousia*, 'absence'; hence it denotes the 'arrival' of someone not at the moment present; and it is especially used in relation to the visit 'of a royal or official personage'.[95] Until evidence for a different meaning is produced, this should be our starting-point.

---

[93] Caird 1965, 20-2; adapted in Caird & Hurst 1994, 365f.

[94] cf. *NTPG* 284f., 342f., 459-64.

[95] LSJ 1343, s.v., with refs. For the ordinary sense of 'arrival', cf. 1 Cor. 16.17; 2 Cor. 7.6, 7; 10.10; Phil. 1.26; 2.12. From this, the most natural meaning for the word as applied to Jesus would be something like 'arrival on the scene', in the sense of 'enthronement'.

What, after all, were the disciples waiting for? They had come to Jerusalem expecting Jesus to be enthroned as the rightful king. This would necessarily involve Jesus taking over the authority which the Temple symbolized. They were now confronted with the startling news that this taking over of authority would mean the demolition, literal and metaphorical, of the Temple, whose demise Jesus had in fact constantly predicted, and which he had already symbolically overthrown in his dramatic (but apparently inconsequential) action in the Temple itself. The disciples now 'heard' his prophetic announcement of the destruction of the Temple as the announcement, also, of his own vindication; in other words, of his own 'coming' – not floating around on a cloud, of course, but of his 'coming' *to Jerusalem as the vindicated, rightful king*. What the disciples had naturally wanted to know was, when would Jesus actually be installed as king? He responded, equally unsurprisingly, with a reworking of scriptural passages about great cities being destroyed, and about the vindication of the true people of Israel's god. All was focused on the central point, that the Temple's destruction would constitute his own vindication. Once grant this premise, and the nightmare of puzzled textual reconstruction is in principle over.

The exegete who wishes to argue a position such as this is in something of a cleft stick. As we have seen, neither the godly traditions of the church nor the (sometimes) less godly traditions of scholarship are used to reading the passage in this way. The godly are likely to accuse me of scholarly trickery, designed to get round what to them seems a clear statement of the future second coming of the Lord. The scholarly are likely to accuse me of pious trickery, getting round the problem that Jesus seems to have been mistaken. I plead guilty to neither charge. I maintain that to read the passage as I suggest is to stand firmly on three things: first, the reconstruction of 'apocalyptic' offered in *NTPG* chapter 10; second, the reconstruction of the worldview of the early church offered in *NTPG* Part IV; third, the reconstruction of Jesus' announcement of the kingdom, and his retelling of its story, which we have set out so far in the present volume. If we take these as our starting-points, the whole passage seems to me (a) to refer clearly to the forthcoming destruction of Jerusalem, and (b) to invest that event with its theological significance. This is emphatically not to 'demythologize' the apocalyptic language concerned. Nor is it to reduce it to a 'mere metaphor'. It is to insist on reading it as it would have been heard in the first century, that is, *both* with its very this-worldly, indeed revolutionary, socio-political reference *and* with its fully symbolical, theological, and even 'mythological' overtones. The event that was coming swiftly upon Jerusalem would be the divine judgment on YHWH's rebellious people, exercised through Rome's judgment on her rebellious subject. It was also the rescue from judgment of Jesus' people, in an event which symbolized dramatically their final escape from exile. All of this spoke powerfully of the vindication of Jesus himself, both as prophet, and as the one who has the right to pronounce upon the Temple, and (in a sense still to be fully explained) as the actual *replacement* for the Temple. This seems to me an historical hypothesis that has a far better chance of success than either of the rival ones mentioned above – and, *a fortiori*, than the fantastic and ever more complex traditio-historical theories that have grown up, since Schweitzer, as an attempt to explain how such an odd chapter came to exist.[96] Once we grant that Schweitzer's position is unnecessary and untenable, most such theories fall with it.[97]

(ii) The Fall of Jerusalem

> And as he came out of the Temple, one of his disciples said to him, 'Look, Teacher, what wonderful stones and what wonderful buildings?' And Jesus said to him, 'Do you not see these great buildings? There will not be left here one stone upon another, that will not be thrown down.' And as he sat on the Mount of Olives opposite the Temple, Peter and James and John and Andrew asked him privately, 'Tell us, when will this be, and what will be the sign when these things are all to be accomplished?'[98]

One of the main reasons, I suppose, why the obvious way of reading the chapter has been ignored for so long must be the fact that in a good deal of Christian theology the fall of Jerusalem has had no theological significance.[99] This has meant not only that Mark 13 is found puzzling, but also that all the references to the same event elsewhere in the gospels – even where it stares

[96] The best attempts are, in my opinion, Wenham 1984; Theissen 1991a, ch. 3.

[97] Among the extraordinary things that have been perpetuated through this line of thought is the very layout of the chapter in two at least of the standard synopses, namely Huck-Lietzmann (1936 [1892]) and Throckmorton (1979 [1949]). Both label Mk. 13.1-4 as 'Prediction of the Destruction of the Temple', joining this with all the other short passages in Jesus' ministry in Jerusalem, and then introduce vv. 5ff. with a flourish of trumpets as a new major section, with the heading 'The Synoptic Apocalypse', beginning with 'The Signs of the Parousia'. (Aland at least has the whole of Mk. 13 under the heading of 'Die synoptische Apokalypse'.) Funk 1985b, 249f., has a similar arrangement, with Mk. 13.1-2 par. as 'Jesus predicts the Destruction of the Temple' and 13.3-13 par. as 'Signs of the End'. The belief that this way of reading the chapter is correct has taken such firm hold on New Testament scholars over such a long period that I sometimes wonder if it can ever be rooted out; but the attempt must be made.

[98] Mk. 13.1-4/Mt. 24.1-3/Lk. 21.5-6. At the end, Mt. has '. . . the sign *of your coming [parousia] and of the close of the age*'. For the sense of the latter phrase see below.

[99] The classic statement of this is in Manson 1931, 281 (discussing Mk. 9.1 and pars.): 'The ruthless suppression by a great military empire of an insane rebellion in an outlying part of its territory has as much – or as little – to do with the coming of the Kingdom of God in power as the suppression of the Indian Mutiny.' This is refuted by Caird & Hurst 1994, 365f. Cf. too Lampe 1984: in the early period, only *Barnabas* makes much of the event.

one in the face, as in Luke 13.1–5 – have been read as general warnings of hellfire in an afterlife, rather than the literal and physical divine-judgment-through-Roman-judgment that we have seen to be characteristic of Jesus' story. The prediction in Mark 13.2 ('There will not be left here one stone upon another, that will not be thrown down.') is neither new nor unexpected. It is the sort of thing that many sectarian Jews of the time might well have thought or said. It is the necessary and predictable focal point of Jesus' whole prophetic ministry. Like Jeremiah, he grieved over the city but could not avoid telling of its coming ruin. Like Josephus, he claimed to see that destruction was inevitable, and interpreted it as divine judgment for Israel's present wickedness. In strange parallelism with the warnings he gave of his own approaching death (we will explore this later), he continued to announce Jerusalem's disaster, and, when faced with the disciples' pardonable enthusiasm for the fantastic buildings before them, it was utterly appropriate that he should bring this strand of his ministry to its climax by dampening their ardour with solemn words of judgment.

The setting given to the following discourse by Matthew and Mark is the Mount of Olives. This can hardly be accidental. The story is not simply to be told in the abstract: as with Jesus' praxis in other ways, the story is symbolically enacted. Jesus seems to intend an allusion to Zechariah 14.4–5. The context is the coming of the divine kingdom (Zechariah 14.9) and the coming great battle of the nations against Jerusalem (14.1–3). Zechariah 14.4–5 speaks of Israel's god standing on the Mount of Olives, and of a great earthquake, after which 'YHWH your god will come, and all the holy ones with him'. There is no earthquake in the synoptic account (though compare Matthew 27.51–2), and Jesus is sitting, not standing; this is enough to suggest that the evangelists have not deliberately invented the scene merely to 'fulfil' Zechariah. Nor does Matthew add, as he might have done, a note saying 'this was done to fulfil the prophecy . . .' But this therefore points all the more to the likelihood of Jesus' choice of the Mount of Olives as the appropriate place from which to utter his last solemn oracles of judgment upon Jerusalem, and his last solemn predictions of the vindication of himself and his followers. He was at least as capable of acting in a symbolically resonant way as the great Hebrew prophets had been; and at least as alert to symbolic resonances, not least the symbolism of place, as were Christian writers a generation or so later.[100] The Mount of Olives was a natural place

---

[100] If the various prophets who led people 'into the wilderness' were apparently aware of the geographical symbolism of their actions; if John the Baptist was aware of the symbolism of the Jordan; if the synoptic evangelists were aware of such symbolism, as redaction-criticism has long insisted (e.g. Conzelmann 1960 [1953]); then is it not bizarre to insist that Jesus was incapable of recognizing and exploiting the symbolism of the Mount of Olives?

for Jesus to be, anyway, half-way between the city itself and Bethany, where he and his followers were spending the nights. The force of the setting then seems to be that this was Jesus' paradoxical retelling of the great story found in Zechariah 14: in predicting Jerusalem's last great struggle, the 'coming' of YHWH, and the final arrival of the divine kingdom, he was acting to fulfil, in his own reinterpreted fashion, the prophecy of Zechariah.

The questions the disciples ask Jesus are explicitly related to this prediction. In Mark (13.4) there is no unclarity about this: 'When will this be, and what will be the sign when these things are about to happen?' In Luke (21.7) it is even clearer: 'When will this be, and what will be the sign when this is about to take place?' We have already seen that Matthew's use of the word *parousia* is not a sign that he has altered this meaning (though it is partly Matthew's version, which in terms of historical reconstruction looks initially the least plausible of the three, that has given scholars, and popular readers and preachers, the idea that the discourse is really 'about' the end of the space-time universe, and the travel downwards to earth of Jesus in a 'second coming').[101] We must, however, stress again: as far as the disciples, good first-century Jews as they were, were concerned, there was no reason whatever for them to be thinking about the end of the space-time universe. There was no reason, either in their own background or in a single thing that Jesus had said to them up to that point, for it even to occur to them that the true story of the world, or of Israel, or of Jesus himself, might include either the end of the space-time universe, or Jesus or anyone else floating down to earth on a cloud. They had not yet even thought of his being taken from them, let alone that he might come back; nor did they have any idea of another figure, earthly, heavenly, or something in between, who would one day come down to earth riding on a literal cloud.[102] Had Jesus wished to introduce so strange and unJewish an idea to them he would have had a very difficult task; as we often find in the gospels, their minds were not exactly at their sharpest in picking up redefinitions even of ideas with which they were already somewhat familiar.

The disciples *were*, however, very interested in a story which ended with Jesus' coming to Jerusalem to reign as king. They *were* looking for the fulfilment of Israel's hopes, for the story told so often in Israel's scriptures to reach its appointed climax. And the 'close of the age' for which they longed was not the end of the space-time order, but the end of the present evil age

---

[101] The *New Jerusalem Bible* insists that Mark 13 only concerns the destruction of Jerusalem, 'as an act of God delivering his people', but suggests that Mt. 24—5 retains the overlap between this idea and 'the final coming of Christ'.

[102] This is the strong point of Vermes' oft-repeated claim, that the 'apocalyptic son of man' is a comparatively modern and non-Jewish invention: cf. e.g. Vermes 1983, ch. 7.

(*ha'olam hazeh*), and the introduction of the (still very much this-worldly) age to come (*ha'olam haba'*) – in other words, the end of Israel's period of mourning and exile and the beginning of her freedom and vindication.[103] Matthew 24.3, therefore, is most naturally read, in its first-century Jewish context, not as a question about (what scholars have come to call, in technical language) the 'parousia', but as a question about Jesus 'coming' or 'arriving' in the sense of his actual enthronement as king, consequent upon the dethronement of the present powers that were occupying the holy city.[104] The disciples were pressing Jesus to give them details of his plan for becoming king, as David had become king, in the city that was at present still rejecting him. They were longing for their own version of the great event for which all Israel had been on tiptoe. Matthew is not, in other words, out on a limb from Mark and Luke at this point.[105] The question at the start of all three versions, seen from within the story the disciples have in their minds, must be read to mean: When will you come in your kingdom?[106] When will the evil age, symbolized by the present Jerusalem regime, be over?

(iii) The Start of the 'Woes', and the Trials of the Disciples

The start of Jesus' answer to the disciples' question is a classic piece of reworked apocalyptic.[107] Completely consistent with his whole approach to the events that were about to take place, he is predicting that the 'Messianic Woes', the birthpangs of the age to come, are about to occur in full force.[108] This is how Israel is to be reborn. The story will take the following form: all manner of strange, dire events will take place, and the disciples will be exposed to the allure of various people who will give themselves out to be YHWH's anointed, commissioned to lead Israel into her glorious future. This already introduces one of the major themes of the chapter in all three synoptic gospels (the references in what follows are to Mark unless otherwise noted). Jesus' disciples must not be deceived, but are to be saved despite all the woes that are to come. They will find themselves hauled before authorities both Jewish and pagan, and at a time when the whole of society is torn with a reign of terror and mutual accusation (13.12) they will find everyone's

---

[103] cf. *NTPG* ch. 10, esp. 299–301.

[104] cf. Lk. 24.21: 'we had hoped that he was the one who would redeem Israel'.

[105] Nor does he divide his chapter into two halves (vv. 4–35, 36–51) on the basis of this double question, the first dealing with Jerusalem and the second with the 'second coming' (against France 1985, 335).

[106] cf. Lk. 23.42, followed by *AcPil.* 10.2.

[107] Mk. 13.5–13/Mt. 24.4–14/Lk. 21.8–19.

[108] cf. *NTPG* 277f.

hand against them. They will fit into none of the regular parties. They must hold firm, and vindication will come (13.13).[109] The scriptural background for the prediction of domestic betrayal is, partly at least, Micah 7.6, which speaks of judgment coming upon Israel and the need to wait patiently for YHWH's deliverance. Through this process Israel will finally be rescued and forgiven:

> The faithful have disappeared from the land,
>   and there is no one left who is upright;
> they all lie in wait for blood,
>   and they hunt each other with nets.
> Their hands are skilled to do evil;
>   the official and the judge ask for a bribe,
> and the powerful dictate what they desire;
>   thus they pervert justice . . .
> Put no trust in a friend,
>   have no confidence in a loved one;
> guard the doors of your mouth
>   from her who lies in your embrace;
> for the son treats the father with contempt,
>   the daughter rises up against her mother,
> the daughter-in-law against her mother-in-law;
>   your enemies are members of your own household.
> But as for me, I will look to YHWH,
>   I will wait for the God of my salvation;
>   my God will hear me.
> Do not rejoice over me, O my enemy;
>   when I fall, I shall rise;
> when I sit in darkness,
>   YHWH will be a light to me.
> I must bear the indignation of YHWH,
>   because I have sinned against him,
> until he takes my side
>   and executes judgment for me.
> He will bring me out to the light;
>   I shall see his vindication.
> Then my enemy will see,
>   and shame will cover her who said to me,
>   'Where is YHWH your God?'
> My eyes will see her downfall;
>   now she will be trodden down
>   like the mire of the streets.[110]

[109] The fact that the Matthaean parallel to this part of Mk. 13 is in Mt. 10 (vv. 16–23) should make us realize just how well it fits into the overall context of Jesus' ministry. It is of course open to those who wish to do so to reason the other way, and to see Mt. 10.16–23 as a post-Easter apocalypse read back into the life of Jesus. Once again the final argument here must be from the overall coherence, or otherwise, of the competing hypotheses, not from small fragments adjudicated individually against the background of suppressed assumptions.

[110] Mic. 7.2–10. In mSot. 9.15, this passage is quoted as part of the condition of Israel at the time of the 'footsteps of the Messiah' (which Danby 306 n.9 describes as 'the end of

The echo of this passage in Mark 13.12 is a classic example of an entire passage being evoked by a single reference.[111] The Micah passage describes the patient endurance of the true people of YHWH, despite betrayal by those close to them, and their eventual vindication in the judgment which falls upon their enemies. This is, in turn, a first-class example of Jesus picking up a story-line from the prophetic tradition and retelling it so as to focus on his own work.

So far, the section has had nothing whatever to do with 'the signs of the parousia' (in the normal scholarly sense), despite being labelled in some such fashion in commentaries, synopses, monographs and articles. It is thoroughly believable as a first-century Jewish prophecy, based on clear passages of scripture, warning of a coming time of national distress, seen as the beginning of the great tribulation that must come upon Israel. Jesus, it appears, has woven into this story a further strand, that of the rescue of Israel from destruction by holding firm to the end; but now the Israel that holds firm, and so is rescued, consists of *his own disciples*. And the great city that oppresses them, from whose imminent judgment they must flee, is not Babylon. It is Jerusalem.

(iv) Specific Signs of Emergency

But there will come a time when it is no longer a matter of holding on, facing torture and betrayal, bearing witness to Jesus' way of being Israel although surrounded by the angry agendas of different warring factions.[112] There will come a time when the appropriate reaction is flight. Jerusalem's doom has been announced, and Jesus' followers must not be caught in the city when it falls. Their vindication will come when the city that has opposed Jesus is destroyed.

It is often said that this passage (together with Luke 19.42–4) reflects Josephus' description of the actual fall of Jerusalem in AD 70, and must therefore have been composed after that time.[113] In fact, as has often been

---

the time of exile'), when, according to various rabbis including the late-C1 Eliezer ben Hyrcanus, Israel must place her trust in 'our father in heaven'.

[111] For this phenomenon, cf. Hays 1989.

[112] Mk. 13.14–23/Mt. 24.15–28/Lk. 21.20–24.

[113] Recently, Funk 1991, 195; cf. Fitzmyer 1985, 1254f., who I believe has not seen the strength of Dodd's argument (see below). Fitzmyer exemplifies the classic problem that scholarship faces in trying to maintain that the passage is a post-70 composition: (a) the passage must refer backwards to the events of 70; (b) the details do not fit the event; therefore (c) Luke cannot have known much about it! This sort of theory can swallow any evidence at all and still come up smiling; but, as with the Cheshire cat, the smile may eventually be all there is to it.

pointed out, there is good reason to doubt this.[114] There are many striking features of Josephus' account of the siege (pestilence, cannibalism and fire) which have no echo in the synoptic tradition; conversely, some features of the synoptic predictions, notably those to do with the fate of the inhabitants, have no counterpart in Josephus.[115] So, too, we do not need Josephus, or indeed even the archaeologists, to inform us that the stones of the city and Temple were not, in fact, all demolished; the evidence of our own eyes will do well enough. It is far more plausible to regard the details of the passage as extrapolations from ancient biblical prophecy than to read them as lame and inaccurate attempts to turn history, after the event, into pseudo-prophecy.

The scriptural background is in fact threefold, and very instructive for what we must hypothesize as the mindset of Jesus, reusing Israel's prophetic heritage, and retelling its story, consistently with his entire set of aims. There are, first and briefly, plenty of allusions to previous destructions of YHWH's people, not least Jerusalem's devastation at the hands of the Babylonians in the sixth century BC. This theme has already been echoed in Mark 13,[116] and now becomes even clearer. The woes on those who will flee with young children look back to Hosea;[117] the shortening of the days, for the sake of the elect, to Isaiah.[118] The coming of false prophets is a regular biblical theme.[119] In particular, the image of everyone running to the mountains before the invading army is reminiscent of Ezekiel's picture of the devastating judgment of Jerusalem at the hands of Babylon.[120] Thus far, Jesus is standing within a regular prophetic tradition, drawing on various parts of it to deepen and intensify his warnings.

Second, more fully, we have passages which align the coming devastation with the Maccabaean crisis. Thus, to begin with:

> After the sixty-two weeks, an anointed one shall be cut off and shall have nothing, and the troops of the prince who is to come shall destroy the city and the sanctuary. Its end shall come with a flood, and to the end there shall be war. Desolations are decreed. He shall make a strong covenant with many for one week, and for half of the week he shall

[114] For what follows, cf. Dodd 1968, 74f.

[115] Lk. 19.44 speaks of dashing children to the ground; Josephus reports that the inhabitants under the age of 17 were sold into slavery (*War* 6.418), but the biblical prophecies resonate with the theme of slaughtered children (e.g. Hos. 10.14; 13.16; Nah. 3.10; cf. Ps. 137.9).

[116] For 13.5 cf. Mic. 3.12; Jer. 7.14; 46.8; Ezek. 24.21.

[117] Mk. 13.17 pars.; Hos. 13.16 [MT 14.1].

[118] Mk. 13.20 par.; Isa. 65.8. In the Isaianic context, judgment is stayed in order that the true covenant people may be delivered, whereupon the judgment will fall upon those Israelites who have followed pagan ways.

[119] Mk. 13.22; Dt. 13; Jer. 6.13f., etc.

[120] Mk. 13.14; Ezek. 7.12–16.

make sacrifice and offering cease; and in their place shall be an abomination that desolates, until the decreed end is poured out upon the desolator.[121]

In so far as it is possible for us to reconstruct the way in which a first-century sectarian Jew would have read this passage, it seems likely that it would be taken as a prophecy of the destruction of the Temple, accompanied by the setting up of pagan symbols, and perhaps pagan worship, in its place.[122] We shall return to this passage presently.

The second Daniel passage picks up echoes of the first:

Forces sent by [a pagan ruler] shall occupy and profane the temple and fortress. They shall abolish the regular burnt offering and set up the abomination that makes desolate. He shall seduce with intrigue those who violate the covenant; but the people who are loyal to their God shall stand firm and take action. The wise among the people shall give understanding to many; for some days, however, they shall fall by sword and flame, and suffer captivity and plunder. When they fall victim, they shall receive a little help, and many shall join them insincerely. Some of the wise shall fall, so that they may be refined, purified, and cleansed, until the time of the end, for there is still an interval until the time appointed.[123]

Once again, the likely first-century reading of this passage would take it to refer to pagan pollution of the Temple, accompanied by tribulation for the true people of YHWH. This theme recurs in the third passage:

Many shall be purified, cleansed, and refined, but the wicked shall continue to act wickedly. None of the wicked shall understand, but those who are wise shall understand. From the time that the regular burnt offering is taken away and the abomination that desolates is set up, there shall be one thousand two hundred and ninety days.[124]

This recurring theme of the 'abomination of desolation' was applied to the action of Antiochus Epiphanes by the author of First Maccabees:

Now on the fifteenth day of Chislev, in the one hundred and forty-fifth year, they erected a desolating sacrilege on the altar of burnt offering. They also built altars in the surrounding towns of Judah, and offered incense at the doors of the houses and in the streets. The books of the law that they found they tore to pieces and burned with fire . . .
But many in Israel stood firm and were resolved in their hearts not to eat unclean food. They chose to die rather than to be defiled by food or to profane the holy covenant; and they did die. Very great wrath came upon Israel.[125]

---

[121] Dan. 9.26-7.
[122] On C1 readings of Daniel cf. *NTPG* 289-95, 312-17.
[123] Dan. 11.31-5.
[124] Dan. 12.10-11.
[125] 1 Macc. 1.54-6, 62-4; cf. 2 Macc. 8.17, and Jos. *Ant.* 18.257-309. Josephus, in telling of Gaius' attempt to put up a statue of himself in the Temple, and the Jews' reaction to the proposal, seems to be consciously echoing the Maccabaean story. This, in other words, would be a comprehensible way of telling a story-with-overtones in the first century.

The passage, which again joins together the pagan pollution of the Temple and the suffering of the righteous within Israel, goes on to describe the rise of the Maccabaean house as (from the writer's perspective) YHWH's answer to the dire situation. The Danielic story was being retold in order to make it clear that the events of 167 BC were to be seen as the fulfilment of prophecy; in other words, so that the heroes and martyrs of that fateful moment could be seen as the true Israel. The writing-up of the Maccabaean revolt was, after all, a polemical act, designed to bolster the new regime by showing the wickedness not only of Antiochus but also of those who had compromised with him. Such an aim is often best furthered by a freshly slanted retelling of the traditional story.

The themes which cluster together in these passages belong closely with one another, and would naturally be read in the first century in terms not of Syrian invasion but of Roman. The outstanding question then becomes: who, in this new situation, are the true people of YHWH, expecting persecution and standing firm under it? And who is the true deliverer, who will fight YHWH's battle and emerge vindicated at the end? It is a question of *roles* within a *story*: granted the shape of the plot, who is now the Agent, who the Helper, and who the Opponent? It is precisely questions like these that Mark 13 and its parallels address. There is no good reason for denying that Jesus himself could, and most probably did, speak of them in this sort of way.

Daniel 9 is the crucial determining reference, with the others being subordinated to it, though their repetition of its central thrust shows how important it was. We should therefore consider it in more detail. In that chapter, Daniel prays (9.4–19) for the restoration and vindication of Jerusalem, at present destroyed and oppressed by Babylon; he prays that YHWH will be faithful and, according to his promise, deliver his faithful people.

The angelic answer to Daniel (9.22–7) sets out a variety of themes. First, there will be an end to transgression, a final atonement, which will usher in the renewed covenant and involve the rebuilding of the city (9.24–5). Second, an anointed one 'shall be cut off and have nothing' (9.26a).[126] Third, 'the troops of the prince who is to come shall destroy the city and the sanctuary', making the sacrificial system to cease and setting up 'an abomination that desolates'. This passage, as we have seen, was read in the second century BC as referring to Antiochus' desecration of the Temple (though what Jews of that period would have made of the cutting off of the anointed one is not easy to guess). Equally clearly, the natural implication in the first century AD would be that the Romans, the present occupying forces,

---

[126] The translation was clearly a problem as early as the LXX, and remains so: cf. Montgomery 1927, 381–3, 401–4; Goldingay 1989, 262.

would destroy the city and the Temple, setting up their own abomination in place of the sacrificial system.[127]

The context and content of Daniel 9 thus point to a complex grid of meaning for Mark 13 and its parallels: YHWH's final faithfulness to the covenant, and his rescue of his faithful ones, is to come about paradoxically through the destruction of the rebuilt city, and also through the cutting off of an abandoned 'anointed one'. These, I suggest, are precisely the themes which Jesus intended to weave into his strange prediction of Jerusalem's destruction.

One final passage ties the predictions of Mark 13 quite tightly to the story of the Maccabees. After Antiochus has desecrated the sanctuary, Mattathias, the father of Judas Maccabaeus, laments the downfall of the great holy place:

> Alas! Why was I born to see this,
>   the ruin of my people, the ruin of the holy city,
> and to live there when it was given over to the enemy,
>   the sanctuary given over to aliens?
> Her temple has become like a person without honour;
>   her glorious vessels have been carried into exile . . .
> And see, our holy place, our beauty,
>   and our glory have been laid waste;
>   the Gentiles have profaned them.[128]

At this point the king's officers try to persuade Mattathias and his sons to offer sacrifice, but they refuse. An unnamed Jew comes forward, however, to offer sacrifice according to the king's command. Mattathias, filled with zeal, kills the man on the altar, kills the officer as well, and tears down the altar:

> Then Mattathias cried out in the town with a loud voice, saying: 'Let every one who is zealous for the law and supports the covenant come out with me!' *Then he and his sons fled to the hills and left all that they had in the town.*[129]

The story continues, of course, with Mattathias' sons continuing his work after his death, cleansing the Temple, and ending up as a new line of priest-kings.

The resonances between this whole story, particularly its punch-line, and Mark 13.14–16 should be clear enough:

---

[127] That the reference need not be a *vaticinium ex eventu* should now hardly need stating, though no doubt different generations of Christians, hearing or reading the passage, would apply it differently to their own situations, as plotted by e.g. Theissen 1991a, ch. 3.

[128] 1 Macc. 2.7–12, cf. 3.45, 50–3.

[129] 1 Macc. 2.15–28. The italicized portion reads in Greek *kai ephugen autos kai hoi huioi autou eis ta ore, kai egkatelipon hosa eichon en te polei.*

> But when you see 'the abomination of desolation' standing where it ought not (let the reader understand), then let those who are in Judaea flee to the mountains; let the one who is on the housetop not go down, nor go in to get anything out of his house; and let the one who is in the field not turn back to get his cloak.

Mark's parenthetical addition may well have crept into the tradition at the time of the crisis over Gaius' statue, but the passage as a whole is comprehensible as being spoken at more or less any time between 167 BC and AD 135 (or at least 70). The force of it is to warn that there is coming a crisis upon Jerusalem, a crisis in which the official Temple cult will be compromised and will need to be torn down. At that time, those who are true members of Israel, loyal to the covenant, must run away to the hills, leaving their possessions in the city.

This is scarcely to be taken as a reference, after the event, to the actual happenings of AD 66–70. For a start, Titus and his legions were occupying the Mount of Olives and Mount Scopus, the two highest hills overlooking Jerusalem; fleeing to the hills would mean surrender and/or death. For another thing, by the time the Romans took the sanctuary itself it was too late to do anything about running away. Thirdly, the tradition of the Christians getting out of Jerusalem and going to Pella hardly counts as fleeing 'to the hills'; to get to Pella they would have had to descend 3,000 feet to the Jordan valley and then travel north for about thirty miles (Pella itself is about three miles east of the Jordan, and twenty miles south of the sea of Galilee). No one in their right mind would describe a flight to Pella as 'to the hills'.[130]

At the same time, the overtones of Jesus' saying should also be clear. The official Temple cult was (in his view, as in the Essenes') so horribly compromised that the only solution was for it to be destroyed. Jesus was claiming the high ground of true covenant loyalty; to defend the sanctuary and cult when they were so corrupt would be disloyalty to YHWH. The way of loyalty was the way of flight. Such flight would not betoken cowardice. It would be undertaken with the intention of regrouping as a body, in order subsequently to be vindicated as the true people, indeed the true leaders. Mattathias' flight to the hills ended with his family becoming the new royal house.

So far, then, the whole of the chapter is to be read not only as a prediction of the destruction of the Temple, but also as an implicit claim that the destruction was coming about because of Israel's apostasy and the Temple's pollution. Jesus' stance is then that of the godly prophet, looking in horror at that which Jerusalem has become; or the godly zealot, encouraging his followers to leave the corrupt shrine and organize a counter-official movement;

---

[130] Euseb. *HE* 3.5.3; cf. *NTPG* 352. On Pella cf. R. H. Smith 1992 (repeating the possible link with Mk. 13.14, but in a looser form); and esp. Lüdemann 1980.

or the would-be Messiah, looking beyond the present crisis to his own establishment as the true king.

The third set of Old Testament allusions evoked by this passage develop this complex theme in a further direction. Instead of seeing Jerusalem as the victim of pagan aggression or corruption, these passages, when put together in the present context, designate Jerusalem herself as Babylon, the enemy of the true people of the covenant god. The prophecies of Isaiah and Jeremiah concerning the downfall of Babylon, and the escape of Israel from the midst of it, leading to the prophecy of Daniel concerning the vindication of the people of god and the destruction of the evil empire, here fit together like a glove. This time the prophetic story-line is well known: it is the story of the kingdom of god, whose 'coming' consists partly in the destruction of the wicked kingdom. But once more (just as in the parable of the prodigal son) the question is: who is who within this story? Which city now takes which role? The answer is so startling that it is worth spelling out just how full and clear the allusions are.[131] The key passages read as follows:

> Wail, for the day of YHWH is near;
>> it will come like destruction from the Almighty! . . .
> Pangs and agony will seize them;
>> they will be in anguish like a woman in labour . . .
> See, the day of YHWH comes,
>> cruel, with wrath and fierce anger,
> to make the earth a desolation,
>> and to destroy its sinners from it.
> For the stars of the heavens and their constellations
>> will not give their light;
> the sun will be dark at its rising,
>> and the moon will not shed its light.
> I will punish the world for its evil,
>> and the wicked for their iniquity;
> I will put an end to the pride of the arrogant,
>> and lay low the insolence of tyrants . . .
> And Babylon, the glory of kingdoms,
>> the splendour and pride of the Chaldeans,
> will be like Sodom and Gomorrah
>> when God overthrew them.[132]

This, then, is what it means to say that 'the sun and the moon will be darkened, and the stars will not give their light' (Mark 13.24). It means: 'Babylon will fall – an earth-shattering event!' Or again, this time with reference to the star that falls from heaven:

---

[131] cf. too above, on Lk. 19.42–4 with its echoes of Hos. 13.16 (judgment on Samaria); Nah. 3.10 (Thebes and Nineveh); Ps. 137.9 (Babylon).

[132] Isa. 13.6, 9–11, 19. Cf. *T. Mos.* 10.1–10, on which cf. *NTPG* 304f.

You will take up this taunt against the king of Babylon . . .

'How are you fallen from heaven,
　O Day Star, son of Dawn!
How are you cut down to the ground,
　you who laid the nations low!
You said in your heart,
　"I will ascend to heaven;
I will raise my throne
　above the stars of God;
I will sit on the mount of assembly
　on the heights of Zaphon;
I will ascend to the tops of the clouds,
　I will make myself like the Most High."
But you are brought down to Sheol,
　to the depths of the Pit.'[133]

Or again, with a reference wider than merely Babylon, but in the same vein:

Their slain shall be cast out,
　and the stench of their corpses shall rise;
　the mountains shall flow with their blood.
All the host of heaven shall rot away,
　and the skies roll up like a scroll.
All their host shall wither
　like a leaf withering on a vine,
　or fruit withering on a fig tree.[134]

The same theme is found in Ezekiel's denunciation of the king of Egypt:

I will strew your flesh on the mountains,
　and fill the valleys with your carcass.
I will drench the land with your flowing blood up to the mountains,
　and the watercourses will be filled with you.
When I blot you out, I will cover the heavens,
　and make their stars dark;
I will cover the sun with a cloud,
　and the moon shall not give its light.
All the shining lights of the heavens I will darken above you,
　and put darkness on your land, says the Lord YHWH.[135]

Joel uses the same language to warn of an approaching cataclysm:

The earth quakes before them,
　the heavens tremble.
The sun and the moon are darkened,
　and the stars withdraw their shining.

[133] Isa. 14.4, 12–15.
[134] Isa. 34.3–4.
[135] Ezek. 32.5–8.

YHWH utters his voice at the head of his army;
> how vast is his host!
> Numberless are those who obey his command.
Truly the day of YHWH is great;
> terrible indeed – who can endure it?

I will show portents in the heavens and on the earth, blood and fire and columns of smoke. The sun shall be turned to darkness, and the moon to blood, before the great and terrible day of YHWH comes. Then everyone who calls on the name of YHWH shall be saved; for in Mount Zion and in Jerusalem there shall be those who escape, as YHWH has said, and among the survivors shall be those whom YHWH calls.

Multitudes, multitudes,
> in the valley of decision!
For the day of YHWH is near
> in the valley of decision.
The sun and the moon are darkened,
> and the stars withdraw their shining.[136]

Darkness, cosmic darkness: this is the dominant image when YHWH acts to judge the Babylons of this world. These richly coloured prophetic stories then give way, still within a context of YHWH's judgment on Babylon, to the command and warning that bids Israel flee from the coming destruction of the great enemy:

Go out from Babylon, flee from Chaldea,
> declare this with a shout of joy, proclaim it,
send it forth to the end of the earth;
> say, 'YHWH has redeemed his servant Jacob!'

Depart, depart, go out from there!
> Touch no unclean thing;
go out from the midst of it, purify yourselves,
> you who carry the vessels of YHWH.
For you shall not go out in haste,
> and you shall not go out in flight;
for YHWH himself will go before you,
> and the God of Israel will be your rear guard.[137]

These passages all tell a story with the same set of motifs: YHWH's victory over the great pagan city; the rescue and vindication of his true people who

---

[136] Joel 2.10-11, 30-2; 3.14-15. We could also add Amos 8.9; Zeph. 1.15.

[137] Isa. 48.20; 52.11-12. The context of the latter passage, particularly the announcement that YHWH is becoming king at last (Isa. 52.7-10), resonates closely with Jesus' proclamation, ministry and self-understanding, though of course the reuse of the passage in Mk. 13 pars. is heavily ironic: in its original form the passage announces the *salvation* of Jerusalem. Here again is the all-important change of roles. Jerusalem has become Babylon; Jesus and his disciples have become Jerusalem.

had been suffering under it; and YHWH's acclamation as king. More or less the same combination reappears in Jeremiah:

> My people have been lost sheep; their shepherds have led them astray, turning them away on the mountains . . .; they have forgotten their fold . . .
>
> Flee from Babylon, and go out of the land of the Chaldeans, and be like male goats leading the flock . . .
>
> Listen! Fugitives and refugees from the land of Babylon are coming to declare in Zion the vengeance of YHWH our God, vengeance for his temple.

> Flee from the midst of Babylon,
>   save your lives, each of you!
> Do not perish because of her guilt,
>   for this is the time of YHWH's vengeance;
>   he is repaying her what is due.
> Babylon was a golden cup in YHWH's hand,
>   making all the earth drunken;
> the nations drank of her wine,
>   and so the nations went mad.
> Suddenly Babylon has fallen and is shattered;
>   wail for her!
> Bring balm for her wound;
>   perhaps she may be healed.
> We tried to heal Babylon,
>   but she could not be healed.
> Forsake her, and let each of us go to our own country;
>   for her judgment has reached up to heaven
>   and has been lifted up even to the skies.
> YHWH has brought forth our vindication;
>   come, let us declare in Zion
>   the work of YHWH our God.

> Come out of her, my people!
>   Save your lives, each of you,
>   from the fierce anger of YHWH!
> Do not be faint-hearted or fearful
>   at the rumours heard in the land –
> one year one rumour comes,
>   the next year another,
> rumours of violence in the land
>   and of ruler against ruler . . .

> You survivors of the sword,
>   go, do not linger!
> Remember YHWH in a distant land,
>   and let Jerusalem come into your mind:
> We are put to shame, for we have heard insults;
>   dishonour has covered our face,
> for aliens have come
>   into the holy places of YHWH's house . . .

I will make her officials and her sages drunk,
    also her governors, her deputies, and her warriors;
they shall sleep a perpetual sleep and never wake,
    says the King, whose name is YHWH of hosts.[138]

When Babylon is destroyed, there is only one proper response for YHWH's people: get out and run. We discover the same set of themes, finally, in two passages in Zechariah:

Up, up! Flee from the land of the north, says YHWH; for I have spread you abroad like the four winds of heaven, says YHWH. Up! Escape from Babylon. For thus said YHWH of hosts (after his glory sent me) regarding the nations that plundered you: Truly, one who touches you touches the apple of my eye.[139]

I will gather all the nations against Jerusalem to battle . . . Then YHWH will go forth and fight against those nations as when he fights on a day of battle. On that day his feet shall stand on the Mount of Olives, which lies before Jerusalem on the east; and the Mount of Olives shall be split in two from east to west by a very wide valley; so that one half of the Mount shall withdraw northward, and the other half southward. And you shall flee by the valley of my mountain, for the valley between the mountains shall reach to Azal; and you shall flee as you fled from the earthquake in the days of King Uzziah of Judah. Then YHWH my God will come, and all the holy ones with him . . . And YHWH will become king over all the earth; on that day YHWH will be one and his name one.[140]

These passages, taken together and in their various parts, are clearly the intended background for several parts of the discourse in Mark 13 and parallels, before we even get to the Danielic allusions. They tell the story of Israel, her god, and the nations in ways that lend themselves perfectly to Jesus' redefinition of Israel around himself; to his announcement that the long-awaited release from exile (the 'kingdom of god') was at hand; and to his identification of the forces opposing the true people of this god, not with Rome, but with present Jerusalem and its hierarchy. His retelling of the prophetic stories, like Susannah's addition to Daniel, has the force of turning the critique of pagan nations against the present Jewish rulers. Jerusalem's fall, and the disciples' flight and escape, will be the final acting out of the predictions that Babylon would fall and Israel escape. This will be her vindication, the sign that her god is indeed king.[141]

---

[138] Jer. 50.6, 8, 28; 51.6–10, 45–6, 50–1, 57.

[139] Zech. 2.6–8.

[140] Zech. 14.2a, 3–5, 9.

[141] This conclusion may be held by some to carry implications for the reading of Rev. 17—19, where some recent commentators (e.g. Massyngberde Ford 1975) have suggested that the great and wicked city is not Rome but Jerusalem (cf. Rev. 11.8). I have discovered that this suggestion arouses anger in some circles, which is not explained simply as annoyance at an exegetical peculiarity (plenty of those are to be found in all the journals, but they merely arouse curiosity). What is at stake here, and for whom?

This context and setting shows the direction in which the imagery of Mark 13.14–23 is moving.[142] It is advice 'more useful to a refugee from military invasion than to a man caught unawares by the last trumpet'.[143] The disciples are not to stay and fight for the physical survival of Jerusalem. They are not to be implicated in the coming war. Jesus will die at the hands of the Romans on the charge of being a Jewish rebel, but they are not to do so. No mistaken sense of loyalty must sway them into trying to bring the kingdom after all by means of the sword. Rather, they are to waste no time: they must run away. Luke (21.20) has cashed out the apocalyptic imagery in Matthew (24.15) and Mark (13.14) in terms of Jerusalem's being surrounded with armies. This, for his gentile readers, makes far more sense: faced with a cryptic allusion to Daniel, they would not be in a position to obey the command of Mark 13.14b, 'Let the reader understand.'[144] Luke's reading of Mark is quite clear: all this language refers to the fall of Jerusalem, which is to be understood against the scriptural background of the predicted destruction of Babylon.[145] We have found nothing in the entire scope of Jesus' language, teaching and ministry to suggest that Luke was thereby misreading Mark, or for that matter reading him differently from Matthew, or that any of them, or their predecessors in the tradition, were putting into Jesus' mind and mouth ideas and words which would have been impossible, anachronistic or unlikely.

On the contrary. What we find in Mark 13 and its parallels is, essentially, a well-known Jewish story retold. It is profoundly similar to the stories that were routinely told within Judaism. It speaks of the true god vindicating his people and judging their enemies. It is the story of the real return from exile; the story, once more, of YHWH returning to judge and save. On the other hand, it is profoundly dissimilar: it speaks, as only some extreme sectarians would speak, of Jerusalem and the Temple as the real enemy, and of a little group, around a prophetic figure, as the true people of Israel. It is profoundly similar to the outlook we find in the early church: similar apocalyptic scenarios were known in the largely gentile groups that made up Paul's congregations and elsewhere.[146] Yet it is also profoundly dissimilar: in its present context, it bursts upon the hearers as a surprise and a warning, not as news they had been anticipating.

---

[142] cf. too Lk. 17.22–37, on which see below.

[143] Caird 1965, 21.

[144] cf. *NTPG* 390–6.

[145] cf. again Dodd 1968, 69–83.

[146] cf. 1 Th. 2.13–16; 2 Th. 1.5–2.12; Rev. *passim*; *Did.* 16.1–8. This multiple and early attestation shows once again that Crossan's official categories are not determinative for his own decisions, since he denies that Jesus was responsible for this group of ideas (1991a, 434).

The Romans, then, would desecrate the sanctuary, in fulfilment of the Danielic warning. They would plant their standards in holy ground, and the little beleaguered community of Jesus' disciples would see it, and know that this was the time to make haste. Unlike its scriptural paradigm, the flight would be horrendous in itself (Mark 13.17–20), but better than staying and going down with the city, caught in the doom of its idolatry. The new Babylon was to be destroyed in an instant, and flight was the only appropriate action, the only way of salvation for Jesus' renewed Israel. Thus far, the shocking story follows the line of the whole narrative that we have reconstructed in the last two chapters.

At that time (13.21–3) there would be false Messiahs. This did not take much guessing. At a time of great national crisis, such as had already happened in 4 BC and AD 6, there would always be those who would set themselves up as YHWH's anointed, and there would always be those who would find them irresistibly attractive.[147] But the church was not to be deceived. If any were expecting a 'second coming' of Jesus to lead the army of liberation, in parallel (as it were) to the subsequent myth of a 'Nero *redivivus*' that circulated among the Roman army, they were to have such thoughts firmly quashed.[148] When the 'son of man' was vindicated, there would be no question, no room for doubt. It would be clear to anyone, whether or not they had eyes to see. Jerusalem's destruction would not be something about which one might debate. It would be like lightning shining from the east to the west. The eagles – the Roman eagles, presumably – would gather round the carcass and pick it clean.[149] The great city that had rejected Jesus' message, his way of peace, would be destroyed. He would thereby be vindicated as a prophet; yes, and more than a prophet.

(v) The Vindication of the Son of Man

But in those days, after that tribulation, the sun will be darkened, and the moon will not give its light, and the stars will be falling from heaven.[150] For the powers of the heavens shall be shaken. And then[151] they shall see 'the son of man coming on the clouds' with

---

[147] cf. Horsley & Hanson 1985; *NTPG* 170–81.

[148] For the rumour, cf. Tac. *Hist.* 2.8. For a recent discussion in terms of the dating of Revelation, cf. Smalley 1994, 40–50.

[149] Mt. 24.27–8/Lk. 17.24, 37.

[150] Lk. adds: 'On the earth distress of nations in perplexity at the roaring of the sea and the waves, men fainting with fear and foreboding of what is coming on the world' (21.25b). The echoes here are of Ps. 65.7 (65.8 MT); Wis. 5.22.

[151] Mt. adds 'the sign of the son of man will appear in heaven, and all the tribes of the earth shall mourn' (24.30). The echoes this time are of Zech. 12.10, whose context is of great mourning in Jerusalem and then victory for the true people of god, especially the house of David.

power and great glory. And he will send out his messengers,[152] and gather in his chosen ones from the four winds, from one end of heaven to the other.[153] From the fig tree learn the parable: when its branch becomes tender and puts forth its leaves, you know that summer is near. So you also, when you see all these things, know that it is near, at the gates. Truly I say to you, that this generation will not pass away until all these things take place. Heaven and earth will pass away, but my words will not pass away.[154]

Our interpretation of this section depends entirely upon the arguments advanced in chapter 10 of *NTPG*.[155] Summarizing the results reached there, we can say: the 'coming of the son of man' does not refer to the 'parousia' in the modern scholarly, and popular, sense of a human figure travelling downwards towards the earth on actual clouds. Nor does the phrase 'son of man' of itself refer to a 'superhuman' figure. Nothing in Daniel, in the rereadings of Daniel in the first century, or in the teaching of Jesus as we have studied it, pushes the reading of Mark 13.26 in that direction. We have already commented on the meaning of the darkening of sun, moon and stars. It is crass literalism, in view of the many prophetic passages in which this language denotes socio-political and military catastrophe, to insist that this time the words must refer to the physical collapse of the space-time world. This is simply the way regular Jewish imagery is able to refer to major socio-political events and bring out their full significance.

As to Mark 13.26 in particular, we may briefly note the following points in relation to the 'coming' of the 'son of man' itself. The word 'coming', so easily misread in English, is in Greek *erchomenon*, and so could mean either 'coming' or 'going'.[156] Even if 'coming' were pressed, that would not advance the cause of those who read the verse as predicting a downward cloudborne movement for the 'son of man', since Daniel 7 conceives the scene from the perspective of heaven, not earth. The 'son of man' figure 'comes' to the Ancient of Days. He comes *from* earth *to* heaven, vindicated after suffering.[157] The Danielic story always was one of vindication and exaltation, and was retold as such in the first century.[158]

---

[152] Mt. adds 'with a trumpet' (24.31), echoing e.g. Isa. 27.13. The word for 'messengers' is *angeloi*; this could mean 'angels', but could equally naturally refer to human messengers.

[153] Lk. omits this last sentence, and instead adds: 'When these things begin, look up, lift up your heads: your redemption is drawing near' (24.28).

[154] Mk. 13.24–31. Significant variations in the pars. (Mt. 24.29–35/Lk. 21.25–33) are noted above.

[155] *NTPG* 280–99.

[156] I cannot resist quoting the remark of one puzzled student, in Vancouver in 1988, who remarked at this point that now *he* didn't know whether he was coming or going.

[157] cf. below, on Mt. 25.31 and Zech. 14.5.

[158] *NTPG* 289–5, 304, 312–17.

The 'coming of the son of man' is thus good first-century metaphorical language for two things: the defeat of the enemies of the true people of god, and the vindication of the true people themselves. Thus, the *form* that this vindication will take, as envisaged within Mark 13 and its parallels, will be precisely the destruction of Jerusalem and the Temple. This is what the whole chapter has been about from the start. Jesus' action in the Temple had pointed in this direction already, as had his cryptic remarks about mountains being cast into the sea. As a prophet, Jesus staked his reputation on his prediction of the Temple's fall within a generation; if and when it fell, he would thereby be vindicated. As the kingdom-bearer, he had constantly been acting, as we shall see later on, in a way which invited the conclusion that he thought he had the right to do and be what the Temple was and did, thereby implicitly making the Temple redundant. The story he had been telling, and by which he had ordered his life, demanded a particular ending. If, then, the Temple remained for ever, and his movement fizzled out (as Gamaliel thought it might[159]), he would be shown to have been a charlatan, a false prophet, maybe even a blasphemer. But if the Temple was to be destroyed and the sacrifices stopped; if the pagan hordes were to tear it down stone by stone; and if his followers did escape from the conflagration unharmed, in a re-enactment of Israel's escape from their exile in doomed Babylon – why, then he would be vindicated, not only as a prophet, but as Israel's representative, as (in some sense) the 'son of man'.

In this context, the imagery of Mark 13.24–5, 27 can be easily understood. These verses, as Caird urged, are not 'flat and literal prose'.[160] They do not speak of the collapse or end of the space-time universe. They are, as we have seen from the passages in Isaiah and Jeremiah quoted above, typical Jewish imagery for events within the present order that are felt and perceived as 'cosmic' or, as we should say, as 'earth-shattering'. More particularly, they are regular Jewish imagery for events that *bring the story of Israel to its appointed climax*. The days of Jerusalem's destruction would be looked upon as days of cosmic catastrophe.[161] The known world would go into convulsions: power struggles and *coups d'état* would be the order of the day; the *pax Romana*, the presupposition of 'civilized' life throughout the then Mediterranean world, would collapse into chaos.[162] In the midst of that chaos Jerusalem would fall. The 'son of man' would thereby be vindicated. That

---

[159] Ac. 5.33–9.

[160] Caird 1965, 22.

[161] Josephus bore witness to this in a different way, by recording the tales of the great gate of the Temple swinging open of its own accord and the angels taking their leave: *War* 6.293–300.

[162] On the *pax Romana*, with all its ambiguities, see Wengst 1987, Part I.

would be the sign that the followers of this 'son of man' would now spread throughout the world: his 'angels', that is, messengers, would summon people from north, south, east and west to come and sit down with Abraham, Isaac and Jacob in the kingdom of YHWH.

The imagery here, once more, evokes the story with which we are already thoroughly familiar, the story of return from exile:

> If you return to YHWH your God, and you and your children obey him with all your heart and with all your soul . . . then YHWH your God will restore your fortunes and have compassion on you, gathering you again from all the people among whom YHWH your God has scattered you. Even if your exile is from the extremity of the heaven unto the extremity of the heaven, from there YHWH your god will gather you, and from there YHWH your god will receive you. YHWH your god will bring you back to your land, which your fathers inherited, and you will inherit it.[163]

The result of 'the vindication of the son of man' – exactly as it ought to be within the controlling story – is that exile will at last be over.[164] The refocusing of this central Jewish hope on to Jesus and his people is made more explicit still by the other clear echo here, of a passage part of which we have already quoted in another connection:

> Up, up! Flee from the land of the north, says YHWH; for I have spread you abroad like the four winds of heaven, says YHWH. Up! Escape to Zion, you that live with daughter Babylon. For thus said YHWH of hosts . . ., regarding the nations that plundered you: Truly, one who touches you touches the apple of my eye. See now, I am going to raise my hand against them, and they shall become plunder for their own slaves. Then you will know that YHWH of hosts has sent me. Sing and rejoice, O daughter Zion! For lo, I will come and dwell in your midst, says YHWH. Many nations shall join themselves to YHWH on that day, and shall be my people; and I will dwell in your midst. And you shall know that YHWH of hosts has sent me to you. YHWH will inherit Judah as his portion in the holy land, and will again choose Jerusalem.[165]

This remarkable passage is heavy with irony in our present context. The promises to Jerusalem, to Zion, are now transferred to Jesus and his people. Meanwhile Jerusalem herself has become the great enemy, the city whose destruction signals the liberation of the true people of god. What is more, when these events take place the prophet who has prophesied them will be well and truly vindicated.

---

[163] Dt. 30.2–5. The LXX of v. 4 renders the Hebrew *biqtse hashamayim*, lit. 'among the ends of the heavens', as *ap' akrou tou ouranou heos akrou tou ouranou*, 'from the end of heaven to the end of heaven', which is echoed more or less exactly in Mt. 24.31b, *ap' akron ouranon heos ton akron auton*, and modified only slightly in Mk. 13.27b, *ap' akrou ges heos akrou ouranou* ('from the end of earth to the end of heaven'). This, in other words, suggests strongly that the Mk. passage refers, not to a 'supernatural' or 'heavenly' event, but to this-worldly activity.

[164] cf. too Ps. 106.47; Isa. 27.13; 2 Macc. 2.7.

[165] Zech. 2.6–12. The 'four winds of heaven' also feature in Dan. 7.2; *Did.* 10.5.

In this context, too, the little parable of the fig tree (Mark 13.28–9) makes perfect sense. Fig trees have already been important, within the story, as eschatological signs.[166] Now they emerge again, not this time bearing leaves which ought to show the presence of fruit, but bearing leaves to show that summer is near. So when the story that Jesus has told – the abomination of desolation, the great tribulation, the chaos of catastrophic world events – comes to pass, this will be to the disciples the sign that they asked for at the start of the chapter.

It should be noted most carefully that the signs do not mean that '*he* is near', as most English translations of Mark 13.29 and its parallels suggest. The Greek is *engus estin*, which can mean '*he* is near', or '*she* is near', or '*it* is near'. In the present context the last of these is both natural and obvious.[167] Luke has paraphrased, just in case (perhaps) anyone should read Mark without understanding: when you see these things, you will know that *the kingdom of god* is near. Here we are in touch, I suggest, with the final moments in Jesus' retelling of the kingdom-story. Luke has rightly brought out the meaning of the entire prediction. When Jerusalem is destroyed, and Jesus' people escape from the ruin just in time, *that will be* YHWH becoming king, bringing about the liberation of his true covenant people, the true return from exile, the beginning of the new world order.

The prediction which follows, that this generation will see the end (Mark 13.30–2), is both thoroughly comprehensible in terms of the whole mindset of Jesus, and thoroughly coherent with the emphasis of the discourse as a whole. This is how the story *must* end. If Jesus is not the last prophet, he is a false prophet. The reference to heaven and earth passing away must not, of course, be taken as an indication that the discourse has after all been about the end of the space-time universe, but as another typical Jewish metaphor such as those in Isaiah or Jeremiah: even though heaven and earth, the things which YHWH created in the beginning, should pass away, unmaking the very word of creation of the sovereign god, yet these words would remain true.[168]

---

[166] Lk. 13.6–9; Mk. 11.12–14, 20–4.

[167] To read 'he is near' in the sense of the 'second coming', with a literalistic understanding of 'the coming of the son of man on a cloud', produces extra problems: why should he be 'at the very gates'? If the answer is that the latter phrase is to be taken metaphorically, I of course agree; but we should then be prepared to acknowledge that the whole passage is a complex web of symbolic metaphor. Only to recognize as metaphor the language that still functions thus in our own world would be the crassest anachronism.

[168] cf. Isa. 51.6; the chapter as a whole concerns the return from exile, and the potential disappearance of heavens and earth is, as in Mk. 13.31/Mt. 24.36/Lk. 21.33, a way of drawing attention to the unshakeableness, by contrast, of the prophetic word, much as in Isa. 40.8 ('the grass withers, the flower fades, but the word of our god shall stand for ever'). Cp. too Jer. 31.36 LXX (I owe this reference to Sylvia Keesmaat).

This is like saying 'Truly, truly, I say to you', only magnified to the furthest degree. There can be no more emphatic statement than this.

How then are we to read the entire passage? There is no need for the common understanding to remain in place a minute longer. Schweitzer, and many subsequent scholars, claimed that Jesus predicted the end of the world within a generation, reinforcing that prediction with the most solemn of declarations, and that he was proved wrong. Many other scholars, believing that Jesus would not have said anything so 'apocalyptic', decided that the early church concocted the passage out of thin air, with the same meaning; the church, too, was proved wrong. This, as we have seen, is a straightforward if devastating misreading of apocalyptic language. The story simply does not work like that. Most popular Christian readings of the text, not least within fundamentalism, have shared Schweitzer's understanding that Jesus predicted the end of the world, but have said that, since this did not happen within a generation, Jesus must have meant something different by 'this generation'.[169] Here we have the solution to the problem of the *timing* of the kingdom, which is of course also raised by such verses as Matthew 10.23 and Mark 9.1.[170] Already present in Jesus' ministry, and climactically inaugurated in his death and resurrection, the divine kingdom will be manifest within a generation, when Jesus and his followers are vindicated in and through the destruction of Jerusalem. The generation that rejects Jesus must be the last before the great cataclysm. There can be no other, because if there were they would need another warning prophet; once the father has sent the son to the vineyard, he can send nobody else. To reject the son is to reject the last chance. The prophecy of 'this generation' is thus closely tied to Jesus' view of his own role within the eschatological process, which we will discuss more fully in the next Part of the book.

(vi) Noah, Lot and the Son of Man

Mark's discourse more or less stops at this point, with only the short paragraph urging watchfulness (see below). But Matthew continues, with material very similar to that which Luke has in his seventeenth chapter; and it will be easier to include Matthew 24.26–8 here as well.[171]

The days of Noah and the days of Lot were both times when devastating judgment fell on those who were failing to heed divine warning.[172] Their

---

[169] Among serious scholars, cf. e.g. Ellis 1966, 246f.; Marshall 1978, 779f. The discussion in Gundry 1993, 790–2 is instructive.

[170] On which, see below, 470.

[171] cf. Lk. 17.22–37; 21.34–6; Mt. 24.26–8, 37–41.

[172] Gen. 5.29—9.17; 19.1–29. Both Noah and Lot were of course well known in sub-

times were perfectly ordinary, with no special signs of imminent disaster: they ate, they drank, they married and were given in marriage. But when YHWH acted in judgment there was no time to waste. Only those who got out and fled – Noah in his boat, Lot and his daughters running away – were saved. Lot's wife looked back and was turned into a pillar of salt. Jesus did not want his disciples to be caught in the coming destruction. They were not to stay for sentimental or nostalgic reasons, or out of a mistaken sense of national or familial solidarity or loyalty. To do so would be to run the risk of being overtaken by the judgment.

While they were waiting for the moment to arrive, however, there would be many voices urging that Israel's vindication was to be found in this or that new movement. They would long to see one of the days of the 'son of man', but would not see it, and would be an open prey to invitations to look at this or that conspiracy or uprising as the way towards vindication. But when it happened there would be no mistaking it: it would be like lightning flashing from east to west, and on that day (once again, this advice would do little for someone caught by the end of the space-time universe!) they should not stop to pack and get ready, but simply run.

At that time there would be division between families and colleagues: one would be taken, another left. It should be noted that being 'taken' in this context means being taken in *judgment*. There is no hint, here, of a 'rapture', a sudden 'supernatural' event which would remove individuals from *terra firma*. Such an idea would look as odd, in these synoptic passages, as a Cadillac in a camel-train. It is a matter, rather, of secret police coming in the night, or of enemies sweeping through a village or city and seizing all they can. If the disciples were to escape, if they were to be 'left', it would be by the skin of their teeth. Luke's version of this discourse comes in his chapter 17, which then leads into the parables of the unjust judge, and the Pharisee and publican, at the start of his next chapter.[173] Israel's god would vindicate his elect, who cry to him day and night. His vindicated elect (18.8, 14),[174] however, would be a group one might not have expected: not the official or self-appointed guardians of Israel's national life, but those who cry to their god for vindication, without presuming to claim that they have kept the whole Torah and so are automatically within 'Israel'. They would be the forgiven ones. Humble in the present, they would be exalted in the future on the day when Israel's god acted. Luke's ending to the discourse in chapter 21

---

sequent Jewish tradition: e.g. *Jub.* 4.33—10.17; 16.5–9.

[173] Lk. 18.1–8, 9–14.

[174] The link between these two ('he will vindicate/grant justice to them'; 'he went home in the right') is sometimes obscured in English translations, but is clear in the Greek, where the same root is used.

belongs here, too. The disciples in that period must not allow their concentration to wander, must not settle down and while away their lives (21.34-6). They must be waiting to stand before the 'son of man', to share in his vindication.

5. Conclusion: Judgment and Vindication

Jesus' story of the kingdom thus followed the pattern of the characteristic Jewish stories of the time. It did this in two senses: first, in that it told the story of how Israel's long exile was finally coming to its close; second, in that it did so subversively, with the present regime in Jerusalem as the target of fierce polemic. Jesus' retelling of the story is not to be squashed down into witty or proverbial aphorisms. It is not to be reduced to timeless moral or doctrinal teaching. He spoke as he acted, as a prophet through whose work YHWH was doing a new thing, indeed *the* new thing for which Israel had waited so long. This (in case anybody should even imagine it) was not, of course, in any sense an anti-Jewish thing to do. Jesus was claiming to be speaking for Israel's true ancestral traditions, denouncing what he saw as deviation and corruption at the very heart of Israel's present life.

This picture possesses the strengths required for any scientific hypothesis, including historical ones.[175] First, it includes the data. If we imagine a different model for Jesus' career from the one we have suggested, much of the material falls apart, and has to be assigned variously all over a purely hypothetical (that is to say, imaginary) early church, much as a computer in distress scatters a splintered file all over its memory. By starting where we have, and following the line of thought through the prophetic praxis and into the stories which brought Jesus' mindset into articulation, we have found a great deal of the material making coherent sense. Second, it does so within an essentially simple framework, which places Jesus credibly within the turbulent world of first-century Judaism. I can imagine people disliking this picture of Jesus; I cannot imagine someone arguing coherently that it could not be historical. The picture, in other words, makes sense, without having loose ends of its own flapping around all over the place. Since the two major criteria for successful hypotheses, which of course balance one another out, are satisfied, we may proceed with some confidence. The third criterion is, of course, whether the hypothesis sheds light on areas other than the original one. That remains to be seen.

One place where such a test cries out to be applied is at the point where, according to the synoptic tradition, Jesus and his contemporaries came into

---

[175] cf. *NTPG* ch. 4, esp. 98-109.

conflict. If telling subversive stories – and the story of the kingdom as we have studied it in these last three chapters is as subversive as anything could be – is likely to provoke dissent and anger, that anger will concentrate itself on places where the retold story, indicative of the rethought mindset, challenges the symbols at the heart of the dominant worldview. There are, of course, other questions raised at this point: what role, for instance, did Jesus think he would play in the events which he saw coming upon Israel? But these questions must remain in the background for the moment. First, we must concentrate on the symbols which characterized Jesus' prophetic work.

Chapter Nine

SYMBOL AND CONTROVERSY

1. Introduction: Kingdom, Symbol, Controversy

(i) The Problem of Symbols

One can close one's eyes to unexpected behaviour. One can stop one's ears against a tale newly told. But if someone burns the flag, something must be done. Controversy, and perhaps even violence, can be expected at the point where, in continuing our journey around the worldview model, we arrive at the quadrant labelled 'symbols', the things which bring the worldview into visibility.[1] The proverbial she-bear robbed of her cubs is not more prone to violence than an otherwise placid human being whose deepest worldview-symbols have been overturned. Praxis may be disturbing. Stories may be subversive. But lay a finger on a cherished symbol, and the fat will be in the fire.

Jesus' behaviour, after all, may have been unusual, to say the least. But healers and wandering holy men were by no means unknown in the ancient world, including ancient Judaism; and they did not arouse great hostility. Jesus' stories were deeply subversive, darkly suggesting that Israel's great hour had come, but not in the way she imagined. But it is perhaps significant that, until the very last of the public parables (the wicked tenants), we do not hear of opposition or anger as the response to one of his teasing narratives. What generates hostility is a clash of symbols. I shall argue in this chapter that Jesus implicitly and explicitly attacked what had become the standard symbols of the second-Temple Jewish worldview; that the symbols of his own work were deeply provocative; and that this redrawing of the symbolic world, as part of his kingdom-announcement, was the cause of actual hostility against him.

The clash of symbolic worlds is regularly linked with the question of why Jesus was executed. There are, broadly, two alternative standard ways of

---

[1] On the place of symbols within worldviews, cf. *NTPG* ch. 5, esp. 122–6; on symbols within the Jewish worldview, cf. *NTPG* ch. 8.

accounting for the death of Jesus. In their extreme forms, they run like this. First, Jesus was a Jewish revolutionary. He espoused the cause of nationalism, seeking 'the kingdom of god' in a fairly traditional 'zealot' sense (with a small 'z'). The Romans, perhaps with the collaboration of some of the Jewish leaders, not surprisingly found this deeply threatening, and executed him as a political trouble-maker and insurrectionist. As we saw in chapter 3, this solution has been tried in many forms and, despite some contemporary political reasons for wanting it to be true, is now largely abandoned.

Second, Jesus was a teacher of a new sort of religion. He believed in the love, grace and mercy of the god of Israel, at a time when those ideas were decidedly unpopular among the Jews. The Pharisees, in particular, objected to his teachings because he opposed the Torah, the foundation of their whole legalistic system. They plotted against him on these strictly religious grounds, until their intentions were implemented by the chief priests who handed Jesus over, on a trumped-up political charge, to the Romans. This solution, widely accepted at a popular level in some form or other, has come under heavy fire in recent years for its gross misrepresentation of Judaism, and for its failure to explain why these religious differences should have led to Jesus' execution.[2]

The first solution offers a political Jesus who offended the Romans; the second, a religious Jesus who offended the Jews. The first solution explains the crucifixion, though not the earlier controversies, at the expense of most of the evidence about Jesus' ministry. The second explains the controversies, though not the crucifixion, at the expense of most of the evidence about first-century Jews. At the historical level, nobody doubts that Jesus was crucified, but a good many doubt that he entered into controversy with the Pharisees in particular. How are we to proceed?

There is an increasing tendency among scholars to see Jesus' action in the Temple as the proximate cause of his death. This has been forcibly argued by Sanders in particular; even Crossan, whose scepticism about such historical links is fairly extreme, allows that this is at least quite possible.[3] This, it should be noted, effectively shifts the ground of the older antithesis of religion and politics, and shifts it, moreover, a long way in the direction of greater historical plausibility. Now we have a *political* Jesus (though not an anti-Roman revolutionary) who offended the *Jews*, specifically the chief

---

[2] See particularly the polemic of Sanders 1985, 1993 against such writers as Jeremias. Whether Sanders is fair to Jeremias (see Meyer 1991; Sanders 1991) is not relevant to my present point, which has to do with extreme positions rather than the careful reporting of scholarly argument.

[3] Crossan 1991a, 354–60.

priests, who were able to turn one kind of political charge (a threat to the Temple) into another kind (a threat to Rome). But this focus seems to leave out of account the apparently 'religious' controversies that the synoptic gospels record as having taken place earlier in Jesus' career. This enables Sanders, in particular, to argue forcibly that Jesus did not engage in controversy with the Pharisees over such 'religious' matters as sabbath and food. Once more, how are we to proceed?

So far, we have seen that Jesus' kingdom-announcement, made in praxis and story, was stating a double positive claim, and a single negative one. Positively, he claimed that Israel was now at last experiencing the real return from exile, and (as we shall see) that YHWH was now at last returning to Zion. Negatively, he claimed (just as, we may stress one more time, the Maccabees, the Pharisees and the Essenes would have claimed) that the judgment of YHWH would shortly fall not only on Gentiles but also on those within Israel who had failed to be truly loyal. His definition of what constituted true loyalty differed, of course, from other definitions on offer, just as the aforementioned groups would have differed from one another at the same point. The *shape* of his claim was thoroughly characteristic of second-Temple renewal movements; the detailed *content* was strikingly different, as were theirs to one another. For, as became increasingly apparent, he was not only claiming that these things – the fulfilment, the coming catastrophe – were somehow being brought about through, and in relation to, his own work. That, too, would have been standard among renewal movements. He was claiming that both fulfilment and catastrophe were being radically *redefined* through his own work.

If this redefinition had been purely a matter of ideas, or of private behaviour, Jesus could have been written off. When it generated a clash of symbols, he had become dangerous. All the signs indicate, I suggest, that exactly this happened at various points throughout his public career.

(ii) Controversy about Controversy

We must now get to the bottom of the debate that has raged on the subject of the synoptic stories of Jesus' controversies with opponents, particularly with the Pharisees. An advance summary of the argument may help at this point.

(i) Traditional readings of the gospels have made Jesus the teacher of a religion of love and grace, of the inner observance of the heart rather than the outward observance of legal codes.

(ii) The same traditional readings have envisaged Jesus opposing the Pharisees, or they him, on the grounds that they supported a religion of outward observances and perceived him to be an antinomian threat.

(iii) This double reading has recently been opposed, particularly by E. P. Sanders, on the grounds of historical implausibility: Jesus did not 'speak against the law', and what he did say would not have been particularly irritating to the Pharisees.

(iv) I shall propose a quite different reading of the controversy-stories, which avoids the critique of the older, caricatured position, to which I do not for a moment subscribe. Jesus announced, in symbol as in word, the kingdom of Israel's god; he attacked the symbols which spoke of an Israel resistant to his kingdom-vision. (One more time: in this he was doing pretty much what the Essenes and Pharisees did to each other.) As a result, some of his contemporaries believed that he was guilty of the offence spelled out in Deuteronomy 13, that is, of 'leading Israel astray'.

(v) The controversy-stories are highly likely to be historical at the core; but their meaning is not the one traditionally assigned to them. They were about eschatology and politics, not religion or morality. Eschatology: Israel's hope was being realized, but it was happening in Jesus' way, and at his initiative. Politics: the kingdom Jesus was announcing was undermining, rather than underwriting, the revolutionary anti-pagan zeal that was the target of much of Jesus' polemic, the cause (according to him) of Israel's imminent ruin, and the focal point of much (Shammaite) Pharisaic teaching and aspiration.

So much by way of summary. A further point of introduction may also be helpful. I argued in the earlier volume that the normal form-critical assumptions about the origin of the controversy-stories in the synoptic gospels ought to be stood on their heads.[4] We may briefly recapitulate as follows.

Received wisdom has suggested that the controversy-stories developed from isolated and detached sayings, quite possibly invented by the early church in response to particular needs. They grew, on this theory, into longer narratives, receiving as they did so fresh colouring from scriptural and other contexts. I have proposed that the opposite is more likely to be the case. Following any striking incident in the life of a figure such as we have already shown Jesus to be, the first audience would tell the story in such a way as to echo Jewish controversy-stories with which they might be familiar. Detached sayings, where they occur, would be the result of the story being passed on,

---

[4] *NTPG* 431f.

later, in contexts where such echoes would not be recognized or appreciated. It is obvious, of course, that the synoptic controversy-stories as we have them share a remarkably similar form. One only has to compare the sprawling and complex narrative of John 6 to see just how well-formed the stories of Mark 2.1—3.6 are. This form certainly reflects the theologically and politically motivated retellings of the very early communities, among which I would include communities during the lifetime of Jesus himself. But there is no reason, within the narrative grammar or hypothetical tradition-history of the stories themselves, to suggest, on grounds of form, that the controversy-stories are essentially later inventions.

In particular, we should note that a good many matters were debated prominently in the early church which have left no record in the gospels at all.[5] There is nothing in the gospels about circumcision; nothing about food offered to idols; about speaking in tongues; about incest; about, in fact, the multitude of matters discussed in 1 Corinthians (a good example, since it is something of a repository of pressing early Christian issues). The only exception, a point at which something discussed in the letter occurs also in the gospel narratives, is divorce; and, precisely at that point, Paul refers explicitly to a word of Jesus.[6]

More recent arguments against the historicity of the controversies emanate from circles that have attempted, often for quite blatant twentieth-century motives, to deny that Jesus clashed at all with his Jewish contemporaries. Within post-holocaust theology, as we saw earlier, this has been part of the attempt to reclaim Jesus as a good first-century Jew who would be horrified at the thought of a 'Christianity' attempting to base itself upon him.[7] This obviously carries with it the necessity to argue a case not just about Jesus, but about the early church: Jesus did not oppose his Jewish contemporaries, but the early church did theirs. There are four varieties of this case, of which the fourth, easily the most important, brings together in itself a further variety of different strands. We must look at them in turn.

1. Perhaps the dominant view of the stories in which Jesus clashes with, or criticizes, the Pharisees is that represented by W. D. Davies. The stories in question (he argues) do not reflect Jesus' day, nor even that of the church up to AD 70. They reflect the post-70 period, when, as the rabbis regrouped at the Synod of Jamnia, the Christians found themselves shut out of the fold

---

[5] Despite the implications of Sanders 1985, 264.

[6] 1 Cor. 7.10f. For this whole discussion cp. *NTPG* 421f. Negative versions of the same argument – issues which continue to be important in the gospels, though they rapidly ceased to be relevant in the expanding church – are highlighted in e.g. Caird 1965, Moule 1967.

[7] Above, ch. 3. The first draft of this chapter was written while I was a guest at the Hebrew University in Jerusalem. I am not about to forget the dangerous ambiguities of the past, or of the present (on which, cf. Ateek 1989; Howard 1993; Ellis 1994).

(probably by the *Birkat ha-Minim*), and responded angrily – by making up sayings of Jesus to denounce the Pharisees (and hence their successors, the rabbis), and by projecting their own controversies back into Jesus' day.[8] This basic outline has become enormously popular in New Testament studies, so that one comes across students innocently supposing that 'Synod of Jamnia, AD 85' is as much a fixed point as 'Fall of Jerusalem, AD 70', and that controversy or conflict between Judaism and Christianity may confidently be dated to some time after this point.

Things are, to put it mildly, by no means that simple. I argued in the earlier volume that the currently favoured picture of Jamnia is almost entirely mythological, and that the evidence for the promulgation of a 'benediction' which suddenly excluded Christians from synagogues is extremely thin.[9] Other recent studies have confirmed that what has been called 'the parting of the ways' was far more complex than scholarship between 1960 and 1990 tended to assume or allow.[10] In fact, the best evidence that we possess for serious and open hostility between Jews – especially Pharisees – and the nascent Christian movement (which was, as of course we must always remember, the *Jewish*-Christian movement) is found in the earliest period for which we have evidence, namely in the letters of Paul. He, by his own admission, had persecuted the very early church with violence and zeal.[11] If we want hard evidence of sharp controversy between Christians and Pharisees we are on much firmer ground in AD 35 (or 45, or 55) than in AD 85.

Persecution of Christians, in fact, did not come initially from pagans. Apart from sporadic and local problems mentioned in Acts, a fierce but brief spell under Nero, and the possibility (it is only that, despite frequent scholarly assertions) of more persecution under Domitian, we do not hear of serious or organized persecution by Gentiles until the second century.[12] It is all from the Jewish side. And the period for which we have the best evidence of persecution of the church by Jews is not after AD 70, but during the first generation of Christianity. Actually, I doubt if anyone would have supported the 'myth of Jamnia' were it not for a natural and laudable desire to undercut

---

[8] cf. e.g. Davies 1964, 1974; Davies & Allison 1988–91. This idea has dominated one stream in Johannine studies, witnessed by Martyn 1979 [1968]: cf. now Smith 1990.

[9] *NTPG* 161–6, 451–2. Lieu 1994, 115 n.22 records 'a general consensus on the impossibility of relating the benediction [i.e. the *Birkat ha-Minim*] directly or exclusively to the rupture between Jews and Christians'.

[10] e.g. Aune 1991; Dunn 1991; 1992a; Bauckham 1993b; Lieu 1994. Collins 1995, 20 speaks of 'the demise of the Jamnia hypothesis'. The diversity between even these works demonstrates already the considerable uncertainties that still surround the whole question.

[11] e.g. Gal. 1.13f., 23 (on which see Wright 1996c); 1 Cor. 15.9; Phil. 3.6; cf. Ac. 8.3; 9.1, 21; 22.4, 19; 26.10f.; cf. 1 Th. 2.14f.; Gal. 4.29; 6.12.

[12] cf. *NTPG* 351–6.

the shallow and non-historical picture of Judaism in general, and Pharisaism in particular, as a shabby, second-rate religion, contrasting sharply with the religion which Jesus is supposed to have taught. That picture has done quite enough damage already, but we must not allow it to do yet more by producing equal and opposite 'corrective' historical distortions.

2. The second variety of arguments against the broad historicity of the controversy-stories may be represented by Geza Vermes.[13] His portrait of Jesus as a Galilean Hasid allows Jesus some individuality or idiosyncrasy, but no real root-and-branch clash with his contemporaries.[14] Vermes, however, marginalizes at the same time Jesus' eschatological claim and actions; and, against almost all other serious recent writers on Jesus, he does not think Jesus did, said or thought very much about the Temple. In particular, he offers no sustained or integrated account of the reasons for Jesus' death. Vermes' portrait answers the first of our sequence of questions ('what sort of a Jew was Jesus?'). But without answers to the others, particularly the third ('why was Jesus executed?'), his theory remains weak and unproven.[15]

3. A third way of arguing that Jesus and the Pharisees were not really opposed to one another is that of the remarkable Jewish scholar Jacob Neusner. Jesus, in his view, was setting up nothing less than a completely different religious system. 'Christianity and Judaism, in their first statements' – and the first Christian statement is, for Neusner, made by Jesus himself – 'really do represent different people talking about different things to different people.'[16] It is interesting to note that Neusner, with this move, ascribes to Jesus what Vermes and others have left to Paul, namely the first attempt to establish something we can call 'Christianity' over against something we can call 'Judaism'. Unlike most other twentieth-century Jewish scholars who have written on the topic, he produces a Jesus who places himself at some distance from, though not in direct controversy with, his Jewish contemporaries. But this picture, though having the apparent contemporary merit of enabling Jewish-Christian dialogue to proceed in a detached way, as it were at arm's length, has little to commend it historically.[17] It may well be,

---

[13] Vermes 1973, 1983, 1993: see ch. 3 for details and further discussion. An earlier argument against Jesus clashing with the Pharisees may be found in Winter 1974 [1961], 174–6, 186. Winter goes so far as to claim, in the latter passage, that Jesus was himself a Pharisee – a view now echoed by Maccoby 1980; this is not noticed by Sanders 1985, 400 n.71.

[14] Vermes 1993, 26: 'His approach to the Torah and his perception of its main message may have borne an individual mark, but neither in general, nor on any particular point, can he be identified as an antinomian teacher.'

[15] Compare the comment of H. Chadwick, reported in Vermes 1983, 13.

[16] Neusner 1989, 290; cf. Neusner 1991, 1993, and similar statements in other works.

[17] cf. *NTPG* 471–6.

as we shall see, that Jesus did and said things which were rightly perceived as revolutionary. But he was not simply offering *an alternative in kind* to Judaism, an entirely different 'religion' in style as well as content. He was claiming, as we have seen all along, to be announcing that the central aspirations of the Jewish people were coming to pass, though not in the way they had expected. He was proposing fulfilment, not mere novelty. And, like all other such proposals within Judaism (and we must stress the word 'within'), it was the character of that proposed fulfilment that led inevitably to controversy.

4. The fourth, and most significant, objection to the synoptic picture of Jesus' clashes with his contemporaries, and with the Pharisees in particular, is offered by E. P. Sanders.[18] In two major books he has presented the following picture:

(i) The Pharisees were a small group, centred upon Jerusalem.[19]

(ii) The Pharisees debated with one another, often sharply, but without violence. Their discussions took for granted that Torah should be kept, and were concerned with the proper manner of that law-keeping. Jesus might have seemed to them a poor legal debater, but they would not have responded to him violently.[20]

(iii) The Pharisees were concerned with their own purity, not with checking up on other people's – which in any case they had no right to do, since they did not in any strict sense 'run things' in the Judaism of the day. Most of the population would, by strict Pharisaic standards, have unwashed hands; but the Pharisees did not go spying on them or plot to kill them.[21]

(iv) Many of Jesus' key teachings in the area of Torah involved an intensification, not an abrogation, of Torah. Nobody would have

---

[18] Sanders 1985, chs. 9, 10; 1993, ch. 14. Sanders is followed in several respects by other scholars, e.g. Fredriksen 1988, 102–10; 1995a & b.

[19] e.g. Sanders 1985, 53, 198, 292, cf. 273: 'the Pharisees . . . did not leave Jerusalem.' This view is not repeated in 1993, perhaps because it has been undermined by such works as Dunn 1988, 266–74 (and cf. *NTPG* 181–203). In his 1985 treatment Sanders was relying heavily on the slender and dubious foundation of Smith 1977 [1956], 1978, criticized in the *NTPG* section just referred to. One example of Pharisees outside Jerusalem: Josephus describes the activity in Galilee of the 'very strict' Eleazar (*Ant.* 20.43–5).

[20] Sanders 1993, 215f., 222f.

[21] Sanders 1985, 265, 291 ('If Jesus disagreed with [the Pharisees] over laws of purity which were peculiar to them, he would have been only one more *'am ha-arets* among many'); cf. 1993, 214, 219. However, in 1993, 44 Sanders allows that the Pharisees 'probably did try to enforce their views' during the Hasmonean period, though he says they apparently did not during the Herodian and post-Herodian period (i.e. the time including the ministry of Jesus). I shall presently question this assumption, as I did in *NTPG* 185–203.

objected if Jesus had managed to prevent murder by preventing hatred, adultery by curbing lust, or greed by reforming tax-collectors.[22]

(v) If Jesus had 'spoken against the law', the early church would not have been so muddled on the issue; Paul would not have needed to write Galatians.[23]

(vi) Though Jesus did not, therefore, 'speak against the law', he 'challenged the adequacy of the Mosaic dispensation' at various points.[24] This, together with his claim to be the spokesman of Israel's god, and his announcement of the kingdom, did generate real opposition, and when his programme finally brought him into conflict with the Temple, this led to his death.[25]

My disagreement with Sanders on these points is oblique, rather than head-on. I am convinced that his final point is basically correct: where conflict occurred, it was because of Jesus' eschatological beliefs and agenda, rather than because of a clash of abstract religious or moral values or teachings. But I do not think that Sanders has followed this insight through in the rest of his analysis.[26] Let us examine each of the first five points in turn.

(i) We do not know for sure how many Pharisees there were in the time of Jesus. The figure of six thousand, often quoted in this context from Josephus *Antiquities* 17.42, refers specifically to the Pharisees who refused to take the oath of allegiance to Caesar, some time in the reign of Herod the Great.[27] In the forty years or so between that incident and the time of Jesus several important political events had taken place, which might well have induced many more to join the movement. We may assume that there were in any case plenty of Pharisees who were not involved with the particular incident in question, and more again who were generally sympathetic to the movement.[28] To risk a modern analogy: the number of ecological activists engaged in one specific anti-nuclear protest in 1956 is not a good indicator of the

---

[22] Sanders 1985, 260–4; 1993, 210–12, 230.

[23] Sanders 1985, 246 (noting that Bultmann made the same point), 249f.; 1993, 220–2. So too e.g. Vermes 1973, 29; Fredriksen 1995a & b. Cf. the nuanced suggestion of a similar argument in Räisänen 1982.

[24] Sanders 1985, 255, 263, 267–9, 293; 1993, 225f. Sanders, following Hengel 1981b [1968], highlights the command 'leave the dead to bury their dead' (Mt. 8.21–2/Lk. 9.59–60) as the best example.

[25] Sanders 1985, 293, 294–318.

[26] Eschatological conflict: Sanders 1985, 263, 267, 269. He claims, though, (1985, 259) that 'the eschatological key does not open every door'. I disagree – once one cuts the eschatological key even more accurately than Sanders has done.

[27] On this point, see *NTPG* 190f., 196f.

[28] Philo *Spec. Leg.* 2.253 refers to 'thousands' (see below).

number engaged in, or sympathetic to, such protests in 1996, following Chernobyl and similar events. So, too, we do not know the geographical spread of Pharisaism at this stage. Granted that Jerusalem was almost certainly their base, the idea that they never went anywhere else should now be abandoned.[29]

(ii) It is true that different schools of Pharisees debated with one another, sometimes hotly, without finding it necessary to think of assassinating each other. (Our evidence, of course, is mostly two hundred or more years later, so we cannot be completely sure; but there is no suggestion that the schools of Hillel and Shammai used actual violence towards one another.) But this is only relevant if we grant that Jesus was offering a set of teachings that appeared, or were intended to appear, as simply a further set of variations on the question, what does it mean to be loyal to Torah and thorough in its observance? The Hillel–Shammai debate was not the only pressure point in first-century Palestine; there were far sharper distinctions between Pharisees and Sadducees, between both of them and the Essenes, and of course between Jews and Samaritans. (We should not forget that, according to one tradition, Jesus himself was accused of being a Samaritan.[30]) And if, instead of a steady-state ethical debate, one posits – as Sanders himself does, and as my whole argument so far suggests – that Jesus was announcing that the climax of Israel's history was fast approaching, with large-scale consequences at every level of Jewish national life, then one can imagine that what was unthinkable in ordinary times might suddenly become thinkable. It is not a matter, in Thomas Kuhn's terminology, of 'normal science', but of a major proposed paradigm shift.[31] If the synoptic scenarios are anything other than a complete fabrication, Jesus was not debating with the Pharisees on their own terms, or about the detail of their own agendas. Two musicians may discuss which key is best for a particular Schubert song. Somebody who proposes rearranging the poem for a heavy metal band is not joining in the discussion, but challenging its very premises.

(iii) I have already argued at some length that the Pharisees' agenda in this period was not simply about (what we think of as) 'purity'.[32] All the evidence suggests that at least the majority of Pharisees, from the Hasmonean and Herodian periods through to the war of AD 66–70, had as their main aim that which purity symbolized: the political struggle to maintain Jewish

---

[29] cf. *NTPG* 195f.

[30] Jn. 8.48; cf. Bauckham 1993b, esp. 139–41.

[31] Kuhn 1970 [1962]. A tragic contemporary analogy: the murder of the Israeli Prime Minister Yitzhak Rabin in November 1995 was the result of his being seen as jeopardizing a major symbol of Jewish identity, namely land. There is all the difference in the world between a legal debate and a clash of symbols.

[32] For what follows, cf. *NTPG* 186–99, with evidence in full.

identity and to realize the dream of national liberation. The Shammaite party, who formed the majority of Pharisees until at least 70, were strongly inclined towards revolution. The 'live and let live' party were the 'lenient' Hillelites, so aptly exemplified by Gamaliel's attitude in Acts 5.33–40; but they were in the minority until at least after 70 (and we must recall that our evidence for the period 70–135 is mostly from later, and thoroughly Hillelite, sources). The 'zeal' we observe in Saul of Tarsus represents the 'severe' Shammaite line, which dominated the Pharisaic agenda in the time of Jesus. Purity (in its very different manifestations such as food laws, handwashing, and so on) was not, in this period, an end in itself, if indeed it was ever really that. It was the symbol, all the more important for a people who perceived themselves under threat, of national identity and national liberation.[33]

Did Pharisees then take any interest in the actions of those outside their own circle? To be sure.[34] They had been known to criticize those in authority, both kings and priests. The Fourth Gospel's picture of Pharisees coming from Jerusalem to check up on John the Baptist, and subsequently on Jesus himself,[35] is supported by the evidence of Saul of Tarsus. He was not content to mind his own business, to maintain his own purity and let others be as impure as they wished. Despite the bitter regret that he speaks of in retrospect, he lets his testimony stand against himself: he persecuted the young church even outside the borders of the Land.[36] Not, again, that he could do this on his own authority. He was not a member of an official 'thought police'. Rather, he sought, and was granted, authority from those who had it, namely, the chief priests. Like Josephus himself, in an expedition we have already had occasion to discuss, he was sent north from Jerusalem to investigate, and to deal with, activities that might prove troublesome and dangerous.[37] This is further supported by a revealing passage in Philo, who describes the self-appointed policing activities of the Pharisees as follows. God, he says, will never release perjurers from their guilt, not least because, for anyone in such categories,

> there are thousands who have their eyes upon him full of zeal for the laws, strictest guardians of the ancestral institutions, merciless to those who do anything to subvert them.[38]

[33] See below, section 2. This is the real answer to Fredriksen 1995b.

[34] cf. esp. *NTPG* 187–97, with primary and secondary refs. and discussions.

[35] Jn. 1.24; 4.1.

[36] 1 Cor. 15.9; Gal. 1.13f. (describing such behaviour, in words that echo Josephus' regular language about the Pharisees, as 'being exceedingly zealous for my ancestral traditions'); Phil. 3.6. See again Wright 1996c.

[37] Jos. *Life* 110: cf. above, 250f.

[38] Philo *Spec. Leg.* 2.253, a passage not discussed by e.g. Sanders 1992b. The 'thousands' is of interest, of course, in relation to the question of the number of Pharisees, discussed above.

We may conclude that the Pharisees, certainly the 'zealous' ones who were the leading group in our period, took a very active interest in the behaviour of those outside their own circle. The fact that their activity was unofficial did not mean it was any the less zealous, or effective.

(iv) It is of course true that, if Jesus intensified the teachings of Torah, those who followed him would not break the Torah itself, and thus would not incur trouble as antinomians. But at this point, as Sanders himself recognizes, the question cannot be simply, did Jesus support the law or undermine it? What was at stake was his implicit, and sometimes explicit, claim: that in and through his own work Israel's god was doing a new thing, or rather *the* new thing, that for which Israel had longed. And when that happened everything would be different. Torah could regulate certain aspects of human behaviour, but it could not touch the heart. That did not constitute a criticism of Torah; Torah operates in its own sphere. But when the promises of scripture were fulfilled, then the heart itself would be changed, and the supreme position of Torah would in consequence be relativized. What was at stake was *eschatology*, in the sense already argued, not a comparison between two styles or patterns of religion.[39]

(v) If Jesus had 'spoken against the law', and had made such speech programmatic for his whole mission, then it would indeed be strange that so many in the early church apparently failed to get the point. But once more things are not that simple.[40] Neither Jesus nor Paul, nor for that matter anyone else in early Christianity, offers a straight yes-or-no, black-or-white answer to questions about 'the Torah' in the abstract. All attempts to make them do so are doomed to failure. The question, again, assumes that what matters is a steady-state scheme of religion and ethics, with something called 'Judaism' proposing one model and Jesus, Paul, or whoever, proposing an alternative. On the contrary. What matters is precisely *the hope of Israel*: Jesus' announcement that the hope was being realized, Paul's belief that in Jesus' cross and resurrection it had indeed been realized, the early church's struggles to work out what it meant to live as the newly constituted people of the one true god. The question is not, what do you think of Torah in the abstract? The question is, what is Israel's god doing with, and for, Israel and the world? And what role does Torah play within that? At this point, ironically, the discussion has, I think, been hijacked by exactly the sort of Protestant dogmatic scheme which Sanders elsewhere, famously, rejects: the celebrated 'question of the law' (is the Torah a good thing or a bad thing?) is raised in that form not in the New Testament but in the somewhat more recent debates between the followers of Luther and of Calvin.

[39] cf. again Sanders 1985, 267–9 and elsewhere.
[40] cf. e.g. Gundry 1993, 370f.

For Paul, the question took the very concrete and practical form: must Gentiles become circumcised in order to be full members of the people of the one true god? As Sanders saw (at least in part) in his celebrated book *Paul and Palestinian Judaism*, what Paul really struck at was the foundational Jewish belief in the inalienable election of Israel as a family, a nation, an *'am*, an *ethnos*.[41] Paul's so-called 'critique of the law' is really a critique of the idea that the people of the one true god can be, in principle, confined to one nation. In so far as Torah was part of the system by which Israel maintained her own superiority, Paul declared that the holy, just and good Torah had itself become demonic. The true god was now calling men and women of every race and nation to belong, on equal terms, to his one family, and in this process Torah had nothing to contribute.[42]

None of these issues, so vital to the work of Paul, was at stake in the ministry of Jesus. The evangelists had plenty of opportunities to have Jesus meet Gentiles, and to discuss the question of the terms upon which they might attain membership of the covenant people, but we find few such meetings, and no such discussions.[43] When we look at various words of Jesus which we *do* find in the gospels – the comment to the Syrophoenician woman, for example, immediately after the controversy story in Mark 7 – what we find is, to say the least, ambivalent in terms of later Pauline debate. 'Dogs under the table' is hardly a Pauline way of speaking about Gentiles, even if the story ends with them being fed anyway. What we find is an entirely different question: what does loyalty to Israel's god mean for a Palestinian Jew faced with the announcement that the long-awaited kingdom is now at last appearing? Jesus' zealous contemporaries would have said: Torah provides the litmus test of loyalty to Israel's god and to his covenant. Jesus said: what counts is following me.

From one angle, of course, once someone like Paul grasped this point, it could lead straight to the radical conclusion, in a very different situation, that therefore any Gentile who followed Jesus was counted a member of the covenant people, irrespective of adherence to Torah. *But the key issue of Torah in Paul's churches was the question of gentile admission, and thus of circumcision; and about that Jesus said not a word.* When the question of food occurs in Galatians 2, the issue is not 'what food may be eaten' (Paul returns an open verdict on that in Romans 14), but 'with whom it may be eaten'. When sabbath-observance is raised in Galatians 4.10, the question is

---

[41] Sanders 1977, e.g. the summary on 551f.

[42] I have explored several of these ideas more fully in Wright 1991. The idea of the single family in Paul is picked up and discussed brilliantly by Boyarin 1994, though his central thesis fails to convince me: see Wright 1995b.

[43] cf. *NTPG* 421.

not whether sabbaths are a good or a bad thing (again, an open verdict appears in Romans 14), but whether gentile Christians should keep them as a matter of status-definition. Paul's question is: now that Gentiles are entering the renewed, eschatological people of God, must they become proselytes, taking on themselves the whole yoke of Torah? It will not do, then, to say, 'if Jesus had spoken against Torah, Paul would not have needed to write Galatians.' Paul was not arguing that Torah was 'a bad thing'; Jesus was not teaching that Torah was 'a good thing'. The nuances of Pauline theology, and of Jesus' proclamation, are not well served by this sort of anachronistic oversimplification. Paul, it might be argued, was thinking through the entire effect of Jesus' kingdom-inauguration, death, and resurrection, in relation to a situation which Jesus himself never faced, and never discussed. Paul would, no doubt, have claimed theological continuity between his own position and that of Jesus.[44] But the radical difference of setting means that he could not put his opponents straight with a simple quotation from the sayings of Jesus. That was hardly his normal style; but in any case no such quotation was available.

Here, then, is the irony of the account offered by Sanders (and by those like Fredriksen who have followed him). He seeks to reject utterly the anachronistic idea that Jesus was teaching a religion, or a theology, which was 'superior' to that of Judaism. He rejects, rightly, any idea that what Jesus found amiss with Pharisaic teaching was 'pettifogging legalism'. He offers, instead, a category which I would myself, in broad terms, endorse: Jesus was announcing 'restoration eschatology'. But Sanders then discusses the question of Jesus and the law within the non-eschatological category of 'patterns of religion'. In those terms, hardly surprisingly, the question is not resolved.

In defending the broad historicity of the gospel accounts of Jesus' clashes with the Pharisees, the picture of Jesus which I am proposing is not one jot or tittle less 'Jewish' than those outlined and rejected above. It is not the case that Davies, Vermes, Neusner, Sanders and others are offering a 'Jewish Jesus', while I am offering something else. The Jesus of whom I speak is every bit as Jewish as Elijah, Jeremiah and John the Baptist, with whom, according to Matthew at least, he was compared. He was a Jewish prophet, and prophets always risked the accusation of disloyalty. As we shall see later in this chapter, that accusation could take a very specific, and threatening, form.

(vi) I completely agree with Sanders that Jesus 'challenged the adequacy of the Mosaic dispensation' at various points, on the grounds that the day for

---

[44] On this long-debated question, see most recently Wenham 1995.

a new dispensation was now dawning. This, in fact, provides the clue to the whole picture. It was precisely Jesus' eschatological programme which led him into opposition with a good many of his contemporaries, and which finally steered him towards the actions which provoked his death. I suggest that this insight should be regarded as the starting-point from which the detailed issues can be worked out. To this task we now turn.

2. Symbols of Israel's Identity: Sabbath, Food, Nation, Land

(i) Introduction: Context and Agendas

What account may we give of the controversies which have themselves become so controversial in contemporary New Testament scholarship?

We must begin where Sanders ends: with eschatology. The main issue between Jesus and his Jewish contemporaries was his claim that the moment had come, that their god was even now inaugurating his kingdom, and that *this* – this praxis, these stories, this person – *was the mode and means of its inauguration*. Thus far, Sanders; and in my view rightly.

But the kingdom-announcement that we have plotted throughout this book was not simply a matter of telling people what time it was. It carried an agenda. Nor was this agenda simply an alternative *halakah*, a set of practical ethics to set alongside those of Shammai and Hillel. It constituted a challenge to Jesus' contemporaries: give up the interpretation of your tradition which has so gripped you, which is driving you towards the cliff-edge of ruin. Embrace instead a different interpretation of your tradition, one which, though it looks like the way of loss, is in fact the way to true victory. And with this announcement and agenda there went a warning: those who fail to come this way are missing their last chance to repent. From here on, those who persist in their destructive interpretation of Israel's traditions will reap the harvest they are sowing. It was this composite announcement, I suggest, that generated the heated exchanges between Jesus and the Pharisees which we find in the synoptic gospels. It issued, even, in plots against Jesus' life. It pointed ahead to what would happen when the same announcement, agenda, and warning ran head-on into the greatest symbol of all, guarded by those who, unlike the Pharisees, had actual power to do something about prophets who said and did the wrong thing at the wrong time.

To understand the inner logic of all this we need to remind ourselves of two points which I argued in *The New Testament and the People of God*, and which I have already restated somewhat in the previous section. The first is vital, though not well known. The second is equally vital, and, though more widely recognized, it is sometimes challenged, and must be spelled out here a little more than, in writing the earlier volume, I had thought necessary.

First, the dominant agenda of the dominant group of Pharisees in Jesus' day was not simply (in our terms) 'religious'. It was just as much (in our terms) 'political'.[45] Zeal for YHWH, the chief characteristic of the hard-line Shammaite Pharisees who formed the strongest Jewish pressure-group prior to AD 70, meant zeal for Torah. One has only to read the books of the Maccabees to see what that meant. The heaven-sent law must be obeyed; there must be no compromise with the idolatrous ways of the nations. This law, moreover, must be defended; force must be used, where necessary, to protect the law and thus guard the life of the true Israel. The great examples of zeal from early days, Phinehas and Elijah, were men whose piety had had a practical, not to say violent, edge. The first killed an Israelite *in flagrante delicto* with a pagan woman. The second put the prophets of Baal to the sword.[46]

We have every reason to suppose that the Shammaite Pharisees kept this tradition alive. Their proverbial strictness in regard to Torah was not simply a matter of religious observances. It was a matter of guarding Israel from paganization, and, more positively, attempting (if and when occasion allowed) to throw off the pagan yoke altogether. It was this agenda which, I suggest, brought Jesus into head-on collision with the dominant Pharisaic movement of his day. For the Shammaite Pharisees, the coming kingdom of YHWH would be a matter of national liberation and the defeat of the pagans. For Jesus, the kingdom was on offer to those who would repent of just that aspiration. It was inevitable that the two would clash. When they did, what was at stake was far more than an argument about the details of how Torah ought to be kept, the niceties of what constituted purity and impurity.

But what is 'purity' all about? This is the second point at issue: there is an all-important connection between purity codes (all focused, ultimately, on the Temple itself) and political conduct and aspirations. To put it simply, the Temple cult, and the observance of sabbaths, of food taboos, and of circumcision were the key things which marked out Jew from Gentile, which (in other words) maintained and reinforced exactly the agenda, both political and religious, of the hard-line Pharisees.[47] These key 'works of Torah' were the constant *leitmotiv* of Jewish (at least, of would-be observant Jewish) existence.

It is important to be clear at this point. I am *not* saying that purity codes are bizarre, legalistic, irrelevant to true piety, or otherwise not in accord with the implicit rules of Protestantism, idealism, or the romantic movement. Far

---

[45] On all this, cf. *NTPG* 186–99; Borg 1984, 4–17.
[46] Num. 25.6–13; 1 Kgs. 18.40. For this tradition, cf. esp. Hengel 1989c [1961], ch. 4.
[47] cf. *NTPG* 237–41; and below, 388.

from it. All societies have purity codes of one sort or another; some are more integrated with a religious structure, some less, but all have them. Nor am I saying, more specifically, that the Jewish purity codes of Jesus' day were bizarre, legalistic, and so on. Paula Fredriksen has criticized some recent writers on Jesus for having him conveniently oppose various features of ancient Judaism which happen to offend certain contemporary sensibilities (in respect of economic inequality, racial prejudice, and even sexism).[48] That critique may or may not be valid; it does not apply to the case I am mounting. I am not saying (though, as we noted in chapter 2, some writers today come perilously close to saying it) that Jesus rejected his own religious culture.[49] I am saying that Jesus offered a fresh interpretation of the scriptural tradition which he shared with his Jewish contemporaries. His was a critique from within. And the object of his critique, I suggest, was the 'zeal' that was leading Israel to ruin – and which was maintained and reinforced by precisely those aspects of Torah which marked out Israel over against her pagan neighbours.

In case there is any doubt on the matter, I cite some witnesses, modern and ancient, for the way in which Torah, not least the purity codes, was regarded as the distinctive badge of the nation of Israel. First, E. P. Sanders:

> There is, however, something which is common to circumcision, Sabbath, and food laws, and which sets them off from other laws: they created a social distinction between Jews and other races in the Greco-Roman world. Further, they were the aspects of Judaism which drew criticism and ridicule from pagan authors. Jewish monotheism also set Jews apart from Gentiles, but it seems not to have drawn the ridicule of pagans in the way that Sabbath, food laws, and circumcision did.[50]

Or, again, discussing Josephus' exaggerated claims for Jewish distinctiveness:

> The argument depends on the fact that the Jews were famous for their loyalty to the law and the tenacity with which it was kept. The idealized picture is based on the reality of general observance.[51]

Keeping the distinctive codes was *the* means of marking Israel out from her pagan neighbours. This is the theme of the opening chapters of 1 Maccabees. Antiochus Epiphanes attempts to bring the Jews into political and religious subjection by forcing them to abandon their ancestral codes:

[48] Fredriksen 1995a & b.
[49] Fredriksen 1995a, 45 and elsewhere.
[50] Sanders 1983a, 102, with 117 n.27; cf., similarly, 1993, 222. Cp. Klausner 1947 [1925], 376: 'The Judaism of that time . . . had no other aim than to save the tiny nation, the guardian of great ideals, from sinking into the broad sea of heathen culture . . .'
[51] Sanders 1985, 396 n.4. For the Josephus material see below.

The king wrote to his whole kingdom that all should be one people, and that all should give up their particular customs. All the Gentiles accepted the command of the king. Many even from Israel gladly adopted his religion; they sacrificed to idols and profaned the sabbath. And the king sent letters by messengers to Jerusalem and the towns of Judah; he directed them to follow customs strange to the land, to forbid burnt offerings and sacrifices and drink offerings in the sanctuary, to profane sabbaths and festivals, to defile the sanctuary and the priests, to build altars and sacred precincts and shrines for idols, to sacrifice swine and other unclean animals, and to leave their sons uncircumcised. They were to make themselves abominable by everything unclean and profane, so that they would forget the law and change all the ordinances.[52]

It could hardly be clearer. The process of assimilation must clear away the four great distinctives: Temple, sabbath, purity and circumcision. Without these, Israel has lost her uniqueness. The initial revolt of Mattathias was aimed at restoring exactly these things; the keynote was 'zeal', especially zeal for Torah:

... a Jew came forward in the sight of all to offer sacrifice on the altar in Modein, according to the king's command. When Mattathias saw it, he burned with zeal and his heart was stirred. He gave vent to righteous anger; he ran and killed him on the altar. At the same time he killed the king's officer who was forcing them to sacrifice, and he tore down the altar. Thus he burned with zeal for the law, just as Phinehas did against Zimri son of Salu.[53]

Now the days drew near for Mattathias to die, and he said to his sons: '. . . Now, my children, show zeal for the law, and give your lives for the covenant of our ancestors . . . My children, be courageous and grow strong in the law, for by it you will gain honour . . . You shall rally around you all who observe the law, and avenge the wrong done to your people. Pay back the Gentiles in full, and obey the commands of the law.'[54]

The same picture emerges from the account in 2 Maccabees:

The king sent an Athenian senator to compel the Jews to forsake the laws of their ancestors and no longer to live by the laws of God; also to pollute the temple in Jerusalem and to call it the temple of Olympian Zeus . . . The altar was covered with abominable offerings that were forbidden by the laws. People could not keep the sabbath, nor observe the festivals of their ancestors, nor so much as confess themselves to be Jews . . . Two women were brought in for having circumcised their children. They publicly paraded them around the city, with their babies hanging at their breasts, and then hurled them down headlong from the wall . . . Eleazar, one of the scribes in high position, . . . was being forced to open his mouth to eat swine's flesh. But he, welcoming death with

---

[52] 1 Macc. 1.41-9.

[53] 1 Macc. 2.23-6. The narrative has itself been affected by the memory of the Phinehas passage: compare 'in the sight of all' with Num. 25.6; 'when Mattathias saw it' with Num. 25.7.

[54] 1 Macc. 2.49-50, 64, 67-8 (on the penultimate phrase, see below, 502-7). The same chapter reveals (2.29-41) the dilemma the rebels found themselves in: when attacked on the sabbath day, should they resist? The vote went for resistance: cf. Jos. *Ant*. 12.274-7, and the similar decision in *War* 2.517f., and cf. Safrai 1976b, 805f.

honour rather than life with pollution, went up to the rack of his own accord, spitting out the flesh.[55]

Temple, sabbath, circumcision and purity of food were thus crucial marks of Jewish identity. Those who threatened that identity attempted to abolish them; those who defended it clung to them tenaciously.

This adherence to the ancestral laws was seen by Philo, too, as the thing which marked out the Jewish nation from all other peoples. Writing against the pretensions of Caligula, he says:

> For he [Caligula] looked with disfavour on the Jews alone because they alone opposed him on principle, trained as they were we may say even from the cradle, by parents and tutors and instructors and by the far higher authority of the sacred laws and also the unwritten customs, to acknowledge one God who is the Father and Maker of the world . . . One nation only standing apart, the nation of the Jews, was suspected of intending opposition, since it was accustomed to accept death as willingly as if it were immortality, to save them from submitting to the destruction of any of their ancestral traditions, even the smallest . . .[56]

The same point is made again and again in Josephus' famous description of the Jewish laws, and the way in which they sustain Israel as a people different at every point from the pagan nations around them:

> My object is not to compose a panegyric upon our nation; but I consider that, in reply to the numerous false accusations which are brought against us, the fairest defence which we can offer is to be found in the laws which govern our daily life . . .
>
> Should anyone of our nation be questioned about the laws, he would repeat them all more readily than his own name. The result, then of our thorough grounding in the laws from the first dawn of intelligence is that we have them, as it were, engraven on our souls . . . To this cause above all we owe our admirable harmony . . . Among us alone will be heard no contradictory statements about God, such as are common among other nations . . .
>
> Practices which, under the name of mysteries and rites of initiation, other nations are unable to observe for but a few days, we maintain with delight and unflinching determination all our lives . . . And from these laws of ours nothing has had power to deflect us, neither fear of our masters, nor envy of the institutions esteemed by other nations. We have trained our courage, not with a view to waging war for self-aggrandizement, but in order to preserve our laws . . .
>
> There is not one city, Greek or barbarian, nor a single nation, to which our custom of abstaining from work on the seventh day has not spread, and where the fasts and the lighting of lamps and many of our prohibitions in the matter of food are not observed.[57]

---

[55] 2 Macc. 6.1-2, 5-6, 10-11, 18-19.

[56] Philo *Leg.* 115-17.

[57] *Apion* 2.147, 178f., 189, 271f., 282; cf. 228 (the Jews stuck to their laws under greater pressure than that which made the Spartans abandon theirs). Josephus does not usually use the word *ethnos* ('nation') in these passages, but merely says 'we' and 'the others'.

And all this, we must note, is a defence not of some abstract system, but of the Jewish nation whose laws these are.[58] These codes – sabbath and other festivals, food laws and taboos most notably among them – were the things which marked out the Jews from their pagan neighbours. The Jews knew it; their neighbours knew it.[59]

Where does all this evidence take us? We have got over the old idea that law-keeping was an early form of Pelagianism, by which Pharisees and others sought to earn their justification or salvation by moral effort. Sanders has expended a good deal of effort in demonstrating that such a picture is thoroughly false to first-century sources, and, though this notion will no doubt reappear from time to time, it must be resisted. We must beware of other caricatures, too, in which Jews are mocked by modern non-Jews, as they were by ancient ones, for their supposedly quaint, comic or bizarre customs. We must instead accept at face value what the Jewish sources them-selves say: these laws, with all their detail and specificity, formed the bound-ary fence around the people of Israel, the nation of the Jews.

This can be reinforced, from the point of view of social anthropology, by a consideration of the role played by purity taboos within the self-awareness of various cultures.[60] Though the original purity codes of Leviticus and Numbers do not make a connection between food taboos and the distinction between Israel and the Gentiles, this connection was clearly endemic in second-Temple Judaism, not at the level of some scholarly projection but at the street-level reality represented by texts such as those cited above. When full allowance has been made for grey areas and blurred edges, those who kept the food taboos and the sabbaths were emphasizing their membership in, or their solidarity with, the nation of the Jews. Those who did not keep them were regarded by the Jews as either renegades (if Jewish), or beyond the pale (if Gentile).

Whether one refers to the Jews in this period as a family, a people, a race, or a nation is not, at the moment, of supreme importance.[61] Of course there are exceptions, the Rahabs and Ruths who are welcomed in from outside, as Josephus stresses.[62] Of course there are plenty of cases when the boundary is blurred. But there is no question that in the first century there was a substan-tial body, not least in Judaea and Galilee, that considered itself Jewish on the

---

[58] *Apion* 2.287–90.

[59] For pagan attitudes to Jewish customs see the massive treatments by Stern 1974–84; 1976; and now Feldman 1993, chs. 3–5. On the care which was taken to avoid compromise with pagan idolatry within the land of Israel cf. e.g. Safrai 1994, 243–54.

[60] cf. Douglas 1966, 1968, 1993. On this point, cp. Goodman 1987, 99f.; Saldarini 1988, 286.

[61] See below, 398–403.

[62] *Apion* 2.209f.

basis, more or less, of shared ancestry, and that considered it its god-given duty to protect that identity by careful observation of the god-given law, particularly the distinctives of sabbath, food, and circumcision, and of the sanctity of the Temple. These formed the clearest marker-posts for the symbolic world of Israel. And, according to the synoptic gospels, three out of these four became occasions of controversy between Jesus and his contemporaries, particularly the Pharisees.

What does this mean? That Jesus himself regarded these laws as bizarre, quaint or comic? Certainly not. That he thought such laws were inhumane, wicked, or otherwise in need of radical reform? Far from it. He did not, in either of those senses, 'speak against the law'. That way of summarizing things is, frankly, far too generalized and in any case anachronistic. Rather, the rigorous application of the law in the way we have observed, as a defence against Gentiles and hence as a reinforcement of national boundaries and aspirations, had become, in Jesus' view, a symptom of the problem rather than part of the solution. The kingdom of the one true god was at last coming into being, and it would be characterized not by defensiveness, but by Israel's being the light of the world; not by the angry zeal which would pay the Gentiles back in their own coin (as Mattathias had advised his sons[63]), but by turning the other cheek and going the second mile. The command to love one's enemies, and the prohibition on violent revolution, constituted not an attack on Torah as such but a radically different interpretation of Israel's ancestral tradition from those currently on offer. Jesus, precisely in affirming Israel's unique vocation to be the light of the world, was insisting that, now that the moment for fulfilment had come, it was time to relativize those god-given markers of Israel's distinctiveness.[64]

It is, no doubt, easy to caricature this emphasis, to imply that it is projected on to Jesus by a contemporary egalitarianism wishing to see its own face at the bottom of the historical well.[65] But that fails to do justice to the picture before us in the texts. Jesus' own demarcation of his followers from the rest of Israel, let alone from the pagan Gentiles, hardly suggests that he was a modern egalitarian born out of due time. His welcome to all and sundry was balanced by the quite sharp exclusivism implied by his controlling categories: those who 'heard his words' and followed him were part of the true people, and those who did not were not.[66] His redefinition of the

[63] 1 Macc. 2.68; see below, 502-7.

[64] This point was already seen clearly enough by Dodd (1968, 94-7).

[65] So Fredriksen 1995 a & b. This is not to say that such a projection does not exist in modern scholarship.

[66] cf. Sanders 1993, 235: '[Jesus] seems to have thought that those who followed him belonged to God's elect.' This is scarcely a back-projection of twentieth-century egalitarianism.

true family was itself a powerful symbolic challenge to a society whose emphasis on the family, the race, the *ethnos* had itself become symbolic. In any case, all such arguments fail once more to pay attention to the strong evidence which meets us at every turn. What Jesus did and said in relation to the symbols of Jewish identity grew not from an intention to propagate a system of religion or ethics, certainly not from an 'opposition' to 'Judaism' conceived as a 'religious system', but from the conviction that the climax of Israel's history was dawning, bringing with it great opportunity and great danger. The opportunity, he believed, lay in his own kingdom-announcement. The danger lay in Israel's obsession with her national existence and liberation, and in the symbols which identified and reinforced it.

I therefore propose that the clash between Jesus and his Jewish contemporaries, especially the Pharisees, must be seen in terms of *alternative political agendas* generated by *alternative eschatological beliefs and expectations*. Jesus was announcing the kingdom in a way which did not reinforce, but rather called into question, the agenda of revolutionary zeal which dominated the horizon of, especially, the dominant group within Pharisaism. It is not to be wondered at, therefore, that he called into question the great emphases on those symbols which had become the focal points of that zeal: sabbath, food taboos, ethnic identity, ancestral land, and ultimately the Temple itself. The symbols had become enacted codes for the aspirations of his contemporaries. Jesus, in challenging them, was not 'speaking against the Torah' *per se*. He was certainly not 'speaking against' the idea of Israel as the chosen people of the one true god. Rather, he was offering an alternative construal of Israel's destiny and god-given vocation, an alternative way of telling Israel's true story, and an alternative to the piety which expressed itself in nationalistic symbols. He was *affirming* Israel's election even as he *redefined* it, just as other Jewish groups and parties did. This was, of course, revolutionary; which was why, in all the stories up to the time of the Temple-incident itself, the message remained veiled and cryptic.

Which is not surprising, when we consider the two symbolic issues over which controversy erupted: sabbath and food.

(ii) Sabbath

There are four stories in the synoptic gospels, and two in John, in which the sabbath is the major issue.[67] Here again I find myself taking issue with the

---

[67] (i) Mk. 2.23-8/Mt. 12.1-8/Lk. 6.1-5; (ii) Mk. 3.1-6/Mt. 12.9-14/Lk. 6.6-11; (iii) Lk. 13.10-17; (iv) Lk. 14.1-6. In John: 5.2-18; 9.1-41. Cf. too *In. Thom.* 2.1-5.

analysis offered by, among others, E. P. Sanders.[68] His position is, once again, easily summarized:

(i) The stories are implausible historically. In the first, Pharisees did not spy on people in cornfields; in the other three, all Jesus did was to speak, which would not have been illegal or objectionable.

(ii) In any case, healing on the sabbath was permissible, if only by extension of the rabbinic teaching which allowed life-saving actions. Jesus might have been regarded as taking a different view of what precisely was permissible, but this would have fallen within the range of current disputes, and nobody would have thought him guilty of a heinous crime.

(iii) The stories are therefore to be seen as retrojections, either of internal debates within the church, or of external debates between church and synagogue.

(iv) In terms of sabbath-observance, Jesus did not 'speak against the law'.

In taking up this question we must comment once more on the Pharisees, their agenda and their activity. Here Sanders, particularly in his earlier treatment, allows himself to caricature:

> Pharisees did not organize themselves into groups to spend their Sabbaths in Galilean cornfields in the hope of catching someone transgressing . . ., nor is it credible that scribes and Pharisees made a special trip to Galilee from Jerusalem to inspect Jesus' disciples' hands.[69]

> Jesus' disciples are picking grain, when suddenly Pharisees appear. But what were they doing in the midst of a grain field on the sabbath? Waiting on the off-chance that someone might pick grain?[70]

Here all that Sanders is really doing is highlighting a point which, though necessary perhaps in terms of an older, opposite caricature, should by now be taken for granted: the Pharisees were not a religious 'thought police', nor did they hold any official jurisdiction under Herod, under the chief priests, or under the Roman authorities. We must, however, give full weight to the passage in Philo quoted above, in which the Pharisees are described as a self-appointed, zealous, and quite effective body in their guarding of ancestral traditions.[71] Even without this, however – even if we were to grant Sanders' point that they did not expect ordinary Jews to conform to their own strict

[68] 1985, 264f.; 1993, 212–18.
[69] Sanders 1985, 265.
[70] Sanders 1993, 214.
[71] Philo *Spec. Leg.* 2.253 (above, 379).

standards of purity, that they did not hunt for ordinary Jews who infringed legal minutiae, or that they travelled from Jerusalem for such purposes – we would have to object. Sanders has once more retreated from his basic thesis, that Jesus was a prophet of restoration eschatology, into a very different argument, to do with non-eschatological religion and ethics. As soon as we return to eschatology, to the announcement of the kingdom, and hence to politics, things look very different.

Contemporary analogies are fraught with danger. But there exist certain persons in modern western society who are elected to no office, hold no government position, carry no authority from the police or the judiciary, and yet who appoint themselves to be the guardians of public morality. From this unofficial position they assume the right to scrutinize and criticize every movement of the royal, the religious, and the politically active – all of whom gnash their teeth but remain powerless. I refer, of course, to journalists. Far be it from me to attack all members of such a noble profession with criticisms appropriate only to some; and yet it cannot go unremarked that some journalists not infrequently bind heavy moral burdens, hard to bear, and lay them on the backs of those whose activities they report, while they themselves do not attempt to lift such burdens with their little finger. This is not a mere digression. It reminds us of two important points. (a) One does not have to be a member of an official thought police in order to have considerable influence within a culture.[72] (b) The self-appointed guardians of public behaviour might not cross the street to inspect the private behaviour of an unknown individual. But they will happily go to the other side of the world, and hide in places far less congenial than Galilean cornfields, in order to take one surreptitious photograph of a princess wearing somewhat less than she would normally put on for the cameras.

To bring this back to the first century. Even if, despite Philo, we were to grant that the average Pharisee would not inspect the hands, or worry about the corn-plucking habits, of an ordinary Jew, we must insist that, in anyone's terms, *Jesus was not an ordinary Jew.* He was a prophet, announcing that Israel's god was becoming king. If a humble monk suddenly becomes Archbishop, or a country boy decides to run for President, all eyes are upon him. If he has already given broad hints of adopting unfashionable or unpopular policies, some of the eyes will be eager for scandal.

In this context – and, anachronistic features apart, it seems to me that the parallel holds quite well – the fact that (a) Jesus was not plucking the corn himself, and that (b) his sabbath healings were performed with a mere word, all seems beside the point. If anything, such details should reinforce our

[72] cf. *NTPG* 195.

suspicions that the stories have not, after all, been made up out of whole cloth to legitimate the practice of the later church. On (a), the close identification of disciple and master is proverbial,[73] and what brought the Pharisees out on that sabbath was precisely that Jesus was the leader and focal point of a new movement. On (b), what matters in relation to the healings is not the detailed regulations laid down by the (largely Hillelite) Mishnah, two hundred years later, for what might or might not be done on the sabbath. What matters is the attitude to the sabbath evinced by someone leading a kingdom-movement.

We are not in a position to recover with any precision the view of sabbath-observance taken by hard-line Shammaites, or their sympathizers, in the Galilee of Jesus' day. We do know that sabbath-keeping was a major symbol of national identity and aspiration. We also know, from a whole plethora of data, that Jesus opposed the prevailing revolutionary aspiration, and claimed the authority of Israel's god and Israel's scriptures in doing so. Hard-line Pharisees would naturally want to check him out for orthodoxy, or rather orthopraxy: did this new kingdom-prophet measure up to the standards required? Was he a stickler, as he ought to be, for Israel's ancestral traditions? Would he, and his movement, lend weight to the revolution, and indeed the correct *sort* of revolution, if and when it came?[74] The signs were not good. If he had spent the week healing, he might have been expected to stop on the sabbath. But he did not. The fact that he could answer his challengers with a legal argument[75] does not mean that the dispute was about the fine-tuned interpretation of Torah, such as might have taken place at any time; merely that, as in several other instances, Jesus was claiming that his (eschatologically motivated) kingdom-praxis could not legally be controverted, however unwelcome its symbolic implications might be.

What, then, about Jesus' response to the corn-plucking charge? The little story about David and his men eating the holy bread[76] is not simply (as Sanders implies) designed to provide a legal parallel in an essentially legal case. It is hardly surprising that the story does not work too well when read in this fashion. It is designed to provide a kingdom-parallel in an essentially kingdom-case. David, at the time of the story, was on the run from Saul. But he was the true king, and in due time he was vindicated by YHWH. Jesus' retelling of this story functions like the parable of the prodigal son, inviting his hearers to discover which role they are playing. Jesus and his followers

---

[73] cf. e.g. Mt. 10.24f.

[74] The War Scroll from Qumran (1QM) shows just how theologically stylized the picture of a forthcoming Holy War against the pagans could be.

[75] Mk. 3.4; Lk. 13.15f.; 14.5.

[76] Mk. 2.25–6/Mt. 12.3–4/Lk. 6.2–4; cf. 1 Sam. 21.1–6.

are like David and his motley crew. The Pharisees are like Saul's servant, Doeg the Edomite, spying on him and then running off to tell the authorities.[77]

This sets the context, too, for the final word in the corn-plucking story. I shall discuss that bane of scholars' lives, 'the son of man', in a subsequent chapter, drawing on my earlier treatment and showing its relevance for Jesus' self-understanding.[78] But, to anticipate, there is excellent evidence that some Jews in the first century already read the phrase, in its Danielic context, as referring in general to the time when YHWH would vindicate Israel over her pagan enemies, and as alluding in particular to the central figure in that vindication, namely, the Davidic king who would spearhead the coming great victory. The phrase itself, of course, is notoriously ambiguous, even cryptic. 'The son of man is lord of the sabbath'; there were doubtless many who heard but did not understand, who looked but never saw. They might have simply heard Jesus say 'I', or 'people in general', or 'one in my position'. That fits well enough with the cryptic tone we have already observed. But, in the light of our whole discussion so far, it fits with the mindset of Jesus that he should refer to himself obliquely, for those with ears to hear, as the one anointed but not yet enthroned, as the one who would be vindicated when YHWH finally did for Israel what he intended to do.

The two Lukan sabbath-stories (13.10–17; 14.1–6) possess the same essential pattern. In the former, the emphasis falls (as often in Luke) on Jesus' mission to restore Israel: this daughter of Abraham, whom the satan bound for eighteen years, is to be loosed from her bond on the sabbath. Here Jesus is portrayed as taking up and transforming the great theme of sabbath as release from work, bringing into immediate presence and sharp focus the theme of sabbath as rest after trouble, as redemption after slavery. Jesus was claiming that Israel's longing – for a great sabbath day when all her enemies would be put to shame, and she herself would rejoice at God's release – was being fulfilled in him. That is why it was not merely generally appropriate that this woman should be healed, and if it happened to be on the sabbath, well and good. The claim was that the sabbath day was the *most appropriate* day, because that day celebrated release from captivity, from bondage, as well as from work.[79] Jesus defined the plight of the woman – bondage to the satan, which as we shall see was part of his description of the plight of Israel

[77] In the Mt. version of the story, there is a further word about the priests in the Temple profaning the sabbath and remaining blameless (12.5). But, as the following verse demonstrates, this too is not simply a legal argument. What matters is the stupendous claim: 'something greater than the Temple is here'.

[78] cf. *NTPG* 291–7; and below, esp. 512–9.

[79] See Dt. 5.15 alongside Ex. 20.11.

in general – in such a way as to make this point clear. And he was claiming that Israel's great coming sabbath day *was already breaking in* in his own ministry. This claim is cognate both with the claim advanced in the Markan sabbath-stories, and with the implication of the resurrection language in two subsequent Lukan parables.[80] It fits with Jesus' redefinition in action, and around himself, of Israel's hope, while also helping to explain why such a claim was felt as a threat, not to petty legalism, but to the whole normal perception of the coming kingdom of god.[81]

The repeated remark about cases which override the sabbath commandment, then,[82] was not simply a lawyer's tactic about justifying precedents. It indicates Jesus' constant determination to set what he was doing, in bringing in the kingdom through his own ministry, within the context of what in fact Israel had known all along, but was currently too blind to see. Wrapped in her own aspirations, she could not recognize the coming of the kingdom when it stood before her in flesh and blood.

The stories have, of course, been foreshortened in the retelling. My guess is that, so far from being made up in the early church to address a new situation, they have been toned down in the early church, as the sharp-edged political situation that gave them birth receded, and other questions took over.[83] The clash of agendas that made the sabbath-controversies what they were in Jesus' ministry was not likely to recur in the same form.[84] We have, once again, double similarity and double dissimilarity. The discussion fits into the first-century Jewish context, but with Jesus challenging prevailing opinion from within a Jewish frame of reference; the stories address the early church, but with a memory of a subtle difference between their meaning for the church and the meaning that they had had in their first occurrence. Sanders persists in discussing the sabbath-incidents as though they are about legal disputes, with the real question being: did Jesus speak or act 'against the law'? I suggest that they were about Jesus' eschatological agenda, with the real question being: did Jesus, as Israel's would-be kingdom-bringer, affirm the key symbols of zealous Israel? The answer to that question was No. Jesus affirmed Israel's election, Israel's belief in her god, and Israel's

---

[80] Mk. 2.23—3.6; Lk. 15.24, 32 (see above, ch 4); 16.31 (above, 255f.).

[81] This time, it is the synagogue ruler who objects. This is interesting from a tradition-historical perspective: no cardboard Pharisees here.

[82] e.g. Lk. 14.5; cf. CD 11.13-14, on which cp. Meier 1994, 756.

[83] For a rabbinic parallel to this move, cf. mYad. 3.5, discussed in *NTPG* 183.

[84] The closest we come is Rom. 14.5-6; Gal. 4.10; Col. 2.16. In none of these is the sabbath-theme anywhere near as important as it is in all four canonical gospels; and in several other major texts about controversy in the early church - e.g. 1 Cor. - it is missing entirely.

eschatological hope. But this status, this theology and this aspiration were to be redefined around a new set of symbols.

All this, I suggest, is powerfully reinforced by Jesus' cryptic comments on the taboos surrounding food.

(iii) Food

The complex story which greets us in Mark's seventh chapter, and Matthew's fifteenth, offers another example of the same basic point. Here, Jesus clashes with some of his contemporaries on the matter of the central symbols by which the Israel of his day defined itself, this time the food laws.[85] Current discussion has again concentrated on the likelihood of Jesus 'speaking against the law' in this instance. The general points that need to be made on this have already been set out above, and we can concentrate on the relevant detail.

The complexity of the passage, in both Mark and Matthew, comes from the fact that it moves swiftly between three distinct issues. It begins with a dispute over handwashing. It continues with Jesus' criticism of the Pharisees for the way in which their traditions nullify scripture. It concludes with a cryptic saying, and then a longer discourse, on the nature of real purity: what matters is not food, but the state of the heart.

It is perfectly possible that three quite separate occasions, or types of occasions, have been combined in this passage. Nothing in our interpretation of Jesus' sayings here hinges on this one way or another. But before we too readily conclude that the mixture of textual weeds among the wheat is evidence that 'a redactor has done this', we should note that the issue binding together the two main discussions (handwashing and food) is of course purity. Behind that, in turn, there stands once more the question: is Jesus, or is he not, loyal to the symbols of Israel's identity? This question turns on the further one: who decides what constitutes such loyalty? Seen from the point of view of these interlocked questions, which belong closely together within Jesus' ministry, the passage offers a clear answer. Jesus disputes the Pharisees' right to make their own interpretations of Torah the litmus test of such loyalty. He claims, instead, that his interpretation is the true one, and theirs the distorted. Moreover, he insists that genuine purity is a matter of the heart, for which the normal purity laws – and hence one of the major definitions of Jewishness and Jewish loyalty – are irrelevant.[86]

---

[85] Mk. 7.1-23/Mt. 15.1-20. Various bits of the narrative are paralleled in non-canonical sources: cf. *P. Oxy. 840.* 2.1-9; *Eger.* 3.1-6; *Thom.* 14.1-5.

[86] On the renewal of the heart see above, 282-7.

This integrated reading, I suggest, once more fits better into the context of Jesus' ministry than into the life of the early church. Mark has to explain the Jewish customs about handwashing to his readers; if they needed such an explanation, it is hardly likely that they were at the same time seriously worried over whether or not to keep the Jewish purity laws.[87] This conclusion is strengthened by the movement from a public, cryptic saying to a private explanation. Once we grasp the highly political, and polemical, significance of Jesus' saying about purity, this sequence makes sense. 'It is not what goes into a person that defiles, but what comes out':[88] this strange saying, which by itself must have been simply a teasing puzzle, was (says Mark), further expounded to Jesus' close followers 'in the house, away from the crowds'.[89] This is, of course, a familiar Markan device, but it is not easily explained as a retrojection of Mark's own setting.[90] For Mark, the abolition, or simple ignoring, of Jewish food taboos was not something that needed to be whispered behind locked doors. By his time it was well out in the open, as indeed it had been from very early on in the church. It looks at this point as though we may be in touch with another tell-tale mark of Jesus' own context. Double dissimilarity (the proposal is scandalous for Jews, the secrecy unnecessary for the early church) is balanced by double similarity (the dispute presupposes the Jewish context; the new outlook was eventually and gradually worked out in the early church, with Mark 7.19b as one important step in that process). It must be regarded as highly likely that Jesus said, cryptically, something much like this.

The parallel with Mark 10.10 is instructive. A Christian in Mark's day, and Mark's church, saying that divorce was forbidden would not have needed to keep this teaching secret. The matter might well have been controversial, but nothing in the context of the early church suggests that it would have been an issue to be discussed only behind closed doors. But if someone in the Jordan valley, in the reign of Herod Antipas, were to proclaim in public that people who divorced and remarried were adulterers, then they were asking for trouble. The last prophet who said things like that had not lived long afterwards.[91] Better to leave the crowds to puzzle over a cryptic saying

---

[87] Mk. 7.3f. See Gundry 1993, 348.

[88] Mk. 7.15/Mt. 15.11/*Thom.* 14.5. Gundry 1993, 364 cogently refutes Crossan's arguments for the originality of the *Thom.* version.

[89] Mk. 7.17. Both this passage and Mt. 15.15 refer to the saying as a 'parable'; cf. Mk. 3.23 for another similar usage, meaning 'cryptic saying' rather than 'narrative with hidden meaning'.

[90] As e.g. Guelich 1989, 374, 377 implies. Cp. 4.10; 4.34; 9.28; 9.33; 10.10; 13.3; and the discussion above, 236–9.

[91] cf., of course, Mk. 6.18, 21–9. I owe my first grasping of this point to a private conversation with Prof. Colin Brown. See above, 284–6.

('What god has joined, humans should not divide'), and explain things to the disciples in private.

So it was with food taboos. If Jesus had said, out on the street, that the time had come when the god-given taboos, which marked out the Jews from their pagan neighbours, were to be made redundant, since in the kingdom which was dawning they would simply not be needed, he might well have started a riot.[92] People had died, in living folk memory, for refusing to eat pork. As we have seen, the whole agenda of the Maccabees, and of those who followed their 'zeal' in Jesus' day, focused on the need to maintain the cultural, and indeed cultic, boundary-markers which insisted that there was one god and that Israel was his people. Jesus was claiming that this one god was redefining Israel around himself and his kingdom-proclamation; that, as part of that work, the purity to which Torah pointed would be achieved by the prophets' dream of a cleansed heart; and that, as a result, the traditions which attempted to bolster Israel's national identity were out of date and out of line.

Actual controversy, I suggest, thus arose over sabbath and food. But there were two other areas in which Jesus challenged the symbols of Israel's worldview, while claiming to speak for her true traditions, and for her god, in announcing the long-awaited kingdom.

(iv) Nation and Family

The first of these was, no doubt, puzzling to Jesus' contemporaries; it is, inevitably, controversial today. In *The New Testament and the People of God* I offered a wide range of sources from the second-Temple period in support of the proposition that the identity (I used the word 'racial') of Israel in this period functioned as itself a worldview-symbol. The terminology has been objected to, but I did not expect the reality to be challenged.[93] Israel in this period was both more and less than a 'race': in other words, outsiders could

---

[92] cf. Sanders 1993, 220: 'Had [Jesus] gone around Galilee, teaching people that it was all right . . . to eat pork, there would have been an enormous outcry.' Quite so. Sanders deduces from the absence of such an outcry that Jesus did no such thing. I suggest that the subtler possibility is the correct one: Jesus taught it cryptically, avoided an outcry, but provoked alarm among those who suspected that there might be disloyalty lurking beneath the surface (so Mt. 15.12–14).

[93] See Fredriksen 1995a & b, criticizing *NTPG* for (among other things) its use of the phrase 'racial purity'. Of course the phrase could, if radically misunderstood, carry extremely negative associations. I intended it as a shorthand for that emphasis on ethnicity, consanguinity, family identity, and national covenant membership, which I, in common with writers of all backgrounds, see everywhere in Jewish sources of all periods (and which, for what it may be worth, I am happy to affirm, along with Paul in e.g. Rom. 9.1–5).

come in, and insiders could move out. But Israel was never simply a voluntary association of people who happened to share territory, customs, and aspirations. Israel gained a vital and central part of her self-identification from her tracing of a common ancestry to Abraham, Isaac and Jacob. Whether one describes this as 'race', 'family', or 'nation', and however much one allows for ways in which the boundaries could be blurred this way and that, the central reality remains.[94]

This ought not, I suggest, to be controversial. One may cite George Foot Moore, one of the most widely respected writers on Judaism this century, who stressed the need of Jews, in the Persian period and beyond, to maintain the clear boundaries of the people of Israel. He wrote:

> In the conditions that existed in Judaea in the age of the restoration and afterwards, an urgent part of the task of the religious leaders was to resist the admixture of heathenism and lapses from Judaism through the intimate relations between Jews and the surrounding peoples, and especially through intermarriage.[95]

This, he pointed out quickly, was no innovation, since it went back to the Pentateuch itself.[96] In addition, it was not unusual in the ancient world: the Romans, Athenians and others had strict laws about intermarriage, some of which made the prohibitions of, for instance, Ezra 10 'appear tame by comparison'.[97] But the Jews, Moore stressed, had more reason than others. Under Persian rule, they did not exist as an independent nation. 'They had only a national religion, and in its preservation lay their self-preservation.'[98]

Nor is this, of course, in any way discreditable (however often people have thought it so):

> The separateness of the Jews, their *amixia*, was one of the prime causes of the animosity toward them, especially in the miscellaneous fusion of people and syncretism of religions in the Hellenistic kingdoms and the Roman world; but it accomplished its end in the survival of Judaism, and therein history has vindicated it.[99]

This national solidarity thus functioned, as we saw in the previous volume, as a major symbol and boundary-marker. Debates come and go about the 'nationality and universality', or as it may be the 'particularism and universalism', of Judaism. Of course, right through the Jewish scriptures and later writings, the whole world comes into view as the concern of the one true god, even while it is clear that this god has called Israel to be his special

[94] For some key texts (there are many more), see *NTPG* 230–2.
[95] Moore 1927–30, 1.19.
[96] Ex. 34.16; Dt. 7.3–4; cf. Ezra 9.11–12.
[97] Moore 1.20.
[98] Moore 1.21.
[99] Ibid. On *amixia*, 'non-mixing', see *NTPG* 230–2, esp. n.63.

people. The apparent tensions between these two beliefs (in shorthand, crea-
tional monotheism and covenantal election) were worked out in many different ways at many different stages, and it is no part of our present purpose
to describe them.[100] What matters is that the election of Israel generated the
symbol of nation or family, which stood alongside the other symbols,
sustaining the whole Jewish worldview in its multiple varieties.[101]

Before demonstrating the way in which Jesus, to put it mildly, set a time-
bomb beside this symbol, it is vital to scotch the suggestion, made by
Fredriksen in her two 1995 articles, that Jesus would thereby have been
objecting to Israel's emphasis on family and common ancestry as though it
were something bad, shabby, or second-rate, and would instead have been
offering a bright new sort of pluralism in religious observance and
allegiance. Such theories do exist, but this is not at all what I am saying. I
am not making Jesus out to have been a religious reformer, still less a postmodern western thinker born out of due time. Rather, I am suggesting (as
Fredriksen herself does) that Jesus was an eschatological prophet, announcing
the kingdom. The reason he did what he did and said what he said was that
he read the signs of the times, believed the kingdom was now dawning in and
through his own work, and realized that some of the symbols of Israel's
worldview had now become (not wicked, or shoddy, but) redundant.

What else can we conclude, from a passage like this?

> When his family heard it, they went out to restrain him, for people were saying, 'He has
> gone out of his mind.' . . . Then his mother and his brothers came; and standing outside,
> they sent to him and called him. A crowd was sitting around him; and they said to him,
> 'Your mother and your brothers and sisters are outside, asking for you.' And he replied,
> 'Who are my mother and my brothers?' And looking at those who sat around him, he

[100] Moore 1.219-34; on the terminology, 219 n.1. See further e.g. Urbach 1981. On
monotheism and election cf. *NTPG* ch. 9.

[101] Throughout the Hebrew Bible Israel is referred to as a *goy*, 'nation', or an *'am*,
'people'; one or other of these stands behind the vast majority of instances of the LXX
ethnos, 'people' or 'nation'. *goy* and *'am* can be used interchangeably, though the former
stresses territorial and political identity (as, e.g., Ps. 83.4), and the latter 'the element of
consanguinity as the basis of union into a people'; this can be an element in *goy* too, though
'am and, still more, *mishpachah* ('family') emphasize the notion of 'common racial origin,
with its basis in consanguinity' (so Clements in *TDOT* 2.427-8). The fact that second-
Temple Judaism did not attain lasting political independence meant that *goy* increasingly
became used for pagan nations. 'Israel did not identify its election with its retaining its status
as a *goy*. As an *'am*, "people," and a *mishpachah*, "family," Israel could remain the people
of Yahweh, and it was only in consequence of this that it hoped to recover once again the
status of a *goy*' (Clements 433). In other words, both the Palestinian Jews who lived under
pagan rule and the Diaspora communities were enabled, by their belief in common ancestry,
to remain as a 'people' despite political and territorial diversity. However many proselytes
there may have been, and however many ethnic Jews assimilated to paganism, the notion of
family identity remained central.

said, 'Here are my mother and my brothers! Whoever does the will of god is my brother and sister and mother.'[102]

In case the force of this be blunted by familiarity, we may note how sharply it cuts against the view summarized by a recent Jewish writer:

> Tannaitic literature is full of comments and statements on the value of family life. The sages . . . tried to invest family life with an aura of holiness. Family life is held in high value in most of the literature of the Second Commonwealth.[103]

Or, again, what about this?

> As he said this, a woman from the crowd lifted up her voice and said to him, 'Blessed is the womb that bore you, and the breasts that nursed you!' But he responded, 'Blessed, rather, are those who hear the word of god and keep it!'[104]

This makes the same point, if anything more sharply. Family identity and pride is as nothing beside the message of the kingdom. This is most strikingly affirmed in the following passage:

> Another of his disciples said to him, 'Lord, permit me first to go and bury my father.' Jesus said to him, 'Follow me, and leave the dead to bury their dead.'[105]

This is, quite frankly, outrageous. Many scholars have pointed out that Jesus is here advocating behaviour that his contemporaries, both Jewish and non-Jewish, would have regarded as scandalous: the obligation to provide a proper burial for one's immediate family was so great as to override almost all other considerations.[106] The only explanation for Jesus' astonishing command is that he envisaged loyalty to himself and his kingdom-movement as creating an alternative family. The same impression is given very strongly by Jesus' quotation of Micah 7.5-6, and the comment which follows:

> Do not think that I have come to bring peace on the earth. I have not come to bring peace, but a sword. For I have come to set a man against his father, and a daughter against her mother, and a daughter-in-law against her mother-in-law; and a man's enemies will be those of his own household. The one who loves father or mother more

[102] Mk. 3.21, 31–5/Mt. 12.46–50/Lk. 8.19–21/*Thom*. 99; cp. Mk. 4.11 & pars.

[103] Safrai 1976a, 748.

[104] Lk. 11.27f./*Thom*. 79. The *Thom*. passage explains the saying by adding Lk. 23.29 ('blessed are the wombs that never bare, and the breasts that never gave suck').

[105] Mt. 8.21–2/Lk. 9.59–60; cp. Lk. 11.27–8/*Thom*. 79.

[106] Hengel 1981b [1968], ch. 1; Sanders 1985, 252–5, both with more details. Cf. mBer. 3.1: 'He whose dead lies unburied before him is exempt from reciting the *Shema'*, from saying the *Tefillah* and from wearing phylacteries.' (Some texts of the Mishnah add: 'and from all the duties enjoined in the Law'.) As Hengel states (1981b [1968], 9f.): 'refusal of burial had always been considered among the Greeks and Jews as an unheard of act of impiety'; cp. Sanders 1985, 253: 'the requirement to care for dead relatives, especially parents, was held very strictly among Jews at the time of Jesus'. Cf. too pp. 346–8 above.

than me is not worthy of me; the one who loves son or daughter more than me is not worthy of me; and whoever does not take up his cross and follow me is not worthy of me.[107]

The same theme, once again, surfaces in the discussion which, in all three synoptics, follows the incident of the rich young ruler:

> There is no-one who has left house, or brothers, or sisters, or mother, or father, or children, or fields, for my sake and the gospel's, who will not receive a hundred times over, now in the present age: houses, and brothers, and sisters, and mothers, and children, and fields – with persecutions; and, in the coming age, the life of the new world.[108]

This theme is embedded very deeply in the tradition of Jesus' sayings (it is probably to be understood, as well, as part at least of the meaning of Jesus' answer to the Sadducees on the subject of the resurrection).[109] It fulfils the criteria of double dissimilarity and double similarity. It is shockingly unlike anything known before, and scarcely reflects the practice of the early church, which seems to have retained some family solidarities. At the same time, it makes sense precisely as a shocking challenge *to* the Jewish world of Jesus' day, and as the root of that multi-ethnicity which came, quite quickly, to be advocated by Paul and others. We may take it that Jesus said, more than once, striking things like this; that, in other words, he regarded loyalty to himself as taking precedence over that family loyalty and identity which was both a universally recognized obligation in the ancient world and a major Jewish cultural and religious identity-symbol.

Once again, we must stress that this does not mean that Jesus thought such a symbol inherently bad, or even second-rate – any more than the rabbi who said that burying the dead took precedence over saying the *Shema* thought that saying the *Shema* was a bad or second-rate activity! What was at stake was eschatological urgency. Just as burying one's dead would normally take precedence over the otherwise admirable and worthy activity of daily prayers, so following Jesus was to take precedence even over the otherwise admirable and worthy cultural symbol of family loyalty. In a world where family identity counted for a good deal more than in today's individualized western culture, the attitude Jesus was urging would result in the disciple

---

[107] Mt. 10.34-9; the parallels in Lk. are 12.51-3; 14.25-7 (a longer version, including wife, brother, sister and even one's self). Also in *Thom.* 55; altered further in *Thom.* 101. The entire context of the Mic. quotation (Mic. 6—7) is worth studying for the many intertextual echoes of Jesus' own work of prophetic warning and promise.

[108] Mk. 10.29-30/Mt. 19.29/Lk. 18.29.

[109] Mt. 22.23-33/Mk. 12.18-27/Lk. 20.27-38: the point is that the Levirate law of marriage, on which the Sadducees' apparent *reductio ad absurdum* is based, only applies when the people of YHWH are constituted by marriage and begetting. Jesus was announcing the dawn of the new age, the time of resurrection, in which this would not be the case.

effectively denying his or her own basic existence.[110] The result was, inevitably, 'a socially deviant life-style away from home',[111] as exemplified in the challenge:

> A scribe came up and said to him, 'Teacher, I will follow you wherever you go.' And Jesus said to him, 'Foxes have holes, and birds of the air their nests; but the son of man has nowhere to lay his head.'[112]

Jesus, therefore, challenged his followers to sit loose to one of the major symbols of the Jewish worldview (which corresponded, of course, to the similar major symbol in many non-Jewish worldviews). Contemporary western individualism has, perhaps, made Jesus' sayings about the family look less striking than they were. As a result, discussion of the clashes between him and his contemporaries has focused on such matters as food taboos, which only come up in one synoptic passage, and away from this vital topic, which occurs all over the place. Jesus' eschatological announcement of the kingdom did not deny the god-givenness of the Jewish symbols, in this case the national and familial identity. But it cut right across them. He was, as we shall see, creating a fictive kinship group – in less technical terms, a new family – around himself.

(v) Possessions

Closely linked with the eschatological call to cut loose from family ties was the similar call to sit loose to possessions. For most people in the ancient world, the most basic possession was land; for Jews, the land was of course the holy land, promised by YHWH to his people.[113] It was because of the Roman registration of the holy land that Judas the Galilean had started his revolt in AD 6.[114] Just as Israel had 'inherited' the land in the first place, land would be the most basic inheritance that a father could leave to his children; the latter phenomenon, indeed, would be given religious depth and significance by the former.[115] This, then, rather than an attack on the first-

---

[110] Mt. 10.39/Lk. 17.33/Jn. 12.25; Mt. 16.25-6/Mk. 8.35-7/Lk. 9.24-5; Lk. 14.26; cp. *Thom.* 55; 67. On the absence of modern 'individualism' in Jesus' world, and the whole system of kinship groups etc. that predominated instead, cf. Malina & Rohrbaugh 1992, 100f.

[111] Malina & Rohrbaugh 1992, 78.

[112] Mt. 8.19-20/Lk. 9.57-8/*Thom.* 86.

[113] Cf. *NTPG* 226f., with refs. On property, cf. Hengel 1974.

[114] cf. esp. Hengel 1989c [1961], 127-44 (and *NTPG* 173).

[115] The Hebrew words for 'inheritance', 'possession' and 'rest' are closely aligned in talking about the land: cf. Janzen 1992, 144f. On the deep-seated unwillingness to part with ancestral land cf. e.g. Alon 1989 [1980], 154f.; Safrai 1994, 308.

century equivalent of twentieth-century materialism, is what was most deeply
at stake when Jesus summoned people to give up their possessions:[116]

> Do not store up for yourselves treasures on earth, where moth and rust consume and
> where thieves break in and steal; but store up for yourselves treasures in heaven, where
> neither moth nor rust consumes and where thieves do not break in and steal. For where
> your treasure is, there your heart will be also.[117]

> Someone in the crowd said to him, 'Teacher, tell my brother to share the inheritance with
> me.' But he said, 'Man, who made me a judge or divider over you?' And he said to
> them, 'Look out – beware of all covetousness; life does not consist in possessions.'[118]

> 'Sell your possessions, and give alms; make for yourselves purses that do not wear out,
> an inexhaustible treasure in heaven, where the thief will not come near, nor the moth
> destroy. For where your treasure is, there will your heart be also.'[119]

> 'Everyone of you that does not set aside all of his possessions cannot be my disciple.'[120]

> 'One thing you lack: go, sell what you have and give to the poor, and come, follow me.'
> But he was grieved at that saying, and went away sorry; for he had great possessions.[121]

This may not have been seen as quite so scandalous as the command to
abandon family loyalties, but it comes somewhere on the same scale. Israel
had been given the land; the different tribes, and families within tribes, had
been allotted their own portion, their own 'inheritance'; maintaining this
inheritance was part of the cultural and religious symbolism of Jesus' world,
especially when, after the exile, the Jews had returned geographically to their
land once again. Parallels in the Israel/Palestine of the late twentieth century
may not be too misleading; they indicate the depth of feeling, and potential
violence, that a challenge to this symbol might evoke. The setting of the second saying quoted above – the demand that Jesus act as arbitrator in a family
property dispute – is scarcely fictitious: nobody in the early church regarded
Jesus as a local magistrate, and the church did not have to meet demands that
it act in this way. Jesus' wry comment about not being 'a judge or divider'
echoes, of course, Exodus 2.14, where Moses is challenged on this point:
Jesus is refusing to be, in that sense, a new Moses, one who will parcel out
the promised land. He has come to bring Israel to her real 'return from
exile'; but, just as this will not underwrite Israel's ethnic aspirations, so it

---

[116] A point missed in the otherwise sensitive discussion of Harvey 1990, ch. 6.

[117] Mt. 6.19–21; cf. Lk. 12.33f.

[118] Lk. 12.13–15; the first part of this dialogue is repeated, and then somewhat altered,
in *Thom.* 72. There follows in Lk. 12.16–21 (paralleled in *Thom.* 63) the parable of the rich
fool. Cf. too the 'god and mammon' saying (Mt. 6.24; Lk. 16.13).

[119] Lk. 12.33–4; cf. Mt. 6.19–21.

[120] Lk. 14.33.

[121] Mk. 10.21–2/Mt. 19.21–2/Lk. 18.22–3.

will not reaffirm her symbolic, and zealously defended, territorial inheritance and possession. On the contrary: the unfaithful tenants will have their vineyard taken away.

Family and property, then, were not for the ancient Jew simply what they are to the modern western world. Both carried religious and cultural significance far beyond personal, let alone 'individual', identity and security. Both functioned symbolically within the total Jewish worldview. To both, Jesus levelled a direct challenge: those who followed him, who were loyal to his kingdom-agenda, would have to be prepared to renounce them, god-given though they were. The reason is not far to seek, in the light of the previous chapters. Family and property were sustaining Jesus' contemporaries in an idolatrous pursuit, in a quest they could not hope to win. They were encouraging Israel to build a tower that could not be completed, to engage in a war, in defence of her land, that she could not win.[122] Both images, in fact, are quite near the bone. Israel's concentration on nation and land was focused in the greatest building programme of the day, and directed towards the greatest war that she would ever fight. Jesus, as we saw, resolutely opposed the move towards a holy war. We shall now see that he opposed the idolization of the great building, too.

3. Symbols of Israel's Identity: The Temple

(i) Introduction

One of the chief gains of the last twenty years of Jesus-research is that the question of Jesus and the Temple is back where it belongs, at the centre of the agenda. Apart from one or two dissident voices,[123] almost all scholars now writing in the field agree on two basic points: Jesus performed a dramatic action in the Temple, and this action was one of the main reasons for his execution. But at this point agreement stops, and questions begin. What precisely did Jesus do in the Temple? Why did he do it? More precisely, what did he *intend* both to symbolize and to accomplish by it? In what way was this action a (or the) cause of his death? Did he foresee this consequence, and, if so, did he go ahead with the action despite it or because of it?

---

[122] Lk. 14.27–32 (tower, war); note that this passage is bracketed by the warnings about sitting loose to the family (14.25–6) and about giving up possessions (14.33). Derrett 1977 sees these allusions, but then obscures them with a more multifaceted reading.

[123] e.g. Vermes 1973, 1993.

These questions underlie a good deal of the rest of this book. In the present section we will make a start by addressing the first pair: what did Jesus do, and why? To come at this we need to recapitulate somewhat, and remind ourselves of the significance of the Temple within the Judaism of Jesus' day.[124]

(ii) The Temple and its Significance

The Temple mount in Jerusalem is still subject to rival claims. Currently in the possession of Islam, every so often a Jewish group will lay siege to it, at least symbolically, with the apparent intention of reclaiming it and rebuilding the Temple after nearly two millennia.[125] Less ambitious Jews, meanwhile, gather regularly to worship at the Western Wall, as close as they can come to the place where the god of Israel promised to dwell with his people. Symbolism of place still carries enormous power.

Some modern scenes encourage anachronistic historiography. This one helps us to avoid one anachronism in particular, namely, the idea that Jesus launched the equivalent of a tourist's protest against the sale of religious trinkets in Westminster Abbey. The Temple was, in Jesus' day, the central symbol of Judaism, the location of Israel's most characteristic praxis, the topic of some of her most vital stories, the answer to her deepest questions, the subject of some of her most beautiful songs. And it was the place Jesus chose for his most dramatic public action. It has long been recognized that the evangelists were alive to the symbolic value of Jerusalem, Mount Zion, and the Temple itself – so much so, in fact, that they were able to weave it as a theme into their writings in a fairly sophisticated manner.[126] It would be very strange if Jesus himself were not equally aware of the significance of the place described by the psalmist as 'the joy of the whole earth'.[127]

There are three aspects of the Temple and its significance which need to be noted in particular: the presence of YHWH, the sacrificial system, and the

---

[124] For what follows, cf. *NTPG* 224-6, and the primary and secondary sources there cited, to which add Meyers 1992, with bibliography; and the rich, evocative and multi-dimensional essay of Meyer 1992a, ch. 11. Certain points in the present treatment respond implicitly to questions and criticisms addressed to *NTPG*.

[125] 'Ours will be the time written of, sung about, talked about as long as the Jewish people will live. Ours will be the generation of the Third Temple . . . Let us go and rebuild Zion.' Resolution of the national executive committee of the Zionist group Habonim, November 1947; quoted in Richler 1995, 154. This ambition continues to be cherished, as reported e.g. in Mairson 1996, 30f.

[126] cf. e.g. Donaldson 1985, on Matthew.

[127] Ps. 48.2. Cf. Sanders 1993, 262: 'I think that it is almost impossible to make too much of the Temple in first-century Jewish Palestine.'

Temple's political significance. First, the Temple was regarded as the dwelling-place of Israel's covenant god:

> God's earthly dwelling place was the tabernacle and afterwards the temple. His great love to Israel is manifest in that, from his throne above the seven heavens, so far away . . ., he came to dwell near his people in the goat-skin tent he bade them set up for him . . . If God has a tabernacle or temple on earth, it is not that he needs a place to dwell in, for his holy house on high was there before the world was created, but, we might put it, because men need some visible thing by which to realize his loving presence.[128]

This point is amplified in Carol Meyers' recent article:

> The Temple in conception was a dwelling place on earth for the deity of ancient Israel . . . The symbolic nature of the Jerusalem Temple . . . depended upon a series of features that, taken together, established the sacred precinct as being located at the cosmic center of the universe, at the place where heaven and earth converge and thus from where God's control over the universe is effected.[129]

This meant, of course, that the closer one came to the Temple, and, within the Temple, the closer one came to the Holy of Holies, the further one moved up a carefully graded scale of purity and its requirements.[130] This underscores the first point: the Temple was the divine dwelling-place, the spot on earth where the living god deigned to dwell.

Second, the Temple was of course the place of sacrifice. It was the place where forgiveness of sins on the one hand, and cleansing from defilement on the other, were believed to be effected.[131] This can be seen dramatically in descriptions of what happened when the sacrificial system came to an end in AD 70:

> The destruction of the Temple in 70 A.D. made an end of the whole system of sacrificial expiation, public and private, and of the universal piaculum, the scapegoat of the Day of Atonement. The loss was keenly felt . . . The story [of Johanan ben Zakkai and Joshua ben Hananiah discussing the destruction of the Temple] illustrates the dismay with which the cessation of sacrifice must have filled many hearts.[132]

Or again, in the words of a more recent writer:

> This *tamid* ['continual'] sacrifice was symbolic not only of the deity's meal, but by extension, of the deity's presence among the people. No greater cultic calamity could be imagined than the loss of this sacrifice, since it symbolized the severing of the divine-human relationship (Dan. 8:11).[133]

---

[128] Moore 1927-30, 1.369f., with rabbinic refs.

[129] Meyers 1992, 351, 539. Cp. too esp. Barker 1991; Meyer 1992a, 231f., 240-51.

[130] The point is made frequently by writers on this topic: e.g. Meyers 1992, 360; D. P. Wright 1992b, 241-3; Sanders 1992b, 70f.

[131] On the distinction, and the close similarities, between these two, see below.

[132] Moore 1927-30, 1.502f.

[133] G. A. Anderson 1992, 878.

Getting to the root meaning and understanding of ancient sacrifices is very difficult. This is not, it should be stressed, because of anything inherently objectionable or alien about them. Animal sacrifice was taken for granted throughout the ancient world; if people today find the idea difficult, that is our problem, and must not be retrojected. Rather, it is because the sources which tell us about sacrifices are usually more concerned to describe what ought to be done than to interpret the significance of the actions.[134] With considerable caution, then, we may suggest the following typology, based on the different types of offerings mentioned in Leviticus 1—7.

The burnt offerings were the regular gift to the deity, which throughout the history of the cult could be spoken of as food for the deity to smell and eat, despite the fact that this was widely recognized as an anthropomorphism (compare Psalm 50.7–15).[135] The 'peace offerings' were the sacrifices, accompanying the burnt offerings, which were eaten by the people, as opposed to the deity; they consequently took on a celebratory character. These two sacrifices were offered regularly, day by day, confirming and celebrating the presence of the deity with his people. Though the other offerings were more specifically aimed at (what may in general be called) 'atonement', these regular daily offerings were also spoken of in this manner. It was for the regular provision of these that the Temple-tax was collected, with the effect that all Israel was responsible, at one remove, for the daily offerings.[136]

If the first two types of offerings enacted and celebrated the presence of the deity, the next two had the effect of restoring the worshipper into fellowship, when this had been fractured by sin or impurity. It is vital to stress that these two things (sin and impurity) are not of course to be identified. A woman incurs impurity through childbirth, but does not thereby sin; a thief is a sinner but may well not have technically contracted impurity.[137] It is none the less important to note that the third sacrifice mentioned in Leviticus, the *hatta't*, normally translated 'sin offering', may equally be rendered as 'purification offering'. It is required *both* in particular cases of sin (Leviticus 4.1–5.13; Numbers 15.22-9; etc.),[138] *and* in several cases of impurity, for

---

[134] cf. G. A. Anderson 1992, 871f., 877-81; Sanders 1992b, ch. 7. I follow these accounts quite closely in what follows.

[135] cf. Sanders 1992b, 106.

[136] See Neusner 1989, citing Ex. 30.16 with mShek. 1.3 and tShek. 1.6.

[137] cf. Sanders 1992b, 71. At the same time, the moral and cultic spheres cannot be neatly separated, as has been done often enough in later, anachronistic readings of, for instance, Paul's view of the law. Cf. e.g. Philo *Spec. Leg.* 3.63, 208f.

[138] The sins in question are 'ignorant' or 'unwilling', i.e. when either one did not know that the action was forbidden or when one knew but did not intend to commit it. Cf. Wright 1991, 221-3.

instance after childbirth (Leviticus 12) or after suffering from a discharge (Leviticus 15). The relation between sin and impurity, and between getting rid of the one and the other, has been the subject of a certain amount of debate, reflected in the discussion of how precisely the sacrifices were supposed to be effective. The ritual seems to have had both an atoning and a purificatory function; so is the point that the sinner is being purged of sin, or that the cultic impurity created by the presence of the impure person, or the sinner, is being removed from the sacred precincts?[139]

The path of wisdom may well be to retain both emphases. In both cases, though for different reasons, the person concerned was not fit to approach the holy place, let alone the deity who dwelt there; the sin/purification offering was therefore offered prior to the burnt offering and peace offering, which as we have seen celebrated the dwelling of the deity with his people.[140] One who has *sinned* within the prescribed limits (i.e. ignorantly or unwillingly) will receive *forgiveness* through offering the sin/purification offering; one who has contracted *impurity* will receive *purification*, by the same means. Repentance and restitution for the sin, and bathing and waiting for sundown, form the first part of forgiveness in the one case, and cleansing in the other. They can, of course, be practised anywhere. But, as Sanders rightly says, 'the act of sacrifice was always the last moment in the correction of either impurity or guilt'.[141]

The fourth sacrifice was the 'guilt offering', which is really 'a special category of sin offering'.[142] Again the meaning is much debated; but the central feature seems to be that this sacrifice dealt with cases where sacred items had been profaned. The offering was a reparation, a restitution to the deity for the specific wrong that had been committed.

These central and regular offerings pointed towards the great national festivals and holy days, and to the sacrifices offered on those occasions.[143]

---

[139] cf. G. A. Anderson 1992, 879f., citing Gese and Janowski as representing the first view and Milgrom the second.

[140] cf. D. P. Wright 1992a, 73: '[That sin/purification offerings] purify the sanctums on behalf of persons reveals the human factor in the dynamics of the sacrifice: that is, when they sin or suffer severe impurity, the sanctuary is soiled . . . Sins and impurity have an intimate connection: the former cause the latter in the sanctuary.'

[141] Sanders 1992b, 116, concluding his example (113–16) of a family coming to the Temple, having during the year had a child (so that the wife needed to complete her post-childbirth purification) and committed a minor felony for which restitution had already been made (so that the husband needed to complete the process of forgiveness). This throws into sharp relief Jesus' announcement of Zacchaeus' forgiveness (Lk. 19.1–10): one would have expected him, in addition to making restitution, to offer a sacrifice in the Temple, and so to complete the process of forgiveness (Sanders 1993, 235).

[142] Sanders 1992b, 107.

[143] cf. Sanders 1992b, 125–43; *NTPG* 233–5.

Whereas sin/purification offerings and guilt offerings had to do with the Jew as an individual, these large occasions related to Israel as a whole. The best-known festival was of course Passover, in which the entire ritual – pilgrimage, recitation of the exodus story, special meal – recalled and celebrated the exodus from Egypt, as the paradigmatic act of Israel's divine liberation from her pagan enemies, focused in the present on the sacrifice of the Passover lamb. Past and present fused together, as did earth and heaven in the Temple itself, into one great act of national celebration and hope.[144] Similarly, the Day of Atonement acted as the corporate national event which corresponded to the regular individual offerings:

> While throughout the year the impurity of individual or community sins may be purged as they arise, once a year a special rite must be performed that cleanses the sanctuary of impurity from deliberate sins and from any other lingering impurity not yet rectified.[145]

As part of this whole process, the sins of the people were confessed over the head of the scapegoat, which was then driven off into the wilderness. Since the whole point of this goat was that it carried away sins, and hence the impurity, from the Temple, it was of course the one animal in the whole annual round of Temple-actions that was not sacrificed.

We may sum up this second main point about the Temple. If it was the place where Israel's god lived (always recognizing, as the central texts do, that 'the heaven and the highest heaven cannot contain' him[146]), it was also the place of sacrifice, where sins and impurities alike could be dealt with, enabling the people, individually and as a nation, to enjoy the unbroken presence of their god.[147]

This god-given scheme of regular sacrifices was designed for regular use day by day, month by month, year by year. But the same texts, notably Leviticus 26 and 1 Kings 9.1–9, speak also of a historical movement. Just as the individual who sins deliberately (as opposed to unwillingly) is to be cut off from the people,[148] so, if the nation sins wilfully and persistently, the result will be exile, and the destruction of the Temple. How then shall the national fellowship with YHWH be restored? At one level, as we saw in chapter 7, the answer is that Israel must repent and seek YHWH with all her heart.[149] This corresponds, more or less, to the individual's repentance and

---

[144] Among recent literature, cf. esp. Bokser 1992, with other refs.

[145] D. P. Wright 1992a, 73. The Day of Atonement is prescribed in detail in Lev. 16, and discussed extensively in mYom.

[146] 1 Kgs. 8.27.

[147] For a further statement of these two basic points, cf. the recent discussion of Grabbe 1992, 538–40.

[148] e.g. Num. 15.30f.; cp. mKer. 1.2; 2.6; 3.2.

[149] See above, 246–58.

restitution. Corresponding to the individual's sacrifice, however, we find two suggestions. In the central section of Isaiah, YHWH's 'servant' will be the true sacrifice, to deal with the sin which has resulted in exile.[150] In the final chapters of Ezekiel and elsewhere (e.g. the Temple Scroll), there will be a new Temple, indicating the restoration of the true cult. The Temple remains the central point of the national hope, the governing eschatology, as well as of the national life and identity; and at the heart of the Temple's existence and significance there stood the sacrificial system.

Thirdly, the Temple possessed enormous political significance. This can be stated quite briefly, but is none the less far-reaching. If the one true and living god has deigned to dwell in this particular building, the people responsible for the building acquire great prestige. The first Temple was not merely an adornment to Solomon's kingship, but a key feature of it; the restored second Temple symbolized a measure of autonomy, despite 'the absence of a crucial element', namely the monarchy.[151] The Maccabaean cleansing of the Temple in 164 BC paved the way for the founding of the Hasmonean dynasty. Herod's grandiose rebuilding of the Temple formed a crucial element in his claim to be king of the Jews.[152] Bar-Kochba, the last of the would-be Messiahs in our period, minted coins depicting the Temple's facade; Hadrian had planned to build a pagan temple on the site, and the Jewish revolutionaries, naturally, aspired to rebuild the true one.[153] The Temple thus functioned as the central political, as well as religious, symbol of Judaism. It pointed not only to YHWH's promise to dwell with his people, and to his dealing with their sins, their impurities, and ultimately with their exile, but also to his legitimation of the rulers who built, rebuilt or ran it. It was bound up inextricably with the royal house, and with royal aspirations. It is for this reason that Jesus' actions in relation to the Temple must be treated with the utmost seriousness. To anyone even vaguely in tune with the relevant symbolism, such actions will inevitably have spoken not just of religion but of royalty.

Of course, by no means all Jews of Jesus' day viewed the Temple of the time with equal enthusiasm. The Essenes, who regarded the Hasmonean high-priestly dynasty as usurpers, refused to take part in the cult, believing that their own community was the god-given substitute, and that in due time,

---

[150] Isa. 53.10: 'When you make his life a guilt-offering' [*'asham*, as in Lev. 5.15 and elsewhere] (cf. below, 605 n.227). The wider context in Isa. describes the coming of the kingdom, the return from exile, the return of YHWH to Zion, and the renewal of the covenant – i.e. the elements which answer to the condition described in Lev. 26; 1 Kgs. 9; etc.

[151] Meyers 1992, 364. Cp. (among many possible refs.) Zech. 6.9–14; *Ps. Sol.* 17.21–34, esp. 22, 30.

[152] Meyers 1992, 364f.; cf. *NTPG* 160, 225–6, 308–9.

[153] Meyers 1992, 367.

when YHWH finally acted, a new Temple would be built.[154] The so-called 'Animal Apocalypse', now part of *1 Enoch*, regarded the offerings in the second Temple as impure, probably reflecting deep dissatisfaction with a corrupt priesthood.[155] The Pharisees, or at least their self-designated successors the rabbis, developed a theology in which their own fellowship and study of Torah functioned as a near-equivalent of the Temple: to study Torah was to be in the presence of Israel's god,[156] and the observation of Torah could even function, according to Johanan ben Zakkai in a later story, in place of the sacrificial system.[157] It is of course difficult to know how much of this surrogate-Temple theology was actually articulated while the Temple was still standing. It seems likely that some teachers in the Diaspora would have taught such a view, but it is also probable that the main emphasis on the study and practice of Torah as actually taking the place of the Temple cult developed in the post-destruction period. Certainly there is every reason to suppose that the belief ascribed to Johanan, even if he did indeed hold it in AD 70, was by no means widely accepted until at least after AD 135, and then, we may suppose, only with a great sense of sorrow and mourning, evidenced in the care lavished by the Mishnah on the details of the (by then non-existent) Temple service.[158] But the possibility clearly existed of thoroughly Jewish theologies in which the Temple itself was at least relativized, if not actively criticized.

If the Essenes were ideologically opposed to the present Temple on the grounds that the wrong people were running it, and the Pharisees were developing a theology in which the blessings normally available in the Temple could be had, by extension, through the Torah, there was also a more popular critique. The poorer classes evidently regarded the Temple as symbolizing the oppression they suffered at the hands of the rich elite. As we saw in a previous discussion, when the revolutionaries took over the Temple at the start of the war, one of their first acts was to burn the record of debts.[159] The unpopularity of the ruling class at this time is well documented, and the widespread dislike of them meant that the first-century Temple, and particularly the way in which it was being run, came in for regular criticism.[160] Jesus' Temple-action belongs on this larger map of disquiet.

---

[154] cf. *NTPG* 205f.; Evans 1992; cp. Collins 1995, 84, with a note about the calendrical differences between the Essenes and the official Jerusalem cult. Herod the Great apparently favoured the Essenes (Jos. *Ant.* 15.371-9; cf. *NTPG* 206), but they do not seem to have returned the compliment, at least as far as Herod's Temple was concerned.

[155] Collins 1995, 84.

[156] mAb. 3.2. Cf. Meyers 1992, 367.

[157] Aboth de R. Nathan 4; cf. *NTPG* 228f.

[158] In the fifth Division of the Mishnah (Kodashim).

[159] Jos. *War* 2.427. On the criticisms of the Temple current at the time see below.

[160] Goodman 1987; see below.

(iii) Jesus' Action in the Temple

What then did Jesus do in the Temple, and why did he do it? This question has been the subject of constant and fascinating discussion in recent years.[161] It is clearly impossible to enter into all the details of this debate. Fortunately, the proposals fall along a spectrum, which can be described quite clearly at a more general level.

The spectrum runs, basically, from 'cleansing' to 'acted parable of destruction'. At one end, many still believe that Jesus disapproved of the Temple cult, or some feature of it, and wanted to reform it (not to abolish it).[162] As we just noted, many Jews were deeply dissatisfied with the present operation of the cult, and the chief priests who ruled it were widely disliked and distrusted.[163] Alternatively, Jesus (it has been suggested) may have had a new theory of purity, which he tried unsuccessfully to institute in the Temple.[164]

At the other end of the spectrum, several writers have recently argued that Jesus acted out, symbolically, the destruction of the Temple itself.[165] For some, this destruction was simply the necessary prelude to rebuilding, and carried no overtones of judgment (Sanders); for others, it was the outworking of divine wrath (Borg: see below); for others, it was the result of the Temple's inherent non-egalitarian and oppressive system (Crossan);[166] for others again, it was the prelude to the establishment of an alternative religious system, starting with the Last Supper (Neusner).[167] Several scholars sketch a position somewhere in the middle: Jesus wanted to reform certain aspects of the Temple, but his action, which spoke of the kingdom coming

---

[161] Every commentary, and almost every recent book on Jesus, devotes space to these texts: particularly notable treatments are Sanders 1985, ch. 1 (followed closely by e.g. Fredriksen 1988, 111–14); Gundry 1993, 639–47. Among other recent studies we may highlight Catchpole 1984; Bauckham 1988; Chilton 1992b, 1994 ch. 2; Matson 1992; Richardson 1992; Meyer 1992a, ch. 11, esp. 261–6. Most of these also cite plentiful earlier literature.

[162] e.g. Richardson 1992; Chilton 1992b, 1994 ch. 2; several articles by Evans (1989a & b, 1992, 1993).

[163] On the criticisms of the Temple current at the time cf., among primary sources, the lament over the evils of the high-priestly families in bPes. 57a; Jos. *Ant.* 20.179–81; 204–7; and the (unfortunately fragmentary) 7th chapter of *T.Mos*, on which see Bauckham 1988, 79f., with note. Other secondary treatments include Goodman 1987; Evans 1989a & b, 1992, 1993.

[164] Chilton 1992b (cf. 1992a). His view is summarized in 1992b, 155, and is followed, with modifications, by Lang 1992, 470.

[165] esp. Sanders 1985, 1993. Barrett 1975 had already made this suggestion.

[166] cf. Crossan 1994, 127–33.

[167] cf. Neusner 1989. Neusner's theory is an interesting cross between Sanders' and Chilton's, with elements of Bauckham as well.

upon Jerusalem, also warned that if this did not happen the result would be ruin;[168] Jesus was offering a sign of forthcoming destruction, and the present corruption of the Temple served as warrant for this.[169] Softer positions are also available. For Catchpole, the 'cleansing' element is to be seen as a later interpretative addition; Jesus' action was simply a sign of the coming kingdom.[170] Borg, in his earlier work, stressed that the Temple-action should be seen as an acted parable of judgment, and that a good deal of the 'apocalyptic' material in the synoptic tradition related to the same theme; he has more recently emphasized the element of socio-economic critique.[171]

Like many events in ancient history, the Temple-action is clearly underdetermined. That is, taken by themselves the questions about what Jesus did and why possess sufficient ambiguity to remain open; there is insufficient data for the full application of the normal criteria for hypotheses.[172] Nevertheless, the plethora of recent theories (of which the previous paragraph offers merely a sample) indicates certain themes which should find a place in any eventual reconstruction: purity, money, sacrificial animals, symbolic destruction, coming kingdom. The apparent great divide between 'reform' and 'destruction' is softened in Sanders' theory, since for him Jesus envisaged a newly built Temple; a fairly drastic method of reform, but still not critical of 'the system' itself. Those who disagree with Sanders at this point still sometimes stress that Jesus did envisage a metaphorical rebuilding, in terms of himself and his community.[173] Even by itself, therefore, the Temple-incident offers the elements for a historical reconstruction (which, like all historical reconstructions, involves entering sympathetically into the worldview of the people concerned).

Nobody, however, supposes that the questions can in fact be taken by themselves. Unless we are to imagine that Jesus' action was purely random and unreflective – which itself would be exceedingly unlikely, granted all the other things we know about him – we must suppose that what he did in the Temple was closely integrated with, perhaps even climactic to, the rest of his work. Whether, therefore, we begin with the Temple-incident and build a

---

[168] Meyer 1979, 170; 1992a, 262–4.

[169] Trumbower 1993, esp. 514. Similarly, though with the emphasis on a particular type of corruption, Bauckham 1988 (see esp. 86, 175 n.82).

[170] Catchpole 1984, summarized at 334.

[171] Borg 1984, 1987a, 1994a, 1994b. See Borg 1994a, 125 n.72: 'Both then and now, I saw the temple as the center of the politics of purity and the temple action as a protest against the politics of purity. However, then I saw the politics of purity (and the temple) as the ideological ground of the national liberation movement; now I see the politics of purity (and the temple) as the ideology of the native ruling elites.'

[172] On hypotheses and their verification cf. esp. *NTPG* 31–46, 98–109.

[173] e.g. Meyer 1979, 1992a & b.

case around it, as Sanders does in a bold and innovative move,[174] or whether we develop a hypothesis on the basis of other evidence and see how the Temple action works in relation to it, as I shall do here, the eventual aim is the same: to see where this awkwardly shaped stone will fit within the building under construction. There is some reason to suppose that it will turn out to be the head corner-stone.[175]

Let us recapitulate. I argued in chapter 5 that Jesus acted as, and saw himself as, a prophet, standing within Israel's long prophetic tradition. One of the things that prophets like Isaiah, Jeremiah and Ezekiel did was to act symbolically, often in relation to Jerusalem and the Temple, sometimes in prediction of its destruction. Isaiah's nakedness, Jeremiah's smashed pot, and Ezekiel's brick come to mind as obvious examples.[176] We have seen that Jesus was capable of acting symbolically, and with deliberate scriptural overtones, in other situations; we should not be surprised if, faced with the central symbol of Israel, he did so here as well. We saw in chapter 8 that his warnings, like Jeremiah's, centred upon the Temple's destruction by the pagans. An action which dramatized this prediction would form, as it were, the climax of his prophetic career.

Further, I argued in chapter 6 that Jesus understood his own vocation as that of a prophet announcing that Israel's god was now at last becoming king. This had two particular focal points: the return of Israel from exile (chapter 6 above), and the return of YHWH to Zion (chapter 14 below). Both of these themes relate closely and obviously to the Temple. When the return happens, the Temple will be properly rebuilt. When YHWH returns to Zion, he will of course come to the Temple; 'but who may abide the day of his coming?' The proclamation of YHWH's kingdom, in both its major themes, thus focused attention on the Temple. If it was, in some sense, to be rebuilt; if YHWH was to return in judgment as well as in mercy; then the present Temple, which in Jesus' day meant Herod's Temple, was under judgment.[177] Its fabulous beauty would not save it. As the Essenes would have affirmed, it was a

---

[174] Sanders 1985, ch. 1.

[175] It is still, predictably, rejected or at least questioned by one or two builders, e.g. Mack 1988, 292; Miller 1991. With the great majority of interpreters, I assume the basic historicity of the event; its multiple coherence with the rest of the picture (including the Temple-ideology set out in e.g. Meyer 1992a, ch. 11) argues strongly in its favour. Some of Miller's questions are, however, quite important, and will be addressed *en passant* in what follows.

[176] Isa. 20.1-6; Jer. 19.1-15; Ezek. 4.1-17. Cf. also Isa. 8.1-4; Jer. 13.1-11; 27.1-15; 32.6-15; Ezek. 12.1-25.

[177] Bauckham 1988, 87 rightly points out that prophecies of the destruction of the Temple regularly refer not merely to demolition but to (divine) judgment (citing Mic. 3.12; Jer. 7.26; *Sib. Or.* 3.265-81; 4.115-18; *Apoc. Abr.* 27; *2 Bar.* 1-8; *4 Bar.* 1-4).

sham, and needed to be destroyed if YHWH was truly to dwell with his people, if the real return from exile was to come about.

Again, I argued in chapter 7 that Jesus engaged in an itinerant ministry, characterized by a welcome to all; by a challenge to follow his way instead of the way of 'zeal'; and by a warning of the consequences for those who refused. This offer of true (though subversive) wisdom, and this warning about the dangers of real (though conventional) folly, likewise focused on the Temple. I argued further, in chapter 8, that Mark 13 and its parallels drew together the strands of previous Temple-warnings, and that it solemnly predicted, in language drawn not least from Jeremiah and Daniel, that the Temple would be destroyed by foreign armies, and that this event should be seen as the outpouring of YHWH's wrath upon his recalcitrant people. The last state of the house would be worse than the first. As the Temple symbolized and drew together the themes of Israel's national life and self-understanding, so Jesus, offering as he was (like some other movements of the time) a new and subversive way of being Israel, naturally conceived of this in terms of the Temple. The house built on sand would fall with a great crash. Only that built on the rock of Jesus' kingdom-announcement would stand.

Finally, in the present chapter we have already seen that Jesus' actions during his Galilean ministry challenged the symbols which were focal points for the thinking, aspirations and actions of a good many of his contemporaries, not least the Pharisees whose zeal for Torah was sustaining the sort of nationalism Jesus was opposing. This was not simply a matter of the purity system, though that played its part; nor was it a matter of Jesus' underwriting of certain twentieth-century ideologies over against first-century ones. It had to do with those symbols which the second-Temple Jewish sources themselves tell us were at the centre of Jewish self-understanding.

The argument of this book so far thus creates a context in which the natural reading of the incident is to see it as an acted parable of judgment. There is a further significant fact: virtually all the traditions, inside and outside the canonical gospels, which speak of Jesus and the Temple speak of its destruction. Mark's fig-tree incident; Luke's picture of Jesus weeping over Jerusalem; John's saying about destruction and rebuilding; the synoptic traditions of the false witnesses and their accusation, and of the mocking at the foot of the cross; *Thomas*' cryptic saying ('I will destroy this house, and no-one will be able to rebuild it'); the charge in Acts that Jesus would destroy the Temple: all these speak clearly enough, not of cleansing or reform, but of destruction.[178] I submit that these cannot all be retrojections, 'prophecies'

---

[178] Mk. 11.12–14/Mt. 21.18–19, cf. Lk. 13.6–9; Lk. 19.41–4; Jn. 2.19; Mk. 14.58/Mt. 26.61; Mk. 15.29/Mt. 27.40; *Thom.* 71; Ac. 6.14.

after the event. Further, the destruction-theme is sufficiently unlike the early Christians' practice of continuing to worship in the Temple for the motif to be regarded as simply a feature of early Christian theology.[179]

All this, I suggest, creates a context within which the conclusion is irresistible: when Jesus came to Jerusalem, he symbolically and prophetically enacted judgment upon it – a judgment which, both before and after, he announced verbally as well as in action. The Temple, as the central symbol of the whole national life, was under divine threat, and, unless Israel repented, it would fall to the pagans. Furthermore, Jesus, by making this claim in this way, perceived himself to be not merely a prophet like Jeremiah, announcing the Temple's doom, but the true king, who had the authority which both the Hasmoneans and Herod had thought to claim.[180] In acting the way he did, 'he conjured up the nation's most compelling traditions at a moment when receiver-competence was at its peak',[181] i.e. when the lookers-on, Passover pilgrims with their hearts set on YHWH's kingdom, would have been most likely to comprehend the multiple symbolic meanings of his action.

On the vexed issue, therefore, of what Jesus did in the Temple and what he meant by it, I take a position which draws together the strengths of the major alternatives:

(i)   Jesus intended to symbolize the imminent destruction of the Temple.

(ii) He believed that Israel's god was in the process of judging and redeeming his people, not just as one such incident among many but as the climax of Israel's whole history.

(iii) The judgment on the Temple would take the form of destruction by Rome, which (like Babylon, according to Jeremiah) would be the agent of the wrath of YHWH.

(iv) The specific reasons for this judgment were, broadly, Israel's failure to obey YHWH's call to be his people (chapters 7, 8 above); more narrowly, Israel's large-scale commitment to national rebellion, coupled with her failure to enact justice within her own society, not least within the Temple-system itself.

(v)   I thus agree with Sanders that Jesus symbolized the destruction of the Temple; but I agree also with Sanders' critics (e.g. Bauckham, Evans) that this was more than a mere intention to replace the present Temple with a new one. It included a critique of the present Temple.

---

[179] On this problem cf. esp. Bauckham 1993b, 143f.; 1995a, 441–50; 1995b.

[180] cf. ch. 11 below.

[181] Meyer 1992a, 263; this gives a positive answer to the question raised by Harvey 1982, 133f.; Sanders 1985, 76, about whether people would have understood the symbolism.

This critique, though, was itself part of Jesus' eschatological programme. That is, after all, what we might expect from a prophet.

We are now in a position to understand the much-discussed passage Mark 11.1–25, and its parallels in Matthew 21.1–22; Luke 19.28–48, and John 12.12–19; 2.13–17. Since the starting-point of our argument was the demonstration of Jesus' self-perception as a prophet, we may begin with the prophetic context which the three synoptic accounts offer. This consists, first, of the composite quotation, from Isaiah 56.7 and Jeremiah 7.11, in Mark 11.17 and parallels;[182] second, of the wider echoes of Zechariah in the whole incident. With many scholars, I am happy to accept that Jesus knew these scriptural passages and intended to evoke and/or act them out.[183]

The context of the Isaiah passage is the prediction of the full return from exile, and all that this would mean:

And the foreigners who join themselves to YHWH,
to minister to him, to love the name of YHWH,
and to be his servants . . .
these will I bring to my holy mountain,
and make them joyful in my house of prayer;
their burnt offerings and their sacrifices
will be accepted on my altar;
for my house shall be called a house of prayer for all peoples.
Thus says YHWH, the god who gathers the outcasts of Israel,
I will gather others to them besides those already gathered.[184]

This passage belongs, clearly enough, with those that predict, as one aspect of Israel's eventual blessing, the ingathering of the Gentiles into the one people of YHWH.[185] It is followed at once, however, by passages strongly critical of the present condition of Israel (56.9–12; 57.1–21). Gentiles are to be welcomed in, but the present people of Israel, especially their supposed leaders and guardians (56.10f.) are under judgment. This offers a natural link into the passage from Jeremiah, which of course forms part of the great sermon denouncing the Temple and warning against an unthinking trust in it:

---

[182] On which see now Chilton & Evans 1994a, 288f.; 319f. They note that the quotations are linked together, in typical Jewish style, by the catchword 'house', which occurs in the part of Jer. 7.11 not quoted ('Has *my house*, which is called by my name, become a den of robbers in your eyes?').

[183] cf. e.g. Sanders 1993, 254 on the Zech. allusion.

[184] Isa. 56.6–8.

[185] cf. *NTPG* 267f. Why do Mt. (21.13) and Lk. (19.46) omit 'for all the nations'? Possibly because, writing after AD 70, there was no prospect of this (see Borg 1984, 349 n.67, with other refs.)? But there was no chance then of its being a house of prayer, either. Perhaps it was because Mt. and Lk. had already begun the process of transforming the event from an acted parable of judgment into a purely economic protest?

Thus says YHWH of hosts, the god of Israel: Amend your ways and your doings, and let me dwell with you in this place. Do not trust in these deceptive words: 'This is the Temple of YHWH, the Temple of YHWH, the Temple of YHWH.'

For if you truly amend your ways and your doings, if you truly act justly one with another, if you do not oppress the alien, the orphan, and the widow, or shed innocent blood in this place, and if you do not go after other gods to your own hurt, then I will dwell with you in this place, in the land that I gave of old to your ancestors forever and ever.

Here you are, trusting in deceptive words to no avail. Will you steal, murder, commit adultery, swear falsely, make offerings to Baal, and go after other gods that you have not known, and then come and stand before me in this house, which is called by my name, and say, 'We are safe!' – only to go on doing all these abominations? *Has this house, which is called by my name, become a den of robbers in your sight?* You know, I too am watching, says YHWH. Go now to my place that was in Shiloh, where I made my name dwell at first, and see what I did to it for the wickedness of my people Israel.

And now, because you have done all these things, says YHWH, and when I spoke to you persistently, you did not listen, and when I called you, you did not answer, therefore I will do to the house that is called by my name, in which you trust, and to the place that I gave to you and to your ancestors, just what I did to Shiloh. And I will cast you out of my sight, just as I cast out all your kinsfolk, all the offspring of Ephraim.[186]

There can be no question about the thrust of this passage. On the one hand, it is a devastating critique of corruption within Jewish society in general. On the other, it is an unambiguous warning that, as a result, the Temple is to be destroyed.

Attention has rightly focused on the 'robbers' in the phrase 'den of robbers'. Older readings of the incident as a dramatic protest against economic exploitation had no apparent difficulty here: the system of money-changing, and of buying and selling animals, constituted (it was said) daylight robbery. It is still assumed by a good many interpreters that the word about a 'den of robbers' means that the synoptic evangelists at least, and probably their sources, saw the incident as a 'cleansing', rather than as an acted parable of destruction.[187] But the context in Jeremiah suggests otherwise. Cleansing is not enough; what is required is destruction – not simply because a new Temple must be built, but because the present one is utterly corrupt.

In fact, the word regularly translated 'robbers' or 'thieves' does not, even without this context, point necessarily, or even primarily, to economic corruption. The Greek word in question (*lestes*) and the Hebrew word behind it in Jeremiah (*parisim*) do not mean 'swindler', but 'one who robs with violence';[188] this does not fit with the charge of economic exploitation, but

---

[186] Jer. 7.3–15. The passage goes on to warn that the valley of Hinnom (= 'Gehenna') will become a mass grave (7.31f.).

[187] So e.g. Sanders 1985, 66f.; 1993, 255f., 260 (suggesting that the evangelists might have lifted the phrase from Jeremiah to make the incident appear politically innocuous).

[188] Harvey 1982, 132f. Chilton & Evans 1994a, 288 n.22 suggest that this is just hyperbole; but see below.

points instead in a rather different direction. The Greek work *lestes* does indeed mean 'one who robs with violence'; but its regular usage in first-century Palestine, as evidenced by dozens of occurrences in Josephus, is in reference to brigands or bandits. Twice he refers to 'caves of *lestai*'; in both cases, these are the brigands, living in the hills, whom Herod the Great wiped out.[189] These 'brigands' or 'bandits' were not mere highway robbers out for what they could get (though no doubt such people existed too). They were revolutionaries. Barabbas, the leader of a murderous civil uprising in Jerusalem, was a *lestes*. So were the two who were crucified with Jesus.[190] Crucifixion was the punishment reserved, not for thieves or swindlers, but for revolutionaries.

The result is a very different charge against the Temple from that of economic trickery – for which, indeed, there is comparatively little evidence in exactly this period.[191] Instead, the evidence, as Borg argued in 1984, 'points decisively to the role of the Temple in resistance toward Rome'.[192] As in Jeremiah's day, the Temple had become the focal point of the hope of national liberation, and hence was regarded as a guarantee of security against the pagans. How then could it symbolize, as Isaiah had indicated it should, the desire of YHWH that all nations should share in the blessings that would accrue to Israel when the kingdom would come, when the real return from exile would take place, and when YHWH himself would return to Zion?[193] This is not to say that there were already, in Jesus' day, violent revolutionaries holed up in the Temple.[194] The point has to do with ideology: the Temple had become, in Jesus' day as in Jeremiah's, the talisman of nationalist violence, the guarantee that YHWH would act for Israel and defend her against her enemies. This ideological point resulted, later, in actions that would otherwise remain inexplicable: after the fall of the Temple, the

---

[189] *Ant.* 14.415f.; 15.345–8; cf. *War* 1.304–11.

[190] Lk. 23.19, with Jn. 18.40; Mk. 15.27 and pars.

[191] See Borg 1984, 348 n.62, with other refs. (and cf. above, 414 n.171. Bauckham 1988, 84f. offers a different interpretation of *lestai*: the priestly aristocracy were using the Temple as a safe haven from which, metaphorically, to launch marauding raids, i.e. to pursue ill-gotten wealth.

[192] Borg 1984, 174. Others who have seen this meaning of 'den of robbers', though they have not agreed in their consequent reconstruction, include Buchanan 1959; Roth 1960; Gaston 1970, 85, 474; Barrett 1975, 15f. Meyer 1992a, 277 n.71, denies the relevance of 'revolutionaries'; but the meaning 'violent ones', which he endorses, makes much the same point.

[193] This reading is different, then, from those which see Jesus attempting to enable Gentiles to share more fully in Temple worship; see the discussion of various views in Sanders 1985, 68f.

[194] As suggested by e.g. Barrett 1975, 16; this is resisted by Gundry 1993, 645, but his objection misses the point I am making.

resistance leaders petitioned Titus to be allowed to leave the city in peace.[195]

Jesus' whole announcement of the kingdom, and the warnings that went with this announcement, were thus sharply and concretely focused in his echoing of Jeremiah's warning of coming destruction. This saying gave the most immediate and direct explanation for the symbolic prophetic action that had just taken place, which otherwise might have remained opaque. The present grievous distortion (from Jesus' point of view) of Israel's national vocation could lead to only one thing: a destruction of the Temple for which the Babylonian invasion, as predicted by Jeremiah, would be the most natural historical backdrop.

The context in Jeremiah offers an explanation, too, for the incident involving the fig tree.[196] Mark, as is well known, 'sandwiched' the Temple action between the cursing of the fig tree and the discovery of its having withered up. He thus clearly intended his readers to get the point (though countless readers have missed it anyway, and some, despite it, have enlisted him as an advocate of 'cleansing' rather than 'destruction'): what Jesus is doing in the Temple is cognate with what he is doing to the fig tree. He has come seeking fruit, and, finding none, he is announcing the Temple's doom. The fig tree action is therefore an acted parable of an acted parable. This is now regularly noted by scholars.[197] But the connection with Jeremiah is not so frequently made. Shortly after the passage quoted above, we find the following:

They have treated the wound of my people carelessly,
saying 'Peace, peace,' when there is no peace.
They acted shamefully, they committed abominations;
yet they were not at all ashamed,
they did not know how to blush.
Therefore they shall fall among those who fall;
at the time when I punish them, they shall be overthrown,
says YHWH.
When I wanted to gather them, says YHWH,
there are no grapes on the vine, nor figs on the fig tree;
even the leaves are withered,
and what I gave them has passed away from them.[198]

---

[195] Jos. *War* 6.323-7, 351-3. (Titus refused, 'indignant that men in the position of captives should proffer proposals to him as victors' (352).)

[196] Mk. 11.12-14, 20-5/Mt. 21.18-22; cf. e.g. Barrett 1975, 13f. On Luke's motives for omitting the story cf. Kinman 1994. Luke, of course, has a parable which points in the same direction (13.6-9), as does the parable of the wicked tenants, which all three synoptists place soon after the Temple-incident (and on which cf. below, 497-501).

[197] On the whole subject cf. Telford 1980.

[198] Jer. 8.11-13; cf. Mic. 7.1 and its surrounding context.

Jesus, in other words, appears to be deliberately evoking the whole context in Jeremiah. The cursing of the fig tree is part of his sorrowful Jeremianic demonstration that Israel, and the Temple, are under judgment.

The word about the mountain being cast into the sea also belongs exactly here.[199] Though the existence of more than one saying in this group suggests that Jesus used to say this sort of thing quite frequently, 'this mountain', spoken in Jerusalem, would naturally refer to the Temple mount. The saying is not simply a miscellaneous comment on how prayer and faith can do such things as curse fig trees. It is a very specific word of judgment: the Temple mountain is, figuratively speaking, to be taken up and cast into the sea.[200]

In addition to Isaiah and Jeremiah, the whole incident cries out to be seen, as various writers have recently argued, within the context of a deliberate re-application of Zechariah.[201] The quasi-royal entry into the city, and Jesus' messianic authority over the Temple (about which more anon), evokes Zechariah 9.9 and 6.12; the warning of a great cataclysm echoes 14.1-5. Further, the whole context speaks of the mighty acts whereby YHWH will set up his kingdom once and for all (14.9), whereupon the Gentiles will come in to worship (14.16-19). In this context, it may be that the action reported by Mark 11.16, where Jesus refused to allow anyone to carry vessels through the Temple (something also forbidden in rabbinic literature[202]), was both part of the 'cleansing' side of the story and, more importantly, another symbol, indicating, by veiled allusion to Zechariah 14.20f., that 'the day' had at last arrived.[203]

With this complex but coherent prophetic material as the necessary back-drop for understanding what Jesus did and why, we can approach the question at the heart of the problem. Why would Jesus banish the traders? If they were not exploiting people economically, or if that was not the main reason

---

[199] Mk. 11.22-4/Mt. 21.21f.; cf. Mt. 17.19f.; Lk. 17.5f.; *Thom.* 48; 1 Cor. 13.2. Even the Jesus Seminar agreed that the multiple attestation made the saying likely, though this was not enough to persuade them that such a politically incorrect saying could emanate from Jesus (Funk & Hoover 1993, 99).

[200] Equally, in a kaleidoscopic twist of prophetic imagery, 'the mountain' could be read, against the background of Zech. 4.7, as the opposition that stands in the way of the Messiah's building of the true Temple. See below, ch. 11.

[201] So Meyer 1992a, 262f.; Sanders 1993, 254; Trumbower 1993, 514, stressing that other first-century figures deliberately acted out scriptural prophecies: e.g. Theudas (*Ant.* 20.97-8), the Egyptian (*War* 2.261-3; *Ant.* 20.168-72), the Samaritan (*Ant.* 18.85-7) - and even Jesus ben Ananias, quoting as he did from Jer. 7.34; 16.9 (*War* 6.300-9).

[202] mBer. 9.5; bBer 54a; 62b.

[203] Difficult though it is to correlate Mk. 11.16 exactly with the different elements in Zech. 14.20f.; cf. Bauckham 1988, 77f.; Gundry 1993, 642f. Bauckham's suggestion (78) that the 'vessels' in question were used to carry the materials for the offerings of flour, oil and wine, and that Jesus was objecting to the monopoly on profits thereby made, is ingenious but, despite some support from mShek. 4.9; 5.4, must remain a guess.

for his action, what purpose would thereby be served? Borg has suggested that in their changing of profane coinage into sacred currency, and their provision of pure, blemish-free animals, 'their activity served and symbolized the quest for holiness understood as separation, a quest at the root of resistance to Rome.'[204] Richardson has argued a case which he himself describes as 'nearly opposite' to that of Borg: the problem was that the Temple coinage consisted of Tyrian shekels, which carried an offensive eagle-symbol; Jesus was thus reacting in favour of the purity system, and against the implicit profanation of the Temple.[205] Bauckham also suggests a financial solution: Jesus was opposed on principle to the Temple-tax (since Jews should not be taxed by their 'father', i.e. YHWH), and to the overpricing of doves (which were supposed to be available cheaply enough for poor people).[206] Chilton, like Richardson, thinks that Jesus was proposing an extension of the purity system, this time involving a change in the way the sacrifices were administered.[207]

I suspect that the answer lies closer to the mechanics of what actually happened in the Temple. Without the Temple-tax, the regular daily sacrifices could not be supplied.[208] Without the right money, individual worshippers could not purchase their sacrificial animals. Without animals, sacrifice could not be offered. Without sacrifice, the Temple had lost its whole *raison d'être*. The fact that Jesus effected only a brief cessation of sacrifice fits perfectly with the idea of a symbolic action. He was not attempting a reform; he was symbolizing judgment. We may remind ourselves of the horror with which Jews contemplated the cessation of the regular sacrifices.[209] Jesus' action symbolized his belief that, in returning to Zion, YHWH would not after all take up residence in the Temple, legitimating its present administration and its place and function within the first-century Jewish symbolic world. Rather, as Josephus himself claims to have realized, the cessation of sacrifice meant that Israel's god would use Roman troops to execute upon the Temple the fate which its own impurity, not least its sanctioning of the ideology of national resistance, had brought upon it.[210] The brief disruption which Jesus

---

[204] Borg 1984, 176.

[205] Richardson 1992: quote from 508 n.5. This proposal is discussed by Chilton 1994, 172–6.

[206] Bauckham 1988; on the tax, see Horbury 1984b; Bauckham 1986.

[207] Chilton 1992a, 1992b; 1994, 172–6.

[208] This is the point Neusner (1989) sees clearly, which enables me to combine the strength of Bauckham's point, and one part of Chilton's (1994, 174) with the theme of judgment.

[209] Dan. 8.11f.; 11.31; 12.11; 1 Macc. 1.45f.; Jos. *War* 6.94f.; mTaan. 4.6.

[210] cf. Jos. *War* 6.96–110. This reported speech of Josephus (from outside the city) to John of Gischala (who was inside), immediately following the cessation of the sacrifices, is most instructive. John, the brigand leader, declares that the city cannot be captured, since it belongs to Israel's god (98). Josephus responds, with lamentation and tears (111), that he

effected in the Temple's normal business symbolized the destruction which would overtake the whole institution within a generation.[211]

I conclude that Jesus' action in the Temple was intended as a dramatic symbol of its imminent destruction; that this is supported by the implicit context of Zechariah's prophecy, and the quotations from Isaiah and Jeremiah; and that Jesus' specific actions of overturning tables, forbidding the use of the Temple as a short-cut, and the cursing of the fig tree, were likewise all designed as prophetic and eschatological symbolism, indicating both the arrival of the kingdom and the doom of the city and Temple that refused it. The reasons for this total action are to be sought in Jesus' agenda, and his critique of his contemporaries, which we have explored in earlier chapters. What he did in Jerusalem was completely consistent with what he had done and said throughout his public work.

Four concluding remarks on the Temple-incident are in order. First, scholars have often puzzled over the fact that Jesus managed to perform such a subversive and shocking action and escape immediate arrest. Troops, both Roman and Jewish, intervened on other occasions; why not this time?[212] The hypothesis I am advancing considerably eases this problem. Jesus' action is to be seen as a swift and striking symbol, rather than either a would-be military coup or an attempt at controlling and reforming the whole system. This does not mean, as Sanders suggests (no doubt with tongue in cheek), that 'perhaps only a few disciples unostentatiously dropped their garments in front of the ass . . ., while only a few quietly murmured "Hosanna".'[213] It means, I suggest, that the action was sudden, dramatic, and powerful – but soon

---

speaks for the traditions of the fathers (107) and in line with the prophets (109) in inviting John to repent (103), even though he sees it is useless, since 'God it is, then, God himself, who with the Romans is bringing the fire to purge his Temple and exterminating a city so laden with pollutions' (110). The fact that the speech is clearly crafted after the event is not important; the sequence of thought demonstrates the coherence of the line of argument we have pursued so far.

[211] Sanders 1993, 259 sees that 'as a good Jewish prophet, [Jesus] could have thought that God would employ a foreign army for this destruction'; but then suggests that, 'as a radical first-century eschatologist, he probably thought that God would do it directly.' In the light of *NTPG* ch. 10, I suggest that this is a false dichotomy. Mairson 1996, 30f. reports a similar non-dichotomy in regard to twentieth-century views about the Temple's rebuilding: the Messiah will build it *and* it will come down from heaven.

[212] e.g. Lk. 13.1-3; Ac. 4.1-4; 21.30-6; Jos. *War* 2.223-7 (= *Ant.* 20.105-12). The last of these is particularly instructive. Cumanus, the fourth procurator (AD 48–52) after Pilate, stationed troops (one company, i.e. 128 soldiers) to overlook the Temple, in order to quell any uprising that might occur during Passover. The indecent behaviour of one of the soldiers provoked a riot, whereupon Cumanus called all his troops to the fortress. The crowd fled in fear, and large numbers were killed.

[213] Sanders 1985, 306. He is referring, strictly speaking, to the entry into Jerusalem, not to the Temple-action; but the point is basically the same.

over. By the time that the attention of the troops was aroused, Jesus would have done what he intended to do, and would have been holding forth to an excited audience while the money-changers scrabbled for their coins and the traders attempted frantically to regain control of their fluttering or stampeding charges. Even supposing the commander had sent for reinforcements, as Cumanus had to do twenty years later, by the time they arrived things might well have quietened down again.[214] Granted that the authorities wanted to avoid trouble (Mark 11.18 and 14.2 are surely right to stress their awareness that public action against someone like Jesus could precipitate trouble, and their desire to avoid it), it is perfectly credible to imagine Jesus performing a dramatic and highly visible symbolic action without being arrested at once. From then on, however, he would of course be a marked man:

> To evoke, even conditionally, the destruction of 'this temple' was to touch not just stone and gold and not only the general well-being but history and hope, national identity, self-understanding, and pride.[215]

Second, if Jesus predicted the Temple's destruction, did he predict also its subsequent rebuilding by YHWH? That is the heart of Sanders' claim:

> On what conceivable grounds could Jesus have undertaken to attack - and symbolize the destruction of - what was ordained by God? The obvious answer is that destruction, in turn, looks towards restoration.[216]

Not everyone will agree that this answer is 'obvious'. The texts in the synoptic gospels which speak of rebuilding are those put in the mouth of the false witnesses at the hearing before the Sanhedrin: 'I will destroy this temple made with hands, and in three days I will build another, made without hands.'[217] There is also, of course, the similar saying in the Johannine version of the incident.[218] It is true, as Sanders is at pains to show, that there are not a few Jewish texts which speak of the eschatological destruction and rebuilding of the Temple.[219] But Sanders rejects what I have argued already is the real motive behind the action, and the sayings: Jesus' analysis of the present plight of Israel in terms of her embracing violent resistance, and so

---

[214] On Cumanus, see the previous note but one.

[215] Meyer 1979, 183 (the whole passage is full of insight). For a similar explanation cf. Gundry 1993, 646. This hypothesis, I submit, cannot be reduced to the either/or of 'major incident, therefore Jesus should have been arrested' or 'not arrested, therefore no real incident': cf. Miller 1991, 248.

[216] Sanders 1985, 71, citing others who have held similar interpretations; 1993, 261f. In the latter book the 'rebuilding' theme is considerably more muted than in the former, being outweighed (correctly, in my opinion) by the emphasis on 'destruction'.

[217] Mk. 14.57f./Mt. 26.60f.

[218] Jn. 2.19.

[219] Sanders 1985, ch. 2 (77–90).

incurring the wrath of YHWH in the form of Roman destruction.[220] Instead, Sanders persists in asserting, on what seems to me a very slender basis, that the only real motive for Jesus' symbolically 'destroying' the Temple is the prospect of its being rebuilt in some fairly literal sense.[221]

I agree wholeheartedly with Sanders that Jesus' action fitted into a programme of eschatological expectation, not reform. I also agree, of course, that Jesus, like Jeremiah, regarded the Temple as god-given; there is no question of his suggesting that it should never have been built in the first place, or that worshipping in it was inherently wrong.[222] He was simply declaring that it was on the way to being redundant. At these points, Sanders and I agree with Schweitzer and his successors, against the nineteenth century on the one hand and the Jesus Seminar (and many others, not least on the fundamentalist fringe) on the other. But I do not think that Jesus' action was motivated by his expectation that YHWH would shortly build a new Temple of bricks and mortar. I think that Jesus saw himself, and perhaps his followers with him, as the new Temple (see below, chapter 13).

Third, there is a link here with Jesus' quotation of Hosea 6.6, 'I desire mercy and not sacrifice'. Israel's god desired mercy, not sacrifice: this text represents a key element in the redefinition.[223] About this passage a short comment is necessary. The quotation is peculiar to Matthew, and a third-century work also attributes it to Johanan ben Zakkai, as a comment upon the destruction of the Temple.[224] This has, not surprisingly, been advanced as evidence that the attribution of the quotation to Jesus is a post-70 invention, in response to the use of the idea by Johanan.[225] I confess that I incline on

---

[220] Sanders 1985, 74 recognizes only one part of this (that any sensible person could see that trouble-making will lead to disaster), and makes a division between the destruction by foreign arms and the destruction by Israel's god – which is untrue both to biblical warrant (e.g. Isa. 10.5f.) and to Josephus' perception of the disaster as caused by Israel's god *and* performed by Rome (*War* 6.110). See n.211 above.

[221] Sanders 1985, 73, 75, 87, 88. On 88 Sanders speaks of 'the connection between disaster, God's chastisement, and the subsequent redemption of a remnant' being 'so firmly fixed in Judaism that we should assume that even a bare statement of destruction would not be altogether misunderstood'. Quite so; but 'the redemption of a remnant' by no means indicates unequivocally 'the rebuilding of the Temple' in a straightforwardly literal sense.

[222] Hence, the early Christians went on worshipping in the Temple (e.g. Lk. 24.45); on this, cf. Bauckham, as in n.179 above. Israel's 'worship' was, for Paul, one of its god-given privileges (Rom. 9.4) – which puts it level with the other privileges which, as he argues throughout Rom., belong to the Messiah and his Jew-plus-Gentile people. Fredriksen 1995b, 90f. caricatures the argument she opposes: I am not suggesting that Jesus 'condemned' the Temple and its worship as 'morally, socially, and religiously wrong'.

[223] Mt. 9.13; 12.7; cf. Mk. 12.33.

[224] *Aboth de R. Nathan* (A) 4.

[225] So Davies & Allison 1988–91, 1.135, following Davies 1964, 306f. and Hill 1977.

this occasion more to the view of Neusner:[226] this story of Johanan, like many others, is probably a projection back from a subsequent debate, perhaps in the time of Bar-Kochba or even later. At that stage, the discussion would not be about whether the Temple's destruction was a tragedy. That was not at issue in the years immediately after AD 70; nobody would have doubted that the destruction was one of the greatest woes ever to befall the nation. The issue, rather, was whether it would be wise now for the Temple to be rebuilt. I find the picture of Johanan, calmly surveying the burned-out shell of the Temple, and quoting Hosea 6 with, as it were, a shrug of the shoulders, less historically credible than the picture of a rabbi in (say) AD 130, afraid that 'the yoke of the kingdom' would mean more trouble, advancing Hosea 6 as a reason for maintaining a low profile with the Romans, a high concentration on Torah, and an indefinite postponement of the Temple's rebuilding. And I find it quite likely that this view would then be ascribed to Johanan ben Zakkai, once the ambiguities of his own time were well past and he could be safely regarded as the founder of rabbinic (largely Hillelite, and certainly non-revolutionary) Judaism. This provides, I suggest, a far better setting for the story.

(There is a point of method here which should not go unremarked. It is strange that one should be invited to take on trust a tradition about Johanan, from a writing manifestly 150 or more years after the event, at a time when rabbinic thought was elevating him and his supposed Jamnian academy to a position they almost certainly never held in their own day, with the comment that great crises evoke significant aphorisms[227] – while being told that Jesus, a master both of biblical lore and of aphorism, who was just as much aware of a crisis in Israel's national life, could not have used the text in his own way and, as Matthew suggests, for a variety of purposes. Sauce for the critical goose is sauce – and perhaps source – for the critical gander.)

The fourth and final point looks on to subsequent discussions. We have already seen that the Temple was completely bound up with Israel's royal ideology.[228] The somewhat shaky line from David and Solomon, through Jehoash, Josiah and Hezekiah, to Zerubbabel, Judas Maccabaeus, Herod the Great, and finally Bar-Kochba, bears witness to this link, as do passages such as Zechariah 6 and *Psalms of Solomon* 17. Did Jesus make this link himself? Was his Temple-action not only prophetic, but deliberately (though no doubt paradoxically) messianic? Did the onlookers get this point? I think the answer

---

[226] Neusner 1970, 114, 130.

[227] So Davies 1964, 307.

[228] *NTPG* 224–6, 307–20; cf. ch. 11 below; and cf. Runnalls 1983; Gundry 1993, 642, with other refs. I find it remarkable that e.g. Catchpole 1984 can regard the Temple-incident as non-messianic.

to all three questions is Yes. This, however, must be the subject of a later discussion (in Part III). Our immediate task must be to step back from the Temple-incident itself and examine the lines that led up to it. We must, in other words, examine Jesus' movement with the question: what were the positive symbols of his own work?

4. Jesus' Symbols of the Kingdom

(i) Introduction: Symbols of 'Return'

We have now seen that Jesus, in true prophetic style, set his face against the central institutions and symbols of Israel. He did so, not because he thought they were bad in themselves, but because he believed they were being wrongly used by his contemporaries to buttress a spurious reading and enacting of the true Jewish worldview. Like the authors of the Scrolls, he was acting radically. He did not aim thereby to depart from 'Judaism', from the traditions of Israel; his aim was to call Israel back to what he saw as the true meaning of those traditions. I shall now argue that the positive symbols of Jesus' own work are not to be seen, as some have recently suggested, as an attempt to establish a non-Jewish way of life, different from 'Judaism' itself. They do not point to an *abandonment* of the underlying Jewish worldview, but rather to a particular *variation* on it. They were intended as true-Jewish symbols, signs of the great renewal for which Israel had longed.

I have argued already that one of the main kingdom-themes informing Jesus' retelling of Israel's story was his belief that the real return from exile, and the real return of YHWH to Zion, were happening in and through his own work. The major symbols of his work strongly reinforce and illuminate this. As often with worldview-symbols, these integrate closely with both praxis and story, and can therefore be treated briefly in the light of chapters 5–8 above.[229] They form a cumulative sequence. Israel's hope was conceived in relation to land, family, Torah and Temple; Jesus subverted the common interpretation of these, and offered his own fresh and positive alternatives.

(ii) Restored Land, Restored People

The prophecies of return from exile, and of the return of YHWH to Zion, saw these events as being marked by the dramatic restoration of creation, focused on the healing of the sick:

---

[229] On the relation between symbols and other worldview-elements, cf. *NTPG* 123–6.

The wilderness and the dry land shall be glad,
the desert shall rejoice and blossom;
like the crocus it shall blossom abundantly,
and rejoice with joy and singing . . .
They shall see the glory of YHWH,
the majesty of our god . . .

Then shall the eyes of the blind be opened,
and the ears of the deaf unstopped;
then shall the lame leap like a deer
and the tongue of the speechless sing for joy . . .

And the ransomed of YHWH shall return,
and come to Zion with singing;
everlasting joy shall be upon their heads;
they shall obtain joy and gladness,
and sorrow and sighing shall flee away.[230]

In the light of our previous arguments, we can say with confidence that Jesus intended his 'mighty works' of healing to be understood symbolically as a fulfilment of this expectation. They were not simply socially or religiously subversive, though clearly they were that as well. They spoke, in the way that symbols can, of return and restoration, of the coming of YHWH to save and heal his people.[231] Thus it was that, when the eschatological prophet John was puzzled by what Jesus was doing, and perhaps by what he was not doing, Jesus replied by alerting John's messengers to the symbolic value of his characteristic praxis:

Go and tell John what you hear and see: the blind are seeing, the lame are walking, the lepers are cleansed and the deaf hear, the dead are being raised up and the poor are hearing the good news. And - blessed is the one who is not offended at me.[232]

The expectation of the restored land has become focused on restored human beings. Jesus offered people 'inheritance', and greater possessions than they would have abandoned; but he regularly construed this in terms of human lives and human communities that were being renewed and restored through the coming of the kingdom.[233] The pearl of great price was available for those who sold everything else;[234] among the things that would have to be sold was the traditional symbol of sacred land itself. It was swallowed up in the eschatological promise. YHWH was now to be king of all the earth.

---

[230] Isa. 35.1-2, 5-6, 10.
[231] On 'mighty works', and the current debates about them, see ch. 5 above.
[232] Mt. 11.4-6/Lk. 7.22-3. See below, 495-7.
[233] cf. Mt. 5.5; Mt. 19.29/Mk. 10.30/Lk. 18.29-30.
[234] Mt. 13.45/*Thom.* 76.

At the same time, Jesus does seem to have had a keen awareness of the symbolism of place. His movement took its origin, after all, from that of John the Baptist, who like several other Jewish prophets of the time was gathering people in the Jordan valley, re-enacting the exodus in which Israel had for the first time come in to possess the land. Jesus' deliberate journey to Jerusalem, his action on the Temple mount, and his discourse on the Mount of Olives, were all designed to evoke, symbolically, those biblical strands of kingdom-expectation which he was claiming to fulfil. The symbol of land was, in that sense, being both affirmed and redefined; the stones would cry out to greet one whose agenda was radically different from popular imagining. Once again we must insist that, if scholars are ready to credit Matthew, say, or Luke with the ability to understand how the geographical symbolism of Israel's traditions could function – and if, equally, John the Baptist and many others were able to understand these same symbols and re-enact them – there is no reason whatsoever to deny Jesus the same skill. Is the real problem, perhaps, that it is less threatening to think of somebody weaving artful tapestries of *ideas* than to think of somebody choosing deliberately to *act* in a symbolic fashion? Jesus, I suggest, did just that.

(iii) The Redefined Family

We saw in the previous section that Jesus drastically challenged the existing familial and national symbolism. In its place, he seems to have gone out of his way to create a fictive kinship, a surrogate family, around himself. 'Here are my mother and my brothers': all those who heard and obeyed the word of Israel's god – by which Jesus clearly meant all those who responded favourably to his kingdom-announcement – constituted a new family, and should treat one another accordingly.[235] Jesus had called for a deep and shocking disloyalty to the human, and nation-defining, family that his hearers knew; it was to be replaced by a total devotion and loyalty to Jesus himself, and to the others who also followed him. One is reminded of Qumran.

The parallel, indeed, makes the symbolic point clearly enough: this was remnant-theology, return-from-exile theology. Instead of the genealogies which marked out the returnees,[236] the symbol of identity for the renewed people was Jesus himself, and his kingdom-announcement. When Jesus told a disciple to 'leave the dead to bury their dead', the alternative he commanded

---

[235] Mk. 3.31–5, etc.; see above, 400–3; cp. *G. Ebi.* 5; *2 Clem.* 9.11. On the importance of kinship ties in Jesus' world cf. e.g. Malina 1993 part IV.

[236] 1 Chr. 1—9; Ezra 2.1–67; 8.1–20; Neh. 7.6–69; 11.3—12.26.

was 'go and announce the kingdom of god'.[237] Jesus and his kingdom-announcement were to override the strictest of normal symbolic obligations. In particular, the call of the twelve said, in language far easier to read than Greek or Aramaic, that this was where YHWH was at last restoring his people Israel.[238] This was the restored, redefined family.

What is more, this family was in principle open to all, beyond the borders of Israel. Land and family were simultaneously rethought in the promise that the eschatological blessing would reach beyond the traditional confines. As the prophets had foretold, many would come from east and west and sit down with Abraham, Isaac and Jacob in the kingdom of god. Once Jesus had symbolically redefined the restored Israel in terms simply of loyalty to himself, this move was in principle open. It is interesting, however, that the evangelists, who all clearly endorsed the mission to the nations, refused to invent symbolic incidents in which Jesus actually enacted this wider implication. Jesus' meetings with Gentiles are few and cryptic, and thus all the more likely to be authentic.[239]

This new family was of course characterized and marked out by one of the best-known features of Jesus' work: his open table-fellowship with anyone who shared his agenda, who wanted to be allied with his kingdom-movement.[240] It has recently been disputed whether Jesus really did include tax-collectors and other notorious characters in his retinue, but this option seems to be a minority view that can be safely left aside.[241] Most writers now agree that eating with 'sinners' was one of the most characteristic and striking marks of Jesus' regular activity.[242] This would not have been of any significance, of course, if Jesus were acting simply as a private individual. But when it is allied with the claim, made in praxis and story, that Jesus was inaugurating the long-awaited kingdom, it becomes deeply symbolic. That is why, as we saw, it aroused controversy. Jesus was, as it were, celebrating the messianic banquet, and doing so with all the wrong people.

Jesus, then, created a new symbol, which drew into itself the symbolism of family and nation that characterized mainstream Israel. Allegiance to Jesus

---

[237] Lk. 9.60; the Mt. version (8.22) simply has 'follow me'.

[238] On the twelve see above, 299f. Nb. Sanders 1985, 101: 'We encounter here historicity of a curious kind: the historicity of a symbol.'

[239] cf. *NTPG* 421f. on Mt. 8.5–13/Lk. 7.1–10; and, for the eschatological expectation, *NTPG* 267f.

[240] Mk. 2.13–17/Mt. 9.9–13/Lk. 5.27–32; Mt. 11.19/Lk. 7.34; Lk. 15.1–2; 19.1–10.

[241] On Horsley's attempt (1987) to distance Jesus from 'collaborators' with Rome, thereby aligning Jesus with movements of social protest, cf. above, 267 n.100.

[242] The throwaway line in Mt. 11.19/Lk. 7.34 is scarcely an invention of the early church; it was only the proximity of the phrase 'son of man' which caused the Jesus Seminar to vote the saying gray rather than pink or red (Funk & Hoover 1993, 180).

himself constituted a new family tie, overriding all others. It is in this light that the next two symbols can be the more readily understood.

(iv) The Redefined Torah

Along with Jesus' redefinition of nation and family, and quite consistent with it, there went his redefinition of Torah. This is a huge topic, and yet the main point here can be stated quite simply. Torah defined Israel: specifically, the works of Torah functioned as symbolic praxis, as the set of badges which demonstrated both to observant Jews and to their neighbours that they were indeed the people of the covenant. For Jesus, the symbolic praxis that would mark out his followers, and which therefore can be classified as, in that sense, redefined Torah, is set out in such places as the Sermon on the Mount, which we have studied elsewhere.[243] In particular, his returned-from-exile people, who had themselves received 'mercy' and 'forgiveness' precisely in being Jesus' people, were now under obligation to demonstrate the same 'mercy' and 'forgiveness' in their new-family relationships. Jesus' table-fellowship virtually replaced the food laws. Forgiveness lay at the heart of the symbolic praxis which was to characterize his redefined Israel.[244]

(v) The Rebuilt Temple

All these redefined symbols came together, hardly surprisingly, in Jesus' alternative Temple-symbolism. We find this in a variety of places in the tradition, which we must look at in somewhat more detail.

The Temple was to Judaea what the Torah was to Galilee. That is an over-simplification, but perhaps a useful one. In fact, of course, until AD 70 the Torah remained firmly in second place, dependent upon the Temple. Nevertheless, in terms of the symbols by which the life of Jewish people in the two areas was ordered, the aphorism holds true. Loyalty to Temple in Judaea functioned in parallel to loyalty to Torah in Galilee.

Jesus' actions and words in the Temple thus functioned symbolically in more or less the same way as his actions and words concerning the Torah. In neither case was there a denial that the institution itself was good, god-given, and to be respected. In both cases there was an assertion that the time had come for the institution to be transcended; in both cases there was an accusation that the institution was currently operating in a way that was destructive

---

[243] Above, ch. 7.
[244] Classically expressed in e.g. Mt. 18.21-35.

both to those involved and, more importantly, to the will of YHWH for his people Israel. In both cases, this was typically Jewish (and typically first-century) critique-from-within. Sanders is right, in other words, to stress that what was at stake in both cases was Jesus' perception that the eschaton was dawning. But he is wrong to minimize or marginalize the critique which Jesus launched, both against his contemporaries and against the symbols which expressed and reinforced their construal of the Jewish worldview. With hindsight from the Temple-action, the significance of Jesus' symbolic actions in the earlier period of his work becomes all the clearer.

One of these key symbolic actions comes to light in the little story, common to all three synoptic gospels, about Jesus' attitude to fasting.[245] John's disciples, and the Pharisees' followers, were fasting, but Jesus and his followers were not. The difference had nothing to do with patterns of religion. It was not that the two fasting groups were concerned with outward observances, while Jesus was concerned only with the inner attitude of the heart. Nor can the fasting groups be dismissed as legalistic ascetics in contrast to Jesus seen as a free-and-easy antinomian. Such an analysis would flatten out the contours of second-Temple Judaism into the bland and anachronistic landscape of moralism. Something quite different was at stake.

Fasting in this period was not, for Jews, simply an ascetic discipline, part of the general practice of piety. It had to do with Israel's present condition: she was still in exile. More specifically, it had to do with commemorating the destruction of the Temple.[246] Zechariah's promise that the fasts would turn into feasts could come true only when YHWH restored the fortunes of his people.[247] That, of course, was precisely what Jesus' cryptic comments implied:

> The wedding guests cannot fast while they have the bridegroom with them, can they? As long as they have the bridegroom with them, they cannot fast . . .
> No one sews a piece of unshrunk cloth on an old cloak; otherwise, the patch pulls away from it, the new from the old, and a worse tear is made. And no one puts new wine into old wineskins; otherwise, the wine will burst the skins, and the wine is lost, and so are the skins; but one puts new wine into fresh skins.[248]

In other words, the party is in full swing, and nobody wants glum faces at a wedding. This is not a piece of 'teaching' about 'religion' or 'morality'; nor is it the dissemination of a timeless truth. It is a claim about eschatology. The

---

[245] Mk. 2.18-22/Mt. 9.14-17/Lk. 5.33-9/*Thom.* 47.1-5; 104.1.

[246] cf. *NTPG* 234f., with refs. to both primary and secondary sources; to these, add Safrai 1976b, 814-16.

[247] Zech. 8.19.

[248] Mk. 2.19, 21f./Mt. 9.15, 16/Lk. 5.34, 36f. Luke describes the latter double saying as a 'parable'; it has become a detached aphorism in *Thom.* 47.4f. (cf. too *Thom.* 104.1-3).

time is fulfilled; the exile is over; the bridegroom is at hand. Jesus' acted symbol, feasting rather than fasting, brings into public visibility his controversial claim, that in his work Israel's hope was being realized; more specifically, that in his work *the Temple was being rebuilt*. Those who had got so used to living in exile that they could not hear the message of liberation were deaf indeed.[249]

The same was true about Jesus' claim to be able to provide forgiveness.[250] This 'forgiveness' should not be thought of as a detached, ahistorical blessing, such as might be offered by anyone at any time. Jesus' offer is not to be construed, as it has been so often, as an attempt to play at 'being god'; nor is it to be rejected as unhistorical on the grounds that such an attempt is unthinkable. Forgiveness was an eschatological blessing; if Israel went into exile because of her sins, then forgiveness consists in her returning: returning to YHWH, returning from exile.[251] Jesus' action and claim indicated that this symbol of return was now becoming a reality. If the authors of the Scrolls believed that their group, being the real returned-from-exile people, had received forgiveness of sins,[252] it is not a large step to think of an eschatological prophet, such as John the Baptist or Jesus, offering his followers the same thing. This brings us to the heart of Jesus' counter-Temple movement:

> This kind of extravagant independence would break the monopoly of the system, with its centre in priesthood and temple.[253]

As a result,

> We are now in a much better position to understand why the scribes came down from Jerusalem to discredit Jesus already in Galilee. His whole ministry there was already undermining the absolute claims of their city and the basis for its control, the temple.[254]

This, too, is the thrust of the little exchange with a scribe, recorded only in Mark:

> The scribe said, 'You are right, teacher: you have said truly that he is one, and that there is none beside him; and that to love him with all the heart and with all the understanding and with all the strength, and to love one's neighbour as oneself, is more than all burntofferings and sacrifices.' And when Jesus saw that he had answered intelligently, he said to him: 'You are not far from the kingdom of god.'[255]

[249] This seems to be the meaning of Luke's addition in 5.39.

[250] Mk. 2.1–13/Mt. 9.1–8/Lk. 5.17–26; Lk. 7.36–50; cf. too Lk. 19.1–10.

[251] cf. esp. Isa. 40.1–2; Lam. 4.22; Dan. 9.1–19; etc.

[252] e.g. 1QH 4.11–12; 5.4; 15.30f. (GM 317, 319, 344).

[253] Meyer 1992a, 257.

[254] Freyne 1988b, 47.

[255] Mk. 12.32–4. Cf. Mt. 9.13; 12.7, quoting Hos. 6.6 (discussed above, 426f.).

In context, this can mean only one thing: the kingdom-behaviour in which Israel's basic confession of faith is truly fulfilled *is worth more than the Temple and its sacrificial system*. And, since Jesus was claiming to offer the renewed heart, the blessing of the new covenant through which people would at last be able to keep the *Shema* by loving their god and neighbour, this conversation resonates symbolically with the rest of the evidence. It indicates that, for Jesus, part of the point of the kingdom he was claiming to inaugurate would be that it would bring with it all that the Temple offered, thereby replacing, and making redundant, Israel's greatest symbol.

Jesus' practice jumps suddenly into startling and symbolic focus when seen in this light. 'My child, your sins are forgiven':[256] that sentence has the effect of a private individual approaching you on the street and offering to issue you with a passport or driving licence – or, perhaps more appropriately in this case, a private individual approaching a prisoner in jail and offering him a royal pardon, signed by himself. From the twentieth-century, late-deist, western-individual perception, it looks simply as if Jesus is behaving as 'god', dispensing forgiveness from a great metaphysical height. That gives a spurious perception of why such symbolic behaviour was shocking. In first-century Jewish reality, the way YHWH forgave sins, as we saw, was ultimately through the officially established and authorized channels of Temple and priesthood.[257] Jesus was claiming, as Sanders has argued, to be in that sense 'speaking for god', claiming by strong implication that he carried in himself the authority normally vested elsewhere.[258]

This should make clear the real nature of Jesus' symbolic clash with those who claimed to speak for Israel's ancestral traditions. Fasting spoke of an Israel still in exile. Sabbath spoke of the great day of rest still to come; also, both to Israel and to the pagans, it announced Israel's determination to remain separate. Food laws, too, spoke of an Israel separate from the nations, eating different food, anxious to reinforce her ethnic, and ultimately her national, boundaries. Jesus' whole work was aimed at announcing that the day of mourning, of exile, of necessary and god-ordained national separateness, was coming to an end. His claim that Israel's god was acting to fulfil the ancient promises in and through his own work was therefore seen to be deeply threatening by the self-appointed guardians of Israel's heritage. In their view, whatever the fulfilment of Israel's destiny might look like, it would not be like this.

---

[256] Mk. 2.5/Mt. 9.2/Lk. 5.20.

[257] Fredriksen 1995b suggests that forgiveness was available anywhere, at any time, within Judaism, whenever someone repented. This is true at one level, but as Sanders makes clear (1992b, 103–18) the transaction was not complete without sacrifice. Fredriksen, it seems, is looking at the question from an essentially post-70 perspective.

[258] e.g. Sanders 1985, 240, 273; 1993, 239.

As we argued earlier, the Pharisees would quite probably have been happy for Jesus to persuade sinners like Zacchaeus or Mary Magdalene to mend their ways. But that was not the issue. The objection of the Pharisees at this point, cognate with the clash of agendas already studied, was that Jesus was claiming to offer something he had no right to offer, on conditions he had no right to set, to people who had no right to receive it. Repentance was a matter of the community, of its official structures, and of reintegration into it for someone who had (for whatever reason) been excluded. That meant going through official channels. It was YHWH's business, and could be done only by his official vicegerents, i.e. the priests, and ultimately through the Temple itself. Jesus, as we saw in chapter 7, was redefining the very notion of repentance. He was claiming the right to regard those who followed him as the true, 'penitent', returned-from-exile Israel.

(Why then, we might ask, did the *priests*, not least the local ones, not object to Jesus? Perhaps they did. Perhaps there was just as much controversy with the priests as with the Pharisees, but that what we have in the gospels is not so much the *invention* of material to fit the needs of the early church, as the *suppression* of potential material that did *not* fit those needs in the Diaspora mission where there were no priests around, or in the post-AD 70 community where there were no priests left. Perhaps Jesus' debates with the Pharisees were seen to be more analogous to (though not identical with) the debates the church faced in those new situations, whereas the matters raised by the priests might not be so relevant. Perhaps, too, many of the priests converted, as Acts indicates (6.7). This suggestion about the history of Jesus-traditions is of course speculative, but no more so than those regularly advanced in support of other hypotheses. It is in fact mild by comparison with some ideas that, despite being groundless, have become 'accepted results of scholarship'.)

Healing, forgiveness, renewal, the twelve, the new family and its new defining characteristics, open commensality, the promise of blessing for the Gentiles, feasts replacing fasts, the destruction and rebuilding of the Temple: all declared, in the powerful language of symbol, that Israel's exile was over, that Jesus was himself in some way responsible for this new state of affairs, and that all that the Temple had stood for was now available through Jesus and his movement. It is not surprising, therefore, that when Jesus came to Jerusalem the place was not, so to speak, big enough for both him and the Temple together. The claim which had been central to his work in Galilee was that Israel's god was now active, through him, to confront evil and so to bring about the real return from exile, the restoration for which Israel had longed; and that Israel's god himself was now returning to Zion in judgment and mercy. The house built on sand, however – the present Temple and all that went with it, and all the hopes of national security which clustered, as in Jeremiah's day, around it – would fall with a great crash. If we understand Jesus' action in the Temple in the way I have suggested, we achieve the very great historical benefit of coherence, at this point, between a good many words and deeds which were most characteristic of Jesus during his itinerant ministry, and the deeds and words which, in Jerusalem, brought that whole prophetic career to its climax.

If, then, we enquire, as we have been doing throughout this chapter, as to Jesus' attitude to the dominant symbols of the Judaism of his day, and as to his own chosen symbols, we find, quite naturally, that Temple and Torah dominate the landscape. Jesus assumed the god-givenness of the institutions. He stood firmly within one of Judaism's oldest traditions, that of offering prophetic critique from within. But the symbolic critique was sharp. Israel's present appropriation of the ancient symbols was leading her headlong into ruin. Jesus was warning of this in the clearest way possible, while at the same time inviting all who would do so to repent and come with him in his way of being Israel, his way of loyalty to YHWH. This, we must stress again, was not an odd thing for a first-century Jew to do. Nor was it odd that he drew his symbolic actions together in a final scenario which encapsulated them all.

(vi) The Symbolic Focus

Put together all the symbols we have outlined so far, and what do we get? We get Jesus feasting with his motley group of followers, as a sign of their healing and forgiveness; Jesus implying that those with him are the true Israel; Jesus enacting the real return from exile, the new exodus; Jesus marking his people out with a new praxis which did for them what Torah did for the pre-eschatological Israel; Jesus forming a counter-Temple movement around himself. If we were to attempt to draw these pictures into one, the scene might look suddenly familiar. It might consist of a young Jewish prophet, reclining at table with twelve followers, celebrating a kind of Passover meal, constituting himself and them as the true Israel, the people of the renewed covenant, and doing so in a setting and context which formed a strange but deliberate alternative to the Temple. The symbols of Jesus' kingdom-announcement, in other words, come together in the upper room.

We shall look at this scene in more detail in chapter 12. Here we may simply note three points.

First, it is completely consistent with the praxis, story and symbols we have studied throughout this Part of the book that Jesus should have celebrated a quasi-Passover of this sort with his followers, as part of his intention to bring in the kingdom.[259] If we have been on historical ground in the interwoven historical reconstruction so far, we might almost have predicted a final prophetic action such as this.

Second, the action in the Temple and the staging of such a meal are, as several recent writers have seen, mutually interpretative.[260] However we 'read' the whole complex of Temple and Last Meal – to that we shall return – it belongs together *as* a complex, an interconnected web of intentional events in which Jesus was enacting, or setting the scene to enact, the coming of the kingdom.

Third, at the heart of Jesus' freshly conceived symbolic universe we find – Jesus himself. His own work, his own presence, his own teaching, even his own impending fate; all these and more cluster together, suggesting that, if it is symbols we are looking for, he himself was the greatest symbol of his own career. It is not simply the case, as in the old caricature which one still sometimes hears trotted out, that Jesus talked about god whereas the early church talked about Jesus. 'If anybody hears my words and does them . . .'; 'If I by the finger of god cast out demons . . .'; 'But I say unto you . . .' Anachronistic western sensibilities may find this somewhat strong meat. Some still try to rescue Jesus from this self-reference, to preserve his humility from such a definite focus on himself.[261] But the profile of the prophet from Nazareth, as it comes into sharper focus, does not allow us to make him in our own image in such a way. He appears much more like we may suppose certain other persons in first-century Judaism to have been: persons who launched movements, who invited people to follow them, who believed, and persuaded others to believe, that through their own work Israel's god would bring in his kingdom. Some such persons, as we have seen, were 'leadership' prophets; some were would-be messiahs.

Those who observed people making such claims, and who disagreed with them, would of course offer an alternative analysis of what was going on. If, once again, it was not at all odd for a charismatic young Jew to speak and act in the way Jesus was speaking and acting, nor was it odd for people to react in the way that they did. Prophets may not perish outside Jerusalem, but it is only providence that prevents them doing so. Anybody acting and speaking as Jesus did was running straight into trouble. People were bound to say he was leading Israel astray; and that, traditionally, was a capital offence.

[259] cf. esp. Mk. 14.25/Mt. 26.29/Lk. 22.18.

[260] cf. e.g. Neusner 1989, 1993; Chilton 1992b.

[261] cf. Funk & Hoover 1993, 32f.: Jesus, having urged humility on his followers, cannot have made special claims for himself. He was, rather, 'like the cowboy hero of the American West exemplified by Gary Cooper . . . self-effacing, modest, unostentatious'. Would such a figure have been a significant historical character?

5. Jesus 'Leading the People Astray'?

The charge that Jesus was 'leading Israel astray' emerges quite clearly in literature from the second century and later. Justin Martyr is aware of the charge;[262] it is clearly reflected in two well-known Talmudic passages.[263] This much is well known. It is not so often suggested that the idea of Jesus as a 'deceiver of the people' is mooted, at least by implication, in the famous passage about Jesus in Josephus' *Antiquities* 18.63f. When what are usually seen as Christian interpolations are removed, the remaining text can, it is true, be read in a positive light, as follows:

> [Jesus] was one who wrought surprising feats and was a teacher of such people as accept the truth gladly. He won over many Jews and many of the Greeks.[264]

But a good case can be made for taking the crucial words in a far more negative sense:

> [Jesus] was a doer of strange deeds, and a deluder of the simple-minded. He led astray many Jews and Greeks.[265]

The same charge is clearly present in John, Luke and Matthew.[266]

The charge goes back, in terms of the Jewish legal system, to Deuteronomy 13. There, three categories of people are listed: the prophet who persuades people to go after other gods; the friend or family member guilty of the same offence; and the scoundrel who leads astray a whole town. In each case the guilty person is to be put to death. Subsequent discussions of this legislation indicate that this was taken extremely seriously, so that normal precautions designed to impede the carrying out of the death penalty would not apply.[267] Although the 'deceiver' is, technically, distinct from the 'false prophet' of Deuteronomy 18 (the false prophet is known because his predictions do not come true, whereas the 'deceiver' performs successful signs and uses them as a ploy to lure people after false gods), the evidence from the second century, when read alongside the relevant passages in the

---

[262] *Dial.* 69.7; cf. Stanton 1994, 166f.

[263] bSanh. 43a; 107b. Cf. Klausner 1947 [1925], 27f.; Horbury 1982a, 57; Stanton 1994, 167. The charge may also be present, by implication at least, in *Ac. Thom.* 48, 96, 102, 106f: so Stanton, 169.

[264] Feldman's translation in the Loeb edn.

[265] cf. Bammel 1974; Stanton 1994, 169-71.

[266] Jn. 7.47, in context of 7.12, 25-7, 40; 10.19-21; Lk. 23.2, 5, 14; Mt. 9.34; 10.25; 12.24-7; 27.63f.; cf. Stanton 1994, 175f.

[267] cf. Neale 1993, 90-4, citing e.g. bSanh. 29a; 33b; etc., and secondary discussions. The 'false prophet' theme turns up, perhaps not surprisingly, in Qumran: cf. 4Q375 1.4-9 (GM 278).

gospels, makes it look very likely that the charges of 'deceiver', 'imposter', 'magician' and 'false prophet' were closely aligned, not least precisely in the case of Jesus.[268]

The recent work on this topic may be summarized, and applied to our present chapter, as follows.[269]

First, it is likely that Jesus was seen by at least some of his Jewish contemporaries in categories taken from Deuteronomy 13. Though a fair bit of the evidence is much later, there is a convergence from several independent sources, which is then corroborated by passages like Mark 3.22, with its parallels (which many think are independent of Mark) in Matthew 12.24 and Luke 11.15.[270] Jesus does seem to have used techniques, in performing cures, which his contemporaries might well have regarded as magical;[271] and anyone doing exorcisms was likely to be regarded as a magician, since exorcism was the commonest form of Jewish magic in the period.[272] Not only is the Deuteronomy 13 background probable; it is quite likely that Jesus was also regarded as a 'rebellious son', in the category of Deuteronomy 21.18-21. The rebel son is described as 'a glutton and a drunkard'; though the Septuagint words at this point are not the same as those in Matthew 11.19 and Luke 7.34, where Jesus is described as 'a glutton and a drunkard, a friend of tax-collectors and sinners', the coincidence is striking, and lends weight to passages such as Mark 3.21, when Jesus' family come to take him away, saying that he is mad.[273]

Second, if Jesus was indeed seen in categories taken from one or more of these passages in Deuteronomy, it can only be because he was indeed doing things for which no other explanation seemed possible. His 'mighty deeds', his 'paradoxes',[274] could not be denied; but their motivation and origin could

---

[268] Stanton 1994, 171-5.

[269] In line with e.g. Stauffer 1960, 74; Jeremias 1971, 78; Bowker 1973, 38-52; Strobel 1980, 80-92; Hengel 1981b [1968], 38-42; Harvey 1982, 59; Sanders 1985, 300f.; the recent articles of Neale 1993 and Stanton 1994; and using material from as yet unpublished lectures by Professor Colin Brown, delivered in Oxford in May 1993.

[270] Those who believe in Q regularly suggest that this is a Mark/Q overlap, resulting in two independent sources: cf. Stanton 1994, 178f.

[271] Aune 1980, 1523-9; Smith 1978, 94-139.

[272] Schürer 3.342f. (Alexander).

[273] This opens up yet another possible dimension of Lk. 15.11-32, where the younger son is precisely a 'rebellious son' – and the parable is told to defend Jesus against the charge of 'receiving sinners and eating with them' (15.2). I owe this point to Professor Colin Brown (cf. too Brown 1984, 288), who alerted me also, on this point, to Derrett 1970, 100-25. Apart from in Dt., the 'rebellious son' theme is echoed in Prov. 23.19-21; 28.7, and referred to in Philo *Ebr.* 13-98; *Mut. Nom.* 206; *Spec. Leg.* 2.232; Jos. *Ant.* 4.264; *Apion* 2.206; 11QT 64; mSanh. 10.4-6; mShab. 9.6 (quoting Dt. 13.17); mAb.Zar. *passim*, esp. 3.3f., also quoting Dt. 13.17.

[274] See above, 187f. This is the word used by Josephus (*Ant.* 18.63) to describe Jesus' 'miracles'.

be seriously called into question. The reason for such questioning, of course, would be that he was, at the same time, teaching things which seemed to imply disloyalty to YHWH. Doing mighty acts while remaining loyal to Israel's traditions would not be problematic, as the existence of other ancient Jewish healers and exorcists indicates. Teaching disloyalty while performing no mighty acts would be threatening, but might not lead to serious action; after all, a great many Jews over the previous two hundred years or more had offered what stricter interpreters regarded as compromised or disloyal teaching, and, though the zealous might gnash their teeth, they did not often take action. What was intolerable was someone whose mighty acts attracted interest, crowds, and a regular following, and whose teaching to that following sounded like radical disloyalty.

Third, this explains at a stroke something that otherwise remains problematic, namely, the mention of plots to kill Jesus. If, after all, he looked like leading a whole town astray, then Deuteronomy 13.12–18 would come into play; it has been suggested that this was why several towns refused to countenance his teaching, since to do so would court disaster for them as well as for him.[275] Suspicion that someone was acting as a 'deceiver' was the one case, according to the Mishnah, in which would-be accusers were allowed to obtain evidence by stealth.[276] When we add this element to the argument advanced above, it appears that there were very good reasons why Pharisees, and perhaps others, might take an unusually close interest in Jesus and his followers, to see if they could detect any tell-tale signs of the disloyalty they already suspected. It is unlikely, as I shall argue later, that this theme explains the entire process which led to Jesus' death.[277] Nevertheless, it seems probable that one important element within the total charge against him was the suspicion that he was guilty of the crime described in Deuteronomy 13. He was a deceiver, leading the people astray.

Fourth, this theme draws together several elements in our entire historical reconstruction so far. We saw in chapter 5 that Jesus' public persona was that of a prophet, not least in that he performed prophetic actions. We saw in chapter 6 that he announced the kingdom of YHWH in what must have been perceived as a thoroughly subversive fashion; we studied in chapters 7 and 8 the agenda which Jesus set before his followers, and the warning that he gave of what would happen if Israel did not follow his way. All of this has built up to the present chapter, in which we have seen that Jesus spoke and acted subversively in relation to Israel's symbols, and that this activity aroused a

---

[275] Stauffer 1960, 74; Neale 1993, 96–100.

[276] mSan. 7.10; cf. Neale 1993, 92f., suggesting a link with Mk. 3.6; 12.13; Lk. 11.54, and citing other discussions.

[277] As has occasionally been argued, e.g. by Strobel 1980. See chs. 11–13 below.

controversy quite unlike the debates between different Pharisaic schools. He was not upholding what had come to be regarded as the inalienable symbols of Israel's nationhood and national aspirations. Instead, he was putting the symbols of his own work into the forefront, claiming in act, even more than in word, that Israel's god was in this way reconstituting his people. The charge that he was a deceiver, leading the people astray, perhaps through magic and false prophecy, fits the bill closely: his onlookers would either have had to conclude something like this or would have had to have become his followers.[278] We can be fairly sure that nobody in the early church invented the idea that Jesus' family said he was mad.[279] It is highly unlikely that anyone would have invented the charge that Jesus did what he did through being in league with the prince of demons.[280] We are here on firm historical ground.

The view from this point is instructive. The portrait of Jesus which emerges from our investigation so far remains thoroughly anchored in first-century Judaism. Indeed, the whole point is that Jesus was claiming to be speaking for Israel's god, her scriptures, and her true vocation. Israel was trusting in her ancestral religious symbols; Jesus was claiming to speak for the reality to which those symbols pointed, and to show that, by her concentration on them, Israel had turned inwards upon herself and was being not only disobedient, but dangerously disobedient, to her god's vision for her, his vocation that she should be the light of the world. Jesus' contemporaries, however, could not but regard someone doing and saying these things as a deceiver. His agenda clashed at every point with theirs. In symbol, as in praxis and story, his way of being Israel, his way of loyalty to Israel's god, was radically different from theirs. His actions in Galilee in relation to Torah pointed to the action he would take in Jerusalem in relation to the Temple; the response he evoked in Galilee pointed to the response he would evoke in Jerusalem. A clash of visions, incarnated in a clash of symbols, led to confrontation. Was this, then, what led to Jesus' death?

We shall tackle that question when we have addressed the prior matter: did Jesus see himself as Messiah? But before we can look at either, we need one more chapter to round off the profile of Jesus as a prophet. We have examined his praxis, his stories, and his symbols. What answers did he give, implicitly and explicitly, to the key questions that comprise the fourth quadrant of the worldview?

[278] Compare Jn. 7.45–52, where exactly this choice is posed.
[279] Mk. 3.21.
[280] Mk. 3.22/Mt. 12.24/Lk. 11.15; cf. Jn. 7.20.

Chapter Ten

THE QUESTIONS OF THE KINGDOM

1. Introduction

The profile of the prophet requires but one more stroke of the pen. We have studied Jesus' characteristic actions, the stories he told, and the ways in which he reorganized his symbolic world. There remain the key questions, the questions which can characterize any worldview: who are we, where are we, what's wrong, what's the solution – and what time is it?[1] What answers might Jesus have given to these questions? The first two can be addressed briefly, drawing together themes that have already been discussed.

Examining Jesus' answers to these worldview questions will clarify and advance our own answer to the first two questions with which this book began: what was Jesus' relation to Judaism, and what were his aims? Answers to these questions will propel us forwards into the third Part of the book.

2. Who Are We?

The short answer Jesus might have given to the question of identity is: we are Israel, the chosen people of the creator god. More specifically, we are the real, the true, Israel, in the process of being redeemed at last by this god, over against the spurious claimants who are either in power or mounting alternative programmes.

This is the message on the edge of every story, at the heart of the symbolic renewal. 'Blessed are those who . . . for theirs is the kingdom of heaven; they shall inherit the earth; they shall see God; they shall be called the sons of God.' 'You have been given to know the secrets of the kingdom.' 'I thank you, Father, for revealing these things to babes.' 'I assign you a

---

[1] See *NTPG* 122-6, esp. 123; and above, 138-43. Since writing *NTPG* I have realized that 'what time is it?' needs adding to the four questions I started with (though at what point in the order could be discussed further). Without it, the structure collapses into the timelessness which characterizes some non-Judaeo-Christian worldviews.

kingdom, so that you may eat and drink at my table in my kingdom, and sit on thrones judging the twelve tribes of Israel.'[2] The call of the twelve makes it clear enough; the thrust of the major stories, such as the prodigal son, emphasizes it from another angle. Jesus and the people around him, his motley group of followers, either constitute the real Israel or they are nothing. They are the returned-from-exile people, the people who at last know YHWH and are known by him, the new-covenant people whose sins are forgiven, at whose coming into existence the angels sing for joy.[3] That is their whole *raison d'être*.

Of course, few first-century Jews in their right minds were prepared to say this in so many words. Those who believed it knew it was a desperate gamble. Those who disbelieved it had every reason to regard the prophet from Nazareth and his followers as purveyors of dangerous nonsense. The ambiguity which many have seen, and which we shall shortly examine, about the *timing* of the kingdom (is it present or future in the ministry of Jesus?) thus appears already in the question of *identity*. All that Jesus and his followers were doing only meant anything if they thought they were, in some sense, the true people of the covenant god; but they were quite unlike what most other Jews had imagined such a people to be. Jesus' own understanding of his and his followers' identity went far beyond the picture of a teacher of miscellaneous truths or maxims. The corporate identity of the new movement belonged firmly within the world of Jewish eschatological expectations.

Within that world, too, there was a strand which, though submerged in some other movements, Jesus brought out and made thematic for his own work. Israel was not the chosen people for her own sake, but for the sake of the world. Part of the identity of Jesus and his followers was that they would inherit this biblical vocation: 'You are the salt of the earth, the light of the world.'[4] The Sermon on the Mount develops the theme: Jesus' followers were to reflect into the world the love of the creator god, who gives sunshine and rain to Israel and the Gentiles alike.[5] Jesus regarded his followers as, in some sense, the eschatological people promised in the scriptures, through whom, in a manner yet to be explicated, the glory of YHWH would be revealed to the world.[6] The disciples may well have had only a very hazy idea of how that would happen; quite probably they thought, if they reflected upon it at all, that the establishment of the kingdom, in some quite

[2] Mt. 5.3–10/Lk. 6.20–3; Mt. 13.11/Mk. 4.11/Lk. 8.10; Mt. 11.25/Lk. 10.21; Mt. 19.28/Lk. 22.29–30.

[3] Lk. 15.7, 10.

[4] Mt. 5.13/Mk. 9.49–50/Lk. 14.34f.; Mt. 5.14–16/Mk. 4.21/Lk. 8.16; 11.33/*Thom.* 33. For the theme in second-Temple Jewish thought cf. *NTPG* 267f.

[5] Mt. 5.43–8/Lk. 6.27–36.

[6] One of the best explorations of this theme remains that of Jeremias 1958.

straightforwardly political sense, would reveal to the nations that YHWH was indeed the king of all the earth. It is notable that, though the gospels are written from the perspective of a well-established gentile mission, they do not inundate Jesus' teaching with anything remotely like a well-developed theology of how Jesus' people would actually *become* the light of the world.[7] This highlights the way in which Jesus' answer to the first worldview question was both clear and nuanced. He and his followers were the eschatological people of the one true god, and as such would be, in a way yet to be explicated, the people through whom this god would make his ways known to the rest of the earth.

3. Where Are We?

As I argued in *The New Testament and the People of God*, and have reinforced in this book, the great majority of Jesus' contemporaries believed that they were still in exile, in all the senses that really mattered. They would have shared the view expressed by Ezra and Nehemiah: though we are back in our own land, we are still slaves.[8] In so far as Jesus' work offers a sense of location and condition, it represents the long-awaited news that the slaves were at last being freed. The meek would inherit the land; the hungry and thirsty would be satisfied.[9]

That said, Jesus seems to have said and done remarkably little on the subject of the Land. As we saw in the previous chapter, what he did say served to undermine adherence to land as a major symbol within the Jewish worldview.[10] He moved freely – and announced the kingdom – not only within Galilee but within the largely gentile Decapolis.[11] He crossed to and fro between Antipas' and Philip's territory (Capernaum and Chorazin were in the one, Bethsaida in the other).[12] He went north, out of Jewish territory, into the district of Tyre and Sidon.[13] He seems to have been well aware of the geographical symbolism of Jerusalem, not least in its relation to Galilee; but, as far as he was concerned, one of the main significances of Jerusalem was that it was the city where prophets were killed.[14] His sense of location

[7] Thus calling into question again the normal form-critical assumption that the gospels reflect first and foremost the life of the early church: cf. *NTPG* 421f.

[8] Ezra 9.8f; Neh. 9.36. Cf. *NTPG* 268–72.

[9] Mt. 5.5f./Lk. 6.21.

[10] Above, 403–5.

[11] Mk. chs. 5, 7. On the character of the Decapolis cf. e.g. Rey-Coquais 1992.

[12] cf. e.g. Mt. 11.21/Lk. 10.13.

[13] Mt. 15.21/Mk. 7.24 (cf. 7.31).

[14] Mt. 23.37/Lk. 13.34.

corresponded, it seems, to his sense of identity and, as we shall see, of timing and purpose. He had not come to rehabilitate the symbol of holy land, but to subsume it within a different fulfilment of the kingdom, which would embrace the whole creation – from which, of course, he drew continually in the narratives and imagery of his teaching and announcement.

More important by far, within Jesus' mindset, was his analysis of Israel's plight, his offer of the solution, and his reading of the signs of the times.

4. What's Wrong?

(i) Introduction

'Violent men are taking it by force.' 'An enemy has done this.' 'This wicked and adulterous generation.' 'You did not know the time of your visitation.' 'He looked round angrily, dismayed by their hardness of heart.'[15] Clearly Jesus thought something was deeply amiss. What was his analysis of the plight to which his kingdom-message was the solution?

Jesus stood, and was conscious of standing, in the long tradition of the Hebrew prophets.[16] Again and again, they castigated Israel for her failure to live up to her calling as the people of YHWH. The charge was a double one. First, Israel had been disloyal to YHWH himself. Second, she had sold out to some form of idolatry, or paganism. Elijah faced a people bent on Baal-worship; Jeremiah, a people who used the Temple as a talisman to protect them from the consequences of their own pagan behaviour. As we have already seen, Jesus' charge against his contemporaries was not dissimilar. They had misread the signs of their own vocation, and were claiming divine backing for a perversion of it. The call to be the light of the world passes easily into a sense of being the children of light, looking with fear and hatred on the children of darkness.[17]

Jesus' analysis of the plight of Israel went beyond the specifics of behaviour and belief to what he saw as the root of the problem: the Israel of his day had been duped by the accuser, the 'satan'.[18] *That which was wrong with the rest of the world was wrong with Israel, too.* 'Evil' could not be located conveniently beyond Israel's borders, in the pagan hordes. It had taken up residence within the chosen people. The battle against evil – the

---

[15] Mt. 11.12; 13.28; 16.4 (etc.); Lk. 19.44.
[16] cf. ch. 5 above.
[17] On this 'dualism' cf. *NTPG* 252-6, 297f.
[18] On this usage see n.33 below.

correct analysis of the problem, and the correct answer to it – was therefore of a different order from that imagined by his contemporaries.

Two words of caution as we explore what this means. First, to say that Jesus regarded the Israel of his day as being in the grip of the satan is, at one level, simply to locate Jesus on the map of first-century Jewish parties and sects. It does not make Jesus in any way anti-Jewish; the very idea is laughable. Even today, not least in Jerusalem, one may see posters and placards in which one group denounces another (often remarkably similar) group as being diabolically inspired. Any claim to speak for the true god may eventually lead to the claim that those who disagree are in league with dark powers. We must again remind ourselves that Jesus was a first-century Jew, not a nineteenth- or twentieth-century western liberal.

Second, Jesus' root-and-branch opposition to the whole tradition of zealous holy war has nothing to do with a twentieth-century liberal dislike of fervent nationalism, loosely and anachronistically projected back on to the first century. Jesus was operating on the basis of a critique *from within* the Jewish culture of his day. There are first-century Jewish analogies to his opposition to violent nationalism. Josephus, not for the first time, comes to mind, warning his contemporaries against war with Rome. Jesus' warnings about the result of Israel's headlong rush to resistance are paralleled in some measure by the strange prophet, also called Jesus, who wandered the walls of Jerusalem during the war, uttering his oracles of woe until silenced by a stone from a Roman catapult.[19] Of course, both parallels are inexact. The ambiguities of Josephus' self-serving and retrospective account cloud the real picture; but the account itself is noteworthy as one way of reconstruing the Jewish hope. Likewise, the unfortunate oracular Jesus offers only a partial analogy: he called no followers, engaged in no programme of action, and met his death not as a result of his oracles but simply as yet another casualty of the siege. They serve, nevertheless, to remind us that there were voices in the first century calling for peace. Jesus of Nazareth was one such. But he believed, as I shall now argue, that the way to peace, blocked by zealotry all around, could only come by his fighting the real battle against the real enemy.

As far as Jesus was concerned, the Israel of his day faced a great battle. This, too, put him in the middle of the map of first-century Judaism (and, indeed, firmly on the map of Messianism, as we shall shortly see); but, as with the Jewish symbols we studied in the previous chapter, Jesus radically redefined the battle that had to be fought. It was because his fundamental agendas collided with those of so many of his contemporaries, particularly

---

[19] Jos. *War* 6.300–9.

Israel's leaders, both *de jure* and self-appointed, that he found himself engaged in controversies of various sorts. I suggest that he understood precisely those controversies as part of *the redefined battle for the kingdom*. Heavy irony swirls in clouds around this formulation: it was because Jesus refused to fight the battle that his contemporaries wanted him to fight that he found himself fighting, from his point of view, the true battle – against them; or rather, he would have said, against the real enemy, whom he perceived to be operating through them.

The tradition and symbol that Jesus was redefining at this point was that of the 'zealous' holy war.[20] As we have seen, this tradition belongs within Israel's story from its very earliest days. One only has to think of the exodus and conquest, of the judges, of David, of Phinehas and Elijah seen as heroes who burned with zeal for YHWH and his law, and who took decisive and violent action against pagans outside Israel and renegades within. The more recent examples included, of course, the Maccabaean heroes (whose memory was kept fresh in the regular celebration of Hanukkah) and legendary figures such as Judith. Those who disapproved of the Hasmonean dynasty, too, had their own well-developed theology of holy war, as witness the War Scroll from Qumran. The various movements of violent resistance which erupted in AD 66–70, and the further strong upsurge which carried the nation to its final disaster in AD 132–5, are strong evidence not just for the nationalist fervour which might accompany any revolutionary movement in any nation at any period of history, but for the very specific Jewish hope that, through the final great battle, the kingdom of YHWH would at last come to be on earth as it was in heaven. This tradition was a firmly fixed part of a major first-century Jewish perception of reality.[21]

Stories of the kingdom of YHWH were thus essentially stories of conflict, and that conflict thus came to play a symbolic role within the worldview as a whole. The true god was not at the moment ruling the world in the way that he intended to do. Evil powers had usurped his authority, and they would have to be defeated if he was to regain his rightful throne. In several strands of first-century Judaism we find that Israel expected either to fight a crucial war or battle, or perhaps to have her god fight it on her behalf – or perhaps (in some traditions) to have the Messiah fight it for her. Anyone telling a new story about the kingdom would have to include this as one element, whether in the form of the battle for the 'man' to stay alive under the tyranny of the 'beasts' (which story could be translated into other imagery, such as the lion waging war against the eagle[22]), the struggle for YHWH's righteous

---

[20] cf. *NTPG* 170–81, upon which the present paragraph draws.
[21] On all this cf. Otto 1984 [1938]; Horsley 1987, esp. 156–60; Hengel 1989c [1961].
[22] 4 Ezra 11–12; cf. *NTPG* 314–6, and below, 512–9.

victory to be won against the evil hordes that ranged themselves against him and his people, the war of the sons of light against the sons of darkness, or in some other form. To this extent at least, I find Horsley's statement to be on target:

> Jesus' overall perspective was that God was bringing an end to the demonic and political powers dominating his society so that a renewal of individual and social life would be possible . . . The language of the end refers not to the end of history or of creation but to the resolution of the historical crisis, and the main hope [in Daniel] is for the deliverance of the people by the (divine) defeat of the Seleucid imperial forces . . . What earlier biblical scholarship labeled as expectations of 'cosmic catastrophe' typical of Jewish apocalypticism would be called, in ordinary contemporary language, eager hopes for anti-imperial revolution to be effected by God . . . Jesus' proclamation and practice of the kingdom of God indeed belonged in the milieu of Jewish apocalypticism. But far from being an expectation of an imminent cosmic catastrophe, it was the conviction that God was now driving the satan from control over personal and historical life, making possible the renewal of the people of Israel. The presence of the kingdom of God meant the termination of the old order.[23]

Horsley thus agrees in principle with the analysis of apocalyptic language I offered in *The New Testament and the People of God*,[24] and applied to Jesus' warnings of coming judgment in chapter 8 of the present book. What I now propose is an extension of that argument: that Jesus used the language of cosmic warfare to *denote* the specific struggles in which he himself engaged, and to *connote* his belief that the inner dimension of these struggles was a battle, indeed ultimately *the* battle, against the powers of darkness. I suggest, in other words, that Jesus believed that he, himself, had to fight the true battle of the people of YHWH, through opposing, not just the pagans (though no doubt he, like most first-century Jews, disapproved of their beliefs and behaviour), not just some renegade Jews, but the whole movement in Jewish life which had embraced exactly this tradition of holy war, and was seeking vigorously to promote it – and which, perhaps, was hoping to recruit him in the cause.[25] He was to fight the battle against those who wished to fight the battle. 'If only you had recognized the things that make for peace! But now they are hidden from your eyes.'[26]

It is not surprising, considering the Jewish context, that, since Jesus was announcing the kingdom, many scholars have held that he was really a Jewish freedom-fighter – and that the gospels have simply hushed up this tradition, changing Christianity into a rather different sort of thing as they did so.[27] Horsley, indeed, is arguing for a fairly mild version of this thesis,

[23] Horsley 1987, 157, 159f.

[24] *NTPG* ch. 10, esp. 280–99.

[25] This is the likely meaning of Mt. 11.12/Lk. 16.16.; see below, 468f.

[26] Lk. 19.42, on which cf. above, 348f.

[27] See chs. 1, 3. The latest argument in this line is that of Eisenman & Wise 1992: Jesus and the earliest Christians were warlike revolutionaries, while Paul was the innovator who

as, in a sense, is Crossan.[28] But the problem with this ought already to be apparent. Not only does the argument fail for lack of evidence and inner logic, as has often been shown.[29] It goes in the diametrically opposite direction to the whole course of Jesus' ministry as we have plotted it so far. It is not that Jesus' agenda was not about 'politics'. That would be at best a half-truth, and the wrong half at that. It is that Jesus in his teaching, and his challenge to Israel, aimed precisely at telling Israel to repent of – her militaristic nationalism. Her aspirations for national liberation from Rome, to be won through a great actual battle, were themselves the tell-tale symptom of her basic disease, and had to be rooted out. Jesus was offering a different way of liberation, a way which affirmed the humanness of the national enemy *as well as* the destiny of Israel, and hence also affirmed the destiny of Israel as the bringer of light to the world, not as the one who would crush the world with military zeal.[30]

Did Jesus therefore abandon the battle, and preach a gospel of being kind to all people, with all the element of fight and struggle taken out? Emphatically not. Once again, we must beware of anachronism. Within the worldview of first-century Jews, and most certainly within the mindset of Jesus, there was a fairly clear perception of an alternative enemy who might have to be fought, a dark power who masterminded attacks on the people of YHWH. One of the key elements in Jesus' perception of his task was therefore his *redefinition* of who the real enemy was; then, where this enemy was actually located; then, what this enemy's strategy was, and how he was to be defeated. If we are serious in our desire to understand how Jesus' mind worked, we cannot ignore this whole theme. It looms large in the gospels. It is comparatively scarce in other early Christian literature, and is very differently treated in non-Christian Jewish literature of the time. At the same time, it is a thoroughly Jewish perception of reality, and makes excellent sense as the presupposition of what we find in early Christianity. It thus meets the test, which is of course only ever applicable in a broad-brush way, of double dissimilarity and double similarity.[31] We can be reasonably certain that here we are in touch with the mindset of Jesus himself. The main strength of the hypothesis is the sense it makes of the evidence as a whole.

---

pointed the young faith towards pacifism. The authors are to be congratulated on finding yet another new way of making Paul the corrupter of the religion of Jesus.

[28] In public and televised debates early in 1996, Crossan's analysis of Jesus' kingdom-preaching emphasized his subversion of Antipas' political, social and economic regime.

[29] See Yoder 1972; Hengel 1971; Bammel & Moule 1984; cf. above, 85, 97f.

[30] cf. esp. Borg 1984; and above, ch. 7.

[31] cf. above, 131–3.

(ii) The Real Enemy Identified: not Rome, but the Satan

Israel's story had sometimes been told in terms of four great empires that had oppressed her. The last one would eventually be destroyed when her god finally acted to bring in his kingdom.[32] In first-century Jewish retellings of this story the fourth kingdom was bound to be Rome. But Rome, from Jesus' point of view, could be at most the penultimate enemy. The pagan hordes surrounding Israel were not the actual foe of the people of YHWH. Standing behind the whole problem of Israel's exile was the dark power known in some Old Testament traditions as the satan, the accuser.[33] The struggle that was coming to a head was therefore cosmic, not merely martial (just as the Temple was the focal point not merely of Israel but of the cosmos; one constantly has to remind oneself of the multi-dimensional way in which first-century Jews understood their world). In this struggle the Gentiles, including the soldiers who might commandeer pack-carrying 'volunteers', were ultimately fellow sufferers. From Jesus' point of view, Israel could not identify Rome as the satan-figure and leave it at that.

This theme comes to a head in three passages in the body of the gospels, flanked by passages at the beginning and end which attempt to hold the various lines together. We must look at them in turn. In each case we discover an implicit story which adds some details to the renewed kingdom-story that Jesus is telling, and systematically subverts the symbol of the holy battle.

(a) The Beelzebul Controversy

The best-known story about Israel's battle and its redefinition comes, in some way or other, in all three synoptic gospels, with echoes in other streams of tradition as well. The discussion arises out of an exorcism. As we suggested earlier, the exorcisms which evidently formed a central part of Jesus' work were not simply the release from bondage of a few tormented souls, but were

[32] Dan. 2, 7; 4 Ezra 11–12; cf. *NTPG* 312-17. Collins (1995, 35) points out that the scheme of four world-empires preparing the way for a fifth, definitive, one was well known to Persian, Hellenistic and Roman writers. He cites, *inter alia*, the *Bahman Yasht*; *Sib. Or.* 4; Dionysius of Halicarnassus 1.2.2-4; Polybius 38.22; Tac. *Hist.* 5.8-9; and, among secondary literature, Mendels 1981. For the successive ages of the world as gold, silver, bronze and iron cf. also Hesiod *Works and Days* 109-201; Ovid *Metamorphoses* 1.89-150. Juv. *Sat.* 13.28-30 regards his own time as a *ninth* 'age', worse yet than iron; on this, cf. Green 1974 [1967], 259, with other literature. Compare too the sequence of kingdoms in 4Q552, 553 (GM 138f.; listed as 4Q547 in Eisenman & Wise 1992, 71-4).

[33] cf. Wink 1984; 1986 ch. 1; Hamilton 1992, with recent bibliography (989); Myers 1990; Pagels 1991, 1994. The Hebrew word *satan* means 'accuser'; I prefer this form, or 'the satan', retaining the biblical ambiguity as to the 'personhood' of this figure.

part of the very fabric of his mission. In the story, Jesus exorcises a blind and dumb demoniac; the onlookers say, 'Can this be the Son of David?' Jesus, however, is accused by the Pharisees of casting out demons by 'Beelzebul, the prince of demons.' He replies with logic ('if the satan casts out the satan, he is divided against himself; how then will his kingdom stand?'); counter-charge ('if I cast out demons by Beelzebul, by whom do your sons cast them out?'); claim ('if it is by the spirit of god that I cast out demons, then the kingdom of god has come upon you'); logic again ('how can one enter a strong man's house and plunder his goods, unless he first binds the strong man? Then indeed he may plunder his house'); and warning ('every sin and blasphemy will be forgiven men, but the blasphemy against the spirit will not be forgiven').[34]

This story highlights three important points. Note, first, how the people's reaction reveals the story within which they were living. Here is someone, they think, fighting a battle with a real enemy, and doing so on our behalf: maybe he is the son of David, the one who fought Israel's battles for her, not least the great one against Goliath.[35] Consider, second, the absolutely secure fact that the early church did not invent the charge that Jesus was possessed by the prince of demons (nor, for that matter, the frequent testimony of demons as to Jesus' messianic identity[36]). This is itself important negative evidence that Jesus did indeed perform exorcisms as a regular, and controversial, part of his ministry, and that this resulted in controversies such as the present one. Reflect, third, that this charge against Jesus is not simply a bit of unpleasant religious propaganda. It is the only way that his opponents could avoid the clear implication of the ministry they were witnessing. Either the redefinition of the kingdom that Jesus claimed to be effecting was real and god-given, or there was a dark power at work in him, stronger yet than the dark powers that had gripped the afflicted individuals. No third option was available. Within the world of first-century Judaism, someone who did such things must be either from the true god or from the enemy.

Indeed, since (as we have seen) Jesus' opponents suspected him of disloyalty to the covenant with YHWH, to the Torah and to the Temple, it is not surprising that they came up with this analysis. In the Torah itself, people who lead Israel astray are frequently thought of as being in league with rival

---

[34] Mt. 12.22–32/Mk. 3.20–30/Lk. 11.14–23; cf. Mt. 9.32–4; 10.25; Lk. 12.10; Jn. 8.48, 52; 10.20; *Thom.* 35, cf. 21; 44. It is the theme, not the precise original words, that concerns us here. For an occurrence of the name Beelzebul, in connection with exorcism, cf. 4Q560 (Garcia Martinez 378), with Penney & Wise 1994.

[35] 1 Sam. 17. Cf. ch. 11, on the messianic battle (below, 484f.).

[36] e.g. Mk. 1.24/Lk. 4.34; Mk. 3.11/Lk. 4.41, cf. Mt. 12.16; Mt. 8.29/Mk. 5.7/Lk. 8.28.

gods.[37] From their point of view, therefore, this was not just a bit of slander, typical scattershot religious polemic. It was a serious theological analysis of the phenomena before them, reflecting one recognizable first-century Jewish worldview. The clash of mindsets represented by this story and counter-story is typical of the battle for Israel's worldview which we are considering in this section.

The only way Jesus could respond to this was by describing his own work as part of the true kingdom-story.[38] In addition to exposing the illogic of their charge, and making a counter-charge of his own, Jesus pointed to the unique quality of his exorcisms.[39] He acted directly, commanding the demons on his own authority.[40] He claimed to be invested with this authority from the covenant god; specifically, in that he was equipped in a new way with the divine spirit.[41] When his commands to the demons were obeyed, there ought to be only one conclusion for the onlookers: Israel's god was at last becoming king. 'The kingdom of god has come upon you.' The battle was already joined, and it was the battle, not with Rome, but with the true accuser, the satan.

Moreover, the battle was being waged successfully. But this could only be so – i.e. the exorcisms could only take effect – if, fourthly, a prior battle had already been won. Jesus was claiming that he had already met the prince of demons and defeated him. This extraordinary and cryptic statement can only be understood in the light of the temptation narrative (see below), and of such passages as Luke 10.18: 'I saw the satan fall like lightning from heaven.'[42] Jesus was claiming, and claiming to demonstrate, that he was being successful in fighting the true battle.

The controversy continues (in Luke, it concludes) with the warning: those who are not joining in this battle are fighting on the enemy side.[43] In Matthew, it continues with the further warning that, in saying what they have, his opponents have put themselves on very risky ground. It is one thing to look at Jesus and say, 'He is mad.' That could be excused. The onlookers had, after all, neither seen, nor expected to see, any such activity as this, and it did not at all look like their expectations of the coming of the kingdom. But it was another thing to look at the working of the spirit of YHWH (this,

[37] See above, pp. 439–42, with refs. there.

[38] Note that in his reply he substitutes 'the satan' for 'Beelzebul': see Lane 1974, 141ff.; Brown 1975–78, 3.472f.

[39] cf. too Mt. 9.33: 'never was anything like this seen in Israel'.

[40] Mk. 1.27/Lk. 4.36.

[41] For 'spirit' in Mt. 12.28, Lk. 11.20 has 'finger', reflecting perhaps Ex. 8.19.

[42] Cp. Isa. 14.12–21; Ezek. 28.1–19. In both cases the downfall of an evil empire (Babylon, Tyre) is spoken of in terms of the myth of the satan and his defeat.

[43] Mt. 12.30/Lk. 11.23; cf. *P. Oxy. 1224.2*.

perhaps, is after all why Matthew has 'spirit' where Luke has 'finger'?) and to say: 'This is the work of the devil.' To say such a thing was to paint oneself into a corner from which there was no escape. Once define the battle for your liberation as the work of the enemy, and you will never be free.[44]

The result of this controversy, whose historicity at least in outline is not to be doubted, is that from Jesus' perspective the battle for the kingdom was being classically redefined, in symbolic action and verbal explanation. The story was being radically retold, so as to focus on the climactic conflict not with Rome, but with the satan. Jesus had already won a decisive victory in this battle; his exorcisms were the implementation of that victory. Acting on his own authority, he was demonstrating the fact that the kingdom was already in some sense present; and, by implication, that he himself was the spirit-equipped agent of that kingdom. Israel's god was already becoming king, in the events of Jesus' ministry.[45]

(b) Who is to be Feared?

The same story of battle and enemy, redefined in much the same way, emerges in another passage:

> I tell you, my friends, do not fear those who kill the body, and after that have no more that they can do. But I will warn you whom to fear: fear him who, after he has killed, has power to cast into Gehenna; yes, I tell you, fear him! Are not five sparrows sold for two pennies? And not one of them is forgotten before god. Why, even the hairs of your head are all numbered. Fear not; you are of more value than many sparrows.[46]

What implicit story are we listening to in this passage? This text, in both Luke and Matthew, is part of the commission to the disciples as they engage on their own work of announcement, warning, and proclamation. Since their mission gained its meaning from the fact that it was an extension of Jesus' own work, the warning presumably reflected and represented Jesus' perception of his own task, of the struggle which he too was facing. Some have seen 'the one who can cast into Gehenna' as YHWH; but this is unrealistic. Jesus did not, to be sure, perceive Israel's god as a kindly liberal grandfather who would never hurt a fly, let alone send anyone to Gehenna.[47] But again

---

[44] cf. above, 452; and cp. Guelich 1989, 180. Mt. continues (12.33–6) with warnings about the present generation and its wickedness. These fit in well within the present theme, as the next section will demonstrate.

[45] The same theme seems to underlie the so-called 'nature miracles'. They are not an invasion by a power unrelated to the world: they symbolize the creator god reclaiming the natural order, defeating the forces of chaos.

[46] Lk. 12.4–7 (par. Mt. 10.28–31).

[47] It should of course be noted again that 'Gehenna' is the name of the smouldering rubbish-heap outside the south-west corner of Jerusalem (cf. above, 183). The extent to

and again – not least in the very next verse of this paragraph – Israel's god is portrayed as the creator and sustainer, one who can be lovingly trusted in all circumstance, not the one who waits with a large stick to beat anyone who steps out of line.[48] Rather, here we have a redefinition of the battle in terms of the identification of the real enemy. The one who can kill the body is the imagined enemy, Rome.[49] Who then is the real enemy? Surely not Israel's own god. The real enemy is the accuser, the satan.[50]

(c) The Seven Other Demons

In Luke, the Beelzebul controversy goes straight on with a further saying, which is placed a few paragraphs later in Matthew:

> When the unclean spirit has gone out of a man, he passes through waterless places seeking rest, but he finds none. Then he says, 'I will return to my house from which I came.' And when he comes he finds it empty, swept, and put in order. Then he goes and brings with him seven other spirits more evil than himself, and they enter and dwell there; and the last state of that man becomes worse than the first. So shall it be also with this evil generation.[51]

Jesus' little story of the wandering and return of the previously exorcised unclean spirit is an important clue to the way in which he saw his exorcisms, and his central battle with the satan, as part of his career as a whole. In the light of the previous passages, I think it highly unlikely that these verses are a sad commentary on the temporary nature of exorcisms: first you drive out the spirit, then it collects a few friends and comes back again. If Jesus really thought that this would be the long-term effect of the exorcisms he was performing, then his claim that he had won a decisive battle, and that he was

---

which it is used in the gospels metaphorically for an entirely non-physical place of torment, and the extent to which, in its metaphorical use, it retains the sense of a physical conflagration such as might accompany the destruction of Jerusalem by enemy forces, ought not to be decided in advance of a full study of Jesus' meaning.

[48] Against e.g. Caird 1963, 160; Marshall 1969; 1978, 513; Fitzmyer 1985, 959; Evans 1990, 515; Davies & Allison 1988-91, 2.206f. Evans notes a further difficulty for the usual view, in that it seems peculiar to describe the creator and lifegiver simply in the negative terms of being able to cast people into Gehenna.

[49] There may still be a hint of the link between Rome and the satan in the story of the Gadarene swine: see Theissen 1983, and e.g. Myers 1990, 190-4.

[50] Perhaps this is a clue to the meaning of the closing phrase of the Lord's Prayer: 'deliver us from the *poneros*', the Evil One (Mt. 6.13/*Did.* 8.2, cf. *Ap. Jas.* 4.1; added by some MSS at the end of Lk. 11.4, but om. by P75, the first hand in א, and others).

[51] Mt. 12.43-5/Lk. 11.24-6. The only substantial difference between the two accounts is that Lk. omits the last sentence.

now conducting exorcisms on that basis, would be called into serious question. Indeed, if this were the case, it would be better not to perform exorcisms at all. Rather, as Matthew's closing sentence, and Luke's context, seems to indicate, this is a kind of *parable* about *Israel*.[52] Here is the link between the exorcisms and the overall mission of Jesus. Just as many of the healings were signs of what Israel's god was wanting to do with her (see chapter 5 above), so the exorcisms themselves were signs that this god wished to deliver Israel herself from the real enemy who is now pitted against her: the satan.

But – this is the force of the strange saying – the problem is that Israel has attempted to get rid of the demon before, and has not succeeded. It is difficult to be sure what is specifically referred to here, but the thrust of the comment should not be in doubt. The mention of the 'house' may well be a clue that Jesus had in mind once more Israel's central institution and symbol, the Temple. There would then be a link with another cryptic saying: 'your house is left to you desolate.'[53] The previous 'exorcism' of Israel presumably refers to one or other of the reform or revolutionary movements, or possibly the rebuilding of the Temple. These, Jesus is saying, did not do the job properly, and left Israel open to further, and worse, internal trouble. If specific movements are in mind, we might perhaps think of the Maccabaean revolt, when 'the house' was 'swept and put in order';[54] or perhaps the Pharisaic movement as a whole, attempting to cleanse the body and soul of Judaism by its zeal for a purity which in some ways reflected that of the Temple; or possibly Herod's massive rebuilding programme, which produced a 'house' that was magnificent but in which (according to Jesus, and probably many of his contemporaries) YHWH had no inclination to make his dwelling. I think the first of these is the most likely, but it does not matter much. Indeed, Jesus might well have been simply referring to reforming movements in general within the Judaism of recent generations. In any case, what he was saying about such movements, and/or some specific examples, was that they could clean up the house for a while, but that they could not prevent the demons returning in force. Nothing short of a new inhabitation of 'the house' would do. This understanding of the saying thus coheres closely with the critique of the Temple which we outlined in chapters 8 and 9, as well as with Jesus' own positive agenda.

---

[52] Lk. 11.29–32 is all about the wickedness of 'this generation'.
[53] Mt. 23.38/Lk. 13.35.
[54] 1 Macc. 4.36–51.

(d) The Initial Victory

But where did Jesus' victory over the powers of evil begin? All three synoptic gospels provide an answer: in a dramatic battle at the outset of Jesus' public career.[55] The fact that the Matthaean and Lukan versions are such stylized and polished literary pieces should not obscure two points. First, some kind of temptation narrative occurs both in Mark and in so-called Q. Second, some kind of experience, early in his career, in which Jesus believed himself to have won an initial decisive victory over the 'real enemy', must be postulated if we are to explain what was said during the Beelzebul controversy. If Jesus claimed that his exorcisms were the putting into effect of a prior decisive battle with the master-demon, it makes sense to ask what form that battle had taken, and when it had happened. One possibility is that Jesus was referring in these terms to a struggle that he had undergone immediately after his baptism.

There are, of course, huge problems with fitting such an episode into a historical treatment. The language is highly charged, the story highly crafted. Subsequent artists' representations of an argument between Jesus and a strange little figure with suspiciously shaped physical extremities have not done much to help twentieth-century readers appropriate the narrative as a serious part of an historical portrait.[56] But it must be said emphatically that again and again in a variety of religious traditions, and certainly within very different parts of the Christian one, those who have believed themselves to be under a vocation to fight battles on behalf of their god have constantly described themselves as being engaged in warfare with unseen forces. How the twentieth century may choose to analyse, psychologize, explain, reduce, or otherwise translate such accounts is no great matter. It may be that, if the mainstream post-Enlightenment worldview is correct, all such language must be seen as evidence of religious neurosis. One might equally well, however, wish to suggest that anyone who conceives of themselves as having a vocation – a common enough human experience – might undergo inner struggles which in many cultures would be most readily described in terms of a battle with a hostile power. What we cannot do, in the twentieth or any other century, is to deny that such self-perceptions did, and still do, characterize people of the sort, broadly speaking, that we are discovering Jesus to have

[55] Mt. 4.1-11/Mk. 1.12-13/Lk. 4.1-13. Mk's account is much briefer; in Lk.'s, the second and third Matthaean temptations are inverted.

[56] cf. Hall 1984 [1974], 298: 'In Romanesque and Gothic art [Satan] is the typical demon of the period with horns, a scaly body, wings, and claws for hands and feet. The Italian Renaissance portrayed him as the "fallen angel" or, in another convention, to illustrate his cunning, as an old man in a monk's habit. The latter generally betrays himself by revealing a cloven hoof or claw under his garments.'

been.[57] It should be no surprise to find a description, however stylized and schematized, of such a battle. It might actually be surprising if we did not.

That said, if such a battle took place it was obviously something essentially private to Jesus. For anyone else to become aware of it, Jesus would have had to have told them. The likelihood or otherwise of this may be variously argued. If it is concluded that the evangelists, or their predecessors (since it is in both Mark and Q), invented the story as a hypothesis to explain the essentially historical phenomena before them, we would still have to ask whether, granted what was said in the previous paragraph, we ought to agree that the hypothesis of such a struggle is a likely one. My own judgment, as I have indicated, is that it is.

The struggle is precisely about the nature of Jesus' vocation and ministry. The pull of hunger, the lure of cheap and quick 'success', the desire to change the vocation to be the light of the world into the vocation to bring all nations under his powerful rule by other means – all of these would easily combine into the temptation to doubt the nature of the vocation of which he had been sure at the time of John's baptism. *If* you are the Son of God . . . There are many different styles of career, ministry, and agenda that Jesus might have adopted. Messiahs came in many shapes and sizes. It was by no means clear from anything in the culture of the time exactly how someone who believed himself to be the eschatological prophet, let alone YHWH's anointed, ought to behave, what his programme should be, or how he should set about implementing it.[58] Finding the way forward was bound to be a battle, involving all the uncertainty and doubt inherent in going out into unknown territory assumed to be under enemy occupation.

When, therefore, we ask how Jesus conceived of the battle which he claimed to have fought as an initially decisive one, the evangelists offer us a suggestion which we cannot lightly dismiss. That the battle had been successful from Jesus' point of view is witnessed by the fact that he had *not* adopted any of the 'messianic' styles offered to him by his culture. We cannot doubt that Jesus was constantly tempted to share, and act in accordance with, the mindset of most Jews of his day. He cannot have been indifferent to the plight of his fellow Jews, as they were systematically crushed, economically, politically and militarily, by Rome. The temptation to be the sort of Messiah that many wanted must have been real and strong. But it was, from the point of view of his mindset, precisely a temptation. He had faced it, and defeated it in principle, and had thereby confirmed the direction for the mission that he should undertake.

---

[57] cf. Borg's account (1994a & b) of Jesus as a 'spirit person' and 'religious ecstatic'.
[58] cf. ch. 11 below.

Thus, in his public activity as we have studied it, Jesus was not engaged in (what we might call) self-aggrandizement. He was not working remarkable signs to impress the public; when people asked him to do so he regarded it as a snare and a delusion, evidence of their hardness of heart.[59] He was not engaged in subversion against Rome, with world domination in view.[60] He was announcing and inaugurating the reign of Israel's god *in a new way*, not reducible to terms of any of these, and indeed explicitly opposed to them all. The victory portrayed in Matthew 4.1–11 is more or less exactly the victory that was acted out in Jesus' career as we have studied it throughout this Part of the book. As part of a strictly historical hypothesis, we are justified in saying that something like this, or at least something that would have given rise to a story like this, almost certainly took place as part of Jesus' mental, emotional and spiritual history. The story he subsequently told about the defeat of the accuser demands it. The symbolic battle with the real enemy had begun, as far as he was concerned, with a private struggle at the outset of his public career. It continued with the controversies between him and his contemporaries, whose subject-matter, as we saw in the previous chapter, was the symbolic world of Israel, and his own subversion of it. Where it would end, we shall discover in good time.

If the real enemy was identified as the satan, not Rome, a further question raises itself: where was this real enemy located?

(iii) The Enemy Relocated: Israel and the Satan

Where did Jesus believe that the satan was active? This question cannot be ignored, and indeed must be clearly grasped if the details of the ministry, of Jesus' proclamation, and of his self-understanding at many points, are to be seen in their proper light.

We may put the question in terms of the narrative logic underlying Jesus' retelling of Israel's story. Stories, as we have seen, characteristically have three key players or sets of players: an agent, a helper or helpers, and an opponent or opponents.[61] Who then is the 'opponent', within Jesus' retelling of the story?

The answer is quite clear. To get the flavour of it, we have only to review quickly several passages which point in the same direction:

---

[59] Mt. 12.38–42/Lk. 11.29–32; Mt. 16.1–4/Mk. 8.11–13; cf. Lk. 11.16; 12.54–6 (cp. *Thom.* 91); 17.20.

[60] We might recall Josephus' passage (*War* 6.312–15) about the Danielic text in which a world ruler would emerge from Israel. See *NTPG* 312–14.

[61] cf. *NTPG* ch. 3 and frequently; in the present vol., 244f. above.

Israel thought of herself as good wheat, ripe for the great harvest; but, when the apocalyptic drama unfolded, weeds would appear among the wheat, sown by 'an enemy'. In the parable's interpretation, the enemy is identified as the devil.

The satan was also, we may assume, responsible for the bad fishes that the dragnet pulled in along with the good.

Israel had cleaned out the 'house', swept it and put it in order, but the demons would return and take possession of it again.

The present generation was wicked and adulterous (as the old prophets had said, Israel has abandoned YHWH as her true bridegroom and has gone after other gods), and was eager for the sort of signs that could only be signs of the wrong sort of kingdom.

The Israel that refused to see Jesus as the heaven-sent answer to her problems was the Israel that had bought into a demonically inspired view of the present situation, and had thus become hard-hearted, blind to where her own aspirations would lead.

The Pharisees, more specifically, were in bondage to mammon.

The satan had bound 'this daughter of Israel'; her release, on the sabbath, was a sign not only that Jesus had come to deliver Israel from real bondage, but also of what that real bondage was.

When Jesus stood before Caiaphas, he identified himself as the representative of the true people of Israel's god, and Caiaphas as the representative of the Beast who was at present opposing that true people.[62]

It is important to see what is, and is not, being said here. One could conceivably read this little catalogue as though it were saying that Jesus was opposed to Israel and all she was and stood for. (Some, perhaps, will be eager to read it that way, so that by caricaturing what the evangelists had said as another example of Christian anti-Judaism they might avoid grasping the larger picture which is emerging.) That would be the opposite of the truth. It was Jesus' contention, as we are seeing throughout this historical reconstruction, that Israel needed rescuing, and that he had come to do it. The enemy from whom she needed rescuing, however, was not an outside enemy, on to whom she could project all her insecurities and ambiguities. To this extent his programme was revolutionary indeed, but revolutionary against Israel's own present leaders, real and self-appointed, rather than against Rome.

The analogy with Qumran may help to show how one who was determined to be loyal to Israel's basic vocation could think in this way. Qumran itself was simply one in a long line of Jewish movements, going back to the very earliest prophets. We think, for example, of Amos, who dared to retell Israel's story in terms of the present regime having become corrupt; or Jeremiah, who dared to see the victory of Israel's enemies and the destruction of the Temple as the work of Israel's god himself. The line continues, as we saw, with Josephus claiming to see Israel's god at work in the

---

[62] Weeds and wheat: Mt 13.34-30, 36-43; dragnet: Mt. 13.47-50; cleansing the house: Lk. 11.24-6; signs: Mt. 12.38-42; Mt. 16.1-4/Mk. 8.11-13/Lk. 11.29-32; cf. Jn. 6.30; mammon: Lk. 16.14f.; satanic bondage: Lk. 13.16; Jesus' answer to Caiaphas: Mt. 26.64/Mk. 14.62/Lk. 22.69 (see below, 524-8, 549-51, 642-4).

destruction of Jerusalem by Rome.[63] Jesus, I suggest, saw the present Jewish rulers and teachers as the dupes of the accuser, and himself and his followers as the true Israel. He told Israel's story, as prophets like Elijah and Michaiah ben Imlach had told it many centuries before, with the present rulers and their tame prophets as the *opponents* of the true people of the covenant god, himself as the *agent*, and the divine spirit as his *helper*.

In terms of Greimas' diagrammatic scheme, we could spell this out as follows. Instead of telling the story in this shape:[64]

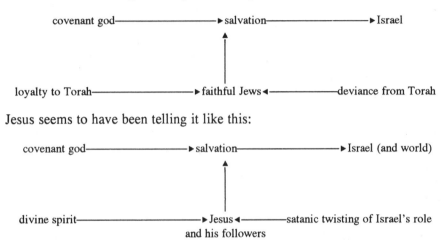

covenant god ────────► salvation ────────────► Israel

loyalty to Torah ──────────► faithful Jews ◄──────────deviance from Torah

Jesus seems to have been telling it like this:

covenant god ────────► salvation ────────────► Israel (and world)

divine spirit ──────────► Jesus ◄──────────satanic twisting of Israel's role
and his followers

(iv) Conclusion: Jesus' Analysis of the Problem

What then must Jesus have thought was going on? How was the story working out? The battle he himself had to fight was with the satan; the satan had made its home in Israel, and in her cherished national institutions and aspirations. The house had been occupied by seven other demons, worse than the first; so it would be with this generation. But, like Jezebel trying to seduce Jehu, the satan was now attempting to lure Jesus himself into making the same mistake as Israel had done.[65] If that turned out not to be possible, the satan would try either to scare him off, or to kill him ahead of time.[66] If we examine Jesus' mindset from this point of view, a good many features of the gospel narratives fall into place.

[63] Above, 64f., 199, 201.
[64] For the mode of narrative analysis see *NTPG* ch. 3.
[65] Mt. 16.23/Mk. 8.33; cf. 2 Kgs. 9.30-7.
[66] cf. Lk. 13.31-5.

This analysis demonstrates, for instance, the hidden dimensions of the controversies studied in the previous chapter. The symbolic clashes must have appeared to Jesus as part of the overarching story. From his point of view, he was fighting Israel's real battle by challenging Israel's idolatrous nationalism, which was passing off its satan-induced worldview as true allegiance to the reign of YHWH. His opponents, meanwhile, especially the Pharisees (during the Galilean ministry) and the chief priests (in Jerusalem) were resisting his attempts, and so challenging the validity of his mission, his vocation, his blueprint for Israel. They rejected his message, his urgent summons to the way of peace, because they rightly perceived that it would mean softening their grip on some cherished, and indeed god-given, national and cultural symbols. One might imagine Josephus, faced with Jesus the Galilean brigand, making a similar analysis of the situation. Further examples of the same phenomenon would be easy to find in other periods as well.

To be sure, all religious polemic tends to make its opponents the dupes of the satan. The Pharisees, according to the sources, tried to do it to Jesus, and if he (by implication at least) paid them back in the same coin that is hardly surprising.[67] What we are studying here, after all, is not how modern western thought would 'like' to see Jesus, but what seems, historically, to have been the case concerning his mindset. And it seems to me that an historical reconstruction like this must include Jesus' suspicion that the satan, having seduced Israel into misconceiving the divine vocation, was trying every possible way to lead him, in turn, down the same path.

A further twist in the story comes with the picture of the disciples. Their ambiguous role, so much discussed in modern literature about the theology and purpose of the evangelists, is of interest here within our study of Jesus himself. The call of the disciples, and the selection of twelve in particular, singles out these men as the spearheads of Jesus' revolutionary movement. They were to be his helpers in the proclamation and inauguration of the kingdom, of the new way of being Israel. But, as Jesus perceived the moment in history at which he found himself (remembering that for a first-century Jew, particularly one who believed himself to be a prophet, the reading of what Israel's god was doing in history was of central importance), he naturally came to see and experience those same disciples, not least the twelve, not least Peter himself, as ambiguous; allies after a fashion, but also a potential threat.

They thought, as one might well imagine, that they were going to Jerusalem to sit on actual physical thrones, and they disputed as to who would get the most important ones.[68] Peter tried to dissuade Jesus from the

---

[67] cf. Johnson 1989; Stanton 1994, 177.

[68] Mt. 20.20-8/Mk. 10.35-45, cf. Lk. 22.24-7; cp. Mt. 18.1-4; Mk. 9.33-7; Lk. 9.46-50.

plan to go to the cross; the satan (Jesus said) had desired to sift him like wheat.[69] Judas became the 'accuser' who was the proximate cause of Jesus' trial and death.[70] Jesus could not, therefore, trust even his closest associates. They had a foot in both camps. Loyal to him in principle (except possibly Judas, though we have no reason for supposing that until near the end his aspirations and hopes were significantly different from those of the rest), they nevertheless still cherished ambitions for the nation of Israel, and for themselves within Israel, which showed that they had not grasped the radical nature of Jesus' agenda.[71] They were thus always liable to let him down at the crucial moment. This theme as a whole, whatever is made of particular sayings, has an excellent claim to be historical, coming as it does in many strands of tradition, and going against the grain of later adulation of early leaders[72] – and, far more important than either of these, making very good sense within the overall hypothesis.

This all points towards the nature of the final battle. Jesus must have realized at some point that, if he was conceiving the task correctly, he would eventually have to fight the battle alone. His reinterpretation of Israel's symbolic battle would ultimately generate a new symbol, more potent than any yet conceived. But even to approach this topic requires that we move to the fourth worldview question.

5. What's the Solution?

If Jesus' analysis of the plight was as I have outlined it, we should expect the solution to be equally radical. At one level, of course, the kingdom of YHWH was itself his proffered solution, with its component elements of the return of the true Israel from exile, the defeat of evil, and the return of YHWH to Zion. Jesus' whole agenda and announcement affirmed this answer to the plight, reworking the answer corresponding to his rethinking of the plight itself. But, if this is one obvious answer, the other one is 'Jesus himself'. He claimed that the kingdom had arrived where he was, and with his activity.

---

[69] Mt. 16.22f./Mk. 8.33, cf. *Ap. Jas.* 5.1–5; Lk. 22.31.

[70] Lk. 22.3, cf. Jn. 6.70; 13.2, 27. That the betrayal by Judas, and the denial by Peter, are historical events is unlikely to be denied except by the most sceptical, or those, like Maccoby 1992, with a particular axe to grind.

[71] cf. Ac. 1.6, which again has a strong *prima facie* case to be seen as historical; Lk. 24.21.

[72] Redaction-critics are now so used to this fact that it is regularly assumed that the early church cherished deep suspicions about the first disciples; these passages are often cited as evidence of splits within early Christianity. Cf. e.g. Weeden 1985 [1968], 1971; Tannehill 1985 [1977]; Best 1986.

He was not announcing it as though he were merely a fly on the wall. His own work – his kingdom-announcement, his prophetic praxis, his celebrations, his warnings, his symbolic activity – all of these were part of the movement through which Israel would be renewed, evil would be defeated, and YHWH would return to Zion at last.

Already we can comment, from this perspective, on the major kingdom-theories that have dominated scholarship in the twentieth century.[73] Schweitzer was right to set Jesus in his first-century background, but disastrously wrong in imagining that this meant an eschatology in which the space-time universe would come to an end. Bultmann was right to see eschatology as central to Jesus' message, but utterly mistaken in thinking that this could be demythologized, without real loss, into the call for individual existentialist decision, leaving first-century affairs on one side in favour of an eternal 'now'. Dodd was right to insist that the kingdom was already present as far as Jesus was concerned, but wrong in reducing this kingdom (not altogether unlike Bultmann) to the level of individual religious or moral experience; wrong, too, in shutting off a future in which this would be manifested in a new way to the world. Brandon, following Reimarus, was right to place Jesus in the setting of first-century Jewish nationalist expectations, but wrong to think that he made them the centre of his own programme instead of the centre of his critique. The normal response to Brandon has been correct: Jesus refused to buy into nationalist politics; but this has often been asserted at the expense of making Jesus somehow 'apolitical'. Jesus' message of judgment on existing Israel, and of a fulfilment of the kingdom which left the nation *qua* nation out of the positive side of the picture, was political to the hilt. Jesus knew this, and acted accordingly.

But how would the story end? Several recent analyses of Jesus' work have left the matter at this point, as though Jesus might have been content simply to press ahead with his work, and to hope that Israel would see sense and come over to his point of view. This not only does violence to several elements in the complex and integrated profile of Jesus in the gospel traditions; it remains historically very unlikely. Two of the main lines of thought about the kingdom in the last two hundred years have made very specific proposals about what Jesus would have regarded as a successful conclusion to his movement. Reimarus and his followers thought in terms of a successful military revolt. Schweitzer, and his, thought in terms of the end of the world, with Jesus either as the true prophet, having predicted the event, or as the 'son of man', who would 'come on the clouds'. If (though we have of course redefined it) we are to retain the eschatological framework of Jesus' agenda –

[73] For the details, see chs. 1–3 above.

if, in other words, we are to resist the idea that he was simply a teacher of timeless truths – we must pose the question all the more sharply: what did Jesus intend should happen next?

We may point up this question as follows. If Jesus' symbolic actions, and his analysis of the plight of the nation, focused on the great battle which had to be fought against the real enemy, the satan, how did Jesus suppose that this battle would take place? The Sermon on the Mount, and the related agendas we studied in chapter 7, suggest the way towards an answer. Evil would be defeated, not by military victory, but by a *doubly* revolutionary method: turning the other cheek, going the second mile, the deeply subversive wisdom of taking up the cross. The agenda which Jesus mapped out for his followers was the agenda to which he himself was obedient. This was how the kingdom would come, how the battle would be won.

We shall explore this more fully in chapter 12. For the moment, we may indicate where the logic of the argument so far has led. Within several Jewish retellings of Israel's story, the great themes of exile and restoration, and of the kingdoms of god and the kingdoms of the world, would reach their climax in a great moment of suffering and vindication. The night would get darker and darker, and then the dawn would come. Israel's tribulations would reach their height, and then redemption would arrive.[74] Daniel would face the lions, and then be exalted. Judith would go into the tent of the enemy commander, and emerge victorious. The Maccabaean martyrs would die horribly, and a new dynasty would be set up within an independent Israel. The son of man would suffer at the hands of the beasts, and then be lifted up to the right hand of the Ancient of Days.[75] The symbol of suffering was itself a key ingredient within the Jewish expectation of the great deliverance, the great victory.

If, then, Jesus was telling a story which belonged genetically within this group of Jewish narratives, as I have argued that he was, there is a strong probability that he envisaged for himself a similar fate of suffering and vindication. The language placed on his lips at various points of the passion narrative probably reflects an awareness of vocation that, historically, had preoccupied him for much longer.[76] In bringing Israel's destiny to its great moment, the story Jesus was telling would include, as part of its climax, the 'woes', the great tribulation, that characterized Israel's vocation in bringing to birth the reign of her god. The 'trials' and the crucifixion were not simply

---

[74] cf. *NTPG* 277–9.

[75] Dan. 6; Jud. 10—16; 2 Macc. 7–8, etc.; Dan. 7.

[76] cf. e.g. Mt. 26.31/Mk. 14.27, quoting 'I will strike the shepherd, and the sheep will be scattered'; Lk. 22.53: 'this is your hour, and the power of darkness.' Cp. too Jn. 14.30, 'the prince of this world is coming'; also Jn. 12.31; 16.11; 19.15.

the last great controversy between him and his opponents. Jesus must have perceived them as the climax of that larger battle of which all the controversies were in fact part. This is where, as we shall see later, Albert Schweitzer glimpsed one of the most important aspects of Jesus' apocalyptic understanding.

All the lines, then, point in one direction, which will occupy us fully in Part III. Jesus saw himself, at least, as a prophet like John the Baptist and Jeremiah; their fate, or even worse, would become his. Jesus was welcoming sinners, keeping company with the unclean; their taint was to infect him at last. He took a stand which brought him into inevitable conflict with the authorities, but he construed that conflict as being not merely with them but with the dark power that, he believed, stood behind them. The climax of the story, of the battle for the kingdom, was therefore, inescapably, that Jesus would die, not as an accident, nor as a bizarre quasi-suicide, a manipulated martyrdom, but as the inevitable result of his kingdom-inaugurating career. But this death, as he conceived it, would be the actual victory of the kingdom, by which the enemy of the people would finally be defeated. Jesus would act out the role of the revolutionary, at the point at which it could no longer be misunderstood. It is therefore not surprising, but entirely natural, to suggest that Jesus, in telling the story of Israel reshaped around himself, predicted his own death. It did not take much insight to see that it was very likely from the beginning. From within Jesus' retelling of the Jewish stories, such a death would carry an obvious, though shocking, interpretation.[77]

Jesus, then, answered the fourth worldview question, at least by implication, with reference to the kingdom and to himself. He retold the story of Israel as his own story. The result was a strange, and doubly subversive, announcement that Israel's god was now at last becoming king, through his (Jesus') own work, his own life, and finally, it seems, through his own death. Having redefined the symbolic battle, he redefined, also, the task that Israel's representative would perform to bring it about. In the process, as we saw in the previous chapter, he must inevitably have been regarded as a traitor, leading Israel astray. He was neither the first nor the last Jewish leader to be pilloried by hard-line orthodox groups for offering a vision which involved the loss of cherished ancestral symbols. This was part of the price he had to pay for his radical redefinition, in praxis, story, symbol and question, of the kingdom of YHWH. It was, after all, part of the profile of a prophet. But he stuck to his message. This, he believed, was how YHWH

---

[77] Mt. 16.21/Mk. 8.31/Lk. 9.22; Mt. 17.22f./Mk. 9.31/Lk. 9.44; Mt. 20.18f./Mk. 10.33f./Lk. 18.31–3; Mt. 20.28/Mk. 10.45; cf. Mt. 17.12. Cp. too Mt. 9.15/Mk. 2.20/Lk. 5.35 (the bridegroom taken away); Mt. 26.11/14.7 ('me you will not always have'); cf. Jn. 12.7. For a pregnant statement of a similar point cf. Schillebeeckx 1979 [1974], 298–312.

would prove himself to be God, not merely a god: by winning the final victory in the ultimate battle.

The answer we have now given to the first four worldview questions points clearly in the direction of a particular answer to the fifth and final one.

6. What Time is it?

If plight and solution pointed to the eschatological coming of the kingdom of YHWH, what stage in this process did Jesus believe himself to be living at? More ink, perhaps, has been spilled on this question than on anything else to do with the kingdom in the work of Jesus. By approaching it as we have done – by five chapters of detailed exposition of the various angles of Jesus' announcement – we may reasonably hope to clarify the matter. After all, Jesus seems to have believed that he could read 'the signs of the times', and to have expected his hearers to do so too.[78]

Our whole argument to this point indicates an irreducibly twofold answer to the question. On the one hand, Jesus clearly believed that with his own work something dramatically new was already happening. The days of preparation were over; Israel's god was now acting in the way he had promised of old. On the other hand, Jesus' work was straining forward for something that was about to happen, that would come to pass so soon that if his hearers were not careful it would burst upon them like a thief in the night. Both elements are strongly present through the various strands of gospel tradition, and to excise one of them because we deem them incompatible is anachronistic criticism of the worst sort. Better by far to hold them together, and to discover the framework of belief and intention within which both make sense.[79]

Analogies with other kingdom-movements will make the point well enough. If we shift the focus away from 'purely theological' matters to questions more germane to first-century Judaism – that is, to questions in which 'theology' was intimately bound up with the social and political hopes of the people – we can understand easily enough how it might have been. David was anointed long before being enthroned. Was he king during that period, or was he not? In Jesus' own century, Judas the Galilean might well have told his followers that, by joining his movement, they were part of the new, and final, reconstitution of Israel, even though there was still the little matter

---

[78] Mt. 16.3 (though the passage is absent from several good MSS); cf. Lk. 12.56.

[79] For this whole debate see the brief discussion, with literature, in ch. 6.2.iii above. Cp. the remark of Evans 1990, 492: the double view (he calls it a 'contradiction') 'lies too deep in the gospel traditions to be eliminated, and must be allowed to stand'.

of throwing off the Roman yoke to be settled. Bar-Kochba went so far as to have coins minted, numbering the years from '1', indicating the beginning of his declaration of independence. He behaved towards his followers as though he were already king. But this 'inaugurated eschatology', too, remained in need of a final victory, which never came. If we had asked Bar-Kochba or his followers whether they were living in the time of the kingdom, their very coins – the only real 'mass media' of the ancient world – would have answered in the affirmative. Denial would have meant disloyalty. But if we concluded from this that they had no future hope, nothing left to aspire to, that their god had established his kingdom once and for all, we would be ludicrously wrong. Once we think historically, the language of a kingdom present yet future, already established yet needing still to win its decisive victory, makes perfect sense.

So it is with Jesus' announcement of the kingdom. 'Since the days of John the Baptist the kingdom has been breaking in'; this is not the announcement of a wholly future kingdom.[80] Indeed, by labelling John as 'Elijah', and by linking his own movement in direct sequence to John's, Jesus leaves his hearers no choice. Either he is an imposter, or he is indeed inaugurating the kingdom. The meaning of the kingdom's 'breaking in' cannot be simply (as the Greek, out of context, would permit) 'has been suffering violence'; this would have been true throughout Israel's long and tragic history.[81] Luke, rendering the same phrase as 'the kingdom *is being preached*' (*euangelizetai* rather than *biazetai*), indicates that this was how he, at least, understood it: the kingdom had burst upon the scene with the arrival of Jesus. The clause which follows, both in Matthew (11.13b) and Luke (16.16b), is cryptic, but can perhaps rightly be read as an ironic, and laconic, comment on the presence of the inbreaking kingdom: yes, and the men of violence are trying either to hijack the movement for their own ends, or, perhaps, to use violence against it. Matthew's version may perhaps lean in the former direction, Luke's in the latter.[82] Matthew's addition of 'Hear, anyone who has

---

[80] Mt. 11.11–15; cp. Lk. 7.28; 16.16. On the Mt. saying cf. Cameron 1984; recently, Davies & Allison 1988–91, 2.253–6; Hagner 1993, 306f., with discussions of other literature.

[81] i.e. *biazetai* is to be read as middle, not passive – despite Davies & Allison 1988–91, 2.255f. It is not necessary (despite most commentators: see Hagner 1993, 307) to read the two relevant clauses as 'roughly synonymous'. Likewise, while I agree that the theme of eschatological distress is not far away, it is not, to my mind, the most obvious referent of this verse.

[82] For detailed discussion of the Mt. text, cf. Davies & Allison 1988–91, 2.254–6; my suggestion is not far from what they describe as the seventh option, and is close to that offered by Pamment 1981, 227f. For Luke 16.16: Johnson 1991, 251 takes it in a positive sense ('everyone is being urged to enter it'; similarly Fitzmyer 1985, 117f.); Nolland 1993, 821 sees it as 'taking vigorous steps to enter'.

ears' (11.15) indicates that he recognizes the saying to be both cryptic and politically loaded. In both cases, the kingdom is certainly already present, but still at risk, needing still to win its final victory.

This is further supported by the vexed and much disputed saying in Luke 17.20-1.[83] In its Lukan form it is a classic *chreia*:[84]

> Being asked by the Pharisees when god's kingdom would come, Jesus answered them by saying: 'The kingdom of god does not come in a way that can be calculated; nor will they say, "See, here!" or "See, there!"; for look, the kingdom of god is *within your grasp*.'

The italicized phrase translates *entos hymon*, an expression that has given rise to much controversy. It has been read as meaning 'within you' in the sense of 'in your heart, as opposed to in your political or material circumstances': that is, the kingdom is an inward, not an outward reality. It has also been read as meaning 'in your midst': that is, the kingdom is already present, here among you. Of these two, the latter is closer to the meaning we would have guessed from the rest of Jesus' work. But philologically the meaning is most likely to be a third option: 'within your grasp'.[85] 'If you had eyes to see,' Jesus seems to be saying, 'you could reach out and take hold of the new reality that is already at work.' This reading is backed up by the following verses (17.22-37). Judgment is coming, and the presence of the kingdom does not mean automatic benefits for those who presume upon them as of right. Rather, it means an opportunity to be seized while there is still time. We should note that, though this saying emphatically means that the kingdom is already present, it also only makes sense if that presence is at least cryptic and hidden. The Pharisees do not think the kingdom is present; nothing in Jesus' ministry corresponds to their vision of what things ought to look like if it were. Luke 17.21 does not therefore support a simplistic 'present kingdom' viewpoint, but the more nuanced blend of present and future which we have seen to characterize Jesus' proclamation throughout.

A third saying which reinforces the sense of the kingdom as a present reality, in which people can share, but which still awaits some sort of final validation, is the word about exorcisms. 'If I by the finger of God cast out demons, then the kingdom of God has come upon you.'[86] This claim not only

---

[83] On this disputed text cf. e.g. Fitzmyer 1985, 1157-63; Nolland 1993, 849-54, both with bibliography. There are partial parallels to the saying in *Thom.* 113 & 3.

[84] cf. *NTPG* 428-35.

[85] So Roberts 1948; Cadbury 1950; Rüstow 1960; followed by Fitzmyer ad loc.

[86] Lk. 11.20/Mt. 12.28; Mt. has 'spirit' for 'finger', and has interestingly preserved the form 'kingdom of god' rather than his more normal 'of heaven' (for the difference in Mt., cf. e.g. Pamment 1981). The Greek of the last phrase is *ephthasen eph' hymas*, literally 'came upon you'. Exegetes now agree that this denotes the emphatic presence, not just the imminent futurity, of the kingdom. For recent discussion cf. e.g. Davies & Allison 1988-91, 2.339-41; Hagner 1993, 343 (Mt.); Fitzmyer 1985, 922; Evans 1990, 492; Nolland 1993, 639-41 (Lk.). See further the previous section of the present chapter.

asserts that the kingdom is present during the ministry of Jesus; it redefines the nature of that kingdom. Clearly, Herod, Pilate and Caiaphas are still holding court; but there is a different enemy who has already suffered a devastating blow, and who will soon be conquered completely. Jesus is already acting as the sovereign one through whom YHWH is even now defeating the enemies of his people. Once again, although the kingdom is clearly a present reality, this saying, in its context, looks forward to the future time when it will be clear that Jesus has not been in league with the prince of demons, but has rather been defeating him and despoiling his kingdom.[87]

The three sayings we have just examined stress the presence of the kingdom, while fully allowing, as the analogy with Bar-Kochba makes clear, for a future final victory. One of the most famous of the 'kingdom'-sayings, however, has this balance the other way round. 'Some standing here will not taste death until they see the kingdom of god.'[88] This constitutes a further clear promise of future victory and vindication. Like the eager followers of the many other prophets and messianic figures who flit through the pages of first-century Jewish history, Jesus' hearers would have understood their leader to be promising them the final victory for which the nation as a whole was longing. The great new exodus would occur: the real 'return from exile', the return of YHWH to Zion, the rebuilding of the Temple, the defeat of the forces of evil – all of this would be contained within the promise. And it would happen within their lifetimes. Political and revolutionary leaders down the ages have said much the same, albeit without the specific first-century Jewish theological overtones. To read this saying as though it were a prediction of Jesus' 'return', or of the 'parousia' in some Schweitzerian end-of-the-world sense, is simply to fail to think historically.

At the same time, in all three accounts the prediction of the coming kingdom follows swiftly upon the quasi-formal acknowledgment of Jesus himself as king, as Messiah.[89] The intervening material constitutes a call to allegiance, with the newly acclaimed 'royal' figure summoning his followers

---

[87] Cf. Caird 1980, 12: 'If Jesus was referring to the final vindication of God's purposes in the reign of justice and peace . . ., it is mere nonsense even to suggest that this was present on earth when Caiaphas was High Priest and Pilate Governor of Judaea. On the other hand, if Jesus was referring to the redemptive sovereignty of God let loose into the world for the destruction of Satan and all his works . . ., it makes nonsense of the whole record of his ministry to argue that for him this lay still in the future.'

[88] Lk. 9.27; Mk. 9.1 (adding 'having come with power'); Mt. 16.28 ('until they see "the son of man" coming in his kingdom', linking the saying closely with the previous verse). Cp. Mt. 10.23 ('you will not have gone through all the towns of Israel before "the son of man" comes'); Mk. 13.30/Mt. 24.34/Lk. 21.32 ('this generation shall not pass away until all is accomplished'). On the latter passage(s) see above, 364f.

[89] Mk. 8.29/Mt. 16.16/Lk. 9.20. Cf. below, ch. 11.

to come with him to the capital, where the kingdom would have to be attained, and to be prepared in doing so for the possibility that they would meet a violent death.[90] Once more, the sequence is thoroughly credible within the context of the Jewish world of the first century. One can imagine Judas the Galilean, Simon or Athronges, Simon bar-Giora, Menahem or Eleazar, or Bar-Kochba himself, speaking in just these terms, and one can imagine their followers thinking very similar thoughts to those which were undoubtedly in the minds of Jesus' followers.[91] Again, therefore, the fact that the full revelation or dawning of the kingdom remains in the future does not negate, but actually rather demands, that something be already acknowledged as present, in this case the Messiahship of Jesus. Only if 'the kingdom' is conceived in non-historical terms, perhaps through some theological scheme, does this seem anything other than completely natural.

We can thus approach the summary statement at the beginning of Mark's and Matthew's account of Jesus' public ministry with some confidence. After John had been arrested, they say, Jesus came into Galilee, announcing the 'gospel', and saying, 'The time is fulfilled; God's kingdom is at hand; repent, and believe the "gospel".'[92]

The crucial phrase here is 'is at hand', in Greek *engiken*. Scholars have been uneasy as to whether to read this as indicating the *presence* of the kingdom ('it is already here'), or the *imminence* of the kingdom ('it is about to dawn'). This debate, of course, is directly affected by what different scholars think the kingdom consisted of. If the kingdom meant the end of the space-time universe, and/or the literal descent to earth, riding on a cloud, of a human figure, this obviously had not happened. That, however, would have made little or no sense to a first-century Jew. If it meant that Herod and Pilate were no longer ruling Judaea, and that instead a Jewish kingdom had been set up under the direct rule of Israel's god, this too – though it would have made excellent sense to Jesus' contemporaries – had obviously not yet happened. The problem, though, is that Jesus spent his whole ministry *redefining* what the kingdom meant. He refused to give up the symbolic language of the kingdom, but filled it with such new content that, as we have seen, he powerfully subverted Jewish expectations.

This shift of meaning in the original context, coupled with scholarly misreading of apocalyptic in the modern one, has produced the real problem, which cannot actually be solved by lexical studies of the Greek word

---

[90] Mk. 8.31-8/Mt. 16.21-7/Lk. 9.22-6.

[91] For these men and movements cf. *NTPG* ch. 7.

[92] Mk. 1.14f.; Mt. 4.17 is nearly parallel. The same announcement is found in Jesus' command to the disciples in Mt. 10.7/Lk. 10.9. On the summons to 'repent and believe' see ch. 7 above.

engiken. Lexicography is ultimately a branch of history, and bears little fruit if separated from its parent stock. Jesus' redefinition of YHWH's kingdom, as we have studied it so far, indicates that in his view the kingdom was indeed present, but that it was not like Israel had thought it would be. Israel's god was becoming king in and through the work of Jesus; this kingdom would reach its climax in the battle which he was going to Jerusalem to fight; within a generation there would be an event which would show that Jesus was right to claim all this. YHWH would be king, and the true Israel would at last be redeemed from her exile. Even before the great events that would inaugurate the kingdom on the public stage and in world history, that kingdom was already present *where Jesus was*. To deny its presence, indeed, would be to undermine the hoped-for future: if it was not, in this sense, already present, what guarantee had Jesus' followers that the final victory was imminent?[93] Jesus' reading of the signs of the times, then, produced an answer to the fifth worldview question which, once we understand him historically, makes perfect sense. His public ministry was itself the true inauguration of the kingdom which would shortly be established.

7. The Prophet and the Kingdom

By way of summing up where we have got to so far, and pointing on to the next Part of the book, we may address the first two questions which, as we saw in chapter 3, focus the current scholarly quest for Jesus. How did Jesus relate to the Judaism of his day, and what were his aims?

Jesus belonged thoroughly within the complex and multiform Judaism of his day.[94] His protests were classic Jewish protests-from-within. His claims (such as we have examined so far) were parallel in form, though different in content, to those of many other Jewish leaders of his day. His activities made sense, and were intended to make sense, within a Jewish worldview. His stories evoked, extended and in part redrew some standard Jewish storylines. The symbols of his own work challenged the permanence of the standard symbols of his Jewish contemporaries, not least through suggesting that, when the time of fulfilment appeared, one of its features would be a necessary reordering of Israel's symbolic universe. Thus his praxis, his

---

[93] If, then, the meaning of *engiken* is pressed as 'has approached, has drawn near' (so e.g. Fitzmyer 1985, 848 (on Lk. 10.9)), this will mean, not that the kingdom is *not* present in the proclamation and actions of Jesus, but that this presence has now approached those to whom the gospel is preached.

[94] cf. Wright 1996a. There must be something called 'Judaism', however pluriform, if the currently fashionable 'Judaisms' is to have any meaning.

stories and his symbols all pointed to his belief and claim that Israel's god was fulfilling his promises and purposes in and through what he himself was doing.

Jesus was neither the first nor the last to make such a claim, though his manner of announcing and embodying it was, so far as we can tell, unparalleled.[95] In a world whose rough-and-tumble of politics, religion, and society threw up a good many possible definitions of what it meant to be Jewish, or to be loyally Jewish, or to be part of the true Israel that would one day be vindicated, there is no question but that Jesus is to be located on the first-century Jewish map along with the very many other movements and groups that came and went at that troubled time. Whether he was, as he claimed, a truly loyal Jew, let alone whether he was indeed the focal point of the true Israel that would one day be vindicated, was of course a matter of debate in his own day, and it has remained so. But Jesus cannot be located, historically, except as one who raised precisely these questions, within first-century Judaism, in an acute form. He was, and remains, 'Jesus the Jew'.[96]

What, then, was he trying to do? What were his 'aims'?[97] This is, of course, the subject of the next Part of this book; but for the moment, on the basis of the argument so far, we can suggest the following.

I have argued that Jesus intended to bring the story of Israel to its god-ordained climax, in and through his own work. His prophetic praxis was designed to challenge his contemporaries to abandon their agendas, including those agendas which appeared to be sanctioned in, or even demanded by, the Torah and the Prophets. He summoned them to follow him in a way of being the people of YHWH which was, according to him, the true though surprising fulfilment of the whole scriptural story. He aimed to bring about a radical shift within, not an abandonment of, the worldview of his hearers. They thought of themselves as Israel, as expecting the fulfilment of YHWH's promises, particularly concerning the great redemption, the restoration, the return from exile, the 'forgiveness of sins'. Jesus offered exactly that; but, as his own stories made clear, what he offered did not look like what they had been expecting. His symbolic actions fleshed out both his rejection of the current ways of conceiving Israel's hope and his own alternative. He aimed, then, to reconstitute Israel around himself, as the true returned-from-exile people; to achieve the victory of Israel's god over the evil that had enslaved his people;

[95] Despite the occasional maverick attempts to set up e.g. the Teacher of Righteousness as a direct parallel: e.g. Clayton 1992.

[96] It is a measure of the impact of the work of Vermes (1973, 1983, 1993) that this phrase – the title of his 1973 book – no longer sounds shocking in the way it did to so many when it was first published.

[97] On 'aims' and 'intentions', and their correlated 'beliefs', cf. *NTPG* 109–12, 125f.

and, somehow, to bring about the greatest hope of all, the victorious return of YHWH to Zion.

If these (so far as we can say at this stage of the argument) were Jesus' aims, what were his more detailed intentions? Clearly, to engage in the itinerant prophetic ministry that we have studied in this profile. He intended to call disciples, twelve in particular. He intended to announce the kingdom in praxis, story and symbol. And, so far as we can see, he achieved these intentions.

But there is one more intention at which we have only glanced to date, and which points us towards the next Part of this book. Jesus intended, it appears, to draw matters to a head in one particular visit to Jerusalem. After all, it was Zion that would hear the 'gospel' from the lips of the god-sent messengers. It was Jerusalem that would rejoice to hear that YHWH had won the victory over Babylon, and that his people were free at last. But to discover the reasons why Jesus focused his work on Jerusalem in this way we must spread out a new canvas. We can say quite a lot, it appears, about the profile of Jesus as a prophet. What can we say, as historians, about the specific vocation to which this prophet was obedient?

Part Three

The Aims and Beliefs of Jesus

Chapter Eleven

JESUS AND ISRAEL:
THE MEANING OF MESSIAHSHIP

1. Introduction

Jesus' prophetic actions, stories, symbols and worldview answers are now before us. Together they present a rounded picture of his mindset, his particular set of variations within the worldview of first-century Judaism. Like all such sketches of worldviews or mindsets, this one points beyond itself to the question of the subject's aims and beliefs. With this, of course, we encounter yet more controversy.

Difficult though the subject is, however, I shall argue that there is a way through. In this Part of the book, more specifically, I shall argue that Jesus applied to himself the three central aspects of his own prophetic kingdom-announcement: the return from exile, the defeat of evil, and the return of YHWH to Zion. These three overlap and dovetail at various points. Indeed, in studying them we shall repeatedly return to some of the same texts and passages. But for the purpose of clarity we may, to some extent, attempt to disentangle them. What is more, this Part of the book does not stand in a linear relationship to the previous Part: I am not suggesting that Jesus' teaching moved from one topic to another in the same way as my discussion does, or that he only began to reveal his aims and beliefs when his kingdom-teaching had been made fully clear. Jesus' aims and beliefs related equally to everything I have so far said about his mindset and his kingdom-announcement; it is we who have to reconstruct them by this circuitous route, not least because of the way debate on the matter has run in the last two hundred years.

We begin with the first aspect of Jesus' kingdom-announcement. I shall argue in the present chapter that Jesus saw himself as the leader and focal point of the true, returning-from-exile Israel. He was the king through whose work YHWH was at last restoring his people. He was the Messiah.

Three things need to be said at once about this claim. First, in case there is anyone left who has not grasped this point, the word 'Messiah', within Jesus' world, does not refer, in itself, to a divine or quasi-divine figure.[1]

---

[1] Since writing this sentence I have read O'Neill 1995; despite great ingenuity, his case

There are puzzling and opaque texts in the Hebrew scriptures which speak of
the king as one speaks of Israel's god.[2] There are passages where the roles of
YHWH and of the king seem to be intertwined.[3] But there is no evidence to
suggest that the various messianic and quasi-messianic figures who flit
through the pages of first-century history thought of themselves, or were
thought of by others, in this fashion. So, when Peter says to Jesus 'You are
the Messiah', and when Caiaphas says the same words but as an ironic question, neither of them should be understood as either stating or asking whether
Jesus thinks he is the incarnate second person of the Trinity. Subsequent
Christian use of the word 'Christ' (the Greek translation of 'Messiah'), and
indeed of the phrase 'son of god', as though they were 'divine' titles has, to
say the least, not helped people to grasp this point; but grasped it must be if
we are to understand Jesus in his historical context.[4]

Getting this straight frees the historian from a good deal of nonsense that
has been propagated in the last hundred years or so. When William Wrede
wrote his book on the 'Messianic secret' in Mark, he simply assumed that
'Messiah', 'Son of Man' and 'Son of God' all meant much the same sort of
thing, and, in particular, that they corresponded to what the early church
came to believe about Jesus as a divine figure. Wrede (who believed, of
course, that Jesus never saw himself as this sort of figure at all) was followed
by Bultmann, and thereafter by many of the most influential New Testament
scholars of the twentieth century. At the same time, of course, Schweitzer
was producing a much more nuanced view of what Messiahship might have
meant to Jesus. But Wrede's view, corresponding as it did to a good deal of
popular usage, continued to hold sway for many years, producing a string of
false either–or distinctions: one still hears people asking earnestly whether
Jesus was, and saw himself as, the 'divine Messiah', or 'whether he was
really, after all, a Palestinian Jew of the first century'. In this debate, as in
some others, the discussion has only recently begun to advance from positions outlined a century ago.[5]

Second, we should be prepared to give up the false historical modesty that
has made so many scholars shy of attributing theological thinking to Jesus
himself. One of the great gains of the last fifty years of scholarship has been
the recognition that Matthew, Mark and Luke – as well as John, Paul and

---

fails to convince at least this reader.

[2] e.g. Ps. 45.7 (45.6 in EVV), in which the same throne seems to belong both to the king
and to YHWH. See below, 624–9.

[3] e.g. Ezek. 34; see ch. 13 below.

[4] The split between 'Jesus' and 'Christ' in book-titles has perpetuated this misleading
view: e.g. De Rosa 1974; Schillebeeckx 1979 [1974], 1980 [1977]; Fredriksen 1988.

[5] On Wrede and Schweitzer cf. chs. 1–3 above.

others – were *theologians*. They were not artless chroniclers or transcribers. They thought deeply and creatively about the Jewish scriptures, about Israel's god, about the achievement of this god in completing the story of those scriptures in Jesus, and about the tasks and problems of their own communities as the people of this god, summoned to a life of loyalty to this Jesus.[6] At the same time, however, scholars have been disarmingly bashful about saying anything similar in relation to Jesus himself. Any deep or creative thoughts or ideas he seems to have had are instantly wished away: oh, we are told, that's simply another aspect of Matthew's (or Mark's, or Luke's, or John's) theology. Jesus must remain, it seems, an unreflective, instinctive, simplistic person, who never thought through what he was doing in the way that several of his contemporaries and followers did. I submit that, historically, the boot is far more likely to be on the other foot.[7] Precisely because Matthew, Mark, Luke and John appear to be creative and intelligent writers and theologians, we must hypothesize, as the common element standing behind all four (not to mention the sources they may or may not have used), some greater, more original, more subtle mind. Who would give shelf-room to a book arguing that all the most majestic and subtle music attributed to Johann Sebastian Bach was in fact the work of his four composing sons, Wilhelm Friedemann, Carl Philipp Emmanuel, Johann Christoph Friedrich, and Johann Christian? We may perhaps be allowed to look forward to a new day, in which Jesus himself is acknowledged, in his own right, as a thinking, reflecting, creative and original theologian.[8]

Third, and following from this, to enquire about how Jesus understood his own role within the historical events he was initiating is not to attempt the impossible, namely to study his psychology. Such attempts are made from time to time,[9] but have not carried much conviction. After all, as pastors, psychiatrists and psychotherapists know, it is hard enough to understand the inner workings of someone's psyche (even supposing we could define such a thing with any precision) when they share one's own culture and language, and when they co-operate with the process and answer one's questions. How

---

[6] cf. *NTPG* chs. 13, 14.

[7] cf. Schweitzer 1954 [1906], 348: 'For, after all, why should not Jesus think in terms of doctrine, and make history in action, just as well as a poor Evangelist can do it on paper, under the pressure of the theological interests of the primitive community.'

[8] This is of course a wider version of a famous argument advanced by C. H. Dodd nearly half a century ago (1965 [1952], 110); though often ignored, it has not been refuted. To the agonized phenomenalist, agreeing in principle but worried that we can never know for *sure* that we are dealing with Jesus and not with the evangelists' theologies, I recommend a good brisk walk, a Brandenburg Concerto, and *NTPG* Part II.

[9] e.g. Miller 1985. Still less convincing are the attempts to psychoanalyse the entire early church: e.g. Lüdemann 1994, ch. 5.

much harder when none of these things are the case. Yet we can ask, and historians often do ask, about people's aims, objectives, motives and beliefs. These things, indeed, are in large measure what 'history' is all about.[10] And when we put aims, objectives, motives and beliefs together we not infrequently find something which combines them, and which may be called 'vocation' or 'ambition'. To study the sense of vocation or ambition possessed by a figure from the past is not to enquire about psychology, but about history. We may or may not be able to answer the question. That depends on the data available. But it can be raised and studied in the same way as any other historical matter.

Two examples will make the point. We know, as a matter of history, that Saul of Tarsus, after a strange and cataclysmic experience on the road to Damascus, believed that he had a vocation from Israel's god to announce Jesus to the pagan world. How do we know that? Not by psychoanalysing Paul; attempts to do so regularly prove a failure. Rather, by the study of history. Paul acted in a way which would be bizarre (in his world) unless he believed himself to have such a vocation, but which, granted the vocation, becomes completely comprehensible. He frequently refers to himself as the apostle to the Gentiles. He seems to have got into trouble for acting and speaking in this way, and to have gone on doing so none the less. We can say, neither by guesswork nor by psychology, but by history, that he really did believe himself to have this vocation.

We also know, as a matter of history, that John the Baptist believed he had a vocation from Israel's god to speak and act as an eschatological prophet, the agent of a renewal that would pave the way for the final great act in the long and stormy drama of YHWH and Israel. Again, this is not a matter of psychology, or indeed of guesswork. We can reason historically to this conclusion from what we know that John said and did, within the context of his time and place. We can be quite confident that he did not simply wake up one morning and decide, for the fun of it, to try splashing water over people and see what happened. He carried on his work fearlessly, at the risk of official opprobrium, imprisonment and death. As historians we can and must say that he believed he had a god-given task and role to which he had to be obedient. History insists that at this point we speak of an awareness of vocation.

If we can say this about two figures who flourished in the years immediately before and after Jesus, it seems absurd not to say the same of Jesus himself. What was the vocation to which he was obedient, or the ambition which led him on? What aims, objectives, motives and beliefs came

[10] cf. *NTPG* ch. 4.

together to make him pursue the course he did?[11] In answer to this question, the present Part of the book proposes the following hypothesis: he believed that it was his own task not only to announce, but also to enact and embody, the three major kingdom-themes, namely, the return from exile, the defeat of evil, and the return of YHWH to Zion. This motivated him to pursue certain identifiable aims and objectives. He acted, in other words, in ways which are puzzling without this hypotheses, but which are clearly explicable on the basis of it. We are not pursuing only a history-of-ideas project, nor proceeding only by the study of Jesus' words. We are investigating the fully-rounded history of what he *did*, and why he thought it made sense.

The present chapter, then, sets out the first part of this hypothesis. Jesus believed that he was embodying, and thus symbolizing in himself, the return of Israel from exile. As such, he believed that the fortunes of the people were drawn together on to himself and his own work. He believed, in short, that he was the Messiah -- though his view of the entire situation, and his vocation within it, meant that he redefined that notion, too.

As with other historical hypotheses, the best way to examine and test this one is to start with the outer framework of the picture and move inwards. We here summarize briefly, not least in the light of writings which have appeared since *The New Testament and the People of God* was written, what was set out in the relevant sections of Parts III and IV of that volume.

2. Messiahship in Judaism and Early Christianity

(i) Messiahship in the Jewish World of Jesus' Day

Whole volumes have been written on the meaning of Messiahship in the Jewish world(s) of Jesus' day. It is thus both unnecessary and impossible to go into great detail about the subject.[12] There are, however, certain fixed points, and something approaching an emerging consensus, which may indicate the right road to pursue.

[11] This move, from public profile to private belief, has some analogies with that made by Ben Meyer in various places, notably *The Aims of Jesus* and his *Anchor Bible Dictionary* article on Jesus (Meyer 1979, 1992b), together with various essays, e.g. 1989, ch. 8.

[12] cf. e.g. Neusner, Green & Frerichs 1987; Charlesworth 1992c (the opening essay of which sets up the question to be addressed quite similarly to my present argument); Gruenwald, Shaked & Stroumsa 1992; Collins 1995. All these volumes cite copious further literature. See too de Jonge 1992; Horsley 1992b & c; Hengel 1995a & b. Karrer 1990 attempts to dissociate the notion of anointing from both royal and priestly ideas, suggesting that it simply designates one who is close to god; but this, in view of the material in the works already referred to, must be judged highly unlikely as the appropriate background for the designation 'Messiah' in reference to Jesus.

To begin with, as I have argued myself, there was no one picture of 'the Messiah' within the Judaism of Jesus' day.[13] The royal and/or messianic movements of the time show considerable freedom and flexibility within a broad concept; the idea of Israel's coming king was one that different movements and different claimants could quite easily reshape around themselves without anyone denouncing them for not having conformed to a commonly recognized ideal or portrait. The varied speculations of the writers of the Scrolls on the one hand, and the bleak story of the Herodian dynasty on the other, demonstrate the wide range of possible options for what the coming king of the Jews might look like. The picture is filled in by the numerous popular messianic movements for which we have evidence, reaching an initial climax with the various figures who emerged during the Jewish War, and a second and final one in the major but abortive Bar-Kochba rebellion. Messiahship, it seems, was whatever people made of it.

We must, however, insist on the relevance of one particular large body of evidence. It is historically spurious, though no doubt comprehensible in terms of idealist metaphysics, to imagine that one can separate out a 'pure' messianic strand of thought (witnessed to by certain salient texts) from the real-life experience of royalty, and would-be royalty, that the Jews had had since the days of the Maccabees.[14] The Hasmonean and Herodian dynasties supplied the actual models of kingship that most people knew; speculations about a coming king were speculations about someone who would replace these suspect dynasties with the true, god-given one. We have only to remind ourselves that 'Messiah' meant, among other things, 'king of the Jews', to be reminded also that in Jesus' day there was at least one person who claimed that title, and who had the power to back up his claim. As we shall see, this explains some of Jesus' most cryptic sayings. One did not lightly, even by implication, issue a direct challenge to a son of Herod the Great.[15]

If these disparate movements had anything in common, it was the expectation, forming the context for whatever messianic figure might emerge, that Israel's long history would at last reach its divinely ordained goal. The long night of exile, the 'present evil age', would give way to the dawn of renewal and restoration, the new exodus, the return from exile, 'the age to come'.

---

[13] *NTPG* 307–20 (summary, 319f.), with other secondary refs.

[14] cp. the wise words of Collins 1995, 41: 'No would-be messiah was motivated only, or primarily, by the desire to act out a textual paradigm. Political and especially social factors provided the obvious occasions of most of the messianic movements of the Roman era.' And again (199): 'The pattern of prophecy and fulfilment was not merely a scribal exercise among the literate few. It had a direct impact on Jewish history in the Roman period.'

[15] Mendels 1992 distinguishes 'ordinary' royal ambitions from 'messianic' ones. I do not think this is possible. The idea of a 'Messiah' is so ill-defined in the period that the discussion must in principle include all royal ambitions and designs. Cf. Mt. 2.1–22.

Where royal hopes were cherished, it was within this setting: the king that would come would be the agent through whom YHWH would accomplish this great renewal. One could also instance a biblical passage like Zechariah 1— 8, where the frequent (if sometimes puzzling) references to messianic figures are firmly set within the context of prophecies of national and cultic restoration. This is precisely the sort of context within which one can understand the crowds' reaction to Jesus as reported in John 6.15: they wanted to seize Jesus and make him king. Where messianic expectations occurred, they formed part of a larger implicit story told, and lived, by Jews of Jesus' day. The king was the focal point of the dream of national liberty.

It is important to stress, therefore, that one does not need, and cannot in any case hope to discover, a fully formed outline picture of 'the Jewish expectation of the Messiah', into which Jesus might or might not fit. Jesus' Jewish world offers instead a flurry of confused elements, some of which may be present in some messianic movements. Sometimes, as in the *Psalms of Solomon* and Qumran, there is considerable concentration on biblical texts; at other times, royal movements (such as Herod's) went ahead without, so far as we know, the need to appeal to scripture.[16] The hope of the nation was central, organizing itself as much around symbols, praxis and stories as around proof-texts.

Among those symbols, carrying 'royal' connotations, the Temple was central.[17] David, the first great king, had had the original idea for the Temple; Solomon, David's son and heir, had built it. Hezekiah and Josiah, two of the greatest pre-exilic kings, had cleansed it and restored it. Rebuilding it was supposed to be part of the post-exilic royal task for the shadowy figures of Zerubbabel and Joshua son of Jehozadak.[18] By cleansing it, Judas Maccabaeus founded a hundred-year priestly, and royal, dynasty. Rebuilding it was a central part of Herod's claim to found a dynasty of his own. Menahem, one of the would-be messiahs of the War period, appeared in the Temple in royal robes, as though to signal the long-awaited coming of divine deliverance; Simon bar Giora appeared, royally apparelled, in the spot where the Temple had stood.[19] Bar-Kochba, as we saw, gave the rebuilding of the Temple such a high priority that he had it stamped on his coins. Temple and kingship went hand in hand.[20]

---

[16] According to Mt. 2.4–6, the aged Herod had to ask the chief priests and scribes 'where the Messiah was to be born'.

[17] cf. ch. 9 above, esp. 406f.

[18] cf. Hag. 2.20–3; Zech. 4.1–10 (apparently combining different but related oracles); 6.9–15.

[19] Jos. *War* 2.444; 7.29.

[20] The attempt of Gundry 1993, 899f. to break the link between Messiah and Temple must be adjudged a failure. Saying that Israel's god is the real Temple-builder is not to deny that the Messiah is also the agent (those who expect the Temple to be rebuilt in our own day

Equally, the king was to be the one who would fight Israel's battles. David had defeated Goliath and the Philistines; the sign that he was going to be king was already clear when the women sang that 'Saul has slain his thousands, and David his tens of thousands'.[21] His true successor, according to the biblical Psalms, would attain his lordship by defeating Israel's enemies.[22] According to the later *Psalms of Solomon*, he would fulfil the Davidic promises of Psalm 2 by smashing the sinners with an iron rod and dashing them in pieces like a potters' vessel.[23] Hezekiah had seen off the Assyrians (though in that case YHWH had done it all by himself); Josiah had died in battle against the national enemy. One of the reasons why Zerubbabel fades from the second-Temple picture may be precisely because he did not even attempt to fight for Israel's freedom. Before Judas Maccabaeus had cleansed the Temple, he had won the great victory over the Syrians. Before Herod started rebuilding it, he had had remarkable military successes against the Parthians and Nabateans. (Part of Herod's unacceptability to many Jews may, of course, have been the way in which he, like the Maccabaeans, consistently co-operated with Rome itself.[24]) Similar tasks were either accomplished or attempted by the would-be Messiahs of the War period, such as Simon bar Giora,[25] and of course Bar-Kochba himself, whose very name ('son of the star') is taken from the warlike prophecy of Numbers 24.17–19:

> I see him, but not now;
> > I behold him, but not near –
> a star shall come out of Jacob,
> > and a scepter shall rise out of Israel;

---

are able to combine the two ideas without any awareness of contradiction). 4QFlor. 1–12 offers an exegesis of 2 Sam. 7.10–14, in which a reference to Ex. 15.17–18 is inserted ('A temple of the Lord will you establish with your hands. YHWH shall reign for ever and ever' [GM 136]); this confirms, rather than undermines, the fact that the text envisages the Davidic Messiah as the builder of the eschatological Temple. Cp. the various Zech. texts (e.g. 3.6–10; 4.5–14; 6.9–13) about king and Temple, on which see Kim 1987a, 138f.; also, the Tg. on Isa. 53.5: 'He [the Messiah] shall build the sanctuary that was polluted because of our transgressions and given up because of our iniquities.' This is not to say, of course, that *all* refs. to destroying or rebuilding the Temple concern a Messiah: cf. e.g. Tob. 14.4; *1 En.* 90.29; 91.13; *Jub.* 1.27–9. Here as elsewhere the argument must concern historical movements and symbols, not just texts.

[21] 1 Sam. 18.7–9; 21.11.

[22] Ps. 110.

[23] *Ps. Sol.* 17.23f.; cf. Ps. 2.9. I find it extraordinary to suppose that this passage refers to 'nonmilitary' victory (Charlesworth 1992b, 20). 17.33, cited in this connection, speaks of the Messiah's not *relying* on military means. Cp. *2 Bar.* 72.2, 6. On this point, cf. *NTPG* 311, n.92; Collins 1995, 54, 203.

[24] cf. 1 Macc. 8. On Herod's status with the Romans cf. Jos. *Ant.* 17.246, where he is described as Caesar's 'friend and ally'; and the other evidence in e.g. Levine 1992b, 163.

[25] cf. Jos. *War* 2.521.

it shall crush the borderlands of Moab,
  and the territory of all the Shethites.
Edom will become a possession,
  Seir a possession of its enemies,
  while Israel does valiantly.
One out of Jacob shall rule,
  and destroy the survivors of Ir.[26]

The praxis that would demonstrate Messiahship thus included leading the victorious battle against Israel's enemies. All of this adds up to a conclusion of obvious importance for the question of Jesus and Messiahship: a Messiah who was executed by the occupying forces was not, after all, the true Messiah. This is not a subtle theological point, though it has huge theological implications. It is merely a truism of first-century politics.

Temple and battle were thus central symbols of a royal vocation. Around these more or less fixed points, capable of sustaining praxis of widely divergent kinds, different movements came and went. Within some of them the underlying story, the central symbols and the royal praxis were expressed in terms of scriptural prophecy. Qumran in particular collected 'messianic' texts, sometimes embedded in more extended writings, sometimes focused in 'testimony' collections.[27] While, even there, we should be clear that such texts were seen as belonging within a story, and as marking out both symbol and praxis, we should also note that they represent the open possibility, within the Judaism of Jesus' day, of scriptural echoes that were, so to speak, ready to be awakened when someone spoke or acted in certain ways.[28]

One echo in particular must be stressed, and properly understood. Several texts from this period speak of the king as 'son of god'. The use of Psalm 2 and 2 Samuel 7 is attested at Qumran in a messianic context, and there are other references which show that 'son of god' as a messianic title was known in various circles in this period.[29] But we must stress that in the first century the regular Jewish meaning of this title had nothing to do with an incipient

---

[26] The tradition of Akiba's naming of Bar-Kochba is preserved in jTaan. 68d. The Numbers prophecy is quoted or alluded to in our period in e.g. 1QSb 5.27; CD 7.19; 4Q175.9–13; 1QM 11.6–7; *TJud.* 24.1–6; Philo *Praem.* 95 (94–7 as a whole is a remarkably warlike passage, predicting the military defeat of Israel's enemies). On all this cf. Collins 1995, 60–4.

[27] The most recent studies of Qumran Messianism are Collins 1995; Schiffman 1994, Part V. See esp. 4Q174, citing 2 Sam. 7, where king and Temple belong closely together, and weaving in Ps. 2 alongside; and 4Q175, in which texts about prophetic, kingly and priestly Messiahs stand side by side.

[28] cf. Collins 1995, 41: 'Actions are also shaped by ideologies, and in Judaism at the turn of the era the available ideologies were predominantly shaped by scriptural traditions.'

[29] Israel as son of god: Ex. 4.22 f.; Jer. 3.19; Wis. 9.7, 18.13; *Sib. Or.* 3.702; 4 Ezra 5.28; *Jub.* 1.25–8; 4QDibHam (=4Q504) 3.4–7 (GM 414); 4Q246 2.1 (GM 138) (cf. Collins 1993b; Hengel 1995b, 39).

trinitarianism; it referred to the king as *Israel's representative*. Israel was the son of YHWH: the king who would come to take her destiny on himself would share this title.

Even from this brief summary of the evidence, the historian is faced with a question. Jesus of Nazareth did not rebuild or adorn the Temple. He did not lead a successful revolution against the Romans. He did not, that is, conform at the level of symbolic praxis (never mind that of textual paradigm) even to the ill-defined popular expectation we are able to chart. So why did his followers insist that he was, after all, the Messiah, the son of the living god?

(ii) Messiahship in Early Christianity

Because insist they did. From its very earliest days, the community of Jesus' followers regarded him as Messiah.[30]

What precisely they meant by this needs to be teased out a bit further. Many have tried to argue that Paul, writing within twenty or so years of Jesus' crucifixion, already used the word *Christos* as a proper name, with its titular significance ('Messiah') being swallowed up by other theological meanings. I believe this to be mistaken.[31] But, even if it were true, the only explanation for it would be that the early Christian movement had been so definite in its application of the *title* to Jesus, surprising as this must have been, that even those who did not agree with the ascription were forced to continue using the word even though, on this hypothesis, it must have been an embarrassment to them. I think, in point of fact, that the mental gymnastics required to sustain this train of thought are themselves an indication that the truth is simpler, and that Paul, in company with all other very early Christians actually known to us (as opposed to those invented by ingenious scholars), believed that Jesus was indeed the true Messiah, and held that belief as a central identifying mark. But my point here is that even if he did not, his continuing use of *Christos* indicates all the more the strength of messianic conviction in the early church.

[30] See e.g. Juel 1988; Hengel 1995b, ch. 1 (a longer version of Hengel 1995a). Charlesworth 1992b, 3f. labels Jewish expectations 'messianology' and Christian beliefs 'christology', thereby suggesting a rigid differentiation between them. I find this unwarranted. Granted that the relation between Jewish and Christian beliefs is not straightforward (ibid., 6), this does not justify us in categorizing them in advance as two automatically separate things – as Charlesworth himself (11) seems to recognize. Certainly the earliest Christians thought their beliefs about Jesus still belonged on the Jewish map.

[31] See the discussion, and the alternative proposals, in Wright 1991, chs. 2, 3.

Christos, in fact, is widespread throughout early Christian writings, and Jesus was known by that word to outsiders like Suetonius and Josephus.[32] Even if we were to argue that its Jewish, national and royal significance had been forgotten quite early on, we would only thereby intensify the question: why did anyone attach this word to Jesus in the first place? In other words, granted that the very early Christian community was Jewish to the core, what caused it to predicate Messiahship of Jesus so firmly that the title stuck even when its original meaning may have been forgotten?

This question needs to be sharpened up by two other considerations. First, to announce a movement as messianic was to court trouble, both from the Roman authorities (for whom Caesar was the only true king) and, as we have seen, from the other claimants to the title 'king of the Jews', namely the Herodian family. Both problems are clearly visible in Acts; yet Jesus' early followers stuck to the word, and the theme. The clash with the authorities, however, does not take place in the way we might have imagined from our knowledge of Jewish history, that is, in the form of a violent confrontation between the new upstart royal house and that of either Caesar or Herod. (We may contrast the messianic movements of 4 BC and AD 6, and of course the Bar-Kochba rebellion.) The closest we come to such a showdown is the strange incident reported by Hegesippus in which some of Jesus' blood-relatives were put on trial by Domitian as though they were part of a royal dynasty.[33] Why, then, did the early Christians label themselves in a way likely to cause trouble? Why, granted that they seem to have worked with a considerably redefined notion of Messiahship and its implications, did they continue to use that word, that model, at all? Once again, why, seeing that Jesus did not do the things a Messiah might have been expected to do, did they ever even begin to use the word in the first place?

Second, a messianic movement without a physically present Messiah posed something of an anomaly, all the more so when the Messiah in question had died the death of a *failed* revolutionary leader. If the early Christians were so keen on having a messianic movement, why did they not choose another Messiah, perhaps from Jesus' family – perhaps Jesus' own brother, James, who was after all the acknowledged leader of the Jerusalem church for the next generation? Granted that they did not do so, what was it that made them launch the claim, scandalous to Jews, incomprehensible to Gentiles, that Jesus was indeed the Messiah?

At this point one regular line of thought has said: it was the resurrection, and only the resurrection, that launched the messianic claim.[34] Up to that point Jesus' movement had not been messianic; Easter made it so.

---

[32] Suet. *Claud.* 25.4 (cf. *NTPG* 355); Jos. *Ant.* 20.200 (cf. *NTPG* 353f.).

[33] Euseb. *HE* 3.19–20; see the discussion in *NTPG* 351f., 356.

[34] This theory passes from Wrede, through Bultmann, to some scholars in the present.

Let us first acknowledge the obvious grain of truth in this suggestion. Without the resurrection – leaving open at the moment what the first disciples thought they meant by that word – it is simply inconceivable that anyone would have regarded Jesus as Messiah, especially if they had not regarded him thus beforehand. But a moment's thought should reveal that this cannot be a complete account of the matter. Not only is it unclear at this stage – especially in the writings of those who have advanced this hypothesis – what precisely happened at Easter; it is certainly not clear that anyone at the time expected the Messiah to die at the hands of the pagans, let alone to be raised from the dead within the midst of ongoing history. Thus, whatever we make of the resurrection itself, there is no surrounding context within which it would make sense to suppose the first disciples saying to themselves: 'We didn't think he was the Messiah – we just thought he was a prophet. But if he's been raised from the dead then we must conclude that he was and is the Messiah, even though he didn't do what we thought a Messiah would do.' One sometimes wonders whether certain scholars would recognize a *reductio ad absurdum* if it came up and bit them on the nose. To change the metaphor, when an argument hits the buffers in this fashion we should be honest and admit that it was travelling on the wrong track.

We may suspect, in fact, that the ease with which the argument 'resurrection, therefore Messiahship' has been accepted during this century has owed not a little to a confusion about both sides of the equation. Granted that the resurrection of Jesus would force his followers to re-evaluate the meaning of his crucifixion, it would not have given to him, his life or his death a 'messianic' meaning *had such a meaning not been in some way present already*. It is this argument, more or less, that has increasingly forced scholars back to the conclusion that there was something at least about Jesus' death, and quite possibly also about his life, that, however surprisingly, must be regarded as messianic.[35] The same argument also puts paid to any easy pre-emptive strike by scholars determined to assert that all 'messianic' material in the gospels must, *ex hypothesi*, be the invention of the early church. If Jesus was so unlike any expected Messiah, and if their own movement was so unlike a messianic movement, why bother to invent passages,

---

[35] Among the first steps back to sanity on this point were taken by Dahl 1974 (the key essay, 'The Crucified Messiah', pp. 10–36, was first published in 1960). More recently, the several works of Ben Meyer have explored the rich possibilities; and such writers as Sanders (1985, 1993), Harvey (1982), Witherington (1990) and Hengel (1995b) have been happy to affirm that Jesus believed himself to be, in some sense, Messiah. Cf. e.g. Hengel 1995b, 41–58, 63–72, and e.g. 217: 'The origin of christology appears unthinkable without the assumption of a messianic claim of Jesus. Christology cannot be based *alone* upon the resurrection appearances' (italics original).

sayings, and above all a title that would be at best beside the point and at worst dangerously misleading?

The criterion of double similarity and double dissimilarity again helps to sharpen up the case.[36] In advance of the detailed argument, we may suggest that the portrait of Jesus as Messiah in the synoptic gospels is not only significantly different from what the Jewish context would have led us to expect (though it makes sense only within, and as a key variant upon, that Jewish setting). It is also significantly different, both in content and in the tone of presentation, from what we find in the early church (though the church's proclamation of Jesus as Messiah makes sense only if we presuppose something like the gospels' picture). In early Christianity, 'Messiahship' quickly becomes part of a larger picture which is announced without hesitation or secrecy, whereas in the gospels it is surrounded by an aura of mystery. As in other cases, the picture the gospels paint is both continuous and discontinuous with non-Christian Judaism on the one hand and the life of the early church on the other, in such a way as to force the historian to postulate that we are here in touch with Jesus himself.

Even a cursory glance at Messiahship within Judaism and the early church, therefore, leads us inexorably back to the question: how did the notion of Messiahship get from the one to the other? Ultimately, the simplest hypothesis must be that it was Jesus himself who caused the transition. Are there, then, any signs that Jesus did after all regard himself, in however paradoxical a sense, as the Messiah, Israel's representative, sent by YHWH to be the spearhead of the great movement of national liberation?

3. Jesus and Kingship: Events in Jerusalem

(i) Introduction

The question, as we have already indicated, cannot be a matter of fitting Jesus neatly into a carefully designed and pre-packaged framework of 'what Jews believed about the Messiah'. No such thing exists. Nor can we simply amass messianic proof-texts from the Hebrew Bible and ask how many of them were present within Jesus' awareness of his own vocation and agenda. Texts matter, but contexts matter even more. Our enquiry must focus, as it has throughout this work, on the praxis, the stories and the symbols – working together, as often as not – which characterize Jesus' career on the one hand and the variegated strands of Jewish messianic belief on the other.

---

[36] cf. above, 131–3.

The somewhat diffuse discussion of these points over the last generation of scholarship has come up with two main focal points: the *titulus* and the Temple. The 'title' on the cross, indicating the reason for Jesus' execution, is widely agreed to be genuinely historical. Jesus died with 'the king of the Jews' written above his head.[37] This is not, after all, so surprising; crucifixion was the regular way of dealing with would-be Messiahs. What is at issue is why anyone thought to lay that charge against Jesus, and why, despite so much apparent evidence to the contrary, it stuck. And the main answer to that question has to do with Jesus' action in the Temple, which most now agree was the proximate cause of his death. These two focal points will thus serve as the framework for our discussion. In what way was Jesus' action in the Temple perceived to be, and/or intended to be, messianic? And in what way did the charge under which Jesus eventually died reflect his own agenda?

(ii) The Temple-Action

Jesus' action in the Temple constitutes the most obvious act of messianic praxis within the gospel narratives. We have already studied the incident in detail in chapter 9 above, where we concluded that it spoke not just of religion but of royalty; and, for that matter, not just of cleansing but of judgment. Jesus was claiming some kind of authority over the Temple and its life. Though the chief priests ruled the Temple *de facto* in this period, the scriptural pattern, which we know to have been alive and well in this period not only from texts but from historical movements, spoke of the Temple's ruler as the true Davidic king.

This was not so much a matter of *teaching* as of *symbolic action*. Jesus, as we have seen often enough, was as capable as any of his contemporaries of deliberately performing actions which had rich symbolic value. Within his own time and culture, his riding on a donkey over the Mount of Olives, across Kidron, and up to the Temple mount spoke more powerfully than words could have done of a royal claim.[38] The allusion to Zechariah (and, with that, several other passages) is obvious:

Rejoice greatly, O daughter Zion!
   Shout aloud, O daughter Jerusalem!
Lo, your king comes to you;
   triumphant and victorious is he,

[37] See e.g., recently, Hengel 1995b, 45–50; and e.g. Bammel 1984; Riesner 1984 [1981], 302f.; Horsley 1994, 413f.
[38] Mt. 21.1–9/Mk. 11.1–10/Lk. 19.28–40/Jn. 12.12–19. Cp. 2 Sam. 15.23–32.

humble and riding on a donkey,
  on a colt, the foal of a donkey.
He will cut off the chariot from Ephraim
  and the war horse from Jerusalem;
and the battle bow shall be cut off,
  and he shall command peace to the nations;
his dominion shall be from sea to sea,
  and from the River to the ends of the earth.[39]

The so-called 'triumphal entry' was thus clearly messianic. This meaning is somewhat laboured by the evangelists, particularly Matthew, but is not for that reason to be denied to the original incident. All that we know of Jewish crowds at Passover-time in this period makes their reaction, in all the accounts, thoroughly comprehensible: they praise their god for the arrival, at last, of the true king.[40] What precisely they meant by this is difficult to assess; that they thought it and said it, there is no good reason to doubt.

Jesus' action in the Temple, however, was equally 'royal'.[41] Once again there are clear scriptural echoes, from passages some of which we know were regarded as explicitly messianic in this period:

[YHWH said to David, through Nathan,] 'When your days are fulfilled and you lie down with your ancestors, I will raise up your offspring after you . . ., and I will establish his kingdom. He shall build a house for my name, and I will establish the throne of his kingdom forever. I will be a father to him, and he shall be a son to me.'[42]

Here is a man whose name is Branch; for he shall branch out in his place, and he shall build the temple of YHWH. It is he that shall build the temple of YHWH; he shall bear royal honour, and shall sit and rule on his throne.[43]

There shall no longer be traders in the house of YHWH of hosts on that day.[44]

[39] Zech. 9.9f.; behind this passage may be echoes of Gen. 49.8–12, of which, in turn, v. 11b may be echoed by Isa. 63.2f. The last couplet of Zech. 9.10 is a quotation from a 'messianic' – by which I mean 'ideally royal' – psalm (72.8). The Mount of Olives location evokes Zech. 14.4, on which see below.

[40] Mt. 21.9/Mk. 11.10/Lk. 19.38/Jn. 12.13. There are almost certainly intentional 'Maccabaean' echoes to the triumphal entry: cf. Farmer 1956, ch. 8; Boers 1989, 89–91. This is not disproved by the non-exact nature of the parallel, as suggested by Witherington 1990, 269 n.18.

[41] Among those who have repeatedly urged this point we may note particularly Betz 1968 [1965], 87–93; Meyer in several works, e.g. 1979, 197–202 (nb. 199: 'the entry into Jerusalem and the cleansing of the temple constituted a messianic demonstration, a messianic critique, a messianic fulfilment event, and a sign of the messianic restoration of Israel'); Hengel 1995b, 55–7. Sanders 1985, 306f.; 1993, 254 disjoins the entry and Temple-action.

[42] 2 Sam. 7.12–14; cf. Collins 1995, 22f., 61–7, 106f., discussing the use of this passage in 4Q174 and elsewhere, in what Collins calls a 'network of interlocking references' (64).

[43] Zech. 6.12f.; cf. Collins 1995, 30f., and his discussion of other 'Branch' texts (60–4).

[44] Zech. 14.21. As Meyer shows (e.g. 1979, 198), Jesus' action will have evoked this text, and, with it, a sense that the decisive moment, and hence also the decisive person, had

It was the king who had ultimate authority over the Temple. He would be its reformer, its rebuilder. Since Jesus' action was aimed at the judgment and reconstitution of this most central symbol, the entire incident must be seen as charged with an explicit messianic claim. This, it must be stressed, belongs to the symbolic praxis of the incident itself, and to the narrative world it claims to evoke. It is not just a matter of 'teaching' in some abstract sense. Someone doing what Jesus did was indicating that Israel's history had reached the point of decisive destruction and rebuilding, and that his own actions were embodying that moment.

This may be seen further by considering the incident in the light of the opening chapters of First Maccabees.[45] Since the festival of Hanukkah was enthusiastically observed in Jesus' day, a far wider circle than simply the literate few would have known the story; the connection of revolt against the pagans, action in the Temple, and the establishment of a royal house was firmly impressed on the popular mind. Briefly, the narrative works as follows. Antiochus Epiphanes, the Syrian megalomaniac king, conquers Jerusalem, officially abolishes the keeping of Torah, and sets up sacrilegious sacrificial worship in the Temple. Mattathias, a priest, refuses to obey the king's edict, and kills a Jew who is offering pagan sacrifice; he 'burns with zeal for the law, just as Phinehas did' (2.26). He and his sons then flee to the hills, where they gather together a force of people eager for the law, and engage in sporadic attacks on pagans and renegades. When Mattathias is about to die, he makes a speech urging his sons to stand firm, to defeat the Gentiles, and to uphold the law. Judas Maccabaeus acts, in fulfilment of royal imagery and prophecy,[46] to regroup Israel; he wins some initial victories. Judas and his army then defeat the Syrians, enter Jerusalem, cleanse the Temple, and restore the true worship. The royal implications of this are not ignored: Judas begins his pre-battle prayer with

> Blessed are you, O Saviour of Israel, who crushed the attack of the mighty warrior by the hand of your servant David, and gave the camp of the Philistines into the hands of Jonathan son of Saul . . .[47]

The story then concludes with the death of Antiochus Epiphanes; the successful defence of the Temple against counter-attack;[48] the treaty between Judas

---

arrived.

[45] cf. esp. Farmer 1956 *passim*. Why was this book so long neglected?

[46] 1 Macc. 3.4: 'like a lion in his deeds, like a lion's cub roaring for prey'; cf. Gen. 49.9f. Cp. too 4 Ezra 11.37; 12.31–4; Rev. 5.5.

[47] 1 Macc. 4.30.

[48] Including the priest's prayer: 'You chose this house to be called by your name, and to be for your people a house of prayer and supplication. Take vengeance on this man and on his army, and let them fall by the sword; remember their blasphemies, and let them live no longer' (1 Macc. 7.37f.).

and Rome; the death of Judas and the succession of his brother Jonathan; Jonathan's rebuilding of Jerusalem, his subsequent activities, and death; the succession of the next brother, Simon; his establishment of what amounts to eschatological peace;[49] his installation as High Priest and leader; and his bequeathing of his role to his sons. In other words, the sequence runs: victory over the pagans, cleansing of the Temple, fulfilment of the promises, and establishment of the new dynasty.

Jesus' symbolic actions inevitably invoked this entire wider context. Jesus was performing *Maccabaean* actions, albeit with some radical differences. This explains, among other things, why the High Priestly family, who regarded themselves as in some senses the successors of the Hasmonean priestly line, found Jesus' action so threatening. It also explains why that action was so inevitably charged with 'royal' overtones. This in turn explains what follows: a glittering series of riddles, all pointing back to the Temple-action and to Jesus' implicit messianic claim.

(iii) Royal Riddles

(a) Destroy and Rebuild

One of the best-attested of these riddles – which one scholar, indeed, has made into the linchpin of his whole interpretation of Jesus' aims at this point – is the dark saying about the destruction and rebuilding of the Temple.[50] Whatever form this originally took, it seems likely that Jesus said this sort of thing more than once.[51] Although Mark claims that the witnesses at the trial were 'false',[52] the parallel tradition in John, the prophecy to the disciples on the Mount of Olives, and the mocking at the cross[53] all reinforce the probability that a saying like this did indeed form part of his explanation of what he had done in the Temple courts. The point at issue for us here is

---

[49] cf. 1 Macc. 14.4–15, echoing various OT prophecies; cf. *NTPG* 429.

[50] Mk. 14.58/Mt. 26.61/Jn. 2.19/*Thom.* 71. Cf. Sanders 1985, 61–76. The *Thom.* saying is best explained as a gnostic revision of the synoptic one: so, rightly, Gundry 1993, 907 and others, against e.g. Crossan 1983, 307f.; Funk & Hoover 1993, 122.

[51] Not only because of the different placing of the incident in Jn., which may of course be variously interpreted, but because of e.g. Mt. 24.1f./Mk. 13.1f./Lk. 21.5f., on which cf. ch. 8 above. Mk. 13 and its pars. may, indeed, be interpreted not least as the prediction of the Temple's destruction on the one hand and Jesus' vindication on the other.

[52] Mk. 14.57. Mt. 26.60 says that other false witnesses came forward, but does not follow Mk. in describing this particular accusation as false.

[53] Mt. 27.40/Mk. 15.29; cf. too Ac. 6.14.

again that this riddling explanation constituted a royal claim.[54] Jesus would do, in some sense or other, what David's son Solomon had done – or, *mutatis mutandis*, what Judas Maccabaeus and his brothers had done. His Temple-action was a claim to royal status.

(b) Say to this Mountain . . .

In Mark and Matthew, Jesus' Temple-action is closely linked with the cursing of the fig tree.[55] As has often been remarked, this has the effect of using one acted symbol to interpret another. In this case, though, the symbol is further interpreted by a riddling saying:

> Whoever says to this mountain, 'Be taken up and cast into the sea', and does not doubt in his heart, but believes that what he says will come to pass, it will happen for him.[56]

We have already commented that 'this mountain', spoken in Jerusalem in the vicinity of the Temple, would naturally refer to the Temple mount itself. There is, however, a biblical allusion which suggests that the saying was also a cryptic messianic riddle. Zechariah 1—8 is all about the return from exile, the restoration of Jerusalem, the return of YHWH to Zion, and the rebuilding of the Temple; and, not surprisingly, about the coming anointed ones, the priest and the king.[57] Zerubbabel is the Davidic figure on whom the prophet rests his hopes for the rebuilding of the Temple, despite all opposition; and, to symbolize that opposition, he uses the image of the great mountain, perhaps (as in other passages in Zechariah 1—8) echoing Isaiah 40, which speaks of the mountains and hills being flattened at the coming of YHWH:

> He said to me, 'This is the word of YHWH to Zerubbabel: Not by might, nor by power, but by my spirit, says YHWH of hosts. What are you, O great mountain? Before Zerubbabel you shall become a plain; and he shall bring out the top stone amid shouts of "Grace, grace to it!"'[58]

I suggest, therefore, that the saying about the mountain has a double thrust. First, it emphasizes that Jesus' action signified the overthrow of the Temple; second, it pointed to Jesus as the one who would at last do what Zerubbabel was supposed to do, that is, to be the true anointed one who would build the true Temple. Whatever the 'mountain' may have signified in Zechariah's

---

[54] So Meyer 1979, 200-2; 1989, 165 (discussing earlier work by Jeremias); 1992a, 72; against Gundry 1993, 899f., on which see above, n.20.

[55] Mt. 21.18-22/Mk. 11.12-14, 20-6. Cf. above, 421f.

[56] Mk. 11.23; abbrev. in Mt. 21.21.

[57] cf., recently, Collins 1995, 30, with other refs.

[58] Zech. 4.6-7; cf. Isa. 40.4; 42.16.

prophecy, it was clearly something that stood in the way of the building of the Temple.[59] Thus, in Jesus' riddle, (a) the present Temple is seen as in opposition to the true one, (b) the present Temple will be destroyed, to make way for the true one, and (c) Jesus is the true anointed one, who will bring out the top stone of the building and thus complete it. Once again, the Temple-action lays claim to royalty.

(c) John the Baptist

The same is true of another riddle which, in all three synoptics, follows close upon the Temple-incident. Jesus is asked a double question: by what authority does he do these things, and who gave him this authority? This is obviously a question about Messiahship. Someone doing what Jesus was doing provokes the thought that he is acting as a would-be Messiah; if so, he is presumably claiming that YHWH has given him this authority.

Jesus replies with a riddle about John the Baptist.[60] Was he sent from heaven – in other words, was he a true prophet – or was he simply another human being without divine authorization?[61] This reply, as the evangelists point out, functioned as a trick counter-question: whichever answer Jesus' interlocutors gave would land them in difficulties. But Jesus' riddle goes deeper than a mere verbal fencing-match.[62] To understand its full thrust, we need to bring into the discussion the other place where John features prominently in Jesus' discourse.

In the period when John was still alive but in prison, and Jesus was already launched into his public career, John sent messengers to ask if Jesus was indeed the one he, John, had hoped.[63] Clearly Jesus could not have simply answered the question by saying 'Yes, I am indeed the Messiah.' Such a reply might or might not have satisfied John; it would certainly have aroused far too much excitement among Jesus' own followers and hearers, and might well have precipitated action from Herod. Instead, Jesus answered with an allusion to Isaiah. The blind see, the lame walk, lepers are cleansed,

---

[59] For various suggestions, cf. e.g. Ackroyd 1968, 173 n.8; Smith 1984, 206.

[60] Mt. 21.23-7/Mk. 11.27-33/Lk. 20.1-8.

[61] On the phrase 'from men' as the opposite of 'from heaven/god', cp. Gal. 1.11f.

[62] Rightly, e.g. Fitzmyer 1985, 1273; Kim 1987b; against e.g. Gundry 1993, 667: 'The whole dialogue has to do with nothing deeper than saving or losing face.' Gundry does say, however (669), that Jesus' authority to cleanse the Temple is supported by John's testimony to him as 'the Stronger One'.

[63] Mt. 11.2-19/Lk. 7.18-35; cf. *Thom.* 46, 78. On this see, in addition to the commentaries, Riesner 1984 [1981], 299-301. 4Q521 (GM 394) offers a clear parallel: see below, 530-3.

the deaf hear, the dead are raised, the poor hear the good news. Blessed, in consequence, is the one who is not offended by Jesus in this work. The implications are clear: this is indeed the messianic age, if only you have eyes to see it. Jesus cannot say more in public. Any claim to be the king of the Jews, in whatever sense, will be a direct threat to Herod, as the following discussion makes clear.[64]

Jesus then speaks even more cryptically to the crowds. Why had they gone out to the wilderness, following John? To see a reed shaken in the wind? Was this the sort of royal movement one might have expected in Galilee? This is where, beneath the careful coding of Jesus' question, the full dimensions of the problem become apparent. Any claim, by John about Jesus or by Jesus about himself, to be the king of the Jews would of course pose a direct challenge, however absurd in terms of actual power, to Herod Antipas. Herod had chosen as his symbol, placed on his coins (instead of a portrait, out of wariness towards Jewish scruple), a typical Galilean reed.[65] (Unlike written texts, coins were a means, indeed the main means, of mass communication, and the symbols on them could function much as well-known political cartoons can in our own day.) Jesus' question, uncoded, means more or less: were you looking for another Herodian-style king? Surely not; you wanted something far greater than that, something more than simply yet another pseudo-aristocrat, lording it over you like a pagan tyrant. And you got it. John was a prophet; indeed, the greatest prophet that ever lived, the one of whom Malachi spoke, the last prophet before the final great day dawned. Well, then: if John was the last of the preparatory prophets, where are we now? The answer is clear, even though it can only be stated cryptically. The one who is least in the kingdom is greater than John. In other words, Jesus himself, the kingdom-bringer, is no mere prophet. He is the one for whom John, and with him the true hopes of Israel, had been waiting. If John is Elijah, this means, without question, that Jesus is the Messiah.[66] The whole discussion of John turns out to be a veiled discussion of Jesus himself. The comment about John to the crowds functions as a further, though allusive, answer to the question John himself had put: yes, Jesus is the one who was to come, and there is no need to look for another.

With this passage in mind, we can return to Jesus' riddle in Jerusalem. It points to a double answer to the question about the authority whereby Jesus had acted in the Temple, and where he got it from.

[64] This, I think, rather than a hypothetical rule forbidding the Messiah to announce himself (O'Neill 1995, ch. 3; cf. Flusser 1959, 107–9), was the obvious reason for the veiled and cryptic nature of Jesus' statements.

[65] cf. Theissen 1991a [1989], 25–59.

[66] So Mt. 11.14 (not in the Lk. par.), with the typical conclusion of 11.15 ('if you have ears, then hear!'). In other words, this is cryptic but vitally important. Cf. Mk. 9.11–13/Mt. 17.10–13.

First, Jesus was implicitly claiming, as in Matthew 11, to be the true successor of the last great prophet. Jesus had been baptized by John; he saw his own work and ministry as the sequel and fulfilment of John's; onlookers would think of his career as in some sense the sequel of John's. John had, in his own way, begun a kingdom-movement, independent of both Herod and the Temple officialdom. Herod had seen that John posed a threat; how much more did Jesus. Jesus' riddle says, as clearly as a riddle can, that the reason he has the authority to act as he has in the Temple is because, as the one to whom John pointed, he is in fact the Messiah. If John was a heaven-sent prophet, he was the last in the line: after him comes the king.[67] John's implicit counter-Temple movement has become, in Jesus, explicit. It has, in other words, become messianic.

Second, Jesus had been *anointed* by the Holy Spirit at the time of John's baptism.[68] He was thus in the same position as David between his anointing by Samuel and his final enthronement. He had the authority to act as he did because YHWH had given it to him, in and through John's baptism.

Any doubts about this interpretation of the riddle about John are dispelled by the further riddles that follow immediately.

(d) Tenants, Servants, Son and Stone

The next riddle, which must be taken as a further cryptic explanation of how Jesus interpreted both his own action and its likely outcome, is the so-called parable of the wicked tenants.[69] From the large number of relevant reflections that this parable might evoke there are three of particular importance for our present purpose.

First, the parable dovetails exactly into the riddle about John. In one sense, Jesus is the last in the prophetic line, coming to Israel to ask for fruit from the vineyard. In another, John was the last in the line; after the last messenger comes the son. In the light of 2 Samuel 7, which as we have seen was known and used in the first century with reference to the Messiah and his role in building the Temple, the natural reading of this is that the final messenger, bringing the last of the prophetic warnings, is also different in kind. He is the Messiah.

---

[67] If Mal. 3.1 stands in the background (cf. Mk. 1.2; Mt. 11.10/Lk. 7.27), this reinforces the train of thought.

[68] This is a fixed point in early Christian tradition about Jesus: cf. Ac. 10.38, with 4.27.

[69] Mt. 21.33-46/Mk. 12.1-12/Lk. 20.9-19/*Thom.* 65-6. For some wider reflections on this parable, cf. *NTPG* 6-11; for the voluminous secondary literature (not least, e.g., Snodgrass 1983) see the commentaries.

Second, the parable tells the story of Israel, culminating in judgment. As in some other parables, Jesus was taking a well-known biblical theme, in this case from Isaiah 5.1–7 and Psalm 80, and developing it further.[70] The retold story functioned as a further explanation of what he had done in the Temple, and, by its echoes of Isaiah, offered a justification for that action, suggesting that the Temple, in Isaiah's day and Jesus', invited prophetic denunciation and, ultimately, divine demolition. The master, who had sent servants and son alike and seen them all rejected, would come and destroy the tenants, and give the vineyard to others.[71] This refers most naturally to the forthcoming destruction of Jerusalem; Jesus' Temple-action was a symbol of the judgment to come. The spoken parable provided the larger narrative framework, drawing on Israel's prophetic tradition and claiming to bring that tradition to its climax, within which the acted parable made sense. The parable thus explained Jesus' action (and, by extension, though this may not be as much to the fore as is sometimes thought, the future action of Israel's god). His Temple-action was a messianic act of judgment.

Third, the parable concludes with the little riddle of the son and the stone. As it stands, this is a simple quotation from Psalm 118.22–3:

> The stone which the builders rejected
> has become the head of the corner;
> this is from the Lord,
> and it is marvellous in our eyes.[72]

The setting of this psalm-reference, however, immediately after the parable of the tenants (a setting which even *Thomas* has preserved) functions to make the quotation into a riddle within a riddle, a teasing question within the teasing question of the larger parable. Several strands of Jesus' understanding of the whole Temple-incident, and of his role within it, come together at this point.

1. The psalm in question is clearly designed to be sung by pilgrims going to the Temple; at this point at least (verses 19–27) it is all about building the Temple, celebrating in the Temple, and ultimately sacrificing in the Temple. Its original context (and we must remember that, with the regular singing of psalms, not least by pilgrims, such contexts would most likely have been as well known as anything in the scriptures) thus makes it extremely apposite within the setting of Jesus' Temple-action at the height of a pilgrim celebration. We should not forget, either, that processing into Jerusalem singing

---

[70] As Black points out (1971, 13f.), Ps. 80 is drawn into play not only by the vineyard imagery but also by the hint of royal imagery (taken as such in the Tg.) in v. 17, which aligns itself with the 'son' theme of the parable.

[71] Mt. 21.41/Mk. 12.9/Lk. 20.16 (not in the *Thom.* par.).

[72] Mt. 21.42/Mk. 12.10f./Lk. 20.17; cf. *Thom.* 66.

songs of praise was as much a 'political' as a 'religious' act. It was what the Maccabees had done after their victories, and their example was followed by those who won the remarkable early victory against the Romans in AD 66.[73]

2. More specifically, the idea of the 'stone' is closely linked with the idea of the new eschatological Temple. I am not aware that Psalm 118.22-3 was interpreted in this way by any of the varieties of Judaism of Jesus' day,[74] but Jesus' own varied use of scriptural rock/stone imagery in relation to the building of the new Temple, interpreted apparently as the new community of the people of YHWH, makes it quite likely that this was his intention here as well, even if the linking of this passage into this (widely attested) theme was original to him.[75] The other obvious passages are from Isaiah and Zechariah. Isaiah 28.16 speaks of YHWH's laying in Zion

> a foundation stone, a tested stone,
> a precious cornerstone, a sure foundation;[76]

Isaiah 8.14 speaks of YHWH himself becoming

> a sanctuary, a stone one strikes against; for both houses of Israel he will become a rock one stumbles over – a trap and a snare for the inhabitants of Jerusalem. And many among them shall stumble; they shall fall and be broken; they shall be snared and taken.[77]

Zechariah 4.7-10, which we examined a moment ago, challenges any opposition to, or obstacles in the way of, Zerubbabel's rebuilding programme:

> What are you, O great mountain? Before Zerubbabel you shall become a plain; and he shall bring out the top stone amid shouts of 'Grace, grace to it!' Moreover, the word of YHWH came to me, saying, 'The hands of Zerubbabel have laid the foundation of this house; his hands shall also complete it. Then you will know that YHWH of hosts has sent

---

[73] 1 Macc. 4.24 (specifying the refrain which comes, among other places, in Ps. 118.1, and throughout Ps. 136); 2 Macc. 15.29; Jos. *War* 2.554. Compare the chant of 'Great is Diana of the Ephesians' in Ac. 19.28, 34.

[74] On the messianic readings of Ps. 118 cf. Jeremias 1966a [1949], 255-61; the first messianic use of the 'stone' here, however, is Rashi (C10) on Mic. 5.1 (*TDNT* 4.273).

[75] cf. Meyer 1979, 183-202. Kim 1987a, 136-40 argues interestingly that various messianic passages in Zech. formed a link in Jesus' mind between 2 Sam. 7 and Ps. 118.

[76] Quoted in 1QS 8.7f. in reference to the eschatological community; cf. too 1QH 6.25f. Cp. Gärtner 1965, 133-7: 'it is a case of a concept which in certain late Jewish traditions was Messianic in character being applied to the collective unity, the community . . .' (134); the texts 'reveal the existence of a special exegetical tradition of the "stone" motif of Isa. xxviii.16, a tradition in which . . . the community is the precious stone and the tested wall of which Scripture speaks. This interpretation is linked, in the texts we have been considering, with a temple symbolism' (136). The Targum on the Psalms explains the 'stone' of Ps. 118.22 as the king or ruler; cf. further SB 1.875f. These 'stone' texts are brought together in 1 Pet. 2.4-8.

[77] This passage is read messianically in bSanh. 38a.

me to you. For whoever has despised the day of small things shall rejoice, and shall see the chosen stone in the hand of Zerubbabel.[78]

The possibility that this combination of ideas, and perhaps of passages, is not far from the meaning of the stone-riddle is strengthened by Luke's, and probably Matthew's, allusion to Isaiah 8 immediately afterwards.[79] The rejected stone that becomes the head of the corner looks very much, in context, like another riddle designed as a cryptic assertion of Jesus' Messiahship and a further explanation of his action in the Temple. Jesus is to be the reality towards which the figure of Zerubbabel was pointing. Judgment will be followed by a strange new rebuilding.

3. The stone which crushes its opponents is yet another biblical stone, this time from a crucial passage in Daniel.[80] Nebuchadnezzar's vision, which Daniel first recounts and then interprets, consists of a statue with a head of gold and feet of clay mixed with iron. A stone is cut out of a mountain, and it smashes the feet of the statue so that the whole edifice is broken to pieces; the stone itself, however, becomes a mountain and fills the whole earth.[81] The interpretation of the stone given in the passage itself is that

> in the days of those kings the god of heaven will set up a kingdom that shall never be destroyed . . . It shall crush all these kingdoms and bring them to an end, and it shall stand for ever.[82]

The passage was regularly interpreted, from at least as early as the first century, to refer to the Messiah, and to the kingdom that would be set up through him.[83] In the previous volume we saw strong evidence that Josephus at least regarded Daniel 2, 7 and 9 as referring together to the great coming day of the messianic kingdom through which Israel would at last rule the world. If these speculations were indeed current in Jesus' day, as seems highly likely, the 'stone' riddle attains a further dimension. Not only does the

---

[78] On the textual problems of the 'chosen stone' in the final phrase, cf. e.g. Ackroyd 1968, 172 n.5.

[79] Lk. 20.18; see the next note.

[80] Dan. 2.34–5, 44–5: explicitly alluded to in Mt. 21.44/Lk. 20.18. Mt. 21.44 is omitted by several MSS, but, as Metzger points out (1971, 58), it is not a simple copy of the Lk. verse, and is not in the most natural place for a scribe to have inserted it.

[81] Dan. 2.31–5. Cf. above, pp. 231f.

[82] Dan. 2.44. The Greek for 'crush' in the Theod. version of v. 44 is *likmesei*, the same word as in Mt. 21.44/Lk. 20.18.

[83] cf. *NTPG* 304; 312–14; cf. e.g. 4 Ezra 13.25–38, a passage closely linked with the messianic text Ps. 2 (cp. Collins 1995, 183–5). Note Josephus' embarrassment (*Ant.* 10.210) at having to deal with this text for his Roman audience. On messianic readings of Dan. 2 in the rabbis, cf. Jeremias in *TDNT* 4.272f.; cf. SB 1.877. On messianic 'stone' passages in Zech., and the close integration of this theme with other features of Jesus' actions and words in Jerusalem, cf. Kim 1987a, 138–40; on the Dan. 2 material, *idem* 142–4.

'stone' speak of the Messiah and the eschatological Temple; it also refers to the victory of this Messiah over the kingdoms that have oppressed the people of YHWH. What is most shocking in this passage – and would completely justify the immediate attempts to have Jesus arrested[84] – is the realization that, in this rereading of prophecy, the present Temple and its present regime were regarded as part of the collection of evil kingdoms. No doubt the Essenes would have agreed. If the revolutionaries read the Daniel text to mean that a world ruler would arise from among the Jews, and if Josephus could reinterpret it (however much with tongue in cheek) to mean that Vespasian would be hailed as Emperor while in Judaea, there is no reason why Jesus should not have reinterpreted it to mean that he was the true Messiah, whose kingdom would be established, and that the present Temple rulers were among the hybrid clay-and-iron feet that would be smashed in the process.

4. In case it may be thought that the interpretative thread has now been stretched beyond breaking point, we may note finally that the 'stone' is in fact also closely linked with the 'son' of the parable. The Aramaic for 'stone' in Daniel 2 is *eben* (the word is the same in Hebrew); the normal Hebrew for 'son', as for instance in 2 Samuel 7, is *ben*. It did not take much skill in biblical interpretation for the pun to be observed and exploited.[85]

The complex riddle comes full circle. The prophetic story of the rejected servants climaxes in the rejected son; he, however, is the messianic stone which, rejected by the builders, takes the chief place in the building. Those who oppose him will find their regime (and their Temple) destroyed, while his kingdom will be established. The psalm text indicates, cryptically, what will later become clear: when the owner of the vineyard acts against the wicked tenants, the son will be vindicated. The whole picture serves as a further, and richer, explanation of what Jesus had been doing in the Temple, and why. I submit that such an essentially elegant and yet richly textured explanation is far more likely to go back to Jesus – who, after all, had long planned and meditated his climactic symbolic action – than to any subsequent thinker or writer.[86]

---

[84] Mt. 21.45f./Mk. 12.12/Lk. 20.19.

[85] So rightly Black 1971, 12f., referring to Lightfoot and Carrington; Snodgrass 1983, 113–18; Kim 1987a, 135. Cf. 4 Ezra 13.36f., 52: the 'mountain carved out without hands' is a clear reference to Dan. 2.34, and is immediately linked with the Messiah, described as 'my Son', and referred to in terms of Ps. 2. The son/stone pun is presumably one explanation for the various messianic interpretations of Daniel's 'stone' in the rabbis (above, n.83). This oblique reference to Dan. 2, seen in the light of the subsequent Danielic references in Mk. 13.26 par., 14.62 par., seems to belong with the messianic reading of the 'son of man' in Dan. 7, on which see below.

[86] Indeed, had a subsequent writer been inclined to 'touch up' the parable, we might well have expected that, among other things, the 'son' would be vindicated more explicitly.

(e) Tribute to Caesar[87]

Jesus' implicit claim, that through his own work YHWH was at last becoming king, invited the question: how does this kingship relate to the rule of Caesar?[88] His further claim (made explicit in the Temple-action), that he himself was the true king, gave this question sharp focus. Would this be the moment when Jesus would be smoked out of his hiding, and reveal himself as a real revolutionary at last? Or would he in the end line up with the ruling elite in their heavily compromised liaison with Rome?[89]

Jesus' Temple-action is bound to have raised questions like these. His onlookers' minds were not *tabulae rasae*. Nor were they those of modern western democrats. They were stocked, kitted out one might say, with stories and symbols about kingdom, slavery, battle, and freedom. Among the older stories, of course, there was the exodus: Pharaoh's unjust rule led to the great moment of liberation. Among the not so old was the Maccabaean revolt: when the pagans seemed to have won, Israel's god acted. Among the very recent was the revolt of Judas the Galilean: loyal Jews should not pay taxes to Caesar, since they have no master, no *despotes*, but YHWH himself.[90] The two Judases, Maccabaean and Galilean, provide the echo-chamber in which questions of kingdom and freedom such as this brief exchange must be heard. Temple, taxes, revolution and Messiahship all went together. Here (the onlookers would think) was another Temple-cleanser, another Galilean.

The question of the tax-money was therefore not simply a trick, designed to frame a charge against Jesus but otherwise unrelated to his Temple-action. Jesus' reply, likewise, should not be read simply as a cunning avoidance of the question, still less as a way of shifting the discussion from 'politics' to 'piety'. Tax and Temple, Caesar and God, are the subject-matter.

---

[87] Mt. 22.15–22/Mk. 12.13–17/Lk. 20.20–6/*Thom.* 100; cf. *P. Eger.* 3. In Mt., this passage is separated from the parable of the tenants by Mt.'s version of the parable of the great supper (Mt. 22.1–14/Lk. 14.16–24). This too, in its context, is a royal and eschatological riddle, explaining Jesus' Temple-action further: the king has made a marriage supper for his son, but those who refuse the invitation will find their city destroyed.

[88] cf. *NTPG* 302–7. Malina & Rohrbaugh 1992, 137f. issue an important warning against imagining that the question, or the answer, can be analysed within the anachronistic distinction between 'politics/economics' on the one hand and 'religion' on the other.

[89] Here, as in Mk. 3.6, the Pharisees join forces with the representatives of the present Jewish would-be 'royal' house, the Herodians (cf. too Mk. 8.15). (Lk. omits the Herodians in all cases; Mt. has them here (i.e. 22.16) but not in the other parallels.) Wengst 1987, 195f. is right to stress that the Herodians would be strongly in favour of paying the tax, since their position depended on Roman patronage; he is wrong, however, to think that at this period the majority of Pharisees would have taken the same line (cf. *NTPG* 185–95). On the right to mint one's own coinage as a symbol of independence, cf. 1 Macc. 15.6.

[90] Jos. *War* 2.118; cf. 2.433; *Ant.* 18.23. Cf. *NTPG* 160, 172–3, 179–80.

'We know that you . . . show no respect of persons.'[91] This preamble assumes that Jesus is not afraid of Caesar, and so will give the revolutionary answer if that is what he believes. That, at least, is what the questioners assume the bystanders will be thinking.[92]

Jesus' pithy reply encapsulates the larger issues of his own doubly revolutionary kingdom-agenda. He began by requesting one of the relevant coins. This took the initiative away from his questioners, forcing them to reveal their own hand first. The coin bore an image and superscription which were, from a strict Jewish point of view, blasphemous.[93] The image was prohibited (even the cynical Antipas, as we saw, had stopped short of using an image of himself on his coins), and the superscription proclaimed Caesar in divine terms, specifically as the son of a god.[94] Jesus' questioners were thus themselves already heavily compromised by possessing such an object.[95]

Jesus then responded with the famous two-line aphorism: give to Caesar what belongs to Caesar, and to God what belongs to God.[96] This has often been taken to imply a neat division of loyalties: state and church, Caesar and God, held in a delicate tension.[97] Alternatively, the saying has been read as a wry, ironic comment, or, indeed, as a direct challenge to zealotry.[98] But there is reason to suppose that both parts of the aphorism are more subtle, and more closely linked to the issues of Temple, Messiah, and Jesus' whole kingdom-announcement, than those options allow.

Jesus' hearers would have been expecting some kind of signal that he was indeed in favour of revolution. It might be cryptic, but in many political

---

[91] Mt. 22.16/Mk. 12.14.

[92] So, rightly, Derrett 1970, 321, following Chrysostom.

[93] Hart 1984, 242 doubts whether Jesus was making this point; but the rhetorical force of the action, preceding the statement, suggests otherwise.

[94] Denoting Tiberius as the (adopted) son of the 'divine Augustus': cf. Hart 1984, 246f.

[95] cf. Malina & Rohrbaugh 1992, 256.

[96] Mt. 22.21/Mk. 12.17/Lk. 20.25/*Thom.* 100.2–3. *Thom.* adds 'and to me what is mine'; as Bruce (1984, 250 n.6) points out, 'god' in *Thom.*, of which this is the only occurrence, probably refers to the demiurge, resulting in an ascending scale (Caesar – god – Jesus). Cf. too Gundry 1993, 696f. Even the Jesus Seminar admits the authenticity of the basic saying (Funk & Hoover 1993, 102, 526 – adding the gratuitous and absurd suggestion that Jesus 'probably slipped the coin into his own purse while they were haggling over what he had told them'). On the saying, cf. esp., in addition to the commentators, Derrett 1970, 313–38 (with survey of earlier interpretations, 318f.); Hart 1984; Bruce 1984; Horsley 1987, 306–17. Derrett's suggestion that the case turns on alternative interpretations of Eccl. 8.2 is ingenious, but I think ultimately unconvincing (so Klemm 1982; Bruce 1984, 260f.).

[97] One example at random: a prospective candidate for the UK Conservative Party, writing in the London *Times* on 9 April 1996, cites the saying in this sense, and suggests that it is the only thing that Jesus would have said to any political rally.

[98] Fitzmyer 1985, 1292–4, arguing for a version of the last: Jesus simply lifts the discussion on to a higher plane. Cf. too Giblin 1971.

situations coded statements are all that one can offer. I suggest that Jesus deliberately framed his answer in terms that could be heard as just such a coded statement, with which he neatly refused the either/or that had been put to him and pointed to his own kingdom-agenda as the radical alternative.

The initial clue is found in a passage probably familiar to Jesus and his audience, if only through the regular celebrations of the Maccabaean heroes at the annual festival of Hanukkah. As the old revolutionary Mattathias was preparing to die, he made a speech to his sons, exhorting them to zeal for the law, and invoking the zealous heroes of old. The speech ends as follows:

> Judas Maccabaeus has been a mighty warrior from his youth; he shall command the army for you and fight the battle against the peoples. You shall rally around you all who observe the law, and avenge the wrong done to your people. *Pay back the Gentiles in full, and obey the commands of the law.*[99]

With that, Mattathias died. The sequel, as we have seen, is that Judas took command, led the revolt, fought the battle, defeated the pagan army, cleansed and restored the Temple, refortified Jerusalem – and established a royal dynasty that lasted for a hundred years. Through Herod's marriage to Mariamne, it was still in existence in Jesus' own day.

Mattathias instructed his sons to give back to the pagans an equal repayment: do to them as they have done to us. The saying is unambiguously revolutionary. The second clause put this in its wider context: obey the commands of the law. There was always a danger that revolutionary fervour would carry the zealous outside the boundaries of Torah. Earlier in the passage, indeed, the revolutionaries had discussed whether they should fight to defend themselves on the sabbath.[100] The Maccabaean saying, then, had a double thrust: your duty towards the pagans is to fight them, and your duty to our god is to keep his commandments. The former was subsumed, ultimately, within the latter. Zeal for YHWH and Torah meant revolution.

I propose that Jesus' cryptic saying should be understood as a coded and subversive echo of Mattathias' last words. His Temple-action, at the head of a kingdom-movement, carrying clear messianic overtones for those with ears to hear, and reinforced by the riddles about destruction and rebuilding, about John the Baptist, and about the 'son' and the 'stone', created a context within which his saying would have meant: Pay Caesar back what he is owed! Render to Caesar what he deserves![101] The *words* Jesus *said* would, *prima facie*, have been heard as revolutionary.

---

[99] 1 Macc. 2.66–8. The LXX of the last sentence (v. 68) begins: *antapodote antapodoma tois ethnesin . . .* The saying in Mt. 22.21 and pars. reads, in various different word-orders, *apodote ta Kaisaros Kaisari.*

[100] 1 Macc. 2.29–41. They decided that they should; cf. Farmer 1956, 72–81.

[101] cf. Derrett 1970, 319, at end of note 2.

When, however, the words are set in context, they acquire a second layer of meaning. Jesus was not in a classroom giving a lecture, or for that matter on a battlefield urging on the troops. He was facing a questioner with a Roman coin in his hand. Suddenly a counterpoint appears beneath the coded revolutionary meaning; faced with the coin, and with the implicit question of revolution, Jesus says, in effect, 'Well then, you'd better pay Caesar back as he deserves!'[102] Had he told them to revolt? Had he told them to pay the tax? He had done neither. He had done both. Nobody could deny that the saying was revolutionary, but nor could anyone say that Jesus had forbidden payment of the tax.[103] Jesus the Galilean envisaged a different sort of revolution from that of Judas the Galilean. He was not advocating compromise with Rome; but nor was he advocating straightforward resistance of the sort that refuses to pay the tax today and sharpens its swords for battle tomorrow.[104]

The second clause of Jesus' saying gives a further two-edged message. 'Give to God what is God's' evokes the call to worship the one true god, echoed in psalm and prophecy throughout Israel's tradition:

Give unto YHWH, you families of the peoples,
    give unto YHWH glory and strength.
Give unto YHWH the glory due to his name;
    bring an offering, and come into his courts.
O worship YHWH in the beauty of holiness,
    tremble before him, all the earth.
Say among the heathen, YHWH is king![105]

To worship in the Temple was also to celebrate YHWH's kingship over the pagans. The context of the quotation is instructive. The passage follows immediately from a standard denunciation of foreign idolatry:

Great is YHWH, and highly to be praised;
    he is more to be feared than all gods.
For all the gods of the heathen are idols,
    but it is YHWH who made the heavens.
Glory and majesty are before him,

---

[102] Cf. NEB's paraphrase of 1 Macc. 2.68: 'Repay the Gentiles in their own coin.'

[103] Of course, that was just what the chief priests did say, perhaps thinking of the 'Maccabaean' understanding of this saying: cf. Lk. 23.2. Wengst 1987, 58–61 argues that Jesus was opposed to all use of money; that he and his followers had given up earning money, and so lived outside the system, including the tax system, entirely. I agree with him that Jesus does not legitimate Caesar's empire; but his solution seems to me problematic in the light of e.g. Lk. 8.3.

[104] The message of the aphorism is thus more subtle, more in tune with the rest of Jesus' agenda (see esp. ch. 7 above), and actually, in its own way, more revolutionary, than is recognized by e.g. Horsley 1987, 316.

[105] Ps. 96.7–10; cf. too e.g. Ps. 29.1–2.

power and honour are in his sanctuary.[106]

Once again Jesus' saying demands to be heard on at least two levels. It could mean simply 'worship the true god as he deserves'. But in context, when Jesus is faced with a coin bearing a blasphemous inscription, the familiar train of thought encapsulated by Psalm 96 suggests that we hear the saying as a deeper challenge. 'Give to God what is God's'; in other words, give to YHWH, and to him alone, the divine honour claimed blasphemously by Caesar. This is not a summons to a detached piety. It is a call to renounce paganism, and to worship and serve the true god and no one else.

Both parts of the saying would most likely have been heard in terms of the orthodox scruples against image-bearing coins. Many of Jesus' Jewish contemporaries regarded such coins as so blasphemous that one should not even look on them, much less possess them.[107] The saying might then carry a note of disgust: 'the only thing to do with something like this is to give it straight back to its pagan owners!'[108] This, again, could be seen as simultaneously a grudging acceptance of the tax and a forthright condemnation of paganism. Paying the tax could, paradoxically, be seen as a necessary part of strict Jewish observance: anything to get rid of these blasphemous coins. No Pharisee or revolutionary would quarrel with that, at least in public.

The saying is thus not simply a coded protest against paganism (in other words, a coded call for revolution). It protests against *Jewish compromise with paganism*. Since Jesus regarded the drive towards revolution as just such a compromise, the saying functions as a further cryptic, riddling challenge to follow him in the real revolution, the real kingdom-movement, the worship of the true god which is parodied not only by the blasphemous worship of Caesar but also by the abuse of the Temple as a talisman of nationalistic ambition. If Tiberius Caesar is, according to the coin, the son of the divine Augustus, Israel is, according to scripture, the son of the creator God YHWH.[109] And, in the context of the 'son and stone' parable, the son of the landowner is, more specifically, the Messiah himself. Yes, Jesus is saying, there is a revolution about to happen, which is the true fulfilment of all your kingdom-dreams; but it will come about in a quite different way, through the

---

[106] Ps. 96.4–6.

[107] cf. bAb. Zar. 3.1 (of a C3 rabbi, Nahum ben Simai); Hippolytus, *Refutatio* 9.21 (of some Essenes). This is one aspect of the wider problem discussed in e.g. Safrai 1994, ch. 3.

[108] cf. Bruce 1984, 259.

[109] Ex. 4.22, etc. It may be that 'and to God the things that are God's' alludes, in part, to the fact that human beings in general are made in the image of the creator, and therefore owe him their whole selves (so e.g. Giblin 1971); but cf. the problems discussed by Gundry 1993, 700. Gundry's alternative ('the things of God' = the divine obligation to follow Jesus in the way of the cross (694)) seems to me, as does Giblin's proposal, too generalized for this quite sharply focused saying.

true self-offering to YHWH of the true Israel. Jesus saw himself as the true Messiah, leading the true kingdom-movement; Israel's true response to YHWH would be to acknowledge him and follow his kingdom-agenda.

The saying thus goes further than Mattathias' second instruction, which was simply to observe the law's commands. It transcends it in exactly the same way as do the 'antitheses' of the Sermon on the Mount.[110] The real revolution would not come about through the non-payment of taxes and the resulting violent confrontation. It would be a matter of total obedience to, and imitation of, Israel's god; this would rule out violent revolution, as Matthew 5 makes clear.[111] Jesus was summoning his hearers to the real revolution, which would come about through Israel reflecting the generous love of YHWH into the whole world. In other words, he was inviting them to follow him in his own royal movement, which was designed to bring in the kingdom in a way very different from that of Judas Maccabaeus two centuries earlier, or Judas the Galilean two decades earlier. Jesus' aphorism, like his kingdom-teaching as a whole, transcended the popular view of the kingdom, subverting the blasphemous claims of Caesar, *and* the compromises of the present Temple hierarchy, *and* the dreams of the revolutionaries.

This riddle, then, relates very closely to its context, in which Jesus' Temple-action was intended, and perceived, as an implicit royal claim.[112] But it could not be reduced to standard terms. Thinking to overthrow Caesar in the name of YHWH and his Torah, the revolutionaries were, in Jesus' view, using Caesar's own weapons. They were the real compromisers. He was claiming the high ground: Render to God that which is God's.

(f) David's Lord and David's Son

The final explicitly royal riddle in Mark 12 and its parallels is found, unusually, in a question put by Jesus himself, to which his interlocutors do not have an answer. If the preceding passages are read, as they often are, as though neither they nor the Temple-incident have any royal connotations, this question bursts upon the reader as a *non sequitur*. But if the sequence of riddles which it concludes do indeed possess, as I have argued, a more or less consistent Messiah-and-Temple theme,[113] it fits very naturally:

[110] Mt. 5.21-48: cf. above, 289-91.

[111] Mt. 5.38-48; cf. above, 290f.

[112] Hence, again, the relevance of Lk. 23.2: Jesus was forbidding the payment of taxes, and giving himself out as Messiah. Luke's reader knows that this is not strictly true, or not in the sense that Jesus' accusers intended Pilate to hear; but they can also see where the idea would have come from.

[113] On Mt. 22.23-33/Mk. 12.18-27/Lk. 20.27-40, cf. above, 402. The discussion of resurrection relates more generally to the 'age to come', a revolutionary concept which the

> How can the scribes say that the Messiah is the son of David? David himself, speaking
> by the holy spirit, says
>> The LORD said to my Lord
>> Sit at my right hand
>> Until I make your enemies
>> A stool for your feet.
> David himself calls him 'Lord'; so how is he his son?[114]

The psalm (110) from which Jesus quotes refers to the enthronement of the
Messiah, to his successful battle against the kings of the earth, and to his
being 'a priest for ever after the order of Melchizedek'.[115] The idea of messianic enthronement belongs with a number of texts in which a figure, possibly messianic, is enthroned alongside YHWH himself. Psalm 110, interestingly, is scarcely referred to in our surviving Jewish texts from the period,
so we may be forced to the conclusion that its widespread use in early
Christianity goes back to Jesus himself.[116] Collins, discussing the recently
published fragment 4Q491, which also speaks of an enthronement among the
gods, suggests that the one who is enthroned may have been 'the eschatological priest/teacher', and says

> The claim that he has a throne in heaven is a validation of his authority, and serves the
> purpose of exhortation in the face of the tribulation of the eschatological battle.[117]

So what might Jesus have meant by asking such a question?[118]

There are two main ways of understanding Jesus' intention.[119] The first,
taken by several scholars, suggests that Jesus is denying that the Messiah is

---

Sadducees, insecure in face of popular desires for the kingdom, were anxious to ridicule.
Jesus' answer to them shows his reaffirmation: yes, revolution is on the way, even if it does
not look exactly like the current expectations suppose. On Mt. 22.34–40/Mk. 12.28–34, cf.
above, 286, 434f., and below, 566f.: the great commandment, when it is fulfilled in the new
covenant dispensation, will render the Temple redundant.

[114] Mk. 12.35–7/Mt. 22.41–5/Lk. 20.41–4.

[115] The phrase 'priest for ever', so important in Heb. 5—7, is applied to Simon Maccabaeus in 1 Macc. 14.41.

[116] For discussion of the use of Ps. 110 in early Christianity, see above all Hay 1973;
Hengel 1995b, ch. 3. Cf. also Juel 1988, 137-9, 162-4; Collins 1995, 142 (aligning this
text with Dan. 7, on which see below), 182. In his ch. 6, Collins discusses esp. 4Q491,
alongside such texts as *3 En.* 10.1; Dan. 7.9, 13 (with Akiba's comment that the 'thrones' of
v. 9 were 'one for God, one for David' (bHag. 14a; bSanh. 38b); cf. Segal 1977, 48f.;
Hengel 1995b, 194-6); *1 En.* 62.5; 69.27, 29; 108.12, etc.; *T. Abr.* 13.1-4; *Ezek. Trag.*
68-89. The absence of pre-Christian messianic use of Ps. 110 is confirmed by the fact that
O'Neill (1995, 112f.), who asserts that it 'must have played a prominent role before the New
Testament', cannot adduce any evidence for this, apart from a possible implication of the
LXX rendering of v. 3, and the possible (in my view, dubious) influence of Ps. 110 on
11QMelch. 2.10f. and *Ps. Sol.* 17 (O'Neill 71f., 96).

[117] Collins 1995, 148f.; cf. Hengel 1995b, 201-3.

[118] cf. too ch. 13 below.

[119] For a good discussion, and a third (unlikely) option, cf. Fitzmyer 1985, 1312-14.

David's son. The same person cannot (it is thought) be both David's lord and David's son, and, since the psalm speaks so clearly of the Messiah as David's lord, Davidic sonship must be excluded. Davidic sonship, however, is so clearly part of the messianic profile in Jewish tradition, going back to 2 Samuel 7, that it seems unlikely that anyone, even Jesus, would have attempted to overturn it with a single counter-text. Indeed, the Messiah-and-Temple nexus, which as we have seen informed Jesus' Temple-action and the subsequent riddles, is explicitly Davidic in its deep traditional roots.

The second reading understands the question to be proposing a drastic re-evaluation of what Davidic sonship *means*, most likely in opposition to the current expectations of a warrior king. But it would be strange to use Psalm 110 for this purpose; it speaks, in no uncertain terms, of the king defeating his enemies in a bloody battle. What is more, we saw in chapter 10 that Jesus *did* think he was engaged in a battle against the true enemies of YHWH and his people, albeit at a different level from the military battles envisaged by his contemporaries. There battle may be redefined, but this point is hardly implicit, let alone explicit, in the psalm as a whole or in the verse quoted.

The question points, rather, to two features of Davidic kingship which, like all these messianic riddles, help to explain Jesus' Temple-action. First, the Psalm goes on to insist that the king is also 'a priest for ever, after the order of Melchizedek' (verse 4): the king, that is, will supersede the present high-priestly regime. We know from Qumran, and from texts like Zechariah 3.1–4.14 and 6.9–14, that there was potential tension between the 'anointed' priestly house and the 'anointed' kingly family. If a would-be king acted in the Temple in such a way as to precipitate a confrontation with the present priestly regime, Psalm 110 was exactly the right text with which to claim legitimation for such an action.

Second, the psalm, particularly the verse quoted here, revises the messianic portrait *so that it included an enthronement scene*, such as we find in the Jewish texts referred to in note 116 above. One of the most obvious points of such a scene is that the one thus enthroned is the judge who will pronounce the doom of YHWH's enemies; Jesus is again explaining the source of his authority, the reason for his sovereign prophetic act of judgment. We are back once again in the tight nexus of Messiah and Temple. By posing this question, Jesus implies that he has gained his authority over the Temple not merely as David's son but, more particularly, as David's lord.

By itself, however, Jesus' question remains dense and cryptic. It needs, and immediately receives in all three synoptic gospels, further fleshing out, which we shall explore in the next section, and in chapter 14.

(g) Royal Riddles: Jesus and the Evangelists

Six royal riddles: at what historical moment, from John the Baptist to the church in AD 100, would they be appropriate? Only, I suggest, within the ministry of Jesus himself. Mark had neither need nor desire to tone down statements that Jesus was Messiah. Whether or not one supposes that his book originally began with what we now call Mark 1.1,[120] the first climax of his work is Peter's confession of Jesus as Messiah, the second is the identical word on the lips of Caiaphas, and his crucifixion scene is dominated by the theme of Jesus' Messiahship.[121] There are certain things that Mark prefers to leave implied rather than stated, but this theme is not one of them.[122] For Matthew and Luke, Jesus' Messiahship is a matter of celebration, not secrecy. The rest of the early church, as we saw, celebrated and announced Jesus' messianic status in a variety of ways. The only time when the cryptic, riddling nature of all these discussions actually makes historical sense is prior to the crucifixion and resurrection of Jesus.[123] Once again, we have double similarity and dissimilarity: the riddles make sense within first-century Judaism, but nobody else said anything quite like this; they are comprehensible as part of the backdrop to early Christianity, but do not make sense (that is, their riddling form becomes unnecessary) after Easter. They belong historically, in other words, where the synoptic evangelists place them: as Jesus' own cryptic but telling explanations of his Temple-action.

(iv) Temple, Messiah and Son of Man

(a) Temple Destroyed, Jesus Vindicated

So far in this chapter we have sketched a picture of Jesus' messianic claim, made symbolically in the Temple and cryptically in a series of riddles. What happens when we integrate this picture with Jesus' prophetic warnings against Jerusalem and the Temple (chapter 8 above), and his prophetic action against the Temple (chapter 9)? The answer is, more or less, Mark 13 and its

---

[120] cf. *NTPG* 390 n.67.

[121] Mk. 8.29; 14.61; 15.1–39.

[122] cf. e.g. Mk. 13.14.

[123] This point belongs closely with those noted at 397f. above about the purity debate in Mk. 7 and the divorce debate in Mk. 10. In neither case does either the evangelist or his source need to be cryptic; in both, the veiled nature of Jesus' comments, and the distinction between what could be said on the street and what could only be said 'in the house', make sense within, and only within, Jesus' own ministry. This argument thus goes beyond the suggestion of plausibility in e.g. Hengel 1995b, 41–58.

parallels.[124] We must now return to this passage once more, this time to see the way in which Jesus' Temple-action is here, too, explained in terms of his Messiahship. So closely do they belong together, in fact, that the destruction of the Temple – predicted already in symbolic action, and here in prophetic oracle – is bound up with Jesus' own vindication, as prophet and also as Messiah. In the eschatological lawcourt scene, he has pitted himself against the Temple. When his prophecy of its destruction comes true, that event will demonstrate that he was indeed the Messiah who had the authority over it. Mark 13.2 and its parallels thus makes explicit the meaning of Mark 11.15–17. 'There will not be one stone upon another that will not be cast down.'

When pressed for explanation, Jesus warns about possible spurious messiahs (13.3-6). He cautions, too, that his followers will be persecuted 'because of my name' (13.13). He introduces once more an explicitly Maccabaean note: 'When you see "the abomination of desolation" standing where it should not, then let those in Judaea flee to the hills' (13.14). The context of 1 Maccabees, described above, should make this clear: something will happen which can only be understood as a re-enactment of the Maccabaean crisis, in which the Syrian 'abomination' precipitated the flight of Mattathias and his sons 'to the hills', as the necessary prelude to their eventual victory, with all its would-be eschatological overtones, and the establishment of their royal house.[125]

Behind this in turn, of course, there stand three passages in Daniel. Taking them in reverse order:

> From the time that the regular burnt offering is taken away and the abomination that desolates is set up, there shall be one thousand two hundred and ninety days.[126]

> For ships of Kittim shall come against him . . . He shall be enraged and take action against the holy covenant. Forces sent by him shall occupy and profane the Temple and fortress. They shall abolish the regular burnt offering and set up the abomination that makes desolate. He shall seduce with intrigue those who violate the covenant; but the people who are loyal to their god shall stand firm and take action.[127]

> After the sixty-two weeks, an anointed one shall be cut off and shall have nothing, and the troops of the prince who is to come shall destroy the city and the sanctuary. Its end shall come with a flood, and to the end there shall be war. Desolations are decreed. He

---

[124] In what follows I shall refer only to Mk. For wider discussion of this passage, see ch. 8 above.

[125] 1 Macc. 1—3. For the 'abomination', cf. 1 Macc. 1.54; the 'flight to the hills', 2.28. Mark's note in 13.14 ('let the reader understand') shows (a) that he took the 'abomination' to refer to Roman invasion and (b) that he thought it dangerous to say so explicitly. Cp. Josephus' coyness about interpreting explicitly apocalyptic oracles which would be seen as anti-Roman (*NTPG* 304).

[126] Dan. 12.11.

[127] Dan. 11.30-2.

shall make a strong covenant with many for one week, and for half of the week he shall make sacrifice and offering cease; and in their place shall be an abomination that desolates, until the decreed end is poured out upon the desolator.[128]

These passages, taken together, clearly stand behind the warnings of Mark 13. Granted our whole argument thus far, there is no reason to doubt that they were used in this way by Jesus himself. They deal with the destruction and desolation of the sanctuary at the hands of the pagans, and in each case they highlight the cessation of the regular sacrifices.[129] Jesus, by temporarily stopping the sacrificial system (chapter 9 above), had symbolically enacted the Temple's destruction. The regular pattern, of Jesus explaining privately to the disciples what had been said or done cryptically in public, is here worked out on a grand scale. And the Danielic texts carry a clear messianic significance: the setting up of the 'abomination' is linked to the activity of the 'anointed one'.[130] The surrounding warnings of suffering and persecution fit the Markan context perfectly, where, once again, Jesus issues a solemn warning about 'false Messiahs' (Mark 13.18–20, 21–3).

This is the context in which we find the famous, and much controverted, passage about the 'son of man':

> But in those days, after that tribulation,
>   'The sun will be darkened
>   and the moon will not give her light;
>   and the stars will be falling from heaven,
>   and the powers in the heavens will be shaken.'
> And then they shall see 'the son of man coming in clouds' with great power and glory.[131]

What Ariadne's thread may we use to guide us through the maze of interpretation that surrounds this passage? We certainly need at least one. There is so much literature on the 'son of man' problem that one can understand those scholars, including Sanders, who say that they do not have a solution to propose; those like Borg and Crossan who simply remove the question from the study of Jesus altogether; and those like an Oxford colleague, better left unnamed, who muttered in a seminar, 'Son of Man? Son of Man? That way lies madness.'[132] I propose three guiding principles that will steer us away from the Minotaur and out into the light.

---

[128] Dan. 9.26f.

[129] Jos. *War* 6.93–5 records the actual cessation, in the August of AD 70.

[130] That Dan. 9, the passage in question, was read messianically in precisely this period, and associated with Dan. 2 and Dan. 7, was argued in detail in *NTPG* 312–19.

[131] Mk. 13.24–6. The quotations are from Isa. 13.10; 34.4; and Dan. 7.13f.

[132] Cf. Sanders 1985, 324, 411 n.8 (but see too Sanders 1993, 246–8); Borg 1984, 221–7; Crossan 1991a, 238–59. The literature on the phrase 'son of man' is notoriously vast and complex. Recent important studies, taking very different positions, and including a wide range of bibliography, include: Moule 1977, 11–22; Casey 1979; Hooker 1979 (cf., earlier, Hooker 1967); Lindars 1983; Kim 1983; Vermes 1983, ch. 7; Horbury 1985; Caragounis

We must grasp, first, the nature of apocalyptic language in general, and Daniel in particular. I set it out in detail in chapter 10 of *The New Testament and the People of God*, and restated it in chapter 8 of the present volume. 'Apocalyptic', I argued, uses 'cosmic' or 'other-worldly' language to describe (what we think of as) 'this-worldly' realities, and to invest them with (what we think of as) their 'theological' or 'spiritual' significance. (The parenthetical disclaimers in the previous sentence hint at the folly of trying to fit the hurricane of first-century Jewish theology into the bottle of late-modern western categories, with their regular false antitheses.) Isaiah 13.10 and 34.4, quoted in Mark 13.24f., speak of the sun being darkened, the stars falling from heaven, and so forth. In their own contexts these passages refer, not to the collapse of the space-time world, but to startling and 'cosmically' significant events, such as the fall of great empires, *within* the space-time world.[133] The dramatic and (to us) bizarre language of much 'apocalyptic' writing is evidence, not of paranoia or a dualistic worldview, as is sometimes anachronistically suggested, but of a creative reuse of Israel's scriptural, and particularly prophetic, heritage. We must never forget that first-century Jews, reading a passage like Daniel 7, would think of being oppressed, not by mythical monsters, but by real Romans. The content of such 'apocalyptic' plays right into the context of Jesus' prophetic ministry. Its language offers itself as the appropriate vehicle for the devastating message he had to announce.

We have been deceived, it seems, by the vividness of metaphor systems other than our own, into attributing to first-century Jews a belief which their actual writings and, equally important, their actual social, political, personal, cultural and religious behaviour all deny. Their expectations remained national, territorial and Temple-centred. Disputes of course raged between those who wanted the present Temple kept and cleansed and those who would have pulled it down and rebuilt it, according to the patterns of Ezekiel or the Temple Scroll; but no Jews whose opinions are known to us thought that their god was about to bring the space-time world, including land and Temple, to a sudden end. A historical understanding of apocalyptic, then, is the first guiding thread.

Second, we must do our best to understand how the 'son of man' figure in Daniel 7 was perceived by various Jewish groups in the first century, and we must read Jesus' so-called 'apocalyptic' discourse in the light of that, rather

---

1986; Hampel 1990; Hare 1990; Borsch 1992; Nickelsburg 1992; Collins 1995, ch. 8. Space prohibits debate with this continuing stream of discussion.

[133] Collins 1995, 105 argues strongly that the phrase 'the end of days' in the Qumran texts does *not* refer to the actual end of the world.

than locating it within the speculations of subsequent Christian and other readers. This can be attempted in three steps.

1. There is an impressive array of evidence to suggest that the Danielic figure of 'one like a son of man', though not necessarily 'messianic' in its original setting, was in fact read in this way, by some Jews at least, in roughly the time of Jesus.[134] What matters here is not the original meaning of the passage; nor the precise usage of a solitary Aramaic phrase in the second century BC or the first century AD; but, rather, the whole narrative sequence of Daniel (especially chapter 7), and the ways in which that narrative could be invoked, echoed or otherwise appropriated among Jesus' near-contemporaries.[135] Thus Daniel 2, 7 and 9, taken together, provided the messianic prophecy that, 'more than anything else, incited the Jews to revolt'.[136] 4 Ezra 11—12 picked up the whole narrative of Daniel 7 and used it in an explicitly messianic oracle, envisaging the Lion of Judah triumphing over the Eagle of Rome. *2 Baruch* 35—40 did the same, with the vine of Israel opposing the cedar of Rome. The so-called 'parables of Enoch' (*1 Enoch* 37—71), which used to be thought possibly post-Christian and therefore not relevant, are increasingly regarded as non-Christian; they reflect a different, but related, messianic development of the Daniel 7 story and picture.[137] Lines 68–89 of the dramatic poem of *Ezekiel the Tragedian* provide a further example of the same phenomenon. These texts do not seem to depend upon one another; they provide good, varied evidence of what appears a widespread expression of hope. The setting remains the national hope of Israel: YHWH would vindicate her against the pagans, rescuing her like a human figure from among monsters – like, you might say, a solitary but faithful Jew delivered from a den of lions. But at the centre of this picture we find the anointed king.[138]

2. If we presuppose *this* picture (as opposed to the various standard literalistic interpretations), then the sequence of thought in Mark 13 not only makes sense; it coheres closely with the messianic evidence we have studied in this chapter so far. Jesus in Mark 13 has already alluded to Daniel 9; when

[134] Collins (1993a, 304–10; 1995, ch. 8) argues that in Daniel itself the figure 'should be understood as a heavenly individual, probably the archangel Michael, rather than as a collective symbol'. I am not concerned to argue against this here, though the parallelism between Dan. 6 and 7 (cf. *NTPG* 294f.) may suggest that the issue is not so simple.

[135] In what follows I draw on *NTPG* 291–7, 312–20.

[136] Jos. *War* 6.312–15; see *NTPG* 312–14.

[137] cf. Charlesworth 1992b, 31, with further secondary refs., on the 'son of man' and 'Messiah' in *1 En.* 48.

[138] cf., similarly, Nickelsburg 1992, 141. Nickelsburg is surely wrong, however, to suggest that the judicial function of the exalted one is an idea foreign to Dan. 7, where the whole scene is precisely forensic, and where the 'one like a son of man' is installed as, so to speak, the executive officer of the central Judge.

we find, shortly afterwards, a quotation from Daniel 7, we are fully justified in assuming that this composite messianic picture is in mind. Nor is it simply a general evocation of vague 'messianic' ideas. The picture is very sharp: this Messiah-figure will bear the brunt of gentile fury, and will be vindicated. When we put this alongside Daniel 9.24–7, the complete picture includes the real end of exile, the final atonement for sin, the anointing of a most holy place,[139] the arrival of an anointed prince, the 'cutting off' of an anointed one, the cessation of the sacrifices, and the setting up of the 'abomination that desolates'. It looks as though the combination of Daniel 7 and 9 provides part of the major theme of Jesus' Temple-discourse, in the middle of which the clear implication is that the Temple's destruction and Jesus' own vindication, *precisely as Messiah*, somehow belong together.

The discourse as a whole then works as follows. Jesus has been asked about the destruction of the Temple. His reply has taken the disciples through the coming scenario: great tribulation, false messiahs arising, themselves hauled before magistrates. They need to know both that Jerusalem is to be destroyed and that they must not stand and fight, but must escape while they can. There will then occur the great cataclysmic event which will be at the same time (a) the final judgment on the city that has now come, with awful paradox, to symbolize rebellion against YHWH; (b) the great deliverance promised in the prophets; and (c) the vindication of the prophet who had predicted the downfall, and who had claimed to be embodying in himself all that Jerusalem and the Temple had previously stood for.

The only appropriate language for such an event – the only language that could do justice to the rushing together of themes which occurs at this point – is the highly charged metaphor and myth of apocalyptic.[140] The beasts will make war upon the son of man, upon YHWH's true Israel; the great Babylon will do its worst; and then will come the moment when the tyrant is overthrown and the true Israel is redeemed, publicly vindicated, shown to be the true people of the creator god. In other words, Jesus and his people will be shown to be in the right. Their claim will be proved true. The city that has opposed him (and them) will reap the inevitable result of choosing the way against which he had solemnly warned, the way of confrontation with Rome, of rebellion against the god of mercy and grace. Thus, in the vindication of the son of man, Jesus' people too will be vindicated: his angels, his messengers, will gather in 'his elect' from the whole world, as befits the people of the one creator god. This belongs completely within the framework of the

[139] Dan. 9.24: some translations have taken this as a holy *one*, i.e. the Messiah, but this is unwarranted (so Goldingay 1989, 260).
[140] cf. Caird 1980, 271 (the last sentence of the book).

Daniel 7 prophecy: when the 'son of man' is vindicated, all peoples, nations and languages will serve him.

3. As we saw in chapter 8, then, there is no suggestion, either from Jesus or from Mark, that the space-time universe is about to come to an end, or that a transcendent figure is about to come floating, cloudborne, towards earth. Jesus identified himself with the true people of Israel, and the Temple with the mainstream of Israel that stood over against him, whose destruction he, like Jeremiah before him, had repeatedly foretold. Mark 13.24–7 does not refer to a *different* event from the one predicted at the start of the chapter (vv. 2, 4). 'The sun will be darkened, and the moon will not give its light': thus might any Jewish prophet speak of a series of events which would possess, as we might say, 'earth-shattering' significance. 'They will see "the son of man coming in clouds" with great power and glory: and he will send out his angels, and gather his elect from the four winds': thus might any Jewish prophet after Daniel speak, to refer to YHWH's vindication of his true people, especially of the true Messiah, and the destruction of the forces that had opposed him and them. And thus, I suggest, Jesus could have spoken, and did speak, and with this intent.

All of this shows how unwise it is to rule out a reference to Daniel 7 in the sayings of Jesus on the grounds that such an allusion would designate Jesus simply as a 'transcendent' figure. The irony is (a) that Daniel 7 has been read as though its first-century readers would have understood it in this way, and then (b) that this meaning has been both wished on to Jesus by pious scholarship, eager to find vestiges of a supernatural glory for the incarnate son of god, and snatched away from him by less pious scholarship, convinced that Jesus could not have spoken thus of himself. The whole debate has suffered the consequences of a failure to read Daniel 7 as it was read in the first century. Thus far, the second guiding thread.

The third guiding thread is, more briefly, the argument of the present book to date. If Jesus really did act, tell stories, reorder symbols and answer the key questions in the way we studied in Part II, then he would naturally have spoken of the Temple's destruction more explicitly, with his close followers and away from the crowds, in language which made it clear that he regarded Herod's Temple, and the regime of Caiaphas and his family, as part of the problem, part of the exilic state of the people of YHWH, rather than as part of the solution. It also makes sense to suppose that, in prophesying the Temple's downfall in symbolic act and solemn oracle, he regarded himself as the one with authority over the Temple, that is, the true Messiah. Taking the argument forward from this point involves recognizing the inner coherence of the whole picture – once, that is, we learn to read the language of apocalyptic, and the coded phrase 'son of man', in a way that is credible within the turbulent world of first-century Jewish kingdom-aspirations.

Plaited together (Ariadne's pigtail, perhaps, rather than Ariadne's thread), these three lines of thought lead us safely away from the never-ending speculation about future would-be 'apocalyptic' figures, such as the supposed 'heavenly son of man' who would 'come' – i.e. 'return', downwards to earth, on a literal cloud. This monstrosity, much beloved (though for different reasons) by both fundamentalists and would-be 'critical' scholars, can be left behind, appropriately enough, in the centre of his mythological maze, where he will no doubt continue to lure unwary travellers to a doom consisting of endless footnotes and ever-increasing epicycles of hypothetical and unprovable *Traditionsgeschichte*. The truly 'apocalyptic' 'son of man' has nothing to do with such a figure. Within the historical world of the first century, Daniel was read as a revolutionary kingdom-of-god text, in which Israel's true representative(s) would be vindicated after their trial and suffering at the hands of the pagans. Jesus, as part of his prophetic work of announcing the kingdom, aligned himself with the 'people of the saints of the most high', that is, with the 'one like a son of man'. In other words, he regarded himself as the one who summed up Israel's vocation and destiny in himself. He was the one in and through whom the real 'return from exile' would come about, indeed, was already coming about. He was the Messiah.

Equally, there is no need to collapse all 'son of man' sayings into the category expounded and indeed popularized by Geza Vermes in particular, namely the 'circumlocutory' use in which 'son of man' merely means 'I', or perhaps 'someone in my position'.[141] This circumlocutory use may indeed have been well known.[142] Jesus himself may have used it on occasion; it may well be the meaning of the phrase in some other passages in the gospels.[143] But we have now established a larger picture than is usual for the interpretation of Mark 13; within that larger picture, we may propose that Jesus could and did reuse Daniel 7, in a way perfectly credible within the first century, to refer to his own coming messianic vindication. Even if Jesus did sometimes use the phrase as a circumlocution, this, in and of itself, has nothing whatever to say about the likelihood or otherwise of his also making more

[141] Vermes 1967, 1973, 1983; Lindars 1983; and others since (cf. e.g. the debate between Bauckham 1985 and Lindars 1985). A balanced position is offered by Collins 1995, 173–5.

[142] Though some still question this: e.g. Fitzmyer 1979; Borsch 1992, 132–5.

[143] e.g. Mt. 8.20/Lk. 9.58 ('foxes have holes; birds have nests; but "the son of man" has nowhere to lay his head'); Mt. 11.19/Lk. 7.34 ('the "son of man" comes eating and drinking'); Mt. 16.13 ('Who do people say that "the son of man" is?', where the pars. in Mk. 8.27/Lk. 9.18 simply have 'I'). But not all the relevant passages work as well (so Caird 1980, 139).

explicit use of Daniel 7, in its wider settings both within Daniel (i.e. including chapters 2 and 9) and within the rereadings of Daniel that took place in the first century. If, as Vermes has to allow, the very early church could have made the link between the Aramaic circumlocution and the Danielic theme of Israel's suffering and vindication, there is no reason why Jesus himself should not have done so as well.[144]

Finally, there is no need to suggest, as has been done often enough since Wrede at least, that Jesus could not, or would not, have referred to himself as the 'son of man', on the grounds that the phrase carries so many overtones of incarnational or trinitarian theology that it becomes unthinkable. My argument so far is that the phrase, with its Danielic associations, would have referred first and foremost to the anointed king through whom YHWH would defeat the pagans. One can quite easily imagine it being predicated of (say) Bar-Kochba.

I come back to where I began.[145] We must not confuse *literary* 'representation' with either *sociological* or *metaphysical* 'representation', or any of these with metaphysical *identification*. At the *literary* level, 'one like a son of man' in Daniel 7 represents 'the people of the saints of the most high'. The phrase 'one like a son of man' thus *refers to* 'the people of the saints of the most high', and *invests* them, by means of apocalyptic imagery, with the status of being the truly human ones who will be exalted over the 'beasts'. As this text was read by suffering Jews in Jesus' day, the 'son of man' became identified as the anointed Messiah; he, of course, would 'represent' the true Israel in the *sociological* sense, standing in her place and fighting her great battle. At a quite different (though, confusingly, still related) level, the language of apocalyptic can suggest a *metaphysical* 'representation': the earthly realm has its counterparts in the heavenly realm. From one point of view, the heavenly court-scene in Daniel 7 functions in this way. The 'heavenly' reality is the vindication, by the 'Ancient of Days', of the 'son of man' over the 'beasts'; this corresponds to the earthly reality, that Israel is suffering at the hands of the pagans, and will be vindicated by her god. To suppose that this would have automatically meant, to a first-century Jew, that Israel, or her human leader, actually *was* a 'heavenly' or 'transcendent' being is to run the risk of a serious category mistake. That is not to say that the categories could not be fused together in new ways: only that to object to Jesus speaking of himself in 'son of man' language taken from Daniel 7, on the grounds that this would involve him in declaring himself to be, unequivocally, 'a transcendent being', misses the point. The

---

[144] Cf. Caird 1980, 139: 'what was linguistically possible for the early Aramaic-speaking church cannot have been linguistically impossible for the Aramaic-speaking Jesus'.

[145] *NTPG* 289–91.

phrase, in its context, *could* be taken in the first century to refer to the Messiah; I have argued that Jesus did take it, and use it, like that. If there is more meaning in it, yet to be uncovered, it is not clear from the Jewish context that anyone would have expected it.

One last argument about the historical probability of attributing this train of thought to Jesus himself. References to the 'son of man' in pre-Christian Jewish literature are few and far between, and there is no precedent at all for 'son of man' imagery being used *against the Temple itself.* This is a *novum* so enormous that we must postulate a context sufficiently strong to bear the weight. The early church defined itself over against non-Christian Judaism in a variety of ways, but is highly unlikely to have initiated this rereading of Daniel. The only context which will do – but which will do very well indeed – is that of the ministry of Jesus himself.

And why not?[146] As in so many other instances, we must be prepared to allow – it seems absurd to have to argue for it, but needs must – that Jesus was himself creative and original in his thinking, his reading of scripture, and his use of imagery. One does not need to possess, or even to postulate, a complete history-of-religions background for everything he seems to have said. In the present case we have exactly what history might lead us to expect: a framework within which a certain range of meaning is easily thinkable; a career in which, at point after point, Israel's story is being rethought and re-imagined around a new centre; and a mind, and vocation, which could remould biblical imagery in a way that, though new in its sharp focus, made sense within its context. That, I suggest, is what we have in Mark 13.26. Jesus' reuse of Daniel 7 in the Temple discourse constitutes, in its wider context, a large-scale messianic riddle to stand beside the miniatures in Mark 12. It underscores once more his action in the Temple and its significance. It draws on to Jesus, in a new and dramatic way, the vocation and destiny to embody in himself that great 'return from exile' which was one of the three main meanings of his announcement of the kingdom.

b) Jesus on Trial

The way is now clear for us to examine, head on, one of the most problematic passages in the whole gospel account, namely, the process that led

---

[146] cf. Collins 1995, 206: 'any explanation must allow Jesus his historic individuality. If he were indistinguishable from other eschatological prophets and messianic pretenders, he could scarcely have had such an impact on history.' Aune 1992a argues for a very early Christian prophetic 'vision report' which drew together Dan. 7 and Ps. 110; would it not be more obvious to suggest that Jesus himself was responsible for this prophetic insight?

specifically to Jesus' death. We shall have more to say about it in the next two chapters, from two further angles; for the present, we must examine its specifically messianic content.[147]

The so-called 'trial narrative' in Mark 14.55–64 and parallels has regularly been subjected to historical critique, on various grounds. (a) It portrays a semi-formal process, which according to the Mishnah should have taken place in the Temple, and during the day – not, as in the accounts before us, in the High Priest's house at night. (b) The story depends on the assumption, which has often been challenged, that the Jewish authorities did not have the right to carry out the death penalty (otherwise why, having found Jesus guilty of a capital offence, would they not have carried out the sentence themselves?). (c) It throws together several later Christian theological themes in an apparently random fashion: the question about the Temple is followed by the question about Jesus being 'Messiah' and 'son of god'; Jesus answers with a reference to the 'son of man'; the High Priest accuses him of blasphemy. Every link in this chain has been scorned as hopelessly weak, producing a succession of *non sequiturs*. (d) It is not clear, within the putative historical context, what it was that Jesus is supposed to have said that was actually blasphemous.[148] Behind all of these, of course, there stands the deeply contentious issue: who was responsible for Jesus' death?

The first of these problems ought not, in fact, to detain us for long.[149] The Mishnah, after all, consists of ideal regulations codified around AD 200, long after the destruction of the Temple and the suppression of the Bar-Kochba revolt, both of which radically altered the situation and character of Judaism. To suppose without more ado that these rules were in force nearly two hundred years earlier, in a different political, religious and cultural situation is like imagining, *mutatis mutandis*, that twentieth-century American laws were already in force under George Washington. (Even if Mishnaic laws had been already in place, we might beg leave to doubt whether they would necessarily have been observed in an emergency, during a major festival, with the chief priests anxiously aware of potential riots and of likely Roman reaction.)

The second question is equally well known: were the Jewish authorities legally allowed to carry out the death penalty?[150] If they had been able to

---

[147] It is out of the question to engage with the huge range of scholarship on issues concerning the hearing before Caiaphas. Brown provides thirteen pages of bibliography on this subject alone (1994, 315–27) and 233 pages of exegesis and historical discussion (328–560).

[148] For details, cf. Brown 1994, 315–560. Sanders 1985, 304f. brackets out Mk. 12 & 13, only to discover that Mk. 14 does not make sense alongside Mk. 11. Rivkin (1978, 1984) insists upon *two* Sanhedrins, one 'religious' and the other 'political'. For criticism, cf. e.g. Brown 1994, 347; for the more likely view, cf. Safrai 1974. Cf., helpfully, Sanders 1985, 311–17.

[149] cf. Brown 1994, 357–63, discussing earlier work.

[150] cf. esp. Brown 1994, 363–72, with other refs.

execute Jesus, the fact that they did not would show that they had not in fact convicted him of a capital crime, and that the Romans bore sole responsibility for his death (with the early church then shifting the blame back on to the Jews). The present state of the question would suggest, however, that the view taken in the gospels is more or less correct. There were occasional extra-legal, zealous acts such as the stoning of Stephen;[151] but officially the Romans had prohibited the Jews from carrying out the death penalty. In any case, the gospel accounts do not in fact shift all the blame from the Romans on to the Jewish authorities. Hardly any of the men in the story, including those who would shortly become the leaders of the young Christian movement, emerge with any credit at all.

Attention must focus, then, on the central problem of Jesus' appearance before Caiaphas. How are we to understand, historically, a story in which so many elements of later theology seem to be embedded? The answer, as so often with tricky historical problems, is that we must begin at both ends.

On the one hand, we have now uncovered plentiful evidence that Jesus, at the climax of his prophetic ministry, engaged in a powerful and implicitly messianic act, in riding into Jerusalem and symbolically enacting the Temple's destruction; and that he explained – if we can call it that – this action in a multiplicity of ways which, taken together, show that he was indeed working within a Temple-and-Messiah frame of thought. He was the true king, who had authority over the Temple. As such, he would be vindicated when his prediction came true, and the Temple was finally destroyed.

On the other hand, we know that, when Jesus was finally executed, the charge against him was that he was a messianic claimant. The title on the cross, whose historicity used to be challenged from time to time, is now generally accepted as historical.[152] Even without it, the crucifixion itself points us to the charge that Jesus was a revolutionary, an insurgent, like the two *lestai* ('brigands') crucified with him. The mocking of Jesus fits exactly: the royal robe, the crown of thorns, the reed instead of the sceptre speak symbolically of a messianic charge.[153] The explicit taunts of the crowd make sense within this picture, bringing together once more the Temple riddles and the messianic claim.[154] Merely threatening the Temple might not have been enough to have Jesus executed; the Essenes had been opposed to the Temple for many years, and the strange prophet called Jesus son of Ananias who

---

[151] Ac. 7.54-60.
[152] cf. recently Hengel 1995b, 47-54, against e.g. Conzelmann and Lindemann. Cf. Suetonius *Caligula* 32.2; *Domitian* 10.1; Cassius Dio 54.3.7; Eusebius *Hist.* 5.1.44.
[153] Mk. 15.16-20 par.
[154] Mk. 15.29-32 par.

proclaimed woe against the city during the war was beaten, but not killed.[155] Only a charge of leading a messianic movement will explain the scenario – which is the more remarkable when we remind ourselves that the earliest Christians did *not* follow the pattern of popular messianic movements, that is, they did not mount a military revolt against Rome. There can be no doubt, historically speaking, that Jesus was executed as a messianic pretender.

The historian is therefore faced with the question: by what steps did matters proceed from Jesus' messianic acts and words in Jerusalem to his 'messianic' death?[156] The gospel accounts offer us what is, after all, a relatively straightforward three-step explanation. The Romans saw Jesus as a would-be Messiah, and hence a threat to Caesar's good order; they saw him thus because the Jewish authorities laid this accusation against him; the Jewish authorities made the accusation because Jesus had first acted like a Messiah and then confessed to the charge. The essential simplicity of this sequence of events, its accounting for the data, and the light it sheds in both directions (backwards to Jesus' earlier actions, forwards not only to the crucifixion but to the nature of early Christianity) suggests that as historians we should abandon it only if we find another scheme which does these jobs even better. So far as I am aware, none which achieves this result has been proposed. The only alternatives are, in effect, variations on Wrede's 'consistent scepticism', which, like a lot of scepticism, goes hand in hand with consistent, and astonishing, credulity. Wrede's followers have broken up the simple account into so many pieces that scholars have gathered twelve baskets full of left-over scraps of tradition from numerous purely imaginary movements and circles in the early church. At this point, I suggest, a use might be found at last for the Enlightenment's scepticism about miracles, not to mention Ockham's razor.

Once we take up the argument from the point we have reached – Jesus' Temple-action, and the riddles and teaching which followed it – the sequence of events becomes, in fact, completely comprehensible. The hearing moves through four stages, each of which makes sense in itself and is coherent with the others.

First, there is – as we might have guessed – the question about the Temple. This takes up nearly half the account in Mark (14.57–61a). Though

---

[155] Jos. *War* 6.300–9, on which cf. Brown 1994, 539f.; Brown is wrong to say (547 n.46) that the Jerusalem authorities wanted this Jesus put to death. On violent opposition to the Essenes from the Jerusalem regime, cf. Brown 1994, 539, with refs. (e.g. 1QpHab. 9.9f.; 11.4–8; 4QpPs37 4.8f.).

[156] cf. Harvey 1982, ch. 2. The inverted commas are a reminder that a crucified Messiah, in Jesus' world, was politically and theologically a contradiction in terms.

Mark describes the witnesses as 'false', he has himself reported that Jesus said things quite similar to their testimony. The difference comes at two points. First, they accuse Jesus of saying that he would *himself* destroy the Temple; up till then, Mark has only reported Jesus saying that the Temple will be destroyed (though his prophetic action might have suggested that he would himself have something to do with it). The accusation sounds like a combination of a garbled report of something Jesus said and an inference drawn from his actions. Second, they say that Jesus claimed he would rebuild the Temple in three days. Apart from the parallel saying in John 2.19, the only other three-day sayings have had to do with Jesus himself, his death and his rising again.[157] Jesus' silence in the face of these accusations is comprehensible. They possess a large grain of truth, but it is mixed with so much confusion that to sort it out would require a complex explanatory discourse, for which this was hardly the moment.

The second stage is the question of Messiahship. For the High Priest to raise this now was utterly natural. If Jesus has been doing and saying things against the Temple, the natural implication is that he thinks he is the anointed one, the Messiah. If he will not answer the preliminary charge, he must face the central question to which it points.

Three things about Caiaphas' question call for comment at this stage. We must remind ourselves, again, that the question 'You are the Messiah, the son of the blessed one?' does *not* mean 'You are the second person of the Trinity?' or 'You are the incarnation of YHWH?' It focuses on Jesus as the would-be Messiah, spoken of as 'son of god' in such texts as Psalm 2 and 2 Samuel 7.[158] The question is clearly contemptuous: anything less like a Messiah than this mute and helpless Jesus it would be hard to imagine. Second, the form of the question (in Greek, and presumably in Aramaic) is, as I have hinted, a statement, only becoming a question with the implied question mark, presumably in the tone of voice, at the end. It is quite possible that Mark intends this, and even that Jesus understood it, as an ironic statement: the High Priest has unwittingly declared Jesus to be Messiah.[159] The riddles have been answered at last, and by YHWH's official representative. Third, the implicit relationship between a Messiah and a High Priest is unclear, but Jesus' claim was probably threatening. The High Priest was also 'anointed'; he had authority over the Temple; some of the Hasmonean High Priests had also been kings. Caiaphas' question must therefore be heard as inviting Jesus to a direct confrontation.

---

[157] Mt. 12.38–42/Lk. 11.29–32 (the sign of Jonah; cf. Mt. 16.1–4; Mk. 8.11f.); and the predictions in Mt. 16.21/Mk. 8.31/Lk. 9.22; Mt. 17.23/Mk. 9.31; Mt. 20.19/Mk. 10.34/Lk. 18.33; cf. Mt. 27.63.

[158] cf. Meyer 1979, 180.

[159] cf. Mk. 8.29, where the same words occur.

The third element in the scene is Jesus' answer. This again is completely comprehensible, granted the argument so far. Behind the three differing synoptic accounts there stands a common pattern. Jesus answers affirmatively, quite possibly by means of letting Caiaphas' words speak for themselves.[160] After Jesus' actions and riddles, it is out of the question to interpret any of the synoptic accounts as implying either reticence about, or denial of, Messiahship. Jesus must, at last, admit openly what he has said up to now in acted and spoken riddles. But he also predicts that he will be vindicated. At one level, this simply backs up the affirmation: 'Yes, and you will see that I am right.' At another level, it invokes two key messianic passages which Jesus has already used in interpreting both his Temple-action and his messianic claim: Daniel 7 and Psalm 110.

The Daniel text, as we saw a few pages back, has nothing to do with a figure 'coming' *from* heaven *to* earth. Despite the widespread opinion that this is what it 'must' mean in the gospels,[161] there is no reason to suppose that on the lips of Jesus, or in the understanding of the earliest traditions, it meant anything other than vindication. It speaks of exaltation: of one who, representing 'the people of the saints of the most high', is raised up from suffering at the hands of the beasts and given a throne to sit on, exercising royal power.[162] Jesus' reference to this passage has nothing to do, as used sometimes to be suggested, with Jesus admitting that Messiahship was a possible way of describing him, but that he preferred the more modest, and by implication humble and suffering, role of 'son of man'.[163] There is nothing particularly modest or understated about the vindication of the 'son of man' in Daniel 7.14, 18 and 27. Taken in conjunction with Daniel 2 and 9, the text belongs quite tightly within Jesus' whole understanding of his work, of the fate of the Temple, and of the coming of the kingdom. He is the true representative of YHWH's people, and will be vindicated as such. The psalm, likewise, speaks of the Messiah's enthronement at YHWH's right hand, as part of the successful war against evil. Both texts, as we have seen, had already been used by Jesus as part of his cryptic messianic profile, his own redefinition of what being the king of the Jews would actually involve. Both texts, taken together with their previous resonances still audible, provide an

[160] Mt. 26.64: 'You said [it]'; Lk. 22.70: 'You say that I am.' These seem to me more historically probable than Mark's simple 'I am'; cf. too Dunn 1992b, 375f. (though I disagree with Dunn's interpretation of this).

[161] cf. e.g. Moule 1977, 18 – suggesting that one must combine an 'upward' and a 'downward' 'coming'. This is ingenious, but, if I am right, unnecessary. Cf. too e.g. Witherington 1995, 230f.

[162] Dan. 7.14, 18, 27 (exaltation to kingly power); 7.9 (thrones, one of which the Ancient of Days occupies).

[163] e.g. Caird 1963, 94f.; Catchpole 1971, 226; Bowker 1977, e.g. 44; 1978, 139–69.

answer not only to the question about Messiahship but also to the question about the Temple: one aspect of Jesus' vindication would be the destruction of the Temple, and, by implication, of its present ruling regime. And both texts, taken together, imply that when all this happens the composite event will constitute the restoration of the kingdom to Israel, the liberation of the people of YHWH from the power of the beasts, the real return from exile.

Jesus' response, then, resonates with ironic power. Now at last, when it can no longer be misunderstood, he can retell the story of Daniel 7 in his own revised version. He is claiming to be the representative of the true people of God. Like the martyrs on trial before pagan tyrants, he is refusing to abandon the ancestral faith and hope, even if it costs him his life. Like Susannah on trial before Jewish judges who turned out to be no better than pagans, he stands before a court who, in his eyes, represent cynical compromise rather than loyalty to YHWH.[164] He therefore declares that Israel's god will vindicate him; and that vindication will include the destruction of the Temple which has come to symbolize and embody the rebellion of Israel against God, her determination to maintain her national exclusivism at the cost of her vocation.

Jesus is not, then, suggesting that Caiaphas will witness the end of the space-time order. Nor will he look out of the window one day and observe a human figure flying downwards on a cloud. It is absurd to imagine either Jesus, or Mark, or anyone in between, supposing the words to mean that. Caiaphas will witness the strange events which follow Jesus' crucifixion: the rise of a group of disciples claiming that he has been raised from the dead, and the events which accelerate towards the final clash with Rome, in which, judged according to the time-honoured test, Jesus will be vindicated as a true prophet.[165] In and through it all, Caiaphas will witness events which show that Jesus was not, after all, mistaken in his claim, hitherto implicit, now at last explicit: he is the Messiah, the anointed one, the true representative of the people of Israel, the one in and through whom the covenant god is acting to set up his kingdom.

Among the other implications which echo out from this explosive statement, there is one which Caiaphas surely did not miss. If Jesus is to be vindicated as the true representative of YHWH's people; and if he, Caiaphas, is presently sitting in judgment on him; then Caiaphas himself, and the regime he represents, are cast in a singularly unflattering light. His court has become part of the evil force which is oppressing the true Israel, and which will be

---

[164] Sus. 56; cf. *NTPG* 220f. Once more, this shows that Jesus' stance is *not* 'anti-Jewish', but is claiming, however controversially, the high ground of true Jewish orthodoxy.

[165] Mk., again, makes the point by having Jesus' prophecy of Peter's denial fulfilled in 14.54, 66–72, in ironic counterpoint to the guards' mocking request for prophecy (v. 65).

overthrown when YHWH vindicates his people. Caiaphas, the High Priest, has become the new Antiochus Epiphanes, the great tyrant oppressing YHWH's people. The Sanhedrin was playing the Fourth Beast to Jesus' Son of Man. The scene, already powerful in theological and political terms, has an added rhetorical dimension. The courtroom is turned inside out: the prisoner becomes the judge, the judge the condemned criminal.

The fourth and final element in the scene – the charge of blasphemy – is the hardest to understand historically. Luke, indeed, has omitted it, streamlining the account: his trial scene ends with Jesus admitting to a messianic claim, which is exactly what the court needs to take him to Pilate and present the charge which, ultimately, will result in Jesus' execution. Matthew and Mark, however, declare that at Jesus' statement of his own coming vindication Caiaphas cries 'Blasphemy!' Why?[166]

Three possible answers may be ruled out at once. Once more, 'Messiah' and 'son of god' did not mean, in Jewish speech of this period, 'the second person of the Trinity'. Most pre-critical readings of the charge are thus excluded – as is the idea that the Messiah was prohibited by law from declaring himself, so that when Jesus did so he had finally been trapped into breaking this commandment (though it is noticeable that in the synoptic tradition Jesus never openly declares himself until this point).[167] Also excluded is the idea that when Jesus said 'I am' (Mark's version of his response), this was taken as a pronunciation of the divine name.

Instead, there are four lines of thought which point towards the charge of blasphemy. The first, of course, is that Jesus has set himself against both the Temple and the anointed High Priest. He has sat in judgment upon the holy place and its appointed guardian. He has pronounced their doom. He will be vindicated, and the dwelling-place of Israel's god will be desolated. He has, in effect, replaced the Temple with himself. How can this be other than blasphemy?[168]

Second, Jesus will be exalted to sit at the right hand of YHWH. Once again, we should restrain ourselves from supposing at once that this makes him a 'transcendent' figure (whatever that means). The king was spoken of thus in another psalm, where the meaning seems to be simply that he is to be YHWH's 'right-hand man', his chief steward in ordering the affairs of Israel and the world.[169] The 'thrones' of Daniel 7.9 were said by Akiba to be 'One

---

[166] cf. Brown 1994, 520–47; see further below, ch. 13.

[167] cf. O'Neill 1995.

[168] Brown 1994, 538–41, while agreeing that opposition to the Temple could have been a reason for a capital charge, disputes whether it would be regarded as blasphemous. He does not, however, consider the extent to which Jesus was implying that he and his movement somehow constituted an alternative Temple.

[169] Ps. 80.17–19, itself a prayer for restoration after exile and the destruction of the Temple: 'Let your hand be upon the man at your right hand; upon the son of man, whom

for God, one for the Messiah' – and we must remind ourselves that *Akiba thought that Bar-Kochba was the Messiah*, the warrior king who would defeat the Romans.[170] To sit on the throne next to YHWH is thus itself first and foremost a *royal* status: just as YHWH ruled Israel and the surrounding nations through David, so he will now rule the world through the Messiah. The Messiah, in other words, will be to the creator god like Joseph was to Pharaoh, or Daniel to Nebuchadnezzar and then to Darius.[171] He will be, in other words, 'the highest of the kings of the earth';[172] but not, or not necessarily or explicitly, a 'transcendent' figure.[173] At the same time, however, Akiba's reading of Daniel 7 is one statement of the idea that there were, after all, 'two powers in heaven', an issue which occasioned serious debate in the century following Jesus' death.[174] This shows that, *within*, not superimposed upon, the reference to a coming great king who would be YHWH's right-hand man, it was possible for some Jews in this period to suggest that such a figure would in some sense share the divine glory – and for some other Jews to object to such a notion. It is certainly not beyond the bounds of possibility both that Jesus intended a reference to this idea and that Caiaphas understood him in these terms, and regarded it as blasphemous.[175]

The third point serves to reinforce this. Jesus' exaltation will be 'on the clouds', as in Daniel 7.13. Clouds, of course, signify theophany. Presumably they serve, in Daniel, as the sign of the presence of the Ancient of Days. At the same time, they indicate that when the 'son of man' is exalted to the throne beside the Ancient One, this too will have a theophanic character.

Fourth, and finally, we argued earlier that Jesus was regarded as a 'false prophet' who was 'leading Israel astray', and that this charge, long held by some of his opponents, lay underneath the questioning before Caiaphas.[176] It is not clear whether this charge of itself could come under the heading of 'blasphemy'; but if someone already regarded as a dangerous heretic, leading Israel to worship other gods, were to declare prophetically that the Temple

---

you made so strong for yourself. Then we will never turn back from you; give us life, and we shall call upon your name. Restore us, YHWH of hosts: let your face shine, and we shall be saved.'

[170] Thrones for YHWH and the Messiah: bHag. 14a; bSanh. 38b. Akiba's endorsement of Bar-Kochba: jTaan. 68d; bSanh. 93b; *Midrash Rabba* 4 on Lam. 2.2. Cf. Schürer 1.543f.

[171] Gen. 41.39–43; Dan. 2.48; 6.3.

[172] Ps. 89.27.

[173] One should not too easily distinguish at this period between 'political' and 'apocalyptic' Messiahship, despite a tradition of discussion which has done so; cf. Reinhartz 1989.

[174] cf. Segal 1977.

[175] cf. Brown 1994, 536–8.

[176] cf. above, 439–42; and Brown 1994, 541–4.

would be destroyed and that he himself would be vindicated in a show of splendour fulfilling Psalm 110 and Daniel 7, the combination of all these elements would be hard to describe *except* as 'blasphemy'.

This fourfold combination, I suggest, explains the charge of 'blasphemy' in ways which fit the historical context.[177] We shall explore the wider implications in chapter 13. For the moment our main point is to underline, for the purposes of the present argument, two features of Jesus' appearance before Caiaphas. First, the whole trial scene is inescapably messianic. Jesus is on trial for actions and words which imply a royal claim, to which he ultimately pleads guilty. Second, his claim of future vindication is itself messianic. Whatever other overtones may be present in his statement, the royal claim is made again in terms which carry the further implication that, when he is vindicated and exalted to his royal throne, this will be the overthrow of evil, the real return from exile. The trial scene thus draws together the key elements of Jesus' prophetic kingdom-announcement, and focuses them on himself. He is the representative of the true people of YHWH.

The whole scene before Caiaphas, then, confirms and draws to a climax the messianic picture already obtained from studying the Temple-action, and the riddles and discourse which followed it. It should now be clear, not only that Jesus was executed by the Romans on a charge of being a messianic pretender, but also that this charge was brought to the Roman authorities by the Jewish leaders, who had extracted from Jesus a confession of what they had already inferred from his actions: he did indeed suppose himself to be the Messiah. From Jesus' answer to Caiaphas to Jesus' death at the hands of the Romans there is a clear, natural line, with the word 'Messiah' written, so to speak, over its head. We are here on firm historical ground.

All this raises the question: was it only in his final arrival in Jerusalem that Jesus acted and spoke messianically? Was this a new idea and belief in the last week or so of his life?

4. Messiahship as the Secret of Jesus' Prophetic Ministry

(i) Caesarea Philippi

All three synoptic gospels report that, while still in Galilee, Jesus' closest followers came to regard him as Messiah. This makes sense, particularly, of the journey to Jerusalem: once Jesus had been seen as the king-in-waiting,

---

[177] Brown 1994, 544–7 lists aspects of Jesus' public ministry which may have been thought 'blasphemous'; the interesting thing about them, of course, is that they do not come up at the trial.

the natural decision was to go to the city which, since the time of David, had been irrevocably associated with Israel's kings.[178] Certain questions, however, remain to be addressed. What precisely did Jesus' followers say about him at that stage, and what did they mean by it? What led them to see Jesus in this light? And, most importantly, what did Jesus himself think, at that stage, about the matter?

The central scene is short and simple.[179] Jesus asks his followers about the general public opinion of him and his work; they tell him that he is thought of as a prophet. But who do *they* think he is? The Messiah.[180] Jesus sternly commands them not to repeat this to anyone.

The disciples, clearly, had some idea of Messiahship, and were keen to fit Jesus into it. The command to secrecy is not to be interpreted as a Markan trick, a subtle explanation of why the early church saw Jesus as Messiah even though nobody had thought of him in that way during his lifetime.[181] Nor is it to be seen as a denial by Jesus of any such status.[182] Nor, once again, is the talk of the suffering 'son of man', which follows this story, to be taken as a rejection of 'Messiah' in favour of a humbler title and role. Rather, it is an indication of what we have already seen: once Jesus was thought of as a potential or would-be Messiah, the movement would swiftly attract attention of the wrong sort. Herod had already heard about Jesus, and reckoned he was a prophet of sorts. If he had known more, he might not have been content with merely 'hoping to see him'.[183] We have already seen that Jesus spoke about Herod, and about John and himself in relation to Herod, in ways which implied an awareness that he was making a claim which Herod would

---

[178] For other movements which aimed to march on Jerusalem, cf. *NTPG* 171-7, with refs.

[179] Mt. 16.13-20/Mk. 8.27-30/Lk. 9.18-21.

[180] The synoptic variations at this point (Mt.: 'the Messiah, the son of the living god'; Lk.: 'God's Messiah') do not alter the basic point, which Mk. has reported in its briefest form.

[181] This line of thought, begun by Wrede nearly a century ago, has long outlived its sell-by date: cf. *NTPG* 391, with other refs.

[182] So, rightly, Meyer 1992b, 787, against e.g. Charlesworth 1992b, 12, who suggests that 'Get thee behind me, Satan!' was Jesus' response to Peter's saying 'You are the Messiah' (cf. Fuller 1965, 109). The theory advanced by O'Neill 1995, ch. 3, that no one except YHWH himself can declare someone to be Messiah, is purely speculative, based on the assumption of that which is then taken to be 'proved'. Nor is it the case that *Ps. Sol.* 17 and 4 Ezra 13.52 deny human beings the right to declare that someone is the Messiah; only YHWH can reveal it, to be sure (as indeed Mt. 11.27/Lk. 10.22; Mt. 16.17 acknowledge), but those who receive the revelation are not thereby automatically forbidden to speak of it. Jesus' response to Peter in Mt. 16.17-19 is normally regarded as secondary; but cf. Meyer 1979, 185-97, reading this, too, as clearly messianic.

[183] Lk. 23.8; cf. Mt. 14.1f./Mk. 6.14-16/Lk. 9.7-9; Lk. 13.31f.

find threatening.[184] Jesus, as we have seen, had some redefinitions of 'Messiahship' in mind; but he accepted the title itself. If he had not, his action in the Temple, and the riddles which surround it, would remain inexplicable.

Are there then signs, within the synoptic accounts of Jesus' ministry prior to the final journey to Jerusalem, that he was engaging, as he was to do in the Temple, in significantly messianic praxis? Are there any riddles that point in the same direction as the cryptic sayings which follow his Temple-action?[185] Once we have grasped the outline of Jesus' kingdom-proclamation as set out in Part II above, the answer to both these questions is Yes.

(ii) Messianic Praxis in the Early Ministry

Jesus' very action in announcing the kingdom could well have been intended, and recognized, as messianic. Assuming what was argued in chapter 6 above, that Jesus' kingdom-proclamation carried an explicitly Isaianic, return-from-exile sense, we may invoke a text from Qumran which identifies the Isaianic kingdom-proclaimer with the Danielic Messiah:

> The messenger [of Isaiah 52.7] is the anointed of the spirit about whom Daniel spoke . . . and the messenger of good who announces salvation is the one about whom it is written that he will send him 'to comfort the afflicted, to watch over the afflicted ones of Zion' [Isaiah 61.2–3].[186]

We cannot be certain how widespread this view may have been, or if Jesus himself explicitly shared it; but the text points to something about Jesus' proclamation, as we studied it earlier, which must now be brought out into the open. Jesus' whole announcement of the kingdom of god indicates that he believed that kingdom to be present where he was, and operative through him personally. He believed that Israel's destiny was reaching its fulfilment in his life, that he was to fight Israel's battles, and that he should summon Israel to regroup, and find new identity, around him. Israel's aspirations, that

---

[184] See above, 495–7.

[185] This question is answered negatively by Collins 1995, 206: the only episode he sees as suggesting royal Messiahship is the triumphal entry. See too Dunn 1992b.

[186] 11Q13 2.18f. (GM 140). Vermes 1995 [1962], 361 suggests that Dan. 9.25 was quoted in the lacuna. Other parts of the text quoted are missing, but the *pesher* interpretation which follows enables accurate restoration. It should be noted that in the previous line, i.e. 11Q13 2.17, 'the mountains' in Isa. 52.7 are interpreted as 'the prophets'; the messenger himself cannot, therefore, be simply an anointed prophet, but must be the Messiah himself, despite Collins 1995, 119 (and cf. Hengel 1995b, 40). Collins 205 questions (following de Jonge 1986, now in de Jonge 1991b) whether the gospel texts support this interpretation in relation to Jesus; the wider context I am sketching suggests strongly that they do.

there should be no king but her own god, were coming to fulfilment, and the way Israelites would discover that fulfilment was in the summons to follow Jesus. This announcement, understood historically, opens up the clear possibility that the proclaimer might be claiming to be Israel's representative king. To say, therefore, as many writers have done, that Jesus preached the kingdom but the church preached Jesus, or that 'the proclaimer became the proclaimed', as though this implied a falsification of the original message, is anachronistic and misleading. The style and manner of Jesus' announcement of the kingdom meant that there always was an implicit self-reference, a christology (of sorts) hidden within the announcement and the invitation, the welcome and the warning.

There are some signs that people began to pick up the implications. 'Can this be the son of David?'[187] It is inconceivable that Jesus, sensitive as he was to the subtleties and allusions of prophetic language and imagery, should have failed to ask the question of himself: if he was called to the vocation of kingdom-bearer, what did that say about his own role and identity? If he had considered the matter and concluded that 'Messiahship' was an idea which he had no wish to embrace, he would, we may suppose, have taken steps to make sure that his styles not only of teaching but also of action would *not* have corresponded with it. There are, in fact, some ways in which this was so, such as his refusal of the military option. But in general, as we look at this question, the answer has to be that he went on doing messianic actions, and backing them up, however cryptically, in words. Once again we are dealing with *paradoxical fulfilment*. The kingdom is present, *and the Messiah is present*, but neither looks like what had been anticipated. The kingdom-announcement opened the possibility that the herald was himself the kingdom-bringer.

When we link this with another Qumran text, the picture comes more fully into focus.

> . . . for the heavens and the earth will listen to his Messiah . . . For he will honour the devout upon the throne of eternal royalty, freeing prisoners, giving sight to the blind, straightening out the twisted . . . and the Lord will perform marvellous acts . . . for he will heal the badly wounded and will make the dead live, he will proclaim good news to the meek, give lavishly to the needy, lead the exiled and enrich the hungry.[188]

This passage finds clear echoes in the accounts of Jesus' healings, not least in one passage which itself carries clear messianic overtones.[189] By implication, the actions with which Jesus was inaugurating the kingdom were themselves

---

[187] Mt. 12.23; cf. 9.27; 15.22; 20.31/Mk. 10.48/Lk. 18.39.

[188] 4Q521 (Frag. 2) 2.1, 7f., 11–13 (GM 394). I agree with Puech 1992, 497 (against Collins 1995, 120–2, 205f.) that the text speaks of the royal Messiah.

[189] Mt. 11.2–6/Lk. 7.18–23, on which cf. above, 495–7.

signs of Messiahship. This is especially so if the exorcisms are seen as messianic, as has recently been argued.[190] Certainly they form part of the battle with the forces of evil which, as we have seen, was both part of Jesus' understanding of his own work and part of the wider Jewish understanding of the royal task.

There are, then, hints that Jesus saw his work from the start as in some sense messianic. These hints are powerfully reinforced when we examine Jesus' praxis in relation to his followers. The choice of twelve (with himself not being *primus inter pares*, but actually calling them into being, and in some sense standing over against them) indicates that he believed himself to be the one through whom the true Israel is being reconstituted.[191] Within that, the choice of three especially close associates – Peter, James and John – has clear echoes in particular of David, who chose three to be his special companions and bodyguard.[192]

Finally, we may return to Jesus' symbolic praxis of feasting with his followers, and of weaving stories around this practice.[193] This is regularly, and rightly, seen as a symbolic evocation of the coming messianic banquet, perhaps already anticipated by the community that awaits the final consummation.[194] Passages such as Isaiah 25, *1 Enoch* 62 and *2 Baruch* 29 are often cited as evidence of this theme; so too, though perhaps more debatably, is the Qumran 'Messianic Rule'.[195] Whether the idea occurs in the rabbis has sometimes been doubted, though the references in *Pirke Aboth* seem to assume it as common knowledge.[196] Outside the gospels, early Christian references to this theme are found in Paul, Revelation and elsewhere.[197]

Jesus' feastings, and the stories he told which reflect this practice, are to be read in this context, as are, perhaps, the accounts of extraordinary feedings of large crowds.[198] Such activity formed a vital part of his symbolic

[190] cf. de Jonge 1991a, 71, referring to 1 Sam. 16.1-13; 16.14-23; Jos. *Ant.* 6.166-8; *Ps.-Philo* 59—60; 11Q11.

[191] This should not be played off against the idea that Jesus himself somehow *represents* Israel, as is done by e.g. Witherington 1995, 230.

[192] 2 Sam. 23.8-17. The parallel in 1QS 8.1-4 is perhaps significant.

[193] cf. above, 431 etc.

[194] For this whole theme, cf. Priest 1992, with other refs. Chilton 1992b, 140 questions whether this theme is as widespread as sometimes imagined.

[195] i.e. 1QSa (the banquet is described in 2.11-22); cf. Priest 1992, 228f. A further scriptural ref. may be found in Zech. 9.15-17, in the 'messianic' context created by 9.9-14.

[196] So Priest 1992, 232, citing mAb. 3.17 (Akiba); 4.16 (Jacob, prob. late C2 AD) (I follow the numbering-system of Danby 1933). It would, of course, be unsurprising if post-135 rabbis screened out such messianic and celebratory ideas.

[197] cf. 1 Cor. 11.23-6; Rev. 19.9, 17-21 (for the background to which, cf. Jer. 12.9; Ezek. 39.17-22); cp. 4 Ezra 2.38 (part of the Christian section).

[198] Meals: e.g. Mt. 9.10-13/Mk. 2.15-17/Lk. 5.29-32; Mt. 11.19/Lk. 7.34; Lk. 15.2; and of course Mt. 26.26-9/Mk. 14.22-5/Lk. 22.15-20. Stories: cf. esp. Mt. 22.1-10/Lk. 14.15-24/*Thom.* 64; and the implicit narratives of Mt. 8.11-12/Lk. 13.28-9; Mt. 9.14-

praxis, as a sign not so much of a generalized social egalitarianism as of his implicit messianic claim. Taken together with the other evidence here assembled, it shows that Jesus was consciously following a 'messianic' programme throughout his work, not simply in his actions in Jerusalem. What is more, this argument advances across the swamp of historical scepticism not by means of the tightrope of isolated sayings, but on the broad and well-built causeway formed out of praxis, stories and sayings taken together as a whole. To the third of these elements – the sayings – we now turn.

(iii) Messianic Sayings in the Early Ministry

The first category of messianic sayings is especially striking. Jesus frequently likens his work to that of a shepherd, especially one who goes looking for lost sheep. He commands the disciples to go to the lost sheep of the house of Israel,[199] and explains his own work in terms of the same task.[200] The disciples themselves are to be like sheep or lambs;[201] they are the 'little flock' to whom the father will give the kingdom.[202] Jesus tells parables about a shepherd and a lost sheep to explain his own ministry of welcome to outcasts, and about a shepherd with sheep and goats to point to the coming crisis and judgment.[203] Mark and Matthew record Jesus as quoting Zechariah 13.7 ('strike the shepherd, and the sheep will be scattered') of himself on the night when he was to be betrayed.[204] Even if one or two of these passages were to be challenged historically, the near-total dissimilarity of this theme with early Christianity, which had quite other things to say about Jesus, is striking negative evidence that the theme goes back to Jesus himself.[205]

All this clearly evokes an important royal theme from the Old Testament, and indeed from further afield.[206] We may compare 2 Samuel 24.17, where

---

17/Mk. 2.18–22/Lk. 5.33-9 (cf. *Thom.* 104); Lk. 22.28–30. The festive meal in Lk. 15.23–32 (contrasting both with the 'riotous living' of 15.13 and the pigs' food of 15.16) is important as the answer to the question of 15.2: cf. ch. 4 above.. Crowds: Mt. 14.13–21/Mk. 6.32-44/Lk. 9.10-17/Jn. 6.1-15; Mt. 15.32-9/Mk. 8.1-10.

[199] Mt. 10.6.

[200] Mt. 12.11f.; 15.24.

[201] Mt. 10.16; Lk. 10.3.

[202] Lk. 12.32. Cf. Mt. 9.36/Mk. 6.34, where the evangelists explain Jesus' compassion on the crowds by saying that they were like sheep without a shepherd.

[203] Mt. 18.12-14; Lk. 15.3-7; *Thom.* 107; Mt. 25.31-46. Cf. too, of course, Jn. 10.

[204] Mt. 26.30/Mk. 14.27.

[205] Exceptions: Heb. 13.20; 1 Pet. 2.25; 5.4.

[206] cf. Collins 1995, 25: 'Throughout the ancient Near East, the ideal king was envisaged as a shepherd, who would rule with wisdom and righteousness.' Cf. too Vancil 1992.

David is responsible for the folly of the census, and the 'sheep', his people, must not be punished for his folly; 1 Kings 22.17, where the death of the king will leave Israel like sheep without a shepherd;[207] Isaiah 44.28, where the pagan King Cyrus is described as YHWH's shepherd; Ezekiel 34.23–4, where the false shepherds will be replaced by 'David, my servant'; and Zechariah 13.7, already mentioned, which, among other 'Davidic' oracles, speaks of the shepherd-king who is smitten and his sheep scattered.[208] In Jeremiah the image could be used for the ruling nobility in general.[209] The imagery is carried on in the post-biblical period, in passages such as this:

> See, Lord, and raise up for them their king,
> the son of David, to rule over your servant Israel
> in the time known to you, O God . . .
>
> His hope will be in the Lord.
> Then who will succeed against him,
> mighty in his actions
> and strong in the fear of God?
> Faithfully and righteously shepherding the Lord's flock,
> he will not let any of them stumble in their pasture.
> He will lead them all in holiness
> and there will be no arrogance among them,
> that any should be oppressed.
> This is the beauty of the king of Israel
> which God knew,
> to raise him over the house of Israel
> to discipline it.[210]

Jesus' use of 'shepherd' imagery, therefore, is comprehensible within this Jewish setting as an evocation of messianic roles and expectations, even while the style he adopted set him apart from other would-be Messiah-figures of the period. So, too, the image is comprehensible as something the early church remembered about Jesus, even though it did not make it a major theme within its own proclamation. We are on good historical ground in saying that this usage not only goes back to Jesus himself, but that it indicates a messianic self-reference in cryptic sayings that accompanied his implicitly messianic praxis. Jesus, in short, was constantly telling a particular *story*, in which the true king of Israel arrives to search for his wayward sheep. This is one sharply focused point of the kingdom-message, in which Israel is to be restored at last after suffering exile at the hands of the pagans and misrule from her own leaders.

[207] cf. 2 Chr. 18.16; Jud. 11.19; 4 Ezra 5.17f. This evokes also the picture of Moses in Num. 27.16f. For Moses and Aaron as YHWH's under-shepherds cf. Ps. 77.20; Isa. 63.11.

[208] cp. too Zech. 11.4f., 7–17.

[209] e.g. Jer. 2.8; 3.15; 10.21; 25.34–8.

[210] *Ps. Sol.* 17.21, 39–42 (quoted from Charlesworth 1985, 667f.).

The same conclusion can be drawn from two cryptic sayings in which Jesus evokes royal traditions to explain his own controversial actions. The first relates to the controversy about Jesus' followers plucking grain on the sabbath.[211] Challenged about his activity, Jesus responded with a parallel: when David was roaming the country with his group of followers, he had the right as the anointed (but not yet enthroned) king to override the normal code of practice. The parallel makes sense only if Jesus somehow believed himself to be in an analogous situation.[212] He had been anointed by YHWH in John's baptism; those hunting him were cast in the role of Saul and his men. The fact that the messianic implication is not drawn out more explicitly by the evangelists (who have no inhibitions about the idea) speaks strongly in its favour – as well as suggesting that the concluding phrase, 'the son of man is lord of the sabbath',[213] may also be intended to carry cryptic messianic meaning.

The second saying compares Jesus and Solomon. The setting is an announcement of judgment on Jesus' contemporaries, comparing them unfavourably with characters from biblical history. The men of Nineveh will denounce this generation, because they repented at Jonah's preaching, and something greater than Jonah is here; the Queen of the South will denounce this generation, because she came from far off to hear the wisdom of Solomon, and something greater than Solomon is here.[214] Solomon, the Temple-builder, is an obvious messianic model. To claim that Jesus is greater than him is to claim that he is the true Messiah; that he will build the eschatological Temple; that through him the Davidic kingdom will be restored. The context also suggests that this Messiah will be the one to whom the nations will come and bow in obedience: through his kingdom the prophecies of messianic worldwide restoration will be fulfilled.[215] The popularity of Solomon as the fictive author of various works (Odes, Psalms, Wisdom and a Testament) is eloquent evidence of his fame in the second-Temple period; for Jesus to compare himself with Solomon, to the latter's disadvantage, was to stake a definite messianic claim. Once again, we do not find any use made of Solomon within the early church outside these passages in the gospels.

In the light of these passages, we can suggest that Luke's placing of a more explicitly messianic statement at the start of Jesus' ministry is not so

[211] Mk. 2.25f./Mt. 12.3f./Lk. 6.3f. See above, 390–6.

[212] There is an interesting parallel to this in the explicitly 'Davidic' career of Simon bar Giora during the war: cf. Jos. *War* 4.503–44, with the discussion of Horsley & Hanson 1985, 119–27, and Horsley 1992b, 288, following Michel 1968.

[213] Mk. 2.28/Mt. 12.8/Lk. 6.5.

[214] Mt. 12.41f./Lk. 11.31f.

[215] cf. e.g. Ps. 72.8–17; 89.20–7; cp. Mt. 8.11/Lk. 7.29.

unthinkable as is sometimes supposed.[216] The passage from Isaiah 61 which Jesus quotes in the synagogue in Nazareth is unambiguously Davidic, and explicitly messianic: YHWH's spirit has anointed the messenger, to bring good tidings to the poor.[217] The announcement is, indeed, far more explicit and public than anything else until the Temple-incident, and this of course is bound to count against it historically; everything else about this stage of Jesus' public ministry treats the theme much more cryptically. This should not, however, be allowed to stand as a final judgment. It could be seen as the exception that proves the rule: if the reaction to Jesus' announcement was as violent as Luke suggests, it would actually help to explain the cryptic and even secret style that Jesus adopted from then on. However much the passage shows clear signs of Lukan editing, an initial messianic announcement, drawing on Isaiah and setting out a controversial kingdom-agenda, is perfectly consistent with the overall picture of Jesus' work we have explored throughout this book.[218]

It should be clear from this that Jesus' awareness of his work as (among other things) messianic did not suddenly begin on his arrival in Jerusalem. Praxis and stories from throughout his public career indicate that he believed himself to have a messianic vocation. Can we go further, and explore the roots of this?

(iv) A Messianic Beginning to the Ministry?

All the gospels suggest that we can. Human awareness of vocation is, no doubt, difficult to describe; nevertheless, in the Hebrew Bible there are various stories of individuals receiving a vocation. Prophets like Samuel, Isaiah, and Jeremiah are called by YHWH. The first two kings of Israel, Saul and David, and for that matter the rebel king of the Northern Kingdom, Jeroboam son of Nebat, all receive a divine call.[219]

All four canonical gospels offer us a 'call' narrative which stands behind the praxis, symbols, stories and teachings of Jesus' public ministry.[220] Any attempt to use this narrative in historical reconstruction is of course fraught with difficulty. But if the hypothesis we have assembled so far in this chapter has any plausibility, it makes sense to enquire after the roots of that vocation

---

[216] Lk. 4.16-30.

[217] The passage demands to be read as an echo of e.g. Isa. 11.1-10.

[218] For recent discussion, cf. e.g. Fitzmyer 1970, 525-40; Nolland 1989, 188-203, both with bibliography.

[219] 1 Sam. 3.2-21; Isa. 6.1-13; Jer. 1.4-12; 1 Sam. 10.1-24 (nb. this was a prophetic, as well as a royal, call: cf. 10.10-13); 16.1-13; 1 Kgs. 11.26-40.

[220] Mt. 3.13-17/Mk. 1.9-11/Lk. 3.21-2/Jn. 1.29-34.

of which Jesus seems to have been so thoroughly aware. Since Jesus' baptism at the hands of John is not historically in doubt; since Jesus referred back to John's baptism when challenged about his exercise of messianic authority;[221] and since at least two strands of tradition offer us a reading of that event in terms of Jesus' messianic vocation,[222] we may, without attempting to enter into details, suggest that it was at this moment that Jesus received either the call to act as Israel's Messiah, or, supposing he had already been aware of such a call, confirmation of this vocation. Psalm 2.7 and Isaiah 42.1, commonly regarded as standing behind the voice heard at Jesus' baptism, point at least in the first instance towards Messiahship as the meaning of the whole incident. Jesus' anointing with the divine spirit can be read as a deliberate allusion to such passages as Isaiah 11.2 (the Messiah's anointing with YHWH's spirit) and 1 Samuel 16.13 (where YHWH's spirit comes powerfully upon David after Samuel has anointed him). However much the text may have been influenced by post-Easter reflection, there is no reason historically to deny that at John's baptism Jesus became aware in a new way of a messianic vocation.[223] Nothing in the overall argument of the present chapter depends on this suggestion, but there is no reason, granted the rest of the argument, why it should be regarded as unlikely.

(v) A Prophetic/Messianic Ministry

All the lines of Jesus' proclamation thus point inward as well as outward. His prophetic message was not the imparting of abstract information or generalized concepts; nor was Jesus, so to speak, simply a disembodied voice; the message was about what Israel's covenant god was doing *within Jesus' own ministry*. 'If I by the finger of God cast out demons, then the kingdom of God has come upon you.' The kingdom was already present where Jesus was, and indeed *because* he was there. Being welcomed into this kingdom consisted in being welcomed into fellowship with Jesus: he was the one around whom Israel was being reconstituted, at whose word she could find forgiveness and healing. The welcome he was offering, and the anger that welcome provoked, made sense only *if Jesus was claiming in some sense to represent Israel in himself*. As a prophet, he gathered followers, and, in his mind at least, they constituted the renewed Israel, the returned-from-exile

[221] Mk. 11.27–33 & par. (above, 495–7).

[222] That is, at least Mk. and Jn.; it may be that Mt. 3.13–17/Lk. 3.21–2 represents a Q tradition partly parallel to Mk., though this is a highly complex question.

[223] For some recent discussions, cf. e.g. Witherington 1990, 148–55; Gundry 1993, 46–53 (both with other lit.).

people of YHWH. This whole scene, summed up here from the previous Part of the book, has encouraged us to ask the question, who did Jesus think he was? The first answer must be: Israel-in-person, Israel's representative, the one in whom Israel's destiny was reaching its climax. He thought he was the Messiah.

Jesus' actions, his message, his warning, and his welcome, make sense only within this framework. If he was not aware of this vocation, we would have to say that, for all his shrewd, quick and thoroughly biblically informed mindset, he was extraordinarily blind to the obvious. We have, however, good reason to decide otherwise. As E. P. Sanders says:

> What he claimed for himself was *tantamount* to claiming kingship . . . The hard evidence is this: he talked about a kingdom; his disciples expected to have a role in it; they considered him their leader; he was crucified for claiming to be king.[224]

I have argued in this section, building on the previous one, that we can go still further than this. Messiahship, and the identification with Israel-in-the-purposes-of-YHWH which it implied, was central to Jesus' self-understanding.

5. Conclusion: Jesus and the Return from Exile

Jesus, then, believed himself to be the focal point of the people of YHWH, the returned-from-exile people, the people of the renewed covenant, the people whose sins were now to be forgiven. He embodied what he had announced. He was the true interpreter of Torah; the true builder of the Temple; the true spokesperson for Wisdom.

All this constituted a striking claim. Not, indeed, to a kingship like that of the Hasmoneans or the Herodians, though Herod might have seen it as that; nor yet to a kingship of the sort aspired to by Judas the Galilean, Simon bar Giora, or Simeon ben Kosiba, though several of Jesus' followers no doubt saw it in those terms, and Jesus was executed as though that had been his intention. It was a claim to a Messiahship which redefined itself around Jesus' own kingdom-agenda, picking up several strands available within popular messianic expectation but weaving them into a striking new pattern, corresponding to none of the options canvassed by others at the time. Jesus' style of Messiahship was sufficiently similar to those in the public mind to get him executed, and for his first followers to see his resurrection as a reaffirmation of him as Messiah, not as something quite different. But it was sufficiently dissimilar to mean that everyone, from his closest followers through to the chief priests, misinterpreted at least to some extent what he was really

---

[224] Sanders 1985, 322 (italics original). Cf., however, Sanders 1993, 240–3.

getting at; and that the movement which did come to birth after his resurrection, though calling itself messianic,[225] cherished agendas and adopted lifestyles quite unlike those of other movements with the same label. If Jesus was a Messiah, he was a Messiah with a great difference. But Messiah was what he claimed to be.

Jesus' redefined notion of Messiahship thus corresponded to his whole kingdom-praxis (chapter 5 above), his kingdom-stories (chapters 6, 7 and 8), and his kingdom-symbols (chapter 9). It offered itself as the central answer to the key kingdom-questions (chapter 10). And it pointed on to a fulfilment of Israel's destiny which no one had imagined or suspected. He came, as the representative of the people of YHWH, to bring about the end of exile, the renewal of the covenant, the forgiveness of sins. To accomplish this, an obvious first-century option for a would-be Messiah would run: go to Jerusalem, fight the battle against the forces of evil, and get yourself enthroned as the rightful king. Jesus, in fact, adopted precisely this strategy. But, as he hinted to James and John, he had in mind a different battle, a different throne. It is to this dark theme that we must now turn.

[225] cf. Ac. 11.26. On the question of why this label was adopted see Cummins 1994, 210–12, in discussion with Taylor 1994.

Chapter Twelve

THE REASONS FOR JESUS' CRUCIFIXION

1. Introduction

Of all the questions regularly asked about Jesus, the question 'Why did Jesus die?' must be among the most frequent. It is certainly the most fascinating – and, as the researcher discovers soon enough, among the most frustrating. It has all the ingredients of a classic: dense and complex sources; the confluence of two great cultures (Jewish and Roman) in a single, swirling drama; characters who still leap off the page, despite the gap of two millennia; tragedies, and tragic ironies, both small and great; gathering stormclouds of philosophy and theology; and, at the centre, a towering but enigmatic figure, who, if the sources are to be believed, had the capacity to evoke anger and admiration in full measure. Small wonder that not only historians and theologians, but also artists and musicians, have returned to the subject times without number.

'Why did Jesus die?', then – the third of the key questions we set ourselves at the start of this book – goes to the heart of our subject.[1] The question 'why', in such a case, involves us inescapably in the study of human intentionality. Why did the Roman authorities consider it appropriate or desirable to execute Jesus? Why did the Jewish authorities consider it right to hand him over to the Romans as deserving of death? And, in the middle of it all, what was Jesus' own intention in the matter? Nor is the question limited by these three aspects. It is also necessary to ask: why did certain first-century Jews, within an exceedingly short time, refer to the death of a messianic pretender – not in itself an uncommon or remarkable event in that time and place – in terms such as 'he loved me and gave himself for me'?[2]

As the historical questions focus at this point, so also do the problems of method. Consistent scepticism once more faces consistent eschatology. Either we know little or nothing about what actually happened, or we know that the ultimate explanation lies in the area of Jesus' beliefs about the imminent

---

[1] See above, ch. 3.2.iii (106-9) for a preliminary discussion and setting of the scene.
[2] Gal. 2.20; cf. too e.g. Phil. 2.6-8; Rom. 5.6-11, and plenty of other examples.

climactic moment in Israel's history.[3] The sources present particular problems; even if Q were admitted as a serious historical source elsewhere in the synoptic gospels, it necessarily falls away here, since Matthew, Mark and Luke overlap.[4] At one level, the texts are full of theological and exegetical reflection; at another, of just the sort of eye-witness detail that suggests that the reflection was caused by the events, not (despite the sceptics) vice versa. After all, if a first-century Jew believed that the events he or she had just witnessed, and indeed taken part in, really were the turning-point of history, they would be unlikely to describe them in the deliberately neutral language of someone writing up an experiment in inorganic chemistry. Changing the science, to distrust the sources because they show evidence of theology and exegesis is like distrusting an astronomer's report because the observations were not conducted during the hours of daylight.

In particular, it must be emphasized that here more than anywhere it is worse than futile to try to separate theology from politics.[5] The tired old split between the Jesus of history and the Christ of faith was never more misleading than at this point. Generations of gospel readers in search of atonement-theology, or at least atonement-homiletics, ignored the actual story the evangelists were telling, with all its rough political edges, in favour of the theological scheme the story was deemed to be inculcating, or at least illustrating. More recent generations of historians, not least those seeking to straighten out dangerous half-truths, have seen the accounts either as nothing but theology (and therefore historically irrelevant) or, worse, as politically motivated theology (and therefore historically damaging). As the eighteenth-century split between these different spheres is increasingly shown to be a mistake, it is time to attempt to put back together that which should not have been separated in the first place.[6]

One feature of the historical/political/theological mix needs special comment. It has become commonplace to claim that the gospel narratives of the

[3] Scepticism: e.g. Crossan 1988a, 1991, 1994, and esp. 1995; Koester 1990, 216–40; 1992, following Bultmann and others, on which cf. Harvey 1982, 16; Hengel 1995b, 41–4. On scepticism in historiography, cf. Meyer 1979, 84f. Eschatology: Schweitzer 1954 [1906], 384–95; and e.g. Farmer 1956; Caird 1965; Wright 1985; de Jonge 1991a, ch. 3; and see below. On rationalizing views, the wry comment of Manson (1953, 76) remains potent forty years later: 'Jesus goes up to Jerusalem to give a course of lecture-sermons on the Fatherhood of God and the Brotherhood of man, and then becomes the victim of an unfortunate miscarriage of justice.' Alter 'lecture-sermons' to 'Cynic aphorisms', allow for a change in fashions as to Jesus' theme, and you have the Jesus Seminar in a nutshell.

[4] This is not to say, of course, that if Q did exist it could not have had a passion narrative; only that, in the nature of the case, we could not know if it did. Seeley 1992 attempts to suggest that Q did take a view on Jesus' death, but that this corresponded, not to Jewish models, but to Stoic/Cynic ideals of the noble death.

[5] See e.g. the protests of Borg 1984, ch. 1; Horsley 1994, esp. 395–8.

[6] cf. ch. 4.2 above.

trials and death of Jesus are strongly coloured by anti-semitism.[7] This, I believe, has not been established. It is of course true that the narratives have been read and exploited in this direction, sometimes devastatingly; but that is a fact about subsequent readers, not necessarily about the stories themselves.[8] When the stories refer to 'the Jews', subsequent gentile Christianity could all too easily forget that Jesus, his family, his followers, the first Christians, and some or all of the writers of the gospels, were themselves Jewish. Paul, whose own Jewishness emerges, often explicitly, with every sentence he writes, can speak of 'the Jews' in general to mean 'non-Christian Jews'.[9] The phrase can be used simply to mean 'Judaeans' as opposed to 'Galileans' and so forth (the word in Greek is after all *Ioudaioi*), and some of the occurrences in John clearly belong here.[10] After all, even the Hebrew Bible can speak of 'the Jews' in this fashion.[11] For much of the narrative we must now examine, the phrase is used by the evangelists to denote the Jewish *leaders*; and it was not only the early Christians who had a quarrel with Caiaphas and his colleagues.

One must therefore guard against attempting to reconstruct history by studying the much later effects of stories and events. To suggest that a story is biased, or to suggest that continuing to tell the same story is likely to perpetuate a biased and perhaps violent point of view, is not to say anything one way or another about its historical value. The fact that lurid tales of British atrocities have goaded generations of Irish republicans to continue their campaign of violence against British rule in Northern Ireland does not (alas), in and of itself, indicate that the tales were false in the first place. The social responsibility of the historian to his or her own day must be balanced with the professional responsibility to follow the evidence wherever it leads. Society is not ultimately served by suppressing truth or inventing falsehood. The stories must speak for themselves. That, I hope, is what they will do in the present chapter.

One further task must be attempted, in line with some recent suggestions.[12] The reasons for Jesus' death must not be tacked on as a separate issue at the end of a discussion of his overall agenda; we must at least raise the question as to whether the two were in fact integrated. It is of course possible that Jesus' death was in that sense an accident, having nothing to do with the

---

[7] e.g., recently, Crossan 1995.

[8] So, rightly, Moule 1987, 177.

[9] e.g. 1 Cor. 1.22; 10.32; 2 Cor. 11.24; 1 Th. 2.14. He can also use the phrase for Jewish Christians, e.g. Gal. 2.13.

[10] e.g. Jn. 11.7f.

[11] e.g. Jer. 32.12.

[12] cf. e.g. Meyer 1979, 218f.; Sanders 1985, 327–35; Wright 1985; Horsley 1994.

aims and agendas that he had been pursuing. But to take that line involves us in saying that *all* the sources are at this point *totally* wrong (as those who take this line readily admit), and that we must simply invent another narrative, however slight, to take their place.[13] But one should only resort to this desperate measure – the methodological equivalent of attempting to ski in bare feet – when all other solutions have failed. The plentiful literature on the topic suggests that we have by no means reached that point yet.

The method by which we may approach the threefold question – the combined intentions of the Romans, the Jewish leaders, and Jesus – must be the same as we have adopted throughout. We possess fixed points at either side of the question: in this case, Jesus' career as a prophet announcing the kingdom, and his death as a messianic pretender. We have seen in the previous chapter that these two overlap: there is a 'prophetic' strand to the hearing before Caiaphas, and there are 'messianic' overtones throughout Jesus' public career. We are in a position to study not merely isolated or detached *sayings* – which always tilt the balance towards sceptical non- or pseudo-reconstruction[14] – but *actions* and *events* which, freighted with symbolic significance, create a context in which stories and sayings can settle down and make themselves at home. In and through it all, we are looking once more for appropriate continuity and discontinuity both with first-century Judaism and with emerging Christianity, though to define precisely what that might mean in this case, ahead of the actual discussion, would be, to say the least, unwise.

Since we have already examined the trial narratives to some degree in the previous chapter, we can be reasonably brief now in covering the same material from a slightly different angle, thus clearing the ground for our discussion of Jesus himself.

2. The Roman Charge

Crucifixion was a powerful symbol throughout the Roman world. It was not just a means of liquidating undesirables; it did so with the maximum degradation and humiliation. It said, loud and clear: we are in charge here; you are our property; we can do what we like with you. It insisted, coldly and brutally, on the absolute sovereignty of Rome, and of Caesar. It told an implicit story, of the uselessness of rebel recalcitrance and the ruthlessness of imperial power. It said, in particular: this is what happens to rebel leaders. Crucifixion was a symbolic act with a clear and frightening meaning.[15]

[13] e.g. Mack 1988, Part III; 1995, ch. 3.
[14] As rightly pointed out by e.g. Meyer 1979, 84f.
[15] On crucifixion see above all Hengel 1977.

All this, though unpleasant, is not controversial. What follows, however, is decidedly so: Jesus was executed as a rebel against Rome. At least, this conclusion is controversial in most orthodox circles. Whenever anyone suggests that Jesus was some kind of a political rebel, the protests are long and loud.[16] The impulse to rescue Jesus from politics, or at least from the wrong sort of politics, may also lie behind the futile attempts to rescue him from Messianism. But the evidence surveyed in the previous chapter leaves us little choice on the last point, and hence on its corollary: when Jesus was crucified, the general impression in Jerusalem that day must have been that he was one more in a long line of would-be, but failed, Messiahs.

However, matters are not as simple as the normal revolutionary theories would suggest, either. There is good reason to suppose that, although Jesus' accusers handed him over, and Pilate executed him, on this charge, *both parties knew he was not guilty of it*, or not in any straightforward sense.[17] It is true that Jesus' kingdom-preaching must have carried, to all his hearers, some sort of revolutionary sense: if YHWH was at last becoming king, all other rulers, from Caesar downwards, would find their power at least relativized. But Jesus' constant redefinition of the kingdom, in praxis as much as in words, meant that anyone who had observed him closely would have been aware that he did not fit the same category as Judas the Galilean had before him, or as Simon bar Giora would do a generation later. And, though the chief priests and Pilate had not, perhaps, done their homework on Jesus very thoroughly, I suggest that they were both aware of some serious differences.

Pilate was not, by any account, a particularly competent or distinguished official.[18] His rule in Judaea was often provocative and bullying. Philo's description of him, though undoubtedly exaggerated for rhetorical effect, is worth quoting. He describes the incident in which Pilate placed golden shields in the Herodian palace, causing offence which was, for Philo, a foretaste of what would have happened had Gaius' plan to erect a statue of himself gone ahead.[19] He tells how a delegation of princes confronted Pilate, threatening to tell Tiberius what was afoot.[20] Pilate's reaction is revealing:

[16] cf. e.g. Hengel 1971; Bammel & Moule 1984, against Brandon 1967 in particular. Horsley 1987, 1994 and in other works attempts to rehabilitate a moderated and non-violent version of Brandon's thesis. So, in some ways, does Crossan 1991a. For the overtones of Jesus' crucifixion as a rebel, cf. e.g. Cullmann 1956, 6, 11f., 22; Farmer 1956, 197.

[17] cf. Sanders 1985, 294f.

[18] On Pilate's rule cf. *NTPG* 174, with refs. to Josephus in particular; Schürer 1.383–7; Brown 1994, 693–705, with plentiful refs.

[19] The description occurs in Philo's quotation (*Leg.* 276–329) of a letter ostensibly from Agrippa I to Caligula.

[20] Philo *Leg.* 299–305; see the discussion in Brown 1994, 701f.

He feared that if they actually sent an embassy they would also expose the rest of his conduct as governor by stating in full the briberies, the insults, the robberies, the outrages and wanton injustices, the executions without trial constantly repeated, the ceaseless and supremely grievous cruelty. So with all his vindictiveness and furious temper, he was in a difficult position. He had not the courage to take down what had been dedicated nor did he wish to do anything which would please his subjects. At the same time he knew full well the constant policy of Tiberius in these matters . . .[21]

Even on the correct assumption that Philo has over-egged the pudding, his picture is not so very different from that of Josephus. The scholarly spectrum of opinion on Pilate is not particularly wide, ranging from those who think he was an unmitigated disaster to those who, like Brown, say merely that he was 'not without very serious faults'.[22] The interesting thing to note for our present discussion is just how similar, underneath the rhetoric, Philo's account of the 'shields' incident is to John's account of Jesus' trial before Pilate. In both incidents, Pilate is caught between his desire not to do what his Jewish subjects want – he intends to snub them if he can – and his fear of what Tiberius will think if news leaks out. 'If you let this man go, you are not Caesar's friend.'[23]

This raises the point at issue in our present discussion. It has been fashionable for some time to say that the evangelists increasingly whitewashed Pilate's character in order to lay the blame for Jesus' death on his Jewish contemporaries.[24] But proponents of this view never quite come to terms with the fact that if John and the rest *were* trying to make Pilate out to be anything other than weak, vacillating, bullying, and caught between two pressing agendas neither of which had anything to do with truth or justice, they did a pretty poor job of it.[25] The later Christian adoption of Pilate as a hero, or even a saint, is many a mile from his characterization in the gospels: the famous scene of Pilate washing his hands must surely be read, both within history and within Matthaean redaction, as merely the high-point of his cynicism. He was the governor; he was responsible for Jesus' death; washing his hands was an empty and contemptuous symbol, pretending that he could

[21] Philo *Leg*. 302f. (quoted from Loeb edn., tr. Colson).

[22] Brown 1994, 704.

[23] Jn. 19.12; cf. Robinson 1985, 265f.; Brown 1994, 843f., both with other refs.

[24] cf. e.g. Winter 1974 [1961], ch. 6. Contrast Horbury 1972, 64f. Robinson 1985, 274 n.204 quotes a fascinating unpublished comment from C. H. Dodd, disputing the idea of an alleged increasing tendency to transfer responsibility from the Romans to the Jews: 'The only "steady growth" is between Mark and Matthew. Luke and John go no further than Mark, John perhaps not so far, and none of them goes any further than the most primitive form of the *kerygma* – or than Paul.'

[25] Lightfoot 1893, 187f. showed well how the 'cynicism, sarcasm and unbelief' and the 'withering scorn' of Pilate is 'painted in deeper colours' by John than by the synoptists.

evade responsibility for something that lay completely within his power.[26] What emerges from the records is not that Pilate wanted to rescue Jesus because he thought he was good, noble, holy or just, but that Pilate wanted to do the opposite of what the chief priests wanted him to do because he always wanted to do the opposite of what the chief priests wanted him to do.[27] That was his regular and settled *modus operandi*.

In this case, however, he was thwarted. The comparatively brief accounts in the synoptic tradition make a lot more sense when placed against the larger screen of the Johannine narrative; taken together, they suggest four things.[28] First, Pilate recognized that Jesus was not the ordinary sort of revolutionary leader, a *lestes* or brigand. If he was a would-be Messiah, he was a highly unusual one. Part of this recognition came, we may suppose, through the prisoner's own equivocation: 'the words are yours', as all four accounts have it.[29] Second, Pilate therefore realized that the Jewish leaders had their own reasons for wanting Jesus executed, and were using the charge of sedition as a convenient excuse. Third, this gave him the opening to do what he would normally expect to do, which was to refuse their request; he tried this, but failed.[30] He failed, fourth, because it was pointed out to him in no uncertain terms that if he did not execute a would-be rebel king he would stand

[26] Mt. 27.24f. On the later Pilate-traditions cf. Brown 1994, 695f. The tragic and horrible later use of Mt. 27.25 ('his blood be on us, and on our children') as an excuse for *soi-disant* 'Christian' anti-semitism is a gross distortion of its original meaning, where the reference is surely to the fall of Jerusalem (cp. Lk. 23.28–31). The legal situation is indicated by mSanh. 4.5: 'in capital cases the witness is answerable for the blood of him [that is wrongfully condemned] and the blood of his posterity [that should have been born to him]' (Danby 1933, 388).

[27] As in the matter of the *titulus*: Jn. 19.21f.

[28] Mt. 27.1–26/Mk. 15.1–15/Lk. 23.1–25/Jn. 18.28—19.16. Cf. Robinson 1985, 254–75; Sherwin-White 1969 [1963], ch. 2. Brown 1994, 721f. has a judicious summing-up which, though somewhat kinder to Pilate, follows a similar line to that adopted here.

[29] Mt. 27.11/Mk. 15.2/Lk. 23.3/Jn. 18.37. The precise meaning of this phrase is of course much debated. Dodd's comment is perhaps pertinent (1968, 89f.): 'It would appear to be intentionally non-committal, meaning something like, "The words are yours", "Have it so if you choose".' He cites the C4 (Greek) *Apostolic Constitutions* 5.14.4, which, commenting on Mt. 26.25, distinguishes explicitly between *su eipas* ('you said [so]') and *nai* ('yes').

[30] According to Mt. 27.15–23/Mk. 15.6–14/Lk. 23.17–23/Jn. 18.39–40, he tried to offer the crowds Jesus' release as part of a Passover custom, but was thwarted by their asking for Barabbas instead. This account has often been queried as part of the evangelists' attempt to shift the blame from Pilate to the Jews, but there is at least as strong a likelihood that it is historical: see, with full details, Brown 1994, 787–820. According to Lk. 23.6–12, Pilate sent Jesus to Herod, presumably so that he could say he acted on Herod's recommendation rather than that of the chief priests. (Parker 1987 proposed Herod as the real mover in the whole process; he is indeed more important in the gospel narratives than often acknowledged, but perhaps not to this extent.) Neither the Barabbas nor the Herod incident materially affects our present enquiry.

accused, himself, of disloyalty to Caesar.[31] Historically, emotionally, politically the sequence makes perfect sense. In terms of the Roman authorities, the answer to the question 'why did Jesus die?' is that Pilate not only put cynical power-games before justice (that was normal), but also, on this occasion, put naked self-interest before both.

This, however, merely heightens the second and third aspects of our question. Why did the chief priests present Jesus to Pilate as a condemned criminal in the first place? And why did Jesus not defend himself against the charge of sedition?

3. The Jewish Charge

The historian's task in examining the Jewish hearing(s) would be a lot easier if we could begin at the end, as we can with the Roman trial. Just as there we are on safe ground with the *titulus* on the cross, from which we can work backwards, so it would be convenient to begin at the end of the Jewish hearing and reconstruct the process by which the court reached its verdict. Sadly, that is precisely what we cannot do, since, as we saw in the previous chapter, the verdict suggested by the synoptic gospels, especially Matthew and Mark, is normally regarded as historically puzzling. We are forced, instead, to work in towards the trial narrative from the two outer fixed points: Jesus' Temple-action on the one hand, and the charge before Pilate (which there is every reason to regard as historical) on the other.[32]

At the surface level, neither move is particularly difficult. Jesus' Temple-action led straightforwardly to the question about Messiahship; his unequivocal claim to Messiahship would translate without difficulty into the charge with which Pilate confronted him: 'Are you the king of the Jews?'[33] But, as with Pilate, we are faced with a curious phenomenon. The Jewish court, to be sure, wanted a charge that they could take to Pilate with some hope of having their conviction, and sentence, ratified and carried out. But they, like Pilate, knew very well that Jesus was not a would-be Messiah of the same sort as Judas the Galilean. If they had thought he was, they would most

[31] One only has to read the account of Tiberius' 'reign of terror' in Tac. *Ann.* 5—6 to understand Pilate's nervousness.

[32] cf. Harvey 1982, ch. 2.

[33] Mt. 27.11/Mk. 15.2/Lk. 23.3/Jn. 18.33. This title reflects 'how a Roman would understand Jesus' in terms of 'an attempt to reestablish the kingship over Judea and Jerusalem exercised by the Hasmoneans . . . and Herod the Great' (Brown 1994, 731). One might add 'or in terms of a populist revolutionary movement, as mentioned by Josephus (e.g. *Ant.* 17.285)' (cf. Sherwin-White 1969 [1963], 24f.). Brown, however, makes unduly heavy weather of the transition from 'Messiah' to 'king of the Jews'.

likely have arrested his followers as well. In fact, however, '*no one* could think that [Jesus] posed an actual threat to the Jewish government . . ., and certainly not to the Roman Empire.'[34] It was just not that sort of movement, and nobody seriously supposed it was. The very clarity of the historical sequence, focused on the idea of Messiahship, merely highlights the real problem: why, then, did the Jewish authorities determine to get rid of Jesus?

Later Jewish tradition, for what it is worth, highlights the motive that, as we saw in chapter 9, emerged as an undertone during the public ministry of Jesus. The Babylonian Talmud puts it like this:

> Jesus was hanged on the eve of Passover. The herald went before him for forty days, saying, 'He is going forth to be stoned because he practised sorcery and enticed and led Israel astray. Let everyone knowing anything in his defence come and plead for him.' But nothing was found in his defence, so he was hanged on the eve of Passover.[35]

In other words, the Jewish tradition, which certainly owes nothing to Christian interpretations of Jesus' death, is clear that Jesus was killed because of crimes punishable by death in Jewish law – specifically, Deuteronomy 13 and similar passages, and their later rabbinic interpretations.[36] This is, perhaps, as close as we come to a fixed point in the Jewish hearings, from which we can work inwards.

But in what ways did they think Jesus was 'leading the people astray'? It is not clear that leading a rebel movement would count in this category, though Josephus of course does his best to blacken the characters, and impugn the motives, of those 'prophetic' leaders he designates as 'brigands'. In any case, as we have seen, it is unlikely that either the chief priests or Pilate regarded Jesus as a serious revolutionary threat. No; as we argued earlier, they invoked Deuteronomy 13 and similar passages because Jesus was following, and advocating, an agenda which involved setting aside some of the most central and cherished symbols of the Judaism of his day, and replacing them with loyalty to himself. More specifically, his attitude to Torah (during his Galilean work) pointed towards his action in the Temple: one can imagine onlookers, aware of what Jesus had done and said in Galilee, saying 'There! I knew he was up to no good!' He appeared, so far as anyone could

---

[34] Sanders 1985, 329 (italics original); cf. 231, 295, 317f. and elsewhere. Sanders stresses that this contrasts Jesus with some other movements that the authorities might have been supposed to regard as parallel.

[35] bSanh. 43a (cf. too 107b). On the whole issue cf. above, 439–42. The apparent oddity of Jesus being stoned *and* hanged is explained by mSanh. 6.4: after stoning, the corpse must be hung on a gibbet, but taken down again before sunset in obedience to Dt. 21.23. The notion of a forty-day appeal for defence is normally discounted, e.g. by Klausner 1947 [1925], 28.

[36] See above, 439–42.

judge, to be speaking and acting in opposition to Torah and Temple, and leading others, by word, example and 'works of power', to do so the same. What could he be, in their eyes, if not a false prophet, performing signs and wonders to lead Israel astray?

The subtext of the hearing before Caiaphas is thus clarified. The surface text, as we saw in the previous chapter, was the framing of a charge which would stick before Pilate, who (as John's account makes clear) would not care a fig about someone 'leading Israel astray', but who would care, or ought to, about someone leading a rebel movement against Rome. The subtext, however, was the determination on the part of the court to find Jesus guilty of a crime in *Jewish* law. The general populus were *wanting* Jesus to be the sort of Messiah whom Pilate, if he caught him, would have to execute – the sort who, like Barabbas, would lead a violent revolution in the city.[37] If the Jewish leaders had found Jesus guilty of being a revolutionary Messiah, and had handed him over to Pilate on that charge, they might well have precipitated the riot they were anxious to avoid.[38] But if they were able to claim that he was guilty of a well-known capital crime in Jewish law, they might win the people over. Further demonstration that this was their aim can be found in the mocking by the Jewish court. Whereas Herod and the Romans taunt Jesus as a would-be Messiah, the Jewish leaders mock him as a would-be *prophet*.[39]

We should not, however, reduce the motivation of the Jewish court simply to the cynical and political. Serious Jewish observers were bound to conclude that Jesus was 'leading Israel astray' in terms of the agendas, and Torah-interpretations, current at the time.[40] Precisely because he would not endorse, but rather opposed, the movement of national resistance, the (Shammaite) majority of Pharisees would find him deeply unsatisfactory.[41] Precisely because he was 'stirring up the people', creating an excitement wherever he went in a highly volatile social and political setting, the chief priests and Sadducees were bound to see him as a serious trouble-maker. John's account of their anxiety bears all the hallmarks of historicity:

> The chief priests and the Pharisees called a meeting of the council, and said, 'What are we to do? This man is performing many signs. If we let him go on like this, everyone

[37] cf. Lk. 23.19, which reads like a sentence from Josephus: Barabbas had committed *phonos* [murder] during a *stasis* [uprising] in the *polis* [city].

[38] As in Mt. 26.5/Mk. 14.2; cf. Lk. 22.2; Jn. 11.47-53. Riots, and Roman repression, at times of festival were nothing new: cf. *NTPG* 172-7, with refs.

[39] Mt. 26.67f./Mk. 14.65/Lk. 22.63-5. Mt. has them call Jesus 'Messiah', but the point of the scene, for him as well, is that Jesus is being taunted as a false prophet.

[40] cf. Klausner 1947 [1925], bk. 8, ch. 3.

[41] On the Pharisees, their groupings, and agendas cf. *NTPG* 181-203, and above, ch. 9.

will believe in him, and the Romans will come and destroy both our holy place and our nation.'[42]

He is performing signs; people will be led away after him; the Temple, and the national life itself, are at risk. These, I suggest, were the real issues underneath the night hearing at the chief priest's house. These issues, too, when coupled with the more obvious accusation that Jesus was a would-be Messiah, gave rise to the charge which, in Luke's account, the assembly put before Pilate:

> We found this man perverting our nation, forbidding us to pay taxes to the emperor, and saying that he himself is the Messiah, a King.[43]

Unless, then, we are to take the route of extreme scepticism and deny that we know anything at all about how and why Jesus was executed, we must say that the combination of charges we now have before us lay at the core of the hearing before the chief priests.

Did they, then, hold an official trial in haste, at night? Sherwin-White argued, not least from circumstantial evidence, that they probably did.[44] They wanted to be able to catch Pilate during working hours – i.e. first thing in the morning – and have the matter settled before the festival proper began.[45] Though certainty at this point is impossible – and is not necessary, either, for the argument of this chapter – I incline to the view that the meeting in John 11, held without Jesus present, was the real 'trial', at which it was agreed (a) that Jesus was a false prophet leading Israel astray, (b) that he was a serious political liability, and (c) that, since it seemed to be a choice between killing him and letting the Temple and nation be jeopardized, he should be killed.[46] All that remained was to extract some sort of confession of guilt in relation both to the Temple and to the charge of false prophecy. That was what the nocturnal hearing succeeded in doing.[47]

Succeeded, indeed, beyond their hopes. The prisoner, in agreeing to the charge of being a would-be Messiah, 'prophesied' his own vindication in such a way that a plausible charge of 'blasphemy' could be added to the list. He had now not only spoken false prophecy against the Temple, thereby

[42] Jn. 11.47f.

[43] Lk. 23.2. Mt. 27.11/Mk. 15.2 demand some such fuller account, since they have Pilate, without any prompting, asking Jesus 'Are you the King of the Jews?'

[44] Sherwin-White 1969 [1963], 44–7.

[45] This assumes that Jesus was executed during the day before Passover: see below.

[46] Cp. Sanders 1985, 317f.

[47] Harvey (1982, 30–2) suggests that the Jewish hearing was political, not judicial: what mattered was not that Jesus was formally convicted of a crime, but that the Jewish gathering heard enough to warrant handing Jesus over to the Romans with the suggestion that the Romans should try him as a would-be Messiah.

placing himself clearly enough in the category condemned by Deuteronomy 13, the category that might convince the crowds that the chief priests' verdict was correct. He had now not only confessed to messianic aspirations, placing himself clearly enough in the category necessary if Pilate was to carry out, despite his normal disregard for the chief priests, the sentence they had passed. He had done these two things in such a way as to prophesy that he, as Messiah, would sit on a throne beside the god of Israel. 'You will see "the son of man" "sitting at the right hand of Power", and "coming on the clouds of heaven".'[48]

Since we have no evidence of anyone before or after Jesus ever saying such a thing of himself, it is not surprising that we have no evidence of anyone framing a blasphemy law to prevent them doing so. But, granted the charge of false prophecy already hanging over him, and the 'two powers' implication that the reference to Daniel 7 suggests, it seems to me likely that the reaction of Caiaphas, as in Matthew 26.65 and Mark 14.63-4, is substantially historical. Among other things, it explains John 19.7, where the chief priests say to Pilate, 'We have a law, and according to that law he ought to die because he has claimed to be the Son of God.'[49] Without the reference to Daniel 7, the phrase 'Messiah, Son of the Blessed' in Mark 14.61 would, as I insisted in the previous chapter, simply mean 'the true Davidic king'. With it, the option is at least open that the phrase is being given a new meaning: 'the one who will sit at the right hand of the god of Israel'. The only remaining objection to the historicity of the scene is, of course, that Jesus would never have said, or meant, any such thing. Discussion of this point must be deferred to the next chapter.

In terms of the Jewish authorities, then, the question 'Why did Jesus die?' evokes a fivefold answer. He was sent to the Roman governor on a capital charge

(i)   because many (not least many Pharisees, but also, probably, the chief priests) saw him as 'a false prophet, leading Israel astray';

(ii)   because, as one aspect of this, they saw his Temple-action as a blow against the central symbol not only of national life but also of YHWH's presence with his people;

(iii)   because, though he was clearly not leading a real or organized military revolt, he saw himself as in some sense Messiah, and could thus become a focus of serious revolutionary activity;

(iv)   because, as the pragmatic focus of these three points, they saw him as a dangerous political nuisance, whose actions might well call down the wrath of Rome upon Temple and nation alike;

[48] Mt. 26.64/Mk. 14.62; cf. Lk. 22.69; see above, 360-5, 524-8.
[49] cf. too Lk. 22.70.

(v)   because, at the crucial moment in the hearing, he not only (as far
           as they were concerned) pleaded guilty to the above charges, but
           also did so in such a way as to place himself, blasphemously,
           alongside the god of Israel.

The leaders of the Jewish people were thus able to present Jesus to Pilate as a
seditious trouble-maker; to their Jewish contemporaries (and later generations
of rabbinic Judaism) as a false prophet and a blasphemer, leading Israel
astray; and to themselves as a dangerous political nuisance. On all counts, he
had to die.

Their verdict was not, of course, a *sufficient* cause of Jesus' death. They
needed Pilate to ratify and carry out the sentence. It was, however, a *neces-*
sary cause of Jesus' crucifixion: Pilate himself would not have brought
charges against Jesus, or, if he had, they would most likely have only
resulted in a flogging.[50] Pilate's decision was both a necessary and a sufficient cause of Jesus' crucifixion. If he had refused to comply, Jesus would
have been flogged and released; once he had agreed, the matter was concluded. This complex nest of causes explains the events; it does justice to the
primary source material; it does not reflect any bias as between Jewish and
Roman authorities, since Pilate emerges at least as badly as Caiaphas; and it
explains, not least by its complexity, the varied emphases found in pagan,
Jewish and early Christian literature.[51]

In both hearings, however, the prisoner had a role to play. He could have
avoided arrest in the first place.[52] He could, perhaps, have chosen to mollify
the Sanhedrin. He could have pointed out to Pilate that he posed no threat to
public order, as his great-great-nephews were later to do before Domitian.[53]
He could, in other words, have played all his cards differently, and might
well have been either acquitted or let off with a lighter punishment. His own
decisions, in other words, were themselves necessary, though insufficient,
causes of his own death. Having examined Pilate and the chief priests, we
must therefore turn our attention to Jesus himself, and ask once more, but
now in relation to his own mindset: why did Jesus die?

[50] On the analogy with Jesus ben Ananias (Jos. *War* 6.302–4); and cf. Lk. 23.16, 22.

[51] Pagan: e.g. Tac. *Ann.* 15.44; Jewish: bSanh. 43a, etc. (see above). (The Roman text
mentions only the Roman involvement, the Jewish text only the Jewish. Neither 'side'
regarded responsibility for Jesus' death as something to be ashamed of.) Early Christian: e.g.
Ac. 2.23; 3.14; 4.10, 27f.; 5.30; 7.52; 10.39; 13.28; 1 Th. 2.14f.

[52] Even granted Judas' betrayal – a topic which, though of considerable interest, is not
relevant to the present investigation.

[53] Eus. *HE* 3.19f.: cf. *NTPG* 351f.; Bauckham 1990, 94–106.

4. The Intention of Jesus (1): The Key Symbol

(i) Introduction

Did Jesus intend to die in something like the manner he did, and if so why? I argued earlier that it makes historical sense to ask this question, instancing three very different figures from roughly Jesus' own period: Seneca, Eleazar, and Ignatius of Antioch.[54] In each case, it not only makes sense to ask what the subject intended; it makes sense to explore the mindset which would sustain such an intention, and the worldview within which such a mindset might originate. It is a task like that which we now approach in relation to Jesus' understanding of his own death.

Albert Schweitzer suggested, nearly a century ago, that one might divide 'Lives of Jesus' into two main groups: those in which Jesus went to Jerusalem in order to 'work', and those in which he went there to die.[55] Schweitzer himself argued strongly for the latter route.[56] Most subsequent scholars have drawn back from it, regarding it (in the words of a recent writer who is otherwise much closer to Schweitzer than many) as implying that Jesus was 'weird'.[57] Since I propose to agree with Schweitzer, in outline though not in detail, it may be as well to say from the start that this counter-argument is flawed. It would of course be 'weird' for a comfortable modern western scholar to act deliberately in such a way as to occasion a capital charge, and then to incriminate him- or herself, partly by silence, and partly by cryptic but damning self-disclosures. But Jesus was not a comfortable modern western scholar.[58] Another worldview dominated his horizon, established his aims and beliefs, and generated his intentions. Four hundred years before him, Socrates had gone to his death rather than ingratiate himself with the Athenian regime; his followers mourned him greatly, but nobody thought him weird, or even inconsistent. Indeed, the point of Socrates' acceptance of the death penalty was that anything else would be radically inconsistent with his whole life and teaching.[59] It should be at least an open question whether

---

[54] Above, 106.

[55] Schweitzer 1954 [1906], 389 n.1.

[56] Recent followers of Schweitzer in this respect include e.g. O'Neill 1980, ch. 4; Bock-muehl 1994, 90; Hengel 1995b, 72.

[57] Sanders 1985, 333 (though what he is criticizing is not strictly Schweitzer's view but what he describes as its 'logical implication').

[58] Sanders (ibid.) claims that Jesus was 'a *reasonable* first-century visionary' (italics original). It all depends, of course, what you mean by 'reasonable'. Surely Sanders, who has done so much to expose the back-projection of certain later assumptions on to the New Testament, does not wish to fall into the same trap himself?

[59] Plato, *Apology*, *Crito* and *Phaedo*. Cf. esp. *Apol.* 40–41: 'I [Socrates] suspect that this thing that has happened to me is a blessing, and we are quite mistaken in supposing death to be an evil . . . I am quite clear that the time had come when it was better for me to die and

Jesus embraced a worldview (not of course the same as that of Socrates) within which his own death would make sense, and would indeed make more sense than anything else.[60]

As in our previous investigations, we must begin with praxis, story and symbol before investigating 'ideas', and the isolated sayings which may or may not disclose them. The idealist tradition, by starting with sayings, tends to lose sight of events and actions within the fog of hypothetical tradition-history. But it is events and actions, and the implicit narratives they disclose, that count within a world that knows the value of symbols. Modern westerners, who live in a world that has rid itself of many of its ancient symbols, and mocks or marginalizes those that are left, have to make a huge effort of historical imagination to enter into a world where a single action can actually *say* something (it is ironic that philosophers within our words-and-ideas culture have had to struggle to reclaim this notion, by means of such concepts as 'speech-acts'[61]). Unless we make the effort, however, we become the prisoners of our own culture, and should give up even trying to be historians. Words focus, limit and sharpen symbolic actions, but do not replace them. And the central symbolic action which provides the key to Jesus' implicit story about his own death is, of course, the Last Supper.

(ii) The Last Supper: Symbol and Significance

(a) Introduction

Jesus' last meal with his followers was a deliberate double drama.[62] As a Passover meal (of sorts), it told the story of Jewish history in terms of divine deliverance from tyranny, looking back to the exodus from Egypt and on to the great exodus, the return from exile, that was still eagerly awaited. But Jesus' meal fused this great story together with another one: the story of Jesus' own life, and of his coming death. It somehow involved him in the god-given drama, not as a spectator, or as one participant among many, but as the central character.

---

be released from my distractions.'

[60] For further discussion of Sanders' objection to Schweitzer, and his counter-proposals, see below.

[61] See the discussion in Thiselton 1980, ch. 5.

[62] For a recent survey of scholarly opinion, and bibliography, cf. O'Toole 1992.

(b) Last Supper and Passover

This presupposes, of course, that the Last Supper was in some sense or other a Passover meal.[63] The synoptic evangelists say as much: they date it; they have Jesus and the disciples speak of 'eating the Passover'; they have the disciples 'preparing the Passover-meal'.[64] John, however, indicates that the meal took place the day *before* the feast; he does not, however, describe the meal, or any symbolic actions concerned with the bread or the wine, but only the footwashing.[65] This fits with the Talmudic evidence, which as we saw had Jesus being executed 'on the eve of the Passover'.[66] Various attempts have been made to resolve this problem. Jesus may have been following a rival (perhaps Essene?) calendar; John has altered the chronology to make the theological point that Jesus is the true Passover lamb, slaughtered at the same time as the lambs were being killed in the Temple in preparation for the evening meal; the synoptists have turned the meal into a Passover meal in obedience to *their* theology or tradition; and so forth.[67] If we are to use the symbolic significance and implicit narrative of the meal as the starting-point for this part of our investigation, the question is of some importance.

It seems to me virtually certain that the meal in question was *some kind of* Passover meal. Several almost incidental details point this way. It was eaten at night, and in Jerusalem; Jesus and his followers normally returned to Bethany for the night, but Passover meals had to be eaten within the city limits, and after dark (days in the Jewish calendar began, of course, at sunset).[68] The meal ended with a hymn, presumably the *Hallel* psalms sung at the end of the Passover meal.[69] The best explanation for Jesus' crucial words is that the head of the household would normally explain certain parts of the Passover meal in relation to the exodus narrative. Likewise, the counter-arguments to the synoptic dating are not especially strong. Thus, for instance, Passover would normally be celebrated by families; but Josephus can speak of it being celebrated by what he calls 'a little fraternity', and in any case, as we have seen, Jesus regarded his followers as a fictive kinship

---

[63] On this whole topic the work of Jeremias 1966a [1949] remains basic. It is impossible here to discuss in detail the many complex issues which his work has raised.

[64] Date: Mt. 26.17/Mk. 14.12/Lk. 22.7. Jesus' words: Mt. 26.18/Mk. 14.14f./Lk. 22.11, 15. Disciples: Mt. 26.17/Mk. 14.12. Preparation: Mt. 26.19/Mk. 14.16/Lk. 22.13.

[65] Jn. 13.1; 18.28; 19.14, 31.

[66] bSanh. 43a: above, 439. This evidence is of course much later, and as we saw contains other elements which label it as secondary.

[67] Alternative calendar: Jaubert 1957. John's lamb-christology: Jn. 1.29, 36; 19.36 (cf. Ex. 12.46; Num. 9.12; 1 Cor. 5.7).

[68] Night: 1 Cor. 11.23; Mt. 26.20/Mk. 14.17; cf. Lk. 22.14. Bethany: Mt. 21.17/Mk. 11.11; Mt. 26.6/Mk. 14.3.

[69] i.e. Pss. 115—118; Mt. 26.30/Mk. 14.26.

group.[70] The only alternative to this conclusion is to adopt a quite radical scepticism about the whole event, which then leaves a major feature of very early Christianity completely inexplicable: Paul 'received' the detailed traditions about the Last Supper in (presumably) his earliest days as a Christian, i.e. in Damascus after his conversion in the early 30s.[71]

At the same time, we have no reason to suppose, granted all we have seen of Jesus' agenda and normal mode of operating, that he would have felt bound to celebrate the festival on the officially appointed day. Scriptural regulations permitted Passover to be kept, in case of necessity, at another time than that laid down, and if Jesus had been eager (as Luke has him imply) to force the issue that lay ahead of him, he might have considered that sufficient reason.[72] Though Jaubert's proposal about Jesus following the Essene (solar) calendar, as opposed to the official (lunar) one, has not received much subsequent support, there is no reason to suppose that Jesus might not have celebrated what we might call a *quasi*-Passover meal a day ahead of the real thing. This, of course, would have meant doing without a lamb (since the priests would not be killing them for Passover until the following day); that would be no bar to treating the meal as a proper Passover, since it was after all what happened in the Diaspora (and, of course, what was to happen throughout the Jewish world after AD 70).[73] Granted that Jesus had, throughout his work, reorganized the symbolic world of his contemporaries around his own life and mission (chapter 9 above), it certainly does not strain credulity to think that he might organize a special quasi-Passover meal a day early. All the lines of our investigation so far point this way, and suggest that Jesus saw the meal as the appropriate way of drawing the symbolism of Passover, and all that it meant in terms of hope as well as of history, on to himself and his approaching fate.[74]

What story did this deeply symbolic meal tell, before any words were spoken?[75] Granted a quasi-Passover setting, the meal itself said two very specific things.

---

[70] cf. Jos. *War* 6.423f.; cf. above, 398–403, 430–2. For discussion of other problems, cf. e.g. O'Toole 1992, 236f.

[71] 1 Cor. 11.23. For a recent discussion of early traditions about the Supper cf. Caird & Hurst 1994, 225–32.

[72] cf. Num. 9.10f., specifying that those who are unclean or absent on Nisan 14 should keep the feast a month later instead; this, according to 2 Chr. 30.2–4, 13–15, was carried out by Hezekiah. For Jesus' eagerness, cf. Lk. 22.15.

[73] cf. mPes. 10.3, reflecting awareness of the change from pre-70 to post-70 Passovers. Cf. Jaubert 1957.

[74] For a similar proposal, cf. Bockmuehl 1994, 92–4.

[75] Sanders 1985, 264 effectively asks the question in the same way, though his answer is somewhat different.

First, like all Jewish Passover meals, the event spoke of leaving Egypt. To a first-century Jew, it pointed to the return from exile, the new exodus, the great covenant renewal spoken of by the prophets. The meal symbolized 'forgiveness of sins', YHWH's return to redeem his people, his victory over Pharaohs both literal and metaphorical; it took place 'in accordance with the scriptures', locating itself within the ongoing story of YHWH's strange saving purposes for Israel as they reached its climax. This was the meal, in other words, which said that Israel's god was about to become king. This, indeed, is not especially controversial.

Second, however, the meal brought Jesus' own kingdom-movement to its climax. It indicated that the new exodus, and all that it meant, was happening *in and through Jesus himself.* This is extremely controversial, and needs to be spelled out in more detail.

The new meaning which Jesus gave to the old meal may be seen when we correlate it with his Temple-action. Both functioned as prophetic symbols, indicating an unexpected fulfilment of Israel's destiny, in which that destiny was being strangely redrawn around Jesus himself. Indeed, from this point of view we might almost suggest that it was *necessary* for Jesus *not* to celebrate the Passover on the regular night; he was precisely not keeping it as simply one more in the sequence, as part of the regular annual Jewish cult, dependent upon the Temple for the necessary sacrificial lamb.[76] If he believed that the kingdom was about to dawn, in other words that YHWH was about to inaugurate the new covenant, the end of exile, the forgiveness of sins, it becomes very likely that he would distinguish this meal from the ordinary Passover meal, while retaining enough of its form for the symbolism to be effective. If he believed that the kingdom was not merely a future event, waiting round some corner yet to be negotiated, but was actually bursting in upon the present moment, it would make sense to anticipate Passover night, celebrating a strange new Passover that would carry a kingdom-in-the-present meaning. And if he really believed that the Temple was due for destruction, that it had been solemnly judged by YHWH and found wanting, he might well regard it as appropriate that he should behave as though already in the Diaspora, already without the Temple, and celebrate his Passover meal without recourse to the system he had denounced, and whose imminent downfall he had predicted.

To calculate the symbolic and narratival significance of Jesus' action in the upper room, therefore, we must place it alongside the Temple-action. The two interpret one another.[77] Thus Jacob Neusner, for instance, has

[76] Though cf. Sanders 1993, 250f. for the opposite view.

[77] We should possibly understand the footwashing scene in Jn. 13.1-20 in this sense. According to the mBer. 9.5, one was supposed to wash the dust of the streets from one's feet before approaching the sacred precincts. Jesus' action, in other words (in addition to all the

argued that the Temple-action and the Last Supper, taken together, indicated that Jesus was in effect intending to replace the Temple, as the symbolic focus of the Judaism, with his own newly instituted quasi-cultic meal.[78] Bruce Chilton, following a similar line of thought, has gone so far as to suggest that what Judas betrayed to the chief priests was that Jesus had performed a scandalous counter-Temple act in celebrating his own Supper as a new and radical alternative.[79] Neusner and Chilton have, I believe, put their finger on a vital point, but I do not think they have drawn from it quite the conclusion that it demands. The intended contrast is not so much between the Temple-system and the regular celebration of a meal instituted by Jesus, so much as between the Temple-system *and Jesus himself*, specifically, his own approaching death. This is not a peculiar idea imported into the picture from outside, but emerges clearly from the cumulative evidence amassed throughout the present book, and particularly in the previous chapter, that Jesus deliberately drew on to himself the whole tradition of Jewish expectation and hope. He saw himself as Messiah, the focal point of the great divine act of liberation. The symbols ordering Israel's life and hope were redrawn, focusing now upon Jesus himself. The final meal which he celebrated with his followers was not, in that sense, free-standing. It gained its significance from his own entire life and agenda, and from the events which, he knew, would shortly come to pass. It was Jesus' chosen way of investing those imminent events with the significance he believed they would carry.[80]

Within this wider context, Jesus' actions with the bread and the cup – which there is excellent warrant to regard as historical[81] – must be seen in the same way as the symbolic actions of certain prophets in the Hebrew scriptures. Jeremiah smashes a pot; Ezekiel makes a model of Jerusalem under siege.[82] The actions carry prophetic power, effecting the events (mostly acts of judgment) which are then to occur. They are at once explained in terms of those events, or rather of YHWH's operating through them. In the same way,

---

other things that commentators normally say about it), could be seen as preparing his followers for something that would actually supersede the Temple. Whether or not we ascribe either the action, or this interpretation of it, to Jesus himself, this theme points us in the same direction as various recent historical studies which have placed the Temple-scene and the upper room in parallel.

[78] Neusner 1989, esp. 290.

[79] Chilton 1992b, 153f.; cf. too 1992a.

[80] Cf. Jeremias 1966a [1949], 260f.

[81] I find it simply incredible that so central and early a tradition as Paul recounts in 1 Cor. 11.23–6 would have been invented wholesale by the early church without a firm basis in Jesus' own actions.

[82] Jer. 19.1–13 (cf. too e.g. 13.1–11; 27.1—28.17; 32.6–15; 35.1–19; etc.); Ezek. 4.1–17 (cf. too 5.1–12; 12.1–25; etc.). Cf. e.g. Beck 1970.

Jesus' central actions during the meal seem to have been designed to reinforce the point of the whole meal: the kingdom-agenda to which he had been obedient throughout his ministry was now at last reaching its ultimate destination. Passover looked back to the exodus, and on to the coming of the kingdom. Jesus intended this meal to symbolize the new exodus, the arrival of the kingdom through his own fate. The meal, focused on Jesus' actions with the bread and the cup, told the Passover story, and Jesus' own story, and wove these two into one.

(c) From Symbol to Word

If the symbolism and implicit story inherent in the action generated and sustained the meal's primary significance, the words spoken brought this into focus and articulation. What precisely was said at Passover meals at this period, and thus the extent to which Jesus may or may not have adjusted the words for his new meaning, is impossible to ascertain. But there is every reason to suppose that the host at a Passover meal, then as now, would retell the story of the exodus, interpreting the actions and the elements of the meal in terms of that story, thereby linking the present company with the children of Israel as they left Egypt.[83] The words of Jesus at the supper would therefore have been seen, not only with later hindsight, but at the time, as performing a similar function. They would have been understood as reinterpreting the meal in relation to himself, claiming that the kingdom-events about to occur were the climax of the long history which looked back to the exodus from Egypt as its formative moment.

Debate will, no doubt, continue about what exactly Jesus said, and in what order, but since in any case we are dealing (a) with a Greek translation of a dense Aramaic original[84] and (b) with sayings which were reused (and perhaps retranslated) again and again in the life of the early church, we should not expect to be able to attain complete precision. What matters is that in the fourfold tradition, all the more impressive for its appearance in at least three independent forms (Mark and Matthew, as so often, seem to stand in closer relation than the others), it emerges that Jesus, in prophetic style, identified the bread with his own body, and the wine with his own blood, and that he spoke about these in language which echoed the context of Passover, sacrifice, and covenant which the meal, in any case, must already

---

[83] cf. e.g. mPes., esp. 10.1–7.

[84] The suggestion that Jesus spoke Hebrew on this occasion is rightly discounted by e.g. Fitzmyer 1985, 1394.

have possessed.[85] The synoptic tradition also indicates that Jesus said something about the climactic events being so close that this would be the last such meal he would share with his followers before the kingdom arrived; this eschatological emphasis is appropriately modified in Paul's new situation.[86]

All this may be spelled out in detail as follows.

1. Jesus' words about the bread identified it with his own body, as Ezekiel identified his brick with Jerusalem. Jesus' action thus indicated prophetically that he was to die, and that his death would be the source of life for his followers. According to the Mishnah, the unleavened bread of Passover was explained by Gamaliel (a contemporary of Jesus) as signifying the redemption from Egypt.[87] Unleavened bread was necessary, in the original story, because of the urgent haste of the exodus. In addition to identifying himself as the means of Israel's redemption, Jesus may have been alluding to the urgency with which his own mission was now at last to be accomplished.

2. Jesus' words about the cup (in Luke, the second cup) identify it, in similar prophetic fashion, with his blood. Behind the four versions there is a common meaning, with some of the accounts making more explicit what is implicit in the Passover setting anyway. The common meaning is that Jesus' coming death will effect the renewal of the covenant, that is, the great return from exile for which Israel had longed.[88] The phrase 'the blood of the covenant', which occurs in some form in all the accounts, echoes Exodus 24.8, in which Moses established the first covenant with the people at Mount Sinai.[89] It also evokes, perhaps equally significantly, Zechariah 9.9–11, which resonates closely with the themes we have studied already in this chapter and the previous one:

Rejoice greatly, O daughter Zion!
   Shout aloud, O daughter Jerusalem!
Lo, your king comes to you;
   triumphant and victorious is he,
humble and riding on a donkey,
   on a colt, the foal of a donkey.
He will cut off the chariot from Ephraim,
   and the war horse from Jerusalem;
and the battle bow shall be cut off,
   and he shall command peace to the nations;

---

[85] Mt. 26.26-8/Mk. 14.22-4/Lk. 22.19-20/1 Cor. 11.23-6. Cp. Jn. 6.51-9. The longer reading of Lk. (including 22.19b-20, omitted by D) is now usually regarded as original: cf. Metzger 1971, 173-7 and the commentaries (e.g. Fitzmyer 1985, 1387f.; still questioned by e.g. Evans 1990, 787f.).

[86] Mt. 26.29/Mk. 14.25/Lk. 22.15-18; cf. 1 Cor. 11.26b.

[87] mPes. 10.5.

[88] On the meaning of 'drinking someone's blood', cf. 2 Sam. 23.13-17.

[89] Ex. 24.6-8.

his dominion shall be from sea to sea,
   and from the River to the ends of the earth.
As for you also, *because of the blood of my covenant with you,*
   I will set your prisoners free from the waterless pit.
Return to your stronghold, O prisoners of hope;
   today I declare that I will restore to you double [or: I am declaring a second time
                                                              that I will return to you].

The covenant is renewed in the context of the messianic victory, which will liberate Israel once and for all from her long exile.[90] As we have already stressed, Jesus' actions at the Last Supper are to be seen in close conjunction with his earlier actions in the Temple, including, as here, his quasi-royal entry. There is no reason to doubt that he intended, in speaking of the final cup of the meal in terms of his own death, to allude to this theme of covenant renewal.[91] It fits precisely with all that we have seen of his agenda so far.

All three synoptic accounts contain a further initial explanation: Jesus' blood will be shed 'on behalf of the many' (Luke has 'on behalf of you'). It has been common to link the Matthaean and Markan version of this to Isaiah 53; the meaning of the saying must then be more fully determined in the light of the larger picture of Jesus' explanatory words, for which see below.

To this, Matthew has added 'for the forgiveness of sins'.[92] Once again we must stress: in its first-century Jewish context, this denotes, not an abstract transaction between human beings and their god, but the very concrete expectation of Israel, namely that the nation would at last be rescued from the 'exile' which had come about because of her sins.[93] Matthew is not suggesting that Jesus' death will accomplish an abstract atonement, but that it will be the means of rescuing YHWH's people from their exilic plight. These words again make explicit the symbolic meaning of the meal.[94]

3. All three synoptists have a version of a saying in which Jesus insists that this will be his last meal with his disciples before the coming of the kingdom. Matthew and Mark refer to subsequent meals in the kingdom; Luke, simply to this being the last pre-kingdom meal.[95] These sayings, of course, make sense only if we postulate the eschatological and apocalyptic setting of Jesus' work for which we have argued throughout. But, within that, they fit extremely well. Jesus' Passover, like the original one, had a strong note of urgency.

[90] The penultimate line clearly refers to the exile, still not undone (so Smith 1984, 259).
[91] cf. Moule 1987, 194.
[92] Mt. 26.28c; cf. Mt. 1.21.
[93] On 'forgiveness' and 'return from exile' see above, 268-74; cp. Jer. 31.31-4, etc.
[94] cf. Meyer 1979, 218f., with other refs.
[95] Mt. 26.29/Mk. 14.25/Lk. 22.16 (eating the Passover); 22.18 (drinking wine). Cf. Hengel 1981a, 72f. Jeremias' suggestion that Jesus fasted at the meal, to pray for the coming of the kingdom (1966a [1949], 207-18), has not commended itself to later scholars.

4. Luke and Paul both include a command that the meal be repeated, and that this repetition be undertaken as a way of remembering Jesus himself.[96] As Jeremias has pointed out, this belongs closely with the words used at Passover meals from that day to this, in which prayer is made that God will remember, and send, the Messiah.[97] The command, though quite comprehensible in the setting we have described, again makes explicit what is in any case implicit in the symbolic action of the meal itself. If Jesus was about to perform the great messianic action, and if his last meal with his followers would function in relation to that action as Passover functioned in relation to the exodus from Egypt, then of course the meal would include the prayer that this messianic action would be successfully accomplished; and of course, as the meal was repeated by Jesus' followers, it would be done not with an eye to YHWH sending the Messiah at last – he had already done that – but with an eye to his remembering the messianic act which Jesus had already accomplished. All this, again, makes sense only once one allows that Jesus really did suppose that he was about to die, and that this was part of the eschatological plan for the fulfilment of YHWH's kingdom-purposes. Once that is supposed, however – and the present chapter argues for doing so on good historical grounds – it fits very well. Jesus' symbolic action deliberately evoked the whole exodus tradition and gave it a new direction.

(d) Conclusion

The great majority of scholars agree that Jesus did celebrate a final meal with his followers on the night before his death, and that this took place at least in the context of Passover week. Building on this strong consensus, I have argued that the meal, as an action, already contained such powerful symbolism, and such a strong retelling of one of Israel's most potent stories, that the endless debates about the words which Jesus may or may not have used at the time ceases to be the central factor in determining the meaning he intended the meal to carry. When we then add the words, even in outline, to the action, there should be no doubt but that Jesus intended to say, with all the power of symbolic drama and narrative, that he was shortly to die, and that his death was to be seen within the context of the larger story of YHWH's redemption of Israel. More specifically, he intended to say that his death was to be seen as the central and climactic moment towards which that story had been moving, and for which the events of the exodus were the crucial and

---

[96] Lk. 22.19b (part of the 'longer' text; see above); 1 Cor. 11.24 (the bread), 25 (the cup).

[97] Jeremias 1966a [1949], 237-55, esp. 252, with refs.

determining backdrop; and that those who shared the meal, not only then but subsequently, were the people of the renewed covenant, the people who received 'the forgiveness of sins', that is, the end of exile. Grouped as they were around him, they constituted the true eschatological Israel.[98]

5. The Intention of Jesus (2): The Sayings and the Symbol

(i) Introduction

Jesus' symbolic action in the upper room, like his action in the Temple, must be set within two contexts: the larger picture of his work which we have built up in Part II, and the larger picture of the Jewish world within which that work made sense. And, just as in relation to the Temple we discovered that a good many of Jesus' sayings, clustered around the incident, functioned as riddles which explained the symbol, so we find in this case several sayings which, though cryptic in themselves, collectively point in one particular direction. Finally, as before, the symbolic action, and the riddles which explain it, create a historical context within which other material can settle down and, through coherence with the larger picture, make itself at home.

How does this work out?

In Part II of this book I argued at length that Jesus was announcing the kingship of YHWH as something which was in the process of *happening*. It was not an idea, a new belief, a different way of regarding one's personal or social existence, only relating tangentially to the time and place of its announcement. It was something which would come to birth within actual history. Jesus' prophetic and symbolic praxis (chapters 5 and 9) constantly pointed in this direction; he told the story of the kingdom (chapters 6-8) as the movement through which Israel's history would reach its long-awaited goal. This all generates the question: what did Jesus think would happen next?

This question, in fact, presses upon any analysis of Jesus and his work. Those who suppose that Jesus was essentially a teacher of timeless truths (whether political, religious or existential) are bound to ask, sooner or later, whether Jesus supposed his message was being widely accepted, and, if not (as seems to have been the case), what he should do next.[99] How much more must we ask it when we have rejected this model and embraced instead the

---

[98] It is thus mistaken to suggest, as does Neusner 1989, 290 (and in several other places), that to see the Last Supper in relation to the Temple-incident suggests that Christianity was founded as a totally different religious tradition to Judaism. Cf. *NTPG* ch. 16.

[99] cf. Barrett 1967, 38.

eschatological picture, with Jesus announcing that the great moment had come? What would the moment look like? How would the kingdom come?

Two strong clues emerge from our consideration of the answers Jesus implicitly gave to the worldview questions (chapter 10), and the story which he held out to his followers (chapter 7). From the former, it emerged that Jesus envisaged some sort of a battle; this was part of the messianic agenda, part of what had to be accomplished if the kingdom was to come. But the enemy against whom the battle would be fought would not be the pagan occupying forces. It would be the real enemy that stood behind them; the accuser, the satan, that had duped YHWH's people into themselves taking the pagan route, seeking to bring YHWH's kingdom by force of arms and military revolt. Jesus seems to have understood his own clashes with Israel's actual and self-appointed rulers and guardians of tradition as part of such a battle (chapter 9). If he were to meet these rulers head-on he would therefore be bound to regard such an encounter as the climactic confrontation between his agenda and theirs, his vocation to bring in the kingdom and their determination to keep Israel on the course which he had denounced. The stories which Jesus told, and the symbols he enacted, were not static or timeless indications of a religious or political system; they were events which were designed to lead to the great Event, the real battle with the real enemy.

But how would such a battle be fought? Here the kingdom-story of chapter 7 is enormously revealing. Jesus summoned his followers to a strange kind of revolution – a double revolution, in fact, through which Israel would become the light of the world, the heaven-sent answer to paganism, not through fighting a military battle like Judas Maccabaeus, but through turning the other cheek, going the second mile, loving her enemies and praying for her persecutors. This agenda was a revolutionary way of being revolutionary. It was not counter-revolutionary in the sense that it supported the *status quo*; it could hardly do that without abandoning the whole Isaianic kingdom-theology upon which it was based, in which YHWH revealed himself as the true king, the true God, in opposition to pagan gods and the regimes they support. Jesus held out the true, subversive wisdom, in opposition to the spurious conventional wisdom of his day. At the heart of that subversive wisdom was the call to his followers to take up the cross and follow him, to become his companions in the kingdom-story he was enacting.

My proposal is that Jesus took his own story seriously – so seriously that, having recommended to his followers a particular way of being Israel-for-the-sake-of-the-world, he made that way thematic for his own sense of vocation, his own belief about how the kingdom would come through his own work.[100] He would turn the other cheek; he would go the second mile; he

[100] After writing this I came upon similar proposals in Manson 1953, 74–7; Farmer 1956, 201f.

would take up the cross. He would be the light of the world, the salt of the earth. He would be Israel for the sake of the world. He would be the means of the kingdom's coming, both in that he would embody in himself the renewed Israel and in that he would defeat evil once and for all. But the way in which he would defeat evil would be the way consistent with the deeply subversive nature of his own kingdom-announcement. He would defeat evil by letting it do its worst to him. Jesus' Jewish context supplied him, as we shall see presently, with several spheres of meaning in which such a line of thought, and of action, would make sense, albeit startling sense.

The particular sense it makes grows from every aspect of Jesus' kingdom-announcement. We saw at the end of chapter 9 that his action in the upper room functioned as the climax of his reconstruction of Israel's symbolic world. We can now see that this symbolic action gained its meaning from the entire thrust of his work, his retelling of the kingdom-story, and his prophetic praxis. Of course, if we remove Jesus from this context, it is easy to ridicule the suggestion that he believed himself called to defeat evil through his own suffering and death. But, as Schweitzer saw, once we put him back into his own world, the world of Jewish apocalyptic eschatology, such a suggestion makes very good sense in itself, and adds the not inconsiderable historical virtue that it draws together the different aspects of Jesus' work into a tight thematic unity. This reading, I suggest, possesses the very great strengths of getting in the data and doing so with an appropriate economy and elegance.

Once we grasp this, the various riddles which circle around Jesus' awareness of where his work was leading him begin to make sense as well. To these we must now turn.

(ii) The Riddles of the Cross

(a) The Rejected Son

We return once more to the key parable which gives theological depth to Jesus' Temple-action.[101] We have already seen that Jesus saw himself as the (messianic) son, coming as the last in the line of the prophets, coming to Israel on behalf of her god. But the truly disturbing thing about the story is of course that the tenants, in rejecting the son, and hence the message from

---

[101] Mt. 21.33-46/Mk. 12.1-12/Lk. 20.9-19; cf. above, esp. 497-501.

his father, kill him, and throw him out of the vineyard.[102] It is this that precipitates the judgment of the vineyard-owner upon his wicked tenants.

As with so much of this material, it is open to anyone to object that the parable has been written up *ex post facto*, and that Jesus could not have told a story about himself, even cryptically, which ended this way. I reply (1) that this begs the question; (2) that the story fits so well with so many strands of Jesus' work and prophetic self-understanding that it is hardly straining historical credibility to ascribe it to him; (3) that the death of the son is not an addition, bolted on to the story from the outside, but belongs at its very climax; (4) that what may be the earliest version, that of Mark, does not have the son being first cast out of the vineyard and then killed (as Matthew does, reflecting perhaps later Christian awareness of Jesus being taken out of the city and then crucified[103]), but rather the reverse, which can hardly be regarded as a Christian retrojection; and (5) that the parable is remarkably free of any later Christian atonement-theology, focusing instead on the close connection between the death of the son and the destruction of the vineyard. I conclude that the prophetic narrative symbolism of this parable belongs to Jesus' awareness that his challenge to the Temple would result in his own death, as the guardians of Israel's traditions refused to respond to the message which he (of course) believed was from YHWH himself.

(b) The Great Commandment

A different viewpoint on the same symbols is provided by the little discussion as to which commandment is the greatest.[104] In its Markan context, this story is not about the relative value of different halakhic codes, though it is conceivable that that is how Matthew took it.[105] Mark continues the story with the scribe's reaction to Jesus' stress on the love of YHWH and of one's neighbour: yes, he says, these commands count for more than all burnt-offerings and sacrifices. Jesus, seeing that he answers shrewdly, replies in return: 'You are not far from the kingdom of god.'[106] This unusually warm commendation of a scribal interlocutor, not the sort of thing one expects to have been invented by the early church, points in the same direction as the other hints we have already examined. Jesus' kingdom-agenda, with the love of YHWH and of neighbour at its heart, suggested that the sacrificial system

---

[102] Mt. 21.39/Mk. 12.8/Lk. 20.15.

[103] cf. Heb. 13.12f.; Rev. 14.20; cp. Ac. 7.58.

[104] Mt. 22.34–40/Mk. 12.28–34. Cf. the similar question and answer in Lk. 10.25–8.

[105] cp. Mt. 22.40 (the end of the story in Mt.) with Mt. 5.17f.; 7.12.

[106] Mk. 12.32–4.

was to be made redundant. This both confirms the meaning of the Temple-action and hints at the meaning of the supper-action. The one was an act of judgment; the other, a pointer towards the Temple's replacement.

(c) Anointing for Burial

All four canonical gospels record the action of a woman in anointing Jesus.[107] Matthew, Mark and John place the incident in the last few days of Jesus' life, Luke much earlier; Matthew and Mark have the woman anoint Jesus' head, Luke and John his feet. The action causes complaint, from the disciples (Matthew), the bystanders (Mark), the Pharisee whose guest Jesus was (Luke), and Judas Iscariot (John). In Matthew, Mark and John Jesus' response to the criticism (we must remember that a good many of his sayings respond to criticism either of himself or his followers; in other words, that the sayings belong with symbolic actions) includes the suggestion that what has been done has been a preparation for his burial.[108] Other overtones may also be present: a hint of a messianic anointing, perhaps,[109] or even the suggestion that the anointing is necessary at this stage because, since Jesus is to die a criminal's death, he may not receive proper anointing later.[110] The saying, though startling in its setting, does not provide the main thrust of the story by itself (which may also indicate its historicity); it is, however, a way of investing the woman's action with such great symbolic value that Jesus adds (in Matthew and Mark) the assurance that wherever the gospel is preached in all the world, what the woman has done will be told as a memorial to her. By itself, this incident, and the saying of Jesus embedded in it, hardly amounts to more than a strange hint. In the context of the symbolic actions in the Temple and the upper room, however, it functions as a further riddle, pointing towards Jesus' awareness of what lay ahead. His own death would somehow initiate a worldwide announcement of the 'good news'.

(d) The Green Tree and the Dry

One of the strangest, and yet ultimately most revealing, of these riddles is a passage peculiar to Luke:

---

[107] Mt. 26.6-13/Mk. 14.3-9/Lk. 7.36-50/Jn. 12.1-8.

[108] Mt. 26.12/Mk. 14.8/Jn. 12.7. The text of the Jn. passage is awkward: lit. 'Let her alone, so that she may keep it for the day of my burial'; among other suggestions, NRSV supplies 'she bought it' before 'so that'. See the discussion in e.g. Barrett 1978 [1955], 413f.

[109] So e.g. Manson 1953, 84f.

[110] So Jeremias 1971, 284 (cf. his 1966b [1936], 107-15).

A great crowd of the people followed him, including some women who were weeping and mourning for him. Jesus turned to them, and said, 'Daughters of Jerusalem, don't weep for me; weep for yourselves and for your children. For behold, the days will come in which people will say, "Blessed are the barren, the wombs that never bore, and the breasts that never gave suck." Then they will begin to say to the mountains, "Fall on us," and to the hills, "Cover us." For if they do this when the wood is green, what will they do when it is dry?'[111]

What could occasion a terrible beatitude such as this, overturning the normal first-century cultural assumption that barrenness was a woman's greatest curse? The answer, in the light of chapter 8 above, must be that Jesus was warning, one last time, of what would happen as a result of Jerusalem rejecting 'the things that make for peace'.[112] She had chosen the way of revolution, of confrontation with Rome; the youngsters playing in the streets in Jesus' day would become the firebrands of the next generation, and would suffer the terrible consequences. The mothers should save their tears for when they would really be needed.

How does the quotation from Hosea 10.8 ('they will say to the mountains, "Fall on us"', etc.) fit in to this?[113] The entire context of the original passage, though normally ignored, is most instructive:

Israel is a luxuriant vine
   that yields its fruit.
The more his fruit increased
   the more altars he built;
as his country improved,
   he improved his pillars.
Their heart is false;
   now they must bear their guilt.
YHWH will break down their altars,
   and destroy their pillars.
For now they will say:
   'We have no king,
for we do not fear YHWH,
   and a king – what could he do for us?'
. . . The high places of Aven, the sin of Israel,
   shall be destroyed.
Thorn and thistle shall grow up
   on their altars.
They shall say to the mountains, Cover us,

---

[111] Lk. 23.27-31. The version in *Thom.* 79 has subtly but decisively altered the emphasis, so that it suggests the voluntary renunciation of conception (so, rightly, e.g. Fitzmyer 1985, 1494; but cf. Soards 1987; Brown 1994, 924). For a full recent discussion of the passage cf. esp. Brown 1994, 920-7.

[112] cf. Lk. 19.42.

[113] The quotation has reversed the two verbs. The verse is also quoted in Rev. 6.16. For the idea cf. Isa. 2.19.

and to the hills, Fall on us.
. . . I will come against the wayward people to punish them;
 and nations shall be gathered against them
 when they are punished for their double iniquity
. . . You have plowed wickedness,
 you have reaped injustice,
 you have eaten the fruit of lies.
Because you have trusted in your power
 and in the multitude of your warriors,
therefore the tumult of war shall rise against your people
 and all your fortresses shall be destroyed,
as Shalman destroyed Beth-arbel on the day of battle
 when mothers were dashed in pieces with their children.
Thus it shall be done to you, O Bethel,
 because of your great wickedness.
At dawn the king of Israel
 shall be utterly cut off.[114]

It is all there: the vine that has become proud and gone to ruin, the judgment on the sanctuary, the rejection of YHWH and of the king, the terrible judgment which will result from trusting in military power, the dire warning to the mothers and their children – and, finally, the death of the king. The application to Jesus' contemporaries fits at every point with the picture we have drawn overall. The judgment of which Jesus was warning the women of Jerusalem was the devastation which would result from the city's rejection of him as the true king, and his message as the true way of peace. His own death at the hands of Rome was the clearest sign of the fate in store for the nation that had rejected him.

With this, we can understand the final cryptic saying. Jesus had announced the divine judgment on Jerusalem, for her failure to repent, for her persistence in militant nationalism. This was not simply a matter of the Jewish leaders judging him, and so pulling down upon their own heads a more severe judgment in turn.[115] It was a matter of the Romans condemning Jesus on a charge of which he was innocent and his compatriots guilty. He was the green tree, they the dry.[116]

[114] Hos. 10.1-3, 8, 10, 13-15.
[115] Brown 1994, 926f. (cf. too Fitzmyer 1985, 1498); this seems peculiar, since it makes the Jewish leaders first the subject, and then the object, of violence, spoiling the saying's parallelism. Johnson 1991, 373f. suggests that the Jewish leaders are the violent ones in both halves of the sentence; but Jesus is dying on a Roman charge and a Roman cross.
[116] For the idea of wet and dry being destroyed together cf. Dt. 29.19; Ezek. 20.47 [MT 21.3]. Various rabbinic uses of the same imagery are collected in SB 2.263f. Leaney 1966 [1958], 283f. suggests that 'the times of the Gentiles' are compared to a tree, at present young and 'green', in the future mature and 'dry'; Evans 1990, 863f. proposes an allusion to the Tammuz-cult. The clearest statement of the view I regard as correct is in Caird 1963, 249f.; this is strongly supported by e.g. Lk. 11.49f.; 13.34f. (see below); 19.41-4; 21.20-4, where in each case the devastation of Jerusalem is to be at the hands of the Romans.

The saying does not carry any sort of atonement-theology such as characterized the church's understanding of Jesus' death from very early on. Indeed, it holds out no hope of rescue, only the warning that what is happening to Jesus is a foretaste of what will happen to many more young Jews in the not too distant future. It belongs, not with even the earliest post-Easter reflection on Jesus' crucifixion, but exactly where Luke places it. Its value in our current quest is therefore simple and powerful. It suggests, in its dark riddling way, that Jesus understood his death as being organically linked with the fate of the nation. He was dying as the rejected king, who had offered the way of peace which the city had rejected; as the representative king, taking Israel's suffering upon himself, though not here even with any hint that Israel would thereby escape. The riddle belongs with the messianic riddles we studied in the previous chapter, yet goes beyond them to point out the fate which the true Messiah would suffer. Having announced the divine judgment upon Temple and nation alike, a judgment which would take the form of awful devastation at the hands of the pagan forces, Jesus was now going ahead of the nation, to undergo the punishment which, above all, symbolized the judgment of Rome on her rebel subjects. If they did this to the one revolutionary who was not advocating rebellion against Rome, what would they do to those who were, and those who followed them?

(e) The Hen and the Chickens

A similar riddle, which again can only be fully understood when heard in relation to Jesus' central symbolic actions, is found in two different contexts in Matthew and Luke:

> Jerusalem, Jerusalem, that kills the prophets and stones those sent to her; how often would I have gathered your children, as a hen gathers her chickens under her wings, and you would not. Behold, your house has been abandoned. I tell you, you will not see me until you say, 'Blessed in the name of the Lord is the one who comes.'[117]

There are three elements to this saying. The first belongs closely with the previous riddle; the second and third integrate this with the wider picture we have been studying, not least with some aspects of the messianic riddles we examined in chapter 11 above.

First, the image of the hen and the chickens envisages a farmyard fire, in which the hen gathers her brood under her wings for safety. When the fire is

---

[117] Mt. 23.37–9/Lk. 13.34–5, with only minimal differences. Note that 'Blessed is the one who comes' (Heb. *baruch ha-ba*) is the normal way of saying 'welcome', so that the final phrase means 'welcome in the name of the Lord'; cf. Jeremias 1966a [1949], 260 n.62. Cp. LXX Ps. 128 [129].8; Sir. 45.15; Gen. 27.7.

over, she may have been scorched to death, but the chickens will be alive, protected under her wings. The picture is familiar in the Hebrew Bible, where it regularly suggests the children of Israel taking shelter under YHWH's wings.[118] This image indicates again that Jesus believed he would suffer the fate that was hanging over Jerusalem; indeed, that he desired to take it upon himself so that she might avoid it. To that extent, it goes beyond the picture of the green tree and dry, suggesting that there had at least been a chance that Jesus might, like Elijah in Ben-Sirach, turn away the divine wrath from Israel.[119] The riddle indicates clearly enough that the chance had come and gone; Jesus' fate and that of Jerusalem remain indissolubly locked together.

The second element brings together Jesus' despair at Israel's failure to seek and find the proffered shelter and the theme of judgment on the Temple in particular. The house has been abandoned. YHWH has left the Temple unprotected, open to enemy devastation. Again the image is familiar and biblical.[120]

The third element, quoting from Psalm 118.26, refers to the welcome offered to pilgrims on their way into Jerusalem. The psalm-verse occurs, of course, just after the passage about the stone which the builders rejected, and which has become the head of the corner[121] – which itself was used in the parable of the wicked tenants as part of the explanation of Jesus' action, coming at the end of the line of rejected prophets. The passages belong closely together and should be seen as mutually interpretative.

Putting the diverse elements together, we may suggest the following meaning. (1) Jesus envisaged himself as the true Temple-builder, coming on no ordinary pilgrimage to Jerusalem. (2) The present Temple, abandoned by YHWH, was under threat of destruction, having refused his message of peace, and his offer of a way of escape. (3) The only hope was to acknowledge him as the true pilgrim, and to welcome him, so that the stone rejected by the builders might indeed become the head of the corner.[122] The riddle thus

[118] Dt. 32.11; Ru. 2.12; Pss. 17.8; 36.7; 57.1; 63.7; 91.4; Isa. 31.5.

[119] Sir. 48.10.

[120] cf. e.g. Jer. 12.7; 22.5; Isa. 64.10f.; Ps. 69.25; 1 Kgs. 9.7–8; Tob. 14.4; and of course Ezek. 8.6; 9.3; 10.1–22; 11.22–3. Fitzmyer 1985, 1037; Johnson 1991, 219 suggest that one might also understand 'house' as referring to the people; Nolland 1993, 742 suggests it should include the city as a whole. These may also be implied, but the Temple-theme in Jesus' riddles about his own messianic vocation (in addition to the regular implication of 'house') is so strong that the Temple itself is the much more natural referent. Sanders (1993, 259) points out that in Mt. 23.21 Jesus refers to YHWH as living in the Temple (not that Sanders thinks much of Mt. 23 is original to Jesus); if this is original, it may indicate Jesus' affirmation of the basic Jewish tradition, which is then followed in v. 38 by its prophetic subversion.

[121] i.e. Ps. 118.22f.

[122] According to Allison 1983, the saying is actually an oracle of hope: this is what Israel must do if she is to be saved. That element may be present, but is heavily modified by the

belongs closely with the messianic riddles we studied in the previous chapter, adding to them the powerful note that this Messiah understood his vocation to include rescuing Jerusalem from the coming devastation by taking it upon himself. She was bent upon refusing, but the offer remained open. Ironically, of course, the crowds in Jerusalem welcomed him (as one might have expected) with Psalm 118.26; but by then it was apparently too late.[123]

(f) The Baptism and the Cup

Working backwards through the synoptic tradition of riddles that explain Jesus' symbolic actions, we reach the strange saying about the fate that awaited Jesus, which he saw as a matter of vocation:

> I came to cast fire upon the earth, and how I wish it were already kindled! I have a baptism to be baptized with, and how I am constrained until it is accomplished![124]

> Can you drink the cup that I drink, or be baptized with the baptism with which I am to be baptized? . . . The cup that I drink you will drink, and you will be baptized with the baptism with which I am baptized, but to sit at my right or at my left is not mine to grant, but is for those for whom it has been prepared.[125]

By themselves, these are necessarily cryptic. In the context we have uncovered, they point unmistakably in one direction. Jesus was aware of a vocation, as part of his messianic work, to bring the battle for the kingdom to its head in an event which could be fully described only in metaphor. The first metaphor here, that of baptism, seems to envisage that Jesus' public career would end in the way it began: not now, though, with an initiation into the renewed people of Israel, but with something else for which that could stand as an appropriate sign and symbol. If John's baptism evoked the exodus; and if Jesus' central and final symbolic act, pointing to his own fate, was a further evocation of the exodus; then it is not unreasonable to see this cryptic reference to a 'baptism' still to be undergone as an allusion to the fate which he would have to suffer, and as investing that fate with exodus-significance.[126] Other uses of 'baptism' and its cognates in the metaphorical

---

preceding 'but you would not'.

[123] Mt. 21.9/Mk. 11.10/Lk. 19.38/Jn. 12.13. On the crowds' reactions to Jesus cf. Farmer 1956, 198–201.

[124] Lk. 12.49–50. Cf. Hengel 1981a, 71: 'What later community could have had any interest in subsequently constructing such an obscure, indeed questionable, saying as [this]?'

[125] Mk. 10.38–40; the Mt. par. (20.22–3) omits the ref. to baptism.

[126] cf. Dunn 1970, 42; cf. Zahl 1983, 328: 'by describing his own mission in terms of judgment, a baptism of catastrophe, Jesus proposed that the judgment fall on him'.

sense of undergoing suffering suggest that this allusion is on target.[127]

The same is true, *mutatis mutandis*, of the 'cup', which occurs again in the Gethsemane narrative.[128] This image is more frequent; and 'drinking the same cup' clearly means 'sharing the same fate'.[129] The cup can denote suffering, even martyrdom,[130] though the context can indicate that it can also be a cup of blessing.[131] Here the context indicates a warning for Jesus' followers, and a strange vocation for himself, to take upon himself the suffering predicted for the people.

As we cautiously allow the riddles to interpret one another, a picture grows up around the central action in the upper room. Jesus knew, somehow, that he was to suffer and die. He interpreted that event through a series of images by which he was saying, not only that this was his god-given lot, but that this was part of the vocation in which his work and Israel's fate were bound up together. We shall explore this further presently.

(g) Riddles and Authenticity

When we examined the messianic riddles which Jesus told in the aftermath of his Temple-action, I argued that their very form was a strong indication of their originality to Jesus himself. The early church was not reticent, or inclined to tell riddles, about his Messiahship; the only place such riddles belong is in Jesus' ministry itself. Something very similar can be said about the riddles that point towards the meaning of Jesus' death.

The early church was not reticent in speaking about Jesus' death, and in developing a rich and multifaceted interpretation of it. The first Christians had no need to speak of it in riddles. The cross was public knowledge, and, though it might be a scandal, it was a nettle that was grasped, not a strange fact that could be alluded to only with cryptic sayings. Putting this the other way around, the riddles are remarkably free of even the beginnings of that early atonement-theology which we see, for instance, so clearly in Paul. Indeed, some of them speak simply of approaching tragic death, without any

[127] The biblical use of flood-imagery for chaos or disaster is well known: e.g. Gen. 6–9; 2 Sam. 22.5; Ps. 69.1-2; 93.3; 124.4-5. For baptism-imagery in relation to suffering cf. e.g. Jos. *War* 4.137; cf. too Ps. 68.3; Job 9.31 in the Aquila version. For further refs. cf. e.g. Delling 1957. On the response to James and John cf. Muddiman 1987.

[128] Mt. 26.39/Mk. 14.36/Lk. 22.42. Cf. Barrett 1967, 46-9.

[129] See the passages cited in SB 1.836-8.

[130] As in *Mt. Isa.* 5.13: 'for me alone the LORD has mixed the cup'. The biblical background for the cup of YHWH's wrath includes e.g. Isa. 51.17, 22, 23 (cf. Job 21.20; Ps. 60.3; Obad. 16); Jer. 25.15-17, 28; 49.12; 51.7; Lam. 4.21; Zech. 12.2.

[131] e.g. Ps. 23.5; 116.13.

sense of a redemption thereby achieved. They do not seem to be later history turned into prophecy: the prediction that James and John would suffer the same fate as Jesus was, so far as we know, only partially accurate.[132] If the story of the two brothers was made up to reflect positions held in the early church, it is very odd that Peter is not mentioned.[133] Nevertheless, though the sayings do not reflect anything that we know of early Christian atonement-theology, we can see how sayings such as these, surrounding Jesus' central symbolic actions, could have been part of the matrix from which that theology developed. They are thus both appropriately dissimilar, and appropriately similar, to the life of the early church.

The same is true (we shall explore this further presently) in relation to the Jewish context of Jesus' work. The riddles we have studied contain numerous links back, in particular, to the world of classical prophecy. But their particular form and direction is unique; we have no other examples of prophets applying to themselves anything like this combination of motifs. These riddles, once more, belong where we find them, namely, on Jesus' own lips. They functioned as cryptic but telling pointers to the event for which the main signpost was the Last Supper. Jesus' own death – the death of the strange non-messianic Messiah – was somehow bound up both with the fate of the whole nation and with the coming of the new exodus in which YHWH would at last establish his kingdom.

(iii) Predictions of the Passion

Working back further from the symbolic act of the Last Supper, and the short riddles which offer little flashes of interpretative insight into why Jesus did what he did on that occasion, we discover a context in which we can at last tackle the more substantial sayings on the subject which the synoptic tradition offers. By themselves, of course, these 'predictions of the passion' are regularly dismissed as *vaticinia ex eventu*, 'prophecies' after the event, reflecting early Christian apologetics and atonement-theology rather than anything characteristic of the mind of Jesus. Approaching them the way we have done offers a new route into Jesus' mindset, and to understanding how, from his point of view, his own death might actually function as part of the means of bringing in the kingdom.

The texts are well known:

---

[132] James was killed by Herod Agrippa I (Ac. 12.2). John's fate is unknown (cf. Taylor 1952, 442, on the relevant Papias traditions) – even if, as Gundry 1993, 584 assumes without argument, he is the person referred to in Rev. 1.9.

[133] So Sanders 1985, 147.

He began to teach them that the son of man must suffer many things, be rejected by the elders, the chief priests and the scribes, and be killed, and after three days be raised.[134]

How then is it written of the son of man, that he should suffer many things and be treated with contempt?[135]

He was teaching the disciples that the son of man will be given into the hands of men, and they will kill him, and that he will rise again three days after his death.[136]

Taking the twelve, he began to tell them what was to happen to him: 'Look, we are going up to Jerusalem; the son of man will be handed over to the chief priests and the scribes, who will condemn him to death, and hand him over to the Gentiles. They will scourge him, spit at him, flog him, and kill him; and after three days he will rise again.'[137]

The son of man came not to be served but to serve, and to give his life as a ransom for many.[138]

You will all fall away because of me this night; for it is written, I will strike the shepherd, and the sheep will be scattered.[139]

For I tell you, this thing that is written must be fulfilled in me: 'And he was numbered among the lawless.' For that which concerns me has its fulfilment.[140]

The hour is at hand, and the son of man is betrayed into the hands of sinners.[141]

All this [Jesus' arrest] has taken place so that the scriptures might be fulfilled.[142]

There are other hints, too: the prophet cannot die except in Jerusalem (but presumably will when he gets there); the bridegroom will be taken away; there will be a time when the disciples will fend for themselves in Jesus' absence.[143] All in all, it is an impressive catalogue.

A great deal depends, of course, on what one deems to be possible, or thinkable, for Jesus himself. There is no problem about the language used here being available to him; no problem about showing that these sayings are very unlike both what we find in the Judaism of the time and what we find in the atonement-theology of the early church. The real problem comes when

[134] Mt. 16.21/Mk. 8.31/Lk. 9.22. Mt. adds 'must go to Jerusalem'.

[135] Mk. 9.12.

[136] Mt. 17.22f./Mk. 9.31/Lk. 9.44 (with variations).

[137] Mt. 20.17–19/Mk. 10.32–4/Lk. 18.31–3.

[138] Mt. 20.28/Mk. 10.45.

[139] Mt. 26.31/Mk. 14.27, quoting Zech. 13.7.

[140] Lk. 22.37.

[141] Mt. 26.45/Mk. 14.41; cf. Lk. 22.22.

[142] Mt. 26.56 (cf. 54)/Mk. 14.49. Goppelt 1981 [1975], 189 professes himself at a loss to know how Conzelmann 1969, 133 can dismiss these sayings so summarily as unhistorical.

[143] Prophet: Lk. 13.33; bridegroom: Mt. 9.15/Mk. 2.20/Lk. 5.35; cf. *Thom.* 104; fending for themselves: Lk. 17.22; Mt. 24.9–14/Mk. 13.9–13/Lk. 21.12–19.

we try to assess whether Jesus could or would have held such ideas in his head; in deciding, that is, the shape of his mindset.

I have already argued that Jesus saw himself as the focal point of Israel's long and tortuous story (and that this was not a particularly unusual thing for persons, under certain circumstances, to think at that time). I have also argued that Jesus acted symbolically, and retold Israel's story, in such a way as to suggest strongly that he believed that this story would reach its climax in the great battle through which evil would be defeated and the people of YHWH rescued once and for all. The riddles we have just studied, in this light, point to a vocation of a particular shape, within which these predictions fit like a glove. The 'son of man' – the representative of the people of the saints of the most high – would find the beasts waging war upon him; but he would be vindicated.

In order to study this further, and to get to the inside of the sayings, we must make a detour. We have got to the point where we must ask: what resources were available to Jesus for reflecting on how the kingdom might come through the suffering and death of Israel's representative?

6. The Intention of Jesus (3): Eschatological Redemption in Judaism

(i) Introduction

To answer this question, we return again to the variegated context of second-Temple Judaism. We proceed down two lines, namely story and symbol, aware of the praxis generated and sustained by these, and of the implicit answers offered as a result to key worldview questions, especially in this case: 'what's the solution?'

(ii) The Controlling Story: Exile and Restoration

We may begin on ground already well prepared. The overarching category within which first-century Jewish reflection could handle the whole question of present suffering and future vindication, of present woe and future redemption, and of the means by which YHWH might bring his people from the one to the other, was that of exile ('the present evil age') and restoration ('the age to come'). I use these terms, of course, as a shorthand; there are, no doubt, different ways of saying the same thing; but once again I must stress: for the bulk of first-century Judaism, the exile was simply not yet over. The promises of Isaiah and the rest had not been fulfilled. As long as

Pilate and Herod – and, for that matter, Caiaphas – were ruling, the kingdom had not yet come. Pagan oppression was the sign of the present evil age; the age to come would bring freedom and peace, when YHWH vindicated his people after their long period of suffering.

Once again, too, we must stress: return from exile, in this period, *meant* 'forgiveness of sins', and vice versa. 'The punishment of your iniquity, O daughter Zion, is accomplished; he will keep you in exile no longer.'[144] As long as Israel was still suffering under foreign rule, the 'sins' that had caused the exile had not been 'forgiven'. Forgiveness was concrete, as it would be for someone in prison: a 'pardon' that did not result in actual release would be no pardon at all. Psalms and prophets alike looked forward to the day when the promises would be fulfilled, when sins would be forgiven, and YHWH would have dealt once and for all with the evil that still oppressed his people.

In particular, the historical and theological theme that dominated the horizon of those longing for the real return from exile was of course the exodus. Celebrated every year at Passover, the exodus created the classic Jewish metanarrative, within which the hope for return from exile made sense, and in terms of which that return was described in some of the classic prophetic texts.[145] It is hard to overestimate the importance of the exodus-story within the historical, political and theological worldview of second-Temple Judaism; and, again and again, that story resonated in a world where most Jews were hoping and praying that it would come true once more, this time for good. That, as we have seen, was the world which Jesus deliberately set out to evoke in his last great prophetic and symbolic action. If we begin here, we are as likely as we shall ever be to track and trace the mindset of Jesus.

(iii) The First Sub-Plot: The Messianic Woes

As we saw in *NTPG*, some second-Temple Jews believed that the great deliverance would come through a period of intense suffering.[146] This functions as a story within the larger story: the time of suffering would be the means through which the apocalyptic drama would attain its goal. Though the theme is not ubiquitous in second-Temple Judaism, it occurs often

[144] Lam. 4.22, summarizing in effect the whole line of thought in Isa. 40—55 (cf. above, 268–74).

[145] e.g. Isa. 51.9-11.

[146] *NTPG* 277f., citing primary and secondary sources; in addition, cf. *Ass. Mos.* 9.1—10.10; *1 En.* 47.1-4. Cf. too the (later) Sifre Dt. 333 on Dt. 32.43.

enough (not least in Qumran, which offers a range of analogies with Jesus and his movement) for us to be able to postulate it with some confidence.

To grasp the significance of this sub-plot within the larger story of new exodus, of exile and restoration, we may return for a moment to Albert Schweitzer. Schweitzer saw the second-Temple expectation of the 'messianic woes' as the vital clue to Jesus' understanding, both of the moment in history at which he was living, and of his own vocation in relation to that moment. For him, the central idea was that of the *peirasmos*, the Testing:

> In order to understand Jesus' resolve to suffer, we must first recognize that the mystery of this suffering is involved in the mystery of the kingdom of god, since the kingdom cannot come until the *peirasmos* has taken place . . . The novelty lies in the form in which [the sufferings] are conceived. The tribulation, so far as Jesus is concerned, is now connected with an historic event: He will go to Jerusalem, there to suffer death at the hands of the authorities . . . In the secret of His passion which Jesus reveals to the disciples at Caesarea Philippi the pre-Messianic tribulation is for others set aside, abolished, concentrated upon Himself alone, and that in the form that they are fulfilled in His own passion and death at Jerusalem. That was the new conviction that had dawned upon Him. He must suffer for others . . . that the Kingdom might come.[147]

This idea, like a good deal that Schweitzer proposed, flew in the face of the theological sensibilities of the early twentieth century, and has for that reason not been much used, or even discussed, in subsequent research. Yet I am persuaded that, with certain important modifications (necessary not least because of our improved knowledge of Jewish apocalyptic), there is a core of historical insight here which should not be lost.

A comment on the likely reaction to such a proposal may be in order. It would of course be extraordinary to think of a cautious western scholar deliberately acting in obedience to a scheme of thought which provided, as it were, the script for a play to be enacted. (Actually, reflecting on the way in which some scholars plan their careers, it may not be so extraordinary as all that.) Western scholars, after all, not only believe in freedom to pursue their research in their own way. They also pride themselves on being detached flies-on-the-wall: observers, not participants. Here, once again, we face the danger of anachronism, imagining Jesus as a great teacher of truths-divorced-from-real-life. Only when we soak ourselves in the history of the time can we escape this imprisonment in our own culture. Schweitzer, I am persuaded, prised the prison door open a crack. I suggest that we push it open further, allowing both history and theology to escape from the clutches of those who have been dominated by anachronism disguised as (apparently sophisticated) scepticism. Only if we follow the first-century evidence where

[147] Schweitzer 1954 [1906], 385–7 (the whole of 384–90 is significant). See too Schweitzer 1925 [1901], ch. 9, esp. 226–36.

it leads, after all, can we be justified in referring to 'Jesus' at all, whether in history or in theology.

My point at the moment is that, within the range of options available to a reflective Jew of the first century who believed himself to be a participant in the long-awaited drama of the kingdom of YHWH, it made a lot of sense to suppose that the kingdom would finally come through a time of intense suffering. We shall apply this to Jesus presently; for the moment we must fill in the picture with a second sub-plot, which likewise functions within the overarching metanarrative of the new exodus, the great return from exile, and which brings the concept of the messianic woes to a sharp point.

(iv) The Second Sub-Plot: Specific or Individual Suffering

The belief in the likelihood, or even the necessity, of suffering as part of the way in which the plan of YHWH would be brought to birth did not remain at a general level in the literature of this period. We can detect several categories of persons for whom specific suffering at the hands of the wicked, or the pagans, might be expected. Such suffering could be interpreted within the eschatological framework we have outlined. It was not arbitrary or random, but formed one sharp edge of the general sufferings of Israel. Within this, there are hints that such suffering *could* be seen, in some sense and in some cases, as part of the means whereby the coming liberation would be accomplished.

One of the most obvious categories of suffering individuals within Israel is that of prophets. The most obvious evidence for this is in the New Testament, where the idea has become proverbial,[148] but it has its roots in the biblical tradition,[149] and is reflected in books such as the *Martyrdom of Isaiah*. In Jesus' own day and experience, of course, the greatest of recent prophets was John the Baptist, and his fate must have weighed heavily upon the mind of the one who looked to him as forerunner.[150] The fearless prophet, opposed and perhaps killed by the Jewish authorities to whom he had spoken the word of YHWH, was a model which can never have been far from the self-understanding of the prophet from Nazareth.

[148] cf. e.g. Mt. 5.11–12/Lk. 6.22–3; Mt. 23.29–36/Lk. 11.47–51; Mt. 23.37/Lk. 13.34 (cf. 13.33); Ac. 7.52; and, of course, the prophets in the parable of the wicked tenants. Cf. Jeremias 1971, 281; de Jonge 1991a, 34–7.

[149] e.g. 2 Chr. 36.15f.; Neh. 9.26; Jer. 2.30; and, for the idea that the prophets (especially true prophets) were always rejected, cf. 1 Kgs. 19.10; 22.8; Ezra 9.10f.; Jer. 26.1–24; Zech. 1.4–6; 7.7–14. Cf. too Ezek. 4.4–6, on which see below.

[150] cf. Schillebeeckx 1979 [1974], 299f. Lk. 13.33 ('no prophet can perish away from Jerusalem') is odd; Jesus regarded John as a prophet, yet he did not perish in Jerusalem.

Quite close to this is the important passage early on in the Wisdom of Solomon. Here, the wicked, out of a sense of the futility of their lives, plot to do evil. Specifically, they plan to kill the righteous man who has shown up their evil ways:

> Let us lie in wait for the righteous man,
> because he is inconvenient to us and opposes our actions;
> he reproaches us for sins against the law . . .
> He professes to have knowledge of God,
> and calls himself a child [or 'servant'] of the Lord . . .
> We are considered by him as something base,
> and he avoids our ways as unclean;
> he calls the last end of the righteous happy,
> and boasts that God is his father.
> Let us see if his words are true,
> and let us test what will happen at the end of his life;
> for if the righteous man is God's child, he will help him,
> and will deliver him from the hand of his adversaries.
> Let us test him with insult and torture,
> so that we may find out how gentle he is,
> and make trial of his forbearance.
> Let us condemn him to a shameful death,
> for, according to what he says, he will be protected.[151]

The writer comments, first, that when this happens Israel's god will hold the souls of the righteous in his hand, at peace though out of human sight; then, that at the appointed time he will raise them from the dead, setting them to rule over the world.[152] The ungodly, meanwhile, will be punished as they deserve.[153] This lesson is then applied more widely, with a further description of the fate which the righteous suffer at the hands of the wicked, and a further description of the bliss that awaits the righteous as a result, before being focused again as a warning to the kings of the earth that what they need more than anything else is Wisdom.[154] As has sometimes been pointed out, the language used to describe the fate of the righteous appears to be drawn from the 'suffering servant' passage in Isaiah 52 and 53, while the scene describing the judgment of the wicked is rooted in such passages as Isaiah 14 (the strange figure whose heaven-storming pride leads to downfall) and Psalm 2 (the Davidic king who routs his enemies).[155] There is good reason to suppose that this passage in the Wisdom of Solomon draws on an exegetical tradition which was used independently by *1 Enoch* and other

---

[151] Wis. 2.12–20.

[152] 3.1–6; 3.7–9.

[153] 3.10–19.

[154] chs. 4—6; on the suffering and vindication of the righteous, 5.4–5; 5.15–16.

[155] cf. Nickelsburg 1992, 140 (e.g. echoes of Ps. 2.4, 9 in Wis. 4.18–19).

second-Temple writings.[156] The value of the passage for our present purpose is thus that it opens a window on a theme which we may cautiously presume to have been more widely known than just among the readers of a particular book.

This supposition is strongly confirmed by the evidence from Qumran. The sufferings of the Teacher of Righteousness are spoken of quite frequently, as for instance in the commentary on Habakkuk:

> Interpreted, [Habakkuk 1.13b] concerns the House of Absalom and the members of its council, who were silent at the time of the chastisement of the Teacher of Righteousness and gave him no help against the Liar . . .[157]

> The interpretation of [Habakkuk 2.15] concerns the Wicked Priest who pursued the Teacher of Righteousness to consume him with the ferocity of his anger in the place of his banishment, in festival time, during the rest of the day of Atonement . . .[158]

But the whole community will also suffer, and thus find their way towards the eventual salvation:

> Interpreted, [Habakkuk 2.4b] concerns all those who observe the Law in the House of Judah, whom God will deliver from the House of Judgment because of their suffering and because of their faith in the Teacher of Righteousness.[159]

> The sons of light and the lot of darkness shall battle together for God's might, between the roar of a huge multitude and the shout of gods and of men, on the day of calamity. It will be a time of suffering for all the people redeemed by God. Of all their sufferings, none will be like this, from its haste until eternal redemption is fulfilled.[160]

Thus, though it is very unlikely that anyone at Qumran thought in terms of a suffering Messiah, it is clear that there was a wider belief that the sufferings of the sect in general, and of one of its founders in particular, were pointers towards the coming liberation, and perhaps part of the means of its arrival.[161] This could sometimes even be expressed in terms of atonement:

> In the Council of the Community there shall be twelve men and three Priests . . . They shall preserve the faith in the Land with steadfastness and meekness and shall atone for sin by the practice of justice and by suffering the sorrows of affliction . . .[162]

---

[156] Nickelsburg 1992, 138–42.

[157] 1QpHab 5.10–11 (Vermes 1995 [1962], 342).

[158] 1QpHab. 11.4–7 (GM 201).

[159] 1QpHab. 8.1–3 (Vermes 1995 [1962], 344). GM 200 translates the key term, however, as 'deeds'.

[160] 1QM 1.11–12 (GM 95). Cf. too e.g. 1QH 11 [=3].6–18 (GM 331f.) (quoted in *NTPG* 277 n.136). Of this psalm, Knibb (1987, 174) writes that 'the concern is entirely with the woes that would inaugurate the messianic age'.

[161] Collins 1995, 123–6 rightly rejects the idea of a 'suffering Messiah' in 4Q451 fr. 9 & 24 (GM 270); Schiffman 1994, 346f. is right to dismiss the suggestion of a 'pierced Messiah' in 4Q285 fr. 5 (GM 124).

[162] 1QS 8.1–4 (Vermes 1995 [1962], 80). For this atoning activity cf. too 1QS 5.6; 9.4;

If Qumran offers further suggestions about the way in which innocent or righteous suffering could be understood within a second-Temple Jewish worldview, the same is true, perhaps more obviously, of the stories of the martyrs, particularly from the time of the Maccabees.[163] What matters here is not so much what actually happened as the way in which the stories of martyrdom were written up retrospectively. We must remember, too, that the Maccabees were celebrated in the big annual festival of Hanukkah, causing their story to be widely known; and that some of Jesus' symbolic actions and explanatory riddles seem deliberately to have evoked Maccabaean action.[164] The sufferings of the martyrs are described in 2 Maccabees as having the effect of dealing with the nation's sins in the present time, so that Israel might receive mercy in the future, unlike the other nations whose sins were mounting up until they were finally to be judged.[165] The martyrs therefore went gladly to their suffering and death, believing that they would be raised to new life in the future.[166] Their sufferings, they claimed, would make a way through the present time of wrath to the salvation which lay beyond, while their tormentors were storing up wrath for themselves:

> Our brothers after enduring a brief suffering have drunk of everflowing life, under God's covenant; but you [the Syrian king Antiochus], by the judgment of God, will receive just punishment for your arrogance. I, like my brothers, give up body and life for the laws of our ancestors, appealing to God to show mercy soon to our nation and by trials and plagues to make you confess that he alone is God, and through me and my brothers to bring to an end the wrath of the Almighty that has justly fallen on our whole nation.[167]

Or, again, in a work more or less contemporary with the time of Jesus:

> You know, O God, that though I might have saved myself, I am dying in burning torments for the sake of the law. Be merciful to your people, and let our punishment suffice for them. Make my blood their purification, and take my life in exchange for theirs.[168]

> Imitate me, brothers; do not leave your post in my struggle or renounce our courageous family ties. Fight the sacred and noble battle for religion. Thereby the just Providence of our ancestors may become merciful to our nation and take vengeance on the accursed tyrant.[169]

---

and cp. jYom. 38b; tYom. 5.6ff.

[163] On the Macc. passages cf. e.g. Hengel 1981a; de Jonge 1988, 174–84, 208–11; 1991a, 45–8. Droge & Tabor 1992 seems to me slanted, to say the least; cf. *NTPG* 364f.

[164] cf. Farmer 1956; and ch. 11 above.

[165] 2 Macc. 6.12–17; cf. 7.18–19.

[166] 2 Macc. 6.30; 7.9, 11, 14, 16–17, 22–3, 29, 30–8.

[167] 2 Macc. 7.36–8.

[168] 4 Macc. 6.27–9; cp. 1.11.

[169] 4 Macc. 9.23–4.

These, then, who have been consecrated for the sake of God, are honoured, not only with this honour, but also by the fact that because of them our enemies did not rule over our nation, the tyrant was punished, and the homeland purified – they having become, as it were, a ransom for the sin of our nation. And through the blood of those devout ones and their death as an atoning sacrifice, divine Providence preserved Israel that previously had been mistreated.[170]

Those who gave over their bodies in suffering for the sake of religion were not only admired by mortals, but also were deemed worthy to share in a divine inheritance. Because of them the nation gained peace . . .[171]

There are three strands of belief which run through these accounts. First, the fate of the martyrs is bound up with the fate of the nation as a whole. Second, as a result, their suffering forms as it were the focal point of the suffering of the nation, continuing the theme of exile-as-the-punishment-for-sin which we find in the great prophetic writings such as Jeremiah, Ezekiel, Isaiah 40—55 and Daniel, but now giving it more precise focus. Third, this representative exilic suffering functions *redemptively*: not only will the martyrs themselves enjoy subsequent heavenly blessing and/or resurrection life, but their sufferings will have the effect of drawing on to themselves the sufferings of the nation as a whole, *so that the nation may somehow escape*.[172] The fact that all these elements are found together in various different passages suggests that this complex theological (and political) train of thought was already well known by the time 4 Maccabees was written, i.e. most likely in the middle of the first century.[173]

This evidence from popular beliefs about prophets, from the Wisdom of Solomon, from Qumran, from the Maccabaean literature, and elsewhere indicates that we are here in touch with a tradition that was reasonably widespread and well known in the period of the second Temple. According to this tradition, the suffering and perhaps the death of certain Jews could function within YHWH's plan to redeem his people from pagan oppression: to win for them, in other words, rescue from wrath, forgiveness of sins, and covenant renewal. This by itself, I suggest, would be enough to give us some

---

[170] 4 Macc. 17.20-2.

[171] 4 Macc. 18.3-4.

[172] The atoning value of sufferings is a regular theme in various subsequent Jewish writings: e.g. Lev. R. 20.7; Sifre Dt. 333 (on Dt. 32.43); Midr. Pss. 118.18; cf. Moore 1927–30, 1.546–52; Schechter 1961 [1909], 307–11; Barrett 1959, 11-15; Montefiore & Loewe 1974 [1938], 225-32; Hengel 1981a, 60-1.

[173] cf. H. Anderson 1992, 453. Similar ideas occur fleetingly in later rabbinic literature, on which see below. Cf. too *T.Ben.* 3.8, which, even in the shorter (Armenian) version, states unequivocally that 'in you will be fulfilled the heavenly prophecy which says that the spotless one will be defiled by lawless men and the sinless one will die for the sake of impious men'. This may, of course, be a Christian interpolation. Cf. Stuhlmacher 1986 [1981], 24, with other refs.; Hengel 1996, 81-3.

substantial clues as to the world of thought within which a prophet and would-be Messiah, in the first third of the first century, might find his own vocation being decisively shaped.

But where did this tradition come from? The language, and frequent biblical allusions, suggest various sources; and, since what we find in the traditions about Jesus sometimes reflects similar passages, we must look at these in a little more detail.

(v) 'According to the Scriptures'

When is an allusion not an allusion? This question forms a powerful undercurrent in a good deal of New Testament study. The historical question (was Paul, or whoever, alluding to a particular text, and if so why) is often intertwined with literary questions about authorial intention and the like; about these things, as the writer to the Hebrews says, we cannot now speak in detail. It is highly probable that writers in second-Temple Judaism alluded to a good many biblical texts, deliberately conjuring up a world of discourse with a word or phrase. It is also highly probable that readers in the twentieth century, alert for such allusions, will hear at least some where none were intended. It is absolutely certain that modern readers who are alert to this danger, and hence unwilling to allow any allusions beyond more or less direct quotations, will radically misread important texts. There are times when the historian needs reminding that history is an art, not a science.[174]

With this uncomfortable introduction, we can proceed to enquire after the biblical roots of the tradition we have been examining. Working backwards, we come first to the book of Daniel. Whenever the Daniel-traditions reached their present form, it is clear both that they were of critical importance at the time of the Maccabaean crisis and that they were read eagerly during the first century as a charter for the revolutionaries who stood within the same Maccabaean tradition of holy revolt against the rule of paganism.[175] We have seen often enough the ways in which early chapters in Daniel were read in the first century, not least as part of the longing for the kingdom of YHWH to be established in place of the rule of the pagans. It is clear that such stories as the three young men in the fiery furnace, and Daniel himself in the lion's den, would have functioned in the Maccabaean period and thereafter as an encouragement to Jews under persecution to hold fast to their ancestral laws,

---

[174] On the whole question of allusion cf. Hays 1989. Hooker 1959, 62–4, 101f. lays down extremely stringent criteria for what will count as a reference to 'the servant' in the NT. On the historical/literary questions cf. *NTPG* chs. 2–4.

[175] cf. Farmer 1956, ch. 6.

even if it meant torture or death. In this context, we find again a close align-
ment between the fate of the nation, not least the Temple itself, and the fate
of the martyrs:

> Forces sent by [the pagan king] shall occupy and profane the temple and fortress. They
> shall abolish the regular burnt offering and set up the abomination that makes desolate.
> He shall seduce with intrigue those who violate the covenant; but the people who are
> loyal to their god shall stand firm and take action. The wise among the people shall give
> understanding to many; for some days, however, they shall fall by sword and flame, and
> suffer captivity and plunder . . . Some of the wise shall fall, so that they may be refined,
> purified, and cleansed, until the time of the end . . .[176]

Much of this, clearly, suggests itself as a source for the themes just
observed, not least in the Wisdom of Solomon and the Maccabaean stories.
Shortly after this passage, the themes are repeated:

> There shall be a time of anguish, such as has never occurred since nations first came into
> existence. But at that time your people shall be delivered, everyone who is found written
> in the book. Many of those who sleep in the dust of the earth shall awake, some to ever-
> lasting life, and some to shame and everlasting contempt. Those who are wise shall shine
> like the brightness of the sky, and those who lead many to righteousness, like the stars
> forever and ever . . . When the shattering of the power of the holy people comes to an
> end, all these things would be accomplished . . . Many shall be purified, cleansed, and
> refined, but the wicked shall continue to act wickedly . . .[177]

Nation and martyr, wisdom and wickedness, 'apocalyptic' and covenant: the
themes belong together within the same overall pattern. The fate of the
Temple and its sacrificial system is closely bound up with the fate of the
'wise' who, as in Wisdom 2—6, are killed but will be vindicated. The 'time
of great anguish' will give birth to the time of deliverance and purification.

Daniel, then, is an obvious source for first-century reflection on the way
in which the fate of nation and martyr hang together. But where do these
ideas in Daniel come from themselves? At one level, the idea of purification
belongs with the Levitical code of sacrifices. In Daniel 12, as in 4 Maccabees
17, we are witnessing the transference to the sphere of human suffering of a
theology which properly, or at least originally, belongs within the world of
Temple and cult:

> Words like 'satisfaction,' 'blood,' 'purification,' 'ransom,' and 'propitiation' clearly
> recapitulate longstanding OT traditions, e.g. the levitical regulations for the Day of
> Atonement (Lev 16; 17:11; etc.) . . .[178]

At another level, the traditions in question exhibit some connections with
second-Temple reflection on the *Akedah*, the so-called 'binding' of Isaac

[176] Dan. 11.31-5.
[177] Dan. 12.1-10.
[178] H. Anderson 1992, 453.

(recounted in Genesis 22). It remains debatable whether this tradition was as clearly developed in our period as later. The issue is not urgent for our own question, since there is no suggestion that Jesus referred to this theme.[179]

There is no debate, however, on the place of the Psalter in forming the worldview and expectation of second-Temple Judaism. The Psalms continued throughout the period to be sung in the regular liturgical and praying life of Israel, not least in the Temple itself. Those going to Jerusalem would use the pilgrim psalms, and those worshipping at a festival the festive ones (the *Hallel* at Passover, for instance). In that the Psalter was collected into its present form long after the Davidic monarchy had ceased to function as such, the regular focus on the promise to David and his heirs was a major way in which the hope for a renewed kingdom was kept alive.[180] Within that, the psalms of lament, which form the bulk of Books I and II of the Psalter (i.e. Psalms 1—41, 42—72), speak again and again of the suffering of the people of YHWH, and of their trust in him to vindicate and deliver them. In one notable instance, an explicitly Davidic psalm becomes, half-way through, a psalm of lament (89.1-37, 38-52). Anyone whose spirituality and thinking had been even partially formed by regular use of the Psalms, and whose life was lived out under pagan oppression, would have no difficulty in making connections between the themes of the poems and their own situation.

A book which, as we have already seen, was arguably of great influence on Jesus, and which contained dark hints about the necessary suffering of the people of YHWH, is of course Zechariah, particularly its second part (chapters 9—14).[181] The writer promises the long-awaited arrival of the true king (9.9-10), the renewed covenant and the real return from exile (9.11-12), the violent defeat of Israel's enemies and the rescue of the true people of YHWH (9.13-17). At the moment, however, Israel are like sheep without a shepherd (10.2); they have shepherds, but they are not doing their job, and will be punished (10.3) as part of the divine plan for the return from exile (10.6-12). The prophet is himself instructed to act as a shepherd, but in doing so to symbolize the worthless shepherds who are currently ruling Israel (11.4-17). There will be a great battle between Israel and the nations, in which 'the house of David shall be like God, like the angel of YHWH, at the head' of the inhabitants of Jerusalem (12.1-9; quotation from verse 8). There will be great mourning for 'one whom they have pierced' (12.10); a 'fountain . . .

---

[179] cf. *NTPG* 273f., and e.g. Hengel 1981a, 61-3 (suggesting that the tradition was already known in Jesus' day); Segal 1984.

[180] e.g. Pss. 2; 18; 20; 21; 45; 72; 89; 101; 110; 132; 144. Ps. 45 is regarded as messianic, and applied to the Teacher of Righteousness, in 4Q171 4.24-7 (GM 206; Vermes 1995 [1962], 352).

[181] On messianic hope in Zech. see recently Collins 1995, 31-4.

for the house of David and the inhabitants of Jerusalem, to cleanse them from sin and impurity' (13.1); a judgment upon the prophets of Israel (13.2–6); and judgment, too, on the shepherd of Israel, who will be struck down, and the sheep scattered (13.7). In another reminiscence of Ezekiel, this will have the effect of destroying two-thirds of the people, while the remaining one-third will be purified, to be in truth the people of YHWH (13.8–9). The book concludes with the great drama in which all the nations will be gathered together to fight against Jerusalem; YHWH will win a great victory, becoming king indeed, judging the nations and sanctifying Jerusalem (14.1–21).

From this (to us) often confusing blur of images certain things stand out. The underlying theme of the passage, as of so much Jewish literature of the period, is the establishment of YHWH's kingship, the rescue of Israel from oppression and exile, and the judgment both of the nations and of wicked leaders within Israel herself. These events will focus on Jerusalem and the Temple; not surprisingly, the royal house of David will clearly have a hand in them, with the king riding into Jerusalem (chapter 9) and being like God at the head of the army (chapter 12). Whatever the actual relationship between the two parts of the book, this theme naturally dovetails with the picture of Zerubbabel in Zechariah 1—8.[182] One of the controlling images in the book is that of the sheep and the shepherd; building no doubt on Ezekiel 34, the prophet sees Israel as the flock, and the king as the shepherd, who eventually shares the fate of the people. The passage about the smitten shepherd is quoted, in a strongly messianic context, in one manuscript of the Qumran Damascus Document;[183] 'they shall look on the one whom they have pierced' (12.10) is taken messianically in a later Talmudic text, which may perhaps refer to Bar-Kochba.[184] These provide slender hints of how some Jews may have read the texts in our period.

A somewhat different biblical passage, which bears analogy both with the traditions described in the previous section and with the symbolic acts and riddling prophecies of Jesus, is found in Ezekiel, where the prophet symbolically undergoes the exile of the people:

> And you, O mortal, take a brick and set it before you. On it portray a city, Jerusalem; and put siegeworks against it, and build a siege-wall against it, and cast up a ramp against it; set camps also against it, and plant battering rams against it all around . . . This is a sign for the house of Israel.
>
> Then lie on your left side, and place the punishment of the house of Israel upon it; you shall bear their punishment for the number of the days that you lie there. For I assign to you a number of days, three hundred and ninety days, equal to the number of the years

[182] cf. Collins 1995, 29–31. Zerubbabel is the likely referent of the 'Branch' prophecy of Zech. 3.8; 6.11f.

[183] CD 19.7–11 (Vermes 1995 [1962], 102; GM 45); cf. Collins 1995, 78–82.

[184] bSukk. 52a (cf. SB 2.583f.).

of their punishment; and so you shall bear the punishment of the house of Israel. When you have completed these, you shall lie down a second time, but on your right side, and bear the punishment of the house of Judah; forty days I assign you, one day for each year . . .[185]

This, too, carries overtones of the Levitical sacrificial system, where the sacrificial animal is said to 'bear' the iniquities of the people.[186] Once again, there is nothing here that could be called a Christian 'atonement-theology'; only a sense that Ezekiel's vocation, first to portray the destruction of Jerusalem in symbolic fashion, and then to undergo in his own person the fate he had just symbolically enacted for the city, has some striking resemblances to the picture we built up earlier, in which Jesus' symbolic actions in the Temple and the upper room, and the riddles with which he explained those actions, pointed to a similar double effect, through which he would undergo the fate he had announced for the Temple.

More important even than Daniel or Ezekiel, as the biblical context for the stories of suffering and martyrdom in the second-Temple period, is the prophecy of Isaiah; particularly chapters 40—55, and particularly, within that, the figure of the servant. This has been a controversial topic, and we must approach the material with care. There are four main points to be made about pre- or non-Christian Jewish readings of this famous passage.[187]

First, the picture of the 'servant', whether in Isaiah 52.13—53.12 or in the other so-called 'servant songs', was only in very modern times abstracted from the message of Isaiah 40—55 as a whole.[188] If we are to stand any chance of understanding how a first-century Jew might have made sense of these passages, one of our first moves must be to read the surrounding contexts. And there we find, not a detached atonement-theology, but the prophecy which we have referred to a number of times in this volume: that YHWH would comfort and restore his people after their exile, would pour out his wrath upon the pagans who had held them captive, and would return in person to Zion to reign as king. Indeed, one of the passages in which these themes are stated most clearly (along with the opening oracle, 40.1–11), is the passage which leads in directly to the fourth servant song, namely 52.7–12 ('How lovely upon the mountains . . .'). Likewise, the chapters (54—55)

---

[185] Ezek. 4.1–6. Commenting on the two actions (laying siege to the brick, and lying prone), Eichrodt (1970 [1965], 85) remarks that 'if the prophet is a type of Yahweh in his first action, he evidently represents Israel in the second'.

[186] cf. e.g. Lev. 10.17; 16.22. It also evokes one of Jesus' warning oracles over Jerusalem (Lk. 19.42-3); cf. Dodd 1968, 76.

[187] On this whole topic see now above all Hengel 1996, in many ways superseding, and in some correcting, the very full treatment in Zimmerli & Jeremias 1967 [1957], 677-700.

[188] cf. Hengel 1996 for the different ways in which the Qumran Isa. scrolls divide the book.

which come after the fourth song celebrate in no uncertain terms Israel's restoration, the renewal of the covenant, and the forgiveness of the sins which led to exile; and chapter 55 throws open the invitation to all and sundry to come and join in the blessing. We would be quite wrong, in other words, to detach the picture of the 'servant' from this wider prophetic (and 'kingdom-of-god') context.

Second, it is fairly widely recognized that Isaiah 40—55, particularly the picture of the suffering righteous servant, was one of the main influences upon the second-Temple writings we examined a moment ago, and indeed on a good many other subsequent Jewish texts. Certainly the Maccabaean texts bear witness to this.[189] Daniel 11—12, in particular, should be regarded as one of the earliest extant interpreters of the servant-figure in Isaiah: it looks as though he saw the martyrs of his own day as at least a partial fulfilment of Isaiah 53.[190] This is hardly surprising. Whenever second-Temple Jews were struggling to make sense of their continued and harsh suffering, it makes sense to suppose that Isaiah offered a large-scale glorious hope, for return from exile and for the coming of the kingdom. Within that perspective, the present suffering of the righteous could be understood as falling somehow within the long-term purposes of YHWH.

Third, there is some evidence that some Jews at least interpreted the 'servant' figure messianically. The 'Branch' of Zechariah 3.8 is described as 'my servant'; a case can be made out for the messianic passages in Zechariah 12 and 13 making allusion to Isaiah;[191] and it can be argued that the subtleties within the two Isaiah scrolls found at Qumran, and within the LXX translations, suggest that those responsible in each case were aware of at least

---

[189] cf. Hengel 1996; and e.g. H. Anderson 1992, 453 (for 4 Macc.); Nickelsburg 1992, 140 (for Wis.); etc. Despite (or perhaps because of) Christian use, Isa. 53 possessed some importance for the later rabbis: cf. e.g. bSot. 14a, joining Isa. 53.12 with Ex. 32.32 and applying it to Moses (possibly in response to Christian use, cf. Moore 1927-30, 1.550 with n.254); jShek. 48c, applying it to 'the men of the Great Assembly'; Sifre Num. 25.13, applying it to Phineas. Isa. 53.4 was used in bSanh. 98b (cf. too 98a), to suggest that the Messiah would be a leper (possibly in ironic deprecation of Messianism; so Collins 1995, 135 n.128, following Urbach). According to Origen *C. Cels.* 1.55, the Jews applied the chapter to the Jewish people as a whole. On the whole question cf. the older work of Neubauer & Driver 1876-77, and the standard studies such as e.g. Jeremias 1950; Zimmerli and Jeremias 1967 [1957]; Hooker 1959, chs. 2, 3; Schürer 2.547-9.

[190] The allusion from Dan. 12.3 ('those who justify the many') to Isa. 53.11 ('he shall justify the many') - observed by e.g. Montgomery 1927, 459, 472f.; Porteous 1965, 171; Lacocque 1979 [1976], 243, 245, 249; Fishbane 1985, 482-99 - is a sign that the whole passage about the suffering righteous ones, from 11.31 to 12.10, may be influenced by Isa. 52.13—53.12. Cf. von Rad's comment (1965 [1960], 315): 'the death of the wise in 11.33, 35, with its purifying effect, is reminiscent of the atoning function of the Isaianic servant.'

[191] So Hengel 1996, 54-7: the sheep which go astray in Isa. 53.6 become the scattered flock of Zech. 13.7.

the possibility of messianic interpretations of some sort or another.[192] The strange 'son of man' figure in *1 Enoch* looks as though it may well be a composite put together out of Daniel 7 and Isaiah 53.[193] It is well known that the Isaiah Targum, which some would date as early as the first century, identifies the 'servant' of 52.11 with the Messiah.[194] There is no reason to suppose that a messianic interpretation would have taken a first-century Jew by surprise.[195]

Fourth, although this messianic identification could be made (as a sharpening up and personalizing of the wider reference to the people as a whole), this does not mean that pre-Christian Judaism as a whole, or in any major part, embraced a doctrine of a *suffering* Messiah, still less a dying one. The Isaiah Targum demonstrates this strikingly: having identified the servant as the Messiah, the subsequent passages about suffering are referred to the sanctuary which was polluted because of Israel's sins (53.5), or to the suffering which the Messiah would inflict upon Israel's enemies (53.7, 9, 11), or to the tribulation through which the exiles would pass to salvation when pagan rule over Israel finally ceased (52.14; 53.3-4, 8), or (a variation on the same theme) to the suffering by means of which the true remnant would be refined and purified (53.10). Only at one point is there a different note: in the Targum's reading of 53.12 it seems to be the Messiah who 'delivered his soul unto death'.[196] Indeed, the use of Isaiah 40—55 as a whole, and in its parts, seldom if ever in pre-Christian Judaism includes *all* those elements which later Christian theology brought together (as, for instance, in 1 Peter 2.21-5): servant, Messiah, suffering, *and* vicarious sin-bearing.[197] It is conceivable that we find the idea of sin-bearing, with reference to Isaiah, in some Jewish texts, but this is far harder to prove than messianic meanings.[198] The main emphasis of the text in our period fell on the sufferings involved in Israel's still-continuing exile. Exile was, after all, the setting and referent of the original prophecy; later Jews, from Daniel's day onwards, would have

[192] cf. Hengel 1996, 63–6 (arguing that the A scroll indicates a *priestly* Messiah); 71–81. The question of whether Isa. 40—55 is used elsewhere in the Scrolls (e.g. 4Q491=4QMᵃ fr. 11, 1.8-18 [GM 117f.], discussed by Hengel 1995b, 201-3; 1996, 83–6; 4Q540/541 [GM 269f.], discussed by Hengel 1996, 66–71) remains open for the time being.

[193] Nickelsburg 1992, 139 (for *1 En.* 62—3); Manson 1953, 173-4, and Black 1992 (for *1 En.* 37—71 in general).

[194] On the Messiah in Tg. Isa. (and, indeed, the dating of the Tg. in question) cf. Chilton 1982, 86–96; 1984a, 197f.

[195] So e.g. Hengel 1981a, 58f., 92f., against e.g. Rese.

[196] Or perhaps 'exposed himself to the risk of death'; cf. North 1948, 11f., with other refs.

[197] Cf. Hooker 1959, 53f., 56-8.

[198] Hengel 1996, conclusion: he cites 4Q540/541 as a possibility. This is not exactly a firm or wide base on which to build.

thought themselves quite justified in reading the passage in relation to their own situation.

What follows from this in terms of the world within which Jesus read the Jewish scriptures, and came to an understanding of his own vocation? There was no such thing as a straightforward pre-Christian Jewish belief in an Isaianic 'servant of YHWH' who, perhaps as Messiah, would suffer and die to make atonement for Israel or for the world. But there was something else, which literally dozens of texts attest: a large-scale and widespread belief, to which Isaiah 40—55 made a substantial contribution, that Israel's present state of suffering was somehow held within the ongoing divine purpose; that in due time this period of woe would come to an end, with divine wrath falling instead on the pagan nations that had oppressed Israel (and perhaps on renegades within Israel herself); that the explanation for the present state of affairs had to do with Israel's own sin, for which either she, or in some cases her righteous representatives, was or were being punished; and that this suffering and punishment would therefore, somehow, hasten the moment when Israel's tribulation would be complete, when she would finally have been purified from her sin so that her exile could be undone at last.[199] There was, in other words, a belief, hammered out not in abstract debate but in and through poverty, exile, torture and martyrdom, that Israel's sufferings might be, not merely a state *from* which she would, in YHWH's good time, be redeemed, but paradoxically, under certain circumstances and in certain senses, part of the means *by* which that redemption would be effected.

(vi) Conclusion: Jesus' Jewish Context

Jesus' world, as we have seen, was structured around rich symbolism and vivid controlling stories. The texts we have just examined offer a set of symbols, and a composite story, within which Jesus' own symbolic act in the Last Supper, and the cryptic and coded riddles and stories with which he explained that act and indeed his whole final journey to Jerusalem, come to life in a fresh way. But I am not arguing that Jesus picked up a package of ideas that was current among Jews of his time and simply applied it to himself. He was challenging existing construals of the tradition, precisely at the point where his contemporaries were expecting a military victory over Israel's enemies; that was part of the whole point. We must not, however,

---

[199] cf. Isa. 40.2: 'Cry to her that she has served her term, that her penalty is paid, that she has received from YHWH's hand double for all her sins'; 54.8: 'In overflowing wrath for a moment I hid my face from you, but with everlasting love I will have compassion on you, says YHWH, your redeemer.'

allow ourselves to be forced on to the horns of the dilemma according to which Jesus is either made to conform to an existing Jewish view or made to 'oppose Judaism' by proposing something totally different. What we find in the gospels, I suggest, is a portrait of Jesus which both reaffirms the deep-rooted Jewish tradition that we have been studying and redefines it around his own vision and vocation of kingdom-bringing. That portrait seems to me, in those terms, very likely to be historically accurate.

There was, then, no such thing as a pre-Christian Jewish version of (what we now think of as) Pauline atonement-theology. There was a variegated and multifaceted story of how the present evil exilic age could be understood, and how indeed it could be brought to an end, through certain persons embodying in themselves the sufferings of Israel. Jesus, therefore, was not offering an abstract atonement theology; he was identifying himself with the sufferings of Israel. We are faced once more with appropriate similarity and dissimilarity. The symbolism and story-telling of Jesus make sense only within this Jewish world, but they play their own strange and unique variation on their dark theme. What Jesus did and said stands out a mile from what early Christianity said about him and his execution, but early Christian atonement-theology is only fully explicable as the post-Easter rethinking of Jesus' essentially pre-Easter understanding. We are back, methodologically, to a position we have been in more than once before. In order to move, as historians, from the Jewish world to the very similar, and yet very different, world of early Christianity, we have to postulate a middle term. The gospels offer us one.

7. The Intention of Jesus (4): The Strange Victory

(i) Introduction

But what precisely does that middle term consist of? How, in other words, can we clarify the mindset of Jesus as he came to terms with his strange vocation? How can we understand his predictions of his own sufferings, within his thoroughly Jewish pre-Easter context?

Let us quickly recapitulate the argument of this chapter so far. Jesus drew his work together in two great symbolic actions, of which the second, the Last Supper, clearly symbolized the new exodus, the renewal of the covenant, and 'the forgiveness of sins', the real return from exile. Around the time of these symbolic actions he told riddles which indicated that he saw his own fate and the fate of the nation as closely interwoven. The destruction hanging over her, and the death that awaited him, were somehow locked together. There are also repeated reports that he spoke quite explicitly (though puzzlingly to his hearers) about his awareness of a vocation to go to Jerusalem and die. Sometimes it seems that this awareness had a scriptural basis. When we place this picture – symbolic action, interpreted through a grid of riddles and stories – within the larger picture of second-Temple Judaism, we find, not an exact fit, but sufficient convergence to suggest the strong possibility of historicity, especially when we reflect on how unlike early Christian atonement-theology the resultant picture turns out to be. Why did Jesus die? Ultimately, because he believed it was his vocation.

I find, therefore, in favour of Schweitzer and against Wrede and his followers; against, too, those like Moule who have taken a cautious middle position.[200] Faced with the choice between consistent scepticism and consistent eschatology, I choose the latter: Jesus constructed his mindset, his variation on the Jewish worldview of his day, on the assumption that he was living in, and putting into operation, the controlling story which the scriptures offered him, which was now reaching its climax. This was not a matter of him plucking from thin air one or two proof-texts which might serve to generate or sustain a few abstract ideas or beliefs. Nor, for that matter, was it a case of him, as an individual, behaving in a manner which we have to designate as 'weird'.[201] It was a matter of his living within the story of YHWH and Israel as it drew towards its goal. Jesus lived in a world where it might well make sense to believe one was called to take upon oneself the fate, the exile, of Israel.

I propose, then, that we can credibly reconstruct a mindset in which a first-century Jew could come to believe that YHWH would act through the suffering of a particular individual in whom Israel's sufferings were focused; that this suffering would carry redemptive significance; *and that this individual would be himself.* And I propose that we can plausibly suggest that this was the mindset of Jesus himself.

This choice of consistent eschatology is far from being arbitrary. It is *not* a matter of choosing 'credulity' over 'scepticism'.[202] It is a matter of scientific, historical judgment. If you go the route of scepticism, you will

[200] Moule 1977, 109 suggests that, though Jesus did not actually intend to die, he deliberately went to Jerusalem knowing that if he did there what his vocation demanded it might very well cost him his life. Following Schweitzer at this general level does not mean going with him all the way, into (e.g.) the trap spotted by Manson 1953, 78, or the position criticized by Sanders 1985, 327–9.

[201] cf. Sanders 1985, 333; see above, 553. Sanders does in fact recognize a possibility not altogether remote from the one I shall propose.

[202] On this spurious set of alternatives, and the importance in all spheres of knowledge of finding the way between them, cf. Polkinghorne 1994, ch. 2, esp. 31.

neither include the data, nor produce simplicity, nor shed light on other cognate areas of research. Choose eschatology, and you will achieve all three.

(ii) Proposal: Eschatology and the Cross

If, that is, you understand the eschatology. I have argued throughout that Jesus did not expect, or proclaim, the end of the space-time universe. Nor did he take the normal option of the military revolutionary. Nor, I have suggested, did he envisage the rebuilding of the Temple, whether by humans or by supernatural agency. Rather, he announced the end of the present evil age; the real, doubly subversive, revolution; and the reconstruction of the people of YHWH on a basis that would leave no future role for the Temple. The hypothesis I now wish to advance draws these three together into one. I propose that Jesus, consistent with the inner logic of his entire kingdom-praxis, -story and -symbolism, told the second-Temple story of the suffering and exile of the people of YHWH in a new form, and proceeded to act it out, finding himself called, like Ezekiel, symbolically to undergo the fate he had announced, in symbol and word, for Jerusalem as a whole.[203]

The picture can be put together step by step. Jesus believed that Israel's history had arrived at its focal point. More: he believed that Israel's *exile* had arrived at its climax. He believed, as we saw in the previous chapter, that he himself was the bearer of Israel's destiny. He was the Messiah, who would take that destiny on himself and draw it to its focal point. As a prophet, after the manner of Elijah, Jeremiah or Ezekiel, he had solemnly announced that Israel – Jerusalem – the Temple – were under judgment. The prophets had come and gone, and been ignored. He came as the last in the line, and they were planning to kill him.

The divine reaction to this, from Jesus' point of view, was not capricious or malevolent. Rather, the prophets, and the Messiah, had been trying to tell the people that there was a way of peace, a way to escape. They were

---

[203] My proposal from this point onwards (cf. Wright 1985) is, I think, substantially new, and there is little point debating in detail with interpretations based on different foundations. I see myself standing on the shoulders of Schweitzer and Caird in particular, though disagreeing with both in certain (different) ways. Hints in the same direction are found in e.g. Farmer 1956, 200–2; Jeremias 1966a [1949], 261; Dahl 1974, 75; Zahl 1983; Antwi 1991; de Jonge 1991a, 42–8. At the epistemological level, I again invoke Polkinghorne 1994 (cf. too Meyer 1979, 81–7): 'Why do I believe in quarks when no fractionally charged particle has ever unequivocally been observed in an experiment? Set your doubts aside for a while and see how belief in confined quarks enables us to understand a variety of phenomena (the hadronic spectrum of octets and decuplets; deep inelastic scatterings) which otherwise would have no underlying intelligibility' (32). Let the reader understand.

extending a lifeline. The prophets had warned Israel of the consequences of compromising with pagan cults; Jesus warned of the consequences of compromising with pagan politics. The Maccabees had denounced, as no better than pagans, those Jews who had compromised with Antiochus Epiphanes; Jesus denounced, as no better than pagans, not only those who compromised with Caesar by playing his power-games, *but also those who compromised with him by thinking to defeat him with his own weapons.* Those who take the sword will perish by the sword. Here is the doubly radical twist in Jesus' telling of the kingdom-story, which marks him out from his Jewish theological, eschatological and political context even while it insists that he is only comprehensible within it. His kingdom-announcement, like all truly Jewish kingdom-announcements, came as the message of the one true God, the God of Israel, in opposition to pagan power, pagan gods, and pagan politics. But, unlike the other kingdom-announcers of his time from Judas the Galilean to Simeon ben Kosiba, Jesus declared that the way to the kingdom was the way of peace, the way of love, the way of the cross. Fighting the battle of the kingdom with the enemy's weapons meant that one had already lost it in principle, and would soon lose it, and lose it terribly, in practice.

And Jesus determined that it was his task and role, his vocation as Israel's representative, to lose the battle on Israel's behalf. Like Jeremiah, he would warn the city of its impending doom even if he was regarded as a traitor for his pains. Like the Maccabaean martyrs, whom he may have had in mind, he would stand up to the tyrant and take the consequences. Like the Teacher of Righteousness, whom he almost certainly did not have in mind, he would confront the Wicked Priest, even if nobody took his part. Like the truly wise man, he would denounce the wicked and let them do their worst to him, believing that the dawning kingdom would see him vindicated. Like the young hotheads who pulled down the eagle from Herod's Temple, he would stand up against the corrupt central symbol of Judaism and face the wrath of its guardians.[204] He took upon himself the totally and comprehensibly Jewish vocation not only of *critique* from within; not only of *opposition* from within; but of *suffering the consequences* of critique and opposition from within. And, with that, he believed – of course! – that YHWH would vindicate him. That too was comprehensibly Jewish.

Yes, but radically new within that framework, and that in two ways. First, Jesus, unlike his predecessors in this paradigm, had announced and was enacting a programme aimed not at nationalistic victory over the pagans, but at making Israel what she was called to be, namely, the light of the world. Indeed, the zeal which characterized both the Maccabees and their successors

---

[204] Jos. *Ant.* 17.149-66; *War* 1.648-55. Cf. *NTPG* 172, 327.

in the first century, making them intensify Torah-observance and draw their boundaries (actual and symbolic) ever tighter, was precisely what Jesus had opposed in his teaching and was now opposing in practice. Israel was called, he believed, to be the people of the creator god *for the world*. Whatever interpretation he put on his own death, therefore, it could not simply correspond to the interpretation the martyrs had put on theirs, namely that they were enabling the nation of Israel to escape from her exile while the rest of the world lurched towards its doom. His symbolic actions had pointed towards a renewal of Israel which broke the boundaries, the wineskins, the taboos, and which incorporated a new set of symbols. His last symbolic action, we may assume, was intended to continue and complete this process.

Second, Jesus therefore not only took upon himself the 'wrath' (which, as usual in Jewish thought, refers to hostile military action) which was coming upon Israel because she had compromised with paganism and was suffering exile. He also took upon himself the 'wrath' which was coming upon Israel *because she had refused his way of peace*. Like the Maccabaean martyrs, he suffered what he saw as the results of Israel's pagan corruption. Israel had flirted with paganism; suffering would come of it, as it always had; the martyrs took it upon themselves. Unlike them, he saw as pagan corruption *the very desire to fight paganism itself*. Israel had become a hotbed of nationalist revolution; suffering would come of it, specifically in the form of Roman swords, falling masonry, and above all crosses planted outside the capital city. He would go, as Israel's representative, and take it upon himself. As in so many of his own parables, he would tell Israel's well-known story one more time, with a radical and multiply subversive twist in its tail. Only he would tell it, not as a wordsmith, swapping aphorisms in the marketplace, but as the king, exiled outside the gate of his own beloved city.

My proposal, then, as the way of making sense of all the data before me, is that Jesus believed it was his god-given vocation to identify with the rebel cause, the kingdom-cause, when at last that identification could not be misunderstood as endorsement. Israel was in exile, suffering at the hands of the pagans; the Roman cross was the bitterest symbol of that ongoing exilic state. He would go ahead of his people, to take upon himself both the fate that they had suffered one way or another for half a millennium at the hands of pagan empires and the fate that his contemporaries were apparently hell-bent upon pulling down on their own heads once for all. The martyr-tradition suggested that this was the way in which Israel would at last be brought through suffering to vindication. Jesus' riddles, binding the fate of the nation to his own fate, suggested strongly that he intended to evoke and enact this tradition. The 'messianic woes' tradition indicated that this suffering and vindication would be climactic, unique, the one-off moment when Israel's history and world history would turn their great corner at last, when YHWH's kingdom would come and his will be done on earth as it was in heaven. The central symbolic act by which Jesus gave meaning to his approaching death suggests strongly that he believed this moment had come. This would be the new exodus, the renewal of the covenant, the forgiveness of sins, the end of exile. It would do for Israel what Israel could not do for herself. It would thereby fulfil Israel's vocation, that she should be the servant people, the light of the world.

(iii) The Cross and the Scriptures

It is within this model of understanding, I suggest, that Jesus' references to the scriptural paradigms standing behind the martyr- and 'messianic woe' traditions make sense. For too long scholarship has asked, as though in a vacuum, whether Jesus thought of himself as 'the servant' or 'the son of man' – as though he lived in a world where only 'ideas' counted, where the symbols and stories of real life, politics, revolt, Torah-observance, Temple cult and the rest were secondary or irrelevant. Within this framework, small wonder that debate has been inconclusive, with those behind crying 'Forward!', and those in front shouting 'Back!'

Once we read the whole historical context, however, *as* history – that is, as the richly woven fabric of praxis, story, symbol and question which make up real life – then everything looks different. It should be beyond doubt that Jesus knew the scriptures intimately; if the Teacher of Righteousness at Qumran could give his followers a new interpretative grid whereby they were able to understand their own situation in the light of their Bible (and vice versa), there is no reason why Jesus should not have done something similar. Part of the evidence for this can be found, as C. H. Dodd observed, in the concentration of very early Christianity on certain particular books and passages, read in certain ways, but found in such diverse writings as to force us to postulate a great creative mind standing behind all the individual strands of early Christianity.[205] Even if this were not so, however, the argument of this book so far makes it virtually certain that Jesus must have thought, and taught, this way.

It then takes very little imagination to work out where some of the focal points of this creative exegesis can be found. The underlying narrative of the book of Daniel as a whole, with chapter 7 unarguably as one of its main focal points; of Zechariah, not least chapters 9—14; of the Psalms, with

---

[205] Dodd 1965 [1952], 109f.

some in particular being of obvious importance; and of Isaiah 40—55 as a
whole, with 52.13—53.12 unarguably as its main focal point: together these
offer grand-scale, deeply poetic, and richly symbolic statements of exile and
restoration, of suffering and vindication, and of the way in which, according
to prophetic promise, YHWH would become king of all the world. Together
they speak of YHWH's once-for-all defeat of evil, and his vindication of his
people, his servant, his Messiah, after their and his terrible, but redemptive,
suffering. Whether or not it is true that Daniel 7 and Isaiah 52—3 had
already been combined in the *Similitudes of Enoch*,[206] there is every reason
to suppose that Jesus himself brought them together, stirring Zechariah 9—14
and certain psalms into the mixture as well, not as isolated or abstracted
proof-texts but as what they manifestly were: climactic statements of the
climactic moment in the long redemptive purposes of YHWH. Each of these
passages was about the coming of the kingdom.[207] Each of them was about
the radical defeat of the powers of evil.[208] Each of them, obviously, was
about the vindication of Israel, and/or her representative. Each of them,
despite popular impressions to the contrary, could be read in the first century
as being about a messianic figure or figures.[209] Since we have already argued
that these constituted the major elements of Jesus' kingdom-announcement,
there is every reason to suppose that he would have felt free to draw on these
texts, in his own way, as passages which in any case stood in the shadows
behind the Maccabaean and other traditions that formed his more immediate
context.

How, more specifically, does Jesus himself seem to have reread these four
crucial parts of scripture, in relation to the vocation which led him to the
upper room, the garden, and the cross?

I have already argued in some detail that Jesus made the book of Daniel
thematic for his whole vocation. He understood it to be referring to the great
climax in which YHWH would defeat the fourth world empire and vindicate
his suffering people. He projected the notion of evil empire on to the present
Jerusalem regime, and identified himself and his movement with the people
who were to be vindicated. This provided him with a messianic self-

---

[206] cf. above, 589f.

[207] Isa. 52.7; Tg. Isa. 53.10 ('they shall look upon the kingdom of their Messiah'; does
this in turn echo Zech. 12.10?); Dan. 7.14, 18, 22, 27; Zech. 14.9 ('YHWH will become
king over all the earth'); Pss. 93; 97; etc.

[208] Isa. 52.7-12 (where the whole point is that YHWH has revealed his power and kingship in defeating Babylon, so that Israel can at last return from exile); Dan. 7.11-12, 26 (as
focal points of the whole book); Zech. 3.1-5; 9.1-8; 9.13-15; 12.3-9; 14.3, 12-15; Ps. 2;
110; etc.

[209] cf. ch. 11 above.

understanding. Did it also, by itself, generate the expectation that he would have to suffer, and that that suffering would somehow be redemptive?

A case can be made out for this view.[210] The overall context of Daniel, in which the sufferings of YHWH's people at the hands of the pagans is such a major theme; and the historical context, from the Maccabees to Jesus, in which the suffering of the martyrs was made so much of; these should guarantee that the figure of the 'son of man' in chapter 7, who is exalted after the fourth beast has 'made war' upon him, should be understood as a suffering figure. We should be cautious, however. Nothing in chapter 7 itself indicates suffering; nothing in the book as a whole, except possibly 11.31–5 and 12.1–3, suggests that the suffering of the martyrs would be redemptive. Any attempt to show that Daniel 7 could by itself generate a picture of one who would suffer redemptively, and to marginalize other texts in which these themes stare us in the face, invites once more the comment of Schweitzer about watering the garden with a leaky bucket when a stream lies right alongside. However, there should be no doubt that the book of Daniel as a whole provided a framework of apocalyptic expectation, messianic hope, and the promise of vindication for faithful Israel the other side of present distress, which contributed substantially towards Jesus' sense of vocation.

Zechariah, too, was undoubtedly of great importance.[211] We saw in the previous chapter that Jesus used the shepherd-image of himself on a number of occasions;[212] Zechariah provided a setting and context within which the sufferings of the sheep were linked with those of the (royal) shepherd. Several of the riddles which we explored as belonging with Jesus' symbolic action at the Last Supper make exactly this connection between the sufferings of Israel and those of the Messiah. When, in this setting, we find Jesus quoting explicitly from Zechariah 13.7 ('smite the shepherd, and the sheep will be scattered'),[213] we should not suspect a cunning insertion by a later exegetically minded Christian theologian, but should see this as an indication of Jesus' own mindset. This is, of course, strikingly confirmed not by isolated sayings but by symbolic actions: Zechariah 9 focuses on the king riding into Jerusalem on a donkey, as the agent of the return from exile and the renewal of the covenant; Zechariah 14, which celebrates the coming of YHWH and his kingdom, ends with the Temple being cleansed of traders. There should be no doubt that Jesus knew this whole passage, and that he saw it as centrally constitutive of his own vocation, at the level not just of ideas but of

---

[210] e.g. Barrett 1959, esp. 13–14.

[211] Among the few writers to have explored this, cf. France 1971, 103–10; Lindars 1973 [1961], 110–34; Kim 1987a.

[212] cf. above, 533–5.

[213] Mt. 26.31/Mk.14.27; cf. Jn. 16.32.

agendas.[214] And this time we find the theme of suffering associated not just with Israel in general but with the shepherd, the Messiah, in particular.

The themes of suffering and kingdom emerge also, as we saw, in the Psalter. We have already observed Jesus' use of the pilgrim Psalm 118 ('the stone which the builders rejected') and of the royal Psalm 110 ('YHWH said to my Lord'). Without venturing down the road of psychology, we can claim as a strong historical probability that Jesus regarded the Psalms as providing a further set of bearings on his vocation, not least as it was focused on his strange royal and pilgrim journey to, and action in, Jerusalem. However, it was a psalm of lament that, according to Matthew and Mark, provided him with one of his last utterances: 'My God, my God, why did you abandon me?'[215] This has of course been the subject of endless discussion, at both the theological and the homiletical levels. For our purposes the critical thing to note is how well the psalm as a whole (never mind the Psalter as a whole) fits with what we have sketched as Jesus' mindset, aims and beliefs. It is, in a sense, the opposite of Psalm 89 (the royal psalm that turns into a lament), turning eventually from shame and despair to an affirmation not only of hope but of the coming kingdom of YHWH:

> My God, my God, why hast thou forsaken me?
> Why art thou so far from helping me, from the words of my groaning?
> O my God, I cry by day, but you do not answer;
> and by night, but find no rest . . .
>
> I will declare your name to my brethren;
> in the midst of the congregation I will praise you:
> You who fear YHWH, praise him!
> All you offspring of Jacob, glorify him;
> stand in awe of him, all you offspring of Israel!
> For he did not despise or abhor the affliction of the afflicted;
> he did not hide his face from me,
> but heard when I cried to him . . .
> The poor shall eat and be satisfied;
> those who seek YHWH shall praise him.
> May your hearts live for ever!
> All the ends of the earth shall remember and turn to YHWH;
> and all the families of the nations shall worship before him.
> For the kingdom is YHWH's,
> And he rules over the nations.
> To him, indeed, shall all who sleep in the earth bow down;
> before him shall bow all who go down to the dust,
> and I shall live for him.

---

[214] cf. too e.g. Mt. 24.30, alluding to Zech. 12.10-12. Zech. 1-8 also furnishes themes for the ministry of Jesus; e.g. 8.19 with the fasting controversy (above, 433f.).

[215] Mt. 27.46/Mk. 15.34; quoted from Ps. 22.1. Lindars (1973 [1961], 89) says that 'the genuineness of this saying, as actually spoken by Jesus, can hardly be disputed'.

My seed shall serve him;
future generations will be told about YHWH,
and proclaim his deliverance to a people yet unborn,
saying that he has done it.[216]

The combination of themes is remarkable, considering our whole reconstruction of Jesus' ministry and mindset. 'The kingdom is YHWH's'; that is the cry of the psalmist who has come through the terrible desolation of the first twenty-one verses to the vindication, the restitution, and indeed the resurrection of the final section. As with Daniel, the suffering is not explicitly said to be redemptive; but it is part of the strange process whereby the kingdom finally dawns. From the historical point of view there is no reason why Jesus should not have carried Psalm 22 (and a good many others) in his head, and why he should not have prayed its first verse as he underwent the agony of crucifixion.[217]

Daniel, Zechariah and the Psalms thus contribute to various elements of Jesus' mindset, his awareness of vocation. The kingdom would come through the suffering of the righteous; the true king would share the suffering of the people. But *redemptive* suffering is not stated explicitly; we only emerge with something that looks like that if we take into account the full context of these books, both literary and historical. That, of course, we must do, as the later use of such texts in martyr-literature, and the still later use in the rabbis, encourages us to do. But there is, as we have seen, one book which, not only in its literary and historical contexts but also in its clear and explicit statements, draws together all the themes we have been studying (the suffering of Israel at the hands of the pagans, and her subsequent vindication as YHWH becomes king of the world and redeems her from exile; the coming of a messianic figure; the *suffering* of a messianic figure), and adds to them a stone which the builders regularly reject but which has a strong claim to be the head of the corner, namely, the claim that the redemption of Israel from exile and the suffering of the messianic figure, are linked precisely as effect and cause. I refer, of course, to Isaiah 40—55.[218]

We begin on solid ground. Isaiah 52.7-12 was, as we have seen, thematic for the whole work of Jesus. The prophetic, heraldic announcement of the

---

[216] Ps. 22.1-2, 22-31.

[217] The psalm has obviously coloured the story of the passion in other ways: e.g. Mt. 27.43/Ps. 22.8; Jn. 19.23-5/Ps. 22.18. But these are best explained on the assumption that Jesus really did utter Ps. 22.1 on the cross.

[218] The debate about Jesus' use, or non-use, of Isa. 53 is long-running and well known. As a small selection, cf. Barrett 1959; Hooker 1959; Jeremias 1967; France 1971; Lindars 1973 [1961], 75-88; Stuhlmacher 1986 [1981], 16-29; Caird & Hurst 1994, 310-16. I am deeply indebted to fellow participants at a conference on this subject at Baylor University, Texas, in February 1996 - not least the central protagonists, Professors Morna Hooker and Otto Betz.

'gospel', telling Zion that her god was becoming king, that he had defeated Babylon and would bring her back from exile, could stand as a summary of all that Jesus was trying to say and accomplish. But if, then, we ask how the message of Isaiah 52.7–12 was to be put into effect, the prophecy as Jesus must have read it had a clear answer. The arm of YHWH, which would be unveiled to redeem Israel from exile and put evil to flight, was revealed, according to Isaiah 53.1, in and through the work of the servant of YHWH.

We have already seen that the 'servant', from chapters 42 to 53, could be seen in the second-Temple period as a reference to the Messiah. This is scarcely surprising, indeed, when we compare the picture of the servant in 42.1–9 with the messianic pictures in Isaiah 9.6–7 and 11.1–10. Indeed, the Isaianic 'herald' himself is seen as a messianic figure in one text from Qumran.[219] The whole passage, equally clearly, speaks of the suffering of YHWH's people at the hands of the pagans, and holds out the constant hope that, because of YHWH's love and loyalty, they will be forgiven their sins and released from exile. One of the main internal dynamics of the whole book is the fluidity of thought, often remarked upon, between Israel herself as the servant and a servant-figure who clearly stands over against Israel.[220] All of this creates a context within which the themes of Jesus' ministry as we have studied them seem to fit like a glove. We thus emerge with the following argument:

(1) Jesus announces and enacts the kingdom of YHWH, doing and saying things which dovetail very closely with the message of Isaiah 40—55 as a whole.

(2) The kingdom-programme of Isaiah 40—55 as a whole is put into effect through the work of the servant, specifically his redemptive suffering.

(3) Jesus acts symbolically as though he intends to put his kingdom-programme into effect through his sharing of Israel's suffering, and speaks as if that is indeed what he intends.

(4) One of the relevant sayings quotes Isaiah 53 directly, and others can most easily be explained as an allusion to it.[221]

---

[219] 11Q13 2.15–20 (GM 140), referring also to Isa. 61; Dan. 9.

[220] As Origen already saw: *C. Cels.* 1.55.

[221] Direct quotation: Lk. 22.37/Isa. 53.12. Allusion: Mk. 9.12/Isa. 53.3 (the only text which explains where 'it is written' that 'the son of man must be treated with contempt', showing also a fusion between Isa. 53 and Dan. 7, like 11Q13's fusion of Isa. 52 and Dan. 9); Mk. 10.45/Isa. 53.10, 12 (cf. Goppelt 1981 [1975], 193–5; Stuhlmacher 1986 [1981], ch. 2; Witherington 1990, 251–6; contrast Seeley 1993); Mk. 14.24/Isa. 53.12. Jeremias 1971, 286f. gives a longer list, including refs. to the Tg. and LXX. These have all of course been discussed *ad nauseam* in the literature; my overall argument is designed to set the debate in a wider context and so, I hope, to avoid getting bogged down.

(5) It is therefore highly probable that, in addition to several other passages which informed his vocation, Jesus regarded Isaiah 53, in its whole literary and historical context, as determinative.

(6) Jesus therefore intended not only to share Israel's sufferings, but to do so as the key action in the divinely appointed plan of redemption for Israel and the world.

This argument is strong, and it is specific. I am not suggesting that Jesus 'regarded himself as "the servant"', as though second-Temple Jews had anticipated modern criticism in separating out the 'servant songs' from the rest of Isaiah 40—55, or as though Jesus had created a 'role' for himself out of a few texts taken out of context. Nor am I saying that the Isaianic pattern was necessarily dominant in Jesus' sense of vocation; it provided one unique and specific element in a more complex whole. Jesus did not speak of Isaiah 53 when faced with Caiaphas; the trial setting called for the judgment scene of Daniel 7, and the question about the Temple called for a statement of messianic enthronement, neither of which were modified or softened by a statement of humble suffering. He did not speak of it directly when instructing his puzzled disciples; if they had understood it, they would not have followed him to Jerusalem. He spoke of it in his actions, particularly in the upper room, and in his readiness to go to the eye of the storm, the place where the messianic woes would reach their height, where the *peirasmos*, the time of testing, would become most acute, and to bear the weight of Israel's exile, dying as her Messiah outside the walls of Jerusalem. We catch echoes of this, rather than direct statements, as Jesus' words cluster round his actions. The son of man must, as it is written, suffer many things, and be treated with contempt; he came to give his life a ransom for many; this is my blood of the covenant, shed for you and for the many for the forgiveness of sins (in other words, for the end of exile); he was numbered with the transgressors. This is not a matter of assuming 'the influence of the Servant' on Jesus, and then finding 'passages which appear to support it'.[222] It is a matter of understanding Jesus' whole kingdom-announcement in the light of several major themes from the Jewish scriptures, and showing that it is absurd, granted the whole picture, to disallow reference, allusion and echo to Isaiah 40—55 in general, and to 52.13—53.12 in particular.

I suggest, then, that Isaiah 40-55 as a whole was thematic for Jesus' kingdom-announcement. His work is not to be understood in terms of the teaching of an abstract and timeless system of theology, not even of atonement-theology, but as the historical and concrete acting out of YHWH's

---

[222] Hooker 1959, 20.

promise to defeat evil and rescue his people from exile, that is, to forgive their sins at last. Within this, the allusions to Isaiah 53 should not be regarded as the *basis* of a theory about Jesus' self-understanding in relation to his death; they may be, rather, the tell-tale signs of a vocation which he could hardly put into words, the vocation to be the 'herald' of Isaiah 40.9 and 52.7, and thence to be, himself, the servant, representing the Israel that was called to be the light of the world but had so signally failed to live up to her calling. The only way that such a vocation could be articulated without distortion was in story, symbol and praxis: all three came together in the Temple, in the upper room, and ultimately on the hill outside the city gate. Jesus' personal reading of Isaiah belongs not so much in the history of ideas, as in the history of vocation, agenda, action and ultimately passion. And he understood this vocation, agenda, action and passion as messianic.

(iv) The Messianic Task

I showed in the previous chapter that two tasks in particular awaited the would-be Messiah. He must cleanse, restore or rebuild the Temple; he must fight and win the battle against Israel's enemies. I now wish to propose, on the basis of my hypothesis so far, that Jesus intended his forthcoming death to accomplish these two tasks, albeit in a manner that was thoroughly, but not surprisingly, redefined.

Neusner has argued, as we saw, that Jesus' Temple-action and his Last Supper must be seen as deliberately mutually interpretative.[223] I agree, but question his conclusion. He suggests that the Supper itself was Jesus' replacement for the Temple cult. However, as we have seen, the symbolism of the Supper was not self-referential. Particularly when explained by Jesus' riddles and stories, never mind his explicit warnings and biblical allusions, it pointed not to itself but to the event which was about to take place; in other words, to Jesus' death.

What then does the parallelism between the Temple-action and the Supper say about Jesus' understanding of his death? It says, apparently, that Jesus intended his death to accomplish that which would normally be accomplished in and through the Temple itself. In other words, Jesus intended that his death should in some sense function sacrificially.[224] This should not surprise us unduly, or be regarded as necessarily meaning that the texts that suggest this viewpoint must be a later Christian retrojection. For a start, the things that point this way are not proof-texts, but actions and events which we have

---

[223] Neusner 1989.
[224] cf. e.g. Jeremias 1971, 290f.; Meyer 1979, 252.

already seen good reason to regard as historically extremely plausible. For another thing, we argued earlier that, during Jesus' ministry, he regularly acted as if he were able to bypass the Temple system in offering forgiveness to all and sundry right where they were.[225] Further, we have already seen that the Maccabaean martyrs were regarded as having, in some sense, offered themselves as a sacrifice through which Israel might be cleansed and purified.[226] We may also point out that near the heart of Isaiah 53 there is a strange phrase which, whatever it may have meant in its original setting, by the first century was certainly taken to refer to a sacrifice:

> When you make his life an offering for sin,
> he shall see his offspring, and shall prolong his days;
> through him the will of the LORD shall prosper.[227]

It is not going beyond the evidence, then, to suggest that Jesus saw his own approaching death in terms of the sacrificial cult. But his would not be one sacrifice among many. The controlling metaphor that he chose for his crucial symbol was not the Day of Atonement, but Passover: the one-off moment of freedom in Israel's past, now to be translated into the one-off moment which would inaugurate Israel's future. In his last great symbolic action, Jesus was implying that he, as Messiah, would establish a reality which would supersede the Temple. He saw his approaching death, therefore, as one key part of his messianic task.

The other part was, of course, the battle. As we discovered in chapter 10, Jesus reconstrued the battle which had to be fought as the battle against the real enemy, the accuser, the satan. He renounced the battle that his contemporaries expected a Messiah to fight, and that several would-be Messiahs in that century were only too eager to fight. He faced, instead, what he seems to have conceived as the battle against the forces of darkness, standing behind the visible forces (both Roman and Jewish) ranged against him.

At one level, he was fighting this battle throughout his ministry, not least when battling with sickness and demon-possession ('this woman, whom the satan bound . . .'; 'If I by the finger of God cast out demons, then the kingdom of God has come upon you'). At another level, he was fighting this battle when he engaged in controversy with those opponents who were bent on driving forward their scheme for national security, national symbols, national hope, in the face of his challenge to a new way of being Israel, of

---

[225] Above, 268–74.

[226] Above, 582f.

[227] Isa. 53.10. The word *asam*, translated in the LXX with *peri hamartias*, the regular phrase for 'sin-offering', may originally have had a wider range of meaning; by the first century we are safe in assuming that the Levitical, i.e. sacrificial, meaning would have been the first, and probably the only, meaning to be 'heard'.

being the light of the world. But at the fundamental level, there were two places were the battle had to be fought.

First, Jesus must have believed that he was fighting the battle against the satan when he came face to face with Caiaphas as his accuser. ('This is your hour,' he said in the garden when the High Priest's servants came to get him, 'and the power of darkness.'[228]) Certainly the Teacher of Righteousness thought he was facing something like evil incarnate when he squared off against the Wicked Priest, and we have no reason to suppose that Jesus would have taken a substantially different view with the High Priest of his day. As we have seen, he seems to have regarded Jerusalem itself, tragically compromised as it was, as the new abode of the satan. His response to Caiaphas meant, among other things, that he was playing David to Caiaphas' Goliath; that he was playing the Danielic 'son of man' to Caiaphas' fourth beast. Small wonder that Caiaphas tore his robe.

Second, granted all we know about Jesus, he must have believed that he was also to fight the real battle, the messianic battle, when he faced the might of Rome, the enemy whom every Messiah for a hundred years either side of Jesus had to confront. The pagan hordes, with all their (to a Jew) blasphemous beliefs and vile practices, were widely regarded as the sons of darkness. Jesus, however, believed he had to fight the darkness itself, not simply its offspring. Hence, Gethsemane, the moment when the vocation was tested to the limit. He could have chosen, then and there, to slip away and establish a private counter-Temple movement, like the Essenes. He could have chosen to call for the twelve legions of angels, or more likely their earthly equivalent; there would have been plenty of people in Jerusalem ready to rally to him. The scene in Gethsemane, involving Jesus in weakness, fear, and (apparently) an agony of doubt, is hard to comprehend as a later Christian invention. It is entirely comprehensible as biography. It was, after all, failed Messiahs who ended up on crosses; the Jesus we have described throughout must have had to wrestle with the serious possibility that he might be totally deluded.

He had, however, already laid down the terms of the battle he had to fight.[229] 'He who saves his life shall lose it; he who loses his life shall save it.' This cryptic and subversive wisdom had always been the challenge he put before his followers; now it was to be revealed as the wisdom by which he

---

[228] Lk. 22.53.

[229] Cf. Farmer 1956, 200–2, and the very suggestive passage in Meyer 1979, 218: 'The faith reflected in the esoteric teachings on repudiation, losing one's life, poverty, and the like followed no pattern of piety attested in contemporary Israel. A deft, assured, original foray into iniquity and redemption, it gave a new and matchless depth to the *'anawim* thematic' [i.e. to the theme of 'the poor'].

was himself to live, and to die. Israel, he had urged, was to be the salt of the earth, the light of the world, through turning the other cheek, going the second mile; now he was to expose his whole body to the Roman lash, and to set off on a forced march with the load the soldiers gave him to carry. And, despite all the overtones of the Maccabaean martyrs which clustered around the event, as he went to his death he seems not to have responded to his pagan torturers in the time-honoured manner. Instead of hurling insults and threats at them, he suffered either in silence or with words of forgiveness; a startling innovation into the martyr-tradition, which sent echoes across early Christianity in such a way as to be, I suggest, inexplicable unless they are substantially historical.[230]

They point, therefore, to the theme which was picked up in very earliest Christianity as the dominant note in Jesus' achievement. All through his public career he had acted on the basis of compassion for the multitudes, for the poor, for the sheep without a shepherd. When questioned as to the greatest commandment in the law, he highlighted the love of God and of one's neighbour. Not much is said in the scriptural text-base concerning the *love* which the Messiah might have for his people, but with Jesus this seemed to be uppermost, once more not simply as an idea but as a reality. We shall explore the roots of this theme in the next chapter, but it would be very odd not to draw attention to it at this point. The earliest Christians regarded Jesus' achievement on the cross as the decisive victory over evil. But they saw it, even more, as the climax of a career in which active, outgoing, healing love had become the trademark and hallmark. It is so easy to turn this point in a sentimental or pietistic direction that a historian may well be shy of raising the matter. But when we put the historical package together in the way that we have, this is the theme that emerges. Ben Meyer put it like this:

> What, in the end, made Jesus operate in this way, what energized his incorporating death into his mission, his facing it and going to meet it?
> The range of abstractly possible answers is enormous . . . But . . . it is above all in the tradition generated by Jesus that we discover what made him operate in the way he did, what made him epitomize his life in the single act of going to his death: He 'loved me and handed himself over for me' . . .; 'having loved his own who were in the world, he loved them to the end' . . . If authenticity lies in the coherence between word (Mark 12.28–34 parr.) and deed (Gal. 2.20; Eph. 5.2; John 13.1; Rev. 1.5), our question has found an answer.[231]

Jesus, therefore, appears to have believed that victory in the real messianic battle would consist in dying at the hands of the Romans, dying the death of the rebel on behalf of the rebels. This was the climax of the way of

---

[230] e.g. 1 Pet. 2.19–25; 3.17f.
[231] Meyer 1979, 252f. (the close of the book).

being Israel which he had urged (without much effect) on his fellow countrymen. This, too, was the implication of his linking of his fate with that of the nation. He had announced judgment, the wrath of Rome no less, on nation and Temple for their failure to be the light of the world, to follow the way of peace. This judgment was not arbitrary; it was the necessary consequence of Israel's determination to follow the path of confrontation with Rome. But the way of the martyr was to take upon himself the suffering that hung over the nation as a whole. The way of the shepherd-king was to share the suffering of the sheep. The way of the servant was to take upon himself the exile of the nation as a whole. As a would-be Messiah, Jesus identified with Israel; he would therefore go ahead of her, and take upon himself precisely that fate, actual and symbolic, which he had announced for nation, city, and Temple. He would do, once and for all, what he had done in smaller, anticipatory actions throughout his public career, as he identified with the poor and sinners, as he came into contact with lepers, corpses and other sources of impurity. 'He has gone in to eat with a sinner' (Luke 19.7) would turn into 'he has gone out to die with the rebels'.

> At last, when there is no risk of misunderstanding, he can identify himself fully with the national aspirations of his people. He cannot preach Israel's national hope, but he can die for it.[232]

Thus

> [Jesus] goes to his death at the hands of a Roman judge on a charge of which he was innocent and his accusers, as the event proved, were guilty. And so, not only in theological truth but in historic fact, the one bore the sins of the many . . .[233]

This, then, was how Jesus envisaged the messianic victory over the real enemy. The satan had taken up residence in Jerusalem, not merely in Rome, and was seeking to pervert the chosen nation and the holy place into becoming a parody of themselves, a pseudo-chosen people intent on defeating the world with the world's methods, a pseudo-holy place seeking to defend itself against the world rather than to be the city set on a hill, shining its light on the world. One more time: this does not mean that Jesus rejected the concepts of chosen nation and holy place. The whole point is that he embraced them; that he discerned, and tried to communicate, what that chosenness, in its scriptural roots, actually meant; and that, discovering the nation as a whole deaf and blind to his plea, he determined to go, himself, to the holy place, and there to do what the chosen people ought to do. He would act on behalf of, and in the place of, the Israel that was failing to be what she was

---

[232] Wright 1985, 87.
[233] Caird 1965, 22 (= Caird & Hurst 1994, 419).

called to be. He would himself be the light of the world. He would be the salt of the earth. He would be set on a hill, unable to be hidden.

He would go, then, to the place where the satan had made his dwelling. He would defeat the cunning plan which would otherwise place the whole divine purpose in jeopardy. He would uphold the honour, the election, the true traditions, of Israel. He would stand, like Mattathias or Judas, against not only the pagans but also the compromisers within the chosen people, more particularly those who wielded power, those who ran the holy place, the shepherds who had been leading the people astray. Jesus, once more, was a first-century Jew, not a twentieth-century liberal.

As such, he must have known that he might have been deeply mistaken. The aims and goals which we must postulate if we are to make sense of his praxis, stories and symbols must have involved him in what we might call a great Pascalian wager, staking all on his vocation and vision. It was, after all, a huge gamble. Messiahs were supposed to defeat the pagans, not to die at their hands. Worse, dying thus actually demonstrated that one was not after all the Messiah; followers of a Messiah who was then crucified knew beyond question that they had backed the wrong horse. Ironically, if Jesus had been the sort of Messiah we may assume many Jews wanted him to be, the strong likelihood is that he would have ended up being crucified just the same. At every point, then, the messianic vocation to which he seems to have given allegiance led him into a dark tunnel, where the only thing left was sheer trust. But we can be confident of what he thought he was thereby going to achieve. He would bring Israel's history to its climax. Through his work, YHWH would defeat evil, bringing the kingdom to birth, and enable Israel to become, after all, the light of the world. Through his work, YHWH would reveal that he was not just a god, but God.

(v) The Victory of God

Jesus, then, went to Jerusalem not just to preach, but to die. Schweitzer was right: Jesus believed that the messianic woes were about to burst upon Israel, and that he had to take them upon himself, solo. I think that Jesus realized this considerably earlier than Schweitzer thought (for him, it was a secondary development, an adjustment of Jesus' earlier vision), but the point is not actually that important. What matters is that, in the Temple and the upper room, Jesus deliberately enacted two symbols, which encapsulated his whole work and agenda. The first symbol said: the present system is corrupt and recalcitrant. It is ripe for judgment. But Jesus is the Messiah, the one through whom YHWH, the God of all the world, will save Israel and thereby the world. And the second symbol said: this is how the true exodus will come about. This is how evil will be defeated. This is how sins will be forgiven.

Jesus knew – he must have known – that these actions, and the words which accompanied and explained them, were very likely to get him put on trial as a false prophet leading Israel astray, and as a would-be Messiah; and that such a trial, unless he convinced the court otherwise, would inevitably result in his being handed over to the Romans and executed as a (failed) revolutionary king. This did not, actually, take a great deal of 'supernatural' insight, any more than it took much more than ordinary common sense to predict that, if Israel continued to attempt rebellion against Rome, Rome would eventually do to her as a nation what she was now going to do to this strange would-be Messiah. But at the heart of Jesus' symbolic actions, and his retelling of Israel's story, there was a great deal more than political pragmatism, revolutionary daring, or the desire for a martyr's glory. There was a deeply theological analysis of Israel, the world, and his own role in relation to both. There was a deep sense of vocation and trust in Israel's god, whom he believed of course to be God. There was the unshakeable belief – Gethsemane seems nearly to have shaken it, but Jesus seems to have construed that, too, as part of the point, part of the battle – that if he went this route, if he fought this battle, the long night of Israel's exile would be over at last, and the new day for Israel and the world really would dawn once and for all. He himself would be vindicated (of course; all martyrs believed that); and Israel's destiny, to save the world, would thereby be accomplished. Not only would he create a breathing space for his followers and any who would join them, by drawing on to himself for a moment the wrath of Rome and letting them escape; if he was defeating the real enemy, he was doing so on behalf of the whole world. The servant-vocation, to be the light of the world, would come true in him, and thence in the followers who would regroup after his vindication. The death of the shepherd would result in YHWH becoming king of all the earth. The vindication of the 'son of man' would see the once-for-all defeat of evil and the establishment of a worldwide kingdom.

Jesus therefore took up his own cross. He had come to see it, too, in deeply symbolic terms: symbolic, now, not merely of Roman oppression, but of the way of love and peace which he had commended so vigorously, the way of defeat which he had announced as the way of victory. Unlike his actions in the Temple and the upper room, the cross was a symbol not of praxis but of passivity, not of action but of passion. It was to become the symbol of victory, but not of the victory of Caesar, nor of those who would oppose Caesar with Caesar's methods. It was to become the symbol, because it would be the means, of the victory of God.

(vi) Conclusion

The line of thought I have been exploring is complex from one point of view, but from another it is essentially very simple. Modern western minds do not, of course, habitually run in grooves like these. From a first-century Jewish point of view, however, it makes excellent if shocking sense. In offering a set of answers to our first three questions (Jesus' interaction with Judaism, his aims throughout his ministry, and the reasons for his death), the case has now been made that we are faced, not with a series of random or scattered events, but with a coherent historical whole. And within the history, as we shall see, there will be plenty of material for theology to go to work, though it may be surprised at what it finds. The silhouette of the cross against a darkened sky is more, not less, evocative for our having studied the portrait of the man who hung there. And the total historical picture, in all its complex simplicity, will challenge the most experienced iconographer.

There remains just one question.

I argued in the previous chapter that Jesus believed he was the focal point of the Israel that would return, at last, from exile. I have argued in this chapter that he believed he was to be the means, in his life and particularly his death, of the radical defeat of evil. Together these make up two of the three elements of the prophetic belief in the coming kingdom of God. What about the third one?

What did Jesus believe about the return of YHWH to Zion?

Chapter Thirteen

THE RETURN OF THE KING

1. Introduction

The countryside we have just traversed is well enough known, though the route I have taken across it is not. It is a different matter with the landscape now before us. Some travellers deny its very existence; others declare it to be inhospitable in the extreme; others have domesticated a small corner of it, thinking thereby to have colonized the whole. My task, then, involves cartography as well as itinerary: making the map as well as following it.

The question before us draws together the three that have occupied us so far (Jesus' relation to Judaism, his agenda, and the reasons for his death), looking at them all together but through a different lens. Jesus saw himself as a prophet announcing and inaugurating the kingdom of YHWH; he believed himself to be Israel's true Messiah; he believed that the kingdom would be brought about by means of his own death at the hands of the pagans. He believed, that is, that the message of the Isaianic herald was coming true at last: Israel's god was becoming king, 'Babylon' was being defeated, and the exile was over at last. This, however, points to one more issue. The Isaianic message centred upon the return of YHWH to Zion. Did that theme find a place in Jesus' agenda and proclamation, and if so how?

As well as belonging with the first three of our questions, this subject points on to the fourth: how did early Christianity begin, and why did it take the shape it did? In particular – and it should be stressed that this is as much a question about Jesus as about the early church – how did it come about that Jesus was *worshipped*, not simply in late and Hellenized Christianity, but in very early, very Jewish, and still insistently monotheist Christianity?[1] Our question, in other words, concerns what is often called 'christology', specifically, what has recently been called 'the christology of Jesus'.[2]

---

[1] cf. e.g. France 1982; Hurtado 1988, 1992; Bauckham 1992; Wright 1991, Part I; and *NTPG* ch. 15, esp. 456-8.

[2] Witherington 1990 (denoting also, however, and quite appropriately, the question of Jesus' Messiahship). It is remarkable that there is no treatment of this topic in, for instance, Chilton & Evans 1994b.

Even where this question has been allowed, the way it has been formed, and the arguments that have been adduced to address it, have often obscured rather than clarified it. I shall attempt a different route. I am not, in other words, intending to survey 'the titles of Jesus' one more time; nor to investigate the nature of Jesus' religious experience, probing for a 'uniqueness' that would somehow 'explain' early Christian views of Jesus. I shall comment on the first of these in a moment; the second, quite frankly, is an attempt to know the unknowable.[3] I want to proceed, as before, on the firmer ground of Jesus' symbolic actions, and the stories and riddles with which he explained them and gave them direction and clarity. This is not, as I have insisted before, a matter of the history of *ideas* alone, but of *actions* which gave practical expression to a *vocation*. And the main argument I have on my side, as I argue both for the existence of a forgotten country and for a manageable route through it, is the close integration which this offers with everything else we have seen in this book so far. Some writers have operated a kind of would-be historical god-of-the-gaps scheme, in which there are certain key things in Jesus' life and work which stand out from the rest, so that while most of what he did can be explained in human terms some parts force us to say 'he did that because he was divine'. This is, of course, reminiscent of the occasional patristic attempts to divide up the things that Jesus did as a human being (hungered, wept, suffered) and the things that he did as 'god' (miracles, resurrection, and so on). But this, like the god-of-the-gaps argument in would-be natural theology, belongs with a metaphysic that is entirely alien to the world of first-century Judaism. It is not a matter of another topic being added on to the outside, like someone drawing a moustache on an Old Master. It is, I hope, more like cleaning away layers of paint superimposed by well-meaning piety and, for that matter, well-meaning impiety, and discovering the true portrait underneath.

Let me stress that I am not asking, in this chapter, whether Jesus actually was or is 'divine', whatever we might mean by that. I am asking about Jesus' own aims and beliefs: the sense of vocation that led him, as a first-century Jew, to do and say what he did and said, and the belief system within which those actions and words made sense. This account of Jesus' aims and beliefs should in principle, of course, dovetail with the mindset we have already studied (that of a prophet announcing the kingdom of YHWH), and with the other aspects of his aims and beliefs (that he intended, as Messiah, to bring about the real return from exile, and the real defeat of evil). It should also make its way as a historical proposal by the means we have frequently utilized, namely that of double similarity, and double dissimilarity, with Judaism

---

[3] cf. Robinson 1984, ch. 11.

614 Part III: The Aims and Beliefs of Jesus

and the early church. I am, in other words, attempting to round off a portrait of Jesus as he was in his lifetime, a portrait which makes sense in itself and which is actually necessary to explain the evidence before us.

There is neither the space nor the need for a detailed history of the research on this topic. The 'New Quest' and its more recent successors have declared the whole subject out of bounds. The 'Third Quest', though it might well have asked whether there was anything within Jesus' own aims and beliefs that functioned as the root of early Christian views about him, by and large has not done so. Harvey is an exception, with his interesting discussion of the concept of 'agency' whereby one person acts on behalf of another, . very often a son for a father.[4] In a good deal of contemporary writing the question hovers just out of sight, like a character in a Beckett play, influencing the action but never actually making a speech. Even if people say proudly that they are historians, and therefore are not interested in such things, that does not make them any the less interested; here Vermes is a good example, pronouncing emphatically on the theological question at the end of a book from which it had been, till then, excluded.[5]

One reason for the decline in discussion of 'the christology of Jesus' – quite apart from the remarkable modesty which suddenly afflicts scholars at this point, balancing out the shamelessness with which they are prepared to invent christologies for everyone else in sight, including some people and groups who are themselves sheer inventions – is the quite proper decline in popularity of research on the *titles* of Jesus. The high-water mark in this industry was perhaps reached with Cullmann's work: forty years on, it remains a remarkable monument to the wrong sort of enquiry.[6] It brought together an essentially history-of-ideas project with an essentially lexicographical method; unfortunately, these two do not add up to history. Where it has been pursued post-Cullmann, it has led simply to a morass of *Religionsgeschichte* in which the unprovability of the theories has been matched only by the impenetrability of the footnotes. Today there is tacit agreement that the study of 'titles' is not the way to proceed – even to the extent of some leading Jesus-scholars relegating them to the margin of their enquiries.[7] Nobody, so far as I know, has thought of a quite different way of addressing the question. I wish to propose one.

My proposal, though large, is quite simple. We saw in chapters 9 and 11 that Jesus' action in the Temple functioned as a deliberate symbol, explained by stories and riddles, whereby he announced YHWH's judgment on the

---

[4] Harvey 1982, ch. 7, etc.; cf. p. 121 n.136.
[5] Vermes 1973, 212f.
[6] Cullmann 1963 [1957].
[7] e.g. Sanders, Crossan.

Temple and proclaimed himself as Messiah. We saw in chapter 12 that Jesus' action in the upper room functioned as a deliberate symbol, explained by further stories and riddles, whereby he drew on to himself the judgment he had predicted for the nation and the Temple, intending thereby to defeat evil and accomplish the great covenant renewal, the new exodus. I shall now argue that these two, taken together and placed within their larger context, constitute a single, though complex, further symbolic action. Jesus' journey to Jerusalem, climaxing in his actions in the Temple and the upper room, and undertaken in full recognition of the likely consequences, was intended to function like Ezekiel lying on his side or Jeremiah smashing his pot. The prophet's action *embodied* the reality. Jesus went to Jerusalem in order to embody the third and last element of the coming of the kingdom. He was not content to *announce* that YHWH was returning to Zion. He intended to enact, symbolize and personify that climactic event.[8]

That Jesus undertook a last journey to Jerusalem is not in doubt. I am proposing that he intended this action, ending in his actions in the Temple and the upper room, to carry a significance which is not normally recognized. In order to make out this case we must look first at the Jewish context within which this symbol would carry meaning, and then at the stories and riddles with which Jesus brought that meaning out.

2. The Jewish World of Meaning

(i) The Hope of YHWH's Return

The Jewish context in question concerns three things: the hope for YHWH's return, the speculation that YHWH's agent would be exalted to share his throne, and the symbolic language used for YHWH's activity in the world. We must look at each in turn.

The second-Temple Jewish hope for YHWH's return has not received as much attention as I believe it should.[9] This hope is, I think, the truth behind the point that Bruce Chilton has stressed in various works: that 'the kingdom of god' denotes the coming of Israel's god in person and in power.[10]

---

[8] This move, from Jesus' representation of Israel to a fully-blown christology, has some analogies with Caird 1982. However, Caird in that article ends with a tantalizing and never-elaborated hint rather than a full proposal.

[9] This should properly have been stressed in *NTPG* ch. 10, where it only received a brief mention (303). Beasley-Murray (1986, Parts I and II) and Glasson (1988) draw attention to this theme, but the former widens it (in my view) inappropriately, and the latter simply applies it to the (post-Jesus) parousia-doctrine.

[10] cf. Chilton 1978, 1982, 1987 [1979]; see the conclusions in the latter work, 283–8 (= 1984b, 124–7). Cf. too Meier 1994, 299: the Jewish hope was 'that God would come on the

Whether or not it is true, as Chilton argues, that Jesus made actual use of an early Jewish commentary on Isaiah (the Isaiah Targum), it is certainly the case that the theme of *announcing* the kingdom, and the phrase 'the kingdom of god' itself, both of which feature in that commentary but not elsewhere in non-Christian Jewish literature, are central features of what we most securely know about Jesus.[11] And in the announcement of the dawning kingdom we find the persistent emphasis that now, at last, YHWH is returning to Zion. He will do again what he did at the exodus, coming to dwell in the midst of his people.[12]

This theme is not usually highlighted in this way. For this reason I shall make the point by setting out the main passages quite fully:

> On that day the branch of YHWH shall be beautiful and glorious, and the fruit of the land shall be the pride and glory of the survivors of Israel . . . Then YHWH will create over the whole site of Mount Zion and over its places of assembly a cloud by day and smoke and the shining of a flaming fire by night. Indeed over all the glory there will be a canopy. It will serve as a pavilion, a shade by day from the heat, and a refuge and a shelter from the storm and rain.[13]

> Then the moon will be abashed, and the sun ashamed;
> for YHWH of hosts will reign on Mount Zion and in Jerusalem,
> and before his elders he will manifest his glory.[14]

> It will be said on that day,
> Lo, this is our god; we have waited for him, so that he might save us.
> This is YHWH, for whom we have waited;
> let us be glad and rejoice in his salvation.
> For the hand of YHWH will rest on this mountain.[15]

> Strengthen the weak hands,
>   and make firm the feeble knees.
> Say to those who are of a fearful heart,
>   'Be strong, do not fear!'
> Here is your God.
>   He will come with vengeance,
> with terrible recompense.
>   He will come and save you.

last day to save and restore his people Israel'; 452: 'the kingdom of God is not primarily a state or place but rather the entire dynamic event of God coming in power to rule his people Israel in the end time.'

[11] cf. Chilton 1982; 1987 [1979], 277, following Stuhlmacher 1968, 142–51.

[12] cf. e.g. Ex. 13.21–2; 14.19; 19.9, 11, 18; 33.12–17; Dt. 33.2.

[13] Isa. 4.2–6. The cloud and fire, of course, link this prophecy to the exodus.

[14] Isa. 24.23.

[15] Isa. 25.9–10. I do not regard Isa. 26.21 as a further statement of this theme, despite Glasson 1988, 259; there it seems as though YHWH is coming *from* the Temple to punish the nations (as, probably, in Mic. 1.3).

Then the eyes of the blind shall be opened,
 and the ears of the deaf unstopped;
then the lame shall leap like a deer,
 and the tongue of the speechless sing for joy . . .
And the ransomed of YHWH shall return,
 and come to Zion with singing;
everlasting joy shall be upon their heads;
 they shall obtain joy and gladness,
 and sorrow and sighing shall flee away.[16]

A voice cries out:
'In the wilderness prepare the way of YHWH,
 make straight in the desert a highway for our god.
Every valley shall be lifted up,
 and every mountain and hill be made low;
the uneven ground shall become level,
 and the rough places a plain.
Then the glory of YHWH shall be revealed,
 and all people shall see it together,
 for the mouth of YHWH has spoken.'

Get you up to a high mountain,
 O Zion, herald of good tidings;
lift up your voice with strength,
 O Jerusalem, herald of good tidings,
 lift it up, do not fear;
say to the cities of Judah,
 'Here is your god!'
See, the Lord YHWH comes with might,
 and his arm rules for him;
his reward is with him,
 and his recompense before him.
He will feed his flock like a shepherd;
 he will gather the lambs in his arms,
and carry them in his bosom,
 and gently lead the mother sheep.[17]

How beautiful upon the mountains
 are the feet of the messenger who announces peace,
 who brings good news, who announces salvation,
 who says to Zion, 'Your god reigns.'
Listen! Your sentinels lift up their voices,
 together they sing for joy;
for in plain sight they see
 the return of YHWH to Zion.
Break forth together into singing,
 you ruins of Jerusalem;

[16] Isa. 35.3–6, 10. Note the combination, in the whole chapter, of the return to Zion of the exiles and of YHWH.
[17] Isa. 40.3–5, 9–11.

for YHWH has comforted his people,
    he has redeemed Jerusalem.
YHWH has bared his holy arm
    before the eyes of all the nations;
and all the ends of the earth shall see
    the salvation of our god.[18]

YHWH saw it, and it displeased him
    that there was no justice.
He saw that there was no one,
    and was appalled that there was no one to intervene;
so his own arm brought him victory,
    and his righteousness upheld him.
He put on righteousness like a breastplate,
    and a helmet of salvation on his head;
he put on garments of vengeance for clothing,
    and wrapped himself in fury as in a mantle . . .
So those in the west shall fear the name of YHWH,
    and those in the east, his glory;
for he will come like a pent-up stream
    that the wind of YHWH drives on.
And he will come to Zion as Redeemer,
    to those in Jacob who turn from transgression, says YHWH.
And as for me, this is my covenant with them, says YHWH: my spirit that is upon you,
and my words that I have put in your mouth, shall not depart out of your mouth . . .[19]

Arise, shine; for your light has come,
    and the glory of YHWH has risen upon you.
For darkness shall cover the earth,
    and thick darkness the people;
but YHWH will arise upon you,
    and his glory will appear over you.
Nations shall come to your light,
    and kings to the brightness of your dawn.[20]

Go through, go through the gates,
    prepare the way for the people;
build up, build up the highway,
    clear it of stones,
      lift up an ensign for the people.
YHWH has proclaimed
    to the end of the earth:
Say to daughter Zion,
    'See, your salvation comes;
his reward is with him,

---

[18] Isa. 52.7–10. The context goes on at once to speak of Israel's hasty departure from Babylon, guarded by her god; and then of the servant who will suffer for the sins of the people.

[19] Isa. 59.15–17, 19–21.

[20] Isa. 60.1–3.

and his recompense before him . . .'

'Who is this that comes from Edom,
 from Bozrah in garments stained crimson?
Who is this so splendidly robed,
 marching in his great might?'
  'It is I, announcing vindication, mighty to save . . .
I have trodden the winepress alone . . .
I looked, but there was no helper;
 I stared, but there was no one to sustain me;
so my own arm brought me victory,
 and my wrath sustained me . . .'
It was no messenger or angel
 but his presence that saved them;
in his love and in his pity he redeemed them;
 he lifted them up and carried them all the days of old . . .
O that you would tear open the heavens and come down,
 so that the mountains would quake at your presence . . .
to make your name known to your adversaries,
 so that the nations might tremble at your presence![21]

For thus says YHWH:
I will extend prosperity to [Jerusalem] like a river,
 and the wealth of the nations like an overflowing stream . . .
You shall see, and your heart shall rejoice;
 your bodies shall flourish like the grass;
and it shall be known that the hand of YHWH is with his servants,
 and his indignation is against his enemies.
For YHWH will come in fire,
 and his chariots like the whirlwind,
to pay back his anger in fury,
 and his rebuke in flames of fire.
For by fire will YHWH execute judgment,
 and by his sword, on all flesh;
 and those slain by YHWH shall be many . . .
For I know their works and their thoughts, and I am coming to gather all nations and
tongues; and they shall come and shall see my glory, and I will set a sign among them.[22]

Then he brought me to the gate, the gate facing east. And there, the glory of the god of
Israel was coming from the east; the sound was like the sound of mighty waters; and the
earth shone with his glory . . . As the glory of YHWH entered the temple by the gate
facing east, the spirit lifted me up, and brought me into the inner court; and the glory of
YHWH filled the Temple.
 While the man was standing beside me, I heard someone speaking to me out of the
Temple. He said to me: Mortal, this is the place of my throne and the place for the soles
of my feet, where I will reside among the people of Israel forever.[23]

[21] Isa. 62.10–11; 63.1, 3, 5, 9; 64.1.
[22] Isa. 66.12, 14–16, 18–19.
[23] Ezek. 43.1–7. This vision, of course, is part of the overall description of the building
of the eschatological Temple.

I will shake all the nations, so that the treasure of all nations shall come, and I will fill this house with glory, says YHWH of hosts . . . The latter glory of this house shall be greater than the former, says YHWH of hosts; and in this place I will give peace, says YHWH of hosts.[24]

Jerusalem shall be inhabited like villages without walls, because of the multitude of people and animals in it. For I will be a wall of fire all around it, says YHWH, and I will be the glory within it . . . Sing and rejoice, O daughter Zion! For lo, I will come and dwell in your midst, says YHWH. Many nations shall join themselves to YHWH on that day, and shall be my people; and I will dwell in your midst. And you shall know that YHWH of hosts has sent me to you. YHWH will inherit Judah as his portion in the holy land, and will again choose Jerusalem.[25]

Thus says YHWH of hosts: I am jealous for Zion with great jealousy, and I am jealous for her with great wrath. Thus says YHWH: I will return to Zion, and will dwell in the midst of Jerusalem; Jerusalem shall be called the faithful city, and the mountain of YHWH of hosts shall be called the holy mountain.[26]

See, a day is coming for YHWH, when the plunder taken from you will be divided in your midst. For I will gather all the nations against Jerusalem to battle . . . Then YHWH will go forth and fight against those nations as when he fights on a day of battle. On that day his feet shall stand on the Mount of Olives . . . then YHWH my god will come, and all the holy ones with him . . . And YHWH will become king over all the earth; on that day YHWH will be one, and his name one . . . Then all who survive of the nations that have come against Jerusalem shall go up year after year to worship the King, YHWH of hosts, and to keep the festival of booths . . .[27]

See, I am sending my messenger to prepare the way before me, and the Lord whom you seek will suddenly come to his Temple. The messenger of the covenant in whom you delight – indeed, he is coming, says YHWH of hosts. But who can endure the day of his coming, and who can stand when he appears? For he is like a refiner's fire and like fuller's soap; he will sit as a refiner and purifier of silver, and he will purify the descendants of Levi and refine them like gold and silver, until they present offerings to YHWH in righteousness. Then the offering of Judah and Jerusalem will be pleasing to YHWH as in the days of old and as in former years.[28]

Our God comes and does not keep silence,
> before him is a devouring fire,
> and a mighty tempest all around him.
He calls to the heavens above
> and to the earth, that he may judge his people . . .[29]

[24] Hag. 2.7, 9; cp. 1.8.
[25] Zech. 2.4-5, 10-12. Notice the explicit exodus-imagery, with YHWH as fire defending his people.
[26] Zech. 8.2-3. The chapter goes on to promise and command that Jerusalem be restored (vv. 4-13), that justice be established within her (14-17), that the fast days, commemorating the Temple's desolation, will become feasts, and (20-3) that the restored Zion, precisely as the home of YHWH, will become the focus of international pilgrimage.
[27] Zech. 14.1-5, 9, 16.
[28] Mal. 3.1-4.
[29] Ps. 50.3-4.

Then shall all the trees of the forest sing for joy
   before YHWH; for he is coming,
   for he is coming to judge the earth.
He will judge the world with righteousness,
   and the peoples with his truth.[30]

Let the floods clap their hands;
   let the hills sing together for joy
   at the presence of YHWH, for he is coming to judge the earth.
He will judge the world with righteousness,
   and the peoples with equity.[31]

This catalogue is impressive in its range and scope, and indicates that the theme would have been well known in the second-Temple period. We may surmise that Jews of those days would also have read stories like the return of the ark of the covenant (1 Samuel 5—7) as a foretaste of what they hoped for. YHWH would return; the promises would be fulfilled; the people would be victorious.

But the geographical return from exile, when it came about under Cyrus and his successors, was not accompanied by any manifestations such as those in Exodus 40, Leviticus 9, 1 Kings 8, or even (a revelation to an individual) Isaiah 6. Never do we hear that the pillar of cloud and fire which accompanied the Israelites in the wilderness has led the people back from their exile. At no point do we hear that YHWH has now gloriously returned to Zion. At no point is the house again filled with the cloud which veils his glory. At no point is the rebuilt Temple universally hailed as the true restored shrine spoken of by Ezekiel. Significantly, at no point, either, is there a final decisive victory over Israel's enemies, or the establishment of a universally welcomed royal dynasty. The closest we come to any of this theologically is the vision of Sirach 24, in which the divine Wisdom, subsequently identified with Torah, comes to dwell in the Temple; the exaltation of the High Priest and the Temple liturgy in Sirach 50 suggests that the author sees the dwelling of Israel's god with his people as a reality in his own day.[32] The closest we come socio-politically is the cleansing of the Temple by Judas Maccabaeus, the defeat of the Syrians, and the establishment of the Hasmonean dynasty; but this, as we saw, remained riddled with ambiguity.[33] So, of course, did the subsequent career of Herod the Great, whose attempt to establish his house as the true royal family was, in retrospect, doomed from the start.[34]

---

[30] Ps. 96.12–13.
[31] Ps. 98.8–9.
[32] cf. *NTPG* 217, 229, 264f.
[33] cf. *NTPG* 158f.
[34] cf. *NTPG* 160, 308f.

Temple, victory and kingship remained intertwined, but the hope they represented remained unfulfilled.

It is therefore not surprising that the scriptural tradition which refers unambiguously to YHWH's return to Zion after the exile is maintained in the post-biblical writings. Passages such as the following go hand in hand with the theme of Israel's continuing exile:

> The god of the universe, the holy great one, will come forth from his dwelling. And from there he will march upon mount Sinai and appear in his camp emerging from heaven with a mighty power . . . Behold, he will arrive with ten million of the holy ones in order to execute judgment upon all . . .[35]

> Then his kingdom will appear throughout his whole creation . . .

> For the heavenly one will arise from his kingly throne.
> Yea, he will go forth from his holy habitation
>   with indignation and wrath on behalf of his sons.

> For god most high will surge forth,
>   the eternal one alone.
> In full view will he come to work vengeance on the nations.
> Yea, all their idols will he destroy.

> For God, who has foreseen all things in the world, will go forth, and his covenant which was established . . .[36]

> '. . . I shall descend and dwell with them in all the ages of eternity.' And he said to the angel of the presence, 'Write for Moses from the first creation until my sanctuary is built in their midst for ever and ever. And the LORD will appear in the sight of all. And everyone will know that I am the God of Israel and the father of all the children of Jacob and king upon Mount Zion for ever and ever. And Zion and Jerusalem will be holy.'[37]

> In the house above which I shall make my name reside [they shall offer] the holocausts . . . continually, from the children of Israel, besides their freewill offerings . . . They shall be for me a people and I will be for them for ever and I shall establish them for ever and always. I shall sanctify my temple with my glory, for I shall make my glory reside over it until the day of creation, when I shall create my temple, establishing it for myself for ever, in accordance with the covenant which I made with Jacob at Bethel.[38]

The notion of Israel's god 'coming' could also be expressed as his 'visiting' his people. This theme, evident in the Scrolls, is known also in early Christian literature, where it is regarded as having been fulfilled in Jesus.[39]

---

[35] *1 En.* 1.3–4, 9; cf. 25.3–5; 90.15; 91.7.

[36] *T. Mos.* 10.1, 3, 7; 12.13.

[37] *Jub.* 1.26–8. The passage immediately preceding speaks, in language reminiscent of Jer. 31 and Ezek. 36, of covenant renewal and return from exile.

[38] 11Q19 (=11Q Temple^a) 29.3–9 (GM 161f.).

[39] 1QS 3.18; 4.19; CD 7.9; 8.2–3 (= 19.15); Lk. 1.68, 78; 7.16; 15.14; cp. Lk. 19.44, 1 Pet. 2.12. The usage of the root *episkeptomai* ('visit') in the latter passages follows that of e.g. LXX Gen. 50.24f.; Ex. 3.16; 4.31; Jud. 8.33, in each of which the reference is to a

There is thus ample evidence that most second-Temple Jews who gave any thought to the matter were hoping for YHWH to return, to dwell once again in the Temple in Jerusalem as he had done in the time of the old monarchy.[40] Robert Webb, in his important study of this theme,[41] has concluded impressively that, of all the figures who were expected to come to the rescue of the Jews in this period, it was YHWH himself whose coming was most regularly anticipated.[42] When other figures such as a Messiah were expected, this did not exclude YHWH's coming, but should be seen as the expression, outworking, or accompaniment of it. And, of course, the presence of the Shekinah glory in the Temple would not mean merely that YHWH had, as it were, taken up official residence. He would also act, most likely through his accredited agents, to judge and to save.[43] This expectation remained basic to Judaism in the time of Jesus.

The hope for the return of YHWH belongs, obviously, very closely with the other two features of the kingdom-expectation, namely the return from exile and the defeat of evil. There is no need, as some have done, to play off the eschatological or 'apocalyptic' notion of the coming kingdom against the idea that kingdom-language refers primarily to Israel's god himself. The latter notion, found especially in the Targum of Isaiah, dovetails perfectly into the eschatological expectation; after all, it is in Isaiah more than anywhere else that the notion of YHWH returning to Zion belongs exactly with the hope for return from exile. The later use of the Targum in rabbinic circles, with their non-eschatological and certainly non-apocalyptic outlook, does not invalidate this. If the Targum of Isaiah was indeed in existence in the first century, and was known and used by Jesus,[44] it would reflect a period quite different from the post-135 rabbinic developments when the revolutionary dreams of the apocalyptic writers were discredited. In that earlier setting, to speak of Israel's god visiting his people in person could not be generalized, abstracted from its eschatological context. If YHWH was visiting his people, that would mean that the exile was over, that evil was defeated, and that sins

---

great act of deliverance.

[40] The evidence, clearly, is much wider than simply bYom. 21b, as Davies 1991 suggests. He claims that Joel 3.17; Ps. 135.21; 11QTemple 29.7–10 (quoted above as evidence for my position!); Mt. 23.21; Jos. *War* 6.299; and mSukk. 5.4 support the view that most second-Temple Jews regarded YHWH as currently resident in the Temple. I do not think any of these passages will bear this weight, even without considering the strength of the evidence to the contrary.

[41] Webb 1991, ch. 7, to which I owe several of the above references.

[42] cf. too Mason 1992.

[43] cf. e.g. Jud. 8.33: 'The Lord will visit/deliver Israel by my hand' (*episkepsetai kyrios ton Israel en cheiri mou*).

[44] cf. Chilton 1982, 1984a.

were forgiven. Conversely, if those things were happening, it would be the sign that YHWH was returning at last.

If YHWH were to act in history, and if he did so through a chosen agent, how might that chosen agent be described? This is the other aspect of first-century Jewish thinking which helps us to understand the context of Jesus' symbolic act and the stories and riddles with which he surrounded it.

(ii) Sharing the Throne of God

We are on firm ground in arguing, as we just have, that most second-Temple Jews expected YHWH to return to Zion, as part of the total redemption of Israel. The other point I wish now to draw out has no such firmness. Nevertheless, there are several texts which seem to point in one particular direction, and this seems to have been picked up by Jesus himself as much as, if not more than, by the early church.

The fundamental point is that, according to some texts from this period, when YHWH acted in history, the agent through whom he acted would be vindicated, exalted, and honoured in a quite unprecedented manner. A proper treatment of this fascinating but confusing topic would take – indeed, does take – at least a full volume in itself,[45] and I must be content with pointing in a general direction with some specific instances.

To begin with, we must note the existence of a complex range of Jewish texts, from widely differing periods, which speculate about the exaltation, and the heavenly enthronement, of a figure who may be either an angel or a human being. These speculations seem to grow from meditation upon, and discussion of, certain key texts, such as Ezekiel 1, in which the prophet receives a vision of YHWH's throne-chariot, and Daniel 7, where 'one like a son of man' is presented to 'the Ancient of Days' and shares his throne. Such speculations formed almost the staple diet of a whole tradition of Jewish mysticism and accompanying theological and cosmological enquiry. This tradition seems to be at least as old as the Qumran texts, since it is reflected in the Melchizedek fragment from Cave 11 and the fragmentary texts of the 'angelic liturgy';[46] it continues for several centuries, being alive and well (for instance) in a book like *3 Enoch*, which is probably to be dated in the fifth or sixth century AD.

---

[45] cf., most recently, Hengel 1995b, ch. 3; and, for fuller treatment of the wider topic, e.g. Gruenwald 1980; Rowland 1982, Part IV; Alexander 1983, 229–53, all with plentiful bibliography. Among basic primary texts are *3 En.* and *T. Job.*

[46] 11Q13; 4Q400–5; 11Q17.

The relationship between two of the primary texts in question is of great interest. Ezekiel 1, the fountain-head of a whole mystical and theological tradition, was itself reworked in Daniel 7: the wheeled throne, the flame of fire, the cloud, the four beasts, and the figure sitting on a throne, all show that we are in the same territory.[47] The differences, however, are also striking: the beasts are wicked, not angelic, and, above all, Daniel's vision implies that there are *two* figures seated on thrones, in place of Ezekiel's single one.[48] This latter move was already anticipated in some measure in Ezekiel 8.2: the Danielic figure is the representative of the kingly power of the one true god, whereas the figure in Ezekiel 8 'is to be regarded as the deity himself described in human form'.[49] In the LXX version of Daniel 7.13 the translator has interpreted 'he came *to* the Ancient of Days' as 'he came *as* the Ancient of Days'.[50] Thus, according to this LXX interpretation,

> the Son of Man is in fact the embodiment of the person of the Ancient of Days. In other words the original scene in Daniel 7, where two figures exist alongside each other in heaven, is changed so that the vice-regent, the Son of Man, takes upon himself the form and character of God himself.[51]

That these texts were read in this way by at least some second-Temple Jews is clear from a number of passages. To begin with an obvious one:

> Thus the Lord commanded the kings and the mighty and the exalted, and those who dwell upon the earth, and said, 'Open your eyes, and raise your horns [or possibly: 'your eyelids'], if you are able to acknowledge the Chosen One. And the Lord of Spirits sat [or possibly: 'set him'] on the throne of his glory, and the spirit of righteousness was poured out on him, and the word of his mouth kills all the sinners and all the lawless, and they are destroyed before him. And on that day all the kings and the mighty and the exalted, and those who possess the earth, will stand up; and they will see and recognise how he sits on the throne of his glory, and the righteous are judged in righteousness before him, and no idle word is spoken before him. And pain will come upon them as upon a woman in labour . . . And pain will take hold of them, when they see that Son of Man sitting on the throne of his glory.[52]

Here one should notice, among other things, that the final phrase draws together Daniel 7 and Psalm 110, and perhaps Zechariah 12.10, in a statement of the exaltation of the Chosen One, the Son of Man, who shares the

---

[47] cf. too *1 En.* 14.14–25.
[48] cf. Rowland 1982, 94–8, pointing out the importance in this connection of Ezek. 8.2.
[49] Rowland 1982, 98.
[50] i.e. reading *hos* rather than Theodotion's *heos*. Cf. Hengel 1995b, 183f.
[51] Rowland 1982, 98.
[52] *1 En.* 62.1–5 (tr. Knibb in Sparks 1984, 243f.). For 'son of man' some mss. have 'son of a woman'. Cf. too e.g. *1 En.* 14.18–21 (on which see e.g. Rowland 1982, 219–22); 45.3; 51.3; 55.4; 61.8; 69.29. The Similitudes of Enoch, from which these passages come, are now widely regarded as non-Christian: cf. e.g. Hengel 1995b, 185f.

throne of the Lord of Spirits. This figure is also described, here and else-where, in language drawn from messianic passages such as Psalm 2 and Isaiah 11, and from the picture of YHWH's servant in Isaiah 40—55. Most scholars now take this section of *1 Enoch* to be pre- or at least non-Christian; it appears, then, to postulate a remarkable exaltation of the agent through whom 'the Lord of Spirits' achieves his purpose.[53]

The tradition unfolding before us takes various forms. Sometimes the texts speak of a mystical journey, attempting to attain to the vision of the one true god himself. Sometimes they speak of an angel who has the name of Israel's god dwelling in him.[54] Sometimes they speak of a human being sharing the throne of Israel's god.[55] Several strands of tradition tell the story of Moses in this fashion;[56] some even speak thus of the martyrs or the pious.[57] In one famous story, which occurs in various forms and periods, the great rabbi Akiba, who hailed Simeon ben Kosiba as Messiah, suggests that the 'thrones' spoken of in Daniel 7.9 are 'one for God, one for David'; even though he was apparently persuaded to modify this opinion (or maybe this is the later tradition preserving his reputation), it seems unlikely that such a position would have been falsely ascribed to one whom later tradition held in such high regard.[58] Other Jewish teachers of the same period (late first and early second centuries AD) seem to have speculated similarly on the possibility of a plurality of 'powers' within 'heaven'.[59] As Rowland points out, another

---

[53] cf. too e.g. *1 En.* 71.13-15 (another rewriting of the scene from Dan. 7).

[54] e.g. *Apoc. Abr.* 10; 17; cf. bSanh. 37b; *3 En.* 12.4f. (where the angel Metatron is called 'the lesser YHWH'), citing Ex. 23.21 ('my name is in him', referring to the angel who guides the children of Israel through the wilderness).

[55] e.g. *1 En.* 71.13-17; *2 En.* 24.1 (late C1 AD); *T. Abr* (rec. A) 11.4-12; 12.4-11; 13.1-8 (C1/2 AD); 4Q491 fr. 11 col. 1 (GM 117f.; cf. Hengel 1995b, 201-3). See further Collins 1995, ch. 6.

[56] e.g. Philo *Vit. Mos.* 1.155-8; Sir. (LXX) 45.2-3; *Artap.* 27.6; *Ezek. Trag.* 68-89, drawing on the imagery of Dan. 7 and Ps. 110; *T. Mos.* 1.14; 11.16-17; cf. Jos. *Ant.* 2.232 (Moses having 'divine beauty'); 3.180 (Moses as a 'divine man'); 3.320 (ranked higher than his human nature); *War* 2.145 (next in awe to God himself). The tradition seems to look back to Ex. 7.1 ('I have made you like God/as a god to Pharaoh'): so Philo *Sacr.* 9 (combining Moses' ascent up Sinai with Ex. 7.1); *Leg. All.* 1.40; *Quod Det.* 161-2; *Migr Abr.* 84; *Mut. Nom.* 19; *Somn.* 2.188-9. On this cf. Meeks 1968; Tiede 1972, 101-240; Fossum 1985; Collins 1995, 145f.; Hengel 1995b, 190f., 196-201. I am indebted on all this to Dr C. Fletcher-Louis, who has also drawn my attention to 4Q374 (GM 278) as a probable further example.

[57] e.g. *T. Job* 33; *T. Ben.* 10.6; cf. e.g. Hengel 1995b, 204-12.

[58] bHag. 14a, cf. bSanh. 38b; cf. e.g. Urbach 1987 [1975, 1979], 998 n.76; Segal 1977; Evans 1991, 222-7; Hengel 1995b, 194-6.

[59] e.g. *3 En.* 16: Elisha ben Abuya has a vision of Metatron enthroned, and declares 'There are indeed two powers in heaven!' – for which he is punished. A different version of the story is found in bHag. 15a. On the idea of 'two powers' cf. too bBer. 33b; bMeg. 25a; and, for '*many*' powers, mSanh. 4.5 (cf. bSanh. 38a).

scriptural passage to which these notions seem to refer is 1 Chronicles 29.23, where Solomon 'sat on the throne of YHWH, succeeding his father David as King'.[60]

It has recently been argued that these all belong within a broad stream of thought and practice, almost a counter-orthodoxy, in which ostensibly monotheistic Jews regarded YHWH as a sort of 'second god'.[61] Even if this overstates the case somewhat, it should be clear that in the first century speculations of this sort were possible. Things like this were thinkable; they were not obviously self-contradictory, nor regarded as necessarily a threat to what second-Temple Jews meant by 'monotheism'. I have argued elsewhere, in fact, that the point of Jewish monotheism was not to offer an analysis of the inner being of the one god, but to mark out the god of Israel as the true god over against the pagan pantheon, and to emphasize the unity of creation and salvation over against dualistic systems of thought.[62] The speculations I have discussed were not denials of Jewish monotheism; they were attempts to find out what that monotheism actually meant in practice.

It is particularly interesting that one of these strands of speculation in particular should be associated with Akiba; for it was Akiba who identified Simeon ben Kosiba as the Messiah, giving him the name 'Bar-Kochba', 'son of the star', alluding to Numbers 24.17. This text, as we saw, was regarded as messianic in other circles in the second-Temple period.[63] True, Akiba is credited with this in only one passage, which has sometimes been regarded as suspect;[64] but, again, the rejection of Messianism in post-135 rabbinic thinking makes it all the more likely that this reference, preserved against the tendency of the tradition (to exonerate a hero like Akiba from complicity in the failed revolt), is historically well founded. And the point should be obvious: when Akiba spoke of the thrones in heaven as being 'one for God, and one for David', this was not, so far as we can tell, a matter of speculation about some future glorious messianic figure. *He had a candidate in mind*: a would-be warrior king, who was to lead the revolt aimed at overthrowing the hated Romans and rebuilding the Temple.[65] Eusebius claims

[60] Rowland 1982, 497 n.66, with other lit. Cf. too 1 Chr. 28.5; 2 Chr. 9.8. In 2 Chr. 13.8 Abijah tells Rehoboam that he cannot withstand 'the kingdom of YHWH in the hand of the sons of David'.

[61] cf. esp. Barker 1992; also 1987, 1991. It is striking that a similar belief emerges in Philo (e.g. *Qu. Gen.* 2.62, where Philo calls the Logos 'a second god', *deuteros theos*; cf. the discussion in *Som.* 1.229f., and, for modern discussion, see e.g. Schürer 3.881–5; Hurtado 1988, 44–8; Barker 1992, ch. 7). Philo's thought-processes here are apparently quite different to those of the rabbis (Segal 1977, 165).

[62] *NTPG* ch. 9, esp. 248–59.

[63] CD 7.19–21; 4QTest. 9–13; 1QM 11.6–7 (GM 38; 137; 104). Cf. Collins 1995, 63f.

[64] jTaan. 68d: cf. e.g. Schäfer 1980.

[65] On the causes and circumstances of the revolt cf. Schürer 1.534–52.

that Bar-Kochba himself 'claimed to be a luminary who had come down to them from heaven and was magically enlightening those who were in misery'.[66] Whether that was so, or whether Eusebius was making an unwarranted deduction from the nickname, when we put together the two things credited to Akiba we arrive at a remarkable position: that one of the greatest rabbis of all time should speak of a human contemporary as one who would share the very throne of Israel's god.

We may speculate on what precisely he might have meant by that.[67] Perhaps he thought that some great angel, some Metatron-like figure, would *represent* the Messiah in the heavenly realm, taking his seat beside the Ancient of Days to indicate that the Messiah had been victorious in the earthly struggle. Or perhaps – which may be another way of saying the same thing – he meant that the Messiah would, in winning the decisive victory over the pagans and rebuilding the Temple, be established as the great earthly king through whom Israel's god would now rule the whole world. There is no reason to suppose that Akiba was a three-decker-universe literalist, who imagined that Israel's god had an actual physical throne somewhere in mid-air, and that Bar-Kochba would mysteriously be lifted up to sit on another one beside him. If he (like his near-contemporary, the author of 4 Ezra) could decode the rich imagery of Daniel 7 so as to make it apply to the political events of his own day, he could certainly use the language of heavenly thrones to *refer to* political events and *invest them* with their 'heavenly', or as we might say 'theological', significance.[68] Seen from that point of view, Akiba might well have meant (in our language): Bar-Kochba is the anointed one, the Messiah, through whom our god will defeat the pagans and rebuild the Temple. He, therefore, is the fulfilment of Daniel's picture of 'one like a son of man' who will be enthroned and sit in judgment over the 'beasts'. He will, in other words, be the vicegerent of Israel's one true god. His victory and his reign will be the victory and reign of our god.

Nor should we suppose for a moment that Akiba was thereby giving up Jewish monotheism. That would be a totally unwarranted slur. We have no reason to suppose that he saw the potential messianic victory of Bar-Kochba as anything other than the supreme victory of the one true god over the pagan gods. Tradition has it, after all, that as he was being tortured to death he

---

[66] Euseb. *HE* 4.6.2 (tr. Lake in LCL); cf. too Jer. *ad Ruf.* 3.31. 'Luminary' translates *phoster*, 'star' or 'heavenly luminary' (such as sun or moon); it is used metaphorically of a king, a generation after Eusebius, by Themistius *Orationes* 16.204c.

[67] cf. Evans 1991, 222–34.

[68] cf. 4 Ezra 11–12, esp. 12.31-4. This vision does not describe, or interpret, the exaltation or enthronement of the 'lion' (i.e. the 'son of man' as interpreted by 4 Ezra); but the next vision (ch. 13) moves further in that direction.

recited the *Shema* until his breath was gone.[69] This is of course the sort of hagiographical detail that pious memory might well invent, but it is unlikely that Akiba would have been regarded with such reverence and respect throughout subsequent generations unless he was known to be 'sound' on the very fundamentals of Judaism. Certainly we must assume that he believed himself to be within the bounds of acceptable theology. Had he been in the least bit flirting with paganism, would he have supported Bar-Kochba in the first place?

The conclusion of this, for the limited purposes of the present discussion, is as follows. Out of a much larger and highly complex set of speculations about the action of Israel's god through various mediator-figures, one possible scenario that some second-Temple Jews regarded as at least thinkable was that the earthly and military victory of the Messiah over the pagans would be seen in terms of the enthronement-scene from Daniel 7, itself a development of the chariot-vision in Ezekiel 1. That is enough to be going on with.

(iii) Symbols for God and God's Activity

I argued in *NTPG* that Jewish thought in our period used various symbols and ideas to communicate the prevailing belief that, though Israel's god was the transcendent creator, dwelling in heaven and not to be contained within earthly categories, he was nevertheless both continually active within the world and specially active within the history of Israel herself.[70] The symbols in question are well known: Shekinah, Torah, Wisdom, Logos and Spirit.

Israel's god dwelt (in principle; and he would do so again) in the Temple; his tabernacling presence ('Shekinah') functioned as had the pillar of cloud and fire in the wilderness. He revealed himself and his will through Torah; for some rabbis at least, when one studied Torah it was as though one was in the Temple itself.[71] He sent his Wisdom to be the guide of human beings; again, for some Jewish writers this Wisdom was to be found both in Torah and in the Temple.[72] Language about the Logos became, for Philo in particular, a way of speaking about the one true god active throughout the cosmos;

[69] bBer. 61b.
[70] *NTPG* ch. 9, esp. 248–59.
[71] mAb. 3.2.
[72] e.g. Sir. 24; cf. *NTPG* 229, 265, with other refs., and Hengel 1995b, 212–14. This is perhaps the place to note that the descent and re-ascent of Wisdom in *1 En.* 42 (cf. *4 Ezra* 5.9f.; *2 Bar.* 48.36; *3 En.* 5.12; 6.3) has nothing to do with a proto-gnostic scheme of salvation, but instead indicates that the divine Wisdom or Shekinah, normally present with YHWH's people, has been withdrawn, leaving them open to hostile action.

once more, we find Logos and Wisdom more or less identified. Finally, the Spirit of YHWH was active both in creation and in inspiring prophets, and was the supreme equipment of the Messiah himself.[73]

Turning this around, we find (not surprisingly, in view of the previous sub-section) that the Messiah is closely related to most of these symbols, these ways of speaking and thinking about the divine activity. He would build, cleanse or rebuild the Temple. He might be a great teacher, or at least a great *enforcer*, of Torah. He might, at a pinch, be identified with the Logos.[74] As Solomon's descendant, he would of course be endowed with Wisdom as well as with the divine Spirit. This does *not* reinstate what I denied in chapter 11, the idea that pre- or non-Christian Jews 'believed that the Messiah was "divine"'. Rather, it emphasizes that the Messiah, if and when he appeared, would be the agent or even the vicegerent of Israel's god, would fight his battles, would restore his people, would rebuild or cleanse the house so that the Shekinah would again dwell in it. Akiba's statement, once we understand it as I have suggested, is perhaps not, after all, as far out of line with other messianic expectations as is sometimes imagined.

The language of Jewish monotheism, in other words, quite naturally developed ways of being true to itself. If it were ever implied that YHWH was totally absent from the creation or Israel, that would be a denial of something absolutely fundamental to Jewish belief and identity; if it were ever implied that something important, let alone salvific, had happened to Israel or the world without YHWH being intimately involved, that too would be a denial of everything that monotheism meant in practice.[75] The one god was not, in other words, a distant absentee landlord. We should not confuse (as I suspect a lot of scholarship has confused) YHWH's geographical abandonment of the Temple with the idea of a great metaphysical gap between him and his creation. If, however, one went to the other extreme, by for instance supposing that YHWH was actually contained without remainder in the Temple, or indeed within the Torah, one would have turned him into a pagan god, an idol. After all, 'heaven and the highest heaven cannot contain thee; how much less this house which I have built'.[76] The language of Shekinah, Torah, Hokmah (Wisdom), Logos, and Spirit were ways of affirming YHWH's intimate involvement with his people and his world, at the same time as affirming also his sovereignty and transcendence over the whole cosmos.

---

[73] Gen. 1.2; Num. 11.17, 23-9; 2 Kgs. 2.9, 15; Neh. 9.20; Isa. 11.2; 42.1; 48.16; 61.1; 63.11.

[74] cf. Philo *Conf. Ling.* 62f., identifying the Messiah also with the 'Branch' of Zech. 6.12 and the first-born son of the 'father'.

[75] cf. e.g. Amos 3.6; Isa. 45.5-7 and frequently.

[76] 1 Kgs. 8.27.

They were, in that sense, ways of talking about the personal presence and action, within creation and within Israel's life, of her transcendent creator god. Ultimately, the deliverance that would come for Israel, rescuing her from foreign domination, restoring her rulers as at the beginning, establishing her in peace and justice for ever – this deliverance, even though wrought through human agents, could and would be the work of YHWH himself. The God of the exodus would reveal himself as the God of the renewed covenant. The great act of deliverance would be the supreme moment in, and the supreme vindication of, the story of monotheism itself.

This summary account of certain Jewish stories and symbols is not, of course, meant to be anything like complete. It is, in any case, mostly dependent on the fuller description in *NTPG* chapters 8–10. It will serve, however, to point up some aspects of the Jewish context within which Jesus' symbolic actions, and his explanatory stories and riddles, could make sense, albeit shocking sense. To these actions and sayings we now return.

3. Jesus' Riddles of Return and Exaltation

(i) Stories of YHWH's Return to Zion

(a) Introduction

I begin by restating my proposal. We have seen Jesus' Temple-action as a symbolic enacting of YHWH's judgment on the Temple, and as a symbolic claim to Messiahship. We have seen his Last Supper as a symbolic enacting of the great exodus, the return from exile which he intended to accomplish in his own death. So, I suggest, we should see his final journey to Jerusalem, climaxing in those two events and in that which followed from them, as the symbolic enacting of the great central kingdom-promise, that YHWH would at last return to Zion, to judge and to save.

In this light, I believe that what J. P. Meier says about Jesus in another context applies just as much if not more here:

> Jesus persists in veiling himself in indirect references and metaphors . . . It is almost as though Jesus were intent on making a riddle of himself . . . Whoever or whatever Jesus was, he was a complex figure, not easily subsumed under one theological rubric or sociological model.[77]

---

[77] Meier 1994, 453f. Cf. too Witherington 1994, 203f., on Jesus as the parabolic embodiment of his own message.

We must therefore examine some of the stories and riddles with which Jesus surrounded and interpreted his journey to Jerusalem. They may hold the key to the secret at the heart of his kingdom-announcement. Reading them this way will inevitably be controversial; I hope it will also be fruitful.

Scholars and simple readers alike have long supposed that parables which speak of a returning king or master are to be read without question as referring to the 'return' of Jesus himself, the so-called 'second coming'. It has then been customary for the ways to divide: did Jesus himself tell these stories? Most scholars today would say that Jesus did not speak of his own 'return', and that therefore such stories are the invention of the early church in the persons of the evangelists or their sources. An alternative response would be to say that Jesus might have spoken of a figure who would come – but that this was a 'son of man' whom he did not identify with himself. Into this complex debate I wish to make a proposal which seems to me to do more justice to all the evidence in its context.

First, I reiterate my earlier point. Jesus did speak of 'the coming of the son of man', but that this whole phrase has to be taken quite strictly in its Danielic sense, in which 'coming' refers to the son of man 'coming' *to the Ancient of Days*. He is not 'coming' *to* earth *from* heaven, but the other way around.[78]

Second, I propose that Jesus did speak of a 'coming' figure in the more usual sense of 'one who comes to Israel'. This coming figure was YHWH himself, as promised in the texts we have set out above. Jesus, I suggest, thought of the coming of YHWH as an event which was bound up with his own career and its forthcoming climax.

The primary evidence for all this is, once more, in the simple announcement of the kingdom. To a Jewish first-century listener, this announcement would itself evoke such passages as Isaiah 40 and 52, whose major theme as we have shown was YHWH's coming, his return, to Zion. But to a twentieth-century reader, long accustomed to reading the gospel through other spectacles, this will sound strange or bizarre. We must therefore engage in the normal historical task of taking off our own spectacles and replacing them, as best we can, with first-century ones.

(b) Talents and Pounds

We have two versions of the famous story of the talents or pounds, and a second-hand report of a third.[79] This is not to be wondered at. It is highly

---

[78] Already argued in *NTPG* 291-7; for the texts, cf. chs. 8 and 11 above.

[79] Mt. 25.14-30/Lk. 19.11-27, with some significant differences, on which see the text. Cf. too *G. Naz.* 18, in which the servants respectively (i) squandered the money, (ii) traded

likely that Jesus used such stories like this on numerous occasions (not just 'twice', as cautious conservative exegetes used to suggest). There is no reason whatever to insist that either Matthew's or Luke's version was 'derived' from the other, or both from a single original.

There are two main differences between Matthew's and Luke's versions. First, trivially, Luke's servants are given 'pounds', not 'talents'; and there are ten of them, each of whom is given one pound, though only three are then singled out for special notice. Second, more importantly, Luke's central character is a nobleman who goes away to be installed as king, is followed by a group of subjects protesting against him, and then returns with kingly power and executes the objectors. This, it is normally and rightly assumed, is a clear reference to the story of Archelaus, son of Herod the Great, who went to Rome in 4 BC to petition Augustus for the kingdom of his father, was followed by a deputation of Jews protesting against him, and was given half the kingdom, with the status of ethnarch.[80] The story thus had, in Luke's retelling, particular local and cultural resonances. I do not believe that this of itself argues either in favour of, or against, authenticity. Nor does its double plot necessarily mean that two stories, originally independent, have been conflated.[81] It merely means that the story would raise certain echoes in the minds of Palestinian hearers in the first century, perhaps more so the earlier it was told (i.e. an audience in 30 would be more likely to get the point than an audience in 90, whose memory would have more recent political upheavals in mind).[82] We must insist on a fairly common-sense point here, which often goes unnoticed: Jesus was just as capable as Luke, or anyone else, of telling stories with two or more points, and of saying things with strong political resonances.[83]

---

and made more, and (iii) hid the money. The first is then judged the most severely. This is a perfectly feasible variation, despite Jeremias' description of it as a 'moralistic perversion' (1963a [1947], 58): it is only 'moralistic' *within the world of the story*, and could easily stand for something quite different in the world of Jesus and his hearers: see below.

[80] Jos. *War* 2.1–38, 80–100; *Ant.* 17.219–49, 299–320. His detractors won in the end, when, ten years later (AD 6), he was deposed after further protests. Archelaus' brothers Antipas and Philip were petitioning at the same time, as had their father before them (*Ant.* 14.370–85), and as did their nephew Agrippa I (*Ant.* 18.238) after them. The allusion to Archelaus is doubted by Derrett 1970, 16; otherwise commentators are almost unanimous in accepting it.

[81] As is frequently suggested e.g. by Caird 1963, 210. For an attempted reconstruction of the 'original' second story, cf. Weinart 1977; for a denial of such a possibility, cf. Evans 1990, 669. For other positions, cf. e.g. Marshall 1978, 701; Fitzmyer 1985, 1230–3.

[82] *Pace* Evans 1990, 669, who sees it as a reworking of the original parable by a writer with literary or historical interests. This would, of course, depend on a late date for Luke, putting it at least after the publication of Josephus' *War*.

[83] Marshall 1978, 702 comments that 'a good deal of the elaboration' (i.e. the parts which were added to the hypothetical 'original') 'is typical of popular story-telling rather than of the theological and stylistic re-working of existing traditions.' Quite so. Was Jesus

What then is this story, in whichever form we find it, actually about? Its setting, clearly, concerns the departure and return of a king, or a master; and its main emphasis falls on the accountability of the servants who are left in charge of property in his absence. Particular stress is laid on the third servant, who is finally punished.[84] But who is the king? And who are the servants?

The king who leaves his subjects tasks to perform, and who then returns to see how they have got on, has of course regularly been read as a code for Jesus, going away and, in due course, returning. The servants are then Jesus' followers, who will be judged on their performance in his absence. This reading then often provides an argument for taking the parable away from Jesus and giving it to the early church, which on a similar exegesis would already have at least ten others. But there are good reasons, negative and positive, for rejecting this whole line of thought, whether in relation to Matthew or Luke or to Jesus himself.[85]

First, in most parables about a king and subjects, or a master and servants, the king or master stands for Israel's god and the subjects or servants for Israel and/or her leaders or prophets. This is so both in Jesus' teaching and in some Jewish parables.[86] 'In Jewish usage the relation of God and Israel was so constantly represented as that of a "lord" and his "slaves" that a hearer of the parable would almost inevitably seek an interpretation along those lines.'[87]

Second, the idea of a king who returns after a long absence fits exactly into the context of the return of YHWH to Zion. The fact that this major theme in second-Temple Jewish eschatology has not usually been highlighted

---

not a 'popular story-teller'? Is there any popular story-teller on record who told stories only once, and then always in the least elaborate form possible?

[84] In both synoptic versions, the description of the third servant takes up 7 verses out of the 17 in the parable. Cf. Dodd 1961 [1935], 111; Talbert 1992, 178. So too in *G.Naz.*, and in Eusebius' discussion of it, the punishment is central.

[85] I am grateful to Catherine Wilson for pointing me in this direction, and for discussing the arguments with me. The standard interpretation is challenged by Johnson 1982: he points out that the parable shows little sign of being directed towards the 'parousia', and that Lk. 19.11 in particular speaks of the awesome consequences of the immediately coming kingdom rather than its indefinite postponement. He does not, however, highlight the theme of YHWH's return to Zion, which I regard as central; he thinks the story refers simply to Jesus as the coming king, highlighting the triumphal entry.

[86] e.g. Lk. 16.1-13; Mk. 12.1-12 and pars.; mAb. 1.3; 2.14, 15, 16; 3.1, 17; 4.22. Several of the mishnaic mini-parables relate directly to Israel's god as the taskmaster, overseer or king who will reward his faithful servants. Other rabbinic examples are discussed in Derrett 1970, 26-9.

[87] Dodd 1961 [1935], 112.

goes some way towards explaining the present state of discussion of the parable, with the puzzles that it has engendered (see the sixth point below).

Third, there are several other smaller parables, which we shall glance at presently, which speak of a master returning to his servants. These have commonly been read as referring to the 'second coming' of Jesus. I shall argue, however, that their primary reference at least is to the events which are predicted in Matthew 24 and its parallels: that is, the fate of Jesus and of Jerusalem *seen in terms of the 'coming* [i.e. the vindication] *of the son of man'*; and that this is closely correlated in turn with the 'arrival' and enthronement of the 'Ancient of Days'. I suggest, therefore, that the best way to read the master/servant parables is in terms of their immediate context in all three synoptics, that is, of Jesus' journey to Jerusalem.

Fourth, although the idea of Jesus' return (the so-called 'second coming') has a place in Luke's writings, it is neither central nor major, and in any case occurs, within the Lukan corpus, only in Acts.[88] It looks much more like a post-Easter innovation than a feature of Jesus' own teaching. Even granted that Jesus' hearers did not always grasp what he said, it strains probability a long way to think of him attempting to explain, to people who had not grasped the fact of his imminent death, that there would follow an indeterminate period after which he would 'return' in some spectacular fashion, for which nothing in their tradition had prepared them.

Fifth, when the 'second coming' is mentioned in early Christian writings, there is no suggestion – as there should be on the normal reading of the parable – of the condemnation of some *within the church*. The closest we come to that in the New Testament is the very difficult passage 1 Corinthians 3.12–17; even there, those who receive negative judgment are still saved, albeit only 'as through fire'. It would, in any case, be very bold to make a so-called Q parable depend for its existence, let alone its meaning, on Paul.

Sixth, on the usual interpretation the Lukan parable in particular does not actually make much sense, as even the proponents of the normal reading recognize.[89] In Luke, the parable is told because Jesus and his followers are getting near Jerusalem, and disciples and crowds alike suppose that the kingdom of God is near (verse 11). If Luke, when editing his material, had wanted to stress that the kingdom (in the sense of Jesus' own 'return') had not in fact come in AD 30 or thereabouts, he might be thought to be pushing on an open door. Luke's point, however, does not concern *timing*, but *effects*. The thrust is not 'no, the kingdom is not coming for a long time'; the

---

[88] e.g. Ac. 1.11; cf. *NTPG* 461–4.

[89] cf. Evans 1990, 666: 'The precise reference of such a parable is not easy to detect.' Fitzmyer 1985, 1232f. creates a generalized 'Lukan' sense which completely ignores the Lukan introduction (v. 11).

point is 'the kingdom is indeed coming – but it will mean judgment, not blessing, for Israel'.[90] It ought to be clear from his next two paragraphs that Luke intends this: in verses 28–40, Jesus approaches Jerusalem in a quasi-royal manner, and in verses 41–4, as the crowd descends the Mount of Olives, he bursts into tears and solemnly announces judgment on the city for failing to recognize 'its time of visitation'. YHWH is visiting his people, and they do not realize it; they are therefore in imminent danger of judgment, which will take the form of military conquest and devastation.[91] This is not a denial of the imminence of the kingdom. It is a warning about what that imminent kingdom will entail. The parable functions, like so many, as a devastating redefinition of the kingdom of god. Yes, the kingdom does mean the return of YHWH to Zion. Yes, this kingdom is even now about to appear. But no, this will not be a cause of celebration for nationalist Israel.

Seventh, despite regular assertions, the Matthaean version of the parable cannot be adduced in support of the regular interpretation, i.e. as concerning Jesus' own return.[92] In Matthew, the other parables in chapter 25 are focused, not on the personal return of Jesus after a long interval in which the church is left behind, but on the great judgment which is coming very soon upon Jerusalem and her current leaders, and which signals the vindication of Jesus and his people as the true Israel. There is, of course, a time-lag to be undergone, but it is not the one normally imagined. It is not the gap between Jesus' going away and his personal return (the 'coming of the son of man' in the literalistic, non-Danielic sense); it is the time-lag, envisaged in Matthew 24, between the ministry of Jesus and the destruction of Jerusalem. This time-lag will be a period in which, in Jesus' absence, his followers will be open prey to the deceit of false Messiahs, and will face a period of great suffering before their vindication dawns.[93]

In both Matthew and Luke, then, the coming of the master/king in judgment on the faithless servant is best read as referring to YHWH's return to Zion, and to the devastating results that this will produce. When expectation

[90] With Dodd 1961 [1935], 112, and Jeremias 1963a [1947], 59 (though without Dodd's or Jeremias' analysis of the reasons for the warning); against e.g. Marshall 1978, 702. Marshall notes that it is hard to see why Luke 'should stress a point which ought to have been obvious to his readers after Easter'; his explanation, that Luke perhaps had to counter a view which identified Easter with the parousia, is entirely gratuitous.

[91] Evans 1990, 669f. thinks that Luke has introduced this theme of Roman judgment on Jerusalem into a parable which previously did not contain it. I agree that Luke intends this theme, but I think it is clear that it was not his invention. On Lk. 19.41–4 see above, 348f. On the language of 'visiting', see above, 622.

[92] According to Jeremias 1963a [1947], 58–63, Mt. and Lk. have taken a parable which expressed Jesus' warning of imminent judgment upon Israel, and have converted it into a 'parousia'-parable.

[93] On Mt. 24.4–28 and pars., see above, ch. 8.

of the coming kingdom is aroused, it is for this that people are longing: that YHWH will come and deliver his people from their enemies, and rule over them as their rightful king. Jesus' parable is, as it were, an expansion of Malachi 3.1-3: the Lord whom you seek shall suddenly come to his Temple – but who can stand before him at his appearing? Israel's aspirations will not be underwritten as they stand. Her hope for national victory over national enemies will remain unfulfilled. Instead,

> He is like a refiner's fire . . .; he will sit as a refiner and purifier of silver . . . Then I will draw near to you for judgment; I will be swift to bear witness against [those who . . .] do not fear me, says YHWH of hosts.[94]

Israel's god is at last returning to his people, to his Temple. But the hope set forth in Isaiah 40—55 must be tempered with the warning of Malachi 3. That is the force of the parable in Matthew and Luke.[95]

What then can we say about the parable in its original telling(s) by Jesus himself?

First, it was a warning that, when YHWH returned to Zion, he would come as judge for those in Israel who had not been faithful to his commission. When YHWH returned, as Israel hoped and longed for him to do, he would come as much to judge as to save, and the judgment would begin with his own household. 'Why do you desire the day of YHWH? It is a day of darkness, not of light.'[96] Israel's hopes of national victory would be set aside; the only people vindicated when their god returned, to act in fulfilment of his promise, would be those who responded to the divine summons now being issued in Jesus' kingdom-announcement.

Second, it was the further warning that this coming of YHWH to Zion was indeed imminent. Ironically, the parable which has most regularly been appealed to as referring to a delay in the coming of the kingdom was originally meant as a warning of imminence. It all depends on where, within the story, the hearer is supposed to be located. It has usually been assumed, quite gratuitously, that the story is told from the perspective of the beginning of the process, when the master is going away. But it is far more likely, in view of the emphasis of the parable, that the 'ideal hearer' is located near the

---

[94] Mal. 3.3-5.

[95] Even the version in *G. Naz.* 18 could be making the same point. Eus. *Theophania* 22 (the only source for the passage), to be sure, treats it in a moralizing way; that was perhaps inevitable, granted that the story spoke of the servant who 'squandered his master's substance with harlots and flute-girls'. But this could still be explained as another way of characterizing the Israel who was squandering her god-given inheritance.

[96] Amos 5.18; the wider context (5.21-7) is, interestingly, a denunciation of the sacrificial system, a challenge to pursue genuine justice and covenant-faithfulness, and a warning about impending judgment by pagan nations.

end of the story, when the master is about to return. This fits with the emphasis of Jesus' entire public career: the moment that counts is even now upon us. YHWH is now at last visiting his people. This 'visitation', a major theme of Jesus' public career in both story and praxis, enables us to locate the parable historically with a fair degree of certainty.

Third, the parable, read in this way, coheres well with several other parables both in form and in thrust. The parable of the sower (compare the sowing imagery in Luke 19.22/Matthew 25.26) ends with the statement that some seed will be fruitful beyond normal expectation, but it places considerable emphasis on the seed that is tragically unfruitful. In the pounds/talents, there are some who are faithful, and who are consequently rewarded, but there will be a servant – and it is on him, as we saw, that the main emphasis falls – who has not obeyed his commission. The steward in Luke 16, and the wicked tenants in Mark 12, will be ejected from their position of trust; in each case, there is a strong probability that Jesus intended a reference to the present Jewish nation and its current leaders. The same fate will befall the unprofitable servant in the present story. The sub-plot in Luke's version fits very well with the sub-plots of certain other parables, notably that of the prodigal son. Those who do not want the king to reign over them are like the older brother who refuses to join in the party. In terms of exile and restoration, they are those who do not want the Temple rebuilt. In the pounds, Jesus implies an analogy between those who rejected Archelaus a generation earlier and those who, in his own day, prefer their own dreams of national independence to the coming of the true king. Just as the king came from Rome to execute vengeance on those who rejected his rule, so 'the son of man' will come – using the Roman armies – to crush rebel Jerusalem. This 'elaboration' of the basic plot coheres completely with the 'warning' tradition in the gospels, which for other reasons may be held to be authentic.[97] It is not a case of a 'simple' story being later 'elaborated'. There is every reason to suppose that, in at least one telling of this sort of story, Jesus himself gave it this particular twist. Such sayings are not *vaticinia ex eventu*. They are theological readings of the current situation, such as we may suppose Jesus to have uttered frequently.

Fourth, at least in its Lukan form the parable contains a hint which links it to the story of the wicked tenants. Within the narrative grammar of that story, the 'coming' of the owner is linked to the 'rejection' of the owner's son. Within the distinct narrative grammar of the pounds, the king who is 'coming' is himself 'rejected' by his subjects. In both cases, the result is judgment. The two are not far apart: the tenants' rejection of the son of

---

[97] See chs. 5, 8 above.

course implies a rejection of the owner himself. When each narrative is placed against the expectation of YHWH's return to Zion, and when that is read in the light of Jesus' own career and announcement, the link becomes even closer. Israel's rejection of YHWH will be acted out in her rejection of Jesus. Like Jesus' other retellings of Israel's stories, this one contains a devastating twist. The Isaianic messenger who appears on the Mount of Olives has a message of woe, not of joy, for Zion. Israel, true to the tragic irony implicit at so many points in her own story, will now reject her rightful king.[98]

Finally, the parable in the sense we have given it coheres completely with Jesus' actions, not least his action in the Temple. He went to Jerusalem to act out, dramatically and symbolically, YHWH's judgment on his rebel people. Unlike the Essenes, he was not content to wage a war of words against the Jerusalem hierarchy from a safe distance. Nor was he satisfied, like the Pharisees, with urging a particular way of Torah-interpretation, and settling for limited co-operation from the hierarchy. He saw the present regime in dual focus: in terms of a servant who had buried the master's money, and in terms of rebel subjects refusing their rightful king. The only appropriate response was judgment.

How, then, did the parable actually work, as a rhetorical event, within the career of Jesus, and particularly in its setting of Jesus' coming to Jerusalem and all that he there accomplished? To answer this we may compare the way in which several other parables *explained Jesus' actions*. The story of the doctor going to the sick, not the healthy, explained why Jesus was associating with tax-collectors. The stories of the sheep, coin and sons explained why he was welcoming sinners. The 'wicked tenants' explained why Jesus did what he did in the Temple. And so on. I propose that this parable should be seen as a key explanatory riddle for Jesus' own action. *He saw his journey to Jerusalem as the symbol and embodiment of YHWH's return to Zion.* It was a new encoding, in an acted narrative, of the widespread and well-known biblical prophecies we set out earlier. The action was prophetic; it was messianic; and it was something more, consonant with both of those but going beyond, into an area where there is no obviously suitable adjective. Jesus was hinting, for those with ears to hear, that as he was riding over the Mount of Olives, celebrating the coming kingdom, and warning Jerusalem that it would mean judgment for those who rejected him and his way of peace, so YHWH was returning to his people, his city and his Temple. But who would abide the day of his coming?

[98] cf. 1 Sam. 8.7; 10.19; 12.12.

(c) Other Stories of the Return of YHWH

If this is the meaning of the parable of the talents/pounds, we may have found a clue to the similar stories elsewhere in the synoptic tradition. Though space forbids a full treatment of all of them, it is not difficult to see that they point in the same direction.

We may take as an excellent example the long passage in Luke 12.35–48, with its various parallels in Matthew and Mark.[99] In the Lukan passage there are three variations on the same theme, indicating most likely that Jesus often told stories of this sort. The master is at a wedding banquet, and the servants must be about their business, with lamps lit, ready when he comes home (Luke 12.35–8). The householder must keep watch, because he does not know what time the thief might break in (12.39–40). The manager in charge of the slaves must look after them properly, because his master will return and judge him according to how he has done his job (12.41–8). The implicit interpretation keeps breaking through to the surface of these smaller parables, even to the disruption of the parabolic story-line: the master will gird himself and wait at table for the servants (12.37),[100] 'the son of man is coming' at an unexpected hour (12.40), and the manager who fails to look after those in his charge will be 'put with the unfaithful'. Our fuller treatment of the judgment-theme in chapter 8 above, coupled with the interpretation of the talents/pounds just given, strongly suggests that the right way to take this whole kaleidoscopic sequence of parables is as further stories about the imminent return of YHWH to Zion, and the awesome consequences which will ensue if Israel is not ready. This composite total event can be referred to in a number of ways, of which one regular one, fully in line with the meaning we have explored earlier, is 'the coming of the son of man'. This is intended to conjure up the whole Danielic scene, in which this figure 'comes' to the Ancient of Days at the time when the Ancient of Days himself 'comes' to take his throne and establish his kingdom.[101]

There should be no doubt at least that Luke intends his readers to understand these sayings in this way. The passage goes on at once with Jesus' urgent desire to precipitate the coming of the kingdom (12.49–50), a coming that will mean division where one might have expected unity (12.51–3). In this context, there is a pressing need to interpret the signs of the times

[99] Mt. 24.36–51; 25.1–13; Mk. 13.33–7. Cf. the (clearly derivative) versions in *Thom.* 21; 103.

[100] Johnson 1991, 206 suggests that this be interpreted in the light of Lk. 22.27 and Jesus' action at the Last Supper.

[101] Most commentators (e.g. Marshall 1978, 532–45) allow 'the coming of the son of man', interpreted in the non-Danielic sense of a future return of Jesus, to dominate the section to the exclusion of the more historically likely meaning.

(12.54-6), to settle with the accuser while there is still time, lest one be convicted, sentenced and imprisoned (12.57-9),[102] and to repent in order to avoid devastating judgment whose main features will be slaughter in the Temple precincts and the crash of falling buildings (13.1-5). The sequence closes with a further story about the returning master, which makes the point as devastatingly as anything else:

> A man had a fig tree planted in his vineyard; and he came looking for fruit on it and found none. So he said to the gardener, 'See here! For three years I have come looking for fruit on this fig tree, and still I find none. Cut it down! Why should it be wasting the soil?' He replied, 'Sir, let it alone for one more year, until I dig around it and put manure on it. If it bears fruit next year, well and good; but if not, you can cut it down.'[103]

This whole sequence is well understood by Caird, who speaks of the way Luke has set together

> the approaching climax of Jesus' ministry and . . . the judgement which is about to overtake the nation of Israel . . . Jesus, Luke would have us understand, was expecting a single great crisis, which would mean death for himself, a searching test for his disciples, and judgement for Israel; and this event, contrary to all appearances of defeat and failure, was to be the great triumph prophesied by Daniel (7.13), in which God would bestow world dominion on the Son of man, the symbolic representative of the people of God.

This, however, was not just Luke's view. It was also Jesus':

> It is hardly credible that [Jesus] should have required his disciples during his lifetime to be on guard night and day for an emergency which, to say the least of it, could not happen until some time after his death. If, however, he did not know when to expect the final and fatal outbreak of official hostility to his ministry, it was inevitable that he should repeatedly and earnestly warn his friends to be ready . . .[104]

Jesus, then, was on his way to Jerusalem; and he intended this journey to be seen in terms of the master coming back to the servants, or the owner to the vineyard. Those who did not read the signs of the times, who did not repent, who did not embrace his way of peace, and of reconciliation with 'the adversary', would be courting a disaster for which Pilate's small-scale act of brutality would be merely a foretaste.

---

[102] Fitzmyer 1985, 1001 is a good example of what happens when these sayings are taken out of their context of the imminent crisis facing Israel in Jesus' ministry and turned into would-be timeless moral lessons: the discourse moves to 'a completely unrelated topic', with only a 'superficial reason' for inclusion at this point. Cp. too Evans 1990, 542f.; though Evans does agree (548) that in 13.5 the destruction of Israel is in view.

[103] Lk. 13.6-9.

[104] Caird 1963, 165f.; cf. 169f. Cf. also Wood 1956 (an article which I came upon late in my research, and which interestingly anticipates some of my own arguments); Johnson 1991, 213f.

In this context, a further dimension to a saying we have already examined comes into view. Having stated that he has a baptism to be baptized with, Jesus clearly envisaged that this would be accomplished in Jerusalem, the city that killed the prophets and stoned messengers sent to it (Luke 13.34). The city had refused his offer of rescue from her imminent plight. YHWH had abandoned her to her fate; she would not see him again until she said 'Blessed in the name of the LORD is the one who comes!'[105] Once again it is Caird's interpretation that commends itself. Jesus was speaking prophetically: Israel's god was the real speaker, hiding his face from his people until they were ready to welcome their Messiah.[106] Behind the riddle of Jesus' own coming to Jerusalem as Messiah there lay a deeper meaning. Jesus was announcing, and embodying, the return of YHWH to Zion.

(ii) Riddles of Exaltation

We have now established a context, within the historical portrait of the aims and beliefs of Jesus, in which we can understand at last some of the most puzzling of the sayings in the gospels. If Jesus intended not only to announce, but also to symbolize and embody, YHWH's return to Zion, we are completely justified in interpreting his sayings about vindication and exaltation within the context of the second-Temple Jewish speculations we examined earlier.

This, indeed, is where some of these riddles positively demand to be set.[107] When Jesus quotes Psalm 110 as part of his own messianic riddle ('How can the scribes say that the Messiah is David's son?'), he is quoting the one passage which can plausibly be advanced, alongside Daniel 7, to explain the 'enthronement' texts in *1 Enoch*.[108] According to the psalm, the Messiah is to share YHWH's throne, sitting at his right hand. This meaning must then be carried over into the trial scene, where in Mark 14.62 and parallels Jesus predicts that Caiaphas and his colleagues will see him vindicated, enthroned as Messiah at YHWH's right hand as in Psalm 110, and 'coming on the clouds of heaven' as in Daniel 7. Just as, according to *1 Enoch*, the rulers of the earth 'will see my elect one sitting on the throne of glory',[109] so the court will see Jesus vindicated and enthroned. It would be a

---

[105] 13.35; cf. above, 570 n.117.
[106] Caird 1963, 174, referring to 'similar expressions of thwarted affection' in Hos. 11.8–9; Isa. 65.1–2.
[107] For the details, see ch. 11 above.
[108] cf. Hengel 1995b, 185–9.
[109] *1 En.* 55.4; 62.3–5.

serious misreading of the Daniel reference, and a serious misjudging of its first-century meaning, to see this as a reference to Jesus flying downwards towards the earth;[110] so, too, it would be a crass literalism to make it refer to a physical 'seeing', by Caiaphas and the rest, of Jesus physically sitting on a throne. Jesus was not suggesting that they would have a Merkabah-style vision of the divine throne-chariot. They would witness something far more telling: the this-worldly events which would indicate beyond any doubt that Israel's god had exalted Jesus, had vindicated him after his suffering, and had raised him to share his own throne.

Here at last, I suggest, we have uncovered the reason why Caiaphas tore his robe and shouted 'Blasphemy!' It was not that Jesus had confessed to being the Messiah. It was not even, or not primarily, that he had spoken against the Temple, although that was serious enough. Claiming to be Messiah, even to be in some sense 'son of god', would not in itself be blasphemous.[111] It was that, in explaining his Temple-action and Temple-statements in terms of Messiahship, he did so by drawing together the two texts which, in several parallel and independent traditions in second-Temple Judaism, pointed towards an enthronement in which the Messiah, or the 'son of man', would share the very throne of Israel's god, would be one of the central figures in a theophany.[112]

We have no means of knowing whether Caiaphas would have been aware of the speculations on this point which we have already studied. (We may remind ourselves that we do not know who in the first century read which non-biblical books; also, that there may have been dozens or even hundreds of texts familiar then and subsequently lost.) Nor do we have any idea whether Jesus had himself been influenced by the non-biblical texts we have studied, or whether his own use was original to himself, albeit parallel to others roughly contemporary.[113] We do not have to settle such matters to make historical sense of the scene. Jesus had claimed that, as the true king, he not only had authority over the Temple, but would share the very throne

[110] Despite the weight of evidence against this, even Hengel (1995b, 185–9) continues, in the tradition of Schweitzer and Bultmann, to read the text this way. For a short statement of the obvious criticism – that the Daniel text never meant that and was never read that way within Judaism – cf. Glasson 1988.

[111] cf. Ac. 6.13f.; 7.48–50. Cf. Sanders 1985, 297f.; 1993, 270–3. Sanders relativizes the Markan account by saying that it focuses on Jesus' 'claiming titles for himself', and prefers to say that he was convicted for his action in the Temple and its implications. Once we acknowledge that the issue was never simply about 'titles', it should be clear that Sanders is perpetrating a false antithesis. Absence of titles does not mean absence of christology.

[112] See the interesting discussions, in several ways parallel to this, in Evans 1991; Bock 1994. Chilton 1992b, 153f. offers an alternative proposal, in line with his wider thesis about Jesus' agenda. Brown 1994, 516–47, provides a full discussion of scholarly views.

[113] Though Witherington (1990, 234–48) suggests that Jesus was influenced by *1 En*.

of Israel's god; and he had done so by evoking texts which resonated with multiple and subversive meaning in the world of his day.

The trial scene, which we have already studied from several angles, now comes into complete focus. At stake was the whole career of Jesus, climaxing in his journey to Jerusalem, which itself exploded in his action in the Temple, and was further explained by his Last Supper. The trial opened, as it was bound to do, with the question about the Temple. Jesus had claimed authority over it, authority indeed to declare its destruction. This could only be because he believed himself to be the Messiah? Yes, answered Jesus: and you will see me vindicated, enthroned at the right hand of Power.[114] The whole sequence belongs together precisely *as* a whole. The final answer drew into one statement the significance of the journey to Jerusalem, the Temple-action, and the implicit messianic claim. Together they said that Jesus, not the Temple, was the clue to, and the location of, the presence of Israel's god with his people.[115] Sociologically, this represented a highly radical Galilean protest against Jerusalem. Politically, it constituted a direct challenge to Caiaphas' power-base and his whole position – and, of course, to those of Caesar and Pilate. Theologically, it was either true or it was blasphemous. Caiaphas wasted no time considering the former possibility.

(iii) Conclusion

When, therefore, we examine the two critical passages (Mark 12.35–7; 14.61–2 and their parallels), not as isolated units, but within the context of Jesus' final journey to Jerusalem and his action in the Temple, and when we set this whole larger unit in the context where it manifestly belongs, namely, the complex and pluriform world of second-Temple Judaism, we discover a total coherence whose historical force is compelling. Double similarity and dissimilarity are once again the order of the day. The picture makes sense only within Judaism, but is without exact parallel there. Early Christian views of Jesus make sense as a development from this position, but they do not repeat it: we do not find Daniel 7 used in this way, with this christological import, in early Christianity outside the reported words of Jesus. The early Christians developed their christology in a number of ways, but not quite like this.[116] Jesus' interpretation of his journey to Jerusalem, and his

---

[114] As is often pointed out (e.g. Hengel 1995b, 187), this circumlocution (following the different one in Mk. 14.61) is a further index of likely historicity.

[115] cf. Neusner 1993, 69: 'the holy place has shifted, now being formed by the circle made up of the master and his disciples.'

[116] For the earliest christology in the NT cf. Wright 1991, Part I.

use in that context of riddles based on Psalm 110 and Daniel 7, are rooted in history.

As with Jesus' other climactic symbolic actions, and their explanation in story and riddle, there are hints earlier in his career that the action and explanation we have been studying was not a new idea which came to him only in the final days of his life. We may briefly survey certain features of his work and teaching which, when seen in the light of the central action and its meaning, turn out to point in the same direction.

4. Vocation Foreshadowed

Jesus told stories to explain his actions; but the stories were about masters and servants, fathers and sons. He talked about YHWH in order to account for his own behaviour. Who is the sower? Who is the prodigal father? Who is the shepherd? Who is the woman searching for her lost coin?

Within Jesus' prophetic and messianic vocation, we can trace the outlines of a deeper vocation that would remain hidden, like so much else, until the very end. He called the twelve into existence; he was not himself *primus inter pares*, the new Reuben, Judah, Levi or Joseph; nor was he even the new Abraham. 'Leave your family and your father's house, and go to the land I will show you'; 'Leave your father and the boat, follow me, and I will make you fishers of men.'[117] He spoke of himself as the bridegroom.[118] His kingdom-banquets were foretastes of the messianic banquet, but also of the great feast that YHWH and Israel would celebrate together once more, following the new wilderness wooing.[119] He invoked the image of the shepherd: a royal symbol, of course, with roots deep in the ancient Israelite traditions of monarchy, but one which also spoke of YHWH himself as the shepherd of his people, taking over from the false shepherds who had been feeding themselves instead of the sheep, and (in several of the relevant passages) thereby bringing about the true homecoming, the moment of covenant renewal.[120] Jesus invoked this image to explain what he was about, to interpret his characteristic actions and words of invitation, welcome, challenge, summons, and warning.

[117] Gen. 12.1; Mk. 1.16-20.
[118] Mt. 9.15/Mk. 2.19-20/Lk. 5.34-5; cf. Mt. 25.1-10.
[119] cf. Hos. 2.14-15 with e.g. Ezek. 16, etc.
[120] Ezek. 34.23f.; 37.24 (David as shepherd; cf. Num. 27.17; 1 Kgs. 22.17; Jer. 3.15; 23.4-5; Mic. 5.2-9; Zech. 11.4-17); 34.1-16 (YHWH as shepherd; cf. Ps. 23.1; 78.52; 80.1; Isa. 40.11; Jer. 31.10; Mic. 7.14; Sir. 18.13). Sheep and shepherd in Jesus' language: Mt. 10.6; 15.24; 18.12-14/Lk. 15.3-7; Mt. 25.32; Mt. 26.31/Mk. 14.27; Lk. 12.32; cf. Mt. 9.36/Mk. 6.34; and of course Jn. 10.1-30 *passim*.

It was perhaps inevitable, then, that he should also speak as though he were the new lawgiver: not just the new Moses, bringing a new Torah from Mount Sinai, but one who gave new instructions on his own authority.[121] This, once more, had nothing to do with a claim that the Torah itself was bad, shoddy, or unworthy. It was an eschatological claim: the moment had arrived for the great renewal, in which Torah would be written on people's hearts. This new dispensation would mean that certain commands would become redundant, like candles in the sunrise; but who would have the authority to declare that this moment had arrived for the holy, god-given Torah? Jesus, apparently; as two leading writers on Jesus and Judaism have declared, Jesus did in this sense 'claim to speak for God', declaring that the Mosaic dispensation was, at the very least, no longer adequate, that a new moment had dawned in which some of its god-given provisions were to be set aside:

> Here is a Torah-teacher who says in his own name what the Torah says in God's name . . . For what kind of torah is it that improves upon the teachings of the Torah without acknowledging the source – and it is God who is the Source – of those teachings? I am troubled not so much by the message, though I might take exception to this or that, as I am by the messenger . . . Sages . . . say things in their own names, but without claiming to improve upon the Torah. The prophet, Moses, speaks not in his own name but in God's name, saying what God has told him to say. Jesus speaks not as a sage nor as a prophet . . . So we find ourselves . . . with the difficulty of making sense, within the framework of the Torah, of a teacher who stands apart from, perhaps above, the Torah . . . We now recognize that at issue is the figure of Jesus, not the teachings at all.[122]

Jesus was not lightly setting Torah aside, as a false prophet urging people to abandon their ancient loyalties and embrace new ones (though that was clearly how he risked being seen, and how some actually did see him). Nor was he blaspheming against Moses, an offence which according to Josephus could have carried the death penalty; though, again, some of what he said might have been interpreted in that way.[123] He was claiming, once more, to be inaugurating the new age in Israel's history, to which the Mosaic law pointed but for which it was not adequate.

We should not be so surprised, then, that when Jesus reinterpreted the ten commandments, in response to the question about attaining the age to come, he replaced the first three commandments with his own invitation, challenge, summons and implied warning: sell all you have, and follow me. Loyalty to Israel's god, astonishingly, would now take the form of loyalty to Jesus; to get rid of ancestral land would be the equivalent of throwing away pagan

---

[121] cf. ch. 7 above; and e.g. Harvey 1982, 168; Brown 1994, 545–7.

[122] Neusner 1993, 30f.; cf., more cautiously, Sanders 1985, 271–4, 293, 298.

[123] Jos. *War* 2.145 (cf. 152).

idols.[124] Just as Jesus acted as if he thought he were the reality to which the Temple pointed, or even the one who had authority over the Temple, so he acted and spoke as if he were in some sense the replacement for Torah, or even the one who had authority over Torah itself.

So, too, Jesus would speak as though he were the spokesman of the divine Wisdom. He was on a journey, like Wisdom in Sirach 24, unable to find rest until he arrived in Jerusalem. Wisdom's search for a home formed a gentler, but ultimately no less effective, prophecy of the return of YHWH to Zion, and Jesus seems to have thought of his great symbolic journey in that way too.[125] Wisdom would be justified by her deeds, and perhaps her children; Israel was now confronted by a greater than Solomon.[126] In particular, Jesus invited his hearers, as Wisdom invited hers, to come to him and find 'rest'.[127] He was, as we saw, offering the eschatological rest towards which the sabbath institution pointed.[128] He was acting and speaking as if the role marked out for the divine Wisdom was one he had to embody himself.

By themselves, I do not think these sayings would be strong enough to bear the weight that is sometimes placed on them. They cannot sustain a complete explanation of Jesus' self-understanding. But they are entirely at home within the wider context of Jesus' symbolic journey to Jerusalem, and his varied explanations of that all-important action. Indeed, it is not easy to suppose them coming into existence except in some such context. Once again, we have no reason outside the synoptic tradition itself to suppose that anyone after Jesus' day made such sayings and symbols central to their understanding of who Jesus was and the role he was playing. It looks as though we are in touch with his own aims and beliefs, his own sense of vocation.

Finally, if Jesus' career came to an end with the charge of blasphemy, occasioned by his action in the Temple and the construal he put upon it, we should not after all be surprised to find that the accusation had been levelled against him in earlier days as well. He announced the forgiveness of sins, which as we saw indicated that he was in some sense bypassing the whole Temple cult.[129] If YHWH's return to Zion was to happen in and through him, he had the right and authority to reconstitute Israel around himself, as the forgiven, i.e. the returned-from-exile, people of the one true god. We must

---

[124] Mt. 19.21/Mk. 10.21/Lk. 18.22. The sabbath command, interestingly, is missing from the incident entirely; or is it taken up in the promise of the age to come?

[125] Mt. 8.18-20/Lk. 9.57-8/*Thom.* 86: cf., suggestively, Witherington 1994, 202f.

[126] Mt. 11.19/Lk. 7.34: cf. Witherington 1990, 51-3; Mt. 12.42/Lk. 11.31.

[127] Mt. 11.28-30/*Thom.* 90, closely parallel to Sir. 6.23-31 (so, rightly, Witherington 1994, 205-8, cf. 143f.).

[128] Neusner 1993, ch. 4, esp. 61f.; Witherington 1994, 207f. Cf. above, 394f.

[129] Mt. 9.1-8/Mk. 2.1-12/Lk. 5.17-26; Lk. 7.48. Cf. above, 268-74.

never forget that the gospels record Jesus' friends as saying that he was mad; it is highly unlikely that the early church invented the charge.[130]

What this all-too-brief survey of the earlier career of Jesus has revealed is an inner coherence between the three things we set out earlier from Jesus' Jewish context. (1) Jesus undertook a symbolic action through which he intended to evoke, and to enact, the long-promised return of YHWH to Zion. (2) In doing so, he saw himself in the role of the strange quasi-messianic figure who would share the very throne of Israel's one true God, and who would attain to that exaltation through suffering and vindication on behalf of Israel, fulfilling her destiny to be the light of the world. (3) Consonant with that vocation, he evoked, in his ministry of kingdom-announcement, of welcome, warning and challenge, three of the central symbols by which Israel had learned to think and speak of her god, particularly of his presence and his actions in her midst: Temple, Torah, and Wisdom. Arguably, he understood his teaching also in terms of the prophetic word of Israel's god; arguably, too, he saw his whole work as being guided, driven along, by YHWH's spirit (what prophet would not?). As a preliminary conclusion to this chapter and Part, then, we can say that Jesus' praxis, stories, symbols and worldview answers thus pointed together, coherently, to a central belief: that the fulfilment of YHWH's promises and purposes, in their rich variety and tight thematic unity, was about to occur; and a central aim: that he would himself act and speak as their embodiment, bringing the promises to fulfilment and the purposes to fruition.

In this light, we can approach the final issue of Jesus' self-understanding (a phrase I have for the most part avoided until now, but which I now use to denote that awareness of vocation which I have been describing) with some hope of success.

Joachim Jeremias made Jesus' experience of Israel's god as *'Abba'*, 'Father', the basis for his attempt to reconstruct Jesus' mindset and self-understanding.[131] Jeremias may have overstated his case somewhat, though he was as well aware as some of his critics that there are some apparent counter-examples to his thesis (that 'Abba' is not found, as an address to Israel's god, in the Palestinian Judaism of Jesus' day), and that 'Abba' was

---

[130] Mk. 3.21; cf. Jn. 10.20. Cf. too the charge of his 'having a demon': Mk. 3.22/Jn. 7.20, etc.

[131] cf. e.g. Jeremias 1967, ch. 1 [=1966b, 15–66]; 1971, 61–8. Cf. e.g. 1967, 52f.: 'All the "My Father" sayings we have discussed deal with the unique revelation and authority which have been given to Jesus . . . Jesus bases his authority on the fact that God has revealed himself to him like a father to his son. "My Father" is thus a word of revelation. It represents the central statement of Jesus' mission.' Schillebeeckx 1979 [1974], 256–71 states the point if anything even more strongly (summary: 269). Cf. Harvey 1982, 168–70; Kim 1983, ch. 5.

not, as is sometimes supposed, a children's word only.[132] Against his major claim, it is doubtful whether one can actually *start* with the expression '*Abba*', found as it is in only one gospel text,[133] and build upon it a whole theory as to the uniqueness of Jesus' experience of, and teaching about, Israel's god. However, it should not be supposed that Jeremias has been disproved completely: there *is* a striking phenomenon to be observed in the prayers of Jesus, and, once we relieve it of the strain of being the loadbearing wall in a much larger construction, it can relax and make a valuable contribution to a different one.

Without going into unnecessary detail (Jeremias' full survey remains largely adequate), we can suggest that Jesus' language about, and address to, Israel's god as 'father' belongs in the first instance with the basic aim and belief that we observed in chapter 11. It evokes the memory of Israel's designation as god's son, with overtones of the exodus in particular;[134] it points, too, to the Messiah as the special son, the one in whom Israel's sonship is focused.[135] All of this, as we saw, is focused quite sharply in the parable of the wicked tenants. Since Jesus believed himself to be the Messiah who would draw Israel's destiny to its climax by embodying the new exodus in himself, it is natural to suppose that he would make a special point of praying in a manner that was consonant with this belief, and teaching his followers to do the same.

What we can now suggest, in the light of the argument of the present chapter so far, is that *within* this meaning, and the messianic vocation it implied, Jesus discovered a deeper one, so that he experienced a peculiar appropriateness in designating Israel's god as 'father'. If it is true, as I have argued, that he acted upon a vocation to do and be for Israel and the world what, according to scripture, only Israel's god can do and be, then we may legitimately enquire whether we have any clues as to what generated, sustained, or at least centrally characterized that vocation. When, asking that question, we discover that Jesus seems to have addressed Israel's god as

---

[132] See above, 262f.; and cf. e.g. Vermes 1973, 210-13; 1983, 41-3; Barr 1988. Vermes quotes bTaan 23b (the story about Hanin, who, being addressed as *Abba* by some children, asked the Master of the Universe to teach them to distinguish the *Abba* who gives rain from the *Abba* who does not) as an example of Palestinian usage. Jeremias (1967, 61f.; 1971, 65f.) points out, however, that in the story *Abba* is used to *denote* Israel's god, but not to *address* him. Jeremias is widely credited with urging that '*Abba* means "Daddy"'; he may be responsible at one remove for this misunderstanding, but he never actually asserted it. Barr, acknowledging this, also admits (39) that Jeremias' wider argumentation remains valid.

[133] Mk. 14.36.

[134] Ex. 4.22, etc. In Wis. 2.13-16 the one who calls himself 'son of god' is probably simply a devout Jew.

[135] 2 Sam. 7.14; Ps. 2.7, 12; 89.26-7.

'father' in a way which, even if not completely unique, is at least very remarkable, we may be near to an answer. And when we find a passage like the following:

> At that time Jesus answered and said: 'I thank you, father, lord of heaven and earth, that you hid these things from the wise and understanding, and revealed them to babes. Yes, father: that was pleasing in your sight. All things have been given me by my father; and no one knows the son except the father, and no-one knows the father except the son, and anyone to whom the son chooses to reveal him.'[136]

– then we may be confirmed in this deduction. As with all that we have discovered in the present chapter, the possibility of Jesus' having a particular intimacy with the one he called 'father' is not, in that sense, a new and strange idea added on to the outside of the rest of the portrait. It appears quite naturally as the inside of the picture, making sense of, and giving depth to, all the rest.[137]

Working back through the gospels, then, we have discovered several themes, by themselves insufficient as the basis for an argument about Jesus' self-understanding, which come into their own when placed in the context of his final great symbolic actions and the explanations with which he surrounded them. Something else I have deliberately avoided until now is any mention, let alone discussion, of the transfiguration.[138] It is, to say the least, not the sort of story that one can make the basis of a historical reconstruction, even of a small part of a case like the present one. But again, however one analyses the account in terms of theology, psychology, biblical allusion, mysticism, anthropology or whatever, the historian of any background will be bound to admit that *if* Jesus thought about his own vocation in the way I have outlined, and *if* an event like the transfiguration took place, then it cannot but have strengthened and given direction to that vocation. And in that light we may just note the words which Jesus is reported to have spoken, in all three synoptic gospels, immediately before the reported event, words which draw together a good deal of what this chapter, and this Part of the book, have been all about:

> If any want to become my followers, let them deny themselves and take up their cross and follow me. For those who want to save their life will lose it, and those who lose their life for my sake, and for the sake of the gospel, will save it. For what will it profit them to gain the whole world and forfeit their life? Indeed, what can they give in return for

---

[136] Mt. 11.25-7/Lk. 10.21-2. Cf., in addition to the commentaries, Jeremias 1971, 56-61; Harvey 1982, 160.

[137] The concept of 'agency', explored usefully by Harvey 1982, ch. 7 and elsewhere (see above, p. 121 n.136), explains much about the father-son picture in the gospels, but does not in my view get to the very heart of it.

[138] Mt. 17.1-9/Mk. 9.2-10/Lk. 9.28-36.

their life? Those who are ashamed of me and of my words in this adulterous and sinful generation, of them the son of man will also be ashamed when he comes in the glory of his father with the holy angels. [And he said to them,] Truly I tell you, there are some standing here who will not taste death until they see that the kingdom of god has come with power.[139]

It should by now be clear how such a passage as this might be read within the paradigm I have advanced. Peter has just declared that Jesus is the Messiah. Jesus has responded by telling the disciples that he must be rejected and killed. He then issues a summons, a warning and a promise, in which all other such 'teaching' is implicitly contained: the disciples must follow him in his doubly risky revolution; they will have to forsake all to do so; the kingdom is about to dawn. The implication is that Jesus saw the coming of the kingdom closely bound up with his own Messiahship, his own forthcoming death, and the journey to Jerusalem which would encapsulate both. He would embody in himself (that is) the return from exile, the defeat of evil, and the return of YHWH to Zion. Once we have understood that entire sequence of thought, as a whole and in its parts, in the way for which I have argued, we can see that, from Jesus' point of view, this was indeed how the 'son of man', who is also here the 'son of god', would be vindicated. This was how YHWH would return to Zion; this was what he would accomplish when he arrived there. This would be the way to the victory of God.

5. Conclusion

We set out in this Part of the book to enquire after Jesus' aims and beliefs. It is time to draw our findings together.

I have argued that Jesus' underlying aim was based on his faith-awareness of vocation.[140] He believed himself called, by Israel's god, to *evoke* the traditions which promised YHWH's return to Zion, and the somewhat more nebulous but still important traditions which spoke of a human figure sharing the divine throne; to *enact* those traditions in his own journey to Jerusalem, his messianic act in the Temple, and his death at the hands of the pagans (in the hope of subsequent vindication); and thereby to *embody* YHWH's return. His intentions, putting those aims into practice, involved the detail of the journey, of his arrival in Jerusalem and action in the Temple, of the Last Supper, of his agonizing wait in the garden, and of his refusal to offer any

---

[139] Mk. 8.34—9.1; par. Mt. 16.24-8/Lk. 9.23-7, with variations that are interesting in themselves but irrelevant to the argument at this point.

[140] 'I was sent to . . .' or 'I came to . . .' is the language of vocation: cf. e.g. Mt. 9.13/Mk. 2.17/Lk. 5.32; Lk. 19.10.

defence of himself before the authorities. He carried out those intentions, believing that he was thereby accomplishing those aims.

Jesus' beliefs, therefore, remained those of a first-century Jew, committed to the coming kingdom of Israel's god. He did not waver in his loyalty to Jewish doctrine. But his beliefs were those of a first-century Jew *who believed that the kingdom was coming in and through his own work.* His loyalty to Israel's cherished beliefs therefore took the form of critique and renovation from within; of challenge to traditions and institutions whose true purpose, he believed (like prophets long before, and radicals in his own day), had been grievously corrupted and distorted; and of new proposals which, though without precedent, were never mere innovation. They always claimed the high ground: fulfilment, completion, consummation.

We can summarize Jesus' beliefs in terms of the three most fundamental Jewish beliefs: monotheism, election, and eschatology.[141]

Jesus believed that there was one God who had made the world, and who had called Israel to be his people; that this one God had promised to be with his people, and guide them to their destiny, their new exodus; that his presence, guidance and ultimately salvation were symbolized, brought into reality, in and through Temple, Torah, Wisdom, Word and Spirit. He was a first-century Jewish monotheist.

He believed that Israel was the true people of the one creator God, called to be the light of the world, called to accomplish her vocation through suffering. He cherished this belief in Israel's special vocation, even as he challenged current interpretations of it.

He believed in the coming kingdom of Israel's god, which would bring about the real return from exile, the final defeat of evil, and the return of YHWH to Zion. He embraced this Jewish hope, making it thematic for his own work.

The difference between the beliefs of Jesus and those of thousands of other Jews of his day amounted simply to this: he believed, also, that all these things were coming true in and through himself. His particular task was to offer a symbolic encoding (or decoding?) of this entire theology and expectation in terms of his own life and work. The words he spoke as Messiah, on the night he was betrayed, would resonate out prophetically as words of Israel's god, spoken about Jesus himself. 'This is my son, my beloved, in whom I am well pleased'; 'This is my son, my beloved, listen to him'; and now 'This is my body, given for you.'[142]

Speaking of Jesus' 'vocation' brings us to quite a different place from some traditional statements of gospel christology. 'Awareness of vocation' is

---

[141] On the pattern and tradition of Jewish belief cf. *NTPG* chs. 9, 10.
[142] Mk. 1.11 par.; 9.7 par.; Lk. 22.19 par.

by no means the same thing as Jesus having the sort of 'supernatural' awareness of himself, of Israel's god, and of the relation between the two of them,
such as is often envisaged by those who, concerned to maintain a 'high'
christology, place it within an eighteenth-century context of implicit Deism
where one can maintain Jesus' 'divinity' only by holding some form of
docetism. Jesus did not, in other words, 'know that he was God' in the same
way that one knows one is male or female, hungry or thirsty, or that one ate
an orange an hour ago. His 'knowledge' was of a more risky, but perhaps
more significant, sort: like knowing one is loved. One cannot 'prove' it
except by living by it. Jesus' prophetic vocation thus included within it the
vocation to enact, symbolically, the return of YHWH to Zion. His messianic
vocation included within it the vocation to attempt certain tasks which,
according to scripture, YHWH had reserved for himself. He would take upon
himself the role of messianic shepherd, knowing that YHWH had claimed this
role as his own. He would perform the saving task which YHWH had said he
alone could achieve. He would do what no messenger, no angel, but only the
'arm of YHWH', the presence of Israel's god, could accomplish.[143] As part of
his human vocation, grasped in faith, sustained in prayer, tested in confrontation, agonized over in further prayer and doubt, and implemented in action,
he believed he had to do and be, for Israel and the world, that which according to scripture only YHWH himself could do and be. He was Israel's Messiah; but there would, in the end, be 'no king but God'.

I suggest, in short, that the return of YHWH to Zion, and the Temple-
theology which it brings into focus, are the deepest keys and clues to gospel
christology.[144] Forget the 'titles' of Jesus, at least for a moment; forget the
pseudo-orthodox attempts to make Jesus of Nazareth conscious of being the
second person of the Trinity; forget the arid reductionism that is the mirror-
image of that unthinking would-be orthodoxy. Focus, instead, on a young
Jewish prophet telling a story about YHWH returning to Zion as judge and
redeemer, and then embodying it by riding into the city in tears, symbolizing
the Temple's destruction and celebrating the final exodus. I propose, as a
matter of history, that Jesus of Nazareth was conscious of a vocation: a vocation, given him by the one he knew as 'father', to enact in himself what, in
Israel's scriptures, God had promised to accomplish all by himself. He would
be the pillar of cloud and fire for the people of the new exodus. He would
embody in himself the returning and redeeming action of the covenant God.

---

[143] Ezek. 34; Isa. 59.15-21; 63.8f. See above, 618f. The 'arm of YHWH' is a major
theme in Isa. 40—55, and seems at 53.1 to be virtually fused with the 'servant of YHWH'.

[144] The present paragraph is another version of one published in Wright 1996d, 28f.

Part Four

Conclusion

Chapter Fourteen

RESULTS

The story of Jesus, as he was in his own setting, is one of the most fascinating chapters of ancient history. His life and agenda, within their own context and compass, bear comparison with any other figure of whom we have knowledge. His teaching, even when abstracted from its setting, kicked and tugged into different shapes, and compelled to serve different agendas, remains shatteringly illuminating. His death stands alongside that of Socrates: the cross and the hemlock have, very largely, 'determined the fabric of western sensibility'.[1]

But that is all: a memory. Herein lies the great puzzle.

Make Jesus a teacher, and you can translate that teaching into other modes. Make him a one-dimensional revolutionary (social, political, military even), and you have a model to imitate. But see him as an eschatological prophet announcing, and claiming to embody, the kingdom of the one true God, and you have a story of a man gambling and apparently losing. Einstein's question, whether God plays dice, acquires a new poignancy.

Schweitzer saw the problem well enough. Place Jesus in his historical (that is, eschatological and apocalyptic) context, and you risk making him massively irrelevant. The very specificity of his teaching, its direction towards the Israel of his own day, makes it more and more like a tract for his own time and less and less like timeless truth. Worse: he promised a kingdom, and it never arrived. For both reasons we have witnessed 'the agonized attempt to save Jesus from apocalyptic': in Schweitzer's day by the pious, anxious to retain Jesus the timeless teacher; in our own by the impious, anxious to reject Jesus the apocalyptic prophet.[2]

Schweitzer grasped this nettle with one hand, and Nietzsche with the other, and declared that the 'spirit' or 'personality' of Jesus was set free, by the very failure of his project, to become relevant, a brooding presence, over all times and places. Jesus would remain a stranger, 'one unknown', but one who still beckons, commands and reveals. Bultmann, however, claimed that

---

[1] Steiner 1996, 361.
[2] Schweitzer 1954 [1906], 400; the mocking phrase is the title of Koch 1972, ch. 6.

this route was not available. The 'personality' of Jesus, he said in a program-matic but wondrously mistaken remark, is unknown to us, but his 'teaching' lives on.[3] Bultmann thus achieved by demythologization what Schweitzer achieved by 'personality', with the significant difference that (to oversimplify for a moment) whereas Schweitzer's Jesus was a man of action, who sum-moned people to *tasks*, Bultmann's was a man of words, who urged people to *think*. Schweitzer's Jesus led him (Schweitzer) to become a medical mission-ary. Bultmann's led him to write a 'New Testament Theology'.

Neither Schweitzer's nor Bultmann's analysis will do. Bultmann's demythologized Jesus simply does not belong in the first century; try reading *Jesus and the Word* straight after reading Josephus. Schweitzer was right to say that 'apocalyptic' was central for Jesus, but wrong to think it meant the end of the world, and wrong to suppose that an eternally valid core of mean-ing could emerge from the failure of the world to end on time. No. Jesus went to Jerusalem to enact and embody the coming kingdom, in which YHWH would be king of all the world. He died the way all failed Messiahs die. If the story ended there, its only real message would be the one Juvenal learned as a schoolboy, writing exercises in rhetoric. Retire from public life altogether; you'll sleep better.[4]

If, in other words, Jesus' praxis, stories and symbols led to crucifixion, one could not even say that he had had several good ideas but had lost at the last throw of the dice. His death, thematically linked as it was to his whole agenda, called the ideas themselves into question. If Jesus was as I have described him, and if his death was the end, it was the end. He becomes like Judas the Galilean or Simeon ben Kosiba, only somewhat more interesting; and that might be merely because the teachings of Judas and Simon have not been preserved. Judas, after all, is described by Josephus as a *sophistes*.

There were, to be sure, ways of coping with the death of a teacher, or even a leader. The picture of Socrates was available, in the wider world, as a model of unjust death nobly borne. The category of 'martyr' was available, within Judaism, for someone who stood up to pagans, and compromising no-better-than-pagans, and died still loyal to YHWH. The category of failed but still revered Messiah, however, did not exist. A Messiah who died at the hands of the pagans, instead of winning YHWH's battle against them, was a deceiver, as the later rabbis (and Christians) said of Bar-Kochba.[5]

Why then did people go on talking about Jesus of Nazareth, except as a remarkable but tragic memory? The obvious answer is the one given by all early Christians actually known to us (as opposed to those invented by

---

[3] Bultmann 1958a [1926], 8–10.
[4] Juv. *Sat.* 1.15–17.
[5] e.g. Lam. R. 2.2; cf. Schürer 1.543f., and above, 627–9.

modern mythographers): Jesus was raised from the dead. This, of course, raises other questions which can only be dealt with in another book: what did they mean by that? What actually happened? Was it something that happened to Jesus, or simply to the disciples? Why did whatever-it-was-that-happened generate the sort of movement that emerged? The resurrection, however we understand it, was the only reason they came up with for supposing that Jesus stood for anything other than a dream that might have come true but didn't. It was the only reason why his life and words possessed any relevance two weeks, let alone two millennia, after his death.

The real problem, therefore, for historians and theologians alike, is not that Jesus expected the end of the world and it failed to happen; nor that the first generation of Christians expected the return of Jesus ('the parousia') within a generation and *it* failed to happen. Those are parodies of the real problem, which is this: Jesus interpreted his coming death, and the vindication he expected after that death, as the defeat of evil; but on the first Easter Monday evil still stalked the earth from Jerusalem to Gibraltar and beyond, and stalks it still. To postpone the effectiveness of his putative victory to an after-life, as has been done so often in the Christian tradition, or to transform it into the victory of true *ideas* over false ones, as has sometimes been done within the idealist tradition, is to de-Judaize Jesus' programme completely. It is to fail to take seriously his stark prayer for the kingdom to come, and God's will to be done, on earth as it is in heaven.

Interestingly, neither of these trivializing options characterized the first generation of Christians. They were indeed concerned with their own, as well as Jesus', resurrection. They were often concerned with articulating and believing the truth. But they announced and celebrated the victory of Jesus over evil as something that had already happened, something that related pretty directly to the real world, their world. There was still a mopping-up battle to be fought, but the real victory had been accomplished. That was the basis of their announcement to the principalities and powers that their time was up.[6] That was the basis of their remarkable joy, which was not merely the tasting of hope in advance, but had to do with past and present as well. To explore this, again, would take us into the area of another book.

The relevance of Jesus, then, becomes radically different depending on whether one accepts or rejects the witness of the early church to his resurrection. Furthermore, even if one does accept that witness, it means radically different things depending on one's view of Jesus prior to his resurrection. If he was a docetic figure, the divine being of so much would-be orthodox christology, his resurrection would simply validate the salvation he had

---

[6] cf. e.g. 1 Cor. 2.6–9; Eph. 3.10; etc.

revealed and offered. It would prove that he was, after all, 'god' (what sort of god?). If he was a teacher of timeless truths, the announcer of the timeless call to decision, or the pioneer of a new way of being-in-the-world, his resurrection would presumably endorse the programme he had articulated; though, interestingly, those who have constructed Jesus-figures like that tend not to include the resurrection in their schemes, except as a metaphor for the rise of Christian faith. But if he was an eschatological prophet/Messiah, announcing the kingdom and dying in order to bring it about, the resurrection would declare that he had in principle succeeded in his task, and that his earlier redefinitions of the coming kingdom had pointed to a further task awaiting his followers, that of *implementing* what he had achieved. Jesus, after all, as a good first-century Jew, believed that Israel functioned to the rest of the world as the hinge to the door; what he had done for Israel, he had done in principle for the whole world. It makes sense, within his aims as we have studied them, to suppose that he envisaged his followers becoming in their turn Isaianic heralds, lights to the world.

But they would be people with a task, not just an idea. To this extent Schweitzer was right, Bultmann wrong. That is why a 'history of ideas' will never get to the bottom either of Jesus or of the early church. The model I outlined in *NTPG*, and in Part I of the present volume, focused deliberately not on questions and answers merely, important though they are as part of the whole, but on actions, and words-as-actions: on praxis and symbol, and the stories which are not 'illustrations' of abstract ideas but are themselves powerful actions, subversive and sustaining. Within that model, 'beliefs' are closely bound up with 'aims'; the aim is not simply to believe as many true things as possible, but to act in obedience, implementing the achievement of Jesus while spurred and sustained by true belief. (I developed the model, not *a priori*, but because I found myself unable to understand Jesus within the history-of-ideas models with which I started. I have done my best to let the subject-matter suggest the method rather than the other way round. That, indeed, is one reason why this book has taken longer to write than I expected.) If, then, 'New Testament Theology' were to be true to itself, it would need to understand itself within the broader category of 'New Testament Agendas'. That, too, needs another book.

I may, perhaps, draw attention to an ironic feature of my argument in the present work. If I am right, the church, not least in its would-be orthodox moments, has regularly read language in which Jesus referred to YHWH's return to Zion (as part of his understanding of what he himself was doing) as referring to the 'second coming'. The irony is threefold. Some parts of the church, not least certain types of Protestantism, have had a far stronger and more enthusiastic belief in the 'second coming' than they have had in the incarnation, which has then only functioned to ensure that Jesus really was a 'divine' or supernatural being whose human history was not after all so relevant to the salvation he offered. Second, those who have rejected the would-be orthodox doctrine, and all that it has entailed in subsequent history, have regularly attacked it as having no historical foundation.[7] Third, those who have desired to explore and understand the incarnation itself have regularly missed what is arguably the most central, shocking and dramatic source material on that subject, which if taken seriously would ensure that the meaning of the word 'god' be again and again rethought around the actual history of Jesus himself.

It is perhaps because of the terror of making this last move that so many have backed away, making reverence an excuse for inauthentic historical method, taking off their historical sandals lest they tread on holy ground, keeping 'god' at a discreet distance by claiming not to know very much about Jesus either. R. H. Lightfoot, in the famous ending to his 1934 Bampton Lectures, is an obvious example.[8] But, even if the prodigal returned home barefoot, he was given shoes to wear when he arrived at his father's house. Stripped of its arrogance, its desire to make off with half of the patrimony and never be seen again, history belongs at the family table. If theology, the older brother, pretends not to need or notice him it will be a sign that he has forgotten, after all, who his father is.

Orthodox theology has often been thus forgetful, and has therefore often cast the Enlightenment in the role of villain. The Enlightenment, it says, was more cunning than any other movement. Was there a forbidden topic? Yes, there was one: investigating the history of Jesus. Very well, let us undertake that: we shall then be like gods, knowing fact from fiction. And so history was driven out of the garden, packed off to the far country, surrounded by thorns and thistles, and given swinehusks to eat.

But supposing history remains one of the father's true sons?

There is a sense in which Reimarus was right and Melanchthon wrong. Christianity does itself a radical disservice when it appeals away from history, when it says that what matters is not what happened but 'what it means for me'. At the same time, though, Reimarus, by being right, turns out two centuries later to have sawn through the branch he looked forward to sitting on. Having appealed to history in the hope that it would destroy Christianity,

[7] cf. e.g. Vermes 1973, 212f.

[8] Lightfoot 1935, 225: 'For all the inestimable value of the gospels, they yield us little more than a whisper of his voice; we trace in them but the outskirts of his ways. Only when we see him hereafter in his fullness shall we know him also as he was on earth. And perhaps the more we ponder the matter, the more clearly we shall understand the reason for it, and therefore shall not wish it otherwise. For probably we are at present as little prepared for the one as for the other.'

his programme in fact puts Christianity in touch once more with roots it had forgotten, allowing the tree access to fresh springs of life. Melanchthon's intention (theological exegesis) can after all be achieved by Reimarus' route (historical study of Jesus). (Whether either of them would approve of the history, or the theology, which results is of course another matter.) The proper response to the 'quest' is not that it should be discontinued in favour of true theology, proclamation or piety. The proper response to all sorts of quests, this one included, is often to say that the right question has been asked, but that a full answer has not yet emerged. We must not back away from history, or seek to keep the theological handbrake on to prevent history running away with us. A truly first-century Jewish theological perspective would teach us to recognize that history, especially the history of first-century Judaism, is the sphere where we find, at work to judge and to save, the God who made the world. Of course this will challenge us radically, in the church as well as outside it. But only if we start out with the presupposition that we already know all there is to be known about God should it puzzle or alarm us.

Lightfoot, turning away from the dangerous glance at the human face of God, said that in the gospels we trace but the outskirts of his ways – which was just as well, he said, since we are as unprepared for that as for the heavenly vision. It has been the burden of this book that the gospels do in fact tell us far more about Jesus than such scholarship had dreamed of, and that, though certain types of orthodoxy may want to recoil from drawing the conclusions, such a response would be self-defeating and profoundly inauthentic. The portrait of Jesus' mindset, aims and beliefs that I have set out suggests, not a terrifying God from whose immediate embodied presence we would shrink, but one whose glory is strangely revealed in the welcome and the warning, the symbol and the story, the threat to the Temple, the celebration in the upper room, and the dark night at noon on Calvary.

Schweitzer said that Jesus comes to us as one unknown. Epistemologically, if I am right, this is the wrong way round. *We* come to *him* as ones unknown, crawling back from the far country, where we had wasted our substance on riotous but ruinous historicism. But the swinehusks – the 'assured results of modern criticism' – reminded us of that knowledge which arrogance had all but obliterated, and we began the journey home. But when we approached, as we have tried to do in this book, we found him running to us as one well known, whom we had spurned in the name of scholarship or even of faith, but who was still patiently waiting to be sought and found once more. And the ring on our finger and the shoes on our feet assure us that, in celebrating his kingdom and feasting at his table, we shall discover again and again not only who he is but who we ourselves are: as unknown and yet well known, as dying and behold we live.

Appendix

'KINGDOM OF GOD' IN EARLY CHRISTIAN LITERATURE

Since the theme of YHWH's kingdom is so central in much of the discussion of this book, it may be helpful to set out the relevant passages in an easily accessible format. Any attempt to give all the following references in full would produce an inventory swollen beyond reasonable bounds. This means that I have had to exercise judgment in summarizing, e.g. where parallel passages exhibit minor variations. Perhaps I should emphasize that I do not intend this list to be polemical: it does not attempt to grind an axe, merely to lay out the phenomena in an easily accessible fashion.

I have divided the passages into those found within the synoptic tradition and those outside it. In the first category, the passages are further subdivided, being listed first by their location in the various traditions, and second by broadly categorized themes.

1. Synoptic Tradition

a. Listed by location

(i) In all three synoptic gospels:

Mt. 12.25-6/Mk. 3.23-6/Lk. 11.17-18: Every kingdom divided against itself is laid waste, and no city or house divided against itself will stand; and if Satan casts out Satan, he is divided against himself; how then will his kingdom stand?

Mt. 13.11/Mk. 4.11/Lk. 8.10: To you it has been given to know the secrets of the kingdom of heaven/god, but to those outside . . .

Mt. 13.31/Mk. 4.30/Lk. 13.18: The kingdom of heaven/god is like a grain of mustard seed . . .

Mt. 16.28/Mk. 9.1/Lk. 9.27: There are some standing here who will not taste death before they see 'the son of man coming in his kingdom'/before they see the kingdom of god come with power/before they see the kingdom of god.

Mt. 18.1-4/Mk. 10.15/Lk. 18.16-17: The disciples came to Jesus, saying, 'Who is the greatest in the kingdom of heaven? And calling to him a child, he put him in the midst of them, and said, 'Truly, I say to you, unleses you turn and become like children, you will never enter the kingdom of heaven. Whoever humbles himself like this child, he is the greatest in the kingdom of heaven. [Mk./Lk.: Whoever does not receive the kingdom of god like a child shall not enter it.]

Cf. too Mt. 19.14: Let the children come to me, and do not hinder them; for to such belongs the kingdom of heaven.

Mt. 19.23f./Mk. 10.23f./Lk. 18.25 It will be hard for a rich man to enter the kingdom of heaven/god.

Mt. 26.29/Mk. 15.43/Lk. 22.16, 18: I shall not drink again of this fruit of the vine until that day when I drink it new with you in my Father's kingdom. [Lk. repeats a similar saying over the bread and cup.]

(ii) In Matthew and Mark:

Mt. 4.17/Mk. 1.15: Repent, for the kingdom of heaven/god is at hand.

Mt. 20.21/Mk. 10.37: Command that these two sons of mine [Mk.: Grant that we . . .] may sit, one at your right hand and one at your left, in your kingdom [for 'kingdom', Mk. has 'glory'].

Mk. 9.47: it is better to enter the kingdom of god with one eye than with two eyes to be thrown into Gehenna. [Cf. Mt. 18.9, where 'life' is parallel to 'kingdom' in Mk.]

(iii) In Matthew and Luke:

Mt. 5.3/Lk. 6.20/*Thom.* 54: Theirs [the poor (Mt.: in spirit)] is the kingdom of heaven.

Mt. 6.33/Lk. 6.31: Seek [Mt.: first] his kingdom.

Mt. 6.10/Lk. 11.2: Thy kingdom come.

Mt. 8.11/Lk. 13.28f.: Many will come from east and west and sit at table with Abraham, Isaac and Jacob in the kingdom of heaven/god, while the sons of the kingdom will be thrown into outer darkness . . . [Lk. adds: you will weep . . . when you see Abraham . . . in the kingdom of god, and you yourselves thrust out.]

Mt. 10.7/Lk. 9.2: preach as you go, saying 'the kingdom of heaven is at hand'. [In Lk., 'he sent them out to preach the kingdom of god.']

Mt. 11.11–12/Lk. 7.28; 16.16, cp. *Thom.* 46: Among those born of women there has risen no one greater than John the Baptist; yet he who is least in the kingdom of heaven is greater than he [par.: Lk. 7.28]. From the days of John the Baptist until now the kingdom of heaven has suffered violence, and men of violence take it by force. [Par.: Lk. 16.16: The law and the prophets were until John; since then the good news of the kingdom of god is preached, and every one enters it violently.]

Mt. 12.28/Lk. 11.20: But if it is by the spirit [Lk: finger] of god that I cast out demons, then the kingdom of god has come upon you.

Mt. 13.33/Lk. 13.20: The kingdom of heaven/god is like leaven . . .

Mt. 22.2: The kingdom of heaven may be compared to a king who gave a marriage feast for his son . . . [Lk. 14.15: one of those who sat at table said 'Blessed is he who shall eat bread in the kingdom of god!' But Jesus replied, 'A man once gave a great banquet . . .]

Lk. 19.11: He proceeded to tell a parable, because he was near to Jerusalem, and because they supposed that the kingdom of god would appear immediately. [Mt. 25.14–30: similar parable, without 'kingdom' introduction, but with 'kingdom' in wider context.]

(iv) In Mark and Luke:

Lk. 22.29–30: I assign you, as my Father assigned to me, a kingdom, so that you may eat and drink at my table in my kingdom, and sit on thrones judging the twelve tribes of

Israel. [Mk. 11.10: similar saying, with 'in the new world' (*palingenesia*) instead of 'kingdom'.]

Mk. 15.43/Lk. 23.51: Joseph of Arimathea was 'looking for the kingdom of god'.

(v) In Matthew only:

Mt. 3.2 (John the Baptist): Repent, for the kingdom of heaven is at hand.

Mt. 4.23: And [Jesus] went about all Galilee teaching in their synagogues and preaching the gospel of the kingdom and healing every disease . . .

Mt. 5.10: Blessed are those who are persecuted for righteousness' sake, for theirs is the kingdom of heaven.

Mt. 5.19f.: Whoever then relaxes one of the least of these commandments and teaches men so, shall be called least in the kingdom of heaven; but he who does them and teaches them shall be called great in the kingdom of heaven. For I tell you, unless your righteousness exceeds that of the scribes and Pharisees, you will never enter the kingdom of heaven.

Mt. 7.21: Not every one who says to me, 'Lord, Lord' shall enter the kingdom of heaven, but he who does the will of my Father who is in heaven.

Mt. 9.35: Jesus went about all the cities and villages, teaching in their synagogues and preaching the gospel of the kingdom, and healing every disease . . .

Mt. 13.19: When anyone hears the word of the kingdom and does not understand it, the evil one comes and snatches away what is sown in his heart . . .

Mt. 13.24: The kingdom of heaven may be compared to a man who sowed good seed in his field . . . [cf. *Thom.* 57.]

Mt. 13.36–43 (3 refs.): (38) The good seed means the sons of the kingdom . . . (41) 'the son of man' will send his angels, and they will gather out of his kingdom all causes of sin . . . (43) Then the righteous will shine like the sun in the kingdom of their Father.

Mt. 13.44–52 (4 refs): (44) The kingdom of heaven is like treasure . . . [cf. *Thom.* 109] (45) like a merchant in search of fine pearls . . . [cf. *Thom.* 76] (47) like a net which was thrown into the sea . . . (52) Every scribe trained for the kingdom of heaven is like a householder who brings out of his treasure what is new and what is old.

Mt. 16.19: I will give you the keys of the kingdom of heaven . . .

Mt. 18.23: The kingdom of heaven may be compared to a king who wished to settle accounts with his servants . . .

Mt. 19.12: There are eunuchs who have made themselves so for the sake of the kingdom of heaven. [Cp. *Thom.* 22, 2 *Clem.* 12.6, below.]

Mt. 20.1: The kingdom of heaven is like a householder who went out early in the morning to hire labourers . . .

Mt. 21.31: Truly I say to you, the tax collectors and the harlots go into the kingdom of god before you.

Mt. 21.43: The kingdom of god will be taken away from you and given to a nation producing the fruits of it.

Mt. 23.13: Woe to you . . . because you shut the kingdom of heaven against men . . .

Mt. 24.14: This gospel of the kingdom will be preached throughout the whole world, as a testimony to all nations . . .

Mt. 25.1: The kingdom of heaven shall be compared to ten maidens . . .

Mt. 25.34: Come, O blessed of my Father, inherit the kingdom prepared for you from the foundation of the world . . .

(vi) In Mark only:

Mk. 4.26: The kingdom of god is as if a man should scatter seed upon the ground . . .
Mk. 12.34: You are not far from the kingdom of god. [Cf. *Thom.* 82 (below).]

(vii) In Luke only:

Lk. 1.33: Of his kingdom there will be no end.
Lk. 4.43: I must preach the good news of the kingdom of god to the other cities also; for I was sent for this purpose.
Lk. 8.1: [Jesus] went on through cities and villages, preaching and bringing the good news of the kingdom of god.
Lk. 9.60: Leave the dead to bury their own dead [= Mt. 8.22]; but as for you, go and proclaim the kingdom of god.
Lk. 9.62: No one who puts his hand to the plough and looks back is fit for the kingdom of god.
Lk. 10.9, 11 (Jesus' instruction to the disciples): Heal the sick and say to them, 'The kingdom of god has come near to you' . . . But whenever . . . they do not receive you, . . . say, 'Even the dust of your town that clings to our feet, we wipe off against you; nevertheless know this, that the kingdom of god has come near.'
Lk. 17.20-1: Being asked by the Pharisees when the kingdom of god was coming, he answered them, 'The kingdom of god is not coming with signs to be observed; nor will they say, "Lo, here it is!" or "There!" for behold, the kingdom of god is *entos hymon*'. [Cf. p. 469: 'within your reach' is more likely than 'in your midst', and either of these than 'within you'. On the saying cp. *P. Oxy.* 654.3; and *Thom.* 3, 113.]
Lk. 18.29: There is no man who has left house or wife or brothers or parents or children, for the sake of the kingdom of god, who will not receive . . . [Mt. 19.29 and Mk. 10.30 have 'for my name's sake'/'for my sake and for the gospel'.]
Lk. 21.31: When you see these things taking place, you know that the kingdom of god is near. [Mt. 24.33/Mk. 13.29 have 'it' (usually translated 'he': cf. p. 364 above).]
Lk. 22.29f.: (see above, under Mk./Lk.)
Lk. 23.42: Jesus, remember me, when you come in your kingdom.

b. Listed by broad categories

(i) summary statements:

Mt. 3.2 (John the Baptist); Mt. 4.17/Mk. 1.15; Mt. 4.23; 9.35; Lk. 4.43; 8.1 (Jesus); Mt. 10.7/Lk. 9.2; Lk. 9.60; 10.9, 11 (disciples); Mt. 24.14 (in the interval before the fall of Jerusalem)

(ii) invitations to, or redefinitions of, the kingdom:

Mt. 5.3/Lk. 6.20; Mt. 5.10; 5.19; 5.20; 6.10/Lk. 11.2; Mt. 6.33/Lk. 6.31; Mt. 12.25-6/Mk. 3.23-6/Lk. 11.17-18; Mt. 12.28/Lk. 11.20; Mt. 16.19; Mt. 18.1, 3, 4/Mk. 10.15/Lk. 18.17 (cf. too Mt. 19.14); Mt. 20.21/Mk. 10.37; Mt. 21.31 (cp. Lk. 11.52); Mk. 12.34 (cf. *Thom.* 82, below); Lk. 22.29f.; Mt. 25.34

(iii) warnings about exclusion from the kingdom:

Mt. 5.20; 7.21; 8.11/Lk. 13.28f.; Mt. 11.11–12/?Lk. 16.16; Mt. 19.12, 14, 23f./Mk. 10.23f., Lk. 18.24–9; Mt. 23.13, Lk. 9.62; Mk. 9.47 (cf. Mt. 18.9, where 'life' is parallel to 'kingdom' in Mk.); Mt. 21.43

(iv) within parabolic redefinition:

Mt. 13.11/Mk. 4.11/Lk. 8.10; Mt. 13.19; Mk. 4.26; Mt. 13.24; Mt. 13.31/Mk. 4.30/Lk. 13.18; Mt. 13.33/Lk. 13.20; Mt. 13.36–43 (3 refs.); Mt. 13.44–52 (4 refs); Mt. 18.23; Mt. 20.1; Mt. 22.2/?Lk. 14.15, 22.2; Lk. 19.11 (cf. Mt. 25.14ff.); Mt. 25.1

(v) the coming of the kingdom:

Mt. 16.28/Mk. 9.1/Lk. 9.27; Lk. 17.20–21; Lk. 22.29–30 (cf. Mk. 11.10); Lk. 21.31; Mt. 25.34; Mt. 26.29/Mk. 15.43/Lk. 22.16, 18

(vi) other:

Lk. 1.33; 23.42; Mk. 15.43/Lk. 23.51

2. John

Jn. 3.3: No one can see the kingdom of god without being born from above.
Jn. 3.5: No one can enter the kingdom of god without being born from water and spirit.
Jn. 18.36f.: My kingdom is not from this world. If my kingdom were from this world, my followers would be fighting to keep me from being handed over to the Judaeans. But as it is, my kingdom is not from here. Pliate asked him, 'So you are a king?' Jesus answered, 'You say that I am a king. For this I was born, and for this I came into the world, to testify to the truth . . .'

3. Acts

Ac. 1.3: He presented himself alive to them, . . . appearing to them during forty days and speaking about the kingdom of god.
Ac. 1.6: Lord, is this the time when you will restore the kingdom to Israel?
Ac. 8.12: But when they believed Philip, who was proclaiming the good news about the kingdom of god and the name of Jesus Christ, they were baptized . . .
Ac. 14.22: [Paul and Barnabas] encouraged [the disciples] to continue in the faith, saying, 'It is through many persecutions that we must enter the kingdom of god.'
Ac. 19.8: [Paul] entered the synagogue [in Ephesus] and for three months spoke out boldly, and argued persuasively about the kingdom of god.
Ac. 20.25: [Paul said to the Ephesian elders] And now I know that none of you, among whom I have gone about proclaiming the kingdom, will ever see my face again.
Ac. 28.23: From morning to evening [Paul] explained the matter to them, testifying to the kingdom of god and trying to convince them about Jesus both from the law of Moses and from the prophets.
Ac. 28.31: [Paul was] proclaiming the kingdom of god and teaching about the Lord Jesus Christ with all boldness and without hindrance.

Cf. too Ac. 4.24 ('Sovereign Lord [*despota*]. . .'); 17.7 ('They are saying that there is another king [*basilea heteron*], Jesus').

4. Pauline Corpus

Ro. 14.17: The kingdom of god is not food and drink but righteousness and peace and joy in the holy spirit.

1 Cor. 4.20: The kingdom of god depends not on [lit. 'is not in'] talk but on power.

1 Cor. 6.9: Wrongdoers will not inherit the kingdom of god

1 Cor. 6.10: None of these [following a long list] will inherit the kingdom of god

1 Cor. 15.24: Then comes the end, when [Christ] hands over the kingdom to god the father, after he has destroyed every ruler and every authority and power

1 Cor. 15.50: Flesh and blood cannot inherit the kingdom of god, nor does the perishable inherit the imperishable.

Gal. 5.21: Those who do such things [following a long list] will not inherit the kingdom of god.

Eph. 5.5: Be sure of this, that no fornicator or impure person . . . has any inheritance in the kingdom of Christ and of god.

Col. 1.13: He has rescued us from the power of darkness and transferred us into the kingdom of his beloved son . . .

Col. 4.11: These [following a list] are the only ones of the circumcision among my co-workers for the kingdom of god, and they have been a comfort to me.[1]

1 Th. 2.12: . . . pleading that you lead a life worthy of god, who calls you into his own kingdom and glory.

2 Th. 1.5: This is evidence of the righteous judgment of god, and is intended to make you worthy of the kingdom of god, for which you are also suffering.

2 Tim. 4.1: In the presence of god and of Christ Jesus, who is to judge the living and the dead, and in view of his appearing and his kingdom, . . .

4.18: The Lord will rescue me from every evil attack and save me for his heavenly kingdom.

Cf. too Rom. 5.17, 21; 6.12–23 (the redeemed 'shall reign'; grace 'shall reign', in contrast to the reign or rule of 'sin'); 1 Cor. 4.8 ('Quite apart from us you have become kings!'); 15.23–8 (the sequence of events in the coming of the kingdom); 1 Tim. 1.17 ('To the King of the ages . . . the only god, be honour and glory'); 6.15 ('He who is the blessed and only sovereign [*dynastes*], the King of kings and Lord of lords . . .').

5. Rest of NT

Heb. 1.8: But of the son he says, 'Your throne, O god, is forever and ever, and the righteous sceptre is the sceptre of your kingdom'.

Heb. 2.9: We see Jesus . . . crowned with glory and honour . . .

Heb. 12.28: Therefore, since we are receiving a kingdom that cannot be shaken, let us give thanks . . .

Jas. 2.5: Has not god chosen the poor in the world to be rich in faith and to be heirs of the kingdom that he has promised to those who love him?

2 Pet. 1.11: For in this way, entry into the eternal kingdom of our Lord and Saviour Jesus Christ will be richly provided for you.

---

[1] This ref. is oddly omitted from the list in Crossan 1991a, 460.

Rev. 1.6: (To him who loves us and freed us from our sins by his blood), and made us to be a kingdom, priests serving his god and Father, to him be glory . . .

Rev. 1.9: I, John, your brother who share with you in Jesus the persecution and the kingdom and the patient endurance . . .

Rev. 5.10: You have made them to be a kingdom and priests serving our god, and they will reign on earth.

Rev. 11.15: The kingdom of the world has become the kingdom of our Lord and of his Messiah, and he will reign forever and ever.

Rev. 11.17: We give you thanks. . . for you have taken your great power and begun to reign.

Rev. 12.10: Now have come the salvation and the power and the kingdom of our god and the authority of his Messiah, for the accuser of our comrades has been thrown down . . .

Rev. 17.14: The Lamb will conquer them, for he is Lord of lords and King of kings, and those with him are called and chosen and faithful.

Rev. 19.6: Hallelujah! For the Lord our god the Almighty reigns.

Rev. 19.16: He has a name inscribed, 'King of kings and Lord of Lords'.

Rev. 20.4: Then I saw thrones, and those seated on them were given authority to judge . . . They came to life and reigned with Christ a thousand years.

Rev. 20.6: They will be priests of god and of Christ, and they will reign with him a thousand years.

Rev. 22.5.: The Lord god will be their light, and they will reign forever and ever.

    Cf. too 2 Pet. 2.1 (referring to Christ as *despotes*, 'master'); Jd. 4 ('Our Master and Lord, Jesus Christ'); Rev. 6.10 ('Sovereign Lord [*despotes*], holy and true').

6. Other Early Christian and Related Literature:

1 Clem. 42.3: the apostles went forth in the assurance of the holy spirit preaching the good news that the kingdom of god was coming.

1 Clem. 50.3: those who were perfected in love by the grace of god have a place among the pious who shall be made manifest at the visitation of the kingdom of Christ [some mss.: of god].

2 Clem. 9.6: Let us then love one another, that we may all attain to the kingdom of god.

2 Clem. 11.7: If then we do righteousness before god we shall enter his kingdom, and shall receive the promises 'which ear hath not heard . . .'

2 Clem. 12.1–6: Let us then wait for the kingdom of god, from hour to hour, in love and righteousness, seeing that we know not the day of the appearing of god. For when the Lord himself was asked by someone when his kingdom would come, he said, 'When the two shall be one, and the outside as the inside, and the male with the female neither male nor female.' Now 'the two are one' when we speak with one another in truth, and there is but one soul in two bodies without dissimulation. And by 'the outside as the inside' he means this, that the inside is the soul, and the outside is the body. Therefore, just as your body is visible, so let your soul be apparent in your good works. And by 'the male with the female neither male nor female' he means this, that when a brother sees a sister he should have no thought of her as female, nor she of him as male. When you do this, he says, the kingdom of my Father will come. [Cf. *Thom.* 22.1–7, below.]

Ignatius *Philad.* 3.3 [quoting 1 Cor. 6.9f.]: Be not deceived, my brethren, if any one follow a maker of schism, he does not inherit the kingdom of god.

Polycarp *Phil.* 5.3 [quoting Gal. 5.17 and 1 Cor. 6.9f.]: Every lust warreth against the spirit, and neither fornicators nor the effeminate nor sodomites shall inherit the kingdom of god, nor they who do iniquitous things.

Barnabas 4.13: Let us never rest as though we were 'called' and slumber in our sins, lest the wicked ruler gain power over us and thrust us out from the kingdom of the Lord.

Hermas *Sim.* 9.15.3: The servant who bears these [wicked] names shall see the kingdom of god, but shall not enter it.

Hermas *Sim.* 9.29.2: such then shall live without doubt in the kingdom of god, because by no act did they defile the commandments of god, but remained in innocence all the days of their lives in the same mind.

Thomas 2.3f.: When they are disturbed, they will marvel, and will reign over all.

Thomas 3.1–3: Jesus said, 'If your leaders say to you, "Look, the kingdom is in the sky," then the birds of the air will precede you. If they say to you, "It is in the sea," then the fish will precede you. Rather, the kingdom is within you and it is outside you.'

Thomas 20.1f.: The disciples said to Jesus, 'Tell us what the kingdom of heaven is like.' He said to them, 'It is like a mustard seed. . .'

Thomas 22.1–7: Jesus said to his disciples, 'These infants being suckled are like those who enter the kingdom.' They said to him, 'Shall we then, as children, enter the kingdom?' Jesus said to them, 'When you make the two one, and when you make the inside like the outside, and the above like the below, and when you make the male and the female one and the same, so that the male not be male nor the female female; and when you fashion eyes in place of an eye, and a hand in place of a hand, and a foot in place of a foot, and a likeness in place of a likeness, then will you enter [the kingdom].'

Thomas 27.1: Jesus said, 'If you do not fast as regards the world, you will not find the kingdom.'

Thomas 46.1–2: Jesus said, 'Among those born of women, from Adam until John the Baptist, there is no one so superior to John the Baptist that his eyes should not be lowered [before him]. Yet I have said, whichever one of you comes to be a child will be acquainted with the kingdom and will become superior to John.'

Thomas 49: Jesus said, 'Blessed are the solitary and elect, for you will find the kingdom. For you are from it, and to it you will return.'

Thomas 82: Jesus said, 'He who is near me is near the fire, and he who is far from me is far from the kingdom.'

Thomas 96.1–2: Jesus said, 'The kingdom of the father is like a certain woman. She took a little leaven, concealed it in some dough, and made it into large loaves.'

Thomas 97.1–2: Jesus said, 'The kingdom of the father is like a certain woman who was carrying a jar full of meal. While she was walking on a road, still some distance from home, the handle of the jar broke and the meal emptied out . . .'

Thomas 98.1–3: Jesus said, 'The kingdom of the father is like a certain man who wanted to kill a powerful man. In his own house he drew his sword and stuck it into the wall in order to find out whether his hand could carry through. Then he slew the powerful man.'

Thomas 99.2–3: Jesus said, 'Those here who do the will of my father are my brothers and my mother. It is they who will enter the kingdom of my father.'

Thomas 107.1–3: Jesus said, 'The kingdom is like a shepherd who had a hundred sheep. One of them, the largest, went astray. He left the ninety-nine and looked for that one until he found it. When he had gone to such trouble, he said to the sheep, "I care for you more than the ninety-nine."'

Thomas 113.1–4: His disciples said to him, 'When will the kingdom come?' [Jesus said,] 'It will not come by waiting for it. It will not be a matter of saying "Here it is" or "There it is." Rather, the kingdom of the father is spread out upon the earth, and men do not see it.'

Thomas 114.2–3: Jesus said, 'I myself shall lead [Mary] in order to make her male, so that she too may become a living spirit resembling you males. For every woman who will make herself male will enter the kingdom of heaven.'

Bibliography

Abbreviations

ABD	*Anchor Bible Dictionary*, ed. David N. Freedman. 6 vols. New York: Doubleday, 1992.
Aland	Aland, K., ed. 1967 [1963]. *Synopsis Quattuor Evangeliorum: Locis Parallelis Evangeliorum Apocryphorum et Patrum Adhibitis*. 2nd edn. Stuttgart: Württembergische Bibelanstalt.
ANF	Ante-Nicene Fathers
cf.	confer
cp.	compare
Epict.	Epictetus (*Disc.* = *Discourses*)
esp.	especially
Euseb.	Eusebius (*HE* = *Historia Ecclesiae*)
Danby	H. Danby, *The Mishnah, Translated from the Hebrew with Introduction and Brief Explanatory Notes*. Oxford: OUP, 1933.
DJG	*Dictionary of Jesus and the Gospels*, ed. J. B. Green, S. McKnight, I. H. Marshall. Downers Grove, Ill., and Leicester: IVP, 1992.
GM	F. García Martínez, *The Dead Sea Scrolls Translated: The Qumran Texts in English*. Leiden: E. J. Brill, 1994.
Herm.	Hermas
Ign.	Ignatius
Jos.	Josephus
JSNTSS	*Journal for the Study of the New Testament* Supplement Series
JSOTSS	*Journal for the Study of the Old Testament* Supplement Series
Juv.	Juvenal (*Sat.* = *Satires*)
LCL	Loeb Classical Library
LSJ	H. G. Liddell and R. Scott, *A Greek-English Lexicon*, new edn. by H. S. Jones. Oxford: OUP, 1940 [1843].
LXX	Septuagint version of the Old Testament (see below)
MT	Masoretic Text (of the Hebrew Bible)
NIDNTT	*The New International Dictionary of New Testament Theology*, ed. Colin Brown. 3 vols. Exeter: Paternoster, 1975-78.
NRSV	New Revised Standard Version (see below)
NT	New Testament
NTA	*New Testament Apocrypha*, ed. E. Hennecke and W. Schneemelcher. 2 vols. London: SCM, 1973, 1974 [1959, 1964].
NTPG	N. T. Wright, *The New Testament and the People of God* (vol. 1 of *Christian Origins and the Question of God*). London: SPCK; Minneapolis: Fortress, 1992.
OT	Old Testament
par(r).	parallel(s) (in the synoptic tradition)
SB	H. L. Strack and P. Billerbeck, *Kommentar zum Neuen Testament aus Talmud und Midrasch*. 6 vols. Munich: C. H. Beck, 1926-56.
SBL	Society of Biblical Literature
SNTSMS	Society for New Testament Studies Monograph Series

Schürer   E. Schürer, *The History of the Jewish People in the Age of Jesus Christ (175 B.C.—A.D. 135)*. Rev. and ed. M. Black, G. Vermes, F. G. B. Millar. 4 vols. Edinburgh: T. & T. Clark, 1973–87.

Suet.   Suetonius

Tac.   Tacitus (*Ann.* = *Annals*; *Hist.* = *Histories*)

TDNT   *Theological Dictionary of the New Testament*, ed. G. Kittel and G. Friedrich. 10 vols. Grand Rapids, Mich.: Eerdmans, 1964–76.

TDOT   *Theological Dictionary of the Old Testament*, ed. G. J. Botterweck and H. Ringgren. Grand Rapids, Mich.: Eerdmans, 1974– .

A
Primary Sources

1. Bible

Biblia Hebraica Stuttgartensia, ed. K. Elliger and W. Rudolph. Stuttgart: Württembergische Bibelanstalt Stuttgart, 1968-76.
Septuaginta: Id est Vetus Testamentum Graece iuxta LXX interpres, ed. A. Rahlfs. 8th edn. 2 vols. Stuttgart: Württembergische Bibelanstalt Stuttgart, 1965 [1935].
Novum Testamentum Graece, ed. B. Aland, K. Aland, J. Karavidopoulos, C. M. Martini, and B. M. Metzger. 27th edn. Stuttgart: Deutsche Bibelgesellschaft, 1993 [1898].
The Holy Bible, Containing the Old and New Testaments with the Apocryphal/Deuterocanonical Books: New Revised Standard Version. New York and Oxford: OUP, 1989.

2. Other Jewish Texts

The Mishnah, Translated from the Hebrew with Introduction and Brief Explanatory Notes by H. Danby. Oxford: OUP, 1933.
The Old Testament Pseudepigrapha, ed. J. H. Charlesworth. 2 vols. Garden City, N. Y.: Doubleday, 1983-85.
The Apocryphal Old Testament, ed. H. F. D. Sparks. Oxford: Clarendon Press, 1984.
The Authorised Daily Prayer Book of the United Hebrew Congregations of the British Commonwealth of Nations, trans. S. Singer. New edn. London: Eyre & Spottiswood, 1962.
Josephus: *Works*, ed. H. St. J. Thackeray, R. Marcus, A. Wikgren and L. H. Feldman. 9 vols. LCL. Cambridge, Mass.: Harvard U. P.; London: Heinemann, 1929-65.
Philo: *Works*, ed. F. H. Colson, G. H. Whitaker, J. W. Earp and R. Marcus. 12 vols. LCL. Cambridge, Mass.: Harvard U. P.; London: Heinemann, 1929-53.
Qumran: *Die Texte aus Qumran*, ed. E. Lohse. Darmstadt: Wissenschaftliche Buchgesellschaft, 1964.
————, trans.: F. García Martínez, *The Dead Sea Scrolls Translated: The Qumran Texts in English*. Leiden: E. J. Brill, 1994.
————, trans.: G. Vermes, *The Dead Sea Scrolls in English*. 4th edn. London: Penguin Books, 1995 [1962].
Rabbinic Literature: cf. Schürer 1.68-118.

3. Other Early Christian and Related Texts

Apostolic Fathers: *The Apostolic Fathers*, ed. and trans. J. B. Lightfoot. 5 vols. London: Macmillan, 1889-90.
————: *The Apostolic Fathers*, ed. and trans. Kirsopp Lake. LCL. 2 vols. London: Heinemann; Cambridge, Mass.: Harvard U. P., 1965.
————: *Early Christian Writings*, trans. Maxwell Staniforth, intr. and ed. by A. Louth. London: Penguin Books, 1968.

Eusebius: *Eusebius. The Ecclesiastical History*, ed. and trans. Kirsopp Lake, H. J. Lawlor and J. E. L. Oulton. LCL. 2 vols. London: Heinemann; Cambridge, Mass.: Harvard U. P., 1973–75.
Hippolytus: in ANF 5.9–259.
Nag Hammadi texts: *The Nag Hammadi Library in English*, ed. J. M. Robinson. Leiden: Brill; San Francisco: Harper & Row, 1977.
New Testament Apocrypha, ed. E. Hennecke and W. Schneemelcher. 2 vols. London: SCM; Philadelphia: Westminster, 1963–65 [1959–64].
————: in *The Complete Gospels: Annotated Scholars Version*, ed. R. J. Miller. Sonoma, Calif.: Polebridge, 1992.
Origen: *Contra Celsum*. in ANF vol. 4.
Thomas: *The Gospel According to Thomas*, ed. A. Guillaumont et al. Leiden: Brill; London: Collins, 1959.

4. Pagan Texts

Dio: *Dio Chrysostom*, ed. and trans. J. W. Cohoon and H. L. Crosbie. 5 vols. LCL. London: Heinemann; Cambridge, Mass.: Harvard U. P., 1932–51.
Epictetus: *The Discourses as reported by Arrian, the Manual, and Fragments*, ed. and trans. W. A. Oldfather. LCL. 2 vols. London: Heinemann; Cambridge, Mass.: Harvard U. P., 1978–79.
Juvenal: *Juvenal and Persius*, trans. G. G. Ramsay. LCL. London: Heinemann; New York: Putnam's, 1920.
————, trans.: *Juvenal. The Sixteen Satires*, trans. and intr. P. Green. London: Penguin Books, 1974 [1967].
Lucian: *Lucian of Samosata*, ed. and trans. A. M. Harmon et al. LCL. London: Heinemann; Cambridge, Mass.: Harvard U. P., 1932.
Pliny the Younger: *C. Plini Caecili Secundi Epistularum Libri Decem*, ed. R. A. B. Mynors. Oxford: OUP, 1963.
————, trans.: *The Letters of the Younger Pliny*, trans. and intr. B. Radice. London: Penguin Books, 1963.
Suetonius: *C. Suetoni Tranquili Opera*, vol. 1. *De Vita Caesarum Libri VIII*. Ed. M. Ihm. Stuttgart: Teubner, 1978 [1908].
————, trans.: *Suetonius. The Twelve Caesars*, trans. R. Graves. London: Penguin Books, 1957.
Tacitus, *Annals*: *Cornelii Taciti Annalium ab Excessu Divi Augusti Libri*, ed. C. D. Fisher. Oxford: Clarendon Press, 1906.
————, trans.: *Tacitus. The Annals of Imperial Rome*, trans. M. Grant. London: Penguin Books, 1956.
Tacitus, *Histories*: *Cornelii Taciti Historiarum Libri*, ed. C. D. Fisher. Oxford: Clarendon Press, n.d.
————, trans.: *Tacitus. The Histories*, trans. K. Wellesley. London: Penguin Books, 1964.
Thucydides: *Thucydidis Historiae*, ed. H. S. Jones. 2 vols. Oxford: OUP, 1898.
————, trans.: *Thucydides: History of the Peloponnesian War*, trans. R. Warner. London: Penguin Books, 1954.

B

Secondary Literature

Achtemeier, Paul J. 1970. 'Toward the Isolation of Pre-Markan Miracle Catenae.' *Journal of Biblical Literature* 89:265-91.

Ackroyd, Peter R. 1968. *Exile and Restoration: A Study of Hebrew Thought of the Sixth Century BC.* London: SCM.

Alexander, Philip S. 1983. '3 (Hebrew Apocalypse Of) Enoch.' In *The Old Testament Pseudepigrapha, Volume 1: Apocalyptic Literature and Testaments*, ed. J. H. Charlesworth, 223-315. Garden City, N. Y.: Doubleday.

————. 1992. '"The Parting of the Ways" from the Perspective of Rabbinic Judaism.' In *Jews and Christians: The Parting of the Ways, A.D. 70 to 135*, ed. J. D. G. Dunn, 1-25. Wissenschaftliche Untersuchungen zum Neuen Testament, vol. 66. Tübingen: Mohr.

Allison, D. C. 1983. 'Matt. 23:39 = Luke 13:35b as a Conditional Prophecy.' *Journal for the Study of the New Testament* 18:75-84.

————. 1985. *The End of the Ages Has Come: An Early Interpretation of the Passion and Resurrection of Jesus.* Philadelphia: Fortress.

————. 1987. 'Jesus and the Covenant: A Response to E. P. Sanders.' *Journal for the Study of the New Testament* 29:57-78.

————. 1994. 'A Plea for Thoroughgoing Eschatology.' *Journal of Biblical Literature* 113:651-68.

Alon, Gedaliah. 1989 [1980]. *The Jews in Their Land in the Talmudic Age (70—640 C.E.).* Cambridge, Mass.: Harvard U. P.

Alter, Robert. 1981. *The Art of Biblical Narrative.* New York: Basic Books.

Anderson, Gary A. 1992. 'Sacrifice and Sacrificial Offerings (OT).' In *ABD* 5:870-86.

Anderson, Hugh. 1992. 'Fourth Maccabees.' In *ABD* 4:452-4.

Anderson, Robert T. 1992. 'Samaritans.' In *ABD* 5:940-7.

Antwi, Daniel J. 1991. 'Did Jesus Consider His Death to Be an Atoning Sacrifice?' *Interpretation* 45:17-28.

Ashton, John. 1991. *Understanding the Fourth Gospel.* Oxford: Clarendon.

Ateek, Naim S. 1989. *Justice and Only Justice: A Palestinian Theology of Liberation.* Maryknoll, N. Y.: Orbis.

Aune, David E. 1980. 'Magic in Early Christianity.' In *Aufsteig und Niedergang der Römischen Welt*, ed. H. Temporini and A. Haase, vol. 2.23, 1507-57. Berlin: De Gruyter.

————. 1983. *Prophecy in Early Christianity and the Ancient Mediterranean World.* Grand Rapids, Mich.: Eerdmans.

————. 1991. 'On the Origins of the "Council of Javneh" Myth.' *Journal of Biblical Literature* 110:491-3.

————. 1992a. 'Christian Prophecy and the Messianic Status of Jesus.' In *The Messiah: Developments in Earliest Judaism and Christianity*, ed. J. H. Charlesworth, 404-22. Minneapolis: Fortress.

————. 1992b. 'Eschatology (early Christian).' In *ABD* 2:594-609.

Austen, Ralph A. 1986. 'Social Bandits and Other Heroic Criminals: Western Models of Resistance and Their Relevance for Africa.' In *Banditry, Rebellion and Social Protest in Africa*, ed. Donald Crummey. London: James Currey; Portsmouth, N.H.: Heinemann.

Bailey, Kenneth E. 1983 [1976, 1980]. *Poet and Peasant/Through Peasant Eyes*. Grand Rapids, Mich.: Eerdmans.

—————. 1991. 'Informal Controlled Oral Tradition and the Synoptic Gospels.' *Asia Journal of Theology* 5(1):34–54.

Bailey, L. 1986. 'Gehenna: The Topography of Hell.' *Biblical Archaeology* 49:187–91.

Baillie, D. M. 1948. *God Was in Christ: An Essay on Incarnation and Atonement*. London: Faber.

Baird, William. 1990. '"One Against the Other": Intra-Church Conflict in 1 Corinthians.' In *The Conversation Continues: Studies in Paul and John in Honor of J. Louis Martyn*, ed. Robert T. Fortna and Beverly R. Gaventa, 116–36. Nashville: Abingdon.

Bammel, Ernst. 1974. 'Zum Testimonium Flavianum (Jos Ant 18,63–64).' In *Josephus-Studien*, ed. O. Betz, K. Haacker, and M. Hengel, 9–22. Göttingen: Vandenhoek & Ruprecht.

—————. 1984. 'The *titulus*.' In *Jesus and the Politics of His Day*, ed. E. Bammel and C. F. D. Moule, 353–64. Cambridge: CUP.

Bammel, Ernst, and Charles F. D. Moule, eds. 1984. *Jesus and the Politics of His Day*. Cambridge: CUP.

Barker, Margaret. 1987. *The Older Testament*. London: SPCK.

—————. 1991. *The Gate of Heaven: The History and Symbolism of the Temple in Jerusalem*. London: SPCK.

—————. 1992. *The Great Angel: A Study of Israel's Second God*. London: SPCK.

Barr, James. 1988. ''Abba Isn't "Daddy".' *Journal of Theological Studies* 39:28–47.

Barrett, C. K. 1959. 'The Background of Mark 10:45.' In *New Testament Essays: Studies in Memory of Thomas Walter Manson, 1893–1958*, ed. A. J. B. Higgins, 1–18. Manchester: Manchester U. P.

—————. 1967. *Jesus and the Gospel Tradition*. London: SPCK.

—————. 1975. 'The House of Prayer and the Den of Thieves.' In *Jesus und Paulus: Festschrift für Werner Georg Kümmel zum 70. Geburtstag*, ed. E. Earle Ellis and E. Grässer, 13–20. Göttingen: Vandenhoek & Ruprecht.

—————. 1978 [1955]. *The Gospel According to St John: An Introduction with Commentary and Notes on the Greek Text*. London: SPCK.

Barth, Karl. 1936–69. *Church Dogmatics*. Edinburgh: T. & T. Clark.

Barton, J. 1986. *Oracles of God*. London: Darton, Longman & Todd.

Bauckham, Richard J. 1978. 'The Sonship of the Historical Jesus in Christology.' *Scottish Journal of Theology* 31:245–60.

—————. 1985. 'The Son of Man: "A Man in My Position" or "Someone"?' *Journal for the Study of the New Testament* 23:23–33.

—————. 1986. 'The Coin in the Fish's Mouth.' In *Gospel Perspectives*. Vol. 6. *The Miracles of Jesus*, ed. D. Wenham and C. Blomberg, 219–52. Sheffield: JSOT Press.

—————. 1988. 'Jesus' Demonstration in the Temple.' In *Law and Religion: Essays on the Place of the Law in Israel and Early Christianity*, ed. B. Lindars, 72–89, 171–6. Cambridge: James Clarke.

—————. 1990. *Jude and the Relatives of Jesus in the Early Church*. Edinburgh: T. & T. Clark.

—————. 1991. 'The Rich Man and Lazarus: The Parable and the Parallels.' *New Testament Studies* 37:225–46.

—————. 1992. 'Jesus, Worship of.' In *ABD* 3:812–19.

————. 1993a. 'Papias and Polycrates on the Origin of the Fourth Gospel.' *Journal of Theological Studies* n.s. 44:24–69.

————. 1993b. 'The Parting of the Ways: What Happened and Why.' *Studia Theologica* 47:135–51.

————. 1995a. 'James and the Jerusalem Church.' In *The Book of Acts in Its Palestinian Setting*, ed. R. J. Bauckham. (*The Book of Acts in Its First Century Setting*, ed. B. W. Winter, vol. 4.) 415–80. Carlisle: Paternoster; Grand Rapids, Mich.: Eerdmans.

————. 1995b. 'James at the Centre.' *European Pentecostal Theological Association Bulletin* 14:22–33.

Beasley-Murray, G. R. 1954. *Jesus and the Future: An Examination of the Criticism of the Eschatological Discourse, Mark 13, with Special Reference to the Little Apocalypse Theory.* London: Macmillan.

————. 1957. *A Commentary on Mark 13.* New York: Macmillan.

————. 1983. 'Second Thoughts on the Composition of Mk. 13.' *New Testament Studies* 29:414–20.

————. 1986. *Jesus and the Kingdom of God.* Grand Rapids, Mich.: Eerdmans.

Beck, N. A. 1970. 'The Last Supper as an Efficacious Symbolic Act.' *Journal of Biblical Literature* 89:192–8.

Beckwith, Roger T. 1985. *The Old Testament Canon of the New Testament Church, and Its Background in Early Judaism.* London: SPCK; Grand Rapids: Eerdmans.

Best, Ernest. 1986. *Disciples and Discipleship: Studies in the Gospel According to Mark.* Edinburgh: T. & T. Clark.

Betz, Hans-Dieter. 1967. 'The Logion of the Easy Yoke and of Rest (Matt 11:28–30).' *Journal of Biblical Literature* 86:10–24.

————. 1985. *Essays on the Sermon on the Mount.* Philadelphia: Fortress.

————. 1992. 'Sermon on the Mount/Plain.' In *ABD* 5:1106–12.

Betz, Otto. 1968 [1965]. *What Do We Know About Jesus?* Trans. M. Kohl. London: SCM.

————. 1987. *Jesus der Messias Israels: Aufsätze zur biblischen Theologie.* Wissenschaftliche Untersuchungen zum Neuen Testament, vol. 42. Tübingen: Mohr.

Black, Matthew. 1971. 'The Christological Use of the Old Testament in the New Testament.' *New Testament Studies* 18:1–14.

————. 1992. 'The Messianism of the Parables of Enoch: Their Date and Contribution to Christological Origins.' In *The Messiah: Developments in Earliest Judaism and Christianity*, ed. J. H. Charlesworth, 145–68. Minneapolis: Fortress.

Blok, Anton. 1972. 'The Peasant and the Brigand: Social Banditry Reconsidered.' *Comparative Studies in Society and History* 14:494–503.

————. 1988 [1974]. *The Mafia of a Sicilian Village 1860–1960: The Study of Violent Peasant Entrepreneurs.* Cambridge: Polity Press.

Blomberg, Craig L. 1990. *Interpreting the Parables.* Leicester: Apollos.

Bock, Darrell L. 1994. 'The Son of Man Seated at God's Right Hand and the Debate Over Jesus' "Blasphemy".' In *Jesus of Nazareth: Lord and Christ. Essays on the Historical Jesus and New Testament Christology*, ed. Joel B. Green and Max Turner, 181–91. Grand Rapids, Mich.: Eerdmans; Carlisle: Paternoster.

Bockmuehl, Markus. 1994. *This Jesus: Martyr, Lord, Messiah.* Edinburgh: T. & T. Clark.

Boers, Hendrikus. 1989. *Who Was Jesus? The Historical Jesus and the Synoptic Gospels.* San Francisco: Harper & Row.

Bokser, Baruch M. 1992. 'Unleavened Bread and Passover, Feasts Of.' In *ABD* 6:755–65.

Booth, Roger P. 1986. *Jesus and the Laws of Purity: Tradition History and Legal History in Mark 7.* Journal for the Study of the New Testament Supplement Series, no. 13. Sheffield: JSOT Press.

Borg, Marcus J. 1984. *Conflict, Holiness and Politics in the Teachings of Jesus.* New York/Toronto: The Edwin Mellen Press.

—————. 1986. 'A Temperate Case for a Non-Eschatological Jesus.' *Foundations and Facets Forum* 2(3):81–102.

—————. 1987a. *Jesus: A New Vision.* San Francisco: Harper & Row.

—————. 1987b. 'The Jesus Seminar and the Passion Sayings.' *Foundations and Facets Forum* 3(2):81–95.

—————. 1987c. 'An Orthodoxy Reconsidered: The "End-of-the-World Jesus"' In *The Glory of Christ in the New Testament: Studies in Christology in Memory of George Bradford Caird*, ed. L. D. Hurst and N. T. Wright, 207–17. Oxford: OUP.

—————. 1994a. *Jesus in Contemporary Scholarship.* Valley Forge, Pa.: TPI.

—————. 1994b. *Meeting Jesus Again for the First Time: The Historical Jesus & the Heart of Contemporary Faith.* San Francisco: HarperSanFrancisco.

Boring, M. E. 1985. 'Criteria of Authenticity: The Lucan Beatitudes as a Test Case' *Foundations and Facets Forum* 1(4):3–38.

—————. 1992. 'Prophecy (Early Christian).' In *ABD* 5:495–502.

Bornkamm, Günther. 1960 [1956]. *Jesus of Nazareth.* Trans. I. McLuskey, F. McLuskey, and J. M. Robinson. Preface by J. M. Robinson. New York: Harper & Row.

Borsch, F. H. 1992. 'Further Reflections on "The Son of Man": The Origins and Development of the Title.' In *The Messiah: Developments in Earliest Judaism and Christianity*, ed. J. H. Charlesworth, 130–44. Minneapolis: Fortress.

Bostock, D. G. 1980. 'Jesus as the New Elisha.' *Expository Times* 92:39–41.

Boucher, Madeleine. 1977. *The Mysterious Parable: A Literary Study.* CBQ Monograph Series, no. 6. Washington: Catholic Biblical Association of America.

Bowden, John. 1988. *Jesus: The Unanswered Questions.* London: SCM.

Bowker, John W. 1973. *Jesus and the Pharisees.* Cambridge: CUP.

—————. 1974. 'Mystery and Parable: Mark iv.1–20.' *Journal of Theological Studies* n.s. 25:300–17.

—————. 1977. 'The Son of Man.' *Journal of Theological Studies* 28:19–48.

—————. 1978. *The Religious Imagination and the Sense of God.* Oxford: Clarendon.

Boyarin, Daniel. 1994. *A Radical Jew: Paul and the Politics of Identity.* Berkeley: University of California Press.

Boyd, Gregory A. 1995. *Cynic Sage or Son of God? Recovering the Real Jesus in an Age of Revisionist Replies.* Wheaton, Ill.: Bridgepoint.

Braaten, Carl E. 1994. 'Jesus and the Church: An Essay on Ecclesial Hermeneutics.' *Ex Auditu* 10:59–71.

Brandon, S. G. F. 1967. *Jesus and the Zealots: A Study of the Political Factor in Primitive Christianity.* Manchester: Manchester U. P.

Braun, Herbert. 1984 [1969]. *Jesus: Der Mann aus Nazareth und seine Zeit.* Tübingen: Mohr.

Breech, James. 1983. *The Silence of Jesus: The Authentic Voice of the Historical Man.* Philadelphia: Fortress.

Brown, Colin. 1969. *Philosophy and the Christian Faith: A Historical Sketch from the Middle Ages to the Present Day.* London: Tyndale Press.

—————, ed. 1975–78. *The New International Dictionary of New Testament Theology.* Exeter: Paternoster.

—————. 1984. *Miracles and the Critical Mind.* Grand Rapids, Mich.: Eerdmans.

—————. 1988 [1985]. *Jesus in European Protestant Thought, 1778–1860.* Grand Rapids: Baker.

Brown, Raymond E. 1994. *The Death of the Messiah: From Gethsemane to the Grave. A Commentary on the Passion Narratives in the Four Gospels.* New York: Doubleday; London: Geoffrey Chapman.

Bruce, Frederick F. 1984. 'Render to Caesar.' In *Jesus and the Politics of His Day*, ed. E. Bammel and C. F. D. Moule, 249–63. Cambridge: CUP.

Buchanan, George W. 1959. 'Mark 11.15-19: Brigands in the Temple.' *Hebrew Union College Annual* 30:169-77.

————. 1984. *Jesus: The King and His Kingdom*. Macon, Ga.: Mercer U. P.

Bultmann, Rudolf. 1957. *History and Eschatology: The Presence of Eternity*. New York: Harper.

————. 1958a [1926]. *Jesus and the Word*. New York: Scribner's.

————. 1958b. *Jesus Christ and Mythology*. New York: Scribner's.

————. 1968 [1921]. *The History of the Synoptic Tradition*. Trans. John Marsh. 2nd edn. Oxford: Blackwell.

Bultmann, Rudolf, Ernst Lohmeyer, Julius Schniewind, Helmut Thielicke, and Austin Farrer. 1961. *Kerygma and Myth: A Theological Defense*. Revised Edition. Ed. Hans Werner Bartsch. New York: Harper.

Burridge, Richard A. 1992. *What Are the Gospels? A Comparison with Graeco-Roman Biography*. SNTSMS vol. 70. Cambridge: CUP.

Butts, J. R. 1987. 'Probing the Polling: Jesus Seminar Results on the Kingdom Sayings.' *Foundations and Facets Forum* 3(1):98-128.

Byrne, Bernard. 1979. *'Sons of God'-'Seed of Abraham': A Study of the Idea of the Sonship of God of All Christians in Paul Against the Jewish Background*. Rome: Biblical Institute Press.

Cadbury, H. J. 1950. 'The Kingdom of God and Ourselves.' *Christian Century* 67:172-3.

————. 1962 [1937]. *The Peril of Modernizing Jesus*. New York: Scribner's.

Caird, George B. 1963. *The Gospel of St. Luke*. London: Penguin Books.

————. 1965. *Jesus and the Jewish Nation*. London: Athlone Press.

————. 1980. *The Language and Imagery of the Bible*. London: Duckworth.

————. 1982. 'Jesus and Israel: The Starting Point for New Testament Christology.' In *Christological Perspectives: Essays in Honor of Harvey K. McArthur*, ed. R. F. Berkey and S. Edwards, 58-68. New York: Pilgrim Press.

Caird, George B., and L. D. Hurst. 1994. *New Testament Theology*. Oxford: OUP.

Cameron, P. S. 1984. *Violence and the Kingdom: The Interpretation of Matthew 11.12*. Arbeiten zum Neuen Testament und zum Judentum, vol. 5. Frankfurt: P. Lang.

Cameron, Ronald D. 1982. *The Other Gospels: Non-Canonical Gospel Texts*. Philadelphia: Westminster.

Capper, Brian J. 1985. *PANTA KOINA: A Study of Earliest Christian Community of Goods in Its Hellenistic and Jewish Context*. Ph.D. Dissertation. Cambridge.

Caragounis, Chrys C. 1986. *The Son of Man: Vision and Interpretation*. Tübingen: Mohr.

Carter, D., and F. A. Hutchison. 1985. 'The Reagan Paradigm.' *Foundations and Facets Forum* 1(4):39-55.

Casey, P. M. 1979. *The Son of Man*. London: SPCK.

Catchpole, David R. 1971. 'The Answer of Jesus to Caiaphas (Matt. xxvi.64).' *New Testament Studies* 17:213-26.

————. 1984. 'The "Triumphal" Entry.' In *Jesus and the Politics of His Day*, ed. E. Bammel and C. F. D. Moule, 319-34. Cambridge: CUP.

————. 1993. *The Quest for Q*. Edinburgh: T. & T. Clark.

Chadwick, Henry. 1959. *The Sentences of Sextus: A Contribution to the History of Early Christian Ethics*. Cambridge: CUP.

Charlesworth, James H., ed. 1983. *The Old Testament Pseudepigrapha*. Vol. 1. *Apocalyptic Literature and Testaments*. Garden City, N. Y.: Doubleday.

————, ed. 1985. *The Old Testament Pseudepigrapha*. Vol. 2. *Expansions of the 'Old Testament' and Legends, Wisdom and Philosophical Literature, Prayers, Psalms and Odes, Fragments of Lost Judaeo-Hellenistic Works*. Garden City, N. Y.: Doubleday.

————. 1988. *Jesus Within Judaism: New Light from Exciting Archaeological Discoveries*. London: SPCK.

————. 1992a. 'Forgiveness (early Judaism).' In *ABD* 2:833-5.

————. 1992b. 'From Messianology to Christology: Problems and Prospects.' In *The Messiah: Developments in Earliest Judaism and Christianity*, ed. J. H. Charlesworth, 3-35. Minneapolis: Fortress.

————, ed. 1992c. *The Messiah: Developments in Earliest Judaism and Christianity*. Minneapolis: Fortress.

Chilton, Bruce D. 1978. 'Regnum Dei Deus Est.' *Scottish Journal of Theology* 31:261-70.

————. 1982. *The Glory of Israel: The Theology and Provenience of the Isaiah Targum*. Journal for the Study of the Old Testament Supplement Series, vol. 23. Sheffield: JSOT Press.

————. 1984a. *A Galilean Rabbi and His Bible*. Wilmington, Del.: Michael Glazier.

————, ed. 1984b. *The Kingdom of God in the Teaching of Jesus*. London: SPCK; Philadelphia: Fortress.

————. 1987 [1979]. *God in Strength: Jesus' Announcement of the Kingdom*. Sheffield: JSOT Press.

————. 1988. 'Jesus and the Repentance of E. P. Sanders.' *Tyndale Bulletin* 39:1-18.

————. 1992a. 'The Purity of the Kingdom as Conveyed in Jesus' Meals.' In *SBL 1992 Seminar Papers*, ed. Eugene H. Lovering, 473-88. Atlanta, Ga.: Scholars Press.

————. 1992b. *The Temple of Jesus: His Sacrificial Program Within a Cultural History of Sacrifice*. University Park, Pa.: Pennsylvania State U. P.

————. 1994. *A Feast of Meanings: Eucharistic Theology from Jesus Through Johannine Circles*. Supplements to *Novum Testamentum*, vol. 72. Leiden: Brill.

Chilton, Bruce, and Craig A. Evans. 1994a. 'Jesus and Israel's Scriptures.' In *Studying the Historical Jesus: Evaluations of the State of Current Research*, ed. Bruce Chilton and Craig A. Evans, 281-335. Leiden: Brill.

————, eds. 1994b. *Studying the Historical Jesus: Evaluations of the State of Current Research*. Leiden: Brill.

Chilton, Bruce D., and J. I. H. MacDonald. 1987. *Jesus and the Ethics of the Kingdom*. London: SPCK.

Clayton, Ken. 1992. *Jesus and the Scrolls: Everyman's Guide to Christianity and the Dead Sea Scrolls*. Wilmslow, Cheshire: Belvedere.

Cleary, M. 1988. 'The Baptist of History and Kerygma.' *Irish Theological Quarterly* 54:211-27.

Collins, John J. 1993a. *Daniel*. Minneapolis: Fortress.

————. 1993b. 'The "Son of God" Text from Qumran.' In *From Jesus to John. Essays on Jesus and New Testament Christology in Honour of Marinus de Jonge*, ed. M. C. de Boer, 65-82. Sheffield: JSOT Press.

————. 1995. *The Scepter and the Star: The Messiahs of the Dead Sea Scrolls and Other Ancient Literature*. New York: Doubleday.

Collins, Raymond F. 1992. 'Mary.' In *ABD* 4:579-82.

Conzelmann, Hans. 1960 [1953]. *The Theology of Luke*. Trans. Geoffrey Buswell. London: Faber & Faber; New York: Harper & Row.

————. 1969. *An Outline of the Theology of the New Testament*. Trans. John Bowden. New York: Harper & Row.

Cranfield, Charles E. B. 1972 [1959]. *The Gospel According to Saint Mark*. Cambridge Greek Testament Commentary. Cambridge: CUP.

Crites, Stephen. 1989 [1971]. 'The Narrative Quality of Experience.' In *Why Narrative? Readings in Narrative Theology*, ed. Stanley Hauerwas and L. Gregory Jones, 65-88. Grand Rapids, Mich.: Eerdmans.

Crossan, J. Dominic. 1973. *In Parables: The Challenge of the Historical Jesus*. New York: Harper & Row.

————. 1983. *In Fragments: The Aphorisms of Jesus*. San Francisco: Harper & Row.

————. 1985. 'Exile, Stealth and Cunning.' *Foundations and Facets Forum* 1(1):59–61.

————. 1988a. *The Cross That Spoke: The Origins of the Passion Narrative*. San Francisco: Harper & Row.

————. 1988b [1975]. *The Dark Interval: Towards a Theology of Story*. 2nd edn. Sonoma, Calif.: Polebridge Press.

————. 1991a. *The Historical Jesus: The Life of a Mediterranean Jewish Peasant*. San Francisco: HarperCollins; Edinburgh: T. & T. Clark.

————, ed. 1991b [1986]. *Jesus Parallels: A Workbook for the Jesus Tradition*. 2nd edn. [1st edn. entitled *Sayings Parallels*] Philadelphia: Fortress.

————. 1992. 'Parable.' In *ABD* 5:146-52.

————. 1994. *Jesus: A Revolutionary Biography*. San Francisco: HarperSanFrancisco.

————. 1995. *Who Killed Jesus? Exposing the Roots of Anti-Semitism in the Gospel Story of the Death of Jesus*. San Francisco: HarperSanFrancisco.

Crummey, Donald, ed. 1986. *Banditry, Rebellion and Social Protest in Africa*. London: James Currey; Portsmouth, N.H.: Heinemann.

Cullmann, Oscar. 1956. *The State in the New Testament*. New York: Scribner's.

————. 1963 [1957]. *The Christology of the New Testament*. London: SCM; Philadelphia: Westminster.

Cummins, S. A. 1994. *Paul and the Crucified Christ in Antioch: Maccabean Martyrdom and Galatians 1 and 2*. D.Phil. Thesis, Oxford University.

Dahl, N. A. 1974. *The Crucified Messiah and Other Essays*. Minneapolis: Augsburg.

Dalman, Gustaf H. 1903. *The Words of Jesus Considered in the Light of Post-Biblical Jewish Writings and the Aramaic Language*. Edinburgh: T. & T. Clark.

————. 1926. 'Viererlei Acker.' *Palästina-Jahrbuch* 22:120-32.

————. 1929. *Jesus-Jeshua: Studies in the Gospels*. London: SPCK.

Danby, Herbert. 1933. *The Mishnah, Translated from the Hebrew with Introduction and Brief Explanatory Notes*. Oxford: OUP.

Daube, David. 1980. 'Typology in Josephus.' *Journal of Jewish Studies* 31:18-36.

Davies, Graham I. 1991. 'The Presence of God in the Second Temple.' In *Templum Amicitiae: Essays on the Second Temple Presented to Ernst Bammel*, ed. W. Horbury, 32-6. JSNTSS vol. 48. Sheffield: JSOT Press.

Davies, Philip R. 1982. *The Damascus Covenant: An Interpretation of the 'Damascus Document'*. JSOTSS vol. 25. Sheffield: JSOT Press.

Davies, S. L. 1983. *The Gospel of Thomas and Christian Wisdom*. New York: Seabury Press.

Davies, W. D. 1964. *The Setting of the Sermon on the Mount*. Cambridge: CUP.

————. 1974. *The Gospel and the Land: Early Christianity and Jewish Territorial Doctrine*. Berkeley: University of California Press.

Davies, W. D., and Dale C. Allison. 1988-91. *A Critical and Exegetical Commentary on the Gospel According to Saint Matthew*. 2 vols so far. Edinburgh: T. & T. Clark.

de Jonge, M. 1986. 'The Earliest Christian Use of *Christos*. Some Suggestions.' *New Testament Studies* 32:321-43.

————. 1988. 'Jesus' Death for Others and the Death of the Maccabaean Martyrs.' In *Text and Testimony (FS A.J. Klijn)*, ed. T. Baarda, A. Hilhorst, G. P. Luttik Luizen, and A. S. van der Woude. Kampen: J. H. Kok.

————. 1991a. *Jesus, the Servant-Messiah*. New Haven and London: Yale U. P.

————. 1991b. *Jewish Eschatology, Early Christian Christology and the Testaments of the Twelve Patriarchs. Collected Essays of Marinus de Jonge*. Leiden: Brill.

————. 1992. 'Messiah.' In *ABD* 4:777-88.

De Rosa, Peter. 1974. *Jesus Who Became Christ*. London: Collins.

Delling, G. 1957. 'ΒΑΠΤΙΣΜΑ, ΒΑΠΤΙΣΘΗΝΑΙ.' *Novum Testamentum* 2:92–115.

Denaux, Adelbert. 1996. Review of Vaage 1994. *Journal of Biblical Literature* 115:136–8.

Derrett, J. D. M. 1970. *Law in the New Testament*. London: Darton, Longman & Todd.

————. 1977. '*Nisi Dominus Aedificaverit Domum*: Towers and Wars.' *Novum Testamentum* 19:241–61.

————. 1973. *Jesus's Audience: The Social and Psychological Environment in Which He Worked*. New York: Seabury.

Dillistone, F. W. 1977. *C. H. Dodd: Interpreter of the New Testament*. London: Hodder & Stoughton.

Dodd, C. H. 1961 [1935]. *The Parables of the Kingdom*. Revised Edition. London: Nisbet; New York: Scribner's.

————. 1965 [1952]. *According to the Scriptures: The Sub-Structure of New Testament Theology*. London: Collins.

————. 1968. *More New Testament Studies*. Manchester: Manchester U. P.

————. 1971. *The Founder of Christianity*. London: Collins.

Donahue, John R. 1988. *The Gospel in Parable: Metaphor, Narrative and Theology in the Synoptic Gospels*. Philadelphia: Fortress.

Donaldson, T. L. 1985. *Jesus on the Mountain: A Study in Matthean Theology*. JSNTSS no. 8. Sheffield: JSOT Press.

Donovan, V. 1982. *Christianity Rediscovered: An Epistle from the Masai*. London: SCM.

Douglas, Mary. 1966. *Purity and Danger: An Analysis of the Concepts of Pollution and Taboo*. London: Routledge & Kegan Paul.

————. 1968. 'Pollution.' In *International Encyclopaedia of Social Sciences*, vol. 12, 333–43.

————. 1993. *In the Wilderness: The Doctrine of Defilement in the Book of Numbers*. Sheffield: Sheffield Academic Press.

Downing, F. Gerald. 1984. 'Cynics and Christians.' *New Testament Studies* 30:584–93.

————. 1987a. *Jesus and the Threat of Freedom*. London: SCM.

————. 1987b. 'The Social Contexts of Jesus the Teacher.' *New Testament Studies* 33:439–51.

————. 1988. *Christ and the Cynics: Jesus and Other Radical Preachers in First-Century Tradition*. Sheffield: Sheffield Academic Press.

————. 1992. *Cynics and Christian Origins*. Edinburgh: T. & T. Clark.

————. 1995. 'Words as Deeds and Deeds as Words.' *Biblical Interpretation* 3(2):129–43.

Downing, John. 1963. 'Jesus and Martyrdom.' *Journal of Theological Studies* n.s. 14:279–93.

Droge, Arthur J., and James D. Tabor. 1992. *A Noble Death: Suicide and Martyrdom Among Christians and Jews in Antiquity*. San Francisco: HarperSanFrancisco.

Drury, John. 1985. *The Parables in the Gospels: History and Allegory*. London: SPCK.

Duling, Dennis C. 1992. 'Kingdom of God, Kingdom of Heaven.' In *ABD* 4:49–69.

Dungan, David L. 1971. *The Sayings of Jesus in the Churches of Paul: The Use of the Synoptic Tradition in the Regulation of Early Church Life*. Oxford: Blackwell.

Dunn, J. D. G. 1970. *Baptism in the Holy Spirit*. London: SCM.

————. 1975. *Jesus and the Spirit: A Study of the Religious and Charismatic Experience of Jesus and the First Christians as Reflected in the New Testament*. London: SCM; Philadelphia: Westminster.

————. 1988. 'Pharisees, Sinners, and Jesus.' In *The Social World of Formative Christianity and Judaism: Essays in Tribute to Howard Clark Kee*, ed. J. Neusner, P. Borgen, E. S. Frerichs, and R. Horsley, 264–89. Philadelphia: Fortress.

————. 1991. *The Partings of the Ways Between Christianity and Judaism and Their Significance for the Character of Christianity*. London: SCM; Philadelphia: TPI.

————, ed. 1992a. *Jews and Christians: The Parting of the Ways, A.D. 70 to 135*. Wissenschaftliche Untersuchungen zum Neuen Testament, vol. 66. Tübingen: Mohr.

————. 1992b. 'Messianic Ideas and Their Influence on the Jesus of History.' In *The Messiah: Developments in Earliest Judaism and Christianity*, ed. J. H. Charlesworth, 365-81. Minneapolis: Fortress.

Edwards, Douglas. 1992. 'The Socio-Economic and Cultural Ethos of the Lower Galilee in the First Century: Implications for the Nascent Jesus Movement.' In *The Galilee in Late Antiquity*, ed. Lee I. Levine, 53-73. New York and Jerusalem: The Jewish Theological Seminary of America.

Eichrodt, Walther. 1970 [1965]. *Ezekiel: A Commentary*. London: SCM.

Eisenman, Robert H., and Michael Wise. 1992. *The Dead Sea Scrolls Uncovered: The First Complete Translation and Interpretation of 50 Key Documents Withheld for Over 50 Years*. Shaftesbury, Dorset and Rockport, Mass.: Element.

Ellis, E. Earle. 1966. *The Gospel of Luke*. London: Nelson.

Ellis, Marc H. 1994. 'The Brokerless Kingdom and the Other Kingdom: Reflections on Auschwitz, Jesus and the Jewish-Christian Establishment.' In *Jesus and Faith: A Conversation on the Work of John Dominic Crossan*, ed. Jeffrey Carlson and Robert A. Ludwig, 100-14. Maryknoll, N. Y.: Orbis.

Epp, Eldon J., and George W. MacRae, eds. 1989. *The New Testament and Its Modern Interpreters*. In *The Bible and Its Modern Interpreters*, ed. Douglas A. Knight. Atlanta, Ga.: Scholars Press.

Evans, Christopher F. 1990. *Saint Luke*. London: SCM.

Evans, Craig A. 1981. 'A Note on the Function of Isaiah vi.9-10 in Mark iv.' *Révue Biblique* 88:234-5.

————. 1985. 'On the Isaianic Background of the Sower Parable.' *Catholic Biblical Quarterly* 47:464-8.

————. 1989a. 'Jesus' Action in the Temple and Evidence of Corruption in the First-Century Temple.' In *SBL 1989 Seminar Papers*, ed. David J. Lull, 522-39. Atlanta, Ga.: Scholars Press.

————. 1989b. 'Jesus' Action in the Temple: Cleansing or Portent of Destruction?' *Catholic Biblical Quarterly* 51:237-70.

————. 1989c. *Life of Jesus Research: An Annotated Bibliography*. Leiden: Brill.

————. 1991. 'In What Sense "Blasphemy"? Jesus Before Caiaphas in Mark 14:61-4.' In *SBL 1991 Seminar Papers*, ed. Eugene H. Lovering, 215-34. Atlanta, Ga.: Scholars Press.

————. 1992. 'Opposition to the Temple: Jesus and the Dead Sea Scrolls.' In *Jesus and the Dead Sea Scrolls*, ed. J. H. Charlesworth, 235-53. New York: Doubleday.

————. 1993. 'Jesus and the "Cave of Robbers": Toward a Jewish Context for the Temple Action.' *Bulletin of Biblical Research* 3:93-110.

Farmer, W. R. 1956. *Maccabees, Zealots, and Josephus: An Inquiry Into Jewish Nationalism in the Greco-Roman Period*. New York: Columbia U. P.

————. 1982. *Jesus and the Gospel*. Philadelphia: Fortress.

Feldman, Louis H. 1993. *Jew and Gentile in the Ancient World: Attitudes and Interactions from Alexander to Justinian*. Princeton, N.J.: Princeton U. P.

Fergusson, David. 1992. *Bultmann*. London: Geoffrey Chapman.

Fernyhough, Timothy. 1986. 'Social Mobility and Dissident Elites in Northern Ethiopia: The Role of Banditry, 1900-69.' In *Banditry, Rebellion and Social Protest in Africa*, ed. Donald Crummey, 151-72. London: James Currey; Portsmouth, N.H.: Heinemann.

Firmage, Edwin. 1992. 'Zoology.' In *ABD*, vol. 6, 1109-67.

Fishbane, Michael. 1985. *Biblical Interpretation in Ancient Israel*. Oxford: OUP.

Fitzmyer, J. A. 1970. *The Gospel According to Luke (I-IX)*. Anchor Bible, vol. 28. New York: Doubleday.

————. 1979. *A Wandering Aramean: Collected Aramaic Essays*. SBL Monograph Series, no. 25. Missoula, Mont.: Scholars Press.

————. 1985. *The Gospel According to Luke (X-XXIV)*. Anchor Bible, vol. 28a. New York: Doubleday.

Flusser, David. 1959. 'Two Notes on the Midrash on 2 Sam. VII.' *Israel Exploration Journal* 9:99-109.

Fortna, Robert T. 1970. *The Gospel of Signs*. SNTSMS vol. 11. Cambridge: CUP.

————. 1988. *The Fourth Gospel and Its Predecessor*. Philadelphia: Fortress.

————. 1992. 'Signs/Semeia Source.' In *ABD* 6:18-22.

Fossum, Jarl E. 1985. *The Name of God and the Angel of the Lord: Samaritan and Jewish Concepts of Intermediaries and the Origin of Gnosticism*. Wissenschaftliche Untersuchungen zum Neuen Testament, vol. II.36. Tübingen: Mohr.

France, R. T. 1971. *Jesus and the Old Testament*. London: Tyndale.

————. 1982. 'The Worship of Jesus: A Neglected Factor in Christological Debate?' In *Christ the Lord: Studies in Christology Presented to Donald Guthrie*, ed. H. H. Rowdon, 17-36. Leicester: IVP.

————.1985. *The Gospel According to Matthew: An Introduction and Commentary*. Leicester: IVP; Grand Rapids, Mich.: Eerdmans.

Fredriksen, Paula. 1988. *From Jesus to Christ: The Origins of the New Testament Images of Jesus*. New Haven and London: Yale U. P.

————. 1995a. 'Did Jesus Oppose the Purity Laws?' *Bible Review* June, 20-47.

————. 1995b. 'What You See is What You Get: Context and Content in Current Research on the Historical Jesus.' *Theology Today* 52:75-97.

Frei, Hans W. 1974. *The Eclipse of Biblical Narrative: A Study in Eighteenth and Nineteenth Century Hermeneutics*. New Haven: Yale U. P.

Freyne, Sean. 1980a. 'The Galileans in the Light of Josephus' *Vita*.' *New Testament Studies* 26:397-413.

————. 1980b. *Galilee from Alexander the Great to Hadrian. a Study of Second Temple Judaism*. Wilmington, Del.: Glazier/Notre Dame U. P.

————. 1987. 'Galilee-Jerusalem Relations in the Light of Josephus' *Life*.' *New Testament Studies* 33:600-9.

————. 1988a. 'Bandits in Galilee: A Contribution to the Study of Social Conditions in First-Century Palestine.' In *The Social World of Formative Christianity and Judaism: Essays in Tribute to Howard Clark Kee*, ed. J. Neusner, P. Borgen, E. S. Frerichs, and R. Horsley, 50-68. Philadelphia: Fortress.

————. 1988b. *Galilee, Jesus and the Gospels: Literary Approaches and Historical Investigations*. Philadelphia: Fortress.

————. 1992. 'Urban-Rural Relations in First-Century Galilee: Some Suggestions from the Literary Sources.' In *The Galilee in Late Antiquity*, ed. Lee I. Levine, 75-91. New York and Jerusalem: The Jewish Theological Seminary of America.

Fuller, Reginald H. 1965. *The Foundations of New Testament Christology*. London: Lutterworth.

Funk, Robert W. 1966. *Language, Hermeneutic, and Word of God: The Problem of Language in the New Testament and Contemporary Theology*. New York: Harper & Row.

————, revised and trans. 1973 (1961). *A Greek Grammar of the New Testament and Other Early Christian Literature*. 5th edn. Chicago and London: The University of Chicago Press.

————. 1985a. 'The Issue of Jesus.' *Foundations and Facets Forum* 1(1):7-12.

————, ed & designed by. 1985b. *New Gospel Parallels*. Vol. 1. *The Synoptic Gospels*. Philadelphia: Fortress.

————, ed & designed by. 1985c. *New Gospel Parallels*. Vol. 2. *John and the Other Gospels*. Philadelphia: Fortress.

————. 1989. 'Unraveling the Jesus Tradition: Criteria and Criticism.' *Foundations & Facets Forum* 5(2):31-62.

————, ed. 1991. *The Gospel of Mark: Red Letter Edition*. Sonoma, Calif.: Polebridge Press.

Funk, Robert W., and Roy W. Hoover. 1993. *The Five Gospels: The Search for the Authentic Words of Jesus*. New York: Macmillan.

Funk, Robert W., Bernard B. Scott, and James R. Butts, eds. 1988. *The Parables of Jesus: Red Letter Edition. A Report of the Jesus Seminar*. Sonoma, Calif.: Polebridge Press.

García Martínez, F. 1994 [1992]. *The Dead Sea Scrolls Translated: The Qumran Texts in English*. Leiden: Brill.

Garnet, Paul. 1977. *Salvation and Atonement in the Qumran Scrolls*. Wissenschaftliche Untersuchungen zum Neuen Testament, vol. II.3. Tübingen: Mohr.

————. 1980a. 'Jesus and the Exilic Soteriology.' In *Studia Biblica 1978*, 111-14. Sheffield: JSOT Press.

————. 1980b. 'Qumran Light on Pauline Soteriology.' In *Pauline Studies: Essays Presented to F. F. Bruce on His 70th Birthday*, ed. Donald A. Hagner and Murray J. Harris, 19-32. Grand Rapids: Eerdmans.

————. 1982. 'Some Qumran Exegetical *cruces* in the Light of Exilic Soteriology.' *Texte und Untersuchungen* 126:201-4. In *Studia Evangelica VII*, Berlin: Akademie-Verlag.

————. 1983. 'The Parable of the Sower: How the Multitudes Understood It.' In *Spirit Within Structure: Essays in Honor of George Johnston on the Occasion of His Seventieth Birthday*, ed. E. J. Furcha, 39-54. Pittsburgh Theological Monographs, New Series, no. 3. Allison Park, Pa.: Pickwick.

Gärtner, Bertil. 1965. *The Temple and the Community in Qumran and the New Testament*. SNTSMS vol. 1. Cambridge: CUP.

Gaston, Lloyd. 1970. *No Stone Upon Another. Studies in the Significance of the Fall of Jerusalem in the Synoptic Gospels*. Supplements to *Novum Testamentum*, no. 23. Leiden: Brill.

Gerhardsson, Birger. 1961. *Memory and Manuscript: Oral Tradition and Written Transmission in Rabbinic Judaism and Early Christianity*. Uppsala: Gleerup.

————. 1964. *Tradition and Transmission in Early Christianity*. Uppsala: Gleerup.

————. 1979. *The Origins of the Gospel Tradition*. London: SCM.

————. 1986. *The Gospel Tradition*. Lund: Gleerup.

Giblin, C. H. 1971. '"The Things of God" in the Question Concerning Tribute to Caesar (Lk 20:25; Mk 12:17; Mt 22:21).' *Catholic Biblical Quarterly* 33:510-27.

Gibson, J. 1981. 'Hoi Telonai Kai Hai Pornai.' *Journal of Theological Studies* 32:423-9.

Glasson, T. F. 1963 [1945]. *The Second Advent: The Origin of the New Testament Doctrine*. 3rd edn. London.

————. 1984 [1977]. 'Schweitzer's Influence - Blessing or Bane?' In *The Kingdom of God*, ed. Bruce D. Chilton, 107-20. London: SPCK; Philadelphia: Fortress.

————. 1988. 'Theophany and Parousia.' *New Testament Studies* 34:259-70.

Goergen, Donald. 1986a. 'The Death and Resurrection of Jesus.' In *A Theology of Jesus*, vol. 2. Wilmington, Del.: Michael Glazier.

————. 1986b. *A Theology of Jesus*. Vol. 1. *The Mission and Ministry of Jesus*. Wilmington, Del.: Michael Glazier.

Goldingay, John E. 1989. *Daniel*. Dallas, Tex.: Word Books.

Goodman, Martin. 1987. *The Ruling Class of Judaea: The Origins of the Jewish Revolt Against Rome A.D. 66-70*. Cambridge: CUP.

Goppelt, Leonhard. 1981 [1975]. *Theology of the New Testament*. Vol. 1. *The Ministry of Jesus in Its Theological Significance*. Grand Rapids, Mich.: Eerdmans.

Goulder, Michael. 1989. *Luke – A New Paradigm*. Sheffield: Sheffield Academic Press.

Goulet-Cazé, M. -O. 1990. 'Le cynisme à l'époque impériale.' In *Aufstieg und Niedergang der Römischen Welt*, ed. H. Temporini and A. Haase, vol. 2.36.4, 2720–2823. Berlin and New York: De Gruyter.

————, ed. 1993. *Le cynisme ancien et ses prolongements*. Paris: Presses Universitaires de France.

Grabbe, Lester L. 1992. *Judaism from Cyrus to Hadrian*. 2 vols. Minneapolis: Fortress.

Grant, Robert M. 1966 [1959]. *Gnosticism and Early Christianity*. 2nd edn. New York: Columbia U. P.

Gray, Rebecca. 1993. *Prophetic Figures in Late Second Temple Jewish Palestine*. New York & Oxford: OUP.

Green, Peter, tr. & ed. 1974 [1967]. *Juvenal. The Sixteen Satires*. London: Penguin Books.

Gruenwald, Ithamar. 1980. *Apocalyptic and Merkavah Mysticism*. Arbeiten zur Geschichte des Antiken Judentums und des Urchristentums, vol. 14. Leiden: Brill.

Gruenwald, Ithamar, Shaul Shaked, and Gedaliahu G. Stroumsa, eds. 1992. *Messiah and Christos. Studies in the Jewish Origins of Christianity Presented to David Flusser on the Occasion of His Seventy-Fifth Birthday*. Tübingen: Mohr.

Guelich, Robert A. 1982. *The Sermon on the Mount*. Waco, Tex.: Word Books.

————. 1989. *Mark 1–8:26*. Dallas, Tex.: Word Books.

Gundry, Robert H. 1993. *Mark: A Commentary on His Apology for the Cross*. Grand Rapids, Mich.: Eerdmans.

Gunneweg, A. H. J. 1983. '"AM HA'ARES – A Semantic Revolution.' *Zeitschrift für die alttestamentliche Wissenschaft* 95:437–40.

Hagner, Donald A. 1984. *The Jewish Reclamation of Jesus: An Analysis and Critique of Modern Jewish Study of Jesus*. Grand Rapids, Mich.: Zondervan.

————. 1993. *Matthew 1–13*. Dallas, Tex.: Word Books.

Hall, John. 1984 [1974]. *Dictionary of Subjects and Symbols in Art*. London: John Murray.

Hamilton, Victor P. 1992. 'Satan.' In *ABD* 5:985–9.

Hampel, V. 1990. *Menschensohn und historischer Jesus. Ein Rätselwort als Schlüssel zum messianischen Selbstvertändnis Jesu*. Neukirchen-Vluyn: Neukirchener Verlag.

Hanks, Thomas D. 1992. 'Poor, Poverty (New Testament).' In *ABD* 5:414–24.

Hare, Douglas R. A. 1990. *The Son of Man Tradition*. Minneapolis: Fortress.

Hart, H. StJ. 1984. 'The Coin of "Render Unto Caesar . . ." (A note on some aspects of Mark 12:13–17; Matt. 22:15–22; Luke 20:20–26).' In *Jesus and the Politics of His Day*, ed. E. Bammel and C. F. D. Moule, 241–8. Cambridge: CUP.

Harvey, Anthony E. 1976. *Jesus on Trial: A Study in the Fourth Gospel*. London: SPCK.

————. 1980. 'The Use of Mystery Language in the Bible.' *Journal of Theological Studies* n.s. 31:320–36.

————. 1982. *Jesus and the Constraints of History: The Bampton Lectures, 1980*. London: Duckworth.

————. 1987. 'Christ as Agent.' In *The Glory of Christ in the New Testament: Studies in Christology in Memory of George Bradford Caird*, ed. L. D. Hurst and N. T. Wright, 239–50. Oxford: Clarendon.

————. 1989. Review of F. G. Downing, *Jesus and the Threat of Freedom* (1987) and *Christ and the Cynics* (1988). *Journal of Theological Studies* n.s. 40:550–3.

————. 1990. *Strenuous Commands: The Ethic of Jesus*. London: SCM; Philadelphia: TPI.

————. 1993. Review of J. D. Crossan, *The Historical Jesus*. *Journal of Theological Studies* 44:226–8.

Hay, David M. 1973. *Glory at the Right Hand: Psalm 110 in Early Christianity*. SBL Monograph Series, no. 18. Nashville: Abingdon.

Hays, R. B. 1989. *Echoes of Scripture in the Letters of Paul*. New Haven and London: Yale U. P.

Healey, Joseph P. 1992. 'Am Ha'arez.' In *ABD* 1:168-9.

Hengel, Martin. 1971 [1970]. *Was Jesus a Revolutionist?* Philadelphia: Fortress.

————. 1973 [1971]. *Victory Over Violence: Jesus and the Revolutionists*. Philadelphia: Fortress.

————. 1974. *Property and Riches in the Early Church: Aspects of a Social History of Early Christianity*. Philadelphia: Fortress.

————. 1977 [1976]. *Crucifixion in the Ancient World and the Folly of the Message of the Cross*. London: SCM; Philadelphia: Fortress.

————. 1981a. *The Atonement: The Origins of the Doctrine in the New Testament*. London: SCM; Philadelphia: Fortress.

————. 1981b [1968]. *The Charismatic Leader and His Followers*. New York: Crossroad Publishing.

————. 1989a. *The 'Hellenization' of Judaea in the First Century After Christ*. London: SCM; Philadelphia: TPI.

————. 1989b. *The Johannine Question*. London: SCM; Philadelphia: TPI.

————. 1989c [1961]. *The Zealots: Investigations Into the Jewish Freedom Movement in the Period from Herod 1 Until 70 A.D.* Edinburgh: T. & T. Clark.

————. 1993. '"Setze dich zu meiner Rechten!" Die Inthronisation Christi zur Rechten Gottes und Psalm 110,1.' In *Le Trône de Dieu*, ed. M. Philoneko, 108-94. Wissenschaftliche Untersuchungen zum neuen Testament, vol. 69. Tübingen: Mohr.

————. 1995a. 'Jesus, the Messiah of Israel: The Debate About the "Messianic Mission" of Jesus.' In *Crisis in Christology: Essays in Quest of Resolution*, ed. W. R. Farmer, 217-40. Livonia, Mich.: Dove Booksellers.

————. 1995b. *Studies in Early Christology*. Edinburgh: T. & T. Clark.

————. 1996. 'Zur Wirkungsgeschichte von Jes 53 in vorchristlicher Zeit.' In *Jeseja 53 und seine Wirkungsgeschichte*, ed. B. Janowski and P. Stuhlmacher, 47-87. Tübingen: Mohr (forthcoming: pagination may alter).

Hick, John. 1993. *The Metaphor of God Incarnate*. London: SCM.

Hill, David. 1977. 'On the Use and Meaning of Hosea vi.6 in Matthew's Gospel.' *New Testament Studies* 24:107-19.

————. 1979. *New Testament Prophecy*. London: Marshall, Morgan & Scott.

Hobsbawm, Eric J. 1965. *Primitive Rebels: Studies in Archaic Forms of Social Movement in the 19th and 20th Centuries*. New York: Norton.

————. 1972. 'Social Banditry: Reply.' *Comparative Studies in Society and History* 14:503-5.

————. 1973a. 'Peasants and Politics.' *Journal of Peasant Studies* 1:3-22.

————. 1973b. 'Social Banditry.' In *Rural Protest: Peasant Movements and Social Change*, ed. H. A. Landsberger, 142-57. New York: Barnes & Noble.

————. 1985 [1969]. *Bandits*. London: Penguin Books.

Hock, Ronald F. 1987. 'Lazarus and Micyllus: Greco-Roman Backgrounds to Luke 16:19-31.' *Journal of Biblical Literature* 106:447-63.

————. 1992. 'Cynics.' In *ABD* 1:1221-6.

Hoehner, Harold W. 1980 [1972]. *Herod Antipas: A Contemporary of Jesus Christ*. Grand Rapids, Mich.: Zondervan.

Hollenbach, Paul W. 1992. 'John the Baptist.' In *ABD* 3:887-99.

Holmberg, B. 1993. 'En Historisk Vändning I Forskningen Om Jesus.' *Svensk Teologisk Kvartalskrift* 69:69-76.

Hooker, M. D. 1959. *Jesus and the Servant: The Influence of the Servant Concept of Deutero-Isaiah in the New Testament*. London: SPCK.

————. 1967. *The Son of Man in Mark*. London: SPCK.

————. 1979. 'Is the Son of Man Problem Really Insoluble?' In *Text and Interpretation: Studies in the New Testament Presented to Matthew Black*, ed. E. Best & R. McL. Wilson, 155–168. Cambridge: CUP.

————. 1982. 'Trial and Tribulation in Mark XIII.' *Bulletin of the John Rylands Library* 65:78–99.

————. 1991. *A Commentary on the Gospel According to St Mark*. Black's New Testament Commentaries. London: A. & C. Black.

Horbury, William. 1972. 'The Passion Narratives and Historical Criticism.' *Theology* 75:58–71.

————. 1982a. 'The Benediction of the *Minim* and Early Jewish-Christian Controversy.' *Journal of Theological Studies* 33:19–61.

————. 1982b. 'I Thessalonians ii.3 as Rebutting the Charge of False Prophecy.' *Journal of Theological Studies* n.s. 33:492–508.

————. 1984a. 'Christ as Brigand in Ancient Anti-Christian Polemic.' In *Jesus and the Politics of His Day*, ed. E. Bammel and C. F. D. Moule, 183–95. Cambridge: CUP.

————. 1984b. 'The Temple Tax.' In *Jesus and the Politics of His Day*, ed. E. Bammel and C. F. D. Moule, 265–86. Cambridge: CUP.

————. 1985. 'The Messianic Associations of "The Son of Man"' *Journal of Theological Studies* 36:34–55.

Horsley, Richard A. 1979. 'Josephus and the Bandits.' *Journal for the Study of Judaism* 10(1):37–63.

————. 1981. 'Ancient Jewish Banditry and the Revolt Against Rome, A.D. 66.' *Catholic Biblical Quarterly* 43:409–32.

————. 1986. 'The Zealots: Their Origin, Relationships and Importance in the Jewish Revolt.' *Novum Testamentum* 28(2):159–92.

————. 1987. *Jesus and the Spiral of Violence: Popular Jewish Resistance in Roman Palestine*. San Francisco: Harper & Row.

————. 1992a [1986]. 'Ethics and Exegesis: "Love Your Enemy" and the Doctrine of Nonviolence.' In *The Love of Enemy and Nonretaliation in the New Testament*, ed. Willard M. Swartley, 72–101. Louisville, Ky.: Westminster/John Knox.

————. 1992b. '"Messianic" Figures and Movements in First-Century Palestine.' In *The Messiah: Developments in Earliest Judaism and Christianity*, ed. J. H. Charlesworth, 276–95. Minneapolis: Fortress.

————. 1992c. 'Messianic Movements in Judaism.' In *ABD* 4:791–7.

————. 1994. 'The Death of Jesus.' In *Studying the Historical Jesus: Evaluations of the State of Current Research*, ed. Bruce Chilton and Craig A. Evans, 395–422. Leiden: Brill.

Horsley, Richard A., and John S. Hanson. 1985. *Bandits, Prophets and Messiahs: Popular Movements at the Time of Jesus*. Minneapolis: Winston Press.

Houlden, J. Leslie. 1992. 'Lord's Prayer.' In *ABD* 4:356–62.

Howard, Geoffrey. 1993. *Weep not for Me*. London: Darton, Longman & Todd.

Huck, Albert, and Hans Lietzmann, eds. 1936 [1892]. *Synopsis of the First Three Gospels*. 9th edn. Tübingen: Mohr.

Hull, John M. 1974. *Hellenistic Magic and the Synoptic Tradition*. London: SCM; Naperville, Ill.: Alec R. Allenson.

Hurtado, Larry W. 1988. *One God, One Lord: Early Christian Devotion and Ancient Jewish Monotheism*. Philadelphia: Fortress.

————. 1992. 'God.' In *Dictionary of Jesus and the Gospels*, ed. Joel B. Green, Scot McKnight, and I. Howard Marshall, 270–6. Downers Grove, Ill. and Leicester: IVP.

Ito, Akio. 1995. 'Romans 2: A Deuteronomistic Reading.' *Journal for the Study of the New Testament* 59:21–37.

Janzen, W. 1992. 'Land.' In *ABD* 4:143–54.

Jaubert, A. 1957. *La Date de la Cène*. Paris: Gabalda.

Jeremias, Joachim. 1950. 'Zum Problem der Deutung von Jes. 53 im palästinischen Spätjudentum.' In *Aux Sources de la Tradition Chrétienne: Mélanges Offerts à M. Maurice Goguel*, 113–19. Neuchâtel.

————. 1958 [1956]. *Jesus' Promise to the Nations*. London: SCM.

————. 1963a [1947]. *The Parables of Jesus*. London: SCM; New York: Scribner's.

————. 1963b [1961]. *The Sermon on the Mount*. Philadelphia: Fortress.

————. 1966a [1949]. *The Eucharistic Words of Jesus*. London: SCM.

————. 1966b. *Abba: Studien zur neutestamentlichen Theologie und Zeitgeschichte*. Göttingen: Vandenhoek & Ruprecht.

————. 1966c [1936]. 'Die Salbungsgeschichte Mk. 14,3–9.' In *Abba: Studien zur neutestamentlichen Theologie und Zeitgeschichte*, 107–15. Göttingen: Vandenhoek & Ruprecht.

————. 1967. *The Prayers of Jesus*. London: SCM; Philadelphia: Fortress.

————. 1971. *New Testament Theology: The Proclamation of Jesus*. New York: SCM; London: Scribner's.

Jeremias, Joachim, and W. Zimmerli. 1967 [1957]. 'παῖς θεοῦ.' In *TDNT*, ed. G. Friedrich, vol. 5, 654–717. Grand Rapids: Eerdmans.

Johnson, L. T. 1982. 'The Lukan Kingship Parable (Lk. 19:11–27).' *Novum Testamentum* 24:139–59.

————. 1989. 'The New Testament's Anti-Jewish Slander and the Conventions of Ancient Polemic.' *Journal of Biblical Literature* 108:419–41.

————. 1991. *The Gospel of Luke*. Collegeville, Minn.: The Liturgical Press.

————. 1995. *The Real Jesus*. San Francisco: HarperSanFrancisco.

Jones, S. Gareth. 1991. *Bultmann: Towards a Critical Theology*. Cambridge: Polity Press.

Juel, Donald. 1988. *Messianic Exegesis: Christological Interpretation of the Old Testament in Early Christianity*. Philadelphia: Fortress.

Jülicher, Adolf. 1910 [1899]. *Die Gleichnisreden Jesu*. Tübingen: Mohr.

Kähler, Martin. 1964 [1892]. *The So-Called Historical Jesus and the Historic, Biblical Christ*. Philadelphia: Fortress.

Karrer, M. 1990. *Der Gesalbte: Die Grundlagen des Christustitels*. Forschungen zur Religion und Literatur des Alten und Neuen Testaments, no. 151. Göttingen: Vandenhoek und Ruprecht.

Käsemann, Ernst. 1964 [1960]. *Essays on New Testament Themes*. London: SCM.

Kee, Howard C. 1983. *Miracle in the Early Christian World*. New Haven: Yale U. P.

————. 1986. *Medicine, Miracle and Magic in New Testament Times*. Cambridge: CUP.

Keesmaat, Sylvia C. 1994. *Paul's Use of the Exodus Tradition in Romans and Galatians*. D.Phil. Dissertation, Oxford University. Oxford.

Kelber, Werner. 1983. *The Oral and Written Gospel*. Philadelphia: Fortress.

Kennedy, G. A. 1984. *New Testament Interpretation Through Rhetorical Criticism*. Chapel Hill, N.C.: University of North Carolina Press.

Kim, Seyoon. 1983. *The Son of Man as the Son of God*. Tübingen: Mohr.

————. 1987a. 'Jesus – The Son of God, the Stone, the Son of Man, and the Servant: The Role of Zechariah in the Self-Identification of Jesus.' In *Tradition and Interpretation in the New Testament: Essays in Honor of E. Earle Ellis*, ed. Gerald F. Hawthorne and Otto Betz, 134–48. Grand Rapids, Mich.: Eerdmans; Tübingen: Mohr.

————. 1987b. 'Die Vollmacht Jesu und der Tempel: Der Sinn der "Tempelreinigung" und der geschichtliche und theologische Kontext des Prozesses Jesu.' In *Aufsteig und Niedergang der Römischen Welt*, ed. H. Temporini & A. Haase, vol. II.26.6. Berlin and New York: de Gruyter.

King, K. 1987. 'Kingdom in the Gospel of Thomas.' *Foundations and Facets Forum* 3(1):48–97.

Kinman, Brent. 1994. 'Lucan Eschatology and the Missing Fig Tree.' *Journal of Biblical Literature* 113:669–78.

Kissinger, Warren S. 1979. *The Parables of Jesus: A History of Interpretation and Bibliography.* Metuchen, N.J.: The Scarecrow Press.

Klausner, Joseph. 1947 [1925]. *Jesus of Nazareth: His Life, Times, and Teaching.* London: George Allen & Unwin.

Klemm, H. G. 1982. 'De Censu Caesaris: Beobachtungen zu J. Duncan M. Derretts Interpretation der Perikope Mark 12:13–17 par.' *Novum Testamentum* 24:234–54.

Kloppenborg, J. S. 1987. *The Formation of Q: Trajectories in Ancient Wisdom Collections.* Philadelphia: Fortress.

—————. 1988. *Q Parallels: Synopsis, Critical Notes, & Concordance.* Sonoma, Calif.: Polebridge Press.

—————. 1992. 'The Theological Stakes in the Synoptic Problem.' In *The Four Gospels. 1992 Festschrift Frans Neirynck*, ed. F. van Segbroeck, C. M. Tuckett, G. van Belle, and J. Verheyden, 93–120. Leuven: Leuven U. P.

Knibb, Michael A. 1976. 'The Exile in the Literature of the Intertestamental Period.' *Heythrop Journal* 17:253–72.

—————. 1987. *The Qumran Community.* Cambridge: CUP.

Knowles, Michael. 1993. *Jeremiah in Matthew's Gospel: The Rejected-Prophet Motif in Matthaean Redaction.* JSNTSS vol. 68. Sheffield: Sheffield Academic Press.

Koch, Klaus. 1972 [1970]. *The Rediscovery of Apocalyptic: A Polemical Work on a Neglected Area of Biblical Studies and Its Damaging Effects on Theology and Philosophy.* London: SCM.

Koester, Helmut. 1982a [1980]. *Introduction to the New Testament.* Vol. 1. *History, Culture and Religion of the Hellenistic Age.* Philadelphia: Fortress; Berlin: de Gruyter.

—————. 1982b. *Introduction to the New Testament.* Vol. 2. *History and Literature of Early Christianity.* Philadelphia: Fortress; Berlin: de Gruyter.

—————. 1990. *Ancient Christian Gospels: Their History and Development.* London: SCM; Philadelphia: TPI.

—————. 1992. 'Jesus the Victim.' *Journal of Biblical Literature* 111:3–15.

Kraft, Robert A., and George W. E. Nickelsburg, eds. 1986. *Early Judaism and Its Modern Interpreters.* In *The Bible and Its Modern Interpreters*, ed. Douglas A. Knight. Atlanta, Ga.: Scholars Press.

Kuhn, Thomas S. 1970 [1962]. *The Structure of Scientific Revolutions.* Chicago: University of Chicago Press.

Kümmel, Werner G. 1972/3 [1970]. *The New Testament: The History of the Investigation of Its Problems.* Nashville: Abingdon; London: SCM.

—————. 1973. *The Theology of the New Testament: According to its Major Witnesses, Jesus–Paul–John.* Nashville: Abingdon; London: SCM.

—————. 1985. *Dreizig Jahre Jesusforschung.* Bonn: Hanstein.

Küng, Hans. 1976. *On Being a Christian.* Garden City, N. Y.: Doubleday.

Lacocque, André. 1979 [1976]. *The Book of Daniel.* London: SPCK.

Ladd, George Eldon. 1966. *Jesus and the Kingdom: The Eschatology of Biblical Realism.* London: SPCK.

—————. 1974a. *The Presence of the Future: The Eschatology of Biblical Realism.* Grand Rapids, Mich.: Eerdmans.

—————. 1974b. *A Theology of the New Testament.* Grand Rapids, Mich.: Eerdmans.

Lambrecht, J. 1983 [1976]. *Once More Astonished: The Parables of Jesus.* New York: Crossroad.

—————. 1985. *The Sermon on the Mount*. Wilmington, Del.: Michael Glazier.

Lampe, Geoffrey W. H. 1984. 'A.D. 70 in Christian Reflection.' In *Jesus and the Politics of His Day*, ed. E. Bammel and C. F. D. Moule, 153–71. Cambridge: CUP.

Lane Fox, Robin. 1986. *Pagans and Christians*. New York: Knopf; London: Penguin Books.

Lane, William L. 1974. *The Gospel of Mark: The English Text with Introduction, Exposition and Notes*. Grand Rapids, Mich.: Eerdmans.

Lang, Bernhard. 1992. 'The Roots of the Eucharist in Jesus' Praxis.' In *SBL 1992 Seminar Papers*, ed. Eugene H. Lovering, 467–72. Atlanta, Ga.: Scholars Press.

Lapide, Pinchas. 1986. *The Sermon on the Mount: Utopia or Program for Action?* Maryknoll, N. Y.: Orbis.

Leaney, A. R. C. 1966 [1958]. *The Gospel According to St Luke*. London: A. & C. Black.

Leivestad, Ragnar. 1973. 'Das Dogma von der Prophetenlosen Zeit.' *New Testament Studies* 19:288–99.

—————. 1987. *Jesus in His Own Perspective: An Examination of His Sayings, Actions, and Eschatological Titles*. Minneapolis: Augsburg.

Levine, Lee I., ed. 1992a. *The Galilee in Late Antiquity*. New York and Jerusalem: The Jewish Theological Seminary of America.

—————. 1992b. 'Herod the Great.' In *ABD* 3:161–69.

Lewis, C. S. 1955 [1942]. *The Screwtape Letters*. London: Fontana.

—————. 1967. *Christian Reflections*. London: Geoffrey Bles.

Liefeld, Walter L. 1967. 'The Wandering Preacher as a Social Figure in the Roman Empire.' Ann Arbor, Mich.: University Microfilms International.

Lieu, Judith. 1994. '"The Parting of the Ways": Theological Construct or Historical Reality?' *Journal for the Study of the New Testament* 56:101–19.

Lightfoot, J. B. 1893. *Biblical Essays*. London: Macmillan.

Lightfoot, Robert H. 1935. *History and Interpretation in the Gospels*. London: Hodder & Stoughton.

Lindars, B. 1973 [1961]. *New Testament Apologetic: The Doctrinal Significance of the Old Testament Quotations*. London: SCM.

—————. 1983. *Jesus Son of Man*. London: SPCK.

—————. 1985. 'Response to Richard Bauckham: The Idiomatic Use of Bar Enasha.' *Journal for the Study of the New Testament* 23:35–41.

Lindsay, D. R. 1993. *Josephus and Faith: πίστις & πιστεύειν as Faith Terminology in the Writings of Flavius Josephus and in the New Testament*. Arbeiten zur Geschichte des Antiken Judentums und des Urchristentums, vol. 19. Leiden: Brill.

Lohfink, Gerhard. 1984. *Jesus and Community*. Trans. J. P. Galvin. Philadelphia: Fortress; New York: Paulist Press.

Lüdemann, Gerd. 1980. 'The Successors of Pre-70 Jerusalem Christianity: A Critical Examination of the Pella-Tradition.' In *Jewish and Christian Self-Definition, Volume One: The Shaping of Christianity in the Second and Third Centuries*, ed. E. P. Sanders, 161–73. Philadelphia: Fortress.

—————. 1994. *The Resurrection of Jesus: History, Experience, Theology*. London: SCM.

Lührmann, D. 1973. 'Pistis im Judentum.' *Zeitschrift für die neutestamentliche Wissenschaft* 64:19–38.

Maccoby, Hyam. 1980 [1973]. *Revolution in Judea. Jesus and the Jewish Resistance*. New York: Taplinger.

—————. 1986. *The Mythmaker: Paul and the Invention of Christianity*. London: Weidenfeld & Nicolson.

—————. 1991. *Paul and Hellenism*. London: SCM; Philadelphia: TPI.

—————. 1992. *Judas Iscariot and the Myth of Jewish Evil*. London: P. Halben.

McGrath, Alister E. 1994 [1986]. *The Making of Modern German Christology 1750–1990.* Leicester: Apollos; Grand Rapids, Mich.: Zondervan.

―――. 1989. 'Christian Ethics.' In *The Religion of the Incarnation*, ed. Robert Morgan, 189–204. Bristol: Bristol Classical Press.

Mack, Burton L. 1985. 'Gilgamesh and the Wizard of Oz: The Scholar as Hero.' *Foundations and Facets Forum* 1(2):3–29.

―――. 1987. 'The Kingdom Sayings in Mark.' *Foundations and Facets Forum* 3(1):3–47.

―――. 1988. *A Myth of Innocence: Mark and Christian Origins.* Philadelphia: Fortress.

―――. 1993. *The Lost Gospel: The Book of Q and Christian Origins.* San Francisco: HarperCollins; Shaftesbury: Element.

―――. 1995. *Who Wrote the New Testament? The Making of the Christian Myth.* San Francisco: HarperSanFrancisco.

MacMullen, Ramsey. 1981. *Paganism in the Roman Empire.* New Haven and London: Yale U. P.

Macquarrie, John. 1990. *Jesus Christ in Modern Thought.* London: SCM; Philadelphia: TPI.

Magonet, Jonathan. 1988. 'Religious Tensions in Counselling.' In *Soul Searching: Studies in Judaism and Psychotherapy*, ed. Howard Cooper, 143–8. London: SCM.

Maier, Johann. 1985. *The Temple Scroll: An Introduction, Translation & Commentary.* JSOTSS no. 34. Sheffield: JSOT Press.

Mairson, Alan. 1996. 'The Three Faces of Jerusalem.' *National Geographic Magazine* April, 2–31.

Maitland, Sara. 1995. *A Big-Enough God: Artful Theology.* London: Mowbray.

Malherbe, Abraham J. 1976. 'Cynics.' In *Interpreter's Dictionary of the Bible, Supplementary Volume*, 201–3. Nashville, Tenn.

―――, ed. 1977. *The Cynic Epistles: A Study Edition.* Missoula, Mont.: Scholars Press.

―――. 1989. *Paul and the Popular Philosophers.* Minneapolis: Fortress.

Malina, Bruce J. 1993. *Windows on the World of Jesus: Time Travel to Ancient Judea.* Louisville, Ky.: Westminster/John Knox.

Malina, Bruce J., and Jerome H. Neyrey. 1988. *Calling Jesus Names: The Social Value of Labels in Matthew.* Sonoma, Calif.: Polebridge Press.

Malina, Bruce J., and Richard L. Rohrbaugh. 1992. *Social-Science Commentary on the Synoptic Gospels.* Minneapolis: Fortress.

Manson, T. W. 1931. *The Teaching of Jesus: Studies of Its Form and Content.* Cambridge: CUP.

―――. 1953. *The Servant-Messiah: A Study of the Public Ministry of Jesus.* Cambridge: CUP.

Marcus, Joel. 1986. *The Mystery of the Kingdom of God.* SBL Dissertation Series, vol. 90. Atlanta, Ga.: Scholars Press.

Marshall, I. Howard. 1969. 'Uncomfortable Words VI. "Fear Him Who Can Destroy Both Soul and Body in Hell"' (Mt. 10:28 RSV).' *Expository Times* 81:276–80.

―――. 1978. *The Gospel of Luke: A Commentary on the Greek Text.* Exeter: Paternoster.

Martyn, J. Louis. 1979 [1968]. *History and Theology in the Fourth Gospel.* Nashville: Abingdon.

Mason, Steve. 1992. 'Fire, Water and Spirit: John the Baptist and the Tyranny of Canon.' *Studies in Religion/Sciences Religieuses* 21:163–80.

Massyngberde Ford, J. 1975. *Revelation: Introduction, Translation and Commentary.* Garden City, N. Y.: Doubleday.

Matson, Mark A. 1992. 'The Contribution to the Temple Cleansing by the Fourth Gospel.' In *SBL 1992 Seminar Papers*, ed. Eugene H. Lovering, 489–506. Atlanta, Ga.: Scholars Press.

Maxtone Graham, Ysenda. 1993. *The Church Hesitant: A Portrait of the Church of England Today*. London: Hodder & Stoughton.

Meeks, Wayne A. 1968. 'Moses as God and King.' In *Religions in Antiquity: Essays in Memory of Erwin Ramsdell Goodenough*, ed. Jacob Neusner, 354-71. Leiden: Brill.

Meier, John P. 1991. *A Marginal Jew: Rethinking the Historical Jesus*. Vol. 1. *The Roots of the Problem and the Person*. New York: Doubleday.

————. 1994. *A Marginal Jew: Rethinking the Historical Jesus*. Vol. 2. *Mentor, Message, and Miracles*. New York: Doubleday.

Melanchthon, Philipp. 1982 [OUP, 1965]. *Melanchthon on Christian Doctrine: Loci Communes 1555*. Ed. and trans. C. L. Manschreck. Grand Rapids, Mich.: Baker Book House.

Mendels, D. 1981. 'The Five Empires. A Note on a Hellenistic Topos.' *American Journal of Philology* 102:330-7.

————. 1992. 'Pseudo-Philo's *Biblical Antiquities*, the "Fourth Philosophy," and the Political Messianism of the First Century C.E.' In *The Messiah: Developments in Earliest Judaism and Christianity*, ed. J. H. Charlesworth, 261-75. Minneapolis: Fortress.

Metzger, B. M. 1971. *A Textual Commentary on the Greek New Testament*. London and New York: United Bible Societies.

Meyer, Ben F. 1979. *The Aims of Jesus*. London: SCM.

————. 1986. *The Early Christians: Their World Mission and Self-Discovery*. Wilmington, Del.: Michael Glazier.

————. 1987. 'The World Mission and the Emergent Realization of Christian Identity.' In *Jesus, the Gospels, and the Church: Essays in Honor of William R. Farmer*, ed. E. P. Sanders, 243-63. Macon, Ga.: Mercer U. P.

————. 1989. *Critical Realism and the New Testament*. Princeton Theological Monograph Series, vol. 17. Allison Park, Pa.: Pickwick Publications.

————. 1991. 'A Caricature of Joachim Jeremias and His Work.' *Journal of Biblical Literature* 110:451-62.

————. 1992a. *Christus Faber: The Master-Builder and the House of God*. Allison Park, Penn.: Pickwick Publications.

————. 1992b. 'Jesus Christ.' In *ABD* 3:773-96.

————. 1993. Review of Crossan 1991. *Catholic Biblical Quarterly* 55:575-6.

Meyer, Marvin W. 1985. 'Making Mary Male: The Categories "Male" and "Female" in the Gospel of Thomas.' *New Testament Studies* 31:554-70.

Meyers, Carol. 1992. 'Temple, Jerusalem.' In *ABD* 6:350-69.

Michel, O. 1967. 'οἶκος κ.τ.λ.' In *TDNT*, vol. 5, 119-59. Grand Rapids, Mich.: Eerdmans.

————. 1968. 'Studien zu Josephus: Simon bar Giora.' *New Testament Studies* 14:402-8.

Milbank, John. 1990. *Theology and Social Theory: Beyond Secular Reason*. Oxford: Blackwell.

Milikowsky, C. 1988. 'Which Gehenna? Retribution and Eschatology in the Synoptic Gospels and in Early Jewish Texts.' *New Testament Studies* 34:238-49.

Millar, Fergus. 1993. *The Roman Near East, 31 BC - AD 337*. Cambridge, Mass., and London: Harvard U. P.

Miller, John W. 1985. 'Jesus' "Age Thirty Transition": A Psychohistorical Probe.' In *SBL 1985 Seminar Papers*, ed. K. H. Richards, 45-56. Atlanta, Ga.: Scholars Press.

Miller, Robert J. 1991. 'The (A)historicity of Jesus' Temple Demonstration: A Test Case in Methodology.' In *SBL 1991 Seminar Papers*, ed. Eugene H. Lovering, 235-52. Atlanta, Ga.: Scholars Press.

————, ed. 1992 [1991]. *The Complete Gospels: Annotated Scholars Version*. Sonoma, Calif.: Polebridge Press.

Montefiore, C. G., and H. Loewe, compilers. 1974 [1938]. *A Rabbinic Anthology*. New York: Schocken Books.

Montgomery, James A. 1927. *A Critical and Exegetical Commentary on the Book of Daniel.* International Critical Commentary. Edinburgh: T. & T. Clark.

Moore, A. L. 1966. *The Parousia in the New Testament.* Supplements to *Novum Testamentum,* no. 13. Leiden: Brill.

Moore, George Foot. 1927-30. *Judaism in the First Centuries of the Christian Era: The Age of the Tannaim.* 3 vols. Cambridge, Mass.: Harvard U. P.

Morgan, Robert. 1987. 'The Historical Jesus and the Theology of the New Testament.' In *The Glory of Christ in the New Testament: Studies in Christology in Memory of George Bradford Caird,* ed. L. D. Hurst and N. T. Wright, 187-206. Oxford: Clarendon.

Moule, C. F. D. 1967. *The Phenomenon of the New Testament: An Inquiry Into the Implications of Certain Features of the New Testament.* London: SCM.

————. 1969. 'Mark 4:1-20 Yet Once More.' In *Neotestamentica et Semitica: Studies in Honour of Matthew Black,* ed. E. E. Ellis and M. Wilcox, 95-113. Edinburgh: T. & T. Clark.

————. 1977. *The Origin of Christology.* Cambridge: CUP.

————. 1984. 'Some Observations on *Tendenzkritik.*' In *Jesus and the Politics of His Day,* ed. E. Bammel and C. F. D. Moule, 91-100. Cambridge: CUP.

————. 1987. 'The Gravamen Against Jesus.' In *Jesus, the Gospels, and the Church: Essays in Honor of William R. Farmer,* ed. E. P. Sanders, 177-95. Macon, Ga.: Mercer U. P.

Muddiman, John. 1987. 'The Glory of Jesus, Mark 10:37.' In *The Glory of Christ in the New Testament: Studies in Christology in Memory of George Bradford Caird,* ed. L. D. Hurst and N. T. Wright, 51-8. Oxford: Clarendon.

Murphy-O'Connor, J. 1990. 'John the Baptist and Jesus: History and Hypotheses.' *New Testament Studies* 36:359-74.

Myers, Ched. 1990 [1988]. *Binding the Strong Man: A Political Reading of Mark's Story of Jesus.* Maryknoll, N. Y.: Orbis.

Neale, D. 1993. 'Was Jesus a *Mesith*? Public Response to Jesus and His Ministry.' *Tyndale Bulletin* 44(1):89-101.

Neill, Stephen C., and N. Thomas Wright. 1988 [1964]. *The Interpretation of the New Testament, 1861-1986.* Oxford: OUP.

Neirynck, F. 1994. 'The Historical Jesus: Reflections on an Inventory.' *Ephemerides Theologicae Lovanienses* 70:221-34.

Neubauer, A., and S. R. Driver. 1876-77. *The Fifty-Third Chapter of Isaiah According to the Jewish Interpreters.*

Neusner, Jacob. 1970. *A Life of Johanan Ben Zakkai.* Studia Post-Biblica, vol. 6. Leiden: Brill.

————. 1989. 'Money-Changers in the Temple: The Mishnah's Explanation.' *New Testament Studies* 35:287-90.

————. 1991. *Jews and Christians: The Myth of a Common Tradition.* London: SCM; Philadelphia: TPI.

————. 1993. *A Rabbi Talks with Jesus: An Intermillenial, Interfaith Exchange.* New York: Doubleday.

Neusner, Jacob, W. S. Green, and E. Frerichs, eds. 1987. *Judaisms and Their Messiahs at the Turn of the Christian Era.* Cambridge: CUP.

Neyrey, Jerome H., ed. 1991. *The Social World of Luke-Acts: Models for Interpretation.* Peabody, Mass.: Hendrickson.

————. 1992. 'A Review of *The Historical Jesus*: The Use of the Social Sciences in Crossan's Reconstruction.' Unpublished Paper. San Francisco.

Nickelsburg, George W. E. 1992. 'Son of Man.' In *ABD* 6:137-50.

Nietzsche, Friedrich. 1909-13. *The Complete Works of Friedrich Nietzsche.* Ed. O. Levy. 18 vols. London: Allen & Unwin.

Noble, Paul R. 1993. 'The *Sensus Literalis*: Jowett, Childs, and Barr.' *Journal of Theological Studies* 44(1):1–23.

Nolland, John. 1989. *Luke 1–9:20*. Dallas, Tex.: Word Books.

———. 1993. *Luke 9:21–18:34*. Dallas, Tex.: Word Books.

North, C. R. 1948. *The Suffering Servant in Deutero-Isaiah: An Historical and Critical Study*. London: OUP.

O'Collins, Gerald. 1995. *Christology: A Biblical, Historical, and Systematic Study of Jesus*. Oxford: OUP.

O'Donovan, Oliver M. T. 1986. *Resurrection and Moral Order: An Outline for Evangelical Ethics*. Leicester: IVP; Grand Rapids, Mich.: Eerdmans.

O'Malley, P. 1979. 'Social Bandits, Modern Capitalism and the Traditional Peasantry. A Critique of Hobsbawm.' *Journal of Peasant Studies* 7:489–99.

O'Neill, John C. 1980. *Messiah: Six Lectures on the Ministry of Jesus*. Cambridge: Cochrane Press.

———. 1991a. *The Bible's Authority: A Portrait Gallery of Thinkers from Lessing to Bultmann*. Edinburgh: T. & T. Clark.

———. 1991b. 'The Lost Written Records of Jesus' Words and Deeds Behind Our Records.' *Journal of Theological Studies* 42:483–504.

———. 1995. *Who Did Jesus Think He Was?* Leiden: Brill.

O'Toole, Robert F. 1992. 'Last Supper.' In *ABD* 4:234–41.

Oakman, Douglas E. 1986. *Jesus and the Economic Questions of His Day*. Studies in the Bible and Early Christianity, vol. 8. Lewiston/Queenston: Edwin Mellen Press.

Ong, Walter J. 1970. *The Presence of the Word: Some Prolegomena for Cultural and Religious History*. New York: Simon & Schuster.

———. 1982. *Orality and Literacy: The Technologizing of the Word*. London and New York: Methuen.

Oppenheimer, A. 1977. *The Am Ha-Aretz. A Study of the Social History of the Jewish People in the Hellenistic-Roman Period*. Leiden: Brill.

Otto, Rudolf. 1984 [1938]. 'The Kingdom of God Expels the Kingdom of Satan.' In *The Kingdom of God*, ed. Bruce D. Chilton, 27–35. London: SPCK; Philadelphia: Fortress.

Overman, J. Andrew. 1990. 'Deciphering the Origins of Christianity.' *Interpretation* 44:193–5.

Pagels, E. 1991. 'The Social History of Satan, the "Intimate Enemy": A Preliminary Sketch.' *Harvard Theological Review* 84:105–28.

———. 1994. 'The Social History of Satan, Part II: Satan in the New Testament Gospels.' *Journal of the American Academy of Religion* 62:17–58.

Painter, John. 1987. *Theology as Hermeneutics: Rudolf Bultmann's Interpretation of the History of Jesus*. Sheffield: The Almond Press.

Pamment, Margaret. 1981. 'The Kingdom of Heaven According to the First Gospel.' *New Testament Studies* 27:211–32.

Parker, Pierson. 1987. 'Herod Antipas and the Death of Jesus.' In *Jesus, the Gospels, and the Church: Essays in Honor of William R. Farmer*, ed. E. P. Sanders, 197–208. Macon, Ga.: Mercer U. P.

Patterson, Stephen J. 1989. 'Fire and Dissension: Ipsissima Vox Jesu in Q 12:49, 51–53?' *Foundations & Facets Forum* 5(2):121–39.

Payne, Philip B. 1980a. 'The Authenticity of the Parable of the Sower and Its Interpretation.' In *Gospel Perspectives: Studies of History and Tradition in the Four Gospels*, ed. R. T. France and David Wenham, vol. 1, 163–207. Sheffield: JSOT Press.

———. 1980b. 'The Seeming Inconsistency of the Interpretation of the Parable of the Sower.' *New Testament Studies* 26:564–8.

Penney, Douglas L., and Michael O. Wise. 1994. 'By the Power of Beelzebub: An Aramaic Inscription Formula from Qumran (4Q560).' *Journal of Biblical Literature* 113:627-50.

Perez, L. A. 1989. *Lords of the Mountain: Social Banditry and Peasant Protest in Cuba 1878-1918.* Pittsburgh, Pa.: University of Pittsburgh Press.

Perkins, Pheme. 1981. *Hearing the Parables of Jesus.* New York: Paulist.

Perrin, N., and D. C. Duling. 1982 [1974]. *The New Testament: An Introduction.* New York: Harcourt Brace Jovanovich.

Perrin, Norman. 1963. *The Kingdom of God in the Teaching of Jesus.* Philadelphia: Fortress.

—————. 1966. 'The Wredestrasse Becomes the Hauptstrasse: Reflections on the Reprinting of the Dodd Festschrift.' *Journal of Religion* 46:296-300.

—————. 1967. *Rediscovering the Teaching of Jesus.* London: SCM.

—————. 1970. *What is Redaction Criticism?* London: SPCK.

—————. 1976. *Jesus and the Language of the Kingdom: Symbol and Metaphor in New Testament Interpretation.* London: SCM; Philadelphia: Fortress.

Pesch, R. 1968. 'Levi-Matthäus (Mc 2,14/Mt 9,9; 10,3): Ein Beitrag zur Lösung eines alten Problems.' *Zeitschrift für die Neutestamentliche Wissenschaft* 59:40-56.

Phillips, Catherine, ed. 1986. *The Oxford Authors: Gerard Manley Hopkins.* Oxford: OUP.

Polkinghorne, John. 1994. *Science and Christian Belief: Theological Reflections of a Bottom-Up Thinker.* London: SPCK.

Porteous, Norman W. 1965. *Daniel: A Commentary.* London: SCM.

Porter, Stanley E. 1993. 'Did Jesus Ever Teach in Greek?' *Tyndale Bulletin* 44:199-235.

Prentis, Richard H. 1996. 'A View from the Old Organ Lofts.' *Friends of Lichfield Cathedral: Annual Report* 59:25-33.

Priest, J. 1992. 'A Note on the Messianic Banquet.' In *The Messiah: Developments in Earliest Judaism and Christianity,* ed. J. H. Charlesworth, 222-38. Minneapolis: Fortress.

Puech, Emile. 1992. 'Une apocalypse messianique (4Q521).' *Revue de Qumran* 15:475-519.

Quell, G. 1967. 'πατήρ κ.τ.λ. [sections A & B].' In *TDNT,* vol. 5, 945-74. Grand Rapids, Mich.: Eerdmans.

Rajak, Tessa. 1983. *Josephus: The Historian and His Society.* London: Duckworth; Philadelphia: Fortress.

Räisänen, H. 1982. 'Jesus and the Food Laws: Reflections on Mark 7.15.' *Journal for the Study of the New Testament* 16:79-100.

Reimarus, H. S. 1970 [1778]. *Fragments.* Ed. Charles H. Talbert. Philadelphia: Fortress.

Reinhartz, A. 1989. 'Rabbinic Perceptions of Simeon Bar Kosiba.' *Journal for the Study of Judaism* 20:171-94.

Remus, Harold E. 1983. *Pagan-Christian Conflict Over Miracle in the Second Century.* Patristic Monograph Series, no. 10. Cambridge, Mass.: The Philadelphia Patristic Foundation.

—————. 1992. 'Miracles (NT).' In *ABD* 4:856-69.

Renan, E. 1863. *La Vie de Jésus.* Paris: Michel Lévy Frères.

Reumann, John. 1989. 'Jesus and Christology.' In *The Bible and Its Modern Interpreters,* ed. Douglas A. Knight, vol. 3. *The New Testament and Its Modern Interpreters,* ed. E. J. Epp and G. W. MacRae, 501-64. Atlanta, Ga.: Scholars Press.

Rey-Coquais, Jean-Paul. 1992. 'Decapolis.' In *ABD* 2:116-21.

Richardson, G. Peter. 1992. 'Why Turn the Tables? Jesus' Protest in the Temple Precincts.' In *SBL 1992 Seminar Papers,* ed. Eugene H. Lovering, 507-23. Atlanta, Ga.: Scholars Press.

Riches, John K. 1980. *Jesus and the Transformation of Judaism.* London: Darton, Longman & Todd.

————. 1988. 'Parables and the Search for a New Community.' In *The Social World of Formative Christianity and Judaism: Essays in Tribute to Howard Clark Kee*, ed. J. Neusner, P. Borgen, E. S. Frerichs, and R. Horsley, 235-63. Philadelphia: Fortress.

Richler, Mordecai. 1995. *This Year in Jerusalem*. Toronto: Vintage Canada.

Riesenfeld, Harald. 1970. *The Gospel Tradition*. Philadelphia: Fortress.

Riesner, Rainer. 1984 [1981]. *Jesus als Lehrer*. Wissenschaftliche Untersuchungen zum Neuen Testament. Tübingen: Mohr.

Rivkin, Ellis. 1978. *A Hidden Revolution*. Nashville: Abingdon.

————. 1984. *What Crucified Jesus?* London: SCM; Nashville: Abingdon.

Roberts, C. H. 1948. 'The Kingdom of Heaven (Lk. xvii.21).' *Harvard Theological Review* 41:1-8.

Robinson, James M. 1959. *A New Quest of the Historical Jesus*. London: SCM.

Robinson, James M., and Helmut Koester. 1971. *Trajectories Through Early Christianity*. Philadelphia: Fortress.

Robinson, John A. T. 1962. *Twelve New Testament Studies*. London: SCM.

————. 1979 [1957]. *Jesus and His Coming: The Emergence of a Doctrine*. London: SCM.

————. 1984. *Twelve More New Testament Studies*. London: SCM.

————. 1985. *The Priority of John*, ed. J. F. Coakley. London: SCM.

Roth, C. 1960. 'The Cleansing of the Temple and Zechariah XIV 21.' *Novum Testamentum* 4:174-81.

Rowland, Christopher C. 1982. *The Open Heaven: A Study of Apocalyptic in Judaism and Early Christianity*. New York: Crossroad.

————. 1991. 'The Second Temple: Focus of Ideological Struggle?' In *Templum Amicitiae: Essays on the Second Temple Presented to Ernst Bammel*, ed. W. Horbury, 175-98. JSNTSS vol. 48. Sheffield: JSOT Press.

Ruether, Rosemary R. 1974. *Faith and Fratricide: The Theological Roots of Anti-Semitism*. New York: Seabury Press.

Runnalls, Donna R. 1983. 'The King as Temple-Builder.' In *Spirit Within Structure: Essays in Honor of George Johnston on the Occasion of His Seventieth Birthday*, ed. E. J. Furcha, 15-37. Allison Park, Pa.: Pickwick Press.

Rüstow, A. 1960. '*Entos hymon estin*: Zur Deutung von Lukas 17.20-21.' *Zeitschrift für die neutestamentliche Wissenschaft* 51:197-224.

Safrai, S. 1974. 'Jewish Self-Government.' In *Compendia Rerum Iudaicarum Ad Novum Testamentum*, vol. 1. *The Jewish People in the First Century: Historical Geography, Political History, Social, Cultural and Religious Life and Institutions*, ed. S. Safrai and M. Stern, 377-419. Philadelphia: Fortress.

————. 1976a. 'Home and Family.' In *Compendia Rerum Iudaicarum Ad Novum Testamentum*, vol. 2. *The Jewish People in the First Century: Historical Geography, Political History, Social, Cultural and Religious Life and Institutions*, ed. S. Safrai and M. Stern. 728-92. Philadelphia: Fortress.

————. 1976b. 'Religion in Everyday Life.' In *Compendia Rerum Iudaicarum Ad Novum Testamentum*, vol. 2. *The Jewish People in the First Century: Historical Geography, Political History, Social, Cultural and Religious Life and Institutions*, ed. S. Safrai and M. Stern, 793-833. Philadelphia: Fortress.

————. 1976c. 'The Synagogue.' In *Compendia Rerum Iudaicarum Ad Novum Testamentum*, vol. 2. *The Jewish People in the First Century: Historical Geography, Political History, Social, Cultural and Religious Life and Institutions*, ed. S. Safrai and M. Stern, 908-44. Philadelphia: Fortress.

Safrai, Ze'ev. 1992. 'The Roman Army in the Galilee.' In *The Galilee in Late Antiquity*, ed. Lee I. Levine, 103-14. New York and Jerusalem: The Jewish Theological Seminary of America.

————. 1994. *The Economy of Roman Palestine*. London and New York: Routledge.

Saldarini, Anthony J. 1988. *Pharisees, Scribes and Sadducees in Palestinian Society*. Wilmington, Del.: Michael Glazier; Edinburgh: T. & T. Clark.

Sanders, E. P. 1977. *Paul and Palestinian Judaism: A Comparison of Patterns of Religion*. Philadelphia: Fortress; London: SCM.

————. 1983a. *Paul, the Law, and the Jewish People*. London: SCM; Philadelphia: Fortress.

————. 1983b. 'Jesus and the Sinners.' *Journal for the Study of the New Testament* 19:5–36.

————. 1985. *Jesus and Judaism*. Philadelphia: Fortress; London: SCM.

————. 1987. 'Jesus and the Kingdom: The Restoration of Israel and the New People of God.' In *Jesus, the Gospels, and the Church: Essays in Honor of William R. Farmer*, ed. E. P. Sanders, 225–39. Macon, Ga.: Mercer U. P.

————. 1990. *Jewish Law from Jesus to the Mishnah: Five Studies*. London: SCM; Philadelphia: TPI.

————. 1991. 'Defending the Indefensible.' *Journal of Biblical Literature* 110:463–77.

————. 1992a. 'Sin, Sinners (NT).' In *ABD* 6:40–7.

————. 1992b. *Judaism: Practice and Belief, 63 BCE – 66 CE*. London: SCM; Philadelphia: TPI.

————. 1993. *The Historical Figure of Jesus*. London: Penguin Books.

Sanders, J. T. 1969. 'Tradition and Redaction in Luke xv.11–32.' *New Testament Studies* 15:433–8.

Sanders, James A. 1992. 'Canon (Hebrew Bible).' In *ABD* 1:837–52.

Schäfer, Peter. 1980. 'Rabbi Aqiva and Bar Kokhba.' In *Approaches to Ancient Judaism*, ed. W. S. Green, 113–30. Chico, Calif.: Scholars Press.

Schechter, S. 1961 [1909]. *Aspects of Rabbinic Theology: Major Concepts of the Talmud*. New York: Schocken Books.

Schiffman, Lawrence H. 1994. *Reclaiming the Dead Sea Scrolls: Their True Meaning for Judaism and Christianity*. New York: Doubleday.

Schillebeeckx, Edward. 1979 [1974]. *Jesus: An Experiment in Christology*. New York: Seabury Press.

————. 1980 [1977]. *Christ: The Christian Experience in the Modern World*. London: SCM.

Schnackenburg, Rudolf. 1990 [1975]. *The Gospel According to St. John*. New York: Crossroad.

————. 1995 [1993]. *Jesus in the Gospels: A Biblical Christology*. Louisville, Ky.: Westminster/John Knox.

Schulz, Siegfried. 1972. *Q. Die Spruchquelle der Evangelisten*. Zürich: Theologischer Verlag.

Schürer, E. 1973–87. *The History of the Jewish People in the Age of Jesus Christ (175 B.C.– A.D. 135)*. Revised and ed. M. Black, G. Vermes, F. Millar, and M. Goodman. 3 vols. Edinburgh: T. & T. Clark.

Schüssler Fiorenza, Elisabeth. 1983. *In Memory of Her: A Feminist Theological Reconstruction of Christian Origins*. New York: Crossroad.

————. 1994. *Jesus. Miriam's Child, Sophia's Prophet: Critical Issues in Feminist Christology*. London: SCM.

Schwarz, D. 1981. '"To Join Oneself to the House of Judah," (Damascus Document IV,11).' *Révue de Qumran* 10:435–46.

Schweitzer, Albert. 1925 [1901]. *The Mystery of the Kingdom of God*. London: A. & C. Black.

————. 1954 [1906]. *The Quest of the Historical Jesus: A Critical Study of its Progress from Reimarus to Wrede*. London: A. & C. Black.

————. 1968a [1967]. *The Kingdom of God and Primitive Christianity*. London: A. & C. Black.

————. 1968b [1930]. *The Mysticism of Paul the Apostle*. London: A. & C. Black; New York: Seabury Press.

Scobie, C. H. H. 1964. *John the Baptist*. London: SCM.

Scott, B. B. 1983. *Jesus, Symbol-Maker for the Kingdom*. Philadelphia: Fortress.

————. 1989. *Hear Then the Parable*. Minneapolis: Fortress.

————. 1990. 'Jesus as Sage: An Innovating Voice in Common Wisdom.' In *The Sage in Israel and the Ancient Near East*, ed. J. G. Gammie and L. G. Perdue, 399–415. Winona Lake, Wis.: Eisenbrauns.

Scott, James M. 1993. 'Paul's Use of Deuteronomistic Tradition.' *Journal of Biblical Literature* 112:645–65.

Seeley, David. 1992. 'Jesus' Death in Q.' *New Testament Studies* 38:222–34.

————. 1993. 'Rulership and Service in Mark 10:41–45.' *Novum Testamentum* 35:234–50.

Segal, Alan F. 1977. *Two Powers in Heaven: Early Rabbinic Reports About Christianity and Gnosticism*. Leiden: Brill.

————. 1984. '"He Who Did not Spare His Own Son . . .": Jesus, Paul and the Akedah.' In *From Jesus to Paul: Studies in Honour of Francis Wright Beare*, ed. P. Richardson & J. C. Hurd, 169–84. Waterloo, Ontario: Wilfrid Laurier U. P.

Segundo, J. L. 1985. *Jesus of Nazareth Yesterday and Today*. Vol. 2. *The Historical Jesus of the Synoptics*. Trans. John Drury. London: Sheed & Ward.

Sellin, G. 1974/1975. 'Lukas als Gleichniserzähler: Die Erzählung vom barmherzigen Samariter (Lk 10:25–27).' *Zeitschrift für die neutestamentliche Wissenschaft* 65:166–89; 66:19–60.

Shaffer, Peter. 1985 [1980]. *Amadeus*. London: Penguin Books.

Shaw, Brent D. 1984. 'Bandits in the Roman Empire.' *Past and Present* 105:5–52.

Sherwin-White, Adrian N. 1969 [1963]. *Roman Society and Roman Law in the New Testament*. Oxford: OUP.

Shogren, Gary S. 1992. 'Forgiveness (NT).' In *ABD* 2:835–8.

Sloan, Robert B. 1977. *The Favorable Year of the Lord: A Study of Jubilary Theology in the Gospel of Luke*. Austin, Tex.: Schola Press.

Smalley, Stephen S. 1994. *Thunder and Love: John's Revelation and John's Community*. Milton Keynes: Nelson Word.

Smith, D. Moody. 1990. 'The Contribution of J. Louis Martyn to the Understanding of the Gospel of John.' In *The Conversation Continues: Studies in Paul and John in Honor of J. Louis Martyn*, ed. Robert T. Fortna and Beverly R. Gaventa, 275–94. Nashville: Abingdon.

Smith, Morton. 1973. *Clement of Alexandria and a Secret Gospel of Mark*. Cambridge, Mass.: Harvard U. P.

————. 1977 [1956]. 'Palestinian Judaism in the First Century.' In *Essays in Greco-Roman and Related Talmudic Literature*, ed. H. Fischel, 183–97. New York: Ktav.

————. 1978. *Jesus the Magician*. London: Gollancz.

Smith, R. H. 1992. 'Pella.' In *ABD* 5:219–21.

Smith, Ralph L. 1984. *Micah–Malachi*. Waco, Tex.: Word Books.

Snodgrass, Klyne. 1983. *The Parable of the Wicked Tenants*. Wissenschaftliche Untersuchungen zum Neuen Testament, no. 27. Tübingen: Mohr.

Soards, M. L. 1987. 'Tradition, Composition, and Theology in Jesus' Speech to the "Daughters of Jerusalem" (Luke 23,26–32).' *Biblica* 68:221–44.

Solomon, Maynard. 1988. *Beethoven Essays*. Cambridge, Mass.: Harvard U. P.

Sommer, Benjamin D. 1996. 'Did Prophecy Cease? Evaluating a Reevaluation.' *Journal of Biblical Literature* 115:31–47.

Sparks, H. F. D., ed. 1984. *The Apocryphal Old Testament*. Oxford: Clarendon.

Stanton, Graham N. 1989. *The Gospels and Jesus*. Oxford: OUP.

————. 1994. 'Jesus of Nazareth: A Magician and a False Prophet Who Deceived God's People?' In *Jesus of Nazareth: Lord and Christ. Essays on the Historical Jesus and New Testament Christology*, ed. Joel B. Green and Max Turner, 164–80. Grand Rapids, Mich.: Eerdmans; Carlisle: Paternoster.

Stauffer, Ethelbert. 1960. *Jesus and His Story*. London: SCM.

Stein, Robert H. 1981. *An Introduction to the Parables of Jesus*. Philadelphia: Westminster.

Steiner, George. 1996. *No Passion Spent: Essays 1978–1996*. London and Boston: Faber.

Stern, Menahem. 1974–84. *Greek and Latin Authors on Jews and Judaism*. Jerusalem: Israel Academy of Sciences and Humanities.

————. 1976. 'The Jews in Greek and Latin Literature.' In *Compendia Rerum Iudaicarum Ad Novum Testamentum*, vol. 2. *The Jewish People in the First Century: Historical Geography, Political History, Social, Cultural and Religious Life and Institutions*, ed. S. Safrai and M. Stern, 1101–59. Philadelphia: Fortress.

Stone, Michael E. 1990. *Fourth Ezra: A Commentary on the Book of Fourth Ezra*. Minneapolis: Augsburg Fortress.

Stowers, Stanley K. 1984. 'Social Status, Public Speaking and Private Teaching: The Circumstances of Paul's Preaching.' *Novum Testamentum* 26:59–82.

Strauss, David Friedrich. 1972 [1835–36]. *The Life of Jesus Critically Examined*. Philadelphia: Fortress.

Strecker, Georg. 1988. *The Sermon on the Mount: An Exegetical Commentary*. Edinburgh: T. & T. Clark.

Strobel, A. 1961. *Untersuchungen zum eschatologischen Verzögerungsproblem, auf Grund der spätjüdisch-urchristlichen Geschichte von Habakuk 2,2 ff*. Supplements to *Novum Testamentum*. Leiden: Brill.

————. 1980. *Die Stunde der Wahrheit*. Tübingen: Mohr.

Stuhlmacher, Peter. 1968. *Das paulinische Evangelium: I. Vorgeschichte*. Forschungen zum Religion und Literatur des Alten und Neuen Testaments, vol. 95. Göttingen: Vandenhoek und Ruprecht.

————. 1986 [1981]. *Reconciliation, Law and Righteousness: Essays in Biblical Theology*. Philadelphia: Fortress.

Sweet, John P. M. 1984. 'The Zealots and Jesus.' In *Jesus and the Politics of His Day*, ed. E. Bammel and C. F. D. Moule, 1–10. Cambridge: CUP.

Talbert, C. H. 1992. *Reading Luke: A Literary and Theological Commentary on the Third Gospel*. New York: Crossroad.

Tannehill, Robert C. 1985 [1977]. 'The Disciples in Mark: The Function of a Narrative Role.' In *The Interpretation of Mark*, ed. W. R. Telford. Philadelphia: Fortress; London: SPCK.

Tatum, W. Barnes. 1982. *In Quest of Jesus: A Guidebook*. Atlanta: John Knox.

Taussig, Hal. 1986. 'The Jesus Seminar and Its Public.' *Foundations and Facets Forum* 2(2):69–78.

Taylor, Justin. 1994. 'Why Were the Disciples First Called "Christians" at Antioch?' *Revue Biblique* 101:75–94.

Taylor, L. 1987. *Bandits and Politics in Peru: Landlord and Peasant Violence in Hualgayoc 1900–30*. Cambridge: Centre of Latin American Studies, University of Cambridge.

Taylor, Vincent. 1952. *The Gospel According to St. Mark: The Greek Text with Introduction, Notes, and Indexes*. London: Macmillan.

Telford, W. R. 1980. *The Barren Temple and the Withered Tree*. JSNTSS vol. 1. Sheffield: JSOT Press.

Thatcher, Adrian. 1993. 'Resurrection and Rationality.' In *The Resurrection of Jesus Christ*, ed. Paul Avis, 171–86. London: Darton, Longman & Todd.

Theissen, Gerd. 1978 [1977]. *Sociology of Early Palestinian Christianity.* [English Title *The First Followers of Jesus*]. Philadelphia: Fortress; London: SCM.

―――――. 1983. *The Miracle Stories of Early Christian Tradition.* Trans. Francis McDonagh. Ed. John Riches. Philadelphia: Fortress.

―――――. 1987 [1986]. *The Shadow of the Galilean: The Quest of the Historical Jesus in Narrative Form.* London: SCM.

―――――. 1991a [1989]. *The Gospels in Context: Social and Political History in the Synoptic Tradition.* Minneapolis: Fortress.

―――――. 1991b. *The Open Door: Variations on Biblical Themes.* London: SCM; Minneapolis: Fortress.

Thielicke, Helmut. 1960. *The Waiting Father: Sermons on the Parables of Jesus.* Cambridge: James Clark.

Thiselton, Anthony C. 1980. *The Two Horizons: New Testament Hermeneutics and Philosophical Description with Special Reference to Heidegger, Bultmann, Gadamer and Wittgenstein.* Exeter: Paternoster.

―――――. 1995. *Interpreting God and the Postmodern Self: On Meaning, Manipulation and Promise.* Edinburgh: T. & T. Clark.

Throckmorton, Burton H., ed. 1979 [1949]. *Gospel Parallels: A Synopsis of the First Three Gospels.* Nashville: Nelson.

Tiede, D. L. 1972. *The Charismatic Figure as Miracle Worker.* SBL Dissertation Series, vol. 1. Missoula, Mont.: Scholars Press.

Tillich, Paul. 1967. *On the Boundary.* London: Collins.

Trumbower, Jeffrey A. 1993. 'The Historical Jesus and the Speech of Gamaliel (Acts 5.35-9).' *New Testament Studies* 39:500-17.

Tuckett, Christopher M. 1989. 'A Cynic Q?' *Biblica* 70:349-76.

―――――. 1992. 'Q (Gospel Source).' In *ABD* 5:567-72.

Urbach, E. E. 1981. 'Self-Isolation or Self-Affirmation in Judaism in the First Three Centuries: Theory and Practice.' In *Jewish and Christian Self-Definition, Volume Two: Aspects of Judaism in the Greco-Roman Period*, ed. E. P. Sanders, A. I. Baumgarten, and Alan Mendelson, 269-98. Philadelphia: Fortress.

―――――. 1987 [1975, 1979]. *The Sages: Their Concepts and Beliefs.* Trans. I. Abrahams. Cambridge, Mass. and London: Harvard U. P.

Vaage, Leif E. 1987. *Q: The Ethos and Ethics of an Itinerant Intelligence.* Unpublished Dissertation. Claremont.

―――――. 1989. 'Q^1 and the Historical Jesus: Some Peculiar Sayings (7.33-34; 9:57-58; 59-60; 14:26-27).' *Foundations and Facets Forum* 5(2):159-76.

―――――. 1994. *Galilean Upstarts: Jesus' First Followers According to Q.* Valley Forge, Pa.: TPI.

van Beeck, F. J. 1994. 'The Quest of the Historical Jesus: Origins, Achievements, and the Specter of Diminishing Returns.' In *Jesus and Faith: A Conversation on the Work of John Dominic Crossan*, ed. Jeffrey Carlson and Robert A. Ludwig, 83-99. Maryknoll, N.Y.: Orbis.

Vancil, Jack W. 1992. 'Sheep, Shepherd.' In *ABD* 5:1187-90.

Vermes, G. 1967. 'The Use of נש בר/נשׁא בר in Jewish Aramaic.' Appendix E. In *An Aramaic Approach to the Gospels and Acts*, by M. Black. 3rd edn., 310-28. Oxford: OUP.

―――――. 1973. *Jesus the Jew: A Historian's Reading of the Gospels.* London: Collins.

―――――. 1981. *The Gospel of Jesus the Jew.* Newcastle: University of Newcastle upon Tyne.

―――――. 1983. *Jesus and the World of Judaism.* London: SCM.

―――――. 1993. *The Religion of Jesus the Jew.* London: SCM.

————. 1995 [1962]. *The Dead Sea Scrolls in English*. 4th edn. London: Penguin Books.

von Rad, Gerhard. 1965 [1960]. *Old Testament Theology*. Vol. 2. *The Theology of Israel's Prophetic Traditions*. New York: Harper & Row; Edinburgh: Oliver & Boyd.

Wallace-Hadrill, J. Michael. 1974. *The Vikings in Francia*. Stanton Lecture.

Wallis, Ian G. 1995. *The Faith of Jesus Christ in Early Christian Traditions*. SNTSMS vol. 84. Cambridge: CUP.

Wansbrough, Henry, ed. 1991. *Jesus and the Oral Gospel Tradition*. JSNTSS vol. 64. Sheffield: Sheffield Academic Press.

Watson, Duane F. 1992. 'Gehenna.' In *ABD* 2:926–8.

Weaver, Dorothy Jean. 1992. 'Transforming Nonresistance: From *Lex Talionis* to "Do not Resist the Evil One".' In *The Love of Enemy and Nonretaliation in the New Testament*, ed. Willard M. Swartley, 32–71. Louisville, Ky.: Westminster/John Knox.

Webb, Robert L. 1991. *John the Baptizer and Prophet: A Socio-Historical Study*. JSNTSS vol. 62. Sheffield: Sheffield Academic Press.

Weeden, T. J. 1971. *Mark – Traditions in Conflict*. Philadelphia: Fortress.

————. 1985 [1968]. 'The Heresy That Necessitated Mark's Gospel.' In *The Interpretation of Mark*, ed. W. R. Telford. Philadelphia: Fortress; London: SPCK.

Weinart, F. D. 1977. 'The Parable of the Throne Claimant [Luke 19:12, 14–15a, 27] Reconsidered.' *Catholic Biblical Quarterly* 39:505–14.

Weiss, Johannes. 1959. *Earliest Christianity: A History of the Period A.D. 30–150*. Vol. 1. New York: Harper & Brothers.

————. 1971 [1892]. *Jesus' Proclamation of the Kingdom of God*. London: SCM.

Wengst, Klaus. 1987 [1986]. *Pax Romana and the Peace of Jesus Christ*. London: SCM.

Wenham, David. 1984. *The Rediscovery of Jesus' Eschatological Discourse*. Gospel Perspectives, vol. 4. Sheffield: JSOT Press.

————. 1989. *The Parables of Jesus: Pictures of Revolution*. London: Hodder & Stoughton.

————. 1995. *Paul: Follower of Jesus or Founder of Christianity?* Grand Rapids, Mich.: Eerdmans.

Wenham, David, and Craig L. Blomberg, eds. 1986. *Gospel Perspectives*. Vol. 6. *The Miracles of Jesus*. Sheffield: JSOT Press.

Wenham, Gordon. 1982. 'Christ's Healing Ministry and His Attitude to the Law.' In *Christ the Lord: Studies in Christology Presented to Donald Guthrie*, ed. Harold H. Rowdon, 115–26. Leicester: IVP.

Wilder, Amos N. 1959. 'Eschatological Imagery and Earthly Circumstance.' *New Testament Studies* 5:229–45.

————. 1971 [1964]. *Early Christian Rhetoric: The Language of the Gospel*. Cambridge, Mass.: Harvard U. P.

————. 1982. *Jesus' Parables and the War of Myths: Essays on Imagination in the Scriptures*. London: SPCK; Philadelphia: Fortress.

Williams, Rowan D. 1994. *Open to Judgment: Sermons and Addresses*. London: Darton, Longman & Todd.

Willis, Wendell, ed. 1987. *The Kingdom of God in 20th-Century Interpretation*. Peabody, Mass.: Hendrikson.

Wilson, A. N. 1992. *Jesus*. London: Sinclair-Stevenson.

Wink, Walter. 1968. *John the Baptist in the Gospel Tradition*. SNTSMS vol. 7. Cambridge: CUP.

————. 1984. *Naming the Powers: The Language of Power in the New Testament*. The Powers, vol. 1. Philadelphia: Fortress.

————. 1986. *Unmasking the Powers: The Invisible Forces That Determine Human Existence*. The Powers, vol. 2. Philadelphia: Fortress.

————. 1992a. *Engaging the Powers: Discernment and Resistance in a World of Domination*. The Powers, vol. 3. Minneapolis: Fortress.

————. 1992b [1988]. 'Neither Passivity Nor Violence: Jesus' Third Way (Matt. 5:38–42 par.).' In *The Love of Enemy and Nonretaliation in the New Testament*, ed. Willard M. Swartley, 102–25. Louisville, Ky.: Westminster/John Knox.

————. 1992c. 'Counterresponse to Richard Horsley.' In *The Love of Enemy and Nonretaliation in the New Testament*, ed. Willard M. Swartley, 133–6. Louisville, Ky.: Westminster/John Knox.

Winter, Paul. 1974 [1961]. *On the Trial of Jesus*. Berlin: De Gruyter.

Wisse, Frederik. 1992. 'Sextus, Sentences Of.' In *ABD* 5:1146–7.

Witherington, Ben. 1985. 'Matthew 5.32 and 19.9 – Exception or Exceptional Situation?' *New Testament Studies* 31:571–6.

————. 1990. *The Christology of Jesus*. Minneapolis: Fortress.

————. 1992. *Jesus, Paul and the End of the World: A Comparative Study in New Testament Eschatology*. Downers Grove, Ill.: IVP; Exeter: Paternoster.

————. 1994. *Jesus the Sage: The Pilgrimage of Wisdom*. Minneapolis: Fortress.

————. 1995. *The Jesus Quest: The Third Search for the Jew of Nazareth*. Downers Grove, Ill.: IVP.

Wood, H. G. 1956. 'Interpreting This Time.' *New Testament Studies* 2:262–6.

Wrede, William. 1971 [1901]. *The Messianic Secret*. London and Cambridge: James Clarke; Greenwood, S. Carolina: Attic.

Wright, C. J. H. 1992. 'Jubilee, Year Of.' In *ABD* 3:1025–30.

————. 1995. *Walking in the Ways of the Lord*. Leicester: Apollos.

Wright, David P. 1992a. 'Day of Atonement.' In *ABD* 2:72–6.

————. 1992b. 'Holiness (OT).' In *ABD* 3:237–49.

Wright, N. T. 1980. 'Justification: The Biblical Basis and Its Relevance for Contemporary Evangelicalism.' In *The Great Acquittal: Justification by Faith and Current Christian Thought*, ed. G. Reid, 13–37. London: Collins.

————. 1982. 'Towards a Third "Quest": Jesus Then and Now.' *ARC* 10:20–7.

————. 1985. 'Jesus, Israel and the Cross.' In *SBL 1985 Seminar Papers*, ed. K. H. Richards, 75–95. Chico, Calif.: Scholars Press.

————. 1986. '"Constraints" and the Jesus of History.' *Scottish Journal of Theology* 39:189–210.

————. 1991. *The Climax of the Covenant: Christ and the Law in Pauline Theology*. Edinburgh: T. & T. Clark; Minneapolis: Fortress.

————. 1992a. *Christian Origins and the Question of God*. Vol. 1. *The New Testament and the People of God*. London: SPCK; Minneapolis: Fortress.

————. 1992b. 'Quest for the Historical Jesus.' In *ABD* 3:796–802.

————. 1992c. *Who Was Jesus?* London: SPCK; Grand Rapids, Mich.: Eerdmans.

————. 1992d. *New Tasks for a Renewed Church*. [USA title: *Bringing the Church to the World*.] London: Hodder & Stoughton; Minneapolis: Bethany House.

————. 1993. 'Taking the Text with Her Pleasure: A Post-Post-Modernist Response to J. Dominic Crossan's *The Historical Jesus: The Life of a Mediterranean Jewish Peasant*.' *Theology* 96:303–10.

————. 1994. 'Gospel and Theology in Galatians.' In *Gospel in Paul: Studies on Corinthians, Galatians and Romans for Richard N. Longenecker*, ed. L. Ann Jervis and Peter Richardson, 222–39. Sheffield: Sheffield Academic Press.

————. 1995a. 'Five Gospels but No Gospel: Jesus and the Seminar. A Critique of the *The Five Gospels: The Search for the Authentic Words of Jesus*, New Translation and Commentary by Robert W. Funk, Roy W. Hoover and the Jesus Seminar (New York: Macmillan, 1993).' In *Crisis in Christology: Essays in Quest of Resolution*, ed. W. R. Farmer, 115–57. Livonia, Mich.: Dove Booksellers.

————. 1995b. 'Two Radical Jews: Daniel Boyarin's *A Radical Jew.*' *Reviews in Religion and Theology* 3:15–23.

————. 1996a. 'Jesus.' In *Early Christian Thought in Its Jewish Context*. Ed. J. P. M. Sweet and John M. G. Barclay, 43–58. Cambridge: CUP.

————. 1996b. *The Lord and His Prayer*. London: SPCK

————. 1996c. 'Paul, Arabia and Elijah (Galatians 1:17).' *Journal of Biblical Literature* 115:683–92.

————. 1996d. 'How Jesus Saw Himself.' *Bible Review* 12 (June):22–9.

Yoder, John H. 1972. *The Politics of Jesus: Vicit Agnus Noster*. Grand Rapids, Mich.: Eerdmans.

Young, Brad H. 1989. *Jesus and His Jewish Parables: Rediscovering the Roots of Jesus' Teaching*. Mahway, N.J.: Paulist.

Young, Norman H. 1985. '"Jesus and the Sinners": Some Queries.' *Journal for the Study of the New Testament* 24:73–5.

Zahl, Paul F. M. 1983. 'The Historical Jesus and Substitutionary Atonement.' *Saint Luke's Journal of Theology* 26:313–32.

Zeitlin, Irving M. 1988. *Jesus and the Judaism of His Time*. Cambridge: Polity Press; Oxford: Basil Blackwell.

Zimmerli, W., and J. Jeremias. 1968. 'παῖς θεοῦ.' In *TDNT*, ed. G. Friedrich, vol. 5, 654–717. Grand Rapids: Eerdmans.

INDEX OF ANCIENT SOURCES

9. Other Early Christian and/or Gnostic Works

INDEX OF MODERN AUTHORS

398, 401, 406, 407,
408, 409, 413, 415,
417, 418, 419, 420,
422, 424, 425, 426,
431, 435, 440, 488,
491, 493, 512, 513,
520, 538, 542, 544,
548, 550, 553, 554,
556, 557, 574, 593,
614, 643, 646
Sanders, J. A., 152
Sanders, J. T., 127
Schechter, S., 583
Schiffman, L. H., 485,
581
Schillebeeckx, E., 7, 21,
24, 25, 26, 42, 103,
121, 466, 478, 579,
648
Schleiermacher, F. D. E.,
17, 47
Schnackenburg, R., 10,
218
Schoonenberg, P., 26
Schopenhauer, A., 4
Schrenk, G., 262
Schulz, S., 41, 42
Schürer, E., 106, 266,
271, 294, 440, 544,
589, 627, 658
Schüssler Fiorenza, E.,
84
Schwarz, D., 278
Schweitzer, A., 3, 4, 5,
6, 7, 13, 16, 17, 18,
19, 20, 22, 23, 25,
26, 28, 29, 47, 66,
75, 80, 81, 82, 83,
84, 95, 96, 100,
102, 103, 113, 114,
117, 122, 123, 139,
174, 207, 208, 209,
213, 216-7, 220,
221, 223, 224, 279,
303, 341, 343, 365,
464, 478, 479, 541,
553, 554, 578, 593,
594, 599, 609, 643,
657, 658, 660, 662
Scobie, C. H. H., 160
Scott, B. B., 29, 174,

176, 225, 311
Scott, J. M., xvii
Seeley, D., 541, 602
Segal, A. F., 508, 527,
586, 626, 627
Segundo, J. L., 26
Sellin, G., 305
Semler, J. S., 16
Shaffer, P., 228
Shaked, S., 481
Sherwin-White, A. N.,
546, 547, 550
Shogren, G. S., 268, 273
Shaw, B. D., 157, 158
Sloan, R. B., 294
Smalley, S. S., 360
Smith, D. Moody, 374
Smith, M., 49, 189, 376,
440
Smith, R. H., 353
Smith, R. L., 495, 561
Snodgrass, K., 231, 501
Soards, M. L., 568
Sommer, B. D., 151, 154
Sparks, H. F. D., 625
Stanton, G. N., 84, 439,
440, 462
Stauffer, E., 440, 441
Stein, R. H., 175
Steiner, G., 657
Stern, M., 388
Stone, M. E., 238
Strack, H., L., 71
Strauss, D. F., 18, 47
Strecker, G., 281, 287
Strobel, A., 440, 441
Stroumsa, G. G., 481
Stuhlmacher, P., 583,
601, 602, 616
Sweet, J. P., 85
Swinburne, A. C., 18

Tabor, J. D., 582
Talbert, C. H., 634
Tannehill, R. C., 463
Tatum, W. B., 5, 13
Taussig, H., 31
Taylor, J., 539
Taylor, L., 157
Taylor, V., 574
Telford, W. R., 25, 421

Thackeray, H. StJ., 263
Theissen, G., 84, 150,
170, 195, 303, 343,
352, 455, 496
Thielicke, H., 129
Thiselton, A. C., 455,
554
Throckmorton, B. H.,
279, 343
Tiede, D. L., 626
Tillich, P., 23, 26
Troeltsch, E., 187
Trumbower, J. A., 414,
422
Tuckett, C., 42, 71

Urbach, E. E., 400, 589,
626

Vaage, L. E., 33, 41, 66,
71, 72, 210
Van Beeck, F. J., 44, 47,
55, 60, 105, 136
Vermes, G., 28, 83, 84,
85, 87, 90, 91, 92,
94, 96, 101, 103,
104, 105, 106, 108,
110, 112, 115, 118,
119, 122, 149, 162,
163, 172, 186, 191,
199, 221, 260, 262,
275, 283, 314, 345,
374, 377, 382, 405,
473, 512, 517, 518,
530, 581, 582, 586,
587, 614, 649, 661

Wallace-Hadrill, J. M.,
87
Wallis, I. G., 259
Wansbrough, H., 133,
135
Watson, D. F., 183, 454
Weaver, D. J., 290
Webb, R. L., 41, 152-5,
160, 161, 163, 164,
167, 168, 616
Weeden, T. J., 463
Weinart, F. D., 633
Weiss, J., 5, 6, 95, 127,
221, 341

INDEX OF SELECTED TOPICS